Meet *PsychSmart*. *PsychSmart* uses a wealth of real-world examples and online tools to create an interactive learning experience designed to reach YOU.

What's Inside?

"Psych at the Movies" suggests feature-length movies related to topics in the chapter.

PSYCH think

"PsychThink" questions distributed throughout each chapter prompt students to think more deeply about a topic discussed in the text. Online interactive challenge questions help students master key concepts.

"Try It!" exercises offer students a chance to apply psychology concepts by answering self-assessment questionnaires.

"Buy It?" segments model critical thinking about psychology and consumer issues.

STUDY TIP

"Study Tips" call attention to important concepts and suggest effective strategies for learning and studying.

"Get Involved" sections extend the study of psychology beyond the classroom.

"From the Perspective of . . ." questions explore the impact of psychology on different professions, such as medicine, marketing, and law.

Did you know?

"Did You Know?" provides short, engaging nuggets of information relevant to the chapter.

i

The McGraw·Hill Companies

Connect
Learn
Succeed™

PSYCHSMART

VICE PRESIDENT, EDITORIAL **Michael J. Ryan**
PUBLISHER **Michael Sugarman**
SENIOR DIRECTOR OF DEVELOPMENT **Dawn Groundwater**
EXECUTIVE EDITOR **Krista Bettino**
DEVELOPMENT EDITOR **Cheri Dellelo**
EDITORIAL COORDINATOR **Chantelle Walker**
EXECUTIVE MARKETING MANAGER **Julia Flohr Larkin**
SENIOR PRODUCTION EDITOR **Mel Valentín**
MANUSCRIPT EDITOR **Patricia Ohlenroth**
PERMISSIONS EDITOR **Marty Moga**
DESIGN MANAGER AND COVER **Cassandra Chu**
INTERIOR DESIGN **Elise Lansdon**
LEAD PHOTO RESEARCH COORDINATOR **Alexandra Ambrose**
PHOTO RESEARCHER **Toni Michaels, PhotoFind, LLC**
ART MANAGER **Robin Mouat**
ILLUSTRATORS **John and Judy Waller**
MEDIA PROJECT MANAGER **Mathew Sletten**
BUYER **Louis Swaim**
COMPOSITION **10/12 Times by Lachina Publishing Services**
PRINTING **38# Consoweb Gloss, Quad/Graphics/Dubuque**
COVER IMAGES **© Henrik Sorensen/Stone/Getty Images**

PSYCHSMART

Published by McGraw-Hill, an imprint of The McGraw-Hill Companies, Inc., 1221 Avenue of the Americas,
New York, NY 10020. Copyright © 2013 by The McGraw-Hill Companies, Inc. All rights reserved. No part
of this publication may be reproduced or distributed in any form or by any means, or stored in a database
or retrieval system, without the prior written consent of The McGraw-Hill Companies, Inc., including,
but not limited to, in any network or other electronic storage or transmission, or broadcast for distance
learning.

2 3 4 5 6 7 8 9 0 QDB/QDB 1 0 9 8 7 6 5 4 3

ISBN: 978-0-07-803528-9
MHID: 0-07-803528-7

Credits: The credits section for this book begins on page 422 and is considered an extension of the
copyright page. Printed in the United States of America.

Library of Congress Cataloging-in-Publication Data

PsychSmart. — 2nd ed.
    p. cm.
    Includes bibliographical references and index.
    ISBN 978-0-07-803528-9 (alk. paper)
    ISBN 0-07-803528-7 (alk. paper)
  1. Psychology.
    BF121.P88 2012
    150—dc23

                                                          2011046969

The Internet addresses listed in the text were accurate at the time of publication. The inclusion of a
Web site does not indicate an endorsement by the authors or McGraw-Hill, and McGraw-Hill does not
guarantee the accuracy of the information presented at these sites.
www.mhhe.com

PSYCHSMART

BRIEF CONTENTS

Ch. 5
LEARNING
STYLES

Ch. 9
HOW DO INFANTS
DEVELOP AFTER
BIRTH?

Ch. 7
CAN YOU LEARN TO BE
A MORE CRITICAL AND
CREATIVE THINKER?

< Ch. 3
HOW DO YOUR
TASTE BUDS
MEASURE UP?

WE LISTENED TO STUDENTS.

Based on extensive student research, we have created a complete learning resource to meet the needs and maximize the workflow of today's college students. Students told us they wanted a briefer text with more visual appeal . . . and a lower price.

WE ALSO LISTENED TO INSTRUCTORS.

We learned about the challenges that they faced in their classrooms every day and what their ideal course materials would look like. They told us they needed an engaging solution for their course needs—but without sacrificing quality and content.

WE RESPONDED.

PsychSmart, written by a team of master teachers, blends core content and psychological research with a wealth of real world examples, plus media and online interactivities to create a dynamic and engaging learning solution for today's students.

About the contributors

Tanya Renner, Professor of Psychology at Kapi'olani Community College, earned a Ph.D. in developmental psychology from the University of California at Berkeley. In addition to teaching introductory psychology, Renner studies effective teaching and learning practices and ways to develop critical thinking skills. A strong advocate for problem-based learning, both as an educator and as a researcher, she also actively supports the use of ePortfolio software as a teaching-learning strategy and participated in a national project headed by the American Council on Education to develop specific strategies for using ePortfolios and for assessing the student learning demonstrated in an ePortfolio.

Robert S. Feldman is a Professor of Psychology and Dean of the College of Social and Behavior Sciences at the University of Massachusetts at Amherst. A winner of the College Distinguished Teacher award and a Fellow of both the American Psychological Association and the Association for Psychological Science, Feldman has written more than 100 books, book chapters, and scientific articles. For much of his career, Feldman has studied lying and deception, culminating in the recent publication of *The Liar in Your Life: The Way to Truthful Relationships.* He holds a Ph.D. from the University of Wisconsin-Madison.

1

INTRODUCTION TO
PSYCHO

COPING WITH DISASTER

It began as a geological event far beneath the ocean floor. But the 8.9-magnitude earthquake, the epicenter of which was off the coast of Japan, spurred a series of events that would reverberate across the world.

First came the shaking, which was so powerful that people were thrown to the ground. Refrigerators flew into the air, books were flung from shelves, brick walls collapsed and disintegrated, and roadways buckled and snapped. Then came the huge waves of a tsunami, inundating towns along the coast of Japan, killing tens of thousands of people. Then several nuclear power plants, lacking electricity, reached near-meltdown conditions. Fires raged, radioactive fuel rods were exposed, and radiation was released into the atmosphere and ocean.

But the real story was not one of disaster, but of how people reacted to the situation. Thousands of volunteers came forward to provide help for the homeless. Brave workers at the nuclear plants stayed on the job and tried to stop the spread of radiation. And people across the globe made donations and sent supplies to help the survivors rebuild their lives.[i]

At its most basic level, the Japanese earthquake and tsunami is a story of people and the human condition. And as such, it raises a host of questions that are primarily psychological in nature. For example:

- How did internal biological activity change for people who were dealing with the disaster?

- How can we reduce people's anxiety and help them cope in the wake of the disaster?

- Is the experience of the disaster linked to later illness?

- How accurately do people remember what they were doing when the quake and tsunami struck?

- Is there a relationship between children's experience of the disaster and their later development?

The field of psychology addresses such questions as these—and many, many more. In this chapter, we begin our examination of psychology, considering the different areas of the field, what makes the study of behavior a science, and many of the various explanations for human behavior and thought that psychologists have put forward.

LOGY

As You READ >>

- What is the science of psychology?
- What are the major specialties in the field of psychology?
- What are the major perspectives used by psychologists?
- What is the scientific method, and do psychologists use theory and research to answer questions of interest?
- What research methods do psychologists use?

>> Psychologists at Work

Why can you almost instantly remember the name of your first-grade teacher after years of not thinking about this person? Why are some people afraid to fly in airplanes? Why do some people think bungee jumping is exhilarating while others find it terrifying? What are the factors that you consider when deciding if you should help someone who has just fallen down? Why do babies cry when their mothers leave the room? Why does drinking a mocha latte make you feel more alert? Why do you keep dreaming that you are back in middle school, and somehow you forgot to put on underwear (again!)? As you try to answer each of these questions, you are doing what psychologists do—trying to understand why we behave and think in certain ways.

Psychology is the scientific study of behavior and mental processes. It encompasses not just what people do but also their thoughts, emotions, perceptions, reasoning processes, memories, and even the biological activities that maintain bodily functioning. Psychologists try to describe, predict, and explain human behavior and mental processes, as well as helping to change and improve the lives of people and the world in which they live. They use scientific methods to find answers that are far more valid and legitimate than those resulting from intuition and speculation, which are often inaccurate.

psychology The scientific study of behavior and mental processes.

THE SUBFIELDS OF PSYCHOLOGY

As the study of psychology has grown, it has given rise to a number of subfields. One way to identify the key subfields is to look at some of the basic questions about behavior that they address.

Behavioral Neuroscience In the most fundamental sense, people are biological organisms. *Behavioral neuroscience* is the subfield of psychology that mainly examines how the brain and the nervous system—and other biological processes—determine behavior. Thus, neuroscientists consider how our bodies influence our behavior. For example, behavioral neuroscientists might want to know what physiological changes occurred as people rushed for their lives when warned that a tsunami was approaching.

Experimental Psychology If you have ever wondered why you are susceptible to optical illusions, how your body registers pain, or how to make the most of your study time, an experimental psychologist can answer your questions. *Experimental psychology* is the branch of psychology that studies the processes of sensing, perceiving, learning, and thinking about the world. (The term *experimental psychologist,* however, is somewhat misleading: Psychologists in every specialty area use experimental techniques.)

Several subspecialties of experimental psychology have become specialties in their own right. One is *cognitive psychology,* which focuses on higher mental processes, including thinking, memory, reasoning, problem solving, judging, decision making, and language. For example, a cognitive psychologist might be interested in what survivors of an earthquake and tsunami remember about their experiences.

Developmental Psychology A baby producing her first smile . . . taking her first steps . . . saying her first word. These universal milestones in development are also singularly special and unique for each person. *Developmental psychology* studies how people grow and change from the moment of conception through death. *Personality* *psychology* focuses on the consistency in people's behavior over time and the traits that differentiate one person from another.

Clinical Psychology Frequent depression, stress, and fears that prevent people from carrying out their normal activities are topics that would interest a health psychologist, a clinical psychologist, and a counseling psychologist. *Health psychology* explores the relationship between psychological factors and physical ailments or disease. For example, health psychologists are interested in assessing how long-term stress (a psychological factor) can affect physical health and in identifying ways to promote behavior that brings about good health.

Clinical psychology deals with the study, diagnosis, and treatment of psychological disorders. Clinical psychologists are trained to provide therapy for problems that range from the crises of everyday life, such as unhappiness over the breakup of a relationship, to more extreme conditions, such as profound, lingering depression.

Like clinical psychologists, counseling psychologists deal with people's psychological problems, but the problems they deal with are more specific. *Counseling psychology* focuses primarily on educational, social, and career adjustment problems. Almost every college has a center staffed with counseling psychologists. This is where students can get advice on the kinds of jobs they might be best suited for, on methods of studying effectively, and on strategies for resolving everyday difficulties, such as problems with roommates and concerns about a specific professor's grading practices.

Social Psychology Our complex networks of social interrelationships are the focus for a number of subfields of psychology. For example, *social psychology* is the study of how people's thoughts, feelings, and actions are affected by others. Social psychologists concentrate on such diverse topics as human aggression, liking and loving, persuasion, and conformity.

Cross-cultural psychology investigates the similarities and differences in psychological functioning in and across various cultures and ethnic groups. For example, cross-cultural psychologists examine how cultures differ in their coping strategies after a major disaster, such as 9/11 or the earthquake and tsunami in Japan.

PSYCH think

> > > Why is one person physically attracted to another? Generate a list of reasons. (Remember that there are no wrong answers.) How might psychologists from each subfield try to answer this question? For example, how would a behavioral neuroscientist's approach be different from an evolutionary psychologist's approach? How might a cross-cultural psychologist investigate physical attractiveness, and how would that approach differ from that of a cognitive psychologist? Based on your list of reasons, what kind of psychologist do you think you could become?

Evolutionary Psychology *Evolutionary psychology* considers how behavior is influenced by our genetic inheritance from our ancestors. The evolutionary approach suggests that the chemical coding of information in our cells not only determines traits such as hair color and race but also holds the key to understanding a broad variety of behaviors that helped our ancestors survive and reproduce.

Behavioral Genetics *Behavioral genetics* seeks to understand how we might inherit certain behavioral traits and how the environment influences whether we actually display such traits (Moffitt & Caspi, 2007; Rende, 2007; Kremen, & Lyons, 2011).

Clinical Neuropsychology *Clinical neuropsychology* unites the areas of neuroscience and clinical psychology. Building on advances in our understanding of the structure and chemistry of the brain, this specialty has already led to promising new treatments for psychological disorders as well as debates over the use of medication to control behavior.

From the perspective of …

AN EDUCATOR You are a high school math teacher and one of your top students suddenly starts to get low grades. When you ask about this, she explains that she has family in Japan and three of them died in the earthquake. To help the student, you can consult with as many psychologists from different specializations as needed. Which ones will you ask for help?

WORKING AT PSYCHOLOGY

Help Wanted: Assistant professor at a small liberal arts college. Teach undergraduate courses in introductory psychology and courses in specialty areas of cognitive psychology, perception, and learning. Strong commitment to quality teaching necessary, as well as evidence of scholarship and research productivity.

Help Wanted: Industrial-organizational consulting psychologist. International firm seeks psychologists for full-time career positions as consultants to management. Candidates must have the ability to establish a rapport with senior business executives and help them to find innovative and practical solutions to problems concerning people and organizations.

Help Wanted: Clinical psychologist with a Ph.D., internship experience, and license. Full-service clinic seeks psychologist to work with multidisciplinary team to provide psychotherapy to individuals and groups. You must also administer psychological tests, be on call for crisis intervention, and develop treatment plans.

As these job listings suggest, psychologists are employed in a variety of settings. Many doctoral-level psychologists are employed by institutions of higher learning (universities and colleges) or are self-employed, usually working as private practitioners treating clients. Other work sites include hospitals, clinics, mental health centers, counseling centers, government human-services organizations, and schools (American Psychological Association, 2007; DeAngelis & Monahan, 2008).

Psychologists: A Portrait Although there is no "average" psychologist in terms of personal characteristics, we can draw a statistical portrait of the profession. Today, close to 300,000 psychologists work in the United States. About half of them are women, and education trends predict that women will soon outnumber men in the field. Almost three fourths of new psychology doctorate degrees are now earned by women (Cynkar, 2007; Frincke & Pate, 2004).

The vast majority of psychologists in the United States are white, limiting the diversity of the field. Only 6% of all psychologists are members of minority groups, which is significant for several reasons. First, the field of psychology is diminished by a lack of the diverse perspectives and talents that minority-group members can provide. Furthermore, their underrepresentation in the profession might deter other minority-group members from entering the field. Finally, because members of minority groups often prefer to receive psychological therapy from treatment providers of their own race or ethnic group, they may be discouraged from seeking treatment because of the rarity of minority psychologists (Bernal et al., 2002; Bryant et al., 2005; Jenkins, A. M., et al., 2003).

The Education of a Psychologist How do people become psychologists? The most common route is to obtain a doctorate, either a *Ph.D.* (doctor of philosophy) or, less frequently, a *Psy.D.* (doctor of psychology). The Ph.D. is a research degree that requires a dissertation based on an original investigation. The Psy.D. is obtained by psychologists who wish to focus on the treatment of psychological disorders. (Psychologists are distinct from psychiatrists, who are physicians—M.D.s—who specialize in the treatment of psychological disorders.)

Both the Ph.D. and the Psy.D. typically take four or five years of work past the bachelor's level. Some fields of psychology involve education beyond the doctorate. For instance, doctoral-level clinical psychologists, who work with people with psychological disorders, typically spend an additional year doing an internship.

About a third of people working in the field of psychology have a master's degree as their highest degree, which they earn after two or three years of graduate study. These psychologists teach, provide therapy, conduct research, or work in specialized programs dealing with drug abuse or crisis intervention. Some work in universities, government, and business, collecting and analyzing data.

Careers for Psychology Majors Although some psychology majors head for graduate school in psychology or an unrelated field, the majority join the workforce immediately after graduation. Most report that the jobs they take after graduation are related to their psychology background.

An undergraduate major in psychology provides excellent preparation for a variety of occupations. Because undergraduates who specialize in psychology develop good analytical skills, are trained to think critically, and are able to synthesize and evaluate information well, employers in business, industry, and the government value their preparation (Kuther, 2003).

>> A Science Evolves

- Seven thousand years ago, people assumed that psychological problems were caused by evil spirits. To allow those spirits to escape from a person's body, ancient healers chipped a hole in a patient's skull with crude instruments—a procedure called trepanning.
- According to the 17th-century philosopher Descartes, nerves were hollow tubes through which "animal spirits" conducted impulses in the same way that water is transmitted through a pipe. When a person put a finger too close to a fire, heat was transmitted to the brain through the tubes.

STUDY TIP

Be sure you can differentiate a Ph.D. (doctor of philosophy) from a Psy.D. (doctor of psychology), as well as psychologists from psychiatrists.

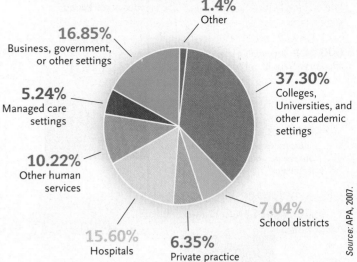

Where Psychologists Work

- 1.4% Other
- 16.85% Business, government, or other settings
- 5.24% Managed care settings
- 10.22% Other human services
- 15.60% Hospitals
- 6.35% Private practice
- 7.04% School districts
- 37.30% Colleges, Universities, and other academic settings

Source: APA, 2007.

Did you know?

What can psychology majors do after graduation? Lots of things! For example, graduates with a bachelor's degree in psychology may find entry-level opportunities in advertising, publishing, business management, law enforcement, and social services, to name a few occupations. For tips on making the most of your time in college, lists of entry level jobs for psychology majors, information about graduate school in psychology, and a whole lot more, check out Margaret Lloyd's Web site: www.psywww.com/careers/index.htm and www.psychdirectory.com.

- Franz Josef Gall, an 18th-century physician, argued that a trained observer could discern intelligence, moral character, and other basic personality characteristics from the shape and the number of bumps on a person's skull. His theory gave rise to the field of phrenology, employed by hundreds of practitioners in the 19th century.

Although these practices might sound far-fetched, in their own times they represented the most advanced thinking about behavior and the brain. Psychology has come a long way since the 18th century, but most of the advances have been recent. As sciences go, psychology is relatively young.

Milestones in Psychology

1690
John Locke introduces idea of *tabula rasa*

◀ **5,000 BCE** Trepanning used to allow the escape of evil spirits

◀ **430 BCE** Hippocrates argues for four temperaments of personality

1879
Wilhelm Wundt inaugurates first psychology laboratory in Leipzig, Germany

1905
Mary Calkins works on memory

1895
Functionalist model formulated

1915
Strong emphasis on intelligence testing

Forerunners of Psychology

1900

First Psychologists

1637
Descartes describes animal spirits

1807
Franz Josef Gall proposes phrenology

1890
Principles of Psychology published by William James

1900
Sigmund Freud develops the psychodynamic perspective

1904
Ivan Pavlov wins Nobel Prize for work on digestion that led to fundamental principles of learning

1920
Gestalt psychology becomes influential

THE ROOTS OF PSYCHOLOGY

The formal beginning of psychology as a scientific discipline is generally considered to be in the late 19th century, when, in Leipzig, Germany, Wilhelm Wundt established the first experimental laboratory devoted to psychological phenomena. When Wundt set up his laboratory in 1879, his aim was to study the building blocks of the mind. He considered psychology to be the study of conscious experience. His perspective, which came to be known as **structuralism**, focused on uncovering the fundamental mental components of perception, consciousness, thinking, emotions, and other kinds of mental states and activities.

To determine how basic sensory processes shape our understanding of the world, Wundt and other structural-

> **structuralism** Wundt's approach, which focuses on uncovering the fundamental mental components of consciousness, thinking, and other kinds of mental states and activities.
>
> **introspection** A procedure used to study the structure of the mind in which subjects are asked to describe in detail what they are experiencing when they are exposed to a stimulus.

ists used a procedure called **introspection**, in which they presented people with a stimulus—such as a bright green object or a sentence printed on a card—and asked them to describe, in their own words and in as much detail as they could, what they were experiencing. Wundt argued that by analyzing their reports, psychologists could come to a better understanding of the structure of the mind.

Over time, psychologists challenged Wundt's approach. They became increasingly dissatisfied with the assumption

1924
John B. Watson, an early behaviorist, publishes *Behaviorism*

1953
B. F. Skinner publishes *Science and Human Behavior*, advocating the behavioral perspective

1980
Jean Piaget, an influential developmental psychologist, dies

2010
New subfields develop such as clinical neuro-psychology and evolutionary psychology

1969
Arguments regarding the genetic basis of IQ fuel lingering controversies

1990 Greater emphasis on multiculturalism and diversity

1950

Modern Psychology

2000

1928
Leta Stetter Hollingworth publishes work on adolescence

1957 Leon Festinger publishes *A Theory of Cognitive Dissonance*, producing a major impact on social psychology

1985 Increasing emphasis on cognitive perspective

1951
Carl Rogers publishes *Client-Centered Therapy*, helping to establish the humanistic perspective

1981 David Hubel and Torsten Wiesel win Nobel Prize for work on vision cells in the brain

2000
Elizabeth Loftus does pioneering work on false memory and eyewitness testimony

1954
Abraham Maslow publishes *Motivation and Personality*, developing the concept of self-actualization

---

that introspection could reveal the structure of the mind. Introspection was not a truly scientific technique, because there were few ways an outside observer could confirm the accuracy of others' introspections. Moreover, people had difficulty describing some kinds of inner experiences, such as emotional responses. Those drawbacks led to the development of a new approach, which largely replaced structuralism.

The perspective that replaced structuralism is known as functionalism. Rather than focusing on the mind's structure, **functionalism** concentrated on what the mind *does* and how behavior functions. Functionalists, whose perspective

became prominent in the early 1900s, asked what role behavior plays in allowing people to adapt to their environments. For example, a functionalist might examine the function of the emotion of fear in preparing us to deal with emergency situations.

Led by the American psychologist William James, the functionalists examined how behavior allows people to satisfy their needs and how our "stream of consciousness" permits us to adapt to our environment. The American educator John Dewey drew on functionalism to develop the field of school psychology, proposing ways to best meet students' educational needs.

Another important reaction to structuralism was the development of gestalt psychology in the early 1900s. **Gestalt psychology** emphasizes how perception is organized. Instead of considering the individual parts that

> **functionalism** An early approach to psychology that concentrated on what the mind does—the functions of mental activity—and the role of behavior in allowing people to adapt to their environments.
>
> **gestalt** (geh-SHTALT) **psychology** An approach to psychology that focuses on the organization of perception and thinking in a "whole" sense rather than on the individual elements of perception.

make up thinking, gestalt psychologists took the opposite tack, studying how people consider individual elements together as units or wholes. Gestalt psychologists proposed that "The whole is different from the sum of its parts"—that is, our perception, or understanding, of objects is greater and more meaningful than the individual elements that make up our perceptions. Gestalt psychologists have made substantial contributions to our understanding of perception.

FOUNDING MOTHERS OF PSYCHOLOGY

As in many scientific fields, social prejudices hindered women's participation in the early development of psychology. Many universities would not even admit women to their graduate psychology programs in the early 1900s.

Despite the hurdles they faced, women made notable contributions to psychology, although their impact on the field was largely overlooked until recently. For example, Margaret Floy Washburn (1871–1939) was the first woman to receive a doctorate in psychology, and she did important work on animal behavior. Leta Stetter Hollingworth (1886–1939) was one of the first psychologists to focus on child development and on women's issues. She collected data to refute the view, popular in the early 1900s, that women's abilities periodically declined during parts of the menstrual cycle (Denmark & Fernandez, 1993; Furumoto & Scarborough, 2002; Hollingworth, 1943/1990).

> Mary Calkins, who studied memory in the early part of the 20th century, became the first female president of the American Psychological Association.

Mary Calkins (1863–1930), who studied memory in the early part of the 20th century, became the first female president of the American Psychological Association. Karen Horney (pronounced "HORN-eye") (1885–1952) focused on the social and cultural factors behind personality, and June Etta Downey (1875–1932) spearheaded the study of personality traits and became the first woman to head a psychology department at a state university. Anna Freud (1895–1982), the daughter of Sigmund Freud, also made notable contributions to the treatment of abnormal behavior, and Mamie Phipps Clark (1917–1983) carried out pioneering work on how children of color grew to recognize racial differences (Horney, 1937; Lal, 2002; Stevens & Gardner, 1982).

In 2005, nearly 72 percent of new Ph.D. and Psy.D.s entering psychology were women. (Cynkar, 2007)

PSYCHOLOGY TODAY

The men and women who laid the foundations of psychology shared a common goal: to explain and to understand behavior using scientific methods. Seeking to achieve the same goal, the tens of thousands of psychologists who followed those early pioneers embraced—and often rejected—a variety of broad perspectives.

The perspectives of psychology offer distinct outlooks and emphasize different factors. Just as we can use more than one map to find our way around a specific region—for instance, a map that shows roads and highways and another map that shows major landmarks—psychologists developed a variety of approaches to understanding behavior. When considered jointly, the different perspectives provide the means to explain behavior in its amazing variety.

Today, the field of psychology includes five major perspectives. These broad perspectives emphasize different aspects of behavior and mental processes. Each takes our understanding of behavior in a somewhat different direction.

The Neuroscience Perspective When we get down to the basics, humans are animals made of skin and bones. The **neuroscience perspective** considers how people and nonhumans function biologically: how individual nerve cells are joined together, how the inheritance of certain characteristics from parents and other ancestors influences behavior, how the functioning of the body affects hopes and fears, which behaviors are reflexive, and so forth. This perspective includes the study of heredity and evolution, which considers how heredity may influence behavior; and behavioral neuroscience, which examines how the brain and the nervous system affect behavior.

> **neuroscience perspective** The approach that views behavior from the perspective of the brain, the nervous system, and other biological functions.

Because every behavior ultimately can be broken down into its biological components, the neuroscience perspective has broad appeal. Psychologists who subscribe to this perspective have made major contributions to the

Major Perspectives of Psychology

Neuroscience
Views behavior from the perspective of biological functioning

Cognitive
Examines how people understand and think about the world

Behavioral
Focuses on observable behavior

Humanistic
Contends that people can control their behavior and that they naturally try to reach their full potential

Psychodynamic
Believes behavior is motivated by inner, unconscious forces over which a person has little control

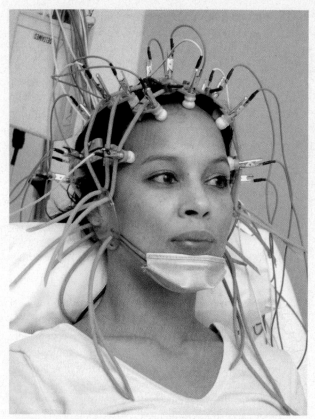

One technique neuroscientists use to study activity in the brain is electroencephalography (EEG). In this painless procedure, electrodes are attached to the scalp and changes in electrical activity are recorded while the person performs specific tasks.

psychology but also in related fields. Although some of the original Freudian principles have been roundly criticized, the contemporary psychodynamic perspective has provided a means not only to understand and treat some kinds of psychological disorders but also to understand everyday phenomena such as prejudice and aggression (Bacal, 2011).

The Behavioral Perspective In contrast to the neuroscience and psychodynamic approaches, the **behavioral perspective** grew out of a rejection of psychology's early emphasis on the inner workings of the mind. Instead, behaviorists suggested that the field should focus on observable behavior that can be measured objectively.

John B. Watson was the first major American psychologist to advocate a behavioral approach. Working in the 1920s, Watson was adamant in his view that one could gain a complete understanding of behavior by studying and modifying the environment in which people operate. In fact, Watson believed that it was possible to elicit any desired type of behavior by controlling a person's environment.

The behavioral perspective was championed by B. F. Skinner, a pioneer in the field. Much of our understanding of how people learn new behaviors is based on the behavioral perspective. As we will see, the behavioral perspective crops up along every byway of psychology. Along with its influence in the area of learning processes, this perspective has made contributions in such diverse areas as treating mental disorders, curbing aggression, resolving sexual problems, and ending drug addiction (Helfand, 2011; Silverman, Roll, & Higgins, 2008).

understanding and betterment of human life, ranging from cures for certain types of deafness to drug treatments for people with severe mental disorders. Furthermore, advances in methods for examining the anatomy and functioning of the brain have permitted the neuroscientfic perspective to extend its influence across a broad range of subfields in psychology.

The Psychodynamic Perspective To many people who have never taken a psychology course, psychology begins and ends with the psychodynamic perspective. Proponents of the **psychodynamic perspective** argue that behavior is motivated by inner forces and conflicts about which we have little awareness or control. They view dreams and slips of the tongue as indications of what a person is truly feeling within a seething cauldron of unconscious psychic activity.

The origins of the psychodynamic view are linked to one person: Sigmund Freud. Freud was a Viennese physician in the early 1900s whose ideas about unconscious determinants of behavior had a revolutionary effect on 20th-century thinking, not just in

Sigmund Freud

The Cognitive Perspective Efforts to understand behavior lead some psychologists directly to the mind. The **cognitive perspective** focuses on how people think, understand, and reason about the world. The emphasis is on learning how people internally comprehend and represent the outside world and how our ways of thinking about the world influence our behavior.

Many psychologists who adhere to the cognitive perspective compare human thinking to the workings of a computer, which takes in information and transforms, stores, and retrieves it. In their view, thinking is *information processing*.

Psychologists who rely on the cognitive perspective ask questions ranging from how people make decisions to whether a person can watch television and study at the same time. The common elements that link cognitive approaches are an emphasis on how people understand and think about the world and an interest in describing the patterns and irregularities in the operation of their minds.

The Humanistic Perspective Rejecting the view that behavior is determined largely by automatically

> Nature (heredity) versus nurture (environment) is one of the major issues that psychologists address.

unfolding biological forces, unconscious processes, or the environment, the **humanistic perspective** instead suggests that all individuals naturally strive to grow, develop, and be in control of their lives and behavior. A major goal of the humanistic perspective is to explore human potential.

According to Carl Rogers and Abraham Maslow, who were central figures in the development of the humanistic perspective, people will strive to reach their full potential if they are given the opportunity to do so. The emphasis of the humanistic perspective is on **free will**, the ability to freely make decisions about one's own behavior and life. The notion of free will stands in contrast to **determinism**, which sees behavior as caused, or determined, by things beyond a person's control.

The humanistic perspective assumes that people have the ability to make their own choices about their behavior rather than relying on societal standards. More than any other approach, it stresses the role of psychology in enriching people's lives and helping them achieve self-fulfillment. By reminding psychologists of their commitment to the individual person in society, the humanistic perspective has had a significant influence on the field (Dillon, 2008; Robbins, 2008).

Don't let the abstract qualities of the different approaches we have discussed lull you into thinking that they are purely theoretical. These perspectives underlie ongoing work of a practical nature, as we discuss throughout this book.

KEY ISSUES IN PSYCHOLOGY

As you consider the many topics and perspectives that make up psychology, ranging from a narrow focus on minute biochemical influences on behavior to a broad focus on social behaviors, you might find yourself thinking that the discipline lacks cohesion. However, the field is more unified than a first glimpse might suggest. For one thing, regardless of what a psychologist's specialty may be, all psychologists use the scientific method to study their topics. Also, they tend to rely on one or more psychological perspectives. For example, a developmental psychologist might use the cognitive perspective to study how children develop the ability to think and reason.

From the perspective of ...

A POLITICAL ANALYST People have very different opinions about Osama Bin Laden. How could you apply psychological perspectives to understand these differences?

---

psychodynamic perspective The approach based on the view that behavior is motivated by unconscious inner forces over which the individual has little control.

behavioral perspective The approach that suggests that observable, measurable behavior should be the focus of study.

cognitive perspective The approach that focuses on how people think, understand, and reason about the world.

humanistic perspective The approach that suggests that all individuals naturally strive to grow, develop, and be in control of their lives and behavior.

free will The idea that behavior is caused primarily by choices that are made freely by the individual.

determinism The idea that people's behavior is produced primarily by factors outside of their willful control.

Key Issues in Psychology

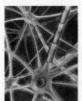    

Issue	Neuroscience	Cognitive	Behavioral	Humanistic	Psychodynamic
Nature (heredity) vs. nurture (environment)	Nature (heredity)	Both	Nurture (environment)	Nurture (environment)	Nature (heredity)
Conscious vs. unconscious determinants of behavior	Unconscious	Both	Conscious	Conscious	Unconscious
Observable behavior vs. internal mental processes	Internal emphasis	Internal emphasis	Observable emphasis	Internal emphasis	Internal emphasis
Free will vs. determinism	Determinism	Free will	Determinism	Free will	Determinism
Individual differences vs. universal principles	Universal emphasis	Individual emphasis	Both	Individual emphasis	Universal emphasis

Can you tell what these dogs are thinking?

Psychologists also agree on what the key issues of the field are. Although there are differences about how best to address them, psychology is a unified science, because psychologists of all perspectives agree that the key issues must be addressed if the field is going to advance. As you contemplate these issues, try not to think of them in "either/or" terms. Instead, consider the opposing viewpoints on each issue as the opposite ends of a continuum, with the positions of individual psychologists typically falling somewhere between the two ends.

- Is Bill Gates smart because his parents were smart? Is it because he went to a progressive school as a young child? Is it both?

    Nature (heredity) versus nurture (environment) is one of the major issues that psychologists address. How much of behavior is due to an individual's genetically determined nature (heredity), and how much is due to nurture, the influences of the physical and social environment in which a child is raised? And what is the interplay between heredity and environment? These questions have deep philosophical and historical roots, and they permeate many topics in psychology.

- After trying on a dress that was two sizes too small, Jazmine asked Lila how she looked. Wanting to be polite, Lila meant to say, "You look great," but unfortunately for both of them, she accidentally said, "You look fat."

    A second major question of interest to psychologists concerns *conscious versus unconscious causes of behavior.* How much of our behavior is produced by forces of which we are fully aware, and how much is due to unconscious activity—mental processes that are not accessible to the conscious mind? For exam-

ple, clinical psychologists adopting a psychodynamic perspective argue that psychological disorders are brought about by unconscious factors, whereas psychologists employing the cognitive perspective suggest that psychological disorders largely are the result of faulty thinking processes.

- Sarah could swear that her dog, Cleo, would weigh in his mind whether he would obey a command. Although sometimes he eagerly came when he was called, other times he seemed to think it over first.

    A third issue is *observable behavior versus internal mental processes.* Should psychology concentrate solely on behavior that can be seen by outside observers, or should it focus on unseen thinking processes? Some psychologists, especially those relying on the behavioral perspective, contend that the only legitimate source of information for psychologists is behavior that can be observed directly. Other psychologists, building on the cognitive perspective, argue that what goes on inside a person's mind is critical to understanding behavior.

- Steve and Hana come from a family with a history of depression. When Steve starts to feel depressed, he claims he can talk himself out of it. When his sister, Hana, begins feeling depressed, she claims she is powerless to stop it.

    Free will versus determinism is a fourth key issue. How much of our behavior is a matter of free will (choices made freely by an individual), and how much is subject to determinism, the notion that behavior is largely produced by factors beyond a person's willful control? For example, some psychologists who specialize in psychological disorders argue that people make intentional choices and that those who display so-called abnormal behavior should be considered responsible for their actions. Other psychologists disagree and contend that such individuals are the victims of forces beyond their control.

- Anyone from anywhere in the world can recognize anger in a person's face. Yet people behave quite differently from one another when riled up. Some start fist fights, some keep their anger inside, and some yell at the dog.

    The fifth key issue concerns *individual differences versus universal principles.* How much of our behavior is a consequence of our unique and special qualities, and how much reflects the culture and society in which we live? How much of our behavior is universally human? Psychologists who take the neuroscience perspective tend to look for universal principles of behavior, such as how the nervous system operates, concentrating on the similarities in our behavioral destinies despite vast differences in our upbringing. In contrast, humanistic psychologists focus more on the uniqueness of every individual. They consider every person's behavior a reflection of distinct and special individual qualities.

PSYCHOLOGY'S FUTURE

What does the future hold for the discipline of psychology? Although the course of scientific development is difficult to predict, several trends seem likely:

- As its knowledge base grows, psychology will become increasingly specialized, and new perspectives will evolve. For example, our growing understanding of the brain and the nervous system, combined with scientific advances in genetics and gene therapy, will allow psychologists to focus on *prevention* of psychological disorders rather than on only their treatment (Cuijpers et al., 2008).
- The evolving sophistication of neuroscientific approaches is likely to have an increasing influence over other branches of psychology. For instance, social psychologists already are increasing their understanding of social behaviors such as persuasion by using brain scans as part of an evolving field known as *social neuroscience* (Bunge & Wallis, 2008; Caccioppo & Decety, 2009).

- Psychology's influence on issues of public interest also will grow. The major problems of our time—such as violence, terrorism, racial and ethnic prejudice, poverty, and environmental and technological disasters—have important psychological aspects (Hobfoll, Hall, & Canetti-Nisim, 2007; Marshall et al., 2007; Seligman & Fowler, 2011).
- Finally, as our communities become more diverse, our differences—embodied in the study of racial, ethnic, linguistic, and cultural factors—will become more important to psychologists providing services and doing research. The result will be a field that can provide an understanding of *human* behavior in its broadest sense (Chang & Sue, 2005; Leong & Blustein, 2000; Quintana, Aboud, & Chao, 2006).

>> The Research Process in Psychology

Birds of a feather flock together.
Opposites attract.

Which of these statements is more accurate? It is hard to say, because we can come up with successful examples of friends and romantic partners who seem to be very similar to each other. We can also come up with examples of friends and partners who seem to be from different planets. Both statements make sense when considered separately.

THE SCIENTIFIC METHOD

If we were to rely on common sense to understand behavior, we'd have considerable difficulty—especially because commonsense views are often contradictory. Psychologists and other scientists meet the challenge of posing appropriate questions and properly answering them by relying on the scientific method. The **scientific method** is the approach used by psychologists to systematically acquire knowledge and understanding about behavior and other phenomena of interest. The scientific method consists of four steps: (1) identifying questions of interest, (2) formulating an explanation, (3) carrying out research

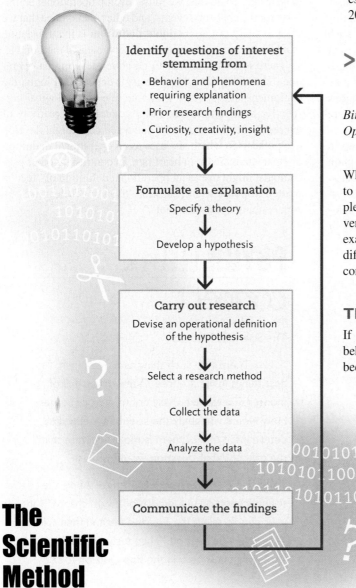

The Scientific Method

Identify questions of interest stemming from
- Behavior and phenomena requiring explanation
- Prior research findings
- Curiosity, creativity, insight

Formulate an explanation
Specify a theory
Develop a hypothesis

Carry out research
Devise an operational definition of the hypothesis
Select a research method
Collect the data
Analyze the data

Communicate the findings

> The scientific method is the approach used by psychologists and other scientists to systematically acquire knowledge and understanding about behavior and other phenomena of interest.

theories Broad explanations and predictions concerning phenomena of interest.

hypothesis A prediction, stemming from a theory, stated in a way that allows it to be tested.

operational definition The translation of a hypothesis into something observable and measurable.

All of us have developed our own informal theories of human behavior, such as "People are basically good" or "People's behavior is usually motivated by self-interest." However, psychologists' theories are more formal and focused. They are established on the basis of a careful study of the psychological literature to identify earlier relevant research and previously formulated theories, as well as psychologists' general knowledge of the field (Guerrero, La Valley, & Farinelli, 2008; Waller, Cray, & Burrows, 2008).

HYPOTHESES: TESTABLE PREDICTIONS

Once a theory is formed, the next step is to carry out research that is designed to test the theoretical explanation. For this step, psychologists need to create a hypothesis. A **hypothesis** is a prediction that can be tested. Hypotheses stem from theories; they help test the underlying soundness of theories.

A hypothesis must be stated in a way that will allow it to be tested. To do this, we must develop operational definitions for the concepts, events, and other phenomena that we want to study. An **operational definition** is the translation of a hypothesis into something observable and measurable.

There is no single way to go about devising an operational definition for a hypothesis; it depends on logic, the equipment and facilities available, the psychological perspective being employed, and ultimately the creativity of the researcher. For example, one researcher might develop a hypothesis in which she uses as an operational definition of "fear" an increase in heart rate. In contrast, another psychologist might use as an operational definition of "fear" a written response to the question "How much fear are you experiencing at this moment?"

designed to support or refute the explanation, and (4) communicating the findings.

THEORIES: BROAD EXPLANATIONS

Psychologists ask questions about the nature and the causes of behavior. They may wish to explore explanations for everyday behaviors. For example, why do we sometimes still wake up early after staying up very late? They may also pose questions that build on findings from previous research. Or they may produce new questions that are based on curiosity, creativity, or insight.

Once a question has been identified, the next step in the scientific method is to develop a theory to explain the observed phenomenon. **Theories** are broad explanations and predictions concerning phenomena of interest. They provide a framework for understanding the relationships among a set of otherwise unorganized facts or principles.

THEORIES OF EVERYTHING

© Roz Chast/The New Yorker Collection/www.cartoonbank.com.

PSYCH think

connect™
WWW.MCGRAWHILLCONNECT.COM/PSYCHOLOGY
The Scientific Method

> > > There's no such thing as a free lunch. The best things in life are free. Our world is full of commonsense ideas like these contradictory adages. How would you apply the scientific method to determine if one of them is more accurate than the other? What question would you ask?

Take the PsychSmart challenge! Apply the scientific method in a simulation. From chapter 1 in your ebook, select the *Exercises* tab and then select "The Scientific Method." Then test yourself by answering question 5 in the Pop Quiz on p. 27.

Hypotheses and the theories behind them help psychologists to pose appropriate questions. With properly stated questions in hand, psychologists proceed to step 3 of the scientific method: research.

PSYCHOLOGICAL RESEARCH METHODS

Research—systematic inquiry aimed at the discovery of new knowledge—is a central component of the scientific method. Research indicates the degree to which hypotheses are accurate. Psychologists can select from a number of alternative research methods. These methods fall into two broad categories: descriptive research and experimental research.

DESCRIPTIVE RESEARCH

Broadly speaking, descriptive research is the systematic collection of information about a person, group, or patterns of behavior. Descriptive research methods include archival research, naturalistic observation, survey research, and case studies.

Archival Research Have divorce rates tapered off in the last 10 years? Are there gender differences in academic performance? In **archival research**, existing data, such as census documents, college records, and newspaper clippings, are examined to test a hypothesis. For example, college records may be used to determine if there are gender differences in academic performance. Government records provide information about divorce rates (Sullivan, Riccio, & Reynolds, 2008).

Archival research is a relatively inexpensive means of testing a hypothesis, because someone else has already collected the basic data. Unfortunately, such records often do not exist. In these instances, researchers may turn to other descriptive research methods, such as naturalistic observation.

Naturalistic Observation Do boys play more aggressively than girls? One way to research this question would be through naturalistic observation. In **naturalistic observation**, the investigator observes some naturally occurring behavior and does not make a change in the situation. For example, a researcher investigating differences in aggressive behavior among boys and girls might observe them on the playground during elementary school recess. The important point to remember about naturalistic observation is that the researcher simply records what occurs, making no modification in the situation that is being observed (Moore, 2002; Rustin, 2006; Schutt, 2001).

Although the advantage of naturalistic observation is obvious—we get a sample of what people do in their "natural habitat"—there is also an important drawback, namely, the inability to control any aspect of the situation. Because naturalistic observation prevents researchers from making changes in a situation, the researchers must wait until the appropriate conditions occur. Furthermore, if people know they are being watched, they may not behave naturally.

Survey Research Do freshman drink more alcohol during the week than seniors do? There is no more straightforward way of finding out what people think, feel, and do than asking them directly. For this reason, surveys are an important research method. In **survey research**, a *sample* of people chosen to represent a larger group of interest (a *population*) is asked a series of questions about their behavior, thoughts, or attitudes. Survey methods have become so sophisticated that even with a very small sample researchers are able to infer with great accuracy how a larger group would respond.

By having freshman and seniors at one school complete a questionnaire about alcohol use, then, could a researcher learn whether one group drinks more than the other? Maybe, but survey research has several potential pitfalls. For one thing, if the sample of people who are surveyed (students at one college or university, for example) is not representative of the broader population of interest (say, all U.S. freshmen and seniors), the results of the survey will have little meaning. In addition, survey respondents may not want to admit to holding socially undesirable attitudes. (Most racists know they are racists and might not want to admit it.) And in some cases, people may not even be consciously aware of what their true attitudes are, or why they hold them.

> **archival research** Research in which existing data, such as census documents, college records, and newspaper clippings, are examined to test a hypothesis.
>
> **naturalistic observation** Research in which an investigator simply observes some naturally occurring behavior and does not make a change in the situation.
>
> **survey research** Research in which people chosen to represent a larger population are asked a series of questions about their behavior, thoughts, or attitudes.

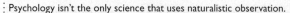
Psychology isn't the only science that uses naturalistic observation.

The Case Study What can the remaining survivors of the holocaust tell us about the emotional effects of surviving very traumatic events? In contrast to a survey, in which many people are studied, a **case study** is an in-depth, intensive investigation of a single individual or a small group. When case studies are used as a research technique, the goal is often not only to learn about the few individuals being examined but also to use the insights gained from the study to improve our understanding of people in general. By interviewing holocaust survivors, for example, psychologists can gain insights into the mechanisms that have helped individuals cope with their trauma.

What are the drawbacks to case studies? If the individuals examined are unique in certain ways, we cannot make valid generalizations to a larger population. Still, such studies sometimes lead the way to new theories and to new treatments for psychological disorders.

case study An in-depth, intensive investigation of an individual or small group of people.

variables Behaviors, events, or other characteristics that can change, or vary, in some way.

correlational research Research in which the relationship between two sets of variables is examined to determine whether they are associated, or "correlated."

Correlational Research

In using the descriptive research methods we have discussed, researchers often want to determine the relationship between two variables. **Variables** are behaviors, events, or other characteristics that can change, or vary, in some way. For example, in a study to determine whether the amount of studying makes a difference in test scores, the variables would be study time and test scores.

In **correlational research**, two sets of variables are examined to determine whether they are associated, or "correlated." The strength and the direction of the relationship between the two variables are represented by a mathematical statistic known as a *correlation* (or, more formally, a *correlation coefficient*), which can range from +1.0 to –1.0.

A *positive correlation* indicates that as the value of one variable increases, we can predict that the value of the other variable will also increase. For example, if we predict that the more time students spend studying for a test, the higher their grades on the test will be, and that the

less they study, the lower their test scores will be, we are expecting to find a positive correlation. (Higher values of the variable "amount of study time" would be associated with higher values of the variable "test score," and lower values of "amount of study time" would be associated with lower values of "test score.") The correlation, then, would be indicated by a positive number, and the stronger the association was between studying and test scores, the closer the number would be to +1.0. For example, we might find a correlation of +.85 between test scores and amount of study time, indicating a strong positive association.

In contrast, a *negative correlation* tells us that as the value of one variable increases, the value of the other decreases. For instance, we might predict that as the number of hours spent studying increases, the number of hours spent in partying decreases. Here we are expecting a negative correlation, ranging between 0 and –1.0. More studying is associated with less partying, and less studying is associated with more partying. The stronger the association between studying and partying is, the closer the correlation will be to –1.0. For instance, a correlation of –.85 would indicate a strong negative association between partying and studying.

Of course, it's quite possible that two variables are unrelated or only slightly related. For instance, we would probably not expect to find a relationship between number of study hours and height. Lack of a relationship would be indicated by a correlation close to 0. For example, if we found a correlation of –.02 or +.03, it would indicate that there is virtually no association between the two variables; knowing how much someone studies does not tell us anything about how tall he or she is.

When two variables are strongly correlated with each other, we are tempted to assume that one variable causes the other. For example, if we find that more study time is associated with higher grades, we might guess that more studying *causes* higher grades. Although this is not a bad guess, it remains just a guess—because finding

PSYCH think

connect™

WWW.MCGRAWHILLCONNECT.COM/PSYCHOLOGY

Correlation

> > > Exercise correlates positively with having more strength (the more you exercise, the more strength you have). And it correlates negatively with depression (the more you exercise, the less likely it is that you are depressed). But it doesn't correlate at all with the number of buildings on your campus! In other words, if you know how much you exercise, that doesn't help you predict how many buildings are on your campus.

Take the PsychSmart challenge! It's YOUR turn to discover some correlations. From chapter 1 in your ebook, select the *Exercises* tab and then select "Correlations." Then test yourself by answering question 9 in the Pop Quiz on p. 27.

that two variables are correlated does not mean that there is a causal relationship between them. The strong correlation suggests that knowing how much a person studies can help us predict how that person will do on a test, but it does not mean that the studying causes the test performance. It might be, for instance, that people who are more interested in the subject matter tend to study more than do those who are less interested, and that the amount of interest, not the number of hours spent studying, predicts test performance. The mere fact that two variables occur together does not mean that one causes the other.

> *The only way psychologists can research cause-and-effect relationships is by carrying out an experiment.*

The inability to demonstrate cause-and-effect relationships is a crucial drawback of correlational research. To establish causality, scientists rely on an alternative technique: the experiment.

EXPERIMENTAL RESEARCH

The *only* way psychologists can establish cause-and-effect relationships through research is by carrying out an experiment. In a formal **experiment**, the researcher investigates the relationship between two (or more) variables by deliberately changing one variable in a controlled situation and observ-

ing the effects of that change on other aspects of the situation. In an experiment, then, the conditions are created and controlled by the researcher, who deliberately makes a change in those conditions in order to observe the effects of that change.

The change that the researcher deliberately makes in an experiment is called the **experimental manipulation**. Experimental manipulations are used to detect relationships between different variables.

Experiments have several steps. First, a hypothesis is stated. For example, "Students who take practice quizzes will get higher test scores than students who do not take the quizzes." For this hypothesis, the experimenter will manipulate who takes the practice quizzes and who does not to see whether those who take practice quizzes get better test scores. This will only make sense if everything else is kept the same for both groups. For example, if the students who do practice quizzes also get more attention from their instructors than those who don't, it would be impossible to know whether improvement in their test scores was due to the practice or the attention or both.

Experimental Groups and Control Groups

Experimental research requires that the responses of at least two groups be compared. One group receives some special **treatment**—the manipulation implemented by the experimenter—and another group receives either no treatment or a different treatment. Any group that receives a treatment is called an **experimental group**; a group that receives no treatment is called a **control group**. (In some experiments there are multiple experimental and control groups, each of which is compared with another group.)

experiment The investigation of the relationship between two (or more) variables by deliberately producing a change in one variable in a situation and observing the effects of that change on other aspects of the situation.

experimental manipulation The change that an experimenter deliberately produces in a situation.

treatment The manipulation implemented by the experimenter.

experimental group Any group participating in an experiment that receives a treatment.

control group A group participating in an experiment that receives no treatment.

"What if these guys in white coats who bring us food are, like, studying us and we're part of some kind of big experiment?"

© Mike Twohy/The New Yorker Collection/ www.cartoonbank.com.

independent variable The variable that is manipulated by an experimenter.

dependent variable The variable that is measured and is expected to change as a result of changes caused by the experimenter's manipulation of the independent variable.

random assignment to condition A procedure in which participants are assigned to different experimental groups or "conditions" on the basis of chance and chance alone.

significant outcome Meaningful results that make it possible for researchers to feel confident that they have confirmed their hypotheses.

replication The repetition of research, sometimes using other procedures, settings, and groups of participants, to increase confidence in prior findings.

By employing both experimental and control groups in an experiment, researchers are able to rule out the possibility that something other than the experimental manipulation produced the results observed in the experiment. Without a control group, we couldn't be sure that some other variable, such as the temperature at the time we were running the experiment, the color of the experimenter's hair, or even the mere passage of time, wasn't causing the changes observed.

For example, consider a medical researcher who thinks she has invented a medicine that cures the common cold. To test her claim, she gives the medicine one day to a group of 20 people who have colds and finds that 10 days later all of them are cured.

Eureka? Not so fast. An observer viewing this flawed study might reasonably argue that the people would have gotten better even without the medicine. What the researcher obviously needed was a control group consisting of people with colds who *don't* get the medicine and whose health is also checked 10 days later. Only if there is a significant difference between experimental and control groups can the effectiveness of the medicine be assessed. Through the use of control groups, then, researchers can isolate specific causes for their findings—and draw cause-and-effect inferences.

Independent and Dependent Variables The **independent variable** is the condition that is manipulated by an experimenter. (You can think of the independent variable as being independent of the actions of those taking part in an experiment; it is controlled by the experimenter.) The **dependent variable** is the variable that is measured and is expected to change as a result of changes caused by the experimenter's manipulation of the independent variable. The dependent variable is dependent on the actions of the *participants* or *subjects*—the people taking part in the experiment. *All* true experiments in psychology have both an independent and a dependent variable.

Random Assignment of Participants To make an experiment a valid test of the hypothesis, a final step must be added to the design: properly assigning participants to a particular experimental group.

The significance of this step becomes clear when we examine various alternative procedures. For example, the experimenters might have assigned just males to the experimental group and just females to the control group. If they had done this, however, any differences they found

between the two groups could not be attributed with any certainty solely to the independent variable, because the differences might just as well have been due to gender. A more reasonable procedure would be to ensure that each group had the same composition in terms of gender; then the researchers would be able to make comparisons across groups with considerably more accuracy.

Participants in each of the experimental groups ought to be comparable, and it is easy enough to create groups that are similar in terms of gender. The problem becomes a bit more tricky, though, when we consider other participant characteristics. How can we ensure that participants in each experimental group will be equally intelligent, extroverted, cooperative, and so forth, when the list of characteristics—any one of which could be important—is potentially endless?

In a simple but elegant procedure called **random assignment to condition**, participants are assigned to different experimental groups, or "conditions," on the basis of chance and chance alone. The experimenter might, for instance, flip a coin for each participant and assign a participant to one group when "heads" came up and to the other group when "tails" came up. The advantage of this technique is that there is an equal chance that participant characteristics will be distributed across the various groups. When a researcher uses random assignment—which in practice is usually carried out using computer-generated random numbers—chances are that each of the groups will have approximately the same proportion of intelligent people, cooperative people, extroverted people, males and females, and so on.

All experiments include the following set of key elements, which are important to keep in mind as you consider whether a research study is truly an experiment:

- An independent variable, the variable that is manipulated by the experimenter
- A dependent variable, the variable that is measured by the experimenter and that is expected to change as a result of the manipulation of the independent variable
- A procedure that randomly assigns participants to different experimental groups, or "conditions," of the independent variable
- A hypothesis that predicts the effect that the independent variable will have on the dependent variable

PSYCH think

> > > How might a researcher use naturalistic observation, case studies, and survey research to examine gender differences in aggressive behavior at the workplace? First state a hypothesis, and then describe your research approaches. What positive and negative features does each method have?

Only if each of these elements is present can a research study be considered a true experiment in which cause-and-effect relationships can be determined.

Even when the results of an experiment seem straightforward, the researcher cannot be sure that the results were truly meaningful until he or she determines whether the results represented a **significant outcome**. Using statistical analysis, researchers can determine whether a numeric difference is a real difference or is due merely to chance. Only when differences between groups are large enough that statistical tests show them to be significant is it possible to conclude that the results support the hypothesis (Cohen, 2002; Cwikel, Behar, & Rabson-Hare, 2000).

Moving Beyond the Study Of course, one experiment does not resolve forever the question of cause and effect. Psychologists—like other scientists—require that findings be **replicated**, or repeated, sometimes using other procedures, in other settings, with other groups of participants, before full confidence can be placed in the results of any single experiment. A procedure called *meta-analysis* permits psychologists to combine the results of many separate studies in one overall conclusion (Cooper & Patall, 2009; Tenenbaum & Ruck, 2007).

In addition to replicating experimental results, psychologists need to test the limitations of their theories and

From the perspective of ...

A DOCTOR Tobacco companies have asserted that no experiment has ever proved that tobacco use causes cancer. Can you explain this claim in terms of the research procedures and designs discussed in this module? What sort of research would establish a cause-and-effect relationship between tobacco use and cancer?

hypotheses to determine under which specific circumstances they do and do not apply. It is critical to continue carrying out experiments to understand the conditions in which exceptions occur and those in which the rule holds (Aronson, 1994; Garcia, S. M., et al., 2002).

>> Research Challenges

You probably realize by now that there are few simple formulas for psychological research. Psychologists must make choices about the type of study to conduct, the measures to take, and the most effective way to analyze the results.

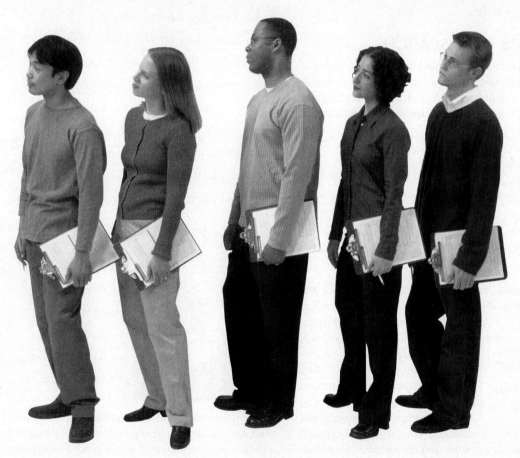

Design of an Experiment to Learn the Effects of the Drug Propanolol on Stress

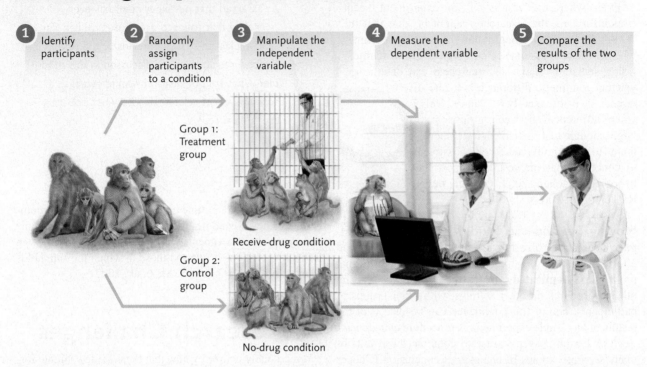

1. Identify participants
2. Randomly assign participants to a condition
3. Manipulate the independent variable
4. Measure the dependent variable
5. Compare the results of the two groups

Group 1: Treatment group

Receive-drug condition

Group 2: Control group

No-drug condition

Even after they have made these essential decisions, they must still consider several critical issues. We turn first to the most fundamental of these issues: ethics.

THE ETHICS OF RESEARCH

Because research has the potential to violate the rights of participants, psychologists are expected to adhere to a strict set of ethical guidelines aimed at protecting participants (APA, 2002). The guidelines involve these safeguards:

- Protection of participants from physical and mental harm
- The right of participants to privacy regarding their behavior
- The assurance that participation in research is completely voluntary
- The necessity of informing participants about the nature of procedures before their participation in the experiment

All experiments, including the minority of studies that involve deception, must be reviewed by an independent panel before being conducted (Fisher et al., 2003; Nagy, 2011; Smith, 2003).

One of psychologists' key ethical principles is **informed consent**. Before participating in an experiment, the participants must sign a document affirming that they have been told the basic outlines of the study and are aware of what their

informed consent A document signed by participants affirming that they have been told the basic outlines of the study and are aware of what their participation will involve.

Do you want to take part in ongoing psychological research? There are hundreds of Web-based studies on everything from "humor in relationships" to "workplace bullying" to "food affecting mood." Hanover College's psych department (http://psych .hanover.edu/research/exponnet .html) maintains a list of participatory online studies conducted by psychological researchers at reputable academic institutions—maybe even yours! Oh, and if you can't get enough— wait a week and go back, because the website is updated very frequently.

get involved!

participation will involve, what risks the experiment may hold, and the fact that their participation is purely voluntary and they may terminate it at any time. Furthermore, after

Research Method	Description	Advantages	Shortcomings
Descriptive and correlational research	Researcher observes a previously existing situation but does not make a change in the situation	Offers insight into relationships between variables	Cannot determine causality
Archival research	Examines existing data to confirm hypothesis	Ease of data collection because data already exist	Dependent on availability of data
Naturalistic observation	Observation of naturally occurring behavior, without making a change in the situation	Provides a sample of people in their natural environment	Cannot control the "natural habitat" being observed
Survey research	A sample is chosen to represent a larger population and asked a series of questions	A small sample can be used to infer attitudes and behavior of a larger population	Sample may not be representative of the larger population; participants may not provide accurate responses to survey questions
Case study	Intensive investigation of an individual or small group	Provides a thorough, in-depth under-standing of participants	Results may not be generalizable beyond the sample
Experimental research	Investigator produces a change in one variable to observe the effects of that change on other variables	Experiments offer the only way to determine cause-and-effect relationship	To be valid, experiments require random assignment of participants to conditions, well-conceptualized inde-pendent and dependent variables, and other careful controls

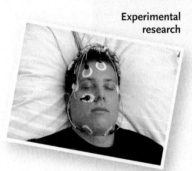
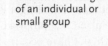

Source: Based on a study by Kaplan & Manuck.

Research Strategies

participation in a study, they must be given a debriefing in which they receive an explanation of the study and the procedures that were involved. The only time informed consent and a debriefing can be eliminated is in experiments in which the risks are minimal, as in a purely observational study in a public place (Barnett et al., 2007; Fallon, 2006; Koocher, Norcross, & Hill, 2005).

SHOULD ANIMALS BE USED IN RESEARCH?

Like those who work with humans, researchers who use non-human animals in experiments have their own set of exacting guidelines to safeguard the animals. Specifically, researchers must make every effort to minimize discomfort, illness, and pain. Procedures that subject animals to distress are permit-ted only when an alternative approach is unavailable and when the research is justified by its prospective value. Along with avoiding causing physical discomfort, researchers are required to promote the *psychological* well-being of some species of research animals, such as primates (Auer et al., 2007; Lutz & Novak, 2005; Rusche, 2003).

But why should animals be used for research in the first place? Is it really possible to learn about human behavior from research on rats, gerbils, and pigeons? The answer is that psychological research that does employ nonhu-mans is designed to answer questions different from those posed in research with humans. For example, the shorter life span of animals (rats live an average of two years) allows researchers to learn about the effects of aging in a relatively short time frame. It is also possible to provide greater exper-imental control over nonhumans and to carry out procedures that might not be possible with people. For example, some studies require large numbers of participants who share similar backgrounds or who have been exposed to particu-lar environments—conditions that could not practically be met with human beings.

Research with animals has provided psychologists with information that has profoundly benefited humans. For instance, it furnished the keys to detecting eye disorders in children early enough to prevent permanent damage, to communicating more effectively with severely retarded children, and to reducing chronic pain in people. Still, the use of research using nonhumans is controversial, involving

PSYCH think

> > > A researcher believes that college professors tend to show female students less attention and respect in the classroom than they show male students. The researcher sets up an experimental study involving observations of classrooms in different conditions. In explaining the study to the professors and students who will participate, what steps should the researcher take to eliminate experimental bias based on both experimenter expectations and participant expectations?

experimental bias Factors that distort how the independent variable affects the dependent variable in an experiment.

placebo A false treatment, such as a pill, "drug," or other substance, without any significant chemical properties or active ingredient.

complex moral and philosophical concerns. Consequently, all research involving nonhumans must be carefully reviewed beforehand to ensure that it is conducted ethically (Hackam, 2007; Herzog, 2005; Plous & Herzog, 2000; Saucier & Cain, 2006; Shankar & Simmons, 2009).

EXPERIMENTAL BIAS

Even the best-laid experimental plans are susceptible to **experimental bias**—factors that distort the way the independent variable affects the dependent variable in an experiment. One of the most common forms of experimental bias is *experimenter expectations*: An experimenter unintentionally transmits cues to participants about the

way they are expected to behave in a given experimental condition. The danger is that those expectations will bring about an "appropriate" behavior—one that otherwise might not have occurred (Rosenthal, 2002, 2003).

A related problem is *participant expectations* about appropriate behavior. People who participate in experiments typically develop their own hypotheses about what the experimenter hopes to learn from the study. If participants form their own hypotheses, they, rather than the experimental manipulation, may produce the effect (Rutherford et al., 2009).

To guard against participant expectations that may bias the results of an experiment, the experimenter may try to disguise the true purpose of the experiment. Participants who do not know that, for instance, helping behavior is being studied in an experiment are more apt to act in a "natural" way than they would if they knew their helping behavior was being examined. For example, suppose we want to know whether experimental participants will help a stranger. If we tell the participants this, they will most likely help the stranger because we told them. To find out if they would help a stranger when no one is watching, we can't tell them what we really want to know until the end of the experiment.

Sometimes it is impossible to hide the actual purpose of research; when that is the case, other techniques are available to prevent bias. Suppose you were interested in testing the ability of a new drug to alleviate the symptoms of severe depression. If you simply gave the drug to half your participants and not to the other half, the participants who were given the drug might report feeling less depressed merely because they knew they were getting a drug. Similarly, the participants who got nothing might report feeling no better because they knew that they were in a no-treatment control group.

To solve this problem, psychologists typically use a procedure in which all the participants receive a treatment, but those in the control group receive only a **placebo**, a false treatment, such as a pill, "drug," or other substance, that

Research involving animals is controversial but, when conducted within ethical guidelines, can yield significant benefits for humans.

has no significant chemical properties or active ingredient. Because members of both groups are kept in the dark about whether they are getting a real or a false treatment, any differences in outcome can be attributed to the quality of the drug and not to the possible psychological effects of being administered a pill or other substance (Crum & Langer, 2007; Rajagopal, 2006; Porto, 2011).

However, there is one more safeguard that a careful researcher must apply in an experiment such as this one. To overcome the possibility that *experimenter* expectations will affect the participant, the person who administers the drug shouldn't know whether it is the true drug or the placebo. By keeping both the participant and the experimenter who interacts with the participant "blind" to the nature of the drug that is being administered, researchers can more accurately assess the effects of the drug. This method is known as the *double-blind procedure.*

Because the field of psychology is based on an accumulated body of research, psychologists must scrutinize the methods, results, and claims of researchers. Several basic questions can help us sort through what is valid and what is not. Among the most important questions to ask are these:

1. *What was the purpose of the research?* Research studies should evolve from a clearly specified theory. Furthermore, we must take into account the specific hypothesis that is being tested. Unless we know what hypothesis is being examined, we cannot judge how successful a study has been.

2. *How well was the study conducted?* Consider who the participants were, how many were involved, what methods were employed, and what problems the researcher encountered in collecting the data. There are important differences, for example, between a case study that reports the anecdotes of a handful of respondents and a survey that collects data from several thousand people.

3. *Are the results presented fairly?* Assess statements on the basis of the actual data they reflect and their logic. For instance, a manufacturer of car X boasts that "no other car has a better safety record than car X." This does not mean that car X is safer than every other car. It just means that no other car has

BUY IT? > > >

Thinking Critically About Research

If you were about to buy a car, it is unlikely that you would stop at the nearest dealership and drive off with the first car a salesperson recommended. Instead, you would probably mull over the purchase, read about different models, consider the alternatives, talk to others about their experiences, and ultimately put in a fair amount of thought before you made such a major purchase.

Many of us are considerably less conscientious when it comes to scientific research. People often jump to conclusions on the basis of incomplete and inaccurate information, and only rarely do they take the time to critically evaluate the research and data to which they are exposed.

been proved safer, although many other cars could be just as safe as car X. Expressed in the latter fashion, the statement doesn't seem worth bragging about.

These three questions can help you assess the validity of research findings—both within and outside the field of psychology. The more you know about how to evaluate research in general, the better you will be able to assess what the field of psychology has to offer.

From the perspective of …

A RESEARCH ANALYST You are hired to study people's attitudes toward health care reform by developing and circulating a questionnaire via the Internet. Is this study likely to accurately reflect the views of the general population? Why or why not?

For REVIEW >>

- **What is the science of psychology?**

  Psychology is the scientific study of behavior and mental processes, encompassing not just what people do but also their biological activities, feelings, perceptions, memory, reasoning, and thoughts. (p. 4)

- **What are the major specialties in the field of psychology?**

  Behavioral neuroscience, cognitive psychology, developmental psychology, personality psychology, health psychology, social psychology and cross-cultural psychology. (pp. 4–6)

- **What are the major perspectives used by psychologists?**

  Neuroscience approach, psychodynamic perspective, behavioral perspective, cognitive approaches, and humanistic perspective. (pp. 11–13)

- **What is the scientific method, and how do psychologists use theory and research to answer questions of interest?**

  The scientific method is the approach psychologists use to understand behavior. It consists of four steps: identifying questions of interest, formulating an explanation, carrying out research that is designed to support or refute the explanation, and communicating the findings. Research in psychology is guided by theories (broad explanations and predictions regarding phenomena of interest) and hypotheses (theory-based predictions stated in a way that allows them to be tested). (pp. 15–17)

- **What research methods do psychologists use?**

  Archival research uses existing records, such as old newspapers or other documents, to test a hypothesis. In naturalistic observation, the investigator acts mainly as an observer, making no change in a naturally occurring situation. In survey research, people are asked a series of questions about their behavior, thoughts, or attitudes. The case study is an in-depth interview and examination of one person or group. (pp. 17–21)

Pop Quiz

1. Match these subfields of psychology with their corresponding issue or question:
   a. behavioral neuroscience
   b. experimental psychology
   c. cognitive psychology
   d. developmental psychology
   e. personality psychology
   f. health psychology
   g. clinical psychology
   h. counseling psychology
   i. educational psychology
   j. school psychology
   k. social psychology
   l. industrial psychology

_____ 1. Joan, a college freshman, is worried about her grades. She needs to learn better organizational skills and study habits to cope with the demands of college.

_____ 2. At what age do children generally begin to acquire an emotional attachment to their fathers?

_____ 3. It is thought that pornographic films that depict violence against women may prompt aggressive behavior in some men.

_____ 4. What chemicals are released in the human body as a result of a stressful event? What are their effects on behavior?

_____ 5. Luis is unique in his manner of responding to crisis situations, with an even temperament and a positive outlook.

_____ 6. The teachers of 8-year-old Jack are concerned that he has recently begun to withdraw socially and to show little interest in schoolwork.

_____ 7. Janetta's job is demanding and stressful. She wonders if her lifestyle is making her more prone to certain illnesses, such as cancer and heart disease.

_____ 8. A psychologist is intrigued by the fact that some people are much more sensitive to painful stimuli than others are.

_____ 9. A strong fear of crowds leads a young woman to seek treatment for her problem.

_____ 10. What mental strategies are involved in solving complex word problems?

_____ 11. What teaching methods most effectively motivate elementary school students to successfully accomplish academic tasks?

_____ 12. Jessica is asked to develop a management strategy that will encourage safer work practices in an assembly plant.

2. The statement "In order to study human behavior, we must consider the whole of perception rather than its component parts" might be made by a person subscribing to which perspective of psychology?

3. Jeanne's therapist asks her to recount a violent dream she recently experienced in order to gain insight into the unconscious forces affecting her behavior. Jeanne's therapist is working from a _____ perspective.

4. "It is behavior that can be observed that should be studied, not the suspected inner workings of the mind." This statement was most likely made by someone with which perspective?

a. cognitive perspective
b. neuroscience perspective
c. humanistic perspective
d. behavioral perspective

5. Match these forms of research to their definition:

a. archival research
b. naturalistic observation
c. survey research
d. case study

_____ 1. directly asking a sample of people questions about their behavior

_____ 2. examining existing records to test a hypothesis

_____ 3. looking at behavior in its true setting without intervening in the setting

_____ 4. doing an in-depth investigation of a person or small group

6. Match each of these research methods with its primary disadvantage:

a. archival research
b. naturalistic observation
c. survey research
d. case study

_____ 1. the researcher may not be able to generalize to the population at large

_____ 2. people's behavior can change if people know they are being watched

_____ 3. the data may not exist or may be unusable

_____ 4. people may lie in order to present a good image

7. A psychologist wants to study the effect of attractiveness on willingness to help a person with a math problem. Attractiveness would be the _____ variable, and the amount of helping would be the _____ variable.

8. Ethical research begins with the concept of informed consent. Before signing up to participate in an experiment, participants should be informed of:

a. the procedure of the study, stated generally
b. the risks that may be involved
c. their right to withdraw at any time
d. all of these

9. The graphs of the data in the online correlation exercise showed:

a. that some variables increase together, but some variables increase as others decrease.
b. how many positive and negative qualities your friends have.
c. that the positive qualities were much stronger than negative ones.
d. that although it is possible to graph correlational data, it is usually very difficult to interpret what the graphs mean.

10. List three benefits of using animals in psychological research.

11. According to a report, a study has shown that men differ from women in their preference for ice cream flavors. This study was based on a sample of two men and three women. What may be wrong with this study?

Answers

TO POP QUIZ QUESTIONS

1. a-4, b-8, c-10, d-2, e-5, f-7, g-9, h-1, i-11, j-6, k-3, l-12
2. gestalt
3. psychodynamic
4. d
5. a-2, b-3, c-1, d-4
6. a-3, b-2, c-4, d-1
7. independent, dependent
8. d
9. a
10. (1) We can study some phenomena in animals more easily than we can in people, because with animal subjects we have greater control over environmental and genetic factors. (2) Large numbers of similar participants can be easily obtained. (3) We can look at generational effects much more easily in animals, because of their shorter life spans, than we can with people.
11. There are far too few participants. Without a larger sample, no valid conclusions can be drawn about ice cream preferences based on gender.

2

NEUROSCIE

BRAIN DIET

Carol Poe, a 60-year-old grandmother from West Virginia, was the second person to receive a new obesity treatment called deep brain stimulation. The procedure involves inserting electrodes into the brain to deliver tiny bursts of electricity to alter the patient's behavior. With obese patients, the idea is to target the hypothalamus, the area of the brain that controls our desire to eat. It works by making the patient feel full.

During the surgery, Carol was asked if she felt hungry or not to help pinpoint the correct position for the electrodes. "I was actually able to experience feelings of hunger and of fullness while the neurosurgeon experimented with the best place to put the electrodes," Carol explained. "Once the electrodes were in the right place, my desire to eat went away. It was amazing going from feeling hungry to feeling full. I'm delighted with what's happened so far. Now I'm hoping to start losing some serious weight."[ii]

Carol Poe had an experience that is difficult even to imagine: She experienced physiological sensations of hunger and fullness that were triggered by direct stimulation of her brain, rather than by the parts of the body where food was being digested.

The ability of surgeons to identify and stimulate such specific areas of the brain is little short of miraculous. The greater miracle, though, is the brain itself. An organ roughly half the size of a loaf of bread, the brain controls our behavior through every waking and sleeping moment. Our movements, thoughts, hopes, aspirations, dreams—our very awareness that we are human—all depend on the brain and the nerves that extend throughout the body, which together make up the nervous system.

NCE AND BEHAVIOR

As You READ >>

- Why do psychologists study the brain and nervous system?
- What are the parts of the nervous system?
- How does the endocrine system affect behavior?
- What are the parts of the brain, and what are their functions?

behavioral neuroscientists (or biopsychologists) Psychologists who specialize in considering the ways in which the biological structures and functions of the body affect behavior.

Because the nervous system plays the leading role in controlling behavior and because humans at their most basic level are biological beings, many researchers in psychology and other fields as diverse as computer science, zoology, and medicine have made the biological underpinnings of behavior their specialty. These experts collectively are called *neuroscientists* (Gazzaniga, Ivry, & Mangun, 2002; Pickersgill, 2011; Posner & DiGiorlamo, 2000).

Psychologists who specialize in considering the ways in which the biological structures and functions of the body affect behavior are known as **behavioral neuroscientists** (or *biopsychologists*). Their research on the brain and other parts of the nervous system enhances our understanding of sensory experiences, states of consciousness, motivation and emotion, development throughout the life span, and physical and psychological health. Moreover, advances in behavioral neuroscience have led to the creation of drugs and other treatments for psychological and physical disorders (Compagni & Manderscheid, 2006; Kosslyn et al., 2002; Plomin, 2003a, b).

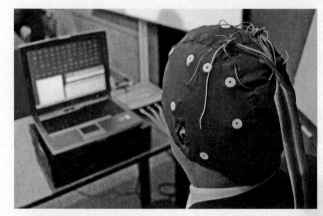

Developing a direct interface between the brain and a computer

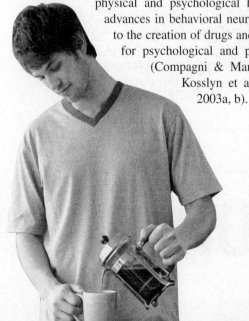

Did you know?

Behavioral neuroscientists have identified an electrical wave the brain makes that can be used to trigger an action in a computer! Can people who are paralyzed use this wave, called the P300, to operate a computer? Researchers are currently working on ways to make this "brain-computer interface" available.

>> Neurons: The Basic Units of the Nervous System

Watching Serena Williams hit a stinging backhand, Dario Vaccaro perform a complex ballet routine, or Derek Jeter swing at a baseball reminds us of the complexity—and wondrous abilities—of the human body. But even the most everyday tasks, such as pouring a cup of coffee or humming a tune, depend on a sophisticated sequence of events in the body. The nervous system is the pathway for the instructions that permit our bodies to carry out such precise activities. Neurons, the cells that make up the nervous system, convey messages throughout the body, enabling us to move, think, experience emotion, and engage in a wide range of other behaviors.

STRUCTURE OF THE NEURON

Imagine that you are driving down the road when suddenly your friend, who is sitting next to you, shouts, "Watch out for that truck!" Immediately you experience strong anxiety, step on the brake, and look around in every direction. This process might seem automatic—but think about it for a moment. How did that information get from your ears into your head and trigger these emotions and behaviors?

Driving a car, playing the piano, or hitting a tennis ball depends on exact muscle coordination. But if we consider *how* the muscles can be activated so precisely, we find that it is up to the brain to communicate and coordinate the complex movements that make up meaningful physical activity.

The brain not only controls movement and other behavior by sending messages to cells throughout the body, but it also receives messages about the body's status on a continuous basis. These messages pass through specialized cells called neurons. **Neurons**, or nerve cells, are the basic units of the nervous system. Their quantity is staggering—perhaps as many as 1 *trillion* neurons are involved in the control of behavior (Boahen, 2005).

Unlike most other cells, neurons have the ability to communicate with other cells and transmit information across relatively long distances. Many of the body's neurons receive signals from our physical surroundings or relay the nervous system's messages to muscles and other cells, but the vast majority of neurons communicate only with other neurons in the elaborate information system that regulates behavior.

Although there are several types of neurons, they all have a similar structure. Like most cells, neurons have a cell body and a nucleus. The nucleus incorporates the hereditary material that determines how a cell functions. Neurons are physically held in place by *glial cells*. Glial cells provide nourishment to neurons, insulate them, help repair damage, and generally support neural functioning (Bassotti et al., 2007; Kettenmann & Ransom, 2005; Yokoyama et al., 2011).

At one end of the neuron's cell body is a cluster of branching fibers called **dendrites** that receive messages from other neurons. On the opposite side of the cell body is a long, slender extension called an **axon**. The axon carries messages received by the dendrites to other neurons. The axon is considerably longer than the rest of the neuron. Although most axons are several millimeters in length, some are as long as 3 feet. Axons end in small bulges called **terminal buttons** that send messages forward to other neurons.

neurons Nerve cells, the basic elements of the nervous system.

dendrite A cluster of fibers at one end of a neuron that receives messages from other neurons.

axon The part of the neuron that carries messages destined for other neurons.

terminal buttons Small bulges at the end of axons that send messages to other neurons.

Dendrites

Cell body

Terminal buttons

Axon (inside myelin sheath)

Movement of electrical impulse

Myelin sheath

Structure of a Neuron

STUDY **TIP**

Remember that *d*endrites *d*etect messages from other neurons; *a*xons carry signals *a*way from the cell body.

Messages travel through a neuron in the form of electrical *impulses*. Generally those impulses move across neurons in one direction only, as if they were traveling on a one-way street. Impulses follow a route that begins with the dendrites, continues into the cell body, and leads ultimately along the axon to adjacent neurons.

To prevent messages from veering off course, most axons are insulated, just as electrical wires must be insulated to prevent current from escaping. The axon insulation, known as a **myelin sheath**, is a protective coating of fat and protein that wraps the axon like a sausage casing. *Myelination,* the process by which neurons become encased in a myelin sheath, begins before birth and continues into young adulthood (Fields, 2008).

HOW NEURONS FIRE

Like a gun, neurons either fire—that is, transmit an electrical impulse along the axon—or don't fire. There is no in-between stage, just as pulling harder on a gun trigger doesn't make the bullet travel faster. Similarly, neurons follow an **all-or-none law**: They are either on or off, with nothing in between the on state and the off state. Once there is enough stimulation, a neuron fires.

Before a neuron fires—that is, when it is in a **resting state**—it has a negative electrical charge of about –70 mil-livolts (a millivolt is one one-thousandth of a volt). When dendrites receive a certain type of message, gates along the cell membrane open briefly to allow positive ions (electrically charged subatomic particles) to rush in at rates as high as 100 million ions per second. The sudden arrival of these positive ions causes the charge within the nearby part of the cell to change momentarily from negative to positive. When the positive charge reaches a critical level, the "trigger" is pulled, and an electrical impulse, known as an action potential, travels along the axon of the neuron.

The **action potential** moves from one end of the axon to the other like a flame traveling along a fuse. As the impulse is transmitted along the axon, the movement of ions causes a change in charge from negative to positive in successive sections of the axon. After the impulse has passed through a particular section of the axon, positive ions are pumped out of that section, and its charge returns to negative while the action potential continues to move along the axon.

Just after an action potential has passed through a section of the axon, the cell membrane in that region cannot admit positive ions again for a fraction of a second, and so a neuron cannot fire again immediately no matter how much stimulation it receives. It is as if the "gun" has to be reloaded after each shot. There then follows a period in which, although it is possible for the neuron to fire, a stronger stimulus is needed than would be needed if the neuron had reached its normal resting state. Eventually, however, the normal resting state is restored, and the neuron is ready to fire once again.

Neurons vary not only in terms of how quickly an impulse moves along the axon but also in their potential rate of firing. Some neurons are capable of firing as many as a thousand times per second; others fire at much slower

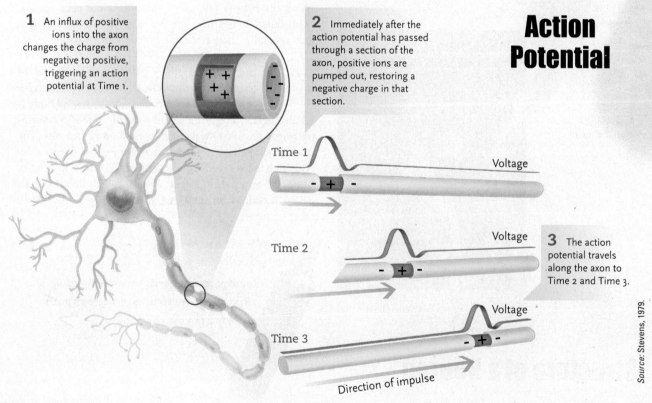

1 An influx of positive ions into the axon changes the charge from negative to positive, triggering an action potential at Time 1.

2 Immediately after the action potential has passed through a section of the axon, positive ions are pumped out, restoring a negative charge in that section.

3 The action potential travels along the axon to Time 2 and Time 3.

Action Potential

Time 1

Time 2

Time 3

Voltage

Direction of impulse

Source: Stevens, 1979.

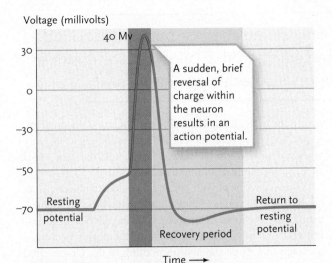

Changes in Electrical Charge in a Neuron During an Action Potential

Voltage (millivolts)

40 Mv

A sudden, brief reversal of charge within the neuron results in an action potential.

Resting potential

Recovery period

Return to resting potential

Time →

rates. The intensity of a stimulus determines how much of a neuron's potential firing rate is reached. A strong stimulus, such as a bright light or a loud sound, leads to a higher rate of firing than a less intense stimulus does. Thus, even though all impulses move at the same strength or speed through a particular axon—because of the all-or-none law—there is variation in the frequency of impulses, providing a mechanism by which we can distinguish the tickle of a feather from the weight of someone standing on our toes.

synapse The space between two neurons where the axon of a sending neuron communicates with the dendrites of a receiving neuron by using chemical messages.

BRIDGING THE GAP BETWEEN NEURONS

If you have ever looked inside a computer, you've seen that each part is physically connected to another part. In contrast, evolution has produced a neural transmission system that at some points has no need for a structural connection between its components. Instead, a chemical connection bridges the gap, known as a synapse, between two neurons. The **synapse** is the space between two neurons where the axon of a sending neuron communicates with the dendrites of a receiving neuron by using chemical messages (Dean & Dresbach, 2006; Fanselow & Poulos, 2005).

How Synapses and Neurotransmitters Work

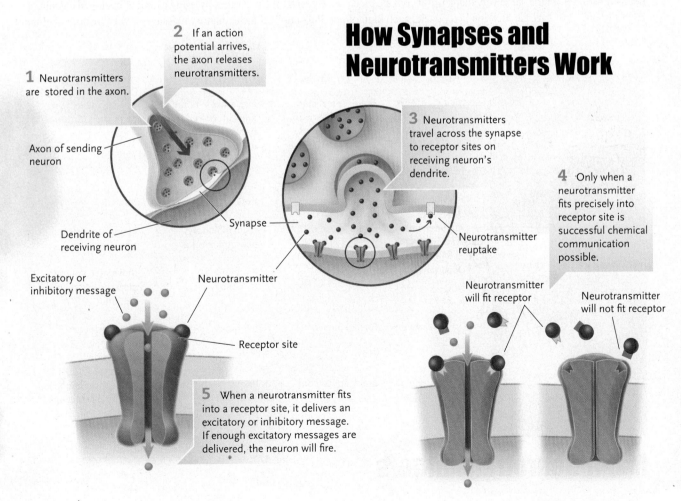

1 Neurotransmitters are stored in the axon.

2 If an action potential arrives, the axon releases neurotransmitters.

3 Neurotransmitters travel across the synapse to receptor sites on receiving neuron's dendrite.

4 Only when a neurotransmitter fits precisely into receptor site is successful chemical communication possible.

Axon of sending neuron

Dendrite of receiving neuron

Synapse

Neurotransmitter reuptake

Excitatory or inhibitory message

Neurotransmitter

Receptor site

Neurotransmitter will fit receptor

Neurotransmitter will not fit receptor

5 When a neurotransmitter fits into a receptor site, it delivers an excitatory or inhibitory message. If enough excitatory messages are delivered, the neuron will fire.

Just as a jigsaw puzzle piece can fit in only one place in a puzzle, each kind of neurotransmitter has a distinctive configuration that allows it to fit into a specific type of receptor site on the receiving neuron.

When a nerve impulse comes to the end of the axon and reaches a *terminal button*, the terminal button releases a chemical courier called a *neurotransmitter*. **Neurotransmitters** are chemicals that carry messages across the synapse to receptor sites on a receiving neuron. Like a boat that ferries passengers across a river, neurotransmitters move across the synapse toward other neurons. The chemical mode of message transmission that occurs between neurons is strikingly different from the means by which communication occurs inside neurons: Although messages are transmitted as electrical impulses *within* a neuron, they are transmitted chemically *between* neurons.

There are several types of neurotransmitters, and not all neurons are capable of receiving the chemical message carried by a particular neurotransmitter. In the same way that a jigsaw puzzle piece can fit in only one specific location in a puzzle, each kind of neurotransmitter has a distinctive configuration that matches a specific type of receptor site on the receiving neuron. Only when a neurotransmitter fits precisely into a receptor site is successful chemical communication possible.

When you look at your email, do you delete the ones that are boring? Do you get some emails that are cool and interesting, so you forward them to your friends? Neurotransmitters are sort of like that. Some of them give neurons a message that gives the neuron nothing to do. Others send a message that encourages the neuron to forward the message to more neurons. When a neurotransmitter matches a receptor site on the receiving neuron, the chemical message it delivers is either excitatory or inhibitory. **Excitatory messages** (cool emails) make it more likely that a receiving neuron will fire and an action potential will travel down its axon and forward the message to other neurons. **Inhibitory messages** (boring emails), in contrast, do just the opposite; they provide chemical information that prevents or decreases the likelihood that the receiving neuron will fire.

Because the dendrites of a neuron receive both excitatory and inhibitory messages simultaneously, the neuron must integrate the messages by using a kind of chemical calculator. Put simply, if the excitatory messages ("fire!") outnumber the

neurotransmitters Chemicals that carry messages across the synapse to the dendrite (and sometimes the cell body) of a receiving neuron.

excitatory message A chemical message that makes it more likely that a receiving neuron will fire and an action potential will travel down its axon.

inhibitory message A chemical message that prevents or decreases the likelihood that a receiving neuron will fire.

Major Neurotransmitters

Name	Location	Effect	Function
Acetylcholine (ACh)	Brain, spinal cord, peripheral nervous system, especially some organs of the parasympathetic nervous system	Excitatory in brain and autonomic nervous system; inhibitory elsewhere	Muscle movement, cognitive functioning
Glutamate	Brain, spinal cord	Excitatory	Memory
Gamma-amino butyric acid (GABA)	Brain, spinal cord	Main inhibitory neurotransmitter	Eating, aggression, sleeping
Dopamine (DA)	Brain	Inhibitory or excitatory	Movement control, pleasure and reward, attention
Serotonin	Brain, spinal cord	Inhibitory	Sleeping, eating, mood, pain, depression
Endorphins	Brain, spinal cord	Primarily inhibitory, except in hippocampus	Pain suppression, pleasurable feelings, appetites, placebos

Dopamine pathways

Serotonin pathways

One important neurotransmitter, *acetylcholine* (or *ACh*, its chemical symbol), is found throughout the nervous system. ACh is involved in our every move, because—among other things—it transmits messages to our skeletal muscles. ACh is also involved in memory capabilities, and diminished production of ACh may be related to Alzheimer's disease (Bazalakova et al., 2007; Mohapel et al., 2005; Van der Zee, Platt, & Riedel, 2011).

> **reuptake** The reabsorption of neurotransmitters by a terminal button.

inhibitory ones ("don't fire!"), the neuron fires. In contrast, if the inhibitory messages outnumber the excitatory ones, nothing happens, and the neuron remains in its resting state (Flavell et al., 2006; Mel, 2002; Rapport, 2005).

Whether a neuron fires or not, the neurotransmitters on its dendrites fall back off into the synapse. At this point, one of three things normally happens. First, some neurotransmitters are broken down by enzymes. Others bind back onto the dendrite and send their message again. Most, however, are reabsorbed back up into the terminal buttons in a process called **reuptake**. This efficient recycling system allows the neuron to repackage the neurotransmitter and use it over and over. The activities involved in reuptake occur at lightning speed, with the process taking just several milliseconds (Helmuth, 2000; Holt & Jahn, 2004).

NEUROTRANSMITTERS: CHEMICAL COURIERS

Neurotransmitters are a particularly important link between the nervous system and behavior. They are vital for normal brain and body functions—so vital, in fact, that a deficiency or an excess of a neurotransmitter can produce severe behavior disorders. More than a hundred chemicals have been found to act as neurotransmitters, and neuroscientists believe that more may ultimately be identified (Penney, 2000; Schmidt, 2006).

The effects of a particular neurotransmitter vary, depending on the area of the nervous system in which it is produced. The same neurotransmitter can act as an excitatory message to a neuron located in one part of the brain and can inhibit firing in neurons located in another part.

Another major neurotransmitter is *dopamine* *(DA)*, which is involved in movement, attention, and learning. The discovery that certain drugs can have a significant effect on dopamine release has led to the development of effective treatments for a wide variety of physical and mental ailments. For instance, Parkinson's disease, a progressive disorder marked by muscle tremors and impaired coordination, is caused by a deficiency of dopamine in the brain. Techniques for increasing the production of dopamine in Parkinson's patients are proving effective (Iversen & Iversen, 2007; Willis, 2005).

*Over*production of dopamine also produces negative consequences. For example, researchers have suggested that schizophrenia and some other severe mental disturbances are affected or perhaps even caused by unusually high levels of dopamine. Drugs that prevent dopamine from binding to dendrites reduce the symptoms displayed by some people diagnosed with schizophrenia (Di Forti, Lappin, & Murray, 2007; Howes & Kapur, 2009; Lyon, 2011; Murray, Lappin, & Di Forti, 2008).

Another neurotransmitter, *serotonin*, is associated with the regulation of sleep, eating, mood, and pain. A grow-

central nervous system (CNS) The part of the nervous system that includes the brain and spinal cord.

spinal cord A bundle of neurons that leaves the brain and runs down the length of the back and is the main means for transmitting messages between the brain and the body.

reflex An automatic, involuntary response to an incoming stimulus.

After being diagnosed with Parkinson's disease, Michael J. Fox became an ardent advocate for research leading to a cure for this disorder of the nervous system.

The runner's high has been attributed to endorphins—neurotransmitters produced in response to stress or pain.

ing body of research suggests that serotonin also plays a role in such diverse behaviors as alcoholism, depression, suicide, impulsivity, aggression, and coping with stress (Carillo et al., 2009; Murphy, Lappin, & Di Forti et al., 2008; Popa et al., 2008).

Endorphins, another class of neurotransmitters, are chemicals produced by the brain that are similar in structure to painkilling drugs such as morphine. The production of endorphins reflects the brain's effort to deal with pain as well as to elevate mood.

Endorphins also may produce the euphoric feelings that runners sometimes experience after long runs. The exertion and perhaps the pain involved in a long run may stimulate the production of endorphins, ultimately resulting in what has been called "runner's high" (Kolata, 2002; Pert, 2002; Stanojevic, Mitic, & Vujic, 2007).

>> The Nervous System: Linking Neurons

In light of the complexity of individual neurons and the neurotransmission process, it should come as no surprise that the connections and the structures formed by the neurons are complicated. Each neuron can communicate with up to 80,000 other neurons, so the total number of possible connections is astonishing. Estimates of the number of neural connections in the brain alone fall in the neighborhood of 10 quadrillion—a 1 followed by 16 zeros—and some experts put the number even higher (Boahen, 2005; Forlenza & Baum, 2004; Kandel, Schwartz, & Jessell, 2000).

Whatever the actual number of neural connections, the human nervous system has both logic and elegance. We turn now to a discussion of its basic structures.

Parts of the Nervous System

The Nervous System

Consists of the brain and the neurons extending throughout the body

Central Nervous System

Consists of the brain and spinal cord

Peripheral Nervous System

Made up of long axons and dendrites, it contains all parts of the nervous system other than the brain and spinal cord

Brain

An organ roughly half the size of a loaf of bread that constantly controls behavior

Spinal Cord

A bundle of nerves that leaves the brain and runs down the length of the back; transmits messages between the brain and the body

Somatic Division (voluntary)

Specializes in the control of voluntary movements and the communication of information to and from the sense organs

Autonomic Division (involuntary)

Concerned with the parts of the body that function involuntarily without our awareness

Sympathetic Division

Acts to prepare the body in stressful emergency situations, mobilizing resources to respond to a threat

Parasympathetic Division

Acts to calm the body after an emergency situation has engaged the sympathetic division; provides a means for the body to maintain storage of energy sources

Did you know?

Do you have a sweet tooth? Some people's brains release endorphins and dopamine when they eat sweets. The release of these neurotransmitters makes them feel good in a way that is similar to the way that taking a drug might feel.

CENTRAL AND PERIPHERAL NERVOUS SYSTEMS

The nervous system consists of the central nervous system and the peripheral nervous system. The **central nervous system (CNS)** includes the brain and the spinal cord. The **spinal cord**, a bundle of neurons about the thickness of a pencil, runs from the brain down the length of the back. The spinal cord is the primary means for transmitting messages between the brain and the rest of the body.

However, the spinal cord is not just a communication channel. It also controls some simple behaviors on its own, without any help from the brain. An example is the way the knee jerks forward when it is tapped with a rubber hammer. This behavior is a type of **reflex**, an automatic, involuntary response to an incoming stimulus. A reflex is also at work when you touch a hot stove and immediately

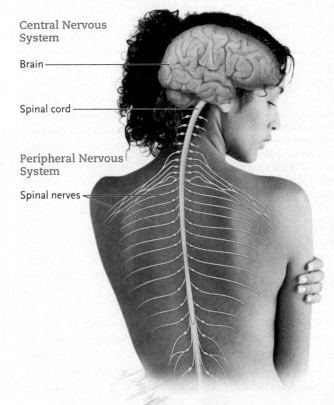

Central Nervous System

Brain

Spinal cord

Peripheral Nervous System

Spinal nerves

withdraw your hand. Although the brain eventually analyzes and reacts to the situation ("Ouch—hot stove—pull away!"), the initial withdrawal is directed only by neurons in the spinal cord.

Three kinds of neurons are involved in reflexes. **Sensory (afferent) neurons** transmit information from the perimeter of the body to the central nervous system. **Motor (efferent) neurons** communicate information from the nervous system to muscles and glands. **Interneurons** connect sensory and motor neurons, carrying messages between the two.

As suggested by its name, the **peripheral nervous system** branches out from the spinal cord and brain and reaches the extremities of the body. Made up of neurons with long axons and dendrites, the peripheral nervous system encompasses all the parts of the nervous system other than the brain and the spinal cord. There are two major divisions—the somatic division and the autonomic division—both of which connect the central nervous system with the sense organs, muscles, glands, and other organs. The **somatic division** specializes in the control of voluntary movements—such as the motion of the eyes to read this sentence or those of the hand to turn this page—and the communication of information to and from the sense organs. In contrast, the **autonomic division** controls the parts of the body that keep us alive—heart, blood vessels, glands, lungs, and other organs that function involuntarily without our awareness. At this moment, the autonomic division of the peripheral nervous system is pumping blood through your body, pushing your lungs in and out, and overseeing the digestion of your last meal.

The autonomic division plays a particularly crucial role during emergencies. Suppose that as you are reading you suddenly sense that a stranger is watching you through the window. As you look up, you see the glint of something that might be a knife. As confusion clouds your mind and fear overcomes your attempts to think rationally, what happens to your body? If you are like most people, you react immediately on a physiological level. Your heart

Glossary

sensory (afferent) neurons Neurons that transmit information from the perimeter of the body to the central nervous system.

motor (efferent) neurons Neurons that communicate information from the nervous system to muscles and glands.

interneurons Neurons that connect sensory and motor neurons, carrying messages between the two.

peripheral nervous system The part of the nervous system that includes the autonomic and somatic subdivisions; made up of neurons with long axons and dendrites, it branches out from the spinal cord and brain and reaches the extremities of the body.

somatic division The part of the peripheral nervous system that specializes in the control of voluntary movements and the communication of information to and from the sense organs.

autonomic division The part of the peripheral nervous system that controls involuntary movement of the heart, glands, lungs, and other organs.

sympathetic division The part of the autonomic division of the nervous system that acts to prepare the body for action in stressful situations, engaging all the organism's resources to respond to a threat.

parasympathetic division The part of the autonomic division of the nervous system that acts to calm the body after an emergency has ended.

get involved!

How fast is your reaction time? Find out! You can test it at http://www.human benchmark.com/tests/reactiontime/index .php and compare your score to others who have visited the site. Two areas of the nervous system that you will use are the brain, where you perceive the stimulus and decide how to respond, and the somatic nervous system, which carries the message to your hand.

rate increases, you begin to sweat, and you develop goose bumps all over your body.

The physiological changes that occur during a crisis result from the activation of one of the two parts of the autonomic nervous system: the **sympathetic division**. The sympathetic division acts to prepare the body for action in stressful situations by engaging all of the organism's resources to run away or to confront the threat. This response is often called the "fight or flight" response.

In contrast, the **parasympathetic division** acts to calm the body after the emergency has ended. When you find, for instance, that the stranger at the window is actually your roommate, who has lost his keys and is climbing in the window to avoid waking you, your parasympathetic division begins to predominate, lowering your heart rate, stopping

> At this moment, the autonomic division of the peripheral nervous system is pumping blood through your body, pushing your lungs in and out, and overseeing the digestion of your last meal.

PSYCH think

> > > How do the parasympathetic and sympathetic nervous systems work together to help you after you have eaten a big meal?

Major Functions of the Autonomic Nervous System

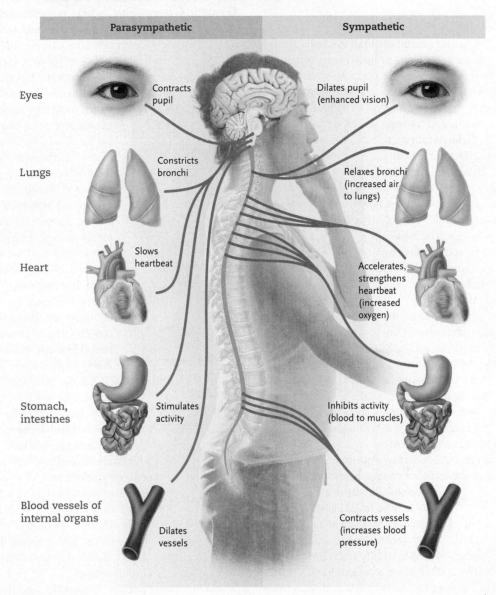

Parasympathetic	Sympathetic

Eyes — Contracts pupil / Dilates pupil (enhanced vision)

Lungs — Constricts bronchi / Relaxes bronchi (increased air to lungs)

Heart — Slows heartbeat / Accelerates, strengthens heartbeat (increased oxygen)

Stomach, intestines — Stimulates activity / Inhibits activity (blood to muscles)

Blood vessels of internal organs — Dilates vessels / Contracts vessels (increases blood pressure)

your sweating, and returning your body to the state it was in before you became alarmed. The parasympathetic division also directs the body to store energy for use in emergencies.

The sympathetic and parasympathetic divisions work together to regulate many functions of the body. For instance, sexual arousal is controlled by the parasympathetic division, but sexual orgasm is a function of the sympathetic division.

EVOLUTION OF THE NERVOUS SYSTEM

The complexities of the nervous system can be better understood if we take the course of evolution into consideration. Why should we care about the evolutionary background of the human nervous system? The answer comes from researchers working in the area of **evolutionary psychology**, the branch of psychology that seeks to identify how behavior is influenced and produced by the genetic inheritance from our ancestors.

Evolutionary psychologists argue that the course of evolution is reflected in the structure and functioning of the nervous system and that evolutionary factors consequently have a significant influence on our everyday behavior. Their work, in conjunction with the research of scientists studying genetics, biochemistry, and medicine, has led to an understanding of how our behavior is affected by heredity,

> **evolutionary psychology** The branch of psychology that seeks to identify behavior patterns that are a result of our genetic inheritance from our ancestors.

our genetically determined heritage. In fact, evolutionary psychologists have spawned a new and increasingly influential field: behavioral genetics.

BEHAVIORAL GENETICS

Our evolutionary heritage manifests itself not only through the structure and the functioning of the nervous system but also through our behavior. In the view of a growing area of study, people's personality and behavioral habits are affected in part by their genetic heritage. **Behavioral genetics** studies the effects of heredity on behavior. Behavioral genetics researchers are finding increasing evidence that cognitive abilities, personality traits, sexual orientation, and psychological disorders are determined to some extent by genetic factors (Kremen, W. S., & Lyons, 2011; Livesley & Jang, 2008; Vernon et al., 2008).

Behavioral genetics lies at the heart of the nature-nurture question, one of the key issues in the study of psychology. Although no one would argue that our behavior is determined *solely* by inherited factors, evidence collected by behavioral geneticists does suggest that our genetic inheritance predisposes us to respond in particular ways to our environment, and even to seek out particular kinds of environments. For instance, research indicates that genetic factors may be related to such diverse behaviors as level of family conflict, schizophrenia, learning disabilities, and general sociability (Ball et al., 2008; Davis, Haworth, & Plomin, 2009; Lakhan & Vieira, 2009).

Like father, like daughter. Laila Ali, daughter of the legendary boxer, Muhammed Ali, became a well-known fighter in her own right. Behavioral geneticists would be interested in the hereditary factors that might have contributed to her success as a boxer.

behavioral genetics The study of the effects of heredity on behavior.

Furthermore, important human characteristics and behaviors are related to the presence (or absence) of particular *genes*, the inherited material that controls the transmission of traits. For example, researchers have found evidence that novelty-seeking behavior is determined, at least in part, by a certain gene (Golimbet et al., 2007; Stedenfeld, 2011).

As we will consider later in the book when we discuss human development, researchers have identified some 25,000 individual genes, each of which appears in a specific sequence on a particular *chromosome,* a rod-shaped structure that transmits genetic information across generations. In 2003, after a decade of effort, researchers identified the sequence of the 3 billion chemical pairs that make up human *DNA,* the basic component of genes. Understanding the basic structure of the human *genome*—the "map" of humans' total genetic makeup—brings scientists a giant step closer to understanding the contributions of individual genes to specific human structures and functioning (Andreasen, 2005; Dale & vonSchantz, 2007; Plomin & Davis, 2009).

Behavioral Genetics, Gene Therapy, and Genetic Counseling Behavioral genetics also holds the promise of developing new diagnostic and treatment techniques for genetic deficiencies that can lead to physical and psychological difficulties. In *gene therapy*, scientists inject into a patient's bloodstream genes meant to cure a particular disease. When the genes arrive at the site of defective genes that are producing the illness, they trigger the production of chemicals that can treat the disease (Eberling et al., 2008; Isacson & Kordower, 2008; Jaffé, Prasad, & Larcher, 2006).

The number of diseases that can be treated through gene therapy is growing, as we will see when we discuss human development. For example, gene therapy is now being used in experimental trials involving people with certain forms of cancer and blindness (Hirschler, 2007; Nakamura, 2004; Wagner et al., 2004).

Advances in behavioral genetics also have led to the development of a profession that did not exist several decades ago: genetic counseling. Genetic counselors help people deal with issues related to inherited disorders. For example, genetic counselors provide advice to prospective parents about the potential risks in a future pregnancy, based on their family history of birth defects and hereditary illnesses. In addition, the counselor considers the parents' age and problems with children they already have. They also can take blood, skin, and urine samples to examine specific chromosomes.

Scientists have already developed genetic tests to determine whether someone is susceptible to certain types of cancer or heart disease, and it may not be long before analysis of a drop of blood can indicate whether a child—or

Did you know?

Genetic tests can reveal more than susceptibility to disease. Recently, researchers have located an "athletic gene." A genetic test can reveal whether a person is better suited for endurance sports or power sports. Do you think it would a good thing or a bad thing to learn about genetic predispositions for various traits and abilities?

A GENETIC COUNSELOR A young couple wants to know the odds of having a baby with an inherited problem. How would you explain to them the potential benefits and dangers of using genetic information to decide whether to have a baby?

potentially an unborn fetus—is susceptible to certain psychological disorders.

How such knowledge will be used is a source of considerable speculation and controversy, controversy that is certain to grow as genetic testing becomes more common (Etchegary, 2004; Malpas, 2008).

>> The Endocrine System: Hormones and Glands

Another of the body's communication systems, the **endocrine system** is a chemical communication network that sends messages throughout the body via the bloodstream. Its job is to secrete **hormones**, chemicals that circulate through the blood and regulate the functioning and growth of the body. The endocrine system also influences—and is influenced by—the functioning of the nervous system. Although the endocrine system is not part of the brain, it is closely linked to the hypothalamus.

As chemical messengers, hormones are like neurotransmitters, although their speed and mode of transmission are quite different. Whereas neural messages are transmitted in thousandths of a second, hormonal communications may take minutes to reach their destination. Furthermore, neural messages move through neurons in specific lines (like a signal carried by wires strung along telephone poles), whereas hormones travel throughout the body, in a manner similar to the way radio waves are transmitted across the entire landscape. Just as radio waves evoke a response only when a radio is tuned to the correct station, hormones flowing through the bloodstream activate only those cells that are receptive and "tuned" to the appropriate hormonal message.

A key component of the endocrine system is the tiny **pituitary gland**, which is found near—and regulated by—the hypothalamus. The pituitary gland has been called the "master gland," because it controls the functioning of the rest of the endocrine system. But the pituitary gland has important functions in its own right. For instance, hormones secreted by the pituitary gland control growth. Extremely short people and unusually tall ones usually have pituitary gland abnormalities. Other endocrine glands affect emotional reactions, sexual urges, and energy levels.

>> The Brain

It is not much to look at. Soft, spongy, mottled, and pinkish-gray in color, weighing about 3 pounds, it hardly can be said to possess much in the way of physical beauty. Despite its physical appearance, however, it ranks as the greatest natural marvel that we know and has a beauty and sophistication all its own. This is the brain.

The brain is responsible for our loftiest thoughts—and our most primitive urges—as well as overseeing the intricate workings of the human body. It would be nearly impossible to design a computer to perform the full range of the brain's capabilities. In fact, it has proved difficult even to come close. The sheer quantity of nerve cells in the brain—numbering in the billions in the average adult—is enough to discourage even the most ambitious computer engineer. Even more astounding than the number of neurons in the brain is the brain's ability to orchestrate complex interconnections among neurons, guiding behavior and giving rise to thoughts, hopes, dreams, and emotions.

> **endocrine system** A chemical communication network that sends messages through the bloodstream to all parts of the body.
>
> **hormone** Substance produced by a gland or tissue and circulated through the blood to regulate the functioning or growth of the body.
>
> **pituitary gland** The major component of the endocrine system, or "master gland," which secretes hormones that control growth and other parts of the endocrine system.

We turn now to a consideration of the particular structures of the brain and the primary functions to which they are related. However, a caution is in order. Although we'll discuss specific areas of the brain in relation to specific behaviors, this approach is an oversimplification. No straightforward one-to-one correspondence exists between a distinct part of the brain and a particular behavior.

SPYING ON THE BRAIN

Do you think you are affectionate? Do you have a special poetic ability? Do you have a heightened sense of color? Are you particularly witty? In the 19th century, you could go see your local phrenologist to gain insight into your personality and other psychological attributes. During your office visit, the phrenologist would feel the bumps on your head to assess your psychological strengths and weaknesses. Phrenologists believed that the shape of your skull was related to the shape of your brain, and the size of various areas of the brain indicated the presence (or

Did you know?

You may improve your brain function by exercising regularly and taking classes such as introductory psychology!

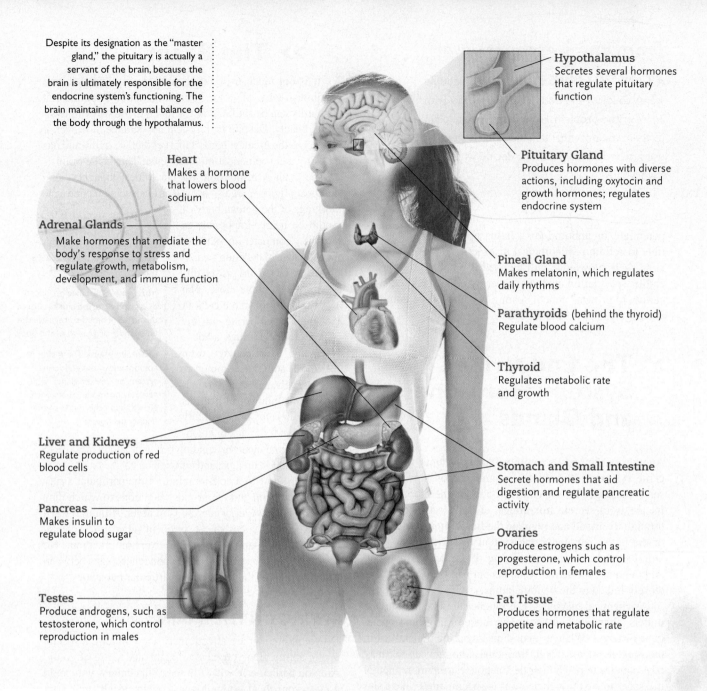

Despite its designation as the "master gland," the pituitary is actually a servant of the brain, because the brain is ultimately responsible for the endocrine system's functioning. The brain maintains the internal balance of the body through the hypothalamus.

Hypothalamus
Secretes several hormones that regulate pituitary function

Pituitary Gland
Produces hormones with diverse actions, including oxytocin and growth hormones; regulates endocrine system

Pineal Gland
Makes melatonin, which regulates daily rhythms

Parathyroids (behind the thyroid)
Regulate blood calcium

Thyroid
Regulates metabolic rate and growth

Stomach and Small Intestine
Secrete hormones that aid digestion and regulate pancreatic activity

Ovaries
Produce estrogens such as progesterone, which control reproduction in females

Fat Tissue
Produces hormones that regulate appetite and metabolic rate

Heart
Makes a hormone that lowers blood sodium

Adrenal Glands
Make hormones that mediate the body's response to stress and regulate growth, metabolism, development, and immune function

Liver and Kidneys
Regulate production of red blood cells

Pancreas
Makes insulin to regulate blood sugar

Testes
Produce androgens, such as testosterone, which control reproduction in males

Major Endocrine Glands

absence) of a variety of moral and intellectual facilities. In other words, bigger bumps meant "more" of a particular trait or behavior.

Although phrenology is no longer considered valid in any way, it shows a desire to link parts of the brain with specific behaviors at a time when the only way to look inside the brain was to cut it open, generally after an individual had died. Although informative, this procedure could hardly tell us much about the functioning of the healthy brain.

Today, brain-scanning techniques provide a window into the living brain. Using these techniques, researchers can take a "snapshot" of the internal workings of the brain without having to open a person's skull. For psychologists, the most important scanning techniques are the electroencephalogram (EEG), positron emission tomography (PET), functional magnetic resonance imaging (fMRI), and transcranial magnetic stimulation imaging (TMS).

One of the oldest imaging techniques, the *electroencephalogram (EEG)*, records electrical activity in the brain through electrodes placed on the head. Although traditionally the EEG produced only a graph of electrical wave patterns, new techniques are now used to transform the

Brain Scanning Techniques

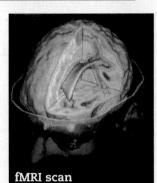

EEG

fMRI scan

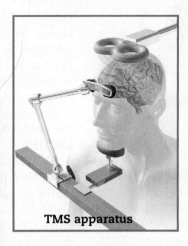

TMS apparatus

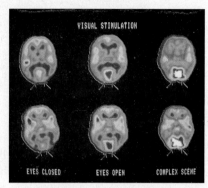

PET scan

brain's electrical activity into a pictorial representation of the brain that allows more precise diagnosis of such disorders as epilepsy and learning disabilities.

Functional magnetic resonance imaging (fMRI) scans provide detailed, three-dimensional computer-generated images of brain structures and activity by aiming a powerful magnetic field at the body. With fMRI, it is possible to produce vivid, detailed images of the functioning of the brain.

Using fMRI scans, researchers can see features of less than a millimeter in size and view changes occurring at intervals of one-tenth of a second. For example, fMRI scans can show the operation of individual bundles of nerves by tracing the flow of blood, opening the way for improved diagnosis of ailments ranging from chronic back pain to certain nervous system disorders, such as stroke, multiple sclerosis, and Alzheimer's. Scans using fMRI are routinely used in planning brain surgery, because they can help surgeons distinguish areas of the brain involved in normal and disturbed functioning (D'Arcy, Bolster, & Ryner, 2007; Mazard et al., 2005; Quenot et al., 2005).

Positron emission tomography (PET) scans show biochemical activity within the brain at a given moment. PET scans begin with the injection of a radioactive (but safe) liquid into the bloodstream, which carries it to the brain. By locating radiation within the brain, a computer can pinpoint the more active regions, providing a striking picture of the brain at work. One application of this technique is to search for brain tumors in people with memory problems (Gronholm et al., 2005; McMurtray et al., 2007).

Transcranial magnetic stimulation (TMS) is one of the newest brain-scanning techniques. By exposing a tiny region of the brain to a strong magnetic field, TMS briefly disrupts electrical activity. Researchers then are able to note the effects of this interruption on normal brain functioning. This procedure is sometimes called a "virtual

lesion," because it produces effects similar to what would occur if areas of the brain were physically cut. The enormous advantage of TMS, of course, is that the virtual cut is only temporary. In addition to identifying areas of the brain that are responsible for particular functions, TMS has been found to be useful in the treatment of certain kinds of psychological disorders, such as depression and schizophrenia (Fitzgerald & Daskalakis, 2008; Pallanti & Bernardi, 2009; Rado, Dowd, & Janicak, 2008).

Future discoveries may yield even more sophisticated methods of examining the brain. For example, the emerging field of optogenetics involves genetic engineering and the use of special types of light to view individual circuits of neurons (Gradinaru et al., 2009; Miesenbock, 2008).

THE CENTRAL CORE: OUR "OLD BRAIN"

Although the capabilities of the human brain far exceed those of the brain of any other species, humans share some basic functions, such as breathing, eating, and sleeping, with more primitive animals. Not surprisingly, those activities are directed by a relatively primitive part of the brain. A portion of the brain known as the **central core** is quite similar in all vertebrates (species with backbones). The central core is sometimes referred to as the "old brain," because its evolution can be traced back some 500 million years to primitive structures found in nonhuman species.

> **central core** The "old brain," which controls basic functions such as eating and sleeping and is common to all vertebrates.

Situated atop the spinal cord at the base of the skull, the central core of the brain houses the hindbrain, the cerebellum, the reticular formation, the thalamus, and the hypothalamus. The *hindbrain* contains the medulla, the pons,

Cerebral cortex
(the "new brain")

Central core
(the "old brain")

Source: Seeley, Stephens, & Tate, 2000.

cerebellum (*ser uh BELL um*) The part of the brain that controls bodily balance.

reticular formation The part of the brain extending from the medulla through the pons and made up of groups of nerve cells that can immediately activate other parts of the brain to produce general bodily arousal.

thalamus The part of the brain located in the middle of the central core that acts primarily to relay information about the senses.

The **cerebellum** is found just above the medulla and behind the pons. Without the cerebellum, we would be unable to walk a straight line without staggering and lurching forward, because it is the job of the cerebellum to control balance. It constantly monitors feedback from the muscles to coordinate their placement, movement, and tension. Drinking too much alcohol seems to depress the activity of the cerebellum, leading to the unsteady gait and movement characteristic of drunkenness. The cerebellum is also involved in several intellectual functions, ranging from the analysis and coordination of sensory information to problem solving (Bower & Parsons, 2003; Paquier & Mariën, 2005; Tian et al., 2011; Vandervert, Schimpf, & Liu, 2007).

The **reticular formation** extends from the medulla through the pons, passing through the middle section of the brain—or *midbrain*—and into the front-most part of the brain, called the forebrain. Like an ever-vigilant guard, the reticular formation can activate other parts of the brain instantly to produce general bodily arousal. If we are startled by a loud noise, for example, the reticular formation can trigger a heightened state of awareness to determine whether a response is necessary. The reticular formation serves a different function when we are sleeping, seeming to filter out background stimuli to allow us to slumber undisturbed.

and the cerebellum. The *medulla* controls a number of critical body functions, the most important of which are breathing and heartbeat. The *pons* lies above the medulla, joining the two halves of the cerebellum. Made up of large bundles of nerves, the pons acts as a transmitter of motor information, coordinating muscles and integrating movement between the right and the left halves of the body. It also plays a role in regulating sleep.

Hidden within the forebrain, the **thalamus** acts primarily as a relay station for information about the senses. Mes-

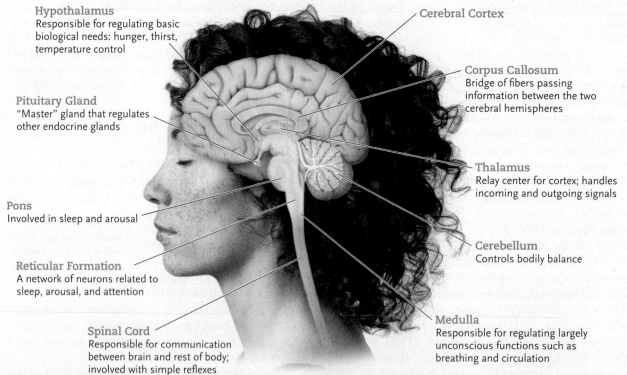

Hypothalamus
Responsible for regulating basic biological needs: hunger, thirst, temperature control

Pituitary Gland
"Master" gland that regulates other endocrine glands

Pons
Involved in sleep and arousal

Reticular Formation
A network of neurons related to sleep, arousal, and attention

Spinal Cord
Responsible for communication between brain and rest of body; involved with simple reflexes

Cerebral Cortex

Corpus Callosum
Bridge of fibers passing information between the two cerebral hemispheres

Thalamus
Relay center for cortex; handles incoming and outgoing signals

Cerebellum
Controls bodily balance

Medulla
Responsible for regulating largely unconscious functions such as breathing and circulation

Johnson & Emmel, 2000.

Major Structures in the Brain

sages from the eyes, the ears, and the skin travel to the thalamus to be relayed to higher parts of the brain. The thalamus also integrates information from higher parts of the brain, sorting it out before sending it on to the cerebellum and medulla.

The **hypothalamus** is located just below the thalamus. Although tiny—about the size of a fingertip—the hypothalamus plays an extremely important role. One of its major functions is to maintain a steady internal environment for the body. The hypothalamus helps keep the body's temperature constant and monitors the amount of nutrients stored in the cells. Equally important, the hypothalamus produces and regulates behavior that is critical to the survival of the species, such as eating, self-protection, and sex.

THE LIMBIC SYSTEM: BEYOND THE CENTRAL CORE

The **limbic system** consists of a series of doughnut-shaped structures that include the *amygdala* and the *hippocampus.* It borders the top of the central core and has connections with the cerebral cortex.

Like the hypothalamus, the limbic system controls a variety of functions relating to emotions and self-preservation, such as eating, aggression, and reproduction. Injury to the limbic system can produce striking changes in behavior. For example, injury to the amygdala, which is involved in fear and aggression, can turn animals that are usually docile and tame into belligerent savages. Conversely, animals that are usually wild and uncontrollable may become meek and obedient following injury to the amygdala (Bedard & Persinger, 1995; Gontkovsky, 2005).

Research examining the effects of mild electric shocks to limbic system structures and other parts of the brain has produced some thought-provoking findings. In one experiment, rats that pressed a bar received mild electric stimulation through an electrode implanted in their brains, which produced pleasurable feelings. Even starving rats on their way to food would stop to press the bar as many times as

they could. Some rats would actually stimulate themselves literally thousands of times an hour—until they collapsed with fatigue (Fountas & Smith, 2007; Olds & Fobes, 1981; Routtenberg & Lindy, 1965).

The extraordinarily pleasurable quality of certain kinds of stimulation has also been experienced by humans who received electrical stimulation to the limbic system as part of their treatment for brain disorders. Although at a loss to describe just what it feels like, these people report the experience to be intensely pleasurable and similar in some respects to sexual orgasm.

The limbic system generally and the hippocampus in particular play an important role in learning and memory, a finding demonstrated in individuals with epilepsy. In an attempt to stop their seizures, surgeons have occasionally removed portions of the limbic system from epileptic patients. One unintended consequence of the surgery is that the patients sometimes have difficulty learning and remembering new information. In one case, a patient who had undergone surgery was unable to remember where he lived, although he had resided at the same address for eight years. Further, even though the patient was able to carry on animated conversations, he was unable, a few minutes later, to recall what had been discussed (Milner, 1966; Rich & Shapiro, 2007).

Functions performed by the limbic system, including self-preservation, learning, memory, and the experience of pleasure, are hardly unique to humans. In fact, the limbic system is sometimes referred to as the "animal brain," because its structures and functions are so similar to those of other mammals. The part of the brain that provides the complex and subtle capabilities that are distinctly human is the cerebral cortex.

hypothalamus A tiny part of the brain, located below the thalamus, that maintains the body's internal balance and regulates such vital behavior as eating, drinking, and sexual behavior.

limbic system The part of the brain that controls eating, aggression, and reproduction.

cerebral cortex The "new brain," responsible for the most sophisticated information processing in the brain; contains four lobes.

THE CEREBRAL CORTEX: OUR "NEW BRAIN"

Although the central core, or "old brain," and the limbic system, or "animal brain," provide essential functions, the structure responsible for the uniquely human ability to think, evaluate, and make complex judgments—indeed, the very capabilities that allow you to read this sentence—resides in the **cerebral cortex**.

The cerebral cortex is referred to as the "new brain" because of its relatively recent evolution. It consists of a mass of deeply folded, rippled, convoluted tissue. Although only about 1/12 of an inch thick, the cortex, if flattened out, would cover an area more than 2 feet square. The folded configuration allows the surface area of the cortex to be considerably greater than it would be if it were smooth and solid. The uneven shape also permits a high level of integration of neurons, allowing sophisticated information processing.

The Limbic System

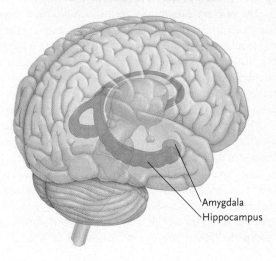

Amygdala
Hippocampus

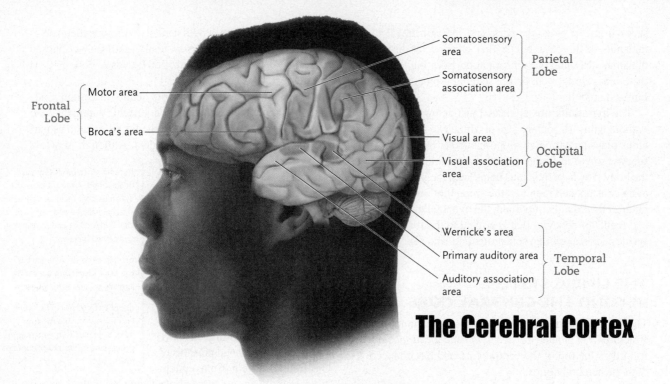

Somatosensory area
Somatosensory association area
Parietal Lobe

Motor area
Frontal Lobe
Broca's area

Visual area
Visual association area
Occipital Lobe

Wernicke's area
Primary auditory area
Auditory association area
Temporal Lobe

The Cerebral Cortex

lobes The four major sections of the cerebral cortex: frontal, parietal, temporal, and occipital.

motor area The part of the cortex that is largely responsible for the body's voluntary movement.

sensory area The brain tissue that corresponds to the different senses, with the degree of sensitivity related to the amount of tissue.

The cortex has four major sections called **lobes**. If we take a side view of the brain, the *frontal lobes* lie at the front center of the cortex, and the *parietal lobes* lie behind them. The *temporal lobes* occupy the lower center portion of the cortex, with the *occipital lobes* behind them. These four sets of lobes are physically separated by deep grooves called *sulci*.

Another way to describe the brain is in terms of the functions associated with a particular area. Three major functional areas are known: the motor area, the sensory area, and the association area. Although we will discuss these areas as though they were separate and independent, remember that behavior is influenced simultaneously by several structures and areas within the brain, operating interdependently.

Every portion of the motor area corresponds to a specific part of the body.

The Motor Area of the Cortex What part of your brain causes your hand to go up when you want to speak in class? The **motor area** of the cortex is largely responsible for voluntary body movements. Every portion of the motor area corresponds to a specific locale within the body. If we were to insert an electrode into a particular part of the motor area of the cortex and apply mild electrical stimulation, there would be involuntary movement in the corresponding part

of the body. If we moved to another part of the motor area and stimulated it, a different part of the body would move.

The motor area is so well mapped that researchers have identified the amount and relative location of brain tissue used to produce movement in specific parts of the human body. For example, the control of movements that are relatively large scale and require little precision, such as the movement of a knee or a hip, is centered in a very small space in the motor area. In contrast, movements that must be precise and delicate, such as facial expressions and finger movements, are controlled by a considerably larger portion of the motor area (Schwenkreis et al., 2007).

The Sensory Area of the Cortex How does your brain know when your nose itches? Sensory neurons in your nose send a message to a region of the brain known as the sensory area for processing. Given the one-to-one correspondence between the motor area and body location, it is not surprising to find a similar relationship between a specific portion of the cortex and the senses.

The **sensory area** of the cortex includes three regions: one that corresponds primarily to body sensations (including touch), one relating to sight, and one relating to sound. For instance, the *somatosensory area* processes sensations of touch and pressure on the skin. As with the motor area, the greater the amount of brain tissue devoted to a specific area of the body, the more sensitive that area of the body.

The senses of sound and sight are also represented in specific areas of the cerebral cortex. An *auditory area* located in the temporal lobe is responsible for hearing. If the auditory area is stimulated electrically, a person will report hearing sounds such as clicks or hums. It also appears that particular locations within the auditory area respond to specific pitches (Bizley et al., 2009; Brown & Martinez, 2007; Hudspeth, 2000; Hyde, Peretz, & Zatorre, 2008).

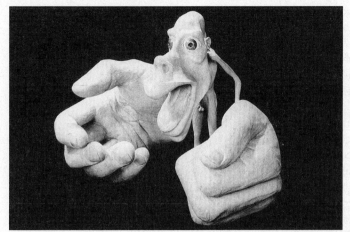

Somatosensory Area

The greater the amount of tissue in the somatosensory area of the brain that is related to a specific body part, the more sensitive is that body part. If the size of our body parts reflected the corresponding amount of brain tissue, we would look like this strange creature.

The *visual area* in the cortex, located in the occipital lobe, responds in a similar way to electrical stimulation. Stimulation by electrodes produces the experience of flashes of light or colors, suggesting that the raw sensory input from the eyes is received in this area of the brain and transformed into meaningful images (Stenbacka & Vanni, 2007; Wurtz & Kandel, 2000).

The Association Areas of the Cortex In a freak accident in 1848, an explosion drove a 3-foot-long iron bar completely through the skull of railroad worker Phineas Gage, where it remained after the accident. Amazingly, Gage survived, and, despite the rod lodged through his head, a few minutes later he seemed to be fine. But he wasn't. Before the accident, Gage was hard-working and cautious. Afterward, he became irresponsible, drank heavily, and drifted from one wild scheme to another. In the words of one of his physicians, "he was 'no longer Gage'" (Della Sala, 2011; Harlow, 1869, p. 14).

What had happened to the old Gage? Although there is no way of knowing for sure, we can speculate that the accident may have damaged the region of Gage's cerebral cortex known as the **association areas**, which generally are considered to be the site of higher mental processes such as thinking, language, memory, and speech (Rowe et al., 2000).

The association areas make up a large portion of the cerebral cortex and consist of the sections that are not directly involved in either sensory processing or directing movement. The association areas control *executive functions,* abilities that relate to planning, goal setting, judgment, and impulse control.

> **association areas** Major regions of the cerebral cortex; sites of higher mental processes, such as thought, language, memory, and speech.

Much of our understanding of the association areas comes from individuals who, like Phineas Gage, have suffered some type of brain injury. These people undergo personality changes that affect their ability to make moral judgments and process emotions, and yet they can still be capable of reasoning logically, performing calculations, and recalling information (Damasio et al., 1994).

Before the accident, Gage was hard-working and cautious. Afterward, he became irresponsible, drank heavily, and drifted from one wild scheme to another.

THE ADAPTABLE BRAIN

Shortly after he was born, Jacob Stark's arms and legs started jerking every 20 minutes. Weeks later he could not focus his eyes on his mother's face. The diagnosis: uncontrollable epileptic seizures involving his entire brain.

His mother, Sally Stark, recalled: "When Jacob was 2¹/₂ months old, they said he would never learn to sit up, would never be able to feed himself. . . . They told us to take him home, love him, and find an institution." (Blakeslee, 1992, p. C3)

Instead, when Jacob was 5 months old surgeons removed 20% of his brain. The operation was a complete success. Three years later Jacob seemed normal in every way, with no sign of seizures.

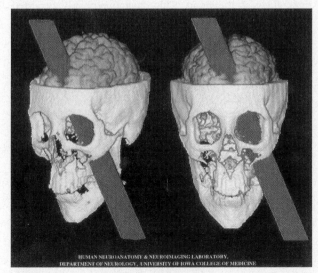

HUMAN NEUROANATOMY & NEUROIMAGING LABORATORY,
DEPARTMENT OF NEUROLOGY, UNIVERSITY OF IOWA COLLEGE OF MEDICINE

Phineas Gage injury model

The surgery that helped Jacob was based on the premise that neurons in part of his brain were misfiring and producing seizures throughout the brain. Surgeons reasoned that if they removed the faulty portion, the remaining parts of the brain, which appeared normal in PET scans, would take over. They correctly bet that Jacob could lead a normal life after surgery, particularly because the surgery was done at so young an age.

The success of Jacob's surgery illustrates that the brain has the ability to shift functions to different locations after injury to a specific area or after surgery. But equally encouraging are some new findings about the *regenerative* powers of the brain and nervous system.

Scientists have learned in recent years that the brain continually reorganizes itself in a process termed **neuroplasticity**. For many years, conventional wisdom held that no new brain cells are created after childhood, but recent research has found otherwise: The interconnections between neurons not only become more complex throughout life, but new neurons apparently also develop in certain areas of the brain during adulthood—a process called *neurogenesis*. In fact, new neurons may become integrated with existing neural connections after some kinds of brain injury during adulthood (Jang, You, & Ahn, 2007; Poo & Isaacson, 2007; Shors, 2009).

The ability of neurons to renew themselves during adulthood has significant implications for the treatment of disorders of the nervous system. For example, drugs that trigger the development of new neurons might be used to counter such diseases as Alzheimer's, a progressive disorder in which neurons die (Eisch et al., 2008; Tsai, Tsai, & Shen, 2007; Waddell & Shors, 2008).

Furthermore, specific experiences can modify the way in which information is processed. For example, if you learn to read Braille, the amount of tissue in your cortex related to sensation in the fingertips will expand. Similarly, if you take up the violin, the area of the brain that receives messages from your fingers will grow—but relating only to the fingers that actually move across the violin's strings (Kolb, Gibb, & Robinson, 2003; Schwartz & Begley, 2002).

PSYCH think

connect™

Parts of the Brain and Their Functions

> > > Which areas of the brain are active during simple tasks? To get an idea, read the following sentence aloud: "Multiple brain areas are active in reading a sentence aloud." Try to think of all the brain areas that were involved in reading the previous sentence. Keep in mind that you had to see the individual letters, recognize the words they spelled, understand what the words mean, speak the words aloud, and listen as you spoke. More complicated than you thought?

Take the PsychSmart Challenge! Test your knowledge of the parts of the brain: From chapter 2 in your ebook, select the *Exercises* tab, and then select "Parts of the Brain and Their Functions." Later, test yourself by answering question 10 in the Pop Quiz on p. 56.

TWO BRAINS OR ONE?

You may have heard people say they are right-brained, because they have a special appreciation for art, or left-brained, because they can solve Sudoku puzzles really quickly. What are they talking about? Do people really favor one side of their brain? Do the different halves of the brain really do different things?

To answer these questions, you need to know about the most recent development, at least in evolutionary terms, in the organization and operation of the human brain: a specialization of the functions controlled by the left and the right sides of the brain. This change probably occurred within the last million years (Hopkins & Cantalupo, 2008; MacNeilage, Rogers, & Vallortigara, 2009; Tommasi, 2009).

The brain is divided into two roughly mirror-image halves. Just as we have two arms, two legs, and two lungs, we have a left brain and a right brain. Because of the way nerves in the brain are connected to the rest of the body, these symmetrical left and right halves, called **hemispheres**, control motion in—and receive sensation from—the side of the body opposite their location. The left hemisphere of the brain, then, generally controls the right side of the body, and the right hemisphere controls the left side of the body. Thus, damage to the right side of the brain is typically indicated by functional difficulties in the left side of the body.

Despite the appearance of similarity between the two hemispheres of the brain, they control somewhat different functions, and they control them in somewhat dif-

Assessing Brain Lateralization

To get a rough sense of your own preferences in terms of brain lateralization, complete this questionnaire.

1. I often talk about my and other's feelings of emotion. True or false? _____
2. I am an analytical person. True or false? _____
3. I methodically solve problems. True or false? _____
4. I'm usually more interested in people and feelings than objects and things. True or false? _____
5. I see the big picture, rather than thinking about projects in terms of their individual parts. True or false? _____
6. When planning a trip, I like every detail in my itinerary worked out in advance. True or false? _____
7. I tend to be independent and work things out in my head. True or false? _____
8. When buying a new car, I prefer style over safety. True or false? _____
9. I would rather hear a lecture than read a textbook. True or false? _____
10. I remember names better than faces. True or false? _____

Scoring: Give yourself 1 point for each of the following responses: 1. False; 2. True; 3. True; 4. False; 5. False; 6. True; 7. True; 8. False; 9. False; 10. True. Maximum score is 10, and minimum score is 0.

The higher your score, the more your responses are consistent with people who are left-brain oriented, meaning that you have particular strength in tasks that require verbal competence, analytic thinking, and processing of information sequentially, one bit of information at a time.

The lower your score, the more your responses are consistent with a right-brain orientation, meaning that you have particular strengths in nonverbal areas, recognition of patterns, music, and emotional expression, and process information globally.

Remember, though, that this is only a rough estimate of your processing preferences and that all of us have strengths in both hemispheres of the brain.

Source: Adapted in part from Morton, B. E. (2003). Asymmetry questionnaire outcomes correlate with several hemisphericity measures. *Brain and Cognition, 51,* 372–374.

ferent ways. Certain behaviors are more likely to reflect activity in one hemisphere than in the other and are said to be **lateralized**.

For example, for most people, language processing occurs mainly on the left side of the brain. In general, the left hemisphere concentrates more on tasks that require verbal competence, such as speaking, reading, thinking, and reasoning. In addition, the left hemisphere tends to process information sequentially, one bit at a time (Banich & Heller, 1998; Hines, 2004; Rogers, 2011; Turkewitz, 1993).

The right hemisphere has its own strengths, particularly in nonverbal areas such as the understanding of spatial relationships, recognition of patterns and drawings, music, and emotional expression. The right hemisphere tends to process information globally, considering it as a whole (Ansaldo, Arguin, & Roch-Locours, 2002; Holowka & Petitto, 2002).

Nonetheless, differences in specialization between the hemispheres of the brain are not great, and the degree and the nature of lateralization vary from one person to another. Furthermore, the two hemispheres function in tandem, working to decipher, interpret, and react to the world.

Moreover, people who suffer damage to the left side of the brain and lose linguistic capabilities often recover the ability to speak, because the right side takes over some of the functions of the left side, especially in young children. The extent of recovery increases the earlier the injury occurs (Gould et al., 1999; Kempermann & Gage, 1999; Johnston, 2004).

HUMAN DIVERSITY AND BRAIN LATERALIZATION

Brain lateralization patterns and brain structure appear to differ in males and females, and even from one culture to another. Let's consider sex differences first. Accumulating evidence points to intriguing gender differences in brain lateralization and brain weight (Boles, 2005; Clements et al., 2006; Kosslyn et al., 2002).

For instance, most males tend to show greater lateralization of language in the left hemisphere. For them, language is clearly a left brain function. In contrast, women display less lateralization, with language abilities apt to be more evenly divided between the two hemispheres. These differences may account, in part, for the superiority often displayed by females on certain measures of verbal skills, such as the beginning of and the fluency of speech (Frings et al., 2006; Petersson et al., 2007).

From the perspective of ...

AN EDUCATOR Brain lateralization is influenced by experience. How could a teacher use this information to help students learn?

Other research suggests that men's brains are somewhat bigger than women's brains are, even after taking differences in body size into account. In contrast, part of the *corpus callosum,* a bundle of fibers that connects the hemispheres of the brain, is proportionally larger in women than in men (Cahill, 2005; Luders et al., 2006; Smith et al., 2007).

Men and women also may process information differently. For example, in one study, fMRI brain scans of men making judgments that discriminate real from false words showed activation of the left hemisphere of the brain, whereas women used areas on both sides of the brain (Rossell et al., 2002).

The meaning of sex differences in brain lateralization is far from clear. Consider one hypothesis related to differences in the proportional size of the corpus callosum. Its greater size in women may permit stronger connections to develop between the parts of the brain that control speech. In turn, this would explain why speech tends to emerge slightly earlier in girls than in boys.

Physical brain differences may be a *reflection* of social and environmental influences rather than a *cause* of differences in men's and women's behavior.

Before we rush to such a conclusion, however, we must consider an alternative hypothesis: The reason verbal abilities emerge earlier in girls may be that infant girls receive greater encouragement to talk than do infant boys. In turn, this greater early experience may foster the growth of certain parts of the brain. If so, physical brain differences may be a *reflection* of social and environmental influences rather than a *cause* of differences in men's and women's behavior. At this point, it is impossible to know which of these alternative hypotheses might be correct (Hamberg, 2005).

Culture also gives rise to differences in brain lateralization. Native speakers of Japanese, for instance, seem to process information regarding vowel sounds primarily in the left hemisphere. In contrast, North and South Americans, Europeans, and individuals of Japanese ancestry who learn Japanese later in life handle vowel sounds principally in the right hemisphere. One explanation proposed for this difference is that certain characteristics of the Japanese language, such as the ability to express complex ideas by using only vowel sounds, result in the development of a specific type of brain lateralization in native speakers (Kess & Miyamoto, 1994; Lin, et al., 2005).

THE SPLIT BRAIN: EXPLORING THE TWO HEMISPHERES

The patient, V. J., had suffered severe seizures. By cutting her corpus callosum, the fibrous portion of the brain that carries messages between the hemispheres, surgeons hoped to create a firebreak to prevent the seizures from spreading. The operation did decrease the frequency and severity of V. J.'s attacks. But V. J. developed an unexpected side effect: She lost the ability to write at will, although she could read and spell words aloud. (Strauss, 1998, p. 287)

People such as V. J., whose corpus callosum has been surgically cut to stop seizures and who are called *split-brain patients,* offer a rare opportunity for researchers investigating the independent functioning of the two hemispheres of the brain. Psychologist Roger Sperry—who won the Nobel

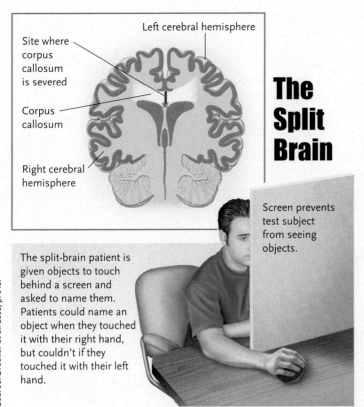

Left cerebral hemisphere

Site where corpus callosum is severed

Corpus callosum

Right cerebral hemisphere

The Split Brain

Screen prevents test subject from seeing objects.

The split-brain patient is given objects to touch behind a screen and asked to name them. Patients could name an object when they touched it with their right hand, but couldn't if they touched it with their left hand.

Source: Brooker et al. 2008, p. 943.

ately transfers information from one hemisphere to the other.)

It is clear from experiments like this one that the right and the left hemispheres of the brain specialize in different sorts of information. At the same time, we must realize that both hemispheres are capable of understanding, knowing, and being aware of the world. The two hemispheres, then, should be regarded as different in terms of the efficiency with which they process certain kinds of information, rather than as two entirely separate brains. The hemispheres work together to allow the full range and richness of thought possible for humans.

CONTROLLING YOUR HEART—AND MIND—THROUGH BIOFEEDBACK

When Tammy DeMichael was involved in a horrific car accident that broke her neck and crushed her spinal cord, experts told her that she was doomed to be a quadriplegic for the rest of her life, unable to move from the neck down. But they were wrong. Not only did she regain the use of her arms, but she also learned to walk 60 feet with a cane (Hess, Houg, & Tammaro, 2007; Lofthouse et al., 2011; Morrow & Wolff, 1991).

The key to DeMichael's astounding recovery: biofeedback. **Biofeedback** is a procedure in which a person learns to control through conscious thought internal physiological processes such as blood pressure, heart and respiration rate, skin temperature, sweating, and the constriction of particular muscles. Although it traditionally had been thought that heart rate, respiration rate, blood pressure, and other bodily functions are under the control of parts of the brain over which we have no influence, psychologists have discovered that these responses are actually susceptible to voluntary control (Cho, Holyoak, & Cannon, 2007; Nagai et al., 2004).

> **biofeedback** A procedure in which a person learns to control through conscious thought internal physiological processes such as blood pressure, heart and respiration rate, skin temperature, sweating, and the constriction of particular muscles.

In biofeedback, a person is hooked up to electronic devices that provide continuous feedback relating to the physiological response in question. For instance, a person interested in controlling headaches through biofeedback might have electronic sensors placed on certain muscles on her head and learn to control the constriction and relaxation of those muscles. Later, when she felt a headache starting, she could relax the relevant muscles and abort the pain (Andrasik, 2007; Nestoriuc et al., 2008).

In DeMichael's case, biofeedback was effective, because not all of the nervous system's connections between the brain and her legs were severed. Through biofeedback, she learned how to send messages to specific muscles, "ordering" them to move. Although it took more than a year, DeMichael successfully regained a large degree of her mobility.

Prize in medicine for his work—developed a number of ingenious techniques for studying how each hemisphere operates (Gazzaniga, 1998; Savazzi et al., 2007; Sperry, 1982).

In one experimental procedure, blindfolded patients touched an object with their right hand and were asked to name it. Because the right side of the body corresponds to the language-oriented left side of the brain, split-brain patients were able to name the object. However, if blindfolded patients touched the object with their left hand, they were unable to name it aloud, even though the information had registered in their brains. When the blindfold was removed, patients could identify the object they had touched. Information can be learned and remembered, then, using only the right side of the brain. (By the way, unless you've had a split-brain operation, this experiment won't work with you, because the bundle of fibers connecting the two hemispheres of a normal brain immedi-

PSYCH think

> > > Before we had sophisticated brain-scanning techniques, we could only probe the brain after people had died, or study the problems people developed after suffering brain damage such as a stroke. If you had been on the scene when the PET and MRI scans were developed, what would you have wanted to study first?

BUY IT? > > >

Can Biofeedback Help with Any Problem?

Although control of physiological processes using biofeedback techniques is not easy to learn, biofeedback has been applied successfully to a variety of ailments, including emotional problems (such as anxiety, depression, phobias, tension headaches, insomnia, and hyperactivity), physical illnesses with a psychological compo-nent (such as asthma, high blood pressure, ulcers, muscle spasms, and migraine headaches), and physical problems (such as spinal cord injuries, strokes, cerebral palsy, and curvature of the spine). Stress reduction is another applica-tion of biofeedback, one that can benefit individuals experiencing severe stress or chronic pain (Kapitz et al., 2010; Vitiello, Bonello, & Pollard, 2007).

But is biofeedback truly effective for all these disorders? If you search the Internet for informa-tion on biofeedback, you'll find websites market-ing biofeedback products to consumers for all sorts of major and minor ailments. They may claim to be "clinically proven," and they may be effective for some people. As you look more deeply into their claims, however, you may notice that some of the devices are based on feedback between your body and the biofeedback appara-tus, and your conscious awareness of the feedback, which is usually the central notion of biofeedback, is not included! Before you spend $100 or more on one of these devices, you might want to consider less expensive alternatives, such as spending time with friends, exercising, meditat-ing (see p. 98), or any of the strategies recom-mended on p. 287 for reducing stress (Lee, S. H. et al., 2007; Yesilyaprak, Kisac, & Sanlier, 2007; Ahmed et al., 2011).

For
REVIEW >>

- **Why do psychologists study the brain and nervous system?**

  Fully understanding human behavior requires knowledge of the biological influences on behavior, especially those originating in the nervous system. Psychologists who study the effects of biological structures and functions on behavior are known as behavioral neuroscientists. (p. 32)

- **What are the basic units of the nervous system?**

  Neurons, the most basic structural units of the nervous system, carry nerve impulses within the brain and from one part of the body to another. Information generally enters a neuron via the dendrites, moves into the cell body, and ultimately travels down the tube-like extension called the axon. (p. 33)

- **How does the endocrine system affect behavior?**

  The endocrine system secretes hormones, chemicals that regulate the functioning of the body, via the bloodstream. The pituitary gland secretes growth hormones and influences the release of hormones by other endocrine glands, and in turn is regulated by the hypothalamus. (pp. 43–47)

- **What are the major parts of the brain, and what are their functions?**

  The central core, or "old brain," is made up of the medulla (which controls functions such as breathing and the heartbeat), the pons (which coordinates the muscles and the two sides of the body), the cerebellum (which controls balance), the reticular formation (which acts to heighten awareness in emergencies), the thalamus (which communicates sensory messages to and from the brain), and the hypothalamus (which maintains the body's internal equilibrium and regulates behavior related to basic survival).

  The cerebral cortex, or "new brain," has areas that control voluntary movement (the motor area); the senses (the sensory area); and thinking, reasoning, speech, and memory (the association areas).

  The limbic system borders on the "old" and "new" brains and is associated with eating, aggression, reproduction, and the experiences of pleasure and pain. (pp. 43–49)

- **How do the two halves of the brain specialize, and how do they work together?**

  The brain is divided into left and right halves, or hemispheres, each of which generally controls the opposite side of the body. The left hemisphere specializes in verbal tasks, such as logical reasoning, speaking, and reading, whereas the right hemisphere specializes in nonverbal tasks, such as spatial perception, pattern recognition, and emotional expression. Nevertheless, both hemispheres are capable of understanding, knowing, and being aware of the world and operate interdependently. (pp. 50–51)

Pop Quiz

1. The _____ is the most basic structural unit of the nervous system.

2. Neurons receive information through their _____ and send messages through their _____.

3. Just as electrical wires have an outer coating, axons are insulated by a coating called the _____ _____.

4. The gap between two neurons is bridged by a chemical connection called a _____.

5. Endorphins are one kind of _____, the chemical "messenger" between neurons.

6. If you put your hand on a red-hot piece of metal, the immediate response of pulling your hand away would be an example of a(n) _____.

7. The central nervous system is composed of the _____ and the _____.

8. In the peripheral nervous system, the _____ division controls voluntary movements, whereas the _____ division controls organs that keep us alive and function without our awareness.

9. Match the name of each brain scan with the appropriate description:
   a. EEG
   b. fMRI
   c. PET

   ____ 1. By locating radiation within the brain, a computer can provide a striking picture of brain activity.

   ____ 2. Electrodes placed around the skull record the electrical signals transmitted through the brain.

   ____ 3. This technique provides a three-dimensional view of the brain by aiming a magnetic field at the body.

10. Match the portion of the brain with its function:
    a. medulla
    b. pons
    c. cerebellum
    d. reticular formation

    ____ 1. maintains breathing and heartbeat

    ____ 2. controls bodily balance

    ____ 3. coordinates and integrates muscle movements

    ____ 4. activates other parts of the brain to produce general bodily arousal

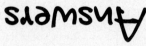

Answers TO POP QUIZ QUESTIONS

1. neuron
2. dendrites, axons
3. myelin sheath
4. synapse
5. neurotransmitter
6. reflex
7. brain, spinal cord
8. somatic, autonomic
9. a-2, b-3, c-1
10. a-1, b-3, c-2, d-4

3

SENSATION

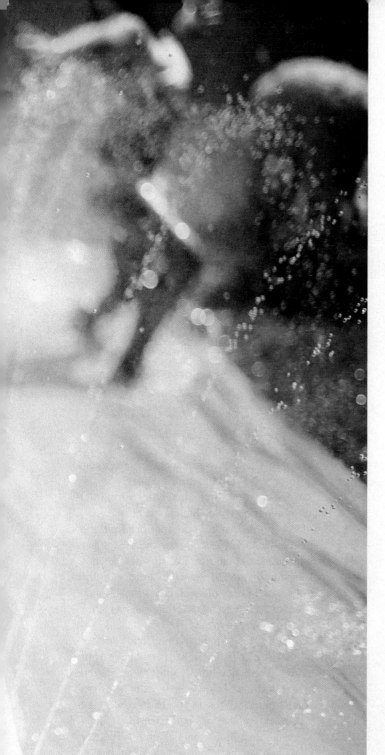

MET ONCE, RECOGNIZED FOREVER

If she meets you once, she'll recognize you the next time she sees you, even if it's decades later.

For a woman known as C.S., recognizing someone she's seen before is routine. In fact, like very few other people she can recognize faces of people she met years ago, sometimes only in passing. These "super-recognizers," as they are called, excel at perceiving and later recalling faces.

One super-recognizer said she had identified another woman on the street who served her as a waitress five years earlier in a different city. Often, super-recognizers are able to recognize another person despite significant changes in appearance, such as aging or a different hair color.

But being a super-recognizer is a mixed blessing. As one woman with this ability says, "It doesn't matter how many years pass, if I've seen your face before, I will be able to recall it." In fact, she sometimes pretends she doesn't recognize a person, "because it seems like I stalk them, or that they mean more to me than they do when I recall that we saw each other once walking on campus four years ago in front of the quad!"[iii]

Most of us are reasonably good at recognizing people's faces, thanks in part to regions of the brain that specialize in perceiving facial patterns. Super-recognizers represent a small minority of people with extraordinary abilities to perceive faces. At the other extreme are people with *faceblindness*, an equally rare disorder that makes it extremely difficult for them to recognize faces at all, even those of friends and family.

Conditions such as super-recognition and faceblindness illustrate how much we depend on our senses and our perceptual abilities to function normally. Our senses offer a window to the world, providing us with not only an awareness, understanding, and appreciation of the world's beauty, but also alerting us to its dangers. Our senses enable us to feel the gentlest of breezes, see flickering lights miles away, and hear the soft murmuring of distant songbirds.

& PERCEPTION

As You
READ >>

- What's the difference between sensation and perception?
- How do we respond to the characteristics of physical stimuli?
- How do our sense organs process stimuli?
- How does perception turn sensory stimuli into meaningful information?

>> Sensation and Perception: Two Sides of the Same Coin

If you are, or someone you know is, a runner, this situation might be familiar to you: When Kyle prepares for a run, he turns on his iPod. He quickly searches for something upbeat to motivate him. After turning down the volume, he skips the first few songs—too slow, too sad. Finally, 50 Cent's "In da Club" starts to play. Perfect! Sensation happens when the sound waves of the music reach Kyle's eardrum and move through his ear to his brain. Perception occurs when he knows he is hearing the music.

In other words, sensation is our first encounter with a raw sensory stimulus, whereas perception is the process by which the brain interprets, analyzes, and integrates that stimulus with other sensory information. Imagine a ringing fire alarm, for instance. If we were considering sensation, we might ask about the loudness of the fire alarm. If we were considering perception, we might ask whether someone recognizes the ringing sound as an alarm and identifies its meaning.

Psychologists who study sensation and perception deal with a wide range of questions, including the ones at the beginning of the chapter and others such as, Why do visual illusions fool us? And how do we distinguish one person from another? We address all these questions and more in this chapter. Let's look first at how our sense organs respond to stimuli.

>> Sensing the World Around Us

As Isabel sat down to Thanksgiving dinner, her father carried the turkey in on a tray and placed it squarely in the center of the table. The noise level, already high from the talking and laughter of family members, grew louder still. As Isabel picked up her fork, the smell of the turkey reached her and she felt her stomach growl hungrily. The sight and sounds of her family around the table, along with the smells and tastes of the holiday meal, made Isabel feel more relaxed than she had since starting school in the fall.

Put yourself in this setting, and consider how different it might be if any one of your senses were not functioning. What if you were blind and unable to see Auntie Mariko's latest tattoo? What if you had no sense of hearing and could not listen to Grandpa and Grandma's annual argument over dark versus white meat? What if you were unable to feel your stomach growl, smell the dinner, or taste the food? Clearly, you would experience the dinner very differently than would someone whose sensory apparatus was intact.

Moreover, the sensations mentioned above barely scratch the surface of sensory experience. Although you might have been taught, as many of us were, that there are just five senses—sight, sound, taste, smell, and touch—that list is incomplete. Human sensory capabilities go well beyond the basic five senses. For example, we are sensitive not merely to touch but also to a considerably wider set of stimuli—pain, pressure, temperature, and vibration, to name a few. In addition, vision has two subsystems—relating to day and night vision—and the ear is responsive to information that allows us not only to hear but also to keep our balance.

To consider how psychologists understand the senses and, more broadly, sensation and perception, we first need a basic working vocabulary. In formal terms, **sensation** is the activation of the sense organs by a stimulus (for example, light or sound). **Perception** is the sorting out, interpretation, analysis, and integration of stimuli carried out by the brain. A **stimulus** is any passing source of physical energy that produces a response in a sense organ.

Stimuli vary in both type and intensity. Different types of stimuli activate different sense organs. For instance, we can differentiate light stimuli (which activate the sense of sight and allow us to see the colors of a tree in autumn) from

: Like this gymnast, we rely on our ears to keep our balance.

sound stimuli (which, through the sense of hearing, permit us to hear the sounds of an orchestra). In addition, stimuli differ in intensity, relating to how strong a stimulus needs to be before we can sense it.

The area of psychology that examines stimulus type and intensity is known as psychophysics. **Psychophysics** is the study of the relationship between the physical aspects of stimuli and our psychological experience of them. Psychophysics played a central role in the development of the field of psychology, and there is still an active group of psychophysics researchers (Chechil, 2003; Gardner, 2005; Hock & Ploeger, 2006; Wolfe, 2011).

ABSOLUTE THRESHOLDS

How do we even detect a sight, a smell, or a sound? This is one of the questions that psychophysics addresses. Think about all the auditory sensory information affecting you at the moment. You may be listening to music; your roommate may be talking on her cellphone; the computer on your desk may be buzzing; the lights overhead may be humming. Although we

---

STUDY TIP

Remember that sensation refers to the activation of the sense organs (a physical response), whereas perception refers to how stimuli are interpreted (a psychological response).

---

sensation The activation of the sense organs by a stimulus (for example, light or sound).

perception The sorting out, interpretation, analysis, and integration of stimuli carried out by the brain.

stimulus Energy that produces a response in a sense organ.

psychophysics The study of the relationship between the physical aspects of stimuli and our psychological experience of them.

This classic picture represents a good example of the differences between sensation and perception. Sensation allows us to see the black-and-white splotches of ink. Perception allows us to recognize the pattern as a picture of a ... Can you figure out what you're looking at? *Source:* James, 1966

are immersed in sensory information, we thrive. Our bodies seem well prepared to deal with an abundance of stimuli.

What is the least amount of stimulation that our senses can detect? The answer to this question lies in the concept of absolute threshold. An **absolute threshold** is the smallest intensity of a stimulus that must be present for our senses to detect it (Aazh & Moore, 2007).

Our senses are extremely responsive to stimuli. For example, the sense of touch is so keen that we can feel a bee's wing fall on our cheek when the wing is dropped from a distance of 1 centimeter. In fact, we might have problems if our senses were any more acute than they are. If our ears were slightly more responsive to noise, for instance, we would be able to hear the sound of air molecules in our ears knocking into the eardrum—a phenomenon that would surely prove distracting and might even prevent us from hearing sounds outside our bodies.

Absolute thresholds are measured under ideal conditions. Normally, noise prevents our senses from detecting stimulation at the absolute thresholds. As defined by psychophysicists, *noise* is background stimulation that interferes with the perception of other stimuli. Noise, then, refers not just to auditory stimuli, as the word suggests, but also to any unwanted stimuli that interfere with other senses.

absolute threshold The smallest intensity of a stimulus that must be present for the senses to detect it.

difference threshold (just noticeable difference) The smallest level of added or reduced stimulation required to sense that a change in stimulation has occurred.

Weber's law A basic law of psychophysics stating that a just noticeable difference is in constant proportion to the intensity of an initial stimulus.

The sense of touch is so acute that we can feel a bee's wing fall on our cheek when the wing is dropped from a distance of one centimeter.

For example, think back to the last time you were at a party in someone's dorm room or apartment. Picture a crowd of talkative people crammed into a small smoke-filled room while loud music plays on the stereo. The din of the crowd and the music makes it hard to hear individual voices, and the smoke makes it difficult to see, or even taste, the food. In this case, the smoke and the crowded conditions would both be considered "noise," because they prevent sensation at more discriminating levels.

DIFFERENCE THRESHOLDS

Suppose you are making spaghetti for your best friend who is visiting from out of town. You don't cook much, and you are trying to spice up the can of tomato sauce you bought at the grocery store. You taste your sauce and note that it needs more salt, so you sprinkle some salt in and stir. You taste the sauce again, but can't taste any difference so you sprinkle in more salt and stir. You taste it one more time and the sauce finally tastes a bit saltier.

You have just demonstrated the **difference threshold**, defined by psychologists as the lowest level of added (or reduced) stimulation required to sense that a *change* in stimulation has occurred. Because the difference threshold is the minimum change in stimulation required to detect the difference between two stimuli, it also is called a **just noticeable difference** (Nittrouer & Lowenstein, 2007).

The stimulus value that constitutes a just noticeable difference depends on the initial intensity of the stimulus. This relationship between changes in the original value of a stimulus and the degree to which a change will be noticed forms one of the basic laws of psychophysics: Weber's law. **Weber's law** (Weber is pronounced vay-bear) states that a just noticeable difference is a *constant proportion* of the intensity of an initial stimulus.

For example, the just noticeable difference for weight is 1:50. Consequently, it takes a 1-ounce increase in a 50-ounce weight to produce a noticeable difference, and it would take a 10-ounce increase to produce a noticeable difference if the initial weight were 500 ounces. In both cases, the same proportional increase is necessary to produce a just noticeable difference—1:50 = 10:500. Similarly, the just noticeable difference for changes in loudness is greater for sounds that

PSYCH think

connect™

WWW.MCGRAWHILLCONNECT.COM/PSYCHOLOGY
Weber's Law

> > > Do you think Weber's law will be true for you? Use your own senses to find out!

Take the PsychSmart challenge! Can Weber's law predict how you will perform in the online simulation? From chapter 3 in your ebook, select the *Exercises* tab, and then select "Weber's Law." Later, test yourself by answering question 2 in the Pop Quiz on p. 85.

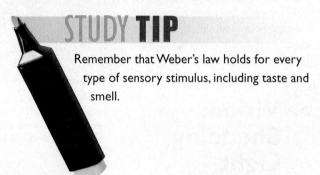
are initially loud than it is for sounds that are initially soft, but the *proportional* increase remains the same.

Weber's law helps explain why a person in a quiet room is more startled by the ringing of a telephone than is a person in an already noisy room. To produce the same amount of reaction in a noisy room, a telephone ring might have to approximate the loudness of a car alarm. Similarly, when the moon is visible during the late afternoon, it appears relatively dim—yet against a dark night sky, it seems quite bright.

SENSORY ADAPTATION

You enter a movie theater and immediately are aware of the popcorn aroma. A few minutes later, you barely notice the smell. The reason you acclimate to the odor is sensory adaptation. **Sensory adaptation** is a reduction in the responsiveness of the sensory neurons after prolonged exposure to unchanging stimuli. This type of adaptation occurs as we become accustomed to a stimulus. In a sense, the brain reduces our sensitivity to the stimulation that it's experiencing (Calin-Jageman & Fischer, 2007; Willert, & Eggert, 2011).

sensory adaptation A reduction in the responsiveness of the sensory neurons after prolonged exposure to unchanging stimuli.

STUDY **TIP**

Remember that Weber's law holds for every type of sensory stimulus, including taste and smell.

Going for a swim on a cold winter's day isn't for everyone, but after the initial plunge, sensory adaptation helps the body adjust to the frigid water—at least for a little while.

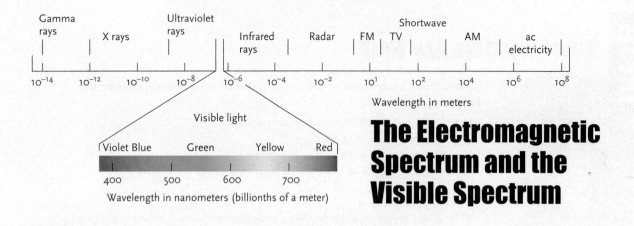

Gamma rays | X rays | Ultraviolet rays | Infrared rays | Radar | FM | TV | Shortwave | AM | ac electricity

10^{-14} 10^{-12} 10^{-10} 10^{-8} 10^{-6} 10^{-4} 10^{-2} 10^{1} 10^{2} 10^{4} 10^{6} 10^{8}

Wavelength in meters

Visible light

Violet Blue | Green | Yellow | Red

400 500 600 700

Wavelength in nanometers (billionths of a meter)

The Electromagnetic Spectrum and the Visible Spectrum

Adaptation also occurs after repeated exposure to a strong stimulus. If you were to hear a loud tone over and over again, for example, eventually it would begin to sound softer. Similarly, although jumping into a cold lake may be temporarily unpleasant, eventually you probably would become accustomed to the temperature.

This apparent decline in sensitivity to sensory stimuli is due to the inability of the sensory nerve receptors to fire off messages to the brain indefinitely. Because these receptor cells are most responsive to *changes* in stimulation, constant stimulation is not effective in producing a sustained reaction.

>> Vision: Shedding Light on the Eye

If, as poets say, the eyes provide a window to the soul, they also provide us with a window on the world. The ability to see permits us to admire and to react to the beauty of a sunset, the configuration of a lover's face, or the words in a book.

Vision starts with light, the physical energy that stimulates the eye. Light is a form of electromagnetic radiation, which is measured in wavelengths. Different wavelengths correspond to different types of energy. The range of wavelengths to which humans are sensitive is called the *visible spectrum.*

Light waves coming from some object outside the body, such as a butterfly, are sensed by the only organ that is capable of responding to the visible spectrum: the eye. Our eyes convert light to a form that can be used by the neurons linking the eyes and the brain. The neurons themselves

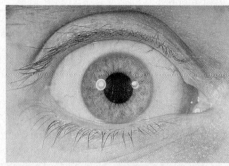

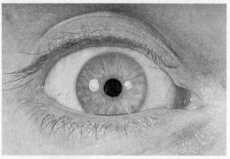

Like the automatic lighting system on a camera, the pupil in the human eye expands to let in more light (*top*) and contracts to block out light (*bottom*).

take up a relatively small percentage of the total eye. Most of the eye is a mechanical device that is similar in many respects to a non-electronic camera that uses film.

Despite the similarities between the eye and a camera, vision involves processes that are far more complex and sophisticated than those of any camera. Furthermore, once an image reaches the neuronal receptors of the eye, the eye/camera analogy ends, because the processing of the visual image in the brain is more reflective of a computer than it is of a camera.

ILLUMINATING THE EYE

The ray of light reflected by an object such as a butterfly first travels through the *cornea*, a transparent, protective window. The cornea, because it is curved, bends (or *refracts*) light as it passes through, playing a primary role in focusing the light more sharply. After moving through the cornea, the light traverses the pupil. The *pupil* is a dark hole in the center of the *iris*, the colored part of the eye, which in humans ranges from a light blue to a dark brown. The size of the pupil depends, in part, on the amount of light in the environment. Generally speaking, the dimmer the surroundings are, the more the pupil opens to allow more light to enter.

Why shouldn't the pupil be open completely all the time, allowing the greatest amount of light into the eye? The answer relates to the basic physics of light. A small pupil greatly increases the range of distances at which objects are in focus. With a wide-open pupil, the range is relatively small, and details are harder to discern. The eye takes advantage of bright light by decreasing the size of the pupil and thereby becoming more discriminating. In dim light the pupil expands to enable us to view the situation

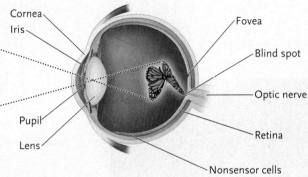

A camera's lens focuses the inverted image on the film in the same way the eye's lens focuses images on the retina

Similarities Between the Human Eye and a Camera

Cornea
Iris
Pupil
Lens

Fovea
Blind spot
Optic nerve
Retina
Nonsensor cells of retina

better—but at the expense of visual detail. (Perhaps one reason candlelight dinners are thought of as romantic is that the dim light prevents one from seeing a partner's physical flaws.) Once light passes through the pupil, it enters the *lens*, which is directly behind the pupil. The lens bends the rays of light so that they are properly focused on the rear of the eye. The lens focuses light by changing its own thickness, a process called *accommodation*: It becomes flatter when viewing distant objects and rounder when looking at closer objects. Have you noticed that some people hold their menus at arm's length when ordering food at a restaurant? The ability of our lenses to accommodate decreases with age and makes it harder to focus on close objects. For this reason, many people start needing reading glasses, bifocal lenses, or longer arms as early as their 40s.

Striking the Retina Having traveled through the pupil and the lens, the image of the butterfly reaches the **retina**, a thin layer of nerve cells at the back of the eye. The retina converts the electromagnetic energy of light to electrical impulses for transmission to the brain. There are two kinds of light-sensitive receptor cells in the retina; their names describe their shapes: rods and cones. **Rods** are thin, cylindrical receptor cells that are highly sensitive to light. **Cones** are cone-shaped, light-sensitive receptor cells that are responsible for sharp focus and color perception, particularly in bright light. The rods and cones are distributed unevenly throughout the retina. Cones are concentrated on the part of the retina called the *fovea*. The fovea is a particularly sensitive region of the retina. If you want to focus on something specific, you will automatically try to center the image on the fovea to see it more sharply.

The rods and cones not only are structurally dissimilar, but they also have different functions. Cones are primarily responsible for the sharply focused perception of color, particularly in brightly lit situations; rods are helpful in dimly lit situations and are largely insensitive to color and details. The rods play a key role in *peripheral vision*—seeing objects that are outside the main center of focus—and in night vision.

retina The part of the eye that converts the electromagnetic energy of light to electrical impulses for transmission to the brain.

rods Thin, cylindrical receptor cells in the retina that are highly sensitive to light.

cones Cone-shaped, light-sensitive receptor cells in the retina that are responsible for sharp focus and color perception, particularly in bright light.

Receptor Cells— Rods and Cones— in the Eye

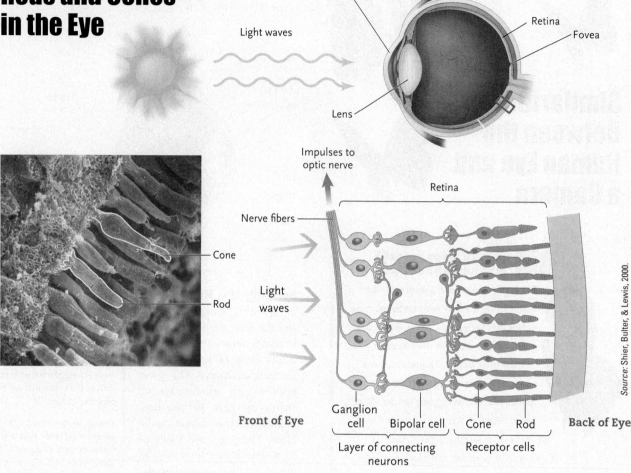

Light waves

Cornea
Retina
Fovea
Lens

Impulses to optic nerve

Nerve fibers

Retina

Cone

Rod

Light waves

Front of Eye

Ganglion cell
Bipolar cell
Cone
Rod
Back of Eye

Layer of connecting neurons

Receptor cells

Source: Shier, Bulter, & Lewis, 2000.

---

optic nerve A bundle of ganglion axons that carry visual information to the brain.

feature detection The activation of neurons in the cortex by visual stimuli of specific shapes or patterns.

Rods and cones also are involved in *dark adaptation*, the phenomenon of adjusting to dim light after being in brighter light. (Think of the experience of walking into a dark movie theater and groping your way to a seat but a few minutes later seeing the seats quite clearly.) The speed at which dark adaptation occurs is a result of the rate of change in the chemical composition of the rods and cones. Although the cones reach their greatest level of adaptation in just a few minutes, it takes the rods 20 to 30 minutes to reach their maximum level. The opposite phenomenon— *light adaptation*, or the process of adjusting to bright light

after exposure to dim light—occurs much more quickly, taking only a minute or so.

Sending an Image to the Brain When light energy strikes the rods and cones, it starts a chain of events that transforms light into neural impulses that can be communicated to the brain. Even before the neural message reaches the brain, however, some initial coding of the visual information takes place.

Stimulation of the nerve cells in the eye triggers a neural response that is transmitted to other nerve cells in the retina called *bipolar cells* and *ganglion cells*. Bipolar cells receive information directly from the rods and cones and communicate that information to the ganglion cells. The ganglion cells collect and summarize visual information, which is then moved out the back of the eyeball and sent to the brain through a bundle of ganglion axons that make up the **optic nerve**.

Because the opening for the optic nerve passes through the retina, no rods or cones exist in that area, and their absence produces a blind spot, an area roughly in the middle of your field of vision where you can't see anything. Normally, however, the blind spot does not interfere with vision, because your brain automatically uses surrounding visual information to fill in the spot.

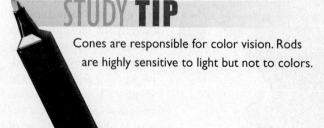

STUDY TIP

Cones are responsible for color vision. Rods are highly sensitive to light but not to colors.

To find your blind spot, close your right eye and look at the haunted house with your left eye. You will see the ghost on the periphery of your vision. Now, while staring at the house, move the page toward you. When the book is about a foot from your eye, the ghost will disappear. At this moment, the image of the ghost is falling on your blind spot. But also note how, when the page is at that distance, not only does the ghost seem to disappear, but the line seems to run continuously through the area where the ghost used to be. This simple experiment shows how we automatically compensate for missing information by using nearby material to complete what is unseen. That's the reason you never notice the blind spot. What is missing is replaced by what is seen next to the blind spot.

Once they have left the eye itself, neural impulses relating to the image move through the optic nerve. As the optic nerve leaves the eyeball, it does not take the most direct route to the part of the brain right behind the eye. Instead, the optic nerves from each eye meet in the brain at a point roughly between the two eyes—called the *optic chiasm* (pronounced *ki-asm*)—where each optic nerve then splits.

When the optic nerves split, the nerve impulses coming from the right half of each retina travel to the right side of the brain, and the impulses arriving from the left half of each retina go to the left side of the brain. Because the image on the retinas is reversed and upside down, however, images coming from the right half of each retina actually originated in the field of vision to the person's left, and the images coming from the left half of each retina originated in the field of vision to the person's right.

Processing the Visual Message By the time a visual message reaches the brain, it has already passed through several stages of processing. The ultimate processing of visual images takes place in the visual cortex of the brain, and it is here that the most complex kinds of processing occur. Psychologists David Hubel and Torsten Wiesel won the Nobel Prize in 1981 for their discovery that many neurons in the cortex are extraordinarily specialized to respond only to visual stimuli of a particular shape or pattern—a phenomenon known as **feature detection**. They found that some cells are activated only by lines of a particular width, shape, or orientation. Other cells are activated only by moving, as opposed to stationary, stimuli (Hubel & Wiesel, 2004; Pelli, Burns, & Farell, 2006).

PSYCH think

> > > Why do you suppose we automatically fill in the blind spot in our vision? Is there some advantage that doing this might give us?

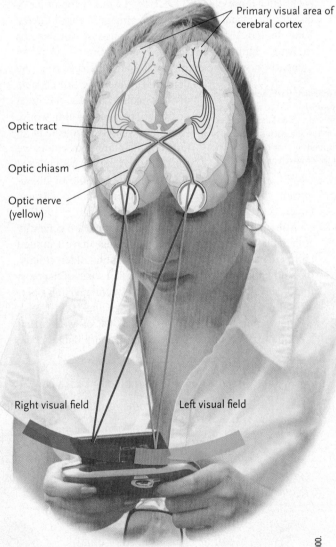

Primary visual area of cerebral cortex

Optic tract

Optic chiasm

Optic nerve (yellow)

Right visual field

Left visual field

Because the optic nerve coming from each eye splits at the optic chiasm, the image to a person's right is sent to the left side of the brain, and the image to the person's left is transmitted to the right side of the brain.

Source: Mader, 2000.

More recent work has added to our knowledge of the complex ways in which visual information coming from individual neurons is combined and processed. Different parts of the brain process nerve impulses in several individual systems simultaneously. For instance, one system relates to shapes, one to colors, and others to movement, location, and depth. Furthermore, different parts of the brain are involved in the perception of specific *kinds* of stimuli, showing distinctions, for example, between the perception of human faces, animals, and inanimate stimuli (Winston, O'Donherty, & Kilner, 2006; Bindemann et al., 2008; Werblin & Roska, 2007; Platek & Kemp, 2009).

COLOR VISION AND COLOR BLINDNESS

Back in elementary school you probably memorized the following set of letters: ROYGBIV. Can you recall what each letter represents? ROYGBIV stands for the order of hues in the visual spectrum (Red, Orange, Yellow, Green, Blue, Indigo, Violet). Although the range of wavelengths to which humans are sensitive is relatively narrow in comparison with the entire electromagnetic spectrum, the portion to which we are capable of responding allows us great flexibility in sensing the world. Nowhere is this clearer than in terms of the number of colors we can discern. A person with normal color vision is capable of distinguishing no less than 7 million different colors (Bruce, Green, & Georgeson, 1997; Rabin, 2004).

trichromatic theory of color vision The theory that there are three kinds of cones in the retina, each of which responds primarily to a specific range of wavelengths.

Although the variety of colors that people are generally able to distinguish is vast, some individuals have a limited ability to perceive color; they are color-blind. Interestingly, the study of color blindness has provided some of the most important clues to understanding how color vision operates (Bonnardel, 2006; Neitz, Neitz, & Kainz, 1996).

Approximately 7% of men and 0.4% of women are color-blind. For most people with color blindness, the

world looks very different. Red fire engines appear yellow, green grass seems yellow, and the three colors of a traffic light all look yellow. In fact, in the most common form of color blindness, all red and green objects are seen as yellow. There are other forms of color blindness as well, but they are quite rare. In yellow-blue blindness, people are unable to tell the difference between yellow and blue. Extremely rare are those people who can't see any color at all, except black, white, and shades of gray.

A person with normal color vision is capable of distinguishing no less than 7 million different colors.

Explaining Color Vision To understand why some people are color-blind, we need to consider the two processes of color vision. The first process is explained by the **trichromatic theory of color vision**. This theory suggests that there are three kinds of cones in the retina, each of which responds primarily to a specific range of wavelengths. One is most responsive to blue-violet colors, one to green, and the third to yellow-red (Brown & Wald, 1964). According to trichromatic theory, perception of color is influenced by the relative strength with which each of the three kinds of cones is activated. If we see a blue sky, the blue-violet cones are primarily triggered, and the others show less activity.

Now consider what happens after you stare at something such as the flag shown on the next page and then look away. If you stare at the black dot on the flag for a minute and then look at a blank sheet of white paper, you'll see an image of the traditional red, white, and blue U.S. flag. Where there was yellow, you'll see blue, and where there were green and black, you'll see red and white. This phenomenon is called an *afterimage*. It occurs because activity in the retina continues even when you are

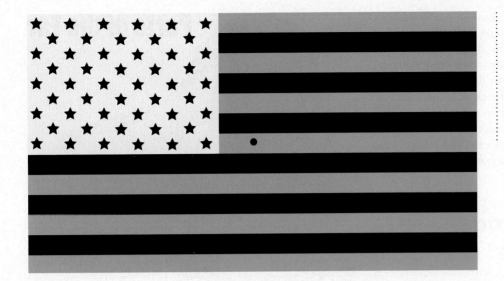

Stare at the dot in this flag for about a minute and then look at a piece of plain white paper. What do you see? Most people see an afterimage that converts the colors in the figure into the traditional red, white, and blue U.S. flag. If you have trouble seeing it the first time, blink once and try again.

no longer staring at the original picture. The trichromatic theory does not explain why the colors in the afterimage are different from those in the original.

Because trichromatic processes do not provide a full explanation of color vision, alternative explanations have been proposed. According to the **opponent-process theory of color vision**, receptor cells are linked in pairs, working in opposition to each other. Specifically, there are a blue-yellow pairing, a red-green pairing, and a black-white pairing. If an object reflects light that contains more blue than yellow, it will stimulate the firing of the cells sensitive to blue, simultaneously discouraging or inhibiting the firing of receptor cells sensitive to yellow—and the object will appear blue. If, in contrast, a light contains more yellow than blue, the cells that respond to yellow will be stimulated to fire while the blue ones are inhibited, and the object will appear yellow (Robinson, D. N., 2007).

The opponent-process theory provides a good explanation for afterimages. When we stare at the yellow in the figure, for instance, our receptor cells for yellow become fatigued and are less able to respond to yellow stimuli. In contrast, the receptor cells for the blue part of the yellow-blue pair are not tired, because they are not being stimulated. When we look at a white surface, the light reflected by it would normally stimulate both the yel-

low and the blue receptors equally. But the fatigue of the yellow receptors prevents this from happening. They temporarily do not respond to the yellow, causing the white light to appear to be blue. Because the other colors in the figure do the same thing relative to their specific opponents, the afterimage produces the opponent colors—for a while. The afterimage lasts only a short time, because the yellow receptors soon recover from their fatigue and begin to perceive the white light more accurately.

> **opponent-process theory of color vision** The theory that receptor cells for color are linked in pairs, working in opposition to each other.

We now know that both trichromatic processes and opponent mechanisms are at work in producing the perception of color vision, but in different parts of the visual sensing system. Trichromatic processes work within the retina itself, whereas opponent mechanisms operate both in the retina and at later stages of neuronal processing (Baraas, Foster, & Amano, 2006; Chen, Zhou, & Gong, 2004; Gegenfurtner, 2003; Puller & Haverkamp, 2011).

As our understanding of the processes that permit us to see has increased, some psychologists have begun to develop new techniques to provide some aspects of vision

STUDY **TIP**

Know the distinctions between the two explanations for color vision—the trichromatic and opponent-process theories.

PSYCH think

> > > Repairing faulty sensory organs through devices such as personal guidance systems and eyeglasses is the goal of much ongoing research. Should researchers also try to improve normal sensory capabilities beyond their "natural" range, so that human visual or audio capabilities are more sensitive than normal? What benefits might this ability bring? What problems might it cause?

to people who are blind. For example, one technology allows light-sensitive chips to be surgically implanted under the retina. Such chips detect light entering the eye and striking them; they then send electrical impulses to the ganglion cells that normally convey visual information from the retina to the nervous system. They therefore function in much the same way as natural photoreceptors would, although the visual information that they can capture and relay to the brain is still limited to simple patterns formed by dots of light (Wickelgren, 2006).

>> Hearing and the Other Senses

The blast-off was easy compared with what the astronaut was experiencing now: space sickness. The constant nausea and vomiting were enough to make her wonder why she had worked so hard to become an astronaut. Even though she had been warned that there was a two-thirds chance that her first experience in space would cause these symptoms, she wasn't prepared for how terribly sick she really felt.

Whether or not the astronaut wishes she could head right back to earth, her experience, a major problem for space travelers, is related to a basic sensory process: the

sound The movement of air molecules brought about by a source of vibration.

eardrum The part of the ear that vibrates when sound waves hit it.

sense of motion and balance. This sense allows people to navigate their bodies through the world and keep themselves upright without falling. Along with hearing—the process by which sound waves are translated into understandable and meaningful forms—the sense of motion and balance resides in the ear.

SENSING SOUND

Although many of us think primarily of the outer ear when we speak of the ear, that structure is only one simple part of the whole. The outer ear acts as a reverse megaphone to collect and bring sounds into the internal portions of the ear. The location of the outer ears on different sides of the head helps with *sound localization*, the process by which we identify the direction from which a sound is coming. Wave patterns in the air enter each ear at a slightly different time, and the brain uses the discrepancy as a clue to the sound's point of origin.

Sound is the movement of air molecules set off by a source of vibration. Sounds, arriving at the outer ear in the form of wavelike vibrations, are funneled into the *auditory*

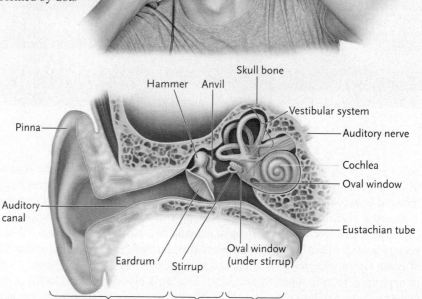

Parts of the Ear

Source: Brooker et al., 2008

canal, a tubelike passage that leads to the eardrum. The **eardrum** is aptly named, because it operates as a miniature drum, vibrating when sound waves hit it. The more intense the sound, the more the eardrum vibrates. These vibrations are transferred into the *middle ear*, a tiny chamber containing three bones (the *hammer*, the *anvil*, and the *stirrup*), which in turn transmit vibrations to the oval win-

Did you know?

Nippon Telegraph and Telephone is developing a technology for us to allow our movements to be controlled remotely! Why would we want to do that? Suppose you were in a new city and wanted to walk to a nearby botanical garden. Wouldn't it be nice to put on a pair of headphones that literally moved you in the right direction? Don't believe it? Check out the video: youtube.com/watch?v=Kf0E9IIkZIU.

A PHYSICIAN A college student is experiencing vertigo, a medical condition in which balance is affected. He gets so dizzy when he stands up that he has nausea and difficulty walking. What would you do to help him?

dow, a thin membrane leading to the inner ear. Because the hammer, anvil, and stirrup act as a set of levers, they not only transmit vibrations but also increase their strength. Moreover, because the opening into the middle ear (the eardrum) is considerably larger than the opening out of it (the *oval window*), the force of sound waves on the oval window becomes amplified. The middle ear, then, acts as a tiny (but powerful) mechanical amplifier.

The *inner ear* is the portion of the ear that changes sound waves into a form in which they can be transmitted to the brain. (As you will see, it also contains the organs that allow us to locate the position of the body and determine how we are moving through space.) When sound enters the inner ear through the oval window, it moves into the **cochlea**, a coiled tube that looks something like a snail and is filled with fluid that vibrates in response to sound. Inside the cochlea is the **basilar membrane**, a structure that runs through the center of the cochlea, dividing it into an upper chamber and a lower chamber. The basilar membrane is covered with **hair cells**. When the hair cells are bent by the vibrations entering the cochlea, the cells send a neural message to the brain (Cho, 2000; Zhou, Liu, & Davis, 2005).

Sorting Out Theories of Sound How does the brain sort out wavelengths of different frequencies and intensities? That is, how do we differentiate Dora the Explorer's voice from Darth Vader's voice or screams at a rock concert from whispers in the library? One clue comes from studies of the basilar membrane, the area in the cochlea that translates physical vibrations into neural impulses. It turns out that sounds affect different areas of the basilar membrane, depending on the frequency of the sound wave. The part of the basilar membrane nearest to the oval window is most sensitive to high-frequency sounds, and the part nearest to the cochlea's inner end is most sensitive to low-frequency sounds. This finding has

STUDY **TIP**

Know the difference between the place theory and the frequency theory of hearing.

led to the **place theory of hearing**, which states that different areas of the basilar membrane respond to different frequencies.

Place theory explains how we differentiate various high pitched sounds (for instance, distinguishing Dora's voice from her pal Boot's voice), but it does not tell the full story of hearing, because very low frequency sounds (for example, Darth Vader's voice) trigger neurons across such a wide area of the basilar membrane that no single site is involved. Consequently, an additional explanation for hearing has been proposed: frequency theory. The **frequency theory of hearing** suggests that the entire basilar membrane acts as a microphone, vibrating as a whole in response to a sound. According to this explanation, the nerve receptors send out signals that are tied directly to the frequency (the number of wave crests per second) of the sounds to which we are exposed, with the number of nerve impulses being a direct function of a sound's frequency. Thus, the higher the pitch of a sound (and therefore the greater the frequency of its wave crests), the greater the number of nerve impulses that are transmitted up the auditory nerve to the brain.

Neither place theory nor frequency theory provides the full explanation for hearing. Place theory provides a better explanation for the sensing of high-frequency sounds, whereas frequency theory explains what happens when low-frequency sounds are encountered. Medium-frequency sounds incorporate both processes (Hirsh & Watson, 1996; Hudspeth, 2000).

After an auditory message leaves the ear, it is transmitted to the auditory cortex of the brain through a complex series of neural interconnections. As the message is transmitted, it is communicated through neurons that respond to specific types of sounds. Within the auditory cortex itself, there are neurons that respond selectively to very specific sorts of sound features, such as clicks and whistles. Some neurons respond only to a specific pattern of sounds, such as a steady tone but not an intermittent one. Furthermore, specific neurons transfer information about a sound's location through their particular pattern of firing (Alho et al., 2006; Middlebrooks et al., 2005; Wang et al., 2005).

Balance: The Ups and Downs of Life Speech perception requires that we make fine discriminations among sounds that are similar in terms of their physical properties. Furthermore, not only are we able to understand *what* is being said from speech, we can use vocal

cochlea (*KOKE-le-uh*) A coiled tube in the ear filled with fluid that vibrates in response to sound.

basilar membrane A vibrating structure that runs through the center of the cochlea, dividing it into an upper chamber and a lower chamber and containing sense receptors for sound.

hair cells Tiny cells covering the basilar membrane that, when bent by vibrations entering the cochlea, transmit neural messages to the brain.

place theory of hearing The theory that different areas of the basilar membrane respond to different frequencies.

frequency theory of hearing The theory that the entire basilar membrane acts like a microphone, vibrating as a whole in response to a sound.

The weightlessness of the ear's otoliths produces space sickness in most astronauts.

cues to determine who is speaking, if they have an accent and thus where they may be from, and even their emotional state. Such capabilities illustrate the sophistication of our sense of hearing (Fowler & Galantucci, 2008; Massaro, 2008; Pell et al., 2009). Several structures of the ear are related more to our sense of balance than to our hearing. Collectively, these structures are known as the vestibular system, which responds to the pull of gravity and allows us to maintain our balance, even when standing in a lurching bus in stop-and-go traffic. The **semicircular canals** of the inner ear consist of three tubes containing fluid that sloshes through them when the head moves, signaling rotational or angular movement to the brain. The pull on our bodies caused by the acceleration of forward, backward, or up-and-down motion, as well as the constant pull of gravity, is sensed by the **otoliths**, tiny, motion-sensitive crystals in the semicircular canals. When we move, these crystals shift like grains of sand on a windy beach. In the reduced-gravity environment of space, the brain's lack of experience in interpreting messages from weightless otoliths is the cause of the space sickness commonly experienced by two thirds of all space travelers (Flam, 1991; Stern & Koch, 1996).

semicircular canals Three tubelike structures of the inner ear containing fluid that sloshes through them when the head moves, signaling rotational or angular movement to the brain.

otoliths Tiny, motion-sensitive crystals within the semicircular canals that sense body acceleration.

SMELL AND TASTE

Until he bit into a piece of raw cabbage on that February evening . . . , Raymond Fowler had not thought much about the sense of taste. The cabbage, part of a pasta dish he was preparing for his family's dinner, had an odd, burning taste, but he did not pay it much attention. Then a few minutes later, his daughter handed him a glass of cola, and he took a swallow. "It was like sulfuric acid," he said. "It was like the hottest thing you could imagine boring into your mouth." (Goode, 1999, pp. D1–D2)

It was evident that something was very wrong with Fowler's sense of taste. After extensive testing, it became clear that he had damaged the nerves involved in his sense of taste, probably because of a viral infection or a medicine he was taking. (Luckily, a few months later his sense of taste returned to normal.)

Smell Even without disruptions in our ability to perceive the world such as those experienced by Fowler, we all know how important the chemical senses of taste and smell are. Although many animals have keener abilities to detect odors than we do, the human sense of smell (*olfaction*) permits us to detect more than 10,000 separate smells. We also have a good memory for smells, and long-forgotten events and memories—good and bad—can be brought back with the mere whiff of cotton candy, baby powder, or the disinfectant used to clean the restrooms in elementary school (Schroers, Prigot, & Fagen, 2007; Stevenson & Case, 2005; Willander & Larsson, 2006).

The sense of smell is activated when the molecules of a substance enter the nasal passages and meet *olfactory cells*, the receptor neurons of the nose, which are spread across the nasal cavity. More than 1,000 separate types of receptors have been identified on those cells so far. Each of these receptors is so specialized that it responds only to a small number of different odors. The responses of the separate olfactory cells are transmitted to the brain, where they are combined into recognition of a particular smell (Marshall, Laing, & Jinks, 2006; Murphy et al., 2004; Zhou & Buck, 2006).

Smell may also act as a hidden means of communication for humans. It has long been known that nonhumans release pheromones, chemicals they secrete into the environment that produce a reaction in other members of the same species, permitting the transmission of messages such as sexual availability. For example, the vaginal secretions of female monkeys contain pheromones that stimulate the sexual interest of male monkeys (Hawkes & Doty, 2009; Holy, Dulac, & Meister, 2000; Touhara, 2007).

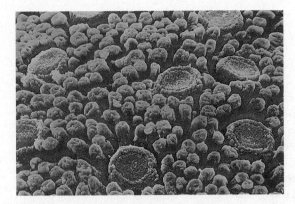

Taste buds may not be much to look at, but they are important for survival. Why do you think the sense of taste might be adaptive?

Taste We are so lucky that we can enjoy the sweetness of jelly beans, the tartness of lemonade, and the saltiness of French fries. We don't consider ourselves as lucky when the bitter aftertaste of certain medicines leaves us longing for a different flavor. The sense of taste (*gustation*) involves receptor cells that respond to four basic qualities: sweet, sour, salty, and bitter. A fifth category, called *umami*, also exists, although there is controversy about whether it qualifies as a fundamental taste. *Umami* is difficult to translate from Japanese, although the English words *meaty* and *savory* come close. Chemically, umami characterizes food that contains amino acids (the substances that make up proteins) (Erickson, 2008; McCabe & Rolls, 2007; Uematsu et al., 2011).

Although the receptor cells for taste are specialized to respond most strongly to a particular type of taste, they also are capable of responding to other tastes as well. Ultimately, every taste is simply a combination of the basic flavor qualities, in the same way that the primary colors blend into a vast variety of shades and hues (Dilorenzo & Youngentob, 2003; Yeomans, Tepper, & Ritezschel, 2007).

The receptor cells for taste are located in roughly 10,000 *taste buds* distributed across the tongue and other parts of the mouth and throat. The taste buds wear out and are replaced every 10 days or so. Otherwise we would lose the ability to taste.

The sense of taste differs significantly from one person to another, largely as a result of genetic factors. Some people, dubbed "supertasters," are highly sensitive to taste; they have twice as many taste receptors as "nontasters," who are relatively insensitive to taste. Supertasters (who, for unknown reasons, are more likely to be female than male) find sweets sweeter, cream creamier, and spicy dishes spicier, and weaker concentrations of flavor are enough to satisfy any cravings they may have. In

The receptor cells for taste are located in roughly 10,000 taste buds, which are distributed across the tongue and other parts of the mouth and throat.

contrast, because they aren't so sensitive to taste, nontasters may seek out relatively sweeter and fattier foods in order to maximize the taste. As a consequence, they may be prone to obesity (Bartoshuk, 2000; Snyder, Fast, & Bartoshuk, 2004; Pickering & Gordon, 2006).

THE SKIN SENSES: TOUCH, PRESSURE, TEMPERATURE, AND PAIN

It started innocently when Jennifer Darling hurt her right wrist during gym class. At first it seemed like a simple sprain. But even though the initial injury healed, the excruciating, burning pain accompanying it did not go away. Instead, it spread to her other arm and then to her legs. The pain, which Jennifer described as similar to "a hot iron on your arm," was unbearable—and never stopped.

The source of Darling's pain turned out to be a rare condition known as "reflex sympathetic dystrophy syndrome," or RSDS. For a victim of RSDS, a stimulus as mild as a gentle breeze or the touch of a feather can produce agony. Even bright sunlight or a loud noise can trigger intense pain.

> **skin senses** The senses of touch, pressure, temperature, and pain.

Pain like Darling's can be devastating, yet a lack of pain can be equally bad. If you never experienced pain, for instance, you might not notice that your arm had brushed against a hot pan, and you would suffer a severe burn. Similarly, without the warning sign of abdominal pain that typically accompanies an inflamed appendix, your appendix might eventually rupture, spreading a fatal infection throughout your body.

In fact, all our **skin senses**—touch, pressure, temperature, and pain—play a critical role in survival, making us aware of potential danger to our bodies. Most of these senses operate through nerve receptor cells located at various depths throughout the skin, distributed unevenly throughout the body. For example, some areas, such as the

Take a Taste Test

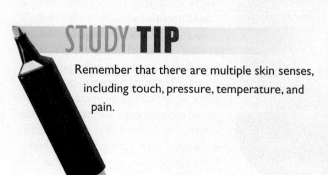

Average tasters lie in between supertasters and nontasters. Bartoshuk and Lucchina lack the data at this time to rate salt reliabilty, but you can compare your results to others taking the test.

1. Taste Bud Count
   Punch a hole with a standard hole punch in a square of wax paper. Paint the front of your tongue with a cotton swab dipped in blue food coloring. Put wax paper on top of your tongue, just to the right of center. With a flashlight and magnifying glass, count the number of pink unstained circles. They contain taste buds.

2. Sweet Taste
   Rinse your mouth with water before tasting each sample. Put 1/2 cup sugar in a measuring cup, and then add enough water to make 1 cup. Mix. Coat front half of your tongue, including the tip, with a cotton swab dipped in the solution. Wait a few moments. Rate the sweetness according to the scale below.

3. Salt Taste
   Put 2 teaspoons of salt in a measuring cup and add enough water to make 1 cup. Repeat the steps listed in #2 above, rating how salty the solution is.

4. Spicy Taste
   Add 1 teaspoon of Tabasco sauce to 1 cup of water. Apply with a cotton swab to first half inch of the tongue, including the tip. Keep your tongue out of your mouth until the burn reaches a peak, then rate the burn according to the scale.

Taste Scale

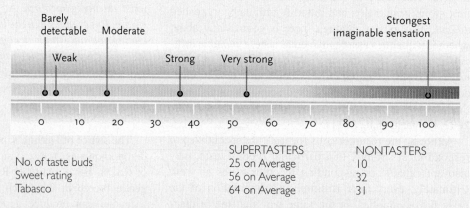

	SUPERTASTERS	NONTASTERS
No. of taste buds	25 on Average	10
Sweet rating	56 on Average	32
Tabasco	64 on Average	31

Adapted from Bartoshuk, L., & Lucchina, L. "Take a taste test," from Brownlee, S., & Watson, T. (1997, January 13). The senses. *U.S. News & World Report*, pp. 51–59. Reprinted by permission of Dr. Linda Bartoshuk.

fingertips, have many more receptor cells sensitive to touch and as a consequence are notably more sensitive than other areas of the body (Gardner & Kandel, 2000).

Probably the most extensively researched skin sense is pain, and with good reason: People consult physicians and take medication for pain more than for any other symptom or condition. Pain costs $100 billion a year in the United States alone (Kalb, 2003; Pesmen, 2006).

STUDY TIP

Remember that there are multiple skin senses, including touch, pressure, temperature, and pain.

Pain is a response to a great variety of different kinds of stimuli. A light that is too bright can produce pain, and sound that is too loud can be painful. One explanation is that pain is an outcome of cell injury; when a cell is damaged, regardless of the source of damage, it releases a chemical called *substance P* that transmits pain messages to the brain.

Skin Sensitivity

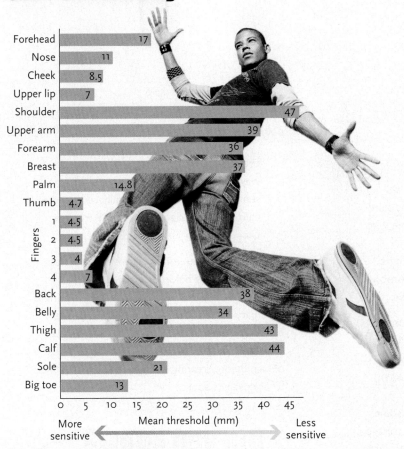

Forehead 17
Nose 11
Cheek 8.5
Upper lip 7
Shoulder 47
Upper arm 39
Forearm 36
Breast 37
Palm 14.8
Thumb 4.7
Fingers
1 4.5
2 4.5
3 4
4 7
Back 38
Belly 34
Thigh 43
Calf 44
Sole 21
Big toe 13

0 5 10 15 20 25 30 35 40 45
Mean threshold (mm)

More sensitive ←——————→ Less sensitive

Kenshalo, *The Skin Senses*, 1968. Springfield, IL: Charles C. Thomas.

Some people are more susceptible to pain than others. For example, some women experience painful stimuli more intensely than men. These gender differences are associated with the production of hormones related to menstrual cycles. In addition, certain genes are linked to the experience of pain—thus we may inherit our sensitivity to pain (Edwards & Fillingim, 2007; Fillingim, 2011; Kim, Clark, & Dionne, 2009; Nielsen et al., 2008; Nielsen, Staud, & Price, 2009).

According to the **gate-control theory of pain**, particular nerve receptors in the spinal cord lead to specific areas of the brain related to pain. When these receptors are activated because of an injury or problem with a part of the body, a "gate" to the brain is opened, allowing us to experience the sensation of pain (Melzack & Katz, 2004).

However, another set of neural receptors can, when stimulated, close the "gate" to the brain, thereby reducing the experience of pain. The gate can be shut in two differ-ent ways. First, other impulses can over-whelm the nerve pathways relating to pain, which are spread throughout the brain. In this case, nonpainful stimuli compete with and sometimes displace the neural mes-sage of pain, thereby shutting off the pain-ful stimulus. This explains why rubbing the skin around an injury (or even listening to distracting music) helps reduce pain. The competing stimuli can overpower the pain-ful ones (Villemure, Slotnick, & Bushnell, 2003).

Psychological factors account for the second way a gate can be shut. Depend-ing on an individual's current emotions, interpretation of events, and previous experience, the brain can close a gate by sending a message down the spinal cord to an injured area, producing a reduction in or relief from pain. Thus, soldiers who are injured in battle may experience no pain—the surprising situation in more than half of all combat injuries. The lack of pain prob-ably occurs because a soldier experiences such relief at still being alive that the brain sends a signal to the injury site to shut down the pain gate (Gatchel & Weisberg, 2000; Pincus & Morley, 2001; Turk, 1994).

Our understanding of pain is incomplete. We do not yet understand, for example, how acupuncture alleviates pain, but scien-tific research has demonstrated that it does work for at least some kinds of pain. It is also possible that the body's own painkillers—called endorphins—as well as positive and negative emotions, play a role in opening and clos-ing the gate (Roy, Pichee, Chen, Peretz, & Rainville, 2009; Witt, Jena, & Brinkhaus, 2006).

> **gate-control theory of pain** The theory that particular nerve receptors in the spinal cord lead to specific areas of the brain related to pain.

HOW OUR SENSES INTERACT

When Matthew Blakeslee shapes hamburger patties with his hands, he experiences a vivid bitter taste in his mouth. Esmerelda Jones (a pseudonym) sees blue when she listens to the note C sharp played on the piano; other notes evoke different hues—so much so that the piano keys are actually color-coded, making it easier for her to remember and play musical scales. (Ramachandran & Hubbard, 2004, p. 53)

The explanation? Both of these people have a rare condition known as *synesthesia*, in which exposure to one sensation (such as sound) evokes an addi-tional one (such as vision).

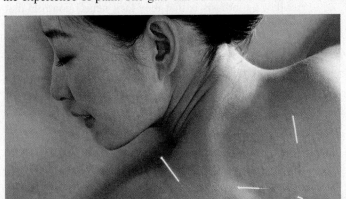

Acupuncture has been used for thousands of years to relieve pain.

BUY IT? > > >

Pain Management

Are you one of the 50 million people in the United States who suffer from persistent pain? What options are available to help people who live with pain on a daily basis?

Psychologists and medical specialists have devised several strategies to fight pain. Among the most important approaches are these:

- *Medication.* Painkilling drugs are the most popular treatment in fighting pain. Medication can be in the form of pills, patches, injections, or liquids (Kalb, 2003; Pesmen, 2006).

- *Nerve and brain stimulation.* Pain can sometimes be relieved by applying a low-voltage electric current to the painful area. In cases of severe pain, electrodes can be implanted surgically into the brain, or a handheld battery pack can stimulate nerve cells to provide direct relief (Campbell & Ditto, 2002; Ross, 2000; Tugay et al., 2007).

- *Light therapy.* Exposure to specific wavelengths of red or infrared light increase the production of enzymes that may promote healing (Evcik et al., 2007; Underwood, 2005).

- *Biofeedback and relaxation techniques.* Using *biofeedback*, people learn to control "involuntary" functions, such as heartbeat and respiration. If the pain involves muscles, as in tension headaches or back pain, sufferers can be trained to relax their bodies systematically (Nestoriuc & Martin, 2007; Vitiello, Bonello, & Pollard, 2007).

- *Cognitive restructuring.* Cognitive treatments are effective for people who believe that "This pain will never stop," "The pain is ruining my life," or "I can't take it anymore" and are thereby likely to make their pain

continued

even worse. By substituting more positive ways of thinking, people can increase their sense of control—and actually reduce the pain they experience (Spanos, Barber, & Lang, 2005; Bogart et al., 2007).

Of course, it's important to investigate these methods carefully before using any particular treatment. Not all the treatments are appropriate for a particular condition. Furthermore, remember that pain is a symptom of something that is amiss. You need to identify the underlying cause of pain before treating it, so seek professional help to discover its source.

Did you know?

Acupuncture has received a great deal of attention in recent years. Scientific research suggests that acupuncture is effective not only for certain types of short-term and chronic pain relief, but other medical problems as well, including dry eye syndrome, dizziness, and maybe even Parkinson's disease (Choi, Yeo, Hong, & Lim, 2011; Hopton & MacPherson, 2010; Park, Ko, Bae, Jung, Moon, Cho, Kim, & Park, 2009).

The origins of synesthesia are a mystery. It is possible that people with synesthesia have unusually dense neural linkages between the different sensory areas of the brain. Another hypothesis is that they lack neural controls that usually inhibit connections between sensory areas (Pearce, 2007; Kadosh, Henik, & Walsh, 2009; Ramachandran, Hubbard, & Butcher, 2004).

Whatever the reason for synesthesia, it is a rare condition. Even so, everyone's senses interact and integrate in a variety of ways. For example, the taste of food is influenced by its texture and temperature. We perceive food that is warmer

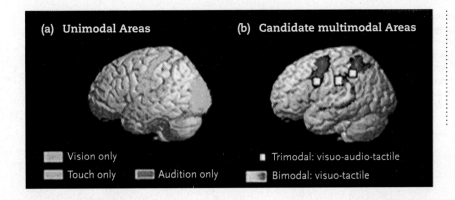

(a) Unimodal Areas

(b) Candidate multimodal Areas

Vision only
Touch only Audition only

Trimodal: visuo-audio-tactile
Bimodal: visuo-tactile

Participants in a study examining sensory interaction were exposed to visual, touch, and auditory stimuli. Although some parts of the brain responded to these stimuli independently (a), other parts responded to the three types of stimuli in an integrated fashion (b). The results illustrate the ways in which various sensory stimuli are integrated. *Source:* Macaluso & Driver, 2005, Figure 1(a).

as sweeter (think of the sweetness of steamy hot chocolate compared with cold chocolate milk). Spicy foods stimulate some of the same pain receptors that are also stimulated by heat—making the use of "hot" as a synonym for "spicy" quite accurate (Balaban, McBurney, & Affeltranger, 2005; Cruz & Green, 2000; Green & George, 2004).

It's important, then, to think of our senses as interacting with one another. For instance, increasing evidence from brain imaging studies show that the senses work in tandem to build our understanding of the world. In short, we engage in multimodal perception, in which the brain collects the information from the individual sensory systems and integrates and coordinates it (Macaluso & Driver, 2005; Paulmann, Jessen, & Kotz, 2009).

Moreover, despite the fact that very different sorts of stimuli activate our individual sensory systems, the senses all react according to the same basic principles that we discussed at the start of this chapter. For example, our responses to visual, auditory, and taste stimuli all follow Weber's law describing our sensitivity to changes in the strength of stimuli.

Ultimately, in some ways our senses are more similar to one another than they are different. Each of them is designed to pick up information from the environment and translate it into useable information. Individually and collectively, our senses help us to understand the complexities of the world, allowing us to navigate through it effectively and intelligently.

>> Perception: Constructing Our Impressions of the World

All of the information that the senses bring to the brain needs to be integrated and understood. Perception is the process of constructing something meaningful from the array of information our senses provide us.

Perception is the process of constructing something meaningful from the array of information our senses provide us.

One of the most important points you should keep in mind about perception is that there is not a 1:1 correspondence between our perceptual representation

Vase-Face Illusion
Is it a vase or the profiles of two people?

When the usual cues we use to distinguish figure from ground are absent, we may shift back and forth between different views of the same figure. If you look at each of these objects long enough, you'll probably experience a shift in what you're seeing.

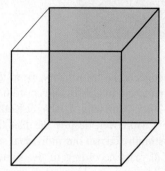

Necker Cube
Is the color portion of the cube the front side or the back?

"I'm turning into my mother"

Understanding this cartoon involves the separation of the figure and ground. If you're having trouble appreciating the humor, stare at the woman on the right and you will see her transformed.

of the world and the physical reality of the world. Perception takes the physical information in the world and interprets it. Why? Because physical information is typically ambiguous. We take the available information our senses provide and interpret physical stimuli based on what we know about the world.

THE GESTALT LAWS OF ORGANIZATION

Some of the most basic perceptual processes can be described by a series of principles that focus on the ways we organize bits and pieces of information into meaningful wholes. Known as **Gestalt laws of organization**, these principles were set forth in the early 1900s by a group of German psychologists who studied patterns, or *Gestalten* (Wertheimer, 1923). Those psychologists discovered a number of principles that are valid for visual—and auditory—stimuli: closure, proximity, similarity, and simplicity.

Gestalt laws of organization
A series of principles that describe how we organize bits and pieces of information into meaningful wholes.

In *closure*, we group elements to form enclosed or complete figures rather than open ones. We use *proximity* by perceiving elements that are closer together as grouped together. Elements that are *similar* in appearance we perceive as grouped together. Finally, in a general sense, the overriding Gestalt principle is *simplicity*: When we observe a pattern, we perceive it in the most basic, straightforward manner that we can. If we have a choice of interpretations, we generally opt for the simpler one.

Although Gestalt psychology no longer plays a prominent role in contemporary psychology, its legacy endures. One fundamental Gestalt principle that remains influential

STUDY **TIP**

The Gestalt laws of organization are classic principles in the field of psychology. Use the four figures below to help you remember them.

Gestalt Diagrams

Gestalt principles of organization characterize our ability to perceive various bits and pieces of information as meaningful patterns.

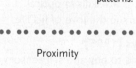

Proximity

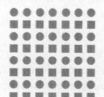

Similarity

Closure

Simplicity

© Paul Noth/The New Yorker Collection/www.cartoonbank.com.

is that two objects considered together form a whole that is different from the simple combination of the objects. Gestalt psychologists argued that the perception of stimuli in our environment goes well beyond the individual elements that we sense. Instead, it represents an active, constructive process carried out within the brain (Humphreys & Müller, 2000; Lehar, 2003; van der Helm, 2006).

TOP-DOWN AND BOTTOM-UP PROCESSING

Ca- yo- re-d t-is -en-en-e, w-ic- ha- ev-ry –hi-d l-tt-r m-ss-ng? It probably won't take you too long to figure out that it says, "Can you read this sentence, which has every third letter missing?"

If perception were based primarily on breaking down a stimulus into its most basic elements, understanding the sentence, as well as other ambiguous stimuli, would not be possible. The fact that you were probably able to recognize such an imprecise stimulus illustrates that perception proceeds along two different avenues, called top-down processing and bottom-up processing.

Picture an adult and a 5-year-old boy watching the popular game show *Wheel of Fortune*. Each works very hard at trying to solve the puzzles, but the adult always wins, not because she is smarter than the child but because she uses the clue (for example, "famous person") and the various letters to decipher B E - - - - E as "Beyoncé." The boy, who is just beginning to read, can't read the clue yet, so he can rely only on recognizing the letters as they are revealed. He sounds out the revealed letters and comes up with words like "beehive." Psychologists would argue that the adult solves the puzzle first because she relies on both top-down processing and bottom-up processing, whereas the child relies much more on bottom-up processing.

In **top-down processing**, perception is guided by higher-level knowledge, experience, expectations, and motivations. You were able to figure out the meaning of the sentence with the missing letters at the beginning of this section because of your prior reading experience and because written English contains redundancies. Not every letter of each word is necessary to decode its meaning. Moreover, your expectations played a role in your being able to read the sentence. You were probably expecting a statement that had *something* to do with psychology, not the lyrics to a Lady Gaga song.

Top-down processing is illustrated by the importance of context in determining how we perceive objects. However, top-down processing cannot occur on its own. Even though top-down processing allows us to fill the gaps in ambiguous and out-of-context stimuli, we would be unable to perceive the meaning of such stimuli without bottom-up processing. **Bottom-up processing** consists of the progression of recognizing and processing information from individual components of a stimulus and moving to the perception of the whole. We would make no headway in our recognition of the sentence without being able to perceive the individual shapes that make up the letters. Some perception, then, occurs at the level of the patterns and features of each of the separate letters.

Top-down and bottom-up processing occur simultaneously and interact with each other in perception. Bottom-up processing permits us to process the fundamental characteristics of stimuli, whereas top-down processing allows us to bring our experience to bear on perception. As psychologists learn more about the complex processes involved in perception, they are developing a better understanding of how the brain continually interprets information from the senses and permits us to make responses appropriate to the environment (Folk & Remington, 2008; Sobel et al., 2007; Westerhausen et al., 2009).

PERCEPTUAL CONSTANCY

Consider what happens as you finish a conversation with a friend and she begins to walk away from you. As you watch her walk down the street, the image on your retina becomes smaller and smaller. Do you wonder why she is shrinking? Of course not. Despite the very real change in the size of the retinal image, you factor into your thinking the knowledge that your friend is moving farther away from you because of perceptual constancy. **Perceptual constancy** is a phenomenon in which physical objects are perceived as unvarying and consistent despite changes in their appearance or in the physical environment. Perceptual constancy leads us to view objects as having an unvarying size, shape, color, and brightness, even if the image on our retina varies. For example, despite the varying images on the retina as an airplane approaches, flies overhead, and disappears, we

top-down processing
Perception that is guided by higher-level knowledge, experience, expectations, and motivations.

bottom-up processing
Perception that consists of the progression of recognizing and processing information from individual components of a stimuli and moving to the perception of the whole.

perceptual constancy
Phenomenon in which physical objects are perceived to have constant shape, color, and size, despite changes in their appearance or in the physical environment.

Top-Down Processing
The power of context helps us perceive the letter B in the top line and the same figure as the number 13 in the bottom line.

Source: Coren & Ward, 1989.

A B C D E F
10 11 12 13 14

Perceptual Constancy

When the moon is near the horizon, it appears much closer to us than it does when it is higher in the sky, and in comparison to the other objects in our field of vision, it looks huge. Perceptual constancy misleads our sense of distance.

Depth Perception

Railroad tracks that seem to join together in the distance illustrate linear perspective.

do not perceive the airplane as changing shape (Garrigan & Kellman, 2008; Redding, 2002; Wickelgren, 2004).

DEPTH PERCEPTION

As sophisticated as the retina is, the images projected onto it are flat and two-dimensional. Yet the world around us is three-dimensional, and we perceive it that way. How do we make the transformation from 2D to 3D?

The ability to view the world in three dimensions and to perceive distance—a skill known as

> **depth perception** The ability to view the world in three dimensions and to perceive distance.

depth perception—is due in part to the fact that we have two eyes. Because there is a certain distance between the eyes, a slightly different image reaches each retina. The brain integrates the two images into one composite view, but it also recognizes the difference in images and uses that difference to estimate the distance of an object from us. The difference in the images seen by the left eye and the right eye is known as *binocular disparity* (Foster et al., 2011; Hibbard, 2007; Kara & Boyd, 2009).

To get a sense of binocular disparity, hold a pencil at arm's length and look at it first with one eye and then with the other. There is little difference between the two views relative to the background. Now bring the pencil just 6 inches away from your face, and try the same thing. This time you will perceive a greater difference between the two views.

The fact that the discrepancy between the images in the two eyes varies according to the distance of objects that we view provides us with a means of determining distance. If we view two objects and one is considerably closer to us than the other is, the retinal disparity will be relatively large, and we will have a greater sense of depth between the two. However, if the two objects are a similar distance from us, the retinal disparity will be minor, and we will perceive them as being a similar distance from us.

In addition to cues that require two eyes, certain cues permit us to obtain a sense of depth and distance with just one eye. These cues are known as *monocular cues*. One monocular cue—*motion parallax*—is the change in position of an object on the retina caused by movement of your body relative to the object. For example, suppose you are a passenger in a moving car, and you focus your eye on a stable object such as a tree. Objects that are closer than the tree will appear to move backward, and the nearer the object is, the more quickly it will appear to move. In contrast, objects beyond the tree will seem to move at a slower speed, but in the same direction as you are going. Your brain is able to use these cues to calculate the relative distances of the tree and other objects.

Similarly, experience has taught us that if two objects are the same size, the one that makes a smaller image on the retina is farther away than is the one that provides a larger image—an example of the monocular cue of *relative size*. But it's not just size of an object that provides information about distance; the quality of the image on the retina helps us judge distance. The monocular cue of *texture gradient* provides information about distance because the details of things that are far away are less distinct (Proffitt, 2006).

Finally, anyone who has ever seen railroad tracks that seem to join together in the distance knows that distant objects appear to be closer together than are nearer ones, a phenomenon called linear perspective. People use *linear perspective* as a monocular cue in estimating distance, allowing the two-dimensional image on the retina to record the three-dimensional world (Bruce, Green, & Georgeson, 1997; Bruggeman, Yonas, & Konczak, 2007; Dobbins et al., 1998; Shimono & Wade, 2002).

PERCEPTUAL ILLUSIONS

If you look carefully at the Parthenon, one of the most famous buildings of ancient Greece, still standing at the top of an Athens hill, the Acropolis, you'll see that it was built with a bulge on one side. If it didn't have that bulge—and quite a few other architectural "tricks" like it, such as columns that incline inward—it would look as if it were crooked and about to fall down. Instead, it appears to stand completely straight, at right angles to the ground.

The fact that the Parthenon appears to be completely upright is the result of a series of visual illusions. **Visual illusions** are physical stimuli that consistently produce errors in perception. In the case of the Parthenon, the building appears to be completely square. However, if it had been built that way, it would look curved. The reason for this is an illusion that makes right angles placed above a line appear as if they were bent. To offset the illusion, the Parthenon was constructed with a slight upward curvature.

> **visual illusions** Physical stimuli that consistently produce errors in perception.

Another visual illusion, the *Müller-Lyer illusion*, has fascinated psychologists for decades. It consists of two lines that are the same length, but one has arrow tips pointing inward and appears to be longer than the other one, which has the arrow tips pointing outward.

Visual Illusion

The Parthenon on the Acropolis in Athens, Greece, is an architectural wonder that looks perfectly straight in the photo.

If the Parthenon had been built with completely true right angles, it would look like this:

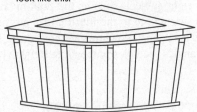

To compensate for this illusion, it was designed to have a slight upward curvature, as illustrated here:
Source: Coren & Ward, 1989, p. 5.

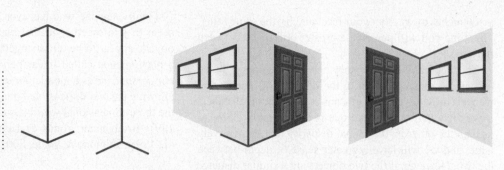

One explanation for the Müller-Lyer illusion suggests that the line with arrow points directed outward is perceived as the relatively close corner of a rectangular object, such as the outside corner of a building. The line with arrow points directed inward is interpreted as the inside corner of a rectangular object, such as a room extending away from us. Our previous experience with distance cues leads us to assume that the outside corner, (left) is closer than the inside corner, (right) and that the inside corner must therefore be longer.

Although all kinds of explanations for visual illusions have been suggested, most concentrate either on the physical operation of the eye or on our misinterpretation of the visual stimulus. For example, one explanation for the Müller-Lyer illusion is that eye movements are greater when the arrow tips point inward, making us perceive the line as longer than it is when the arrow tips face outward. In contrast, a different explanation for the illusion suggests that we unconsciously attribute particular significance to each of the lines (Gregory, 1978; Redding & Hawley, 1993). We tend to perceive one line as if it were the relatively close outside corner of a rectangular object, such as the outside corner of a room. In contrast, when we view the other line, we perceive it as the relatively more distant inside corner of a rectangular object, such as the inside corner of a room. Because previous experience leads us to assume that the outside corner is closer than the inside corner, and since both lines are actually the same length, we assume that the one that appears to be closer is actually shorter.

Despite the complexity of the latter explanation, a good deal of evidence supports it. For instance, cross-cultural studies show that people raised in areas where there are few right angles—such as the Zulu in Africa—are much less susceptible to the illusion than are people who grow up where most structures are built using right angles and rectangles (Segall, Campbell, & Herskovits, 1966).

CULTURE AND PERCEPTION

In the late 1950s, anthropologist Colin Turnbull studied the life of the Mbuti Pygmies, who lived their entire lives in dense forests. One afternoon, Turnbull asked a Pygmy named Kenge to accompany him on a trip to the mountains. This trip required a long drive across the vast plains of the Congo. Kenge had never stepped out of the forest, so he tentatively accepted Turnbull's offer. As they were driving, Turnbull pointed out some buffalo in the far distance. Kenge could not believe these brown specks were buffalo and forcefully argued they must be insects. As they drove closer to the buffalo, the images of the buffalo gradually increased in size. Kenge thought Turnbull was performing witchcraft to make these animals grow. After several similar experiences that day, Kenge began to accept that objects in the distance look smaller than they do close up and started to reconsider his ideas about perceptual constancy. Kenge did, however, return to the forest claiming that the plains were a "bad country" (Turnbull, 1961).

Kenge's experience demonstrates that the culture in which we are raised has clear consequences for how we perceive the world. Consider, for instance, the so-called devil's tuning fork (on this page), a mind-boggling drawing in which the center tine of the fork alternates between appearing and disappearing.

Try to make your own drawing of the devil's tuning fork on a piece of paper. Chances are that the task is nearly impossible for you—unless you are a member of an African culture that has had little exposure to Western cultures. Westerners automatically interpret the drawing as something that cannot exist in three dimensions, and they therefore are inhibited from reproducing it. Some African peoples, in contrast, do not make the assumption that the figure is "impossible" and instead view it in two dimensions, a perception that enables them to copy the figure with ease (Deregowski, 1973).

Kenge's experiences also demonstrate that cultural differences are also reflected in depth perception. A Western

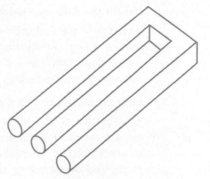

The "devil's tuning fork" has three prongs—or does it have two?

viewer of the drawing of the hunter below would interpret the hunter as aiming for the antelope in the foreground, while an elephant stands under the tree in the background. In contrast, in one study in which the drawing was used, members of an isolated African tribe interpreted the scene very differently by assuming that the hunter is aiming at the elephant. Westerners use the difference in sizes between the two animals as a cue that the elephant is farther away than the antelope (Hudson, 1960).

Does this mean that basic perceptual processes differ among people of different cultures? No. Variations in learning and experience produce cross-cultural differences in perception, while the underlying psychological processes involved in perception are similar (McCauley & Henrich, 2006).

Although visual illusions may seem like mere psychological curiosities, they actually illustrate something fundamental about perception. There is a basic connection between our prior knowledge, needs, motivations, and expectations about how the world is put together and the way we perceive it. Our view of the world is very much an outcome, then, of fundamental psychological factors. Furthermore, each person perceives the environment in a way that is unique and special (Knoblich & Sebanz, 2006; Repp & Knoblich, 2007).

Is the man aiming for the elephant or the antelope? Westerners assume that the differences in size between the two animals indicate that the elephant is farther away, and therefore the man is aiming for the antelope. In contrast, members of some African tribes, not used to depth cues in two-dimensional drawings, assume that the man is aiming for the elephant.

From Fig. 1 (p. 186) of Hudson, W. (1960). Pictorial depth perception in sub-cultural groups in Africa. *Journal of Social Psychology, 52,* 183–208, reprinted by permission of the publisher (Taylor & Francis Group, http://www .informaworld.com).

For REVIEW >>

- **What's the difference between sensation and perception?**

  Sensation is the activation of the sense organs by any source of physical energy. In contrast, perception is the process by which we sort out, interpret, analyze, and integrate stimuli to which our senses are exposed. (p. 60)

- **How do we respond to the characteristics of physical stimuli?**

  The absolute threshold is the smallest amount of physical intensity at which a stimulus can be detected. The difference threshold, or just noticeable difference, is the smallest change in the level of stimulation required to sense that a change has occurred. According to Weber, a just noticeable difference is a constant proportion of the intensity of an initial stimulus. Sensory adaptation occurs when we become accustomed to a constant stimulus and change our evaluation of it. Repeated exposure to a stimulus results in an apparent decline in sensitivity to it. (pp. 61–64)

- **How do our sense organs process stimuli?**

  Vision depends on sensitivity to light, electromagnetic waves in the visible part of the spectrum that are either reflected off objects or produced by an energy source. The eye shapes the light into an image that is transformed into nerve impulses and interpreted by the brain.

  Sound, motion, and balance are centered in the ear. Sounds, in the form of vibrating air waves, enter through the outer ear and travel through the auditory canal and the eardrum into the middle ear. In the inner ear, hair cells on the basilar membrane change the sound waves into nerve impulses that are transmitted to the brain.

  The skin senses are responsible for the experiences of touch, pressure, temperature, and pain. (pp. 63–77)

- **How does perception turn sensory stimuli into meaningful information?**

  Perception is a constructive process in which people try to construct a meaningful interpretation. The Gestalt laws of organization describe the way in which we organize bits and pieces of information into meaningful wholes. In top-down processing, perception is guided by higher-level knowledge, experience, expectations, and motivations. In bottom-up processing, perception consists of the progression of recognizing and processing information from individual components of a stimuli and moving to the perception of the whole. Perceptual constancy permits us to perceive stimuli as unvarying in size, shape, and color despite changes in the environment or the appearance of the objects being perceived. (pp. 77–83)

Pop Quiz

1. _____ is the stimulation of the sense organs; _____ is the sorting out, interpretation, analysis, and integration of stimuli by the sense organs and the brain.

2. If you were to do this activity on Weber's law again, it is likely that you would _____.
   a. get a better score.
   b. not do as well because of the fatigue effect.
   c. maybe get a better score, but it depends on how soon the test could be repeated.
   d. get the same results.

3. The proper sequence of structures that light passes through in the eye is the _____, _____, _____, and _____.

4. Match each type of visual receptor with its function.
   a. rods
   b. cones
   _____ 1. used for dim light, largely insensitive to color
   _____ 2. detect color, good in bright light

5. _____ theory states that there are three types of cones in the retina, each of which responds primarily to a different color.

6. The _____ theory of hearing states that the entire basilar membrane responds to a sound, vibrating more or less, depending on the nature of the sound.

7. The three fluid-filled tubes in the inner ear that are responsible for our sense of balance are known as the _____ _____.

8. The _____-_____ theory states that when certain skin receptors are activated as a result of an injury, a "pathway" to the brain is opened, allowing pain to be experienced.

9. Match each of the following organizational laws with its meaning:
   a. closure
   b. proximity
   c. similarity
   d. simplicity
   _____ 1. Elements close together are grouped together.
   _____ 2. Patterns are perceived in the most basic, direct manner possible.
   _____ 3. Groupings are made in terms of complete figures.
   _____ 4. Elements similar in appearance are grouped together.

10. Processing that involves higher functions such as expectations and motivations is known as _____, whereas processing that recognizes the individual components of a stimulus is known as _____.

11. Match the monocular cues with their definitions.
    a. relative size
    b. linear perspective
    c. motion parallax
    _____ 1. Straight lines seem to join together as they become more distant.
    _____ 2. An object changes position on the retina as the head moves.
    _____ 3. If two objects are the same size, the one producing the smaller retinal image is farther away.

12. The exercise on depth perception would probably work just as well if
    a. the background was changed to some other setting.
    b. there were more three-dimensional objects than two-dimensional objects.
    c. you were good at drawing and could make really convincing pictures.
    d. there were more two-dimensional objects than three-dimensional objects.

Answers TO POP QUIZ QUESTIONS

1. Sensation; perception
2. d
3. cornea, pupil, lens, retina
4. a-1, b-2
5. Trichromatic
6. frequency
7. semicircular canals
8. gate-control
9. a-3, b-1, c-4, d-2
10. top-down, bottom-up
11. a-3, b-1, c-2
12. a

Sensation & Perception • 85

4

STATES OF CO

OUT OF CONTROL

Annie Fuller knew she was in trouble a year ago when in the space of a few hours she managed to drink a male coworker more than twice her size under the table. Of course, she'd been practicing for a quarter of her life by then; at 47, she was pouring a pint of bourbon, a 12-pack of beer, and a couple of bottles of wine into her 115-pound body each day. She had come to prefer alcohol to food, sex, or the company of friends and loved ones. Her marriage had ended, and she had virtually stopped leaving the house except to work and to drink. Fuller had tried and failed enough times over the years to know that she would not be able to sober up on her own.[iv]

Annie Fuller was an alcoholic—a person who abuses alcohol to the point where it causes serious life problems. Like Annie, many alcoholics develop a resistance to alcohol, which means they have to consume ever greater quantities of it to achieve the same effects. What those effects are, why people find them so pleasurable, and why some people become alcoholics are some of the questions we will address.

In this chapter, we consider a range of topics about states of consciousness. Among these, sleeping and dreaming occur naturally for most of us. In contrast, drug and alcohol use, hypnosis, and meditation are methods of deliberately altering our subjective understanding of both our physical surroundings and our private internal world.

There are many different ways to understand consciousness. Did you know, for example, that while you are asleep you are still monitoring your environment?

SCIOUSNESS

- What is consciousness?
- What happens when we sleep?
- What do dreams mean?
- What kind of consciousness do hypnotized people experience?
- How do different drugs affect consciousness?

Consciousness is the awareness of the sensations, thoughts, and feelings we experience at a given moment. In *waking consciousness*, we are awake and fully aware of our thoughts, emotions, and perceptions. All other states of consciousness are considered *altered states of consciousness*, although psychologists make a distinction between altered states of consciousness that occur naturally, such as sleep and dreaming, and those that result from the use of alcohol and other drugs.

> **consciousness** The awareness of the sensations, thoughts, and feelings we experience at a given moment.
>
> **stage 1 sleep** The state of transition between wakefulness and sleep, characterized by relatively rapid, low-amplitude brain waves.

>> Sleep and Dreams

Mike Trevino, 29, slept 9 hours in 9 days in his quest to win a 3,000-mile, cross-country bike race. For the first 38 hrs and 646 miles, he skipped sleep entirely. Later he napped—with no dreams he can remember—for no more than 90 minutes a night. Soon he began to imagine that his support crew was part of a bomb plot. "It was almost like riding in a movie. I thought it was a complex dream, even though I was conscious," says Trevino, who finished second. (Springen, 2004, p. 47)

Trevino's case is unusual—in part because he was able to function with so little sleep for so long—and it raises many questions about sleep and dreams. Can we live without sleep? What *is* sleep anyway? And what are dreams?

THE STAGES OF SLEEP

Many people consider sleep a time of tranquility when we set aside the tensions of the day and spend the night in uneventful slumber. However, a scientific look at sleep shows that a good deal of brain and physical activity occurs throughout the night (Gorfine & Zisapel, 2009).

While we sleep, our mental and physical states change all night long. Measures of electrical activity in the brain show that the brain is active throughout the night. It produces electrical signals with systematic, wavelike patterns that change in height (or amplitude) and speed (or frequency). There is also significant physical activity in muscle and eye movements.

As the wavelike electrical patterns change, we move through a series of distinct stages of sleep during a night's rest. There are five stages, known as *stage 1* through *stage 4* and *REM sleep*. We move through these stages in cycles lasting about 90 minutes. (Actually, these 90-minute cycles are typical only of young, healthy adults who do not abuse drugs.) Each of these sleep stages is associated with a unique pattern of brain waves.

When people first go to sleep, they move from a waking state in which they are relaxed with their eyes closed into **stage 1 sleep**, which has relatively rapid, low-amplitude brain waves. This stage is a transition between wakefulness and sleep and lasts only a few minutes.

Sleep Quiz

Although sleeping is something we all do for a significant part of our lives, myths and misconceptions about the topic abound. To test your own knowledge of sleep and dreams, try answering the following questions before reading further.

1. Some people never dream. True or false? _____
2. Most dreams are caused by body sensations such as an upset stomach. True or false? _____
3. It has been proved that people need eight hours of sleep to maintain mental health. True or false? _____
4. When people do not recall their dreams, it is probably because they are secretly trying to forget them. True or false? _____
5. Depriving someone of sleep will inevitably cause the individual to become mentally imbalanced. True or false? _____
6. If we lose some sleep we will eventually make up all the lost sleep the next night or another night. True or false? _____
7. No one has been able to go more than 48 hours without sleep. True or false? _____
8. Everyone is able to sleep and breathe at the same time. True or false? _____
9. Sleep enables the brain to rest because little brain activity takes place during sleep. True or false? _____
10. Drugs have been proved to provide a long-term cure for sleeplessness. True or false? _____

Scoring: This is an easy set of questions to score for every item is false. But don't lose any sleep if you missed them. They were chosen to represent the most common myths regarding sleep.

Source: Palladino & Carducci (1984).

From Palladino, J. J., & Carducci, B. J. (1984). Students' knowledge of sleep and dreams. *Teaching of Psychology, 11,* 189–191. Copyright © 1984. Reproduced with permission of Sage Publications Inc. Journals in the format Textbook via Copyright Clearance Center.

The Sleep Cycle

Stage 1
Light sleep. Muscle activity slows. Occasional muscle twitching.

Stage 2
Breathing and heart rate slows down. Slight decrease in body temperature.

Stage 3
Deep sleep begins. Brain begins to generate slow delta waves.

Stage 4
Very deep sleep. Rhythmic breathing. Limited muscle activity. Brain produces delta waves.

Rapid eye movement (REM)
Brainwaves speed up and dreaming occurs. Muscles relax and heart rate increases. Breathing is rapid and shallow.

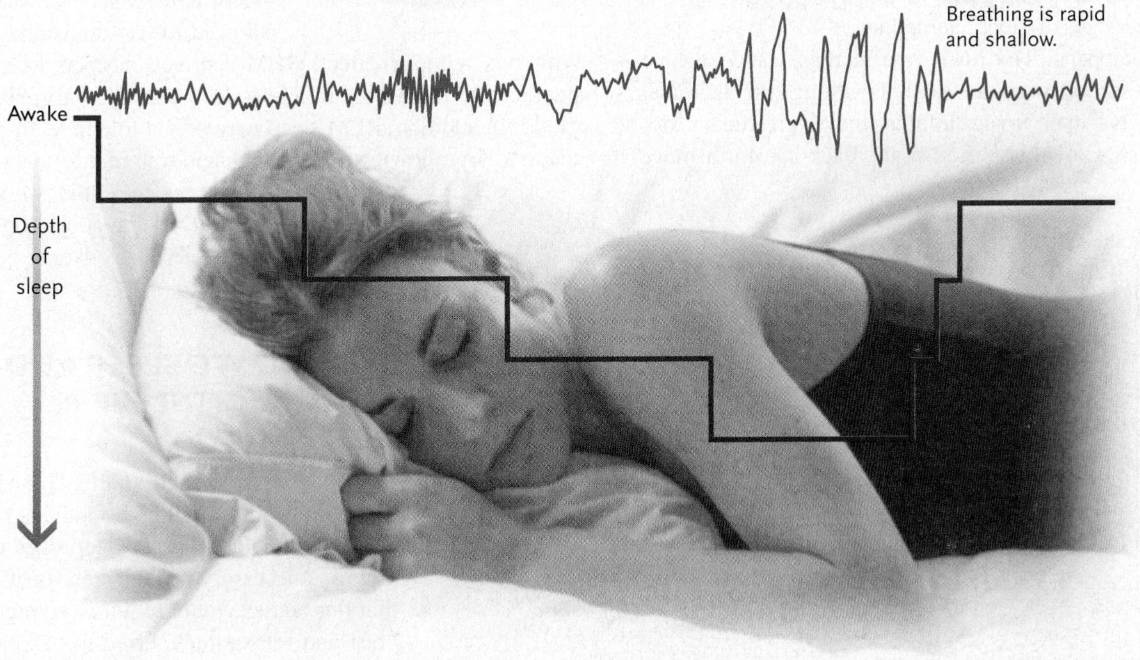

Awake

Depth of sleep

Source: Hobson, 1989.

stage 2 sleep A sleep deeper than that of stage 1, characterized by a slower, more regular wave pattern, along with momentary interruptions of "sleep spindles."

stage 3 sleep A sleep characterized by slow brain waves, with greater peaks and valleys in the wave pattern than in stage 2 sleep.

stage 4 sleep The deepest stage of sleep, during which we are least responsive to outside stimulation.

rapid eye movement (REM) sleep Sleep occupying 20% of an adult's sleeping time, characterized by increased heart rate, blood pressure, and breathing rate; erections; eye movements; and the experience of dreaming.

During stage 1, images sometimes appear, as if we were viewing still photos, although this is not true dreaming. Stage 1 occurs only when we first fall asleep.

As sleep becomes deeper, we enter **stage 2 sleep**. Young adults in their early 20s spend about half of their sleep time in this stage. Stage 2 is characterized by a slower, more regular wave pattern with momentary interruptions of sharply pointed wave spikes called *sleep spindles*. It becomes increasingly difficult to awaken a person from sleep as stage 2 progresses.

In **stage 3 sleep**, the brain waves become slower, with higher peaks and lower valleys in the wave pattern. By the time sleepers arrive at **stage 4 sleep**, the pattern is even slower and more regular. In stage 4, we are least responsive to efforts to wake us up and are quite possibly aggravated if the attempt is successful.

Stage 4 sleep typically occurs during the early part of the night. In the first half of the night, sleep is dominated by stages 3 and 4. In the second half, we spend more time in stages 1 and 2—as well as a fifth stage, when dreaming occurs.

REM SLEEP: THE PARADOX OF SLEEP

Several times a night, when sleepers have cycled back to a shallower state of sleep, something curious happens. The heart rate increases and becomes irregular, blood pressure rises, breathing rate increases, and males—even male infants—have erections. Most characteristic of this period is the back-and-forth move-

ment of the eyes, as if the sleeper were watching an action-filled movie. This period of sleep is called **rapid eye movement**, or **REM**, **sleep** and it contrasts with stages 1 through 4, which are collectively labeled *non-REM* (or *NREM*) sleep. REM sleep occupies a little over 20% of adults' total sleeping time.

Paradoxically, while all this activity is occurring, the major muscles of the body appear to be paralyzed. In addition, and most important, REM sleep correlates positively with dreaming. In other words, REM is usually accompanied by dreams, which—whether or not people remember them—are experienced by *everyone* during some part of the night. Although some dreaming occurs in non-REM stages of sleep, dreams are most likely to occur in the REM period, when they are the most vivid and most easily remembered (Conduit, Crewther, & Coleman, 2004; Lu et al., 2006; Titone, 2002).

There is good reason to believe that REM sleep plays a critical role in everyday human functioning. People deprived of REM sleep—by being awakened every time they begin to display the physiological signs of that stage—show a *rebound effect* when allowed to rest undisturbed. With this rebound effect, REM-deprived sleepers spend significantly more time in REM sleep than they normally would. In addition, REM sleep may play a role in learning and memory, allowing us to rethink and restore information and emotional experiences that we've had during the day (Nishida et al., 2009; Rivera-Garcia et al., 2011; Walker & van der Helm, 2009).

WHY DO WE SLEEP AND HOW MUCH SLEEP IS NECESSARY?

Sleep is a requirement for normal human functioning. Surprisingly, though, we don't know exactly what sleep does or why it is necessary. It seems reasonable that our bodies would require a tranquil "rest and relaxation" period to become

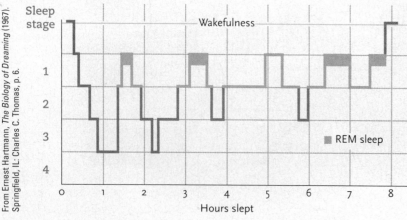

From Ernest Hartmann, *The Biology of Dreaming* (1967). Springfield, IL: Charles C. Thomas, p. 6.

Sleep stage

Wakefulness

REM sleep

Hours slept

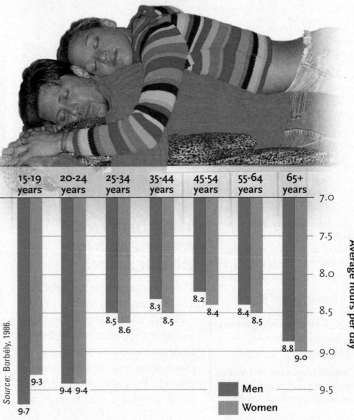

Number of Hours People Sleep Each Night

revitalized. Indeed, experiments with rats show that total sleep deprivation results in death (Rechtschaffen et al., 2002). Further, studies of sleep deprivation in humans show that we experience weakened immune systems, difficulty concentrating, and are more easily irritated (Hui et al., 2007; Palma et al., 2007).

There are several explanations for why we sleep. One explanation, based on an evolutionary perspective, suggests that sleep permitted our ancestors to conserve energy at night, a time when food was relatively hard to come by. Consequently, they were better able to forage for food when the sun was up. A second explanation for why we sleep is that sleep restores and replenishes our brains and bodies. For instance, the reduced activity of the brain during non-REM sleep may give neurons in the brain a chance to repair themselves. Furthermore, the onset of REM sleep stops the release of neurotransmitters called *monoamines*, and so permits receptor cells to get some necessary rest and to increase their sensitivity during periods of wakefulness (McNamara, 2004; Siegel, 2003; Steiger, 2007). Finally, sleep may be essential because it assists physical growth and brain development in children. For example, the release of growth hormones is associated with deep sleep (Peterfi et al., 2010).

	15-19 years	20-24 years	25-34 years	35-44 years	45-54 years	55-64 years	65+ years
Men	9.3	9.4	8.5	8.3	8.2	8.4	8.8
Women	9.7	9.4	8.6	8.5	8.4	8.5	9.0

Source: Borbély, 1986.

These explanations remain speculative, and there is still no definitive answer that explains why sleep is essential. Scientists have also been unable to establish just how much sleep is absolutely required. Most people sleep between seven and eight hours each night. In addition, there is wide variability among individuals, with some people needing as little as three hours of sleep. Sleep requirements also vary over the course of a lifetime: As they age, people generally need less and less sleep (Gangwisch et al., 2008).

People who participate in sleep deprivation experiments, in which they are kept awake for stretches as long as 200 hours, show no lasting effects. It's no fun—they feel weary and irritable, can't concentrate, and show a loss of creativity, even after only minor deprivation. They also show a decline in logical reasoning ability. However, after being allowed to sleep uninterruptedly, they bounce back and are able to perform normally after just a few days (Dinges et al., 1997; McClelland & Pilcher, 2007; Veasey et al., 2002).

In short, as far as we know, most people suffer no permanent consequences of temporary sleep deprivation. But even a temporary lack of sleep can make us feel edgy, slow our reaction time, and lower our performance on academic and physical tasks. In addition, we put ourselves, and others, at risk when we do routine activities, such as driving, when we're very sleepy (Anderson & Home, 2006; Kong, Soon, & Chee, 2011; Morad et al., 2009; Philip et al., 2005).

Airlines whose pilots fly for many hours with little sleep put the safety of their flight crews and passengers at risk.

What Do People Dream About?

Percentage of respondents reporting at least one thematic event

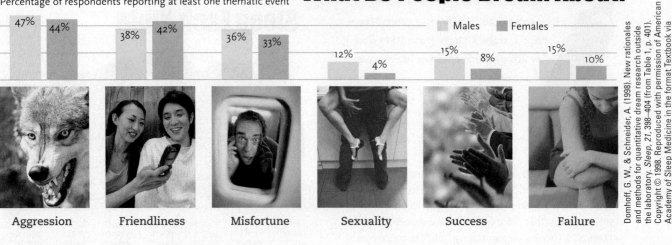

☐ Males ☐ Females

| Aggression | Friendliness | Misfortune | Sexuality | Success | Failure |
| 47% 44% | 38% 42% | 36% 33% | 12% 4% | 15% 8% | 15% 10% |

unconscious wish fulfillment theory Sigmund Freud's theory that dreams represent unconscious wishes that dreamers desire to see fulfilled.

latent content of dreams According to Freud, the "disguised" meanings of dreams, hidden by more obvious subjects.

manifest content of dreams According to Freud, the apparent story line of dreams.

THE FUNCTION AND MEANING OF DREAMING

The average person experiences 150,000 dreams by the age of 70. Although dreams tend to be subjective to the person having them, there are some common elements that frequently occur in everyone's dreams. Typically, people dream about everyday events, such as going to the supermarket, working, and preparing a meal. Students dream about going to class; professors dream about teaching. Dental patients dream of getting their teeth drilled; dentists dream of drilling the wrong tooth. The English have tea with the queen in their dreams; in the United States, people go to a bar with the president (Domhoff, 1996; Schredl, & Piel, 2005; Taylor & Bryant, 2007).

Over the years, scientists and others have come up with theories to explain why we dream. Each theory tends to focus on one reason. There may, however, be a number of reasons why we dream, so we may need more than one theory to fully understand how dreams work.

Do Dreams Have Hidden Meaning? Sigmund Freud viewed dreams as a guide to the unconscious (Freud, 1900). In his **unconscious wish fulfillment theory**, he proposed that dreams represent unconscious wishes that dreamers desire to see fulfilled. However, because these wishes are threatening to the dreamer's conscious awareness, the actual wishes—called the **latent content of dreams**—are disguised. The true subject and meaning of a dream has little to do with its apparent story line, which Freud called the **manifest content of dreams**.

To Freud, interpreting a dream's manifest content was necessary to understand the true (latent) meaning of the dream. As people described their dreams to him, Freud tried to associate symbols in the manifest content with the latent content. He argued that certain symbols and their meanings were universal. For example, to Freud, dreams in which a person is flying symbolized a wish for sexual intercourse.

THE FAR SIDE® BY GARY LARSON

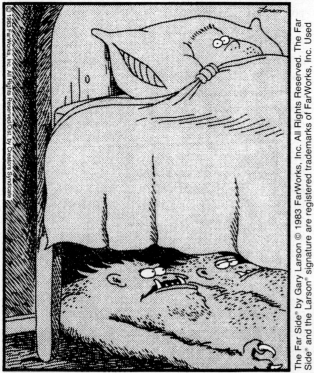

"I've got it again, Larry ... an eerie feeling like there's something on top of the bed."

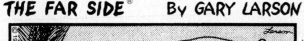

STUDY TIP

The chart at the top of page 93 summarizes the differences between the three main explanations of dreaming.

Three Theories of Dreams

Theory	Basic Explanation	Meaning of Dreams	Is Meaning of Dream Disguised?
Unconscious wish fulfillment theory (Freud)	Dreams represent unconscious wishes the dreamer wants to fulfill	Latent content reveals unconscious wishes	Yes, by manifest content of dreams
Dreams-for-survival theory	Information relevant to daily survival is reconsidered and reprocessed	Clues to everyday concerns about survival	Not necessarily
Activation-synthesis theory	Dreams are the result of random activation of various memories, which are tied together in a logical story line	Dream scenario that is constructed is related to dreamer's concerns	Not necessarily

Many psychologists reject Freud's view that dreams typically represent unconscious wishes and that particular objects and events in a dream are symbolic. Instead, they consider the direct, overt action of a dream to be the dream's meaning. For example, a dream in which we are walking down a long hallway to take an exam for which we haven't studied does not relate to unconscious, unacceptable wishes. Instead, it may just mean that we are concerned about an impending test (Cartwright, Agargum, & Kirkby, 2006; Duesbury, 2011; Nikles et al., 1998; Picchioni et al., 2002).

Dreams-for-Survival Theory According to the **dreams-for-survival theory**, dreams permit us to reconsider information that is critical for our daily survival. In this view, dreaming is an inheritance from our animal ancestors, whose small brains were unable to sift through all the information they received during waking hours. Consequently, dreaming provided a mechanism for processing information 24 hours a day.

According to this theory, dreams represent concerns about our daily lives, illustrating our uncertainties, indecisions, ideas, and desires. Dreams are seen as consistent with everyday living and represent key concerns growing out of our daily experiences (Ross, 2006; Winson, 1990).

Research supports the dreams-for-survival theory, suggesting that certain dreams permit people to focus on and consolidate memories, particularly those related to motor skills. For example, rats seem to dream about mazes that they learned to run through during the day, at least according to the patterns of brain activity produced while they are sleeping (Kenway & Wilson, 2001; Kuriyama, Stickgold, & Walker, 2004; Smith, 2006; Stickgold et al., 2001).

Activation-Synthesis Theory Drawing on the neuroscience perspective, psychiatrist J. Allan Hobson has proposed the **activation-synthesis theory** of dreams. The activation-synthesis theory focuses on the random

> **dreams-for-survival theory** The theory suggesting that dreams permit information that is critical for our daily survival to be reconsidered and reprocessed during sleep.
>
> **activation-synthesis theory** Hobson's theory that the brain produces random electrical energy during REM sleep that stimulates memories lodged in various portions of the brain.

PSYCH think

connect™

WWW.MCGRAWHILLCONNECT.COM/PSYCHOLOGY
Freudian Interpretation of Dreams

> > > Suppose that a new "miracle pill" allows a person to function with only one hour of sleep per night. However, because a night's sleep is so short, a person who takes the pill will never dream again. Knowing what you do about the functions of sleep and dreaming, what would be some advantages and drawbacks of such a pill from a personal standpoint? Would you take such a pill?

Take the PsychSmart challenge! Learn about the mysterious symbols Freud used to interpret dreams. Before you watch this video, write down your views about dreams and symbols. After watching the video, review your explanation and note where your ideas have changed. What changed them? If nothing changed, explain why. From chapter 4 in your ebook, select the *Exercises* tab. Then select "Freudian Interpretation of Dreams." Complete the exercise, then test yourself by answering question 5 in the Pop Quiz on p. 109.

electrical energy that the brain produces during REM sleep, possibly as a result of changes in the production of particular neurotransmitters. This electrical energy randomly stimulates memories stored in the brain. Because we have a need to make sense of our world even while asleep, the brain takes these chaotic memories and weaves them into a logical story line, filling in the gaps to produce a rational scenario (Hobson, 2005; Porte & Hobson, 1996).

Activation-synthesis theory has been refined by the activation information modulation (AIM) theory. According to AIM, dreams are initiated in the brain's pons, which sends random signals to the cortex. Areas of the cortex that are involved in particular waking behaviors are related to the content of dreams. For example, areas of the brain related to vision are involved in the visual aspects of the dream, while areas of the brain related to movement are involved in aspects of the dream related to motion (Hobson, 2007).

Activation-synthesis and AIM theories do not entirely reject the view that dreams reflect unconscious wishes. They suggest that the particular scenario a dreamer produces is not random but instead is a clue to the dreamer's fears, emotions, and concerns. Hence, what starts out as a random process culminates in something meaningful. For example, suppose your visual memory of a horse is stimulated, and your auditory memory of a cat's meow is stimulated, and your emotional memory of sadness is stimulated. And let's say that your biggest worry right now is your mother's health. Your brain's attempt to make sense of these sensations and your anxiety might result in a storyline like this: You dream you are walking a horse toward your mother but the horse meows and turns into a cat, which makes you very sad.

SLEEP DISTURBANCES

At one time or another, almost all of us have difficulty sleeping—a condition known as insomnia. It could be due to a particular situation, such as the breakup of a relationship, concern about an upcoming test, or the loss of a job. Some cases of insomnia, however, have no obvious cause. Some people are simply unable to fall asleep easily, or they go to sleep readily but wake up frequently during the night. About one in three people will experience insomnia at some point in their lives (Bains, 2006; Cooke & Ancoli-Israel, 2006; Henry et al., 2008).

Other sleep problems are less common than insomnia, although they are still widespread. For instance, some 20 million people suffer from *sleep apnea,* a condition in

which a person has difficulty breathing while sleeping. The result is disturbed, fitful sleep, because the person is constantly reawakened when the lack of oxygen becomes great enough to trigger a waking response. Some people with apnea wake as many as 500 times during the course of a night, although they may not even be aware that they woke up. Not surprisingly, sleep disrupted by apnea results in extreme fatigue the next day. Sleep apnea also may play a role in *sudden infant death syndrome (SIDS),* a mysterious killer of seemingly normal infants who die while sleeping (Aloia & Arendt, 2007; Gami et al., 2005; Sparks & Rizzo, 2009).

Narcolepsy is uncontrollable sleeping that occurs for short periods while a person is awake. No matter what the activity—holding a heated conversation, exercising, or driving—a narcoleptic will suddenly fall asleep. People with narcolepsy go directly from wakefulness to REM sleep, skipping the other stages. The causes of narcolepsy are not known, although there could be a genetic component, because narcolepsy runs in families (Billiard, 2008; Ervik, Abdelnoor, & Heier, 2006; Mahmood & Black, 2005; Nishino, 2007; Vignatelli, 2011).

We know relatively little about night terrors, sleeptalking, and sleepwalking, three sleep disturbances that are

Some people with apnea wake as many as 500 times during the course of a night, without being aware of it.

Circadian Rhythms

7:00 A.M.
- Hay fever symptoms are worst

8:00 A.M.
- Risk for heart attack and stroke is highest
- Symptoms of rheumatoid arthritis are worst
- Helper T lymphocytes are at their lowest daytime level

Noon
- Level of hemoglobin in the blood is at its peak

6:00 A.M.
- Onset of menstruation is most likely
- Insulin levels in the bloodstream are lowest
- Blood pressure and heart rate begin to rise
- Levels of the stress hormone cortisol increase
- Melatonin levels begin to fall

3:00 P.M.
- Grip strength, respiratory rate, and reflex sensitivity are highest

4:00 A.M.
- Asthma attacks are most likely to occur

4:00 P.M.
- Body temperature, pulse rate, and blood pressure peak

2:00 A.M.
- Levels of growth hormone are highest

6:00 P.M.
- Urinary flow is highest

9:00 P.M.
- Pain threshold is lowest

1:00 A.M.
- Pregnant women are most likely to go into labor
- Immune cells called helper T lymphocytes are at their peak

11:00 P.M.
- Allergic responses are most likely

usually harmless. All occur during stage 4 sleep and are more common in children than in adults. Small children who have night terrors may scream, bringing terrified parents running. But typically these children will not understand why the parents have come and will not recall why they screamed. Sleeptalkers and sleepwalkers usually have a vague consciousness of the world around them, and a sleepwalker may be able to walk with agility around obstructions in a crowded room. Unless a sleepwalker wanders into a dangerous environment, sleepwalking typically poses little risk (Baruss, 2003; Guilleminault et al., 2005; Lee-Chiong, 2006).

CIRCADIAN RHYTHMS

Cycling back and forth between wakefulness and sleep is an example of the body's circadian rhythms. **Circadian rhythms** (from the Latin *circa diem*, or "about a day") are physiological fluctuations that take place on a daily basis. Sleeping and waking, for instance, occur naturally to the beat of an internal pacemaker that works on a cycle of about 24 hours. Several other bodily functions, such as body temperature, hormone production, and blood pressure, also follow circadian rhythms (Beersma & Gordijn, 2007; Blatter & Cajochen, 2007; Karatsoreos et al., 2011; Saper et al., 2005).

Circadian cycles involve a variety of behaviors. For instance, sleepiness occurs throughout the day in regular patterns, with most of us getting drowsy in mid-afternoon—regardless of whether we have eaten a heavy lunch. By making an afternoon siesta part of their everyday habit, people in several cultures take advantage of the body's natural inclination to sleep at this time (Reilly & Waterhouse, 2007; Takahashi et al., 2004; Wright, 2002).

Psych at the Movies

Akiro Kurosawa's Dreams (1990)
A series of stories based on actual bizarre and magical dreams of the director.

Waking Life (2001)
The fascinating encounters and conversations a man encounters in a lucid dream.

The Fountain (2006)
As this odyssey crosses time and space, it challenges some of our most basic notions of our own awareness and existence.

Inception (2010)
This sci-fi thriller offers a mind-bending scenario of a dream within a dream within a dream.

Requiem for a Dream (2000)
Two stories are paralleled in this highly disturbing movie: a young man's escalating dependence and addiction to illegal street drugs, and his mother's physician-condoned abuse of prescription drugs.

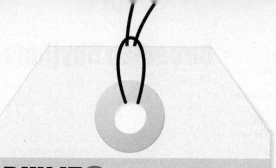

Getting a Good Night's Sleep

Do you have trouble sleeping? You're not alone—70 million people in the United States have sleep problems. But before you run out and buy a "white noise" CD or a special bed or an expensive gadget to analyze your sleep patterns, consider some free alternatives. Psychologists studying sleep disturbances have a number of suggestions for overcoming insomnia (Benca, 2005; Edinger et al., 2001; Finley & Cowley, 2005). Here are some ideas:

- *Exercise during the day (at least six hours before bedtime) and avoid naps.* Not surprisingly, it helps to be tired before going to sleep!
- *Choose a regular bedtime and stick to it.* Going to sleep at the same time everyday helps your natural internal rhythms regulate your body.
- *Avoid drinks with caffeine after lunch.* The effects of beverages such as coffee, tea, and some soft drinks can linger for as long as 8 to 12 hours after they are consumed.
- *Drink a glass of warm milk at bedtime.* Milk contains the chemical tryptophan, which helps people fall asleep.
- *Try not to sleep.* This approach works because people often have difficulty falling asleep because they are trying so hard. A better strategy is to go to bed only when you feel tired. If you don't get to sleep within 10 minutes, leave the bedroom and do something else, returning to bed only when you feel sleepy. Continue this process all night if necessary. But get up at your usual hour in the morning, and don't take any naps during the day. After three or four weeks, most people become conditioned to associate their beds with sleep—and fall asleep rapidly at night (Sloan et al., 1993; Smith, 2001; Ubell, 1993).

People cannot be hypnotized against their will.

For long-term problems with sleep, you might consider visiting a sleep disorders center. For information on accredited clinics, consult the American Academy of Sleep Medicine at www.aasmnet.org.

>> Hypnosis and Meditation

You are feeling relaxed and drowsy. You are getting sleepier. Your body is becoming limp. Your eyelids are feeling heavier. Your eyes are closing; you can't keep them open anymore. You are totally relaxed. Now, place your hands above your head. But you will find they are getting heavier and heavier—so heavy you can barely keep them up. In fact, although you are straining as hard as you can, you will be unable to hold them up any longer.

An observer watching this scene would notice a curious phenomenon. Many of the people listening to the voice are dropping their arms to their sides. The reason for this strange behavior? These people have been hypnotized.

HYPNOSIS: A TRANCE-FORMING EXPERIENCE?

People under **hypnosis** appear to be in a trancelike state of heightened susceptibility to the suggestions of others. In some respects, it appears that they are asleep. Yet other aspects of their behavior contradict this notion, because they are attentive to the hypnotist's suggestions and may carry out bizarre or silly suggestions.

How is someone hypnotized? Typically, the process follows a series of four steps. First, a person is made comfortable in a quiet environment. Second, the hypnotist explains what is going to happen, such as telling the person that he or she will experience a pleasant, relaxed state. Third, the hypnotist tells the person to concentrate on a specific object or image, such as the hypnotist's moving finger or an image of a calm lake. The hypnotist may have the person concen-

trate on relaxing different parts of the body, such as the arms, legs, and chest. Fourth, once the subject is in a highly relaxed state, the hypnotist may make suggestions that the person interprets as being produced by hypnosis, such as "Your arms are getting heavy" and "Your eyelids are more difficult to open." Because the person begins to experience these sensations, he or she believes they are caused by the hypnotist and becomes susceptible to the suggestions of the hypnotist.

Despite their compliance when hypnotized, people do not lose all will of their own. They will not perform antisocial behaviors, and they will not carry out self-destructive acts if they realize the acts are destructive. People will not reveal hidden truths about themselves, and they are capable of lying. Moreover, despite popular misconceptions, people cannot be hypnotized against their will (Gwynn & Spanos, 1996; Raz, 2007).

There are wide variations in people's susceptibility to hypnosis. About 5 to 20% of the population cannot be hypnotized at all, and some 15% are very easily hypnotized. Most people fall somewhere in between. Moreover, the ease with which a person is hypnotized correlates with a number of other characteristics. People who are readily hypnotized are also easily absorbed while reading books or listening to music, becoming unaware of what is happening around them, and they often spend an unusual amount of time daydreaming. In sum, then, they show a high ability to concentrate and to become completely focused on what they are doing (Benham, Woody, & Wilson, 2006; Kirsch & Braffman, 2001; Rubichi et al., 2005).

STUDY TIP

The question of whether hypnosis represents a different state of consciousness or is similar to normal waking consciousness is an unresolved issue in psychology.

A Different State of Consciousness? One view of hypnosis says that it represents a state of divided consciousness. According to famed hypnosis researcher Ernest Hilgard, hypnosis brings about a dissociation, or division, of consciousness into two simultaneous components. In one stream of consciousness, hypnotized people are following the commands of the hypnotist. Yet on another level of consciousness, they are acting as "hidden observers," aware of what is happening to them. For instance, hypnotic subjects may appear to be following the hypnotist's suggestion about feeling no pain, yet they may be conscious of the pain on some level (Fingelkurts, Fingelkurts, & Kallio, 2007; Hilgard, 1992; Kallio & Revonsuo, 2003).

> **hypnosis** A trancelike state of heightened susceptibility to the suggestions of others.

On the other side of this controversial issue are psychologists who believe that hypnosis occurs during normal waking consciousness. They argue that altered brain wave patterns are not sufficient to demonstrate a qualitative difference, because no other specific physiological changes occur when people are in trances. Furthermore, little support exists for the contention that adults can recall memories of childhood events accurately while hypnotized. That lack of evidence suggests that there is nothing qualitatively special about the hypnotic trance (Hongchun & Ming, 2006; Hunter, 2011; Lynn et al., 2003; Lynn, Fassler, & Knox, 2005; Wagstaff, 2009).

More recent models suggest that the hypnotic state may best be viewed as involving normal waking consciousness, but with some important differences (Jamieson, 2007; Kihlstrom, 2005; Lynn et al., 2000).

As arguments about the true nature of hypnosis continue, though, one thing is clear: Hypnosis has been used successfully to solve practical human problems. In fact, psychologists working in many different areas have found hypnosis to be a reliable, effective tool for pain control, smoking reduction, improvement of athletic performance, and treatment of psychological disorders (Accardi & Milling, 2009; Carmody et al, 2008).

MEDITATION: REGULATING OUR OWN CONSCIOUSNESS

When traditional practitioners of the ancient Eastern religion of Zen Buddhism want to achieve greater spiritual

insight, they turn to meditation, a technique that has been used for centuries to alter consciousness. **Meditation** is a learned technique for focusing attention that brings about an altered state of consciousness. A popular meditation practice is to repeat a *mantra*—a sound, word, or syllable—over and over. In other forms of meditation, the focus may be on a picture, flame, or specific part of the body. Still other forms of meditation, including some styles of yoga, engage the body and mind in mutual, concentrated focus. Regardless of the type, the key to meditation is to concentrate so thoroughly that the meditator reaches a different state of consciousness.

After meditation, people often report feeling thoroughly relaxed. They sometimes relate that they have gained new insights into themselves and their problems. The long-term practice of meditation may even improve health because of the physiological changes it produces. For example, during meditation, oxygen usage decreases, heart rate and blood pressure decline, and brain-wave patterns change (Barnes et al., 2004; Lee, Kleinman, & Kleinman, 2007; Travis et al., 2009).

meditation A learned technique for refocusing attention that brings about an altered state of consciousness.

Anyone can achieve relaxation through meditation by following a simple procedure. The fundamentals include sitting in a quiet room with the eyes closed, breathing deeply and rhythmically, and repeating a word or sound—such as the word *one*—over and over. Practiced twice a day for 20 minutes, the technique is effective in bringing about relaxation (Aftanas & Golosheykin, 2005; Benson et al., 1994).

CROSS-CULTURAL ROUTES TO ALTERED STATES OF CONSCIOUSNESS

A group of Native American Sioux men sit naked in a steaming sweat lodge as a medicine man throws water on sizzling rocks to send billows of scalding steam into the air.

From the perspective of …

A PHYSICIAN Would you recommend meditation in addition to prescription drugs as a way to help your patients cope with stress-related illness? How would meditation alone be helpful?

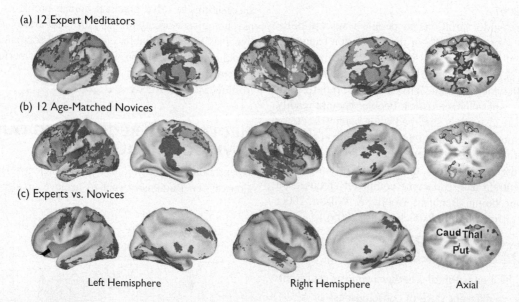

(a) 12 Expert Meditators

(b) 12 Age-Matched Novices

(c) Experts vs. Novices

Left Hemisphere   Right Hemisphere   Axial

To understand the long-term effects of meditation, researchers compared the brain activation of novice and experienced meditators. These fMRI brain scans show the regions of brain activation in (a) expert meditators who had between 10,000 and 54,000 hours of practice in meditating and (b) novice meditators who had no experience mediating, and they also show (c) the comparison between the two. In (c), red hues show greater activation in the experts, and blue hues show greater activation for the novices. The findings suggest that long-term meditation produces significant changes in regions of the brain related to concentration and attention.

Aztec priests smear themselves with a mixture of crushed poisonous herbs, hairy black worms, scorpions, and lizards. Sometimes they drink the potion.

During the 16th century, a devout Hasidic Jew lies across the tombstone of a celebrated scholar. As he murmurs the name of God repeatedly, he seeks to be possessed by the soul of the dead wise man's spirit. If successful, he will attain a mystical state, and the deceased's words will flow out of his mouth.

Each of these rituals has a common goal: suspension from the bonds of everyday awareness and access to an altered state of consciousness. Although they may seem exotic from the vantage point of many Western cultures, these rituals represent an apparently universal effort to alter consciousness (Bartocci, 2004; Irwin, 2006).

Some scholars suggest that the quest to alter consciousness represents a basic human desire (Siegel, 1989). Whether or not we accept this view, it is clear that variations in states of consciousness share several characteristics across a variety of cultures. Alterations in states of consciousness can lead to changes in thinking, which may become shallow, illogical, or otherwise different from normal. In addition, people's sense of time can become disturbed, and their perceptions of the physical world and of themselves may change. They may lose self-control and do things that they would never do otherwise. Finally, they may feel a sense of *ineffability*—the inability to understand an experience rationally or describe it in words (Finkler, 2004; Martindale, 1981; Travis, 2006).

Of course, recognizing that efforts to produce altered states of consciousness are widespread throughout the world's societies does not answer a fundamental question: Is the experience of unaltered states of consciousness similar across different cultures?

Because humans are pretty much alike in the ways our brains and bodies are wired, we might assume that the basic experience of consciousness is similar across cultures. However, the ways in which certain aspects of consciousness are interpreted and viewed vary widely among different cultures. For instance, Arabs perceive time as moving more slowly than do North Americans, who tend to be more hurried (Alon & Brett, 2007; Haynes, Nixon, & West, 2007).

PSYCH think

connect™
WWW.MCGRAWHILLCONNECT.COM/PSYCHOLOGY
Drug Effects

> > > Why do you think people in almost every culture use various ways to alter their states of consciousness?

Take the PsychSmart challenge! Send drugs into the brain and see what happens. From chapter 4 in your ebook, select the *Exercises* tab. Next, select "Drug Effects." After doing the exercise, answer question 9 in the Pop Quiz on p. 109 to review.

>> Drug Use: The Highs and Lows of Consciousness

Drugs of one sort or another are a part of almost everyone's life in the United States. From infancy on, many people take vitamins, aspirin, cold-relief medicine, and the like, and surveys find that 80% of American adults have taken an over-the-counter pain reliever in the last six months.

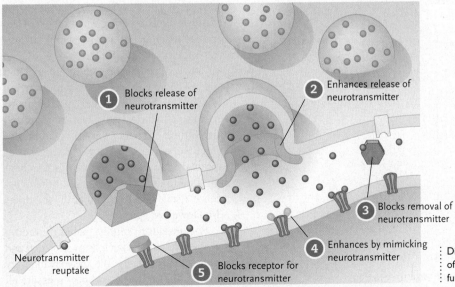

1 Blocks release of neurotransmitter

2 Enhances release of neurotransmitter

3 Blocks removal of neurotransmitter

4 Enhances by mimicking neurotransmitter

5 Blocks receptor for neurotransmitter

Neurotransmitter reuptake

Different drugs affect different parts of the nervous system and brain and function in one of these specific ways.

Drug addiction is among the most difficult of all behaviors to modify, even with extensive treatment.

Coffee is an integral part of social rituals in cultures around the world.

Nonetheless, these drugs rarely produce an altered state of consciousness (Dortch, 1996).

In contrast, some substances, known as psychoactive drugs, lead to an altered state of consciousness. **Psychoactive drugs** influence a person's emotions, perceptions, and behavior. Yet even this category of drugs is common in most of our lives. If you have ever had a cup of coffee or sipped a beer, you have taken a psychoactive drug. A large number of individuals have used other drugs that are more dangerous than one mug of coffee or beer. For instance, surveys find that 41% of high school seniors have used an illegal drug in the last year. In addition, 30% report having been drunk on alcohol. The figures for the adult population are even higher (Johnston et al., 2009).

psychoactive drugs Drugs that influence a person's emotions, perceptions, and behavior.

addictive drugs Drugs that produce a physiological or psychological dependence in the user so that withdrawal from them leads to a craving for the drug that, in some cases, may be nearly irresistible.

Of course, the effects of drugs vary widely, in part because they affect the nervous system in very different ways. Some drugs alter the limbic system, and others affect the operation of specific neurotransmitters. For example, some drugs block or enhance the release of neurotransmitters, others block the receipt or the removal of a neurotransmitter from the synapse, and still others mimic the effects of a particular neurotransmitter.

Typically, the most dangerous drugs are addictive. **Addictive drugs** produce a physiological and/or psychological dependence in the user, and withdrawal from them leads to a craving for the drug that, in some cases, may be nearly irresistible. In *biologically based* addictions, the body becomes so accustomed to functioning in the presence of a drug that it cannot function without it. *Psychologically based* addictions are those in which people believe that they need the drug to cope with the stresses of daily living. Although we generally associate addiction with drugs such as heroin, everyday sorts of drugs, such as caffeine (found in coffee) and nicotine (found in cigarettes), are also addictive (Li et al., 2007).

Why do people take drugs in the first place? There are many reasons, ranging from the perceived pleasure of the experience itself, to the escape that a drug-induced high affords from the everyday pressures of life, to an attempt to achieve a religious or spiritual state. However, other factors having little to do with the nature of the experience itself also lead people to try drugs (McDowell & Spitz, 1999).

For instance, highly publicized drug use by role models such as movie stars and professional athletes, the easy availability of some illegal drugs, and peer pressure all

Drug Use by High School Seniors

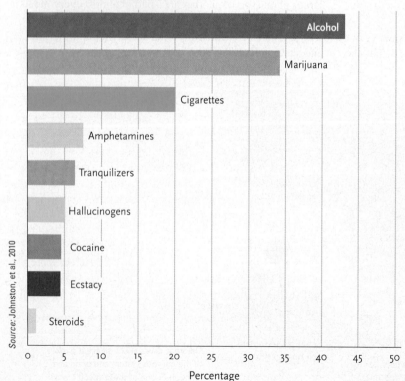

Source: Johnston, et al., 2010

Percentage

Levels of Caffeine in Common Beverages and Drugs

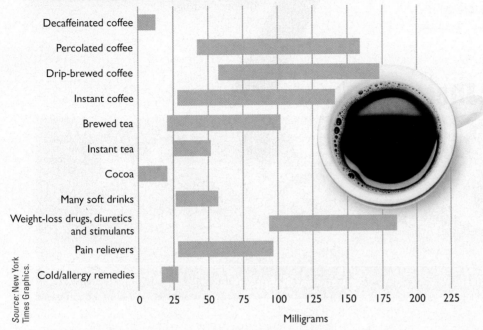

Source: New York Times Graphics.

Milligrams

play a role in the decision to use drugs. In some cases, the motive is simply the thrill of trying something new. Finally, genetic factors may predispose some people to be more susceptible to drugs and to become addicted to them. Regardless of the forces that lead a person to begin using drugs, drug addiction is among the most difficult of all behaviors to modify, even with extensive treatment (Lemonick, 2000; Mosher & Akins, 2007; Ray & Hutchison, 2007; Thompson, Goldsmith, & Tran, 2011).

Because of the difficulty in treating drug problems, there is little disagreement that the best hope for dealing with the overall societal problem of substance abuse is to prevent people from becoming involved with drugs in the first place. However, there is little accord on how to accomplish this goal (Clayton, Segress, & Caudill, 2008; D'Amico et al., 2009).

STIMULANTS: DRUG HIGHS

It's one o'clock in the morning, and you still haven't finished reading the last chapter of the text on which you will be tested in the morning. Feeling exhausted, you turn to the one thing that may help you stay awake for the next two hours: a cup of strong black coffee.

If you have ever found yourself in this situation, you have resorted to a major *stimulant*, caffeine, to stay awake. *Caffeine* is one of a number of **stimulants**, drugs whose

effect on the central nervous system causes a rise in heart rate, blood pressure, and muscular tension. Caffeine is present not only in coffee, but it is also an important ingredient in energy drinks, tea, soft drinks, and chocolate as well.

Caffeine produces several reactions. The major behavioral effects are an increase in attentiveness and improved reaction time. Caffeine can also brighten one's mood, most likely by mimicking the effects of a natural brain chemical, adenosine. Too much caffeine, however, can result in nervousness and insomnia. People can develop a physiological dependence on the drug. Regular users who suddenly stop drinking coffee may experience headaches or depression. Many people who drink large amounts of coffee on weekdays have headaches on weekends because of a sudden drop in the amount of caffeine they are consuming (Clayton & Lundberg-Love, 2009; Ganio et al., 2011; Hammond & Gold, 2008; Kendler, Myers, & Gardner, 2006).

Nicotine, found in cigarettes, is another common stimulant. Besides stimulating the central nervous system, nicotine increases levels of the neurotransmitter dopamine in the brain, making the smoker feel good. After a while, the smoker's brain learns to rely on nicotine to release adequate levels of dopamine. Smokers become dependent on nicotine, and those who suddenly stop smoking develop a strong craving for the drug. This mechanism is similar to the ones activated by cocaine and heroin, which are also highly addictive (Haberstick, Timberlake, & Ehringer, 2007; Ray et al., 2008).

Amphetamines Dexedrine and Benzedrine, also known as uppers, speed, black beauties, bumble bees, copilots, and bennies, belong to a class of strong stimulants known as *amphetamines*. In small quantities, amphetamines—which stimulate the central nervous system—produce a sense of energy and alertness, talkativeness, heightened confidence,

> **stimulants** Drugs that have an arousal effect on the central nervous system, causing a rise in heart rate, blood pressure, and muscular tension.

The average person over the age of 14 drinks 2½ gallons of pure alcohol over the course of a year.

STUDY **TIP**

This summary will help you learn the effects of specific drugs.

Drugs and Their Effects

Drugs	Effects	Withdrawal Symptoms	Risks
Stimulants			
Cocaine Amphetamines	Increased confidence, mood elevation, sense of energy and alertness, decreased appetite, anxiety, irritability, insomnia, transient drowsiness, delayed orgasm	Apathy, general fatigue, prolonged sleep, depression, disorientation, suicidal thoughts, agitated motor activity, irritability, bizarre dreams	Elevated blood pressure, increase in body temperature, face picking, suspiciousness, bizarre and repetitious behavior, vivid hallucinations, convulsions, possible death
Depressants			
Alcohol Sedatives	Anxiety reduction, impulsiveness, dramatic mood swings, bizarre thoughts, suicidal behavior, slurred speech, disorientation, slowed mental and physical functioning, limited attention span	Weakness, restlessness, nausea and vomiting, headaches, nightmares, irritability, depression, acute anxiety, hallucinations, seizures, possible death	Confusion, decreased response to pain, shallow respiration, dilated pupils, weak and rapid pulse, coma, possible death
Rohypnol	Anxiety reduction, muscle relaxation, amnesia, sleep	Seizures	Seizures, coma, incapacitation, inability to resist sexual assault
Narcotics			
Heroin Morphine	Anxiety and pain reduction, apathy, difficulty in concentration, slowed speech, decreased physical activity, drooling, itching, euphoria, nausea	Anxiety, vomiting, sneezing, diarrhea, lower back pain, watery eyes, runny nose, yawning, irritability, tremors, panic, chills and sweating, cramps	Depressed levels of consciousness, low blood pressure, rapid heart rate, shallow breathing, convulsions, coma, possible death
Hallucinogens			
Cannabis	Euphoria, relaxed inhibitions, increased appetite, disoriented behavior	Hyperactivity, insomnia, decreased appetite, anxiety	Severe reactions rare but include panic, paranoia, fatigue, bizarre and dangerous behavior, decreased testosterone over long-term; immune-system effects
MDMA (Ecstasy)	Heightened sense of oneself and insight, feelings of peace, empathy, energy	Depression, anxiety, sleeplessness	Increase in body temperature, memory difficulties
LSD	Heightened aesthetic responses; vision and depth distortion; heightened sensitivity to faces and gestures; magnified feelings; paranoia, panic, euphoria	Not reported	Nausea and chills; increased pulse, temperature, and blood pressure; slow, deep breathing; loss of appetite; insomnia; bizarre, dangerous behavior

and a mood "high." They increase concentration and reduce fatigue. Amphetamines also cause a loss of appetite, increased anxiety, and irritability. When taken over long periods of time, amphetamines can cause feelings of being persecuted and a general sense of suspiciousness. People taking amphetamines may lose interest in sex. If taken in too large a quantity, amphetamines overstimulate the central nervous system to such an extent that they may cause convulsions and death (Carhart-Harris, 2007).

Methamphetamine is a white, crystalline drug that U.S. police now say is the most dangerous street drug. Commonly known as "ice," "crank," or "meth," this drug is highly addictive and relatively cheap, and it produces a strong, lingering high. It has made addicts of people across the social spectrum, ranging from soccer moms to urban professionals to poverty-stricken inner-city residents. Once addicted, users take it more and more frequently and in increasing doses. Long-term use of this drug can lead to brain damage (Sharma, Sjoquist, & Ali, 2007; Halkitis, 2009; Kish et al., 2009).

Cocaine Although the use of cocaine has declined over the last decade, this stimulant and its derivative, crack, still represent a serious concern. Cocaine is inhaled or "snorted" through the nose, smoked, or injected directly into the bloodstream. It is rapidly absorbed into the body and takes effect almost immediately.

When used in relatively small quantities, cocaine produces feelings of profound psychological well-being, increased confidence, and alertness. Cocaine produces this "high" through the neurotransmitter dopamine, which is one of the chemicals that are related to ordinary feelings of pleasure. Normally when dopamine is released, excess amounts of the neurotransmitter are reabsorbed by the releasing neuron through the process of reuptake. However, when cocaine enters the brain, it blocks reabsorption of leftover dopamine. As a result, the brain is flooded with dopamine-produced pleasurable sensations (Jarlais, Arasteh, & Perlis, 2007; Redish, 2004).

However, there is a steep price to be paid for the pleasurable effects of cocaine. The brain may become permanently rewired, triggering a psychological and physical addiction in which users grow obsessed with obtaining the drug. Over time, users deteriorate mentally and physically. In extreme cases, cocaine can cause hallucinations; a common one is of insects crawling over one's body. Ultimately, an overdose of cocaine can lead to death (George & Moselhy, 2005; Little et al., 2009; Paulozzi, 2006).

DEPRESSANTS: DRUG LOWS

In contrast to the initial effect of stimulants—increased arousal of the central nervous system—the effect of **depressants** is to impede the nervous system by inhibiting the firing of neurons. Small doses of depressants result in at least temporary feelings of *intoxication*—drunkenness—along with a sense of euphoria and joy. When large amounts are taken, however, speech becomes slurred and muscle control

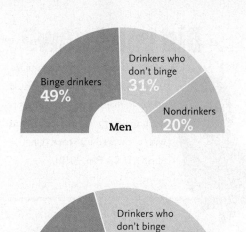

Men

Binge drinkers 49%

Drinkers who don't binge 31%

Nondrinkers 20%

Women

Binge drinkers 41%

Drinkers who don't binge 40%

Nondrinkers 19%

Drinking Habits of College Students

Source: Wechsler et al., 2003.

becomes disjointed, making motion difficult. Ultimately, heavy users may lose consciousness entirely.

Alcohol The most common depressant in the United States is alcohol, which is used by more Americans than any other drug. Based on liquor sales, the average person over the age of 14 drinks 2½ gallons of pure alcohol over the course of a year. This works out to more than 200 drinks per person. Although alcohol consumption has declined steadily over the last decade, surveys of college students show that more than three-fourths of them have had a drink within the last 30 days (Jung, 2002; Midanik, Tam, & Weisner, 2007).

One of the more disturbing trends is the high frequency of binge drinking among college students. For men, binge drinking is defined as having five or more drinks in one sitting. For women, who generally weigh less than men and whose bodies absorb alcohol less efficiently, binge drinking is defined as having four or more drinks at one sitting (Mokdad, Brewer, & Naimi, 2007; Norman, 2011).

Around 50% of male college students and 40% of female college students say they engaged in binge drinking at least once within the previous two weeks. Some 17% of female students and 3% of male students admitted drinking on 10 or more occasions during the previous 30 days. Furthermore, even light drinkers were affected by the high rate of alcohol use: Two-thirds of lighter drinkers said that they had had their studying or sleep disturbed by drunk students, and a quarter of the women said they had been the target of an unwanted sexual advance by a drunk classmate (Grucza, Norberg, & Beirut, 2009; Read et al., 2008; Wechsler et al., 1994, 2000, 2002).

> **depressants** Drugs that slow down the nervous system.

and stress, feelings of happiness, and loss of inhibitions (Sayette, 1993; Steele & Josephs, 1990).

As the dose of alcohol increases, however, the depressive effects become more pronounced. People may feel emotionally and physically unstable. They also show poor judgment and may act aggressively. Moreover, memory is impaired, brain processing of spatial information is diminished, and speech becomes slurred and incoherent. Eventually they may fall into a stupor and pass out. If they drink enough alcohol in a short time, they may die of alcohol poisoning (Murphy et al., 1998; Thatcher & Clark, 2006; Zeigler et al., 2005).

Although most Americans fall into the category of casual users, 14 million people in the United States—one in every 13 adults—have a drinking problem. *Alcoholics* are people with alcohol-abuse problems who come to rely on alcohol and continue to drink even though it causes serious health and other life problems. In addition, they become increasingly immune to the intoxicating effects of alcohol. Consequently, alcoholics must drink progressively more to experience the initial positive feelings that alcohol produces.

Some alcoholics must drink constantly in order to feel well enough to function in their daily lives. Others drink inconsistently, but occasionally go on binges in which they consume large quantities of alcohol.

It is not clear why certain people become alcoholics and develop a tolerance for alcohol, while others do not. There

It used to be that U.S. women were somewhat lighter drinkers than men, but the gap between the sexes is narrowing for older men and women and there is no difference between the sexes for teenagers. Women are more susceptible to the effects of alcohol, and alcohol abuse may harm the women's brains more than men's (Mancinelli, Binetti, & Ceccanti, 2007; Mann et al., 2005; Wuethrich, 2001).

Although alcohol is a depressant, most people claim that it increases their sense of sociability and well-being. The discrepancy between the actual and the perceived effects of alcohol lies in the initial effects it produces in the majority of individuals who use it: the release of tension

>> TRY IT!

Consider Your Drinking Style

If you drink alcohol, do you have a style of use that is safe and responsible? Read the statements below and rate the extent to which you agree with them, using the following scale:

**1 = Strongly disagree   2 = Disagree   3 = Neutral   4 = Agree
5 = Strongly agree**

	1	2	3	4	5
1. I usually drink alcohol a few times a week.					
2. I sometimes go to class after I've been drinking alcohol.					
3. I frequently drink when I'm alone.					
4. I have driven while under the influence of alcohol.					
5. I've used a fake ID card to purchase alcohol.					
6. I'm a totally different person when I'm drinking alcohol.					
7. I often drink so much that I feel drunk.					
8. I wouldn't want to go to a party where alcohol wasn't being served.					
9. I avoid people who don't like to drink alcohol.					
10. I sometimes urge others to drink more alcohol.					

Scoring: The lower your score (that is, the more 1s and 2s), the better able you are to control your alcohol consumption and the more likely it is that your alcohol use is responsible. The higher your score (that is, the more 4s and 5s), the greater is your use and reliance on alcohol, and the more likely it is that your alcohol consumption may be reckless. If your score is over 40, you may have an alcohol problem and should seek professional help to control your alcohol usage.

may be a genetic cause, although the question whether there is a specific inherited gene that produces alcoholism is controversial. What is clear is that the chances of becoming an alcoholic are considerably higher if alcoholics are present in earlier generations of a person's family. However, not all alcoholics have close relatives who are alcoholics. In these cases, environmental stressors are suspected of playing a larger role (Nurnberger & Bierut, 2007; Whitfield et al., 2004; Zimmermann et al., 2007).

Sedatives Sedatives, including barbiturates, benzodiazepines, and nonbenzodiazepines, are depressant drugs that reduce irritability and have a calming effect. Barbiturates, such as Nembutal, Seconal, and phenobarbital, are older prescription drugs that have a high potential for addiction. Prescribed to induce sleep or reduce stress, barbiturates, such as Seconal and phenobarbital, produce a sense of relaxation. They have a high potential for abuse and overdose.

A newer class of drugs, the benzodiazepines have largely replaced barbiturates for short-term treatment of anxiety, insomnia, seizures, and alcohol withdrawal. Like barbiturates, benzodiazepines, which include Xanax and Valium, are prescription drugs to be used only under a doctor's supervision.

Another benzodiazepine, Rohypnol, is a short-acting sedative that is sometimes called the "date rape drug." When mixed with alcohol, it can prevent victims from resisting sexual assault. Sometimes people who are unknowingly given the drug are so incapacitated that they have no memory of the assault (Britt & McCance-Katz, 2005). Rohypnol cannot be prescribed or sold legally in the United States.

Nonbenzodiazepines such as Ambien and Lunesta differ chemically from the benzodiazepines but produce similar effects. Generally prescribed to treat insomnia, these drugs are also less likely to produce physical dependence than benzodiazepines and barbiturates.

NARCOTICS

Narcotics are drugs that increase relaxation and relieve pain and anxiety. Two of the most powerful narcotics, *morphine* and *heroin*, are derived from the poppy seed pod. Although morphine is used medically to control severe pain, heroin is illegal in the United States. This status has not prevented its widespread use.

> **narcotics** Drugs that increase relaxation and relieve pain and anxiety.

Heroin can be inhaled or injected directly into the bloodstream with a hypodermic needle (Maxwell, Bohman, & Spense, 2004). The immediate effect has been described as a "rush" of positive feeling, similar in some respects to a sexual orgasm—and just as difficult to describe. After the rush, a heroin user experiences a sense of well-being and peacefulness that lasts three to five hours. When the effects of the drug wear off, however, the user feels extreme anxiety and a desperate desire to repeat the experience.

Drinks consumed in two hours	Alcohol in blood (percentage)	Typical effects
2	0.05	Judgment, thought, and restraint weakened; tension released, giving carefree sensation
3	0.08	Tensions and inhibitions of everyday life lessened; cheerfulness
4	0.10	Voluntary motor action affected, making hand and arm movements, walk, and speech clumsy
7	0.20	Severe impairment—staggering, loud, incoherent, emotionally unstable, 100 times greater traffic risk; exuberance and aggressive inclinations magnified
9	0.30	Deeper areas of brain affected, with stimulus-response and understanding confused; stuporous; blurred vision
12	0.40	Incapable of voluntary action; sleepy, difficult to arouse; equivalent of surgical anesthesia
15	0.50	Comatose; centers controlling breathing and heartbeat anesthetized; death increasingly probable

Effects of Alcohol

Note: A drink refers to a typical 12-ounce bottle of beer, a 1.5-ounce shot of hard liquor, or a 5-ounce glass of wine. These quantities are only rough benchmarks. The effects vary significantly depending on an individual's height, recent food intake, genetic factors, and even psychological state.

Moreover, larger amounts of heroin are needed each time to produce the same pleasurable effect. These last two properties fit the criteria for physical and psychological addiction: The user is constantly either shooting up or attempting to obtain ever-increasing amounts of the drug. Eventually, the life of the addict revolves around heroin.

From the perspective of...

THE CHILD OF AN ALCOHOLIC PARENT You have some friends who like to abuse alcohol. When they tell you they are thinking about starting a family, how would you explain to them the effects of alcohol abuse on family relationships?

Because of the powerful feelings of physical pleasure the drug produces, heroin addiction is particularly difficult to cure (van den Brink & van Ree, 2003). One treatment that has shown some success is replacing heroin with methadone. *Methadone* is a synthetic chemical that satisfies a heroin user's physiological cravings for the drug without providing the "high" that accompanies heroin. When heroin users receive regular doses of methadone, they may be able to function relatively normally. The use of methadone has one significant drawback, however: Although it removes the psychological dependence on heroin, it replaces it with a physiological dependence on methadone. Researchers are attempting to identify non-addictive chemical substitutes for heroin as well as substitutes for other addictive drugs that do not replace one addiction with another (Amato et al., 2005; Joe, Flynn, & Broome, 2007; Verdejo, Toribio, & Orozco, 2005). *Oxycodone* (sold as the prescription drug *OxyContin*) is a type of pain-reliever that has led to a significant amount of abuse. Many well-known people (including Courtney Love and Rush Limbaugh) have become dependent on it.

Hallucinogens: Psychedelic Drugs
What do some mushrooms, jimsonweed, and morning glories have in common? Besides being fairly common plants, each can be a source of a powerful **hallucinogen**, a drug that is capable of producing hallucinations, or changes in the perceptual process.

hallucinogen A drug that is capable of producing hallucinations, or changes in the perceptual process.

Marijuana. The most common hallucinogen in widespread use today is *marijuana*, whose active ingredient—tetrahydrocannabinol (THC)—is found in a common weed, cannabis. Marijuana is typically smoked in cigarettes or pipes, although it can be cooked and eaten. Just over 32% of high school seniors and 11% of eighth-graders report having used marijuana in the last year (Johnston et al., 2009).

The effects of marijuana vary from person to person, but they typically consist of feelings of euphoria and general well-being. Sensory experiences seem more vivid and intense, and a person's sense of self-importance seems to grow. Memory may be impaired, causing users to feel pleasantly "spaced out." However, the effects are not universally positive. Individuals who use marijuana when they feel depressed can end up even more depressed, because the drug tends to magnify both good and bad feelings.

There are clear risks associated with long-term, heavy marijuana use. Researchers are actively investigating the mechanisms underlying dependence on marijuana. Some evidence suggests that there are similarities in the way marijuana and drugs such as cocaine and heroin affect the brain. Furthermore, there is some evidence that heavy use at least temporarily decreases the production of the male sex hormone testosterone, potentially affecting sexual activity and sperm count (Haney, 2008; Iverson, 2000; Lane et al., 2007; Rossato, Pagano, & Vettor, 2008).

In addition, marijuana smoked during pregnancy may have lasting behavioral effects on children who are exposed prenatally, although the results are inconsistent. Heavy use also affects the ability of the immune system to fight off germs and increases stress on the heart, although it is unclear how strong these effects are.

How marijuana smoking by itself can harm the lungs is being studied. When marijuana smoking is combined with tobacco smoking, it appears the negative effects from the tobacco smoke are magnified (Tan et al., 2009).

Despite the risks associated with it, marijuana has several medical uses. It helps to prevent nausea from chemotherapy, treat some AIDS symptoms, and relieve muscle spasms for people with spinal cord injuries. In a controversial move,

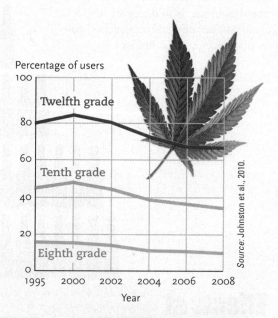

Source: Johnston et al., 2010.

Teenage Marijuana Use

several states have made the use of the drug legal if it is prescribed by a physician—although it remains illegal under U.S. federal law (Chapkis & Webb, 2008; Cohen, 2009; Iverson, 2000; Seamon et al., 2007).

MDMA (Ecstasy) and LSD. Two powerful hallucinogens are *MDMA ("Ecstasy")* and *lysergic acid diethylamide (LSD, or "acid")*. Both drugs affect the operation of the neurotransmitter serotonin in the brain, causing an alteration in brain-cell activity and perception (Aghajanian, 1994; Buchert et al., 2004; Cloud, 2000).

Ecstasy users report a sense of peacefulness and calm. People on the drug report experiencing increased empathy and connection with others, as well as feeling more relaxed, yet energetic. Although the data are not conclusive, some researchers have found declines in memory and performance on intellectual tasks associated with Ecstasy use, and such findings suggest that there may be long-term changes in serotonin receptors in the brain (El-Mallakh & Abraham, 2007; Jones et al., 2008; Montgomery et al., 2005).

LSD, which is structurally similar to serotonin, produces vivid hallucinations. Perceptions of colors, sounds, and shapes are altered so much that even the most mundane experience—such as looking at the knots in a wooden table—can seem moving and exciting. Time perception is distorted, and objects and people may be viewed in a new way. Some users report that LSD increases their understanding of the world. For others, the experience brought on by LSD can be terrifying, particularly if users have had emotional difficulties in the past. Furthermore, people occasionally experience flashbacks, in which they hallucinate long after they initially used the drug (Baruss, 2003; Wu, Schlenger, & Galvin, 2006).

IDENTIFYING DRUG AND ALCOHOL PROBLEMS

In a society bombarded with commercials for drugs that are guaranteed to do everything from curing the common cold to giving new life to "tired blood," it is no wonder that drug-related problems are a major social issue. Yet many people with drug and alcohol problems deny they have them, and even close friends and family members may fail to realize when occasional social use of drugs or alcohol has turned into abuse.

Certain signs indicate when use becomes abuse (National Institute on Drug Abuse, 2000). Among them are these:

- Always getting high to have a good time
- Being high more often than not
- Getting high to get oneself going

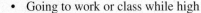

- Going to work or class while high
- Missing or being unprepared for class or work because you were high
- Feeling badly later about something you said or did while high
- Driving a car while high
- Coming in conflict with the law because of drugs
- Doing something while high that you wouldn't do otherwise
- Being high in nonsocial, solitary situations
- Being unable to stop getting high
- Feeling a need for a drink or a drug to get through the day
- Becoming physically unhealthy
- Failing at school or on the job
- Thinking about liquor or drugs all the time
- Avoiding family or friends while using liquor or drugs

Any combination of these symptoms indicates the possibility of a serious drug problem. Because drug and alcohol dependence are almost impossible to cure on one's own (Room, Babor, & Rehm, 2005), people who suspect that they have a problem should seek immediate attention from a psychologist, physician, or counselor.

For REVIEW >>

- **What is consciousness?**

  Consciousness is a person's awareness of the sensations, thoughts, and feelings at a given moment. Waking consciousness can vary from active to passive states. Altered states of consciousness include naturally occurring sleep, dreaming, and drug-induced states. (p. 88)

- **What happens when we sleep, and what do dreams mean?**

  The brain is active throughout the night, and sleep proceeds through a series of stages identified by unique patterns of brain waves. REM (rapid eye movement) sleep is characterized by an increase in heart rate, a rise in blood pressure, an increase in the rate of breathing, and, in males, erections. Dreams occur during this stage. According to Freud, dreams have both a manifest content (an apparent story line) and a latent content (a true but hidden meaning). The dreams-for-survival theory suggests that information relevant to daily survival is reconsidered in dreams. The activation-synthesis theory proposes that dreams are a result of random electrical energy that haphazardly stimulates different memories, which then are woven into a coherent story line. (pp. 88–96)

- **Hypnotized people experience what kind of consciousness?**

  Hypnosis produces significant behavioral changes, including increased concentration and suggestibility, heightened ability to recall and construct images, lack of initiative, and acceptance of suggestions that clearly contradict reality. (pp. 96–99)

- **How do different drugs affect consciousness?**

  Stimulants cause arousal in the central nervous system. Two common stimulants are caffeine and nicotine. More dangerous are cocaine and amphetamines, which in large quantities can lead to convulsions and death. Alcohol and other depressants decrease arousal in the central nervous system. They can cause intoxication along with feelings of euphoria. Alcohol's initial effects of released tension and positive feelings yield to depressive effects as the dose of alcohol increases. Morphine and heroin are narcotics, drugs that produce relaxation and relieve pain and anxiety. Because of their addictive qualities, morphine and heroin are particularly dangerous. Hallucinogens are drugs that produce hallucinations or other changes in perception. The most frequently used hallucinogen is marijuana, which has several long-term risks. Two other hallucinogens are LSD and Ecstasy. (pp. 99–107)

Pop Quiz

1. _____ is the term used to describe our understanding of the world external to us, as well as our own internal world.

2. _____ _____ are internal bodily processes that occur on a daily cycle.

3. Freud's theory of unconscious _____ _____ states that the actual wishes an individual expresses in dreams are disguised because they are threatening to the person's conscious awareness.

4. Match the theory of dreaming with its definition.
   a. Dreams permit important information to be reprocessed during sleep.
   b. The manifest content of dreams disguises the latent content of the dreams.
   c. Electrical energy stimulates random memories, which are woven together to produce dreams.
   ____ 1. activation-synthesis theory
   ____ 2. dreams-for-survival theory
   ____ 3. dreams as wish fulfillment

5. The video on Freudian dream interpretation described _____
   a. how free association is used to interpret the unconscious meaning of dreams.
   b. why psychoanalysis is an essential part of understanding the latent meaning of dreams.
   c. how projective tests are used to interpret the unconscious meaning of dreams.
   d. how dreamwork changes the unconscious meaning of dreams into acceptable form.

6. _____ is a state of heightened susceptibility to the suggestions of others.

7. A friend tells you, "I once heard of a person who was murdered by being hypnotized and then told to jump from the Golden Gate Bridge!" Could such a thing have happened? Why or why not?

8. _____ is a learned technique for focusing attention to bring about an altered state of consciousness.

9. The activity on drug effects showed that
   a. some people are more susceptible to becoming addicted to drugs.
   b. some drugs make neuron receptors more sensitive.
   c. drug effects sometimes appear to be very small or might even be invisible on a brain scan.
   d. brain structures such as the temporal lobe respond in different ways to drugs.

10. Match the type of drug to an example of that type.
    a. LSD
    b. heroin
    c. Dexedrine, or speed
    ____ 1. narcotic
    ____ 2. amphetamine
    ____ 3. hallucinogen

11. Classify each drug listed as a stimulant (S), depressant (D), hallucinogen (H), or narcotic (N).
    1. nicotine
    2. cocaine
    3. alcohol
    4. morphine
    5. marijuana

12. The effects of LSD can recur long after the drug has been taken. True or false?

Answers
TO POP QUIZ QUESTIONS

1. Consciousness
2. Circadian rhythms
3. wish fulfillment
4. 1-c, 2-a, 3-b
5. d
6. Hypnosis
7. no; people who are hypnotized cannot be made to perform self-destructive acts
8. Meditation
9. b
10. 1-b, 2-c, 3-a
11. 1-S, 2-S, 3-D, 4-N, 5-H
12. true

5

LEARNING

I WAS A BLACKBERRY ADDICT

Senator Thad Cochran of Mississippi, like almost every politician on the Hill, got a BlackBerry after 9/11 for security purposes. But he gave it back. "I was always distracted," Cochran said. "I couldn't concentrate. Every time the light came on or it beeped, I felt this compulsion to stop everything I was doing." Though he doesn't begrudge his colleagues for their Black-Berry addiction, Cochran says the result is that during meetings on the Hill almost everyone is "always checking messages" or typing, he says. "It just beeps or buzzes, all the time, and people get up and leave the room."[v]

Are you like Senator Cochran, reaching for your cell phone or BlackBerry the moment it beeps or vibrates? Do you know people who stop in midsentence when their cell phone rings to answer it?

You might have heard jokes about people being addicted to their "crackberries," but actually their behavior isn't an addiction at all; it's just a very well-learned response. This learning came about because of the same processes that allow us to learn to read a book, drive a car, study for a test, or perform any of the numerous activities that make up our daily routine. Each of us must acquire and then refine our skills and abilities through learning.

Psychologists have approached the study of learning from several angles. Some study how our natural responses become associated with events in the environment, such as salivating when we smell food cooking or feeling hungry when the lunch bell rings. Others consider how learning is a consequence of rewarding or punishing circumstances. Finally, several other approaches focus on the cognitive aspects of learning, or the thought processes that shape learning.

As You READ >>

- What is the role of reward and punishment in learning?
- How can the information from this chapter be used to change undesired behaviors?
- Does thinking matter at all in learning?

For behavioral psychologists, **learning** is a relatively permanent change in behavior that is brought about by experience. From the beginning of life, humans are primed for learning. Infants exhibit a primitive type of learning called *habituation*, defined by psychologists as the decrease in a behavioral response to a stimulus that occurs after repeated presentations of the same stimulus. Young infants, for example, may initially show interest in a novel stimulus, such as a brightly colored toy, but they will soon lose interest if they see the same toy over and over. Habituation permits us to ignore things that have stopped providing new information. Adults exhibit habituation, too: Newlyweds soon stop noticing that they are wearing a wedding ring.

learning A relatively permanent change in behavior brought about by experience.

Although philosophers have speculated on the foundations of learning since the time of Aristotle, the first systematic research on learning in the West was done at the beginning of the twentieth century, when Ivan Pavlov (does the name ring a bell?) developed a framework for learning called classical conditioning.

>> Classical Conditioning

In Hawaii, there is a popular snack called *li hing mui*. If you just say these three words out loud around people who grew up in Hawaii, many will start to salivate. If you are not from Hawaii, you probably have no reaction to the words *li hing mui*. Is there a word or phrase or event that makes you salivate? Maybe McDonald's golden arches make you salivate. If so,

Times Square in New York City is a favorite destination for tourists, who can't help but notice all the large neon signs, crowded streets, noise, and unfamiliar smells, all stimuli to which long-time residents are habituated.

you are displaying a basic form of learning called classical conditioning. *Classical conditioning* helps explain such diverse phenomena as shivering when you look outside at night and see snow, and getting sweaty palms and a racing heart while watching a movie that has scary music, dark scenes, and sudden scene changes.

WHAT IS CLASSICAL CONDITIONING?

Ivan Pavlov (1849–1936), a Russian physiologist, never intended to do psychological research. In 1904 he won the Nobel Prize for his work on digestion, a testament to his contribution to that field. Yet Pavlov is remembered not for his physiological research but for his experiments on learning—work that he began quite accidentally (Marks, 2004; Samoilov & Zayas, 2007).

Pavlov had been studying the secretion of stomach acids and salivation in dogs in response to the ingestion of varying amounts and kinds of food. While doing that, he observed a curious phenomenon: Sometimes stomach secretions and salivation would begin in the dogs when they had not yet eaten any food. The mere sight of the experimenter who normally brought the food, or even the sound of the experimenter's footsteps, was enough to produce salivation in the dogs. Pavlov's genius lay in his ability to recognize the implications of this discovery. He saw that the dogs were responding not only on the basis of a biological need (hunger) but also as a result of learning—or, as it came to be called, classical conditioning. **Classical conditioning** is a type of learning in which a neutral stimulus (such as the experimenter's footsteps) comes to elicit a response after being paired with a stimulus (such as food) that naturally brings about that response.

To demonstrate classical conditioning, Pavlov (1927) attached a tube to a dog's mouth so that he could measure precisely the dog's salivation. He then rang a bell and, just a few seconds later, allowed the dog to eat its food. This pairing occurred repeatedly and was carefully planned so that, each time, exactly the same amount of time elapsed between the presentation of the bell and the food. At first the dog would salivate only when the food was in its mouth, but soon it began to salivate at the sound of the bell. In fact, even when Pavlov stopped giving the food to the dog, the dog still salivated after hearing the sound. The dog had been classically conditioned to salivate to the bell.

The basic processes of classical conditioning that underlie Pavlov's discovery are straightforward, although the terminology he chose is not simple. Before conditioning, there are two unrelated stimuli: the ringing of a bell and food. We know that normally the ringing of a bell does not lead to salivation, although it may lead to some other type of response, such as pricking up the ears. The bell is therefore called the **neutral stimulus**, because it is a stimulus that, before conditioning, does not naturally bring about the response in which we are interested. We also have food, which naturally causes a dog to salivate—the response we want to condition. The food is considered an **unconditioned stimulus**, or **UCS**, because food placed in a dog's mouth automatically causes salivation to occur. The reflexive response that the food elicits (salivation) is called an **unconditioned response**, or **UCR**. This is a natural, inborn, reflexive response that is not associated with previous learning.

One way to tell if a stimulus is a UCS is to consider whether every normal human would experience the UCR. If the answer is yes, then it is likely a UCS. For example, would any healthy human experience sweating in extremely hot and humid weather? The answer is yes. In this case, the extreme heat and humidity are the UCS and sweating is the UCR. Unconditioned responses are always brought about by the presence of unconditioned stimuli.

Returning to Pavlov's study, the bell is rung each time the dog is about to receive food. The goal of conditioning is for the dog to associate the bell with the unconditioned stimulus (meat) and therefore to bring about the same response as the unconditioned stimulus. After a number of pairings of the bell and meat, the bell alone causes the dog to salivate.

> **classical conditioning** A type of learning in which a neutral stimulus comes to bring about a response after it is paired with a stimulus that naturally brings about that response.
>
> **neutral stimulus** A stimulus that, before conditioning, does not naturally bring about the response of interest.
>
> **unconditioned stimulus (UCS)** A stimulus that naturally brings about a particular response without having been learned.
>
> **unconditioned response (UCR)** A response that is natural and needs no training (for example, salivation at the smell of food).

For many people who grew up in Hawaii, *li hing mui*, a salty sweet or sour snack, is a mouth-watering treat. For anyone else, it may or may not be something you can learn to enjoy.

1 **Before conditioning** The ringing bell does not bring about salivation, making it a neutral stimulus.

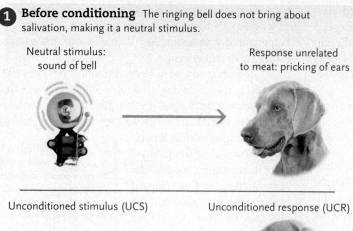

Neutral stimulus: sound of bell

Response unrelated to meat: pricking of ears

Unconditioned stimulus (UCS)

Unconditioned response (UCR)

Meat

Salivation

2 **During conditioning** The bell is rung just before presentation of the meat.

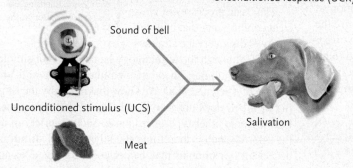

Neutral stimulus

Unconditioned response (UCR)

Sound of bell

Unconditioned stimulus (UCS)

Salivation

Meat

3 **After conditioning** The ringing bell alone stimulates salivation, making it a conditioned stimulus and salivation the conditioned response.

Conditioned stimulus (CS)

Conditioned response (CR)

Sound of bell

Salivation

Classical Conditioning

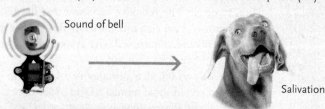

STUDY TIP

To understand the process of classical conditioning, you need to know the difference between the CS and the UCS and their relationship to the CR and the UCR.

When conditioning is complete, the bell is no longer a neutral stimulus but has become a **conditioned stimulus**, or **CS**. At this point, we say that acquisition has occurred. **Acquisition** is the process of learning to associate the neutral stimulus with a UCS. Salivation in response to the conditioned stimulus (bell) is considered a **conditioned response**, or **CR**. After conditioning, then, the conditioned stimulus evokes the conditioned response.

Although the terminology Pavlov used to describe classical conditioning may seem confusing, the following summary can help make the relationships between stimuli and responses easier to understand and remember:

- Conditioned = learned
- Unconditioned = not learned (inborn, genetically programmed)
- An *un*conditioned stimulus leads to an *un*conditioned response.
- *Un*conditioned stimulus–*un*conditioned response pairings are *un*learned and *un*trained.
- During conditioning, a previously neutral stimulus is transformed into the conditioned stimulus.
- A conditioned stimulus leads to a conditioned response, and a conditioned stimulus–conditioned response pairing is a consequence of learning and training.
- An unconditioned response and a conditioned response are similar (such as salivation in Pavlov's experiment), but the unconditioned response occurs naturally and is typically stronger, whereas the conditioned response is learned and usually less intense.

HOW DO CONDITIONING PRINCIPLES APPLY TO HUMAN BEHAVIOR?

Although the first conditioning experiments were carried out with animals, classical conditioning principles were soon found to explain many aspects of everyday human behavior. Recall, for instance, the earlier illustration of how people may salivate at the sight of McDonald's golden arches. The cause of this reaction is classical conditioning: The previously neutral arches have become associated with the food from inside the restaurant that has been eaten on previous occasions (the unconditioned stimulus), causing the arches to become a conditioned stimulus that brings about the conditioned response of salivation.

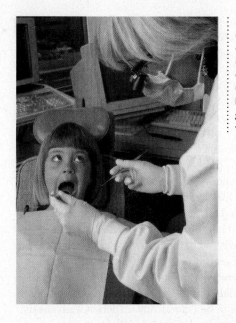

Avoiding the dentist because of a previous unpleasant experience isn't uncommon. That's how stimulus generalization works.

In the study, the experimenters sounded a loud noise whenever Little Albert touched a white, furry rat. The noise (the unconditioned stimulus) evoked fear (the unconditioned response). After just a few pairings of noise and rat, Albert began to show fear of the rat by itself, bursting into tears when he saw it. The rat, then, had become a CS that brought about the CR, fear. Furthermore,

conditioned stimulus (CS) A once-neutral stimulus that has been paired with an unconditioned stimulus to bring about a response formerly caused only by the unconditioned stimulus.

acquisition A process of learning to associate a neutral stimulus with a UCS.

conditioned response (CR) A response that, after conditioning, follows a previously neutral stimulus (for example, salivation at the ringing of a bell).

Sometimes emotional responses are learned through classical conditioning processes. For instance, how do some of us develop fears of mice, cockroaches, and other creatures that are typically harmless? In a now infamous case study, psychologist John B. Watson and colleague Rosalie Rayner (1920) showed that classical conditioning could be one cause of such fears by conditioning an 11-month-old infant named Albert to be afraid of rats. "Little Albert," like any healthy infant with normal hearing, initially was frightened by loud noises (UCS) but had no fear of rats (neutral stimulus).

From the perspective of...

A PARENT Violent images in the media can actually link emotions, such as fear and anger, with stimuli through classical conditioning. Children are particularly susceptible to this process and may react with more fear or anger than normal in a real-life situation (Bushman & Huesmann, 2006).

the effects of the conditioning lingered: Five days later, Albert reacted with some degree of fear not only when shown a rat, but when shown objects that looked similar to the white, furry rat, including a white rabbit, a white sealskin coat, and even a white Santa Claus mask.

Would Little Albert have continued to be afraid of white, furry things throughout his life? Probably not. We will never know, for sure, however, because he died at the age of six (Beck, Levinson, & Irons, 2009).

Learning through classical conditioning occurs throughout our lives. For example, you may be one of many who do not go to a dentist as often as you should because of prior associations of dentists with pain. In this case, the UCS would be the drill hitting a nerve in your tooth, and the UCR would be pain. What is the CS? In extreme cases, classical conditioning can lead to the development of *phobias*, which are intense, irrational fears that we will consider later in the book.

Can classical conditioning improve your performance on exams? If you have test anxiety, it's worth a try. You can condition yourself to relax as a response to a specific song. Choose a relaxing song to which you don't normally listen. Listen to this song only in a peaceful, relaxing environment for 5–15 minutes every day. Practice deep breathing exercises (taking deep and slow breaths, counting them as you go) while listening. Don't listen to this song at any other time. Do this for a couple of weeks and then listen to the song without the breathing exercises. Are you more relaxed just from listening to the music? If so, you have conditioned yourself and listening to this song right before a test may help you relax so you can focus on the test.

get involved!

Classical conditioning also accounts for pleasant experiences. That is, certain events trigger the release of neurotransmitters that help us feel pleasure. The runner's high, for example, occurs when endorphins are released in response to jogging a long distance. The UCS is the extended jogging, and the UCR is the release of endorphins. The CS could be any number of things, including the smell or sight of running clothes or shoes. Classical conditioning, then, may explain many of the reactions we have to stimuli in the world around us.

EXTINCTION OF A CONDITIONED RESPONSE

What would happen if a dog that had become classically conditioned to salivate at the ringing of a bell never again received food when the bell was rung? The answer lies in one of the basic phenomena of learning: extinction. **Extinction** occurs when a previously conditioned response decreases in frequency and eventually disappears.

To produce extinction, one needs to end the association between conditioned stimuli and unconditioned stimuli. For instance, if we had trained a dog to salivate (CR) at the ringing of a bell (CS), we could produce extinction by repeatedly ringing the bell but *not* providing food. At first the dog would continue to salivate when it heard the bell, but after a few times the amount of salivation would probably decline, and the dog would eventually stop responding to the bell altogether. At that point, we could say that the response had been extinguished. In sum, extinction occurs when the conditioned stimulus is presented repeatedly without the unconditioned stimulus.

Once a conditioned response has been extinguished, has it vanished forever? Not necessarily. Pavlov discovered this phenomenon when he returned to his dog a few days after the conditioned behavior had seemingly been extinguished. If he rang a bell, the dog once again salivated—an effect known as **spontaneous recovery**, or the reemergence of an extinguished conditioned response after a period of rest and with no further conditioning.

Spontaneous recovery helps explain why it is so hard to overcome drug addictions. For example, cocaine addicts who are thought to be "cured" can experience an irresistible impulse to use the drug again if they are subsequently confronted by a stimulus with strong connections to the drug, such as a white powder (Díaz & De la Casa, 2011; DiCano & Everitt, 2002; Plowright, Simonds, & Butler, 2006; Rodd et al., 2004).

GENERALIZATION AND DISCRIMINATION

Despite differences in color and shape, to most of us a rose is a rose is a rose. The pleasure we experience at the beauty, smell, and grace of the flower is similar for different types of roses. Pavlov noticed a similar phenomenon. His dogs often salivated not only at the ringing of the bell that was used during their original conditioning but also at the sound of a buzzer as well.

Such behavior is called stimulus generalization. **Stimulus generalization** is a process in which after a stimulus has been conditioned to produce a particular response, stimuli that are similar to the original stimulus produce the same response. The greater the similarity between two

extinction A basic phenomenon of learning that occurs when a previously conditioned response decreases in frequency and eventually disappears.

spontaneous recovery The reemergence of an extinguished conditioned response after a period of rest and with no further conditioning.

stimulus generalization Occurs when a conditioned response follows a stimulus that is similar to the original conditioned stimulus; the more similar the two stimuli are, the more likely generalization is to occur.

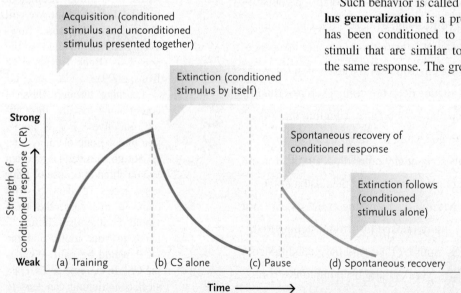

Acquisition (conditioned stimulus and unconditioned stimulus presented together)

Extinction (conditioned stimulus by itself)

Spontaneous recovery of conditioned response

Extinction follows (conditioned stimulus alone)

Strong

Weak

Strength of conditioned response (CR)

(a) Training   (b) CS alone   (c) Pause   (d) Spontaneous recovery

Time ⟶

Acquisition, Extinction, and Spontaneous Recovery in Classical Conditioning

stimuli, the greater the likelihood of stimulus generalization. Stimulus generalization helps us understand why people who have been stung by a bee will cringe when they see a wasp or maybe even an ordinary housefly. Little Albert, who, as we mentioned earlier, was conditioned to be fearful of white rats, grew afraid of other furry white things as well. However, according to the principle of stimulus generalization, it is unlikely that he would have been afraid of a black dog, because its color would have differentiated it sufficiently from the original fear-evoking stimulus.

> Stimulus generalization helps us understand why people who have been stung by a bee will cringe when they see a wasp or maybe even an ordinary housefly.

The conditioned response elicited by the new stimulus is usually not as intense as the original conditioned response, although the more similar the new stimulus is to the old one, the more similar the new response will be. It is unlikely, then, that Little Albert's fear of the Santa Claus mask was as great as his learned fear of a rat.

Stimulus discrimination, in contrast, occurs if two stimuli are sufficiently distinct from each other that one evokes a conditioned response but the other does not. Stimulus discrimination is the ability to differentiate between stimuli. For example, my dog Cleo comes running into the kitchen when she hears the sound of the electric can opener, which she has learned is used to open her dog food when her dinner is about to be served. But she does not race into the kitchen at the sound of the food processor, which is similar. In other words, she discriminates between the stimuli of can opener sound and food processor sound. Similarly, our ability to discriminate between the behavior of a growling dog and that of one whose tail is wagging can lead to adaptive behavior—avoiding the growling dog and petting the friendly one.

PSYCH think

> > > How would you have helped Little Albert get over his fear?

>> Operant Conditioning

Very good . . . What a clever idea . . . Fantastic . . . I agree . . . Thank you . . . Excellent . . . Super . . . Right on . . . This is the best paper you've ever written; you get an A . . . You are really getting the hang of it . . . I'm impressed . . .

You're getting a raise . . . Have a cookie . . . You look great . . . I love you . . .

Few of us mind being the recipient of any of these comments. But what is especially noteworthy about them is that each of these simple statements can be used, through a process known as operant conditioning, to bring about powerful changes in behavior and to teach the most complex tasks. Operant conditioning is the basis for many of the most important kinds of human, and animal, learning.

Operant conditioning is learning in which a voluntary response becomes more likely to occur again or less likely, depending on its favorable or unfavorable consequences. For example, if some money fell down out of the sky every time you finished reading a page in your textbook, would you be more likely to read more pages in your book? If so, the money would be considered a favorable consequence that strengthened your reading response.

Unlike classical conditioning, in which the original behaviors are the natural, involuntary biological responses to the presence of a stimulus such as food, water, or pain, operant conditioning applies to *voluntary* responses, which an organism performs deliberately to produce a desirable outcome. The term *operant* emphasizes this point: We operate on the environment to produce a desirable result. Operant conditioning is at work when we learn that working industriously can bring about a raise or that studying hard results in good grades.

As with classical conditioning, the basis for understanding operant conditioning was laid by work with animals. We turn now to some of that early research.

> **stimulus discrimination** The process that occurs if two stimuli are sufficiently distinct from each other that one evokes a conditioned response but the other does not; the ability to differentiate between stimuli.
>
> **operant conditioning** Learning in which a voluntary response is strengthened or weakened, depending on its favorable or unfavorable consequences.

HOW OPERANT CONDITIONING WORKS

B.F. Skinner (1904–1990), one of the 20th century's most influential psychologists, inspired a whole generation of psychologists studying operant conditioning. Skinner became interested in specifying how behavior varies as a result of alterations in the environment. To illustrate, let's consider what happens to a rat in the typical Skinner box, a chamber with a highly controlled environment that Skinner designed to study operant conditioning processes with laboratory animals (Pascual & Rodríguez, 2006).

Suppose you want to teach a hungry rat to press a lever that is in its box. At first the rat will wander around the box, exploring the environment in a relatively random fashion. At some point, however, it will probably press the lever by chance, and when it does, you have set up the box so that the rat will receive a food pellet. The first time this happens, the rat will not learn the connection between pressing a lever and receiving food and will continue to explore the box. Sooner or later the rat will press the lever again and receive a pellet, and in time the frequency of the pressing response will increase. Eventually, the rat will press the lever continually until it satisfies its hunger, thereby demonstrating that it has learned that receiving food is contingent on pressing the lever.

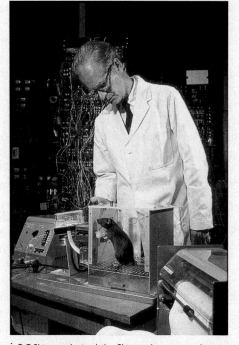
B.F. Skinner devised the Skinner box to condition rats to press a lever in order to obtain food.

What kind of stimuli can act as reinforcers? Bonuses, toys, and good grades can serve as reinforcers—if they strengthen the probability of the response that occurred before their introduction. What makes something a reinforcer depends on individual preferences. Although a chocolate bar can act as a reinforcer for one person, an individual who dislikes chocolate may find 75 cents more desirable. The only way we can know if a stimulus is a reinforcer for a particular organism is to observe whether the frequency of a previously occurring behavior increases after the presentation of the stimulus.

Of course, we are not born knowing that 75 cents can buy a candy bar. Rather, through experience we learn that money is a valuable commodity because of its association with stimuli, such as food and drink, that are naturally reinforcing. This fact suggests a distinction between primary reinforcers and secondary reinforcers. A *primary reinforcer* satisfies some biological need and works naturally, regardless of a person's prior experience. Food for a hungry person, warmth for a cold person, and relief for a person in pain all would be classified as primary reinforcers. A *secondary reinforcer*, in contrast, is a stimulus that becomes reinforcing because of its association with a primary reinforcer. For instance, we know that money is valuable because we have learned that it allows us to obtain other desirable objects, including primary reinforcers such as food and shelter. Money thus becomes a secondary reinforcer (Moher et al., 2008).

Positive Reinforcers, Negative Reinforcers, and Punishment In many respects, reinforcers can be thought of in terms of rewards; both a reinforcer and a reward increase the probability that a preceding response will occur again. But the term *reward* is limited to *positive* occurrences, and this is where it differs from a reinforcer—for it turns out that reinforcers can be positive (added to a situation) or negative (subtracted from a situation).

A **positive reinforcer** is a stimulus *added* to the environment that brings about an increase in a preceding response.

Did you know?

Stroke victims are being taught to speak again through operant conditioning. Rewarding phrases such as "good job" help to improve their ability to use language (Sigurðardóttir & Sighvatsson, 2006).

Reinforcement: The Central Concept of Operant Conditioning Skinner called the process that leads the rat to continue pressing the key "reinforcement." **Reinforcement** is the process by which a stimulus increases the probability that a preceding behavior will be repeated. In other words, pressing the lever is more likely to occur again because of the rewarding stimulus of food.

In a situation such as this one, the food is called a reinforcer. A **reinforcer** is any stimulus that increases the probability that a preceding behavior will occur again. Hence, food is a reinforcer, because it increases the probability that the behavior of pressing (formally referred to as the *response* of pressing) will take place.

reinforcement The process by which a stimulus increases the probability that a preceding behavior will be repeated.

reinforcer Any stimulus that increases the probability that a preceding behavior will occur again.

positive reinforcer A stimulus added to the environment that brings about an increase in a preceding response.

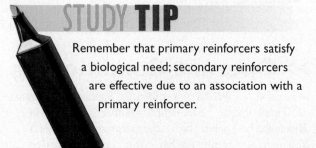

STUDY **TIP**

Remember that primary reinforcers satisfy a biological need; secondary reinforcers are effective due to an association with a primary reinforcer.

If food, water, money, or praise is provided after a response, it is more likely that that response will occur again in the future. The paychecks that workers get at the end of the week, for example, increase the likelihood that they will return to their jobs the following week.

In contrast, a **negative reinforcer** refers to an unpleasant stimulus whose *removal* leads to an increase in the probability that a preceding response will be repeated. For example, if you have an itchy rash (an unpleasant stimulus) that is relieved when you apply a certain brand of ointment, you are more likely to use that ointment the next time you have an itchy rash. Using the ointment, then, is negatively reinforcing, because it removes the unpleasant itch. Similarly, if your iPod volume is so loud that it hurts your ears when you first turn it on, you are likely to reduce the volume level. Lowering the volume is negatively reinforcing, and you are more apt to repeat the action in the future when you first turn it on. Negative reinforcement, then, teaches the individual that taking an action removes an undesirable condition that exists in the environment. Like positive reinforcers, negative reinforcers increase the likelihood that preceding behaviors will be repeated (Magoon & Critchfield, 2008).

Reinforcement *increases* the frequency of the behavior preceding it; punishment *decreases* the frequency of the behavior preceding it.

Note that negative reinforcement is not the same as punishment. **Punishment** refers to a stimulus that *decreases* the probability that a prior behavior will occur again. Unlike negative reinforcement, which produces an *increase* in behavior, punishment *reduces* the likelihood of a prior response.

Let's consider something unpleasant that might happen in your environment: nagging by your housemates or parents. Your mother nagging you to clean your room could be an unpleasant stimulus. If you clean your room to make the nagging stop, you are more likely to repeat this behavior in the future. In this way your room-cleaning behavior has been strengthened. Suppose, however, that your housemate nags you every time you turn up the volume on the TV. To avoid getting nagged, you might stop turning up the volume so loud. In this case, your loud-volume behavior decreases to avoid the punishment of nagging. In the first case, the specific behavior is apt to increase because of the negative reinforcement; in the second, it is likely to decrease because of the punishment.

There are two types of punishment: positive punishment and negative punishment, just as there are positive reinforcement and negative reinforcement. In both cases, "positive" means adding something, and "negative" means removing (subtracting) something. *Positive punishment* weakens a response through the application of an unpleasant stimulus. For instance, getting a ticket for speeding or spending ten years in jail for armed robbery is positive punishment. In contrast, *negative punishment* consists of taking away something pleasant. For instance, when a teenager is told she is "grounded" and will no longer be able to use the family car because of her poor grades, or when an employee is informed that he has been demoted with a cut in pay because of a poor job evaluation, negative punishment is being administered. Both positive and negative punishment result in a decrease in the likelihood that a previous behavior will be repeated.

These rules can help you distinguish among the concepts of positive and negative reinforcement and punishment:

- Reinforcement *increases* the frequency of the behavior preceding it; punishment *decreases* the frequency of the behavior preceding it.
- A positive stimulus is added to a situation. It may mean getting something desirable (a positive reinforcement), such as an A on a test, or getting something undesirable (a positive punishment), such as being laughed at by other kids at school.

> **negative reinforcer** An unpleasant stimulus whose *removal* leads to an increase in the probability that a preceding response will be repeated in the future.
>
> **punishment** A stimulus that decreases the probability that a previous behavior will occur again.

Reinforcement and Punishment

Intended Result	When stimulus is added, the result is . . .	When stimulus is removed or terminated, the result is . . .
Reinforcement (increase in behavior)	**Positive reinforcement**  Example: Giving a raise for good performance Result: *Increase* in response of good performance	**Negative reinforcement**  Example: Applying ointment to relieve an itchy rash leads to a higher future likelihood of applying the ointment Result: *Increase* in response of using ointment
Punishment (decrease in behavior)	**Positive punishment**  Example: Arresting a teenager when she steals a CD Result: *Decrease* in frequency of response of stealing	**Negative punishment**  Example: Teenager's access to car restricted by parents due to teenager's breaking curfew Result: Decrease in response of breaking curfew

- A negative stimulus is taken away from a situation. It may mean getting rid of something undesirable (a negative reinforcement), such as no longer having cravings for a cigarette, or losing something desirable (a negative punishment), such as losing access to your cell phone.

The Pros and Cons of Punishment: Why Reinforcement Beats Punishment Is punishment an effective way to modify behavior? There are situations in which punishment may be a reasonable choice. For instance, a parent may not have a second chance to warn a child not to run into a busy street, and so punishing the first incidence of this behavior may prove to be wise. Moreover, the use of punishment to suppress behavior, even temporarily, provides an opportunity to reinforce a person for subsequently behaving in a more desirable way.

STUDY **TIP**

The differences between positive reinforcement, negative reinforcement, positive punishment, and negative punishment are trickier than you might think, so pay special attention to the list and the summary chart in the figure above.

There are some rare instances in which punishment can be the most humane approach to treating certain severe disorders. For example, some children suffer from *autism*, a psychological disorder that can lead them to abuse themselves by tearing at their skin or banging their heads against the wall, injuring themselves severely in the process. In such cases—and when all other treatments have failed—punishment in the form of a quick but intense electric shock has been used to prevent self-injurious behavior. Such punishment is used only to keep the child safe and to buy time until positive reinforcement procedures can be initiated (Ducharme, Sanjuan, & Drain, 2007; Matson & LoVullo, 2008; Toole et al., 2004).

Punishment has several disadvantages that make its routine use questionable. For one thing, punishment is frequently ineffective, particularly if it is not delivered shortly after the undesired behavior or if the individual is able to leave the setting in which the punishment is being given. An employee who is reprimanded by the boss may quit; a teenager who loses the use of the family car may borrow a friend's car instead. In such instances, the initial behavior that is being punished may be replaced by one that is even less desirable.

Even worse, physical punishment can convey to the recipient the idea that physical aggression is permissible and perhaps even desirable. A father who yells at and hits his son for misbehaving teaches the son that aggression is an appropriate, adult response. The son soon may copy his father's behavior by acting aggressively toward others. In addition,

In what ways is punishment ineffective?

Schedules of Reinforcement The world would be a different place if poker players never played cards again after the first losing hand, fishermen quit fishing as soon as they missed a catch, or telemarketers never made another phone call after their first hang-up. The fact that such unreinforced behaviors continue, often with great frequency and persistence, illustrates that reinforcement need not be received continually for behavior to be learned and maintained. In fact, behavior that is reinforced only occasionally can ultimately be learned better than can behavior that is always reinforced.

When we refer to the frequency and timing of reinforcement that follows desired behavior, we are talking about **schedules of reinforcement**. Behavior that is reinforced every time it occurs is said to be on a **continuous reinforcement schedule**; if it is reinforced some but not all of the time, it is on a **partial** (or **intermittent**) **reinforcement schedule**. Learning occurs more rapidly when the behavior is continuously reinforced. Imagine, for example, that you are trying to teach your cat to greet you every time you come home. The cat will learn much more quickly that it is going to get a reward when it greets you if you give it a reward every single time it greets you. Later, once a behavior is learned, it will last longer if you stop giving reinforcement all the time. If you reinforce the cat's greeting only sometimes, that is, if you use a partial reinforcement schedule to maintain its behavior, it will be more likely to keep on greeting you long after you stop giving it a reward (Casey, Cooper-Brown, & Wacher, 2006; Gottlieb, 2004; Reed, 2007; Staddon & Cerutti, 2003).

Why should intermittent reinforcement result in stronger, longer-lasting learning than continuous reinforcement does? We can answer the question by examining how we might behave when using a candy vending machine

schedules of reinforcement Different patterns of frequency and timing of reinforcement following desired behavior.

continuous reinforcement schedule Reinforcing of a behavior every time it occurs.

partial (or intermittent) reinforcement schedule Reinforcing of a behavior sometimes but not all of the time.

physical punishment is often administered by people who are themselves angry or enraged. It is unlikely that individuals in such an emotional state will be able to think through what they are doing or control carefully the degree of punishment they are inflicting. Ultimately, those who resort to physical punishment run the risk that they will grow to be feared. Punishment can also reduce the self-esteem of recipients unless they can understand the reasons for it (Leary et al., 2008; Miller-Perrin, Perrin, & Kocur, 2009; Smith, Springer, & Barrett, 2011; Zolotor et al., 2008).

Finally, punishment does not convey any information about what an alternative, more appropriate behavior might be. To be useful in bringing about more desirable behavior in the future, punishment must be accompanied by specific information about the behavior that is being punished, along with specific suggestions concerning a more desirable behavior. Punishing a child for staring out the window in school could merely lead her to stare at the floor instead. Unless we teach her appropriate ways to respond, we have merely managed to substitute one undesirable behavior for another. If punishment is not followed up with reinforcement for subsequent behavior that is more appropriate, little will be accomplished.

In short, reinforcing desired behavior is a more effective technique for modifying behavior than using punishment. Both in and out of the scientific arena, reinforcement usually beats punishment (Hiby, Rooney, & Bradshaw, 2004; Pogarsky & Piquero, 2003; Sidman, 2006).

PSYCH think

> > > Given the scientific findings we have just discussed, what would you tell parents who ask if the routine use of physical punishment is likely to be a useful strategy for helping their children learn to love learning? Do you think your answer might change based on differences in cultural background and experience?

NEXT
STIMULUS
20 MILES

WEYANT

© Christopher Weyant/The New Yorker Collection/www.cartoonbank.com.

In formal terms, we can see the difference between the two reinforcement schedules: Partial reinforcement schedules (such as those provided by slot machines) maintain performance longer than do continuous reinforcement schedules (such as those established in candy vending machines) before *extinction*—the disappearance of the conditioned response—occurs (Bouton, 2011).

Certain kinds of partial reinforcement schedules produce stronger and lengthier responding before extinction than do others. Although many different partial reinforcement schedules have been examined, they can most readily be put into two categories: schedules that consider the *number of responses* made before reinforcement is given, called *fixed-ratio* and *variable-ratio schedules*, and those that consider the *amount of time* that elapses before reinforcement is provided, called *fixed-interval* and *variable-interval schedules* (Gottlieb, 2006; Pellegrini et al., 2004; Reed & Morgan, 2008; Svartdal, 2003).

In a **fixed-ratio schedule**, reinforcement is given only after a specific number of responses. For instance, a rat might receive a food pellet every tenth time it pressed a lever; here, the ratio would be 1:10. Similarly, garment workers are generally paid on fixed-ratio schedules: They receive a specific number of dollars for every blouse they sew. Because a greater rate of production means more reinforcement, people on fixed-ratio schedules are apt to work as quickly as possible.

In a **variable-ratio schedule**, reinforcement occurs after a varying number of responses rather than after a fixed number. Although the specific number of responses necessary to receive reinforcement varies, the number of responses usually hovers around a specific average. A good example of a variable-ratio schedule is a telephone salesperson's job. She might make a sale during the third, eighth, ninth, and twentieth calls without being successful during any call in between. Although the number of responses that must be made before making a sale varies, it averages out to a 20 percent success rate. Under these circumstances, you might expect that the salesperson would try to make as many calls as possible in as short a time as possible. This is the case with all variable-ratio schedules, which lead to a high rate of response and resistance to extinction.

In contrast to fixed-ratio and variable-ratio schedules, in which the crucial factor is the number of responses, fixed-*interval* and variable-*interval* schedules focus on the amount of time that has elapsed since a person or animal was rewarded. One example of a fixed-interval schedule is a weekly paycheck. For people who receive regular, weekly paychecks, it typically makes relatively little difference exactly how much they produce in a given week.

Because a **fixed-interval schedule** provides reinforcement for a response only if a fixed time period has elapsed,

fixed-ratio schedule A schedule by which reinforcement is given only after a specific number of responses are made.

variable-ratio schedule A schedule by which reinforcement occurs after a varying number of responses rather than after a fixed number.

fixed-interval schedule A schedule that provides reinforcement for a response only if a fixed time period has elapsed, making overall rates of response relatively low.

compared with a Las Vegas slot machine. When we use a vending machine, prior experience has taught us that every time we put in the appropriate amount of money, the reinforcement, a candy bar, ought to be delivered. In other words, the schedule of reinforcement is continuous. In comparison, a slot machine offers intermittent reinforcement. People who use these machines learn that after putting in their cash, most of the time they will not receive anything in return. At the same time, though, they know that they will occasionally win something.

Now suppose that, unknown to us, both the candy vending machine and the slot machine are broken, and so neither one is able to dispense anything. It would not be very long before we stopped depositing coins into the broken candy machine. Probably at most we would try only two or three times before leaving the machine in disgust. But the story would be quite different with the broken slot machine. Here, money might be dropped into the machine for a considerably longer time, even though there would be no payoff.

STUDY TIP

Remember that the different schedules of reinforcement affect the rapidity with which a response is learned and how long it lasts after reinforcement is no longer provided.

Outcomes of Reinforcement Schedules

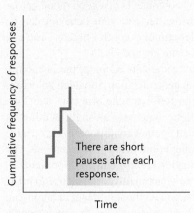

Fixed-ratio schedule

Cumulative frequency of responses

There are short pauses after each response.

Time

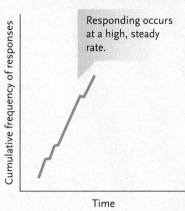

Variable-ratio schedule

Cumulative frequency of responses

Responding occurs at a high, steady rate.

Time

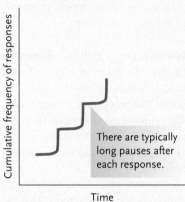

Fixed-interval schedule

Cumulative frequency of responses

There are typically long pauses after each response.

Time

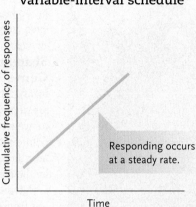

Variable-interval schedule

Cumulative frequency of responses

Responding occurs at a steady rate.

Time

overall rates of response are relatively low. This is especially true in the period just after reinforcement, when the wait time before another reinforcement is relatively long. Students' study habits often exemplify this reality. If the periods between exams are relatively long (meaning that the opportunity for reinforcement for good performance is given fairly infrequently), some students often study minimally or not at all until the day of the exam draws near. Just before the exam, however, those students begin to cram for it, signaling a rapid increase in the rate of their studying response. As you might expect, immediately after the exam there is a rapid decline in the rate of responding, with few of those students opening a book the day after a test. Fixed-interval schedules produce the kind of "scalloping effect" shown in the graphic above (Saville, 2009).

One way to decrease the delay in responding that occurs just after reinforcement, and to maintain the desired behavior more consistently throughout an interval, is to use a variable-interval schedule. In a **variable-interval schedule**, the time between reinforcements varies around some average rather than being fixed. For example, a professor who gives surprise quizzes that vary from one every three days to one every three weeks, averaging one every two weeks, is using a variable-interval schedule. Compared to the study habits we observed with a fixed-interval schedule, students' study habits under such a variable-interval schedule would most likely be very different. Students would be apt to study more regularly, because they would never know when the next surprise quiz was coming. Variable-interval schedules, in general, are more likely to produce relatively steady rates of responding than are fixed-interval schedules, with responses that take longer to extinguish after reinforcement ends.

variable-interval schedule A schedule by which the time between reinforcements varies around some average rather than being fixed.

PSYCH think

connect™

WWW.MCGRAWHILLCONNECT.COM/PSYCHOLOGY

Schedules of Reinforcement

> > > How might operant conditioning be applied in the classroom to increase the likelihood that children will complete their homework more frequently?

Take the PsychSmart challenge! Learn how to use psychology to motivate people. From chapter 5 in your ebook, select the *Exercises* tab. Then select "Schedules of Reinforcement." After doing the exercise, test your understanding of reinforcement schedules by answering question 8 in the Pop Quiz on p. 135.

: Do your study habits follow a fixed-interval schedule?

Discrimination and Generalization in Operant Conditioning

It does not take a child long to learn that sharing toys gets rewarded with a cookie and refusing to share results in a time out. The same operant conditioning principles account for the way that a pigeon can learn to peck a key when a green light goes on, but not when a red light appears. Just as in classical conditioning, then, operant learning involves the phenomena of discrimination and generalization.

One process by which people learn to discriminate stimuli is known as stimulus control training. In *stimulus control training*, a behavior is reinforced in the presence of a specific stimulus, but not in its absence. For example,

> shaping The process of teaching a complex behavior by rewarding closer and closer approximations of the desired behavior.

one of the most difficult discriminations many people face is determining when someone's friendliness is not mere friendliness but a signal of romantic interest. People learn to make the discrimination by observing the presence of certain nonverbal cues—such as increased eye contact and touching—that indicate romantic interest. When such cues are absent, people learn that no romantic interest is indicated. In this case, the nonverbal cue acts as a discriminative stimulus, one to which an organism learns to respond during stimulus control training. A *discriminative stimulus* signals the likelihood that reinforcement will follow a response. For example, if you

wait until your roommate is in a good mood before you ask to borrow her car, your behavior can be said to be under stimulus control because you can discriminate among her moods.

Just as in classical conditioning, the phenomenon of stimulus generalization, in which an organism learns a response to one stimulus and then exhibits the same response to slightly different stimuli, occurs in operant conditioning. If you have learned that being polite helps you to get your way in a certain situation (reinforcing your politeness), you are likely to generalize your response to other situations. Sometimes, though, generalization can have unfortunate consequences, as when people behave negatively toward all members of a racial group because they have had an unpleasant experience with one member of that group.

Shaping: Reinforcing What Doesn't Come Naturally Consider the difficulty of using only operant conditioning to teach people to repair an automobile transmission. You would have to wait until they performed a desired behavior before providing reinforcement. It would probably take them a very long time to accidentally stumble on the correct behavior.

There are many complex behaviors, ranging from auto repair to zoo management, that we would not expect to occur naturally as part of anyone's spontaneous behavior. Since these behaviors would never occur naturally, there would be no opportunity to reinforce them. However, there is a procedure, known as shaping, that can be used to guide someone toward the desired behavior. **Shaping** is the process of teaching a complex behavior by rewarding closer and closer approximations of the desired behavior. In shaping, you start by reinforcing any behavior that is at all similar to the behavior you want the person (or animal) to learn. Later, you reinforce only responses that are closer to the behavior you ultimately want to teach. Finally, you reinforce only the desired response. Each step in shaping, then, moves only slightly beyond the previously learned behavior, permitting the person to link the new step to the behavior learned earlier (Krueger & Dayan, 2009).

> Shaping is the process of teaching a complex behavior by rewarding closer and closer approximations of the desired behavior.

Shaping allows other species to learn complex responses that might never occur naturally, ranging from lions jumping through hoops, dolphins rescuing divers lost at sea, or rodents finding hidden land mines. Shaping also underlies the learning of many complex human skills. For instance, the ability to participate in a college psychology class is shaped from the first childhood experiences in a classroom. Behaviors such as attention and concentration, for example, are much less apparent in a preschool than they are in a college classroom. Over the years, we are rewarded for closer and closer approximations of desirable attention and concentration behaviors (Meyer & Ladewig, 2008).

Comparing Classical and Operant Conditioning We've considered classical conditioning and operant conditioning as two completely different processes. And there are a number of key distinctions between the two forms of learning. For example, the key concepts in classical conditioning are the associations between stimuli and the *reflexive* responses we experience, whereas in operant conditioning the key concept is making a *voluntary* response to obtain reinforcement.

BEHAVIOR ANALYSIS AND BEHAVIOR MODIFICATION

Two people who had been living together for three years began to fight frequently. The issues of disagreement ranged from who was going to do the dishes to the quality of their love life.

Disturbed, the couple went to a *behavior analyst,* a psychologist who specializes in behavior-modification techniques. He asked both partners to keep a detailed written record of their interactions over the next two weeks.

When they returned with the data, he carefully reviewed the records with them. In doing so, he noticed a pattern: Each of their arguments had occurred just after one or the other had left a household chore undone, such as leaving dirty dishes in the sink or draping clothes on the only chair in the bedroom.

Concept	Classical Conditioning	Operant Conditioning
Basic principle	Building associations between a conditioned stimulus and conditioned response.	Reinforcement *increases* the frequency of the behavior preceding it; punishment *decreases* the frequency of the behavior preceding it.
Nature of behavior	Based on involuntary, natural, innate behavior. Behavior is elicited by the unconditioned or conditioned stimulus.	Organism voluntarily operates on its environment to produce a desirable result. After behavior occurs, the likelihood of the behavior occurring again is increased or decreased by the behavior's consequences.
Order of events	Before conditioning, an unconditioned stimulus leads to an unconditioned response. After conditioning, a conditioned stimulus leads to a conditioned response.	Reinforcement leads to an increase in behavior; punishment leads to a decrease in behavior.
Example	 After a physician gives a child a series of painful injections (an unconditioned stimulus) that produce an emotional reaction (an unconditioned response), the child develops an emotional reaction (a conditioned response) whenever she sees the physician (the conditioned stimulus).	 A student who, after studying hard for a test, earns an A (the positive reinforcer), is more likely to study hard in the future. A student who, after going out drinking the night before a test, fails the test (punishment) is less likely to go out drinking the night before the next test.

Classical and Operant Conditioning Compared

Using the data the couple had collected, the behavior analyst asked both partners to list all the chores that could possibly arise and assign each one a point value depending on how long it took to complete. Then he had them divide the chores equally and agree in a written contract to fulfill the ones assigned to them. If either failed to carry out one of the assigned chores, he or she would have to place $1 per point in a fund for the other to spend. They also agreed to a program of verbal praise, promising to reward each other verbally for completing a chore.

Both partners agreed to try the program for a month and to keep careful records of the number of arguments they had during that period. To their surprise, the number declined rapidly.

This case provides an illustration of **behavior modification**, a formalized technique for promoting the frequency of desirable behaviors and decreasing the incidence of unwanted ones. Using the basic principles of learning theory, behavior-modification techniques have proved to be helpful in a variety of situations.

> **behavior modification** A formalized technique for promoting the frequency of desirable behaviors and decreasing the incidence of unwanted ones.

For example, people with severe mental retardation have started dressing and feeding themselves for the first time in their lives as a result of behavior modification. Behavior modification has also helped people lose weight, quit smoking, and behave more safely (Delinsky, Latner, & Wilson, 2006; Ntinas, 2007; Wadden, Crerand, & Brock, 2005; Kalarchian et al., 2011).

The techniques used by behavior analysts are as varied as the list of processes that modify behavior. They include reinforcement scheduling, shaping, generalization training, and extinction. Participants in a behavior-change program do, however, typically follow a series of similar basic steps:

- *Identifying goals and target behaviors.* The first step is to define *desired behavior*. Is it an increase in time spent studying? A decrease in weight? An increase in the use of language? A reduction in the amount of aggression displayed by a child? The goals must be stated in observable terms and must lead to specific targets. For instance, a goal might be "to increase study time," whereas the target behavior would be "to study at least two hours per day on weekdays and an hour on Saturdays."
- *Designing a data-recording system and recording preliminary data.* To determine whether behavior has changed, one must collect data before any changes are made in the situation. This information provides a *baseline* against which future changes can be measured.
- *Selecting a behavior-change strategy.* The most crucial step is to select an appropriate strategy. Because all the principles of learning can be employed to bring about behavior change, a "package" of treatments is normally used. This might include the systematic use of positive reinforcement for desired behavior (verbal praise or something more tangible, such as food), as well as a program of extinction for undesirable behavior (ignoring a child who throws a tantrum). Selecting

the right reinforcers is critical, and it may be necessary to experiment a bit to find out what is important to a particular individual.
- *Implementing the program.* Probably the most important aspect of program implementation is consistency. It is also important to reinforce the intended behavior. For example, suppose a mother wants her daughter to spend more time on her homework, but as soon as the child sits down to study, she asks for a snack. If the mother gets a snack for her, she is likely to be reinforcing her daughter's delaying tactic, not her studying.
- *Keeping careful records after the program is implemented.* Another crucial task is record keeping. If the target behaviors are not monitored, there is no way of knowing whether the program has actually been successful.
- *Evaluating and altering the ongoing program.* Finally, the results of the program should be compared with baseline data to determine the program's effectiveness. If the program has been successful, the procedures employed can be phased out gradually. For instance, if the program called for reinforcing every instance of picking up one's clothes from the bedroom floor, the reinforcement schedule could be modified to a fixed-ratio schedule in which every third instance was reinforced. However, if the program has not been successful in bringing about the desired behavior change, consideration of other approaches might be advisable.

Behavior-change techniques based on these general principles have enjoyed wide success and have proved to be one of the most powerful means of modifying behavior. Clearly, it is possible to employ the basic notions of learning theory to improve our lives.

>> Cognitive Approaches to Learning

Consider what happens when people learn to drive a car. They don't just get behind the wheel and stumble around until they randomly put the key into the ignition and, later, after many false starts, accidentally manage to get the car to move forward, thereby receiving positive reinforcement. This is how it would work if conditioning were the only type of learning. In real life, however, conditioning is only part of how we learn complex behaviors. For example, we already know the basic elements of driving from prior experience as passengers, when we likely noticed how the key was inserted into the ignition, the car was put in drive, and the gas pedal was pressed to make the car go forward.

Clearly, not all learning can be explained by operant and classical conditioning paradigms. In fact, activities like learning to drive a car imply that some kinds of learning must involve higher-order processes in which people's thoughts and memories and the way they process information account for their responses. In order to understand and explain the full range of human learning, such

Learning to drive a car is an example of a cognitive approach to learning.

situations force us to go beyond the concepts of learning as the unthinking, mechanical, and automatic acquisition of associations between stimuli and responses, as in classical conditioning, or the presentation of reinforcement, as in operant conditioning.

Some psychologists view learning in terms of the thought processes, called *cognitions*, that underlie it—an approach known as **cognitive learning theory**. Although psychologists working from the cognitive learning perspective do not deny the importance of classical and operant conditioning, they have developed approaches that focus on the unseen mental processes that occur during learning, rather than concentrating solely on external stimuli, responses, and reinforcements. For example, two types of learning that cannot be explained by operant or classical conditioning concepts are latent learning and observational learning.

LATENT LEARNING

Early evidence for the importance of cognitive processes comes from a series of animal experiments that revealed a type of cognitive learning called latent learning. In **latent learning**, a new behavior is learned but not demonstrated until some incentive is provided for displaying it (Tolman & Honzik, 1930). In short, latent learning occurs without reinforcement.

In the studies demonstrating latent learning, psychologists examined the behavior of rats in a maze such as the one shown on page 128. In one experiment, rats were randomly assigned to one of three experimental conditions. One group of rats was allowed to wander around the maze

once a day for 17 days without ever receiving a reward. Understandably, those rats made many errors and spent a relatively long time reaching the end of the maze. A second group, however, was always given food at the end of the maze. Not surprisingly, those rats learned to run quickly and directly to the food box, making few errors.

A third group of rats started out in the same situation as the unrewarded rats, but only for the first 10 days. On the 11th day, a critical experimental manipulation was introduced: From that point on, the rats in this group were given food for completing the maze. The results of this manipulation were dramatic. The previously unrewarded rats, which had earlier seemed to wander about aimlessly, showed such reductions in running time and declines in error rates that their performance almost immediately matched that of the group that had received rewards from the start.

To cognitive theorists, it seemed clear that the unrewarded rats had learned the layout of the maze early in their explorations; they just never displayed their latent learning until the reinforcement was offered. Instead, those rats seemed to develop a *cognitive map* of the maze—a mental representation of spatial locations and directions.

People, too, develop cognitive maps of their surroundings. For example, latent learning may permit you to know the location of a kitchenware store at a local mall you've frequently visited, even if you've never entered the store and don't even like to cook.

> **cognitive learning theory** An approach to the study of learning that focuses on the thought processes that underlie learning.
>
> **latent learning** Learning in which a new behavior is acquired but is not demonstrated until some incentive is provided for displaying it.

The possibility that we develop our cognitive maps through latent learning presents something of a problem for strict operant conditioning theorists. If we consider the results of the maze-learning experiment, for instance, we cannot clearly see what reinforcement permitted the rats

STUDY TIP

Remember that the cognitive learning approach focuses on the *internal* thoughts and expectations of learners, whereas classical and operant conditioning approaches focus on *external* stimuli, responses, and reinforcement.

Once a day for 17 days rats were allowed to run through a maze. Rats that were never rewarded (unrewarded control condition) consistently made the most errors. Those that received food for finishing the maze each time (rewarded control condition) made far fewer errors. The experimental group was initially unrewarded but began to be rewarded on the tenth day. Soon their error rate fell to about the same level as that of the rewarded controls. Apparently, this group had developed a cognitive map of the maze and demonstrated their latent learning when they were rewarded for completing the maze successfully.

Finish

Two-way curtain

One-way door

Start

Latent Learning in Rats

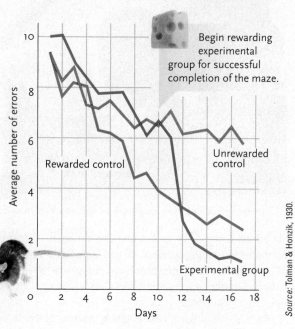

Average number of errors

Begin rewarding experimental group for successful completion of the maze.

Rewarded control

Unrewarded control

Experimental group

Days

Source: Tolman & Honzik, 1930.

that initially received no reward to learn the layout of the maze, because there was no obvious reinforcer present. Instead, the results support a cognitive view of learning, in which changes occur in unobservable mental processes (Beatty, 2002; Frensch & Rünger, 2003; Laria et al., 2009; Stouffer & White, 2006).

observational learning
Learning by observing the behavior of another person, or model.

OBSERVATIONAL LEARNING: LEARNING THROUGH IMITATION

Let's return for a moment to the case of a person learning to drive. How can we account for instances in which an individual with no direct experience in carrying out a particular

Albert Bandura

behavior learns the behavior and then performs it? To answer this question, psychologists have focused on another aspect of cognitive learning: observational learning.

According to psychologist Albert Bandura and colleagues, a major part of human learning consists of **observational learning**, which is learning by watching the behavior of another person, or *model*. Because of its reliance on observation of others—a social phenomenon—the perspective taken by Bandura is often referred to as a *social cognitive* approach to learning (Bandura, 1999, 2004; Buchanan & Wright, 2011).

Bandura dramatically demonstrated the ability of models to stimulate learning in a classic experiment. In the study, young children saw a film of an adult wildly hitting a 5-feet-tall inflatable punching toy called a Bobo doll (Bandura, Ross, & Ross, 1963a, 1963b). Later the children were given the opportunity to play with the Bobo doll themselves, and, sure enough, most displayed the same kind of behavior, in some cases mimicking the aggressive behavior almost identically.

Observational learning is particularly important in acquiring skills in which the operant conditioning technique of shaping is inappropriate. Piloting an airplane and performing brain surgery, for example, are behaviors that could hardly be learned by using trial-and-error methods without grave cost—literally—to those involved in the learning process.

Not all behavior that we witness is learned or carried out, of course. One crucial factor that determines whether we

Did you know?

Learning actually rewires your brain. New neural connections are formed when you learn something for the first time. These connections become stronger the more you use what you have learned, and this makes it easier for you to access those memories.

This child is learning by modeling the behavior of his father.

later imitate a model is whether the model is rewarded for his or her behavior. If we observe a friend being rewarded for putting more time into her studies by receiving higher grades, we are more likely to imitate her behavior than we would if her behavior resulted only in being stressed and tired. Models who are rewarded for behaving in a particular way are more apt to be mimicked than are models who receive punishment. Observing the punishment of a model, however, does not necessarily stop observers from learning the behavior. Observers can still describe the model's behavior—they are just less apt to perform it (Bandura, 1977, 1986, 1994).

Observational learning provides a framework for understanding a number of important issues relating to the extent to which people learn simply by watching the behavior of others. For instance, does watching violence on television cause us to become more violent?

VIOLENCE IN TELEVISION AND VIDEO GAMES: DOES THE MEDIA'S MESSAGE MATTER?

In an episode of *The Sopranos* television series, fictional mobster Tony Soprano murdered one of his associates. To make identification of the victim's body difficult, Soprano and one of his henchmen dismembered the body and dumped the body parts.

A few months later, two real-life half brothers in Riverside, California, strangled their mother and then cut her head and hands from her body. Victor Bautista, 20, and Matthew Montejo, 15, were caught by police after a security guard noticed that the bundle they

STUDY TIP

A key point of observational learning approaches is that the behavior of models who are rewarded for a given behavior is more likely to be imitated than behavior in which the model is punished for the behavior.

were attempting to throw in a dumpster had a foot sticking out of it. They told police that the plan to dismember their mother was inspired by *The Sopranos* episode (Martelle, Hanley, & Yoshino, 2003).

Like other "media copycat" killings, the brothers' cold-blooded brutality raises a critical issue: Does observing violent and antisocial acts in the media lead viewers to behave in similar ways? Because research on modeling shows that people frequently learn and imitate the aggression that they observe, this issue has tremendous potential for application to everyday life.

Early research on media violence helped uncover the importance of *types* of media violence and *types* of viewers. Today, the questions being addressed tend to focus on specific aspects of violence and aggressive behavior and specific types of viewers who may be more easily affected (Gunter, 2008). For example, researchers have found that the more exposure to media violence children experienced, the more likely they were to use physical aggression to defend themselves (Gentile, Mathieson, & Crick, 2011). Surprisingly, though, media exposure did *not* correlate with a greater tendency to initiate physical aggression (Adachi, & Willoughby, 2011; Lee et al., 2011).

Another way to document important differences among viewers is to look for variations in brain structure and/or function. For example, if media violence affects people differently, will we see different patterns of brain activity for those who have greater exposure to media violence? One study found that adolescents with no history of mental disorders or inappropriate aggression and less exposure to media violence showed greater activity in the amygdala than adolescents who had higher exposure rates to media violence and exhibited a disruptive behavioral disorder (Kalnin et al., 2011). Of course, we need to be wary when interpreting this finding because we cannot tell for certain whether the difference in brain activity is the cause of the different exposure and susceptibility to violent behavior or perhaps the result of it.

From the perspective of ...

A CRIMINOLOGIST How might a criminologist determine whether a suspect had knowledge of a crime by using the principles of learning?

Violent video games have been linked with actual aggression. In one of a series of studies by psychologist Craig Anderson and his colleagues, for example, college students who frequently played violent video games, such as *Postal* or *Doom*, were more likely to have been involved in delinquent behavior and aggression than were their peers. Frequent players also had lower academic achievement (Anderson et al., 2004; Anderson & Dill, 2000; Bartholow et al., 2004; Carnagey, 2009; Swing & Anderson, 2002, 2007).

Several aspects of media violence may contribute to real-life aggressive behavior (Bushman & Anderson, 2001; Johnson et al., 2002). For one thing, experiencing violent media content seems to lower inhibitions against carrying out aggression—watching television portrayals of violence or using violence to win a video game makes aggression seem a legitimate response to particular situations. Exposure to media violence also may distort our understanding of the meaning of others' behavior, predisposing us to view even nonaggressive acts by others as aggressive. Finally, a continuous diet of aggression may leave us desensitized to violence, and what previously would have repelled us now produces little emotional response. Our sense of the pain and suffering brought about by aggression may be diminished (Bartholow, Bushman, & Sestir, 2006; Carnagey, Anderson, & Bushman, 2007; Weber, Ritterfeld, & Kostygina, 2006).

> The more exposure to media violence children experienced, the more likely they were to use physical aggression to defend themselves.

DOES CULTURE INFLUENCE HOW WE LEARN?

When a member of the Chilcotin Indian tribe teaches her daughter to prepare salmon, at first she allows the girl only to observe the entire process. A little later, she permits her child to try out some basic parts of the task. Her response to questions is noteworthy. For example, when the daughter asks about how to do "the backbone part," the mother's response is to repeat the entire process with another salmon. The reason? The mother feels that one cannot learn the individual parts of the task apart from the context of preparing the whole fish (Tharp, 1989).

It should not be surprising that children raised in the Chilcotin tradition, which stresses instruction that starts by communicating the entire task, may have difficulty with traditional Western schooling. In the approach to teaching most characteristic of Western culture, tasks are broken down into their component parts. Only after each small step is learned is it thought possible to master the complete task.

Do the differences in teaching approaches between cultures affect how people learn? Some psychologists, taking a cognitive perspective on learning, suggest that people develop particular *learning styles*, characteristic ways of approaching material, based on both their cultural background and their personal, unique pattern of abilities (Anderson & Adams, 1992; Barmeyer, 2004; Li, 2011; Wilkinson & Olliver-Gray, 2006).

Learning styles differ along several dimensions. For example, one central dimension concerns relational versus analytical approaches to learning. People with a *relational learning style* master material best through exposure to a

Analytical versus Relational Approaches to Learning

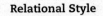

Relational Style	Analytical Style
1 Perceive information as part of total picture	Able to dis-embed information from total picture (focus on detail)
2 Exhibit improvisational and intuitive thinking	Exhibit sequential and structured thinking
3 More easily learn materials that have a human, social content and are characterized by experimental/cultural relevance	More easily learn materials that are inanimate and impersonal
4 Have a good memory for verbally presented ideas and information, especially if relevant	Have a good memory for abstract ideas and irrelevant information
5 Are more task-oriented concerning nonacademic areas	Are more task-oriented concerning academics
6 Are influenced by authority figures' expression of confidence or doubt in students' ability	Are not greatly affected by the opinions of others
7 Prefer to withdraw from unstimulating task performance	Show ability to persist at unstimulating tasks
8 Style conflicts with the traditional school environment	Style matches most school environments

Source: Anderson & Adams, 1992.

full unit or phenomenon. Parts of the unit are comprehended only when their relationship to the whole is understood. For example, a student learning about operant conditioning would participate in several different operant conditioning experiences and by doing so come to understand the individual elements such as reinforcement and punishment.

In contrast, those with an *analytical learning style* do best when they can carry out an initial analysis of the principles and components underlying a phenomenon or situation. By developing an understanding of the fundamental principles and components, they are best able to understand the full picture. For example, a student learning about operant conditioning would learn first about each element, reinforcement, punishment, schedules of reinforcement, and so on, and then put them altogether to understand the concept.

According to James Anderson and Maurianne Adams, particular minority groups in Western societies display characteristic learning styles. For instance, they argue that Caucasian females and African-American, Native-American, and Hispanic-American males and females are more apt to use a relational style of learning than Caucasian and Asian-American males, who are more likely to employ an analytical style (Adams et al., 2000; Anderson & Adams, 1992; Richardson, 2011).

The conclusion that members of particular ethnic and gender groups have similar learning styles is controversial. Because there is so much diversity within each particular racial and ethnic group, critics argue that generalizations about learning styles cannot be used to predict the style of any single individual, regardless of group membership.

Still, it is clear that values about learning, which are communicated through a person's family and cultural background, have an effect on how successful students are in school. One theory suggests that members of minority groups who were voluntary immigrants are more apt to be successful in school than those who were brought into a majority culture against their will. For example, Korean children in the United States—the sons and daughters of voluntary immigrants—perform quite well, as a group, in school. In contrast, Korean children in Japan, who were often the sons and daughters of people who were forced to immigrate during World War II, essentially as forced laborers, do less well in school. The theory suggests that the motivation to succeed is lower for children in forced immigration groups (Foster, 2005; Ogbu, 1992, 2003).

PSYCH think

> > > The relational style of learning sometimes conflicts with the traditional school environment. Could a school be created that takes advantage of the characteristics of the relational style? How? Are there types of learning for which the analytical style is clearly superior?

Personal Styles

What's Your Receptive Learning Style? Read each of the following statements and rank them in terms of their usefulness to you as learning approaches. Base your ratings on your personal experiences and preferences, using the following scale:

1 = Not at all useful   2 = Not very useful   3 = Neutral   4 = Somewhat useful   5 = Very useful
Scoring information is on the next page.

	1	2	3	4	5
1. Studying alone					
2. Studying pictures and diagrams to understand complex ideas					
3. Listening to class lectures					
4. Performing a process myself rather than reading or hearing about it					
5. Learning a complex procedure by reading written directions					
6. Watching and listening to film, computer, or video presentations					
7. Listening to a book or lecture on tape					
8. Doing lab work					
9. Studying teachers' handouts and lecture notes					
10. Studying in a quiet room					
11. Taking part in group discussions					
12. Taking part in hands-on classroom demonstrations					
13. Taking notes and studying them later					
14. Creating flash cards and using them as a study and review tool					
15. Memorizing and recalling how words are spelled by spelling them "out loud" in my head					
16. Writing key facts and important points down as a tool for remembering them					
17. Recalling how to spell a word by seeing it in my head					
18. Underlining or highlighting important facts or passages in my reading					
19. Saying things out loud when I'm studying					
20. Recalling how to spell a word by "writing" it invisibly in the air or on a surface					
21. Learning new information by reading about it in a textbook					
22. Using a map to find an unknown place					
23. Working in a study group					
24. Finding a place I've been to once by just going there without directions					

Scoring: The statements reflect four receptive learning styles:

Read/write learning style. If you have a read/write learning style, you prefer information that is presented visually in a written format. You feel most comfortable reading, and you may recall the spelling of a word by thinking of how the word looks. You probably learn best when you have the opportunity to read about a concept rather than listening to a teacher explain it.

Visual/graphic learning style. Students with a visual/graphic learning style learn most effectively when material is presented visually in a diagram or picture. You might recall the structure of a chemical compound by reviewing a picture in your mind, and you benefit from instructors who make frequent use of visual aids such as videos, maps, and models. Students with visual learning styles find it easier to see things in their mind's eye—to visualize a task or concept—than to be lectured about them.

Auditory/verbal learning style. Have you ever asked a friend to help you put something together by having her read the directions to you while you worked? If you did, you may have an auditory/verbal learning style. People with auditory/verbal learning styles prefer listening to explanations rather than reading them. They love class lectures and discussions, because they can easily take in the information that is being talked about.

Tactile/kinesthetic learning style. Students with a tactile/kinesthetic learning style prefer to learn by doing—touching, manipulating objects, and doing things. For instance, some people enjoy the act of writing because of the feel of a pencil or a computer keyboard—the tactile equivalent of thinking out loud. Or they may find that it helps them to make a three-dimensional model to understand a new idea.

To find your primary learning style, disregard your 1, 2, and 3 ratings. Add up your 4 and 5 ratings for each learning style (i.e., a "4" equals 4 points and a "5" equals 5 points). Use the following to link the statements to the learning styles and to write down your summed ratings:

Learning Style Statements Total (Sum) of Rating Points
Read/write 1, 5, 9, 13, 17, and 21
Visual/graphic 2, 6, 10, 14, 18, and 22
Auditory/verbal 3, 7, 11, 15, 19, and 23
Tactile/kinesthetic 4, 8, 12, 16, 20, and 24

The total of your rating points for any given style will range from a low of 0 to a high of 30. The highest total indicates your main receptive learning style. Don't be surprised if you have a mixed style, in which two or more styles receive similar ratings.

For REVIEW >>

- What is learning?

  Learning is a relatively permanent change in behavior resulting from experience. Classical conditioning is a form of learning that occurs when a neutral stimulus—one that normally brings about no relevant response—is repeatedly paired with a stimulus (called an unconditioned stimulus) that brings about a reflexive, untrained response. By studying salivation in dogs, Pavlov determined that conditioning occurs when the neutral stimulus is repeatedly presented just before the unconditioned stimulus. After repeated pairings, the neutral stimulus elicits the same response that the unconditioned stimulus brings about. When this occurs, the neutral stimulus has become a conditioned stimulus, and the response a conditioned response. Watson applied Pavlov's principles to condition a human infant called "Little Albert" to fear a white rat. Little Albert also came to fear other white furry objects, demonstrating stimulus generalization. Learning is not always permanent. Extinction occurs when a previously learned response decreases in frequency and eventually disappears. (pp. 112–117)

- What is the role of reward and punishment in learning?

  In operant conditioning, a voluntary behavior is strengthened or weakened through reinforcement or punishment. Skinner's work with animals showed that reinforcing or rewarding behavior increases the probability that the behavior will be repeated. Reinforcers can be positive or negative. In contrast to reinforcement, positive and negative punishment decreases or suppresses a target behavior. (pp. 117–126)

- How can the information from this chapter be used to change undesired behaviors?

  Behavior modification is a method for applying the principles of learning theory to promote the frequency of desired behaviors and to decrease or eliminate unwanted ones. (pp. 125–126)

- Does thinking matter at all in learning?

  Cognitive approaches to learning consider learning in terms of thought processes, or cognition. Latent learning and the apparent development of cognitive maps support cognitive approaches. Learning also occurs when we observe the behavior of others. The major factor that determines whether an observed behavior will actually be performed is the nature of the reinforcement or punishment a model receives. Learning styles vary with cultural background and reflect an individual's unique pattern of abilities. (pp. 126–131)

Pop Quiz

1. _____ involves changes brought about by experience, whereas maturation describes changes resulting from biological development.

   Refer to this passage to answer questions 2 through 5:

   > The last three times little Theresa visited Dr. Lopez for check-ups, he administered a painful preventive immunization shot that left her in tears. Today, when her mother takes her for another checkup, Theresa begins to sob as soon as she comes face to face with Dr. Lopez, even before he has had a chance to say hello.

2. The painful shot that Theresa received during each visit was a(n) _____ _____ that elicited the _____ _____ , her tears.

3. Dr. Lopez is upset because his presence has become a _____ _____ for Theresa's crying.

4. Fortunately, Dr. Lopez gave Theresa no more shots for quite some time. Over that period she gradually stopped crying and even came to like him. _____ had occurred.

5. _____ conditioning describes learning that occurs as a result of reinforcement.

6. Match the type of operant learning with its definition.
   a. positive reinforcement
   b. negative reinforcement
   c. positive punishment
   d. negative punishment
   ____ 1. an unpleasant stimulus is presented to decrease behavior
   ____ 2. an unpleasant stimulus is removed to increase behavior
   ____ 3. a pleasant stimulus is presented to increase behavior
   ____ 4. a pleasant stimulus is removed to decrease behavior

7. Match the type of reinforcement schedule with its definition.
   a. fixed-ratio
   b. variable-interval
   c. fixed-interval
   d. variable-ratio
   ____ 1. reinforcement occurs after a set time period
   ____ 2. reinforcement occurs after a set number of responses
   ____ 3. reinforcement occurs after a varying time period
   ____ 4. reinforcement occurs after a varying number of responses

8. The schedules of reinforcement activity taught me that
   a. some people like to get rewarded at the same time each week and some like to be surprised.
   b. giving big rewards may make people more motivated; it depends on their personality.
   c. some people are really easy to get along with and others are more rigid.
   d. most people want lots of little rewards, but a few prefer to get one big reward.

9. In the shaping activity,
   a. I had to alternate between giving positive and negative reinforcement.
   b. the first behavior I reinforced was different from the last one.
   c. there were three birds to train.
   d. I used a model bird that the bird I was training was supposed to imitate.

10. In cognitive learning theory, it is assumed that people develop a(n) _____ about receiving a reinforcer when they behave a certain way.

11. In _____ learning, a new behavior is learned but is not shown until appropriate reinforcement is presented.

12. Bandura's theory of _____ learning states that people learn through watching a(n) _____—another person displaying the behavior of interest.

Answers TO POP QUIZ QUESTIONS

1. Learning
2. unconditioned stimulus, unconditioned response
3. conditioned stimulus
4. Extinction
5. Operant
6. 1–c, 2–b, 3–a, 4–d
7. 1–c, 2–a, 3–b, 4–d
8. a
9. b
10. expectation
11. latent
12. observational, model

6

MEMORY

REMEMBERING IT ALL

Meet Jill Price at one of her favorite Los Angeles restaurants, and she'll scoot into a booth and start to reminisce. "On Wednesday, December 11, 1996, my friend and I came here hunting for the perfect crab cake," she says. She also remembers Saturday, November 4, 1995 (she saw on TV that Israeli Prime Minister Yitzhak Rabin was killed), and Friday, September 20, 1985 (her first visit to the eatery; she wore a large hat). "It's all flashing through my head," she says matter-of-factly. "I'm totally in the moment. I just have a split screen of my past, too."

What Price, 42, has is the first-ever diagnosed case of highly superior autobiographical memory, which forces her to recall every day of her life from the age of 14. Given a date, she can tell you on what day of the week it fell, what she did and any historical event she heard of that day. "It's like I walk around with a video camera," says Price. "My memories are nonstop and involuntary."[vi]

While we might think that having perfect recall for all the events in our lives would be a blessing, Jill Price's experience suggests otherwise. Her extremely rare condition (called *hyperthymestic syndrome*) affects the part of her memory that stores experiences related to life events. She has perfect, vivid memories of virtually every day of her life, memories both good and bad. And while it's pleasant for her to relive her fond memories, she can't escape the pain of the bad ones (Parker, Cahill, & McGaugh, 2006; Price, 2008).

Price's condition illustrates the complexity and the mystery of the phenomenon we call memory. Memory allows us to retrieve a vast amount of information. We are able to remember the name of a friend with whom we haven't talked for years and recall the details of a picture that hung in our bedroom as a child. At the same time, though, memory failures are common. We forget where we left the keys to the car and fail to answer an exam question about material we studied only a few hours earlier. Why?

As You READ >>

- What is memory?
- Why do we recall some memories better than others?
- Why do we forget information?

>> The Foundations of Memory

You are playing a game of Trivial Pursuit, and winning the game comes down to one question: On what body of water is Mumbai located? As you rack your brain for the answer, several fundamental processes relating to memory come into play. You may never, for instance, have been exposed to information regarding Mumbai's location. Or if you have been exposed to it, it may simply not have registered in a meaningful way. In other words, the information might not have been recorded in your memory. The initial process of recording information in a form usable to memory, a process called *encoding*, is the first stage in remembering something. **Encoding** is the process by which we put information into our memory.

Even if you had been exposed to the information and originally knew the name of the body of water, you may still be unable to recall it during the game because of a failure to retain it. Memory specialists speak of **storage**, the maintenance of material saved in memory. If the material is not stored adequately, it cannot be recalled later.

> **encoding** The process by which we put information into our memory.
>
> **storage** The process by which we maintain material saved in memory.
>
> **retrieval** The process by which we access memories that have been in storage.
>
> **memory** The process by which we encode, store, and retrieve information.

Memory also depends on the process of *retrieval*. **Retrieval** is the process by which we access memories that have been in storage. Material in memory storage has to be located and brought into awareness to be useful. Your failure to recall Mumbai's location, then, may rest on your inability to retrieve information that you learned earlier.

In sum, psychologists consider **memory** to be the process by which we encode, store, and retrieve information. Each of the three parts of this definition—encoding, storage, and retrieval—represents a different process. You can think of these processes as being analogous to a computer's keyboard (encoding), hard drive (storage), and software that accesses the information for display on the screen (retrieval). Only if all three processes have operated will you successfully recall the body of water on which Mumbai is located: the Arabian Sea.

Does this camera use encoding, storage, and retrieval?

Three Basic Processes of Memory

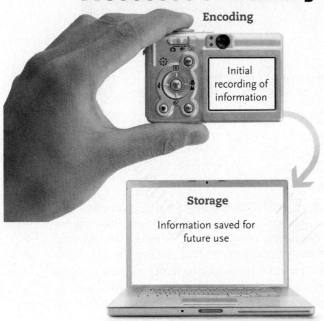

Encoding

Initial recording of information

Storage

Information saved for future use

Retrieval

Recovery of stored information

STUDY **TIP**

Although the three types of memory are discussed as separate memory stores, these are not mini-warehouses located in specific areas of the brain. Instead, they represent three different memory systems with different characteristics.

Recognizing that memory involves encoding, storage, and retrieval gives us a start in understanding the concept. But how does memory actually function? How do we explain what information is initially encoded, what gets stored, and how it is retrieved?

According to the *three-system approach to memory* that dominated memory research for several decades, there are different memory storage systems or stages through which information must travel if it is to be remembered (Atkinson & Shiffrin, 1968, 1971). Historically, the approach has been extremely influential in the development of our understanding of memory, and—although new theories have augmented it—it still provides a useful framework for understanding how information is recalled.

The three-system memory theory focuses on storage and proposes three separate stages of memory storage. **Sensory memory** refers to the initial, momentary storage of sensory information that lasts only an instant. In a second stage, **short-term memory** holds information for up to 25 seconds and stores it according to its meaning rather than as mere sensory stimulation. The third type of storage system is **long-term memory**. Information is stored in long-term memory on a relatively permanent basis, although it may be difficult to retrieve.

sensory memory The initial, momentary storage of information, lasting only an instant.

short-term memory Memory that holds information for up to 25 seconds.

long-term memory Memory that stores information on a relatively permanent basis, although it may be difficult to retrieve.

SENSORY MEMORY

A momentary flash of lightning, the sound of a twig snapping, and the sting of a pinprick all represent stimulation of exceedingly brief duration, but they may nonetheless provide important information that can require a response. Such stimuli are initially—and fleetingly—stored in sensory memory, the first repository of the information the world presents to us. Actually, there are several types of sensory memories, each related to a different source of sensory information. For instance, *iconic memory* reflects information from the visual system. *Echoic memory* stores auditory information coming from the ears. In addition, there are corresponding memories for each of the other senses.

Sensory memory can store information for only a very short time. If sensory information does not pass into short-term memory, it is lost for good. For instance, iconic memory seems to last less than a second, and echoic memory typically fades within 2 or 3 seconds. Yet sensory memory is highly precise: Sensory memory can store an

A momentary flash of lightning leaves a visual memory, a fleeting but exact replica of the sensory stimulus.

Three-System Approach to Memory

Repetitive rehearsal (retains information in short-term memory)

Elaborative rehearsal (moves information into long-term memory)

Sensory information →

Sensory memories
Sight (iconic)
Sound (echoic)
Other sensory memories

→ **Short-term memory** →

Long-term memory

Forgetting
typically within 1 second

Forgetting
within 25 seconds

almost exact replica of each stimulus to which it is exposed (Baldwin & Ash, 2011; Darwin, Turvey, & Crowder, 1972; Deouell, Parnes, & Pickard, 2006; Long & Beaton, 1982; Sams et al., 1993).

In sum, sensory memory operates as a kind of snapshot that stores information—which may be of a visual, auditory, or other sensory nature—for a brief moment in time. But it is as if each snapshot, immediately after being taken, is destroyed and replaced with a new one. Unless the information in the snapshot is transferred to some other type of memory, it is lost.

Sensory memory operates as a kind of snapshot that stores sensory information for a brief moment in time.

SHORT-TERM MEMORY

Because the information that is stored briefly in sensory memory consists of representations of raw sensory stimuli, it is not meaningful to us. If we are to make sense of it and possibly retain it, the information must be encoded so that it can be transferred to the next stage of memory: short-term memory. Short-term memory is the memory store in which information first has meaning, although the maximum length of retention there is relatively short (Hamilton & Martin, 2007).

chunk A meaningful grouping of stimuli that can be stored as a unit in short-term memory.

The specific processes by which sensory memories are transformed into short-term memories are not clear. One area of investigation concerns how paying attention to iconic sensory memory results in persistence of sensory information in the primary visual cortex (Serences, Ester, Vogel, & Awh, 2009). Much remains to be learned about this process. What is clear, however, is that unlike sensory memory, which holds a relatively full and detailed—if short-lived—representation of the world, short-term memory has incomplete representational capabilities. Apparently, short-term memory needs to reduce the incoming information to the parts that are meaningful and important. For example, if you look up from your book, you will experience a lot of visual stimulation. As soon as you pay attention to and think about part of it, that information will enter your short-term memory.

In fact, the specific amount of information that can be held in short-term memory has been identified as seven items, or "chunks," of information, with variations up to plus or minus two chunks. A **chunk** is a meaningful grouping of stimuli that can be stored as a unit in short-term memory. According to George Miller (1956), a chunk can be individual letters or numbers, permitting us to hold a seven-digit phone number (such as 226-4610) in short-term memory.

But a chunk also may consist of larger categories, such as words or other meaningful units. For example, consider the following list of 21 letters:

P B S F O X C N N A B C C B S M T V N B C

Because the list exceeds seven chunks, it is difficult to recall the letters after one exposure. But suppose they were presented as follows:

PBS FOX CNN ABC CBS MTV NBC

In this case, even though there are still 21 letters, you'd be able to store them in short-term memory, since they represent only seven chunks.

Chunks can vary in size from single letters or numbers to categories that are far more complicated. The specific nature of what constitutes a chunk varies according to one's past experience. For example, expert chess players are able to remember larger configurations of chess pieces than inexperienced players can, because the experts chunk pieces in different (and larger) ways (Baldwin & Ash, 2011; deGroot, 1978; Oberauer, 2007).

Although it is possible to remember seven or so relatively complicated sets of information entering short-term memory, the information cannot be held there very long. Just how brief is short-term memory? If you've ever looked

Look at this chessboard for about five seconds, and then, after covering up the board, try to draw the position of the pieces on a blank chessboard or a piece of paper. Unless you are an experienced chess player, you are likely to have great difficulty with this task. Yet chess masters do this quite well (deGroot, 1966). They can reproduce correctly 90 percent of the pieces on the board, not because they have superior memories but because they see the board in terms of chunks, or meaningful units, and reproduce the positions of the chess pieces by using those units.

up a telephone number in a phone directory, repeated the number to yourself, put away the directory, and then forgotten the number after you've tapped the first three numbers into your phone, you know that information does not remain in short-term memory very long. Most psychologists believe that information in short-term memory is lost after 15 to 25 seconds—unless it is transferred to long-term memory (Buchsbaum & D'Esposito, 2009; Jonides et al., 2008; Ranganath & Blumenfeld, 2005).

HOW NOT TO REMEMBER NAMES

Hi! Remember me?

O.K. He has a button nose. That rhymes with Sutton. Willie Sutton. Willie Sutton robbed banks. "Banks" rhymes with Hanks. Tom Hanks. His name is Tom. No. His name is Hank. No, Tom. Hank. Wait. "Hank" sounds weird. I've got it: FRANK! No... not Frank...

From the perspective of ...

A MARKETING SPECIALIST Just repeating the name of your product in your ads might help consumers recognize your product when they go shopping. How could you use elaborative rehearsal to increase the chances that they would want to buy your product?

it is kept current in short-term memory, but it will not necessarily be placed in long-term memory. Instead, as soon as we stop punching in the phone numbers, the number is likely to be replaced by other information and completely forgotten.

rehearsal The repetition of information that has entered short-term memory.

In contrast, if the information in short-term memory is rehearsed using a process called elaborative rehearsal, it is much more likely to be transferred into long-term memory. *Elaborative rehearsal* occurs when the information is considered and organized in some fashion. The organization might include expanding the information to make it fit into a logical framework, linking it to another memory, turning it into an image, or transforming it in some other way. For example, a list of vegetables to be purchased at a store could be woven together in memory as items being used to prepare an elaborate salad, could be linked to the items bought on an earlier shopping trip, or could be thought of in terms of the image of a farm with rows of each item.

Rehearsal The transfer of material from short- to long-term memory proceeds largely on the basis of **rehearsal**, the repetition of information that has entered short-term memory. Rehearsal accomplishes two things. First, as long as the information is repeated, it is maintained in short-term memory. More important, however, rehearsal allows us to transfer the information into long-term memory (Kvavilashvili & Fisher, 2007).

Whether the transfer is made from short- to long-term memory seems to depend largely on the kind of rehearsal that is carried out. If the information is simply repeated over and over again—as we might do with a telephone number while we rush from the phone book to the phone—

Working Memory Rather than seeing short-term memory as an independent way station into which memories arrive, either to fade or to be passed on to long-term memory, many contemporary memory theorists conceive of short-term memory as far more active. In this view, short-term memory is like an information processing system that manages both new material gathered from sensory memory and older material that is constantly being drawn from long-term storage. In this increasingly influential view, short-term memory is referred to as **working memory** and defined as a set of temporary memory stores that actively manipulate and rehearse information (Bayliss et al., 2005a, 2005b; Hofmann, Friese, & Schmeichel, 2011; Unsworth & Engle, 2005).

Working memory is thought to contain a *central executive* processor that is involved in reasoning and decision making. The central executive coordinates three distinct storage-and-rehearsal systems: the *visual store*, the *verbal store*, and the *episodic buffer*. The visual store specializes in visual and spatial information, whereas the verbal store holds and manipulates material relating to speech, words, and numbers. The episodic buffer contains information that represents episodes or events (Baddeley, 2001; Bröder & Schiffer, 2006; Rudner & Rönnberg, 2008).

Working memory permits us to keep information in an active state briefly so that we can do something with the information. For instance, we use working memory when we're doing a multistep arithmetic problem in our heads, storing the result of one calculation while getting ready to move to the next stage. (I make use of my working memory when I figure a 20% tip in a restaurant by first calculating 10% of the total bill and then doubling it.) Although working memory aids in the recall of information, it uses a significant amount of cognitive resources during its operation. In turn, this can make us less aware of our surroundings—something that has implications for the debate about the use of cell phones while driving. If a phone conversation requires thinking, it will burden working memory and leave drivers dangerously less aware of their surroundings (Sifrit, 2006; Strayer & Drews, 2007).

working memory A set of active, temporary memory stores that actively manipulate and rehearse information.

declarative memory Memory for factual information: names, faces, dates, and the like.

> If a phone conversation requires thinking, it will burden working memory and leave drivers dangerously less aware of their surroundings.

LONG-TERM MEMORY

Material that makes its way from short-term memory to long-term memory enters a storehouse of almost unlimited capacity (Jonides et al., 2008). The information in long-term memory is filed and cross-referenced with other memories so that we can retrieve it when we need it.

Evidence of the existence of long-term memory, as distinct from short-term memory, comes from a number of sources. For example, people with certain kinds of brain damage have no lasting recall of new information received after the damage occurred, although people and events stored in memory before the injury remain intact (Milner, 1966). Because information that was encoded and stored before the injury can be recalled and because short-term memory after the injury appears to be operational—new material can be recalled for a very brief period—we can infer that there are two distinct types of memory storage: one for short-term and one for long-term storage.

The distinction between short- and long-term memory is also supported by the *serial position effect*, in which the ability to recall information in a list depends on where in the list an item appears. For instance, often a *primacy effect* occurs, in which items presented early in a list are remembered better. There is also a *recency effect*, in which items presented late in a list are remembered best (Bonanni et al., 2007; Tan & Ward, 2008; Tydgat & Grainger, 2009).

LONG-TERM MEMORY MODULES

Just as short-term memory is often conceptualized in terms of working memory, many contemporary researchers now regard long-term memory as having several different components, or *memory modules*. Each of these modules represents a different memory system in the brain (Jonides et al., 2003).

One major distinction within long-term memory is that between declarative memory and procedural memory. **Declarative memory** is memory

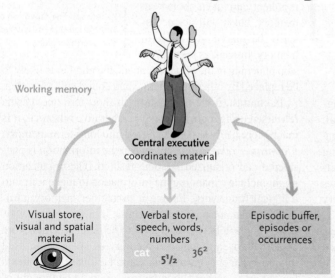

Model of Working Memory

Working memory

Central executive
coordinates material

| Visual store, visual and spatial material | Verbal store, speech, words, numbers | Episodic buffer, episodes or occurrences |

cat $5^1/_2$ 36^2

Source: Adapted from Baddeley, Chincotta, & Adlam, 2001

for factual information: names, faces, dates, and facts, such as "a bike has two wheels." In contrast, **procedural memory** (or *nondeclarative memory*) refers to memory for skills and habits, such as how to ride a bike or hit a baseball. Information about *things* is stored in declarative memory; information about *how to do things* is stored in procedural memory (Bauer, 2008; Brown & Robertson, 2007; Feldhusen, 2006; Fosshage, 2011).

Declarative memory can be subdivided into semantic memory and episodic memory. **Semantic memory** is memory for general knowledge and facts about the world, as well as memory for the rules of logic that are used to deduce other facts. Because of semantic memory, we remember that the ZIP code for Beverly Hills is 90210, that Hawaii is in the Pacific Ocean, and that *memoree* is the incorrect spelling of *memory*. Thus, semantic memory is somewhat like a mental almanac of facts (Nyberg & Tulving, 1996; Tulving, 2002).

The ability to remember specific skills and the order in which they are used is called procedural memory. If driving a car involves procedural memory, is texting while driving safe?

PSYCH think

> > > People say that you never forget how to ride a bicycle. Why would this be true? [Hint: Where is this kind of memory stored?]

In contrast, **episodic memory** is memory for events that occur in a particular time, place, or context. For example, recall of who helped you balance when you were learning to ride a bike, a first kiss, or arranging a surprise 21st birthday party for someone is based on episodic memories. Episodic memories relate to particular contexts. For example, remembering *when* and *how* we learned that 2 × 2 = 4

would be an episodic memory; the fact itself (that 2 × 2 = 4) is a semantic memory.

Episodic memories can be surprisingly detailed. Consider, for instance, how you'd respond if you were asked to identify what you were doing on a specific day two years ago. Impossible? You may think otherwise as you read the exchange on the next page between a researcher and a participant in a study who was asked, in a memory experiment, what he was doing "on Monday afternoon in the third week of September two years ago."

procedural memory Memory for skills and habits, such as riding a bike or hitting a baseball, sometimes referred to as *nondeclarative memory*.

semantic memory Memory for general knowledge and facts about the world, as well as memory for the rules of logic that are used to deduce other facts.

episodic memory Memory for events that occur in a particular time, place, or context.

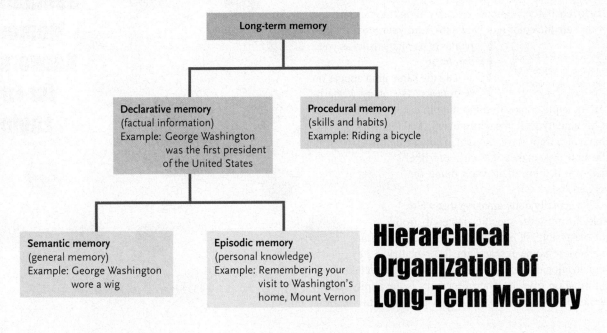

Long-term memory

Declarative memory
(factual information)
Example: George Washington was the first president of the United States

Procedural memory
(skills and habits)
Example: Riding a bicycle

Semantic memory
(general memory)
Example: George Washington wore a wig

Episodic memory
(personal knowledge)
Example: Remembering your visit to Washington's home, Mount Vernon

Hierarchical Organization of Long-Term Memory

PARTICIPANT: Come on. How should I know?

EXPERIMENTER: Just try it anyhow.

PARTICIPANT: OK. Let's see: Two years ago . . . I would be in high school in Pittsburgh . . . That would be my senior year. Third week in September—that's just after summer—that would be the fall term . . . Let me see. I think I had chemistry lab on Mondays. I don't know. I was probably in chemistry lab. Wait a minute—that would be the second week of school. I remember he started off with the atomic table—a big fancy chart. I thought he was crazy trying to make us memorize that thing. You know, I think I can remember sitting . . . (Lindsay & Norman, 1977)

Episodic memory, then, can provide information about events that happened long in the past (Reynolds & Takooshian, 1988). But semantic memory is no less impressive, permitting us to dredge up tens of thousands of facts ranging from the date of our birthday to the knowledge that $1 is less than $5.

SEMANTIC NETWORKS

Try to recall, for a moment, as many things as you can think of that are the color red. Now pull from your memory the names of as many fruits as you can recall.

semantic networks Mental representations of clusters of interconnected information.

Did the same item appear on both tasks? For many westerners, an apple comes to mind in both cases, since it fits equally well in each category. And the fact that you might have thought of an apple on the first task makes it even more likely that you'll think of it when doing the second task.

It's actually quite amazing that we're able to retrieve specific material from the vast store of information in our long-term memories. Some researchers theorize that a key organizational tool that allows us to recall detailed information from long-term memory is the ability to create associations between different pieces of information.

In this view, knowledge is stored in **semantic networks**, mental representations of clusters of interconnected information (Collins & Loftus, 1975; Collins & Quillian, 1969; Cummings, Ceponiene, & Koyama, 2006).

If you grew up in the United States, for example, consider what would be the associations in your memory relating to fire engines, the color red, and a variety of other semantic concepts. Thinking about a particular concept leads to recall of related concepts. For example, seeing a fire engine may activate our recollections of other kinds of emergency vehicles, such as an ambulance, which in turn may activate recall of the related concept of a vehicle. And thinking of a vehicle may lead us to think about a bus that we've seen in the past. Activating one memory triggers the activation of related memories in a process known as *spreading activation* (Foster et al., 2008; Kreher et al., 2008).

THE NEUROSCIENCE OF MEMORY

Can we pinpoint a location in the brain where sensory, short-term, and long-term memories reside? Is there a single site that corresponds to a particular memory, or is memory distributed in different regions across the brain? Do memories leave an actual physical trace that scientists can view?

The search for the *engram,* the term for the physical memory trace that corresponds to a memory, has proved to be a major puzzle to psychologists and other neuroscientists interested in memory. Using advanced brain scanning procedures in their efforts to determine the neuroscientific basis of memory formation, investigators have learned that certain areas and structures of the brain specialize in different types of memory-related activities. The *hippocampus*, a part of the brain's limbic system, plays a central role in the consolidation of declarative memories. Located within the brain's *medial temporal lobes*, just behind the eyes, the hippocampus aids in the initial encoding of information,

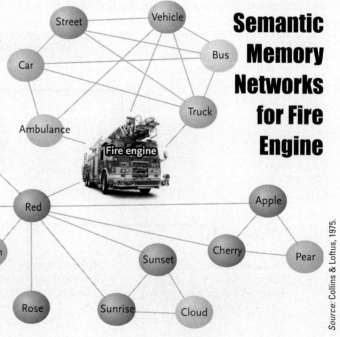

Semantic Memory Networks for Fire Engine

Source: Collins & Loftus, 1975.

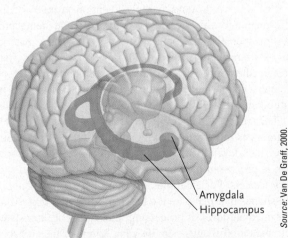

"The matters about which I'm being questioned, Your Honor, are all things I should have included in my long-term memory but which I mistakenly inserted in my short-term memory."

Ed Fisher © Ed Fisher/The New Yorker Collection/www.cartoonbank.com.

acting as a kind of neurological e-mail system. That information is subsequently passed along to the cerebral cortex of the brain, where it is actually stored (Govindarajan, Kelleher, & Tonegawa, 2006; Lavenex & Lavenex, 2009; Peters et al., 2007).

The *amygdala*, another part of the limbic system, also plays an important role in memory. The amygdala is especially involved with memories involving emotion (Buchanan & Adolphs, 2004; Hamann, 2001; Talmi et al., 2008). For example, if you are frightened by a large Doberman, you're likely to remember the event vividly—an outcome related to the functioning of the amygdala. Encountering the Doberman, or any large dog, in the future is likely to reactivate the amygdala and bring back the unpleasant memory, for a while, at least.

Amygdala
Hippocampus

Source: Van De Graff, 2000.

Memory Consolidation in the Brain

>> Recalling Long-Term Memories

An hour after his job interview, Ricardo was sitting in a coffee shop, telling his friend Laura how well it had gone, when the woman who had interviewed him walked in. "Well, hello, Ricardo. How are you doing?" Trying to make a good impression, Ricardo began to make introductions but suddenly realized he could not remember the name of the interviewer. Stammering, he desperately searched his memory, but to no avail. "I *know* her name," he thought to himself, "but here I am, looking like a fool. I can kiss this job good-bye."

> **tip-of-the-tongue phenomenon** The inability to recall information that one realizes one knows—a result of the difficulty of retrieving information from long-term memory.

Have you ever tried to remember someone's name, convinced that you knew it but unable to recall it no matter how hard you tried? This common occurrence—known as the **tip-of-the-tongue phenomenon**—exemplifies how difficult it can be to retrieve information stored in long-term memory (Brennen, Vikan, & Dybdahl, 2007; Cleary, 2006; Schwartz, 2001, 2002, 2008).

RETRIEVAL CUES

Perhaps recall of names and other memories is not perfect, because there is so much information stored in long-term memory. Because the material that makes its way to long-term memory is relatively permanent, the capacity of long-term memory is vast. For instance, if you are like the average college student, your vocabulary includes some 50,000 words, you know hundreds of mathematical "facts," and you are able to conjure up images with no trouble at all. In fact, simply cataloging all your memories would probably take years of work. Given this enormous amount of information, it is amazing that you can

Did you know?

"Wait, wait—don't tell me!" If you have experienced the tip-of-the-tongue phenomenon, research suggests that you *should* let someone tell you (or you should look it up) instead of straining to remember a word, because the longer you try, the more likely you will forget it again in the future. It is likely that you will think of many incorrect words while trying to come up with the right one, and these can become associated with, and thus clutter, your memory pathway to the word (Warriner & Humphreys, 2008).

If someone asked you to name the members of your soccer team from 10 years ago, you might not be able to remember them off the top of your head. But a photo would probably be enough of a retrieval cue to enable you to recall most of the other players' names.

recall Memory task in which specific information must be retrieved.

recognition Memory task in which individuals are presented with a stimulus and asked whether they have been exposed to it in the past or to identify it from a list of alternatives.

levels-of-processing theory The theory of memory that emphasizes the degree to which new material is mentally analyzed.

immediately recall the way your childhood home looked.

How do we sort through this vast array of material and retrieve specific information at the appropriate time? One way is through retrieval cues. A *retrieval cue* is a stimulus that allows us to recall more easily information that is in long-term memory. It may be a word, an emotion, or a sound; whatever the specific cue, a memory will suddenly come to mind when the retrieval cue is present. For example, the smell of roasting turkey may evoke memories of Thanksgiving or family gatherings.

Retrieval cues guide people through the information stored in long-term memory in much the same way that a search engine such as Google or Yahoo! guides people

through the Internet (Noice & Noice, 2002; Schneider & Logan, 2009). They are particularly important when we are making an effort to *recall* information, as opposed to being asked to *recognize* material stored in memory. In **recall**, a specific piece of information must be retrieved—such as that needed to remember what you wore to your sister's wedding or to write an essay on a test. In contrast, **recognition** occurs when people are presented with a stimulus and asked whether they have been exposed to it previously, or are asked to identify it from a list of alternatives.

As you might guess, recognition is generally a much easier task than recall. Recall is more difficult, because it consists of a series of processes: a search through memory, retrieval of potentially relevant information, and then a decision regarding whether the information you have found is accurate. If the information appears to be correct, the search is over, but if it does not, the search must continue. In contrast, recognition is simpler, because it involves fewer steps (Leigh, Zinkhan, & Swaminathan, 2006; Miserando, 1991). This is why many students think a multiple choice test is easier—they have only to recognize which choice is the correct one. In contrast, recall might be a short answer question on an exam. Which do you find easier?

LEVELS OF PROCESSING

One determinant of how well memories are recalled is the way in which material is first perceived, processed, and understood. The **levels-of-processing theory** emphasizes the degree to which new material is mentally analyzed. It suggests that the amount of information processing that occurs when material is initially encountered is central in determining how much of the information is ultimately remembered. According to this approach, the depth of information processing during exposure to material—meaning the degree to which it is analyzed and considered—is critical; the greater the intensity of its initial processing is, the more likely we are to remember it (Craik, 1990; Craik & Lockhart, 2008; Troyer, Häfliger, & Cadieux, 2006).

Because we do not pay close attention to much of the information to which we are exposed, very little mental processing typically takes place, and we forget new material almost immediately. However, information to which we pay greater attention is processed more thoroughly. Therefore, it enters memory at a deeper level—and is less apt to be forgotten than is information processed at shallower levels.

The theory goes on to suggest that there are considerable differences in the ways in which information is processed at various levels of memory. At shallow levels, information is processed merely in terms of its physical and sensory aspects. For example, we may pay attention only to the shapes that make up the letters in the word *dog*. At an intermediate level of processing, the shapes are translated into meaningful units—in this case, letters of the alphabet. Those letters are considered in the context of words, and specific phonetic sounds may be attached to the letters.

At the deepest level of processing, information is analyzed in terms of its meaning. We may see it in a wider

context and draw associations between the meaning of the information and broader networks of knowledge. For instance, we may think of dogs not merely as animals with four legs and a tail but also in terms of their relationship to cats and other mammals. We may form an image of our own dog, thereby relating the concept to our own lives. According to the levels-of-processing approach, the deeper the initial level of processing of specific information is, the longer the information will be retained.

There are considerable practical implications to the notion that recall depends on the degree to which information is initially processed. For example, the depth of information processing is critical when learning and studying course material. Rote memorization of a list of key terms for a test is unlikely to produce a lasting memory, because processing occurs at a shallow level. In contrast, thinking about the meaning of the terms and reflecting on how they relate to information that one currently knows results in far more effective long-term retention (Conway, 2002; Wenzel, Zetocha, & Ferraro, 2007).

> Rote memorization of a list of key terms for a test is unlikely to produce a lasting memory, because processing occurs at a shallow level.

Explicit memory, or conscious recall of information, benefits from frequent rehearsal.

EXPLICIT AND IMPLICIT MEMORY

If you've ever had surgery, you probably hoped that the surgeons were focused completely on the surgery and gave you their undivided attention while slicing into your body. The reality in most operating rooms is quite different, though. Surgeons may be chatting with nurses about a new restaurant or something else unrelated to your surgery.

If you are like most patients, you are left with no recollection of the conversation that occurred while you were under anesthesia. However, it is very possible that, although you had no conscious memories of the discussions on the merits of the restaurant, on some level you probably did recall at least some information. In fact, careful studies have found that people who are anesthetized during surgery sometimes demonstrate later that they have memories of snippets of conversations they heard during surgery, but they have no *conscious* recollection of when they were exposed to the information (Kihlstrom et al., 1990; Sebel, Bonke, & Winogard, 1993).

The discovery that people have memories about which they are unaware has been an important one. It has led to speculation that two forms of memory, explicit and implicit, may exist side by side. **Explicit memory** refers to intentional or conscious recollection of information. When we try to remember a name or date we have encountered or learned about previously, we are searching our explicit memory.

In contrast, **implicit memory** refers to memories of which people are not consciously aware but that can affect subsequent performance and behavior. Skills that operate automatically and without thinking, such as jumping out of the path of an automobile coming toward us as we walk down the side of a road, are stored in implicit memory. Similarly, a feeling of vague dislike for an acquaintance, without knowing why we have that feeling, may be a reflection of implicit memories. Perhaps the person reminds us of

explicit memory Intentional or conscious recollection of information.

implicit memory Memories of which people are not consciously aware but that can affect subsequent performance and behavior.

someone else in our past that we didn't like, even though we are not aware of the memory of that other individual (Coates, Butler, & Berry, 2006; Tulving, 2000; Uttl, Graf, & Consentino, 2003; Voss & Paller, 2008).

Implicit memory is closely related to the prejudice and discrimination people exhibit toward members of minority groups (Banaji & Greenwald, 1994). As we first discussed in the chapter regarding the conducting of psychological research, even though people may say and even believe they harbor no prejudice, assessment of their implicit memories may reveal that they have negative associations about members of minority groups. Such associations can influence people's behavior without their being aware of their underlying beliefs (Greenwald, Nosek, & Banaji, 2003; Greenwald, Nosek, & Sriram, 2006; Hofmann et al., 2008; Spataro, Mulligan, & Rossi-Arnaud, 2011).

One way that memory specialists study implicit memory is through experiments that use priming. **Priming** is a phenomenon in which exposure to a word or a concept (called a *prime*) later makes it easier to recall related information. Priming effects occur even when people have no conscious memory of the original word or concept (Schacter & Badgaiyan, 2001; Shacter, Dobbins, & Schnyer, 2004; Toth & Daniels, 2002).

The typical experiment designed to illustrate priming helps clarify the phenomenon. In priming experiments, participants are rapidly exposed to a stimulus such as a word, an object, or perhaps a drawing of a face. The second phase of the experiment is done after an interval ranging from several seconds to several months. At that point, participants are exposed to incomplete perceptual information that is related to the first stimulus, and they are asked whether they recognize it. For example, the new material may consist of the first letter of a word that had been presented earlier or a part of a face that had been shown earlier. If participants are able to identify the stimulus more readily than they identify stimuli that have not been presented earlier, priming has taken place (Fazio, 2003). Clearly, the earlier stimulus has been remembered—although the material resides in implicit memory, not explicit memory.

The same thing happens to us in our everyday lives. Suppose several months ago you watched a documentary on the planets, and the narrator described the moons of Mars,

focusing on its moon named Phobos. You promptly forget the name of the moon, at least consciously. Then, several months later, you're completing a crossword puzzle that you have partially filled in, and it includes the letters *obos*. As soon as you look at the set of letters, you think of Phobos and suddenly recall for the first time since your initial exposure to the information that it is one of the moons of Mars. The sudden recollection occurred because your memory was primed by the letters *obos*.

In short, when information that we are unable to consciously recall affects our behavior, implicit memory is at work. Our behavior may be influenced by experiences of which we are unaware—an example of what has been called "retention without remembering" (Horton et al., 2005).

FLASHBULB MEMORIES

Where were you on February 1, 2003? You will most likely draw a blank until this piece of information is added: February 1, 2003, was the date the Space Shuttle *Columbia* broke up in space and fell to Earth.

You probably have little trouble recalling your exact location and a variety of other trivial details that occurred when you heard about the shuttle disaster, even though the incident happened a few years ago. Your ability to remember details about this fatal event illustrates a phenomenon known as flashbulb memory. **Flashbulb memories** are memories related to a specific, important, or surprising event that are so vivid they represent a sort of snapshot of the event.

Several events that can lead to flashbulb memories are common among college students. For example, involvement in a car accident, meeting one's roommate for the first time, and the night of high school graduation are all typical flashbulb memories (Bohn & Berntsen, 2007; Romeu, 2006; Talarico, 2009).

Of course, flashbulb memories do not contain every detail of an original scene. For example, people over the age of 55 may remember exactly where they were when they heard that President John F. Kennedy had been shot.

priming A phenomenon in which exposure to a word or concept (called a *prime*) later makes it easier to recall related information, even when there is no conscious memory of the word or concept.

flashbulb memories Memories centered on a specific, important, or surprising event that are so vivid it is as if they represented a snapshot of the event.

get **involved!**

Nosek, Banaji, and Greenwald of Harvard University have created Project Implicit, an online research project that will teach you about your own implicit memory while incorporating your responses into their research. There are over 90 different Implicit Associations Tests that you can choose to answer. Be ready to be surprised at your results! Try it at https://implicit.harvard.edu/implicit/.

Where were you the night that Barack Obama was elected president of the United States? Do you have a flashbulb memory for this event?

the World Trade Center in New York was attacked by suicidal terrorists? Do you remember watching television that morning and seeing images of the first plane, and then the second plane, striking the towers?

If you do, you are among the 73% of Americans who recall viewing the initial television images of both planes on September 11. However, that recollection is wrong: In fact, television broadcasts showed images only of the second plane on September 11. No video of the first plane was available until early the following morning, September 12, when it was shown on television (Begley, 2002).

Flashbulb memories illustrate a more general phenomenon about memory: Memories that are exceptional are more easily retrieved (although not necessarily accurately) than are those relating to events that are commonplace. The more distinctive a stimulus is, and the more personal relevance the event has, the more likely we are to recall it later (Berntsen & Thomsen, 2005; Shapiro, 2006; Talarico & Rubin, 2007).

Even with a distinctive stimulus, however, we may not remember where the information came from. *Source amnesia* occurs when we have a memory for some material but cannot recall where we encountered it before. For example, source amnesia can explain situations in which we meet someone we know but can't remember where we met them initially.

But it is unlikely that they recall what their friends were wearing or what was served for lunch that day.

Furthermore, the details recalled in flashbulb memories are often inaccurate. For example, do you remember when

College Students' Most Common Flashbulb Memories

From David C. Rubin, "The Subtle Deceiver: Recalling Our Past," *Psychology Today*, September 1985, pp. 39–46. Reprinted with permission from *Psychology Today* magazine, (Copyright © 1985 Sussex Publishers, LLC.).

Being in or witnessing a car accident

Met a roommate for the first time

Night of high school graduation

Night of your senior prom

An early romantic experience

Public speaking

Receipt of college admissions letter

First date–when you met him or her

First airplane flight

Moment you opened your SAT scores

0   10   20   30   40   50   60   70   80   90

Percentage of sample reporting that event resulted in "flashbulb memories"

> The more distinctive a stimulus is, and the more personal relevance the event has, the more likely we are to recall it later.

CONSTRUCTIVE PROCESSES IN MEMORY

As we have seen, although it is clear that we can have detailed recollections of significant and distinctive events, it is difficult to gauge the accuracy of such memories. In fact, it is apparent that our memories reflect, at least in part, **constructive processes**, processes in which memories are influenced by the meaning we give to events. When we retrieve information, then, the memory that is produced is affected not just by the direct prior experience we have had with the stimulus but also by our guesses and inferences about its meaning.

constructive processes
Processes in which memories are influenced by the meaning we give to events.

The notion that memory is based on constructive processes was first put forward by Frederic Bartlett, a British psychologist. He

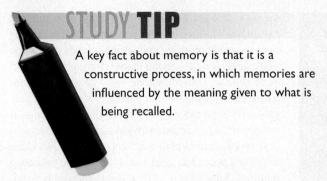

STUDY **TIP**

A key fact about memory is that it is a constructive process, in which memories are influenced by the meaning given to what is being recalled.

suggested that people tend to remember information in terms of **schemas**, organized bodies of information stored in memory that bias the way new information is interpreted,

schemas Organized bodies of information stored in memory that bias the way new information is interpreted, stored, and recalled.

stored, and recalled (Bartlett, 1932). For example, you probably have a schema for what to do and what to expect when you eat at a restaurant. Suppose your schema includes a host and a server, and suppose that you go out to a new restaurant that has only servers who also seat customers. Later, if someone asks, you may construct your memory using your schema and incorrectly "remember" seeing both a host and a server. Our reliance on schemas means that memories often consist of a general reconstruction of previous experience.

Bartlett argued that schemas are based not only on the specific material to which people are exposed but also on their understanding of the situation, their expectations about the situation, and their awareness of the motivations underlying the behavior of others.

One of the earliest demonstrations of schemas came from a classic study that involved a procedure similar to a common children's game in the United States, "telephone," in which information from memory is passed sequentially from one person to another. In the study, a participant viewed a drawing in which there were a variety of people of differing racial and ethnic backgrounds on a subway car, one of whom—a white person—was shown with a razor in his hand (Allport & Postman, 1958). The first participant was asked to describe the drawing to someone else without looking back at it. Then that person was asked to describe it to another person (without looking at the drawing), and then the process was repeated with still one more participant.

The report of the last person differed in significant, yet systematic, ways from the initial drawing. Specifically, many people described the drawing as depicting an African American with a knife—an incorrect recollection, given that the drawing showed a razor in the hand of a Caucasian person. The transformation of the Caucasian's razor into an African American's knife clearly indicates that the participants held a schema that included the unwarranted prejudice that African Americans are more violent than Caucasians and thus more apt to be holding a knife. In short, our expectations and knowledge—and prejudices—

affect the reliability of our memories (McDonald & Hirt, 1997; Newby-Clark & Ross, 2003).

Memory in the Courtroom For Calvin Willis, the inadequate memories of two people cost him more than two decades of his life. Willis was the victim of mistaken identity when a young rape victim picked out his photo as the perpetrator of the rape. On that basis, he was tried, convicted, and sentenced to life in prison. Twenty-one years later, DNA testing showed that Willis was innocent, and the victim's identification wrong (Corsello, 2005).

Unfortunately, Willis is not the only victim to whom apologies have had to be made; many cases of mistaken identity have led to unjustified legal actions. Research on eyewitness identification of suspects, as well as on memory for other details of crimes, has shown that eyewitnesses are apt to make important errors when they try to recall details of criminal activity—even if they are highly confident about their recollections (Thompson, 2000; Wells, Olson, & Charman, 2002; Zaragoza, Belli, & Payment, 2007).

One reason is the effect of the weapons used in crimes. When a criminal perpetrator displays a gun or a knife, it acts as a perceptual magnet, attracting the eyes of the witnesses. As a consequence, witnesses pay less attention to other details of the crime and are less able to recall what actually occurred (Brewer & Wells, 2011; Martire & Kemp, 2011; Pickel, 2009; Steblay et al., 2003; Zaitsu, 2007).

One reason eyewitnesses are prone to memory-related errors is that the specific wording of questions posed to them by police officers or attorneys can affect the way they recall information, as a number of experiments illustrate. For example, in one experiment the participants were shown a film of two cars crashing into each other.

PSYCH think

connect™
WWW.MCGRAWHILLCONNECT.COM/PSYCHOLOGY
Eyewitness Fallibility

> > > An eyewitness's memory for details of crimes can contain important errors. How could a lawyer use this information when evaluating an eyewitness's testimony? Should eyewitness accounts be permissible in a court of law?

Take the PsychSmart challenge! How good are your eyewitness memory skills? This activity will test your ability to notice details. From chapter 6 in your ebook, select the *Exercises* tab. Then select "Eyewitness Fallibility." Review by answering Pop Quiz question 9 on p. 160.

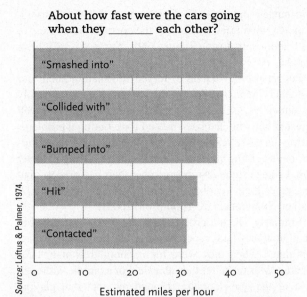

About how fast were the cars going when they _____ each other?

"Smashed into"

"Collided with"

"Bumped into"

"Hit"

"Contacted"

Source: Loftus & Palmer, 1974.

Estimated miles per hour

Accuracy of Eyewitness Testimony Affected by Interviewer's Word Choice

Some were then asked the question, "About how fast were the cars going when they *smashed* into each other?" On average, they estimated the speed to be 40.8 miles per hour. In contrast, when another group of participants was asked, "About how fast were the cars going when they *contacted* each other?" the average estimated speed was only 31.8 miles per hour (Loftus & Palmer, 1974).

The problem of memory reliability becomes even more acute when children are witnesses, because increasing evidence suggests that children's memories are highly vulnerable to the influence of others (Douglas, Goldstein, & Bjorklund, 2000; Loftus, 1993; Loftus & Cahill, 2007). For instance, in one experiment, 5- to 7-year-old girls who had just had a routine physical examination were shown

Did you know?

One eyewitness might be wrong, as was the case for Calvin Willis, but what about two? If two women accused Joseph Abbitt of rape, could they both be mistaken? After spending 14 years in prison for two rapes, the DNA evidence proved conclusively that Abbitt was innocent.

an anatomically explicit doll. The girls were shown the doll's genital area and asked, "Did the doctor touch you here?" Three of the girls who did not have a vaginal or anal exam said that the doctor had in fact touched them in the genital area, and one of those three made up the detail "The doctor did it with a stick" (Saywitz & Goodman, 1990).

Children's memories are especially susceptible to influence when the situation is highly emotional or stressful. For example, in trials in which there is significant pretrial publicity or in which alleged victims are questioned repeatedly, often by untrained interviewers, the memories of the alleged victims may be influenced by the types of questions they are asked (Goodman & Quas, 2008; Lamb & Garretson, 2003; Quas, Malloy, & Melinder, 2007; Scullin, Kanaya, & Ceci, 2002).

Repressed memories are recollections of events that are initially so shocking that the mind responds by pushing them into the unconscious. Supporters of the notion of repressed memory suggest that some repressed memories may remain hidden, possibly throughout a person's lifetime, unless they are triggered by some current circumstance, such as the probing that occurs during psychological therapy (Sabbagh, 2009).

However, memory researcher Elizabeth Loftus maintains that some repressed memories may well be inaccurate or even wholly false—representing *false memory*. For example, false memories develop when people are unable

From the perspective of ...

A JUROR Knowing what you now know about the fallibility of people's memories even when they are trying to be honest, how would you determine the innocence or guilt of a defendant?

to recall the source of a memory of a particular event about which they have only vague recollections. When the source of the memory becomes unclear or ambiguous, people may become confused about whether they actually experienced the event or whether it was imagined (Bernstein & Loftus, 2009a; Loftus, 2004; Wade, Sharman, & Garry, 2007).

There is great controversy regarding the legitimacy of repressed memories (Geraerts et al., 2007; Ost, 2006; Sabbagh, 2009). Many therapists give great weight to the authenticity of repressed memories, and their views are supported by research showing that specific regions of the brain help keep unwanted memories out of awareness, as well as research showing that at least some repressed memories are accurate. On the other side of the issue are researchers who maintain that there is insufficient scientific support for the existence of such memories. There is also a middle ground: memory researchers who suggest that false memories are a result of normal information processing. The challenge for those on all sides of the issue is to distinguish truth from fiction (Anderson et al., 2004; Bernstein & Loftus, 2009b; Brown & Pope, 1996; Strange, Clifasefi, & Garry, 2007).

Autobiographical Memory Your memory of experiences in your own past is likely to be partly truth and partly fiction. The same constructive processes that make us inaccurately recall the behavior of others also interfere with the accuracy of autobiographical memories. **Autobiographical memories** are our recollections of cir-

autobiographical memories Our recollections of circumstances and episodes from our own lives.

Autobiographical Memories of Grades Recalled by College Students

Percentage of grades recalled accurately

Source: Bahrick et al., 1996.

Original grade assigned

cumstances and episodes from our own lives. Autobiographical memories encompass the episodic memories we hold about ourselves (Rubin, 1999; Sumner, Griffith, & Mineka, 2011; Sutin & Robins, 2007).

For example, we tend to forget information about our past that is incompatible with the way in which we currently see ourselves. One study found that adults who were well adjusted but who had been treated for emotional problems during the early years of their lives tended to forget important but troubling childhood events, such as being in foster care. College students misremember their bad grades—but remember their good ones (Kemps & Tiggemann, 2007; Walker, Skowronski, & Thompson, 2003).

Similarly, when a group of 48-year-olds were asked to recall how they had responded on a questionnaire they had completed when they were high school freshman, their accuracy was no better than chance. For example, although 61% of the questionnaire respondents said that playing sports and other physical activities was their favorite pastime, only 23% of the adults recalled it accurately (Offer et al., 2000).

It is not just certain kinds of events that are distorted; particular periods of life are remembered more easily than others are. For example, when people reach late adulthood, they remember periods of life in which they experienced major transitions, such as attending college and working at their first job, better than they remember their middle-age years (Cordnoldi, De Beni, & Helstrup, 2007).

Cultural Influences on Memory Travelers who have visited areas of the world in which there is no written language often return with tales of people with phenomenal memories. For instance, storytellers in some preliterate cultures can recount long chronicles that recall the names and activities of people over many generations. Those feats led experts to argue initially that people in preliterate societies develop a different, and perhaps better, type of memory than do those in cultures that employ a written language. They suggested that in a society that lacks writing, people are motivated to recall information with accuracy, especially information relating to tribal histories and traditions that would be lost if they were not passed down orally from one generation to another (Berntsen & Rubin, 2004; Daftary & Meri, 2002).

Today, memory researchers dismiss that view. For one thing, preliterate peoples don't have an exclusive claim to amazing memory feats. Some Hebrew scholars memorize thousands of pages of text and can recall the locations of particular words on the page. Similarly, poetry singers in the Balkans can recall thousands of lines of poetry. Even in cultures in which written language exists, then, astounding feats of memory are possible (Rubin et al., 2007; Strathern & Stewart, 2003).

Memory researchers now suggest that there are both similarities and differences in memory across cultures. One current theory says that basic memory processes such as short-term memory capacity and the structure of long-term memory—the "hardware" of memory—are universal

What's Your Memory Style?

What's your dominant memory style? Do you most easily remember sounds, sights, or the way things feel? Or perhaps you easily remember all of these? Read the statements below and circle the response choice that most closely describes your habits.

To help recall lectures, I …

V. Read the notes I took during class.

A. Close my eyes and try to hear what the instructor said.

K. Try to place myself back in the lecture room and feel what was going on at the time.

To remember a complex procedure, I …

V. Write down the steps I have to follow.

A. Listen carefully and repeatedly to the instructions.

K. Do it over and over again.

To learn sentences in a foreign language, I do best if I …

V. Read them on paper to see how they're written.

A. Hear them in my head until I can say them aloud.

K. See someone speaking them and then practice moving my mouth and hands the way the speaker did.

If I have to learn a dance move, I like …

V. To see a diagram of the steps before trying it.

A. Someone to coach me through it while I try it.

K. To watch it once and then give it a try.

When I recall a very happy moment, I tend to …

V. Visualize it in my head.

A. Hear the sounds that I heard when experiencing it.

K. Feel with my hands and rest of my body what I felt at the time.

When I have to remember driving directions, I usually …

V. See a map of the route in my mind.

A. Repeat the directions aloud to myself.

K. Feel my hands steering and the car driving along the correct route.

Answer Key: If you chose mostly Vs, your main memory style is visual; your preference is to remember things in terms of the way they appear.

If you chose mostly As, your main memory style is auditory; your preference is to recall material in terms of sound.

If you chose mostly Ks, your main memory style is kinesthetic; your preference is to remember using your sense of touch.

Keep in mind that this questionnaire gives only a rough idea of how we usually use our memories. Remember: All of us use all of the memory styles during the course of each day.

Storytellers in many cultures can recount hundreds of years of history in vivid detail. This amazing ability is due less to basic memory processes than to the ways in which storytellers acquire and retain information.

and operate similarly in people in all cultures. In contrast, cultural differences can be seen in the way information is acquired and rehearsed—the "software" of memory. Culture determines how people frame information initially, how much they practice learning and recalling it, and the strategies they use to try to recall it (Mack, 2003; Rubin et al., 2007; Wang & Conway, 2006).

>> Forgetting: When Memory Fails

All of us who have experienced even routine instances of forgetting—such as not remembering where you first met someone or that you were supposed to pick up your brother at 5 p.m.—understand the very real consequences of memory failure. At such times, we may wish fervently that we had Jill Price's incredible memory. We would never have to be embarrassed because we had forgotten someone's name or an important appointment. We would never have to miss another question on an exam. The irony is that memory failure is essential to remembering important information.

The ability to forget inconsequential details about experiences, people, and objects helps us avoid being burdened and distracted by trivial stores of meaningless data. Forgetting permits us to form general impressions and recollections. For example, the reason our friends consistently look familiar to us is because we're able to forget their clothing, facial blemishes, and other transient features that change from one occasion to the next. Instead, our memories are based on a summary of various critical features—a far more economical use of our memory capabilities.

In the late 19th century, German psychologist Hermann Ebbinghaus (1885, 1913) conducted research on forgetting that laid the foundation for future studies. Using himself as the only participant in his study, Ebbinghaus memorized lists of three-letter nonsense syllables—meaningless sets of two consonants with a vowel

decay The loss of information in memory through its nonuse.

"He must have forgotten something."
© Frank Cotham/The New Yorker Collection/www.cartoonbank.com.

in between, such as FIW and BOZ. By measuring how easy it was to relearn a given list of the nonsense syllables after varying periods of time had passed since the initial learning, he found that forgetting occurs systematically. The most rapid forgetting occurs in the first nine hours, particularly in the first hour. After nine hours, the rate of forgetting slows and declines little, even after the passage of many days.

Despite his primitive methods, Ebbinghaus's basic conclusions have been upheld. There is almost always a strong initial decline in memory, followed by a more gradual drop over time. Furthermore, relearning of previously mastered material is almost always faster than starting from scratch, whether the material is academic information or a motor skill such as serving a tennis ball (Wixted & Carpenter, 2007).

WHY WE FORGET

Why do we forget? One reason is that we may not have paid attention to the material in the first place—a failure of *encoding*. For example, if you grew up in the United States, you probably have been exposed to thousands of pennies during your life. Despite this experience, you may not have a clear sense of the details of the coin. Consequently, the reason for your memory failure is that

> Memory failure is essential to remembering important information.

you probably never encoded the information into long-term memory initially. Obviously, if information was not placed in memory to start with, there is no way the information can be recalled (Nickerson & Adams, 1979).

But what about material that has been encoded into memory and yet can't be remembered later? Several processes account for memory failures, including decay, interference, and cue-dependent forgetting.

Decay is the loss of information through nonuse. This explanation for forgetting assumes that *memory traces*, the physical changes that take place in the brain when new material is learned, simply fade away over time (Grann, 2007).

Although there is evidence that decay does occur, it doesn't completely explain forgetting. Often there is no relationship between how long ago a person was exposed to information and how well that information is recalled. If decay was responsible for all

Ebbinghaus's Forgetting Curve

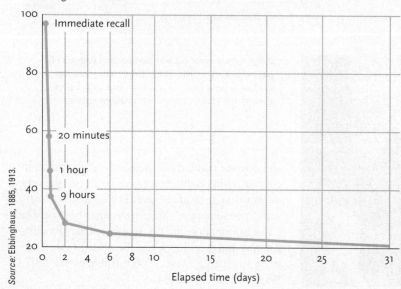

Percentage of retention

Source: Ebbinghaus, 1885, 1913.

- 100 — Immediate recall
- 80
- 60 — 20 minutes
- 40 — 1 hour / 9 hours
- 20

Elapsed time (days): 2 4 6 8 10 15 20 25 31

(a)   (b)   (c)   (d)

(e)   (f)   (g)

One of these pennies is the real thing. Can you find it? Why is this task harder than it seems at first? Source: Nickerson & Adams, 1979

If you don't have a penny handy, the correct answer is "A."

forgetting, we would expect that the more time that has elapsed between the initial learning of information and our attempt to recall it, the harder it would be to remember it, because there would be more time for the memory trace to decay. Yet people who take several consecutive tests on the same material often recall more of the initial information when taking later tests than they did on earlier tests. If decay were operating, we would expect the opposite to occur (Payne, 1986).

Because decay does not fully account for forgetting, memory specialists have proposed an additional mechanism: **interference**. In interference, information in memory disrupts the recall of other information (Naveh-Benjamin, Guez, & Sorek, 2007; Pilotti, Chodorow, & Shono, 2009).

Finally, forgetting may occur because of **cue-dependent forgetting**, forgetting that occurs when there are insufficient retrieval cues to rekindle information that is in memory (Tulving & Thompson, 1983). For example, you may not be able to remember where you lost a set of keys until you mentally walk through your day, thinking of each place you visited. When you think of the place where you lost the keys—say, the library—the retrieval cue of the library may be sufficient to help you recall that you left them on the desk in the library. Without that retrieval cue, you might be unable to recall the location of the keys.

Some retrieval cues are tied to the physical or emotional context in which the memory was made. In one study, for example, divers were taught something while on land or

SHOPPING

underwater. Later, they were tested either on land or underwater. Their scores were highest when they were tested in the same context in which they learned the material (Baddeley, Eysenck, & Anderson, 2009; Godden & Baddeley, 1975).

Most research suggests that interference and cue-dependent forgetting are key processes in forgetting (Bower, Thompson, & Tulving, 1994; Mel'nikov, 1993). We forget things mainly because new memories interfere with the retrieval of old ones or because appropriate retrieval cues are unavailable, not because the memory trace has decayed.

PROACTIVE AND RETROACTIVE INTERFERENCE

There are actually two sorts of interference that influence forgetting: proactive and retroactive. In **proactive interference**, information learned earlier disrupts the recall of newer material. Suppose, as a student of foreign languages, you first learned French in the tenth grade, and then in the eleventh grade you took Spanish. When in the twelfth grade you take a college achievement test in Spanish, you may find you have difficulty recalling the Spanish translation of a word because all you can think of is its French equivalent (Bunting, 2006).

In contrast, **retroactive interference** refers to difficulty in the recall of information because of later exposure to different material. If, for example, you have difficulty on a French achievement test because of your more recent exposure to Spanish, retroactive interference is to blame. One way to remember the

interference The phenomenon by which information in memory disrupts the recall of other information.

cue-dependent forgetting Forgetting that occurs when there are insufficient retrieval cues to rekindle information that is in memory.

proactive interference Interference in which information learned earlier disrupts the recall of newer material.

retroactive interference Interference in which there is difficulty in the recall of information learned earlier because of later exposure to different material.

STUDY **TIP**

Memory loss through decay comes from nonuse of the memory; memory loss through interference is due to the presence of other information in memory.

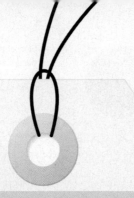

BUY IT? > > >

Improving Your Memory

Have you ever heard of ginkgo biloba? Supplements containing gingko biloba, a substance derived from the leaves of the gingko biloba tree, are marketed as nonprescription memory enhancers. Do they work? Research evidence from controlled studies does not support the claims that ginkgo biloba increases the ability to remember or focus attention (Solomon et al., 2002).

There are, however, some effective strategies for studying and remembering course material that do not involve drugs or other supplements.

- *Rely on organizational cues.* To help recall material you read in textbooks, try organizing the material in memory the first time you read it. Organize your reading on the basis of any advance information you have about the content and about its arrangement. You will then be able to make connections and see relationships among the various facts and process the material at a deeper level, which in turn will later aid recall.
- *Use the keyword technique.* If you are studying a foreign language, try the *keyword technique* of pairing a foreign word with a common English word that has a similar sound. This English word is known as the *keyword.* For example, to learn the Spanish word for duck (*pato,* pronounced *pot-o*), you might choose the keyword *pot;* for the Spanish word for horse (*caballo,* pronounced *cob-eye-yo*), the keyword might be *eye.* Once you have

continued

thought of a keyword, imagine the Spanish word "interacting" with the English keyword. You might envision a duck taking a bath in a pot to remember the word *pato,* or a horse with a large, bulging eye in the center of its head to recall *caballo* (Carney & Levin, 1998; Wyra, Lawson, M. J., & Hungi, 2007).

- *Use elaborative rehearsal.* Although practice does not necessarily make perfect, it helps. Making meaningful connections provides a framework for remembering. By studying and rehearsing material after mastering it—a process called *overlearning*—people show better long-term recall than they show if they stop practicing after their initial learning of the material.
- *Take effective notes.* "Less is more" is perhaps the best advice for taking lecture notes that facilitate recall. Rather than trying to jot down every detail of a lecture, it is better to listen and think about the material, and take down the main points. In effective note taking, thinking about the material when you first hear it is more important than writing it down. This is one reason why borrowing someone else's notes is a bad idea; you will have no framework in memory that you can use to understand them (Feldman, R. S., 2010).

Remember, there may not be shortcuts to a better memory, but careful encoding and rehearsal are proven techniques for improving memory.

difference between proactive and retroactive interference is to keep in mind that *pro*active interference progresses in time—the past interferes with the present—whereas *retro*active interference retrogresses in time, working backward as the present interferes with the past (Jacoby et al., 2007).

Although the concepts of proactive and retroactive interference illustrate how material may be forgotten, they

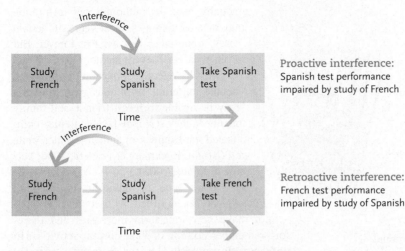

Proactive interference: Spanish test performance impaired by study of French

Retroactive interference: French test performance impaired by study of Spanish

Proactive and Retroactive Interference

Alzheimer's is the fourth leading cause of death among adults in the United States.

PSYCH think

> > > What are the implications of proactive and retroactive interference for learning multiple foreign languages? Would earlier language training in a different language help or hinder learning a new language?

do not explain whether forgetting is caused by the actual loss or modification of information or by problems in the retrieval of information. Most research suggests that material that has apparently been lost because of interference can eventually be recalled if appropriate stimuli are presented (Anderson, 1981; Tulving & Psotka, 1971; Wixted, 2005), but the question has not been fully answered.

MEMORY DYSFUNCTIONS

First you notice that you're always misplacing things, or that common nouns are evading you as stubbornly as the names of new acquaintances. Pretty soon you're forgetting appointments and getting flustered when you drive in traffic. On bad days you find you can't hold numbers in your mind long enough to dial the phone. You try valiantly to conceal your lapses, but they become ever more glaring. You crash your car. You spend whole mornings struggling to dress yourself properly. And even as you lose the ability to read or play the piano, you're painfully aware of what's happening to you (Cowley, 2000, p. 46).

These memory problems are symptomatic of **Alzheimer's disease**, an illness characterized in part by severe memory problems. Alzheimer's is the fourth leading cause of death among adults in the United States, affecting an estimated 5 million people. In the beginning, Alzheimer's symptoms appear as simple forgetfulness of things such as appointments and birthdays. As the disease progresses, memory loss becomes more profound, and even the simplest tasks—such as using a telephone—are forgotten. Ultimately, victims may lose their ability to speak or comprehend language, and physical deterioration sets in, leading to death.

> **Alzheimer's disease** An illness characterized in part by severe memory problems.
>
> **amnesia** Memory loss that occurs without other mental difficulties.

The causes of Alzheimer's disease are not fully understood. Increasing evidence suggests that Alzheimer's results from an inherited susceptibility to a defect in the production of the protein beta amyloid, which is necessary for normal nerve cell function. When the synthesis of beta amyloid goes awry, large clumps of cells form, triggering inflammation and the deterioration of neurons in the brain (Detoledo-Morrell, Stoub, & Wang, 2007; Horínek, Varjassyová, & Hort, 2007; Selkoe, 2008; Wilson et al., 2011).

Alzheimer's disease is one of a number of memory dysfunctions. Another is **amnesia**, memory loss that

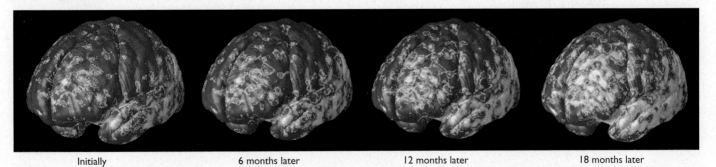

Initially   6 months later   12 months later   18 months later

This series of brain images clearly shows the changes caused by Alzheimer's disease over 18 months, with the normal tissue (in purple) retreating during that time.

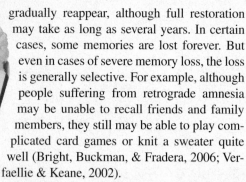

Psych at the Movies

The Curious Case of Benjamin Button (2008)
The main character in this romantic drama has a life so different from everyone else's that he can't rely on normal experiences to help him make sense of his life and his memories.

The Bourne Identity (2002)
A CIA assassin suffers from a form of amnesia in which he has lost all memory of self-identifying information, but he retains procedural memory for such things as hand-to-hand combat skills.

The Notebook (2004)
A man regularly visits his wife, who is institutionalized with Alzheimer's disease. He spends hours reading the story of their young romance to her, during the rare moments when she thinks coherently and recognizes him.

Eternal Sunshine of the Spotless Mind (2004)
Are we better off with or without our more difficult memories? Would you erase memories if you could? The main characters in this movie are faced with this decision.

Hunting Down Memory (2009)
A real-life case of retrograde amnesia is the subject of this intriguing documentary about a Norwegian man who has lost all memory of his life from birth to age 27.

gradually reappear, although full restoration may take as long as several years. In certain cases, some memories are lost forever. But even in cases of severe memory loss, the loss is generally selective. For example, although people suffering from retrograde amnesia may be unable to recall friends and family members, they still may be able to play complicated card games or knit a sweater quite well (Bright, Buckman, & Fradera, 2006; Verfaellie & Keane, 2002).

A second type of amnesia—*anterograde amnesia*—is exemplified by people who cannot make new long-term memories and therefore remember nothing of their current activities. In **anterograde amnesia**, loss of memory occurs for events that follow an injury. Information cannot be transferred from short-term to long-term memory, resulting in the ability to remember only short-term memories in the present for about 20 seconds. People with this condition usually remember long-term memories that were stored before the injury (Gilboa, Winocur, & Rosenbaum, 2006).

From the perspective of . . .

A SPOUSE What strategies would you use to insure the safety of a spouse with Alzheimer's? How could you maximize their quality of life?

retrograde amnesia Amnesia in which memory is lost for occurrences prior to a certain event.

anterograde amnesia Amnesia in which memory is lost for events that follow an injury.

occurs without other mental difficulties. The type of amnesia immortalized in countless Hollywood films involves a victim who receives a blow to the head and is unable to remember anything from his or her past. In reality, amnesia of this type, known as retrograde amnesia, is quite rare. In **retrograde amnesia**, memory is lost for occurrences prior to a certain event. Usually, lost memories

Did you know?

Patients with anorexia nervosa tend to focus on negative memories, but they don't appear to use effective coping strategies to handle these memories. Instead, they cope by forgetting the specific details of painful autobiographical events (Kovács, Szabó, & Pászthy, 2011).

For REVIEW >>

- **What is memory?**

Memory is the process by which we encode, store, and retrieve information. Memory can be thought of as a three-stage process. Sensory memories are very brief, but they are precise, storing a nearly exact replica of a stimulus. Roughly seven (plus or minus two) chunks of information can be transferred and held in short-term memory for up to 25 seconds; if they are not transferred to long-term memory, they are then lost. Memories are transferred into long-term storage by encoding the information for meaning and other strategies, such as elaborative rehearsal. Long-term memory includes declarative memory and procedural memory. Declarative memory is divided into episodic memory and semantic memory. (pp. 138–145)

- **Why do we recall some memories better than others?**

Retrieval cues, such as emotions, sights, and sounds, are a major strategy for recalling information successfully. The levels-of-processing approach to memory suggests that the way in which information is initially perceived and analyzed determines the success with which it is recalled; the deeper the initial processing, the greater the recall. Flashbulb memories are memories centered on a specific, important event. The more distinctive a memory is, the more easily it can be retrieved. Memory is a constructive process, such that our memories are influenced by the meaning we give to events. Eyewitnesses are apt to make substantial errors when they try to recall the details of crimes. The problem of memory reliability becomes even more acute when the witnesses are children. (pp. 145–153)

- **Why do we forget information?**

Several processes account for memory failure, including decay, interference (both proactive and retroactive), and cue-dependent forgetting, as well as Alzheimer's disease and amnesia.

Alzheimer's disease is an illness characterized in part by a progressive loss of memory. Amnesia, another type of memory loss that occurs without other mental difficulties, can take two forms: retrograde amnesia and anterograde amnesia. (pp. 154–158)

Pop Quiz

1. Match the type of memory with its definition:

   a. long-term memory

   b. short-term memory

   c. sensory memory

   _____ 1. holds information up to 25 seconds.

   _____ 2. stores information on a relatively permanent basis.

   _____ 3. direct representation of a stimulus.

2. There appear to be two types of declarative memory: _____ memory, for knowledge and facts, and _____ memory, for personal experiences.

3. Some memory researchers believe that long-term memory is stored as associations between pieces of information in _____ networks.

4. While with a group of friends at a dance, Eva bumps into a man she dated last month, but when she tries to introduce him to her friends, she cannot remember his name. What is the term for this occurrence?

5. _____ is the process of retrieving a specific item from memory.

6. A friend of your mother's tells you, "I know exactly where I was and what I was doing when I heard that John Lennon was killed." What is this type of memory phenomenon called?

7. _____ __ _____ theory states that the more a person analyzes a statement, the more likely he or she is to remember it later.

 8. An important conclusion to be drawn from the levels of processing activity is that

   a. focusing on visual and auditory information is much more effective for remembering than is encoding for meaning.

   b. visual imagery is very effective for building memory capacity.

   c. I will probably remember things better if I think about what they mean.

   d. I should practice the first five levels of processing every night, but the next five need to be practiced only once a week.

9. The eyewitness fallibilty exercise provided a review of

   a. the three-stage theory of memory.

   b. the theory of working memory, including the central executive.

   c. the differences between procedural and declarative memory.

   d. episodic memory.

10. If, after learning the history of the Middle East for a class two years ago, you now find yourself unable to recall what you learned, you are experiencing memory _____, caused by nonuse.

11. Difficulty in accessing a memory because of the presence of other information is known as _____.

12. _____ interference occurs when material is difficult to retrieve because of subsequent exposure to other material; _____ interference refers to difficulty in retrieving material as a result of the interference of previously learned material.

7

THINKING,

Eureka!

Clifford Matson's "Eureka!" moment arrived the day the silverfish invaded his bathroom.

Dr. Matson, tall, white-haired, and retired after 50 years of practicing dentistry in his hometown of Junction City, Oregon, was fretting about the insects skittering around the bathroom. Then, several seemingly unrelated thoughts collided in his mind.

One was about the pesky silverfish. One concerned a book he was reading about neem trees, tropical trees grown in India and Burma that have seeds with their own natural pesticides. The third thought arrived when Dr. Matson noticed the small cork squares separating the double-pane windows in the bathroom.

A couple of drops of neem oil on one of those little cork squares ought to be just the ticket to get rid of silverfish, Dr. Matson thought. He tried it, and the silverfish died. Then he tried the neem oil–soaked cork squares on cockroaches, and they bit the dust as well.

Two years ago, the U.S. Patent and Trademark Office granted Dr. Matson Patent No. 6,093,413 for Cork-EZ, an adhesive-backed piece of cork the size of a Scrabble square that delivers a natural pesticide derived from cedar bark.[vii]

Clifford Matson has big plans for his invention. But whether or not Cork-EZ revolutionizes the extermination field, it is clear that Matson has that elusive quality that marks successful inventors: creativity.

Where does Matson's creativity come from? More generally, how do people use information to devise innovative solutions to problems? And how do people think about, understand, and through language describe the world?

Answers to these questions come from **cognitive psychology**, the broad area of psychology that focuses on the study of higher mental processes, including thinking, language, problem solving, knowing, reasoning, judging, and decision making. We cover these topics in this chapter, along with intelligence, intelligence testing, and factors associated with creativity. Memory, the subject of chapter 6, is another process of interest to cognitive psychologists.

LANGUAGE, AND INTELLIGENCE

- What is thinking?
- How do people approach and solve problems?
- How does language develop?
- How is intelligence defined and conceptualized?
- What are the major approaches to measuring intelligence in the West, and what do intelligence tests measure?

>> Thinking and Reasoning

What are you thinking about at this moment?

The mere ability to pose such a question underscores the distinctive nature of the human capacity for thinking. No other species contemplates, analyzes, recollects, or plans the way humans do. Psychologists define **thinking** as the manipulation of mental representations of information. A representation may take the form of a word, a concept, a visual image, a sound, or any other type of sensory data stored in memory. Thinking transforms a specific representation of information into new and different forms, allowing us to answer questions, solve problems, and reach goals.

Although a clear sense of what exactly occurs when we think remains elusive, an understanding of the nature of the fundamental elements involved in thinking is growing. We begin by considering our use of mental images and concepts, the building blocks of thought.

cognitive psychology The branch of psychology that focuses on the study of higher mental processes, including thinking, language, memory, problem solving, knowing, reasoning, judging, and decision making.

thinking The manipulation of mental representations of information.

mental images Representations in the mind that resemble the object or event being represented.

MENTAL IMAGES

Think of your best friend.

Chances are that some kind of visual image comes to mind when you are asked to think of her or him, or any other person or object, for that matter. To some cognitive psychologists, such mental images constitute a major part of thinking.

Mental images are representations in the mind of an object or an event. They are not just visual representations; our ability to "hear" a tune in our heads is also considered a mental image. In fact, every sensory modality may produce a corresponding mental image (De Beni, Pazzaglia, & Gardini, 2007; Gardini et al., 2009; Kosslyn, 2005).

Research has found that our mental images have some of the properties of the actual stimuli they represent. For example, it takes the mind longer to scan mental images of large objects than of small ones, just as the eye takes longer to scan an actual large object than an actual small one. Similarly, we are able to manipulate and rotate mental images of objects, just as we are able to manipulate and rotate them in the real world (Iachini & Giusberti, 2004; Mast & Kosslyn, 2002; Zacks, 2008).

Some experts see the production of mental images as a way to improve various skills. For instance, many athletes use mental imagery in their training. Basketball players may try to produce vivid and detailed images of the court, the basket, the ball, and the noisy crowd. They may visualize themselves taking a foul shot, watching the ball, and hearing the swish as it goes through the net. And it works: The use of mental imagery can lead to improved performance in sports (Mamassis & Doganis, 2004; Thompson, Hsiao, & Kosslyn, 2011).

CONCEPTS

If someone asks you what is in your kitchen cabinet, you might answer with a detailed list of items ("a jar of peanut butter, three boxes of macaroni and cheese, six unmatched dinner plates," and so forth). More likely, though, you would respond by naming some broader categories, such as "food" and "dishes."

Using such categories reflects the operation of concepts. **Concepts** are mental groupings of similar objects, events, or people. Concepts enable us to organize complex phenomena into simpler, and therefore more easily usable, cognitive categories (Connolly, 2007; Goldstone & Kersten, 2003; Murphy, 2005).

Concepts help us classify newly encountered objects on the basis of our past experience. For example, when we see someone tapping a small, handheld screen, we recognize that it's most likely a smart phone, even if we've never seen that model before. Ultimately, concepts influence behavior; we would assume, for instance, that it might be appropriate to pet an animal after determining that it is a dog, whereas we would behave differently after classifying the animal as a wolf.

When cognitive psychologists first studied concepts, they focused on those that were clearly defined by a unique set of properties or features. For example, an equilateral triangle is a closed shape that has three sides of equal length. If an object has these characteristics, it is an equilateral triangle; if it does not, it is not an equilateral triangle.

Other concepts—often those with the most relevance to our everyday lives—are more ambiguous and difficult to define. For instance, broader concepts such as "table" and "bird" have a set of general, relatively loose characteristic features that might overlap with other concepts. For example, consider the table used in table tennis (also called ping pong). Is the table a piece of furniture? Or is it more appropriately considered a piece of game equipment? When we consider these more ambiguous concepts, we usually think in terms of examples called **prototypes**. Prototypes are typical, highly representative examples of a concept that correspond to our mental image or best exam-

Many athletes, such as Serena Williams, use mental imagery to focus on a task, a process they call "getting in the zone." What other occupations might require the use of strong mental imagery?

ple of the concept (Rosch, 1975). For instance, although a robin and an ostrich are both examples of birds, those who grew up around robins and not around ostriches are more likely to think of a robin when asked for an example of a bird. Consequently, for those people who think that robin is the best example of a bird, we would say that robin is a prototype of the concept "bird." Similarly, when we think of the concept of a table, those of us who are likely to think of a coffee table before we think of a drafting table, would have "coffee table" closer to our prototype of a table.

ALGORITHMS AND HEURISTICS

When faced with making a decision, we often turn to various kinds of cognitive shortcuts, known as algorithms and heuristics, to help us. An **algorithm** is a rule that, if applied appropriately, guarantees a solution to a problem. We can use an algorithm even if we cannot understand why it works. For example, you may know that you can find the length of the third side of a right triangle by using the formula $a^2 + b^2 = c^2$, although you may not have the foggiest notion of the mathematical principles behind the formula.

A **heuristic** is a cognitive shortcut that *may* lead to a correct solution. Unlike algorithms, heuristics often allow

> **concepts** Mental groupings of similar objects, events, or people.
>
> **prototypes** Typical, highly representative examples of a concept.
>
> **algorithm** A rule that, if applied appropriately, guarantees a solution to a problem.
>
> **heuristic** A cognitive shortcut that may lead to a solution.

Which one of these two images matches your prototype for "phone"? The one on the left is the first telephone, invented by Alexander Graham Bell.

us to reach a solution more quickly, but the solution may not be correct. For example, when I play tic-tac-toe, I follow the heuristic of placing an X in the center square when I start the game. This tactic doesn't guarantee that I will win, but experience has taught me that it will increase my chances of success. Similarly, some students follow the heuristic of preparing for a test by ignoring the assigned textbook reading and studying only their lecture notes—a strategy that may or may not pay off.

Although heuristics often help people to solve problems and to make decisions, certain kinds of heuristics are more likely to lead to inaccurate conclusions. For example, we sometimes use the *representativeness heuristic*, a rule we apply when we judge people by the degree to which they represent a certain category or group of people. Suppose, for instance, you are the owner of a fast-food store that has been robbed many times by teenagers. Using the concept of a prototype discussed above, we could guess that you have developed over time a prototype for the appearance and age of a person who is going to rob your store. The representativeness heuristic (that is, using your prototype category) would lead you to raise your guard each time someone of this age group enters your store (even though, statistically, it is unlikely that any given teenager will rob the store) (Fisk, Bury, & Holden, 2006; Nilsson, Juslin, & Olsson, 2008).

The *availability heuristic* involves judging the probability of an event on the basis of how easily the event can be recalled from memory. According to this heuristic, we assume that events we remember easily are likely to

Although you might not realize it, you use heuristics every day.

> Some students follow the heuristic of preparing for a test by ignoring the assigned textbook reading and studying only their lecture notes—a strategy that may or may not pay off.

have occurred more frequently in the past—and are more likely to occur in the future—than events that are harder to remember.

For instance, the availability heuristic makes us more afraid of dying in a plane crash than in an auto accident, despite statistics clearly showing that airplane travel is much safer than auto travel. Similarly, although 10 times more people die from falling out of bed than from lightning strikes, we're more afraid of being hit by lightning. The reason is that plane crashes and lightning strikes receive far more publicity, and they are therefore more easily remembered (Caruso, 2008; Fox, 2006; Kluger, 2006; Oppenheimer, 2004).

SOLVING PROBLEMS

According to an old legend, a group of Vietnamese monks guard three towers on which sit 64 golden rings. The monks believe that if they succeed in moving the rings from the first tower to the third according to a series of rigid rules, the world as we know it will come to an end. (Should you prefer that the world remain in its present state, there's no need for immediate concern: it would take $2^{64} - 1$ moves to solve the problem, and if we assume that each move takes 1 second, the solution would take close to 600 billion years.)

In the Tower of Hanoi puzzle, a much simpler version of the task facing the monks, three disks are placed on three posts as in the figure at the top of the next page. The goal of the puzzle is to move all three disks to the third post, arranged in the same order, by using as few moves as possible. There are two restrictions: Only one disk can be moved at a time, and no disk can ever cover a smaller one during a move.

Why are cognitive psychologists interested in the Tower of Hanoi problem? Because the way people go about solving such puzzles helps illuminate how people solve complex, real-life problems. Psychologists have found that problem solving typically involves three steps: preparing to create solutions, producing solutions, and evaluating the solutions that have been generated.

PSYCH think

connect

WWW.MCGRAWHILLCONNECT.COM/PSYCHOLOGY
Heuristics

> > > How might the availability heuristic contribute to prejudice based on race, age, and gender? Can awareness of this heuristic prevent prejudice?

Take the PsychSmart challenge! Find out how you use heuristics. From chapter 7 in your ebook, select the *Exercises* tab. Then select "Heuristics." After you complete the exercise, answer Pop Quiz question 2 on p. 191.

Tower of Hanoi Puzzle

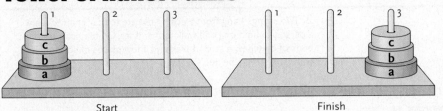

Start   Finish

Can you solve the Tower of Hanoi puzzle? The goal of the puzzle is to move all three disks from the first post to the third and still preserve the original order of the disks, using the fewest number of moves possible while following the rules that only one disk at a time can be moved and no disk can cover a smaller one during a move. The solution lists the moves in sequence.

Solution: Move C to 3, B to 2, C to 2, A to 3, C to 1, B to 3, and C to 3.

Steps in problem solving

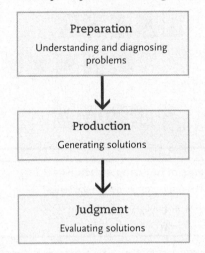

Preparation
Understanding and diagnosing problems

↓

Production
Generating solutions

↓

Judgment
Evaluating solutions

Preparation: Understanding and Diagnosing Problems When approaching a problem like the Tower of Hanoi, most people begin by trying to understand the problem thoroughly. If the problem is an unusual one, they probably will pay special attention to any restrictions placed on coming up with a solution—such as the rule about moving only one disk at a time in the Tower of Hanoi problem. If, by contrast, the problem is a familiar one, they are apt to spend considerably less time in this preparation stage.

Problems vary from well defined to ill defined (Evans, 2004; Kim, & Grunig, 2011; Vartanian, 2009; Reitman, 1965). In a *well-defined problem*—such as a mathematical equation or the solution to a jigsaw puzzle—both the nature of the problem itself and the information needed to solve it are available and clear. Thus, we can make straightforward judgments about whether a potential solution is appropriate. With an *ill-defined problem*, such as how to increase morale on an assembly line or to bring peace to the Middle East, not only may the specific nature of the problem be unclear, but the information required to solve the problem may be even less obvious.

Typically, a problem falls into one of the three categories: arrangement, inducing structure, and transformation, as shown in the figure on page 168. Solving each type requires somewhat different kinds of psychological skills and knowledge (Chronicle, MacGregor, & Ormerod, 2004; Spitz, 1987).

Arrangement problems require the problem solver to rearrange or recombine elements in a way that will satisfy a certain criterion. Usually, several different arrangements can be made, but only one or a few of the arrangements will produce a solution. Anagram problems and jigsaw puzzles are examples of arrangement problems (Coventry et al., 2003).

In *problems of inducing structure*, a person must identify the existing relationships among the elements presented and then construct a new relationship among them. In such a problem, the problem solver must determine not only the relationships among the elements but also the structure and size of the elements involved. In the example shown (on the next page), a person must first determine that the solution requires the numbers to be considered in pairs (14-24-34-44-54-64). Only after identifying that part of the problem can a person determine the solution rule (the first number of each pair increases by one, while the second number remains the same).

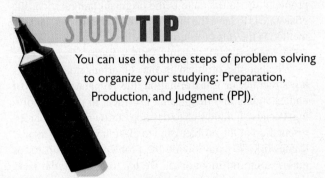
Winnowing out non-essential information is often a critical step in the preparation stage of problem solving.

Categories of Problems (Answers can be found on p. 169)

Arrangement problems

1. Anagrams: Rearrange the letters in each set to make an English word:

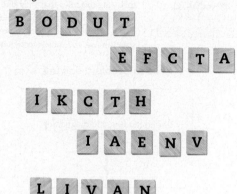

B O D U T

E F C T A

I K C T H

I A E N V

L I V A N

2. Two strings hang from a ceiling but are too far apart to allow a person to hold one and walk to the other. On the floor are a book of matches, a screwdriver, and a few pieces of cotton. How could the strings be tied together?

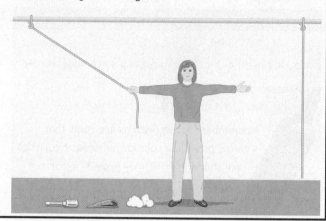

Problems of inducing structure

1. What number comes next in the series?

1 4 2 4 3 4 4 4 5 4 6 4

2. Complete these analogies:

baseball is to bat as tennis is to _____

merchant is to sell as customer is to _____

Transformation problems

1. Water jars: A person has three jars with the following capacities:

Jar A: 28 ounces   Jar B: 7 ounces   Jar C: 5 ounces

How can the person measure exactly 11 ounces of water?

2. Ten coins are arranged in the following way. By moving only two of the coins, make two rows that each contains six coins.

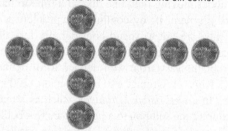

The Tower of Hanoi puzzle represents the third kind of problem—*transformation problems*—which consist of an initial state, a goal state, and a method for changing the initial state into the goal state. In the Tower of Hanoi problem, the initial state is the original configuration, the goal state is to have the three disks on the third peg, and the method is the rules for moving the disks (Emick & Welsh, 2005; Majeres, 2007; Mataix-Cols & Bartres-Faz, 2002).

Whether the problem is one of arrangement, inducing structure, or transformation, the preparation stage of understanding and diagnosing is critical in problem solving, because it allows us to develop our own cognitive representation of the problem and to place it within a personal framework. We may divide the problem into subparts or ignore some information as we try to simplify the task. Winnowing out nonessential information is often a critical step in the preparation stage of problem solving.

Our ability to represent a problem—and the kind of solution we eventually come to—depends on the way a problem is phrased, or framed. Consider, for example, if

Did you know?

If you want to convince someone to use sunscreen, the odds of succeeding are higher if you use positive framing ("It helps keep your skin looking young") compared to negative framing ("If you don't, you could develop skin cancer") (APA, 1999).

you were a cancer patient having to choose between surgery and radiation and were given the two sets of treatment options shown in the figure (on the next page) (Chandran & Menon, 2004; Tversky & Kahneman, 1987). When the options are framed in terms of the likelihood of survival, only 18% of participants in a study chose radiation

L. E. Bourne & R. L. Dominowski, *Cognitive Processes*, 1st ed., © 1979. Printed and electronically reproduced by permission of Pearson Education, Inc., Upper Saddle River, New Jersey.

(Answers to problems on p. 168)

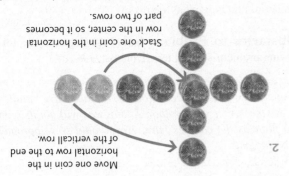

2. Move one coin in the horizontal row to the end of the vertical row. Stack one coin in the horizontal row in the center, so it becomes part of two rows.

Transformation problems

1. Fill jar A; empty into jar B once and into jar C twice. What remains in jar A is 11 ounces.

Problems of inducing structure

1. 7

2. racket, buy

Arrangement problems

1. DOUBT, FACET, THICK, NAIVE, ANVIL.

2. The screwdriver is tied to one of the strings. This makes a pendulum that can be swung to reach the other string.

---

over surgery. However, when the choice was framed in terms of the likelihood of dying, 44% chose radiation over surgery—even though the outcomes are identical in both sets of framing conditions.

Production: Generating Solutions The second step in problem solving is the production of possible solutions. If a problem is relatively simple, we may already have a direct solution stored in long-term memory, and all we need to do is retrieve the appropriate information. If we cannot retrieve or do not know the solution, we must generate possible solutions and compare them with information in long- and short-term memory.

When all else fails, we can solve problems through trial and error, but we tend to resist this approach in favor of any possible heuristics. Wouldn't you get frustrated if forced to try solving a problem by trial and error instead of using shortcuts? Thomas Edison invented the light bulb only because he tried thousands of different kinds of materials for a filament before he found one that worked (carbon). Another difficulty with trial and error is that some problems are so complicated that it would take a lifetime to try out every possibility. For example, according to some estimates, there are some 10^{120} possible sequences of chess moves (10^{120} is equal to 1 followed by 120 zeros) (Fine & Fine, 2003).

In place of trial and error, complex problem solving often involves the use of heuristics, cognitive shortcuts that can generate solutions. Probably the most frequently applied heuristic in problem solving is a **means-ends analysis**, which involves repeated tests for differences between the desired outcome and what currently exists. Consider this simple example (Chrysikou, 2006; Huber, Beckmann, & Herrmann, 2004; Newell & Simon, 1972): I want to take my son to preschool. What's the difference between what I have and what I want? One of distance. What changes distance? My automobile. My automobile won't work. What is needed to make it work? A new battery. What has new batteries? An auto repair shop . . .

> **means-ends analysis** Repeated testing for differences between the desired outcome and what currently exists.

In a means-end analysis, each step brings the problem solver closer to a resolution. Although this approach is

---

Problem: Surgery or radiation?

Survival Frame

Surgery: Of 100 people having surgery, 90 live through the post-operative period, 68 are alive at the end of the first year, and 34 are alive at the end of five years.

Radiation: Of 100 people having radiation therapy, all live through the treatment, 77 are alive at the end of one year, and 22 are alive at the end of five years.

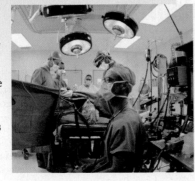

Far more patients choose surgery

Mortality Frame

Surgery: Of 100 people having surgery, 10 die during surgery, 32 die by the end of the first year, and 66 die by the end of five years.

Radiation: Of 100 people having radiation therapy, none die during the treatment, 23 die by the end of one year, and 78 die by the end of five years.

Far more patients choose radiation

often effective, if the problem requires indirect steps that temporarily *increase* the discrepancy between a current state and the solution, means-ends analysis can be counterproductive. For example, sometimes the fastest route to the summit of a mountain requires a mountain climber to backtrack temporarily; a means-end approach—which implies that the mountain climber should always forge ahead and upward—is ineffective in such instances.

Another heuristic commonly used to generate solutions is to divide a problem into intermediate steps, or *subgoals*, and solve each of those steps. For instance, in our Tower of Hanoi problem, we could choose several obvious subgoals, such as moving the largest disk to the third post.

If solving a subgoal is a step toward the ultimate solution to a problem, identifying subgoals is an appropriate strategy. In some cases, however, forming subgoals is not all that helpful and may actually increase the time needed to find a solution. For example, some mathematics problems are so complex that it takes longer to identify the appropriate subdivisions than to solve the problems by other means (Fishbach, Dhar, & Zhang, 2006; Kaller et al., 2004; Reed, 1996).

Judgment: Evaluating the Solutions The final stage in problem solving is judging the adequacy of a solution. Often this is a simple matter: If the solution is clear—as in the Tower of Hanoi problem—we will know immediately whether we have been successful (Varma, 2007).

If the solution is less concrete or if there is no single correct solution, evaluating solutions becomes more difficult. In such instances, we must decide which alternative solution is best. Unfortunately, we often quite inaccurately estimate the quality of our own ideas. For instance, a team of drug researchers working for a specific company may consider their remedy for an illness to be superior to all others, overestimating the likelihood of their success and downplaying the approaches of competing drug companies (Eizenberg & Zaslavsky, 2004).

Theoretically, we can make accurate choices among alternative solutions by being methodical and using valid information. Yet, as we see next, several kinds of obstacles

> **functional fixedness** The tendency to think of an object only in terms of its typical use.
>
> **mental set** The tendency for old patterns of problem solving to persist.

to and biases in problem solving affect the quality of the decisions and judgments we make.

Obstacles to Problem Solving Consider the following problem-solving test (Duncker, 1945):

You are given a set of tacks, candles, and matches, each in a small box, and told your goal is to place three candles at eye level on a nearby door, so that wax will not drip on the floor as the candles burn. How would you approach this challenge?

If you have difficulty solving the problem, you are not alone. Most people cannot solve it when it is presented with the objects shown *inside* the boxes. However, if the objects were presented *beside* the boxes, just resting on the table, chances are that you would solve the problem much more readily.

The difficulty you probably encountered in solving this problem stems from its presentation, which is misleading at the initial preparation stage. Actually, significant obstacles to problem solving can exist at each of the three major stages. Although cognitive approaches to problem solving suggest that thinking proceeds along fairly rational, logical lines as a person confronts a problem and considers various solutions, several factors can hinder the development of creative, appropriate, and accurate solutions.

- *Functional Fixedness.* The difficulty most people experience with the candle problem is caused by **functional fixedness**, the tendency to think of an object only in terms of its typical use. For instance, functional fixedness probably leads you to think of this book as something to read, instead of its potential use as a doorstop or as kindling for a fire. In the candle problem, because the objects are first presented inside the boxes, functional fixedness leads most people to see the boxes simply as containers for the objects they hold rather than as a potential part of the solution. They do not envision another function for the boxes.
- *Mental Set.* Functional fixedness is an example of a broader phenomenon known as **mental set**, the tendency for old patterns of problem solving to persist. A

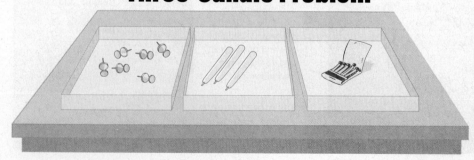

Three-Candle Problem

The problem here is to place three candles at eye level on a nearby door so that the wax will not drip on the floor as the candles burn—using only the materials in the figure. The solution appears on p. 172.

malfunctioned in 1979, a disaster that almost led to a nuclear meltdown, the plant operators immediately had to solve a problem of the most serious kind. Several monitors gave contradictory information about the source of the problem: One suggested that the pressure was too high, leading to the danger of an explosion; others indicated that the pressure was too low, which could lead to a meltdown. Although the pressure was, in fact, too low, the supervisors on duty relied on the one monitor—which turned out to be faulty—that suggested that the pressure was too high. Once they had made their decision and acted on it, they ignored the contradictory evidence from the other monitors (Wickens, 1984).

The operators' mistake exemplifies **confirmation bias**, in which problem solvers favor initial hypotheses and ignore contradictory information that supports alternative hypotheses or solutions. Even when we find evidence that contradicts a solution we have chosen, we are apt to stick with our original hypothesis.

Confirmation bias occurs for several reasons. For one thing, rethinking a problem that appears to be solved already takes extra cognitive effort, so we are apt to stick with our first solution. For another, we give greater weight to subsequent information that supports our initial position than to information that is not supportive of it (Evans & Feeney, 2004; Parmley, 2007; Rassin, 2008).

> **confirmation bias** The tendency to favor information that supports one's initial hypotheses and ignore contradictory information that supports alternative hypotheses or solutions.

classic experiment (Luchins, 1946) demonstrated this phenomenon. As you can see in the figure at the bottom of page 172, the object of the task is to use the jars in each row to measure out the designated amount of liquid. (Try it to get a sense of the power of mental set before moving on.)

If you have tried to solve the problem, you know that the first five rows are all solved in the same way: First fill the largest jar (B), and then from it fill the middle-size jar (A) once and the smallest jar (C) two times. What is left in B is the designated amount. (Stated as a formula, the designated amount is B–A–2C.) The demonstration of mental set comes in the sixth row of the problem, a point at which you probably encountered some difficulty. If you are like most people, you tried the formula and were perplexed when it failed. Chances are, in fact, that you missed the simple (but different) solution to the problem, which involves merely subtracting C from A. Interestingly, people who were given the problem in row 6 *first* had no difficulty with it at all.

- *Inaccurate Evaluation of Solutions.* When the nuclear power plant at Three Mile Island in Pennsylvania

CREATIVITY AND PROBLEM SOLVING

Despite obstacles to problem solving, many people adeptly discover creative solutions to problems. One enduring question that cognitive psychologists have sought to answer is

"I'll be happy to give you innovative thinking. What are the guidelines?"

© Leo Cullum/The New Yorker Collection/www.cartoonbank.com.

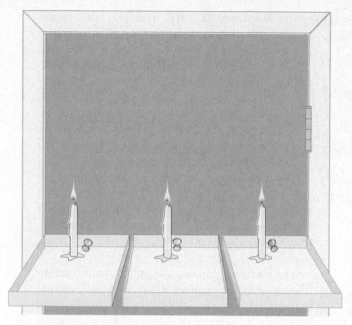

: Solution to the 3-candle problem on page 170.

creativity The ability to generate original ideas or solve problems in novel ways.

divergent thinking The ability to generate unusual, yet nonetheless appropriate, responses to problems or questions.

convergent thinking The ability to produce responses that are based primarily on knowledge and logic.

what factors underlie **creativity**, the ability to generate original ideas or solve problems in novel ways.

Although identifying the stages of problem solving helps us understand how people approach and solve problems, it does little to explain why some people come up with better solutions than others do. For instance, even the possible solutions to a simple problem often show wide discrepancies. Consider, for example, how you might respond to the question "How many uses can you think of for a newspaper?"

Now compare your solution with this one proposed by a 10-year-old boy:

Given jars with these capacities (in ounces):

	A	B	C	Obtain:
1.	21	127	3	100
2.	14	163	25	99
3.	18	43	10	5
4.	9	42	6	21
5.	20	59	4	31
6.	28	76	3	25

You can read it, write on it, lay it down and paint a picture on it . . . You could put it in your door for decoration, put it in the garbage can, put it on a chair if the chair is messy. If you have a puppy, you put newspaper in its box or put it in your backyard for the dog to play with. When you build something and you don't want anyone to see it, put newspaper around it. Put newspaper on the floor if you have no mattress, use it to pick up something hot, use it to stop bleeding, or to catch the drips from drying clothes. You can use a newspaper for curtains, put it in your shoe to cover what is hurting your foot, make a kite out of it, shade a light that is too bright. You can wrap fish in it, wipe windows, or wrap money in it . . . You put washed shoes in newspaper, wipe eyeglasses with it, put it under a dripping sink, put a plant on it, make a paper bowl out of it, tie it on your feet for slippers. You can put it on the sand if you had no towel, use it for bases in baseball, make paper airplanes with it, use it as a dustpan when you sweep, ball it up for the cat to play with, wrap your hands in it if it is cold. (Ward, Kogan, & Pankove, 1972)

This list shows extraordinary creativity. Unfortunately, it is much easier to identify *examples* of creativity than to determine its causes. Several factors, however, seem to be associated with creativity (Isaksen, Dorval, & Treffinger, 2011; Kaufman & Baer, 2005; Schepers & van den Berg, 2007; Simonton, 2003).

One of these factors is **divergent thinking**, the ability to generate unusual, yet appropriate, responses to problems or questions. This type of thinking contrasts with **convergent thinking**, which produces responses that are based primar-

A Classic Mental Set

In this classic demonstration of mental set, the goal is to use the jars in each row to measure out the designated amount of liquid. After you've figured out the solution for the first five rows, you'll probably have trouble with the sixth row—even though the solution is actually easier. In fact, if you had tried to solve the problem in the sixth row first, you probably would have solved it right away.

ily on knowledge and logic. For instance, in reply to the question "What can you do with a newspaper?" someone relying on convergent thinking might say "You read it." In contrast, "You use it as a dustpan" is a more divergent—and creative—response (Cropley, 2006; Runco, 2006; Schepers & van den Berg, 2007).

Another aspect of creativity is its cognitive complexity, or preference for elaborate, intricate, and complex stimuli and thinking patterns. For instance, creative people often have a wider range of interests, are more independent, and are more interested in philosophical or abstract problems than are less creative individuals (Barron, 1990; Richards, 2006).

One factor that is *not* closely related to creativity is intelligence, as it is defined and measured in the West. Traditional intelligence tests, which ask focused questions that have only one acceptable answer, tap convergent thinking skills. Such tests may penalize highly creative people for their divergent thinking. This may explain why researchers consistently find that creativity is only slightly related to school grades and intelligence when intelligence is measured using traditional intelligence tests (Hong, Milgram, & Gorsky, 1995; Nusbaum & Silvia, 2011; Sternberg & O'Hara, 2000).

>> Language

'Twas brillig, and the slithy toves
Did gyre and gimble in the wabe:
All mimsy were the borogoves,
And the mome raths outgrabe.

Although few of us have ever come face to face with a tove, we have little difficulty in discerning that in Lewis Carroll's (1872) poem "Jabberwocky," the expression *slithy toves* contains an adjective, *slithy*, and the noun it modifies, *toves*.

> **language** The communication of information through symbols arranged according to systematic rules.

Our ability to make sense out of nonsense, if the nonsense follows typical rules of language, illustrates the complexity of both human language and the cognitive processes that underlie its development and use. The use of **language**—the communication of information through symbols arranged according to systematic rules—is an important cognitive ability, one that is indispensable if we are to communicate with one another. Not only is language central to communication, it is also closely tied to the very way in which we think about and understand the world. Without language, our ability to transmit information, acquire knowledge, and cooperate with others would be tremendously hindered. No wonder psychologists have devoted considerable attention to studying language (Hoff, 2008; Reisberg, 2009; Stapel & Semin, 2007).

GRAMMAR: THE RULES OF LANGUAGE

To understand how language develops and relates to thought, we first need to review some of the formal elements of language. The basic structure of language rests on **grammar**, the system of rules that determine how our thoughts can be expressed in words.

Grammar deals with three major components of language: phonology, syntax, and semantics. **Phonology** is the study of the smallest basic units of speech, called **phonemes**, that affect meaning, and of the way we use those sounds to form words and produce meaning. For instance, the *a* sound in *fat* and the *a* sound in *fate* represent two different phonemes in English (Hardison, 2006).

Linguists have identified more than 800 different phonemes among all the world's languages. Although English speakers use just 52 phonemes to produce words, other languages use from as few as 15 to as many as 141. Differences in phonemes are one reason people have difficulty learning other languages. For example, to a Japanese speaker, whose native language does not have an *r* phoneme, pronouncing such English words as *roar* present some difficulty (Dimitropoulou, Duñabeitia, & Carreiras, 2011; Gibbs, 2002; Iverson et al., 2003). Similarly, for a native English speaker, it is difficult to hear the difference between the two sounds made by the letter "*p*." Consider the way the *p* sounds in the word *pull*. It you say *pull* while holding a candle in front of your mouth, the flame will be moved by your breath. Now say the word *spell*. Notice that the flame does not move. If you grew up speaking Thai, you are familiar with both of these sounds. If you grew up speaking Spanish first, it is likely you use the *p* as in *spell* whenever you make a *p* sound. Even more challenging than hearing the difference for Native English speakers is the problem of making the sound of the *p* in *spell* without using a preceding *s*. Try it. You know you are getting close when you can say *pull* with a lit candle in front of your mouth and the flame is not pushed by the air leaving your mouth.

Syntax refers to the rules that indicate how words and phrases can be combined to form sentences. Every language has intricate rules that guide the order in which words may be strung together to communicate meaning. English speakers have no difficulty recognizing that "TV down the turn" is not a meaningful sequence, whereas "Turn down the TV" is. To understand the effect of one type of syntax rule in English, consider the changes in meaning caused by the different word orders in the following three utterances: "John kidnapped the boy," "John, the kidnapped boy," and "The boy kidnapped John" (Eberhard, Cutting, & Bock, 2005; Robert, 2006). In other languages, such as Russian, changing the word order does not change the basic meaning of a sentence. They use prefixes, suffixes, and other devices to change our understanding of who does an action and who/what received an action.

grammar The system of rules that determine how our thoughts can be expressed through language.

phonology The study of the smallest units of speech, called phonemes.

phonemes The smallest units of speech.

syntax Ways in which words and phrases can be combined to form sentences.

semantics The rules governing the meaning of words and sentences.

babble Meaningless speechlike sounds made by children from around the age of 3 months through 1 year.

The third major component of language is **semantics**, the meanings of words and sentences. Semantic rules allow us to use words to convey the subtlest nuances. In English, we can again use word order to make the distinction between "The truck hit Laura" (which we would be likely to say if we had just seen the vehicle hitting Laura) and "Laura was hit by a truck" (which we would probably say if someone asked why Laura was missing class while she recuperated) (Pietarinen, 2006; Richgels, 2004). Frequently, the shading of meanings is accomplished in English by the use of words that are similar in meaning, but not identical. Consider, for example, the difference in these two sentences: "Mary loved John." "Mary adored John."

Despite the complexities of language, most of us acquire the basics of grammar without even being aware that we have learned its rules. (And our knowledge of these rules likely remains unconscious, which is why most of us probably did not enjoy classes in grammar when we were in school.) Moreover, even though we may have difficulty explicitly stating the rules of grammar, our linguistic abilities are so sophisticated that we can utter an infinite number of different statements. How do we acquire these abilities?

LANGUAGE DEVELOPMENT

To parents, the sounds of their infant babbling and cooing are music to their ears (except, perhaps, at three o'clock in the morning). These sounds also serve an important function. They mark the first step on the road to the development of language.

Babbling Children **babble**—make speechlike but meaningless sounds—from around the age of 3 months through 1 year. While babbling, babies may produce, at one time or another, sounds found in all languages, not just the one to which they are exposed. Even infants who are unable to hear but who are exposed to sign language from birth "babble," using their hands (Locke, 2006; Majorano & D'Odorico, 2011; Pettito, 1993).

An infant's babbling increasingly resembles the specific language spoken in the infant's environment. Young infants can distinguish among all 869 phonemes that have been

While babbling, babies may produce sounds found in all languages.

Young children master the basic rules of grammar in their native language without being taught them and acquire a large enough vocabulary by age 5 to hold up their end of a simple conversation.

Producing Language By the time children are approximately 1 year old, they stop producing sounds that are not in the language to which they have been exposed. It is then a short step to the production of actual words. In English, these are typically short words that start with a consonant sound such as *b, d, m, p,* and *t*—this helps explain why *mama* and *dada* are so often among babies' first words. Of course, even before they produce their first words, children can understand a fair amount of the language they hear. Language comprehension precedes language production.

After the age of 1 year, children begin to learn more complicated forms of language. Their vocabulary increases sharply and, by age 2, the average child has a vocabulary of more than 50 words. Just six months later, that vocabulary has grown to several hundred words. At first, they produce two-word combinations, called **telegraphic speech**, because these primitive sentences sound as if they were part of a telegram, in which words not critical to the message are left out. Rather than saying, "I showed you the book," a child using telegraphic speech may say, "Show book," and "That's my sister's shoe" may become "Sissy shoe." Gradually, children use less telegraphic speech and produce increasingly complex sentences (Volterra et al., 2003).

By age 3, many children have learned to make plurals by adding *s* to nouns and to form the past tense by adding *-ed* to verbs. These skills also lead to errors, because children carefully apply rules they have just figured out. They **overgeneralize** these rules, using them even when doing so results in an error. Thus, although it is correct to say "he walked" for the past tense of *walk*, the *-ed* rule doesn't work quite so well when children say "he runned" for the past tense of *run* (Gershkoff-Stowe, Connell, & Smith, 2006; Howe, 2002; Kidd & Lum, 2008; Rice et al., 2004).

By age 5, children have acquired the basic rules of language. However, they do not attain until later a full vocabulary and the ability to comprehend and use subtle grammatical rules. For example, a 5-year-old boy who sees a blindfolded doll and is asked, "Is the doll easy

> **telegraphic speech** Sentences in which words not critical to the message are left out.
>
> **overgeneralization** The phenomenon by which children apply language rules even when the application results in an error.

identified across the world's languages. However, after the age of 6 to 8 months, that ability begins to decline. Infants begin to "specialize" in the language to which they are exposed as neurons in their brains reorganize to respond only to the specific phonemes the infants routinely hear.

Some theorists argue that a *sensitive period* exists for language development early in life, in which a child is especially responsive to language cues and most easily acquires language. In fact, if children are not exposed to language during this sensitive period, later they will have great difficulty overcoming this deficit (Bates, 2005; Shafer & Garrido-Nag, 2007).

From the perspective of ...

A SPEECH THERAPIST A very concerned young couple has brought their 30-month-old child to see you. The father tells you that his child speaks ungrammatically, sometimes using only two words and sometimes adding weird endings to words. For example, just last night the child said, "Two childs finded it." What would you tell these parents and what would you recommend to them?

Cases in which abused children have been isolated from contact with others support the theory of such sensitive periods. In one case, for example, a girl named Genie was exposed to virtually no language from the age of 20 months until she was rescued at age 13 years. She was unable to speak at all. Despite intensive instruction, she learned only some words and was never able to master the complexities of language (Rymer, 1994; Veltman & Browne, 2001).

Did you know?

Being fluent in two languages makes it easier to switch back and forth mentally between different perspectives, which is an important critical thinking skill (Prior & MacWhinney, 2010).

or hard to see?" would have great trouble answering the question. In fact, if he were asked to make the doll easier to see, he would probably try to remove the doll's blindfold. By the time they are 8 years old, however, children have little difficulty understanding this question, because they realize that the doll's blindfold has nothing to do with an observer's ability to see the doll (Chomsky, 1969; Hoff, 2003).

THEORIES OF LANGUAGE ACQUISITION

Humans make enormous strides in language development during childhood. However, the reasons for this rapid growth are far from obvious. Psychologists have offered two major explanations, one based on learning theory and the other based on innate processes.

Learning Theory Approaches The **learning-theory approach** suggests that language acquisition follows the principles of reinforcement and conditioning discovered by psychologists who study learning (see chapter 5). For example, a child who says "mama" receives hugs and praise from her mother, which reinforce the behavior of saying "mama" and make its repetition more likely. This view suggests that children first learn to speak by being rewarded for making sounds that approximate speech. Ultimately, through a process of shaping, language becomes more and more like adult speech (Ornat & Gallo, 2004; Skinner, 1957).

In support of the learning-theory approach to language acquisition, the more that parents speak to their young children, the more proficient the children become in language use. In addition, by the time they are 3 years old, children who hear higher levels of linguistic sophistication in their parents' speech show a greater rate of vocabulary growth, vocabulary use, and even general intellectual achievement than do children whose parents' speech is more simple (Hart & Risley, 1997).

The learning-theory approach is less successful in explaining how children acquire language rules. Children are reinforced not only when they use language correctly but also when they use it incorrectly. For example, parents answer a child's "Why the dog won't eat?" as readily as they do the correctly phrased question, "Why won't the dog eat?" Listeners understand both sentences equally well. Learning theory, then, cannot fully explain language acquisition.

learning-theory approach (to language development) The theory suggesting that language acquisition follows the principles of reinforcement and conditioning.

nativist approach (to language development) The theory that a genetically determined, innate mechanism directs language development.

universal grammar Noam Chomsky's theory that all the world's languages share a common underlying structure.

language-acquisition device A neural system of the brain hypothesized by Noam Chomsky to permit understanding of language.

: How do we acquire language?

Did you know?

The ability to read facial expressions is so central to verbal comprehension that over 900 digital emoticons (smiley face, wink, and so on) have been developed for use when communicating by e-mail. =:o

Nativist Approaches Pointing to such problems with learning-theory approaches to language acquisition, linguist Noam Chomsky (1968, 1978, 1991) provided a groundbreaking alternative. Chomsky argued that humans are born with an innate linguistic capability that emerges primarily as a function of maturation. According to his **nativist approach** to language, all the world's languages share a common underlying structure called a **universal grammar**. Chomsky suggested that the human brain has a neural system, a **language-acquisition device**, that not only lets us understand the structure that language provides but also gives us strategies and techniques for learning the unique characteristics of our native language (Lidz & Gleitman, 2004; McGilvray, 2004; White, 2007).

Chomsky used the concept of the language-acquisition device as a metaphor, and he did not identify a specific area of the brain in which it resides. However, evidence

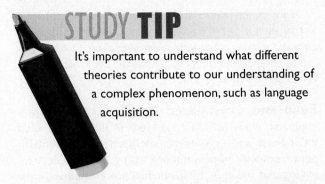

collected by neuroscientists suggests that the ability to use language, which was a significant evolutionary advance in human beings, is tied to specific neurological developments (Sahin, Pinker, & Halgren, 2006; Sakai, 2005; Willems & Hagoort, 2007).

For example, scientists have discovered a gene related to the development of language abilities that may have emerged as recently—in evolutionary terms—as 100,000 years ago. Furthermore, it is clear that specific sites within the brain are closely tied to language and that the shape of the human mouth and throat are tailored to the production of speech. And there is evidence that features of some languages, such as Chinese, Vietnamese, Navajo, and other tonal languages in which pitch is used to convey meaning, are tied to specific genes (Chandra, 2007; Dediu & Ladd, 2007; Gontier, 2008; Grigorenko, 2009; Hauser, Chomsky, & Fitch, 2002).

Interactionist Approaches Because both of these approaches help us understand different aspects of language acquisition, many theorists take an **interactionist approach** to language development. The interactionist approach suggests that language development is produced through a combination of genetically determined predispositions and environmental circumstances that help teach language.

Specifically, proponents of the interactionist approach suggest that the brain's hardwired language-acquisition device that Chomsky and geneticists point to provides the hardware for our acquisition of language, whereas the exposure to language in our environment that learning theorists observe allows us to develop the appropriate software. But the issue of exactly how language is acquired remains hotly contested (Hoff, 2008; Pinker & Jackendoff, 2005; Waxman, 2009).

>> Intelligence

Members of the Trukese tribe in the South Pacific often sail a hundred miles in open ocean waters. Although their destination may be just a small dot of land less than a mile wide, the Trukese are able to navigate precisely toward it without the aid of a compass, chronometer, sextant, or any of the other sailing tools that are used by Western navigators.

They are able to sail accurately, even when the winds do not allow a direct approach to the island and they must take a zigzag course (Gladwin, 1964; Mytinger, 2001).

How are the Trukese able to navigate so effectively? If you asked them, they could not explain it. They might tell you that they use a process that takes into account the rising and setting of the stars and the appearance, sound, and feel of the waves against the side of the boat. But at any given moment as they are sailing along, they could not identify their position or say why they are doing what they are doing in terms that would make sense to someone with a Western understanding of navigation. Similarly, they could not explain to us the navigational theory underlying their sailing technique.

If we gave Trukese sailors a Western standardized test of navigational knowledge and theory or, for that matter, a traditional test of intelligence, they might do poorly on it, but it wouldn't be very smart on our part to think that meant that the Trukese were unintelligent: Despite their inability to explain to us how they do it, they are able to navigate successfully through the open ocean waters. From their perspective, we might be the unintelligent ones, because we cannot understand their explanations and we cannot, therefore, accomplish navigation without all sorts of unnecessary gadgets, such as sextants and computers.

For years psychologists have grappled with the issue of devising a general definition of intelligence that takes cultural differences into account. Laypersons have fairly clear ideas of what intelligence is, although their ideas are grounded in their cultures. Westerners commonly view intelligence as the ability to form categories and debate rationally. In contrast, people in Eastern cultures and some African communities often view intelligence more in terms of understanding and relating to one another

> **interactionist approach (to language development)** The view that language development is produced through a combination of genetically determined predispositions and environmental circumstances that help teach language.

What does the Trukese people's method of navigation, without maps or instruments, tell us about the nature of intelligence?

(Brislin, Worthley, & MacNab, 2006; Nisbett, 2003; Sternberg, 2005, 2007).

The definition of intelligence that psychologists employ contains some of the same elements found in the layperson's conception. To psychologists, **intelligence** is the capacity to understand the world, think rationally, and use resources effectively when faced with challenges. Although psychologists recognize that intelligence occurs in a specific context, as demonstrated by the examples above and this definition, research lags behind this understanding; it is not yet clear exactly what intelligence is and how it can be measured.

Do you see yourself as a good writer, but you're not really good at math? Are you more comfortable writing a computer program than taking a dance class? Do your friends, parents, and teachers tell you that you are really smart in many different areas?

One basic issue regarding intelligence is this: If you are an intelligent person, are you generally better at most things than someone who would not be considered intelligent? Or, is it the case that we can be brilliant in a few areas and pretty slow in others? As you read this next section, try to keep an open mind, because when there are various theories that get a lot of attention, typically they all turn out to have some truth in them.

intelligence The capacity to understand the world, think rationally, and use resources effectively when faced with challenges.

g or g-factor The single, general factor for mental ability assumed to underlie intelligence in some early theories of intelligence.

fluid intelligence Intelligence that reflects information-processing capabilities, reasoning, and memory.

crystallized intelligence The accumulation of information, skills, and strategies that are learned through experience and can be applied in problem-solving situations.

theory of multiple intelligences Gardner's intelligence theory that proposes that there are eight distinct spheres of intelligence.

THEORIES OF INTELLIGENCE

Early psychologists interested in intelligence hypothesized that there was a single, general factor for mental ability, which they called *g*, or the *g*-factor. This general intelligence factor was thought to underlie performance in every aspect of intelligence, and it was the *g*-factor that was presumably being measured on tests of intelligence (Colom, Jung, & Haier, 2006; Haier et al., 2009; Spearman, 1927).

More recent theories see intelligence in a different light. Rather than viewing intelligence as a unitary entity, they consider it to be a multidimensional concept that includes different types of intelligence (Stankov, 2003; Sternberg & Pretz, 2005; Tenopyr, 2002).

Fluid and Crystallized Intelligence Some psychologists study two different kinds of intelligence: fluid intelligence and crystallized intelligence. **Fluid intelligence** reflects information-processing capabilities: reasoning and memory. Fluid intelligence encompasses the ability to reason abstractly. If we were asked to solve an analogy, group a series of letters according to some criterion or remember a set of numbers, we would be using fluid intelligence. We use fluid intelligence when we're trying to rapidly solve a puzzle (Di Fabio & Palazzeschi, 2009; Kane & Engle, 2002; Saggino et al., 2006).

In contrast, **crystallized intelligence** is the accumulation of information, skills, and strategies that people have learned through experience and that they can apply in problem-solving situations. It reflects our ability to call up information from long-term memory. We would be likely to rely on crystallized intelligence, for instance, if we were asked to participate in a discussion about the solution to the causes of poverty, a task that allows us to draw on our own past experiences and knowledge of the world. In contrast to fluid intelligence, which reflects a more general kind of intelligence, crystallized intelligence is more a reflection of the culture in which a person is raised. The differences between fluid intelligence and crystallized intelligence become especially evident in late adulthood, when people show declines in fluid, but not crystallized, intelligence (Aartsen, Martin, & Zimprich, 2002; Buehner, Krumm, & Ziegler, 2006; Tranter & Koutstaal, 2008).

Gardner's Multiple Intelligences Psychologist Howard Gardner has taken an approach very different from traditional thinking about intelligence. Gardner argues that rather than asking "How smart are you?" we should be asking a different question: "How are you smart?" In answering the latter question, Gardner has developed a **theory of multiple intelligences** (Gardner, 2000).

"To be perfectly frank, I'm not nearly as smart as you seem to think I am."

© W.B. Park/The New Yorker Collection/www.cartoonbank.com.

Musical intelligence

1

Skills in tasks involving music. Case example:

When he was 3, Yehudi Menuhin was smuggled into San Francisco Orchestra concerts by his parents. By the time he was 10 years old, Menuhin was an international performer.

Logical-mathematical intelligence

3

Skills in problem solving and scientific thinking. Case example:

Barbara McClintock, who won the Nobel Prize in medicine, describes one of her break-throughs, which came after thinking about a problem for half an hour . . . : "Suddenly I jumped and ran back to the (corn) field. At the top of the field (the others were still at the bottom) I shouted, 'Eureka, I have it!'"

Spatial intelligence

5

Skills involving spatial configurations, such as those used by artists and architects. Case example:

Natives of the Truk Islands navigate at sea without instruments. During the actual trip, the navigator must envision mentally a reference island as it passes under a particular star and from that he computes the number of segments completed, the proportion of the trip remaining, and any corrections in heading.

Intrapersonal intelligence

7

The knowledge of the internal aspects of oneself; access to one's own feelings and emotions. Case example:

In her essay "A Sketch of the Past," Virginia Woolf displays deep insight into her own inner life through these lines, describing her reaction to several specific memories from her childhood that still, in adulthood, shock her: "Though I still have the peculiarity that I receive these sudden shocks, they are now always welcome; after the first surprise, I always feel instantly that they are particularly valuable. And so I go on to suppose that the shock-receiving capacity is what makes me a writer."

Gardner's Multiple Intelligences

Bodily kinesthetic intelligence

2

Skills in using the body in the solution of problems or in the construction of products or displays, exemplified by dancers, athletes, actors, and surgeons. Case example:

Fifteen-year-old Babe Ruth played third base. During one game, his team's pitcher was doing very poorly and Babe loudly criticized him from third base. Brother Matthias, the coach, called out, "Ruth, if you know so much about it, you pitch!" Ruth said later that at the very moment he took the pitcher's mound, he knew he was supposed to be a pitcher.

Linguistic intelligence

4

Skills involved in the production and use of language. Case example:

At the age of 10, T. S. Eliot created a magazine called *Fireside*, to which he was the sole contributor.

Interpersonal intelligence

6

Skills in interacting with others, such as sensitivity to the moods, temperaments, motivations, and intentions of others. Case example:

When Anne Sullivan began instructing the deaf and blind Helen Keller, her task was one that had eluded others for years. Yet, just two weeks after beginning her work with Keller, Sullivan achieved great success.

Naturalist intelligence

8

The ability to identify and classify patterns in nature. Case example:

Dr. Temple Grandin, Professor of Animal Science at Colorado State University, is an internationally acclaimed designer of humane strategies and equipment for handling cattle. She is autistic and finds it easier to understand cows than humans.

Source: Adapted from *Multiple Intelligences: New Horizons* by H. Gardner. © 2006 by Howard Gardner.

Gardner argues that we have at a minimum eight different forms of intelligence, each relatively independent of the others: musical, bodily kinesthetic, logical-mathematical, linguistic, spatial, interpersonal, intrapersonal, and naturalist. In Gardner's view, each of the multiple intelligences is linked to an independent system in the brain. Furthermore, he suggests that there may be even more types of intelligence, such as *existential intelligence*, which

Piloting a helicopter requires both fluid intelligence and crystallized intelligence. Which of the two kinds of intelligence do you think is more important for this line of work?

involves identifying and thinking about the fundamental questions of human existence. The Dalai Lama might exemplify this type of intelligence (Gardner, 1999, 2000).

Although Gardner illustrates his conception of the specific types of intelligence with descriptions of well-known people, we all have the same eight kinds of intelligence—in different degrees. Moreover, although the eight basic types of intelligence are presented individually, Gardner suggests that these intelligences are interdependent. Normally, any activity encompasses several kinds of intelligence working together.

The concept of multiple intelligences has led to the development of intelligence test questions for which more than one answer can be correct; these provide an opportunity for test takers to demonstrate different kinds of intelligence. In addition, many educators, embracing the concept of multiple intelligences, have designed classroom curricula that are meant to draw on different aspects of intelligence (Douglas, Burton, & Reese-Durham, 2008; Kelly & Tangney, 2006; Tirri & Nokelainen, 2008).

Information-Processing Approach One of the newer contributions to understanding intelligence comes from the work of cognitive psychologists who take an *information-processing approach*. They assert that the way people store material in memory and use that material to solve intellectual tasks provides the most accurate measure of intelligence. Consequently, rather than focusing on the structure of intelligence or its underlying content or dimensions, information-processing approaches examine the *processes* involved in producing intelligent behavior (Hunt, 2005; Neubauer & Fink, 2005; Pressley & Harris, 2006).

For example, research shows that people with high scores on tests of intelligence spend more time on the initial encoding stages of problems, identifying the parts of a problem and retrieving relevant information from long-term memory, than do people with lower scores. This initial emphasis on recall-

ing relevant information pays off in the end; those who use this approach are more successful in finding solutions than are those who spend relatively less time on the initial stages (Deary & Der, 2005; Hunt, 2005; Sternberg, 1990).

Other information-processing approaches examine the sheer speed of processing. For example, research shows that the speed with which people are able to retrieve information from memory is related to verbal intelligence. In general, people with high scores on measures of verbal intelligence react more quickly on a variety of information-processing tasks, ranging from reactions to flashing lights to distinguishing between letters. The speed of information processing, then, may underlie some differences in intelligence (Gontkovsky & Beatty, 2006; Helmbold, Troche, & Rammsayer, 2007; Jensen, 2005; Sheppard & Vernon, 2008).

Practical Intelligence and Emotional Intelligence Consider the following situation:

An employee who reports to one of your subordinates has asked to talk with you about waste, poor management practices, and possible violations of both company policy and the law on the part of your subordinate. You have been in your present position only a year, but in that time you have had no indications of trouble about the subordinate in question. Neither you nor your company has an "open door" policy, so it is expected that employees should take their concerns to their immediate supervisors before bringing a matter to the attention of anyone else. The employee who wishes to meet with you has not discussed this matter with her supervisors because of its delicate nature. (Sternberg, 1998, p. 17)

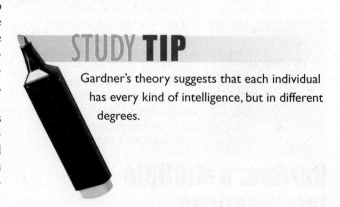

STUDY **TIP**

Gardner's theory suggests that each individual has every kind of intelligence, but in different degrees.

Your response to this situation has a lot to do with your future success in a business career, according psychologist Robert Sternberg. The question is one of a series designed to evaluate your practical intelligence. **Practical intelligence** is intelligence related to overall success in living (Muammar, 2007; Sternberg, 2000, 2002b; Sternberg & Hedlund, 2002; Wagner, 2002).

Traditional intelligence tests were developed to predict academic performance, not success in one's career. Sternberg points to evidence showing that most of these traditional measures of intelligence do not, in fact, do a very good job of predicting *career* success (McClelland, 1993). Specifically, although successful business executives usually score at least moderately well on intelligence tests, the rate at which they advance and their ultimate business achievements are only minimally associated with traditional measures of their intelligence.

Sternberg argues that career success requires a very different type of intelligence from that needed for academic success. Whereas academic success is based on knowledge of a specific information base obtained from reading and listening, practical intelligence is learned mainly through observation of others' behavior. People who are high in practical intelligence are able to learn general norms and principles and apply them appropriately. Consequently, practical intelligence tests measure the ability to employ broad principles in solving everyday problems (Stemler et al., 2009; Stemler & Sternberg, 2006; Sternberg & Pretz, 2005).

In addition to practical intelligence, Sternberg argues there are two other basic, interrelated types of successful intelligence: analytical intelligence and creative intelligence. Analytical intelligence focuses on abstract but traditional types of problems measured on IQ tests, whereas creative intelligence involves the generation of novel ideas and products (Benderly,

2004; Sternberg, Grigorenko, & Kidd, 2005; Sternberg, Kaufman, & Pretz, 2004).

Some psychologists broaden the concept of intelligence even further to include emotions. They define **emotional intelligence** as the set of skills that underlie the accurate assessment, evaluation, expression, and regulation of emotions (Humphrey, Curran, & Morris, 2007; Mayer, Salovey, & Caruso, 2004, 2008).

Emotional intelligence underlies the ability to get along well with others. It provides us with an understanding of what other people are feeling and experiencing and permits us to respond appropriately to others' needs. Emotional intelligence is the basis of empathy for others, self-awareness, and social skills.

Abilities in emotional intelligence may help explain why people with only modest scores on traditional intelligence tests can be quite successful. High emotional intelligence may enable an individual to tune into others' feelings, permitting a high degree of responsiveness to people around us.

Although the notion of emotional intelligence makes sense, it has yet to be quantified in a rigorous manner. Still, the notion of emotional intelligence reminds us that there are many ways to demonstrate intelligent behavior—just as there are multiple views of the nature of intelligence (Barrett & Salovey, 2002; Brackett, Rivers, & Salovey, 2011; Fox & Spector, 2000).

practical intelligence According to Sternberg, intelligence related to overall success in living.

emotional intelligence The set of skills that underlie the accurate assessment, evaluation, expression, and regulation of emotions.

intelligence tests Tests devised to quantify a person's level of intelligence.

Healthcare is one field where high emotional intelligence can be a valuable asset. In what other fields might emotional intelligence be beneficial?

MEASURING INTELLIGENCE

Given the variety of approaches to the components of intelligence, we should not be surprised that measuring intelligence has proved challenging. Psychologists who study intelligence have focused much of their attention on the development of **intelligence tests** and have relied on such tests to quantify a person's level of intelligence. These tests have proved to be of great benefit in identifying students in need of special attention in school, diagnosing cognitive difficulties, and helping people make optimal educational and vocational choices. At the same time, their use has proved controversial and raised important social and educational issues.

PSYCH think

> > > What role might emotional intelligence have in the classroom? How might emotional intelligence be tested? Should emotional intelligence be a factor in determining academic promotion to the next grade?

Historically, the first effort at intelligence testing in the West was based on an uncomplicated, but completely wrong, assumption: that the size and shape of a person's head could be used as an objective measure of intelligence. The idea was put forward by Sir Francis Galton (1822–1911), an eminent English scientist whose ideas in other domains proved to be considerably better than his notions about intelligence.

Galton's motivation to identify people of high intelligence stemmed from personal prejudices. He sought to demonstrate the natural superiority of people of high social class (including him) by showing that intelligence is inherited. He hypothesized that head configuration, being genetically determined, is related to brain size and therefore is related to intelligence.

mental age The age for which a given level of performance is average or typical.

Galton's theories were proved wrong on virtually every count. Head size and shape do not correlate with intellectual performance, and subsequent research has found little relationship between brain size and intelligence. However, Galton's work did have at least one desirable result: He was the first person to suggest that intelligence could be quantified and measured in an objective manner (Jensen, 2002).

The Development of IQ Tests The intelligence tests developed by the French psychologist Alfred Binet (1857–1911) provided the foundation for modern intelligence tests. His tests followed from a simple premise: If performance on certain tasks or test items improved with *chronological*, or physical, age, performance could be used to distinguish more intelligent children from less intelligent ones within a particular age group. On the basis of this principle, Binet devised the first formal intelligence test, which was designed to identify the "dullest" students in the Paris school system in order to provide them with remedial aid.

Binet began by presenting tasks to same-age students who had been labeled "bright" or "dull" by their teachers. If a task could be completed by the bright students but not by the dull ones, he retained that task as a proper test item; otherwise it was discarded. In the end he came up with a test that distinguished between the bright and dull groups, and—with further work—one that distinguished among children in different age groups (Binet & Simon, 1916; Sternberg & Jarvin, 2003).

On the basis of the Binet test, children were assigned a score relating to their **mental age**, the age for which a given level of performance is average or typical. For example, if the average 8-year-old answered, say, 45 items correctly on a test, anyone who answered 45 items correctly would be assigned a mental age of 8 years. Consequently, whether the person taking the test was 20 years old or 5 years old, he or she would have the same mental age of 8 years (Cornell, 2006).

STUDY TIP

Traditional intelligence measures relate to academic performance; practical intelligence relates to success in life; and emotional intelligence relates to emotional skills.

Assigning a mental age to students provided an indication of their general level of performance. However, it did not allow for adequate comparisons among people of different chronological ages. By using mental age alone, for instance, we might assume that an 18-year-old responding at a 20-year-old's level would be demonstrating the

Major Approaches to Intelligence

Approach	Characteristics
Fluid and crystallized intelligence	Fluid intelligence relates to reasoning, memory, and information-processing capabilities; crystallized intelligence relates to information, skills, and strategies learned through experience
Gardner's multiple intelligences	Eight independent forms of intelligence
Information-processing approaches	Intelligence is reflected in the ways people store and use material to solve intellectual tasks
Practical intelligence	Intelligence in terms of nonacademic, career, and personal success
Emotional intelligence	Intelligence that is the basis of empathy for others, self-awareness, and social skills

same degree of intelligence as a 5-year-old answering at a 7-year-old's level, when actually the 5-year-old would be displaying a much greater relative degree of intelligence.

A solution to the problem came in the form of the **intelligence quotient**, or **IQ**, a score that takes into account an individual's mental *and* chronological ages. Historically, the first IQ scores employed the following formula, in which *MA* stands for mental age and *CA* for chronological age:

$$\text{IQ score} = (MA/CA) \times 100$$

Using this formula, we can return to the earlier example of an 18-year-old performing at a mental age of 20 and calculate an IQ score of $(20/18) \times 100 = 111$. In contrast, the 5-year-old performing at a mental age of 7 comes out with a considerably higher IQ score: $(7/5) \times 100 = 140$.

As a bit of trial and error with the formula will show you, anyone who has a mental age equal to his or her chronological age will have an IQ equal to 100. Moreover, people with a mental age that is greater than their chronological age will have IQs that exceed 100.

Although the basic principles behind the calculation of an IQ score still hold, today IQ scores are figured in a different manner and are known as *deviation IQ scores*. First, the average test score for everyone of the same age who takes the test is determined, and that average score is assigned an IQ of 100. Then, with the aid of statistical techniques that calculate the differences (or "deviations") between each score and the average, IQ scores are assigned.

When IQ scores from large numbers of people are plotted on a graph, they form a *bell-shaped curve* (see graph on next page). Approximately two-thirds of all individuals fall within 15 IQ points of the average score of 100. As scores increase or fall beyond that range, the percentage of people in a category falls considerably.

Contemporary IQ Tests Remnants of Binet's original intelligence test are still with us, although the test has been revised significantly. Now in its fifth edition and called the *Stanford-Binet Intelligence Scale,* the test consists of a series of items that vary in nature according to the age of the person being tested (Roid, Nellis, & McLellan, 2003). For example, young children are asked to copy figures or answer questions about everyday activities. Older people are asked to solve analogies, explain proverbs, and describe similarities that underlie sets of words.

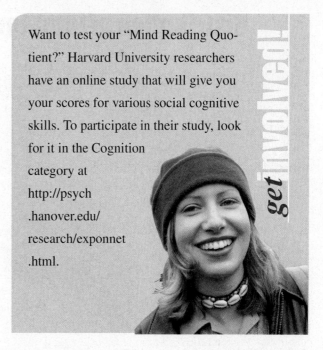

The test is administered orally, and includes both verbal and nonverbal assessments. An examiner begins by finding a mental age level at which a person is able to answer all the questions correctly and then moves on to successively more difficult problems. When a mental age level is reached at which no items can be answered, the test is over. By studying the pattern of correct and incorrect responses, the examiner is able to compute an IQ score for the person being tested.

> **intelligence quotient (IQ)**
> A score that takes into account an individual's mental and chronological ages.

The IQ tests most frequently used in the United States were devised by psychologist David Wechsler and are known as the Wechsler Adult Intelligence Scale–IV, or more commonly the WAIS-IV (for adults), and a children's version, the Wechsler Intelligence Scale for Children–IV, or WISC-IV. Both the WAIS-IV and the WISC-IV measure verbal comprehension, perceptual reasoning, working memory, and processing speed.

The verbal and nonverbal scales include questions of very different types. Verbal tasks consist of more traditional kinds of problems, including vocabulary definition and comprehension of various concepts. In contrast, the nonverbal part involves the timed assembly of small objects and the arrangement of pictures in a logical order. Although an individual's scores on the verbal and nonverbal sections of the test are generally within close range of each other, the scores of a person with a language deficiency or a background of severe environmental deprivation or brain injury may show a relatively large discrepancy between the two sections. By providing separate scores, the WAIS-IV and WISC-IV give a more precise picture of a person's specific abilities compared with other IQ tests (Kaufman & Lichtenberger, 1999, 2000). Since the publication of the WAIS and WISC, the Stanford-Binet has been modified so that it, too, now provides subscores.

STUDY TIP

The traditional formula for IQ scores is the ratio of mental age divided by chronological age, multiplied by 100, but the actual calculation of IQ scores today is done in a more sophisticated manner.

Distribution of Intelligence

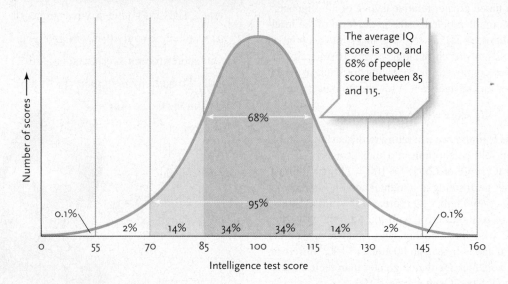

The average IQ score is 100, and 68% of people score between 85 and 115.

Number of scores →

68%

95%

0.1%
2%
14%
34%
34%
14%
2%
0.1%

0   55   70   85   100   115   130   145   160

Intelligence test score

Achievement and Aptitude Tests IQ tests are not the only kind of tests that you might have taken during the course of your schooling. Two other kinds of tests, related to intelligence but intended to measure somewhat different phenomena, are achievement tests and aptitude tests. An **achievement test** is a test designed to determine a person's level of knowledge in a specific subject area. Rather than measuring general ability, as an intelligence test does, an achievement test concentrates on the specific material a person has learned. High school students sometimes take specialized achievement tests in specific areas such as world history and chemistry as a college entrance requirement; lawyers must pass an achievement test (in the form of the bar exam) in order to practice law.

An **aptitude test** is designed to predict a person's ability in a particular area or line of work. Most of us take one or the other of the best-known aptitude tests in the process of pursuing admission to college: the SAT and the ACT. The SAT and ACT are meant to predict how well people will do in college, and the scores have proved in recent years to be moderately correlated with college grades (Hoffman, 2001).

Although in theory the distinction between aptitude tests and achievement tests is precise, it is difficult to develop an aptitude test that does not rely at least in part on past achievement. For example, the SAT has been strongly criticized for being less an aptitude test (predicting college success) than an achievement test (assessing prior performance).

Reliability and Validity of Tests When we use a ruler, we expect to find that it measures an inch in the same

achievement test A test designed to determine a person's level of knowledge in a given subject area.

aptitude test A test designed to predict a person's ability in a particular area or line of work.

reliability The property by which tests measure consistently what they are trying to measure.

way it did the last time we used it. When we weigh ourselves on the bathroom scale, we hope that the variations we see on the scale are due to changes in our weight and not to errors on the part of the scale (unless the change in weight is in an unwanted direction!).

In the same way, we want psychological tests to have **reliability**—to measure consistently what they are trying to measure. Each time a test is administered, a test-taker should achieve the same results—assuming that nothing about the person has changed relevant to what is being measured.

Suppose, for instance, that when you first took the SAT exams, you scored 400 on the verbal section of the test. Then, after taking the test again a few months later, you scored 700. Upon receiving your new score, you might well stop celebrating for a moment to question whether the test is reliable, for it is unlikely that your abilities could have changed enough to raise your score by 300 points (Coyle, 2006).

Sample Items from the Wechsler Adult Intelligence Scale (WAIS-IV)

Name	Goal of Item	Example
Information	Assess general information	Who wrote *Tom Sawyer*?
Comprehension	Assess understanding and evaluation of social norms and past experience	Why is copper often used for electrical wires?
Arithmetic	Assess math reasoning through verbal problems	Three women divided 18 golf balls equally among themselves. How many golf balls did each person receive?
Similarities	Test understanding of how objects or concepts are alike, tapping abstract reasoning	In what way are a circle and a triangle alike?
Figure weights	Test perceptual reasoning	Problems require test-taker to determine which possibility balances the final scale.
Matrix reasoning	Test spatial reasoning	Test-taker must decide which of the five possibilities replaces the question mark and completes the sequence.
Block design item	Test understanding of relationship of parts to whole	Problems require test-taker to reproduce a design in fixed amount of time.

But suppose your score changed hardly at all, and both times you received a score of about 400. You couldn't complain about a lack of reliability. However, if you knew your verbal skills were above average, you might be concerned that the test did not adequately measure what it was supposed to measure. In sum, the question has now become one of validity rather than reliability. A test has **validity** when it actually measures what it is supposed to measure.

Knowing that a test is reliable is no guarantee that it is also valid. For instance, Sir Francis Galton assumed that skull size is related to intelligence, and he was able to measure skull size with great reliability. However, the measure of skull size was not valid—it had nothing to do with intelligence. In this case, then, we have reliability without validity.

Usually, if a test is unreliable, it cannot be valid. Given the assumption that all other factors—motivation to score well, knowledge of the material, health, and so forth—are similar, if a person scores high the first time he or she takes a specific test and low the second time, the test cannot be measuring what it is supposed to measure. Therefore, the test is both unreliable and not valid.

> **validity** The property by which tests actually measure what they are supposed to measure.

Test validity and reliability are prerequisites for accurate assessment of intelligence—as well as for other measurement tasks carried out by psychologists. For example, personality psychologists' measures of personality and social psychologists' measures of attitudes must meet the tests of validity and reliability for the results to be meaningful (Feldt, 2005; Phelps, 2005; Yao, Zhour, & Jiang, 2006).

Suppose you take a test and the psychologist tells you that your score is 300. Is 300 a high score? A low score? Is it average? What do you need to know to answer these questions?

If we assume that a test is both valid and reliable, one additional step is necessary to interpret the meaning of a specific test-taker's score: the establishment of norms. **Norms** are standards of test performance that permit the comparison of one person's score on a test to the scores of others who have taken the same test. For example, a norm permits test-takers to know that they have scored, say, in the top 15% of those who have taken the test previously. Tests for which norms have been developed are known as *standardized tests*. So let's suppose that the average score on the test you took is 450. What does that tell you?

Test designers develop norms by calculating the average score achieved by a specific group of people for whom the test has been designed. Then the test designers can determine the extent to which each person's score differs from the scores of the other individuals who have taken the test in the past and provide future test-takers with a qualitative sense of their performance. An example of this is shown in the graph of intelligence test scores on page 184.

The samples of test-takers who are employed in the establishment of norms are critical to the norming process. The people used to determine norms must be representative of the individuals to whom the test is directed. In other words, say for example all the test-takers were geniuses with IQs over 200. *Their* average score was 450. You might not feel so bad about your score of 300 because they were not a representative group of college students.

VARIATIONS IN INTELLECTUAL ABILITY

Millions of children and adults in the United States have been identified as far enough below average in intelligence that they can be regarded as having a serious deficit. Individuals with low IQs (people with mental retardation or intellectual disabilities) as well as those with unusually high IQs (the intellectually gifted) require special attention if they are to reach their full potential.

Mental Retardation (Intellectual Disabilities)

Mental retardation occurs in 1% to 3% of the population. There is wide variation in the characteristics of people with mental retardation, in part because of the breadth of the definition. **Mental retardation** (or **intellectual disabilities**, as it is increasingly being called) is a disability characterized by significant limitations both in intellectual functioning and in conceptual, social, and practical adaptive skills (American Association of Mental Retardation, 2002).

Although below-average intellectual functioning can be measured in a relatively straightforward manner—using

norms Standards of test performance that permit the comparison of one person's score on a test with the scores of other individuals who have taken the same test.

mental retardation (intellectual disabilities) A condition characterized by significant limitations both in intellectual functioning and in conceptual, social, and practical adaptive skills.

fetal alcohol syndrome A major cause of mental retardation, occurring when the mother uses alcohol during pregnancy.

standard IQ tests—gauging limitations in adaptive behavior is more difficult. Ultimately, this imprecision leads to a lack of uniformity in how experts apply the label *mental retardation*. Furthermore, it has resulted in significant variation in the definition of abilities of people who are categorized as mentally retarded, ranging from those who can be taught to work and function with little special attention to those who virtually cannot be trained and must receive institutional treatment throughout their lives (Detterman, Gabriel, & Ruthsatz, 2000; Greenspan, 2006).

Most people with mental retardation have relatively minor deficits and are classified as having *mild retardation*. These individuals, who have IQ scores ranging from 55 to 69, constitute some 90% of all people with mental retardation. Although their development is typically slower than that of their peers, they can function independently by adulthood and are able to hold jobs and have families of their own (Bates et al., 2001; Murphy, Clegg, & Almack, 2011; Smith, 2006).

At greater levels of retardation—*moderate retardation* (IQs of 40 to 54), *severe retardation* (IQs of 25 to 39), and *profound retardation* (IQs below 25)—the difficulties are more pronounced. For people with moderate retardation, deficits are obvious early, with language and motor skills lagging behind those of peers. Although these individuals can hold simple jobs, they need to have a moderate degree of supervision throughout their lives. Individuals with severe and profound mental retardation are generally unable to function independently and typically require care for their entire lives (Garwick, 2007).

The most common preventable cause of mental retardation is fetal alcohol syndrome, caused by a mother's use of alcohol while pregnant.

What produces mental retardation? In nearly one third of the cases there is an identifiable cause related to biological or environmental factors. The most common preventable cause of retardation is **fetal alcohol syndrome**, produced by a mother's use of alcohol while pregnant. Increasing evidence shows that even small amounts of alcohol intake can produce intellectual deficits. One in every 750 infants is born with fetal alcohol syndrome in the United States (Manning & Hoyme, 2007; Murthy et al., 2009; West & Blake, 2005).

Down syndrome, another major biological cause of mental retardation, results when a person is born with 47 chromosomes instead of the usual 46. In most cases, there is an extra copy of the 21st chromosome, which leads to problems in how the brain and body develop. In other cases of mental retardation, an abnormality occurs in the structure of a chromosome. Birth complications, such as a temporary lack of oxygen, may also cause retardation. In some cases, mental retardation occurs after birth or following a head injury, a

Most individuals with Down syndrome have mild to moderate mental retardation. Like this student at the Mexican School of Down Art, they can be productive members of society.

stroke, or infections such as meningitis (Bittles, Bower, & Hussain, 2007; Hazlett et al., 2011; Plomin, 2005).

However, the majority of cases of mental retardation are classified as **familial retardation**, meaning that no apparent biological defect exists but there is a history of retardation in the family. Whether the family background of retardation is caused by environmental factors, such as extreme continuous poverty leading to malnutrition, or by some underlying genetic factor is usually impossible to determine (Zigler, Finn-Stevenson, & Hall, 2002).

Important advances in the care and treatment of those with retardation have been made in the last three decades. Much of this change was instigated by the Education for All Handicapped Children Act of 1975 (Public Law 94-142). In this federal law, Congress stipulated that people with retardation are entitled to a full education and that they must be educated and trained in the *least restrictive environment*. The law increased the educational opportunities for individuals with mental retardation, facilitating their integration into regular classrooms as much as possible—a process known as *mainstreaming* (Aussilloux & Baghdadli, 2006; Gibb et al., 2007; Katsiyannis, Zhang, & Woodruff, 2005).

The Intellectually Gifted Another group of people—the intellectually gifted—differ from those with average intelligence as much as do individuals with mental retardation, although in a different manner. Accounting for 2%–4% of the population, the **intellectually gifted** have IQ scores greater than 130.

Although the stereotype associated with the gifted suggests that they are awkward, shy social misfits who are unable to get along well with peers, most research indicates that just the opposite is true. The intellectually gifted are most often outgoing, well adjusted, healthy, popular people who are able to do most things better than the average person can (Gottfredson & Deary, 2004; Lubinski et al., 2006; Mueller, 2009).

For example, in a famous study by psychologist Lewis Terman that started in the early 1920s, 1,500 children who had IQ scores above 140 were followed for the rest of their lives. From the start, the members of this group were more physically, academically, and socially capable than their nongifted peers. In addition to doing better in school, they also showed better social adjustment than average. All these advantages paid off in terms of career success: As a group, the gifted received more awards and distinctions, earned higher incomes, and made more contributions in art and literature than typical individuals did. Perhaps most important, they reported greater satisfaction in life than did the nongifted (Campbell, & Feng, 2011; Hegarty, 2007).

Of course, not every member of the group Terman studied was successful. Furthermore, high intelligence is not a homogeneous quality; a person with a high overall IQ is not necessarily gifted in every academic subject but may excel in just one or two. A high IQ is not a universal guarantee of success (Clemons, 2006; Shurkin, 1992; Winner, 2003).

> **familial retardation** Mental retardation in which no apparent biological defect exists, but there is a history of retardation in the family.
>
> **intellectually gifted** The 2% to 4% of the population who have IQ scores greater than 130.

GROUP DIFFERENCES IN INTELLIGENCE

Kwang is often washed with a pleck tied to a

(a) rundel.
(b) flink.
(c) pove.
(d) quirj.

If you found this kind of item on an intelligence test, you would probably complain that the test was totally absurd and had nothing to do with your intelligence or anyone else's—and rightly so. How could anyone be expected to respond to items presented in a language that was so unfamiliar?

STUDY TIP

Remember that in most cases of intellectual disability, there is no apparent biological deficiency, but a history of mental retardation exists in the family.

Yet to some people, even more reasonable questions may appear just as nonsensical. Consider the example of a child raised in a city who is asked about procedures for milking cows, or someone raised in a rural area who is asked about subway ticketing procedures. Obviously, the previous experience of the test-takers would affect their ability to answer correctly. And if such types of questions were included on an IQ test, a critic could rightly contend that the test had more to do with prior experience than with intelligence.

Although IQ tests do not include questions that are so clearly dependent on prior knowledge as questions about cows and subways, the background and experiences of test-takers do have the potential to affect results. In fact, the issue of devising fair intelligence tests that measure knowledge unrelated to culture and family background and experience is central to explaining an important and persistent finding: Members of certain racial and cultural groups consistently score lower on traditional intelligence tests than do members of other groups. For example, as a group, blacks tend to average 10 to 15 IQ points lower than whites. Does this variation reflect a true difference in intelligence, or are the questions biased in regard to the kinds of knowledge they test? Clearly, if whites perform better because of their greater familiarity with the kind of information that is being tested, their higher IQ scores are not necessarily an indication that they are more intelligent than members of other groups (Fagan & Holland, 2007; Morgan, Marsiske, & Whitfield, 2008; Templer & Arikawa, 2006).

There is good reason to believe that some standardized IQ tests contain elements that discriminate against minority-group members whose experiences differ from those of the white majority. In other words, people who tend to do better on IQ tests have more in common culturally with the people who created the tests. Consider the question "What should you do if another child grabbed your hat and ran off with it?" Most white middle-class children answer that they would tell an adult, and this response is scored as correct. However, a reasonable response might be to chase the person and fight to get the hat back, the answer that is chosen by many urban black children—but one that is scored as incorrect (Aiken, 1997; Kamin, 2006; Miller-Jones, 1991; Reynolds & Ramsay, 2003).

culture-fair IQ test A test that does not discriminate against the members of any minority group.

heritability A measure of the degree to which a characteristic is related to genetic, inherited factors.

NATURE, NURTURE, AND IQ

In an attempt to produce a **culture-fair IQ test**, one that does not discriminate against the members of any minority group, psychologists have tried to devise test items that assess experiences common to all cultures or emphasize questions that do not require language usage. However, test-makers have found this difficult to do, because past experiences, attitudes, and values almost always affect respondents' answers.

For example, children raised in Western cultures group things on the basis of what they *are* (such as putting *dog* and *fish* into the category of *animal*). In contrast, members of the Kpelle tribe in Africa see intelligence demonstrated by grouping things according to what they *do* (grouping *fish* with *swim*). Similarly, children in the United States asked to memorize the position of objects on a chessboard perform better than do African children living in remote villages if household objects familiar to the U.S. children are used. But if rocks are used instead of household objects, the African children do better. In short, it is difficult to produce a test that is truly culture-fair (Sandoval et al., 1998; Serpell, 2000; Valencia & Suzuki, 2003).

The efforts of psychologists to produce culture-fair measures of intelligence relate to the lingering controversy over differences in intelligence between members of minority and majority groups. In attempting to identify whether there are real intellectual differences between such groups, psychologists have had to confront the broader issue of determining the relative contribution to intelligence of genetic factors (heredity) and experience (environment)—the nature-nurture issue that is one of the basic issues of psychology.

Richard Herrnstein, a psychologist, and Charles Murray, a sociologist, fanned the flames of the debate with the publication of their book *The Bell Curve* in the mid-1990s (Herrnstein & Murray, 1994). They argued that an analysis of IQ differences between whites and blacks demonstrated that although environmental factors played a role, there were also basic genetic differences between the two races. They based their argument on a number of findings. For instance, on average, whites score 15 points higher than do blacks on traditional IQ tests even when socioeconomic status (SES) is taken into account. According to Herrnstein and Murray, middle- and upper-SES blacks score lower than do middle- and upper-SES whites, just as lower-SES blacks score lower on average than do lower-SES whites. Intelligence differences between blacks and whites, they concluded, could not be attributed to environmental differences alone.

Moreover, intelligence in general shows a high degree of **heritability**, a measure of the degree to which a characteristic can be attributed to genetic, inherited factors (for example, Miller & Penke, 2007; Petrill, 2005; Plomin, 2009). The closer the genetic link between two related people, the greater the correspondence of IQ scores. For example, the correlation for spouses, who are geneti-

Efforts to produce culture-fair measures of intelligence relate to the lingering controversy over differences in intelligence between members of minority and majority groups.

From Table 1 (p. 410) from Henderson, N. D. (1982). Human behavior genetics. *Annual Review of Psychology*, 33, 403–440. Copyright © 1982. Reproduced with permission of Annual Reviews, Inc. in the format Textbook via Copyright Clearance Center.

Relationship between IQ and Closeness of Genetic Relationship

Relationship	Genetic overlap	Rearing	Correlation
Monozygotic (identical) twins	100%	Together	0.86
Dizygotic (fraternal) twins	50%	Together	0.62
Siblings	50%	Together	0.41
Siblings	50%	Apart	0.24
Parent-child	50%	Together	0.35
Parent-child	50%	Apart	0.31
Adoptive parent-child	0%	Together	0.16
Unrelated children	0%	Together	0.25
Spouses	0%	Apart	0.29

The difference between these two correlations shows the impact of the environment.

The relatively low correlation for unrelated children raised together shows the importance of genetic factors.

cally unrelated and have been reared apart, is relatively low, whereas the correlation for identical twins reared together is high. Using data such as these, Herrnstein and Murray argued that differences between races in IQ scores were largely caused by genetically based differences in intelligence.

Many psychologists strongly refuted the arguments laid out in *The Bell Curve*. One criticism is that even when attempts are made to hold socioeconomic conditions constant, wide variations remain among individual households. Furthermore, no one can convincingly assert that the living conditions of blacks and whites are identical even when their socioeconomic status is similar. In addition, as we discussed earlier, there is reason to believe that traditional IQ tests may discriminate against lower-SES urban blacks by asking for information pertaining to experiences they are unlikely to have had (American Psy-

chological Association Task Force on Intelligence, 1996; Hall, 2002; Horn, 2002; Nisbett, 2007).

Moreover, blacks who are raised in economically enriched environments have similar IQ scores to whites in comparable environments. For example, a study by Sandra Scarr and Richard Weinberg (1976) examined black children who had been adopted at an early age by white middle-class families of above-average intelligence. The IQ scores of those children averaged 106—about 15 points above the average IQ scores of unadopted black children in the study. Other research shows that the racial gap in IQ narrows considerably after a college education, and cross-cultural data demonstrate that when racial gaps exist in other cultures, it is the economically disadvantaged groups that typically have lower scores. In short, the evidence that genetic factors play the major role in determining racial differences in IQ is not compelling (Cahill, 2011; Fagan & Holland, 2007; Nisbett, 2009; Sternberg, Grigorenko, & Kidd, 2005).

Furthermore, drawing comparisons between different races on any dimension, including IQ scores, is an imprecise, potentially misleading, and often fruitless venture. By far, the greatest discrepancies in IQ scores occur among all *individuals*, not among different racial/ethnic *groups* of people. There are blacks who score high on IQ tests and whites who score low, just as there are whites who score high and blacks who score low. For the concept of intelligence to aid in the betterment of society, we must examine how *individuals* perform, not the groups to which someone decides they belong (Angoff, 1988; Fagan & Holland, 2002, 2007).

The more critical question to ask is not whether hereditary or environmental factors primarily underlie intelligence, but whether there is anything we can do to maximize the intellectual development of each individual. If we can find ways to do this, we will be able to make changes in the environment—which may take the form of enriched home and school environments—that can lead each person to reach his or her potential.

PSYCH think

connect

WWW.MCGRAWHILLCONNECT.COM/PSYCHOLOGY

Gardner's Theory of Multiple Intelligences

> > > Do you think there is any way to develop a standardized test that accurately measures all types of intelligence?

Take the PsychSmart challenge! Discover your multiple intelligences. From chapter 7 in your ebook, select the *Exercises* tab. Then select "Gardner's Multiple Intelligences." After doing the exercise, answer Question 12 on p. 191 to test your mastery of the theory of multiple intelligences.

STUDY **TIP**

Remember that there is much more variation in IQ scores among individuals than in scores among different racial/ethnic groups.

For REVIEW >>

- **What is thinking?**

  Thinking is the manipulation of mental representations of information. Thinking transforms such representations into novel and different forms, permitting people to answer questions, solve problems, and reach goals. Mental images, concepts, and prototypes enable us to think about and understand the complex world in which we live. (pp. 164–166)

- **How do people approach and solve problems?**

  Problem solving typically involves three stages: preparation, production of solutions, and evaluation of solutions. Strategies for solving problems include simple trial and error and, for more complex problems, algorithms and heuristics. Factors that hinder effective problem solving include mental set, inappropriate use of algorithms and heuristics, and confirmation bias. (pp. 166–173)

- **How does language develop?**

  Infants understand their native language before they begin speaking it. Babbling is the first stage of language production, followed by one-word utterances. After 1 year of age, children use two-word combinations, increase their vocabulary, and use telegraphic speech. By age 5, acquisition of language rules is relatively complete. Learning theorists suggest that language is acquired through reinforcement and conditioning. In contrast, the nativist approach suggests that an innate language-acquisition device guides language development. The interactionist approach argues that language development stems from a combination of genetically determined predispositions for language and environmental circumstances. (pp. 173–177)

- **How is intelligence defined and conceptualized?**

  Because intelligence can take many forms, defining it is challenging. One commonly accepted view is that intelligence is the capacity to understand the world, think rationally, and use resources effectively when faced with challenges. Among the various conceptions of intelligence proposed by researchers are fluid and crystallized intelligence; Gardner's eight spheres of intelligence; information-processing models; practical intelligence; and emotional intelligence. (pp. 177–182)

- **What are the major approaches to measuring intelligence in the West, and what do intelligence tests measure?**

  Intelligence tests have traditionally compared a person's mental age and chronological age to yield an IQ, or intelligence quotient, score. Specific tests of intelligence include the Stanford-Binet test, the Wechsler Adult Intelligence Scale–IV (WAIS-IV), and the Wechsler Intelligence Scale for Children–IV (WISC-IV). Achievement tests and aptitude tests are other types of standardized tests. (pp. 181–186)

Pop Quiz

1. _____ are mental groupings of similar objects, events, or people.

2. The purpose of the heuristics activity was to
   a. teach me how to use the best heuristic for a given situation.
   b. help me remember the different types of heuristics and how they work.
   c. show me that I use heuristics without realizing it.
   d. motivate me to learn how to use as many heuristcs as I can.

3. Solving a problem by trying to reduce the difference between the current state and the goal state is known as a _____.

4. Thinking of an object only in terms of its typical use is known as _____ _____. A broader, related tendency for old problem-solving patterns to persist is known as a _____ _____.

5. Match the component of grammar with its definition.
   a. rules showing how words can be combined into sentences
   b. rules governing the meaning of words and sentences
   c. the study of the sound units that affect speech
   _____ 1. syntax
   _____ 2. phonology
   _____ 3. semantics

6. _____ _____ refers to the phenomenon in which young children omit non-essential portions of sentences.

7. A child knows that adding -ed to certain words puts them in the past tense. As a result, instead of saying "He came," the child says "He comed." This is an example of _____.

8. _____ is a measure of intelligence that takes into account a person's chronological and mental ages.

9. _____ tests predict a person's ability in a specific area; _____ tests determine the specific level of knowledge in an area.

10. _____ _____ _____ is the most common preventable cause of mental retardation.

11. A(n) _____ - _____ test tries to use only questions appropriate to all the people taking the test.

12. According to the exercise on multiple intelligences, one practical application of Gardner's theory has been
   a. an increased interest in the performing arts.
   b. the assessment of different intelligences for each child so that teaching can be individually tailored to each child's strengths.
   c. the assessment of each type of intelligence in order to help people figure out what career will best suit them.
   d. the use of more varied teaching techniques.

8

MOTIVATION

FALLING OFF THE DIET WAGON

When Kirstie Alley stepped on the scale for the first time in 15 months, she had a hunch that it wouldn't be pretty. "I thought I weighed 190, but I got on the scale and started screaming," recalls Alley. "It said 228 lbs., which is my highest weight ever." But looking back, Alley, 58, is hardly shocked that her body . . . had ballooned beyond 200 lbs. yet again. . . . She had not worked out and even banished her gym equipment to the garage. As for her diet, her small, low-calorie portions gave way to Chinese takeout and pasta drenched in butter. "I fell off the horse," says the 5' 8" star . . . I just sort of went wild."[viii]

Actress Kirstie Alley's notorious up-and-down battle with obesity—at one point she dieted down to 145 pounds, only to gain back the weight—is just one very public example of the struggles that millions of people have maintaining an appropriate weight. But why do the natural mechanisms that regulate our other bodily functions often fail when it comes to regulating our eating behavior? Psychologists specializing in the study motivation might ask this kind of question. They seek to discover the desired goals—the motives—that guide behavior. For example, loneliness might motivate us to spend time with friends.

While motivation concerns the forces that direct future behavior, emotion pertains to the feelings we experience throughout our lives. The study of emotions focuses on our internal experiences at any given moment. All of us feel a variety of emotions: happiness at succeeding at a difficult task, sadness over the death of a loved one, anger at being treated unfairly. Psychologists who research emotions have developed a number of different theories about the nature of emotions and how they function.

We begin this chapter by examining the major conceptions of motivation and discussing how different motives and needs jointly affect behavior. We consider motives that are biologically based and universal in the animal kingdom, such as hunger, as well as motives that appear to be unique to humans, such as the need for achievement.

We then turn to emotions. We consider the roles and the functions that emotions play in people's lives and discuss several theoretical approaches that attempt to explain how and why people understand and experience their emotions. Finally, we look at how nonverbal behavior communicates emotions.

AND EMOTION

- How do our needs guide and energize behavior?
- What factors affect hunger and sexual behavior?
- What are our needs for achievement? For affiliation? For power?
- Does everyone experience emotions in the same way?
- How do we communicate our feelings nonverbally?

>> Explaining Motivation

In just a moment, 27-year-old Aron Ralston's life changed. An 800-pound boulder dislodged in a narrow canyon where Ralston was hiking in an isolated Utah canyon, pinning his lower arm to the ground.

For the next five days, Ralston lay in the rugged and isolated canyon, unable to escape. An experienced climber who had search-and-rescue training, he had ample time to consider his options. He tried unsuccessfully to chip away at the rock, and he rigged up ropes and pulleys around the boulder in a vain effort to move it.

Finally, out of water and nearly dehydrated, Ralston reasoned there was only one option left, short of dying. In acts of incredible bravery, Ralston broke two bones in his forearm, applied a tourniquet, and used a dull pocketknife to amputate his arm beneath the elbow.

Freed from his entrapment, Ralston climbed down from where he had been pinned and then hiked five miles, where a Dutch family gave him aid and flagged down a rescue helicopter (Cox, 2003; Lofholm, 2003).

Aron Ralston had to amputate his own right arm with a dull knife in order to free himself from a boulder and escape Blue John Canyon. Where did he find the motivation?

motivation The factors that direct and energize the behavior of humans and other organisms.

instincts Inborn patterns of behavior that are biologically determined rather than learned.

What motivation lay behind Ralston's profound courage?

To answer questions like this, psychologists employ the concept of **motivation**, the factors that direct and energize

the behavior of humans and other organisms. Motivation has biological, cognitive, and social aspects, and the complexity of the concept has led psychologists to develop a variety of approaches. All of these theoretical perspectives seek to explain the energy that guides people's behavior in specific directions.

INSTINCT APPROACHES

When psychologists first tried to explain motivation, they turned to **instincts**, inborn patterns of behavior that are biologically determined rather than learned. According to instinct approaches to motivation, people and animals are born preprogrammed with sets of behaviors essential to their survival. Those instincts provide the energy that channels behavior in appropriate directions.

By definition, instinctual behaviors are rigid patterns of behavior that every member of a species (or all females and all males in the case of sexual behavior) will carry out in exactly the same way. These behaviors occur in an unchanging sequence that cannot be altered and they must be exactly the same. Salmon provide a famous example: They all choose practically the same moment to swim back to the river where they were born. They then swim upstream to reproduce, even though these behaviors result in their death. Humans, on the other hand, don't do *anything* in exactly the same way, even when we try (Bernard, 1924; Hankins, 1925; & LaPierre, 1938). Eating is an example of something humans do that is similar to an instinct. First, we chew. Then, we swallow. But even this sequence

The seasonal migration of birds is instinctual behavior. In contrast, the motivation underlying human behavior is complex and can be difficult to explain.

can be altered. For example, when we swallow an aspirin, we don't necessarily chew it first.

A major problem with trying to use the concept of instinct to explain motivation is that human behaviors are far more complex than those of many other animal species, and we don't appear to have any true instincts. As a result, newer explanations have replaced conceptions of motivation based on instincts.

DRIVE-REDUCTION APPROACHES

After rejecting instinct theory, some psychologists proposed simple drive-reduction theories of motivation to take its place (Hull, 1943). **Drive-reduction approaches** suggest that a lack of some basic biological requirement such as water produces a drive to obtain that requirement (in this case, the thirst drive).

In drive-reduction theories, **drive** is defined as motivational tension, or arousal, that energizes behavior to fulfill a need. Many basic drives, such as hunger, thirst, sleep, and sex, are related to biological needs of the body or of the species as a whole. These are called *primary drives*. Primary drives contrast with secondary drives, in which behavior fulfills no obvious biological need. In *secondary drives*, prior experience and learning bring about needs. For instance, some people have strong needs to achieve academically and professionally. We can say that their achievement need is reflected in a secondary drive that motivates their behavior (McKinley et al., 2004; Seli, 2007).

We usually try to satisfy a primary drive by reducing the underlying need. For example, we become hungry after not eating for a few hours and may raid the refrigerator, especially if the next scheduled meal is not imminent. If the weather turns cold, we put on extra clothing or raise the setting on the thermostat to keep warm. If our bodies need liquids to function properly, we experience thirst and seek out water.

Although drive-reduction theories provide a good description of how primary drives motivate behavior, they cannot address behaviors for which the goal is not to reduce a drive but rather to maintain or even to increase the level of excitement or arousal. For instance, some behaviors seem to be

motivated by nothing more than curiosity, such as rushing down the street to watch firefighters investigate an alarm. Similarly, many people pursue thrilling activities such as riding a roller coaster or steering a raft down the rapids of a river. Such behaviors contradict the idea that people seek to reduce all drives, as drive-reduction approaches would indicate (Begg & Langley, 2001; Rosenbloom & Wolf, 2002).

Both curiosity and thrill-seeking behavior, then, shed doubt on drive-reduction approaches as a complete explanation for motivation. In both cases, rather than seeking to reduce an underlying drive, people appear to be motivated to increase their overall level of stimulation and activity. To explain this phenomenon, psychologists have devised yet a third theoretical perspective: arousal approaches to motivation.

What motivates people to engage in thrill-seeking behavior, such as skydiving?

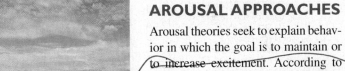

drive-reduction approaches to motivation Theories suggesting that a lack of a basic biological requirement such as water produces a drive to obtain that requirement (in this case, the thirst drive).

drive Motivational tension, or arousal, that energizes behavior to fulfill a need.

arousal approaches to motivation The belief that we try to maintain certain levels of stimulation and activity, increasing or reducing them as necessary.

AROUSAL APPROACHES

Arousal theories seek to explain behavior in which the goal is to maintain or to increase excitement. According to **arousal approaches to motivation**, each person tries to maintain a certain level of stimulation and activity. As with the drive-reduction model, this model suggests that if our stimulation and activity levels become too high, we try to reduce them. But, in contrast to the drive-reduction model, the arousal model also suggests that if levels of stimulation and activity are too low, we will try to increase them by seeking stimulation.

People vary widely in the optimal level of arousal they seek out, with some people looking for especially high levels of arousal. For example, people who participate in daredevil sports, high-stakes gamblers, and criminals who pull off high-risk robberies may be exhibiting a particularly high need for arousal (Cavenett & Nixon, 2006; Zuckerman, 2002; Zuckerman & Kuhlman, 2000).

Do You Seek Out Sensation?

How much stimulation do you crave in your everyday life? You will have an idea after you complete the following questionnaire, which lists some items from a scale designed to assess your sensation-seeking tendencies. Circle either *A* or *B* in each pair of statements. If neither *A* nor *B* accurately describes you, choose the one that better describes your inclination. Try to answer all items.

1. A I would like a job that requires a lot of traveling.
   B I would prefer a job in one location.
2. A I am invigorated by a brisk, cold day.
   B I can't wait to get indoors on a cold day.
3. A I get bored seeing the same old faces.
   B I like the comfortable familiarity of everyday friends.
4. A I would prefer living in an ideal society in which everyone was safe, secure, and happy.
   B I would have preferred living in the unsettled days of our history.
5. A I sometimes like to do things that are a little frightening.
   B A sensible person avoids activities that are dangerous.
6. A I would not like to be hypnotized.
   B I would like to have the experience of being hypnotized.
7. A The most important goal of life is to live it to the fullest and to experience as much as possible.
   B The most important goal of life is to find peace and happiness.
8. A I would like to try parachute jumping.
   B I would never want to try jumping out of a plane, with or without a parachute.
9. A I enter cold water gradually, giving myself time to get used to it.
   B I like to dive or jump right into the ocean or a cold pool.
10. A When I go on a vacation, I prefer the comfort of a good room and bed.
    B When I go on a vacation, I prefer the change of camping out.
11. A I prefer people who are emotionally expressive, even if they are a bit unstable.
    B I prefer people who are calm and even-tempered.
12. A A good painting should shock or jolt the senses.
    B A good painting should give one a feeling of peace and security.
13. A People who ride motorcycles must have some kind of unconscious need to hurt themselves.
    B I would like to drive or ride a motorcycle.

compare with those of others.
your sensation-seeking tendencies
give you an indication of how
Still, the questionnaire will at least
seeking scores tend to decrease.
people get older, their sensation-
seeking tendencies. Moreover, as
rough estimate of your sensation-
questionnaire provides only a
Keep in mind that this

12–13 very high
10–11 high
6–9 average
4–5 low
0–2 very low sensation seeking

the following scoring key:
number of points and then use
your total score by adding up the
7A, 8A, 9B, 10B, 11A, 12A, 13B. Find
responses: 1A, 2A, 3A, 4B, 5A, 6B,
point for each of the following
Scoring: Give yourself one

"Do you seek out sensation?"
questionnaire from Marvin Zuckerman,
"The Search for High Sensation,"
Psychology Today, February 1978,
pp. 30–46. Reprinted with permission from
Psychology Today magazine, (Copyright
© 1978 Sussex Publishers, LLC.).

INCENTIVE APPROACHES

When a luscious dessert appears on the table after a filling meal, its appeal has little or nothing to do with the biological need for more food or the maintenance of arousal. Rather, if we choose to eat the dessert, such behavior is motivated by the external stimulus of the dessert itself, which acts as an anticipated reward. This reward, in motivational terms, is an *incentive.*

Incentive approaches to motivation suggest that motivation stems from the desire to obtain valued external goals, or incentives. In this view, the desirable properties of external stimuli—whether grades, money, affection, or food—account for a person's motivation.

Although the theory seeks to explain why we may succumb to an incentive (such as a mouthwatering dessert) even though we lack internal cues (such as hunger), it is an incomplete theory because it does not explain why we sometimes seek out food, for example, when no food (incentive) is available. In other words, we sometimes behave as if we're being motivated only by biological drives. Consequently, many psychologists believe that the internal drives proposed by drive-reduction theory work in tandem with the external incentives of incentive theory to "push" and "pull" behavior, respectively. Thus, at the same time that we seek to satisfy our underlying hunger needs (the push of drive-reduction theory), we may be drawn to food that appears very appetizing (the pull of incentive theory). Rather than contradicting each other, then, drives and incentives may work together in motivating behavior (Berridge, 2004; Jeffrey & Adomdza, 2011; Lowery, Fillingim, & Wright, 2003; Pinel, Assanand, & Lehman, 2000).

incentive approaches to motivation Theories suggesting that motivation stems from the desire to obtain valued external goals, or incentives.

COGNITIVE APPROACHES

Cognitive approaches to motivation suggest that motivation is a product of our thoughts, expectations, and goals—our cognitions. For instance, the degree to which students are motivated to prepare for a test is based, in part, on the expectation of how well studying will pay off in terms of a good grade.

Cognitive theories of motivation draw a key distinction between intrinsic and extrinsic motivation. Intrinsic motivation causes us to par-

PSYCH think

> > > Which approaches to motivation can you use to improve your own motivation to study and learn? How can we adjust school policies to increase students' motivation to succeed?

ticipate in an activity for our own enjoyment rather than for any concrete, tangible reward that it will bring us. In contrast, extrinsic motivation causes us to do something for money, a grade, or some other concrete, tangible reward. For example, when a physician works long hours because she loves medicine, intrinsic motivation is prompting her; if she works hard to make a lot of money, extrinsic motivation underlies her efforts (Lepper, Corpus, & Iyengar, 2005; Shaikholeslami & Khayyer, 2006; Finkelstien, 2009).

We are more apt to persevere, work harder, and produce work of higher quality when motivation for a task is intrinsic rather than extrinsic. In fact, in some cases providing rewards for desirable behavior (thereby increasing extrinsic motivation) actually may decrease intrinsic motivation (Henderlong & Lepper, 2002; James, 2005; Grant, 2008).

MASLOW'S HIERARCHY OF NEEDS

What do Eleanor Roosevelt, Abraham Lincoln, and Albert Einstein have in common? The common thread, according to a model of motivation devised by

---

Self-actualization is an ongoing process of self-fulfillment in which people realize their highest potentials, each in his or her own unique way.

---

psychologist Abraham Maslow, is that each of them fulfilled the highest levels of motivational needs underlying human behavior.

Maslow's model places motivational needs in a hierarchy and suggests that before more sophisticated, higher-order needs can be met, certain primary needs must be satisfied (Maslow, 1970, 1987).

Using a pyramid to represent the model, Maslow placed the more fundamental, lower-order needs at the base and the higher-level needs at the top. For a specific higher-order need to guide behavior, a person must first fulfill the more basic needs in the hierarchy.

The most basic needs in Maslow's model are primary physiological drives: needs for water, food, sleep, sex, and the like. Safety needs come next in the hierarchy; Maslow suggests that people need a relatively safe, secure environment in order to function effectively. After meeting these basic lower-order needs, a person can consider satisfying higher-order needs, such as the needs for love and a sense of belonging, esteem, and self-actualization.

Imagine, for a moment, that you live in a war-torn country. Your village experiences the rapid fire of automatic weapons on a fairly regular basis, your water has been poisoned, and

cognitive approaches to motivation Theories suggesting that motivation is a product of people's thoughts and expectations—their cognitions.

Higher-order needs

Maslow's Hierarchy of Needs

Self-actualization
A process of self-fulfillment

Esteem
The need to develop a sense of self-worth

Love and belongingness
The need to obtain and give affection

Safety needs
The need for a safe and secure environment

Physiological needs
The primary drives: needs for water, food, sleep, and sex

Lower-order needs

Source: After Maslow, 1970.

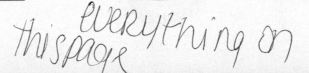

your crops have been destroyed. Which of the following are you going to be most motivated to do: find a place to be safe from the bullets, find true love, or get a haircut? Maslow's theory predicts that we would seek safety before we could focus on higher–level needs such as love and self-esteem.

Love and belongingness needs include the needs to obtain and to give affection and to be a contributing member of some group or society. After fulfilling these needs, a person strives for esteem. In Maslow's thinking, esteem relates to the need to develop a sense of self-worth by recognizing that others know and value one's competence.

Once these four sets of needs have been fulfilled—no easy task—a person can strive for the highest-level need, self-actualization. **Self-actualization** is an ongoing process of self-fulfillment in which people realize their highest potentials, each in his or her own unique way. The important thing is that people feel at ease with themselves and satisfied that they are using their talents to the fullest (Laas, 2006; Piechowski, 2003; Reiss & Havercamp, 2005).

Although research has not validated the specific order of Maslow's stages, and although it is difficult to measure self-actualization objectively, Maslow's model is important for two reasons: It highlights the complexity of human needs, and it emphasizes the idea that until more basic biological needs are met satisfactorily, people will be relatively unconcerned with higher-order needs. So if people are starving, their first interest will be in obtaining food (Hanley & Abell, 2002; Ojha & Pramanick, 2009; Samantaray, Srivastava, & Misra, 2002).

Maslow's hierarchy of needs has spawned other approaches to motivation. For example, Edward Deci and Richard Ryan (2008) have considered human needs in terms of psychological well-being. They suggest in their *self-determination theory* that people have the three basic

self-actualization A process of self-fulfillment in which people realize their highest potential, each in his or her own unique way.

Where on Maslow's pyramid would you place these Jain monks, whose spiritual beliefs require an ascetic lifestyle, including a limited diet and detachment from people and possessions?

needs of competence, autonomy, and relatedness. Competence is the need to produce desired outcomes, while autonomy is the perception that we have control over our own lives. Finally, relatedness is the need to be involved in close, warm relationships with others. In the view of self-determination theory, these three psychological needs are innate and universal across cultures, and they are as essential as basic biological needs (Jang et al., 2009; Nansteenkiste et al., 2009).

APPLYING MOTIVATION APPROACHES

The various theories of motivation provide us with several different perspectives. Which provides the fullest account of motivation? Actually, many of the approaches we've considered are complementary, rather than contradictory. Employing more than one approach can help us understand motivation in a particular instance.

Consider, for example, Aron Ralston's hiking accident, described earlier. His interest in climbing in an isolated and potentially dangerous area may be explained by arousal

STUDY **TIP**

Review the distinctions between the different explanations for motivation (instinct, drive reduction, arousal, incentive, cognitive, and Maslow's hierarchy of needs).

approaches to motivation. From a cognitive perspective, we recognize his careful consideration of various strategies to extricate himself from the boulder. Maslow might point out that his basic needs were not being met while he was trapped, so he made choices based on the motivation to satisfy food, water, and shelter needs.

In short, applying multiple approaches to motivation in a given situation provides a broader understanding than we might obtain with a single approach. We'll see this again when we consider specific motives—such as the needs for food, achievement, affiliation, and power—and draw on several of the theories for the fullest account of what motivates behavior.

From the perspective of ...

A PAROLE OFFICER How could you apply Maslow's hierarchy of needs to help your parolees motivate themselves to find ways to live crime-free?

How might different motivation approaches explain a young person's decision to volunteer for military service?

>> Human Needs and Motivation

In the United States, approximately one in four girls and one in ten boys suffer from eating and weight control disorders (Austin, Ziyadeh, Forman, Prokop, Keliher, & Jacobs, 2008). These disorders, which usually appear during adolescence, can bring about extraordinary weight loss and other forms of physical deterioration. Extremely dangerous, they sometimes result in death.

Why are some people subject to such disordered eating, which revolves around the motivation to avoid weight gain at all costs? And why do so many other people engage in overeating, which leads to obesity? To answer such questions as these, we must consider some of the specific needs that underlie behavior (Milyavskaya & Koestner, 2011).

HUNGER AND EATING

Two thirds of the people in the United States are overweight, and the rest of the world is not far behind: In 2008, the World Health Organization estimated that 1.5 billion people worldwide were overweight and 1 in 3 of those were obese (WHO, 2011). Overweight is defined using a measure called the Body Mass Index (BMI), which is based on a ratio of weight to height. People with a BMI of 25 or greater are considered overweight. **Obesity** is defined as having a BMI greater than or equal to 30. According to the World Health Organization, worldwide obesity has reached epidemic proportions, accompanied by increases in heart disease, diabetes, cancer, and premature deaths (Hill, Catenacci, & Wyatt, 2005; Stephenson & Banet-Weiser, 2007).

> **obesity** Body weight with a BMI greater than or equal to 30.

Did you know?

Diet foods and diet soft drinks can work *against* your diet! Research suggests that consumption of artificial sweeteners may lead to more calorie consumption and weight gain (Swithers & Davidson, 2008).

Biological Factors in the Regulation of Hunger In contrast to human beings, other species are unlikely to become obese. Internal mechanisms regulate not only the quantity of food they take in but also the kind of food they desire. For example, rats that have been deprived of particular foods seek out alternatives that contain the specific nutrients their diet is lacking, and many species, given the choice of a wide variety of foods, select a well-balanced diet (Bouchard & Bray, 1996; Jones & Corp, 2003; Woods et al., 2000).

Complex mechanisms tell us whether we require food or should stop eating. It's not just a matter of an empty stomach causing hunger pangs and a full one alleviating those pangs. (Even individuals who have had their stomachs removed still experience the sensation of hunger.) One important factor is changes in the chemical composition of the blood. For instance, changes in levels of glucose, a kind of sugar, regulate feelings of hunger. The hormone insulin leads the body to store excess sugar in the blood as fats and carbohydrates. The hormone *ghrelin* communicates to the brain feelings of hunger. The production of ghrelin increases according to meal schedules, as well as the sight or smell of food, producing the feeling that tells us we're hungry and should eat (Kojima & Kangawa, 2008; Teff, 2007; Wren & Bloom, 2007).

The brain's *hypothalamus* monitors glucose levels. Increasing evidence suggests that the hypothalamus carries the primary responsibility for monitoring food intake. Injury to the hypothalamus has radical consequences for eating

Find Your Body Mass Index

To calculate your body mass index, follow these steps:

1. Indicate your weight in pounds: _____ pounds
2. Indicate your height in inches: _____ inches
3. Divide your weight (item 1) by your height (item 2), and write the outcome here: _____
4. Divide the result above (item 3) by your height (item 2), and write the outcome here: _____
5. Multiply the number above by 703, and write the product here: _____ This is your body mass index.

Example: For a person who weighs 210 pounds and who is 6 feet tall, divide 210 pounds by 72 inches, which equals 2.917. Then divide 2.917 by 72 inches (item 3), which yields .041. Multiplying .041 (from item 4) by 703 yields a BMI of 28.5.

Interpretation:

• Underweight = less than 18.5
• Normal weight = 18.5–24.9
• Overweight = 25–29.9
• Obesity = BMI of 30 or greater

Keep in mind that a BMI greater than 25 may or may not be due to excess body fat. For example, professional athletes may have little fat but weigh more than the average person, because they have greater muscle mass.

---

behavior, depending on the site of the injury. For example, rats whose *lateral hypothalamus* is damaged may literally starve to death. They refuse food when it is offered, and unless they are force-fed, they eventually die. Rats with an injury to the *ventromedial hypothalamus* display the opposite problem: extreme overeating. Rats with this injury can increase in weight by as much as 400%. Similar phenomena occur in humans who have tumors of the hypothalamus (Fedeli et al., 2009; Seymour, 2006; Woods & Seeley, 2002).

weight set point The particular level of weight that the body strives to maintain.

metabolism The rate at which food is converted to energy and expended by the body.

Although the important role that the hypothalamus plays in regulating food intake is clear, the exact way this organ operates is still unclear. One hypothesis suggests that injury to the hypothalamus affects the **weight set point**, or the particular level of weight that the body strives to maintain, which in turn regulates food intake. Acting as a kind of internal weight thermostat, the hypothalamus calls for either greater or less food intake (Berthoud, 2002; Capaldi, 1996; Woods et al., 2000).

In most cases, the hypothalamus does a good job. Even people who are not deliberately monitoring their weight show only minor weight fluctuations in spite of substantial day-to-day variations in how much they eat and exercise. However, injury to the

> People with a high metabolic rate can eat virtually as much as they want without gaining weight, whereas others, with low metabolism, may eat literally half as much yet gain weight readily.

hypothalamus can alter the weight set point, and a person then is motivated to meet the internal goal by increasing or decreasing food consumption. Even temporary exposure to certain drugs can alter the weight set point (Cabanac & Frankhan, 2002; Hallschmid et al., 2004; Khazaal et al., 2008).

Genetic factors determine the weight set point, at least in part. People seem destined, through heredity, to have a particular **metabolism**, the rate at which food is converted to energy and expended by the body. People with a high metabolic rate can eat virtually as much as they want without gaining weight, whereas others, with low metabolism, may eat literally half as much yet gain weight readily (Jequier, 2002; Westerterp, 2006).

Social Factors in Eating You're having dinner with relatives at your aunt's home and you've just emptied your plate. You feel completely stuffed. Suddenly your aunt passes you the roast beef platter and encourages you to have another helping. Even though you are full and don't like roast beef very much, you take another serving and eat it all.

Along with internal biological factors, external social factors, based on societal rules and on what psychologists have learned about appropriate eating behavior, also play an important role in when and how much we eat. Take, for example, the simple fact that some people customarily eat breakfast, lunch, and dinner at approximately the same times every day. Because they tend to eat on schedule every day, they feel hungry as the usual hour approaches, sometimes quite independently of what their internal cues are telling them. Similarly, they put roughly the same amount of food on their plates every day, even though the amount of exercise they may have had, and consequently their need for energy replenishment, varies from day to day.

Other social factors relate to our eating behavior as well. Some of us head for the refrigerator after a difficult day, seeking solace in a pint of Heath Bar Crunch ice cream. Why? Perhaps when we were children, our parents gave us food when we were upset. Eventually, we may have learned, through the basic mechanisms of classical and operant conditioning, to associate food with comfort and consolation. Similarly, we may learn that eating, which focuses our attention on immediate pleasures, provides an escape from unpleasant thoughts. Consequently, we may eat when we feel distressed (Bulik et al., 2003; Elfhag, Tynelius, & Rasmussen, 2007; Macht & Simons, 2011; O'Connor & O'Connor, 2004).

The Roots of Obesity

Given that both biological and social factors influence eating behavior, determining the causes of obesity has proved to be a challenging task. Researchers have followed several paths.

Some psychologists suggest that greater sensitivity to external eating cues based on social factors, coupled with lower insensitivity to internal hunger cues, produces obesity. Others argue that overweight people have higher weight set points than other people do. Because their set points are unusually high, their attempts to lose weight by eating less may make them especially sensitive to external, food-related cues and therefore more apt to overeat, perpetuating their obesity (Cooper, 2011; Tremblay, 2004; West, Harvey-Berino, & Raczynski, 2004).

But why may some people's weight set points be higher than those of others? One biological explanation is that obese individuals have a higher level of the hormone *leptin*, which appears to be designed, from an evolutionary standpoint, to "protect" the body against weight loss. The body's

Until recently, school cafeterias served a lot of foods that are high in fat and calories. This situation no doubt contributed to an epidemic of childhood obesity. Now schools are required to offer fresher, healthier options.

weight-regulation system thus appears to be designed more to protect against losing weight than to protect against gaining it. This explanation is consistent with the observation that it's easier to gain weight than to lose it (Ahiima & Osei, 2004; Levin, 2006; Yanovski & Yanovski, 2011; Zhang et al., 2005).

Another biologically based explanation for obesity relates to fat cells in the body. Starting at birth, the body stores fat either by increasing the number of fat cells or by increasing the size of existing fat cells. Furthermore, any loss of weight past infancy does not decrease the number of fat cells; it affects only their size. Consequently, people are stuck with the number of fat cells they inherit from an early age, and the rate of weight gain during the first four months of life is related to being overweight during later childhood (Stettler et al., 2002).

According to the weight-set-point hypothesis, the presence of too many fat cells from earlier weight gain may result in the set point's becoming "stuck" at a higher level than is desirable. In such circumstances, losing weight becomes a difficult proposition, because one is constantly at odds with one's own internal set point when dieting (Freedman, 1995; Leibel, Rosenbaum, & Hirsch, 1995).

Not everyone agrees with the set-point explanation for obesity. Pointing to the rapid rise in obesity over the last several decades in the United States, some researchers suggest that the body does not try to maintain a fixed weight set point. Instead, they suggest, the body has a *settling point*, determined by a combination of our genetic heritage and the nature of the environment in which we live. If high-fat/high-sugar foods are prevalent in our environment and we are genetically predisposed to obesity, we settle into an equilibrium that maintains relatively high weight. In contrast, if our environment is nutritionally healthier, a genetic predisposition to obesity will not be triggered, and we settle into an equilibrium in which our weight is lower (Comuzzie & Allison, 1998; Pi-Sunyer, 2003).

Eating Disorders

Eating disorders are among the 10 most frequent causes of disability in young women. One devastating weight-related disorder is **anorexia nervosa**. In this severe eating disorder, people may refuse to eat while denying that their behavior and appearance—which can become skeleton-like—are unusual. Some 10% of people with anorexia literally starve themselves to death (Clausen et al., 2011; Striegel-Moore & Bulik, 2007).

Anorexia nervosa mainly afflicts females between the ages of 12 and 40, although both men and women of any

anorexia nervosa A severe eating disorder in which people may refuse to eat while denying that their behavior and appearance—which can become skeleton-like—are unusual.

bulimia A disorder in which a person binges on large quantities of food, followed by efforts to purge the food through vomiting or other means.

age may develop it. People with the disorder typically come from stable homes, and they are often successful, attractive, and relatively affluent. The disorder often occurs after serious dieting, which somehow gets out of control. Life begins to revolve around food: Although people with the disorder eat little, they may cook for others, go shopping for food frequently, or collect cookbooks (Jacobs et al., 2009; Myers, 2007; Polivy, Herman, & Boivin, 2005).

A related problem is **bulimia**, a disorder in which an individual binges on large quantities of food, for instance, consuming an entire gallon of ice cream and a whole pie in a single sitting. After such a binge, the person experiences guilt and depression and often induces vomiting or takes laxatives to eliminate the food—behavior known as purging. Though the weight of a person with bulimia often remains normal, constant binging-and-purging cycles and the use of drugs to induce vomiting or diarrhea can cause health problems and may lead to heart failure (Couturier & Lock, 2006; Mora-Giral et al., 2004).

PSYCH think

> > > Movies, TV shows, commercials, best-selling books, music videos—all of these give us messages about how we should look and how much we should weigh. If you don't like those messages, what can you do about it?

Exercising to excess in an attempt to become thinner is an eating disorder known as *exercise bulimia*. Unlike people with anorexia, people with exercise bulimia don't control their weight by refusing to eat. Instead, they focus on purging the calories that they do consume; but whereas individuals with bulimia purge by vomiting or using laxatives, those with exercise bulimia purge by monitoring and working off every calorie they eat. As with other eating disorders, people with exercise bulimia can acquire a frail, sickly, and even skeletal appearance while still seeing themselves as overweight and being preoccupied with the fear of eating more calories than they are burning off (Abraham et al., 2007; Heywood & McCabe, 2006).

Since exercise is usually beneficial to health and many people such as competitive athletes exercise very frequently or for long periods of time, when does exercising become a disorder? One indicator is exercise that goes beyond the point of benefit to where the excessive activity starts doing more harm than good. For example, a person with exercise

PSYCH think

> > > Why is exercise bulimia considered an *eating* disorder instead of an *exercise* disorder?

bulimia may sustain sports injuries such as muscle sprains or joint injuries, yet nevertheless continue working out despite the pain (Hrabosky et al., 2007).

Another indicator is a compulsion to exercise—people with exercise dependency tend to feel anxious and guilty about missing a workout and let their exercise activities interfere with their work and with their social lives. Some researchers suggest that it is this compulsion rather than the actual quantity of exercise that indicates the presence of a disorder (Adkins & Keel, 2005; Hausenblas & Downs, 2002).

Eating disorders represent a growing problem: Estimates show that between 1% and 4% of high school-age and college-age women have either anorexia nervosa or bulimia. As many as 10% of women suffer from bulimia at some point in their lives. Furthermore, an increasing number of men are diagnosed with eating disorders; an estimated 10% to 13% of all cases occur in males (Kaminski et al., 2005; Park, 2007; Swain, 2006).

Males and females alike may also suffer from binge eating disorder, in which people eat large amounts of food. Unlike bulimia, however, they do not purge the food. This disorder may be more prevalent in men and women than both anorexia and bulimia combined (Hudson, Hiripi, Harrison & Kessler, 2007).

Brain scans from people with eating disorders show that they process information about food differently than healthy individuals do.

What are the causes of eating disorders? Some researchers suspect a biological cause such as a chemical imbalance in the hypothalamus or pituitary gland, perhaps brought on by genetic factors. Furthermore, brain scans from people with eating disorders

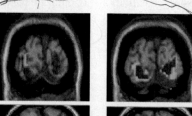
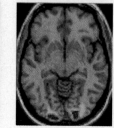

In a study comparing patients with anorexia and healthy individuals, participants viewed images of different foods so researchers could observe their cognitive processing. Comparison of fMRI scans of patients with anorexia (*left column*) and healthy participants (*right column*) showed significant differences in their reactions to the food stimuli. *Source:* Santel et al., 2006, Figure 4.

BUY IT? > > >

Losing Weight Successfully

Although 60% of the people in the United States say they want to lose weight, it's an uphill struggle for most of them. Most people who diet eventually regain the weight they have lost, and so they try one weight loss plan after another, getting caught in a seemingly endless cycle of weight loss and gain (Cachelin & Regan, 2006; Mann, 2007; Newport & Carroll, 2002; Parker-Pope, 2003).

If you want to lose weight, you should keep several things in mind (Gatchel & Oordt, 2003; Heshka et al., 2003):

- *There is no easy route to weight control.* You will have to make permanent changes in your life to lose weight without gaining it back. The most obvious strategy—cutting down on the amount of food you eat—is just the first step toward a lifetime commitment to changing your eating habits.

- *Keep track of what you eat and what you weigh.* Unless you keep careful records, you won't really know how much you are eating.

- *Eat "big" foods.* Eat fiber and foods that are bulky and heavy but low in calories, such as grapes and soup. Such foods trick your body into thinking you've eaten more and thus decrease hunger.

- *Cut out television.* One reason for the epidemic of obesity in the United States is the number of hours spent viewing television. Not only does watching television preclude other activities that burn calories (even walking around the house is helpful), people often eat junk food while sitting in front of the TV (Hu et al., 2003).

continued

- *Exercise.* Exercise for at least 30 consecutive minutes three times each week. When you exercise, you use up fat stored in your body as fuel for muscles, which is measured in calories. As you use up this fat, you will probably lose weight. Almost any activity helps burn calories.

- *Decrease the influence of external, social stimuli on your eating behavior.* Serve yourself smaller portions of food, and leave the table before you see what is being served for dessert. Don't even buy snack foods such as nachos and potato chips; if they're not readily available in the kitchen cupboard, you're not apt to eat them. Wrap refrigerated foods in aluminum foil so that you cannot see the contents and be tempted every time you open the refrigerator.

- *Avoid fad diets.* No matter how popular they are at a particular time, extreme diets, including liquid diets, usually don't work in the long run and can be dangerous to your health.

- *Avoid taking any of the numerous diet pills advertised on television that promise quick and easy results.*

- *Maintain good eating habits.* When you have reached your desired weight, maintain the new habits you have learned to avoid gaining back the weight you have lost.

- *Set reasonable goals.* Even small changes in behavior—such as walking 15 minutes a day or eating a few less bites at each meal—can prevent weight gain (Hill et al., 2003).

Brazilian fashion model Ana Carolina Reston died at age 21 of anorexia complications. Following the deaths of Reston and other models, the fashion industry began changing its standards to promote a healthier image. Spain's Madrid fashion show now requires models to have a body mass index of at least 18 in order to participate.

become preoccupied with their weight and take to heart the cliché that one can never be too thin. This may explain why, as countries become more developed and Westernized, and dieting becomes more popular, eating disorders increase. Finally, some psychologists suggest that the disorders result from overly demanding parents or other family problems (Couturier & Lock, 2006; Grilo et al., 2003; Kluck, 2008).

The complete explanations for anorexia nervosa and bulimia remain elusive. These disorders most likely stem from both biological and social causes, and successful treatment probably needs to encompass several strategies, including therapy and dietary changes (Cooper & Shafran,

show that they process information about food differently than healthy individuals do (Klump & Culbert, 2007; Polivy & Herman, 2002; Santel et al., 2006).

androgens Male sex hormones secreted by the testes.

Others believe that the cause has roots in society's valuation of slenderness and the parallel notion that obesity is undesirable. These researchers maintain that people with anorexia nervosa and bulimia

Did you know?

Aerobic exercise isn't good just for losing weight or being healthy or having fun. If you are a healthy young adult who has a tendency to feel tired, doing low intensity aerobic exercise three times a week may help you feel more energetic (Puetz, Flowers, & O'Connor, 2008).

2008; Mintle, 2011; O'Brien & LeBow, 2007; Wilson, Grilo, & Vitousek, 2007).

If you or a family member needs advice or help with an eating problem, contact the National Eating Disorders Association at www.nationaleatingdisorders.org.

SEXUAL MOTIVATION

Compared to the sexual behavior of other species, human sexual behavior is rather complicated, although the underlying biology is not all that different from that of related species. In males, for example, the *testes* begin to secrete **androgens**, which are sex hormones that occur in higher levels in males, at puberty. Not only do androgens produce secondary sex characteristics, such as the growth of body hair and a deepening of the voice, they also increase the sex drive. Because the level of androgen production by the testes is fairly constant, men are capable of (and interested in) sexual activities without any regard to biological cycles. Given the proper stimuli leading to arousal, men can engage in sexual behavior at any time (Goldstein, 2000).

Women show a different pattern. When they reach maturity at puberty, the two female ovaries begin to produce estrogens and **progesterone**, sex hormones that occur in higher levels in females. However, those hormones are not produced consistently; instead, their production follows a cyclical pattern. The greatest output occurs during **ovulation**, when an egg is released from the ovaries, making the chances of fertilization by a sperm cell highest. While in nonhumans the period around ovulation is the only time the female is receptive to sex, humans are different. Although there are variations in reported sex drive, women are receptive to sex throughout their cycles (Leiblum & Chivers, 2007).

Masturbation: Solitary Sex If you listened to physicians 75 ago, you would have been told that **masturbation**, sexual self-stimulation, often using the hand to rub the genitals, would lead to a wide variety of physical and mental disorders, ranging from hairy palms to insanity. If those physicians had been correct, however, most of us would be wearing gloves to hide the sight of our hair-covered palms—for masturbation is one of the

Cutaway Side Views of the Female and Male Sex Organs

Female

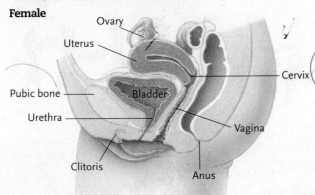

Ovary
Uterus
Cervix
Pubic bone
Bladder
Urethra
Vagina
Clitoris
Anus

Male

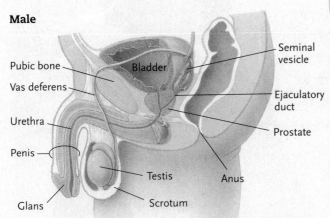

Pubic bone
Bladder
Seminal vesicle
Vas deferens
Ejaculatory duct
Urethra
Prostate
Penis
Anus
Testis
Glans
Scrotum

most frequently practiced sexual activities. In the United States, some 94% of males and 63% of females have masturbated at least once, and among college students, the frequency ranges from "never" to "several times a day" (Hunt, 1974; Laqueur, 2003; Michael et al., 1994; Polonsky, 2006).

Despite the high incidence of masturbation, attitudes toward it still reflect some of the negative views of yesteryear. For instance, one survey found that around 10% of people who masturbated experienced feelings of guilt, and 5% of the males and 1% of the females considered their behavior perverted (Arafat & Cotton, 1974). Despite these negative attitudes, however, most experts on sex view masturbation as a healthy and legitimate—and harmless—sexual activity. In addition, masturbation is seen as providing a means of learning about one's own sexuality and a way of discovering changes in one's body such as the emergence of precancerous lumps (Coleman, 2002; Herbenick et al., 2009; Levin, 2007).

Heterosexuality People often believe that the first time they have sexual intercourse they have achieved one of life's major milestones. However, **heterosexuality**, sexual attraction and behavior directed to the other sex, consists of far more than male-female intercourse. Kissing, petting, caressing, massaging, and other forms of sex play are all components of heterosexual behavior. Still, the focus of sex researchers has been on the act of intercourse, especially in terms of its first occurrence and its frequency (Holtzman & Kulish, 1996; Janssen, 2007).

Premarital Sex Until fairly recently, premarital sexual intercourse, at least for women, was considered one of the major taboos in our society. Traditionally, women in Western societies have been warned that "nice girls don't do it"; men have been told that although premarital sex is okay for them, they should marry virgins. This view that premarital sex is permissible for males but not for females is called the **double standard** (Liang, 2007).

Although the majority of adults in the United States once believed that premarital sex was always wrong, there has been a dramatic change in public opinion. For example, the percentage of middle-age people who say sex before marriage is "not wrong at all" has increased considerably, and overall 60% of Americans say premarital sex is okay. More than half say that living together before marriage is morally acceptable (Harding & Jencks, 2003; Thornton & Young-DeMarco, 2001).

estrogens Class of female sex hormones.

progesterone A female sex hormone secreted by the ovaries.

ovulation The point at which an egg is released from the ovaries.

masturbation Sexual self-stimulation.

heterosexuality Sexual attraction and behavior directed to the other sex.

double standard The view that premarital sex is permissible for males but not for females.

extramarital sex Sexual activity between a married person and someone who is not his or her spouse.

homosexuals Persons who are sexually attracted to members of their own sex.

bisexuals Persons who are sexually attracted to people of the same sex and the other sex.

Changes in attitudes toward premarital sex were matched by changes in actual rates of premarital sexual activity. For instance, the most recent figures show that just over one-half of women between the ages of 15 and 19 have had premarital sexual intercourse. These figures are close to double the number of women in the same age range who reported having intercourse in 1970. Clearly, the trend over the last several decades has been toward more women engaging in premarital sexual activity (Jones, Darroch, & Singh, 2005).

Among males, there has also been an increase in the incidence of premarital sexual intercourse, although change has not been as dramatic as it has been for females—probably because the rates for males were higher to begin with. For instance, the first surveys of premarital intercourse carried out in the 1940s showed an incidence of 84% across males of all ages; recent figures put the figure at closer to 95%. Moreover, the average age of males' first sexual experience has been declining steadily. Almost half of males have had sexual intercourse by the age of 18, and by the time they reach age 20, 88% have had intercourse. There also are race and ethnicity differences: African Americans tend to have sex for the first time earlier than do Puerto Ricans, who have sex earlier than whites do. Racial and ethnic differences probably reflect differences in socioeconomic opportunities and family structure (Arena, 1984; Hyde, Mezulis, & Abramson, 2008; Singh et al., 2000).

Marital Sex To judge by the number of articles about sex in heterosexual marriages, one would think that sexual behavior was the number one standard by which marital bliss is measured. Married couples are often concerned that they are having too little sex, too much sex, or the wrong kind of sex (Harvey, Wenzel, & Sprecher, 2005).

Although there are many different dimensions along which sex in marriage is measured, one is certainly the frequency of sexual intercourse. What is typical? As with most other types of sexual activities, there is no easy answer to the question, because there are such wide variations in patterns between individuals. In one study, 43% of married couples reported having sexual intercourse a few times a month and 36% of couples said they had sex two or three times a week. With increasing age and length of marriage,

the frequency of intercourse declines. Still, sex continues into late adulthood, with almost half of people reporting that they engage in sexual activity at least once a month and that its quality is high (Michael et al., 1994; Powell, 2006).

Although early research found **extramarital sex** to be widespread, the current reality appears to be otherwise. According to surveys in the United States, 85% of married women and more than 75% of married men are faithful to their spouses. Furthermore, the median number of sex partners, inside and outside marriage, since the age of 18 for men was six, and for women two. Accompanying these numbers is a high, consistent degree of disapproval of extramarital sex, with nine of ten people saying that it is "always" or "almost always" wrong (Daines, 2006; Michael et al., 1994; Whisman & Snyder, 2007).

Homosexuality and Bisexuality Homosexuals are sexually attracted to members of their own sex, whereas **bisexuals** are sexually attracted to people of the same sex and the other sex. Many male homosexuals prefer the term *gay* and female homosexuals the label *lesbian*, because these terms refer to a broader array of attitudes and lifestyles than the term *homosexual*, which focuses on the sexual act.

At http://psych.hanover.edu/research/exponnet.html, you can find a variety of online research projects on emotion and other topics of interest to psychologists. You can help by participating in one of these projects and contributing your data to the study. At the same time, you can learn more about the way psychologists gather information and try to find out how emotions work. It's a win-win prospect.

get involved!

The number of people who choose same-sex sexual partners at one time or another is considerable. Estimates suggest that around 20% to 25% of males and about 15% of females have had at least one gay or lesbian experience during adulthood. The exact number of people who identify themselves as exclusively homosexual has proved difficult to gauge, with some estimates as low as 1.1% and some as high as 10%. Most experts suggest that between 5% and 10% of both men and women are exclusively gay or lesbian during extended periods of their lives (Firestein, 1996; Hunt, 1974; Sells, 1994).

Although people often view homosexuality and heterosexuality as two completely distinct sexual orientations, the issue is not that simple. Pioneering sex researcher Alfred Kinsey acknowledged this when he considered sexual orientation along a scale or continuum, with "exclusively homosexual" at one end and "exclusively heterosexual" at the other. In the middle were people who showed both homosexual and heterosexual behavior. Kinsey's approach suggests that sexual orientation is dependent on a person's sexual feelings and behaviors and romantic feelings (Kinsey, Pomeroy & Martin, 1948; Kinsey, Pomeroy, Martin, & Gebhard, 1953; Weinberg, Williams, & Pryor, 1991).

Causes of Sexual Orientation What determines whether people become homosexual or heterosexual? Although there are a number of theories, none has proved completely satisfactory.

Some explanations for sexual orientation are biological in nature, suggesting that there are genetic causes. Evidence for a genetic origin of sexual orientation comes from studies of identical twins, which have found that when one twin identified himself or herself as homosexual, the occurrence of homosexuality in the other twin was higher than it was in the general population. Such results occur even for twins who have been separated early in life and who therefore are not necessarily raised in similar social environments (Gooren, 2006; Hamer et al., 1993; Kirk, Bailey, & Martin, 2000; Turner, 1995).

Hormones also may play a role in determining sexual orientation. For example, research shows that women

exposed to DES, or diethylstilbestrol (a synthetic estrogen), before birth (their mothers took the drug to avoid miscarriage) were more likely to be homosexual or bisexual (Meyer-Bahlburg, 1997).

Some evidence suggests that differences in brain structures may be related to sexual orientation. For instance, the structure of the anterior hypothalamus, an area of the brain that governs sexual behavior, differs in male homosexuals and heterosexuals. Similarly, other research shows that, compared with heterosexual men or women, gay men have a larger anterior commissure, which is a bundle of neurons connecting the right and left hemispheres of the brain (Byne, 1996; LeVay, 1999; 2011).

However, research suggesting that biological causes are at the root of sexual orientation is not conclusive, because most findings are based on only small samples of individuals. Still, the possibility is real that some inherited or biological factor exists that predisposes people toward heterosexuality or homosexuality, if certain environmental conditions are met (Rahman, Kumari, & Wilson, 2003; Teodorov et al., 2002; Veniegas, 2000).

Little evidence suggests that sexual orientation is brought about by child-rearing practices or family dynamics. Although proponents of psychoanalytic theories once argued that the nature of the parent-child relationship can produce homosexuality (for example, Freud, 1922/1959), research evidence does not support such explanations (Isay, 1994; Roughton, 2002).

Because of the difficulty in finding a consistent explanation, we can't answer the question of what determines sexual orientation. It does seem unlikely that any single factor orients a person toward homosexuality or heterosexuality. Instead, it seems reasonable to assume that a combination of biological and environmental factors is involved (Bem, 1996; Hyde & Grabe, 2008).

Although we don't know at this point exactly why people develop a certain sexual orientation, one thing is clear: There is no correlation between sexual orientation and psychological adjustment. Gays, lesbians, and bisexuals generally enjoy the same quality of mental and physical health that heterosexuals do, although the discrimination they experience may produce higher rates of some disorders, such as depression (Poteat & Espelage, 2007). Heterosexuals,

"Frankly, I've repressed my sexuality so long I've actually forgotten what my orientation is."

© Robert Mankoff/The New Yorker Collection/ www.cartoonbank.com.

STUDY **TIP**

The determinants of sexual orientation have proven difficult to pinpoint. It is important to know the variety of explanations that have been put forward.

THE NEEDS FOR ACHIEVEMENT, AFFILIATION, AND POWER

Although hunger may be one of the more potent primary drives in our day-to-day lives, powerful secondary drives that have as yet no clear biological basis also motivate us. Among the more prominent of these is the need for achievement.

The Need for Achievement The **need for achievement** is a stable, learned characteristic in which a person obtains satisfaction by striving for and attaining a level of excellence (McClelland et al., 1953). People with a high need for achievement seek out situations in which they can compete against some standard—be it grades, money, or winning at a game—and prove themselves successful. But they are not indiscriminate when it comes to picking their challenges: They tend to avoid situations in which success will come too easily (which would be unchallenging) and situations in which success is unlikely. Instead, people high in achievement motivation generally choose tasks that are of intermediate difficulty (Speirs Neumeister, K. L., & Finch, 2006).

transsexuals Persons who believe they were born with the body of the other gender.

need for achievement A stable, learned characteristic in which a person obtains satisfaction by striving for and attaining a level of excellence.

bisexuals, and homosexuals also hold similar kinds of attitudes about themselves, independent of sexual orientation. For such reasons, the American Psychological Association and most other mental health organizations have endorsed efforts to reduce discrimination against gays and lesbians, such as permitting gays and lesbians the right to legally marry (Cochran, 2000; Morris, Waldo, & Rothblum, 2001; Perez, DeBord, & Bieschke, 2000).

Transsexualism **Transsexuals** are people who believe they were born with the body of the other gender. In fundamental ways, transsexualism represents less a sexual difficulty than a gender issue involving one's sexual identity (Heath, 2006; Meyerowitz, 2004).

Transsexuals sometimes seek sex-change operations in which their existing genitals are surgically removed and the genitals of the desired sex are fashioned. Several steps, including intensive counseling and hormone injections, along with living as a member of the desired sex for several years, precede surgery, which is, not surprisingly, highly complicated. The outcome, though, can be quite positive (Lobato, Koff, & Manenti, 2006; O'Keefe & Fox, 2003; Stegerwald & Janson, 2003).

Transsexualism is part of a broader category known as transgenderism. The term *transgenderism* encompasses not only transsexuals but also people who view themselves as a third gender, transvestites (who dress in the clothes of the other gender), and others who believe that traditional male-female gender classifications inadequately characterize them (Hyde & Grabe, 2008; Hyde, Mezulis, & Abramson, 2008; Prince, 2005).

Transsexuals are distinct from individuals who are known as *intersex* or by the older term *hermaphrodite*. An intersex person is someone who is born with an atypical combination of sexual organs, or chromosomal or gene patterns. In some cases, they are born with both male and female sexual organs, or the organs are ambiguous. It is an extremely rare condition, found in 1 in 4,500 births. Intersexism involves a complex mix of physiological and psychological issues (Lehrman, 2007; Diamond, 2009).

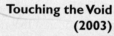

Psych at the Movies

Touching the Void (2003)
Joe is injured while tied to Simon during their descent of Siula Grande in Peru. Simon has to cut the rope to prevent both of them from dying. He believes Joe died, but this is the story of Joe's incredible motivation to survive.

Bridget Jones's Diary (2001)
Sometimes we eat for reasons other than hunger. The main character in this movie, Bridget Jones, binges when she is depressed.

Gandhi (1982)
This story of one man's amazing courage demonstrates qualities of a self-actualizing leader who used nonviolence to defy British rule in India.

The World Unseen (2007)
This story of two women, who discover that sexual motivation doesn't always follow the rules, takes place in South Africa, where the rules are rigidly upheld.

No Strings Attached (2011)
This is the story of friends with benefits, who get into trouble when emotions get in the way.

In contrast, people with low achievement motivation tend to be motivated primarily by a desire to avoid failure. As a result, they seek out easy tasks, being sure to avoid failure, or seek out very difficult tasks for which failure has no negative implications, because almost anyone would fail at them. People with a high fear of failure stay away from tasks of intermediate difficulty, because they may fail where others have been successful (Martin & Marsh, 2002; Morrone & Pintrich, 2006; Puca, 2005).

A high need for achievement generally produces positive outcomes, at least in success-oriented cultures in Western society. For instance, people motivated by a high need for achievement are more likely to attend college than are their low-achievement counterparts; and once they are in college, they tend to receive higher grades in classes that are related to their future careers. Furthermore, high achievement motivation correlates with future economic and occupational success (McClelland, 1985; Thrash & Elliot, 2002).

STUDY TIP

A key feature of people with a high need for achievement is that they prefer tasks of *moderate* difficulty.

MEASURING ACHIEVEMENT MOTIVATION

How can we measure a person's need for achievement? The measuring instrument used most frequently is the *Thematic Apperception Test (TAT)* (Spangler, 1992). In the TAT, an examiner shows a series of ambiguous pictures. The examiner tells participants to write a story that describes what is happening, who the people are, what led to the situation, what the people are thinking or wanting, and what will happen next. Researchers then use a standardized scoring system to determine the amount of achievement imagery in people's stories. For example, someone who writes a story in which the main character strives to beat an opponent, studies in order to do well at some task, or works hard in order to get a promotion shows clear signs of an achievement orientation. The inclusion of such achievement-related imagery in the participants' stories is assumed to indicate an unusually high degree of concern with—and therefore a relatively strong need for—achievement (Tuerlinckx, DeBoeck, & Lens, 2002).

> **need for affiliation** An interest in establishing and maintaining relationships with other people.
>
> **need for power** A tendency to seek impact, control, or influence over others, and to be seen as a powerful individual.

The Need for Affiliation Few of us choose to lead our lives as hermits. Why? One reason is that most people have a **need for affiliation**, an interest in establishing and maintaining relationships with other people. Individuals with a high need for affiliation write TAT stories that emphasize the desire to maintain or reinstate friendships and show concern over being rejected by friends.

People who have higher affiliation needs are particularly sensitive to relationships with others. They desire to be with their friends more of the time, and alone less often, compared with people who are lower in the need for affiliation. However, gender is a greater determinant of how much time is actually spent with friends: Regardless of their affiliative orientation, female students spend significantly more time with their friends and less time alone than male students do (Cantwell & Andrews, 2002; Johnson, 2004; Semykina & Linz, 2007).

The Need for Power If your fantasies include becoming president of the United States or running Microsoft, your dreams may reflect a high need for power. The **need for power**, a tendency to seek impact, control, or influence over others and to be seen as a powerful individual, is an additional type of motivation (Lee-Chai & Bargh, 2001; Winter, 2007; Zians, 2007).

As you might expect, people with strong needs for power are more apt to belong to organizations and seek office than are those low in the need for power. They also tend to work in professions in which their power needs may be fulfilled, such as business management and—you may or may not be surprised—teaching (Jenkins, 1994). In addition, they seek to display the trappings of power. Even in college, they are more likely to collect prestigious possessions, such as electronic equipment and sports cars.

How is gender correlated with the need for affiliation?

>> Understanding Emotional Experiences

At one time or another, all of us have experienced the strong feelings that accompany both very pleasant and very negative experiences. Perhaps we have felt the thrill of getting a sought-after job, the joy of being in love, the sorrow over someone's death, or the anguish of inadvertently hurting someone. We also have less intense feelings throughout our daily lives: the pleasure of a friendship, the enjoyment of a movie, and the embarrassment of breaking a borrowed item.

Despite the varied nature of these feelings, they all represent emotions. Although everyone has an idea of what an emotion is, formally defining the concept has proved to be an elusive task. Here, we'll use a general definition: **Emotions** are feelings that generally have both physiological and cognitive elements and that influence behavior.

emotions Feelings that generally have both physiological and cognitive elements and that influence behavior.

Think, for example, about how it feels to be happy. First, we obviously experience a feeling that we can differentiate from other emotions. We likely also experience some identifiable physical changes in our bodies: Perhaps the heart rate increases, or we find ourselves "jumping for joy." Finally, the emotion probably encompasses cognitive elements: Our understanding and evaluation of the meaning of what is happening prompts our feelings of happiness.

We can, however, also experience an emotion without the presence of cognitive elements. For instance, we may react with fear to something but have no idea why we are fearful, or we may experience pleasure over sexual excitation without having cognitive awareness or understanding of just what it is about the situation that is exciting.

THE FUNCTIONS OF EMOTIONS

Imagine what it would be like if we didn't experience emotion—no depths of despair, no depression, no remorse—but at the same time no happiness, joy, or love. Obviously, life would be considerably less satisfying, even dull, if we lacked the capacity to sense and express emotion.

But what purpose do emotions serve beyond making life interesting? Psychologists have identified several key functions that emotions play in our daily lives (Frederickson & Branigan, 2005; Frijda, 2005; Gross, 2006; Kappas, 2011; Siemer, Mauss, & Gross, 2007). Among the most important are these:

- *Preparing us for action.* Emotions act as a link between events in our environment and our responses. If you saw an angry dog charging toward you, your emotional reaction (fear) would be associated with physiological arousal of the sympathetic division of the autonomic nervous system, the activation of the "fight-or-flight" response.
- *Shaping our future behavior.* Emotions promote awareness that helps us make appropriate responses. For instance, your emotional response to unpleasant events teaches you to avoid similar circumstances in the future.
- *Helping us interact more effectively with others.* We often communicate the emotions we experience through our verbal and nonverbal behaviors, making our emotions obvious to observers. These behaviors can act as a signal to observers, allowing them to understand better what we are experiencing and to help them predict our future behavior.

DETERMINING THE RANGE OF EMOTIONS

If we were to list the words in the English language that have been used to describe emotions, we would end up with at least 500 examples (Averill, 1975). The list would range from such obvious emotions as *happiness* and *fear* to less common ones, such as *adventurousness* and *pensiveness*.

One challenge for psychologists has been to sort through this list to identify the most important, fundamental emotions. Theorists have hotly contested the issue of cataloging emotions and have come up with different lists, depending on how they define the concept of emotion. In fact, some reject the question entirely, saying that *no* set of emotions should be singled out as most basic, and that emotions are best understood by breaking them down into their component parts. Other researchers argue for looking at emotions in terms of a hierarchy, dividing them into positive and negative categories, and then organizing them into increasingly narrower subcategories (Dillard & Shen, 2007; Manstead, Frijda, & Fischer, 2003).

Hierarchy of Emotions

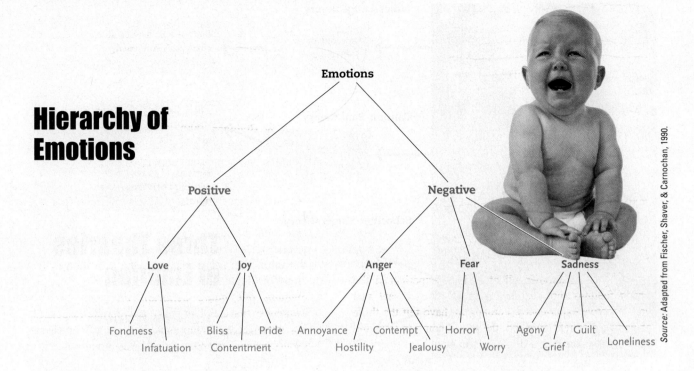

Source: Adapted from Fischer, Shaver, & Carnochan, 1990.

Emotions
- Positive
  - Love
    - Fondness
    - Infatuation
  - Joy
    - Bliss
    - Contentment
    - Pride
- Negative
  - Anger
    - Annoyance
    - Hostility
    - Contempt
    - Jealousy
  - Fear
    - Horror
    - Worry
  - Sadness
    - Agony
    - Grief
    - Guilt
    - Loneliness

Still, most researchers suggest that a list of basic emotions would include, at a minimum, happiness, anger, fear, sadness, disgust, and surprise. Other lists are broader, including emotions such as contempt, guilt, and joy (Ekman, 1994a; Shweder & Heidt, 1994; Tracy & Robins, 2004).

One difficulty in defining a basic set of emotions is that significant differences exist in the ways various cultures experience and express emotion. For instance, Germans talk of *Schadenfreude,* a feeling of pleasure over another person's difficulties, and the Japanese experience *hagaii,* a mood of vulnerable heartache colored by frustration. In Tahiti, *musu* refers to a feeling of reluctance to yield to unreasonable demands made by one's parents.

Finding *Schadenfreude, hagaii,* or *musu* in a particular culture doesn't mean that the members of other cultures are incapable of experiencing such emotions. It does suggest, though, that fitting a particular emotion into a linguistic category to describe that emotion may make it easier to discuss, contemplate, and perhaps experience (Li, Wang, & Fischer, 2004; Kuppens et al., 2006; Russell & Sato, 1995).

PSYCH think

> > > If researchers learned how to control emotional responses so that specific emotions could be caused or prevented, which emotions do you think people might want to avoid? To enjoy more often? Would it be wise to avoid emotions such as anger and fear?

THE ROOTS OF EMOTIONS

I've never been so angry before; I feel my heart pounding, and I'm trembling all over . . . I don't know how I'll get through the performance. I feel like my stomach is filled with butterflies . . . That was quite a mistake I made! My face must be incredibly red . . . When I heard the footsteps in the night, I was so frightened that I couldn't catch my breath.

If you examine our language, you will find that there are literally dozens of ways to describe how we feel when we experience an emotion. The language we use to describe emotions is, for the most part, based on the physical symptoms that are associated with a particular emotional experience (Kobayashi, Schallert, & Ogren, 2003; Manstead & Wagner, 2004; Spackman, Fujiki, & Brinton, 2006).

Consider, for instance, the experience of fear. Imagine that it is late on New Year's Eve. You are crossing a major boulevard and suddenly, out of nowhere, a large truck comes barreling down the road and is headed directly toward you. You quickly look around and decide which direction to run to avoid getting hit.

While you are assessing the situation and deciding what to do, something dramatic will be happening to your body. The most likely reactions, which are associated with activation of the autonomic nervous system, include an increase in your rate of breathing, an acceleration of your heart rate, a widening of your pupils (to increase visual sensitivity), and a dryness in your mouth as the functioning of your salivary glands, and in fact of your entire digestive system, slows dramatically. At the same time, though, your sweat glands probably become more active, because increased sweating helps you rid yourself of the excess heat produced in response to any emergency activity.

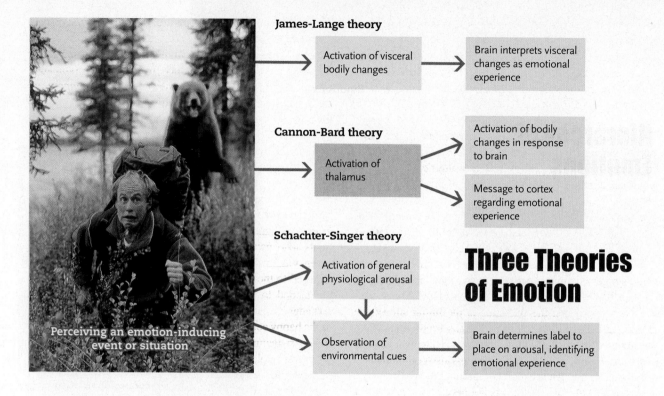

James-Lange theory

Activation of visceral bodily changes → Brain interprets visceral changes as emotional experience

Cannon-Bard theory

Activation of thalamus → Activation of bodily changes in response to brain

Message to cortex regarding emotional experience

Schachter-Singer theory

Activation of general physiological arousal → Observation of environmental cues → Brain determines label to place on arousal, identifying emotional experience

Perceiving an emotion-inducing event or situation

Three Theories of Emotion

Of course, all these physiological changes are likely to occur without your awareness. At the same time, though, the emotional experience accompanying them will be obvious to you: You most surely would report being fearful.

Although it is easy to describe the general physical reactions that accompany emotions, defining the specific role that those physiological responses play in the experience of emotions has proved to be a major puzzle for psychologists. As we shall see, some theorists suggest that specific bodily reactions *cause us to experience a particular emotion—we experience fear, for instance, because* the heart is pounding and we are breathing deeply. In contrast, other theorists suggest that the physiological reaction results from the experience of an emotion. In this view, we experience fear, and as a result the heart pounds and our breathing rate increases.

James-Lange theory of emotion The idea that emotional experience is a reaction to bodily events occurring as a result of an external situation ("I feel sad because I am crying").

The James-Lange Theory of Emotion William
James and Carl Lange were two of the first researchers to explore the nature of emotions. James and Lange characterized emotional experience as a reaction to bodily events that occur reflexively in response to some situation or event in the environment. This view is summarized in James's statement, "we feel sorry because we cry, angry because we strike, afraid because we tremble" (James, 1890).

James and Lange suggested that crying at a loss leads us to feel sorrow, that striking out at someone who frustrates us results in our feeling anger, that trembling at a menac-

ing threat causes us to feel fear. In their view, for every major emotion there is an accompanying physiological or "gut" reaction by our internal organs—called a *visceral experience*. It is this specific pattern of visceral response that leads us to label the emotional experience.

In sum, James and Lange proposed that we experience emotions as a result of physiological changes that produce specific sensations. The brain interprets these sensations as specific kinds of emotional experiences. This view has come to be called the **James-Lange theory of emotion** (Cobos et al., 2002; Laird & Bresler, 1990).

The James-Lange theory has some serious drawbacks. For the theory to be valid, visceral changes would have to occur relatively quickly, because we experience some emotions—such as fear when hearing a stranger rapidly approaching on a dark night—almost instantaneously. This kind of emotional experience occurs even before certain physiological changes can be set into motion.

The James-Lange theory poses another difficulty: Physiological arousal does not invariably produce emotional experience. For example, a person who is jogging has an increased heartbeat and respiration rate, as well as many of the other physiological changes associated with certain emotions. Yet joggers typically do not think of such changes in terms of emotions. There cannot be a one-to-one correspondence, then, between visceral changes and emotional experience. Visceral changes by themselves may not be sufficient to produce emotion.

Finally, our internal organs produce a relatively limited range of sensations. Although some types of physiological changes are associated with specific emotional experiences, it is difficult to imagine how each of the myriad emotions that people are capable of experiencing could be the result of a unique visceral change. Many emotions actually are associated with relatively similar sorts of visceral changes, a fact that contradicts the James-Lange theory (Cameron, 2002; Davidson, Deuser, & Sternberg, 1994).

The Cannon-Bard Theory In response to the difficulties inherent in the James-Lange theory, Walter Cannon, and later Philip Bard, suggested an alternative view. In what has come to be known as the **Cannon-Bard theory of emotion** (Cannon, 1929), they rejected the view that physiological arousal alone leads to the perception of emotion. Instead, the theory assumes that both physiological arousal *and* the emotional experience are produced simultaneously by the same nerve stimulus, which Cannon and Bard suggested emanates from the thalamus in the brain.

The theory states that after we perceive an emotion-producing stimulus, the thalamus is the initial site of the emotional response. Next, the thalamus sends a signal to the autonomic nervous system, thereby producing a visceral response. At the same time, the thalamus also communicates a message to the cerebral cortex regarding the nature of the emotion being experienced. It is not necessary for different emotions to have unique physiological patterns associated with them, then, as long as the message sent to the cerebral cortex differs according to the specific emotion.

The Cannon-Bard theory seems to have been accurate in rejecting the view that physiological arousal alone accounts for emotions. But more recent research has led to some important modifications of the theory. For one thing, we now understand that the amygdala and other structures in the limbic system, not the thalamus, play a major role in emotional experience. In addition, the simultaneous occurrence of the physiological and emotional responses, which is a fundamental assumption of the Cannon-Bard theory, has yet to be demonstrated conclusively. This ambiguity has allowed room for yet another theory of emotions: the Schachter-Singer theory.

The Schachter-Singer Theory Suppose that, as you are being followed down a dark street, you notice a man on the other side of the street being followed by another suspicious-looking figure. The man turns and sees his pursuer. Now assume that instead of reacting with fear, the man begins to laugh and seems gleeful. Would his reactions make you less fearful? Might you decide there is nothing to fear, and start feeling jovial yourself?

According to an explanation that focuses on the role of cognition, the **Schachter-Singer theory of emotion**, this might very well happen. This approach to explaining emotions emphasizes that we identify the emotion we are experiencing by observing our environment and comparing ourselves with others (Schachter & Singer, 1962).

Schachter and Singer's classic experiment found evidence for this hypothesis. In the study, half of the participants were told that they would receive an injection of a vitamin and the other half were told that they would receive an injection of epinephrine. In reality, they were all given epinephrine, a drug that causes an increase in physiological arousal, including higher heart and respiration rates and a reddening of the face, responses that typically occur during strong emotional reactions. The members of both groups were then placed individually in a situation in which a confederate of the experimenter acted in one of two ways. In one condition he acted as if he were angry and hostile, and in the other condition he behaved as if he were exuberantly happy.

The purpose of the experiment was to determine how the participants would react emotionally to the confederate's behavior. When they were asked to describe their own emotional state at the end of the experiment, the participants who believed they were given vitamins and who were exposed to the angry confederate tended to report that they felt angry, while those exposed to the happy confederate tended to report feeling happy. Those who were told they received epinephrine tended to report simply feeling the effects of the injection. In sum, the results suggest that participants who thought they were given vitamins turned to the environment and the behavior of others for an explanation of the physiological arousal they were experiencing.

> **Cannon-Bard theory of emotion** The view that both physiological arousal and emotional experience are produced simultaneously by the same nerve stimulus.
>
> **Schachter-Singer theory of emotion** The idea that emotions are determined jointly by a nonspecific kind of physiological arousal and its interpretation, based on environmental cues.

The results of the Schachter-Singer experiment, then, supported a cognitive view of emotions, in which emotions are determined jointly by a relatively nonspecific kind of physiological arousal *and* the labeling of that arousal on the basis of cues from the environment. Later research has found that arousal is not as nonspecific as Schachter and Singer assumed. When the source of physiological arousal is unclear, however, we may look to our surroundings to determine just what we are experiencing.

Making Sense of the Multiple Perspectives on Emotion As new approaches to emotion continue to develop, it is reasonable to ask why so many theories of emotion exist and, perhaps more important, which one provides the most complete explanation. Actually, we have only scratched the surface. There are almost as many explanatory theories of emotion as there are individual emotions (for example, Frijda, 2005; Herzberg, 2009; Manstead, Frijda, & Fischer, 2003; Prinz, 2007).

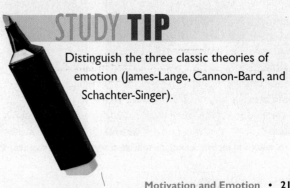

STUDY TIP

Distinguish the three classic theories of emotion (James-Lange, Cannon-Bard, and Schachter-Singer).

Why are theories of emotion so plentiful? For one thing, emotions are not a simple phenomenon but are intertwined closely with motivation, cognition, neuroscience, and other related branches of psychology. For example, evidence from brain imaging studies shows that even when people come to supposedly rational, non-emotional decisions—such as moral or philosophical judgments—emotions come into play (Greene et al., 2001).

In short, emotions are complex phenomena, encompassing both biological and cognitive aspects, and, at this time, no single theory fully explains all the facets of emotional experience. Furthermore, contradictory evidence of one sort or another challenges each approach, and so no theory has proved invariably accurate in its predictions.

> At this time, no single theory fully explains all the facets of emotional experience.

This abundance of perspectives on emotion is not a cause for despair—or unhappiness, fear, or any other negative emotion. It simply reflects the fact that psychology is an evolving, developing science. As we gather more evidence, the specific answers to questions about the nature of emotions will become clearer.

CULTURAL DIFFERENCES IN EXPRESSIONS OF EMOTION

Consider, for a moment, the six photos displayed below. Can you identify the emotions being expressed by the person in each of the photos? You don't have to be an expert on facial expressions to see that these expressions display six of the basic emotions: happiness, anger, sadness, surprise, disgust, and fear. Hundreds of studies of nonverbal behavior show that these emotions are consistently distinct and identifiable, even by untrained observers (Ekman & O'Sullivan, 1991; Leu, Wang, & Koo, 2011).

Interestingly, these six emotions are not unique to Western cultures; rather, they constitute basic human emotions that are expressed universally, regardless of where individuals have been raised and what learning experiences they have had. Psychologist Paul Ekman convincingly demonstrated this point when he studied the members of an isolated New Guinea jungle tribe who had had almost no contact with Westerners (Ekman, 1972). The people of the tribe did not speak or understand English, had never seen a movie, and had had very limited experience with Caucasians before Ekman's arrival. Yet their nonverbal responses to emotion-evoking stories, as well as the ways in which they identified basic emotions, were quite similar to those of Westerners.

Being so isolated, the New Guineans could not have learned from Westerners to recognize or produce similar facial expressions. Instead, their similar abilities and manner of responding emotionally appear to be innate. Although one could argue that similar experiences in both cultures led the members of each one to learn similar types of nonverbal behavior, this appears unlikely, because the

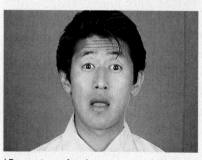

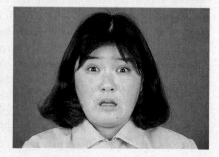

Expressions of six basic emotions: happiness, anger, sadness, surprise, disgust, and fear.

two cultures are so very different. The expression of basic emotions, then, seems to be universal (Ekman, 1994b; Izard, 1994; Matsumoto, 2002).

Why do people across cultures express emotions similarly? A hypothesis known as the **facial-affect program** gives one explanation. The facial-affect program—which is assumed to be universally present at birth—is analogous to a computer program that turns on when a particular emotion is experienced. When set in motion, the "program" activates a set of nerve impulses that make the face display an appropriate expression. Each primary emotion produces a unique set of muscular movements, forming different kinds of expressions. For example, the emotion of happiness is universally displayed by movement of a muscle that raises the corners of the mouth—forming what we would call a

"And just exactly what is that expression intended to convey?"

© Gahan Wilson/The New Yorker Collection/www.cartoonbank.com.

smile (Ekman, 2003; Kendler et al., 2008; Kim, Kim, & Kim, 2007; Kohler et al., 2004).

The importance of facial expressions is illustrated by an intriguing idea known as the **facial-feedback hypothesis**. According to this hypothesis, facial expressions not only *reflect* emotional experience but also help *determine* how people experience and label emotions (Izard, 1990). Basically, "wearing" an emotional expression provides muscular feedback to the brain that helps produce an emotion congruent with that expression. For instance, the muscles activated when we smile may send a message to the brain indicating the experience of happiness—even if there is nothing in the environment that would produce that particular emotion. Some theoreticians have gone further, suggesting that facial expressions are *necessary* for an emotion to be experienced (Rinn, 1984, 1991). According to this view in its extreme form, if no facial expression is present, the emotion cannot be felt.

facial-affect program Activation of a set of nerve impulses that make the face display the appropriate expression.

facial-feedback hypothesis The hypothesis that facial expressions not only reflect emotional experience but also help determine how people experience and label emotions.

Support for the facial-feedback hypothesis comes from a classic experiment carried out by psychologist Paul Ekman and colleagues (Ekman, Levenson, & Friesen, 1983). In the study, professional actors were asked to follow very explicit instructions regarding the movements of muscles in their faces. You might try this example yourself:

- Raise your brows and pull them together.
- Raise your upper eyelids.
- Now stretch your lips horizontally back toward your ears.

After carrying out these directions—which, as you may have guessed, are meant to produce an expression of fear—the actors' heart rates rose and their body temperatures fell, physiological reactions that characterize fear. Overall, facial expressions representing the primary emotions produced physiological effects similar to those accompanying the genuine emotions in other circumstances (Keillor et al., 2002; Soussignan, 2002).

Did you know?

Your face can give you away when you lie! Certain microexpressions (expressions that flash so quickly they are largely outside our control) have been associated with lying. Training law enforcement and security to read microexpressions may be a more reliable method for detecting liars than the old-fashioned polygraph (Anderson, 2005).

[For REVIEW >>

- **What is motivation and how does it influence behavior?**

  Motivation relates to the factors that direct and energize behavior. Drive is the motivational tension that energizes behavior to fulfill a need. Arousal approaches suggest that we try to maintain a particular level of stimulation and activity. Incentive approaches focus on the positive aspects of the environment that direct and energize behavior. Cognitive approaches focus on the role of thoughts, expectations, and understanding of the world in producing motivation. Maslow's hierarchy of needs include physiological, safety, love and belongingness, esteem, and self-actualization needs. Only after the more basic needs are fulfilled can a person strive to satisfy higher-order needs. (pp. 194–198)

- **What factors affect hunger and sexual behavior?**

  Eating behavior is motivated by biological and social factors. The hypothalamus in the brain appears to regulate food intake. Social factors, such as mealtimes, cultural food preferences, and other learned habits, also play a role in the regulation of eating, determining when, what, and how much one eats. A greater sensitivity to social cues and a lower insensitivity to internal cues may contribute to obesity. In addition, obesity may be caused by an unusually high weight set point—the weight the body attempts to maintain—and genetic factors. Sexual behavior has a biological basis, but almost any kind of stimulus can produce sexual arousal, depending on a person's previous experience. Self-stimulation, or masturbation, is one of the most frequently practiced sexual activities. Attitudes toward masturbation have traditionally been negative even though no negative consequences have been detected. Heterosexuality is the most common sexual orientation, although the number of people who choose same-sex sexual partners at one time or another is considerable. From 5% to 10% of men and women are estimated to be exclusively homosexual during extended periods of their lives. No explanation for why some people are heterosexual and others are homosexual has been confirmed; among the possibilities are genetic or biological factors, childhood and family influences, and previous learning experiences and conditioning. (pp. 199–208)

- **What are our needs for achievement? For affiliation? For power?**

  Need for achievement refers to the stable, learned characteristic of striving for excellence. The need for affiliation is a concern with establishing and maintaining relationships with others, whereas the need for power is a tendency to seek to exert influence on others. (pp. 208–209)

- **Does everyone experience emotions in the same way?**

  Emotions are broadly defined as feelings that may affect behavior and generally have both a physiological component and a cognitive component. Emotions prepare us for action, shape future behavior, and help us interact more effectively with others. Although numerous theories of emotion have been proposed, none of them alone provides a clear-cut explanation that is fully supported by research. (pp. 210–214)

- **How do we communicate our feelings nonverbally?**
  A person's facial expressions reveal emotions. Expressions of emotion are universal and can be recognized by people from different cultures. One explanation for this similarity is that an innate facial-affect program activates specific muscle movements representing the emotion being experienced. The facial-feedback hypothesis suggests that facial expressions not only reflect, but also produce, emotional experiences. (pp. 214–215)

Pop Quiz

1. _____ are forces that guide a person's behavior in a certain direction.

2. Biologically determined, inborn patterns of behavior are known as _____.

3. According to Maslow, a person with no job, no home, and no friends can become self-actualized. True or false?

4. Match the following terms with their definitions.
   a. leads to refusal of food and starvation
   b. responsible for monitoring food intake
   c. causes extreme overeating
   _____ 1. hypothalamus
   _____ 2. lateral hypothalamic damage
   _____ 3. ventromedial hypothalamic damage

5. _____ is the rate at which energy is produced and expended by the body.

6. The increase in premarital sex in the United States in the last 40 years has been greater for women than for men. True or false?

7. A young girl who is rejected by one of her peers seeks to regain her friendship. What type of motivation is Debbie displaying in her story?
   a. need for achievement
   b. need for motivation
   c. need for affiliation
   d. need for power

8. The _____ - _____ theory of emotions states that emotions are a response to instinctive bodily events.

9. Your friend—a psychology major—tells you, "I was at a party last night. From the time I arrived till the time I left, my general level of arousal increased. Since I was at a party where people were enjoying themselves, I assume I must have felt happy." What theory of emotion does your friend subscribe to?

10. What are the six basic emotions that can be identified from facial expressions?

11. One of the major points that was made in the Detection of Deception activity was that
   a. the brain cannot make the eyes smile when you put on a fake smile.
   b. lie detection using a polygraph is still very imperfect.
   c. hand and eye movements always match when you are telling the truth.
   d. most liars have to practice a lot to become convincing.

Answers
TO POP QUIZ QUESTIONS

1. Motives
2. instincts
3. false; lower-order needs must be fulfilled before self-actualization can occur
4. 1-b, 2-a, 3-c
5. Metabolism
6. true
7. c
8. James-Lange
9. Schachter-Singer
10. surprise, sadness, happiness, anger, disgust, and fear
11. a

9

DEVELOPM

TWICE-BORN BABY

Keri and Chad McCartney were looking forward to learning whether their baby was a boy or a girl. But the moment an image swam onto the screen at a Texas doctor's office, the technician fell silent. When Keri, 40, and Chad, 39, a pastor, peered closer, they saw a bulge below the fetus. "What's that?" they asked. "Well, it's a mass," came the answer.

Then Dr. Debra Williams delivered difficult news: The tailbone attachment was a rare tumor, present in 1 out of 35,000 pregnancies, that draws on the fetal blood supply. The baby's odds of survival were less than 10%.[ix]

But Keri and Chad's daughter Marcie did survive. In a risky intervention, surgeons temporarily removed their daughter from Keri's uterus and cut out most of the tumor. They then put her back into her mother's uterus to finish developing normally until she finally could be delivered—a second time—10 weeks later.

The medical advances that permitted Marcie to survive are just some of the many that have improved children's lives, not only in the prenatal period but throughout their life span. Marcie's story also serves as an introduction to one of the broadest and most important areas of psychology: developmental psychology. This branch of psychology studies the patterns of growth and change that occur throughout life. It deals with issues ranging from new ways of conceiving children, to learning how to raise children, to understanding the milestones of life that we all face.

Developmental psychologists study the interaction between the unfolding of biologically predetermined patterns of growth and a constantly changing, dynamic environment. They ask how our genetic background affects our behavior throughout our lives and how environmental influences, events, and experiences work with—or against—genetic capabilities to shape us throughout our lives.

ENT

- How do infants grow and develop before birth?
- What do newborn babies actually know, and how can we tell?
- How do children learn to get along with and understand other people?
- What are the real psychological challenges of adolescence?
- In what ways do people continue to develop and to grow after they reach adulthood?

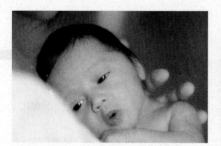

>> Nature and Nurture

How many bald, 6-foot-six, 250-pound volunteer fire-fighters in New Jersey wear droopy mustaches, aviator-style eyeglasses, and a key ring on the right side of the belt?

The answer is two: Gerald Levey and Mark Newman. They are twins who were separated at birth. Each twin did not even know the other existed until they were reunited—in a fire station—by a fellow firefighter who knew Newman and was startled to see his double, Levey, at a firefighters' convention.

The lives of the twins, although separate, took remarkably similar paths. Levey went to college, studying forestry; Newman planned to study forestry in college but instead took a job trimming trees. Both had jobs in supermarkets. One had a job installing sprinkler systems; the other installed fire alarms.

Both men are unmarried and find the same kind of woman attractive: "tall, slender, long hair." They share similar hobbies, enjoying hunting, fishing, going to the beach, and watching old John Wayne movies and professional wrestling. Both like Chinese food and drink the same brand of beer. Their mannerisms are also similar—for example, each one throws his head back when he laughs. And, of course, there is one more thing: They share a passion for fighting fires.

The similarities we see in twins Gerald Levey and Mark Newman vividly raise one of the fundamental questions posed by **developmental psychology**, the study of the patterns of growth and change that occur throughout life.

developmental psychology The branch of psychology that studies the patterns of growth and change that occur throughout life.

nature–nurture issue The issue of the degree to which environment and heredity influence behavior.

The question is this: How can we distinguish between the *environmental* causes of behavior (the influence of parents, siblings, family, friends, schooling, nutrition, and all the other experiences to which a child is exposed) and *hereditary* causes (those based on the genetic makeup of an individual that influence growth and development throughout life)? This question sums up the **nature–nurture issue**. In this context, nature refers to hereditary factors, and nurture to environmental influences.

Although the question was first posed as a nature-*versus*-nurture issue, developmental psychologists today agree that *both* nature and nurture interact to produce specific developmental patterns and outcomes. Consequently, the question has evolved into *How and to what degree* do environment and heredity both produce their effects? No one grows up free of environmental influences, nor does anyone develop without being affected by his or her inherited *genetic makeup*. However, the debate over the relative influence of the two factors remains active, with different approaches

Gerald Levey and Mark Newman, identical twins raised apart.

and different theories of development emphasizing the environment or heredity to a greater or lesser degree (Belsky & Pluess, 2009; Gottesman & Hanson, 2005; Rutter, 2006).

For example, some developmental theories rely on basic psychological principles of learning and stress the role that learning plays in producing changes in behavior in a developing child. Such theories emphasize the role of the environment in development. In contrast, other developmental theories emphasize the influence of one's physiological makeup and functioning on development. These theories stress the role of heredity and *maturation*—the unfolding of biologically predetermined patterns of behavior—in producing developmental change. Maturation can be seen, for instance, in the development of sex characteristics (such as breasts and body hair) that occurs at the start of adolescence. Furthermore, behavioral geneticists, who study the effects of heredity on behavior by looking for genetic commonalities among families and corresponding behaviors, and evolutionary psychologists, who look for behavior patterns over large groups of people that may result from the genetic inheritance of our ancestors, have highlighted the importance of heredity in influencing human behavior (Buss, 2003a, b; Ilies, Arvey, & Bouchard, 2006; Reif & Lesch, 2003).

Characteristics Strongly Influenced by Heredity

Despite their differences over theory, developmental psychologists concur on some points. They agree that genetic factors not only provide the potential for specific behaviors or traits to emerge but also place limitations on the emergence of such behavior or traits. For instance, heredity defines people's general level of intelligence, setting an upper limit that—regardless of the quality of the environment—people cannot exceed. Heredity also places limits on physical abilities; humans simply cannot run at a speed of 60 miles an hour, nor will they grow as tall as 10 feet, no matter what the quality of their environment (Dodge, 2004; Pinker, 2004).

Developmental psychologists also agree that in most instances environmental factors play a critical role in enabling people to reach the potential capabilities that their genetic background makes possible. If Albert Einstein had received no intellectual stimulation as a child and had not been sent to school, it is unlikely that he would have reached his genetic potential. Similarly, a great athlete such as baseball star Derek Jeter would have been unlikely to display much physical skill if he had not been raised in an environment that nurtured his innate talent and gave him the opportunity to train and perfect his natural abilities.

PSYCH think

> > > How would you use environmental experiences to help children develop to their full genetic potential?

The relationship between heredity and environment is far from simple. As a consequence, developmental psychologists typically take an *interactionist* position on the nature–nurture issue, suggesting that a combination of hereditary and environmental factors influences development. Developmental psychologists face the challenge of identifying the relative strength of each of these influences on the individual, as well as that of identifying the specific changes that occur over the course of development (McGregor & Capone, 2004; Moffitt, Caspi, & Rutter, 2006).

Developmental psychologists use several approaches to study the ways in which genetic heritage and the environment interact to influence behavior. In one approach, researchers can experimentally control the genetic makeup of laboratory animals by carefully breeding them for specific traits. Then if they place genetically identical

Physical Characteristics	Intellectual Characteristics	Emotional Characteristics and Disorders
Height	Memory	Shyness
Weight	Intelligence	Extraversion
Obesity	Age of language acquisition	Emotionality
Tone of voice	Reading disability	Neuroticism
Blood pressure	Mental retardation	Schizophrenia
Tooth decay		Anxiety
Athletic ability		Alcoholism
Alcoholism		
Firmness of handshake		
Age of death		
Activity level		

animals in different types of environments, they can identify which behaviors stay the same across the different environments and which behaviors change. Theoretically, those behaviors that do not change very much would be more influenced by genes. For example, if genetically identical animals placed in very different environments all still show a similar degree of curiosity, researchers would conclude that curiosity is strongly influenced by genetic heritage.

: Nonhuman research helps us better understand
: the influences of nature and nurture.

Human twins serve as another important source of information about the relative effects of genetic and environmental factors. If **identical twins** (those who begin life with the same genes) display different patterns of development, those differences have to be attributed to variations in the environment in which the twins were raised. The most useful data come from identical twins (such as Gerald Levey and Mark Newman) who are adopted at birth by different sets of adoptive parents and raised apart in differing environments. Studies of nontwin siblings who are raised in totally different environments also shed some light on the issue. Because they have relatively similar genetic backgrounds, siblings who show similarities as adults provide strong evidence for the importance of heredity (Sternberg, 2002a; Vitaro, Brendgen, & Arseneault, 2009).

identical twins Twins who begin life with the same genes.

cross-sectional research A research method that compares people of different ages at the same point in time.

longitudinal research A research method that investigates behavior as participants age.

Researchers can also take the opposite tack. Instead of concentrating on people with similar genetic backgrounds who are raised in different environments, they may consider people raised in similar environments who have totally dissimilar genetic backgrounds. If they find similar courses of development in, for example, two adopted children who have different genetic backgrounds and have been raised in the same family, they have evidence for the importance of environmental influences on development. Moreover, psychologists can carry out research involving animals with dissimilar genetic backgrounds; by experimentally varying the environment in which they are raised, they can determine the influence of environmental factors (independent of heredity) on development (Greven, Rijsdijk, & Plomin, 2011; Petrill & Deater-Deckard, 2004).

DEVELOPMENTAL RESEARCH TECHNIQUES

Developmental psychologists use a variety of methods to measure behavior and how it changes over time. **Cross-sectional research** is a popular technique that compares people of different ages at the same point in time. Cross-

sectional studies provide information about differences in development among different age groups (Creasey, 2005; Huijie, 2006).

Suppose, for instance, we are interested in the development of intellectual ability in adulthood. To carry out a cross-sectional study, we might compare a sample of 25-, 45-, and 65-year-olds who all take the same IQ test. We then can determine whether average IQ test scores differ in each age group.

Cross-sectional research has limitations, however. For instance, we cannot be sure that the differences in IQ scores we might find in our example are due to age differences alone. Instead, the scores may reflect differences in the educational attainment of the cohorts represented. A *cohort* is a group of people who grow up at similar times, in similar places, and in similar conditions. In the case of IQ differences, any age differences we find in a cross-sectional study may reflect educational differences among the cohorts studied: People in the older age group, for example, may belong to a cohort that was less likely to attend college than were the people in the younger groups.

A longitudinal study, the second major research strategy used by developmental psychologists, provides one way around this problem. **Longitudinal research** traces the behavior of one or more participants as the participants age. Longitudinal studies assess *change* in behavior over time, whereas cross-sectional studies assess *differences* among groups of people.

For instance, consider how we might investigate intellectual development during adulthood by using a longitudinal research strategy. First, we might give an IQ test to a group of 25-year-olds. We'd then come back to the same people 20 years later and retest them at age 45. Finally, we'd return to them once more when they were 65 years old and test them again.

By examining changes at several points in time, we can clearly see how individuals develop. Unfortunately, longitudinal research requires an enormous expenditure of time (as the researcher waits for the participants to get older), and participants who begin a study at an early age may drop out, move away, or die as the research continues. Moreover,

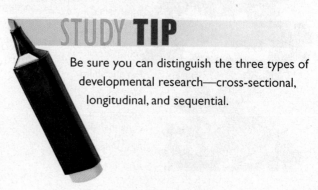

STUDY TIP

Be sure you can distinguish the three types of developmental research—cross-sectional, longitudinal, and sequential.

participants who take the same test at several points in time may become "test-wise" and perform better each time they take it, having become more familiar with the test.

To make up for the limitations in both cross-sectional and longitudinal research, investigators have devised an alternative strategy. Known as **sequential research**, it combines cross-sectional and longitudinal approaches by taking a number of different age groups and examining them at several points in time. For example, investigators might use a group of 3-, 5-, and 7-year-olds, examining them every six months for a period of several years. This technique allows a developmental psychologist to tease out the specific effects of age changes from other possibly influential factors.

Most traits result from a combination of genes, which operate together and interact with environmental influences.

>> Prenatal Development

Our increasing understanding of the first stirrings of life spent inside a mother's womb has permitted significant medical advances, such as those that help infants born more than 10 weeks ahead of schedule, survive the first critical weeks after birth and to go on to become healthy, energetic individuals. Yet our knowledge of the biology of *conception*—when a male's sperm penetrates a female's egg—and its aftermath makes the start of life no less remarkable.

Let's consider how an individual is created by looking first at the genetic endowment that the fertilized cell receives at the moment of conception.

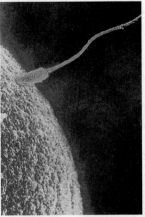

Conception occurs when a male's sperm cell penetrates a female's egg cell.

BASIC GENETICS

The one-cell entity established at conception contains 23 pairs of **chromosomes**, rod-shaped structures that contain all basic hereditary information. One member of each pair is from the mother, and the other is from the father. Each chromosome contains thousands of **genes**—the basic units through which genetic information is transmitted. Either individually or in combination, genes produce the specific characteristics of each person. Composed of sequences of *DNA (deoxyribonucleic acid)* molecules, genes carry the biological instructions for creating a human being.

Humans have some 25,000 different genes. Some genes control the development of systems common to all members

of the human species—the heart, circulatory system, brain, lungs, and so forth; others shape the characteristics that make each human unique, such as facial configuration, height, and eye color. The child's sex is also determined by a specific combination of genes. Specifically, a child usually inherits an X chromosome from its mother and either an X or a Y chromosome from its father. When it receives an XX combination, it develops as a female; with an XY combination, it develops as a male. Male development is triggered by a single gene on the Y chromosome, and without the presence of that specific gene (or when it malfunctions), the individual will develop as a female.

> **sequential research** A research method that combines cross-sectional and longitudinal research by considering a number of different age groups and examining them at several points in time.
>
> **chromosomes** Rod-shaped structures that contain all basic hereditary information.
>
> **genes** The parts of the chromosomes through which genetic information is transmitted.
>
> **zygote** The new cell formed by the union of an egg and sperm.

As behavioral geneticists have discovered, genes are also at least partially responsible for a wide variety of personal characteristics, including intelligence, personality traits, and psychological disorders. Of course, few of these characteristics are determined by a single gene. Instead, most traits result from a combination of genes, which operate together and interact with environmental influences (Haberstick et al., 2005; Plomin & McGuffin, 2003; Ramus, 2006).

EARLIEST DEVELOPMENT

When an egg becomes fertilized by the sperm, the resulting one-celled entity is called a **zygote**. Sometimes two eggs are fertilized and two zygotes develop into nonidentical (dizygotic) twins. When a single zygote splits into two, two embryos develop into identical (monozygotic) twins. The zygote starts out as a microscopic speck. Three days after fertilization, though, the zygote increases to around 32 cells, and within a week it has grown to 100–150 cells. These first two weeks are known as the *germinal period*.

Two weeks after conception, the developing individual enters the *embryonic period*, which lasts from week 2 through week 8, and the developing human is now called an **embryo**. As an embryo develops through an intricate, preprogrammed process of cell division, it grows 10,000 times larger by 4 weeks of age, attaining a length of about one-fifth of an inch. At this point, it has developed a beating heart, a brain, an intestinal tract, and a number of other organs. Although all these organs are at a primitive stage of development, they are clearly recognizable. Moreover, by week 8, the embryo is about an inch long, and has discernible arms and legs and a face.

From week 8 and continuing until birth, the developing individual enters the *fetal period* and is called a **fetus**. At the start of this period, it begins to respond to touch. At 16 to 18 weeks, its movements become strong enough for the mother to sense them. About the same time, hair may begin to grow on the fetus's head, and the facial features become similar to those the child will display at birth. The major organs begin functioning, although the fetus could not survive outside the mother's womb. In addition, a lifetime's worth of brain neurons are produced—although it is unclear whether the brain is capable of thinking at this early stage.

embryo A developed zygote that has a heart, a brain, and other organs.

fetus A developing individual, from 8 weeks after conception until birth.

By week 24, a fetus has many of the characteristics it will display as a newborn. In fact, when an infant is born prematurely at this age, it can open and close its eyes; suck; cry; look up, down, and around; and even grasp objects placed in its hands, although it is still unable to survive for long outside the mother.

The fetus continues to develop before birth. It begins to grow fatty deposits under the skin, and it gains weight. At prenatal age 28 weeks, the fetus weighs less than 3 pounds and is about 16 inches long. It may be capable of learning: One study found that the infants of mothers who had repeatedly read aloud the Dr. Seuss story *The Cat in the Hat* before giving birth preferred the sound of that story to other stories after they were born (Schenone et al., 2010; Spence & DeCasper, 1982).

Before birth, a fetus passes through several *sensitive periods*. A sensitive period is the time when organisms are exceptionally receptive to certain kinds of stimuli. For example, fetuses are especially affected by their mothers' use of drugs at certain times before birth. If they are exposed to a specific drug before or after a sensitive period, the drug may have relatively little effect, but if exposure comes during a sensitive period, the effect will be significant (Konig, 2005; Uylings, 2006; Werker & Tees, 2005).

Sensitive periods can also occur after birth. For instance, some language specialists suggest that there is a period in which children are especially receptive to developing language. If children are not exposed to appropriate linguistic stimuli, their language development may be impaired (Innocenti, 2007; Sohr-Preston & Scaramella, 2007).

In the final weeks of pregnancy, the fetus continues to gain weight and grow. At the end of the normal 38 weeks of pregnancy the fetus typically weighs 7 pounds and is about 20 inches in length. However, the story is different for *preterm infants*, who are born before week 38. Because they have not been able to develop fully, they are at higher risk for illness, future problems, and death. For infants who have been in the womb for more than 30 weeks, the prospects are relatively good. However, for those born between weeks 24 and 30, the story is often less positive. Such newborns, who may weigh as little as 2 pounds at birth, are in grave danger, because they have immature organs. Babies born before 24 weeks have less than a 50-50 chance of survival. If they do survive—and it takes extraordinary medical intervention to assure this—they may later experience significant developmental delays.

Genetic Influences on the Fetus The process of fetal growth that we have just described reflects normal development, which occurs in 95% to 98% percent of all pregnancies. In the other 2% to 5% of cases, children are born with serious birth defects. A major cause of such defects is faulty genes or chromosomes. Here are some of the more common genetic and chromosomal difficulties.

- *Phenylketonuria (PKU).* A child born with the inherited disease phenylketonuria cannot produce an enzyme that is required for normal development. This deficiency results in an accumulation of poisons that eventually cause profound mental retardation. The disease is treatable, however, if it is caught early.

These remarkable photos of a live embryo at age 4 weeks (*left*) and a fetus at 15 weeks (*right*) illustrate the degree of physical development that occurs in 11 weeks.

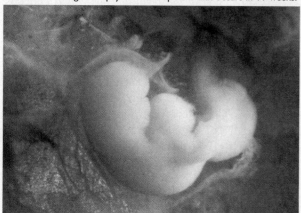

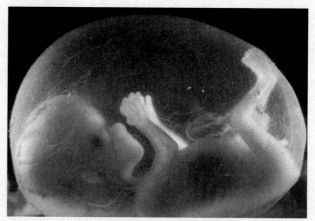

Most infants today are routinely tested for PKU, and children with the disorder can be placed on a special diet that allows them to develop normally (Christ et al., 2006; Goldstein & Reynolds, 2011; Ievers-Landis et al., 2005; Widaman, 2009; Waisbren, 2011).

- *Sickle-cell anemia.* About 10% of the African-American population has the possibility of passing on sickle-cell anemia, a disease that gets its name from the abnormally shaped red blood cells it causes. Children with the disease may have episodes of pain, yellowish eyes, stunted growth, and vision problems, and heart problems can lead to premature death in middle age (Selove, 2007; Taras & Potts-Datema, 2005).
- *Tay-Sachs disease.* Children born with Tay-Sachs disease, a disorder most often found in Jews of eastern European ancestry, usually die by age 3 or 4 because of the body's inability to break down fat. If both parents carry the genetic defect that produces the fatal illness, their child has a one in four chance of being born with the disease (Leib et al., 2005; Weinstein, 2007).
- *Down syndrome.* Down syndrome, one of the causes of mental retardation, occurs when the zygote receives an extra chromosome on the 21st pair at the moment of conception. Down syndrome is related to the mother's age; mothers who are younger than 18 or over 35 have a higher risk than other women do of having a child with the syndrome (Roizen & Patterson, 2003; Sherman et al., 2007).

Prenatal Environmental Influences Genetic factors are not the only causes of difficulties in fetal development. Environmental influences—the *nurture* part of the nature–nurture equation—also affect the fetus. Some of the more profound consequences are brought about by **teratogens**, environmental agents such as a drug, chemical, or virus, that produce a birth defect. Among the major prenatal environmental influences on the fetus are these:

- *Mother's nutrition.* What a mother eats during her pregnancy can have important implications for the health of her baby. Seriously undernourished mothers cannot provide adequate nutrition to a growing fetus, and they are likely to give birth to underweight babies. Poorly nourished babies are also more susceptible to disease, and a lack of nourishment may have an adverse effect on their mental development (Everette, 2008; Najman et al., 2004; Zigler, Finn-Stevenson, & Hall, 2002).

Environment and Prenatal Development

Environmental Factor	Possible Effect on Prenatal Development
Rubella (German measles)	Blindness, deafness, heart abnormalities, stillbirth
Syphilis	Mental retardation, physical deformities, maternal miscarriage
Addictive drugs	Low birth weight, addiction of infant to drug, with possible death after birth from withdrawal
Nicotine	Premature birth, low birth weight and length
Alcohol	Mental retardation, lower-than-average birth weight, small head, limb deformities
Radiation from X rays	Physical deformities, mental retardation
Inadequate diet	Reduction in growth of brain, smaller-than-average weight and length at birth
Mother's age—younger than 18 at birth of child	Premature birth, increased incidence of Down syndrome
Mother's age—older than 35 at birth of child	Increased incidence of Down syndrome
DES (diethylstilbestrol)	Reproductive difficulties and increased incidence of genital cancer in children of mothers who were given DES during pregnancy to prevent miscarriage
AIDS	Possible spread of AIDS virus to infant; facial deformities; growth failure
Accutane	Mental retardation and physical deformities

- *Mother's illness.* Several diseases that have a relatively minor effect on the health of a mother can have devastating consequences for a developing fetus if they are contracted during a sensitive period of embryonic or fetal development. For example, rubella (German measles), syphilis, diabetes, and high blood pressure may each produce a permanent effect on the fetus.
- *Mother's use of drugs.* Mothers who take illegal, physically addictive drugs such as cocaine run the risk of giving birth to babies who are similarly addicted. Their newborns suffer painful withdrawal symptoms and sometimes show permanent physical and mental impairment as well. Even legal drugs, such as the acne medication, accutane, can have a tragic effect when taken by a pregnant woman (who may not know that she has become pregnant) (Ikonomidou et al, 2000; Schecter, Finkelstein, & Koren, 2005).

> **teratogens** Environmental agents such as a drug, chemical, virus, or other factor that produce a birth defect.

- *Alcohol.* Alcohol is extremely dangerous to fetal development. For example, 1 out of every 750 infants is born with fetal alcohol syndrome (FAS), a condition resulting in below-average intelligence, growth delays, and facial deformities. FAS is now the primary preventable cause of mental retardation. Even mothers who use small amounts of alcohol during pregnancy place their child at risk. *Fetal alcohol effects* (FAE) is a condition in which children display some, although not all, of the problems of FAS owing to their mother's consumption of alcohol during pregnancy (Henderson, Kesmodel, & Gray, 2007; Mooney & Valkinskaya, 2011; Murthy et al., 2009; Niccols, 2007; Mooney & Valkinskaya, 2011; Murthy et al., 2009).

- *Nicotine use.* Pregnant mothers who smoke put their children at considerable risk. Smoking while pregnant can lead to miscarriage and infant death. For children who do survive, the negative consequences of mother's tobacco use can last a lifetime, including a higher risk of respiratory disease, ear infections, and even psychological disorders (Haslam & Lawrence, 2004; Rogers, 2009; Shea & Steiner, 2008).

Several other environmental factors have an impact on the child before and during birth. Keep in mind, however, that although we have been discussing the influences of genetics and environment separately, neither factor works alone. Furthermore, despite the emphasis here on some of the ways in which development can go wrong, the vast majority of births occur without difficulty.

>> Infancy and Childhood

His head was molded into a long melon shape and came to a point at the back. . . . He was covered with a thick greasy white material known as "vernix," which made him slippery to hold, and also allowed him to slip easily through the birth canal. In addition to a shock of black hair on his head, his body was covered with dark, fine hair known as "lanugo." His ears, his back, his shoulders, and even his cheeks were furry. . . . His skin was wrinkled and quite loose, ready to scale in creased places such as his feet and hands. . . . His ears were pressed to his head in unusual positions—one ear was matted firmly forward on his cheek. His nose was flattened and pushed to one side by the squeeze as he came through the pelvis. (Brazelton, 1969, p. 3)

What kind of creature is this? Although the description hardly fits that of the adorable babies seen in baby food ads, it depicts a normal, completely developed child just after the moment of birth. The newborn arrives in the world in a form that hardly meets the standards of beauty by which we typically measure babies.

reflexes Unlearned, involuntary responses that occur automatically in the presence of certain stimuli.

THE EXTRAORDINARY NEWBORN

Several factors cause a newborn's strange appearance. The trip through the mother's birth canal may have squeezed the incompletely formed bones of the skull together and squashed the nose into the head. The skin secretes *vernix,* a white, greasy covering, for protection before birth, and the baby may have *lanugo,* a soft fuzz, over the entire body for a similar purpose. The infant's eyelids may be puffy with an accumulation of fluids because of the upside-down posi-

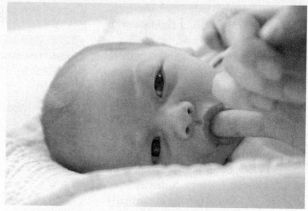

The sucking reflex is one of several innate responses that are critical to a newborn's survival.

tion during birth. All these features change during the first two weeks of life, as the newborn takes on a more familiar appearance. Even more impressive are the capabilities a newborn begins to display right after birth—capabilities that grow at an astounding rate over the ensuing months.

Reflexes A newborn enters the world with a number of **reflexes**—unlearned, involuntary responses that occur automatically in the presence of certain stimuli. Critical for survival, many of these reflexes unfold naturally as part of an infant's ongoing maturation. The *rooting reflex,* for instance, causes newborns to turn their heads toward things that touch their cheeks—such as the mother's nipple or a bottle. Similarly, a *sucking reflex* prompts infants to suck at things that touch their lips. Among other reflexes are a *gag reflex* (to clear the throat), the *startle reflex* (a group of movements in which an infant flings out the arms, fans the fingers, and arches the back in response to a sudden noise), and the *Babinski reflex* (a baby's toes fan out when the outer edge of the sole of the foot is stroked).

Infants lose these primitive reflexes after the first few months of life, replacing them with more complex and organized behaviors. Although at birth a newborn is capable of only jerky, limited voluntary movements, during the first year of life the ability to move independently grows enormously. The typical baby rolls over by the age of about 3 months, sits without support at about 6 months, stands alone at about 11 months, and walks at just over a year old. Not only does the ability to make large-scale movements (such as moving an arm or leg) improve during this time, fine-muscle movements (for example, using a finger to push a toy) become increasingly sophisticated.

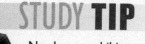

STUDY **TIP**

Newborns exhibit several reflexes—unlearned, involuntary responses—including the rooting, sucking, gag, startle, and Babinski reflexes.

Development of the Senses When parents peer into the eyes of their newborn, is the child able to return their gaze? Although it was thought for some time that newborns can see only a hazy blur, most current findings indicate that the capabilities of newborns are far more impressive. Although their eyes have a limited capacity to focus on objects that are not within a 7- to 8-inch distance from the face, newborns can follow objects moving within their field of vision. They also show the rudiments of depth perception, as they react by raising their hands when an object appears to be moving rapidly toward the face (Gelman & Kit-Fong Au, 1996; Maurer et al., 1999).

You might think that it would be hard to figure out just how well newborns can see, because their lack of both language and reading ability clearly prevents them from saying what direction the E on a vision chart is facing. However, researchers have devised a number of ingenious methods, relying on the newborn's biological responses and innate reflexes, to test perceptual skills.

For instance, infants who see a novel stimulus typically pay close attention to it, and, as a consequence, their heart rates increase. But if they repeatedly see the same stimulus, their attention to it decreases, and the heart rate returns to a slower rate. This phenomenon is known as **habituation**, the decrease in the response to a stimulus that occurs after repeated presentations of the same stimulus. By studying habituation, developmental psychologists can tell when a child who is too young to speak can detect and discriminate a stimulus (del Rosal, Alonso, & Moreno, 2006; Gurnwald et al., 2003; Hannon & Johnson, 2005; Kaufman & Needham, 2011).

> **habituation** The decrease in response to a stimulus that occurs after repeated presentations of the same stimulus.

Through the use of such research techniques, we now know that infants' visual perception is remarkably sophisticated from the start of life. At birth, babies prefer patterns with contours and edges over less distinct patterns, indicating that they can respond to the configuration of stimuli. Furthermore, even newborns are apparently born with the understanding that objects stay the same size even when the image on the retina changes size as the object moves closer and farther away (Moore, Goodwin, & George, 2007; Norcia et al., 2005).

In fact, newborns can discriminate facial expressions—and even imitate them. Newborns who see an adult with a happy, sad, or surprised facial expression can produce a good imitation of the adult's expression. Even very young infants, then, can respond to the emotions and moods that their caregivers' facial expressions reveal. This capability provides the foundation for social interaction skills in children (Grossman, Striano, & Friederici, 2007; Lavelli & Fogel, 2005; Meltzoff, 1996).

Other visual abilities grow rapidly after birth. By the end of their first month, babies can distinguish some colors from others, and after 4 months they can

From the perspective of ...

A GENETIC COUNSELOR What advice would you give expectant parents whose fetus has tested positive for Down syndrome? What strategies could you suggest for maximizing their child's prenatal development?

Milestones of Physical Development, Birth to Age 2

| 3.2 months: Rolling over | 3.3 months: Grasping rattle | 5.9 months: Sitting without support | 7.2 months: Standing while holding on | 8.2 months: Grasping with thumb and finger |

| 11.5 months: Standing alone well | 12.3 months: Walking well | 14.8 months: Building tower of two cubes | 16.6 months: Walking up steps | 23.8 months: Jumping in place |

Source: Frankenburg et al., 1992.

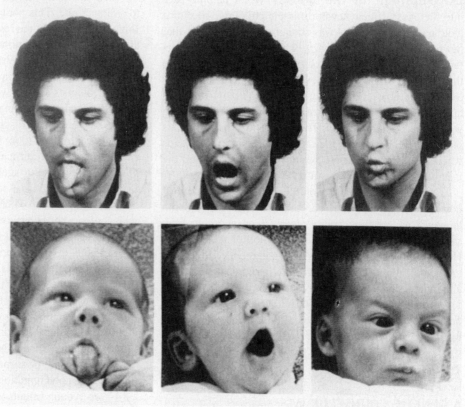

The young infant is clearly imitating the expressions of the adult model, rehearsing for future social interactions.

Source: Courtesy of Dr. Tiffany Field.

focus on near or far objects. By age 4 or 5 months they are able to recognize two- and three-dimensional objects. By the age of 7 months, neural systems related to the processing of information about facial expressions show a high degree of sophistication, causing babies to respond differently to specific facial expressions (Johnson, 2004; Leppanen et al., 2007; Nakato et al., 2011; Striano & Vaish, 2006).

In addition to vision, infants display other impressive sensory capabilities. Newborns can distinguish different sounds to the point of being able to recognize their own mothers' voices and at least some aspects of the language spoken in their home before they are born (Kisilevsky, et al., 2009).

Did you know?

All new babies cry, but apparently they don't all cry in the same way. One recent study found that the language spoken while the fetus was developing made a difference: French newborns had a different melody to their cries than German newborns (Mampe, Friederici, Christophe, & Wermke, 2009).

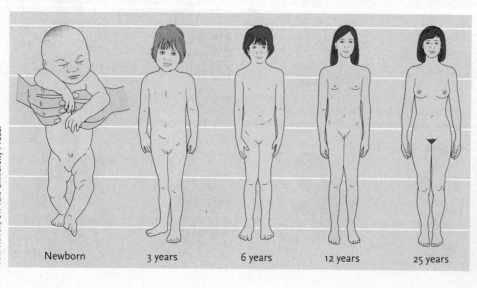

Adapted from Figure 5 from W. J. Robbins, *Growth* (1929). New Haven, CT: Yale University Press.

Newborn   3 years   6 years   12 years   25 years

Head Size Relative to Body Size, Birth to Age 25

Average Height and Weight of U.S. Males and Females, Birth to Age 20

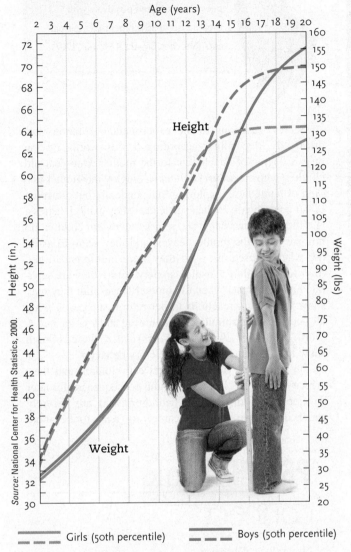

Age (years)

Height (in.) / Weight (lbs) chart, with axes showing Age 2–20, Height 30–72 in., Weight 20–160 lbs.

Source: National Center for Health Statistics, 2000.

Height

Weight

——— Girls (50th percentile)   ——— Boys (50th percentile)

INFANCY THROUGH MIDDLE CHILDHOOD

During infancy and childhood, until the start of adolescence around age 11 or 12, development proceeds rapidly in physical, social, and cognitive domains. Physical growth

> Attachment, the positive emotional bond that develops between a child and a specific individual, is central to social development in infancy.

provides the most obvious sign of children's development. During the first year of life, children typically triple their birth weight, and their height increases by about half. This rapid growth slows down as the child gets older—think how gigantic adults would be if that rate of growth were constant—and from age 3 to the beginning of adolescence at around age 13, growth averages a gain of about 5 pounds and 3 inches a year.

The physical changes that occur as children develop are not just a matter of increasing height and weight. The relationship of the size of the various body parts to one another changes dramatically as children age. For example, the head of a fetus (and a newborn) is disproportionately large, but it soon becomes more proportional in size to the rest of the body as growth occurs mainly in the trunk and legs.

> **attachment** The positive emotional bond that develops between a child and a specific individual.

DEVELOPMENT OF SOCIAL BEHAVIOR

As anyone who has seen an infant smiling at the sight of his or her mother can guess, at the same time that infants grow physically and hone their perceptual abilities, they also develop socially. The nature of a child's early social development provides the foundation for social relationships that will last a lifetime.

Relationships with Caregivers Attachment, the positive emotional bond that develops between a child and a specific individual, is the most important form of social development that occurs during infancy. The earliest studies of attachment, carried out by animal ethologist Konrad Lorenz (1966), focused on newborn goslings. Under normal circumstances, goslings instinctively follow their mother, the first moving object they perceive after birth. Lorenz found that goslings whose eggs were raised in an incubator and who viewed him immediately after hatching would follow his every movement, as if he were their mother. He labeled this process *imprinting*, behavior that takes place during a critical period and involves attachment to the first moving object that is observed.

Our understanding of attachment progressed when psychologist Harry Harlow, in a classic study, gave infant monkeys the choice of cuddling a wire

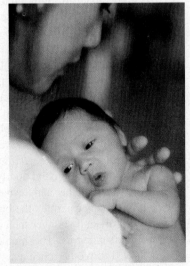

The close attachment bonds that form between infants and their primary caregivers are the most important social relationships of an individual's early life.

In Harlow's classic study, baby monkeys preferred the soft, terry-cloth "mother" even though the wire "mother" provided their food.

Source: Harry Harlow Primate Laboratory / University of Wisconsin.

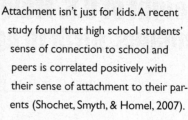
"monkey" that provided milk or a soft, terry-cloth "monkey" that was warm but did not provide milk. Their choice was clear: They spent most of their time clinging to the warm cloth "monkey," although they made occasional forays to the wire monkey to nurse. The cloth monkey provided greater comfort to the infants than did milk (Blum, 2002; Harlow & Zimmerman, 1959; Whipple, Bernier, & Mageau, 2011).

Building on this pioneering work with nonhumans, developmental psychologists have suggested that human attachment grows through the responsiveness of infants' caregivers to the signals the babies provide, such as crying, smiling, reaching, and clinging. The greater the responsiveness of the caregiver to the child's signals, the more likely it is that the child will develop a trusting bond and become securely attached. Full attachment eventually develops as a result of the complex series of interactions between caregiver and child. In the course of these interactions, the infant plays as critical and active a role as the caregiver in the formation of the bond. Infants who respond positively to a caregiver produce more positive behavior on the part of the caregiver, which in turn produces an even stronger degree of attachment in the child. Developmental psychologists have devised a relatively straightforward way to measure attachment. Developed by Mary Ainsworth, the *Ainsworth strange situation* consists of a sequence of events involving a child and (typically) his or her mother. Initially, the mother and the baby enter an unfamiliar room, and the mother permits the baby to explore while she sits down. An adult stranger then enters the room, after which the mother leaves. The mother returns, and the stranger leaves. The mother once again leaves the baby alone, and the stranger returns. Finally, the stranger leaves, and the mother returns (Ainsworth et al., 1978; Combrink-Graham & McKenna, 2006; Izard & Abe, 2004).

Babies' reactions to the experimental situation vary drastically, depending, according to Ainsworth, on the baby's degree of attachment to the mother. One-year-old children who are *securely attached* employ the mother as a kind of home base, exploring independently but returning to her occasionally. When she leaves, they exhibit distress, and they go to her when she returns. *Avoidant* children do not cry when the mother leaves, and they seem to avoid her when she returns, as if they were indifferent to her. *Ambivalent* children display anxiety before they are separated and are upset when the mother leaves, but they may show ambivalent reactions to her return, such as seeking close contact but simultaneously hitting and kicking her. A fourth reaction is *disorganized-disoriented*; these children show inconsistent, often contradictory behavior.

The nature of attachment between children and their primary caregivers has far-reaching consequences for later development. For example, children who are securely attached to their primary caregivers tend to be more

PSYCH think

connect™

WWW.MCGRAWHILLCONNECT.COM/PSYCHOLOGY
Naturalistic Observation

> > > The bonds that develop between parent and infant are not always perfectly happy and trusting. How might temperament, parenting style, and genetics affect the ability of a parent and infant to develop a secure attachment?

Take the PsychSmart Challenge! Can you figure out which baby demonstrates the most secure attachment? From chapter 1 in your ebook, select the *Exercises* tab. Then, select "Naturalistic Observation." After completing the activity, answer question 4 in the Pop Quiz on p. 255 to confirm your understanding of the attachment study.

socially and emotionally competent than are their less securely attached peers, and others find them more cooperative, capable, and playful. Furthermore, children who are securely attached at age 1 show fewer psychological difficulties when they grow older compared with avoidant and ambivalent youngsters. As adults, children who are securely attached tend to have more successful romantic relationships. However, being securely attached at an early age does not guarantee good adjustment later, and, conversely, children who lack secure attachment do not always have difficulties later in life (Hardy, 2007; Mikulincer & Shaver, 2005; Roisman et al., 2005).

Although early developmental research focused largely on the mother-child relationship, more recent research has highlighted the father's role in parenting, and with good reason: The number of fathers who are primary caregivers for their children has grown significantly, and fathers play an increasingly important role in their children's lives. For example, in almost 13% of families with children, the father is the parent who stays at home to care for preschoolers (Day & Lamb, 2004; Halford, 2006; Parke, 2004).

When fathers interact with their children, their play often differs from that of mothers. Fathers engage in more physical, rough-and-tumble sorts of activities, whereas mothers play more verbal and traditional games, such as peekaboo. Despite such behavioral differences, the nature of attachment between fathers and children compared with that between mothers and children can be similar. In fact, children can form multiple attachments simultaneously (Borisenko, 2007; Diener et al., 2008; Pellis & Pellis, 2007).

Relationships with Peers

By the time they are 2 years old, children have become less dependent on their parents and more self-reliant, increasingly preferring to play with friends. Initially, play is relatively independent: Even though they may be sitting side by side, 2-year-olds pay more attention to toys than to one another when playing. They soon begin to actively interact, however, modifying one another's behavior and later exchanging roles during play (Colwell & Lindsey, 2005; Lindsey & Colwell, 2003).

Cultural factors also affect children's styles of play. For example, Korean American children engage in a higher degree of parallel play—playing independently even when they are next to each other—than do their Anglo-American counterparts, while Anglo-American preschoolers are involved in more pretend play (Bai, 2005; Drewes, 2005; Suizzo & Bornstein, 2006).

As children reach school age, their social interactions begin to follow set patterns, as well as becoming more frequent. Children may engage in elaborate games involving teams and rigid rules. This play serves purposes other than mere enjoyment. It allows children to become increasingly competent in their social interactions with others. Through play they learn to take the perspective of other people and to infer others' thoughts and feelings, even when those thoughts and feelings are not directly expressed (Royzman, Cassidy, & Baron, 2003).

In short, social interaction helps children to interpret the meaning of others' behavior and to develop the capacity to respond appropriately. Furthermore, children learn physical and emotional self-control: They learn to avoid hitting a playmate who beats them at a game, to be polite, and to control their emotional displays and facial expressions (for example, smiling even when receiving a disappointing gift). Situations that provide children with opportunities for social interaction, then, may enhance their social development (Feldman, 1993; Talukdar & Shastri, 2006; Whitebread et al., 2009).

Parenting Styles Parents' child-rearing practices are critical in shaping their children's social competence. According to classic research by developmental psychologist Diana Baumrind, there are four main categories of parenting styles. Rigid and punitive, **authoritarian parents** value unquestioning obedience from their children. They have strict standards and discourage expressions of disagreement. **Permissive parents** give their children relaxed or inconsistent direction and, although warm, require little of them. In contrast, **authoritative parents** are firm, setting limits for their children. As the children get older, these parents try to reason and explain things to them. They also set clear goals and encourage their children's independence. Finally, **uninvolved parents** show little interest in their children. Emotionally detached, they view parenting as nothing more than providing food, clothing, and shelter for children. At their most extreme, uninvolved parents are guilty of neglect, a form of child abuse (Baumrind, 2005; Carlo et al., 2011; Lagacé-Séguin & d'Entremont, 2006; Winsler, Madigan, & Aquilino, 2005).

As you might expect, the four kinds of child-rearing styles correlate with very different

authoritarian parents Parents who are rigid and punitive and value unquestioning obedience from their children.

permissive parents Parents who give their children relaxed or inconsistent direction and, although they are warm, require little of them.

authoritative parents Parents who are firm, set clear limits, reason with their children, and explain things to them.

uninvolved parents Parents who show little interest in their children and are emotionally detached.

Fathers today are more likely to be the primary caregivers for their young children than was the case when psychologists started studying attachment. More recent studies show that the nature of attachment between fathers and children can be similar to that of mothers and children.

Parenting Style	Parent Behavior	Type of Behavior Produced in Child
Authoritarian	Rigid, punitive, strict standards (example: "If you don't clean your room, I'm going to take away your iPod for good and ground you.")	Unsociable, unfriendly, withdrawn
Permissive	Lax, inconsistent, undemanding (example: "It might be good to clean your room, but I guess it can wait.")	Immature, moody, dependent, low self-control
Authoritative	Firm, sets limits and goals, uses reasoning, encourages independence (example: "You'll need to clean your room before we can go out to the restaurant. As soon as you finish, we'll leave.")	Good social skills, likable, self-reliant, independent
Uninvolved	Detached emotionally, sees role only as providing food, clothing, and shelter (example: "I couldn't care less if your room is a pigsty.")	Indifferent, rejecting behavior

Baumrind's Four Styles of Parenting

temperament The basic, innate disposition that emerges early in life.

psychosocial development Development of individuals' interactions and understanding of one another and of their knowledge and understanding of themselves as members of society.

kinds of behavior in children (with many exceptions, of course). Children of authoritarian parents tend to be unsociable, unfriendly, and relatively withdrawn. In contrast, permissive parents' children show immaturity, moodiness, dependence, and low self-control. The children of authoritative parents fare best. With high social skills, they are likable, self-reliant, independent, and cooperative. Worst off are the children of uninvolved parents; they feel unloved and emotionally detached, and their physical and cognitive development is impeded. Children with low social skills face peer rejection that can have lasting results (Berk, 2005; Snyder, Cramer, & Afrank, 2005; Saarni, 1999).

Before we congratulate authoritative parents and condemn authoritarian, permissive, and uninvolved ones, we should note that in many cases nonauthoritative parents also have perfectly well-adjusted children. Moreover, children are born with a particular **temperament**—a basic, innate

Did you know?

Culture matters, but not as much as you might think when it comes to parenting styles. One study found that children who have authoritarian parents, whether in the United States or China, tend to have the same kinds of problems (Pomerantz & Wang, 2009).

disposition. Some children are naturally easygoing and cheerful, whereas others are irritable and fussy, or pensive and quiet. The kind of temperament a baby is born with may in part bring about specific kinds of parental child-rearing styles (Coplan, Reichel, & Rowan, 2009; Majdandzic & van den Boom, 2007; Miner & Clarke-Stewart, 2008).

Erikson's Theory of Psychosocial Development In tracing the course of social development, some theorists have considered how the challenges of society and culture change as an individual matures. Following this path, psychoanalyst Erik Erikson developed one of the more comprehensive theories of social development. Erikson (1963) viewed the developmental changes occurring throughout life as a series of eight stages of psychosocial development, of which four occur during childhood. **Psychosocial development** involves changes in the way in which people understand themselves, one another, and the world around them over the course of a lifetime.

Erikson suggests that passage through each of the stages necessitates the resolution of a crisis or conflict. Accordingly, Erikson represents each stage as a pairing of the most positive and most negative aspects of the crisis of that period. Although each crisis is never resolved entirely—life becomes increasingly complicated as we grow older—it has to be resolved sufficiently to equip us to deal with demands made during the stages of development that follow.

In the first stage of psychosocial development, the **trust-versus-mistrust stage** (ages birth to 1½ years), infants develop feelings of trust if their physical requirements and psychological needs for attachment are consistently met and their interactions with the world are generally positive. In contrast, inconsistent care and unpleasant interactions with others can lead to mistrust and leave an infant unable to meet the challenges required in the next stage of development.

In the second stage, the **autonomy-versus-shame-and-doubt stage** (ages 1½ to 3 years), toddlers develop independence and autonomy if exploration and freedom are encouraged, or they experience shame, self-doubt, and unhappiness if they are overly restricted and protected. As you can imagine, it will be difficult for children to feel free to explore in safety if they have not developed basic trust with one or more of their primary caregivers. According to Erikson, the key to the development of autonomy during this period is that the child's caregivers provide the appropriate amount of control. If parents provide too much control, children cannot assert themselves and develop their own sense of control over their environment; if parents provide too little control, the children become overly demanding and controlling.

> Erikson's theory of psychosocial development is one of the few theories that encompass the entire life span.

Next, children face the crises of the **initiative-versus-guilt stage** (ages 3 to 6). In this stage, children's desire to act independently conflicts with the guilt that comes from the unintended and unexpected consequences of such behavior. Children in this period come to understand that they are persons in their own right, and they begin to make decisions about their behavior. If parents react positively to children's attempts at independence, they will help their children resolve the initiative-versus-guilt crisis positively.

The fourth and last stage of childhood is the **industry-versus-inferiority stage** (ages 6 to 12). During this period, increasing competency in all areas, whether social interactions or academic skills, characterizes successful psychosocial development. In contrast, difficulties in this stage lead to feelings of failure and inadequacy.

According to Erikson, children develop autonomy between the ages of 1½ to 3 years if their caregivers give them an opportunity to explore without too many restrictions.

Erikson's theory suggests that psychosocial development continues throughout life, and he proposes four more crises that are faced after childhood (described on pp. 242–243). Although his theory has been criticized on several grounds (for example, some of the concepts are vague and/or not easy to measure), it remains influential and is one of the few theories that encompass the entire life span.

Cognitive Development: Children's Thinking About the World Suppose you had two drinking glasses of different shapes—one short and broad and one tall and thin. Now imagine that you filled the short, broad one with soda about halfway and then poured the liquid from that glass into the tall one. The soda would appear to fill about three-quarters of the second glass. If someone asked you whether there was more soda in the second glass than there had been in the first, what would you say?

You might think that such a simple question hardly deserves an answer; of course, there is no difference in the amount of soda in the two glasses. However, most 4-year-olds would be likely to say that there is more soda in the second glass. If you then poured the soda back into the short glass, they would say there is now less soda than there was in the taller glass.

Why are young children confused by this problem? The reason is not immediately obvious. Anyone who has observed preschoolers must be impressed by how far they have progressed

trust-versus-mistrust stage According to Erikson, the first stage of psychosocial development, occurring from birth to age 1½ years, during which time infants develop feelings of trust or lack of trust.

autonomy-versus-shame-and-doubt stage The period during which, according to Erikson, toddlers (ages 1½ to 3 years) develop independence and autonomy if exploration and freedom are encouraged, or shame and self-doubt if they are restricted and overprotected.

initiative-versus-guilt stage According to Erikson, the period during which children ages 3 to 6 years experience conflict between independence of action and the sometimes negative results of that action.

industry-versus-inferiority stage According to Erikson, the last stage of childhood, during which children age 6 to 12 years may develop positive social interactions with others or may feel inadequate and become less sociable.

No theory of cognitive development has been more influential than that of Swiss psychologist Jean Piaget.

from the early stages of development. They speak with ease, know the alphabet, count, play complex games, use computers, tell stories, and communicate ably. Yet despite this seeming sophistication, there are deep gaps in children's understanding of the world. Some theorists have suggested that children cannot understand certain ideas and concepts until they reach a certain stage of **cognitive development**—the process by which a child's understanding of the world changes as a function of age and experience. In contrast to Erikson's theory of psychosocial development discussed previously, theories of cognitive development seek to explain the intellectual advances that occur during development. These advances include quantitative and qualitative changes. Quantitative development refers to growth that adds more to what already is in place. In physical development, for example, children grow taller as they develop. In intellectual development, children tend to develop longer attention spans as they grow.

cognitive development The process by which a child's understanding of the world changes as a function of age and experience.

Qualitative development refers to changes that instead of adding more abilities result in different ones. For example, walking is a physical development that occurs after crawling, but walking is not simply *more* crawling. Quali-

tative changes in intellectual development enhance the ability to think.

Now stop reading for a moment, and consider what you are planning to do this weekend. How many items did you hold in your mind while thinking about your plans? As we will see in the following discussion of Piaget's theory, children's ability to think about different concepts depends on how many items they can hold in mind. At first, they can't hold any!

Piaget's Theory of Cognitive Development No theory of cognitive development has been more influential than that of Swiss psychologist Jean Piaget. Piaget (1970) suggested that children around the world proceed through

Piaget's Theory of Cognitive Development

Sensorimotor Stage

Development of object permanence, development of motor skills, little or no capacity for symbolic representation

Birth to 2 Years

Preoperational Stage

Development of language and symbolic thinking, egocentric thinking

2 to 7 Years

Concrete Operational Mastery Stage

Development of conservation and concept of reversibility

7 to 12 Years

Formal Operational Stage

Development of logical and abstract thinking

12 Years through Adulthood

a series of four stages in a fixed order. He maintained that these stages differ not only in the *quantity* of information acquired at each stage but also in the *quality* of knowledge and understanding as well. Taking an interactionist point of view, he suggested that movement from one stage to the next occurs when a child reaches an appropriate level of maturation *and* is exposed to relevant types of experiences. Piaget assumed that, without having such experiences, children could not reach their highest level of cognitive growth.

Piaget proposed four stages: sensorimotor, preoperations, concrete operations, and formal operations. During the **sensorimotor stage**, from birth to age 2, children base their understanding of the world primarily on touching, sucking, chewing, shaking, and manipulating objects. In the initial part of the stage, children have a limited ability to think about the world using images, language, or other kinds of symbols. Consequently, infants lack what Piaget calls **object permanence**, the ability to hold in mind a mental representation of things and ideas. Without this ability, infants cannot have the awareness that objects—and people—continue to exist even if they are out of sight.

How do we know that children lack object permanence? Although we cannot ask infants, we can observe their reactions when a toy they are playing with is hidden under a blanket. Until the age of about 9 months, children will make no attempt to locate the hidden toy. However, soon after that age they will begin an active search for the missing object, indicating that they have developed a mental representation of the toy. Object permanence, then, is a critical development during the sensorimotor stage.

The most important development during the **preoperational stage**, beginning about age 2 and lasting till age 7, is the use of language. Children develop internal representational systems that allow them to describe people, events, and feelings. They even use symbols in play, pretending, for example, that a book pushed across the floor is a car.

Although children use more advanced thinking in this stage than they did in the earlier sensorimotor stage, their thinking is still qualitatively different to that of adults. We see this when we observe a preoperational child using **egocentric thought**, a way of thinking in which the child views the world entirely from his or her own perspective. Preoperational children do not understand that other people have a different perspective and knowledge. Thus, children's stories and explanations to adults can be maddeningly uninformative, as they are delivered without any context. For example, a preoperational child may start a story with "He wouldn't let me go," neglecting to mention who "he" is or where the storyteller wanted to go. We also see egocentric thinking when children at the preopera-

Children who have not mastered the principle of conservation assume that the volume of a liquid increases when it is poured from a short, wide container into a tall, thin one.

tional stage play hiding games. For instance, 3-year-olds frequently hide with their faces against a wall, covering their eyes—although they are still in plain view. It seems to them that if *they* cannot see, then no one else will be able to see them.

In addition, preoperational children have not yet developed the ability to understand the **principle of conservation**, which is the knowledge that quantity is unrelated to the arrangement and physical appearance of objects. Children who have not mastered this concept do not know that the amount, volume, or length of an object does not change when its shape or configuration changes. The question about the two glasses—one short and broad and the other tall and thin—with which we began our discussion of cognitive development illustrates this point clearly. Children who do not understand the principle of conservation invariably state that the amount of liquid changes as it is poured back and forth. They cannot comprehend that a transformation in appearance does not imply a transformation in amount. Instead, it seems as reasonable to the child that there is a change in quantity as it does to the adult that there is no change.

In a number of other ways, some quite startling, the failure to understand the principle of conservation affects children's responses. Research demonstrates that principles that are obvious to and unquestioned by adults may be completely misunderstood by children during the preoperational period.

Mastery of the principle of conservation, at around age 7, marks the beginning of Piaget's **concrete operational stage**, although children do not fully understand some aspects of conservation, such as conservation of weight and volume, until they are older.

During the concrete operational stage, which spans the ages of 7 to 12, children develop the ability to think in a more logical manner and begin to overcome some of the egocentrism of the preoperational period. One of the major principles children learn during this stage is reversibility, the idea that some changes can be undone by reversing an earlier action. For example, they

sensorimotor stage According to Piaget, the stage from birth to 2 years, during which a child has little competence in representing the environment by using images, language, or other symbols.

object permanence The awareness that objects—and people—continue to exist even if they are out of sight.

preoperational stage According to Piaget, the period from 2 to 7 years of age that is characterized by language development.

egocentric thought A way of thinking in which a child views the world entirely from his or her own perspective.

principle of conservation The knowledge that quantity is unrelated to the arrangement and physical appearance of objects.

concrete operational stage According to Piaget, the period from 7 to 12 years of age that is characterized by logical thought and a loss of egocentrism.

Principles of Conservation

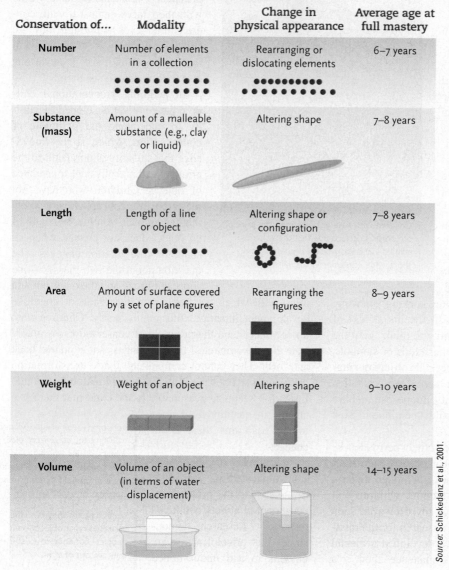

Conservation of...	Modality	Change in physical appearance	Average age at full mastery
Number	Number of elements in a collection	Rearranging or dislocating elements	6–7 years
Substance (mass)	Amount of a malleable substance (e.g., clay or liquid)	Altering shape	7–8 years
Length	Length of a line or object	Altering shape or configuration	7–8 years
Area	Amount of surface covered by a set of plane figures	Rearranging the figures	8–9 years
Weight	Weight of an object	Altering shape	9–10 years
Volume	Volume of an object (in terms of water displacement)	Altering shape	14–15 years

Source: Schickedanz et al., 2001.

incorporates logical techniques for resolving problems.

The way in which children approach the "pendulum problem" devised by Piaget (Piaget & Inhelder, 1958) illustrates the emergence of formal operational thinking. The problem solver is asked to figure out what determines how fast a pendulum swings. Is it the length of the string, the weight of the pendulum, or the force with which the pendulum is pushed? (For the record, the answer is the length of the string.)

Children in the concrete operational stage approach the problem haphazardly, without a logical or rational plan of action. For example, they may simultaneously change the length of the string and the weight on the string and the force with which they push the pendulum. Because they are varying all the factors at once, they cannot tell which factor is the critical one. In contrast, people in the formal operational stage approach the problem systematically. Acting as if they were scientists conducting an experiment, they examine the effects of changes in one variable at a time. This ability to rule out competing possibilities characterizes formal operational thought.

Although formal operational thought emerges during the teenage years, some individuals use this type of thinking only infrequently. Moreover, it appears that many individuals never reach this stage at all; most studies show that only 40% to 60% of college students and adults fully reach it, with some estimates running as low as 25% of the general population (Keating & Clark, 1980). No other theorist has given us as comprehensive a theory of cognitive development as Piaget did. In general, most developmental psychologists agree that Piaget provided us with a fairly accurate account of age-related changes in cognitive development. Still, many contemporary theorists suggest that stage theories such as Piaget's do not accurately predict children's cognitive development. For instance, children are not always consistent in their performance of tasks that—if Piaget's theory is accurate—ought to be performed equally well at a specific stage (Feldman, 2003, 2004).

Piaget also underestimated the age at which infants and children can understand specific concepts and principles. In fact, they seem to be more sophisticated in their cognitive abilities than Piaget believed. For instance, some evidence

formal operational stage
According to Piaget, the period from age 12 to adulthood that is characterized by abstract thought.

can understand that when someone rolls a ball of clay into a long sausage shape, that person can re-create the original ball by reversing the action. Children can even conceptualize this principle in their heads, without having to see the action performed before them; at this point, they can hold two ideas in mind simultaneously.

Although children make important advances in their logical capabilities during the concrete operational stage, their thinking still displays one major limitation: They are largely bound to the concrete, physical reality of the world. For the most part, they have difficulty understanding questions of an abstract or hypothetical nature.

Piaget's **formal operational stage** produces a new kind of thinking that is abstract, formal, and logical. During the period from age 12 to adulthood, thinking is no longer tied to events that individuals observe in the environment but

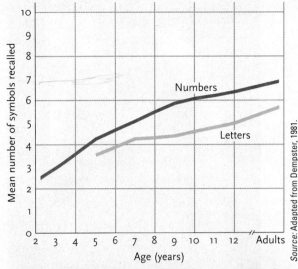

Source: Adapted from Dempster, 1981.

Memory Span Increases with Age for Both Numbers and Letters

suggests that infants as young as 5 months have a rudimentary understanding of arithmetic (McCrink & Wynn, 2007; van Marle & Wynn, 2009; Wynn, Bloom, & Chiang, 2002).

Furthermore, some developmental psychologists suggest that cognitive development proceeds in a more continuous fashion than Piaget's stage theory implies. They propose that cognitive development is primarily quantitative in nature, rather than qualitative. In this view, although there are differences in when, how, and to what extent a child can use specific cognitive abilities—reflecting quantitative changes—the underlying cognitive processes change relatively little with age (Case & Okamoto, 1996; Gelman & Baillargeon, 1983).

Information-Processing Approaches: Charting Children's Mental Programs If cognitive development does not proceed as a series of stages, as Piaget suggested, how can we explain the enormous growth in children's cognitive abilities? Many developmental psychologists attribute cognitive development to changes in **information processing**, the way in which people take in, use, and store information (Cashon & Cohen, 2004; Lacerda, von Hofsten, & Heimann, 2001; Munakata, 2006).

According to this approach, quantitative changes occur in children's ability to organize and manipulate information. From this perspective, children become increasingly adept at information processing, much as a computer program may become more sophisticated as a programmer modifies it on the basis of experience. Information-processing approaches consider the kinds of "mental programs" that children invoke when approaching problems.

Several significant changes occur in children's information-processing capabilities. The speed at which children can scan, recognize, and compare stimuli increases with age. As they grow older, children can pay attention to stimuli longer and discriminate among different stimuli more readily, and they are less easily distracted (Myerson et al., 2003; Van den Wildenberg & Van der Molen, 2004).

Both short-term and long-term memory also improve dramatically with age. Preschoolers can hold only two or three chunks of information in short-term memory, 5-year-olds can hold four, and 7-year-olds can hold five. (Adults are able to keep seven, plus or minus two, chunks in short-

term memory.) The size of chunks held in short-term memory also grows with age, as does the sophistication and organization of knowledge stored in long-term memory. Still, long-term memory capabilities are impressive at a very early age: even before they can speak, infants can remember for months events in which they actively participated (Bayliss et al., 2005b; Cowan et al., 2003).

Finally, improvement in information processing relates to advances in **metacognition**, an awareness and understanding of one's own cognitive processes. Metacognition involves the planning, monitoring, and revising of cognitive strategies. Younger children, who lack an awareness of their own cognitive processes, often do not realize their incapabilities. Thus, when they misunderstand others, they may fail to recognize their own errors. It is only later, when metacognitive abilities become more sophisticated, that children are able to know when they *don't* understand. Such increasing sophistication reflects a change in children's *theory of mind*, their knowledge and beliefs about the way the mind operates (Bernstein, Loftus, & Meltzoff, 2005; Lockl & Schneider, 2007; Matthews & Funke, 2006).

> **information processing** The way in which people take in, use, and store information.
>
> **metacognition** An awareness and understanding of one's own cognitive processes.

Vygotsky's Sociocultural View of Cognitive Development According to Russian developmental psychologist Lev Vygotsky, the culture in which we are raised significantly affects our cognitive development; we cannot understand cognitive development without taking into account the social aspects of learning. Vygotsky argues that cognitive development occurs as a consequence of social interactions in which children work with others to jointly solve problems. Through such interactions,

Adults and older children promote cognitive development in young children by helping them to complete new tasks. Vygotsky called this kind of support scaffolding.

haps by demonstrating a few times, until Maria could do the subtraction problems on her own. Vygotsky claims that scaffolding not only promotes the solution of specific problems but also aids in the development of overall cognitive abilities (Schaller & Crandall, 2004).

More than other approaches to cognitive development, Vygotsky's theory considers how an individual's specific cultural and social context affects intellectual growth. The way in which children understand the world grows out of interactions with parents, peers, and other members of a specific culture (Kozulin et al., 2003; John-Steiner & Mahn, 2003).

Vygotsky's approach compliments Piaget's theory and the information-processing perspectives. These theories contribute in different ways to our understanding of the complex and intriguing process of cognitive development and its biological and environmental underpinnings.

>> Adolescence

Joseph Charles, Age 13: Being 13 is very hard at school. I have to be bad in order to be considered cool. I sometimes do things that aren't good. I have talked back to my teachers and been disrespectful to them. I do want to be good, but it's just too hard. (Gibbs, 2005, p. 51)

Trevor Kelson, Age 15: "Keep the Hell Out of my Room!" says a sign on Trevor's bedroom wall, just above an unmade bed, a desk littered with dirty T-shirts and candy wrappers, and a floor covered with clothes. Is there a carpet? "Somewhere," he says with a grin. "I think it's gold." (Fields-Meyer, 1995, p. 53)

Lauren Barry, Age 18: "I went to a National Honor Society induction. The parents were just staring at me. I think they couldn't believe someone with pink hair could be smart. I want to be a high-school teacher, but I'm afraid that, based on my appearance, they won't hire me."

Although Joseph, Trevor, and Lauren have never met, they share anxieties that are common to adolescence—concerns about friends, parents, appearance, independence, and their futures. **Adolescence**, the developmental stage between childhood and adulthood, is a crucial period. It is a time

zone of proximal development (ZPD)
According to Vygotsky, the level at which a child can almost, but not fully, comprehend or perform a task on his or her own.

adolescence The developmental stage between childhood and adulthood.

children's cognitive skills increase, and they gain the ability to function intellectually on their own. More specifically, he suggests that children's cognitive abilities increase when they encounter information that they are ready to learn. He called this readiness to learn the **zone of proximal development (ZPD)**, the level at which a child can almost, but not fully, comprehend or perform a task on his or her own. When children receive information that falls within the ZPD, they can increase their understanding or master a new task. In contrast, if the information lies outside children's ZPD, the children will not be able to master it (Maynard & Martini, 2005; Rieber & Robinson, 2006; Vygotsky, 1926/1997; Warford, 2011).

In short, cognitive development occurs when parents, teachers, or skilled peers assist a child by presenting information that is both new and within the ZPD. This type of assistance, called *scaffolding*, provides support for learning and problem solving that encourages independence and growth. For example, suppose 5-year-old Maria is ready to learn that subtraction is the reverse of addition. Her older brother could give her some apples and encourage her to use them to do some addition problems. Then he could provide scaffolding for subtraction, per-of profound changes and, occasionally, turmoil. Considerable biological change occurs as adolescents attain sexual and physical maturity. At the same time, and rivaling these physiological changes, important social, emotional, and cognitive changes occur as adolescents strive for independence and move toward adulthood.

Because many years of schooling precede most people's entry into the workforce in Western societies, the stage of adolescence is fairly long, beginning just before the teenage years and ending just after them. No longer children but considered by our society to be not quite adults, adolescents must cope with a period of rapid physical, cognitive, and social change.

PHYSICAL CHANGES

If you think back to the start of your own adolescence, the changes you probably remember best are physical ones. A spurt in height, the growth of breasts in girls, deepening voices in boys, the development of body hair, and intense sexual feelings cause curiosity, interest, and sometimes embarrassment for young adolescents.

The physical changes that occur at the start of adolescence result largely from the secretion of various hormones, and they affect virtually every aspect of an adolescent's life. Not since infancy has development been so dramatic. Weight and height increase rapidly, owing to a growth spurt that typically begins around age 10 for girls and age 12 for boys. Adolescents may grow as much as 5 inches in one year.

Puberty, the period when the sexual organs mature, begins at about age 11 or 12 for girls, when menstruation starts. There are wide variations, however. Some girls experience *menarche,* the onset of menstruation as early as age 8 or 9 or as late as age 16. In Western cultures, the average age at which adolescents reach sexual maturity has been steadily decreasing over the last century, most likely as a result of improved nutrition and medical care (Finlay, Jones, & Coleman, 2002; Tanner, 1990).

For boys, the onset of puberty is marked by their first ejaculation, known as *spermarche*. Spermarche usually occurs around the age of 13. At first, relatively few sperm are produced during an ejaculation, but the amount increases significantly within a few years.

The age at which puberty begins has implications for the way adolescents feel about themselves—as well as the way others treat them. Early-maturing boys have a distinct advantage over later-maturing boys. They do better in athletics, are generally more popular with peers, and have more positive self-concepts (Becker & Luthar, 2007; Ge et al., 2003).

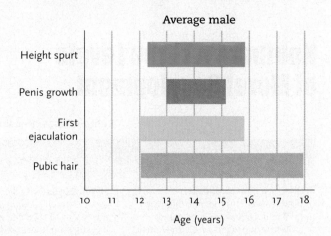

Average male

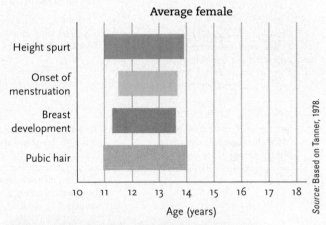

Average female

Source: Based on Tanner, 1978.

Physical Development in Adolescence

The picture differs for girls. Although early-maturing girls are more sought after as dates and have better self-esteem than do later-maturing girls, some consequences of early physical maturation may be less positive. For example, early breast development may set them apart from their peers and be a source of ridicule (Franko & Striegel-Moore, 2002; Nadeem & Graham, 2005; Olivardia & Pope, 2002).

> **puberty** The period at which maturation of the sexual organs occurs, beginning about age 11 or 12 for girls and 13 or 14 for boys.

Late physical maturation may produce certain psychological difficulties for both boys and girls. Boys who are smaller and less coordinated than their more mature peers tend to feel ridiculed and less attractive. Similarly, late-maturing girls may be at a disadvantage in middle school and early high school. They may hold relatively low social status and be overlooked in dating (Lanza & Collins, 2002).

In Western cultures, the average age at which adolescents reach sexual maturity has been steadily decreasing over the last century, most likely as a result of improved nutrition and medical care.

Kohlberg's Three Levels of Moral Development

Sample Moral Reasoning of Subjects

Level	In Favor of Stealing the Drug	Against Stealing the Drug
Level 1 Preconventional morality: At this level, the concrete interests of the individual are considered in terms of rewards and punishments.	"If you let your wife die, you will get in trouble. You'll be blamed for not spending the money to save her, and there'll be an investigation of you and the druggist for your wife's death."	"You shouldn't steal the drug because you'll be caught and sent to jail if you do. If you do get away, your conscience will bother you thinking how the police will catch up with you at any minute."
Level 2 Conventional morality: At this level, people approach moral problems as members of society. They are interested in pleasing others by acting as good members of society.	"If you let your wife die, you'll never be able to look anybody in the face again."	"After you steal the drug, you'll feel bad thinking how you've brought dishonor on your family and yourself; you won't be able to face anyone again."
Level 3 Postconventional morality: At this level, people use moral principles which are seen as broader than those of any particular society.	"If you don't steal the drug, and if you let your wife die, you'll always condemn yourself for it afterward. You won't be blamed and you'll have lived up to the outside rule of the law, but you won't have lived up to your own conscience and standards of honesty."	"If you steal the drug, you won't be blamed by other people, but you'll condemn yourself because you won't have lived up to your own conscience and standards of honesty."

D. Goslin (Ed.), *Handbook of Socialization Theory and Research* (1969). Chicago: Rand McNally.

Clearly, the rate at which physical changes occur during adolescence can affect the way in which people are viewed by others and the way they view themselves. Just as important as physical changes, however, are the psychological and social changes that unfold during adolescence.

MORAL AND COGNITIVE DEVELOPMENT

In a European country, a woman is near death from a special kind of cancer. The one drug that the doctors think might save her is a medicine that a medical researcher has recently discovered. The drug is expensive to make, and the researcher is charging 10 times the cost, or $5,000, for a small dose. The sick woman's husband, Henry, approaches everyone he knows in hopes of borrowing money, but he can get together only about $2,500. He tells the researcher that his wife is dying and asks him to lower the price of the drug or let him pay later. The researcher says, "No, I discovered the drug, and I'm going to make money from it." Henry is desperate and considers stealing the drug for his wife.

What would you tell Henry to do?

Did you know?

Westerners are likely familiar with the Golden Rule: Do unto others as you would have them do unto you. In contrast, Huang (2005) proposes a Daoist-Confucian Copper Rule: Do (or don't do) unto others as they would (or would not) have us do unto them.

Kohlberg's Theory of Moral Development In the view of psychologist Lawrence Kohlberg, the advice you give Henry reflects your level of moral development. According to Kohlberg, people pass through a series of stages in the evolution of their sense of justice and in the kind of reasoning they use to make moral judgments (Kohlberg, 1984). Largely because of the various cognitive limitations that Piaget described, preadolescent children tend to think either in terms of concrete, unvarying rules ("It is always wrong to steal" or "I'll be punished if I steal") or in terms of the rules of society ("Good people don't steal" or "What if everyone stole?").

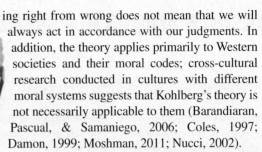
Adolescents, however, can reason on a higher plane, having typically reached Piaget's formal operational stage of cognitive development. Because they are able to comprehend broad moral principles, they can understand that morality is not always black and white and that conflict can exist between two sets of socially accepted standards.

Kohlberg (1984) suggests that the changes in moral reasoning can be understood best as a three-level sequence. His theory assumes that people move through the levels in a fixed order and that they cannot reach the highest level until about age 13—primarily because of limitations in cognitive development before that age. However, many people never reach the highest level of moral reasoning. In fact, Kohlberg found that only a relatively small percentage of adults rise above the second level of his model (Hedgepeth, 2005; Kohlberg & Ryncarz, 1990; Powers, 2006).

Although Kohlberg's theory has had a substantial influence on our thinking about moral development, the research support is mixed. One difficulty with the theory is that it pertains to moral *judgments*, not moral *behavior*. Know-

ing right from wrong does not mean that we will always act in accordance with our judgments. In addition, the theory applies primarily to Western societies and their moral codes; cross-cultural research conducted in cultures with different moral systems suggests that Kohlberg's theory is not necessarily applicable to them (Barandiaran, Pascual, & Samaniego, 2006; Coles, 1997; Damon, 1999; Moshman, 2011; Nucci, 2002).

One glaring shortcoming of Kohlberg's research is that he primarily used male participants. Furthermore, psychologist Carol Gilligan (1996) argues that, because of men's and women's distinctive socialization experiences, a fundamental difference exists in the way each gender views moral behavior. According to Gilligan, men view morality primarily in terms of broad principles, such as justice and fairness. In contrast, women see it in terms of responsibility toward individuals and willingness to make sacrifices to help a specific individual within the context of a particular relationship. Compassion for individuals is a more salient factor in moral behavior for women than it is for men.

Because Kohlberg's model defines moral behavior largely in terms of abstract principles such as justice, Gilligan finds that it inadequately describes the moral development of females. She suggests that women's morality centers on individual well-being and social relationships—a morality of *caring*. In her view, compassionate concern for the welfare of others represents the highest level of morality.

The fact that Gilligan's conception of morality differs greatly from Kohlberg's suggests that gender plays an important role in determining what a person sees as moral. Although the research evidence is not definitive, it seems plausible that their differing conceptions of what constitutes moral behavior may lead men and women to regard the morality of a specific behavior in different ways (Jorgensen, 2006; Sherblom, 2008; Walker & Frimer, 2009).

ADOLESCENT SOCIAL DEVELOPMENT

"Who am I?" "How do I fit into the world?" "What is life all about?"

Questions such as these assume special significance during the teenage years, as adolescents seek to find their

STUDY TIP

The difference between Kohlberg's theory and Gilligan's approach to moral development is significant, with Kohlberg's theory focusing on stages of development in males and Gilligan's resting on gender differences.

Erikson's Stages of Psychosocial Development

1 Trust Versus Mistrust

Approximate age:
Birth–1½ years

Positive outcomes: Feelings of trust from environmental support

Negative outcomes: Fear and concern regarding others

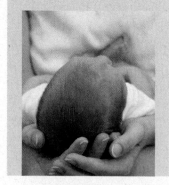

2 Autonomy Versus Shame and Doubt

Approximate age:
1½–3 years

Positive outcomes: Self-sufficiency if exploration is encouraged

Negative outcomes: Doubts about self, lack of independence

3 Initiative Versus Guilt

Approximate age:
3–6 years

Positive outcomes: Discovery of ways to initiate actions

Negative outcomes: Guilt from actions and thoughts

4 Industry Versus Inferiority

Approximate age:
6–12 years

Positive outcomes: Development of sense of competence

Negative outcomes: Feelings of inferiority, no sense of mastery

5 Identity Versus Identity Confusion

Approximate age:
Adolescence

Positive outcomes: Awareness of uniqueness of self, knowledge of role to be followed

Negative outcomes: Inability to identify appropriate roles in life

6 Intimacy Versus Isolation

Approximate age:
Early adulthood

Positive outcomes: Development of loving, sexual relationships and close friendships

Negative outcomes: Fear of relationships with others

7 Generativity Versus Stagnation

Approximate age:
Middle adulthood

Positive outcomes: Sense of contribution to continuity of life

Negative outcomes: Trivialization of one's activities

8 Integrity Versus Despair

Approximate age:
Late adulthood

Positive outcomes: Sense of unity in life's accomplishments

Negative outcomes: Regret over lost opportunities of life

identity-versus-role-confusion stage According to Erikson, a time in adolescence of major testing to determine one's unique qualities.

identity The distinguishing character of the individual: who each of us is, what our roles are, and what we are capable of.

place in the broader social world. As we will see, this quest takes adolescents along several routes.

Erikson's Theory of Psychosocial Development

Erikson's theory of psychosocial development emphasizes the search for identity during the adolescent years. As was noted earlier, psychosocial development encompasses the way people's understanding of themselves, of one another, and of the world around them changes during the course of development (Erikson, 1963).

The fifth stage of Erikson's theory (introduced above), **identity-versus-role-confusion**, encompasses adolescence. During this stage, a time of major testing, people try to determine what is unique about themselves. They attempt to discover who they are, what their strengths are, and what kinds of roles they are best suited to play for the rest of their lives—in short, their **identity**. Unsuccessful navigation of this stage leaves a person confused about the most appropriate role to play in life. He or she may lack a stable identity, adopt an unacceptable role such as that of a social deviant, and/or have difficulty maintaining close personal relationships later in life (Goldstein, 2006; Updegraff et al., 2004; Vleioras & Bosma, 2005).

THE WORLD'S FIRST GENETICALLY ENGINEERED HUMAN HITS ADOLESCENCE

We buy you the best genes in the world—FOR THIS?

So, I got my nose pierced. So what, man?

I remember checking "genius" on the order form—AND NOW LOOK!

© Roz Chast/The New Yorker Collection/www.cartoonbank.com.

During the identity-versus-role-confusion period, adolescents feel pressured to decide what to do with their lives. Because this pressure comes at a time of major physical changes as well as important changes in what society expects of them, adolescents can find the period to be an especially difficult one. The identity-versus-role-confusion stage has another important characteristic: declining reliance on adults for information, with a shift toward using the peer group as a source of social judgments. The peer group becomes increasingly important, enabling adolescents to form close, adult-like relationships and helping them clarify their personal identities. According to Erikson, the identity-versus-role-confusion stage marks a pivotal point in psychosocial development, paving the way for continued growth and the future development of personal relationships.

During early adulthood, people enter the **intimacy-versus-isolation stage**. Spanning the period of early adulthood (from postadolescence to the early 30s), this stage focuses on developing close relationships with others. Difficulties during this stage result in feelings of loneliness and a fear of close relationships, whereas successful resolution of the crises of the stage results in the possibility of forming relationships that are intimate on a physical, intellectual, and emotional level.

Development continues during middle adulthood as people enter the **generativity-versus-stagnation stage**. Generativity is the ability to contribute to one's family, community, work, and society, and to assist the development of the younger generation. Success in this stage results in a person's feeling positive about the continuity of life, whereas difficulties lead a person to feel that his or her activities are trivial or stagnant and have done nothing for upcoming generations. In fact, if a person has not successfully resolved the identity crisis of adolescence, he or she may still be foundering in identifying an appropriate career, for example.

Finally, the last stage of psychosocial development, the **ego-integrity-versus-despair** stage, spans later adulthood

and continues until death. Now a sense of accomplishment signifies success in resolving the difficulties presented by this stage of life; failure to resolve the difficulties results in regret over what might have been achieved but was not.

Notably, Erikson's theory suggests that development does not stop at adolescence but continues throughout adulthood, a view that a significant amount of research now confirms. For instance, a 22-year study by psychologist Susan Whitbourne found considerable support for the fundamentals of Erikson's theory, determining that psychosocial development continues through adolescence and adulthood. In sum, adolescence is not an end point but rather a way station on the path of psychosocial development (McAdams et al., 1997; Whitbourne et al., 1992).

Although Erikson's theory provides a broad outline of identity development, critics have pointed out that his approach is anchored in male-oriented concepts of individuality and competitiveness. In an alternative conception, psychologist Carol Gilligan suggests that women may develop identity through the establishment of relationships. In her view, a primary component of women's identity is the construction of caring networks among themselves and others (Gilligan, 2004).

Adolescent Suicide Although the vast majority of teenagers pass through adolescence without major psychological difficulties, some experience unusually severe psychological problems. Sometimes those problems become so extreme that adolescents take their own lives. Suicide is the third leading cause of death for adolescents (after accidents and homicide) in the United States. More teenagers and young adults die from suicide than from cancer, heart disease, AIDS, birth defects, stroke, pneumonia and influenza, and chronic lung disease combined (CDC, 2004).

A teenager commits suicide every 90 minutes in the United States. Furthermore, the reported rate of suicide may actually be understated, because medical personnel hesitate to report suicide as a cause of death. Instead, they frequently label a death as an accident in an effort to protect the survivors. Overall, as many as 200 adolescents may attempt suicide for every 1 who does take his or her own life (Brausch & Gutierrez, 2009; Centers for Disease Control, 2000).

Male adolescents are five times more likely to commit suicide than are females, although females *attempt* suicide more often than males do. The rate of adolescent suicide is significantly greater among whites than among nonwhites. However, the suicide rate of African-American males has increased much more rapidly than has that of white males over the last two decades. Native Americans have the highest suicide rate of any ethnic group in the United

intimacy-versus-isolation stage According to Erikson, a period during early adulthood that focuses on developing close relationships.

generativity-versus-stagnation stage According to Erikson, a period in middle adulthood during which we take stock of our contributions to family and society.

ego-integrity-versus-despair stage According to Erikson, a period from late adulthood until death during which we review life's accomplishments and failures.

States, and Asian Americans have the lowest rate (Boden, Fergusson, & Horwood, 2007; Centers for Disease Control, 2004; Gutierrez et al., 2005).

Although the question of why so many adolescents commit suicide remains unanswered, several factors put adolescents at risk. One factor is depression, characterized by unhappiness, extreme fatigue, and—a variable that seems especially important—a profound sense of hopelessness. In other cases, adolescents who commit suicide are perfectionists, inhibited socially and prone to extreme anxiety when they face any social or academic challenge (Caelian, 2006; Centers for Disease Control, 2004b; Richardson et al., 2005).

Family background and adjustment difficulties are also related to suicide. A long-standing history of conflicts between parents and children may lead to adolescent behavior problems, such as delinquency, dropping out of school, and aggressive tendencies. In addition, teenage alcoholics and abusers of other drugs have a relatively high rate of suicide (Bidwell, 2011; Winstead & Sanchez, 2005).

Several warning signs indicate when a teenager's problems may be severe enough to warrant concern about the possibility of a suicide attempt. They include these signs:

- School problems, such as missing classes, truancy, and a sudden change in grades
- Frequent incidents of self-destructive behavior, such as careless accidents
- Loss of appetite or excessive eating
- Withdrawal from friends and peers
- Sleeping problems
- Signs of depression, tearfulness, or overt indications of psychological difficulties, such as hallucinations
- A preoccupation with death, an afterlife, or what would happen "if I died"

PSYCH think

connect™
WWW.MCGRAWHILLCONNECT.COM/PSYCHOLOGY
Suicide Risk Factors

> > > In what ways could school cultures help or hurt students who are going through adolescence? For example, what kinds of school policies might provide more support for adolescents who are at risk for suicide?

Take the PsychSmart Challenge! Can you tell which teen might be at risk for suicide? From chapter 9 in your ebook, select the *Exercises* tab. Next, select "Suicide Risk Factors." Then, keeping in mind that being at risk for suicide doesn't mean that a person will ever attempt suicide, answer question 9 in the Pop Quiz on p. 255.

- Putting affairs in order, such as giving away prized possessions or making arrangements for the care of a pet
- An explicit announcement of thoughts of suicide

If you know someone who shows signs that he or she is suicidal, urge that person to seek professional help. You may need to take assertive action, such as enlisting the assistance of family members or friends. Talk of suicide is a serious signal for help, not a confidence to be kept.

U.S. Suicide Rates by Age and Sex (per 100,000 people)

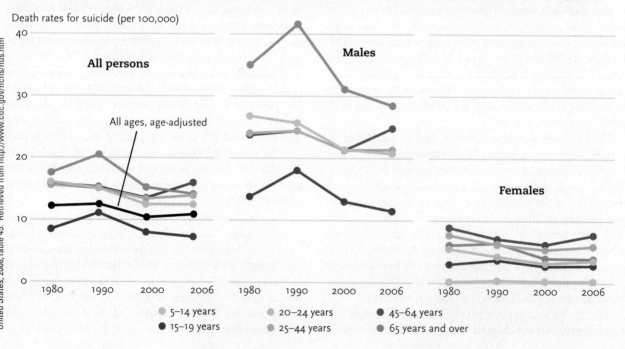

Source: Based on data from National Center for Health Statistics (2009). *Health, United States, 2008,* Table 45. Retrieved from http://www.cdc.gov/nchs/hus.htm

For immediate help with a suicide-related problem, call 1-800-273-8255, a national hotline staffed with trained counselors, visit the website at www.suicidepreventionlifeline.org, or call 911.

Rites of Passage: Coming of Age Around the World

It is not easy for male members of the Awa tribe in New Guinea to make the transition from childhood to adulthood. First come whippings with sticks and prickly branches, both for the boys' own past misdeeds and in honor of those tribesmen who were killed in warfare. In the next phase of the ritual, adults jab sharpened sticks into the boys' nostrils. Then they force a 5-foot length of vine into the boys' throats, until they gag and vomit. Finally, tribesmen cut the boys' genitals, causing severe bleeding.

Although the rites that mark the coming of age of boys in the Awa tribe might horrify insulated Westerners, the Awa isn't the only culture that practices coming-of-age rituals. Other cultures have less fearsome, but no less important, ceremonies marking the passage from childhood to adulthood. For instance, when a girl first menstruates in traditional Apache tribes, the event is marked by dawn-to-dusk chanting. Western religions, too, have several types of celebrations, including bar and bat mitzvahs at age 13 for Jewish boys and girls and confirmation ceremonies for children in many Christian denominations (Magida, 2006).

In most societies, males, but not females, are the focus of coming-of-age ceremonies. The renowned anthropologist Margaret Mead remarked, only partly in jest, that the preponderance of male ceremonies might reflect the fact that "the worry that boys will not grow up to be men is much more widespread than that girls will not grow up to be women" (1949, p. 195). It may be, however, that most cultures place greater emphasis on male rites than on female ones because, for females, the transition from childhood is marked by a definite, biological event: menstruation. For males, in contrast, no single event can be used to pinpoint entry into adulthood. Thus, men are forced to rely on culturally determined rituals to acknowledge their arrival into adulthood.

For Latina teens, quinceañera (meaning *15 years*) celebrations signify the transition to adulthood.

Early adulthood is when most individuals focus on their jobs and careers.

>> Adulthood

Psychologists generally agree that early adulthood begins around age 20 and lasts until about age 40 to 45, with middle adulthood beginning then and continuing until around age 65. Despite the importance of these periods of life in terms of both the accomplishments that occur during them and their overall length (together they span some 44 years), they have been studied less than has any other stage. For one reason, the physical changes that occur during these periods are less apparent and more gradual than are those at other times during the life span. In addition, the diverse social changes that arise during this period defy simple categorization.

The variety of changes that occur in early adulthood have led many developmental psychologists to view the start of the period as a transitional phase called *emerging adulthood*. Emerging adulthood is the period that extends from the late teenage years into the mid-twenties. During emerging adulthood, people are no longer adolescents, but they haven't fully taken on the responsibilities of adulthood. Instead, they are still engaged in determining who they are and what their life and career paths should be (Bukobza, 2009; Lamborn & Groh, 2009; Schwartz, Côté, & Arnett, 2005).

The view that adulthood is preceded by an extended period of emerging adulthood reflects the reality that industrialized countries have shifted away from manufacturing economies to ones that focus on technology and information, which require a greater amount of time spent in education and training. Furthermore, the age at which most people marry and have children has risen significantly (Arnett, 2007).

As we discuss the changes that occur through emerging adulthood, early adulthood, middle adulthood, and ultimately late adulthood, keep in mind the demarcations between the periods are fuzzy. However, the changes are certainly no less profound than they were in earlier periods of development.

THE PEAK OF HEALTH

For most people, early adulthood marks the peak of physical health. From about 18 to 25 years of age, people's strength is greatest, their reflexes are quickest, and their chances of dying from disease are slim. Moreover, reproductive capabilities are at their highest level.

: Physically, most individuals reach their peak in young adulthood.

Around age 25, the body becomes slightly less efficient and more susceptible to disease. Overall, however, ill health remains the exception; most people stay remarkably healthy during early adulthood. (Can you think of any machine other than the body that can operate without pause for so long a period?)

During middle adulthood people gradually become aware of changes in their bodies. People often experience weight gain, as their eating habits continue unchanged while they begin to get less exercise. Furthermore, the sense organs gradually become less sensitive, and reactions to stimuli are slower. But generally, the physical declines that occur during middle adulthood are minor and often unnoticeable (DiGiovanna, 1994).

One important biological change that occurs to both women and men during middle adulthood pertains to reproductive capabilities. On average, during their late 40s or early 50s, women approach **menopause**, at which point they stop menstruating and are no longer fertile. Because menopause is accompanied by a significant reduction in the production of estrogen, a female hormone, women sometimes experience symptoms such as hot flashes, sudden sensations of heat. Sometimes, in industrialized cultures, these symptoms are treated through *hormone therapy (HT)*, in which menopausal women take synthetic hormones.

menopause The period during which women stop menstruating and are no longer fertile.

Menopause was once blamed for a variety of psychological symptoms, including depression and memory loss. However, it is not yet clear how the erratic changes in hormonal levels that characterize menopause are related to such difficulties. Current cross-cultural research shows that women's reactions to menopause vary significantly across cultures, and suggests that the more a society values old age, the less difficulty its women have during menopause (Beyene, Gillis, & Lee, 2007; Elliot, Berman, & Kim, 2002). Without more information, however, we can only speculate as to the cause-and-effect relationship between these two variables.

For men, the aging process during middle adulthood is somewhat subtler. There are no physiological signals of increasing age equivalent to the end of menstruation in women; that is, no male menopause exists. In fact, men remain fertile and are capable of fathering children until

well into late adulthood. However, some gradual physical decline occurs: Sperm production decreases, and the frequency of orgasm tends to decline. Once again, though, any psychological difficulties associated with these changes are usually brought about not so much by physical deterioration as by the inability of an aging individual to meet the exaggerated standards of youthfulness.

ADULT SOCIAL DEVELOPMENT

Social developmental transitions in adulthood are qualitative and profound. During this period, people typically launch themselves into careers, marriage, and families, all of which require significant adjustment.

Entry into early adulthood is usually marked by leaving one's childhood home and entering the world of work. People envision life goals and make career choices. Their lives often center on their careers, which form an important part of their identity (Levinson, 1990, 1992; Vaillant & Vaillant, 1990).

In their early 40s, people may begin to question their lives as they enter a period called the *midlife transition*. The idea that life will end at some point becomes increasingly influential in their thinking, and they may question their past accomplishments (Gould, 1978). Facing signs of physical aging and feeling dissatisfaction with their lives, some individuals experience what has been popularly labeled a *midlife crisis*.

In most cases, though, the passage into middle age is relatively calm. Most 40-year-olds view their lives and accomplishments positively enough to proceed relatively smoothly through midlife, and the 40s and 50s are often a particularly rewarding period. Rather than looking to the future, people concentrate on the present, and their involvement with their families, friends, and other social groups takes on new importance (Whitbourne, 2000, 2010).

Finally, during the last stages of adulthood people become more accepting of others and of their own lives and are less concerned about issues or problems that once bothered them. People come to accept the fact that death is inevitable, and they try to understand their accomplishments in terms of the broader meaning of life. Although people may begin, for the first time, to label themselves as "old," many also develop a sense of wisdom and feel freer to enjoy life (Baltes & Kunzmann, 2003; Miner-Rubino, Winter, & Stewart, 2004; Ward-Baker, 2007).

Marriage, Children, and Divorce In the typical fairy tale, a dashing young man and a beautiful young woman marry, have children, and live happily ever after. However, that scenario does not match the realities of love and marriage in the 21st century. Today, it is just as likely that the man and the woman would first live together, then marry and have children, but ultimately divorce. (Or the partners could be same-sex.)

The percentage of U.S. households made up of unmarried couples has increased dramatically over the last two decades. At the same time, the average age at which mar-

Young adulthood is a time of developmental transitions, when many people begin careers, marry, and start a family.

riage takes place is higher than at any time since the turn of the 20th century. These changes have been dramatic, and they suggest that the institution of marriage has changed considerably from earlier historical periods.

When people do marry, the probability of divorce is high, especially for younger couples. Even though divorce rates have been declining since they peaked in 1981, about half of all first marriages end in divorce. Before they are 18 years old, two-fifths of children will experience the breakup of their parents' marriages. Moreover, the rise in divorce is not just a U.S. phenomenon: The divorce rate has accelerated over the last several decades in most industrialized countries. In some countries, the increase has been enormous. In South Korea, for example, the divorce rate quadrupled from 11% to 47% in the 12-year period ending in 2002 (Lankov, 2004; Olson & DeFrain, 2005; Schaefer, 2000).

Changes in marriage and divorce trends have doubled the number of single-parent households in the United States over the last two decades. Almost 25% of all family households are now headed by one parent, compared

with 13% in 1970. If present trends continue, almost three-fourths of American children will spend some portion of their lives in a single-parent family before they turn 18. For children in minority households, the numbers are even higher. Almost 60% of all black children and more than a third of Hispanic children live in homes with only one parent. Furthermore, in most single-parent families, it is the mother, rather than the father, with whom the children reside—a phenomenon that is consistent across racial and ethnic groups throughout the industrialized world (U.S. Bureau of the Census, 2000).

What are the economic and emotional consequences for children living in homes with only one parent? Single-parent families are often economically less well off, and this economic disadvantage has an effect on children's opportunities. Over a third of single-mother families with children have incomes below the poverty line. In addition, good child care at an affordable price is often hard to find. Furthermore, for children of divorce, the parents' separation is often a painful experience that may result in obstacles to their establishing close relationships later in life. Children may blame themselves for the breakup or feel pressure to take sides (Liu, He, & Wu, 2007; U.S. Bureau of the Census, 2000; Wallerstein et al., 2000).

Nevertheless, most evidence suggests that children from stable, single-parent families are no less well adjusted than are those from stable, two-parent families. In fact, children may be more successful growing up in a harmonious single-parent family than in a two-parent family that engages in continuous conflict (Clarke-Stewart et al., 2000; Harold et al., 1997; Kelly, 2000; Olson & DeFrain, 2005).

Changing Roles of Men and Women One of the major changes in family life in the last two decades has been the evolution of men's and women's roles. More women than ever before act simultaneously as wives, mothers, and wage earners—in contrast to women in traditional marriages, in which the husband is the sole wage earner and the wife assumes primary responsibility for care of the home and children.

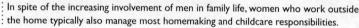
In spite of the increasing involvement of men in family life, women who work outside the home typically also manage most homemaking and childcare responsibilities.

Close to 75% of all married women with school-age children are now employed outside the home, and 55% of mothers with children under age 6 are working. In the mid-1960s, only 17% of mothers of 1-year-olds worked full-time; now, more than half are in the labor force (Halpern, 2005; U.S. Bureau of the Census, 2001).

Most married working women are not free of household responsibilities. Even in marriages in which the spouses hold jobs that have similar status and require similar hours, the distribution of household tasks between husbands and wives has not changed substantially. Working wives are still more likely than husbands to feel responsible for traditional homemaking tasks such as cooking and cleaning. In contrast, husbands still view themselves as responsible primarily for household tasks such as repairing broken appliances and doing yard work (Ganong & Coleman, 1999; Juster, Ono, & Stafford, 2002).

GROWING OLD

I've always enjoyed doing things in the mountains—hiking or, more recently, active cliff-climbing. The more difficult the climb, the more absorbing it is. The climbs I really remember are the ones I had to work on. Maybe a particular section where it took two or three tries before I found the right combination of moves that got me up easily—and, preferably, elegantly. It's a wonderful exhilaration to get to the top and sit down and perhaps have lunch and look out over the landscape and be so grateful that it's still possible for me to do that sort of thing. (Lyman Spitzer, age 74, quoted in Kotre & Hall, 1990, pp. 358–359)

If you can't quite picture a 74-year-old man rock-climbing, some rethinking of your view of late adulthood may be in order. In spite of the societal stereotype of "old age" as a time of inactivity and physical and mental decline,

gerontologists, specialists who study aging, are beginning to paint a very different portrait of late adulthood.

By focusing on the period of life that starts at around age 65, gerontologists are making important contributions to clarifying the capabilities of older adults. Their work is demonstrating that significant developmental processes continue even during old age. And as life expectancy increases, the number of people who reach older adulthood will continue to grow substantially. Consequently, developing an understanding of late adulthood has become a critical priority for psychologists (Birren, 1996; Moody, 2000, Schaie, 2005).

The Aging Body Napping, eating, walking, conversing. It probably doesn't surprise you that these relatively nonstrenuous activities represent the typical pastimes of late adulthood. But it is striking that these activities are identical to the most common leisure activities reported in a survey of college students (Harper, 1978). Although the students cited more active pursuits—such as sailing and playing basketball—as their favorite activities, in actuality they engaged in such sports relatively infrequently, spending most of their free time napping, eating, walking, and conversing.

Although the leisure activities in which older adults engage may not differ all that much from the ones that younger people pursue, many physical changes are, of course, brought about by the aging process. The most obvious are those of appearance—hair thinning and turning gray, skin wrinkling and folding, and sometimes a slight loss of height as the thickness of the disks between vertebrae in the spine decreases—but subtler changes also occur in the body's biological functioning. For example, sensory capabilities decrease as a result of aging: Vision, hearing, smell, and taste become less sensitive. Reaction time slows, and physical stamina changes (Madden, 2007; Schieber, 2006; Stenklev & Laukli, 2004).

Olivia Patricia "Pat" Thomas celebrates after blowing out her candles at her 112th birthday party in Williamsville, N.Y. In June 2009, Thomas turned 114. As increasing numbers of people are living into their 90s and beyond, the study of late adulthood has become a priority for psychologists.

What are the reasons for these physical declines? **Genetic preprogramming theories of aging** suggest that human cells have a built-in time limit to their reproduction. These theories suggest that after a certain time cells stop dividing or become harmful to the body—as if a kind of automatic self-destruct button had been pushed. In contrast, **wear-and-tear theories of aging** suggest that the mechanical functions of the body simply work less efficiently as people age. Waste by-products of energy production eventually accumulate, and mistakes are made when cells divide. Eventually the body, in effect, wears out, just as an old automobile does (Hayflick, 2007; Ly et al., 2000; Miquel, 2006; Schaie, & Willis, 2011).

It may be that both the genetic preprogramming and the wear-and-tear views contribute to natural aging. It is clear, however, that physical aging is not a disease but a natural biological process. Many physical functions do not decline with age. For example, sex remains pleasurable well into old age (although the frequency of sexual activity decreases), and some people report that the pleasure they derive from sex increases during late adulthood (DeLamater & Sill, 2005; Gelfand, 2000).

Thinking in Late Adulthood At one time, many gerontologists would have agreed with the popular view that older adults are forgetful and confused. Most research today indicates that this assessment is far from accurate, however.

When older people are compared with young adults, differences can be exaggerated if the older ones have health problems that may affect cognitive functioning. Older people are often less healthy than younger ones, and when only *healthy*

genetic preprogramming theories of aging Theories that suggest that human cells have a built-in time limit to their reproduction, and that after a certain time they are no longer able to divide.

wear-and-tear theories of aging Theories that suggest that the mechanical functions of the body simply stop working efficiently.

STUDY TIP

Two major theories of aging—the genetic preprogramming and the wear-and-tear views—explain some of the physical changes that take place in older adults.

Some decline in cognitive functioning occurs in late adulthood, but abilities based on accumulated knowledge and experience may actually improve as people age.

older adults are compared to healthy younger adults, intellectual differences are far less evident. Furthermore, the average number of years in school is often lower in older adults (for historical reasons) than in younger ones, and older adults may be less motivated to perform well on intelligence tests than younger people. Finally, traditional IQ tests may be inappropriate measures of intelligence in late adulthood. Older adults sometimes perform better on tests of practical intelligence than do younger individuals (Dixon & Cohen, 2003; Willis & Schaie, 1994).

Still, some declines in intellectual functioning during late adulthood do occur, although the pattern of age differences is not uniform for different types of cognitive abilities. In general, skills relating to *fluid intelligence* (which involves information-processing skills such as speed of memory retrieval, calculations, and analogy solving) show declines in late adulthood. In contrast, skills relating to *crystallized intelligence* (intelligence based on the accumulation of knowledge, skills, and strategies learned through experience) remain steady and in some cases even improve (Kaufman, Johnson, & Liu, 2008; Rozencwajg et al., 2005; van Hooren, Valentijn, & Bosma, 2007).

Alzheimer's disease A progressive brain disorder that leads to a gradual and irreversible decline in cognitive abilities.

Even when changes in intellectual functioning do occur during late adulthood, people often are able to compensate for any decline. They can still learn; they may just need more time to master what they choose to learn. Furthermore, teaching older adults strategies for dealing with new

problems can prevent declines in performance (Cavallini, Pagnin, & Vecchi, 2003; Peters et al., 2007; Saczynski, Willis, & Schaie, 2002).

Are Older Adults Forgetful? One of the characteristics we commonly associate with late adulthood is forgetfulness. How accurate is this assumption?

Most evidence suggests that memory deficits are not an inevitable part of the aging process. For instance, research shows that older people in cultures in which older adults are held in high esteem, such as mainland China, are less likely to show memory losses than are those living in cultures in which the expectation is that memory will decline. Similarly, when older people in Western societies are reminded of the advantages of age (for example, "age brings wisdom"), they tend to do better on tests of memory (Dixon, Rust, & Feltmate, 2007; Hess, Hinson, & Statham, 2004; Levy, 1996).

In the past, older adults with severe cases of memory decline, accompanied by other cognitive difficulties, were said to suffer from senility. *Senility* is a broad, imprecise term typically applied to older adults who experience progressive deterioration of mental abilities, including memory loss, disorientation to time and place, and general confusion. Once thought to be an inevitable state that accompanies aging, senility is now viewed by most gerontologists as a label that has outlived its usefulness. Rather than senility being the cause of certain symptoms, the symptoms are deemed to be caused by some other factor.

Some cases of memory loss are caused by disease. For instance, **Alzheimer's disease** is a progressive brain disorder that leads to a gradual and irreversible decline in cognitive abilities. Nineteen percent of people age 75 to 84 have Alzheimer's, and almost 50% of people over age 85 are affected by the disease. Unless a cure is found, some 14 million people will experience Alzheimer's by 2050—more than three times the current number (Alzheimer's Association, 2009; Feinberg, 2002; Hurt et al., 2005; Rogers, 2007).

Alzheimer's occurs when production of the *beta amyloid precursor protein* goes awry, producing large clumps of cells that trigger inflammation and deterioration of nerve cells. The brain shrinks, neurons die, and several areas of the hippocampus and frontal and temporal lobes deteriorate. So far, there is no cure for Alzheimer's (Behrens, Lendon, & Roe, 2009; Medeiros et al., 2007; Wilson et al., 2011; Wolfe, 2006).

In other cases, cognitive declines may be caused by temporary anxiety and depression, which can be treated success-

Age-Related Changes in Intellectual Skills

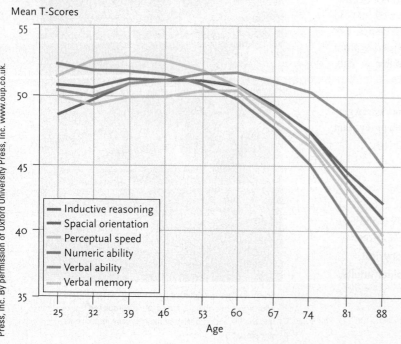

Mean T-Scores

Legend:
- Inductive reasoning
- Spacial orientation
- Perceptual speed
- Numeric ability
- Verbal ability
- Verbal memory

X-axis: Age (25, 32, 39, 46, 53, 60, 67, 74, 81, 88)
Y-axis: Mean T-Scores (35–55)

Schaie, K. W. (2005). Longitudinal studies. In *Developmental Influences on Adult Intelligence: The Seattle Longitudinal Study*, Figure 5.7a (p. 127). Copyright © 2005 by Oxford University Press, Inc. By permission of Oxford University Press, Inc. www.oup.co.uk.

From the perspective of . . .

A MIDDLE-AGED COUPLE One of your parents has recently been diagnosed with Alzheimer's. Using research on aging and theoretical approaches, what strategies will you use to help your parent?

fully, or may even be due to overmedication. The danger is that people with such symptoms may receive no treatment, thereby continuing their decline (Sachs-Ericsson et al., 2005; Selkoe, 1997).

In sum, declines in cognitive functioning in late adulthood, for the most part, are not inevitable. The key to maintaining cognitive skills may lie in intellectual stimulation. Like most people, older adults need a stimulating environment in order to hone and to maintain their skills (Bosma et al., 2003; Glisky, 2007; Hertzog et al., 2008).

The Social World of Late Adulthood Just as the view that old age predictably means mental decline has proved to be wrong, so has the view that late adulthood inevitably brings loneliness. People in late adulthood most often see themselves as functioning members of society, with only a small number of them reporting that loneliness is a serious problem (Binstock & George, 1996; Jylha, 2004).

Certainly, late adulthood brings significant challenges. People who retire after having worked all of their adult lives experience a major shift in the role they play. Moreover, many older people must face the death of their spouse. The death of a partner means the loss of a companion, confidante, and lover. It can also bring about changes in economic well-being.

People approach aging in different ways. According to the **disengagement theory of aging**, aging is accompanied by a gradual withdrawal from the world on physical, psychological, and social levels. Such disengagement serves an important purpose, providing an opportunity for increased reflectiveness and decreased emotional investment in others at a time of life when social relationships will inevitably be ended by death (Adams, 2004; Wrosch, Bauer, & Scheier, 2005).

Because little research supports disengagement theory, alternative theories have been suggested. According to the **activity theory of aging**, people who age most successfully are those who maintain the interests, activities, and level of social interaction they experienced during middle adulthood. Activity theory argues that late adulthood should reflect a continuation, as much as possible, of the activities in which people participated during the earlier part of their lives (Crosnoe & Elder, 2002; Nimrod & Kleiber, 2007).

Although most research is supportive of activity theory, not all people in late adulthood need a life filled with activities and social interaction to be happy; as in every stage of life, some older adults are just as satisfied leading a relatively inactive, solitary existence. What may be more important is how people view the aging process: Evidence shows that positive self-perceptions of aging are associated with increased longevity (Levy et al., 2002; Levy & Myers, 2004).

Regardless of how people age, most engage in a process of **life review**, in which they examine and evaluate their lives. Remembering and reconsidering what has occurred in the past, people in late adulthood often come to a better understanding of themselves, sometimes resolving lingering problems and conflicts, and facing their lives with greater wisdom and serenity.

disengagement theory of aging A theory that suggests that aging produces a gradual withdrawal from the world on physical, psychological, and social levels.

activity theory of aging A theory that suggests that the elderly who are most successful while aging are those who maintain the interests and activities they had during middle age.

life review The process by which people examine and evaluate their lives.

© Roz Chast/The New Yorker Collection/www.cartoonbank.com.

ADJUSTING TO DEATH

At some time in our lives, we all face death—not only our own demise but also the deaths of friends and loved ones. Although there is nothing more inevitable in life, for many people death remains a frightening, emotion-laden topic. Certainly, little is more stressful than the death of a loved one or the contemplation of our own imminent death, and preparing for death is one of our most crucial developmental tasks (Aiken, 2000).

A generation ago, talking about death was taboo. The topic was never mentioned to dying people, and gerontologists had little to say about it. That changed, however, with the pioneering work of Elisabeth Kübler-Ross (1969), who brought the subject of death into the open. Based on her observations of people as they dealt with their own impending death, she developed a theory that we generally move through five broad stages when we cope with grief, loss, and death:

- *Denial.* In this stage, people resist the idea that they are dying. Even if told that their chances for survival are small, they refuse to admit that they are facing death.
- *Anger.* After moving beyond the denial stage, dying people become angry—angry at people around them who are in good health, angry at medical professionals for being ineffective, angry at God.
- *Bargaining.* Anger leads to bargaining, in which the dying try to think of ways to postpone death. They may decide to dedicate their lives to religion if God saves them; they may say, "If only I can live to see my son married, I will accept death then."
- *Depression.* When dying people come to feel that bargaining is of no use, they move to the next stage: depression. They realize that their lives really are coming to an end, leading to what Kübler-Ross calls "preparatory grief" for their own deaths.
- *Acceptance.* In this stage, people accept impending death. Usually they are unemotional and uncommunicative; it is as if they have made peace with themselves and are expecting death with no bitterness.

Keep in mind that not everyone and not every culture experiences each of these stages in the same way. In fact, Kübler-Ross's stages pertain only to people who are fully aware that they are dying and have the time to evaluate their impending death. Furthermore, vast differences occur in the way individuals react to impending death. The specific cause and duration of dying, as well as the person's culture, sex, age, and personality and the type of support received from family and friends, all have an effect on how people respond to death (Carver & Scheier, 2002; Coyle, 2006).

get involved!

A great active way to learn more about people of different ages is to work and interact with such individuals. Many colleges and universities have offices or Web sites listing diverse volunteer, service learning, and community-based research opportunities within the local communities. Possibilities for offering your service include daycare centers, youth organizations, assisted living residences, homeless shelters, hospitals, hospice organizations, and schools. As you teach, or coach, or conduct a survey, or perhaps serve food, you will be gaining invaluable experience as well as building your resume.

How Do You Feel About Death?

To assess your feelings about death, complete the following questionnaire. For statements 1 through 11, use these scale labels:

1 = never; 2 = rarely; 3 = sometimes; 4 = often

1. I think about my own death. _____
2. I think about the death of loved ones. _____
3. I think about dying young. _____
4. I think about the possibility of my being killed on a busy road. _____
5. I have fantasies of my own death. _____
6. I think about death just before I go to sleep. _____
7. I think of how I would act if I knew I were to die within a given period of time. _____
8. I think of how my relatives would act and feel upon my death. _____
9. When I am sick, I think about death. _____
10. When I am outside during a lightning storm, I think about the possibility of being struck by lightning. _____
11. When I am in a car, I think about the high incidence of traffic fatalities. _____

For statements 12 through 30, use these scale labels:

1 = strongly disagree   2 = disagree   3 = agree   4 = strongly agree

12. I think people should first become concerned about death when they are old. _____
13. I am much more concerned about death than those around me. _____
14. Death hardly concerns me. _____
15. My general outlook just doesn't allow for morbid thoughts. _____
16. The prospect of my own death arouses anxiety in me. _____
17. The prospect of my own death depresses me. _____
18. The prospect of the death of my loved ones arouses anxiety in me. _____
19. The knowledge that I will surely die does not in any way affect the conduct of my life. _____
20. I envisage my own death as a painful, nightmarish experience. _____
21. I am afraid of dying. _____
22. I am afraid of being dead. _____
23. Many people become disturbed at the sight of a new grave, but it does not bother me. _____
24. I am disturbed when I think about the shortness of life. _____
25. Thinking about death is a waste of time. _____
26. Death should not be regarded as a tragedy if it occurs after a productive life. _____
27. The inevitable death of humanity poses a serious challenge to the meaningfulness of human existence. _____
28. The death of the individual is ultimately beneficial because it facilitates change in society. _____
29. I have a desire to live on after death. _____
30. The question of whether or not there is a future life worries me considerably. _____

Scoring: If you rated any of these items—12, 14, 15, 19, 23, 25, 26, and 28—as 1, change these ratings to 4; those you rated as 2, change to 3; those you rated as 3, change to 2; and those you rated as 4, change to 1. Add up your ratings.

Average scores on the scale typically range from about 68 to 80. If you scored about 85, death is something that seems to produce some degree of anxiety. Scores lower than 68 suggest that you experience little fear of death.

Reproduced with permission of author and publisher from: Dickstein, L. S. Death concern: measurement and correlates. *Psychological Reports*, 1972, 30, 563–571. © Psychological Reports 1972.

For
REVIEW >>

- **How do infants grow and develop before birth?**

  At conception, a male sperm and a female egg unite, with each contributing to the new individual's genetic makeup. A newborn baby normally enters the world after 38 weeks of pregnancy. Genes affect a wide array of personal characteristics as well as physical characteristics. Genetic abnormalities produce birth defects such as phenylketonuria (PKU), sickle-cell anemia, Tay-Sachs disease, and Down syndrome. Among the environmental influences on fetal growth are the mother's nutrition, illnesses, and drug intake. (pp. 223–226)

- **What do newborn babies actually know, and how can we tell?**

  Newborns infants have reflexes, unlearned, involuntary responses that occur automatically in the presence of certain stimuli. These reflexes disappear a few months after birth. Sensory abilities develop rapidly in infants. Relatively soon after birth infants can distinguish color, depth, sound, tastes, and smells. (pp. 226–228)

- **How do children learn to get along with and understand other people?**

  Attachment—the positive emotional bond between a child and a specific individual—is central to social development in infancy. Measured in the laboratory by means of the Ainsworth strange situation, attachment relates to later social and emotional adjustment. As children become older, the nature of their social interactions with peers changes. Initially play occurs relatively independently, but it becomes increasingly cooperative. According to Erikson, eight stages of psychosocial development involve people's changing interactions and understanding of themselves and others over the course of their lifetime. During childhood, the four stages are trust-versus-mistrust (birth to $1\frac{1}{2}$ years), autonomy-versus-shame-and-doubt ($1\frac{1}{2}$ to 3 years), initiative-versus-guilt (3 to 6 years), and industry-versus-inferiority (6 to 12 years). (pp. 229–233)

- **What are the real psychological challenges of adolescence?**

  Adolescence, the developmental stage between childhood and adulthood, begins with the onset of puberty, the point at which sexual maturity occurs. The age at which puberty begins has implications for the way people view themselves and the way others see them. Moral judgments during adolescence increase in sophistication, according to Kohlberg. Although Kohlberg's model adequately describes males' moral development, Gilligan suggests that women view morality in terms of caring for individuals rather than in terms of broad, general principles of justice. According to Erikson's model of psychosocial development, adolescence may be accompanied by an identity crisis. Adolescence is followed by three more stages of psychosocial development that cover the remainder of the life span. (pp. 238–245)

- **In what ways do people continue to develop and grow after they reach adulthood?**

  Early adulthood marks the peak of physical health. Physical changes occur relatively gradually in men and women as they age. One major physical change occurs at the end of middle adulthood for women: They begin menopause, after which they are no longer fertile. During middle adulthood, people typically experience a midlife transition in which the notion that life is not unending becomes more important. In some cases this may lead to a midlife crisis. People in their 50s realize that their lives and accomplishments are fairly well set, and they try to come to terms with them. Among the important developmental milestones during adulthood are marriage, family changes, and divorce. Another important determinant of adult development is work. (pp. 245–248)

Pop Quiz

1. Developmental psychologists are interested in the effects of both _____ and _____ on development.

2. Match each of the following terms with its definition.
   a. basic unit through which genetic information is passed
   b. fertilized egg
   c. rod-shaped structure containing genetic information
   _____ 1. zygote
   _____ 2. gene
   _____ 3. chromosome

3. The emotional bond that develops between a child and its caregiver is known as _____.

4. One important attachment indicator to watch for, according to the expert in the naturalistic observation activity, is _____.
   a. blinking
   b. whom the child gives toys to
   c. giggling
   d. eye contact

5. Match the parenting style with its definition.
   a. rigid; highly punitive; demanding obedience
   b. gives little direction; lax on obedience
   c. firm but fair; tries to explain parental decisions
   d. emotionally detached and unloving
   _____ 1. permissive
   _____ 2. authoritative
   _____ 3. authoritarian
   _____ 4. uninvolved

6. Match the stage of development with the thinking style characteristic of that stage.
   a. sensorimotor
   b. formal operational
   c. preoperational
   d. concrete operational
   _____ 1. egocentric thought
   _____ 2. object permanence
   _____ 3. abstract reasoning
   _____ 4. conservation; reversibility

7. Delayed maturation typically provides both males and females with a social advantage. True or false?

8. Erikson believed that during adolescence, people must search for _____, whereas during early adulthood, the major task is _____.

9. Which statement is true?
   a. Teenagers aren't really at risk for suicide—what you hear on the news is just hype.
   b. There are specific behaviors and feelings that correlate with being at risk for suicide.
   c. People who talk about committing suicide usually just want attention and aren't really at risk for suicide.
   d. There are many different sad stories, but all point to being at risk for suicide.

10. Rob recently turned 40 and surveyed his goals and accomplishments. Although he has accomplished a lot, he realized that many of his goals will not be met in his lifetime. This stage is called a(n) _____ _____.

11. During old age, a person's _____ intelligence continues to increase, whereas _____ intelligence may decline.

12. In Kübler-Ross's _____ stage, people resist the idea of death. In the _____ stage, they attempt to make deals to avoid death, and in the _____ stage, they passively await death.

PERSONAL

WHO IS THE REAL MADOFF?

To some, Bernard L. Madoff was an affable, charismatic man who moved comfortably among power brokers on Wall Street and in Washington. He secured a long-standing role as an elder statesman on Wall Street, allowing him to land on important boards and commissions where his opinions helped shape securities regulations. And his employees say he treated them like family.

There was, of course, another side to Mr. Madoff. Reclusive, at times standoffish and aloof, this Bernard rarely rubbed elbows in Manhattan's cocktail circuit or at Palm Beach balls. This Bernard was quiet, controlled, and closely attuned to his image down to the most minute details.[x]

Which was the real Bernard Madoff? Was he the powerful, charismatic Wall Street businessman? Or was he the self-conscious, detail-oriented recluse? And perhaps most important, were there any signs that Madoff was secretly operating a fraudulent investment scheme that ultimately cheated thousands of people out of billions of dollars? Many people, like Madoff, have different sides to their personalities, appearing one way to some and quite differently to others.

To some extent, we all have different sides to our personalities. For example, do you behave differently when relaxing with your close friends than when at work? Would your friends be surprised if they could see your reaction when your parents called you to another room and then scolded you for something? While we tend to have a great deal of stability in our personalities, different aspects come out in different situations. As we'll see, personality psychology is the study of the psychological makeup of individuals and how it influences their interactions with others and with their physical environment.

ITY

As You READ >>

- How do psychologists think about personality?
- What are the major features of the different psychological approaches to personality?
- How can psychologists most accurately measure personality?
- What are the major types of personality measures?

>> What Is Personality?

How would you describe your best friend to someone you've just met? Apart from describing her physical characteristics (maybe she's 5'7" and has brown hair and green eyes), would you add some personal qualities, such as happy and easy-going or sympathetic and conscientious but shy?

personality The pattern of enduring characteristics that produce consistency and individuality in a given person.

Most of us would agree that individuals have certain lasting characteristics, such as a happy disposition, that make their behavior fairly predictable from one day to the next. Indeed, psychologists define **personality** as the pattern of enduring characteristics that produce consistency and individuality in a given person. Personality encompasses the behaviors that make each of us unique and that differentiate us from others. It is also personality that leads us to act consistently over extended periods of time.

Like other areas of psychology, personality psychology includes several different perspectives. Here we consider a number of them. We begin with psychodynamic theories of personality, which emphasize the role of the unconscious mind. Next, we consider approaches that focus on identifying fundamental personality traits (including sociability and conscientiousness); theories that view personality as a set of learned behaviors; biological and evolutionary perspectives on

personality; and approaches, known as humanistic theories, that highlight the uniquely human aspects of personality. We end with a discussion of personality measurement and applications of personality tests.

>> Psychodynamic Approaches to Personality

The college student was intent on making a good first impression on an attractive woman he had spotted across a crowded room at a party. As he walked toward her, he mulled over a line he had heard in an old movie the night before: "I don't believe we've been properly introduced yet." To his horror, what came out was a bit different. After threading his way through the crowded room, he finally reached the woman and blurted out, "I don't believe we've been properly seduced yet."

Although this student's error may seem to be merely an embarrassing slip of the tongue, according to some personality theorists such a mistake is not an error at all (Motley, 1987). Instead, *psychodynamic personality theorists* might argue that the error illustrates one way in which behavior is triggered by inner forces that are beyond our awareness. These hidden drives, shaped by childhood experiences, play an important role in energizing and directing everyday behavior.

Psychodynamic approaches to personality are based on the idea that personality is motivated by inner forces and conflicts about which people have little awareness and over which they have no control. The most important pioneer of the psychodynamic approach was Sigmund Freud. A number of Freud's followers, including Carl Jung, Karen Horney, and Alfred Adler, refined Freud's theory and developed their own psychodynamic approaches.

FREUD'S PSYCHOANALYTIC THEORY: MAPPING THE UNCONSCIOUS MIND

Sigmund Freud, an Austrian physician, developed **psychoanalytic theory** in the early 1900s. According to Freud's theory, conscious experience is only a small part of our psychological makeup and experience. He argued that much of our behavior is motivated by the **unconscious**, a part of the personality that contains the memories, knowledge, beliefs, feelings, urges, drives, and instincts of which the individual is not aware.

Like the unseen mass of a floating iceberg, the contents of the unconscious far surpass in quantity the information in our conscious awareness. Freud maintained that to understand personality, we must expose what is in the unconscious. But because the unconscious disguises the meaning of the material it holds, the content of the unconscious cannot be observed directly. It is therefore necessary to interpret clues to the unconscious—slips of the tongue, fantasies, and dreams—to understand the unconscious processes that direct behavior. A slip of the tongue such as the one quoted earlier (sometimes termed a *Freudian slip*) may be interpreted as revealing the speaker's unconscious sexual desires.

To Freud, much of our personality is determined by our unconscious. Some of the unconscious is made up of the *preconscious*, which contains material that is not threatening and is easily brought to mind, such as the knowledge that $2 + 2 = 4$. But deeper in the unconscious are instinctual drives, the wishes, desires, demands, and needs that are hidden from conscious awareness because of the conflicts and pain they would cause if they were part of our everyday lives. The unconscious provides a "safe haven" for our recollections of threatening events.

Structuring Personality: Id, Ego, and Superego
To describe the structure of personality, Freud developed a comprehensive theory that held that personality consists of three separate but interacting components: the id, the ego, and the superego. Freud suggested that the three

Freud's Model of Personality

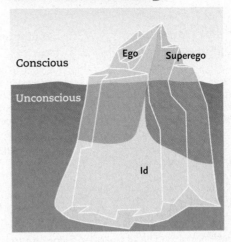

structures can be diagrammed to show how they relate to the conscious and the unconscious.

Although the three components of personality described by Freud may appear to be actual physical structures in the nervous system, they are not. Instead, they represent abstract conceptions of a general *theoretical model* of personality that describes the interaction of forces that motivate behavior.

If personality consisted only of primitive, instinctual cravings and longings, it would have just one component: the id. The **id** is the raw, unorganized, inborn part of personality. From the time of birth, the id is driven by primal urges to satisfy hunger, sex, aggression, and irrational impulses. These urges are fueled by "psychic energy," which, according to the theory, is limited. For instance, if the id is using up most of the psychic energy, then there may not be enough for the ego and superego to do their jobs.

psychodynamic approaches to personality Approaches that assume that personality is motivated by inner forces and conflicts about which people have little awareness and over which they have no control.

psychoanalytic theory Freud's theory that unconscious forces act as determinants of personality.

unconscious A part of the personality that contains the memories, knowledge, beliefs, feelings, urges, drives, and instincts of which the individual is not aware.

id The raw, unorganized, inborn part of personality whose sole purpose is to reduce tension created by primitive drives related to hunger, sex, aggression, and irrational impulses.

STUDY TIP

Remember that the three parts of personality in Freud's theory—the id, the ego, and the superego—are abstract conceptions and *not* physical structures in the brain.

Freud's Psychosexual Stages of Personality Development

1
Oral Stage
Age: Birth to 12–18 months

Source of pleasure: Interest in oral gratification from sucking, eating, mouthing, biting

Adult fixation: Smoking, eating, talking, sarcasm

2
Anal Stage
Age: 12–18 months to 3 years

Source of pleasure: Gratification from expelling and withholding feces; coming to terms with society's controls relating to toilet training

Adult fixation: Unusual rigidity, orderliness, or extreme sloppiness

3
Phallic Stage
Age: 3 to 5–6 years

Source of pleasure: Interest in the genitals, coming to terms with sexual conflict that leads to identification with same-sex parent

Adult fixation: Attraction to people like one's opposite-sex parent

4
Latency Stage
Age: 5–6 years to adolescence

Source of pleasure: Sexual concerns largely unimportant

Adult fixation: Does not apply

5
Genital Stage
Age: Adolescence to adulthood

Source of pleasure: Reemergence of sexual interests and establishment of mature sexual relationships

Adult fixation: Does not apply

---

ego The part of the personality that provides a buffer between the id and the outside world.

superego According to Freud, the final personality structure to develop; it represents the rights and wrongs of society as handed down by a person's parents, teachers, and other important figures.

psychosexual stages Developmental periods that children pass through during which they encounter conflicts between the demands of society and their own sexual urges.

fixations Conflicts or concerns that persist beyond the developmental period in which they first occur.

identification The process of wanting to be like another person as much as possible, imitating that person's behavior and adopting similar beliefs and values.

The id operates according to the *pleasure principle*, in which the goal is the immediate reduction of tension and the maximization of satisfaction. However, in most cases reality prevents the fulfillment of the demands of the pleasure principle: We cannot always eat when we are hungry, and we can discharge our sexual drives only when the time and the place are appropriate. To account for this fact of life, Freud suggested a second component of personality, which he called the ego.

The **ego**, which begins to develop soon after birth, strives to balance the desires of the id and the realities of the objective, outside world. In contrast to the pleasure-seeking id, the ego operates according to the *reality principle*, in which instinctual energy is restrained to maintain the safety of the individual and to help integrate the person into society. In a sense, then, the ego is the "executive" of personality: It makes decisions, controls actions, and allows thinking and problem solving of a higher order than the id's capabilities permit.

The **superego**, the final personality structure to develop in childhood, represents the rights and wrongs of society as taught and modeled by a person's parents, teachers, and other significant individuals. The superego includes the *conscience*, which prevents us from behaving in a morally improper way by making us feel guilty if we do wrong. The superego helps us to control impulses coming from the id, making our behavior less selfish and more virtuous.

Both the superego and the id are unrealistic in that they do not consider the practical realities imposed by society.

The superego, if left to operate without restraint, would create perfectionists unable to make the compromises that life requires. An unrestrained id would create a primitive, pleasure-seeking, thoughtless individual seeking to fulfill every desire without delay. As a result, the ego must mediate between the demands of the superego and the demands of the id.

Developing Personality: Psychosexual Stages
Freud also provided us with a view of how personality develops through a series of five **psychosexual stages**, during which individuals encounter conflicts between the demands of society and their own sexual urges. The five psychosexual stages of personality development in Freud's theory—oral, anal, phallic, latency, and genital—suggest how personality develops as people age.

The sequence Freud proposed is noteworthy, because it explains how experiences and difficulties during a particular childhood stage may predict specific characteristics in the adult personality. This theory is also unique in associating each stage with a major biological function, which Freud assumed to be the focus of pleasure in a given period.

According to Freud, failure to resolve the conflicts at a particular stage can result in **fixation**, the persistence of conflicts or concerns beyond the developmental period in which they first occur. Such conflicts may be due to having needs ignored or (conversely) being overindulged during the earlier period.

According to Freud, one of the most important hurdles of personality development arises during the phallic stage (ages 3 to 5 or 6), when children unconsciously develop a sexual interest in their opposite-sex parent and see the same-sex parent as a rival. To resolve such unacceptable feelings, they come to identify with the same-sex parent. Freud defined **identification** as the process of wanting to be like another person as much as possible, imitating that person's behavior and adopting similar beliefs and values.

Defense Mechanisms
Freud's efforts to describe and theorize about the underlying dynamics of personality and

its development were motivated by very practical problems that his patients faced in dealing with *anxiety*, an intense, negative emotional experience. According to Freud, anxiety is a danger signal to the ego. Although anxiety can arise from realistic fears—such as seeing a poisonous snake about to strike—it can also occur in the form of *neurotic anxiety*, in which irrational impulses emanating from the id threaten to burst through and become uncontrollable.

According to Freud, anxiety is a danger signal to the ego.

Because anxiety, obviously, is unpleasant, Freud believed that people develop a range of defense mechanisms to deal with it. Defense mechanisms are *unconscious* strategies that people use to reduce anxiety by concealing its source from themselves.

The primary defense mechanism is **repression**, in which unacceptable or unpleasant id impulses are pushed back into the unconscious. Repression is the most direct method of dealing with anxiety; instead of handling an anxiety-producing impulse on a conscious level, we simply ignore it. For example, a college student who feels hatred for her mother may repress those personally and socially unacceptable feelings. The feelings remain lodged within the unconscious, because acknowledging them would provoke anxiety. Similarly, memories of childhood abuse may be repressed. Although such memories may not be consciously recalled, according to Freud they can affect later behavior, and they may be revealed through dreams or slips of the tongue or symbolically in some other fashion.

If repression is ineffective in keeping anxiety at bay, we might use other defense mechanisms. Freud, and later his daughter Anna Freud (who became a well-known psychoanalyst), formulated an extensive list of potential defense mechanisms (Conte & Plutchik, 2004; Cramer, 2007; Hentschel et al., 2004; Yu, 2011).

All of us employ defense mechanisms to some degree, according to Freudian theory, and they can serve a useful purpose by protecting us from unpleasant information. Yet some people fall prey to them to such an extent that they must constantly direct a large amount of psychic energy toward hiding and rechanneling unacceptable impulses. When this occurs, everyday living becomes difficult. In such cases, the result is a mental disorder produced by anxiety—what Freud called "neurosis" (a term rarely used by psychologists today, although it endures in everyday conversation).

> **repression** The primary defense mechanism in which unacceptable or unpleasant id impulses are pushed back into the unconscious.

Freud's Defense Mechanisms

Defense Mechanism	Explanation	Example
Repression	Unacceptable or unpleasant impulses are pushed back into the unconscious.	A woman is unable to recall that she was raped.
Regression	People behave as if they were at an earlier stage of development.	A boss has a temper tantrum when an employee makes a mistake.
Displacement	The expression of an unwanted feeling or thought is redirected from a more threatening powerful person to a weaker one.	A brother yells at his younger sister after a teacher gives him a bad grade.
Rationalization	People provide self-justifying explanations in place of the actual, but threatening, reason for their behavior.	A student who goes out drinking the night before a big test rationalizes his behavior by saying the test isn't all that important.
Denial	People refuse to accept or acknowledge an anxiety-producing piece of information.	A student refuses to believe that he has flunked a course.
Projection	People attribute unwanted impulses and feelings to someone else.	A man who is unfaithful to his wife and feels guilty suspects that his wife is unfaithful.
Sublimation	People divert unwanted impulses into socially approved thoughts, feelings, or behaviors.	A person with strong feelings of aggression becomes a soldier.
Reaction formation	Unconscious impulses are expressed as their opposite in consciousness.	A mother who unconsciously resents her child acts in an overly loving way toward the child.

Evaluating Freud's Legacy Freud's theory has had a significant effect on the field of psychology—and even more broadly on Western philosophy and literature. The ideas of the unconscious, defense mechanisms, and childhood roots of adult psychological difficulties have been accepted by many people.

However, many contemporary personality psychologists have leveled significant criticisms against psychoanalytic theory. Among the most important is the lack of compelling scientific data to support it. Although individual case studies *seem* supportive, we lack conclusive evidence showing that the personality is structured and operates along the lines Freud laid out. The lack of evidence is due, in part, to the fact that Freud's conception of personality is built on unobservable abstract concepts. Moreover, it is not clear that the stages of personality that Freud laid out provide an accurate description of personality development. We also know now that important changes in personality can occur in adolescence and adulthood—something that Freud did not believe happened. Instead, he argued that personality largely is set by adolescence (Hayslip et al., 2006).

The vague nature of Freud's theory also makes it difficult to predict how certain developmental difficulties will be displayed in an adult. For instance, if a person is fixated at the anal stage, according to Freud, he or she may be unusually messy—or unusually neat. Freud's theory offers no way to predict how the difficulty will be exhibited (Crews, 1996; Macmillan, 1996). Furthermore, Freud can be faulted for arguing that women have weaker superegos

neo-Freudian psychoanalysts Psychoanalysts who were trained in traditional Freudian theory but who later rejected some of its major points.

collective unconscious According to Jung, a common set of ideas, feelings, images, and symbols that we inherit from our ancestors, the whole human race, and even animal ancestors from the distant past.

than men do and in some ways unconsciously yearn to be men (the concept of penis envy).

Finally, Freud made his observations and derived his theory from a limited population. His theory was based almost entirely on case studies of upper-class Austrian women living in the strict, puritanical era of the early 1900s who had come to him seeking treatment for psychological and physical problems. How far one can generalize beyond this population is a matter of considerable debate.

Still, Freud generated an important method of treating psychological disturbances called *psychoanalysis*. As we will see when we discuss treatment approaches to psychological disorder, psychoanalysis remains in use today (Heller, 2005; Messer & McWilliams, 2003; Riolo, 2007).

Moreover, Freud's emphasis on the unconscious has been partially supported by current research on dreams and implicit memory. As we first noted when we discussed dreaming, advances in neuroscience are not inconsistent with some of Freud's arguments. Furthermore, cognitive and social psychologists have found increasing evidence that unconscious processes help us think about and evaluate our world, set goals, and choose a course of action (Derryberry, 2006; Litowitz, 2007; Turnbull & Solms, 2007).

THE NEO-FREUDIAN PSYCHOANALYSTS

Freud laid the foundation for important work done by a series of successors who were trained in traditional Freudian theory but later rejected some of its major points. These theorists are known as **neo-Freudian psychoanalysts**.

> Jung rejected Freud's view of the primary importance of unconscious sexual urges.

The neo-Freudians placed greater emphasis than Freud had on the functions of the ego, suggesting that it has more control than does the id over day-to-day activities. They focused more on the social environment and minimized the importance of sex as a driving force in children's and adults' lives. They also paid greater attention to the effects of society and culture on personality development.

Jung's Collective Unconscious One of the most influential neo-Freudians, Carl Jung (pronounced "yoong"), rejected Freud's view of the primary importance of unconscious sexual urges. Instead, he looked at the primitive urges of the unconscious more positively, arguing that they represented a more general, and positive, life force that encompasses an inborn drive motivating creativity and more positive resolution of conflict (Cassells, 2007; Finn, 2011; Lothane, 2005).

Jung suggested that we have a universal **collective unconscious**, a common set of ideas, feelings, images, and symbols that we inherit from our relatives, the whole human race, and even nonhuman animal ancestors from the distant past. This collective unconscious is shared by everyone and is displayed in behavior that is common across diverse cultures—such as love of mother, belief in a supreme being, and even behavior as specific as fear of snakes (Drob, 2005; Hauke, 2006; Oehman & Mineka, 2003).

Jung went on to propose that the collective unconscious contains **archetypes**, universal symbolic representations of a particular person, object, or experience. For instance, a mother archetype, which contains reflections of our ancestors' relationships with mother figures, is suggested by the prevalence of mothers in art, religion, literature, and mythology. (Think of the Virgin Mary, Earth Mother, wicked stepmothers in fairy tales, Mother's Day, and so forth.) Jung also suggested that an unconscious feminine archetype affects how men behave, whereas an unconscious male archetype influences women's behavior (Bair, 2003; Jung, 1961; Smetana, 2007).

To Jung, archetypes play an important role in determining our day-to-day reactions, attitudes, and values. For example, Jung might explain the popularity of the *Star Wars* movies as being due to their use of broad archetypes of good (Luke Skywalker) and evil (Darth Vader).

Although no reliable research evidence confirms the existence of the collective unconscious—and even Jung acknowledged that such evidence would be difficult to produce—Jung's theory has had significant influence in areas beyond psychology, including business and the arts (Bayne, 2005; Furnham & Crump, 2005; Gladwell, 2004).

In terms of Jung's theory, Harry Potter and Lord Voldemort represent archetypes of good and evil.

From the perspective of …

A DISTRICT ATTORNEY How could you use Jung's archetypes to sway a jury? Which archetypes would be most effective?

Horney's Feminist Perspective Karen Horney (pronounced "HORN-eye") was one of the earliest western psychologists to champion women's issues and is sometimes called the first feminist psychologist. Horney suggested that personality develops in the context of social relationships and depends particularly on the relationship between parents and child and how well the child's needs are met. She rejected Freud's suggestion that women have penis envy, asserting that what women envy most in men is not their anatomy but the independence, success, and freedom that women often are denied (Horney, 1937; Miletic, 2002; Smith, 2007).

Horney was also one of the first to stress the importance of cultural factors in the determination of personality. For example, she suggested that society's rigid gender roles for women lead them to experience ambivalence about success, fearing that they will make enemies if they are too successful. Her conceptualizations, developed

in the 1930s and 1940s, laid the groundwork for many of the central ideas of feminism that emerged decades later (Eckardt, 2005; Jones, 2006).

Adler and the Other Neo-Freudians

Alfred Adler, another important neo-Freudian psychoanalyst, also considered Freudian theory's emphasis on sexual needs misplaced. Instead, Adler proposed that the primary human motivation is a striving for superiority, not in terms of superiority over others but in a quest for self-improvement and perfection (Hjertaas, 2004; Rosov, 1993).

Adler used the term **inferiority complex** to describe situations in which adults have not been able to overcome the feelings of inferiority they developed as children, when they were small and limited in their knowledge about the world. Early social relationships with parents have an important effect on children's ability to outgrow feelings of personal inferiority and instead to orient themselves toward attaining more socially useful goals, such as improving society.

archetypes According to Jung, universal symbolic representations of a particular person, object, or experience (such as good and evil).

inferiority complex According to Adler, a problem affecting adults who have not been able to overcome the feelings of inferiority that they developed as children, when they were small and limited in their knowledge about the world.

Karen Horney was one of the earliest proponents of women's issues in psychology.

Other neo-Freudians included Erik Erikson, whose theory of psychosocial development we discussed in chapter 9, and Freud's daughter, Anna Freud. Like Adler and Horney, Erikson and Anna Freud focused less than Freud did on inborn sexual and aggressive drives and more on the social and cultural factors behind personality.

>> Trait Approaches to Personality

If someone asked you to characterize another person, you would probably come up with a list of that individual's personal qualities, as you see them. In fact, much of our own understanding of others' behavior is based on the premise that people possess certain traits that are consistent across different situations. For example, we generally assume that if someone is outgoing and sociable in one situation, he or she is outgoing and sociable in other situations (Gilbert et al., 1992; Gilbert, Miller, & Ross, 1998; Mischel, 2004). But how would you know which of those qualities are most important to an understanding of that person's behavior?

Personality psychologists have asked similar questions. To answer them, some have developed a model of personality centered on traits. **Traits** are consistent personality characteristics and behaviors displayed in different situations. **Trait theories** attempt to identify the consistencies in individuals' behavior.

> **traits** Consistent personality characteristics and behaviors displayed in different situations.
>
> **trait theory** A model of personality that seeks to identify the basic traits necessary to describe personality.

Trait theorists do not assume that some people have a trait and others do not; rather, they propose that all people possess certain traits, but that the degree to which a particular trait applies to a specific person varies and can be quantified (Olson, 2006). For instance, you may be relatively friendly, whereas I may be relatively unfriendly. But we both have a "friendliness" trait, although your degree of "friendliness" is higher than mine. The major challenge for trait theorists taking this approach has been to identify the specific primary traits necessary to describe personality.

Did you know?

Your Facebook profile may tell others more about you than you realize. A very recent study found when people were allowed to view someone's profile, they were fairly accurate in their assessment of that person's personality (Back et al., 2010).

ALLPORT'S TRAIT THEORY

Personality psychologist Gordon Allport was faced with a problem crucial to all trait approaches: identifying the principal traits. Allport eventually suggested that there are three fundamental categories of traits: cardinal, central, and secondary (Allport, 1961, 1966). A *cardinal trait* is a single characteristic that directs most of a person's activities. For example, a totally selfless person may direct all her energy toward humanitarian activities; an intensely power-hungry person may be driven by an all-consuming need for control.

Most people, however, do not develop a single, comprehensive cardinal trait. Instead, they possess a handful of central traits that make up the core of personality. *Central traits*, such as honesty and sociability, are the major characteristics of an individual. According to Allport, they usually number from five to ten in any one person. Finally, *secondary traits* are characteristics that affect behavior in fewer situations and are less influential than central or cardinal traits. For instance, a mild reluctance to eat meat and a casual interest in modern art might be considered secondary traits (Glicksohn & Nahari, 2007; Nicholson, 2003).

FACTOR ANALYSIS

Later attempts to identify primary personality traits have centered on a statistical technique known as factor analysis (Kim & Mueller, 1978; Lee & Ashton, 2007). *Factor analysis* is a statistical method of identifying associations among a large number of variables to reveal more general patterns. For example, a personality researcher might administer a questionnaire to many participants, asking them to describe themselves by referring to an extensive list of traits. By statistically combining responses and computing which traits are associated with one another in the same person, a researcher can identify the most fundamental patterns or combinations of traits—called *factors*—that underlie participants' responses.

Using factor analysis, personality psychologist Raymond Cattell (1965) suggested that 16 pairs of *source traits* represent the basic dimensions of personality. Using those source traits, he developed the Sixteen Personality Factor Questionnaire, or 16 PF, a measure that provides scores for each of the source traits (Cattell, Cattell, & Cattell, 1993, 2000).

Did you know?

Are you a dog person? A cat person? Using the Big Five, personality differences have been identified, based on the species of pet preferred. Dog people tended to score higher on extraversion, agreeableness, and conscientiousness. Cat people tended to score higher on openness and neuroticism (Gosling, Sandy, & Potter, 2010).

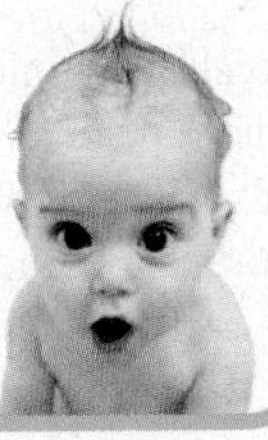

Another trait theorist, psychologist Hans Eysenck (1995), also used factor analysis to identify patterns of traits, but he came to a very different conclusion about the nature of personality. He found that personality could best be described in terms of just three major dimensions: *extraversion, neuroticism*, and *psychoticism*. The extraversion dimension relates to the degree of sociability, whereas the neurotic dimension encompasses emotional stability. Finally, psychoticism refers to the degree to which reality is distorted. By evaluating people along these three dimensions, Eysenck was able to predict behavior accurately in a variety of situations (Eysenck, 1991).

THE BIG FIVE FACTORS OF PERSONALITY

For the last two decades, the most influential trait approach contends that five traits or factors—called the "Big Five"—lie at the core of personality. Using modern factor analytic statistical techniques, a host of researchers have identified a similar set of five factors that underlie personality. The five factors are *openness to experience, conscientiousness, extraversion, agreeableness*, and *neuroticism* (emotional stability) (Costa & McCrae, 2008; John & Srivastava, 1999; McCrae & Costa, 1990).

The "Big Five" traits are found in a number of areas. For example, the "Big Five" are descriptive of different populations of people, including children, college students, older adults, and speakers of different languages. Cross-cultural research conducted in areas ranging from Europe to the Middle East to Africa also has been supportive (Joshanloo & Afshari, 2011; McCrae et al., 2005; Schmitt, Allik, & McCrae, 2007; Schmitt et al., 2008).

The growing consensus is that the "Big Five" currently represent the best description of personality traits (Costa & McCrae, 2008). Still, the debate over the specific number and kinds of traits—and even the usefulness of trait approaches in general—remains a lively one (Fleeson, 2004).

STUDY TIP

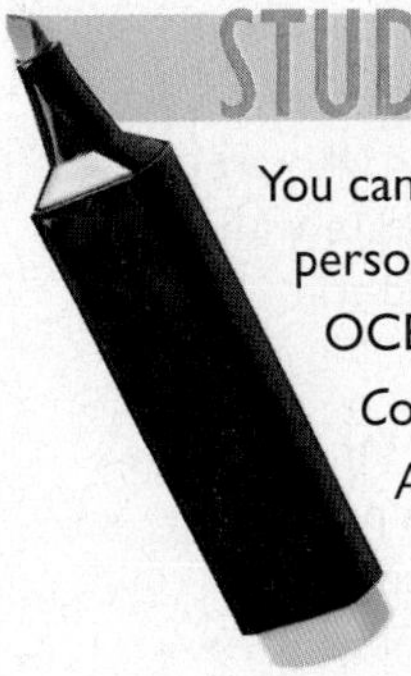

You can remember the "Big Five" set of personality traits by using the acronym OCEAN (Openness to experience, Conscientiousness, Extraversion, Agreeableness, and Neuroticism).

The Big Five Personality Factors and Dimensions of Sample Traits

Openness to experience
Independent—Conforming
Imaginative—Practical
Preference for variety—Preference for routine

Conscientiousness
Careful—Careless
Disciplined—Impulsive
Organized—Disorganized

Extraversion
Talkative—Quiet
Fun-loving—Sober
Sociable—Retiring

Agreeableness
Sympathetic—Fault-finding
Kind—Cold
Appreciative—Unfriendly

Neuroticism (Emotional Stability)
Stable—Tense
Calm—Anxious
Secure—Insecure

Source: Adapted from Pervin, 1990, Chapter 3, and McCrae & Costa, 1986, p. 1002.

Eysenck's Three Dimensions of Personality

Extraversion	Neuroticism	Psychoticism
Sociable	Anxious	Aggressive
Lively	Depressed	Cold
Active	Guilt feelings	Egocentric
Assertive	Low self-esteem	Impersonal
Sensation-seeking	Tense	Impulsive

Source: Eysenck, 1990.

of personality rather than an explanation of behavior. In the view of some critics, then, traits do not provide explanations for behavior; they merely describe it (Fleeson, 2004).

>> Learning Approaches to Personality

The psychodynamic and trait approaches concentrate on the "inner" person—the fury of an unobservable but powerful id or a hypothetical set of traits. In contrast, early behavioral approaches to personality focused on the "outer" person. To a strict behaviorist, personality was simply the sum of learned responses to the external environment. Internal events such as thoughts, feelings, and motivations were ignored, because they were irrelevant. Although the existence of personality was not denied, these theorists said that personality was best understood by looking at features of a person's environment.

SKINNER'S BEHAVIORIST APPROACH

According to the most influential learning theorist, B. F. Skinner (who carried out pioneering work on operant conditioning), personality was a collection of learned behavior patterns (Skinner, 1975). Similarities in responses across different situations were caused by similar patterns of reinforcement that had been received in such situations in the past. If I am sociable both at parties and at meetings, it is because I have been reinforced for displaying social behaviors—not because I am fulfilling an unconscious wish based on experiences during my childhood or because I have an internal trait of sociability.

EVALUATING TRAIT APPROACHES TO PERSONALITY

Trait approaches have several virtues. They provide a clear, straightforward characterization of people's behavioral consistencies. Furthermore, traits allow us to readily compare one person with another. Because of these advantages, trait approaches to personality have had an important influence on the development of several useful personality measures (Funder, 1991; Larsen & Buss, 2006; Wiggins, 2003).

However, trait approaches also have some drawbacks. For example, we have seen that various trait theories describing personality come to very different conclusions about which traits are the most fundamental and descriptive. The difficulty in determining which of the theories is the most accurate has led some personality psychologists to question the validity of trait conceptions of personality in general. Even if we can identify a set of primary traits, we are left with little more than a label or description

social cognitive approaches to personality Theories that emphasize the influence of a person's cognitions—thoughts, feelings, expectations, and values—as well as observation of others' behavior, in determining personality.

SOCIAL COGNITIVE APPROACHES

Modern approaches of personality that are grounded in behaviorist theories have found it necessary to stop rejecting the importance of what is "inside" a person and to stop focusing solely on the "outside." These theories, called collectively **social cognitive approaches**, emphasize the influence of cognition—thoughts, feelings, expectations, and values—as well as observation of others' behavior, on personality. According to Albert Bandura, one of the main proponents of this point of view, people can foresee

Did you know?

Birth order appears to affect personality in various ways. For example, first-born children tend to like more structure, such as rules to follow, when challenged to solve problems (Skinner & Fox-Francoeur, 2010).

the possible outcomes of certain behaviors in a specific setting without actually having to carry them out. This understanding comes primarily through *observational learning*—viewing the actions of others and observing the consequences (Bandura, 1986, 1999).

For instance, children who view a model behaving in an aggressive manner tend to copy the behavior if the consequences of the model's behavior are seen to be positive. If, in contrast, the model's aggressive behavior has resulted in no consequences or negative consequences, children are considerably less likely to act aggressively (Bandura, 1986, 1992). According to social cognitive approaches, then, personality develops through repeated observation and imitation of the behavior of others.

People with high self-efficacy have higher aspirations and greater persistence in working to attain goals and ultimately achieve greater success than do those with lower self-efficacy.

Self-Efficacy Bandura's approach places particular emphasis on **self-efficacy**, belief in one's personal capabilities. Self-efficacy underlies people's faith in their ability to carry out a specific behavior or produce a desired outcome. People with high self-efficacy have higher aspirations and greater persistence in working to attain goals and ultimately achieve greater success than do those with lower self-efficacy (Bandura & Locke, 2003; Betz, 2007; Glickler, 2006).

For example, someone who has studied hard while in college and has gotten high grades is likely to have a high sense of self-efficacy with regard to succeeding in college. In contrast, someone who studied a lot but did not get good grades probably would not have a strong sense of self-efficacy for college success.

How Much Consistency Exists in Personality? Another social-cognitive theorist, Walter Mischel, takes a different approach to personality from that of Albert Bandura. He rejects the view that personality consists of broad traits that lead to substantial consistencies in behavior across different situations. Instead, he sees personality as considerably more variable from one situation to another (Mischel, 2009).

In this view, particular situations give rise to particular kinds of behavior. Some situations are especially influential (think of a movie theater, where everyone displays pretty much similar behavior, sitting quietly and observing the film). Other situations permit variability in behavior (a party, for example, where some people may be dancing, while others are eating and drinking).

From this perspective, personality cannot be considered without taking the particular context of the situation into account—a view known as *situationism*. In his *cognitive-affective processing system (CAPS)* theory, Mischel argues that people's thoughts and emotions about themselves and the world determine how they view, and then react, in particular situations. Personality is thus seen as a reflection of how people's prior experiences in different situations affect their behavior (Shoda & Mischel, 2004, 2006).

Self-Esteem Our behavior also reflects the view we have of ourselves and the way we value the various parts of our personalities. **Self-esteem** is the component of personality that encompasses our positive and negative self-evaluations. Unlike self-efficacy, which focuses on our views of whether we are able to carry out a task, self-esteem relates to how we feel about ourselves.

Although people have a general level of self-esteem, it is not one dimensional. We may see ourselves positively in one domain but negatively in others. For example, a good student may have high self-esteem in academic domains but lower self-esteem in sports (Gentile et al., 2009; Salmela-Aro & Nurmi, 2007; Swann, Chang-Schneider, & Larsen McClarty, 2007; vanDellen et al., 2011).

Almost everyone goes through periods of low self-esteem (after, for instance, an undeniable failure), but some people are chronically low in self-esteem. For them, failure seems to be an inevitable part of life. In fact, low self-esteem may lead to a cycle of failure in which past failure breeds future failure.

self-efficacy Belief in one's personal capabilities. Self-efficacy underlies people's faith in their ability to carry out a particular behavior or produce a desired outcome.

self-esteem The component of personality that encompasses our positive and negative self-evaluations.

From the perspective of...

AN EDUCATOR How might you encourage your students' development of self-esteem and self-efficacy? Which would be more important—or are both essential?

Consider, for example, students with low self-esteem who are studying for a test. Because of their low self-esteem, they expect to do poorly on the test. In turn, this belief raises their anxiety level, making it increasingly difficult to study and perhaps even leading them not to work as hard. Because of these attitudes, the ultimate outcome is that they do, in fact, perform badly on the test, and this outcome has a negative effect on their sense of self-efficacy. Failure reinforces their low self-esteem, and the cycle is perpetuated. In short, low self-esteem and low self-efficacy can lead to a cycle of failure that is self-destructive.

EVALUATING LEARNING APPROACHES TO PERSONALITY

Because they ignore the internal processes that are uniquely human, early learning theorists such as Skinner were accused of oversimplifying personality to such an extent that the concept became meaningless. In the eyes of their critics, reducing behavior to a series of stimuli and responses, and excluding thoughts and feelings from the realm of personality, left behaviorists practicing an unrealistic and inadequate form of science.

Nonetheless, learning approaches had a major impact on the study of personality. For one thing, they offered a strategy for gathering evidence that helped make personality psychology an objective, scientific venture by focusing on observable behavior and the environment. In addition, they produced important, successful means of treating a variety of psychological disorders. The degree of success of these treatments is a testimony to the merits of learning theory approaches to personality.

>> Biological and Evolutionary Approaches to Personality

Approaching the question of what determines personality from a different direction, **biological and evolutionary approaches to personality** suggest that important components of personality are inherited. Building on the work of behavioral geneticists, researchers using biological and evolutionary approaches argue that personality is determined at least in part by our genes, in much the same way that our height is largely a result of genetic contributions from our ancestors. The evolutionary perspective assumes that personality traits that led to the reproductive success of our ancestors are more likely to be preserved and passed on to subsequent generations (Buss, 2001, 2009).

biological and evolutionary approaches to personality Theories that suggest that important components of personality are inherited.

The importance of genetic factors in personality is illustrated by studies of twins. For instance, personality psychologist Auke Tellegen and colleagues at the University of Minnesota examined the personality traits of pairs of twins who were genetically identical but were raised apart from each other (Tellegen et al., 1988, 2004). In the study, each twin was given a battery of personality tests, including one that measured 11 key personality characteristics.

The results of the personality tests indicated that in major respects the twins were quite similar in personality, despite having been separated at an early age. Moreover, certain traits were more heavily influenced by heredity than were others. For example, social potency (the degree to which a person assumes mastery and leadership roles in social situations) and traditionalism (the tendency to follow authority) had particularly strong genetic components, whereas achievement and social closeness had relatively weak genetic components.

Does the identification of specific genes linked to personality mean that we are destined to have certain types of personalities?

Some researchers contend that specific genes are related to personality. For example, people with a longer dopamine-4 receptor gene are more likely to be thrill seekers than are those without such a gene. These thrill seekers tend to be extroverted, impulsive, quick-tempered, and always in search of excitement and novel situations (Golimbet, V. E., et al., 2007; Hopwood et al., 2011; Ray et al., 2009; Robins, 2005).

Does the identification of specific genes linked to personality mean that we are destined to have certain types of personalities? Hardly. First, it is unlikely that any single gene is linked to a specific trait. For instance, the dopamine-4 receptor accounts for only around 10% of the variation in novelty seeking between different individuals. In other words, there are many reasons why people might be thrill seekers, and most of them appear to be environmental

Biological and evolutionary approaches to personality seek to explain the consistencies in personality that are found in some families.

Percentage (degree to which heredity influences each characteristic)

61% **Social potency**	Is masterful; a forceful leader who likes to be the center of attention
60% **Traditionalism**	Follows rules and authority; endorses high moral standards and strict discipline
55% **Stress reaction**	Feels vulnerable and sensitive; is given to worrying and easily upset
55% **Absorption**	Has a vivid imagination readily captured by rich experience; relinquishes sense of reality
55% **Alienation**	Feels mistreated and used, that "the world is out to get me"
54% **Well-being**	Has a cheerful disposition; feels confident and optimistic
51% **Harm avoidance**	Shuns the excitement of risk and danger; prefers the safe route even if it is tedious
48% **Aggression**	Is physically aggressive and vindictive; has taste for violence; is "out to get the world"
46% **Achievement**	Works hard; strives for mastery; puts work and accomplishment ahead of other things
43% **Control**	Is cautious and plodding; is rational and sensible; likes carefully planned events
33% **Social closeness**	Prefers emotional intimacy and close ties; turns to others for comfort and help

Source: Tellegan et al., 1988.

People are born with particular temperaments, dispositions that are consistent throughout childhood.

Genetic Influences on Personality

and/or due to other genes (Keltikangas-Järvinen et al., 2004; Lahti et al., 2005).

More importantly, our genes interact with our environment. In order to truly understand how our personalities are shaped, then, we need to look at how our environments affect our genetic heritage and at how our genes affect the environments in which we live.

Although an increasing number of personality theorists are taking biological and evolutionary factors into account, no comprehensive, unified theory that considers biological and evolutionary factors is widely accepted. Still, it is clear that certain personality traits have significant genetic components and that heredity and environment interact to determine personality (Bouchard, 2004; Ebstein, Benjamin, & Belmaker, 2003; South & Krueger, 2008).

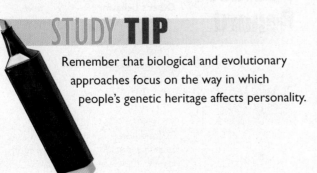

STUDY TIP

Remember that biological and evolutionary approaches focus on the way in which people's genetic heritage affects personality.

>> Humanistic Approaches to Personality

Where, in all the approaches to personality that we have discussed, is an explanation for the selflessness of a Nelson Mandela, the creativity of a Michelangelo, or the brilliance and perseverance of an Einstein? An understanding of such unique individuals—as well as more ordinary sorts of people who have some of the same attributes—comes from humanistic theory. **Humanistic approaches to personality** emphasize people's inherent goodness and their tendency to move towards higher levels of functioning. It is this conscious, self-motivated ability to change and improve, along with people's unique creative impulses, that humanistic theorists argue make up the core of personality (Pennington, 2003).

> **humanistic approaches to personality** Theories that emphasize people's innate goodness and desire to achieve higher levels of functioning.

ROGERS AND THE NEED FOR SELF-ACTUALIZATION

The major proponent of the humanistic point of view is Carl Rogers (1971). Along with other humanistic theorists,

| MOB PSYCHOLOGIST |

"So, while extortion, racketeering, and murder may be bad acts, they don't make you a bad person."

© Robert Mankoff/The New Yorker Collection/www.cartoonbank.com.

such as Abraham Maslow, Rogers maintains that all people have a fundamental need to move in the direction of **self-actualization**, a way of living in which people realize their highest potential, each in a unique way.

Becoming self-actualizing may be a lifelong process for some people, whereas others may never reach this stage. A more basic need, according to Rogers, is peoples' need for positive regard, which reflects the desire to be loved and respected. Because others provide this positive regard, we grow dependent on them. We begin to see and judge ourselves through the eyes of other people, relying on their values and being preoccupied with what they think of us.

According to Rogers, one outgrowth of placing importance on the opinions of others is that a conflict may grow between people's experiences and their *self-concepts*, the set of beliefs they hold about what they are like as individuals. If the discrepancies are minor, so are the consequences. But if the discrepancies are great, they will lead to psychological disturbances in daily functioning, such as the experience of frequent anxiety.

For example, suppose you believe that you are a generous person. If you occasionally observe that others think your contributions are less than generous, you might count this as a minor discrepancy. But suppose everyone criticized you for being greedy and stingy. This would be a large discrepancy. If you continued to believe you were generous in the face of all that evidence to the contrary, you might develop serious anxiety.

Rogers suggests that one way of overcoming the discrepancy between experience and self-concept is through the receipt of unconditional positive regard from another person—a friend, a spouse, or a therapist. **Unconditional positive regard** refers to an attitude of acceptance and respect on the part of an observer, no matter what a person says or does. This acceptance, says Rogers, gives people the opportunity to evolve and grow both cognitively and emotionally and to develop more realistic self-concepts.

self-actualization A state of self-fulfillment in which people realize their highest potential, each in a unique way.

unconditional positive regard An attitude of acceptance and respect on the part of an observer, no matter what a person says or does.

You may have experienced the power of unconditional positive regard when you confided in someone, revealing embarrassing secrets, because you knew the listener would still love and respect you, even after hearing the worst about you (Marshall, 2007; Snyder, 2002).

In contrast, you can think of *conditional positive regard* as love that comes with strings attached. In such cases, others withdraw their love and acceptance if you do something of which they don't approve. The result is that you experience a discrepancy between who you are and what others wish you would be, and this can lead to anxiety and frustration.

The Need for Unconditional Positive Regard

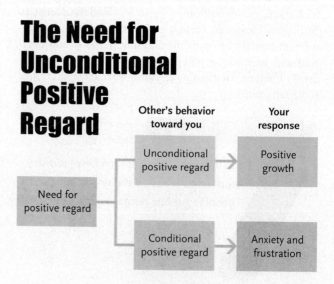

	Other's behavior toward you	Your response
Need for positive regard	Unconditional positive regard	Positive growth
	Conditional positive regard	Anxiety and frustration

EVALUATING HUMANISTIC APPROACHES

Humanistic approaches have been criticized for making the assumption that people are basically "good"—a notion that is unverifiable—and, equally important, for using nonscientific values to build supposedly scientific theories. On the other hand, humanistic theories have been important in highlighting the uniqueness of human beings and guiding the development of a significant form of therapy designed to alleviate psychological difficulties (Bauman & Kopp, 2006; Cain, 2002; South & Krueger, 2008).

>> Comparing Approaches to Personality

In light of the multiple approaches we have discussed, you may be wondering which of the theories provides the most accurate description of personality. Given the complexity of human personality, it makes sense that psychologists would develop a variety of theories that tackle the question from different angles. Each theory is built on different assumptions and focuses on somewhat different aspects of personality. When taken together, however, these apparently independent theories show us the factors that will need to be explained before we can claim to understand how personality works, how it is developed, and how it may be changed.

>> Assessing Personality

Psychologists interested in assessing personality must be able to define the most meaningful ways of discriminating between one person's personality and another's. To do this, they use **psychological tests**, measures devised to assess behavior objectively. With the results of such tests, psychologists can help people better understand themselves and make decisions about their lives. Psychological tests are also employed by researchers interested in the causes and the consequences of personality (Aiken, 2000; Hambleton, 2006; Kaplan & Saccuzzo, 2001).

psychological tests Standard measures devised to assess behavior objectively; used by psychologists to help people make decisions about their lives and understand more about themselves.

Like the assessments developed to measure intelligence, all psychological tests must have reliability and validity. *Reliability* refers to the measurement consistency of a test. If a test is reliable, it yields the same result each time it is administered to a specific person or group. In contrast, unreliable tests give different results each time they are administered.

Summary of Five Approaches to Personality

Theoretical Approach and Major Theorists	Conscious versus Unconscious Determinants of Personality	Hereditary Factors (Nature) versus Environmental Factors (Nurture)	Free Will versus Determinism	Stability versus Modifiability
Psychodynamic (Freud, Jung, Horney, Adler)	Emphasizes the unconscious	Stresses innate, inherited structure of personality while emphasizing importance of childhood experience	Stresses determinism, the view that behavior is directed and caused by factors outside one's control	Emphasizes the stability of characteristics throughout a person's life
Trait (Allport, Cattell, R. B., Eysenck)	Disregards both conscious and unconscious	Approaches vary	Stresses determinism, the view that behavior is directed and caused by factors outside one's control	Emphasizes the stability of characteristics throughout a person's life
Learning (Skinner, Bandura)	Disregards both conscious and unconscious	Focuses on the environment	Stresses determinism, the view that behavior is directed and caused by factors outside one's control	Stresses that personality remains flexible and resilient throughout one's life
Biological and evolutionary (Tellegen)	Disregards both conscious and unconscious	Stresses the innate, inherited determinants of personality	Stresses determinism, the view that behavior is directed and caused by factors outside one's control	Emphasizes the stability of characteristics throughout a person's life
Humanistic (Rogers, Maslow)	Stresses the conscious more than unconscious	Stresses the interaction between both nature and nurture	Stresses the freedom of individuals to make their own choices	Stresses that personality remains flexible and resilient throughout one's life

SELF-REPORT MEASURES OF PERSONALITY

Psychologists use **self-report measures** to ask people about a small sample of their behavior. This sampling of self-report data is then used to infer the presence of particular personality characteristics.

One of the best examples of a self-report measure, and one of the most frequently used personality tests (Sellbom & Ben-Porath, 2006), is the **Minnesota Multiphasic Personality Inventory-2 (MMPI-2)**. Although the original purpose of this measure was to identify people with specific sorts of psychological difficulties, MMPI-2 has been found to predict a variety of other behaviors. For instance, MMPI scores have been shown to be good predictors of whether college students will marry within 10 years and will get an advanced degree. Police departments use the test to measure whether police officers are likely to use their weapons. Psychologists in Russia administer a modified form of the MMPI to their astronauts and Olympic athletes (Butcher, 2005; Sellbom & Ben-Porath, 2006; Sellbom, Fischler, & Ben-Porath, 2007; Williams & Butcher, 2011).

The test consists of a series of 567 items to which a person responds "true," "false," or "cannot say." The questions cover a variety of issues, ranging from mood ("I feel useless at times") to opinions ("People should try to understand their dreams") to physical and psychological health ("I am bothered by an upset stomach several times a week" and "I have strange and peculiar thoughts").

There are no right or wrong answers. Instead, interpretation of the results rests on the pattern of responses.

self-report measures A method of gathering data about people by asking them questions about a sample of their behavior.

Minnesota Multiphasic Personality Inventory-2 (MMPI-2) A widely used self-report test that identifies people with psychological difficulties and is employed to predict some everyday behaviors.

For meaningful conclusions to be drawn, tests also must be valid. Tests have *validity* when they actually measure what they are designed to measure. If a test is constructed to measure sociability, for instance, we need to know that it actually measures sociability, not some other trait.

Suppose you took a test and were told you had earned a 325. Is that a good score? Is it very low? Average? To address this issue, psychological tests are given to samples of people in order to establish *norms*, that is, standards of test performance that permit the comparison of one person's score on a test with the scores of others who have taken the same test. For example, a norm permits test takers who have received a certain score on a test to know that they have scored in the top 10% of all those who have taken the test.

>> TRY IT!

The Life Orientation Test – Revised

Use the following scale to answer the items below:

**0 = strongly disagree   1 = disagree   2 = neutral   3 = agree
4 = strongly agree**

1. In uncertain times, I usually expect the best.
2. It's easy for me to relax.
3. If something can go wrong for me, it will.
4. I'm always optimistic about my future.
5. I enjoy my friends a lot.
6. It's important for me to keep busy.
7. I hardly ever expect things to go my way.
8. I don't get upset too easily.
9. I rarely count on good things happening to me.
10. Overall, I expect more good things to happen to me than bad.

Scoring: First, reverse your answers to questions 3, 7, and 9. Do this by changing a 0 to a 4, a 1 to a 3, a 3 to a 1, and a 4 to a 0 (answers of 2 stay as 2). Then sum the reversed scores, and add them to the scores you gave to questions 1, 4, and 10. (Ignore questions 2, 5, 6, and 8, which are filler items.)

The total score you get is a measure of a particular orientation to life: your degree of optimism. The higher your score, the more positive and hopeful you generally are about life. For comparison purposes, the average score for college students is 14.3, according to the results of a study by Scheier, Carver, and Bridges (1994). People with a higher degree of optimism generally deal with stress better than do those with lower scores.

The test yields scores on ten separate scales, plus three scales meant to measure the validity of the respondent's answers (Bacchiochi, 2006; Butcher, 2005; Stein & Graham, 2005). The authors of the MMPI-2 used a procedure known as **test standardization** to determine what specific patterns of responses indicate. To create the test, the authors asked groups of psychiatric patients with a specific diagnosis, such as depression or schizophrenia, to complete a large number of items. They then determined which items best differentiated members of those groups from a comparison group of normal participants, and included those specific items in the final version of the test.

Let's take an interplanetary travel example for fun. Suppose a group of people who had visited Mars were tested, and that several items (for example, "I really enjoy eating breakfast") were answered "true" more often by the Mars visitors than by people in the other groups. This would mean we could discern a unique pattern of responses for the Mars visitors. Then, if someone took the test and answered in the Mars visitor pattern, that person would be predicted to belong to the group of people who had visited Mars. By systematically carrying out this procedure on groups with different diagnoses, the test authors were able to devise a number of subscales that identified different forms of abnormal behavior.

PROJECTIVE METHODS

In a **projective personality test** a person is shown an ambiguous stimulus and asked to describe it or tell a story about it. The responses are considered to be "projections" of the individual's personality.

The best-known projective test is the **Rorschach test**. Devised by Swiss psychiatrist Hermann Rorschach (1924), the test involves showing people a series of symmetrical stimuli, or "inkblots," and asking what the figures represent to them. Their responses are recorded, and through a complex set of clinical judgments on the part of the examiner, people are classified by their personality type. For instance, respondents who see a bear in one inkblot are thought to have a strong degree of emotional control, according to the scoring guidelines developed by Rorschach (Pineda et al., 2011; Silverstein, 2007; Weiner, 2004).

The **Thematic Apperception Test (TAT)** is another well-known projective test. The TAT consists of a series of pictures about which a person is asked to write a story. The stories are then used to draw inferences about the writer's personality characteristics (Langan-Fox & Grant, 2006; Weiner, 2004).

Tests with stimuli as ambiguous as those used in the Rorschach and TAT require particular skill and care in their interpretation—too much, in many critics' estimation. The Rorschach in particular has been criticized for requiring too much inference on the part of the examiner, and attempts to standardize scoring have frequently failed. Furthermore, many critics question the validity of the information provided by the Rorschach about underlying personality traits. Despite such problems, both the Rorschach and the TAT are widely used, especially in clinical settings, and their proponents suggest that their reliability and validity are good enough to provide useful inferences about personality (Garb et al., 2005; Society for Personality Assessment, 2005; Wood et al., 2003).

From the perspective of ...

A POLICE CHIEF Hiring new police officers involves many different kinds of tests, including psychological fitness tests. What personality traits would you want to encourage in your police force? What traits would you rather not see?

test standardization A technique used to validate questions in personality tests by studying the responses of people with known diagnoses.

projective personality test A test in which a person is shown an ambiguous stimulus and asked to describe it or tell a story about it.

Rorschach test A test that involves showing a series of symmetrical visual stimuli to people who then are asked what the figures represent to them.

Thematic Apperception Test (TAT) A test consisting of a series of pictures about which a person is asked to write a story.

get involved!

There are many personality research projects that need your data and that will repay you with information about your performance on their personality inventories. Go to http://psych .hanover.edu/research/exponnet .html, scroll down to the section on Personality, and click on one (or more) projects that look interesting to you. (Caveat: Before sharing personal information anywhere online, first make sure you are on a secure and reputable site.)

"Rorschach! What's become of you?"

STUDY **TIP**

In projective tests such as the Rorschach and Thematic Apperception Test (TAT), researchers present an ambiguous stimulus and ask a person to describe or tell a story about it, and use the responses to make inferences about personality.

BEHAVIORAL ASSESSMENT

If you were a psychologist subscribing to a learning approach to personality, you would be likely to object to the inferential nature of projective tests. Instead, you would be more apt to use **behavioral assessment**—direct measures of an individual's behavior designed to describe personality characteristics. An effort is made to ensure that behavioral assessment is carried out objectively, quantifying behavior as much as possible. For example, an observer may record the number of social contacts that a person initiates, the number of questions asked, or the number of aggressive acts. Another method is to measure the duration of events: the duration of a temper tantrum in a child, the length of a conversation, the amount of time spent working, or the time spent in cooperative behavior.

behavioral assessment Direct measures of an individual's behavior used to describe personality characteristics.

Behavioral assessment is particularly appropriate for observing—and eventually remedying—specific behavioral difficulties, such as profound shyness in children. It provides a means of assessing the specific nature and incidence of a problem and subsequently allows psychologists to determine whether intervention techniques have been successful.

PSYCH think

> > > What do you think are the key characteristics of personality? Do the assessments described here target those characteristics?

BUY IT? > > >

Assessing Personality Assessments

Many companies, including manufacturing giants like General Motors and technology companies like Microsoft, employ personality tests to help determine who gets hired. For example, potential Microsoft employees have been asked brain teasers such as "If you had to remove 1 of the 50 U.S. states, which would it be?" Other employers ask questions that are even more subjective, such as "How would you describe November?" With such questions, it's not always clear that the tests are reliable or valid (McGinn, 2003).

Before relying too heavily on the results of such personality testing as a potential employee, employer, or consumer of testing services, you should keep several points in mind:

- *Understand what the test claims to measure.* Standard personality measures are accompanied by information that discusses how the test was developed, to whom it is most applicable, and how the results should be interpreted. Read any explanations of the test; they will help you understand the results.

- *Base no decision only on the results of any one test.* Test results should be interpreted in the context of other information—academic records, social interests, and home and community activities.

- *Remember that test results are not always accurate.* The results may be in error; the test may be unreliable or invalid. You may, for example, have had a "bad day" when you took the test, or the person scoring and interpreting the test may have made a mistake. You should not place too much significance on the results of a single administration of any test.

In sum, remember that human behavior—particularly your own—is complex. Just as there is currently no single, all-encompassing theory of personality, no single test provides an understanding of the intricacies of someone's personality (Gladwell, 2004; Hogan, Davies, & Hogan, 2007; Paul, 2004).

For REVIEW >>

- **How do psychologists think about personality?**

  Personality is defined as the pattern of enduring characteristics that produce consistency and individuality in a given person. (p. 258)

- **What are the major features of the different psychological approaches to personality?**

  The psychodynamic approaches focus on the unconscious foundations of personality. Freud's psychoanalytic theory laid the foundation for the psychodynamic approaches. Freud proposed that personality consists of the pleasure-seeking id, the realistic ego, and the superego, or conscience. In addition, Freud suggested that personality develops through a series of psychosexual stages, each of which is associated with a primary biological function. Defense mechanisms, according to Freudian theory, are unconscious strategies with which people reduce anxieties relating to impulses from the id. Neo-Freudian psychoanalytic theorists built on Freud's work, although they placed greater emphasis on the role of the ego and paid more attention to the role of social factors in determining behavior. (pp. 258–264)

  Trait approaches have been used to identify relatively enduring dimensions along which people differ from one another—dimensions known as traits. Learning approaches to personality concentrate on observable behavior. To a strict learning theorist, personality is the sum of learned responses to the external environment. Biological and evolutionary approaches to personality focus on the way in which personality characteristics are inherited. Humanistic approaches emphasize the inherent goodness of people. They consider the core of personality in terms of a person's ability to change and improve. (pp. 264–271)

- **How can psychologists most accurately assess personality?**

  Psychological tests such as the MMPI-2 are standard assessment tools that measure behavior objectively. They must be reliable (measuring what they are trying to measure consistently) and valid (measuring what they are supposed to measure). (pp. 271–272)

- **What are the major types of personality measures?**

  Self-report measures ask people about a sample range of their behaviors. These reports are used to infer the presence of particular personality characteristics. Projective personality tests (such as the Rorschach and the Thematic Apperception Test) present an ambiguous stimulus, and the test administrator infers information about the test taker from his or her responses. Behavioral assessment is based on the principles of learning theory. It employs direct measurement of an individual's behavior to determine characteristics related to personality. (pp. 272–274)

Pop Quiz

1. Match each section of the personality (according to Freud) with its description.
   a. determines right from wrong on the basis of cultural standards
   b. operates according to the "reality principle"; energy is redirected to integrate the person into society
   c. seeks to reduce tension brought on by primitive drives
   _____ 1. ego
   _____ 2. id
   _____ 3. superego

2. Which of the following represents the proper order of personality development, according to Freud?
   a. oral, phallic, latency, anal, genital
   b. anal, oral, phallic, genital, latency
   c. oral, anal, phallic, latency, genital
   d. latency, phallic, anal, genital, oral

3. _____ _____ is the term Freud used to describe unconscious strategies used to reduce anxiety.

4. The activity on defense mechanisms demonstrates that _____ and that I might not have understood this as well if I didn't do the Interactivity.
   a. there are many different kinds of defense mechanisms and each one has its own specific meaning and purpose
   b. people really aren't aware that they're using a defense mechanism—it really is unconscious
   c. since people use defense mechanisms in their own way, you can never really know for sure which one they are actually using
   d. using defense mechanisms helps keep our society safer from violence

5. Ivan's determination to succeed is the dominant force in all his activities and relationships. According to Gordon Allport's theory, this is an example of a _____ trait. In contrast, Desiree's fondness for old western movies is an example of a _____ trait.

6. A person who enjoys activities such as parties and hang gliding might be described by Eysenck as high on what trait?

7. Proponents of which approach to personality would be most likely to agree with the following statement? "Personality can be thought of as learned responses to a person's upbringing and environment."
   a. humanistic
   b. biological and evolutionary
   c. learning
   d. trait

8. Which approach to personality emphasizes the innate goodness of people and their desire to grow?
   a. humanistic
   b. psychodynamic
   c. learning
   d. biological and evolutionary

9. The Q-sort personality assessment technique used in the activity on your ideal self has you _____.
   a. sort your favorite activities into categories
   b. prioritize your career and family goals
   c. match your moods and feelings with different animals and then get an analysis based on your choices
   d. sort your traits and behaviors.

10. _____ is the consistency of a personality test; _____ is the ability of a test to actually measure what it is designed to measure.

11. _____ are standards used to compare scores of different people taking the same test.

12. Tests such as the MMPI-2, in which a small sample of behavior is assessed to determine larger patterns, are examples of _____.
    a. cross-sectional tests
    b. projective tests
    c. achievement tests
    d. self-report tests

Answers
TO POP QUIZ QUESTIONS

1. 1-b, 2-c, 3-a
2. c
3. Defense mechanisms
4. b
5. cardinal, secondary
6. extraversion
7. c
8. a
9. d
10. Reliability, validity
11. Norms
12. d

11

HEALTH PSYC

STRESS, CO

NEVER A MOMENT'S REST

Louisa Denby's day began badly: She slept through her alarm and had to skip breakfast to catch the bus to campus. Then, when she went to the library to catch up on the reading she had to do before taking a test the next day, the one article she needed was missing. The librarian told her that replacing it would take 24 hours. Feeling frustrated, she walked to the computer lab to print out the paper she had completed at home the night before.

The computer wouldn't read her disk. She searched for someone to help her, but she was unable to find anyone who knew any more about computers than she did.

It was only 9:42 a.m., and Louisa had an aching headache. Apart from that pain, she was conscious of only one feeling: stress.

It's not hard to understand why Louisa Denby was experiencing stress. For people like her—and that probably includes most of us—the intensity of juggling multiple roles leads to feelings of never having sufficient time. In some cases, this takes a toll on both physical and psychological well-being.[xi]

Stress and how we cope with it have long been central topics of interest for psychologists. In recent years, however, the focus has broadened as psychology has come to view stress in the broader context of one of psychology's newer subfields: health psychology. In the pages that follow, we discuss the ways in which psychological factors affect health. We first focus on the causes and consequences of stress, as well as on the means of coping with it. Next, we explore the psychological aspects of several major health problems, including heart disease, cancer, depression, and ailments resulting from smoking. Finally, we examine various stress management strategies and the correlates of happiness.

HOLOGY:
PING, AND WELL-BEING

- How is health psychology a relationship between medicine and psychology?
- What is stress, how does it affect us, and what are some common coping strategies?
- How do our attitudes, beliefs, and behaviors interact with stress-related health problems?
- What specific attitudes and behaviors can we adopt to minimize the unpleasant effects of stress and maximize our well-being?

health psychology The branch of psychology that investigates the psychological factors related to wellness and illness, including the prevention, diagnosis, and treatment of health problems.

psychophysiological disorders Medical problems influenced by an interaction of psychological, emotional, and physical difficulties.

stress A person's response to events that are threatening or challenging.

Health psychology investigates the psychological factors related to wellness and illness, including the prevention, diagnosis, and treatment of medical problems. For example, health psychologists investigate the effects of psychological factors such as stress on illness. They also study prevention: how more healthful behavior may help people avoid and reduce serious health problems.

Many of the findings in recent years have forced us to change our thinking about the relationship between psychological factors and medical illness. As recently as 25–30 years ago, for example, most psychologists and health-care providers probably would have laughed at the notion that a discussion group could improve a cancer patient's chances of survival. Today, however, such methods have gained increasing acceptance.

Growing evidence suggests that psychological factors have a substantial effect both on major health problems that were once seen in purely physiological terms. One class of physical problems, known as **psychophysiological disorders**, often result from or are worsened by stress (Siegel, 2005). Once referred to as psychosomatic disorders (a term dropped because people assumed that the disorders were somehow

: Even pleasant events can produce significant stress.

unreal), psychophysiological disorders are medical problems that are influenced by an interaction of psychological, emotional, and physical difficulties (Siegel & Davis, 2008). The more common psychophysiological disorders range from such major problems as high blood pressure to usually less serious conditions, such as headaches, backaches, skin rashes, indigestion, fatigue, and constipation. Stress has even been positively correlated with the common cold (Andrasik, 2006; Cohen et al., 2003).

>> Stress and Coping

Most of us need little introduction to the phenomenon of **stress**, people's response to events that threaten or challenge them. Whether it is a paper or an exam deadline, a family problem, or even the possibility of a natural disaster such as a flood or a tornado, life is full of circumstances and events that challenge us. Even enjoyable events—such as planning a party or beginning a sought-after job—can produce stress, although unpleasant events often result in greater detrimental consequences than do pleasant ones.

All of us face stress. Some health psychologists believe that daily life actually involves a series of repeated sequences of perceiving a stressor, considering ways to cope with it, and ultimately adapting to it with greater or lesser success. Typically, these adaptations are so small that we don't even

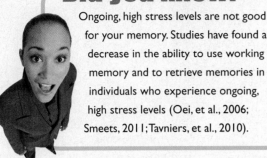

Did you know?

Ongoing, high stress levels are not good for your memory. Studies have found a decrease in the ability to use working memory and to retrieve memories in individuals who experience ongoing, high stress levels (Oei, et al., 2006; Smeets, 2011; Tavniers, et al., 2010).

notice them. When the stressor is more severe or lasts a long time, however, we must make a major effort to adapt. Our attempts to overcome extreme or continuing stress may produce biological and psychological responses that result in health problems (Boyce & Ellis, 2005; Dolbier, Smith, & Steinhardt, 2007; Lundberg, 2011).

THE NATURE OF STRESSORS: MY STRESS IS YOUR PLEASURE

Stress is a personal thing. Although certain kinds of events, such as the death of a loved one or participation in military combat, are universally stressful, other situations may or may not be stressful to a specific person.

Consider, for instance, bungee jumping. Some people would find jumping off a bridge while attached to a slender rubber tether extremely stressful. However, there are individuals who see such an activity as challenging and fun-filled. Whether bungee jumping is stressful depends in part, then, on a person's perception of the activity.

For people to consider an event stressful, they must perceive it as threatening or challenging and must not have access to all of the resources needed to deal with it effectively. Consequently, the same event may at some times be stressful and at other times provoke no stressful reaction at all. A young man may experience stress when he is turned down for a date—if he attributes the refusal to his unattractiveness or unworthiness. But if he attributes it to some factor unrelated to his self-esteem, such as a previous commitment by the person he asked, the experience of being refused may create no stress at all. Hence, a person's interpretation of events plays an important role in determining what is stressful (Folkman & Moskowitz, 2000; Friborg et al., 2007; Giacobbi, et al., 2005).

A person's interpretation of events plays an important role in determining what is stressful.

Categorizing Stressors What kinds of events tend to be seen as stressful? There are three general types of

PSYCH think

connect™

WWW.MCGRAWHILLCONNECT.COM/PSYCHOLOGY
Stress and Coping

> > > How do you handle the stress in your life? Do you take direct action? Do you problem-solve by thinking through the issues? Do you take time out to get away from an ongoing stressor?

Take the PsychSmart challenge! What does the "Stress and Coping" activity tell you about your own coping strategies? From chapter 11 in your ebook, select the *Exercises* tab. Then, select "Stress and Coping." After completing the activity, answer Pop Quiz question 2 on p. 298 to check your understanding of the results.

stressors: cataclysmic events, personal stressors, and daily hassles.

Cataclysmic events are strong stressors that occur suddenly and typically affect many people simultaneously. Disasters such as tornadoes and plane crashes, as well as terrorist attacks, are examples of cataclysmic events that can affect hundreds or thousands of people simultaneously.

> **cataclysmic events** Strong stressors that occur suddenly, affecting many people at once (for example, natural disasters).
>
> **personal stressors** Major life events, such as the death of a family member, that have immediate negative consequences that generally fade with time.

Although it might seem that cataclysmic events would produce potent, lingering stress, in many cases they do not. In fact, cataclysmic events involving natural disasters may produce less stress in the long run than do events that initially are not as devastating. One reason is that natural disasters have a clear resolution. Once they are over, people can look to the future knowing that the worst is behind them. Moreover, the stress induced by cataclysmic events is shared by others who also experienced the disaster. Such sharing permits people to offer one another social support and a firsthand understanding of the difficulties that others are going through (Benight, 2004; Hobfoll et al., 1996; Yesilyaprak, Kisac, & Sanlier, 2007).

The second major category of stressor is the personal stressor. **Personal stressors** include such major life events as the death of a parent or spouse, the loss of one's job, a major personal failure, or even something positive such as getting married. Typically, personal stressors produce an immediate major reaction that soon tapers off. For example, stress arising from the death of a loved one tends to be greatest just after the time of death, but people begin to feel less stress and are better able to cope with the loss over time (Compas & Wagner, 1991).

Daily hassles are the third major category of stressors. Exemplified by being interrupted too often or having too many things to do, daily hassles are the minor irritations of life that most of us face time and time again. Another type of daily hassle is a long-term, chronic problem, such as experiencing dissatisfaction with school or a job, being in an unhappy relationship, or living in crowded quarters without privacy (Bhatia & Dey, 2011; McIntyre, Korn, & Matsuo, 2008; Weinstein et al., 2004).

By themselves, daily hassles do not require much coping or even a response on the part of the individual, although they certainly produce unpleasant emotions and moods. Yet they add up—and ultimately they may take as great a toll as a single, more stressful incident does. In fact, the *number* of daily hassles people face is positively correlated with psychological symptoms and health problems such as flu, sore throat, and backaches.

The flip side of hassles is *uplifts*, the minor positive events that make us feel good—even if only temporarily. Uplifts range from relating well to a companion to finding one's surroundings pleasing. What is especially intriguing about uplifts is that they are negatively correlated with people's psychological health: The greater the number of uplifts we experience, the fewer the psychological symptoms we report (Chamberlain & Zika, 1990; Jain, Mills, & Von Känel, 2007; Ravindran et al., 2002).

daily hassles Everyday annoyances, such as being stuck in traffic, that cause minor irritations and may have long-term ill effects if they continue or are compounded by other stressful events.

Everyone confronts daily hassles such as heavy traffic. At what point do daily hassles become more than mere irritants?

tions by the adrenal glands, an increase in heart rate and blood pressure, and changes in how well the skin conducts electrical impulses. On a short-term basis, these responses may be adaptive, because they produce an "emergency reaction" in which the body prepares to defend itself through activation of the sympathetic nervous system. Those responses may allow more effective coping with the stressful situation (Akil & Morano, 1996; McEwen, 1998).

However, continued exposure to stress results in a decline in the body's overall level of biological functioning because of the constant secretion of stress-related hormones. Over time, stressful reactions can promote deterioration of body tissues such as blood vessels and the heart. Ultimately, we become more susceptible to disease as our ability to fight off infection is lowered (Brydon et al., 2004; Dean-Borenstein, 2007; Ellins et al., 2008).

On a psychological level, high levels of stress prevent people from adequately coping with life. Their view of the environment can become clouded (for example, a minor criticism made by a friend is blown out of proportion). Moreover, at the highest levels of stress, emotional responses may be so extreme that people are unable to act at all. People under a lot of stress also become less able to deal with new stressors.

In short, stress affects us in multiple ways. It may increase the risk that we will become ill, it may directly cause illness, it may make us less able to recover from a disease, and it may reduce our ability to cope with future stress (Gurunjj & Roethel-Wendorf, 2009).

The High Cost of Stress Stress can produce both biological and psychological consequences. Often the most immediate reaction to stress is a biological one. Exposure to stressors generates a rise in hormone secre-

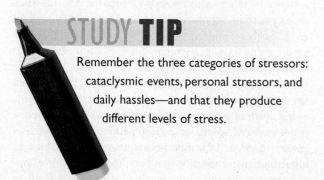

STUDY TIP

Remember the three categories of stressors: cataclysmic events, personal stressors, and daily hassles—and that they produce different levels of stress.

The General Adaptation Syndrome Model

The effects of long-term stress are illustrated in a series of stages proposed by Hans Selye (pronounced "ZELL-yay"), a pioneering stress theorist (Selye, 1976, 1993). This model,

Stressor

1 Alarm and mobilization
Meeting and resisting stressor.

2 Resistance
Coping with stress and resistance to stressor.

3 Exhaustion
Negative consequences of stress (such as illness) occur when coping is inadequate.

Source: Selye, 1976.

Selye's General Adaptation Syndrome (GAS)

the **general adaptation syndrome (GAS)**, suggests that the physiological response to stress follows the same set pattern regardless of the cause of stress.

The GAS has three phases. The first stage—*alarm and mobilization*—occurs when people become aware of the presence of a stressor. On a biological level, the sympathetic nervous system becomes energized, helping a person cope initially with the stressor.

However, if the stressor persists, people move into the second response stage: *resistance*. During this stage, the body is actively fighting the stressor on a biological level. During resistance, people use a variety of means to cope with the stressor—sometimes successfully but at a cost of some degree of physical or psychological well-being. For example, a student who faces the stress of failing several courses might spend long hours studying, seeking to cope with the stress.

If the coping strategies used in the resistance phase are not enough to resolve the stressor, people enter the last stage of the GAS: *exhaustion*. During the exhaustion stage, a person's ability to adapt to the stressor declines to the point where negative consequences of stress appear: physical illness and psychological symptoms in the form of an inability to concentrate, heightened irritability, or, in severe cases, disorientation and a loss of touch with reality. In a sense, people wear out, and their physical resources to fight the stressor are used up. For example, when villagers suddenly find themselves in

the middle of a war, they may respond initially with alarm and quickly move into resistance. However, their best efforts to cope are unlikely to slow down the bullets and bombs, and they will eventually become exhausted.

How do people move out of the third stage after they have entered it? In some cases, exhaustion allows people to avoid a stressor. For example, people who become ill from overwork may be excused from their duties for a time, giving them a temporary respite from their responsibilities. At least for a time, then, the immediate stress is reduced (Brooks, McCabe, & Schneiderman, 2011).

Although the GAS has had a substantial impact on our understanding of stress, Selye's theory has not gone unchallenged. For example, whereas the theory suggests that regardless of the stressor, the biological reaction is similar, some health psychologists disagree. They believe that people's biological responses are specific to the way they appraise a stressful event. If a stressor is seen as unpleasant but not unusual, then the biological response may be different from that if the stressor is seen as unpleasant, out of the ordinary, and unanticipated. This perspective has led to an increased focus on coping strategies (Gaab, et al., 2005; Harvey et al., 2010).

> **general adaptation syndrome (GAS)** A theory developed by Selye that suggests that a person's response to a stressor consists of three stages: alarm and mobilization, resistance, and exhaustion.

Did you know?

A 2011 survey by CareerCast (careercast.com) found the top five least stressful jobs are: audiologist, dietician, software engineer, computer programmer, and dental hygienist.

COPING WITH STRESSORS

Stress is a normal part of life—and not necessarily a completely bad part. For example, without stress, we might not be sufficiently motivated to complete the activities we need to accomplish. However, it is also clear that too much stress can take a toll on physical and psychological health. How do people deal with stress? Is there a way to reduce its negative effects?

How Stressful Is Your Life?

Test your level of stress by answering these questions and adding up your score. Questions apply to the previous month only. The key below will help you determine the extent of your stress.

0 = never; 1 = almost; 2 = sometimes; 3 = fairly often; 4 = very often

_____ 1. How often have you been upset because of something that happened unexpectedly?

_____ 2. How often have you felt that you were unable to control the important things in your life?

_____ 3. How often have you felt nervous and "stressed"?

_____ 4. How often have you felt confident about your ability to handle your personal problems?

_____ 5. How often have you felt that things were going your way?

_____ 6. How often have you been able to control irritations in your life?

_____ 7. How often have you found that you could not cope with all the things that you had to do?

_____ 8. How often have you felt that you were on top of things?

_____ 9. How often have you been angered because of things that were outside your control?

_____ 10. How often have you felt difficulties were piling up so high that you could not overcome them?

How You Measure Up

Stress levels vary among individuals—compare your total score to the averages below:

Age

18–29	14.2
30–44	13.0
45–54	12.6
55–64	11.9
65 & over	12.0

Gender

Men	12.1
Women	13.7

Marital Status

Widowed	12.6
Married or living with a partner	12.4
Single or never wed	14.1
Divorced	14.7
Separated	16.6

Source: Cohen, S., 1999.

---

coping The efforts to control, reduce, or learn to tolerate the challenges and/or threats that lead to stress.

Efforts to control, reduce, or learn to tolerate the threats and/or challenges that lead to stress are known as **coping**. We habitually use certain coping responses to deal with stress. Most of the time, we're not aware of these responses—just as we may be unaware of the minor stressors of life until they build up to harmful levels (Wrzesniewski & Chylinska, 2007).

We also have other, more direct, and potentially more positive ways of coping with stress, which fall into two main categories (Baker & Berenbaum, 2007; Folkman & Moskowitz, 2000, 2004):

"Today, we examined our life style, we evaluated our diet and our exercise program, and we also assessed our behavioral patterns. Then we felt we needed a drink."

of a problem that cannot be solved, avoidant coping may be a healthy choice (Penley, Tomaka, & Wiebe, 2002; Stanton et al., 2000).

Avoidant coping can also include less effective forms of coping, such as the use of wishful thinking to reduce stress or using more direct escape routes, such as drug use, alcohol use, and overeating. An example of wishful thinking to avoid a test would be to say to oneself, "Maybe it will snow so hard tomorrow that the test will be canceled." Alternatively, a person might get drunk to avoid a problem. When avoidant coping results in a postponement of dealing with a stressful situation, this can make the problem even worse (Glass et al., 2009; Hutchinson, Baldwin, & Oh, 2006; Roesch et al., 2005).

- *Emotion-focused coping.* In emotion-focused coping, people try to manage their emotions in the face of stress, seeking to change the way they feel about or perceive a problem. Examples of emotion-focused coping include strategies such as accepting sympathy from others and looking at the bright side of a situation.
- *Problem-focused coping.* Problem-focused coping involves thinking about ways to modify the stressful problem or source of stress and then taking action. Problem-focused strategies lead to changes in behavior or to the development of a plan of action to deal with stress. Starting a study group to improve poor classroom performance is an example of problem-focused coping. In addition, one might take a time-out from stress by creating positive events. For example, taking a day off from caring for a relative with a serious, chronic illness to go to a health club or spa can bring significant relief from stress.

People often employ several types of coping strategies simultaneously. Many will use problem-focused coping strategies in situations that they perceive they can change. However, when a situation is believed to be unchangeable, for example, if a parent is terminally ill, problem-focused coping may not be as effective as emotion-focused coping. A grieving daughter might watch a comedy in order to laugh at the jokes and temporarily distance herself from the pain of losing her parent. Using emotions to get a break from a painful situation is one form of *avoidant coping*, which is when people reduce stress through various forms of escape. In the case

Psych at the Movies

Black Swan (2010)
A young woman strives to be a perfect ballerina, which can be a very stressful undertaking. As the pressure builds, the woman's coping strategies fail her.

Alice in Wonderland (2010)
Daily hassles take on a whole new meaning in this award-winning film, which follows teenaged Alice as she copes with the unexpected in Wonderland.

Everything Must Go (2010)
This story of an alcoholic who is kicked out by his wife provides an excellent example of avoidant coping strategies, including denial and substance abuse.

Where the Heart Is (2000)
This film is loosely based on the true story of an abandoned young pregnant woman who delivered her baby at a Walmart. She and her child benefit from her development of a strong social support network, consisting of a pseudo-family and friends.

Wilby Wonderful (2004)
One of the main characters in this quirky Canadian film, a workaholic real estate agent, demonstrates the classic Type A behavior pattern.

>> Psychological Aspects of Illness and Stress

I feel that it is absolutely necessary to be my own best advocate, and the best place to learn how to do that is in a group of other well-educated patients and their caregivers. We know what life post-diagnosis is like, and we help each other in ways that no docs, nurses, clergy, well-meaning friends and family possibly can. We laugh, we cry, we bitch, and we push and pull each other! We mourn the losses, celebrate small and large victories, and we educate ourselves and others. But most importantly—we embrace each other and our lives. (Anonymous blog post, 2010)

psychoneuroimmunology (PNI) The study of the relationship among psychological factors, the immune system, and the brain.

Type A behavior pattern A cluster of behaviors involving hostility, competitiveness, time urgency, and feeling driven.

Type B behavior pattern A cluster of behaviors characterized by a patient, cooperative, noncompetitive manner.

Health psychologists recognize that good health and the ability to cope with illness are affected by psychological factors such as thoughts, emotions, and the ability to manage stress. They have paid particular attention to the immune system, the complex of organs, glands, and cells that constitute our bodies' natural line of defense in fighting disease. In fact, health psychologists are among the primary investigators in a growing field called **psychoneuroimmunology**, or **PNI**, the study of the relationship among psychological factors, the immune system, and the brain. PNI has led to discoveries such as the existence of an association between

From the perspective of . . .

A HUMAN RESOURCES MANAGER How would you help your employees use coping strategies effectively when confronted with a stressor? How could you help them use problem-focused coping more often?

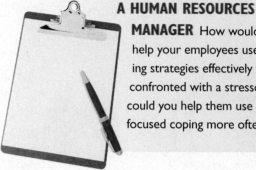

a person's emotional state and the success of the immune system in fighting disease (Byrne-Davis & Vedhara, 2008; Dickerson et al., 2004; Kemeny, 2007).

While the relationships between stress, physical health and illness, and emotional factors are complex and not yet well understood, current research is helping to show exactly how stress and the immune system interact and how prolonged stress can damage the immune response (Broman, 2005; Segerstrom, 2010; Tausk, Elenkov, & Moynihan, 2008).

Why is stress so damaging to the immune system? One reason is that stress may overstimulate the immune system. Rather than fighting invading bacteria, viruses, and other foreign invaders, it may begin to attack the body, damaging healthy tissue. When that happens, it can lead to disorders, such as arthritis, and an allergic reaction. Stress can also decrease the immune system response, permitting viruses that cause colds to reproduce more easily or allowing cancer cells to spread more rapidly (Cohen, Hamrick, & Rodriguez, 2002; Dougall & Baum, 2004; Segerstrom & Miller, 2004).

In this section, we'll consider the psychological components of five different health problems in which stress has been implicated—heart disease, cancer, depression, post-traumatic stress disorder, and smoking.

Major Consequences of Stress

Source: Adapted from Baum, 1994.

Stress

Direct physiological effects	Harmful behaviors
•Elevated blood pressure •Decrease in immune system functioning •Increased hormonal activity •Psychophysiological conditions	•Increased smoking, alcohol abuse •Decreased nutrition •Decreased sleep •Increased drug abuse

THE As, Bs, AND Ds OF CORONARY HEART DISEASE

Many of us feel angry, frustrated, or competitive at one time or another, but for some people these feelings represent a pervasive, characteristic set of personality traits known as the Type A behavior pattern. The **Type A behavior pattern** is a cluster of behaviors involving hostility, competitiveness, time urgency, and feeling driven. In contrast, the **Type B behavior pattern** is characterized by a patient, cooperative, noncompetitive, and nonaggressive manner. It's important to keep in mind that Type A and Type B represent the ends of a continuum, and most people fall somewhere in between the two endpoints. Few people are purely a Type A or a Type B.

It's important to distinguish between Type A (hostility, competitiveness), Type B (patience, cooperativeness), and Type D (distressed) behaviors.

The importance of the Type A behavior pattern lies in its links to coronary heart disease. Men who display the Type A pattern develop coronary heart disease twice as often and suffer significantly more fatal heart attacks than do those classified as having the Type B pattern. Moreover, the Type A pattern predicts who is going to develop heart disease at least as well as—and independently of—any other single factor, including age, blood pressure, smoking habits, and cholesterol levels in the body (Beresnevaité, Taylor, & Bagby, 2007; Rosenman et al., 1994; Wielgosz & Nolan, 2000).

Hostility is the key component of the Type A behavior pattern that is related to heart disease. Although competition, time urgency, and feelings of being driven may produce stress and potentially other health and emotional problems, they aren't linked to coronary heart disease in the way that hostility is (Boyle et al., 2005; Ohira et al., 2007; Williams et al., 2000).

Why is hostility so toxic? The key reason is that hostility produces excessive physiological arousal in stressful situations. That arousal, in turn, results in increased production of the hormones epinephrine and norepinephrine, as well as increases in heart rate and blood pressure. Such an exaggerated physiological response ultimately produces an increased incidence of coronary heart disease (Demaree & Everhart, 2004; Eaker et al., 2004; Myrtek, 2007).

Keep in mind that not everyone who displays Type A behaviors is destined to have coronary heart disease. For one thing, a firm association between Type A behaviors and coronary heart disease has not been established for women; most findings pertain to males, not to females, in part because until recently, most research was done on men. In addition, other types of negative emotions, besides the hostility found in Type A behavior, appear to be related

From the perspective of …

A NURSE PRACTITIONER What type of advice would you give to your patients about the connections between personality and disease? For example, would you encourage Type A people to become "less Type A" in order to decrease their risk of heart disease?

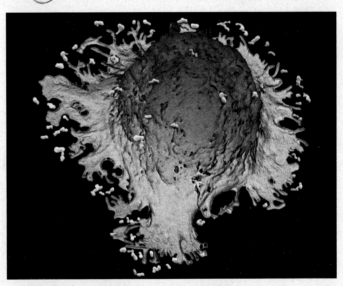

Psychological factors affect the ability to fight off disease. In this highly enlarged view, a cell from the body's immune system engulfs and destroys disease-producing bacteria.

Stress can decrease the immune system response, permitting viruses that cause colds to reproduce more easily or allowing cancer cells to spread more rapidly.

PSYCH think

connect™

WWW.MCGRAWHILLCONNECT.COM/PSYCHOLOGY

Type A Behavior

> > > Most of us fall somewhere in the middle between Type A and Type B, which means that we are neither Type A nor Type B. Why do you think we try to fit ourselves into these two categories if they seldom apply?

Take the PsychSmart challenge! Do you fit the Type A category? From chapter 11 in your ebook, select the *Exercises* tab. Then, select "Type A Behavior." After completing this activity, check your understanding of the Type A behavior pattern by answering Pop Quiz question 5 on p. 298.

Taking a course in car repair would be one way to cope with frequent car breakdowns or with the loss of a job in a shrinking company.

to heart attacks. For example, psychologist Johan Denollet has found evidence that what he calls *Type D*—for "distressed"—behavior is linked to coronary heart disease.

Relationship Between Patient Attitude and Cancer Survival

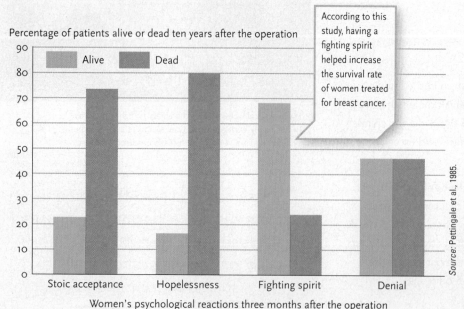

Percentage of patients alive or dead ten years after the operation

According to this study, having a fighting spirit helped increase the survival rate of women treated for breast cancer.

Source: Pettingale et al., 1985.

Women's psychological reactions three months after the operation

PSYCH think

> > > Is there a danger of "blaming the victim" when we argue that the course of cancer can be improved if a person with the disease holds positive attitudes or beliefs, particularly when we consider people with cancer who are not recovering? Is it wrong to blame the victim in this case?

In his view, insecurity, anxiety, and the negative outlook displayed by Type Ds puts them at risk for repeated heart attacks (Denollet, 2005; Schiffer et al., 2005; Spindler et al., 2009; Williams et al., 2011).

PSYCHOLOGICAL ASPECTS OF CANCER

Hardly any disease is feared more than cancer. Many people think of cancer in terms of lingering pain and suffering (Feuerstein, 2007; White & Macleod, 2002). Although a diagnosis of cancer is not as grim as it once was—several kinds of cancer have a high cure rate if detected early enough (Feuerstein, 2007)—cancer remains the second leading cause of death in the United States after coronary heart disease (O'Hair, Thompson, & Sparks, 2005). Although the processes involved in the spread of cancer are physiological, accumulating evidence suggests that the emotional responses of cancer patients to their disease may have a critical effect on its course. For example, one experiment found that people who adopt a fighting spirit are more likely to recover than are those who pessimistically suffer and resign themselves to death (Pettingale et al., 1985). The study analyzed the survival rates of women who had undergone the removal of a breast because of cancer (Greer, 1999).

The results suggested that the survival rates were related to the psychological response of the women three months after surgery. Women who stoically accepted their fate, trying not to complain, and those who felt the situation was hopeless and that nothing could be done showed the lowest survival rates; most of those women were dead after 10 years. In comparison, the survival rates of women who showed a fighting spirit (predicting that they would overcome the disease and planning to take steps to prevent its recurrence) and the survival rates of women who (erroneously) denied that they had ever had cancer (saying that the breast removal was merely a preventive step) were significantly higher. In sum, according to this study, cancer patients with a positive attitude were more likely to survive than were those with a more negative one.

However, other research contradicts the notion that the course of cancer is affected by patients' attitudes and emotions. For example, some findings show that although a "fighting spirit" leads to better coping, the long-term survival rate is no better than it is for patients with a less positive attitude (Rom, Miller, & Peluso, 2009; Watson et al., 1999).

> One experiment found that people who adopt a fighting spirit are more likely to recover from cancer than are those who pessimistically suffer and resign themselves to death.

What is increasingly clear, however, is that certain types of psychological therapy have the potential for extending the lives of cancer patients. For example, the results of one study showed that women with breast cancer who received psychological treatment lived at least a year and a half longer, and experienced less anxiety and pain, than did women who did not participate in therapy. Research on patients with other health problems, such as heart disease, also has found that therapy can be beneficial, both psychologically and medically (Butler et al., 2009; Frasure-Smith, Lesperance, & Talajic, 2000; Spiegel, 1996).

DEPRESSION

It is normal to feel sadness from time to time. However, sadness sometimes turns into a clinical disorder known as major depression. When this happens, someone who is sad will also have serious difficulties with concentration, making decisions, and getting along with others. Although there are a

variety of causes of depression, stress has been identified as one causal factor. Furthermore, there is strong evidence that a stressful situation that leads to a feeling of helplessness correlates with depression (Banasr, 2010; Leonard & Myint, 2009).

Have you ever faced an intolerable situation that you just couldn't resolve, and you finally simply gave up and accepted things the way they were? If so, you may have experienced one of the possible consequences of being in an environment in which control over a situation is not possible—a state that produces learned helplessness. **Learned helplessness** occurs when people conclude that unpleasant or aversive stimuli cannot be controlled— a view of the world that becomes so ingrained that they cease trying to remedy the aversive circumstances, even if at some later point they actually could exert some influence on the situation (Aujoulat, Luminet, & Deccache, 2007; Seligman, 1975, 2007).

> **learned helplessness** A state in which people conclude that unpleasant or aversive stimuli cannot be controlled—a view of the world that becomes so ingrained that they cease trying to remedy the aversive circumstances, even if they actually can exert some influence.

Victims of learned helplessness have concluded that there is nothing they can do to change the conditions in their lives that are intolerable. People who perceive that they have little or no control experience more physical symptoms and depression than those who feel a sense of control over a situation (Bjornstad, 2006; Chou, 2005; Schultz, 2007). In other words, people whose life experiences have led them to believe they cannot cope with stressors, either emotionally or in terms of problem solving, are at risk for developing depression.

POST-TRAUMATIC STRESS DISORDER (PTSD)

Some victims of major catastrophes and severe personal stressors experience post-traumatic stress disorder (PTSD),

Survivors of natural disasters are at greater risk for heart disease. Not only does stress affect risk-related behavior such as smoking and poor eating habits, but it can also lead to increased blood pressure, inflammation, and damage to the blood vessels, including the coronary arteries (Underwood, 2005).

in which a person has experienced a significantly stressful event that has long-lasting effects that may include vivid flashbacks or dreams of the event. An episode of PTSD may be triggered by an otherwise innocent stimulus, such as the sound of a honking horn that leads someone to reexperience a past event that produced considerable stress (Paris, 2000).

Terrorist attacks also produce high incidences of PTSD. For example, 11% of people in New York City had some form of PTSD in the months after the September 11 terrorist attacks. But the responses varied significantly with a resident's proximity to the attacks—the closer someone lived to the World Trade Center, the greater the likelihood of PTSD (Lee, Isaac, & Janca, 2007; Marshall et al., 2007; Susser, Herman, & Aaron, 2002).

Symptoms of post-traumatic stress disorder also include emotional numbing, sleep difficulties, interpersonal problems, alcohol and drug abuse, and in some cases suicide. About 16% of soldiers returning from Iraq show symptoms of PTSD (Kaplan et al., 2007; Magruder & Yeager, 2009; Pole, 2007). Furthermore, civilians may also have PTSD, especially those who have experienced child abuse or rape, rescue workers who face overwhelming situations, and victims of sudden natural disasters or accidents that produce feelings of helplessness and shock (Friedman, 2006; Hoge & Castro, 2006; Marmar, 2009). As with other stressors, PTSD has also been shown to affect immune system functioning (Heim & Pace, 2011; Uddin et al., 2010).

Although smoking is prohibited in an increasing number of places, it remains a significant social problem.

SMOKING

Would you walk into a convenience store and buy an item with a label warning you that its use could kill you? Although most people would probably answer no, millions make such a purchase every day: a pack of cigarettes. Furthermore, they do this despite clear, well-publicized evidence that smoking is linked to cancer, heart attacks, strokes, bronchitis, emphysema, and a host of other serious illnesses. Smoking is the greatest preventable cause of death in the United States; one in five U.S. deaths is caused by smoking. Worldwide, close to 5 million people die each year from the effects of smoking (Ezzati, 2005).

Why People Smoke Why do people smoke despite all the evidence showing that it is bad for their health? It is not that they are somehow unaware of the link between smoking and disease; surveys show that most smokers agree with the statement "Cigarette smoking frequently

causes disease and death." And almost three quarters of the 48 million smokers in the United States say they would like to quit. Still, 700,000 people a year take up the habit (Wetter et al., 1998; Price, 2008).

Heredity seems to determine, in part, whether people will become smokers, how much they will smoke, and how easily they can quit. Genetics also influences how susceptible people are to the harmful effects of smoking. However, although genetics plays a role in smoking, most research suggests that environmental factors are the primary cause of the habit (Fernander, Shavers & Hammons, 2007; Morley et al., 2007). Smoking at first may be seen as "cool" or sophisticated, as a rebellious act, or as facilitating calm performance in stressful situations. Greater exposure to smoking in media such as film also leads to a higher risk of becoming an established smoker. In addition, smoking a cigarette is sometimes viewed as a "rite of passage" for adolescents, undertaken at the urging of friends and viewed as a sign of growing up (Heatherton & Sargent, 2009; Sargent et al., 2007; Wills et al., 2008).

Ultimately, smoking becomes a habit. People begin to label themselves smokers, and smoking becomes part of their self-concept. Moreover, they become dependent physiologically as a result of smoking, because nicotine, a primary ingredient of tobacco, is highly addictive. A complex relationship develops among smoking, nicotine levels, and a smoker's emotional state, in which a certain nicotine level becomes associated with a positive emotional state. As a result, people smoke in an effort to regulate *both* emotional states and nicotine levels in the

Did you know?

The nicotine content of cigarettes increased by about 11% between 1998 and 2005.

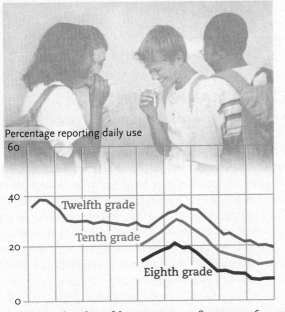

Percentage reporting daily use

Use of Tobacco by Teenagers

Source: Monitoring the Future Study, 2010.

blood (Amos, Wiltshire, & Haw, 2006; Kassel et al., 2007; Ursprung, Sanouri, & DiFranza, 2009).

Quitting Smoking Because smoking has both psychological and biological components, it is a difficult habit to break (Dodgen, 2005). Long-term successful treatment typically occurs in just 15% of those who try to stop smoking, and once smoking becomes a habit, it is as hard to stop as an addiction to cocaine or heroin. In fact, some of the biochemical reactions to nicotine are similar to those to cocaine, amphetamines, and morphine. Many people try to quit smoking but fail. The average smoker tries to quit 8 to 10 times before being successful, and even then many relapse. Even long-time quitters can fall off the wagon: About 10% relapse after more than one year of avoiding cigarettes (Dani & Montague, 2007; Dohnke, Weiss-Gerlach, & Spies, 2011; Foulds, 2006; Grady & Altman, 2008; Vanasse, Niyonsenga, & Courteau, 2004).

Among the most effective tools for ending the smoking habit are drugs that replace the nicotine found in cigarettes. Whether in the form of gum, patches, nasal sprays, or inhalers, these products provide a dose of nicotine that reduces dependence on cigarettes (Vagg & Chapman, 2005). Another approach is exemplified by the drugs Zyban and Chantrix, which, rather than replacing nicotine, reduce the pleasure from smoking and suppress withdrawal symptoms that smokers experience when they try to stop (Brody, 2008; Garwood & Potts, 2007; Shiffman, 2007).

Behavioral strategies, which view smoking as a learned habit and concentrate on changing the smoking response, can also be effective. Initial "cure" rates of 60% have been reported, and one year after behavioral treatment more than half of those who quit have not resumed smoking. Counseling, either individually or in groups, also increases the rate of success in breaking the habit. The best treatment seems to be a combination of nicotine replacement and counseling. What doesn't work? Going it alone: Only 5% of smokers who quit cold-turkey on their own are successful (Noble, 1999; Rock, 1999; Woodruff, Conway, & Edwards, 2007).

Ultimately, the most effective means of reducing smoking may be changes in societal norms and attitudes toward the habit. For instance, many cities and towns have made smoking in public places illegal, and legislation banning smoking in places such as college classrooms and buildings—based on strong popular sentiment—is being passed with increasing frequency. In addition, smokers are more likely to quit when their friends are quitting (Hamilton, Biener, & Brennan, 2007; Christakis & Fowler, 2008).

The long-term effect of the barrage of information regarding the negative consequences of smoking on people's health has been substantial; overall, smoking has declined over the last two decades, particularly among males (Druss, 2005; Keltner & Grant, 2006). Still, more than one-fourth of students enrolled in high school are active smokers by the time they graduate, and there is evidence that the decline in smoking is leveling off. Among these students, around 10% become active smokers as early as the eighth grade (Fichtenberg & Glantz, 2006; Johnston et al., 2009).

Promoting Smoking Throughout the World

A Jeep decorated with the Camel logo pulls up to a high school in Buenos Aires. A woman begins handing out free cigarettes to 15- and 16-year-olds during their lunch recess.

At a video arcade in Taipei, free American cigarettes are strewn atop each game. At a disco filled with high school students, free packs of Salems are on each table (Ecenbarger, 1993, p. 50).

As the number of smokers has declined in the United States, cigarette manufacturers have turned to new markets in an effort to increase the number of people who smoke. In the process, they have employed some dubious marketing techniques.

For instance, a few years ago the RJ Reynolds tobacco company developed a line of candy-flavored Camel Exotic Blend cigarettes with names such as TwistaLime and Warm Winter Toffee. These cigarettes were clearly targeted at the U.S. youth market. One study indicated that 17-year-olds made up the largest group of smokers of these cigarettes. Outraged by the manufacturer's blatant efforts to entice teens and young adults to take up smoking, Congress outlawed the sale of flavored tobacco (except for menthol) in 2009 (Harris, 2009; Klein et al., 2008).

Because of legal constraints on smoking in the United States, manufacturers have turned their sights to other parts of the world, where they see a fertile market of nonsmokers.

Although they must often sell cigarettes more cheaply than they do in the United States, the huge number of potential smokers still makes it financially worthwhile for the tobacco companies. The United States is the world's largest exporter of cigarettes (Bartecchi, MacKenzie, & Schrier, 1995; Brown, 2001).

The United States is the world's largest exporter of cigarettes.

Clearly, the push into worldwide markets has been successful. In some Latin American cities, as many as 50% of teenagers smoke. Children as young as age 7 smoke in Hong Kong, and 30% of children smoked their first whole cigarette before the age of 10 in India, Ghana, Jamaica, and Poland. The World Health Organization predicts that smoking will prematurely kill some 200 million of the world's children and that ultimately 10% of the world's population will die as a result of smoking. Of everyone alive today, 500 million will eventually die from tobacco use (Mackay & Eriksen, 2002).

One reason for the increase in smoking in developing countries is that their governments make little effort to discourage smoking. In fact, many governments are in the tobacco business and rely on revenues from tobacco sales. For example, the world's largest manufacturer of cigarettes is the China National Tobacco Corporation, which is owned by the Chinese government (Marsh, 2008).

>> Promoting Health and Wellness

When Stuart Grinspoon first noticed the small lump in his arm, he assumed it was just a bruise from the touch football game he had played the previous week. But as he thought about it more, he considered more serious possibilities and decided that he'd better get it checked out at the university health service. But the visit was less than satisfactory. A shy person, Stuart felt embarrassed talking about his medical condition. Even worse, after answering a string of questions, he couldn't even understand the physician's diagnosis and was too embarrassed to ask for clarification.

Stuart Grinspoon's attitudes toward health care are shared by many Americans. We approach physicians the same way we approach auto mechanics. When something goes wrong with the car, we want the mechanic to figure out the problem and then fix it. In the same way, when something isn't working right with our bodies, we want a diagnosis of the problem and then a (we hope, quick) repair.

Yet such an approach ignores the fact that—unlike auto repair—good health care requires taking psychological factors into account. Health psychologists have sought to determine the factors involved in the promotion of good health and, more broadly, a sense of well-being and happiness. Let's take a closer look at two areas they have tackled: developing successful stress management behaviors and identifying the correlates of well-being and happiness.

STRESS MANAGEMENT

What can we do to manage the stress in our lives? There are a variety of behaviors that have been shown to promote health even in the face of severe stressors. Research suggests that we take certain steps to manage stress. First, we need to make an effort to acknowledge the stress in our lives and how it is affecting us. Specifically, what stressors are currently having an impact? Do they make it hard to sleep or to eat regular, healthy meals? Do they make it hard to relax?

Second, we need to assess how we are coping with those stressors. Are they seen as a challenge or a threat? If a stressor is seen as a threat, how can it be reappraised as a challenge or made less threatening? It sounds simple, but if someone feels threatened, it usually isn't possible to just change the appraisal. This is where friends, family, mentors, and/or professional consultation with a clinical psychologist might be a good idea, because they can help you deal with the stressor.

A third stress management strategy is to consider what kinds of coping we are using and whether these coping strategies are the best choices. For example, suppose your teacher didn't believe that you had to go to the hospital to help out when your father was in an accident. If you used avoidant coping, perhaps you assumed your teacher would just figure it out and start being reasonable. In this instance, such coping would not be the best choice because this wishful thinking may not work.

A fourth strategy is to consider how well you are taking care of your basic needs. Are you getting enough sleep? Are you eating well? Do you get regular exercise? Do you give

Social support helps to buffer stressful events in life, but many people find it difficult to meet others in their area. Typically, a college or university will sponsor clubs for students who share common interests. If you don't find any clubs at your college that work for you, you could start your own!

get involved!

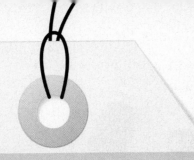

BUY IT? > > >

Tips for Stress Management

How can we deal with the stress in our lives? Effective coping depends on the nature of the stressor and the degree to which it can be controlled, but here are some general guidelines (Aspinwall & Taylor, 1997; Folkman & Moskowitz, 2000):

- *Turn a threat into a challenge.* When a stressful situation might be controllable, treat the situation as a challenge, focusing on ways to control it. If your car is always breaking down, you might take a course in auto mechanics and learn to deal directly with the car's problems.

- *Make a threatening situation less threatening.* "Look for the silver lining in every cloud." When a stressful situation seems to be uncontrollable, try changing your appraisal of the situation and modifying your attitude toward it (Smith & Lazarus, 2001; Cheng & Cheung, 2005).

- *Change your goals.* For an uncontrollable situation, adopt new goals that fit the situation. For example, a dancer who has been in an automobile accident and has lost full use of her legs may no longer have a career in dance but might try to become a choreographer instead.

- *Take physical action.* Changing your physiological reaction to stress can help with coping. For example, biofeedback and exercise can be effective in reducing stress (Hamer, Taylor, & Steptoe, 2006; Langreth, 2000).

- *Prepare for stress before it happens.* When possible, practice *proactive coping*, anticipating and preparing for stress. For example, in anticipation of finals week, you can try to arrange your schedule so you have more time to study (Aspinwall & Taylor, 1997; Bode et al., 2007).

yourself time to relax and enjoy time with friends? These sorts of stress management strategies have been demonstrated to help people in a variety of stressful situations (Brown et al., 2010; Stauder et al., 2009; Williams et al., 2010).

Social support is especially important. Our relationships with others often help us cope with stress. Researchers have found that social support, the knowledge that we are part of a mutual network of caring, interested others, enables us to experience lower levels of stress and be better able to cope with the stress we experience (Bolger, N. & Amarel, 2007; Cohen, 2004; Martin & Brantley, 2004).

> **social support** A mutual network of caring, interested others.

The social and emotional support that people provide one another helps them to deal with stress in several ways. For instance, such support demonstrates that a person is an important and valued member of a social network. Similarly, other people can provide information and advice about appropriate ways of dealing with stress (Day & Livingstone, 2003; Lindorff, 2005).

Finally, people who are part of a social support network can provide actual goods and services to help others in stressful situations. For instance, they can supply temporary living quarters to a person whose house has burned down, or they can offer study help to a student who is experiencing stress because of poor academic performance (Albrektsen & Ovamstrom, 2003; Natvig, Takizawa et al., 2007).

Recent research is also beginning to identify how social support affects brain processing. One experiment found that areas of the brain related to stress were activated less when social support was available. Such support might include simply being able to hold the hand of another person (Coan, Schaefer, & Davidson, 2006).

Being your own best advocate includes taking care of yourself by making sure you get enough sleep and eat a healthy diet. It also means that when you need medical attention you communicate with and visit your health-care provider.

Communicating Effectively with Health-care Providers Too often we assume the doctor must know best and we keep quiet instead of asking about our options. And when the doctor prescribes a medication, we often do not understand what it is for and how much to take. Researchers have found that half of all patients are unable to report accurately how long they are to continue taking a medication prescribed for them, and about a quarter do not even know the purpose of the drug (Atkinson, 1997; Halpert, 2003; Svarstad, 1976).

PSYCH think

> > > How do you think stress might hinder communication between physicians and patients?

A Patient Talks to Her Physician

The following excerpt from a case study used at the Harvard Medical School is an example of poor interviewing technique on the part of the physician.

Patient: I can hardly drink water.

Doctor: Um-hum.

Patient: Remember when it started? . . . It was pains in my head. It must have been then.

Doctor: Um-hum.

Patient: I don't know what it is. The doctor looked at it . . . said something about glands.

Doctor: Ok. Um-hum, aside from this, how have you been feeling?

Patient: Terrible.

Doctor: Yeah.

Patient: Tired . . . there's pains . . . I don't know what it is.

Doctor: Ok. . . . Fever or chills?

Patient: No.

Doctor: Ok. . . . Have you been sick to your stomach or anything?

Patient: (Sniffles, crying) I don't know what's going on. I get up in the morning tired. The only time I feel good . . . maybe like around suppertime . . . and everything (crying) and still the same thing.

Doctor: Um-hum. You're getting the nausea before you eat or after? (Goleman, 1988, p. B16)

Although the frequent "um-hums" suggest that the physician is listening to the patient, in fact he does not encourage the patient to disclose more pertinent details. Even more, late in the interview, the physician ignores the patient's emotional distress and coldly continues through the list of questions.

Sometimes patient-physician communication difficulties occur because the material that must be communicated is too technical for patients, who may lack fundamental knowledge about the body and basic medical practices. The amount of physician-patient communication also is related to the sex of a physician and patient. Overall, female primary care physicians provide more patient-centered communications than do male primary care physicians. Furthermore, patients often prefer same-sex physicians (Bertakis, 2009; Bertakis, Franks, & Epstein, 2009; Kiss, 2004; Roter, Hall, & Aoki, 2002; Schnatz et al., 2007; Street & Haidet, 2011).

Cultural values and expectations also contribute to communication barriers between patients and their physicians. Providing medical advice is even more difficult when the native language and/or culture of the doctor and patient are different (Culhane-Pera, Borkan, & Patten, 2007; Ho et al., 2004; Whaley, 2000).

What can you do to improve communication with health-care providers? Here are some tips provided by physician Holly Atkinson (Atkinson, 2003):

- Make a list of health-related concerns before you visit a health-care provider.
- Before a visit, write down the names and dosages of every drug you are currently taking.
- Determine if your provider will communicate with you via e-mail and under what circumstances.
- If you find yourself intimidated, take along an advocate—a friend or relative—who can help you communicate more effectively.
- Take notes during the visit.

You should also pay attention to the way information is framed, because research shows that framing will affect your understanding and behavior. *Positively framed messages*

Did you know?

Social support from friends and family (in the form of encouraging words, cheering, and so on) could make the difference for a winning performance in sports.

"There's no easy way I can tell you this, so I'm sending you to someone who can."

that by investigating **subjective well-being**, people's evaluations of their lives in terms of both their thoughts and their emotions. Considered another way, subjective well-being is the measure of how happy people are (Diener, Lucas, & Oishi, 2002; Dolan & White, 2007; Kesebir & Diener, 2008; Strobel, Tumasjan, & Sporrle, 2011; Tsaousis, Nikolaou, & Serdaris, 2007).

> **subjective well-being** People's own evaluation of their lives in terms of both their thoughts and their emotions.

Patients' satisfaction with their medical care is linked to how well and how accurately physicians communicate the nature of their medical problems and treatments.

---

suggest that a change in behavior will lead to a gain, emphasizing the benefits of carrying out a health-related behavior. For instance, suggesting that skin cancer is curable if it is detected early and that you can reduce your chances of getting the disease by using a sunscreen places information in a positive frame. In contrast, *negatively framed messages* highlight what you can lose by not performing a behavior. For instance, a physician might say that if you don't use sunscreen, you're more likely to get skin cancer, which can kill you if it's not detected early.

What type of message is more effective? According to psychologists Alex Rothman and Peter Salovey, it depends. When you hear a positively framed message, you are more likely to be motivated to engage in preventive behaviors, such as wearing sunscreen. If the message you hear is framed negatively, you are more likely to be watchful for symptoms (Apanovich, McCarthy, & Salovey, 2003; Lee & Aaker, 2004; McCaul, Johnson, & Rothman, 2002).

THE CORRELATES OF HAPPINESS

What makes for a good life?

This is a question that philosophers and theologians have pondered for centuries, and now health psychologists are turning their spotlight on the question. They are doing

From the perspective of...

A HEALTH-CARE PROVIDER How would you try to better communicate with your patients? How might your techniques vary, depending on the patient's background, gender, age, and culture?

What Are the Characteristics of Happy People?
Research on the subject of well-being shows that happy people share several characteristics (Myers, 2000; Diener & Seligman, 2002; Otake, Shimai, & Tanaka-Matsumi, 2006):

- *Happy people have high self-esteem.* Particularly in Western cultures, which emphasize the importance of individuality, people who are happy like themselves. They see themselves as more intelligent and better able to get along with others than the average person. In fact, they often hold *positive illusions* or moderately inflated views of themselves as good, competent, and desirable (Boyd-Wilson, McClure, & Walkey, 2004; Taylor et al., 2000).
- *Happy people have a firm sense of control.* They feel more in control of events in their lives, unlike those who feel they are the pawns of others and who experience learned helplessness (Myers & Diener, 1995).
- *Happy individuals are optimistic.* Their optimism permits them to persevere at tasks and ultimately to achieve more. In addition, their health is better (Peterson, 2000).
- *Happy people are generally made happy by the same sorts or activities, regardless of gender.* Most of the time, adult men and women achieve the same level of happiness from the same things, such as hanging out with friends. But there are some differences: For example, women get less pleasure from being with their parents than men. The explanation? For women, time spent with their parents more closely resembles work, such as helping them cook or pay the bills. For men, it's more likely to involve recreational activities, such as watching a football game with their fathers (Kreuger, 2007).
- *Happy people like to be around other people.* They tend to be extroverted and have a supportive network of close relationships (Diener & Seligman, 2002).

Faces Scale: "Which face comes closest to expressing how you feel about your life as a whole?"

20%   46%   27%   4%   2%   1%   0%

Most people in the United States rate themselves as happy, whereas only a small minority indicate that they are "not too happy."

From Andrews, F. M., & Withey, S. B. (1976). *Social Indicators of Well-Being: Americans' Perceptions of Life Quality* (p. 376). © 1976 Plenum Press, New York. With kind permission of Springer Science+Business Media B.V.

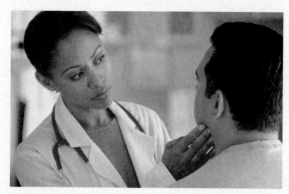

Positively framed messages suggest that a change in behavior will lead to a health-related gain.

Perhaps most important, most people are at least moderately happy most of the time. In both national and international surveys, people living in a wide variety of circumstances report being happy. Furthermore, life-altering events that one might expect would produce long-term spikes in happiness, such as winning the lottery, probably won't make you much happier than you already are, as we discuss next (Diener & Biswas-Diener, 2008; Tov, W. & Diener, 2007).

Does Money Buy Happiness? If you were to win the lottery, would you be happier?

Probably not. At least that's the implication of health psychologists' research on subjective well-being. That research shows that although winning the lottery brings an initial surge in happiness, a year later winners' level of happiness seems to return to what it was before. The converse phenomenon occurs for people who have had serious injuries in accidents: Despite an initial decline in happiness, in most cases victims return to their prior levels of happiness after the passage of time (Diener & Biswas-Diener, 2002; Nissle & Bschor, 2002; Spinella & Lester, 2006).

Why is the level of subjective well-being so stable? One explanation is that people have a general *set point* for happiness, a marker that establishes the tone for one's life. Although specific events may temporarily elevate or depress one's mood (a surprise promotion or a job loss, for example), ultimately people return to their general level of happiness.

Although the theory doesn't yet include an explanation for how people's happiness set points are initially established, some evidence suggests that the set point is determined at least in part by genetic factors. Specifically, identical twins who grow up in widely different circumstances turn out to have very similar levels of happiness (Diener, Lucas, & Scollon, 2006; Kahneman, Diener, & Schwarz, 1998; Scollon & King, 2011).

Most people's well-being set point is relatively high. For example, some 30% of people in the United States rate themselves as "very happy," and only one in 10 rates himself or herself as "not too happy." Most people declare themselves to be "pretty happy."

Few differences exist between members of different demographic groups. Men and women report being equally happy, and African Americans are only slightly less likely than European Americans to rate themselves as "very happy." Furthermore, happiness is hardly unique to U.S. culture. Even countries that are not economically prosperous have, on the whole, happy residents (Diener & Clifton, 2002; Suh, 2002; Suhail & Chaudhry, 2004).

The bottom line: Money does *not* seem to buy happiness. Despite the ups and downs of life, most people tend to be reasonably happy, and they adapt to the trials and tribulations—and joys and delights—of life by returning to a steady-state level of happiness. That habitual level of happiness can have profound—perhaps life-prolonging—implications (Diener & Seligman, 2004; Hecht, 2007).

STUDY **TIP**

Remember the concept that individuals have a set point (a general, consistent level) for subjective well-being.

For REVIEW >>

- **How is health psychology a union between medicine and psychology?**

  The field of health psychology considers how psychology can be applied to the prevention, diagnosis, and treatment of medical problems. (p. 280)

- **What is stress, how does it affect us, and how can we best cope with it?**

  Stress is a response to threatening or challenging environmental conditions. People encounter stressors—the circumstances that produce stress—of both a positive and a negative nature. General classes of events that provoke stress are cataclysmic events, personal stressors, and daily hassles. Stress produces immediate physiological reactions. In the short term those reactions may be adaptive, but in the long term they may have negative consequences, including the development of psychophysiological disorders. Stress can be reduced by developing a sense of control over one's circumstances. Coping with stress can take a number of forms, including the use of emotion-focused or problem-focused coping strategies. (pp. 280–285)

- **How can our attitudes and beliefs affect health-related problems such as coronary heart disease, cancer, and smoking?**

  Hostility, a key component of the Type A behavior pattern, is linked to coronary heart disease. The Type A behavior pattern is a cluster of behaviors involving hostility, competitiveness, time urgency, and feeling driven. Increasing evidence suggests that people's attitudes and emotional responses affect the course of cancer through links to the immune system. In post-traumatic stress disorder (PTSD), a person who has experienced a highly stressful event may reexperience the event in vivid flashbacks or dreams. Smoking, the leading preventable cause of health problems, is hard to quit, even though most smokers are aware of the dangerous consequences of the behavior. (pp. 286–292)

- **How does our rapport with a physician affect our health?**

  Although patients would often like physicians to base a diagnosis only on a physical examination, communicating one's problem to the physician is equally important. Patients may find it difficult to communicate openly with their physicians because of the high social prestige of physicians and the technical nature of medical information. (pp. 292–295)

- **How does a sense of well-being develop?**

  Subjective well-being, the measure of how happy people are, is highest in people with high self-esteem, a sense of control, optimism, and a supportive network of close relationships. (pp. 295–296)

Pop Quiz

1. _____ is defined as a response to challenging or threatening events.

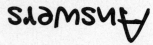2. The Stress and Coping activity showed _____.
   a. how stressed out I am
   b. a comparison of my stress level to other college students
   c. how likely I am to become ill in the coming year due to stress
   d. how often I use each of three coping strategies

3. Match each portion of the GAS with its definition.
   a. ability to adapt to stress diminishes; symptoms appear
   b. activation of sympathetic nervous system
   c. various strategies are used to cope with a stressor
   _____ 1. alarm and mobilization
   _____ 2. exhaustion
   _____ 3. resistance

4. Stressors that affect a single person and produce an immediate major reaction are known as
   a. personal stressors.
   b. psychic stressors.
   c. cataclysmic stressors.
   d. daily stressors.

5. Doing the activity on Type A behavior gave me a better understanding of the _____.
   a. genetic heritage of Type A behavior
   b. kinds of behaviors and attitudes that are linked with heart disease
   c. environmental factors that may lead to Type A behavior
   d. interaction of the effects of environment and genetics that determine Type A behavior

6. The Type A behavior pattern is known to directly cause heart attacks. True or false?

7. A cancer patient's attitude and emotions may affect that person's _____ system, helping or hindering the patient's fight against the disease.

8. Smoking is used to regulate both nicotine levels and emotional states in smokers. True or false?

9. Health psychologists are most likely to focus on which of the following problems with health care?
   a. incompetent health-care providers
   b. rising health-care costs
   c. ineffective communication between physician and patient
   d. scarcity of medical research funding

10. If you want people to floss more to prevent gum disease, the best approach is to _____.
    a. use a negatively framed message
    b. use a positively framed message
    c. have a dentist deliver a message on the pleasures of flossing
    d. provide people with free dental floss

11. Winning the lottery is likely to _____.
    a. produce an immediate and long-term increase in the level of well-being
    b. produce an immediate, but not lingering, increase in the level of well-being
    c. produce a decline in well-being over the long run
    d. lead to an increase in greed over the long run.

Answers TO POP QUIZ QUESTIONS

1. Stress
2. d
3. 1-b, 2-a, 3-c
4. a
5. b
6. false
7. immune
8. true
9. c
10. a
11. b

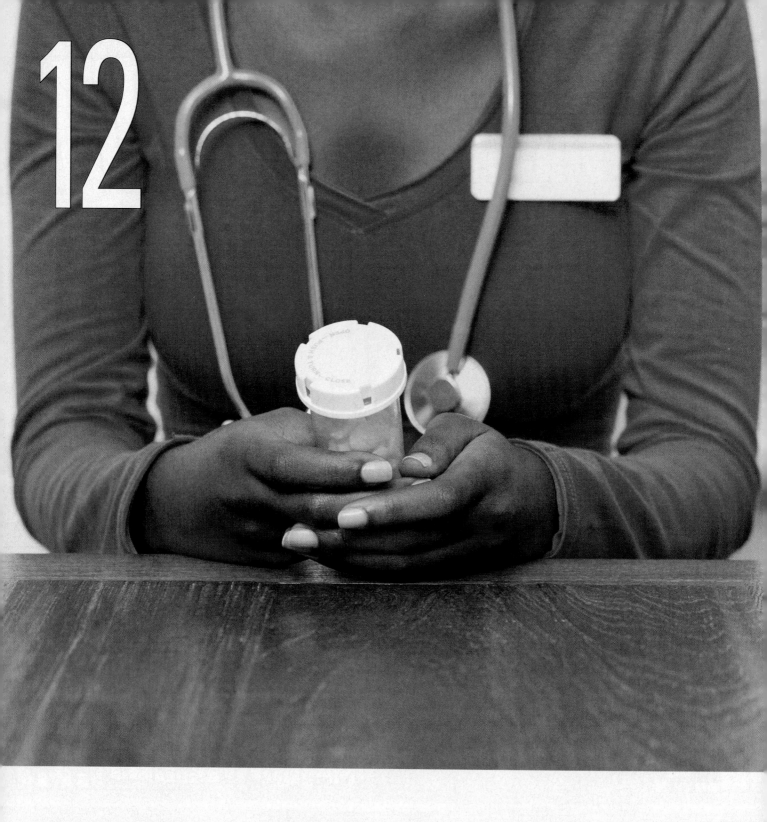

PSYCHOLO

LILY

If you had a cup of coffee with Lily (a pseudonym), you wouldn't get much sense of how much she has suffered. She is 50 but could pass for 30. . . . She is friendly but not terribly expressive, and she carries an aura of self-protection. . . .

As a teenager, Lily felt little self-confidence. "Junior high and high school just sucks, right?" she said, laughing. "But I had a propensity to take it a little more seriously." With the help of therapy, she made it through high school and college, but in her late 20s, she became dissatisfied with her job selling specialty equipment. One October day, as she headed out for a mountain-biking trip, she looked at the sky and had the feeling that something was wrong. Bleakness massed around her quickly, much faster than it had when she was younger. Soon, nothing gave Lily much joy.

She recalled a talk show on which girls had discussed cutting themselves as a release, a way to relieve depression. "I was so numb," she said. "I just wanted to feel something—anything." So she took a knife from the kitchen and cut deeply into her left arm.[xii]

Lily suffered from borderline personality disorder, a psychological disorder that afflicts an estimated 6% of the population. As we'll discuss later in the chapter, it is characterized by difficulties in forming a clear sense of self-identity, relationship problems, mood swings, and high rates of self-injury.

Lily's difficulties raise many questions. What triggered her disorder? How did genetic factors interact with stressors in her life to result in this disorder? Could it have been prevented? And more generally, how do we distinguish normal from abnormal behavior? How can Lily's behavior be categorized and classified in such a way as to pinpoint the specific nature of her problem?

We address the issues raised by Lily's case in this chapter. We begin by discussing the difference between normal and abnormal behavior, which can be surprisingly indistinct. We then turn to a consideration of the most significant kinds of psychological disorders. Next, we consider ways of evaluating behavior—one's own and that of others—to determine whether seeking help from a mental health professional is warranted. Finally, we describe the various approaches to therapy.

GICAL DISORDERS AND TREATMENT

- What theories do psychologists use to explain psychological disorders?
- What are the major categories of psychological disorders?
- How can we tell when it's time to get professional help for ourselves or someone else?
- What types of treatment are available for psychological disorders?

>> Defining and Diagnosing Abnormal Behavior

Psychologists typically define **abnormal behavior** broadly, considering it to be behavior that causes people to experience distress and prevents them from functioning in their daily lives (Nolen-Hoeksema, 2007). Because of the imprecision of this definition, it's best to view abnormal behavior and normal behavior as marking two ends of a continuum rather than as absolute states. Behavior should be evaluated in terms of gradations, ranging from fully normal functioning to extremely abnormal behavior (Wilmshurst, 2009). Daily behavior of humans typically falls somewhere between these extremes.

abnormal behavior Behavior that causes people to experience distress and prevents them from functioning in their daily lives.

biomedical perspective The perspective that suggests that when an individual displays symptoms of abnormal behavior, the root cause will be found in a physical examination of the individual, which may reveal a hormonal imbalance, a chemical deficiency, or a brain injury.

psychoanalytic perspective The perspective that suggests that abnormal behavior stems from childhood conflicts over opposing wishes regarding sex and aggression.

PERSPECTIVES ON ABNORMALITY: FROM SUPERSTITION TO SCIENCE

Throughout much of human history, people linked abnormal behavior to superstition and witchcraft. Particularly in the West, individuals who displayed abnormal behavior were accused of being possessed by demons. Authorities "treated" abnormal behavior by attempting to drive out the source of the problem. This typically involved whip-

> It's best to view abnormal behavior and normal behavior as marking two ends of a continuum rather than as absolute states.

ping, immersion in hot water, starvation, or other forms of torture in which the cure was often worse than the affliction (Berrios, 1996; Howells & Osborn, 1984).

Contemporary Western approaches to abnormal behavior are grounded in scientific theory and evidence. The perspectives used to understand psychological disorders today suggest not only different causes of abnormal behavior but different treatment approaches as well. Some perspectives seem to offer better explanations for specific disorders than others do. Here we survey the biomedical, psychoanalytic, behavioral, and cognitive perspectives.

Biomedical Perspective When people display the symptoms of tuberculosis, medical professionals can generally find tubercular bacteria in their body tissue. Similarly, the **biomedical perspective** suggests that when an individual displays symptoms of abnormal behavior, the fundamental cause will be found through a physical examination of the individual, which may reveal a hormonal imbalance, a chemical deficiency, or a brain injury. Indeed, when we speak of mental "illness," "symptoms" of abnormal behavior, and mental "hospitals," we are using terminology associated with the biomedical perspective.

Psychoanalytic Perspective Whereas the biomedical perspective suggests that biological causes are at the root of abnormal behavior, the **psychoanalytic perspective**,

Perspectives on Psychological Disorders

Perspective	Description
Biomedical perspective	Assumes that physiological causes are at the root of psychological disorders
Psychoanalytic perspective	Argues that psychological disorders stem from childhood conflicts
Behavioral perspective	Assumes that abnormal behaviors are learned responses
Cognitive perspective	Assumes that cognitions (people's thoughts and beliefs) are central to psychological disorders

based on Freud's psychoanalytic theory, holds that abnormal behavior stems from childhood conflicts over opposing wishes regarding sex and aggression. According to Freud, children pass through a series of stages in which sexual and aggressive impulses take different forms and produce conflicts that require resolution. If these childhood conflicts are not dealt with successfully, they remain unresolved in the unconscious and eventually bring about abnormal behavior during adulthood. To uncover the roots of people's disordered behavior, the psychoanalytic perspective scrutinizes their early life history.

Behavioral Perspective Both the biomedical and the psychoanalytic perspectives look at abnormal behaviors as *symptoms* of an underlying problem. In contrast, the **behavioral perspective** views the behavior itself as the problem. Using the basic principles of classical and operant conditioning and social learning, behavioral theorists see both normal and abnormal behaviors as responses to various stimuli, responses that have been learned through past experience and that are guided in the present by stimuli in the individual's environment. To explain why abnormal behavior occurs,

we must analyze how an individual has learned abnormal behavior and observe the circumstances in which it is displayed.

Cognitive Perspective Rather than considering only external behavior, as in traditional behavioral approaches, the **cognitive perspective** assumes that *cognitions* (people's thoughts and beliefs) are central to a person's abnormal behavior. A primary goal of treatment using the cognitive perspective is to explicitly teach new, more adaptive ways of thinking. For instance, suppose that you develop the erroneous belief that, whenever you take an exam, "doing well on this exam is crucial to my entire future." Through therapy, you might learn to hold the more realistic, and less anxiety-producing, thought: "my entire future is not dependent on this one exam." By changing cognitions in this way, psychologists working within a cognitive framework help people free themselves from thoughts and behaviors that are potentially maladaptive (Clark, 2004; Everly & Lating, 2007).

From the perspective of …

AN EMPLOYER A key and highly-paid employee of yours is arrested for shoplifting. What sort of explanation for this behavior would be provided by *each* perspective on abnormality: the biomedical perspective, the psychoanalytic perspective, the behavioral perspective, and the cognitive perspective?

CLASSIFYING ABNORMAL BEHAVIOR: THE *DSM*

Over the years, mental health professionals have developed many different classification systems that vary in terms of their utility and the degree to which they have been accepted. However, one standard system, devised by the American Psychiatric Association, has emerged in the United States. Most professionals today use this classification system, known as the ***Diagnostic and Statistical Manual of Mental Disorders, Fourth Edition, Text Revision (DSM-IV-TR)***, to diagnose and classify abnormal behavior.

DSM-IV-TR presents comprehensive and relatively precise definitions for more than 200 disorders, divided into 17 major categories. The intent is that, by following the criteria

behavioral perspective The perspective that looks at the behavior itself as the problem.

cognitive perspective The perspective that suggests that people's thoughts and beliefs are a central component of abnormal behavior.

Diagnostic and Statistical Manual of Mental Disorders, Fourth Edition, Text Revision (DSM-IV-TR) A system, devised by the American Psychiatric Association, used by most professionals to diagnose and classify abnormal behavior.

"First off, you're not a nut, you're a legume."

Major Categories of Psychological Disorders

Categories of Disorders	Examples
Anxiety Problems in which anxiety impedes daily functioning	Generalized anxiety disorder, panic disorder, phobic disorder, obsessive-compulsive disorder, post-traumatic stress disorder
Somatoform Psychological difficulties displayed through physical problems	Hypochondriasis, conversion disorder
Dissociative The splitting apart of crucial parts of personality that are usually integrated	Dissociative identity disorder (multiple personality), dissociative amnesia, dissociative fugue
Mood Emotions of depression or euphoria that are so strong they intrude on everyday living	Major depression, bipolar disorder
Schizophrenia and psychotic disorders Declines in functioning, thought and language disturbances, perception disorders, emotional disturbances, residual subtypes and withdrawal from others	Disorganized, paranoid, catatonic, undifferentiated, residual subtypes
Personality Problems that create little personal distress but that lead to an inability to function as a normal member of society	Antisocial (sociopathic) personality disorder, narcissistic personality disorder
Sexual Problems related to sexual arousal from unusual objects or problems related to functioning	Paraphilia, sexual dysfunction
Substance-related Problems related to drug dependence and abuse	Alcohol, cocaine, hallucinogens, marijuana
Cognitive Disorders	Alzheimer's Disease, amnesia

DIAGNOSTIC AND STATISTICAL MANUAL OF MENTAL DISORDERS

FOURTH EDITION
TEXT REVISION

DSM-IV-TR

AMERICAN PSYCHIATRIC ASSOCIATION

presented in the *DSM-IV-TR* classification system, diagnosticians can identify the specific problem that an individual is experiencing.

DSM-IV-TR is designed to be primarily descriptive and avoids suggesting an underlying cause for an individual's behavior and problems. For instance, the term *neurotic*—a label that is commonly used by people in their everyday descriptions of abnormal behavior—is not listed as a *DSM-IV-TR* category. Because the term *neurosis* refers to problems associated with a specific cause based in Freud's theory of personality, it is not included in *DSM-IV-TR*.

DSM-IV-TR has the advantage, then, of providing a descriptive system that does not specify the cause of or reason for a problem. Instead, it paints a picture of the behavior that is being displayed. Why should this approach be important? For one thing, it allows communication between mental health professionals of diverse backgrounds and theoretical approaches. In addition, precise classification enables researchers to explore the causes of a problem. Without reliable descriptions of abnormal behavior, researchers would be hard-pressed to find ways to investigate the disorder. Finally, *DSM-IV-TR* provides a kind of conceptual shorthand with which professionals can describe the behaviors that tend to manifest simultaneously in an individual (Frances, First, & Pincus, 2002; Røysamb et al., 2011; Widiger & Clark, 2000).

The Shortcomings of DSM When clinical psychologist David Rosenhan and eight colleagues sought admission to separate mental hospitals across the United States in the 1970s, each stated that he or she was hearing voices—"unclear voices" that said "empty," "hollow," and "thud"—and each was immediately admitted to the hospital. However, the truth was that they were conducting a study, and none of them was really hearing voices. Aside from this misrepresentation, *everything* else they did and said represented their true behavior, including the responses they gave during extensive admission interviews and their answers to the battery of tests they were asked to complete. In fact, as soon as they were admitted, they said they no longer heard any voices. In short, each of the imposters acted in a "normal" way (Rosenhan, 1973).

We might assume that Rosenhan and his colleagues would have been quickly discovered as the impostors they were, but this was not the case. Instead, each of them was diagnosed as severely abnormal on the basis of observed behavior. Mental health professionals labeled most as suffering from schizophrenia and kept them in the hospital for 3 to 52 days, with the average stay being 19 days. When they were discharged, most of the "patients" left with the label *schizophrenia—in remission*, implying that the abnormal behavior had only temporarily subsided and could recur at any time. Most disturbing, no one on the hospital staff identified any of the impostors as such—although some of the real patients figured out the ruse.

The results of Rosenhan's classic study illustrate that placing labels on individuals powerfully influences the way mental health workers perceive and interpret their actions. It also points out that determining who is psychologically disordered is not always a clear-cut or accurate process.

Although *DSM-IV-TR* was developed to provide more accurate and consistent diagnoses of psychological disorders, it has not been entirely successful. For instance, critics charge that it relies too much on the medical perspective. Because it was drawn up by psychiatrists—who are physicians—some condemn it for viewing psychological disorders primarily in terms of the symptoms of an underlying physiological disorder. Moreover, critics suggest that *DSM-IV-TR* compartmentalizes people into inflexible, all-or-none categories, rather than considering the degree to which a person displays psychologically disordered behavior (Samuel & Widiger, 2006; Schmidt, Kotov, & Joiner, 2004).

Other concerns with *DSM-IV-TR* are more subtle, but equally important. For instance, some critics argue that labeling an individual as abnormal provides a dehumanizing, lifelong stigma. (Think, for example, of political contenders whose candidacies have been terminated by the disclosure that they received treatment for psychological disorders.) Furthermore, after an initial diagnosis has been made, mental health professionals, who may concentrate on the initial diagnostic category, could overlook other diagnostic possibilities (Duffy et al., 2002; Quinn, Kahng, & Crocker, 2004; Szasz, 1994).

Despite the drawbacks inherent in any labeling system, *DSM-IV-TR* has significantly influenced the way in which U.S. mental health professionals view psychological disorders. It has increased both the reliability and the validity of diagnostic categorization. In addition, it offers a logical way to organize examination of the major types of mental disturbance (Milling, Chau & Mills-Baxter, 2006; Widiger & Mullins-Sweatt, 2008).

PSYCH think

> > > Do you agree that *DSM* should be updated every several years? Why or why not?

>> Major Categories of Psychological Disorders

Now that we understand something about abnormality and the classification of psychological disorders, we can turn our attention to several categories of disorders. Within each category we consider some of the specific disorders, including their major symptoms and some possible causes. Keep in mind that, although we'll be discussing these disorders in an objective manner, each represents a very human set of difficulties that influence, and in some cases considerably disrupt, people's lives.

ANXIETY DISORDERS

All of us, at one time or another, experience *anxiety*, a feeling of apprehension or tension, in reaction to stressful situations. This type of anxiety is a normal reaction to stress that often helps, rather than hinders, our daily functioning. But some people experience anxiety in situations in which there is no external reason or cause for such distress. When anxiety occurs without external justification and begins to interfere with people's daily functioning, mental health professionals consider it maladaptive. Mental health professionals categorize persistent anxiety that impairs daily functioning as **anxiety disorder**. The four major types of anxiety disorders are phobic disorder, panic disorder, generalized anxiety disorder, and obsessive-compulsive disorder.

anxiety disorder The occurrence of anxiety without an obvious external cause, affecting daily functioning.

phobias Intense, irrational fears of specific objects or situations.

Phobic Disorder

It's not easy moving through the world when you're terrified of electricity. "Donna," 45, a writer, knows that better than most. Get her in the vicinity of an appliance or a light switch or—all but unthinkable—a thunderstorm, and she is overcome by a terror so blinding she can think of nothing but fleeing. That, of course, is not always possible, so over time, Donna has come up with other answers. When she opens the refrigerator door, rubber-sole shoes are a must. If a light bulb blows, she will tolerate the dark until someone else changes it for her. Clothes shopping is done only when necessary, lest static on garments send her running from the store. And swimming at night is absolutely out of the question, lest underwater lights electrocute her. (Kluger, 2001, p. 51)

Donna suffers from a **phobia**, an intense, irrational fear of a specific object or situation. For example, claustrophobia is a fear of enclosed places, acrophobia is a fear of high places, xenophobia is a fear of strangers, social phobia is the fear of being judged or embarrassed by others, and—as in Donna's case—electrophobia is a fear of electricity.

The objective danger posed by an anxiety-producing stimulus (which can be just about anything) is typically small or nonexistent. However, to someone suffering from the phobia, the danger is great, and a full-blown panic attack may follow exposure to the stimulus. Phobic disorders differ from generalized anxiety disorders and panic

Types of Phobias

Agoraphobia Fear of places where help might not be available in case of emergency

Example: Person becomes housebound because any place other than the person's home arouses extreme anxiety symptoms.

Specific phobia

Animal type Fear of specific animals or insects
Example: Person has extreme fear of dogs, cats, or spiders.

Natural environment type Fear of events or situations in the natural environment
Example: Person has extreme fear of storms, heights, or water.

Situational type Fear of public transportation, tunnels, bridges, elevators, flying, driving
Example: Person becomes extremely claustrophobic in elevators.

Blood injection-injury type
Fear of blood, injury, injections
Example: Person panics when viewing a child's scraped knee.

Social phobia Fear of being judged or embarrassed by others

Example: Person avoids all social situations and becomes a recluse for fear of encountering others' judgment.

Source: Adapted from Nolen-Hoeksema, 2007.

Acrophobia, the fear of heights, is a relatively common phobia.

disorders in that they involve a specific, identifiable stimulus that sets off the anxiety reaction.

Phobias may have only a minor effect on people's lives if those who suffer from them can avoid the stimuli that trigger fear. Unless they are firefighters or window washers, for example, people with a fear of heights may experience little daily stress from the phobia (although it may prevent them from living on a high floor in an apartment). However, a *social phobia*, or a fear of strangers, presents a more serious problem. In one extreme case, a Washington woman left her home just three times in thirty years—once to visit her family, once for a medical operation, and once to purchase ice cream for a dying companion (Adler, 1984; Kimbrel, 2007; Lueken et al., 2011).

panic disorder Anxiety disorder that takes the form of panic attacks lasting from a few seconds to as long as several hours.

generalized anxiety disorder The experience of long-term, persistent anxiety and worry.

Panic Disorder In another type of anxiety disorder, **panic disorder**, *panic attacks* occur that last from a few seconds to several hours. Unlike phobias, which are stimulated by specific objects or situations, panic disorders do not have any identifiable stimuli. Instead, during an attack, anxiety suddenly—and often without warning—rises to a peak, and an individual feels a sense of impending, unavoidable doom. Although the physical symptoms differ from person to person, they may include heart palpitations, shortness of breath, unusual amounts of sweating, faintness and dizziness, gastric sensations, and sometimes a sense of imminent death. After such an attack, many sufferers understandably tend to feel exhausted (Laederach-Hofmann & Messerli-Buergy, 2007; Rachman & deSilva, 2004).

Panic attacks seemingly come out of nowhere and are unconnected to any specific stimulus. Because they don't know what triggers their feelings of panic, victims of panic attacks may become fearful of going places. In fact, some people with panic disorder develop a complication called *agoraphobia*, the fear of being in a situation in which escape is difficult and in which help for a possible panic attack would not be available. In extreme cases, people with agoraphobia never leave their homes (Herrán, Carrera, & Sierra-Biddle, 2006; Marcaurelle, Belanger, & Marchand, 2005; Reinecke et al., 2011; Wittchen et al., 2008).

In addition to the physical symptoms, panic disorder affects how information is processed in the brain. For instance, people with panic disorder have reduced reactions in the anterior cingulate cortex to stimuli (such as viewing a fearful face) that normally produce a strong reaction in those without the disorder. It may be that recurring high levels of emotional arousal experienced by individuals with panic disorder desensitizes them to emotional stimuli (Pillay et al., 2006, 2007).

Most common psychological disorders in the United States

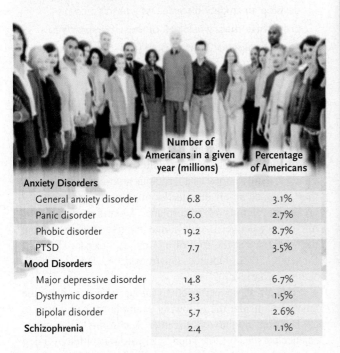

	Number of Americans in a given year (millions)	Percentage of Americans
Anxiety Disorders		
General anxiety disorder	6.8	3.1%
Panic disorder	6.0	2.7%
Phobic disorder	19.2	8.7%
PTSD	7.7	3.5%
Mood Disorders		
Major depressive disorder	14.8	6.7%
Dysthymic disorder	3.3	1.5%
Bipolar disorder	5.7	2.6%
Schizophrenia	2.4	1.1%

Comedian Howie Mandel has talked openly about his struggles with Obsessive Compulsive Disorder (OCD). Although he has developed coping strategies, he still cannot bring himself to shake hands. His alternative is to bump fists.

Generalized Anxiety Disorder People with **generalized anxiety disorder** experience long-term, persistent anxiety and uncontrollable worry. Sometimes their concerns are about identifiable issues involving family, money, work, or health. In other cases, though, people with the disorder feel that something dreadful is about to happen but can't identify the reason, experiencing "free-floating" anxiety.

Because of persistent anxiety, people with generalized anxiety disorder cannot concentrate or set their worry and fears aside; their lives become centered on their worry. Furthermore, their anxiety is often accompanied by physiological symptoms such as muscle tension headaches, dizziness, heart palpitations, and insomnia (Starcevic et al., 2007).

Obsessive-Compulsive Disorder In **obsessive-compulsive disorder**, people are plagued by unwanted thoughts, called obsessions, and/or feel that they must carry out actions, termed *compulsions*, against their will.

An **obsession** is a persistent, unwanted thought or idea that keeps recurring. For example, a student may be unable to stop thinking that she has neglected to put her name on a test and may think about it constantly for the two weeks it takes to get the paper back. A man may go on vacation and wonder the whole time whether he locked his house. A woman may hear the same tune running through her head over and over. In each case, the thought or idea is unwanted and difficult to put out of mind. Of course, many people

suffer from mild obsessions from time to time, but usually such thoughts persist only for a short period. For people with serious obsessions, however, the thoughts persist for days or months and may consist of bizarre, troubling images (Hollander et al., 2011; Lee & Kwon, 2003, 2005; Rassin & Muris, 2007).

As part of an obsessive-compulsive disorder, people may also experience **compulsions**, irresistible urges to repeatedly carry out some act that seems strange and unreasonable, even to them. Whatever the compulsive behavior is, people experience extreme anxiety if they cannot carry it out, even if it is something they want to stop. The acts may be relatively trivial, such as repeatedly checking the stove to make sure all the burners are turned off, or more unusual, such as continually washing oneself (Clark, 2007; Frost & Steketee, 2002; Moretz & McKay, 2009).

For example, consider this passage from the autobiography of a person with obsessive-compulsive disorder:

I thought my parents would die if I didn't do everything in exactly the right way. When I took my glasses off at night I'd have to place them on the dresser at a particular angle.

obsessive-compulsive disorder A disorder characterized by obsessions or compulsions.

obsession A persistent, unwanted thought or idea that keeps recurring.

compulsion An irresistible urge to repeatedly carry out some act that seems strange and unreasonable.

Sometimes I'd turn on the light and get out of bed seven times until I felt comfortable with the angle.

If the angle wasn't right, I felt that my parents would die. The feeling ate up my insides. If I didn't grab the molding on the wall just the right way as I entered or exited my room; if I didn't hang a shirt in the closet perfectly; if I didn't read a paragraph a certain way; if my hands and nails weren't perfectly clean, I thought my incorrect behavior would kill my parents (Summers, 2000, p. 42).

Although such compulsive rituals lead to some immediate reduction of anxiety, in the long term the anxiety returns. In fact, people with severe cases lead lives filled with unrelenting tension (Goodman, Rudorfer, & Maser, 2000; Penzel, 2000).

The Causes of Anxiety Disorders We've considered the four major types of anxiety disorders, but there are others as well. For instance, *posttraumatic stress disorder* (in which a person reexperiences a stressful event in vivid flashbacks or dreams; chapter 11) is classified as an anxiety disorder.

Because there are so many different kinds of anxiety disorders, it is unlikely that any single theory would explain them all. From a biomedical perspective, genetic factors clearly are part of the picture. For example, if one member of a pair of identical twins has panic disorder, there is a 30% chance that the other twin will have it also (Gelernter & Stein, 2009; Hettema, 2005). Furthermore, a person's characteristic level of anxiety is related to a specific gene involved in the production of the neurotransmitter serotonin. This is consistent with findings indicating that certain chemical deficiencies in the brain appear to produce some kinds of anxiety disorder (Beidel & Turner, 2007; Chamberlain et al., 2008; Holmes et al., 2003).

Some researchers believe that an overactive autonomic nervous system may be at the root of panic attacks. Specifically, they suggest that poor regulation of the brain's locus ceruleus may lead to panic attacks, which cause the limbic system to become overstimulated. In turn, the overstimulated limbic system produces chronic anxiety, which ultimately leads the locus ceruleus to generate still more panic attacks (Balaban, 2002; Davies et al., 2008).

There are also biological causes at work in obsessive-compulsive disorder (OCD). For example, researchers have found differences in the brains of those with the disorder, with certain areas of the brain showing greater activity compared to those without the disorder (Christian et al., 2008). Psychologists who employ the behavioral perspective have taken a different approach that emphasizes environmental factors. They consider anxiety to be a learned response to stress. For instance, suppose a dog bites a young girl. When the girl next sees a dog, she is frightened and runs away—a behavior that relieves her anxiety and thereby reinforces her avoidance behavior. After repeated encounters with dogs in which she is reinforced for her avoidance behavior, she may develop a full-fledged phobia regarding dogs.

Finally, the cognitive perspective suggests that anxiety disorders grow out of inappropriate and inaccurate thoughts and beliefs about circumstances in a person's world. For example, people with anxiety disorders may view a friendly puppy as a ferocious and savage pit bull, or they may see an air disaster looming every moment they are in the vicinity of an airplane. According to the cognitive perspective, people's maladaptive thoughts about the world are at the root of an anxiety disorder (Frost & Steketee, 2002; Ouimet, Gawronski, & Dozois, 2009; Wang & Clark, 2002).

Each of these perspectives alone offers part of the answer. Consider the following example to see how these explanations might work together. According to the neuroscience perspective, the young girl who was bitten by a dog might have a greater tendency to develop an anxiety disorder, in this case a phobia of dogs, because of her genetic heritage and/or because of her brain chemistry. Further, after she has learned to be afraid as described by the behaviorialists, she would probably come to view friendly dogs as dangerous, which would be a cognitive issue.

MOOD DISORDERS

From the time I woke up in the morning until the time I went to bed at night, I was unbearably miserable and seemingly incapable of any kind of joy or enthusiasm. Everything—every thought, word, movement—was an effort. Everything that once was sparkling now was flat. I seemed to myself to be dull, boring, inadequate, thick brained, unlit, unresponsive, chill skinned, bloodless, and sparrow drab. I doubted, completely, my ability to do anything well. It seemed as though my mind had slowed down and burned out to the point of being virtually useless. (Jamison, 1995, p. 110)

We all experience shifts in mood. Sometimes we are happy, perhaps even euphoric; at other times we feel upset, saddened, or depressed. Such changes in mood are a normal part of everyday life. In some people, however, moods are so pronounced and lingering—like the feelings described above by writer (and psychiatrist) Kay Redfield Jamison—that they interfere with the ability to function effectively. In extreme cases, a mood may become life-threatening, and in others it may cause the person to lose touch with reality. Situations such as these represent **mood disorders**, disturbances in emotional experience that are strong enough to intrude on everyday living.

Major Depression President Abraham Lincoln, Queen Victoria, and newscaster Mike Wallace all suffered from periodic attacks of **major depression**, a severe psychological disorder that interferes with concentration, decision making, and sociability. Major depression is one of the more common forms of mood disorders. Some 15 million people in the United States suffer from major depression, and, at any one time, 6% to 10% of the U.S. population is clinically depressed. Almost one in five people in the United States experiences major depression at some point in life, and 15% of college students have received a diagnosis of depression. The cost of depression is more than $80 billion a year in lost productivity (Scelfo, 2007; Simon et al., 2008; Winik, 2006).

Women are twice as likely to be diagnosed with major depression as men, with one-fourth of all females apt to encounter it at some point during their lives (Whiffen & Demidenko, 2006). Furthermore, although no one is sure why, the rate of reported depression is going up throughout the world (Bhugra & Mastrogianni, 2004; Compton et al., 2006; Lecrubier, 2001). Results of in-depth interviews conducted in the United States, Puerto Rico, Taiwan, Lebanon, Canada, Italy, Germany, and France indicate that reported incidents of depression have increased significantly over previous rates in each country. In some countries, the likelihood that individuals will have major depression at some point in their lives is three times higher than it was for earlier generations (Kendler, Gatz, & Gardner, 2006; Miller, 2003; Staley, Sanacora, & Tamagnan, 2006).

> **mood disorder** A disturbance in emotional experience that is strong enough to intrude on everyday living.
>
> **major depression** A severe form of depression that interferes with concentration, decision making, and sociability.

When psychologists speak of major depression, they do not mean the sadness that comes from experiencing one of life's disappointments or hardships, something that we all have experienced. Some depression is normal after the breakup of a long-term relationship, the death of a loved one, or the loss of a job. It is normal even after less serious problems, such as losing a favorite possession or not winning the lottery.

People who suffer from major depression experience similar sorts of feelings as those who are experiencing a normal mood shift, but their feelings are much stronger. They may feel useless, worthless, and lonely and may think the future is hopeless and that no one can help them. They may lose their appetite and have no energy. Moreover, they may experience such feelings for months or even years. They may cry uncontrollably, have sleep disturbances, and be at risk for suicide.

Portrait of Dr. Gachet by Vincent Van Gogh.

The severe depth and the long duration of such behavior are the hallmarks of major depression (Cadwallader, 1991; Coyne, 1976; Mialet, Pope & Yurgelun, 1996; Tse & Bond, 2004).

Mania and Bipolar Disorder

Depression leads to the depths of despair; mania, in contrast, leads to emotional heights. **Mania** is an extended state of intense, wild elation. People experiencing mania feel intense happiness, power, invulnerability, and energy. They may become involved in wild schemes, believing they will succeed at anything they attempt.

> **mania** An extended state of intense, wild elation.
>
> **bipolar disorder** A disorder in which a person alternates between periods of euphoric feelings of mania and periods of depression.

Typically, people sequentially experience periods of mania and depression (Johnson, Fulford, & Eisner, 2009). This alternation of mania and depression is called **bipolar disorder** (a condition previously known as manic-depressive disorder). The swings between highs and lows may occur a few days apart or may alternate over a period of months or years. In addition, in bipolar disorder, periods of depression are usually longer than periods of mania (Nivoli et al., 2011; Zarate & Manji, 2009). In the *DSM-IV-TR*, a distinction is made between Bipolar I, where a person will alternate between mania and depression, and Bipolar II, which includes at least one episode of hypomania (less intense than mania) and episodes of depression. Recent research has indicated that although Bipolar II may appear to be less severe, the suicide rate for people with this disorder may be similar to that of those with Bipolar I (Novick, Swartz, & Frank, 2010).

Causes of Mood Disorders

Because they represent a major mental health problem, mood disorders—and, in particular, depression—have received a good deal of study. Several approaches have been used to explain the disorders.

Some mood disorders have genetic and biochemical roots. In fact, most neuroscience evidence suggests that bipolar disorder has biological origins. For instance, bipolar disorder (and some forms of major depression) clearly runs in some families. Additionally, several neurotransmitters, including serotonin and norepinephrine, have been implicated in depression (Kato, 2007; Plomin & McGuffin, 2003; Popa et al., 2008).

Further evidence from the neuroscience perspective comes from brain imaging studies that suggest that people with depression experience a general blunting of emotional reactions. For example, one study found that the brains of people with depression showed significantly less activation when these people viewed photos of human faces displaying strong emotions than did those of people without the disorder (Gotlib et al., 2004).

Cognitive explanations of mood disorders have benefited greatly from Martin Seligman's (Seligman, 1975; Seligman & Maier, 1967) seminal work with dogs. Based on that work, he suggests that depression is largely a response to learned helplessness. *Learned helplessness* is a learned expectation that events in one's life are uncontrollable and that one cannot escape from the situation. One theoretical explanation of learned helplessness suggests that people simply give up fighting aversive events and submit to them, thereby producing depression. Other

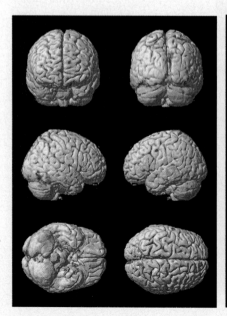
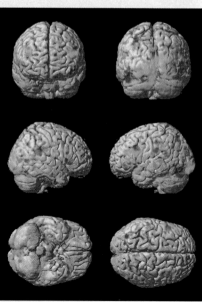

Brain imaging studies suggest that people with depression experience a general blunting of emotional reactions. In one study, represented here, the brains of individuals with depression (*left*) showed significantly less activation in response to photos of sad, angry, and fearful faces than did those of people without the disorder (*right*). *Source:* Ian Gotlib, Stanford Mood and Anxiety Disorders Laboratory, 2004.

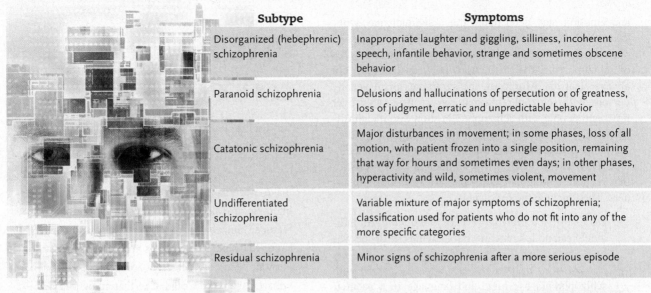

Subtype	Symptoms
Disorganized (hebephrenic) schizophrenia	Inappropriate laughter and giggling, silliness, incoherent speech, infantile behavior, strange and sometimes obscene behavior
Paranoid schizophrenia	Delusions and hallucinations of persecution or of greatness, loss of judgment, erratic and unpredictable behavior
Catatonic schizophrenia	Major disturbances in movement; in some phases, loss of all motion, with patient frozen into a single position, remaining that way for hours and sometimes even days; in other phases, hyperactivity and wild, sometimes violent, movement
Undifferentiated schizophrenia	Variable mixture of major symptoms of schizophrenia; classification used for patients who do not fit into any of the more specific categories
Residual schizophrenia	Minor signs of schizophrenia after a more serious episode

Subtypes of Schizophrenia

cognitive theories suggest that depression results from hopelessness, a combination of learned helplessness and an expectation that negative outcomes in one's life are inevitable (Bjornstad, 2006; Kwon & Laurenceau, 2002; Maier & Watkins, 2000).

The various theories of depression have not provided a complete answer to an elusive question that has dogged researchers: Why is depression diagnosed in approximately twice as many women as men—a pattern that is similar across cultures?

One explanation suggests that the stress experienced by women may be greater than that experienced by men at certain points in their lives—such as when a woman must simultaneously earn a living and be the primary caregiver for her children (Stephens & Townsend, 1997). In addition, women have a higher risk for physical and sexual abuse, typically earn lower wages than men, report greater unhappiness with their marriages, and generally experience chronic negative circumstances. Furthermore, women and men may respond to stress with different coping mechanisms. For instance, men may abuse drugs, but women respond with depression (Antonucci et al., 2002; Holden, 2005; Nolen-Hoeksema, 2007).

Biological factors may also explain some women's depression. For example, because the rate of female depression begins to rise during puberty, hormones have been suggested as a factor that causes women to be more vulnerable to the disorder (Hyde, Mezulis & Abramson, 2008). In addition, 25% to 50% of women who take oral contraceptives report symptoms of depression, and

depression that occurs after the birth of a child has been linked to hormonal changes (Bloch et al., 2006; Serrano & Warnock, 2007). It is clear, ultimately, that researchers have discovered no definitive solutions to the puzzle of depression, and there are many alternative theories. Most likely, a complex interaction of several factors causes mood disorders.

SCHIZOPHRENIA

Things that relate, the town of Antelope, Oregon, Jonestown, Charlie Manson, the Hillside Strangler, the Zodiac Killer, Watergate, King's trial in L.A., and many more. In the last 7 years alone, over 23 Star Wars scientists committed suicide for no apparent reason. The AIDS cover-up, the conference in South America in 87 had over 1,000 doctors claim that insects can transmit it. To be able to read one's thoughts and place thoughts in one's mind without the person knowing it's being done. Realization is a reality of bioelectromagnetic control, which is thought transfer and emotional control, recording individual brainwave frequencies of thought, sensation, and emotions (Nolen-Heoksema, 2007, pp. 385–386).

This excerpt illustrates the efforts of a person with schizophrenia, one of the more severe forms of mental disturbance, to hold a conversation with a clinician. People with schizophrenia account for by far the largest percentage of those hospitalized for mental disorders. They are also in many respects the least likely to recover from their psychological difficulties (Awad & Voruganti, 2007; Keller, Fischer, & Carpenter, 2011).

Schizophrenia refers to a class of disorders in which severe distortion of reality occurs. Thinking, perception,

> **schizophrenia** A class of disorders in which severe distortion of reality occurs.

Why is depression diagnosed in approximately twice as many women as men?

and emotion may deteriorate; the individual may withdraw from social interaction; and the person may display bizarre behavior. Although there are several types of schizophrenia, the distinctions between them are not always clear-cut. Moreover, the symptoms displayed by persons with schizophrenia may vary considerably over time, and people with schizophrenia show significant differences in the pattern of their symptoms even when they are labeled with the same diagnostic category. Nonetheless, *DSM-IV-TR* describes a number of characteristics that reliably distinguish schizophrenia from other disorders. They include the following:

- *Decline from a previous level of functioning.* An individual can no longer carry out activities he or she was once able to do.

- *Disturbances of thought and speech.* People with schizophrenia use logic and language in a peculiar way. Their thinking often does not make sense, and their information processing logic is frequently faulty, something referred to as a formal thought disorder. They also do not follow conventional linguistic rules (Penn et al., 1997). Consider, for example, the following response to the question "Why do you think people believe in God?"

Uh, let's, I don't know why, let's see, balloon travel. He holds it up for you, the balloon. He don't let you fall out, your little legs sticking down through the clouds. He's down to the smokestack, looking through the smoke trying to get the balloon gassed up you know. Way they're flying on top that way, legs sticking out. I don't know, looking down on the ground, heck, that'd make you so dizzy you just stay and sleep you know, hold down and sleep there. I used to be sleep outdoors, you know, sleep outdoors instead of going home. (Chapman & Chapman, 1973, p. 3)

As this selection illustrates, although the basic grammatical structure may be intact, the substance of thinking characteristic of schizophrenia is often illogical, garbled, and lacking in meaningful content (Heinrichs, 2005; Holden, 2003).

- *Delusions.* People with schizophrenia often have delusions, which are firmly held, unshakable beliefs with no basis in reality. Among the common delusions experienced by people with schizophrenia are the beliefs that they are being controlled by someone else, they are being persecuted by others, and their thoughts are being broadcast so that others know what they are thinking (Coltheart, Langdon, & McKay, 2007; Startup, Bucci, & Langdon, 2009).

- *Hallucinations and perceptual disorders.* People with schizophrenia do not perceive the world as most other people do. They also may have *hallucinations,* the experience of perceiving things that do not exist. Furthermore, they may see, hear, or smell things differently than other people do and may not even have a sense of their bodies in the way that others do; they

PSYCH think

connect™

WWW.MCGRAWHILLCONNECT.COM/PSYCHOLOGY

Schizophrenia

> > > Do the conversational excerpts of people with schizophrenia sound familiar? Would they make more sense if we thought they were narrating their dreams? Have you ever had a dream that featured similar bizarre leaps of scene and conversation? This possibility raises an intriguing question: How do we know when we are awake and when we are dreaming? Could it be that some people with schizophrenia have lost the ability to tell the difference?

Take the PsychSmart challenge! How do mental health professionals identify and categorize the symptoms of schizophrenia? From chapter 12 in your ebook, select the *Exercises* tab. Then, select "Schizophrenia." Complete the activity to get a better perspective on the behaviors associated with this disorder, and then answer Pop Quiz question 7 on p. 333 to check your understanding of schizophrenia.

may have difficulty determining where their bodies stop and the rest of the world begins (Botvinick, 2004; Copolov et al., 2003; Thomas et al., 2007).

- *Emotional disturbances.* People with schizophrenia sometimes show a lack of emotion in which even the most dramatic events produce little or no emotional response. Conversely, they may display emotion that is inappropriate to a situation (Combs, Basso, Wanner & Ledet, 2008; Kring & Earnst, 2003; Kring & Moran, 2008). For example, a person with schizophrenia may laugh uproariously at a funeral or react with anger when being helped by someone.

- *Withdrawal.* People with schizophrenia tend to have little interest in others. They tend not to socialize or hold real conversations with others, although they may talk at another person. In the most extreme cases they do not even acknowledge the presence of other people, appearing to be in their own isolated world (Combs et al., 2008; Combs & Mueser, 2007).

Types of Schizophrenia The symptoms of schizophrenia are classified into two types by *DSM-IV-TR.* Positive-symptom schizophrenia is indicated by the *presence* of disordered behavior such as hallucinations,

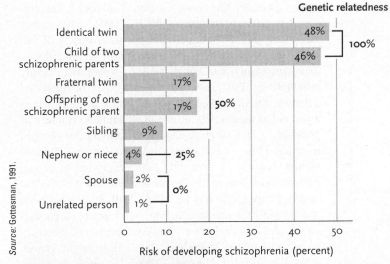

Source: Gottesman, 1991.

Genetic relatedness

Identical twin	48%
Child of two schizophrenic parents	46%
Fraternal twin	17%
Offspring of one schizophrenic parent	17%
Sibling	9%
Nephew or niece	4%
Spouse	2%
Unrelated person	1%

100% (Identical twin, Child of two schizophrenic parents)
50% (Fraternal twin, Offspring of one schizophrenic parent)
25% (Nephew or niece)
0% (Spouse)

Risk of developing schizophrenia (percent)

0 10 20 30 40 50

Risk of Developing Schizophrenia, Based on Genetic Relatedness to a Person with Schizophrenia

delusions, and emotional extremes. In contrast, negative-symptom schizophrenia shows an *absence or a loss* of normal functioning, such as social withdrawal or blunted emotions. Schizophrenia researchers sometimes speak of *Type I schizophrenia*, in which positive symptoms are dominant, and *Type II schizophrenia,* in which negative symptoms are more prominent (Buchanan et al., 2007; Levine & Rabinowitz, 2007).

The distinction between Type I and Type II schizophrenia is important, because it suggests that two different processes might trigger schizophrenia, the cause of which remains one of the greatest mysteries facing psychologists who deal with disordered behavior.

Solving the Puzzle of Schizophrenia The predominant approach used to explain the onset of schizophrenia today, the *predisposition model of schizophrenia,* incorporates a number of biological and environmental factors. This model suggests that individuals may inherit a predisposition or an inborn sensitivity to schizophrenia that makes them particularly vulnerable to stressful factors

in the environment, such as social rejection or dysfunctional family communication patterns (Combs et al., 2008). The stressors may vary, but if they are strong enough and are coupled with a genetic predisposition, the result is the onset of schizophrenia. Similarly, a strong genetic predisposition may lead to the onset of schizophrenia even when the environmental stressors are relatively weak.

One indication that genetic factors seem to be involved in producing at least a susceptibility to developing schizophrenia is that schizophrenia is more common in some families than in others. For example, the closer the genetic link between a person with schizophrenia and another individual, the greater the likelihood that the other person will experience the disorder (Brzustowicz et al., 2000; Gottesman & Hanson, 2005; Plomin & McGuffin, 2003).

If genetics alone were responsible for schizophrenia, the chance of both of two identical twins having schizophrenia would be 100% instead of just under 50%, because identical twins begin life with the same genetic makeup. Moreover, attempts to find a link between schizophrenia and a particular gene have been only partly successful. Apparently, genetic factors alone do not produce schizophrenia (Franzek & Beckmann, 1996; Lenzenweger & Dworkin, 1998).

Other theories look toward environmental influences, such as the emotional and communication patterns of the families of people with schizophrenia. For instance, some researchers suggest that schizophrenia results from high levels of expressed emotion (McCleary & Sanford, 2002). *Expressed emotion* is an interaction style characterized by criticism, hostility, and emotional intrusiveness by family members. Other researchers suggest that faulty communication patterns lie at the heart of schizophrenia (Lobban, Barrowclough, & Jones, 2006; Miklowitz & Tompson, 2003). An important point to remember is that the models used today associate schizophrenia with several kinds of biological and environmental factors. It is increasingly clear that no single factor, but a combination of interrelated variables, produces schizophrenia (McDonald & Murray, 2004; Meltzer, 2000; Opler et al., 2008).

PERSONALITY DISORDERS

I had always wanted lots of things; as a child I can remember wanting a bullet that a friend of mine had brought in to show the class. I took it and put it into my school bag and when my friend noticed it was missing, I was the one who stayed after school with him and searched the room, and I was the one who sat with him and bitched about the other kids and how one of them took his bullet. I even went home with him to help him break the news to his uncle, who had brought it home from the war for him. (Duke & Nowicki, 1979, pp. 309–310)

STUDY **TIP**

In Type I schizophrenia, positive symptoms such as hallucinations, delusions, and emotional extremes are dominant; in Type II schizophrenia, negative symptoms, characterized by an absence or a loss of normal functioning, are dominant.

This excerpt provides a graphic first-person account of a person with a personality disorder. *DSM-IV-TR* characterizes a **personality disorder** by a set of inflexible, maladaptive behavior patterns that keep a person from functioning appropriately in society. Personality disorders differ from the other problems we have discussed, because people affected by them often have little sense of personal distress associated with the psychological maladjustment. In fact, people with personality disorders frequently lead seemingly normal lives. However, just below the surface lies a set of rigid, unhealthy personality traits that do not permit these individuals to function as productive members of society (Clarkin & Lenzenweger, 2004; Friedman, Oltmanns, & Turkheimer, 2007; Millon & Davis, 1996, 1999).

The most widely publicized type of personality disorder, illustrated by the case above, is classified in *DSM-IV-TR* as **antisocial personality disorder** (sometimes referred to as a sociopathic personality). Individuals with this disturbance show no regard for the moral and ethical rules of society or the rights of others. They may seem at first to be quite intelligent, charming, and highly persuasive. On closer examination, however, they often turn out to be manipulative and deceptive. In fact, some of the best con artists have antisocial personalities.

People with this disorder may also be impulsive and lack the ability to withstand frustration. Moreover, they lack any guilt or anxiety about their wrongdoing. When those with antisocial personality disorder behave in a way that injures someone else, they understand intellectually that they have caused harm but feel no remorse (Goodwin & Hamilton, 2003; Hilarski, 2007; Lykken, 1995).

personality disorder A disorder characterized by a set of inflexible, maladaptive behavior patterns that keep a person from functioning appropriately in society.

antisocial personality disorder A disorder in which individuals show no regard for the moral and ethical rules of society or the rights of others.

borderline personality disorder A disorder in which individuals have difficulty developing a secure sense of who they are.

It is estimated that about 1 in every 200 people has antisocial personality disorder (NIMH, 2007). What causes this constellation of problem behaviors? A variety of factors have been suggested, ranging from an inability to experience emotions appropriately to problems in family relationships. For example, in many cases of antisocial behavior, the individual has come from a home in which a parent has died or left, or one in which there is a lack of affection, a lack of consistency in discipline, or outright rejection. Other explanations concentrate on sociocultural factors, because an unusually high proportion of people with antisocial personalities comes from lower socioeconomic groups (Millon et al., 1996). Still, no one has been able to pinpoint the specific causes of antisocial personalities, and it is likely that some combination of factors is responsible (Costa & Widiger, 2002; Nigg & Goldsmith, 1994; Rosenstein & Horowitz, 1996).

From the perspective of ...

A PSYCHOLOGIST Personality disorders are often not apparent to others, and many people with these problems seem to live basically normal lives. Because these people often appear from the outside to function well in society, why should they be considered psychologically disordered?

People diagnosed with **borderline personality disorder** have difficulty developing a secure sense of who they are. As a consequence, they tend to rely on relationships with others to define their identity. The problem with this strategy is that rejections are devastating. Furthermore, people with this disorder distrust others and have difficulty controlling their anger. Their emotional volatility leads to impulsive and self-destructive behavior, including self-mutilation. Individuals with borderline personality disorder often feel empty and alone and they have difficulty cooperating with others. They may form intense, sudden, one-sided relationships, demanding the attention of another person and then feeling angry when they don't receive it. Some cognitive theorists suggest that this disorder may be linked to environments where others have discounted or criticized their emotional reactions, and they may not have learned to regulate their emotions effectively (Hopwood et al., 2009; King-Casas et al., 2008; Links, Eynan, & Heisel, 2007).

Another example of a personality disturbance is the **narcissistic personality disorder**, which is characterized by an exaggerated sense of self-importance. Those with the disorder expect special treatment from others, while at the same time disregarding others' feelings. In some ways, in fact, the main attribute of the narcissistic personality is an inability to experience empathy for other people.

The *DSM-IV-TR* includes several other categories of personality disorder, ranging in severity from individuals who may simply be regarded by others as eccentric, obnoxious, or difficult to people who act in a manner that is criminal and dangerous to others. Although they are not out of touch with reality in the way that people with schizophrenia are, many people with personality disorders lead lives that put them on the fringes of society (Millon, Davis, & Millon, 2000; Trull & Widiger, 2003).

OTHER DISORDERS

Keep in mind that the various forms of psychological disorders described in *DSM-IV-TR* cover much more ground than we have been able to discuss in this chapter. Some relate to topics previously considered in other chapters. For example, *psychoactive substance-use disorder* relates to problems that arise from the use and abuse of drugs. Furthermore, *alcohol use disorders* are among the most serious and widespread problems (Chanon & Boettiger, 2009; Stimson et al., 2007). Both psychoactive substance-use disorder and alcohol use disorder co-occur with many other psychological disorders, such as mood disorders, posttraumatic stress disorder, and schizophrenia, complicating treatment considerably (Salgado, Quinlan, & Zlotnick, 2007).

Other disorders are specific to childhood. One of these is *attention-deficit hyperactivity disorder (ADHD)*, a disorder marked by inattention, impulsiveness, a low tolerance for frustration, and generally a great deal of inappropriate activity. Another is autism, a severe developmental disability that impairs children's ability to communicate and relate to others. Autism usually appears in the first three years and typically continues throughout life. About 1 in 110 children are now thought to have the disorder, and its prevalence has risen significantly in the last decade. Whether the increase is the result of an actual rise in the incidence of autism or is due to better reporting is a question of intense debate among researchers (Barkley, 2005; Rice, 2009; Smith, Barkley, & Shapiro, 2006; Swanson, Harris, & Graham, 2003).

Another widespread problem is *eating disorders*. They include such disorders as *anorexia nervosa* and *bulimia*, which we considered in the chapter on motivation and emotion (chapter 8), as well as *binge-eating disorder*, characterized by binge eating without behaviors designed to

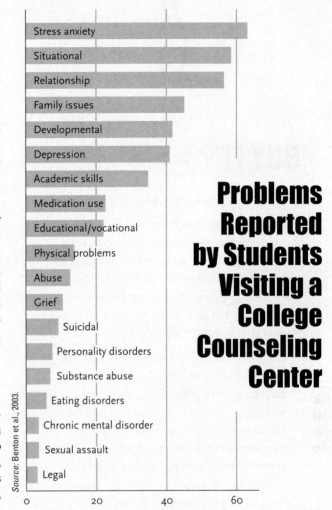

Problems Reported by Students Visiting a College Counseling Center

Source: Benton et al., 2003.

Percentage of students reporting problem

prevent weight gain. Finally, *sexual disorders*, in which one's sexual activity is unsatisfactory, are another important class of problems. They include *sexual desire disorders, sexual arousal disorders,* and *paraphilias,* atypical sexual activities that may include nonconsenting partners.

narcissistic personality disorder A personality disturbance characterized by an exaggerated sense of self-importance.

Organic mental disorders are problems that have a purely biological basis, such as Alzheimer's disease and some types of mental retardation. There are other disorders that we have not mentioned at all, and each of the classes we have discussed can be divided into several subcategories (Kopelman & Fleminger, 2002; Pratt et al., 2003; Reijonen et al., 2003).

PSYCHOLOGICAL DISORDERS IN PERSPECTIVE

How common are the kinds of psychological disorders we've been discussing? Here's one answer: About half of the people you meet in the United States are likely to suffer, at some point during their life, from a psychological disorder.

BUY IT? > > >

Deciding When You Need Help

How do you know when you or someone you know needs the help of a mental health professional? The following list of symptoms offers a rough set of guidelines for determining when the normal problems of everyday living have escalated beyond your ability to deal with them by yourself (Engler & Goleman, 1992):

- Long-term feelings of distress that interfere with your sense of well-being, competence, and ability to function effectively in daily activities
- Occasions in which you experience overwhelmingly high stress, accompanied by feelings of inability to cope with the situation
- Prolonged depression or feelings of hopelessness, especially when they do not have any clear cause (such as the death of someone close)
- Withdrawal from other people
- Thoughts of inflicting harm on oneself or suicide
- A fear or phobia that prevents you from engaging in everyday activities
- Inability to interact effectively with others, preventing the development of friendships and loving relationships

If you decide to seek therapy, you're faced with a daunting task. Choosing a therapist is not a simple matter. One place to begin the process of identifying a therapist is at the "Help Center" of the American Psychological Association at http://locator.apa.org or 1-800-964-2000. And, if you start therapy, you and your therapist should agree on clear, specific, and attainable goals for treatment.

About half of the people you meet in the United States are likely to suffer, at some point during their life, from a psychological disorder.

That's the conclusion drawn from a massive study on the prevalence of psychological disorders (Kessler, Berglund, & Demler, 2005). In that study, researchers conducted face-to-face interviews with more than 8,000 men and women between the ages of 15 and 54 years. The sample was designed to be representative of the population of the United States. According to results of the study, 48% of those interviewed had experienced a disorder at some point in their lives. In addition, 30% experienced a disorder in any particular year, and the number of people who experienced simultaneous multiple disorders (known as *comorbidity*) was significant (Kessler & Wang, 2008; Merikangas et al., 2007; Welkowitz et al., 2000).

The most common disorder reported in the study was depression, with 17% of those surveyed reporting at least one major episode. Ten percent had suffered from depression during the current year. The next most common disorder was alcohol dependence, which occurred at a lifetime incidence rate of 14%. In addition, 7% of those interviewed had experienced alcohol dependence in the last year. Other frequently occurring psychological disorders were drug dependence, disorders involving panic (such as an overwhelming fear of talking to strangers and terror of heights), and posttraumatic stress disorder.

Although some researchers think that the estimates of severe disorders may be too high (Narrow et al., 2002), the national findings are consistent with studies of college students and their psychological difficulties. For example, in one study of the problems of students who visited a college counseling center, more than 40% of students reported being depressed. These figures include only students who sought help from the counseling center, not those who did not seek treatment. Consequently, the figures are not representative of the entire college population (Benton et al., 2003).

The prevalence of psychological disorders is a problem not only in the United States; according to the World Health Organization, mental health difficulties are also a global concern. Throughout the world, psychological disorders are widespread. Furthermore, there are economic disparities in treatment, such that more affluent people with mild disorders receive more and better treatment than do poor people who have more severe disorders. In fact, psychological disorders make up 14% of global illness, and 90% of people in developing countries receive no care at all for their disorders (Jacoby et al., 2007; The WHO World Mental Health Survey Consortium, 2004; Wang et al., 2007).

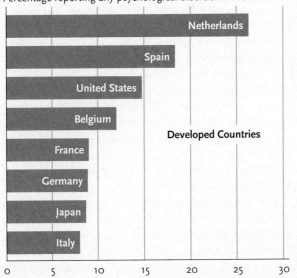

Percentage reporting any psychological disorder in the last 12 months

Netherlands
Spain
United States
Belgium
France
Germany
Japan
Italy

Developed Countries

0   5   10   15   20   25   30

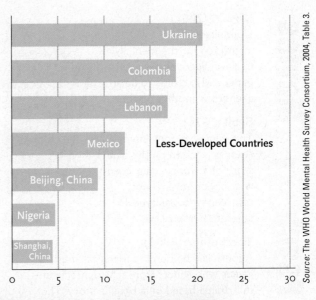

Ukraine
Colombia
Lebanon
Mexico
Beijing, China
Nigeria
Shanghai, China

Less-Developed Countries

0   5   10   15   20   25   30

Source: The WHO World Mental Health Survey Consortium, 2004, Table 3.

Prevalence of Psychological Disorders Worldwide

Also, keep in mind that the incidence of specific disorders varies significantly in other cultures. For instance, cross-cultural surveys show that the incidence of major depression varies significantly from one culture to another. The probability of having at least one episode of depression is only 1.5% in Taiwan and 2.9% in Korea, compared with 11.6% in New Zealand and 16.4% in France. Such notable differences underscore the importance of considering the cultural context of psychological disorders (Horwath & Weissman, 2000; Tseng, 2003; Weissman et al., 1997).

THE SOCIAL AND CULTURAL CONTEXT OF PSYCHOLOGICAL DISORDERS

In considering the nature of the psychological disorders described in *DSM-IV-TR*, keep in mind that the specific disorders reflect turn-of-the-21st-century Western cultures. The classification system provides a snapshot of how its authors viewed mental disorder when it was published. In fact, the development of the most recent version

PSYCH think

> > > Are there problem behaviors in today's society that might end up listed as disorders in the *DSM* of tomorrow? What are they and why might they be listed?

From the perspective of ...

A COLLEGE COUNSELOR What kinds of educational materials about psychological disorders would you make available to college students? What guidelines would you use in choosing materials that are sensitive to cultural differences?

of *DSM* was a source of great debate, in part reflecting issues that divide society.

For example, two disorders caused particular controversy during the revision process. One, known as *self-defeating personality disorder*, was ultimately removed from the appendix, where it had appeared in the previous revision. The term *self-defeating personality disorder* had been applied to cases in which people who were treated unpleasantly or demeaningly in relationships neither left nor took other action. It was typically used to describe people who remained in abusive relationships.

Although some clinicians argued that it was a valid category, one that they observed in clinical practice, the disorder seemed to lack enough research evidence to support its designation as a disorder in *DSM*. Furthermore, some critics complained that use of the label had the effect of condemning targets of abuse for their plight—a blame-the-victim phenomenon—and as a result, the category was removed from the manual.

A second and even more controversial category was "premenstrual dysphoric disorder." That disorder is characterized by severe, incapacitating mood changes or depression related to a woman's menstrual cycle. Some critics argued that the classification simply labels normal

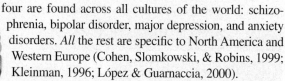
female behavior as a disorder. Former U.S. Surgeon General Antonia Novello suggested that what "in women is called PMS [premenstrual syndrome, a similar classification] in men is called healthy aggression and initiative" (Cotton, 1993, p. 270). Advocates for including the disorder prevailed, however, and "premenstrual dysphoric disorder" appears in the appendix of *DSM-IV-TR* (Hartung & Widiger, 1998; Pearlstein & Steiner, 2008).

Such controversies underline the fact that our understanding of abnormal behavior reflects the society and culture in which we live. Future revisions of *DSM* may include a different catalog of disorders. Even now, other cultures might include a list of disorders that look very different from the list that appears in the current *DSM*, as we discuss next. If we use the *DSM* to guide our judgments, then a person who hears voices of the recently deceased will probably be considered to be a victim of a psychological disturbance. Yet some Plains Indians routinely hear the voices of the dead calling to them from the afterlife, and this is considered normal in their culture.

This is only one example of the role of culture in labeling behavior as "abnormal." In fact, among all the major adult disorders included in the *DSM* categorization, just four are found across all cultures of the world: schizophrenia, bipolar disorder, major depression, and anxiety disorders. *All* the rest are specific to North America and Western Europe (Cohen, Slomkowski, & Robins, 1999; Kleinman, 1996; López & Guarnaccia, 2000).

Furthermore, even though disorders such as schizophrenia are found throughout the world, cultural factors influence the specific symptoms of the disorder. Hence, catatonic schizophrenia, in which an individual appears to be frozen in the same position, sometimes for days, is rare in North America and Western Europe. In contrast, in India, 80% of people with schizophrenia are catatonic.

Other cultures have disorders that do not appear in the West. For example, in Malaysia, a behavior called *amok* is characterized by a wild outburst in which a person, usually quiet and withdrawn, kills or severely injures another. *Koro* is a condition found in Southeast Asian males who develop an intense panic that the penis is about to withdraw into the abdomen. (Cohen, Slomkowski, & Robins, 1999; López & Guarnaccia, 2000).

In sum, we should not assume that the *DSM* provides the final word on psychological disorders. The disorders it includes are very much a creation and function of Western cultures at a particular moment in time, and its categories should not be seen as universally applicable (Tseng, 2003).

>> Treatment of Psychological Disorders

Next thing I know I am waking up. I am back on an upper floor of Massachusetts General Hospital, in the unit where I slept last night. I feel light-headed, groggy, the way you do when anesthesia is wearing off and you are floating in the abyss between sleep and wakefulness. I vaguely recall the anesthesiologist having had me count to ten, but I never got beyond three or four. I remember Charlie Welch and his ECT [electroconvulsive therapy] team, but am not sure I got the treatment. One clue is a slight headache, which they told me ECT might cause but which could have come from the anesthesia. Another is the goo on my hair, where they must have attached the electrodes.

There is one more sign that I did in fact have my first session of seizure therapy: I feel good—I feel alive. (From Dukakis, K., & Tye, L. (2006). Shock: The Healing Power of Electroconvulsive Therapy. New York: Avery, p. 119.)

The procedure that has brought new life to the former first lady of Massachusetts Kitty Dukakis is just one of many approaches to the treatment of psychological disorders. All the different approaches, ranging from one-meeting informal counseling sessions to long-term drug therapy to more invasive procedures such as ECT, have a

Gabriel Byrne (*right*) plays a psychotherapist in the HBO drama *In Treatment*. *In Treatment*'s writers used their experiences in therapy as source material for the show.

common objective: the relief of psychological disorders and the ultimate aim of enabling individuals to achieve richer, more meaningful, and more fulfilling lives within the context of their culture.

Many approaches to treating psychological disorders focus on treating the individual person; others focus on treating the social system (especially family) in which dysfunctional issues have arisen. Despite their diversity, those therapies that focus on individuals tend to fall into two main categories: psychologically based and biologically based therapies. Psychologically based therapy, or **psychotherapy**, is treatment in which a trained professional—a therapist—uses psychological techniques to help someone overcome psychological difficulties and disorders, resolve problems in living, or bring about personal growth. In psychotherapy, the goal is to produce psychological change in a person (called a "client" or "patient") through discussions and interactions with the therapist. In contrast, **biomedical therapy** relies on drugs and medical procedures to improve psychological functioning.

As we describe the various approaches to therapy, keep in mind that although the distinctions may seem clear-cut, the classifications and procedures overlap a good deal. In fact, many therapists today use a variety of methods with an individual patient, taking an *eclectic approach to therapy*. Assuming that both psychological and biological processes often produce psychological disorders, eclectic therapists may draw from several perspectives simultaneously to

STUDY TIP

To better understand psychodynamic therapy, review Freud's psychoanalytic theory, discussed in the chapter on personality.

address both the psychological and the biological aspects of a person's problems (Berman, Jobes, & Silverman, 2006; Goin, 2005).

PSYCHOTHERAPIES

Therapists use some 400 different varieties of psychotherapy, approaches to therapy that focus on psychological factors. Although diverse in many respects, all psychological approaches see treatment as a way of solving psychological problems by modifying individuals' behavior and helping them gain a better understanding of themselves and their past, present, and future.

Most psychotherapists employ one of four major approaches to therapy (Sampson, McCubbin & Tyrer, 2006): psychodynamic, behavioral, cognitive, and humanistic treatments. These approaches are based on the models of personality and psychological disorders developed by psychologists. Here we'll consider the psychodynamic, behavioral, cognitive, and humanistic approaches, as well as interpersonal psychotherapy and group therapy, and the effectiveness of psychotherapy.

Psychodynamic Approaches to Therapy Psy-**chodynamic therapy** seeks to bring unresolved past conflicts and unacceptable impulses from the unconscious into the conscious, where clients may deal with the problems more effectively. Psychodynamic approaches are based on Freud's psychoanalytic approach to personality, which holds that individuals employ *defense mechanisms*, psychological strategies to protect themselves from unacceptable unconscious impulses (Gabbard, 2009; Huprich, 2009; Kudler et al., 2009).

The most common defense mechanism is repression, which pushes threatening conflicts and impulses back into the unconscious. However, since unacceptable conflicts and impulses can never be completely buried, some of the anxiety associated with them can produce abnormal behavior in the form of what Freud called *neurotic symptoms* (Huprich, 2009).

How do we rid ourselves of the anxiety produced by unconscious, unwanted impulses and drives? To Freud, the answer was to confront the conflicts and impulses by bringing them out of the unconscious part of the mind and into the conscious part. Freud assumed that this technique would reduce anxiety stemming from past conflicts and that the client could then participate in his or her daily life more effectively.

psychotherapy Treatment in which a trained professional—a therapist—uses psychological techniques to help a person overcome psychological difficulties and disorders, resolve problems in living, or bring about personal growth.

biomedical therapy Therapy that relies on drugs and other medical procedures to improve psychological functioning.

psychodynamic therapy Therapy that seeks to bring unresolved past conflicts and unacceptable impulses from the unconscious into the conscious, where clients may deal with the problems more effectively.

A psychodynamic therapist, then, faces the challenge of finding a way to assist an individual's attempts to explore and understand the unconscious. The technique that has evolved has a number of components, but basically it consists of guiding clients to consider and discuss their past experiences, in explicit detail, from the time of their first memories. This process assumes that clients will eventually stumble on long-hidden crises, traumas, and conflicts that are producing anxiety in their adult lives. It's the therapist's role to recognize these issues and help the client to "work through"—understand and rectify—those difficulties (Gabbard, 2009; Huprich, 2009).

Psychoanalysis: Freud's Therapy

Classic Freudian psychodynamic therapy, called *psychoanalysis*, tends to be a lengthy and expensive affair. **Psychoanalysis** is Freudian psychotherapy in which the goal is to release hidden unconscious thoughts and feelings in order to reduce their power in controlling behavior.

In psychoanalysis, clients may meet with a therapist frequently, sometimes for as much as 50 minutes a day, 4 to 6 days a week, for several years. In their sessions, they often use a technique developed by Freud called *free association*. Psychoanalysts using this technique tell clients to say aloud whatever comes to mind, regardless of its apparent irrelevance or senselessness, and the analysts attempt to recognize and label the connections between what a client says and the client's unconscious. Therapists also use *dream interpretation*, examining dreams to find clues to unconscious conflicts and problems. Moving beyond the surface description of a dream (called the *manifest content*), therapists seek its underlying meaning (the *latent content*), thereby revealing the true unconscious meaning of the dream (Auld, Hyman, & Rudzinski, 2005; Bodin, 2006; Cabaniss et al., 2011; Galatzer-Levy & Cohler, 1997).

Because of the close interaction between client and psychoanalyst, the relationship between the two often becomes emotionally charged and takes on a complexity unlike most other relationships. Clients may come to think of the analyst as a symbol of a significant other in their past, perhaps a parent or a lover, and apply some of their feelings for that person to the analyst—a phenomenon known as transference. Specifically, **transference** is the unconscious transfer to a psychoanalyst of feelings of love or anger that had been originally directed at parent or other authority figures (Evans, 2007; Steiner, 2008; Van Beekum, 2005).

Contemporary Psychodynamic Approaches

Few people have the time, money, or patience to participate in years of traditional psychoanalysis. Moreover, no conclusive evidence shows that psychoanalysis, as originally conceived by Freud in the 19th century, works better than other, more recent forms of psychodynamic therapy (de Maat et al., 2009; Huprich, 2009).

Today, psychodynamic therapy tends to be of shorter duration, usually lasting no longer than 3 months or 20 sessions. The therapist takes a more active role than Freud would have liked, controlling the course of therapy and prodding and advising the client with considerable directness. Finally, the therapist puts less emphasis on a client's past history and childhood, concentrating instead on an individual's current relationships and specific complaints (Charman, 2004; Goode, E., 2003b; Wolitzky, 2006).

Evaluating Psychodynamic Therapy

Even with its current modifications, psychodynamic therapy has its critics. In its longer versions, it can be time-consuming and expensive, especially in comparison with other forms of psychotherapy, such as behavioral and cognitive approaches. Furthermore, less articulate clients may not do as well as more verbal ones do (de Maat et al., 2009; Huprich, 2009).

Ultimately, the most important concern about psychodynamic treatment is whether it actually works, and there is no simple answer to this question. Psychodynamic treatment techniques have been controversial since Freud introduced them. Part of the problem is the difficulty in establishing whether clients have improved after psychodynamic therapy. Determining effectiveness depends on reports from the therapist or the clients themselves, reports that are obviously open to bias and subjective interpretation (de Maat et al., 2009; Huprich, 2009).

Furthermore, critics have questioned the entire theoretical basis of psychodynamic theory, maintaining that constructs such as the unconscious have not been scientifically confirmed. Despite the criticism, for some people, the psychodynamic treatment approach provides solutions to difficult psychological issues and effective treatment for psychological disturbance. It also permits the potential development of an unusual degree of insight into one's life (Ablon & Jones, 2005; Anestis, Anestis, & Lilienfeld, 2011; Bond, 2006; Clay, 2000).

"And when did you first realize you weren't like other precipitation?"

© Michael Maslin/The New Yorker Collection/www.cartoonbank.com.

BEHAVIORAL APPROACHES TO THERAPY

Perhaps, when you were a child, your parents rewarded you with an ice cream cone when you were especially good . . . or sent you to your room if you misbehaved. Sound principles back up such a child-rearing strategy: Good behavior is maintained by reinforcement, and unwanted behavior can be eliminated by punishment, concepts that are explained in chapter 5.

Behavioral approaches to treatment would seek to modify the behavior of this couple, rather than focusing on the underlying causes of behavior.

These principles represent the underpinnings of **behavioral treatment approaches**. Building on the basic processes of learning, behavioral treatment approaches make this fundamental assumption: Both abnormal behavior and normal behavior are *learned*. People who act abnormally either have failed to learn the skills they need to cope with the problems of everyday living or have acquired faulty skills and patterns that are being maintained through some form of reinforcement. To modify abnormal behavior, then, proponents of behavioral approaches propose that people must learn new behavior to replace the faulty skills they have developed and unlearn their maladaptive behavior patterns (Krijn et al., 2004; Norton & Price, 2007).

Behavioral psychologists do not need to delve into people's pasts or their psyches. Rather than viewing abnormal behavior as a symptom of an underlying problem, they consider the abnormal behavior as the problem in need of modification. The goal of therapy is to change people's behavior to allow them to function more effectively. In this view, then, there is no problem other than the maladaptive behavior itself, and if one can change that behavior, treatment is successful.

Classical Conditioning Treatments Suppose you bite into your favorite candy bar and find that not only is it infested with ants but that you've also swallowed a bunch of them. You immediately become sick to your stomach and throw up. Your long-term reaction? You never eat that kind of candy bar again, and it may be months before you eat any type of candy. You have learned, through the basic process of classical conditioning, to avoid candy so that you will not get sick and throw up.

This simple example illustrates how a person can be classically conditioned to modify behavior. Behavior therapists use this principle when they employ **aversive conditioning**, a form of therapy that reduces the frequency of undesired behavior by pairing an aversive, unpleasant stimulus with undesired behavior. For example, behavior therapists might use aversive conditioning by pairing alcohol with a drug that causes severe nausea and vomiting. After the two have been paired a few times, the person associates the alcohol alone with vomiting and finds alcohol less appealing.

Although aversion therapy works reasonably well in inhibiting substance-abuse problems such as alcoholism and certain kinds of sexual disorder, critics question its long-term effectiveness (Mann, 2004; McLellan & Childress, 1985). Also, important ethical concerns surround aversion techniques that employ such potent stimuli as electric shock, which therapists use only in the most extreme cases, such as client self-mutilation (Kishore, R. and Dutt, K., 1986). Nonetheless, aversion therapy offers an important procedure for eliminating maladaptive responses for some period of time—a respite that provides, even if only temporarily, an opportunity to encourage more adaptive behavior patterns (Bordnick et al., 2004; Delgado, Labouliere, & Phelps, 2006).

Another treatment to grow out of classical conditioning is systematic desensitization. In **systematic desensitization**, gradual exposure to an anxiety-producing stimulus is paired with relaxation to extinguish the response of anxiety (Choy, Fyer, & Lipsitz, 2007; Dowling, Jackson, & Thomas, 2008; Pagoto, Kozak, & Spates, 2006).

Suppose, for instance, you were extremely afraid of flying. The very thought of being in an airplane would make you begin to sweat and shake, and you couldn't get yourself near enough to an airport to know how you'd react if you actually had to fly somewhere. Using systematic desensitization to treat your problem, you would first be trained in relaxation techniques by a behavior therapist, learning to relax your body fully.

The next step would involve constructing a *hierarchy of fears*—a list, in order of increasing severity, of the things you associate with your fears. For instance, your hierarchy might resemble this one:

1. Watching a plane fly overhead.
2. Going to an airport.
3. Buying a ticket.
4. Stepping into the plane.
5. Seeing the plane door close.
6. Having the plane taxi down the runway.
7. Taking off.
8. Being in the air.

> **behavioral treatment approaches** Treatment approaches that build on the basic processes of learning, such as reinforcement and extinction, and assume that normal and abnormal behavior are both learned.
>
> **aversive conditioning** A form of therapy that reduces the frequency of undesired behavior by pairing an aversive, unpleasant stimulus with undesired behavior.
>
> **systematic desensitization** A behavioral technique in which gradual exposure to an anxiety-producing stimulus is paired with relaxation to extinguish the response of anxiety.

How to Achieve the Relaxation Response

Step 1 Pick a focus word or short phrase that's firmly rooted in your personal belief system. For example, a nonreligious individual might choose a neutral word like *one* or *peace* or *love*. A Christian person desiring to use a prayer could pick the opening words of Psalm 23, *The Lord is my shepherd*; a Jewish person could choose *Shalom*.

Step 2 Sit quietly in a comfortable position.

Step 3 Close your eyes.

Step 4 Relax your muscles.

Step 5 Breathe slowly and naturally, repeating your focus word or phrase silently as you exhale.

Step 6 Throughout, assume a passive attitude. Don't worry about how well you're doing. When other thoughts come to mind, simply say to yourself, "Oh, well," and gently return to the repetition.

Step 7 Continue for 10 to 20 minutes. You may open your eyes to check the time, but do not use an alarm. When you finish, sit quietly for a minute or so, at first with your eyes closed and later with your eyes open. Then do not stand for one or two minutes.

Step 8 Practice the technique once or twice a day.

From *Meditation* by Herbert Benson, M.D., Benson-Henry Institute for Mind Body Medicine. Reprinted with permission from Dr. Herbert Benson.

Once you had developed this hierarchy and had learned relaxation techniques, you would learn to associate the two sets of responses. To do this, your therapist might ask you to put yourself into a relaxed state and then imagine yourself in the first situation identified in your hierarchy. Once you could consider that first step while remaining completely relaxed, you would move on to the next situation, eventually moving up the hierarchy in gradual stages until you could imagine yourself being in the air without experiencing anxiety. Then you would be asked to make a visit to an airport and ultimately would take a flight.

Although systematic desensitization has proven to be a successful treatment, today it is often replaced with a less complicated form of therapy called exposure. **Exposure** is a behavioral treatment for anxiety in which people are confronted, either suddenly or gradually, with a stimulus that they fear. However, unlike systematic desensitization, relaxation training is omitted. Exposure allows the maladaptive response of anxiety or avoidance to extinguish, and research shows that this approach is generally as effective as systematic desensitization (Bush, 2008; Havermans et al., 2007; Hoffmann, S. G., 2007).

In most cases, therapists use *graded exposure* (exposing the patient to a hierarchy of fears) in which clients are exposed to a feared stimulus in gradual steps. For example, an individual who is afraid of dogs might first view a video of dogs. Gradually, as the client becomes comfortable with images of dogs, the exposure escalates to seeing a live, leashed dog across the room, and then actually petting and touching the dog (Berle, 2007; Means & Edinger, 2007).

exposure A behavioral treatment for anxiety in which people are confronted, either suddenly or gradually, with a stimulus that they fear.

From the perspective of . . .

A GRANDPARENT Your grandchild has developed a phobia of butterflies. How could you use systematic desensitization to help her overcome this irrational fear?

PSYCH think

connect
WWW.MCGRAWHILLCONNECT.COM/PSYCHOLOGY
Systematic Desensitization

> > > Phobias such as fear of flying and fear of spiders are comparatively common. Behavior therapies have been shown to be very effective in eliminating phobias, but many people seem to prefer to simply avoid the object of their phobia rather than be treated. Why do you think we keep our phobias when we don't have to?

Take the PsychSmart challenge! Help Albert get over his phobia of rats with systematic desensitization. From chapter 12 in your ebook, select the *Exercises* tab. Next, select "Systematic Desensitization." Then answer Pop Quiz question 11 on p. 333 to check your knowledge of this technique.

A "Fearless Peer" who models appropriate and effective behavior can help children overcome their fears.

Exposure has proved to be an effective treatment for a number of problems, including phobias, anxiety disorders, and even impotence and fear of sexual contact. Through this technique, people can learn to enjoy the things they once feared (Choy, Fyer, & Lipsitz, 2007; Franklin, March, & Garcia, 2007; Powers & Emmelkamp, 2008).

Operant Conditioning Techniques Some behavioral approaches make use of the operant conditioning principles that we discussed earlier in the book (learning; chapter 5). These approaches are based on the concept that rewarding people for carrying out desirable behavior increases the likelihood that they will repeat the behavior and that punishing or ignoring undesirable behavior eventually extinguishes it.

One example of the systematic application of operant conditioning principles is the *token system*, which rewards a person for desired behavior with a token, such as a poker chip or some kind of play money. Although it is most frequently employed in institutional settings for individuals with relatively serious problems, and sometimes with children as a classroom management technique, the system resembles what parents do when they give children money for being well behaved—money that the children can later exchange for something they want. The desired behavior may range from simple things, such as keeping one's room neat, to personal grooming and interacting with other people. In institutions, patients can exchange tokens for some object or activity, such as snacks, new clothes, or, in extreme cases, being able to sleep in one's own bed rather than in a sleeping bag on the floor (Kadzin, 1988; McKinley et al., 1988).

Contingency contracting, a variant of the token system, has proved quite effective in producing behavior modification (D'Eramo & Francis, 2004; Francis, 1995). In *contingency contracting*, the therapist and the client (or teacher and student, or parent and child) draw up a written agreement. The contract states a series of behavioral goals the client hopes to achieve. It also specifies the positive consequences for the client if the client reaches goals—usually an explicit reward such as money or additional privileges. Contracts frequently state negative consequences if the client

does not meet the goals. For example, clients who are trying to quit smoking might write out a check to a cause they have no interest in supporting (for instance, the National Rifle Association if they are strong supporters of gun control). If the client smokes on a given day, the therapist will mail the check.

Behavior therapists also use *observational learning*, the process in which the behavior of other people is modeled, to systematically teach people new skills and ways of handling their fears and anxieties. For example, modeling helps when therapists are teaching basic social skills such as maintaining eye contact during conversation and acting assertively. Similarly, children with dog phobias have been able to overcome their fears by watching another child—called the "Fearless Peer"—repeatedly walk up to a dog, touch it, pet it, and finally play with it. Modeling, then, can play an effective role in resolving some kinds of behavior difficulties, especially if the model receives a reward for his or her behavior (Bandura, Grusec, & Menlove, 1967; Egliston & Rapee, 2007; Goubert et al., 2011; Greer, Dudek-Singer, Gautreaux, 2006).

Evaluating Behavior Therapy Behavior therapy works especially well for eliminating anxiety disorders, treating phobias and compulsions, establishing control over impulses, and learning complex social skills to replace maladaptive behavior. More than any of the other therapeutic techniques, it provides methods that nonprofessionals can use to change their own behavior. Moreover, it is efficient, because it focuses on solving carefully defined problems (Barlow, 2007; Richard & Lauterbach, 2006).

Critics of behavior therapy believe that because this therapy emphasizes changing external behavior, people do not necessarily gain insight into thoughts and expectations that may be fostering their maladaptive behavior (Farmer & Chapman, 2008; Miltenberger, 2008). Yet neuroscientific evidence shows that behavioral treatments can produce actual changes in brain functioning, suggesting that behavioral treatments can produce changes beyond external behavior (Miltenberger, 2008).

COGNITIVE APPROACHES TO THERAPY

If you assumed that illogical thoughts and beliefs lie at the heart of psychological disorders, wouldn't the most direct treatment route be to teach people new, more adaptive modes of thinking? The answer is yes, according to psychologists who take a cognitive approach to treatment.

Cognitive treatment approaches teach people more adaptive ways of thinking by changing their dysfunctional cognitions about the world and themselves. Unlike behavior therapists, who focus on modifying external behavior, cognitive therapists attempt to change the way people think, as well as their behavior. Because

cognitive treatment approaches Treatment approaches that teach people to think in more adaptive ways by changing their dysfunctional cognitions about the world and themselves.

they often use basic principles of learning, their methods are sometimes referred to as the **cognitive-behavioral approach** (Beck & Rector, 2005; Butler et al., 2006; Friedberg, 2006).

Cognitive therapists teach clients more adaptive ways of thinking.

Although cognitive treatment approaches take many forms, they all share the assumption that anxiety, depression, and negative emotions develop from maladaptive thinking. Accordingly, cognitive treatments seek to change the thought patterns that lead to getting "stuck" in dysfunctional ways of thinking. Therapists systematically teach clients to challenge their assumptions and adopt new approaches to old problems (Freeman et al., 2004; Perkins, Conklin, & Levine, 2008).

Cognitive therapy is relatively short-term, usually lasting a maximum of 20 sessions. Therapy tends to be highly structured and focused on concrete problems. Therapists often begin by teaching the theory behind the approach and then continue to take an active role throughout the course of therapy, acting as teacher, coach, and partner (Freeman et al., 2004).

Another influential form of therapy that builds on a cognitive perspective is that of Aaron Beck (Beck, 1995, 2004). Beck's *cognitive therapy* aims to change people's illogical thoughts about themselves and the world. Playing the role of teacher, the cognitive therapist urges clients to obtain information on their own that will lead them to discard their inaccurate thinking through a process of cognitive appraisal. In *cognitive appraisal,* clients are asked to evaluate situations, themselves, and others in terms of their memories, values, beliefs, thoughts, and expectations. During the course of treatment, therapists help clients discover

cognitive-behavioral approach A treatment approach that incorporates basic principles of learning to change the way people think.

humanistic therapy Therapy in which the underlying rationale is that people have control of their behavior, can make choices about their lives, and are essentially responsible for solving their own problems.

ways of thinking more appropriately about themselves and others (Beck, Freeman, & Davis, 2004; Moorey, 2007; Rosen, 2000).

Evaluating Cognitive Approaches to Therapy

Cognitive approaches to therapy have proved successful in dealing with a broad range of disorders, including anxiety disorders, depression, substance abuse, and eating disorders. Furthermore, the willingness of cognitive therapists to incorporate additional treatment approaches (for example, combining cognitive and behavioral techniques in cognitive behavioral therapy) has made this approach a particularly effective form of treatment (Bhar et al., 2008; Ishikawa et al., 2007; Mitte, 2005).

At the same time, critics have pointed out that the focus on helping people to think more rationally ignores the fact that life is, in reality, sometimes irrational. Changing one's assumptions to make them more reasonable and logical thus may not always be helpful—even assuming that it is possible to bring about true cognitive change. Still, the success of cognitive approaches has made it one of the most frequently employed therapies (Beck, 2005; Leahy, 2003).

HUMANISTIC THERAPY

As you know from your own experience, a student cannot master the material covered in a course without some hard work, no matter how good the teacher and the textbook are. *You* must take the time to study, memorize the vocabulary, and learn the concepts. Nobody else can do it for you. If you choose to put in the effort, you'll succeed; if you don't, you'll fail. The responsibility is primarily yours.

Humanistic therapy draws on this philosophical perspective of self-responsibility in developing treatment techniques. The many different types of therapy that fit into this category have a similar rationale: We have control of our own behavior, we can make choices about the kinds of lives we want to live, and it is up to us to solve the difficulties we encounter in our daily lives.

Humanistic therapists believe that people naturally are motivated to strive for self-actualization. As we discussed in the chapter on motivation, *self-actualization* is the term that clinical psychologist Abraham Maslow used to describe the state of self-fulfillment in which people realize their highest potentials, each in their own unique way.

Instead of acting in the more directive manner of some psychodynamic and behavioral approaches, humanistic therapists view themselves as guides or facilitators. Therapists using humanistic techniques seek to help people to understand themselves and to find ways to come closer to the ideal they hold for themselves. In this view, psychological disorders result from the inability to find meaning in life and from feelings of loneliness and a lack of connection to others (Cain, 2002).

Humanistic approaches have produced many therapeutic techniques. Among the most important is person-centered therapy.

Person-Centered Therapy

Consider the following therapy session excerpt:

ALICE: I was thinking about this business of standards. I somehow developed a sort of a knack, I guess, of— well—habit—of trying to make people feel at ease around me, or to make things go along smoothly . . .

THERAPIST: In other words, what you did was always in the direction of trying to keep things smooth and to make other people feel better and to smooth the situation.

ALICE: Yes. I think that's what it was. Now the reason why I did it probably was—I mean, not that I was a good little Samaritan going around making other people happy, but that was probably the role that felt easiest for me to play . . .

THERAPIST: You feel that for a long time you've been playing the role of kind of smoothing out the frictions or differences or whatnot . . .

ALICE: M-hm.

THERAPIST: Rather than having any opinion or reaction of your own in the situation. Is that it? (Rogers, 1951, pp. 152–153)

The therapist does not interpret or answer the questions the client has raised. Instead, the therapist clarifies or reflects what the client has said (for example, "In other words, what you did . . ."; "You feel that . . ."; "Is that it?"). This therapeutic technique, known as *nondirective counseling*, is at the heart of person-centered therapy, which was first practiced by Carl Rogers in the mid-20th century (Raskin & Rogers, 1989; Rogers, 1951, 1980).

Person-centered therapy (also called *client-centered therapy*) aims to enable people to reach their potential for self-actualization. By providing a warm and accepting environment, therapists hope to motivate clients to air their problems and feelings. In turn, this enables clients to make realistic and constructive choices and decisions about the things that bother them in their current lives (Bohart, 2006; Bozarth, Zimring, & Tausch, 2002; Kirschenbaum, 2004).

Instead of directing the choices clients make, therapists provide what Rogers calls *unconditional positive regard*— expressing acceptance and understanding, regardless of the feelings and attitudes the client expresses. By providing this support, therapists hope to create an atmosphere that enables clients to come to decisions that can improve their lives (Kirschenbaum & Jourdan, 2005; Vieira & Freire, 2006).

Furnishing unconditional positive regard does not mean that therapists must approve of everything their clients say or do. But they do need to communicate that they are caring and *empathetic*—understanding of a client's emotional experiences (Fearing & Clark, 2000).

Person-centered therapy is rarely used today in its purest form. Contemporary approaches tend to be somewhat more directive, with therapists nudging clients toward insights rather than merely reflecting their statements. However, therapists still view clients' insights as central to the therapeutic process (Presbury, McKee, & Echterling, 2007; Raskin & Rogers, 1989; Tudor, 2008).

Evaluating Humanistic Therapies

The idea that psychological disorders result from restricted growth potential appeals philosophically to many people (Rice & Greenberg, 1992; Whitton, 2003). In the supportive atmosphere that humanistic therapists create, clients can discover solutions to difficult psychological problems.

However, humanistic treatments lack specificity, a problem that has troubled their critics. Humanistic approaches are not very precise and are probably the least scientifically and theoretically developed type of treatment. Moreover, this form of treatment works best for the same type of highly verbal client who profits most from psychoanalytic treatment.

INTERPERSONAL THERAPY

Interpersonal therapy (IPT) considers therapy in the context of social relationships. Although its roots stem from psychodynamic approaches, interpersonal therapy concentrates more on the here and now with the goal of improving a client's current relationships. It typically focuses on interpersonal issues such as conflicts with others, social skills issues, role transitions (such as divorce), and grief (Braaten, 2011; Weissman, Markowitz, & Klerman, 2007).

Interpersonal therapy is more active and directive than traditional psychodynamic approaches, and sessions are more structured. The approach makes no assumptions about the underlying causes of psychological disorders but focuses on the interpersonal context in which a disorder is developed and maintained. It also tends to be shorter than traditional psychodynamic approaches, typically lasting only 12 to 16 weeks. During those sessions, therapists make concrete suggestions on improving relations with others, offering recommendations and advice.

Because interpersonal therapy is short and structured, researchers have been able to demonstrate its effectiveness more readily than longer-term types of therapy. Evaluations of the approach have shown that interpersonal therapy is especially effective in dealing with depression,

person-centered therapy
Therapy in which the goal is to reach one's potential for self-actualization.

interpersonal therapy (IPT)
Short-term therapy that focuses on the context of current social relationships.

anxiety, addictions, and eating disorders (Grigoriadis & Ravitz, 2007; Miller et al., 2008; Salsman, 2006).

GROUP THERAPY AND FAMILY THERAPY

Although most treatment takes place between a single individual and a therapist, some forms of therapy involve groups of people seeking treatment. In **group therapy**, several unrelated people meet with a therapist to discuss some aspect of their psychological functioning.

People typically discuss with the group their problems, which often center on a common difficulty, such as alcoholism or a lack of social skills. The other members of the group provide emotional support and dispense advice on ways in which they have coped effectively with similar problems (Alonso, Alonso, & Piper, 2003; Rigby & Waite, 2007; Scaturo, 2004).

Groups vary greatly in terms of the particular model they employ; there are psychoanalytic groups, humanistic groups, and groups corresponding to the other therapeutic approaches. Furthermore, groups also differ in regard to the degree of guidance the therapist provides. In some, the therapist is quite directive, whereas in others, the members of the group set their own agenda and determine how the group will proceed (Beck & Lewis, 2000; Stockton, Morran, & Krieger, 2004).

group therapy Therapy in which people meet with a therapist to discuss problems with a group.

family therapy An approach that focuses on the family and its dynamics.

spontaneous remission Recovery without treatment.

Because in group therapy several people are treated simultaneously, it is a much more economical means of treatment than individual psychotherapy. However, critics argue that group settings lack the individual attention inherent in one-to-one therapy and that especially shy and withdrawn individuals may not receive the attention they need in a group setting (Olivares-Olivares, Rosa-Alcazar, & Olivares-Rodriguez, 2008; Takahashi & Washington, 1991).

Family Therapy One specialized form of group therapy is family therapy. As the name implies, **family therapy** involves two or more family members, one (or

: In group therapy, people with psychological problems
: meet with a therapist to talk about their problems.

more) of whose problems led to treatment. But rather than focusing simply on the members of the family who present the initial problem, family therapists consider the family as a unit, to which each member contributes. By meeting with the entire family simultaneously, family therapists try to understand how the family members interact with one another (Cooklin, 2000; Strong & Tomm, 2007).

Many family therapists believe that family members fall into rigid roles or set patterns of behavior, with one person acting as the scapegoat, another as a bully, and so forth. In their view, that system of roles perpetuates family disturbances. One goal of this type of therapy, then, is to get the family members to adopt new, more constructive roles and patterns of behavior (Minuchin, 1999; Sori, 2006; Sprenkle & Moon, 1996).

EVALUATING PSYCHOTHERAPY

Is therapy effective? This question requires a complex response. Identifying the most appropriate form of treatment is a controversial, and still unresolved, task for mental health professionals. Even before considering whether one form of therapy works better than another, we need to determine whether therapy in *any* form effectively alleviates psychological disturbances.

Until the 1950s, most people simply assumed that therapy was effective. But in 1952, psychologist Hans Eysenck published an influential study in which he concluded that people would go into **spontaneous remission**, recovery without treatment, if they were simply left alone. Eysenck's review stimulated a continuing stream of better controlled, more carefully crafted studies on the effectiveness of psychotherapy, and today most psychologists agree: Therapy works (Fraser & Solovey, 2007). Several comprehensive reviews indicate that therapy brings about greater improvement than does no treatment at all, with the rate of spontaneous remission being fairly low (for example, Carr, 2009; Corcoran & Pillai, 2009; de Maat et al., 2009; Moore et al., 2009; Venning et al., 2009). In most

"So, would anyone in the group care to respond to what Clifford has just shared with us?"

© Tom Cheney/The New Yorker Collection/
www.cartoonbank.com.

cases, then, the symptoms of abnormal behavior do not go away by themselves if left untreated—although the issue continues to be hotly debated (Lutz et al., 2006; Seligman, 1996; Westen, Novotny, & Thompson-Brenner, 2004).

Other research, using various techniques, also supports the notion that therapy helps. Some have used *meta analysis*, where data from a large number of studies are statistically combined. In another example, a massive survey of 186,000 individuals found that respondents felt they had benefited substantially from psychotherapy. However, there was little difference in "consumer satisfaction" on the basis of the specific type of treatment they had received (Cuijpers et al., 2008; Malouff, Thorsteinsson, & Schutte, 2007; Seligman, 1995).

In short, converging evidence allows us to draw several conclusions about the effectiveness of psychotherapy (Pachankis & Goldfried, 2007; Seligman, 1996; Strupp & Binder, 1992):

- *For most people, psychotherapy is effective.* This conclusion holds over different lengths of treatment, specific kinds of psychological disorders, and various types of treatment. Thus, the question "Does psychotherapy work?" appears to have been answered convincingly: It does (Payne & Marcus, 2008; Seligman, 1996; Spiegel, 1999; Westen, Novotny, & Thompson-Brenner, 2004).

- *However, psychotherapy doesn't work for everyone.* As many as 10% of people treated show no improvement or deteriorate (Boisvert & Faust, 2003; Coffman et al., 2007; Lilienfeld, 2007; Pretzer & Beck, 2005).

- *No single form of therapy works best for every problem, and certain specific types of treatment are better, although not invariably, for specific types of problems.* For example, cognitive therapy works especially well for panic disorders, and exposure therapy relieves specific phobias effectively. However, there are exceptions to these generalizations, and often the differences in success rates for different types of treatment are not substantial (Miller & Magruder, 1999; Westen, Novotny, & Thompson-Brenner, 2004).

- *Most therapies share several basic similar elements.* Despite the fact that the specific methods used in different therapies are very different from one another, there are several common themes that lead them to be effective. These elements include the opportunity for a client to develop a positive relationship with a therapist, an explanation or interpretation of a client's symptoms, and confrontation of negative emotions. The fact that these common elements exist in most therapies makes it difficult to compare one treatment with another (Norcross, 2002; Norcross, Beutler & Levant, 2006).

Because no single type of psychotherapy is invariably effective for every individual, some therapists use an eclectic approach to therapy. In an *eclectic approach to therapy*, therapists use a variety of techniques, integrating several perspectives, to treat a person's problems. By employing more than one approach, therapists can choose the appropriate mix of treatments to match the specific needs of the individual. Furthermore, therapists with certain personal characteristics may work better with particular individuals and types of treatments, and racial and ethnic factors may also be related to the success of treatment (Chambless et al., 2006; Cheston, 2000; Hayes, 2008).

People's environmental and cultural backgrounds are important considerations during treatment for psychological disorders. In the United States, for example, behavior that may signal psychological disorder in one socioeconomic group may simply be adaptive in people from other racial and socioeconomic groups. For instance, characteristically suspicious and distrustful people may be displaying a survival strategy to protect them from psychological and physical injury, rather than suffering from a psychological disturbance (Paniagua, 2000; Pottick et al., 2007; Tseng, 2003).

In fact, therapists must question some basic assumptions of psychotherapy when dealing with clients who are from a different racial and/or ethnic background than the therapist. For example, some cultures place much greater emphasis on the group, the family, and society. When a member of one of these groups faces a critical decision, the family helps make it—a cultural practice suggesting that family members should also play a role in psychological treatment (Leitner, 2007; McCarthy, 2005; Ponterotto, Gretchen, & Chauhan, 2001). Because therapists themselves are from different cultures and ethnic groups, they have different degrees of understanding of cultural beliefs and expectations of other groups. Sometimes, then, referral of a potential client to a therapist who is more familiar with that person's cultural background might be advisable.

BIOMEDICAL THERAPY

If you get a kidney infection, your doctor gives you an antibiotic, and with luck, about a week later your kidney should be as good as new. If your appendix becomes inflamed, a surgeon removes it, and your body functions normally once more. Could a comparable approach, focusing on the body's physiology, be effective for psychological disturbances?

According to biological approaches to treatment, the answer is yes. Therapists routinely use biomedical therapies (Markowitz & Patrick, 2008). This approach suggests that rather than focusing on a client's psychological conflicts or past traumas, or on environmental factors that may produce abnormal behavior, focusing treatment directly on brain chemistry and other neurological factors may be more appropriate. To do this, therapists can use drugs, electric shock, or surgery to provide treatment.

Drug Therapy Drug therapy, the control of psychological disorders through drugs, works by altering the operation of neurotransmitters and neurons in the brain. Some drugs operate by inhibiting neurotransmitters or receptor

> **drug therapy** Control of psychological disorders through the use of drugs.

Class of Drug	Effects of Drug	Primary Action of Drug	Examples
Antipsychotic Drugs, Atypical Antipsychotic Drugs	Reduction in loss of touch with reality, agitation	Block dopamine receptors	Antipsychotic: Chlorpromazine (Thorazine), clozapine (Clozaril), haloperidol (Haldol) Atypical Antipsychotic: rizperadine, olanzapine
Antidepressant Drugs			
Tricyclic antidepressants	Reduction in depression	Permit rise in neurotransmitters such as norepinephrine	Trazodone (Desyrel), amitriptyline (Elavil), desipramine (Norpamin)
MAO inhibitors	Reduction in depression	Prevent MAO from breaking down neurotransmitters	Phenelzine (Nardil), tranylcypromine (Parnate)
Selective serotonin reuptake inhibitors (SSRIs)	Reduction in depression	Inhibit reuptake of serotonin	Fluoxetine (Prozac), Luvox, Paxil, Celexa, Zoloft, nefazodone (Serzone)
Mood Stabilizers			
Lithium	Mood stabilization	Can alter transmission of impulses within neurons	Lithium (Lithonate), Depakote, Tegretol
Antianxiety Drugs	Reduction in anxiety	Increase activity of neurotransmitter GABA	Benzodiazepines (Valium, Xanax)

Drug Treatments for Psychological Disorders

neurons, reducing activity at particular synapses, the sites where nerve impulses travel from one neuron to another. Other drugs do just the opposite: They increase the activity of certain neurotransmitters or neurons, allowing particular neurons to fire more frequently.

Probably no greater change has occurred in mental hospitals than the successful introduction in the mid-1950s of **antipsychotic drugs**—drugs used to reduce severe symptoms of disturbance, such as loss of touch with reality and agitation (Stroup, Kraus, & Marder, 2006). Previously, the typical mental hospital wasn't very different from the stereotypical 19th-century insane asylum, giving mainly custodial care to screaming, moaning, clawing patients who displayed bizarre behaviors. Suddenly, in just a matter of days after hospital staff members administered antipsychotic drugs, the wards became considerably calmer environments in which professionals could do more than just try to get patients through the day without causing serious harm to themselves or others.

This dramatic change came about through the introduction of the drug *chlorpromazine*. Along with other similar drugs, chlorpromazine rapidly became the most popular and successful treatment for schizophrenia. Today drug therapy is the preferred treatment for most cases of severely abnormal behavior and, as such, is used for most patients hospitalized with psychological disorders (Sharif et al., 2007). The newest generation of antipsychotics, referred to as *atypical antipsychotics,* which have fewer side effects, include *rizperidone, olanzapine*, and *paliperidone* (Lublin,

antipsychotic drugs Drugs that temporarily reduce such psychotic symptoms as agitation, hallucinations, and delusions.

antidepressant drugs Medications that improve mood and promote a feeling of well-being in severely depressed individuals.

Eberhard, & Levander, 2005; Nasrallah et al., 2008; Savas, Yumru, & Kaya, 2007).

How do antipsychotic drugs work? Most block dopamine receptors at the brain's synapses. Atypical antipsychotics affect both serotonin and dopamine levels in certain parts of the brain, such as those related to planning and goal-directed activity (Advokat, 2005; Sawa & Snyder, 2002).

Despite the effectiveness of antipsychotic drugs, they do not produce a "cure" in the same way that an antibiotic cures an infection. Most of the time, when the drug is withdrawn, the symptoms reappear. Furthermore, such drugs can have long-term side effects, such as dryness of the mouth and throat, dizziness, and sometimes tremors and loss of muscle control, which may continue after drug treatments are stopped (Voruganti et al., 2007).

As their name suggests, **antidepressant drugs** are a class of medications used in cases of severe depression to improve the moods of clients. They are also sometimes used for other disorders, such as anxiety disorders and bulimia (Hedges et al., 2007; Walsh et al., 2006).

Most antidepressant drugs work by changing the concentration of specific neurotransmitters in the brain. For example, *tricyclic drugs* increase the availability of norepinephrine at the synapses of neurons, whereas *MAO inhibitors* prevent the enzyme monoamine oxidase (MAO) from breaking down neurotransmitters. Newer antidepressants—such as Lexapro—are *selective serotonin reuptake inhibitors (SSRIs)*. SSRIs target the neurotransmitter serotonin, permitting it to linger at the synapse. Some antidepressants produce a combination of effects. For instance, nefazodone (Serzone) blocks serotonin at some receptor sites but not others, whereas bupropion (Wellbutrin and Zyban) affect the norepinephrine and dopamine systems (Dhillon, Yang, & Curran, 2008; Lucki & O'Leary, 2004; Robinson, 2007).

Finally, there are some newer drugs on the horizon. For instance, scientists have found that the anesthetic ketamine blocks the neural receptor NMDA, which affects the neurotransmitter glutamate. Glutamate plays an important role in mood regulation and the ability to experience pleasure, and researchers believe that ketamine blockers may prove to be useful in the treatment of depression (Skolnick, Popik, & Trullas, 2009).

The overall success rates of antidepressant drugs is good. Unlike antipsychotic drugs, antidepressants can produce lasting, long-term recovery from depression. In many cases, even after clients stop taking the drugs, their depression does not return. Yet antidepressant drugs may produce side effects such as drowsiness and faintness, and there is evidence that SSRI antidepressants can increase the risk of suicide in children and adolescents (Gibbons et al., 2007; Leckman & King, 2007; Olfson & Marcus, 2008).

Mood stabilizers are used to treat mood disorders. For example, the drug *lithium*, a form of mineral salts, has been used successfully to control bipolar disorder. Although no one knows definitely why, lithium and other mood stabilizers such as divalproex sodium (*Depakote*) and carbamazepine (*Tegretol*) effectively reduce manic episodes. But they do not effectively treat depressive phases of bipolar disorder, so antidepressants are usually prescribed during those phases (Abraham & Calabrese, 2007; L. Smith et al., 2007; Salvi et al., 2008).

Lithium and similar drugs have a quality that sets them apart from other drug treatments: They can be a *preventive* treatment, blocking future episodes of manic depression. Often, people who have had episodes of bipolar disorder can take a daily dose of lithium to prevent a recurrence of their symptoms. Most other drugs are useful only when symptoms of psychological disturbance occur (Keck & McElroy, 2007; Pary et al., 2006).

Antianxiety drugs, as the name implies, reduce the level of anxiety a person experiences and increase feelings of well-being. They are prescribed not only to reduce general tension in people who are experiencing temporary difficulties but also to aid in the treatment of more serious anxiety disorders (Zito, 1993).

Antianxiety drugs such as Xanax and Valium are among the medications most frequently prescribed by physicians.

In fact, more than half of all U.S. families have someone who has taken such a drug at one time or another.

Although the popularity of antianxiety drugs suggests that they hold few risks, they can produce a number of potentially serious side effects. For instance, they can cause fatigue, and long-term use can lead to dependence. Moreover, when taken in combination with alcohol, some antianxiety drugs can be lethal. But a more important issue concerns their use to suppress anxiety. Almost every therapeutic approach to psychological disturbance views continuing anxiety as a signal of some other sort of problem. Thus, drugs that mask anxiety may simply be hiding other difficulties. Consequently, rather than confronting their underlying problems, people may be hiding from them through the use of antianxiety drugs (Pandit, Argyropoulos, & Nutt, 2001).

Electroconvulsive Therapy (ECT) First introduced in the 1930s, **electroconvulsive therapy (ECT)** is a procedure used in the treatment of severe depression. In this procedure, an electric current of 70 to 150 volts is briefly administered to a patient's head, causing a loss of consciousness and often causing seizures. Health professionals usually sedate patients and give them muscle relaxants before administering the current, and such preparations help reduce the intensity of muscle contractions produced during ECT. Typically, a patient receives about 10 such treatments in the course of a month, but some patients continue with maintenance treatments for months afterward (Freudenreich, & Goff, 2011; Greenberg & Kellner, 2005; Stevens & Harper, 2007).

ECT is a controversial technique. Apart from the obvious distastefulness of a treatment that evokes images of electrocution, side effects are common. For instance, after treatment, patients often experience disorientation, confusion, and sometimes memory loss that may remain for months. Furthermore, ECT often does not produce long-term improvement; one study found that without follow-up medication, depression returned in most individuals who had undergone ECT treatments. Finally, even when ECT does work, we do not know why, and some critics believe it may cause permanent brain damage (Gardner & O'Connor, 2008; Kato, 2009; Sackeim et al., 2001).

In light of the drawbacks to ECT, why do therapists use it at all? Basically, in many severe cases of depression, it offers the only quickly effective treatment—as in the case of Kitty Dukakis, whose treatment was described previously in this chapter. For instance, it may prevent depressed, suicidal individuals from committing suicide, and it can act more quickly than antidepressive medications (Kellner et al., 1997).

The use of ECT has risen in the last decade, with more than 100,000 people undergoing it each year. Still, ECT

mood stabilizers Drugs used to treat mood disorders that prevent manic episodes of bipolar disorder.

antianxiety drugs Drugs that reduce the level of anxiety a person experiences, essentially by reducing excitability and increasing feelings of well-being.

electroconvulsive therapy (ECT) A procedure used in the treatment of severe depression in which an electric current of 70 to 150 volts is briefly administered to the head.

tends to be used only when other treatments have proved ineffective, and researchers continue to search for alternative treatments (Eranti & McLoughlin, 2003; Fink, 2000; Pandya, Pozuelo, & Malone, 2007).

One new and promising alternative to ECT is **transcranial magnetic stimulation (TMS)**. TMS creates a precise magnetic pulse in a specific area of the brain. By activating particular neurons, TMS has been found to be effective in relieving the symptoms of depression in a number of controlled experiments. However, the therapy can produce side effects, such as seizures and convulsions, and it is still considered experimental (Lefaucheur et al., 2007; Kim, Pesiridou, & O'Reardon, 2009; Leo & Latif, 2007).

Psychosurgery If ECT strikes you as a questionable procedure, the use of **psychosurgery**—brain surgery in which the object is to reduce symptoms of mental disorder—probably appears even more dubious. A technique used only rarely today, psychosurgery was introduced as a "treatment of last resort" in the 1930s.

The initial form of psychosurgery, a *prefrontal lobotomy*, consisted of surgically destroying or removing parts of a patient's frontal lobes, which, surgeons thought, controlled emotionality. In the 1930s and 1940s, surgeons performed the procedure on thousands of people, often with little precision. For example, in one common technique, a surgeon would jab an ice pick under a patient's eyeball and swivel it back and forth (El-Hai, 2005; Ogren & Sandlund, 2007).

Often psychosurgery did improve a patient's behavior—but not without drastic side effects. Along with remission of the symptoms of the mental disorder, patients sometimes experienced personality changes, becoming bland, colorless, and unemotional. In other cases, patients became aggressive and unable to control their impulses. In the worst cases, the patient died as a result of the surgery (Mashour, Walker, & Martuza, 2005).

With the introduction of effective drug treatments—and the obvious ethical questions regarding the appropriateness of forever altering someone's personality—psychosurgery became nearly obsolete. However, it is still used in very rare cases when all other procedures have failed and the individual's behavior presents a high risk to himself and others. For example, surgeons sometimes use a more precise form of psychosurgery called a *cingulotomy* in rare cases of obsessive-compulsive disorder in which they destroy tissue in the *anterior cignulate* area of the brain. In another technique, *gamma knife surgery*, beams of radiation are used to destroy areas of the brain related to obsessive-compulsive disorder (Carey, 2009c; Lopes et al, 2009; Shah et al., 2008; Wilkinson, 2009).

Biomedical Therapies in Perspective In some respects, no greater revolution has occurred in the field of

transcranial magnetic stimulation (TMS) A depression treatment in which a precise magnetic pulse is directed to a specific area of the brain.

psychosurgery Brain surgery once used to reduce the symptoms of mental disorder but rarely used today.

mental health than biological approaches to treatment. As previously violent, uncontrollable individuals have been calmed by the use of drugs, mental hospitals have been able to concentrate more on actually helping them and less on custodial functions. Similarly, people whose lives have been disrupted by depression or bipolar episodes have been able to function normally, and other forms of drug therapy have also shown remarkable results.

The use of biomedical therapy for everyday problems is rising. For example, one survey of users of a college counseling service found that from 1989 to 2001, the proportion of students receiving treatment who were taking medication for psychological disorders increased from 10% to 25% (Benton et al., 2003).

Furthermore, new forms of biomedical therapy are promising. For example, the newest treatment possibility—which remains experimental at this point—is gene therapy. As we discussed when considering behavioral genetics, specific genes may be introduced to particular regions of the brain. These genes then have the potential to reverse or even prevent biochemical events that give rise to psychological disorders (Lymberis et al., 2004; Sapolsky, 2003; Tuszynski, 2007).

Despite their current usefulness and future promise, biomedical therapies do not represent a cure-all for psychological disorders. For one thing, critics charge that such therapies merely provide relief of the *symptoms* of mental disorder; as soon as the drugs are withdrawn, the symptoms return. Although it is considered a major step in the right direction, biomedical treatment may not solve the underlying problems that led to therapy in the first place (Alonso, 2004). Biomedical therapies also can produce side effects, ranging from minor to serious physical reactions to the development of *new* symptoms of abnormal behavior.

Still, biomedical therapies—sometimes alone and more often in conjunction with psychotherapy—have permitted millions of people to function more effectively (Stroup et al., 2006). Furthermore, although biomedical therapy and psychotherapy appear distinct, research shows that biomedical therapies ultimately may not be as different from talk therapies as one might imagine, at least in terms of their consequences.

Specifically, measures of brain functioning as a result of drug therapy compared with psychotherapy show little difference in outcomes. For example, one study compared the reactions of clients with major depression who received either an antidepressant drug or psychotherapy. After six weeks of either therapy, activity in the portion of the brain related to the disorder—the basal ganglia—had changed in similar ways, and that area appeared to function more normally. Although such research is not definitive, it does suggest that at least for some disorders, psychotherapy may be just as effective as biomedical interventions—and vice versa. Research also makes it clear that no single treatment is effective universally, and that each type of treatment has both advantages and disadvantages (DeRubeis, Hollon, & Shelton, 2003; Greenberg & Goldman, 2009; Hollon, Thase, & Markowitz, 2002; Pinquart, Duberstein, & Lyness, 2006).

> Unlike other approaches, community psychology aims to prevent or minimize the incidence of psychological disorders.

Community Psychology The approaches to treatments discussed so far have a common element: They are "restorative," aimed at alleviating psychological difficulties that already exist. Unlike those approaches, **community psychology** aims to prevent or minimize the incidence of psychological disorders.

Community psychology came of age in the 1960s, when mental health professionals developed plans for a nationwide network of community mental health centers. The hope was that those centers would provide low-cost mental health services, including short-term therapy and community educational programs.

In another development, the population of mental hospitals has plunged as drug treatments made physical restraint unnecessary (Dixon & Goldman, 2003). This resulted in the transfer of former mental patients out of institutions and into the community—a process known as **deinstitutionalization**. It was encouraged by the growth of the community psychology movement. Proponents of deinstitutionalization wanted to ensure not only that deinstitutionalized individuals received proper treatment but also that their civil rights were maintained (Perry et al., 2011; St. Dennis et al., 2007; Wolff, 2002).

Unfortunately, the promise of deinstitutionalization has not been met, largely because insufficient resources are provided to deinstitutionalized clients. What started as a worthy attempt to move people out of mental institutions and into the community ended, in many cases, with former patients

While deinstitutionalization has had many successes, it has also contributed to the release of mental patients into the community with little or no support. As a result, many have become homeless.

being dumped into the community without any real support. Many became homeless—between a third and a half of all homeless adults are thought to have a major psychological disorder—and some became involved in illegal acts caused by their disorders. In short, many people who need treatment do not get it, and in some cases care for people with psychological disorders has simply shifted from one type of treatment site to another (Dumont & Dumont, 2008; Price, 2009; Shinn et al., 2007).

> **community psychology** A branch of psychology that focuses on the prevention and minimization of psychological disorders in the community.
>
> **deinstitutionalization** The transfer of former mental patients from institutions to the community.

However, the community psychology movement has had some positive outcomes. Telephone "hot lines" are now common. At any time of the day or night, people experiencing acute stress can call a trained, sympathetic listener who can provide immediate—although obviously limited—treatment (Cauce, 2007; Reese, Conoley, & Brossart, 2002; Paukert, Stagner, & Hope, 2004).

College and high school crisis centers are another innovation that grew out of the community psychology movement. Modeled after suicide prevention hot-line centers (services that enable potential suicide victims to call and speak to someone about their difficulties), crisis centers give callers an opportunity to discuss life crises with a sympathetic listener, who is often a volunteer.

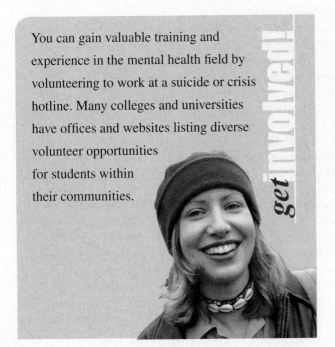

You can gain valuable training and experience in the mental health field by volunteering to work at a suicide or crisis hotline. Many colleges and universities have offices and websites listing diverse volunteer opportunities for students within their communities.

get involved!

For REVIEW >>

- **What theories do psychologists use to explain psychological disorders?**

  The medical perspective views abnormality as a symptom of an underlying disease. Psychoanalytic perspectives suggest that abnormal behavior stems from childhood conflicts in the unconscious. Behavioral approaches view abnormal behavior not as a symptom of an underlying problem but as the problem itself. The cognitive approach suggests that abnormal behavior is the result of faulty cognitions (thoughts and beliefs). In this view, abnormal behavior can be remedied by changing one's flawed thoughts and beliefs. (pp. 302–305)

- **What are the major categories of psychological disorders?**

  Anxiety disorders are present when a person experiences so much anxiety that it affects daily functioning. Mood disorders are characterized by emotional states of depression or euphoria so strong that they intrude on everyday living. Schizophrenia is one of the more severe forms of mental illness. Symptoms of schizophrenia include declines in functioning, thought and language disturbances, perceptual disorders, emotional disturbance, and withdrawal from others. People with personality disorders experience little or no personal distress, but they do suffer from an inability to function as normal members of society. These disorders include antisocial personality disorder, borderline personality disorder, and narcissistic personality disorder. (pp. 305–318)

- **How can we tell when it's time to get professional help for ourselves or someone else?**

  The signals that indicate a need for professional help include long-term feelings of psychological distress, feelings of inability to cope with stress, withdrawal from other people, thoughts of inflicting harm on oneself or suicide, prolonged feelings of hopelessness, chronic physical problems with no apparent causes, phobias and compulsions, paranoia, and an inability to interact with others. (p. 316)

- **What types of treatment approaches are available for psychological disorders?**

  Psychoanalytic treatment approaches seek to bring unresolved past conflicts and unacceptable impulses from the unconscious into the conscious, where clients may deal with the problems more effectively. Behavioral approaches to treatment view abnormal behavior as the problem, rather than as a symptom of some underlying cause. This view suggests that the outward behavior must be changed by means of aversive conditioning, systematic desensitization, observational learning, or other behavioral therapy. Cognitive treatment approaches consider the goal of therapy to be helping a person restructure a faulty belief system into a more realistic, rational, and logical view of the world. Humanistic therapy is based on the premise that people have control of their behavior, that they can make choices about their lives, and that it is up to them to solve their problems. Interpersonal therapy focuses on interpersonal relationships and strives for immediate improvement during short-term therapy. Drug therapy, the best example of biomedical treatment, can dramatically reduce the symptoms of mental disturbance. Antipsychotic drugs effectively reduce psychotic symptoms. Antidepressant drugs reduce depression so successfully that they are used widely. Antianxiety drugs, or minor tranquilizers, are among the most frequently prescribed medications of any sort. Nondrug biomedical treatments include electroconvulsive therapy (ECT), used in severe cases of depression and psychosurgery, which typically consists of surgically destroying or removing certain parts of the brain. (pp. 318–330)

Pop Quiz

1. Virginia's mother thinks that her daughter's behavior is clearly abnormal, because, despite being offered admission to medical school, Virginia decides to become a waitress. What approach is Virginia's mother using to define abnormal behavior?

2. Which of the following statements is a strong argument against the biomedical perspective on abnormality?
   a. Physiological abnormalities are almost always impossible to identify.
   b. There is no conclusive way to link past experience and behavior.
   c. The medical perspective rests too heavily on the effects of nutrition.
   d. Assigning behavior to a physical problem takes responsibility away from the individual for changing his or her behavior.

3. Angel is painfully shy. According to the behavioral perspective, the best way to deal with his "abnormal" behavior is to _____.
   a. treat the underlying physical problem
   b. use the principles of learning theory to modify his shy behavior
   c. express a great deal of caring
   d. uncover his negative past experiences through hypnosis

4. Vi is terrified of elevators. She could be suffering from a(n) _____.
   a. obsessive-compulsive disorder
   b. phobic disorder
   c. panic disorder
   d. generalized anxiety disorder

5. An overpowering urge to carry out a strange ritual is called a(n) _____.

6. States of extreme euphoria and energy paired with severe depression characterize _____ disorder.

7. The activity on schizophrenia showed _____.
   a. how much schizophrenia disrupts a person's life
   b. how medication has made an amazing difference in the lives of people with schizophrenia
   c. how five different people were able to find five different solutions to their schizophrenia
   d. that schizophrenia is usually connected with other mental disorders such as depression and borderline personality disorder

8. The latest version of *DSM* is considered to be the conclusive guideline on defining psychological disorders. True or false?

9. In what culture is catatonic schizophrenia most common?

10. According to Freud, people use _____ _____ as a means of preventing unwanted impulses from intruding on conscious thought.

11. The message of the activity on systematic desensitization is that _____.
    a. the severity of a phobia determines which type of therapy will be necessary
    b. we can learn to love what we used to fear
    c. systematic desensitization can be combined with other therapies to cure phobias
    d. even though it is old-fashioned, systematic desensitization is more effective than exposure therapy

SOCIAL PSY

A GIFT OF LIFE

Ten weeks pregnant, Katie Purdom had just picked up daughter Victoria Leigh, 4, from preschool in Lebanon, Kentucky, on a misty afternoon . . . when a neighbor's dog ran in front of her SUV. She swerved to avoid it, causing the car to flip over and land in a 4-ft.-deep creek; her seat belt locked, Katie was pinned, as was Victoria, who was belted into her booster seat in back. "The water was coming in everywhere," says Katie, 31, a non-swimmer who works in the bakery at a local Wal-Mart. "Tori kept saying, 'I'm cold, Momma, help!' It was terrifying." As she tried to reach back to hold her child's face above the rising water, Katie heard a man's voice: It was Perry Bland, 52, who had spotted them while driving on the route he's covered for 27 years. With calming words, he pulled out his plastic letter opener and started to saw away at the seat belts. Ten minutes later both mother and daughter were free, having escaped with only minor scratches. Now seven months along with a baby boy, Katie says, "I owe Perry our lives." Perry, who has become something of a local celebrity, is just thankful it all worked out. "I still get choked up," he says. "I know how close it could have been."[xiii]

What led Perry Bland to behave so heroically? Was it simply the circumstances, or was it something about the kind of person Bland was? What, in general, drives some people to help others—and conversely, why do other people show no concern for the welfare of others? More broadly, how can we improve social conditions so that people can live together in harmony?

CHOLOGY

- What are attitudes, how do they influence behavior, and how can they be changed?
- How do we influence one another?
- Where do stereotypes come from?
- Why are we attracted to certain people? How do relationships develop?
- What makes some people aggressive and others kind and helpful?

Social psychology is the scientific study of how our thoughts, feelings, and actions are affected by others. Social psychologists consider the kinds of behaviors in which we engage with others and how and why our behaviors and attitudes can change when we are with others. They examine how the nature of situations in which we find ourselves influences our behavior in important ways.

The broad scope of social psychology is conveyed by the kinds of questions social psychologists ask, such as: How can we convince people to change their attitudes or adopt new ideas and values? In what ways do we come to understand what others are like? How are we influenced by what others do and think? Why do some people display so much violence, aggression, and cruelty toward others that people throughout the world live in fear of annihilation at their hands? And why, in comparison, do some people place their own lives at risk to help others? In exploring these and other questions, we also discuss strategies for confronting and solving a variety of problems and issues that all of us face—ranging from achieving a better understanding of persuasive tactics to forming more accurate impressions of others.

We begin with a look at how our attitudes shape our behavior and how we form judgments about others. We discuss how we are influenced by others, and we consider prejudice and discrimination, focusing on their roots and the ways in which we can reduce them. After examining what social psychologists have learned about the ways in which people form friendships and relationships, we'll conclude with a look at the determinants of aggression and helping—two opposing sides of human behavior.

> **social psychology** The scientific study of how people's thoughts, feelings, and actions are affected by others.
>
> **attitudes** Evaluations of a particular person, behavior, belief, or concept.

>> Attitudes and Social Cognition

What do Shaquille O'Neal, Rachael Ray, and Eli Manning have in common?

Each has appeared in advertisements designed to mold or change our thinking about something. Commercials are part of the barrage of messages we receive each day from sources as varied as politicians, sales staff in stores, and celebrities, all of which are meant to influence us.

PERSUASION: CHANGING ATTITUDES

Persuasion is the process of changing attitudes, one of the central concepts of social psychology. **Attitudes** are evalua-

Companies use athletes such as basketball star LeBron James to persuade us to buy their products. Can celebrities really affect the purchasing habits of consumers?

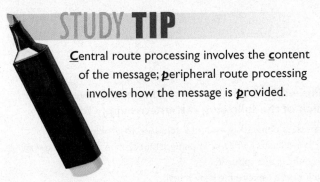

tions of a particular person, behavior, belief, or concept. For example, you probably hold attitudes toward the U.S. president (a person), abortion (a behavior), affirmative action (a belief), or architecture (a concept) (Brock, T. C., & Green, M. C., 2005; Hegarty & Massey, 2007; Simon & Hoyt, 2008).

The ease with which we can change our attitudes depends on a number of factors, including:

- *Message source.* The characteristics of a person who delivers a persuasive message, known as an *attitude communicator*, have a major impact on the effectiveness of that message. Communicators who are physically and socially attractive produce greater attitude change than those who are less attractive. Moreover, the expertise and trustworthiness of a communicator are related to the effectiveness of a message—except in situations in which the audience believes the communicator has an ulterior motive (Ariyanto, Hornsey, & Gallois, 2006; McClure, Sutton, & Sibley, 2007; Messner, Reinhard, & Sporer, 2008).

- *Characteristics of the message.* It is not just who delivers a message that affects attitudes but also what the message is like. Generally, two-sided messages—which include both the communicator's position and the one he or she is arguing against—are more effective than one-sided messages, given the assumption that the arguments for the other side can be effectively refuted and the audience is knowledgeable about the topic. In addition, fear-producing messages ("If you don't practice safer sex, you'll get AIDS") are generally effective when they provide the audience with a means for reducing the fear. However, if the fear that is aroused is too strong, messages may evoke people's defense mechanisms and be ignored (Perloff, 2003).

- *Characteristics of the target.* Once a communicator has delivered a message, characteristics of the target of the message may determine whether the message will be accepted. For example, the more we are exposed to ideas presented as news reports, even unbelievable ones, the more likely we are to accept them as true (Gibbons, Lukowski, Walker, 2005).

Routes to Persuasion Recipients' receptiveness to persuasive messages depends on the type of information-processing they use. Social psychologists have discovered two primary information-processing routes to persuasion: central route and peripheral route processing (Cacioppo & Petty, 1989; Petty et al., 2005). **Central route processing** occurs when the recipient thoughtfully considers the issues and arguments involved in persuasion. In central route processing, people are swayed in their judgments by the logic, merit, and strength of arguments.

In contrast, **peripheral route processing** occurs when people are persuaded on the basis of factors unrelated to the nature or quality of the content of a persuasive message. Instead, factors that are irrelevant or extraneous to the issue, such as who is providing the message, how long the arguments are, or the emotional appeal of the arguments, influence them (Petty et al., 2005; Warden, Wu, & Tsai, 2006; Wegener et al., 2004).

In general, people who are highly involved and motivated use central route processing to comprehend a message. However, if a person is uninvolved, unmotivated, bored, or distracted, the nature of the message becomes less important, and peripheral factors become more critical. Although both central route and peripheral route processing lead to attitude change, central route processing generally leads to stronger, more lasting attitude change.

central route processing Message interpretation characterized by thoughtful consideration of the issues and arguments used to persuade.

peripheral route processing Message interpretation characterized by consideration of the source and related general information rather than of the message itself.

Two Routes to Persuasion

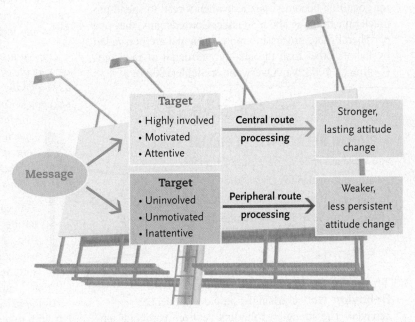

The Need for Cognition

This simple questionnaire will give you a general idea of the level of your need for cognition. Which of the following statements apply to you?

1. I really enjoy a task that involves coming up with new solutions to problems.
2. I would prefer a task that is intellectual, difficult, and important to one that is somewhat important but does not require much thought.
3. Learning new ways to think doesn't excite me very much.
4. The idea of relying on thought to make my way to the top does not appeal to me.
5. I think only as hard as I have to.
6. I like tasks that require little thought once I've learned them.
7. I prefer to think about small, daily projects rather than long-term ones.
8. I would rather do something that requires little thought than something that is sure to challenge my thinking abilities.
9. I find little satisfaction in deliberating hard and for long hours.
10. I don't like to be responsible for a situation that requires a lot of thinking.

Scoring: The more you agree with statements 1 and 2, and disagree with the rest, the greater the likelihood that you have a high need for cognition.

Source: Cacioppo, Berntson, & Crites, Jr. (1996).

Are some people more likely than others to use central route processing rather than peripheral route processing? The answer is yes. People who have a high *need for cognition*, a person's habitual level of thoughtfulness and cognitive activity, are more likely to employ central route processing (Cacioppo, Berntson, & Crites, 1996; Curşeu, 2011; Dai & Wang, 2007).

People who have a high need for cognition enjoy thinking, philosophizing, and reflecting on the world. Consequently, they tend to reflect more on persuasive messages by using central route processing and are likely to be persuaded by complex, logical, and detailed messages. In contrast, those who have a low need for cognition become impatient when forced to spend too much time thinking about an issue. Consequently, they use peripheral route processing more often and are persuaded by factors other than the quality and detail of messages (Dollinger, 2003; Van Overwalle & Siebler, 2005).

cognitive dissonance The conflict that occurs when a person holds two contradictory attitudes or thoughts (referred to as cognitions).

From the perspective of …

A PUBLIC RELATIONS SPECIALIST Suppose you were assigned to develop a TV public relations campaign for a well-known manufacturer that wanted to improve its public image. How could you use theories of persuasion to reach the greatest number of people?

The Link Between Attitudes and Behavior Not surprisingly, attitudes influence behavior. The strength of the link between particular attitudes and behavior varies, but generally people strive for consistency between their attitudes and their behavior. Furthermore, people hold fairly consistent attitudes. For instance, you would probably not hold the attitude that eating meat is immoral and still have a positive attitude toward hamburgers (Ajzen, 2002; Conner et al., 2003; Levi, Chan, & Pence, 2006).

Often our behavior shapes our attitudes.

Ironically, the consistency that leads attitudes to influence behavior also works the other way around—often our behavior shapes our attitudes. Consider, for instance, the following incident:

You've just spent what you feel is the most boring hour of your life, turning pegs for a psychology experiment. Just as you finally finish and are about to leave, the experimenter asks you to do him a favor. He tells you that he needs a helper for future experimental sessions to introduce subsequent participants to the peg-turning task. Your specific job will be to tell them that turning the pegs is an interesting, fascinating experience. Each time you tell this tale to another participant, you'll be paid $1.

If you agree to help the experimenter, you may be setting yourself up for a state of psychological tension called cognitive dissonance. According to social psychologist Leon Festinger (1957), **cognitive dissonance** occurs when a person holds two contradictory attitudes or thoughts (referred to as *cognitions*).

If you participate in the situation just described, you are left with two contradictory thoughts: (1) I believe the task is boring, but (2) I said it was interesting with little justification ($1). These two thoughts should arouse dissonance. How can you reduce cognitive dissonance? You cannot deny having said that the task is interesting without breaking with reality. Relatively speaking, it is easier to change your attitude toward the task—and thus the theory predicts that participants will reduce dissonance by adopting more positive attitudes toward the task (Cooper, 2007; Cooper, Mirabile, & Scher, 2005; Rydell, McConnell, & Mackie, 2008).

A classic experiment (Festinger & Carlsmith, 1959) confirmed this prediction. The experiment followed essentially the same procedure outlined earlier, in which a participant was offered $1 to describe a boring task as interesting. In addition, in a comparison condition, some participants were offered $20 to say that the task was interesting. The reasoning behind this condition was that $20 was enough money to give participants in this condition a good reason to convey incorrect information; dissonance would not be aroused, and less attitude change would be expected. The results supported this notion. More of the participants who were paid $1 changed their attitudes (becoming more positive toward the peg-turning task) than did participants who were paid $20. (If you are thinking that $20 wouldn't be enough money to matter, keep in mind that this was in the 1950s, when $20 might have bought someone a week's worth of groceries.)

We now know that cognitive dissonance theory accounts for many everyday events involving attitudes and behavior. For example, smokers who know that smoking leads to lung cancer hold contradictory cognitions: (1) I smoke, and (2) smoking leads to lung cancer. The theory predicts that these two thoughts will lead to a state of cognitive dissonance. More important, it predicts that—assuming that they don't change their behavior by quitting smoking—smokers will be motivated to reduce their dissonance by one of the following methods: (1) modifying one or both of the cognitions, (2) changing the perceived importance of one cognition, (3) adding cognitions, or (4) denying that the two cognitions are related to each other. Hence, a smoker may decide that he really doesn't smoke all that much or that he'll quit soon (modifying the cognition), that the evidence linking smoking to cancer is weak (changing the importance of a cognition), that the amount of exercise he gets compensates for the smoking (adding cognitions), or that there is no evidence linking smoking and cancer (denial). Any of these techniques would help to reduce dissonance (see, for example, Peretti-Watel, Halfen, & Grémy, 2007).

social cognition The cognitive processes by which people understand and make sense of others and themselves.

schemas Sets of cognitions about people and social experiences.

SOCIAL COGNITION: UNDERSTANDING OTHERS

When we meet someone for the first time, we tend to form an impression of that person. What we think of a stranger may or may not be positive, and it may or may not be accurate, but that first impression tends to influence our interpretation of that individual's behavior from then on. Learning how we come to understand what others are like and how we explain the reasons underlying others' behavior has been a continuing focus in social psychology.

Understanding What Others Are Like Consider for a moment the enormous amount of information about other people to which we are exposed. How do we decide what is important and what is not? How do we make judgments about the characteristics of others? Social psychologists interested in this question study **social cognition**—the way people understand and make sense of others and themselves. Those psychologists have learned that individuals have highly developed **schemas**, sets of cognitions about people and social experiences. Those schemas organize information

Two contradictory cognitions

1. "I smoke."
2. "Smoking leads to cancer."

Dissonance

Modifying one or both cognitions ("I really don't smoke too much.")

Changing perceived importance of the cognition ("The evidence is weak that smoking causes cancer.")

Adding additional cognitions ("I exercise so much that it doesn't matter that I smoke.")

Denying that cognitions are related ("There is no evidence linking smoking and cancer.")

Cognitive Dissonance and Smoking

stored in memory, represent in our minds the way the social world operates, and give us a framework to recognize, categorize, and recall information relating to such social stimuli as people and groups (Brewer & Hewstone, 2003; Mancuso et al., 2011; Moskowitz, 2004; Smith & Semin, 2007).

We typically hold schemas for specific types of people. Our schema for "teacher," for instance, generally consists of a number of characteristics: knowledge of the subject matter he or she is teaching, a desire to impart that knowledge, and an awareness of the student's need to understand what is being said. Or we may hold a schema for "mother" that includes the characteristics of warmth, nurturance, and caring. Regardless of their accuracy, schemas are important, because they organize the way in which we recall, recognize, and categorize information about others. Moreover, they help us predict what others are like on the basis of relatively little information, because we tend to fit people into schemas even when we do not have much concrete evidence to go on (Bargh & Chartrand, 2000; Ruscher, Fiske, & Schnake, 2000).

Impression Formation

How do we decide that Sayreeta is a flirt, Jacob is obnoxious, or Hector is a really nice guy? The earliest work on social cognition examined *impression formation*, the process by which an individual organizes information about another person to form an overall impression of that person.

In a classic early study, students learned that they were about to hear a guest lecturer (Kelley, 1950). Students were randomly assigned to two groups. Those in the first group were told that the lecturer was "a rather warm person, industrious, critical, practical, and determined," while those in the second group that he was "a rather cold person, industrious, critical, practical, and determined."

The simple substitution of "cold" for "warm" caused drastic differences in the way the students in each group perceived the lecturer, even though he gave the same talk in the same style in each condition. Students who had been told he was "warm" rated him considerably more positively than students who had been told he was "cold."

central traits The major traits considered in forming impressions of others.

attribution theory The theory of personality that seeks to explain how we decide, on the basis of samples of an individual's behavior, what the specific causes of that person's behavior are.

tively than students who had been told he was "cold."

The findings from this experiment led to additional research on impression formation that focused on the way in which people pay particular attention to certain unusually important traits—known as **central traits**—to help them form an overall impression of others. According to this work, the presence of a central trait alters the meaning of other traits (Jussim, 1989; Neuberg, 1989). Hence, the description of the lecturer as "industrious" presumably meant something different when it was associated with the central trait "warm" than it meant when it was associated with "cold" (Glicksohn & Nahari, 2007; Widmeyer & Loy, 1988).

We make such impressions remarkably quickly. In just a few seconds, using what have been called "thin slices of

PSYCH think

connect™
WWW.MCGRAWHILLCONNECT.COM/PSYCHOLOGY
First Impressions and Attraction

> > > You see Annette, a new coworker, act in a way that seems abrupt and curt. You conclude that Annette is unkind and unsociable. The next day you see Annette acting kindly toward another worker. Are you likely to change your impression of Annette? Why or why not?

Take the PsychSmart challenge! Is your judgment affected by your first impressions? Find out how important first impressions are in our judgments of people around us. From chapter 13 in your ebook, select the *Exercises* tab. Next select "First Impressions and Attraction." After doing the activity, answer Pop Quiz question 3 about this activity on p. 359.

behavior" (Ambady & Rosenthal, 1992), we are able to make judgments of people that are often very accurate and that match those of people who make judgments based on longer samples of behavior (Carney, Colvin, & Hall, 2007; Holleran, Mehl, & Levitt, 2009; Pavitt, 2007).

Of course, as we gain more experience with people and see them exhibiting behavior in a variety of situations, our impressions of them become more complex. However, because our knowledge of others usually has gaps, we still tend to fit individuals into personality schemas that represent particular "types" of people. For instance, we may hold a "gregarious person" schema, made up of the traits of friendliness, aggressiveness, and openness. The presence of just one or two of those traits may be sufficient for us to assign a person to a particular schema.

Even when schemas are not entirely accurate, they serve an important function: They allow us to develop expectations about how others will behave. Those expectations permit us to plan our interactions with others more easily and serve to simplify a complex social world (Wang & Ross, 2007).

Attribution Processes

At one time or another, most of us have puzzled over the reasons behind someone's behavior. Perhaps it was interpreting the sudden change in mood of a college roommate, or it may have been in more formal circumstances, such as being a judge on a student judiciary board in a cheating case. In contrast to theories of social cognition, which describe how people develop an overall impression of others' personality traits, **attribution theory** seeks to explain how we decide, on the basis

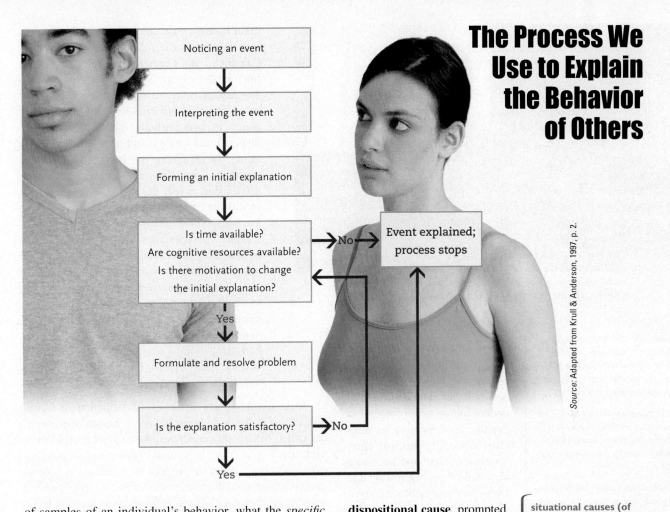

Source: Adapted from Krull & Anderson, 1997, p. 2.

The Process We Use to Explain the Behavior of Others

Flow chart:
Noticing an event → Interpreting the event → Forming an initial explanation → Is time available? Are cognitive resources available? Is there motivation to change the initial explanation? → (No) Event explained; process stops / (Yes) Formulate and resolve problem → Is the explanation satisfactory? → (No) loops back / (Yes) Event explained; process stops

of samples of an individual's behavior, what the *specific* causes of that person's behavior are.

The general process we use to determine the causes of behavior and other social occurrences proceeds in several steps. After first noticing that something unusual has happened—for example, tennis star Roger Federer has played a terrible tennis match—we try to interpret the meaning of the event. This leads us to formulate an initial explanation (maybe Federer stayed up late the night before the match). Depending on the time available, the cognitive resources on hand (such as the attention we can give to the matter), and our motivation (determined in part by how important the event is), we may choose to accept our initial explanation or seek to modify it (Federer was sick, perhaps). If we have the time, cognitive resources, and motivation, the event triggers deliberate problem solving as we seek a fuller explanation. During the problem formulation and resolution stage, we may try out several possibilities before we reach a final explanation that seems satisfactory to us (Brown, 2006; Malle, 2004).

In seeking an explanation for behavior, we try to answer the question: Is the cause situational or dispositional? **Situational causes** originate in the environment. For instance, someone who knocks over a quart of milk and then cleans it up probably does the cleaning not because he or she is necessarily a neat person but because the *situation* requires it. In contrast, a person who spends hours shining the kitchen floor probably does so because he or she is a neat person. In this case, the behavior has a **dispositional cause**, prompted by the person's disposition (his or her internal traits or personality characteristics).

Attribution Biases: To Err Is Human If we always processed information in the rational manner that attribution theory suggests, the world might run a lot more smoothly. Unfortunately, although attribution theory generally makes accurate predictions, people do not always process information about others in as logical a fashion as the theory seems to suggest. In fact, research reveals consistent biases in the ways people make attributions. Typical ones include these:

- *The halo effect.* Harry is intelligent, kind, and loving. Is he also conscientious? If you were to guess,

situational causes (of behavior) Perceived causes of behavior that are based on environmental factors.

dispositional causes (of behavior) Perceived causes of behavior that are based on internal traits or personality factors.

STUDY **TIP**

The central question in making an attribution is whether the cause of behavior is due to situational or dispositional factors.

: The assumed-similarity bias leads us to believe that others
: hold similar attitudes, opinions, and likes and dislikes.

halo effect A phenomenon in which an initial understanding that a person has positive traits is used to infer other uniformly positive characteristics.

assumed-similarity bias The tendency to think of people as being similar to oneself, even when meeting them for the first time.

self-serving bias The tendency to attribute personal success to personal factors (skill, ability, or effort) and to attribute failure to factors outside oneself.

fundamental attribution error A tendency to over-attribute others' behavior to dispositional causes and the corresponding minimization of the importance of situational causes.

your most likely response probably would be yes. Your guess reflects the **halo effect**, a phenomenon in which an initial understanding that a person has positive traits is used to infer other uniformly positive characteristics. The opposite would also hold true. Learning that Harry was unsociable and argumentative would probably lead you to assume that he was lazy as well. However, because few people have either uniformly positive or uniformly negative traits, the halo effect often leads to misperceptions of others (Dennis, 2007; Goffin, Jelley, & Wagner, 2003).

- *Assumed-similarity bias.* How similar to you—in terms of attitudes, opinions, and likes and dislikes—are your friends and acquaintances? Most people believe that their friends and acquaintances are similar to them. But this belief extends to a general tendency—known as the **assumed-similarity bias**—for people to think of others as being similar to them, even when they are meeting for the first time. Given the diversity of people in the world, this assumption often reduces the accuracy of our judgments (Lemay & Clark, 2008; Lemay, Clark, Feeney, 2007; West & Kenny, 2011).

- *The self-serving bias.* When their teams win, coaches usually feel that the success is due to their coaching. But when they coach a losing team, coaches may think it's due to the poor skills of their players. Similarly, if you get an A on a test, you may think it's due to your hard work, but if you get a poor grade, it's due to the professor's inadequacies. The reason is the **self-serving bias**, the tendency to attribute success to per-

sonal factors (skill, ability, or effort) and attribute failure to external factors (Krusemark, Campbell, & Clementz, 2008; Shepperd, Malone, & Sweeny, 2008).

- *The fundamental attribution error.* One of the more common attribution biases is the tendency to over-attribute others' behavior to dispositional causes and the corresponding failure to recognize the importance of situational causes. Known as the **fundamental attribution error**, this tendency is prevalent in Western cultures (Miller, 1984; Ross, 1977). We tend to exaggerate the importance of personality characteristics (dispositional causes) in producing others' behavior, minimizing the influence of the environment (situational factors). For example, we are more likely to jump to the conclusion that someone who is often late to work is too lazy to take an earlier bus (a dispositional cause) than to assume that the lateness is due to situational factors, such as that she must wait for her babysitter to arrive before she can leave to catch the bus.

Social psychologists' awareness of attribution biases has led, in part, to the development of a new branch of economics called behavioral economics. *Behavioral economics* is concerned with how individuals' biases can irrationally affect economic decisions. Rather than viewing people as rational, thoughtful decision makers who impartially weigh choices to draw conclusions, behavioral economists focus on the irrationality of judgments (Ariely & Norton, 2010).

Attributions in a Cultural Context Attribution biases do not affect all of us in the same way. The culture

PSYCH think

connect
WWW.MCGRAWHILLCONNECT.COM/PSYCHOLOGY
Fundamental Attribution Error

> > > We explain our own and each other's behaviors all the time. If we found out that we make the fundamental attribution error on a regular basis, could we choose to stop making that error?

Take the PsychSmart Challenge! Will you make the fundamental attribution error? From chapter 13 in your ebook, select the *Exercises* tab. Then select "Fundamental Attribution Error." After completing this activity, answer Pop Quiz question 4 on p. 359 to test your understanding of this important concept.

in which we are raised clearly plays a role in how we attribute others' behavior.

Take, for example, the fundamental attribution error, the tendency to overestimate the importance of personal, dispositional factors and under-attribute situational factors in determining the causes of others' behavior. The error is pervasive in Western cultures and not in Eastern societies. For instance, adults in India were more likely to use situational attributions than dispositional ones in explaining events. These findings are the opposite of those for the United States, and they contradict the fundamental attribution error (Lien et al., 2006; Miller, 1984).

One reason for the difference may lie in the norms and values of Eastern society, which emphasize social responsibility and societal obligations to a greater extent than in Western societies. Cultural differences in attributions may have profound implications. For example, parents in Asia tend to attribute good academic performance to effort and hard work (situational factors). In contrast, parents in Western cultures tend to deemphasize the role of effort and attribute school success to innate ability (a dispositional factor). As a result, Asian students in general may strive harder to achieve and ultimately outperform U.S. students in school (Lien et al., 2006; Stevenson, Lee, & Mu, 2000).

The difference in thinking between people in Asian and Western cultures is a reflection of a broader difference in the way the world is perceived. Asian societies generally have a *collectivistic orientation,* a worldview that promotes the notion of interdependence. People with a collectivistic orientation generally see themselves as parts of a larger, interconnected social network and as responsible to others. In contrast, people in Western cultures are more likely to hold an *individualist orientation* that emphasizes personal identity and the uniqueness of the individual. They focus more on what sets them apart from others and what makes them special (Markus et al., 2007; Markus & Kitayama, 2003; Wang, 2004).

Children in Asian societies may perform exceptionally well in school, because their culture emphasizes academic success and perseverance.

>> Social Influence and Groups

You have just transferred to a new college and are attending your first class. When the professor enters, the students all immediately begin singing as they fall to their knees and sway side to side. You've never encountered such behavior, and it makes no sense to you. Is it more likely that you will (1) jump up to join the rest of the class or (2) remain seated?

On the basis of what research has told us about **social influence**, the process by which the actions of an individual or group affect the behavior of others, a person would almost always choose the first option. As you undoubtedly know from your own experience, pressures to conform can be painfully strong and can bring about changes in behavior that otherwise never would have occurred (Bentley, Ormerod, & Batty, 2011; Brehm, Kassin, & Fein, 2005).

Why can conformity pressures in groups be so strong? For one reason, groups, and other people generally, play a central role in our lives. As defined by social psychologists, a **group** consists of two or more people who (1) interact with one another; (2) perceive themselves as part of a group, and (3) are interdependent— that is, the events that affect one group member affect other members, and the behavior of members has significant consequences for the success of the group in meeting its goals (Brehm et al., 2005).

> **social influence** The process by which the actions of an individual or group affect the behavior of others.
>
> **group** Two or more people who interact with one another; perceive themselves as part of a group, and are interdependent.

Groups develop and hold *norms,* expectations regarding behavior appropriate to the group. Furthermore, we understand that not adhering to group norms can result in retaliation from other group members, ranging from being ignored to being overtly derided or even being rejected or excluded by the group. Thus, people conform to meet the expectations of the group (Baumeister, Twenge, & Nuss, 2002; Jetten, Hornsey, & Adarves-Yorno, 2006).

Groups exert considerable social influence over individuals, ranging from the mundane, such as the decision to

STUDY TIP

To differentiate among the three types of social pressure—conformity, compliance, and obedience—you need to know the nature and the strength of the social pressure brought to bear on a person.

wear a certain kind of jeans, to extreme cases, such as the cruelty of guards at the Abu Ghraib prison in Iraq. We'll consider three types of social pressure: conformity, compliance, and obedience.

CONFORMITY: FOLLOWING WHAT OTHERS DO

Conformity is a change in behavior or attitudes brought about by a desire to follow the beliefs or standards of other people. Subtle or even unspoken social pressure results in conformity.

The classic demonstration of pressure to conform comes from a series of studies carried out in the 1950s by Solomon Asch (Asch, 1951). In the experiments, the participants thought they were taking part in a test of perceptual skills with six other people. The experimenter showed the participants one card with three lines of varying length and a second card that had a fourth line that matched one of the first three. The task was seemingly straightforward: Each of the participants had to announce aloud which of the first three lines was identical in length to the "standard" line on the second card. Because the correct answer was always obvious, the task seemed easy.

Indeed, the participants all agreed on the first few trials. But then something odd began to happen. From the perspective of the participant in the group who answered last on each trial, all the answers of the first six participants seemed to be wrong—unanimously wrong. And this pattern persisted. Over and over again, the first six participants provided answers that contradicted what the last participant believed to be correct. The last participant faced the dilemma of whether to follow his own perceptions or follow the group by repeating the answer everyone else was giving.

As you might have guessed, this experiment was more contrived than it appeared. The first six participants were actually confederates (paid employees of the experimenter) who had been instructed to give unanimously erroneous answers in many of the trials. And the study had nothing to do with perceptual skills. Instead, the issue under investigation was conformity.

conformity A change in behavior or attitudes brought about by a desire to follow the beliefs or standards of other people.

status The social rank held within a group.

social supporter A group member whose dissenting views make nonconformity to the group easier.

Asch found that in about one-third of the trials, the participants conformed to the unanimous but erroneous group answer, with about 75% of all participants conforming at least once. However, he found strong individual differences. Some participants conformed nearly all the time, whereas others never did.

Since Asch's pioneering work, literally hundreds of studies have examined conformity, and we now know a great deal about the phenomenon. Significant findings focus on:

- *The characteristics of the group.* The more attractive a group is to its members, the greater is its ability to produce conformity. Furthermore, a person's relative **status**, the social rank held within a group, is critical: The lower a person's status in the group, the greater the power of the group over that person's behavior (Hogg & Hains, 2001).
- *The situation in which the individual is responding.* Conformity is considerably higher when people must respond publicly than it is when they can do so privately, as the founders of the United States noted when they authorized secret election ballots (Bond, 2005).
- *The kind of task.* People working on ambiguous tasks and questions (ones having no clear answer) are more susceptible to social pressure (see, for example, Fein, et al., 2007). Asked to give an opinion, such as what type of clothing is fashionable, a person will more likely yield to conformist pressures than he or she will if asked a question of fact. In addition, tasks at which an individual is less competent than others in the group make conformity more likely. For example, a person who is an infrequent computer user may feel pressure to conform to an opinion about computer brands when in a group of experienced computer users.
- *Unanimity of the group.* Groups that unanimously support a position show the most pronounced conformity pressures. But what of the case in which people with dissenting views have an ally in the group, known as a **social supporter**, who agrees with them? Having just one person present who puts forward the minority point of view is sufficient to reduce conformity (Goodwin, Costa, & Adonu, 2004; Levine & Moreland, 2006; Prislin, Brewer, & Wilson, 2002).

Conforming to a social role can have powerful consequences for behavior.

Conformity to Social Roles Another way in which conformity influences behavior is through social roles. *Social roles* are the behaviors that are associated with people in a given position. For example, the role of "student" comprises such behaviors as studying, listening to an instructor, and attending class. Like theatrical roles, social roles tell us what behavior is associated with a given position.

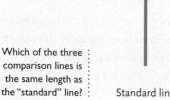

Which of the three comparison lines is the same length as the "standard" line?

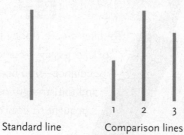

Standard line   Comparison lines

Sometimes, though, social roles influence us so profoundly that we engage in behavior in entirely atypical—and damaging—ways. This fact was brought home in an influential experiment conducted by Philip Zimbardo and colleagues (Zimbardo, 1973). In the study, the researchers set up a mock prison, complete with cells, solitary confinement cubicles, and a small recreation area. The researchers then advertised for students who were willing to spend two weeks in a study of prison life. Once they identified the study participants, the students were randomly assigned by a flip of a coin to be either a prisoner or a prison guard. Neither prisoners nor guards were told how to fulfill their roles (Zimbardo, 1973, 2007; Zimbardo, Maslach, & Haney, 2000).

After just a few days in this mock prison, the students assigned to be guards became abusive to the prisoners, waking them at odd hours and subjecting them to arbitrary punishment. They withheld food from the prisoners and forced them into hard labor. In contrast, the students assigned to the prisoner role soon became docile and submissive to the guards. They became extremely demoralized, and one slipped into a depression so severe he was released after just a few days. In fact, after only six days of captivity, the remaining prisoners' reactions became so extreme that the study was ended.

The experiment (which, it's important to note, drew criticism on both methodological and ethical grounds) provided a clear lesson: Conforming to a social role can have a powerful consequence on the behavior of even normal, well-adjusted people, inducing them to change their behavior in sometimes undesirable ways. This phenomenon may explain how the situation in which U.S. Army guards at the Iraq Abu Ghraib prison found themselves could have led to their abusive behavior toward the prisoners (Haney & Zimbardo, 2009; Zimbardo, 2007).

COMPLIANCE: SUBMITTING TO DIRECT SOCIAL PRESSURE

When we refer to conformity, we usually mean a phenomenon in which the social pressure is subtle or indirect. But in some situations social pressure is much more obvious, with direct, explicit pressure to endorse a particular point of view or behave in a certain way. Social psychologists call the type of behavior that occurs in response to direct social pressure **compliance**.

Several specific techniques represent attempts to gain compliance, including these:

- *Foot-in-the-door technique.* A salesperson comes to your door and asks you to accept a small sample. You agree, thinking you have nothing to lose. A little later comes a larger request, which, because you have already agreed to the first one, you have a hard time turning down.

  The salesperson in this case is using a tried-and-true strategy that social psychologists call the *foot-in-the-door technique.* In the foot-in-the-door technique, you ask a person to agree to a small request and later

ask that person to comply with a more important one. It turns out that compliance with the more important request increases significantly when the person first agrees to the smaller favor.

Why does the foot-in-the-door technique work? One theoretical explanation suggests that involvement with the small request leads to an interest in an issue, and taking an action—any action—makes the individual more committed to the issue, thereby increasing the likelihood of future compliance (Beaman, 1983). Another explanation revolves around people's self-perceptions. By complying with the initial request, individuals may come to see themselves as people who provide help when asked. Then, when confronted with the larger request, they agree in order to avoid cognitive dissonance, as described earlier. Although we don't know if either of these two explanations is more accurate or if another theory might provide better answers, it is clear that the foot-in-the-door strategy is effective (Bloom, McBride, & Pollak, 2006; Burger & Caldwell, 2003; Guéguen et al., 2008).

- *Door-in-the-face technique.* A fund-raiser asks for a $500 contribution. You laughingly refuse, telling her that the amount is way out of your league. She then asks for a $10 contribution. What do you do? If you are like most people, you'll probably be a lot more compliant than you would be if she hadn't asked for the huge contribution first. In this tactic, called the *door-in-the-face technique,* someone makes a large request, expecting it to be refused, and follows it with a smaller one. This strategy, which is the opposite of the foot-in-the-door approach, has also proved to be effective (Ebster & Neumayr, 2008; Pascual & Gueguen, 2005, 2006; Turner et al., 2007).

  The use of this technique is widespread. You may have tried it at some point, perhaps by asking your parents for a large increase in your allowance and later settling for less. Similarly, television writers, by sometimes sprinkling their scripts with obscenities that they know will be cut out by network censors, hope to keep key phrases intact (Cialdini & Sagarin, 2005).

- *That's-not-all technique.* In this technique, a salesperson offers you a deal at an inflated price. But immediately after the initial offer, the salesperson offers an incentive, discount, or bonus to clinch the deal.

  Although it sounds transparent, this practice can be quite effective. In one study, the experimenters set up a booth and sold cupcakes for 75 cents each. In one condition, the experimenters directly told customers

> **compliance** Behavior that occurs in response to direct social pressure.

that the price was 75 cents. But in another condition, they told customers that the price was originally $1 but had been reduced to 75 cents. As we might predict, more people bought cupcakes at the "reduced" price—even though it was identical to the price in the other experimental condition (Burger, Reed, & DeCesare, 1999; Pratkanis, 2007).

- *Not-so-free sample.* If you ever receive a free sample, keep in mind that it comes with a psychological cost. Although they may not couch it in these terms, salespeople who provide samples to potential customers do so to instigate the norm of reciprocity. The *norm of reciprocity* is the well-accepted societal standard dictating that we should treat other people as they treat us. Receiving a *not-so-free sample*, then, suggests the need for reciprocation—in the form of a purchase, of course (Burger et al., 2009; Cialdini, 2006; Park & Antonioni, 2007).

From the perspective of ...

A CANDIDATE FOR STUDENT BODY PRESIDENT What concerns do you have about the ways your opponents might try to manipulate students' opinions to get their votes? What could you do to help students better understand the issues?

Obedience Compliance techniques are used to gently lead people toward agreement with a request. In some cases, however, requests aim to produce **obedience**, a change in behavior in response to the commands of others. Although obedience is considerably less common than

> **obedience** A change in behavior in response to the commands of others.

conformity and compliance, it does occur in several specific kinds of relationships (Nowak, Vallacher & Miller, 2003). For example, we may show obedience to our bosses, teachers, or parents merely because of the power they hold to reward or punish us.

To acquire an understanding of obedience, consider for a moment how you might respond if a stranger said to you:

I've devised a new way of improving memory. All I need is for you to teach people a list of words and then give them a test. The test procedure requires only that you give learners a shock each time they make a mistake on the test. To administer the shocks you will use a "shock generator" that gives shocks ranging from 15 to 450 volts. You can see that the switches are labeled from "slight shock" through "danger: severe shock" at the top level, where there are three red Xs. But don't worry; although the shocks may be painful, they will cause no permanent damage.

Presented with this situation, you would be likely to think that neither you nor anyone else would go along with the stranger's unusual request. Clearly, it lies outside the bounds of what we consider good sense.

Or does it? Suppose the stranger asking for your help were a psychologist conducting an experiment. Or suppose the request came from your teacher, your employer, or your military commander—all people in authority with a seemingly legitimate reason for the request.

If you still believe it's unlikely that you would comply—think again. The situation presented above describes a classic experiment conducted by social psychologist Stanley Milgram in the 1960s. In the study, an experimenter told participants to give increasingly stronger shocks to another person as part of a study on learning. In reality, the experiment had nothing to do with learning; the real issue under consideration was the degree to which participants would comply with the experimenter's requests. In

fact, the "learner" supposedly receiving the shocks was a confederate who never really received any punishment (Milgram, 2005).

Most people who hear a description of Milgram's experiment feel that it is unlikely that *any* participant would give the maximum level of shock—or, for that matter, any shock at all. Even a group of psychiatrists to whom the situation was described predicted that fewer than 2% of the participants would fully comply and administer the strongest shocks (Milgram, 1963, 1974).

However, the actual results contradicted both experts' and nonexperts' predictions. Some 65% of the participants eventually used the highest setting on the shock generator—450 volts—to shock the learner. This obedience occurred even though the learner, who had mentioned at the start of the experiment that he had a heart condition, demanded to be released, screaming, "Let me out of here! Let me out of here! My heart's bothering me. Let me out of here!" Despite the learner's pleas, most participants continued to administer the shocks.

Why did so many individuals comply with the experimenter's demands? The participants, who were extensively interviewed after the experiment, said they obeyed primarily because they believed that the experimenter would be responsible for any potential ill effects that befell the learner. The participants accepted the experimenter's orders, then, because they thought that they personally could not be held accountable for their actions—they could always blame the experimenter (Blass, 1996, 2004).

Milgram's experiment forces us to ask ourselves this question: Would we be able to withstand the intense power of authority?

Although most participants in the Milgram experiment later agreed that the knowledge gained from the study outweighed the discomfort they may have felt, the experiment has been criticized for creating an extremely trying set of circumstances for the participants, thereby raising serious

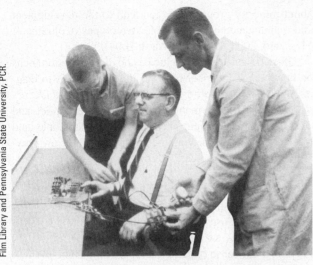

Source: Copyright 1965 by Stanley Milgram. From the film *Obedience*, distributed by the New York University Film Library and Pennsylvania State University, PCR.

The "learner" in Milgram's experiment was connected to a "shock generator" by electrodes attached to the skin—or so the study participants were led to believe.

ethical concerns. (For ethical reasons, the experiment could not be conducted today.) Other critics have suggested that Milgram's methods were ineffective in creating a situation that actually mirrored real-world obedience. For example, how often are people placed in a situation in which someone orders them to continue hurting a victim, while the victim's protests are ignored (Blass, 2000, 2004)?

Despite these concerns, Milgram's research remains the strongest laboratory demonstration of obedience. And partial replications of Milgram's work, conducted in an ethically defensible way, find similar results, adding support for the original work (Blass, 2009; Burger, 2009; Post, 2011).

Furthermore, we need only consider actual instances of obedience to authority to witness some frightening real-life parallels. For instance, after World War II the major defense that Nazi officers gave to excuse their participation in atrocities during the war was that they were "only following orders." Milgram's experiment, which was motivated in part by his desire to explain the behavior of everyday Germans during World War II, forces us to ask ourselves this question: Would we be able to withstand the intense power of authority?

PSYCH think

> > > What are the ethical concerns with the Milgram experiment? What sorts of effects might the experiment have had on participants? Do you think the experiment would have had similar results if it had been conducted not in a laboratory setting, but among members of a social group (such as a fraternity or a sorority) with strong pressures to conform?

>> Stereotypes, Prejudice, and Discrimination

What do you think when someone says, "He's African American," "She's Chinese," "That's a woman driver," "He's a white guy"?

If you're like most people, you'll probably automatically form some sort of impression of what each person is like. Most likely your impression is based on a **stereotype**, a set of generalized beliefs and expectations about a specific group and its members. Stereotypes, which may be negative or positive, grow out of our tendency to categorize and organize the vast amount of information we encounter in our everyday lives. All stereotypes share the common feature of oversimplifying the world: We view individuals not in terms of their unique, personal characteristics but in terms of characteristics we attribute to all the members of a particular group.

Stereotypes can lead to **prejudice**, a negative (or positive) evaluation of a group and its members. For instance, racial prejudice occurs when a member of a racial group is evaluated in terms of race and not because of his or her own characteristics or abilities. Although prejudice can be positive ("I love the Irish"), social psychologists have focused on understanding the roots of negative prejudice ("I hate immigrants").

Common stereotypes and forms of prejudice involve racial, religious, gender, and ethnic groups. Over the years, various groups have been called "lazy" or "shrewd" or "cruel" with varying degrees of regularity by those who are not members of that group. Even today, despite major progress toward reducing legally sanctioned forms of prejudice, such as school segregation, stereotypes remain (Eberhardt et al., 2004; Hunt, Seifert, & Armenta, 2006; Jackson, 2011; Pettibrew, 2004).

Although usually backed by little or no evidence, stereotypes can have harmful consequences. Acting on negative stereotypes results in **discrimination**—behavior directed toward individuals on the basis of their membership in a particular group. Discrimination can lead to exclusion from jobs, neighborhoods, and educational opportunities and may result in lower salaries and benefits for members of specific groups. Discrimination can also result in more favorable treatment to favored groups, as when an employer hires a job applicant of her own racial group because of the applicant's race.

Stereotyping not only leads to overt discrimination but also can cause members of stereotyped groups to behave in ways that reflect the stereotype through a phenomenon known as the *self-fulfilling prophecy*. Self-fulfilling prophecies are expectations about the occurrence of a future

stereotype A set of generalized beliefs and expectations about a particular group and its members.

prejudice A negative (or positive) evaluation of a particular group and its members.

discrimination Behavior directed toward individuals on the basis of their membership in a particular group.

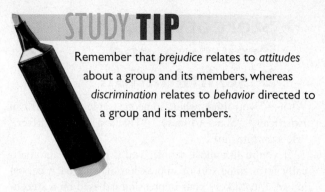
event or behavior that act to increase the likelihood that the event or behavior will occur. For example, if people think that members of a specific group lack ambition, they may treat them in a way that actually brings about a lack of ambition (Madon, Willard, & Guyll, 2006; Oskamp, 2000; Seibt & Förster, 2005).

THE FOUNDATIONS OF PREJUDICE

No one has ever been born disliking a specific racial, religious, or ethnic group. People learn to hate, in much the same way that they learn the alphabet.

According to *observational learning approaches* to stereotyping and prejudice, the behavior of parents, other adults, and peers shapes children's feelings about members of various groups. For instance, bigoted parents may commend their children for expressing prejudiced attitudes. Likewise, young children learn prejudice by imitating the behavior of adult models. Such learning starts at an early age: Children as young as 6 months old demonstrate awareness of different skin colors, and by 3 years of age they begin to show preferences for members of their own race (Bronson & Merryman, 2009; Dovidio & Gaertner, 2006; Ponterotto, Utsey, & Pedersen, 2006).

The mass media also provide information about stereotypes, not just for children but for adults as well. When inaccurate portrayals are the primary source of information about minority groups, they can lead to the development and maintenance of unfavorable stereotypes (Coltraine & Messineo, 2000; Do, 2006; Ward, 2004).

Other explanations of prejudice and discrimination focus on how being a member of a specific group helps to magnify one's sense of self-esteem. According to *social identity theory*, we use group membership as a source of pride and self-worth. Social identity theory suggests that people tend to be *ethnocentric,* viewing the world from their own perspective and judging others in terms of their group membership. Slogans such as "gay pride" and "black is beautiful" illustrate that the groups to which we belong furnish us with a sense of self-respect (Hogg, 2006; Tajfel & Turner, 2004).

However, the use of group membership to provide social respect produces an unfortunate outcome. In an effort to maximize our sense of self-esteem, we may come to think that our own group (our *ingroup*) is better than groups to which we don't belong (our *outgroups*). Consequently, we inflate the positive aspects of our ingroup—and, at the same time, devalue outgroups. Ultimately, we come to view members of outgroups as inferior to members of our ingroup (Tajfel & Turner, 2004). The end result is prejudice toward members of groups of which we are not a part.

MEASURING PREJUDICE AND DISCRIMINATION: THE IMPLICIT ASSOCIATION TEST

Could you be prejudiced and not even know it? The answer, according to the researchers who developed the *Implicit Association Test,* is probably yes. People are often careful about revealing their true attitudes about members of various groups, not only to others but also to themselves. Even though they may truly believe that they are unprejudiced, the reality is that they actually routinely differentiate between people on the basis of race, ethnicity, and sexual orientation.

The Implicit Association Test, or IAT, is an ingenious measure of prejudice that permits a more accurate assessment of people's discrimination between members of different groups. It was developed, in part, as a reaction to the difficulty in finding a questionnaire that would reveal prejudice. Direct questions such as "Would you prefer interacting with a member of Group X rather than Group Y?" typically identify only the most blatant prejudices, because people try to censor their responses (Greenwald et al., 2006; Rudman & Ashmore, 2007).

In contrast, the IAT makes use of the fact that people's automatic reactions often provide the most valid indicator of what they actually believe. Having grown up in a culture that teaches us to think about members of particular groups in specific ways, we tend to absorb associations about those groups that are reflective of the culture (Lane, K. A. et al., 2007).

: Like father, like son?

Sometimes we are aware of the ways that social experiences influence us, and sometimes we are not. For example, you might have attitudes or engage in behaviors that reveal a bias towards a group of people and not be aware of it. Would you like to find out about conscious or unconscious biases that you may have? To find out, take an Implicit Associations Test at https://implicit.harvard .edu/implicit.

The results of the IAT show that almost 90% of the people who take the test have a pro-white implicit bias, and more than two-thirds of non-Arab, non-Muslim test-takers display implicit biases against Arab Muslims. Moreover, more than 80% of heterosexuals display an implicit bias against gays and lesbians (Wittenbrink & Schwarz, 2007).

Of course, having an implicit bias does not mean that people will overtly discriminate, a criticism that has been made of the test. Yet it does mean that the cultural lessons to which we are exposed have a considerable unconscious influence on us.

> People are often careful about revealing their true attitudes about members of various groups, not only to others but also to themselves.

REDUCING PREJUDICE AND DISCRIMINATION

How can we diminish the effects of prejudice and discrimination? Psychologists have developed several strategies that have proved effective.

- *Increasing contact between the target of stereotyping and the holder of the stereotype.* In a ground-breaking 1954 ruling, the United States Supreme Court ruled that school segregation, in which whites and blacks attended separate schools, was unconstitutional. One rationale for the ruling was social psychological evidence that segregation had harmful consequences for the self-esteem and academic performance of minority students. By desegregating schools, the hope was that the contact in school between students of different races ultimately would reduce prejudice and discrimination.

  Research has shown consistently that increasing the amount of interaction between people can reduce negative stereotyping. But only certain kinds of contact are likely to reduce prejudice and discrimination. Situations in which contact is relatively intimate, the individuals are of equal status, or participants must cooperate with one another or are dependent on one another are more likely to reduce stereotyping (Dovidio, Gaertner, & Kawakami, 2003; Pettigrew & Tropp, 2006; Ruggs, Martinez, & Hebl, 2011; Tropp & Pettigrew, 2005).

- *Making values and norms against prejudice more conspicuous.* Sometimes just reminding people about the values they already hold regarding equality and fair treatment of others is enough to reduce discrimination. Similarly, people who hear others making strong, vehement antiracist statements are subsequently more likely to strongly condemn racism (Czopp & Monteith, 2006; Ponterotto, Utsey, & Pedersen, 2006; Tropp & Bianchi, 2006).

- *Providing information about the targets of stereotyping.* Probably the most direct means of changing stereotypical and discriminatory attitudes is education: teaching people to be more aware of the positive characteristics of targets of stereotyping. For instance, when the meaning of puzzling behavior is explained to people who hold stereotypes, they may come to appreciate the significance of the behavior (Banks, 2006; Isbell & Tyler, 2003; Nagda, Tropp, & Paluck, 2006).

From the perspective of ...

A PRISON WARDEN How might overt forms of prejudice and discrimination toward disadvantaged groups be reduced in a state or federal prison?

>> Positive and Negative Social Behavior

Are people basically good or bad? Is it human nature to be loving, considerate, unselfish, and noble? Or is humankind essentially violent and cruel?

Social psychologists have taken different approaches to try to answer these questions. Here we consider what they have learned about what attracts us to others and about two conflicting sides of human behavior—aggression and helping.

LIKING AND LOVING: INTERPERSONAL ATTRACTION AND THE DEVELOPMENT OF RELATIONSHIPS

Nothing is more important in most people's lives than their feelings for others (McAdams, 1989). Unsurprisingly, then, liking and loving have become a major focus of interest for social psychologists. Known more formally as the study of **interpersonal attraction**, or **close relationships**, this area addresses the factors that lead to positive feelings for others.

How Do I Like Thee? Let Me Count the Ways By far the greatest amount of research has focused on liking, probably because it is easier and infinitely less expensive for investigators to conduct short-term experiments to produce states of liking in strangers who have just met than to instigate and observe loving relationships over long periods. Consequently, research has given us a good deal of knowledge about the factors that initially attract two people to each other. The important factors considered by social psychologists are the following:

- *Proximity.* If you live in a dormitory or an apartment, consider the friends you made when you first moved in. Chances are that you became friendliest with those who lived geographically closest to you. In fact, this is one of the more firmly established findings in the literature on interpersonal attraction: Proximity leads to liking (Burgoon et al., 2002; Smith & Weber, 2005).

> **interpersonal attraction (or close relationship)** Positive feelings for others; liking and loving.

- *Mere exposure.* Repeated exposure to a person is often sufficient to produce attraction. Interestingly, repeated exposure to any stimulus—a person, picture, compact disc, or virtually anything—usually makes us like the stimulus more. Becoming familiar with a person can evoke positive feelings; we then transfer the positive feelings stemming from familiarity to the person himself or herself (Butler & Berry, 2004; Zajonc, 2001).
- *Similarity.* Folk wisdom tells us that birds of a feather flock together. However, it also maintains that opposites attract. Social psychologists have come up with a clear verdict regarding which of the two statements is correct: We tend to like those who are similar to us. Discovering that others have similar attitudes, values, or traits promotes our liking for them. Furthermore, the more similar others are, the more we like them (Bates, 2002; Montoya & Insko, 2008; Umphress, Smith-Crowe, & Brief, 2007).

"I'm attracted to you, but then I'm attracted to me, too"

© Richard Cline/The New Yorker Collection/www.cartoonbank.com.

- *Physical attractiveness.* For most people, the equation *beautiful = good* is true. As a result, physically attractive people are more popular than are physically unattractive ones, if all other factors are equal. This finding, which contradicts the values that most people say they hold, is apparent even in childhood—with nursery-school-age children rating their peers' popularity on the basis of attractiveness—and continues into adulthood. Indeed, physical attractiveness may be the single most important element promoting initial liking in college dating situations, although its influence eventually decreases when people get to know each other better (Little, Burt, & Perrett, 2006; Luo & Zhang, 2009; Zebrowitz & Montepare, 2005).

These factors alone, of course, do not account for liking. For example, in one experiment that examined the desired qualities in a friendship, the top-rated qualities in a same-sex friend included sense of humor, warmth and kindness, expressiveness and openness, an exciting personality, and similarity of interests and leisure activities (Sprecher & Reagan, 2002; Whitchurch, Wilson, & Gilbert, 2011).

How Do I Love Thee? Let Me Count the Ways

Whereas our knowledge of what makes people like one another is extensive, our scientific understanding of romantic love is more limited in scope and recently acquired. As a first step, researchers tried to identify the characteristics that distinguish between liking and loving. They discovered that love is not simply a greater quantity of liking, but a qualitatively different psychological state. For instance, at least in its early stages, romantic love includes relatively intense physiological arousal, an all-encompassing interest in another individual, fantasizing about the other, and relatively rapid swings of emotion. Similarly, romantic love,

PSYCH think

> > > Is there any aspect of love that cannot be studied by science? How would you define *falling in love*? How would you study it?

unlike liking, includes elements of passion, closeness, fascination, exclusiveness, sexual desire, and intense caring. We idealize partners by exaggerating their good qualities and minimizing their imperfections (Garza-Guerrero, 2000; Murray, Holmes, & Griffin, 2004).

Other researchers have theorized that there are two main types of love: passionate love and companionate love. **Passionate (or romantic) love** represents a state of intense absorption in someone. It includes intense physiological arousal, psychological interest, and caring for the needs of another. In contrast, **companionate love** is the strong affection we have for those with whom our lives are deeply involved. The love we feel for our parents, other family members, and some close friends falls into the category of companionate love (Loving, Crockett, & Paxson, 2009; Masuda, 2003; Regan, 2006).

Psychologist Robert Sternberg makes an even finer differentiation between types of love. He proposes that love consists of three parts:

- *Decision/commitment,* the initial thoughts that one loves someone and the longer-term feelings of commitment to maintain love
- *Intimacy component,* feelings of closeness and connectedness
- *Passion component,* the motivational drives relating to sex, physical closeness, and romance.

According to Sternberg, these three components combine to produce the different types of love. He suggests that different combinations of the three components vary over the course of relationships. For example, in strong, loving relationships the level of commitment peaks and then remains stable. Passion, in contrast, peaks quickly and then declines and levels off relatively early in most relationships. In addition, relationships are happiest in which the strengths of the various components are similar for both partners (Sternberg, Hojjat, & Barnes, 2001; Sternberg, 2004a, 2006).

Liking and loving clearly show a positive side of human social behavior. Now we turn to behaviors that are just as much a part of social behavior: aggression and helping behavior.

AGGRESSION AND PROSOCIAL BEHAVIOR

Drive-by shootings, carjackings, and abductions are just a few examples of the violence that seems all too common today. Yet we also find examples of generous, unselfish, thoughtful behavior that suggest a more optimistic view of humankind. Rigoberta Menchú Tum, an indigenous Guatemalan who campaigns tirelessly for civil rights on behalf of indigenous peoples and who won the Nobel Peace Prize in 1992, may epitomize this type of behavior. Or contemplate the simple kindnesses of life: lending a valued compact disc, stopping to help a child who has fallen off her bicycle, or merely sharing a candy bar with a friend. Such instances of helping are no less characteristic of human behavior than are the distasteful examples of aggression.

> **passionate (or romantic) love** A state of intense absorption in someone that includes intense physiological arousal, psychological interest, and caring for the needs of another.
>
> **companionate love** The strong affection we have for those with whom our lives are deeply involved.

Hurting Others: Aggression We need look no further than the daily paper or the nightly news to be bombarded with examples of aggression, both on a societal level (war, invasion, assassination) and on an individual level (crime, child abuse, and the many petty cruelties humans are capable of inflicting on one another). Is such aggression an inevitable part of the human condition? Or is aggression primarily a product of particular circumstances that, if changed, could lead to its reduction?

The difficulty of answering such knotty questions becomes apparent as soon as we consider how best to define the term *aggression*. Depending on the way we define the word, many examples of inflicted pain or injury may or may not qualify as aggression. For instance, a rapist is clearly acting with aggression toward his victim. It is less certain that a physician carrying out an emergency medical procedure without an anesthetic, thereby causing incredible pain to the patient, should be considered aggressive.

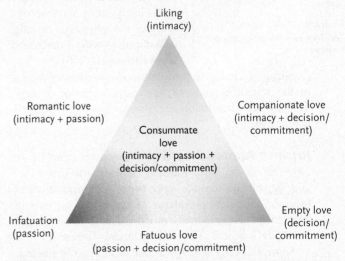

Sternberg's Three Types of Love

Understand Your Relationship Style

Each of us has a general manner in which we approach close relationships with others. Read the three statements below, and determine which best describes you:

1. I find it relatively easy to get close to others and am comfortable depending on them and having them depend on me. I don't often worry about being abandoned or about someone getting too close to me.

2. I am somewhat uncomfortable being close to others; I find it difficult to trust them completely and to allow myself to depend on them. I am nervous when anyone gets too close, and often love partners want me to be more intimate than I feel comfortable being.

3. I find that others are reluctant to get as close as I would like. I often worry that my partner doesn't really love me or won't want to stay with me. I want to merge completely with another person, and this desire sometimes scares people away.

The choice you make suggests the general style of emotional bonds that you develop with others.

If you thought the first statement described you best, it is probably easy for you to develop close ties with others. Around 55% of people describe themselves in this way.

If statement 2 describes you best, you probably have a more difficult time getting close to others, and you may have to work harder to develop close ties with other people. About 25% of people place themselves in this category.

Finally, if statement 3 describes you best, you, along with the 20% of people who describe themselves in this way, aggressively seek out close relationships. However, these relationships are probably a source of concern to you.

Keep in mind that this is an inexact assessment and presents only a very rough estimate of your general approach to close relationships. But your response can be helpful in answering these questions: Are you generally satisfied with your relationships? Would you like to change them in some way?

Most social psychologists define aggression in terms of the intent and the purpose behind the behavior. **Aggression** is intentional injury or harm to another person (Anderson, 2004). By this definition, the rapist is clearly acting aggressively, whereas the physician causing pain during a medical procedure is not (Berkowitz, 2001).

aggression The intentional injury of, or harm to, another person.

catharsis The process of discharging built-up aggressive energy.

Social psychologists have developed several approaches to the scientific study of aggressive behavior, including instinct, frustration-aggression, and observational learning theories.

Instinct Approaches If you have ever punched an adversary in the nose, you may have experienced a certain satisfaction, despite your better judgment. Instinct theories, noting the prevalence of aggression not only in humans but also in animals, propose that aggression is primarily the outcome of innate—or inborn—urges.

Sigmund Freud (1920) was one of the first to suggest, as part of his theory of personality, that aggression is a primary instinctual drive. Konrad Lorenz, an ethologist (a scientist who studies animal behavior), expanded on Freud's notions by arguing that humans, along with members of other species, have a fighting instinct, which in earlier times ensured protection of food supplies and weeded out the weaker of the species (Lorenz, 1966, 1974). Lorenz's instinct approach led to the controversial notion that aggressive energy constantly builds up within an individual until the person finally discharges it in a process called **catharsis**. The longer the energy builds up, says Lorenz, the greater will be the amount of the aggression displayed when it is discharged.

However, little research has found evidence for the existence of a pent-up reservoir of aggression that needs to be released. In fact, some studies flatly contradict the notion of catharsis, leading psychologists to look for other explanations for aggression (Bushman, Wang, & Anderson, 2005; Scheele & DuBois, 2006; Shaver & Mikulincer, 2011; Verona & Sullivan, 2008).

Frustration-Aggression Approaches Frustration-aggression theory suggests that *frustration* (the reaction to the thwarting or blocking of goals) produces anger, leading to a readiness to act aggressively. Whether actual aggression occurs depends on the presence of *aggressive cues*, stimuli that have been associated in the past with actual aggression or violence and that will trigger aggression again (Berkowitz, 2001).

What kinds of stimuli act as aggressive cues? They can range from the most explicit, such as the presence of weapons, to more subtle cues, such as the mere mention of the name of an individual who behaved violently in the past. For example, angered participants in experiments behave significantly more aggressively when in the presence of a gun than a comparable situation in which no guns are present. Similarly, frustrated participants who view a violent movie are more physically aggressive toward a confederate with the same name as the star of the movie than they are toward a confederate with a different name. It appears, then, that frustration does lead to aggression, at least when aggressive cues are present (Berkowitz, 2001; Marcus-Newhall, Pederson, & Carlson, 2000).

Observational Learning Approaches Do we learn to be aggressive? The observational learning (sometimes called social learning) approach to aggression says that we do. Taking an almost opposite view from instinct theories, which focus on innate explanations of aggression, observational learning theory emphasizes that social and environmental conditions can teach individuals to be aggressive. The theory sees aggression not as inevitable, but rather as a learned response that can be understood in terms of rewards and punishments.

Observational learning theory pays particular attention not only to direct rewards and punishments that individuals themselves receive but also to the rewards and punishments that models—individuals who provide a guide to appropriate behavior—receive for their aggressive behavior. According to observational learning theory, people observe the behavior of models and the subsequent consequences of that behavior. If the consequences are positive, the behavior is likely to be imitated when observers find themselves in a similar situation (Askew & Field, 2008; Green & Osborne, 1985).

Suppose, for instance, a girl hits her younger brother when he damages one of her new toys. Whereas instinct theory would suggest that the aggression had been pent up and was now being discharged and frustration-aggression theory would examine the girl's frustration at no longer being able to use her new toy, observational learning theory would look to previous situations in which the girl had viewed others being rewarded for their aggression. For example, perhaps she had watched a friend get to play with a toy after he painfully twisted it out of the hand of another child.

Observational learning theory has received wide research support. For example, nursery-school-age children who have watched an adult model behave aggressively and then receive reinforcement for it later display similar behavior themselves if they have been angered, insulted, or frustrated after exposure. Furthermore, a significant amount of research links watching television shows containing violence with subsequent viewer aggression (Carnagey, Anderson, & Bartholow, 2007; Greer, Dudek-Singer, & Gautreaux, 2006; Winerman, 2005).

Helping Others Turning away from aggression, we move now to the opposite—and brighter—side of human nature: helping behavior. Helping behavior, or **prosocial behavior** as it is more formally known, has been considered under many different conditions. However, the question that psychologists have looked at most closely relates to bystander intervention in emergency situations (Latane & Darley, 1968, 1970; Latane & Nida, 1981; Levine & Crowther, 2008). Why does someone help a person in need?

One critical factor is the number of other people present. When more than one person witnesses an emergency situation, a sense of **diffusion of responsibility** can arise among the bystanders. Diffusion of responsibility is the tendency for people to feel that responsibility for acting is shared, or diffused, among those present. The more people who are present in an emergency, the less personally responsible each individual feels—and therefore the less help he or she provides (Barron & Yechiam, 2002; Blair, Thompson, & Wuensch, 2005; Gray, 2006).

Although most research on helping behavior supports the diffusion-of-responsibility explanation, other factors

> **prosocial behavior** Helping behavior.
>
> **diffusion of responsibility** The tendency for people to feel that responsibility for acting is shared, or diffused, among those present.

From the perspective of ...

A SOCIAL PSYCHOLOGIST How would you interpret the aggression between religious groups in Egypt using each of the three main approaches to the study of aggression: instinct approaches, frustration-aggression approaches, and observational learning approaches? Which of the approaches fits the situation in Egypt best?

Is This Aggression?

To see for yourself the difficulties involved in defining aggression, consider each of the following acts and determine whether it represents aggressive behavior—according to your own definition of aggression.

1. A spider eats a fly. Yes_____ No_____
2. Two wolves fight for the leadership of the pack. Yes_____ No_____
3. A soldier shoots an enemy at the front line. Yes_____ No_____
4. The warden of a prison executes a convicted criminal. Yes_____ No_____
5. A man viciously kicks a cat. Yes_____ No_____
6. A man, while cleaning a window, knocks over a flower pot, which, in falling, injures a pedestrian. Yes_____ No_____
7. Mr. X, a notorious gossip, speaks disparagingly of many people of his acquaintance. Yes_____ No_____
8. A man mentally rehearses a murder he is about to commit. Yes_____ No_____
9. An angry son purposely fails to write to his mother, who is expecting a letter and will be hurt if none arrives. Yes_____ No_____
10. An enraged boy tries with all his might to inflict injury on his antagonist, a bigger boy, but is not successful in doing so. His efforts simply amuse the bigger boy. Yes_____ No_____
11. A senator does not protest the escalation of bombing to which she is normally opposed. Yes_____ No_____
12. A farmer beheads a chicken and prepares it for supper. Yes_____ No_____
13. A hunter kills an animal and mounts it as a trophy. Yes_____ No_____
14. A physician gives a flu shot to a screaming child. Yes_____ No_____
15. A boxer gives his opponent a bloody nose. Yes_____ No_____
16. A Girl Scout tries to assist an elderly woman but trips her by accident. Yes_____ No_____
17. A bank robber is shot in the back while trying to escape. Yes_____ No_____
18. A tennis player smashes her racket after missing a volley. Yes_____ No_____
19. A person commits suicide. Yes_____ No_____
20. A cat kills a mouse, parades around with it, and then discards it. Yes_____ No_____

Source: Benjamin (1985).

are clearly involved in helping behavior. According to a model of the helping process, the decision to give aid involves four basic steps (Garcia et al., 2002; Latané and Darley, 1970):

- *Noticing a person, event, or situation that may require help.*
- *Interpreting the event as one that requires help.* Even if we notice an event, it may be sufficiently ambiguous for us to interpret it as a nonemergency situation. It is here that the presence of others first affects helping behavior. The presence of inactive others may indicate to us that a situation does not require help—a judgment we do not necessarily make if we are alone.
- *Assuming responsibility for helping.* It is at this point that diffusion of responsibility is likely to occur if others are present. Moreover, a bystander's particular expertise is likely to play a role in determining whether he or she helps. For instance,

STUDY TIP

Understand the distinction between the instinctual, frustration-aggression, and observational learning approaches to aggression.

if people with training in medical aid or lifesaving techniques are present, untrained bystanders are less likely to intervene, because they feel they have less expertise.

- *Deciding on and implementing the form of helping.* After we assume responsibility for helping, we must decide how to provide assistance. Helping can range from very indirect forms of intervention, such as calling the police, to more direct forms, such as giving first aid or taking the victim to a hospital. Most social psychologists use a *rewards-costs approach* for helping to predict the nature of the assistance a bystander will choose to provide. The general notion is that the rewards for helping, as perceived by the bystander, must outweigh the costs if helping is to occur, and most research tends to support this notion (Bartlett & DeSteno, 2006; Koper & Jaasma, 2001; Lin & Lin, 2007).

After determining the nature of the assistance needed, the actual help must be implemented. A rewards-costs analysis suggests that we are most likely to use the least costly form of implementation. However, this is not always the case: In some situations, people behave altruistically. **Altruism** is helping behavior that is beneficial to others but clearly requires self-sacrifice. For example, people who helped strangers escape from the burning World Trade Center towers

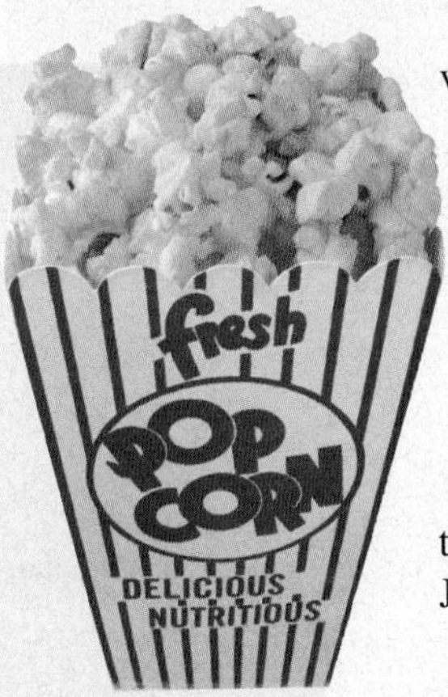

altruism Helping behavior that is beneficial to others but clearly requires self-sacrifice.

The more people who are present in an emergency, the less personally responsible each individual feels—and therefore the less help he or she provides.

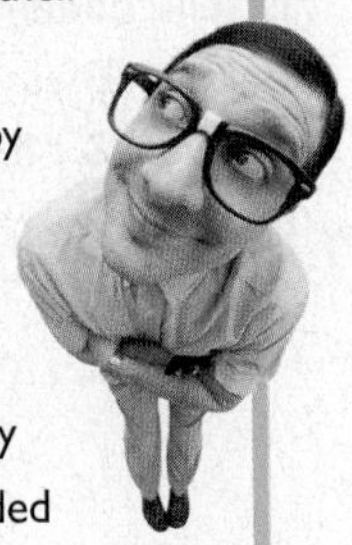

The Helping Process

Noticing a person, event, or situation that may require help

↓

Interpreting the event as one that requires help

↓

Assuming responsibility for helping

↓

Deciding on and implementing the form of helping

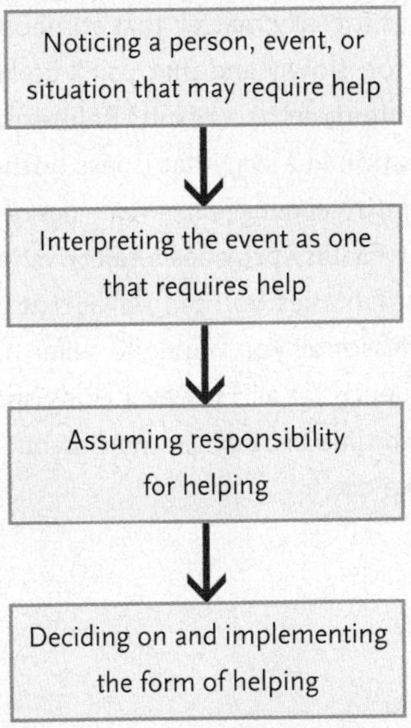

Latané, Bibb; Darley, John M., *The Unresponsive Bystander: Why Doesn't He Help?* 1st ed., © 1970. Printed and electronically reproduced by permission of Pearson Education, Inc., Upper Saddle River, NJ.

BUY IT? > > >

Dealing Effectively with Anger

At one time or another, almost everyone feels angry. The anger may result from a frustrating situation, or it may be due to the behavior of another individual. The way we deal with anger may determine the difference between a promotion and a lost job or a broken relationship and one that mends itself.

How can we manage our anger? Social psychologists who have studied the topic suggest several good anger management strategies that maximize the potential for positive consequences (Nelson & Finch, 2000). Among the most useful strategies are the following:

- *Look again at the anger-provoking situation from the perspective of others.* By taking others' points of view, you may be able to understand the situation better, and with increased understanding you may become more tolerant of the apparent shortcomings of others.
- *Minimize the importance of the situation.* Does it really matter that someone is driving too slowly and that you'll be late to an appointment as a result? Reinterpret the situation in a way that is less bothersome.
- *Fantasize about getting even—but don't act on it.* Fantasy provides a safety valve. In your fantasies, you can yell at that unfair professor all you want and suffer no consequences at all. However, don't spend too much time brooding: Fantasize, but then move on.

continued

- *Relax.* By teaching yourself the kinds of relaxation techniques used in systematic desensitization (discussed in chapter 12, psychological disorders), you can help reduce your reactions to anger. In turn, your anger may dissipate.
- *Focus on your own feelings when communicating the problem.* Verbally attacking someone isn't productive. If you really want to see the problem solved, say how you feel. But beware: Saying that you feel something doesn't mean you are really discussing your feelings. For example, saying "I feel that you are a liar" is an opinion, not a feeling. "I feel very unhappy about the way you wrapped my car around a telephone pole" is an example of a genuine expression of what you are feeling.
- *Wait until you are calm before trying to talk about the problem.* When you are upset, your blood has higher levels of stress hormones and sugar. It pays to wait until your blood levels have returned to normal and you can communicate calmly and clearly.

No matter which of these strategies you try, above all, don't ignore your anger. People who always try to suppress their anger may experience a variety of consequences, such as self-condemnation, frustration, and even physical illness (Burns, Quartana, & Bruehl, 2007; Gardner & Moore, 2008; Quartana & Burns, 2007).

⋮ Altruism is often the only bright side of a natural disaster.

during the 9/11 terrorist attack, putting themselves at mortal risk, would be considered altruistic (Batson & Powell, 2003; Krueger, Hicks, & McGue, 2001; Manor & Gailliot, 2007; Marshall, 2011).

People who intervene in emergency situations tend to possess certain personality characteristics that differentiate them from nonhelpers. For example, helpers are more self-assured, sympathetic, and emotionally understanding, and they have greater *empathy* (a personality trait in which someone observing another person experiences the emotions of that person) than are nonhelpers (Graziano et al., 2007; Stocks, Lishner, & Decker, 2009; Walker & Frimer, 2007). However, most social psychologists agree that no single set of attributes differentiates helpers from nonhelpers. For the most part, temporary situational factors (such a person's mood) determine whether we will intervene in a situation requiring aid (Dovidio et al., 2006; Eisenberg, Guthrie, & Cumberland, 2002).

For REVIEW >>

• What are attitudes, how do they influence behavior, and how can they be changed?

Attitudes are evaluations of a particular person, behavior, belief, or concept. Attitudes can be changed by others, through persuasion. The two primary information-processing routes—central route processing and peripheral route processing—determine our receptiveness to persuasion. When an individual simultaneously holds two cognitions—attitudes or thoughts—that contradict each other, cognitive dissonance occurs. To resolve the contradiction, we either change our thinking or deny there's a contradiction, thereby reducing cognitive dissonance.

Our attitudes about other people are part of social cognition. Often the impressions we form of people influence the way we interpret their behavior. Attribution theory suggests that we use situational or dispositional factors to understand the causes of behavior. (pp. 336–343)

• How do we influence one another?

Social influence is the area of social psychology concerned with situations in which the actions of an individual or group affect the behavior of others. Conformity refers to changes in behavior or attitudes that result from a desire to follow the beliefs or standards of others. Compliance is behavior that results from direct social pressure. Obedience is a change in behavior in response to the commands of others. (pp. 343–347)

- Where do stereotypes come from?

  Stereotypes are generalized beliefs and expectations about a specific group and its members. Stereotyping can lead to prejudice and self-fulfilling prophecies. Prejudice is the negative (or positive) evaluation of a particular group and its members. Stereotyping and prejudice can lead to discrimination, behavior directed toward individuals on the basis of their membership in a particular group. According to observational learning approaches, children learn stereotyping and prejudice by observing the behavior of parents, other adults, and peers. Social identity theory suggests that group membership is used as a source of pride and self-worth, and this may lead people to think of their own group as better than others. (pp. 347–349)

- Why are we attracted to certain people? How do relationships develop?

  The primary determinants of liking include proximity, exposure, similarity, and physical attractiveness. Loving is distinguished from liking by the presence of intense physiological arousal, an all-encompassing interest in another, fantasies about the other, rapid swings of emotion, fascination, sexual desire, exclusiveness, and strong feelings of caring. Love can be categorized as passionate or companionate. In addition, love has several components: intimacy, passion, and decision/commitment. (pp. 350–351)

- What makes some people aggressive, and others kind and helpful?

  Aggression is intentional injury of or harm to another person. Explanations of aggression include instinct approaches, frustration-aggression theory, and observational learning. Helping behavior in emergencies is determined in part by the phenomenon of diffusion of responsibility, which results in a lower likelihood of helping when more people are present. Deciding to help is the outcome of a four-stage process consisting of noticing a possible need for help, interpreting the situation as requiring aid, assuming responsibility for taking action, and deciding on and implementing a form of assistance. (pp. 351–357)

Pop Quiz

1. An evaluation of a particular person, behavior, belief, or concept is called a(n) _____.

2. One brand of peanut butter advertises its product by describing its taste and nutritional value. It is hoping to persuade customers through _____ route processing. In ads for a competing brand, a popular actor happily eats the product—but does not describe it. This approach hopes to persuade customers through _____ route processing.

3. The activity on first impressions and attraction demonstrated how _____.
   a. the order of presentation of information about a person can affect first impressions
   b. the physical appearance of a date (through pictures of each person) can profoundly affect the first impression
   c. first impression can be based on myth and fiction, rather than on fact
   d. cultural values, family, and peers can affect our perceptions of attraction

4. A key point of the activity on the fundamental attribution error is _____.
   a. that the fundamental attribution error is something that used to affect us much more than it does today
   b. that the fundamental attribution error is committed more often by adults than by children
   c. that we know more about our own situation so we tend to say our own behaviors depend on the situation
   d. how closely our tendency to make the fundamental attribution error mirrors our susceptibility to first impressions

5. Sopan was happy to lend his textbook to a fellow student who seemed bright and friendly. He was surprised when his classmate did not return it. His assumption that the bright and friendly student would also be responsible reflects the _____ effect.

6. A _____ _____ , or person who agrees with the dissenting viewpoint, is likely to reduce conformity.

7. Who pioneered the study of conformity?
   a. Skinner
   b. Asch
   c. Milgram
   d. Fiala

8. Which of the following techniques asks a person to comply with a small initial request to enhance the likelihood that the person will later comply with a larger request?
   a. door-in-the-face
   b. foot-in-the-door
   c. that's-not-all
   d. not-so-free sample

9. The negative (or positive) evaluation of a group and its members is called _____.
   a. stereotyping
   b. prejudice
   c. self-fulfilling prophecy
   d. discrimination

10. Paul is a store manager who does not expect women to succeed in business. He therefore offers important, high-profile responsibilities only to men. If the female employees fail to move up in the company, it could be an example of a _____-_____ prophecy.

11. Which of the following sets are the three components of love proposed by Sternberg?
   a. passion, closeness, sexuality
   b. attraction, desire, complementarity
   c. passion, intimacy, decision/commitment
   d. commitment, caring, sexuality

12. If a person in a crowd does not help in an apparent emergency situation because many other people are present, that person has fallen victim to the phenomenon of _____ _____ _____.

Answers

TO POP QUIZ QUESTIONS

1. attitude
2. central, peripheral
3. a
4. c
5. halo
6. social supporter
7. b
8. b
9. b
10. self-fulfilling
11. c
12. diffusion of responsibility

The number following the definitions indicates the page where the term was identified. Consult the index for further page references.

A

abnormal behavior Behavior that causes people to experience distress and prevents them from functioning in their daily lives. **302**

absolute threshold The smallest intensity of a stimulus that must be present for the senses to detect it. **62**

achievement test A test designed to determine a person's level of knowledge in a given subject area. **184**

action potential An electric nerve impulse that travels through a neuron's axon when it is set off by a "trigger," changing the neuron's charge from negative to positive. **34**

activation-synthesis theory Hobson's theory that the brain produces random electrical energy during REM sleep that stimulates memories lodged in various portions of the brain. **93**

activity theory of aging A theory that suggests that the elderly who are most successful while aging are those who maintain the interests and activities they had during middle age. **251**

addictive drugs Drugs that produce a physiological or psychological dependence in the user so that withdrawal from them leads to a craving for the drug that, in some cases, may be nearly irresistible. **100**

adolescence The developmental stage between childhood and adulthood. **238**

aggression The intentional injury of, or harm to, another person. **352**

algorithm A rule that, if applied appropriately, guarantees a solution to a problem. **165**

all-or-none law The rule that neurons are either on or off. **34**

altruism Helping behavior that is beneficial to others but clearly requires self-sacrifice. **355**

Alzheimer's disease A progressive brain disorder that leads to a gradual and irreversible decline in cognitive abilities. **157, 251**

amnesia Memory loss that occurs without other mental difficulties. **157**

androgens Male sex hormones secreted by the testes. **204**

anorexia nervosa A severe eating disorder in which people may refuse to eat while denying that their behavior and appearance—which can become skeleton-like—are unusual. **201**

anterograde amnesia Amnesia in which memory is lost for events that follow an injury. **158**

antianxiety drugs Drugs that reduce the level of anxiety a person experiences, essentially by reducing excitability and increasing feelings of well-being. **329**

antidepressant drugs Medications that improve mood and promote a feeling of well-being in severely depressed individuals. **328**

antipsychotic drugs Drugs that temporarily reduce such psychotic symptoms as agitation, hallucinations, and delusions. **328**

antisocial personality disorder A disorder in which individuals show no regard for the moral and ethical rules of society or the rights of others. **314**

anxiety disorder The occurrence of anxiety without an obvious external cause, affecting daily functioning. **305**

aptitude test A test designed to predict a person's ability in a particular area or line of work. **184**

archetypes According to Jung, universal symbolic representations of a particular person, object, or experience (such as good and evil). **263**

archival research Research in which existing data, such as census documents, college records, and newspaper clippings, are examined to test a hypothesis. **17**

arousal approaches to motivation The belief that we try to maintain certain levels of stimulation and activity, increasing or reducing them as necessary. **195**

association areas Major regions of the cerebral cortex; sites of higher mental processes, such as thought, language, memory, and speech. **49**

assumed-similarity bias The tendency to think of people as being similar to oneself, even when meeting them for the first time. **342**

attachment The positive emotional bond that develops between a child and a specific individual. **229**

attitudes Evaluations of a particular person, behavior, belief, or concept. **336**

attribution theory The theory of personality that seeks to explain how we decide, on the basis of samples of an individual's behavior, what the specific causes of that person's behavior are. **340**

authoritarian parents Parents who are rigid and punitive and value unquestioning obedience from their children. **231**

authoritative parents Parents who are firm, set clear limits, reason with their children, and explain things to them. **231**

autobiographical memories Our recollections of circumstances and episodes from our own lives. **152**

autonomic division The part of the peripheral nervous system that controls involuntary movement of the heart, glands, lungs, and other organs. **40**

autonomy-versus-shame-and-doubt stage The period during which, according to Erikson, toddlers (ages 1½ to 3 years) develop independence and autonomy if exploration and freedom are encouraged, or shame and self-doubt if they are restricted and overprotected. **233**

aversive conditioning A form of therapy that reduces the frequency of undesired behavior by pairing an aversive, unpleasant stimulus with undesired behavior. **321**

axon The part of the neuron that carries messages destined for other neurons. **33**

B

babble Meaningless speechlike sounds made by children from around the age of 3 months through 1 year. **174**

basilar membrane A vibrating structure that runs through the center of the cochlea, dividing it into an upper chamber and a lower chamber and containing sense receptors for sound. **71**

behavior modification A formalized technique for promoting the frequency of desirable behaviors and decreasing the incidence of unwanted ones. **126**

behavioral assessment Direct measures of an individual's behavior used to describe personality characteristics. **274**

behavioral genetics The study of the effects of heredity on behavior. **42**

behavioral neuroscientists (or biopsychologists) Psychologists who specialize in considering the ways in which the biological structures and functions of the body affect behavior. **32**

behavioral perspective The approach that focuses on observable, measurable behavior and ways to change problem behaviors. **13, 303**

behavioral treatment approaches Treatment approaches that build on the basic processes of learning, such as reinforcement and extinction, and assume that normal and abnormal behavior are both learned. **321**

biofeedback A procedure in which a person learns to control through conscious thought internal physiological processes such as blood pressure, heart and respiration rate, skin temperature, sweating, and the constriction of particular muscles. **53**

biological and evolutionary approaches to personality Theories that suggest that important components of personality are inherited. **268**

biomedical perspective The perspective that suggests that when an individual displays symptoms of abnormal behavior, the root cause will be found in a physical examination of the individual, which may reveal a hormonal imbalance, a chemical deficiency, or a brain injury. **302**

biomedical therapy Therapy that relies on drugs and other medical procedures to improve psychological functioning. **319**

bipolar disorder A disorder in which a person alternates between periods of euphoric feelings of mania and periods of depression. **310**

bisexuals Persons who are sexually attracted to people of the same sex and the other sex. **206**

borderline personality disorder A disorder in which individuals have difficulty developing a secure sense of who they are. **314**

bottom-up processing Perception that consists of the progression of recognizing and processing information from individual components of a stimuli and moving to the perception of the whole. **79**

bulimia A disorder in which a person binges on large quantities of food, followed by efforts to purge the food through vomiting or other means. **202**

C

Cannon-Bard theory of emotion The view that both physiological arousal and emotional experience are produced simultaneously by the same nerve stimulus. **213**

case study An in-depth, intensive investigation of an individual or small group of people. **18**

cataclysmic events Strong stressors that occur suddenly, affecting many people at once (for example, natural disasters). **281**

catharsis The process of discharging built-up aggressive energy. **352**

central core The "old brain," which controls basic functions such as eating and sleeping and is common to all vertebrates. **45**

central nervous system (CNS) The part of the nervous system that includes the brain and spinal cord. **38**

central route processing Message interpretation characterized by thoughtful consideration of the issues and arguments used to persuade. **337**

central traits The major traits considered in forming impressions of others. **340**

cerebellum (*ser uh BELL um*) The part of the brain that controls bodily balance. **46**

cerebral cortex The "new brain," responsible for the most sophisticated information processing in the brain; contains four lobes. **47**

chromosomes Rod-shaped structures that contain all basic hereditary information. **223**

chunk A meaningful grouping of stimuli that can be stored as a unit in short-term memory. **140**

circadian rhythms Physiological fluctuations that occur on approximately a 24-hour cycle. **95**

classical conditioning A type of learning in which a neutral stimulus comes to bring about a response after it is paired with a stimulus that naturally brings about that response. **113**

cochlea (*KOKE-le-uh*) A coiled tube in the ear filled with fluid that vibrates in response to sound. **71**

cognitive approaches to motivation Theories suggesting that motivation is a product of people's thoughts and expectations—their cognitions. **197**

cognitive-behavioral approach A treatment approach that incorporates basic principles of learning to change the way people think. **324**

cognitive development The process by which a child's understanding of the world changes as a function of age and experience. **234**

cognitive dissonance The conflict that occurs when a person holds two contradictory attitudes or thoughts (referred to as cognitions). **338**

cognitive learning theory An approach to the study of learning that focuses on the thought processes that underlie learning. **127**

cognitive perspective The perspective that suggests that people's thoughts and beliefs are a central component of normal and abnormal behavior. **13, 303**

cognitive psychology The branch of psychology that focuses on the study of higher mental processes, including thinking, language, memory, problem solving, knowing, reasoning, judging, and decision making. **164**

cognitive treatment approaches Treatment approaches that teach people to think in more adaptive ways by changing their dysfunctional cognitions about the world and themselves. **323**

collective unconscious According to Jung, a common set of ideas, feelings, images, and symbols that we inherit from our ancestors, the whole human race, and even animal ancestors from the distant past. **262**

community psychology A branch of psychology that focuses on the prevention and minimization of psychological disorders in the community. **331**

companionate love The strong affection we have for those with whom our lives are deeply involved. **351**

compliance Behavior that occurs in response to direct social pressure. **345**

compulsion An irresistible urge to repeatedly carry out some act that seems strange and unreasonable. **307**

concepts Categorizations of objects, events, or people that share common properties. **165**

concrete operational stage According to Piaget, the period from 7 to 12 years of age that is characterized by logical thought and a loss of egocentrism. **235**

conditioned response (CR) A response that, after conditioning, follows a previously neutral stimulus (for example, salivation at the ringing of a bell). **115**

conditioned stimulus (CS) A once-neutral stimulus that has been paired with an unconditioned stimulus to bring about a response formerly caused only by the unconditioned stimulus. **115**

cones Cone-shaped, light-sensitive receptor cells in the retina that are responsible for sharp focus and color perception, particularly in bright light. **65**

confirmation bias The tendency to favor information that supports one's initial hypotheses and ignore contradictory information that supports alternative hypotheses or solutions. **171**

conformity A change in behavior or attitudes brought about by a desire to follow the beliefs or standards of other people. **344**

consciousness The awareness of the sensations, thoughts, and feelings we experience at a given moment. **88**

constructive processes Processes in which memories are influenced by the meaning we give to events. **149**

continuous reinforcement schedule Reinforcing of a behavior every time it occurs. **121**

control group A group participating in an experiment that receives no treatment. **19**

convergent thinking The ability to produce responses that are based primarily on knowledge and logic. **172**

coping The efforts to control, reduce, or learn to tolerate the threats that lead to stress. **285**

correlational research Research in which the relationship between two sets of variables is examined to determine whether they are associated, or "correlated." **18**

creativity The ability to generate original ideas or solve problems in novel ways. **172**

cross-sectional research A research method that compares people of different ages at the same point in time. **222**

crystallized intelligence The accumulation of information, skills, and strategies that are learned through experience and can be applied in problem-solving situations. **178**

cue-dependent forgetting Forgetting that occurs when there are insufficient retrieval cues to rekindle information that is in memory. **155**

culture-fair IQ test A test that does not discriminate against the members of any minority group. **188**

D

daily hassles Everyday annoyances, such as being stuck in traffic, that cause minor irritations and may have long-term ill effects if they continue or are compounded by other stressful events. **282**

decay The loss of information in memory through its nonuse. **154**

declarative memory Memory for factual information: names, faces, dates, and the like. **142**

deinstitutionalization The transfer of former mental patients from institutions to the community. **331**

dendrite A cluster of fibers at one end of a neuron that receive messages from other neurons. **33**

dependent variable The variable that is measured and is expected to change as a result of changes caused by the experimenter's manipulation of the independent variable. **20**

depressants Drugs that slow down the nervous system. **103**

depth perception The ability to view the world in three dimensions and to perceive distance. **80**

determinism The idea that people's behavior is produced primarily by factors outside of their willful control. **13**

developmental psychology The branch of psychology that studies the patterns of growth and change that occur throughout life. **220**

Diagnostic and Statistical Manual of Mental Disorders, Fourth Edition, Text Revision (DSM-IV-TR) A system, devised by the American Psychiatric Association, used by most professionals to diagnose and classify abnormal behavior. **303**

difference threshold (just noticeable difference) The smallest level of added or reduced stimulation required to sense that a change in stimulation has occurred. **62**

diffusion of responsibility The tendency for people to feel that responsibility for acting is shared, or diffused, among those present. **353**

discrimination Behavior directed toward individuals on the basis of their membership in a particular group. **347**

disengagement theory of aging A theory that suggests that aging produces a gradual withdrawal from the world on physical, psychological, and social levels. **251**

dispositional causes (of behavior) Perceived causes of behavior that are based on internal traits or personality factors. **341**

divergent thinking The ability to generate unusual, yet nonetheless appropriate, responses to problems or questions. **172**

double standard The view that premarital sex is permissible for males but not for females. **205**

dreams-for-survival theory The theory suggesting that dreams permit information that is critical for our daily survival to be reconsidered and reprocessed during sleep. **93**

drive Motivational tension, or arousal, that energizes behavior to fulfill a need. **195**

drive-reduction approaches to motivation Theories suggesting that a lack of a basic biological requirement such as water produces a drive to obtain that requirement (in this case, the thirst drive). **195**

drug therapy Control of psychological disorders through the use of drugs. **327**

E

eardrum The part of the ear that vibrates when sound waves hit it. **70**

ego The part of the personality that provides a buffer between the id and the outside world. **260**

egocentric thought A way of thinking in which a child views the world entirely from his or her own perspective. **235**

ego-integrity-versus-despair stage According to Erikson, a period from late adulthood until death during which we review life's accomplishments and failures. **243**

electroconvulsive therapy (ECT) A procedure used in the treatment of severe depression in which an electric current of 70 to 150 volts is briefly administered to the head. **329**

embryo A developed zygote that has a heart, a brain, and other organs. **224**

emotional intelligence The set of skills that underlie the accurate assessment, evaluation, expression, and regulation of emotions. **181**

emotions Feelings that generally have both physiological and cognitive elements and that influence behavior. **210**

endocrine system A chemical communication network that sends messages through the bloodstream to all parts of the body. **43**

episodic memory Memory for events that occur in a particular time, place, or context. **143**

estrogens Class of female sex hormones. **205**

evolutionary psychology The branch of psychology that seeks to identify behavior patterns that are a result of our genetic inheritance from our ancestors. **41**

excitatory message A chemical message that makes it more likely that a receiving neuron will fire and an action potential will travel down its axon. **36**

experiment The investigation of the relationship between two (or more) variables by deliberately producing a change in one variable in a situation and observing the effects of that change on other aspects of the situation. **19**

experimental bias Factors that distort how the independent variable affects the dependent variable in an experiment. **24**

experimental group Any group participating in an experiment that receives a treatment. **19**

experimental manipulation The change that an experimenter deliberately produces in a situation. **19**

explicit memory Intentional or conscious recollection of information. **147**

exposure A behavioral treatment for anxiety in which people are confronted, either suddenly or gradually, with a stimulus that they fear. **322**

extinction A basic phenomenon of learning that occurs when a previously conditioned response decreases in frequency and eventually disappears. **116**

extramarital sex Sexual activity between a married person and someone who is not his or her spouse. **206**

F

facial-affect program Activation of a set of nerve impulses that make the face display the appropriate expression. **215**

facial-feedback hypothesis The hypothesis that facial expressions not only reflect emotional experience but also help determine how people experience and label emotions. **215**

familial retardation Mental retardation in which no apparent biological defect exists, but there is a history of retardation in the family. **187**

family therapy An approach that focuses on the family and its dynamics. **326**

feature detection The activation of neurons in the cortex by visual stimuli of specific shapes or patterns. **66**

fetal alcohol syndrome A major cause of mental retardation in newborns, occurring when the mother uses alcohol during pregnancy. **186**

fetus A developing individual, from 8 weeks after conception until birth. **224**

fixations Conflicts or concerns that persist beyond the developmental period in which they first occur. **260**

fixed-interval schedule A schedule that provides reinforcement for a response only if a fixed time period has elapsed, making overall rates of response relatively low. **122**

fixed-ratio schedule A schedule by which reinforcement is given only after a specific number of responses are made. **122**

flashbulb memories Memories centered on a specific, important, or surprising event that are so vivid it is as if they represented a snapshot of the event. **148**

fluid intelligence Intelligence that reflects information-processing capabilities, reasoning, and memory. **178**

formal operational stage According to Piaget, the period from age 12 to adulthood that is characterized by abstract thought. **236**

free will The idea that behavior is caused primarily by choices that are made freely by the individual. **13**

frequency theory of hearing The theory that the entire basilar membrane acts like a microphone, vibrating as a whole in response to a sound. **71**

functional fixedness The tendency to think of an object only in terms of its typical use. **170**

functionalism An early approach to psychology that concentrated on what the mind does—the functions of mental activity—and the role of behavior in allowing people to adapt to their environments. **9**

fundamental attribution error A tendency to over-attribute others' behavior to dispositional causes and the corresponding minimization of the importance of situational causes. **342**

G

gate-control theory of pain The theory that particular nerve receptors in the spinal cord lead to specific areas of the brain related to pain. **75**

general adaptation syndrome (GAS) A theory developed by Selye that suggests that a person's response to a stressor consists of three stages: alarm and mobilization, resistance, and exhaustion. **283**

generalized anxiety disorder The experience of long-term, persistent anxiety and worry. **306**

generativity-versus-stagnation stage According to Erikson, a period in middle adulthood during which we take stock of our contributions to family and society. **243**

genes The parts of the chromosomes through which genetic information is transmitted. **223**

genetic preprogramming theories of aging Theories that suggest that human cells have a built-in time limit to their reproduction, and that after a certain time they are no longer able to divide. **249**

gestalt (*geh-SHTALT*) **psychology** An approach to psychology that focuses on the organization of perception and thinking in a "whole" sense rather than on the individual elements of perception. **9**

Gestalt laws of organization A series of principles that describe how we organize bits and pieces of information into meaningful wholes. **78**

g **or g-factor** The single, general factor for mental ability assumed to underlie intelligence in some early theories of intelligence. **178**

grammar The system of rules that determine how our thoughts can be expressed. **174**

group Two or more people who interact with one another; perceive themselves as part of a group, and are interdependent. **343**

group therapy Therapy in which people meet with a therapist to discuss problems with a group. **326**

H

habituation The decrease in response to a stimulus that occurs after repeated presentations of the same stimulus. **227**

hair cells Tiny cells covering the basilar membrane that, when bent by vibrations entering the cochlea, transmit neural messages to the brain. **71**

hallucinogen A drug that is capable of producing hallucinations, or changes in the perceptual process. **106**

halo effect A phenomenon in which an initial understanding that a person has positive traits is used to infer other uniformly positive characteristics. **342**

health psychology The branch of psychology that investigates the psychological factors related to wellness and illness, including the prevention, diagnosis, and treatment of medical problems. **280**

hemispheres Symmetrical left and right halves of the brain that control the side of the body opposite to their location. **50**

heritability A measure of the degree to which a characteristic is related to genetic, inherited factors. **188**

heterosexuality Sexual attraction and behavior directed to the other sex. **205**

heuristic A cognitive shortcut that may lead to a solution. **165**

homosexuals Persons who are sexually attracted to members of their own sex. **206**

hormone Substance produced by a gland or tissue and circulated through the blood to regulate the functioning or growth of the body. **43**

humanistic approaches to personality Theories that emphasize people's innate goodness and desire to achieve higher levels of functioning. **269**

humanistic perspective The approach that suggests that all individuals naturally strive to grow, develop, and be in control of their lives and behavior. **13**

humanistic therapy Therapy in which the underlying rationale is that people have control of their behavior, can make choices about their lives, and are essentially responsible for solving their own problems. **324**

hypnosis A trancelike state of heightened susceptibility to the suggestions of others. **97**

hypothalamus A tiny part of the brain, located below the thalamus, that maintains the body's internal balance and regulates such vital behavior as eating, drinking, and sexual behavior. **47**

hypothesis A prediction, stemming from a theory, stated in a way that allows it to be tested. **16**

I

id The raw, unorganized, inborn part of personality whose sole purpose is to reduce tension created by primitive drives related to hunger, sex, aggression, and irrational impulses. **259**

identical twins Twins who are genetically identical. **222**

identification The process of wanting to be like another person as much as possible, imitating that person's behavior and adopting similar beliefs and values. **260**

identity The distinguishing character of the individual: who each of us is, what our roles are, and what we are capable of. **242**

identity-versus-role-confusion stage According to Erikson, a time in adolescence of major testing to determine one's unique qualities. **242**

implicit memory Memories of which people are not consciously aware but that can affect subsequent performance and behavior. **147**

incentive approaches to motivation Theories suggesting that motivation stems from the desire to obtain valued external goals, or incentives. **196**

independent variable The variable that is manipulated by an experimenter. **20**

industry-versus-inferiority stage According to Erikson, the last stage of childhood, during which children age 6 to 12 years may develop positive social interactions with others or may feel inadequate and become less sociable. **233**

inferiority complex According to Adler, a problem affecting adults who have not been able to overcome the feelings of inferiority that they developed as children, when they were small and limited in their knowledge about the world. **263**

information processing The way in which people take in, use, and store information. **237**

informed consent A document signed by participants affirming that they have been told the basic outlines of the study and are aware of what their participation will involve. **23**

inhibitory message A chemical message that prevents or decreases the likelihood that a receiving neuron will fire. **36**

initiative-versus-guilt stage According to Erikson, the period during which children ages 3 to 6 years experience conflict between independence of action and the sometimes negative results of that action. **233**

instincts Inborn patterns of behavior that are biologically determined rather than learned. **194**

intellectually gifted The 2% to 4% of the population who have IQ scores greater than 130. **187**

intelligence The capacity to understand the world, think rationally, and use resources effectively when faced with challenges. **178**

intelligence quotient (IQ) A score that takes into account an individual's mental and chronological ages. **183**

intelligence tests Tests devised to quantify a person's level of intelligence. **181**

interactionist approach (to language development) The view that language development is produced through a combination of genetically determined predispositions and environmental circumstances that help teach language. **177**

interference The phenomenon by which information in memory disrupts the recall of other information. **155**

interneurons Neurons that connect sensory and motor neurons, carrying messages between the two. **40**

interpersonal attraction (or close relationship) Positive feelings for others; liking and loving. **350**

interpersonal therapy (IPT) Short-term therapy that focuses on the context of current social relationships. **325**

intimacy-versus-isolation stage According to Erikson, a period during early adulthood that focuses on developing close relationships. **243**

introspection A procedure used to study the structure of the mind in which subjects are asked to describe in detail what they are experiencing when they are exposed to a stimulus. **8**

J

James-Lange theory of emotion The idea that emotional experience is a reaction to bodily events occurring as a result of an external situation ("I feel sad because I am crying"). **212**

L

language The communication of information through symbols arranged according to systematic rules. **173**

language-acquisition device A neural system of the brain hypothesized by Noam Chomsky to permit understanding of language. **176**

latent content of dreams According to Freud, the "disguised" meanings of dreams, hidden by more obvious subjects. **92**

latent learning Learning in which a new behavior is acquired but is not demonstrated until some incentive is provided for displaying it. **127**

lateralization The dominance of one hemisphere of the brain in specific functions, such as language. **50**

learned helplessness A state in which people conclude that unpleasant or aversive stimuli cannot be controlled—a view of the world that becomes so ingrained that they cease trying to remedy the aversive circumstances, even if they actually can exert some influence. **289**

learning A relatively permanent change in behavior brought about by experience. **112**

learning-theory approach (to language development) The theory suggesting that language acquisition follows the principles of reinforcement and conditioning. **176**

levels-of-processing theory The theory of memory that emphasizes the degree to which new material is mentally analyzed. **146**

life review The process by which people examine and evaluate their lives. **252**

limbic system The part of the brain that controls eating, aggression, and reproduction. **47**

lobes The four major sections of the cerebral cortex: frontal, parietal, temporal, and occipital. **48**

longitudinal research A research method that investigates behavior as participants age. **222**

long-term memory Memory that stores information on a relatively permanent basis, although it may be difficult to retrieve. **139**

M

major depression A severe form of depression that interferes with concentration, decision making, and sociability. **309**

mania An extended state of intense, wild elation. **310**

manifest content of dreams According to Freud, the apparent story line of dreams. **92**

masturbation Sexual self-stimulation. **205**

means-ends analysis Repeated testing for differences between the desired outcome and what currently exists. **169**

meditation A learned technique for refocusing attention that brings about an altered state of consciousness. **98**

memory The process by which we encode, store, and retrieve information. **138**

menopause The period during which women stop menstruating and are no longer fertile. **246**

mental age The average age of individuals who achieve a particular level of performance on a test. **182**

mental images Representations in the mind that resemble the object or event being represented. **164**

mental retardation (intellectual disabilities) A condition characterized by significant limitations both in intellectual functioning and in conceptual, social, and practical adaptive skills. **186**

mental set The tendency for old patterns of problem solving to persist. **170**

metabolism The rate at which food is converted to energy and expended by the body. **200**

metacognition An awareness and understanding of one's own cognitive processes. **237**

Minnesota Multiphasic Personality Inventory-2 (MMPI-2) A widely used self-report test that identifies people with psychological difficulties and is employed to predict some everyday behaviors. **272**

mood disorder A disturbance in emotional experience that is strong enough to intrude on everyday living. **309**

mood stabilizers Drugs used to treat mood disorders that prevent manic episodes of bipolar disorder. **329**

motivation The factors that direct and energize the behavior of humans and other organisms. **194**

motor area The part of the cortex that is largely responsible for the body's voluntary movement. **48**

motor (efferent) neurons Neurons that communicate information from the nervous system to muscles and glands. **40**

myelin sheath A protective coat of fat and protein that wraps around axons. **34**

N

narcissistic personality disorder A personality disturbance characterized by an exaggerated sense of self-importance. **315**

narcotics Drugs that increase relaxation and relieve pain and anxiety. **105**

nativist approach (to language development) The theory that a genetically determined, innate mechanism directs language development. **176**

naturalistic observation Research in which an investigator simply observes some naturally occurring behavior and does not make a change in the situation. **17**

nature–nurture issue The issue of the degree to which environment and heredity influence behavior. **220**

need for achievement A stable, learned characteristic in which a person obtains satisfaction by striving for and attaining a level of excellence. **208**

need for affiliation An interest in establishing and maintaining relationships with other people. **209**

need for power A tendency to seek impact, control, or influence over others, and to be seen as a powerful individual. **209**

negative reinforcer An unpleasant stimulus whose *removal* leads to an increase in the probability that a preceding response will be repeated in the future. **119**

neo-Freudian psychoanalysts Psychoanalysts who were trained in traditional Freudian theory but who later rejected some of its major points. **262**

neurons Nerve cells, the basic elements of the nervous system. **33**

neuroplasticity The ability of the brain to adapt by adding neurons, making new connections between neurons, and reorganizing information-processing areas. **50**

neuroscience perspective The approach that views behavior from the perspective of the brain, the nervous system, and other biological functions. **11**

neurotransmitters Chemicals that carry messages across the synapse to the dendrite (and sometimes the cell body) of a receiving neuron. **36**

neutral stimulus A stimulus that, before conditioning, does not naturally bring about the response of interest. **113**

norms Standards of test performance that permit the comparison of one person's score on a test with the scores of other individuals who have taken the same test. **186**

O

obedience A change in behavior in response to the commands of others. **346**

obesity Body weight that is more than 20% above the average weight for a person of a particular height. **199**

object permanence The awareness that objects—and people—continue to exist even if they are out of sight. **235**

observational learning Learning by observing the behavior of another person, or model. **128**

obsession A persistent, unwanted thought or idea that keeps recurring. **307**

obsessive-compulsive disorder A disorder characterized by obsessions or compulsions. **307**

operant conditioning Learning in which a voluntary response is strengthened or weakened, depending on its favorable or unfavorable consequences. **117**

operational definition The translation of a hypothesis into specific, testable procedures that can be measured and observed. **16**

opponent-process theory of color vision The theory that receptor cells for color are linked in pairs, working in opposition to each other. **69**

optic nerve A bundle of ganglion axons that carry visual information to the brain. **66**

otoliths Tiny, motion-sensitive crystals within the semicircular canals that sense body acceleration. **72**

overgeneralization The phenomenon by which children apply language rules even when the application results in an error. **175**

ovulation The point at which an egg is released from the ovaries. **205**

P

panic disorder Anxiety disorder that takes the form of panic attacks lasting from a few seconds to as long as several hours. **306**

parasympathetic division The part of the autonomic division of the nervous system that acts to calm the body after an emergency has ended. **40**

partial (or intermittent) reinforcement schedule Reinforcing of a behavior sometimes but not all of the time. **121**

passionate (or romantic) love A state of intense absorption in someone that includes intense physiological arousal, psychological interest, and caring for the needs of another. **351**

perception The sorting out, interpretation, analysis, and integration of stimuli by the sense organs and brain. **61**

perceptual constancy Phenomenon in which physical objects are perceived to have constant shape, color, and size, despite changes in their appearance or in the physical environment. **79**

peripheral nervous system The part of the nervous system that includes the autonomic and somatic subdivisions; made up of neurons with long axons and dendrites, it branches out from the spinal cord and brain and reaches the extremities of the body. **40**

peripheral route processing Message interpretation characterized by consideration of the source and related general information rather than of the message itself. **337**

permissive parents Parents who give their children relaxed or inconsistent direction and, although they are warm, require little of them. **231**

personality The pattern of enduring characteristics that produce consistency and individuality in a given person. **258**

personality disorder A disorder characterized by a set of inflexible, maladaptive behavior patterns that keep a person from functioning appropriately in society. **314**

personal stressors Major life events, such as the death of a family member, that have immediate negative consequences that generally fade with time. **281**

person-centered therapy Therapy in which the goal is to reach one's potential for self-actualization. **325**

phobias Intense, irrational fears of specific objects or situations. **305**

phonemes The smallest units of speech. **174**

phonology The study of the smallest units of speech, called phonemes. **174**

pituitary gland The major component of the endocrine system, or "master gland," which secretes hormones that control growth and other parts of the endocrine system. **43**

place theory of hearing The theory that different areas of the basilar membrane respond to different frequencies. **71**

placebo A false treatment, such as a pill, "drug," or other substance, without any significant chemical properties or active ingredient. **24**

positive reinforcer A stimulus added to the environment that brings about an increase in a preceding response. **118**

practical intelligence According to Sternberg, intelligence related to overall success in living. **181**

prejudice A negative (or positive) evaluation of a particular group and its members. **347**

preoperational stage According to Piaget, the period from 2 to 7 years of age that is characterized by language development. **235**

priming A phenomenon in which exposure to a word or concept (called a *prime*) later makes it easier to recall related information, even when there is no conscious memory of the word or concept. **148**

principle of conservation The knowledge that quantity is unrelated to the arrangement and physical appearance of objects. **235**

proactive interference Interference in which information learned earlier disrupts the recall of newer material. **155**

procedural memory Memory for skills and habits, such as riding a bike or hitting a baseball, sometimes referred to as *nondeclarative memory*. **143**

progesterone A female sex hormone secreted by the ovaries. **205**

projective personality test A test in which a person is shown an ambiguous stimulus and asked to describe it or tell a story about it. **273**

prosocial behavior Helping behavior. **353**

prototypes Typical, highly representative examples of a concept. **165**

psychoactive drugs Drugs that influence a person's emotions, perceptions, and behavior. **100**

psychoanalysis Freudian psychotherapy in which the goal is to release hidden unconscious thoughts and feelings in order to reduce their power in controlling behavior. **320**

psychoanalytic perspective The perspective that suggests that abnormal behavior stems from childhood conflicts over opposing wishes regarding sex and aggression. **302**

psychoanalytic theory Freud's theory that unconscious forces act as determinants of personality. **259**

psychodynamic approaches to personality Approaches that assume that personality is motivated by inner forces and conflicts about which people have little awareness and over which they have no control. **259**

psychodynamic perspective The approach based on the view that behavior is motivated by unconscious inner forces over which the individual has little control. **13**

psychodynamic therapy Therapy that seeks to bring unresolved past conflicts and unacceptable impulses from the unconscious into the conscious, where clients may deal with the problems more effectively. **319**

psychological tests Standard measures devised to assess behavior objectively; used by psychologists to help people make decisions about their lives and understand more about themselves. **271**

psychology The scientific study of behavior and mental processes. **4**

psychoneuroimmunology (PNI) The study of the relationship among psychological factors, the immune system, and the brain. **286**

psychophysics The study of the relationship between the physical aspects of stimuli and our psychological experience of them. **61**

psychophysiological disorders Medical problems influenced by an interaction of psychological, emotional, and physical difficulties. **280**

psychosexual stages Developmental periods that children pass through during which they encounter conflicts between the demands of society and their own sexual urges. **260**

psychosocial development Development of individuals' interactions and understanding of one another and of their knowledge and understanding of themselves as members of society. **232**

psychosurgery Brain surgery once used to reduce the symptoms of mental disorder but rarely used today. **330**

psychotherapy Treatment in which a trained professional—a therapist—uses psychological techniques to help a person overcome psychological difficulties and disorders, resolve problems in living, or bring about personal growth. **319**

puberty The period at which maturation of the sexual organs occurs, beginning about age 11 or 12 for girls and 13 or 14 for boys. **239**

punishment A stimulus that decreases the probability that a previous behavior will occur again. **119**

R

random assignment to condition A procedure in which participants are assigned to different experimental groups or "conditions" on the basis of chance and chance alone. **20**

rapid eye movement (REM) sleep Sleep occupying 20% of an adult's sleeping time, characterized by increased heart rate, blood pressure, and breathing rate; erections; eye movements; and the experience of dreaming. **90**

recall Memory task in which specific information must be retrieved. **146**

recognition Memory task in which individuals are presented with a stimulus and asked whether they have been exposed to it in the past or to identify it from a list of alternatives. **146**

reflex An automatic, involuntary response to an incoming stimulus. **38, 226**

rehearsal The repetition of information that has entered short-term memory. **141**

reinforcement The process by which a stimulus increases the probability that a preceding behavior will be repeated. **118**

reinforcer Any stimulus that increases the probability that a preceding behavior will occur again. **118**

reliability The property by which tests measure consistently what they are trying to measure. **184**

replication The repetition of research, sometimes using other procedures, settings, and groups of participants, to increase confidence in prior findings. **20**

repression The primary defense mechanism in which unacceptable or unpleasant id impulses are pushed back into the unconscious. **261**

resting state The state in which there is a negative electrical charge of about -70 millivolts within a neuron. **34**

reticular formation The part of the brain extending from the medulla through the pons and made up of groups of nerve cells that can immediately activate other parts of the brain to produce general bodily arousal. **46**

retina The part of the eye that converts the electromagnetic energy of light to electrical impulses for transmission to the brain. **65**

retroactive interference Interference in which there is difficulty in the recall of information learned earlier because of later exposure to different material. **155**

retrograde amnesia Amnesia in which memory is lost for occurrences prior to a certain event. **158**

reuptake The reabsorption of neurotransmitters by a terminal button. **37**

rods Thin, cylindrical receptor cells in the retina that are highly sensitive to light. **65**

Rorschach test A test that involves showing a series of symmetrical visual stimuli to people who then are asked what the figures represent to them. **273**

S

Schachter-Singer theory of emotion The idea that emotions are determined jointly by a nonspecific kind of physiological arousal and its interpretation, based on environmental cues. **213**

schedules of reinforcement Different patterns of frequency and timing of reinforcement following desired behavior. **121**

schemas Organized bodies of information stored in memory that bias the way new information is interpreted, stored, and recalled. **150**

schemas Sets of cognitions about people and social experiences. **339**

schizophrenia A class of disorders in which severe distortion of reality occurs. **311**

scientific method The approach through which psychologists systematically acquire knowledge and understanding about behavior and other phenomena of interest. **15**

self-actualization A state of self-fulfillment in which people realize their highest potential, each in a unique way. **198, 270**

self-efficacy Belief in one's personal capabilities. Self-efficacy underlies people's faith in their ability to carry out a particular behavior or produce a desired outcome. **267**

self-esteem The component of personality that encompasses our positive and negative self-evaluations. **267**

self-report measures A method of gathering data about people by asking them questions about a sample of their behavior. **272**

self-serving bias The tendency to attribute personal success to personal factors (skill, ability, or effort) and to attribute failure to factors outside oneself. **342**

semantic memory Memory for general knowledge and facts about the world, as well as memory for the rules of logic that are used to deduce other facts. **143**

semantic networks Mental representations of clusters of interconnected information. **144**

semantics The rules governing the meaning of words and sentences. **174**

semicircular canals Three tubelike structures of the inner ear containing fluid that sloshes through them when the head moves, signaling rotational or angular movement to the brain. **72**

sensation The activation of the sense organs by a source of physical energy. **61**

sensorimotor stage According to Piaget, the stage from birth to 2 years, during which a child has little competence in representing the environment by using images, language, or other symbols. **235**

sensory adaptation An adjustment in sensory capacity after prolonged exposure to unchanging stimuli. **63**

sensory (afferent) neurons Neurons that transmit information from the perimeter of the body to the central nervous system. **40**

sensory area The brain tissue that corresponds to the different senses, with the degree of sensitivity related to the amount of tissue. **48**

sensory memory The initial, momentary storage of information, lasting only an instant. **139**

sequential research A research method that combines cross-sectional and longitudinal research by considering a number of different age groups and examining them at several points in time. **223**

shaping The process of teaching a complex behavior by rewarding closer and closer approximations of the desired behavior. **124**

short-term memory Memory that holds information for 15 to 25 seconds. **139**

significant outcome Meaningful results that make it possible for researchers to feel confident that they have confirmed their hypotheses. **20**

situational causes (of behavior) Perceived causes of behavior that are based on environmental factors. **341**

skin senses The senses of touch, pressure, temperature, and pain. **73**

social cognition The cognitive processes by which people understand and make sense of others and themselves. **339**

social cognitive approaches to personality Theories that emphasize the influence of a person's cognitions—thoughts, feelings, expectations, and values—as well as observation of others' behavior, in determining personality. **266**

social influence The process by which the actions of an individual or group affect the behavior of others. **343**

social psychology The scientific study of how people's thoughts, feelings, and actions are affected by others. **336**

social support A mutual network of caring, interested others. **293**

social supporter A group member whose dissenting views make nonconformity to the group easier. **344**

somatic division The part of the peripheral nervous system that specializes in the control of voluntary movements and the communication of information to and from the sense organs. **40**

sound The movement of air molecules brought about by a source of vibration. **70**

spinal cord A bundle of neurons that leaves the brain and runs down the length of the back and is the main means for transmitting messages between the brain and the body. **38**

spontaneous recovery The reemergence of an extinguished conditioned response after a period of rest and with no further conditioning. **116**

spontaneous remission Recovery without treatment. **326**

stage 1 sleep The state of transition between wakefulness and sleep, characterized by relatively rapid, low-amplitude brain waves. **88**

stage 2 sleep A sleep deeper than that of stage 1, characterized by a slower, more regular wave pattern, along with momentary interruptions of "sleep spindles." **90**

stage 3 sleep A sleep characterized by slow brain waves, with greater peaks and valleys in the wave pattern than in stage 2 sleep. **90**

stage 4 sleep The deepest stage of sleep, during which we are least responsive to outside stimulation. **90**

status The social rank held within a group. **344**

stereotype A set of generalized beliefs and expectations about a particular group and its members. **347**

stimulants Drugs that have an arousal effect on the central nervous system, causing a rise in heart rate, blood pressure, and muscular tension. **101**

stimulus Energy that produces a response in a sense organ. **61**

stimulus discrimination The process that occurs if two stimuli are sufficiently distinct from each other that one evokes a conditioned response but the other does not; the ability to differentiate between stimuli. **117**

stimulus generalization Occurs when a conditioned response follows a stimulus that is similar to the original conditioned stimulus; the more similar the two stimuli are, the more likely generalization is to occur. **116**

stress A person's response to events that are threatening or challenging. **280**

structuralism Wundt's approach, which focuses on uncovering the fundamental mental components of consciousness, thinking, and other kinds of mental states and activities. **8**

subjective well-being People's own evaluation of their lives in terms of both their thoughts and their emotions. **295**

superego According to Freud, the final personality structure to develop; it represents the rights and wrongs of society as handed down by a person's parents, teachers, and other important figures. **260**

survey research Research in which people chosen to represent a larger population are asked a series of questions about their behavior, thoughts, or attitudes. **17**

sympathetic division The part of the autonomic division of the nervous system that acts to prepare the body for action in stressful situations, engaging all the organism's resources to respond to a threat. **40**

synapse The space between two neurons where the axon of a sending neuron communicates with the dendrites of a receiving neuron by using chemical messages. **35**

syntax Ways in which words and phrases can be combined to form sentences. **174**

systematic desensitization A behavioral technique in which gradual exposure to an anxiety-producing stimulus is paired with relaxation to extinguish the response of anxiety. **322**

T

telegraphic speech Sentences in which words not critical to the message are left out. **175**

temperament The basic, innate disposition that emerges early in life. **232**

teratogens Environmental agents such as a drug, chemical, virus, or other factor that produce a birth defect. **225**

terminal buttons Small bulges at the end of axons that send messages to other neurons. **33**

test standardization A technique used to validate questions in personality tests by studying the responses of people with known diagnoses. **273**

thalamus The part of the brain located in the middle of the central core that acts primarily to relay information about the senses. **46**

Thematic Apperception Test (TAT) A test consisting of a series of pictures about which a person is asked to write a story. **273**

theories Broad explanations and predictions concerning phenomena of interest. **16**

theory of multiple intelligences Gardner's intelligence theory that proposes that there are eight distinct spheres of intelligence. **178**

thinking The manipulation of mental representations of information. **164**

tip-of-the-tongue phenomenon The inability to recall information that one realizes one knows—a result of the difficulty of retrieving information from long-term memory. **145**

top-down processing Perception that is guided by higher-level knowledge, experience, expectations, and motivations. **79**

trait theory A model of personality that seeks to identify the basic traits necessary to describe personality. **264**

traits Consistent personality characteristics and behaviors displayed in different situations. **264**

transcranial magnetic stimulation (TMS) A depression treatment in which a precise magnetic pulse is directed to a specific area of the brain. **330**

transference The transfer of feelings to a psychoanalyst of love or anger that had been originally directed to a client's parents or other authority figure. **320**

transsexuals Persons who believe they were born with the body of the other gender. **208**

treatment The manipulation implemented by the experimenter. **19**

trichromatic theory of color vision The theory that there are three kinds of cones in the retina, each of which responds primarily to a specific range of wavelengths. **68**

trust-versus-mistrust stage According to Erikson, the first stage of psychosocial development, occurring from birth to age 1½ years, during which time infants develop feelings of trust or lack of trust. **233**

Type A behavior pattern A cluster of behaviors involving hostility, competitiveness, time urgency, and feeling driven. **286**

Type B behavior pattern A cluster of behaviors characterized by a patient, cooperative, noncompetitive manner. **286**

U

unconditional positive regard An attitude of acceptance and respect on the part of an observer, no matter what a person says or does. **270**

unconditioned response (UCR) A response that is natural and needs no training (for example, salivation at the smell of food). **113**

unconditioned stimulus (UCS) A stimulus that naturally brings about a particular response without having been learned. **113**

unconscious A part of the personality that contains the memories, knowledge, beliefs, feelings, urges, drives, and instincts of which the individual is not aware. **259**

unconscious wish fulfillment theory Sigmund Freud's theory that dreams represent unconscious wishes that dreamers desire to see fulfilled. **92**

uninvolved parents Parents who show little interest in their children and are emotionally detached. **231**

universal grammar Noam Chomsky's theory that all the world's languages share a common underlying structure. **176**

V

validity The property by which tests actually measure what they are supposed to measure. **185**

variable-interval schedule A schedule by which the time between reinforcements varies around some average rather than being fixed. **123**

variable-ratio schedule A schedule by which reinforcement occurs after a varying number of responses rather than after a fixed number. **122**

variables Behaviors, events, or other characteristics that can change, or vary, in some way. **18**

visual illusions Physical stimuli that consistently produce errors in perception. **81**

W

wear-and-tear theories of aging Theories that suggest that the mechanical functions of the body simply stop working efficiently. **249**

Weber's law A basic law of psychophysics stating that a just noticeable difference is in constant proportion to the intensity of an initial stimulus. **62**

weight set point The particular level of weight that the body strives to maintain. **200**

working memory A set of active, temporary memory stores that actively manipulate and rehearse information. **142**

Z

zone of proximal development (ZPD) According to Vygotsky, the level at which a child can almost, but not fully, comprehend or perform a task on his or her own. **238**

zygote The new cell formed by the union of an egg and sperm. **223**

A

Aartsen, M. J., Martin, M., & Zimprich, D. (2002). Gender differences in level and change in cognitive functioning: Results from the longitudinal aging study Amsterdam. *Gerontology, 50*, 35–38.

Aazh, H., & Moore, B. C. J. (2007). Dead regions in the cochlea at 4 kHz in elderly adults: Relation to absolute threshold, steepness of audiogram, and pure-tone average. *Journal of the American Academy of Audiology, 18*, 97–106. Abboud, L. (2005, July 27). The next phase in psychiatry. *The Wall Street Journal*, pp. D1, D5.

Ablon, J. S., & Jones, E. E. (2005). On analytic process. *Journal of the American Psychoanalytic Association, 53*, 541–568.

Aboitiz, F., Garcia, R., & Brunetti, E. (2006). The origin of Broca's area and its connections from an ancestral working memory network. In Y. Grodzinsky, & K. Amunts, *Broca's region*. New York: Oxford University Press.

Abraham, P. F., & Calabrese, J. R. (2007). Review of: Lithium treatment of mood disorders: A practical guide, 6th rev. ed. *Bipolar Disorders, 9*, 548.

Abraham, S. F., Boyd, C., Luscombe, G., Hart, S., & Russell, J. (2007). When energy in does not equal energy out: Disordered energy control. *Eating Behaviors, 8*, 350–356.

Abramowitz, J. S., Olatunji, B. O., & Deacon, B. J. (2007). Health anxiety, hypochondriasis, and the anxiety disorders. *Behavior Therapy, 38*, 86–94.

Abrams, R. L., Klinger, M. R., & Greenwald, A. G. (2002). Subliminal words activate semantic categories (not automated responses). *Psychonomic Bulletin & Review, 9*, 100–106.

Abt, S. (1999, July 26). Armstrong wins tour and journey. *The New York Times*, pp. D1, D4.

Accardi, M., & Milling, L. (2009). The effectiveness of hypnosis for reducing procedure-related pain in children and adolescents: A comprehensive methodological review. *Journal of Behavioral Medicine, 32*, 328–339.

Adachi, P. C., & Willoughby, T. (2011). The effect of violent video games on aggression: Is it more than just the violence? *Aggression and Violent Behavior, 16*, 55–62.

Adams, B., & Parker, J. D. (1990). Maternal weight gain in women with good pregnancy outcome. *Obstetrics and Gynecology, 76*, 1–7.

Adams, K. B. (2004). Changing investment in activities and interests in elders' lives: Theory and measurement. *International Journal of Aging and Human Development, 58*, 87–108.

Adams, L., & Russakoff, D. (1999, June 12). Dissecting Columbine's cult of the athlete. *The Washington Post*, A1.

Adams, M., Zuniga, X., Hackman, H. W., Castaneda, C. R., & Blumenfeld, W. J. (2000). *Readings for diversity and social justice: An anthology on racism, sexism, anti-Semitism, heterosexism, classism, and ableism*. New York: Routledge.

Adams, W. L. (2006). The truth about photographic memory. *Psychology Today*, March 1. Accessed from www.psychologytoday.com/articles/pto-20060323-000001.html.

Adams-Byers, J., Squilkr Witsell, S., & Moon, S. M. (2004). Gifted students' perceptions of the academic and social/emotional effects of homogeneous and heterogeneous grouping. *Gifted Child Quarterly, 48*, 7–20.

Addolorato, G., Leggio, L., Abenavoli, L., & Gasbarrini, G. (2005). Neurobiochemical and clinical aspects of craving in alcohol addiction: A review. *Addictive Behaviors, 30*, 1209–1224.

Addus, A. A., Chen, D., & Khan, A. S. (2007). Academic performance and advisement of university students: A case study. *College Student Journal, 41*, 316–326.

Adkins, E., & Keel, P. (2005). Does "excessive" or "compulsive" best describe exercise as a symptom of bulimia nervosa? *International Journal of Eating Disorders, 38*, 24–29.

Adler, J. (1984, April 23). The fight to conquer fear. *Newsweek*, pp. 66–72.

Adolphs, R. (2002). Neural systems for recognizing emotion. *Current Opinion in Neurobiology, 12*, 169–177.

Advokat, C. (2005). Differential effects of clozapine versus other antipsychotics on clinical outcome and dopamine release in the brain. *Essential Psychopharmacology, 6*, 73–90.

Aftanas, L., & Golosheykin, S. (2005). Impact of regular meditation practice on EEG activity at rest and during evoked negative emotions. *International Journal of Neuroscience, 115*, 893–909.

Aghajanian, G. K. (1994). Serotonin and the action of LSD in the brain. *Psychiatric Annals, 24*, 137–141.

Agras, W. S., Berkowitz, R. I. (1996). Behavior therapy. In R. E. Hales & S. C. Yudofsky (Eds.), *The American Psychiatric Press synopsis of psychiatry*. Washington, DC: American Psychiatric Press.

Ahiima, R. S., & Osei, S. Y. (2004). Leptin signaling. *Physiology and Behavior, 81*, 223–241.

Aiken, L. (1996). *Assessment of intellectual functioning* (2nd ed.). New York: Plenum.

Aiken, L. (1997). *Psychological testing and assessment* (9th ed.). Needham Heights, MA: Allyn & Bacon.

Aiken, L. (2000a). *Dying, death, and bereavement* (4th ed.). Mahwah, NJ: Erlbaum.

Aiken, L. (2000b). *Personality: Theories, assessment, research, and applications*. Springfield, IL: Charles C. Thomas.

Ainsworth, M. D. S., Blehar, M. C., Waters, E., & Wall, S. (1978). *Patterns of attachment: A psychological study of the strange situation*. Hillsdale, NJ: Erlbaum.

Ajzen, I. (2002). Residual effects of past on later behavior: Habituation and reasoned action perspectives. *Personality and Social Psychology Review, 6*, 107–122.

Akil, H., & Morano, M. I. (1996). The biology of stress: From periphery to brain. In S. J. Watson (Ed.), *Biology of schizophrenia and affective disease*. Washington, DC: American Psychiatric Press.

Akirav, I., Raizel, H., & Maroun, M. (2006). Enhancement of conditioned fear extinction by infusion of the GABA-sub(A) agonist muscimol into the rat prefrontal cortex and amygdala. *European Journal of Neuroscience, 23*, 758–764.

Alho, K., Vorobyev, V. A., Medvedev, S. V., Pakhomov, S. V., Starchenko, M. G., Terganiemi, M., et al. (2006). Selective attention to human voice enhances brain activity bilaterally in the superior temporal sulcus. *Brain Research, 1075*, 142–150.

Allan, G. (2004). Being unfaithful: His and her affairs. In J. Duncombe, K. Harrison., G. Allan, & D. Marsden (Eds.), *The state of affairs: Explorations in infidelity and commitment*. Mahwah, NJ: Lawrence Erlbaum Associates Publishers.

Allison, B. Z., Wolpaw, E. W., & Wolpaw, J. R. (2007). Brain-computer interface systems: Progress and prospects. *Expert Review of Medical Devices, 4*, 463–474.

Allport, G. W. (1961). *Pattern and growth in personality*. New York: Holt, Rinehart and Winston.

Allport, G. W. (1966). Traits revisited. *American Psychologist, 21*, 1–10.

Allport, G. W., & Postman, L. J. (1958). The basic psychology of rumor. In E. D. Maccoby, T. M. Newcomb, & E. L. Hartley (Eds.), *Readings in social psychology* (3rd ed.). New York: Holt, Rinehart and Winston.

Allwood, M. A. (2007). The relations of violence exposure, trauma symptoms and aggressive cognitions to youth violent behavior. *Dissertation Abstracts International: Section B: The Sciences and Engineering, 67*, 5387.

Aloia, M. S., Smith, K., & Arendt, J. T. (2007). Brief behavioral therapies reduce early positive airway pressure discontinuation rates in sleep apnea syndrome: Preliminary findings. *Behavioral Sleep Medicine, 5*, 89–104.

Alon, I., & Brett, J. M. (2007). Perceptions of time and their impact on negotiations in the Arabic-speaking Islamic world. *Negotiation Journal, 23*, 55–73.

Alonso, A., Alonso, S., & Piper, W. (2003). Group psychotherapy. In G. Stricker & T. A. Widiger, et al. (Eds.), *Handbook of psychology: Clinical psychology* (Vol. 8). New York: Wiley

Alonso, Y. (2004, May). The biopsychosocial model in medical research: The evolution of the health concept over the last two decades. *Patient Education and Counseling, 53*(2), 239–244.

Alzheimer's Association. (2011). *2011 Alzheimer's Disease Facts and Figures Report: Quick Facts*. Chicago: Alzheimer's Association.

Amabile, T., Barsade, S., Mueller, J., and Staw, B. (2005). Affect and creativity at work. *Administrative Science Quarterly, 50*, 267–403.

Amato, L., Davoili, M., Perucci, C. A., Ferri, M., Faggiano, F., & Mattick R. P. (2005). An overview of systematic reviews of the effectiveness of opiate maintenance therapies: Available evidence to inform clinical practice and research. *Journal of Substance Abuse Treatment, 28*, 321–329.

Ambady, N., & Rosenthal, R. (1992, March). Thin slices of expressive behavior as predictors of interpersonal consequences: A meta-analysis. *Psychological Bulletin, 111*(2), 256–274.

American Association of Mental Retardation (AAMR). (2002). *Mental retardation: Definition, classification, and systems of supports* (10th ed.). Washington, DC: AAMR.

American Insomnia Association (2005). Causes of insomnia. In L. Vande Creek (Ed.), *Innovations in clinical practice: Focus on adults*. Sarasota, FL: Professional Resource Press/Professional Resource Exchange.

American Psychological Association (APA). (1993a). *Employment survey*. Washington, DC: American Psychological Association.

American Psychological Association (APA). (1993b, January/February). Subgroup norming and the Civil Rights Act. *Psychological Science Agenda, 5*, 6.

American Psychological Association (APA). (1999, March 21). It's not what you say, it's how you say it: Message framing motivates beach-goers to use sunscreen. Retrieved from www.apa.org/releases/sunscreen.html.

American Psychological Association (APA). (2002, August 21). *APA ethics code, 2002*. Washington, DC: American Psychological Association.

American Psychological Association (APA). (2007). *Psychology, careers for the twenty-first century*. Washington, DC: American Psychological Association.

American Psychological Association (APA). (2007). *Where psychologists work*. Washington, DC: American Psychological Association.

American Psychological Association Research Office. (2007). Employment characteristics of APA members by membership status, 2000 (Table 4). In 2000 APA Directory Survey, Washington, DC: American Psychological Association.

American Psychiatric Association Task Force on DSM-IV (2000). *Diagnostic and statistical manual of mental disorders* (4th ed. Text Revision). Arlington, VA: American Psychiatric Association.

American Psychological Association Task Force on Intelligence. (1996). *Intelligence: Knowns and unknowns*. Washington, DC: American Psychological Association.

Amos, A., Wiltshire, S., & Haw, S. (2006). Ambivalence and uncertainty: Experiences of and attitudes towards addiction and smoking cessation in the mid-to-late teens. *Health Education Research, 21*, 181–191.

Anand, G., & Burton, T. M. (2003, April 11). Drug debate: New antipsychotics pose a quandary for FDA, doctors. *The Wall Street Journal*, pp. A1, A8.

Anastasi, A., & Urbina, S. (1997). *Psychological testing* (7th ed.). Englewood Cliffs, NJ: Prentice Hall.

Anderson, C. (2004). Aggression. In E. Borgatta (Ed.), *The encyclopedia of sociology* (rev. ed.). New York: Macmillan.

Anderson, C., & Home, J. A. (2006). Sleepiness enhances distraction during monotonous task. *Sleep: Journal of Sleep and Sleep Disorders Research, 29*, 573–576.

Anderson, C. A., & Dill, K. E. (2000). Video games and aggressive thoughts, feelings, and behavior in the laboratory and in life. *Journal of Personality and Social Psychology, 78*, 772–790.

Anderson, C. A., Carnagey, N. L., Flanagan, M., Benjamin, A. J., Jr., Eubanks, J., & Valentine, J. C. (2004). Violent video games: Specific effects of violent content on aggressive thoughts and behavior. In M. P. Zanna (Ed.), *Advances in experimental social psychology* (Vol. 36). San Diego, CA: Elsevier Academic Press.

Anderson, J. (2000). *Learning and memory: An integrated approach* (2nd ed.). Hoboken, NJ: John Wiley & Sons Inc.

Anderson, J. A., & Adams, M. (1992). Acknowledging the learning styles of diverse student populations: Implications for instructional design. *New Directions for Teaching and Learning, 49*, 19–33.

Anderson, J. R. (1981). Interference: The relationship between response latency and response accuracy. *Journal of Experimental Psychology: Human Learning and Memory, 7*, 311–325.

Anderson, Q. (2005). Lying faces. ScienCentral. www.sciencentral.com/articles/view.php3?language=english&type=article&article_id=218392481.

Andersson, M., Wehling, E., Hugdahl, K. & Lundervold, A. (2006). Age and gender effect in information processing: A dichotic listening study. *Alzheimer's and Dementia, 2*, S377–S378.

Andrasik, F. (2006). Psychophysiological disorders: Headache as a case in point. In F. Andrasik, *Comprehensive handbook of personality and psychopathology: Vol. 2: Adult psychopathology.* Hoboken, NJ: John Wiley & Sons.

Andrasik, F. (2007). What does the evidence show? Efficacy of behavioural treatments for recurrent headaches in adults. *Neurological Science, 28, Supplement*, S70–S77.

Andreasen, N. C. (2005). *Research advances in genetics and genomics: Implications for psychiatry.* Washington, DC: American Psychiatric Publishing.

Anestis, M. D., Anestis, J. C., & Lilienfeld, S. O. (2011). When it comes to evaluating psychodynamic therapy, the devil is in the details. *American Psychologist, 66*, 149–151.

Angoff, W. H. (1988). The nature-nurture debate, aptitudes, and group differences. *American Psychologist, 43*, 713–720.

Ansaldo, A. I., Arguin, M., & Roch Locours, L. A. (2002). The contribution of the right cerebral hemisphere to the recovery from aphasia: A single longitudinal case study. *Brain Languages, 82*, 206–222.

Antonucci, T. C., Lansford, J. E., Akiyama, H., Smith, J., Baltes, M. M., Takahashi, K., et al. (2002). Differences between men and women in social relations, resource deficits, and depressive symptomatology during later life in four nations. *Journal of Social Issues, 58*, 767–783.

Antony, M. M., Brown, T. A., & Barlow, D. H. (1992). Current perspectives on panic and panic disorder. *Current Directions in Psychological Science, 1*, 79–82.

Apanovich, A. M., McCarthy, D., & Salovey, P. (2003). Using message framing to motivate HIV testing among low-income, ethnic minority women. *Health Psychology, 22*, 88–94.

Apkarian, A. V., Bushnell, M. C., Treede, R. D., & Zubeita, J. K. (2005). Human brain mechanisms of pain perception and regulation in health and disease. *European Journal of Pain, 9*, 463–484.

Aponte, J. F., & Wohl, J. (2000). *Psychological intervention and cultural diversity.* Needham Heights, MA: Allyn & Bacon.

Arafat, I., & Cotton, W. L. (1974). Masturbation practices of males and females. *Journal of Sex Research, 10*, 293–307.

Arambula, P., Peper, E., Kawakami, M., & Gibney, K. H. (2001). The physiological correlates of Kundalini yoga meditation: A study of a yoga master. *Applied Psychophysiology & Biofeedback, 26*, 147–153.

Arbuthnott, A., & Sharpe, D. (2009). The effect of physician–patient collaboration on patient adherence in non-psychiatric medicine. *Patient Education and Counseling, 77*, 60–67.

Archambault, D. L. (1992). Adolescence: A physiological, cultural, and psychological no man's land. In G. W. Lawson & A. W. Lawson (Eds.), *Adolescent substance abuse: Etiology, treatment, and prevention.* Gaithersburg, MD: Aspen.

Arena, J. M. (1984, April). A look at the opposite sex. *Newsweek on Campus*, p. 21.

Ariely, D., & Norton, M. I. (2010). Conceptual consumption. *Annual Review of Psychology, 60*, 475–499.

Ariyanto, A., Hornsey, M. J., & Gallois, C. (2006). Group-directed criticism in Indonesia: Role of message source and audience. *Asian Journal of Social Psychology, 9*, 96–102.

Arlin, P. K. (1989). The problem of the problem. In J. D. Sinnott (Ed.), *Everyday problem solving: Theory and applications.* New York: Praeger.

Armstrong, T. (2000). *Multiple intelligences in the classroom* (2nd ed.). Washington, DC: Association for Supervision & Curriculum Development.

Armstrong, T. (2003). *The multiple intelligences of reading and writing: Making the words come alive* (2nd ed.). Washington, DC: Association for Supervision & Curriculum Development.

Arnett, J. J. (2007). Afterword: Aging out of care—Toward realizing the possibilities of emerging adulthood. *New Directions for Youth Development, 113*, 151–161.

Aronson, E. (1994). *The social animal.* New York: Macmillan.

Aronson, J., & Steele, Claude M. (2005). Stereotypes and the fragility of academic competence, motivation, and self-concept. In A. J. Elliot & C. S. Dweck (Eds.), *Handbook of competence and motivation.* New York: Guilford Publications.

Asch, S. E. (1951). Effects of group pressure upon the modification and distortion of judgments. In H. Guetzkow (Ed.), *Groups, leadership, and men.* Pittsburgh: Carnegie Press.

Askew, C., & Field, A. (2008, October). The vicarious learning pathway to fear 40 years on. *Clinical Psychology Review, 28*(7), 1249–1265.

Aslin, R. (2009). The role of learning in cognitive development: Challenges and prospects. *Learning and the infant mind* (pp. 286–295). New York: Oxford University Press.

Aspinwall, L. G., & Taylor, S. E. (1997). A stitch in time: Self-regulation and proactive coping. *Psychological Bulletin, 121*, 417–436.

Atkinson, H. (Ed.). (1997, January 21). Understanding your diagnosis. *HealthNews*, p. 3.

Atkinson, H. G. (2003, August). Are you a "good" patient? *HealthNews*, p. 5.

Atkinson, J. W., & Feather, N. T. (1966). *Theory of achievement motivation.* New York: Krieger.

Atkinson, R. C., & Shiffrin, R. M. (1968). Human memory: A proposed system and its control processes. In K. W. Spence & J. T. Spence (Eds.), *The psychology of learning and motivation: Advances in research and theory* (Vol. 2) (pp. 80–195). New York: Academic Press.

Atkinson, R. C., & Shiffrin, R. M. (1971). The control of short-term memory. *Scientific American, 225*, 82–90.

Atran, S. (2003). Genesis of suicide terrorism. *Science, 299*, 1534–1539.

Auer, J. A., Goodship, A., Arnoczky, S., Pearce, S., Price, J., Claes, L., von Rechenberg, B., Hofmann-Amtenbrinck, M., Schneider, E., Muller-Terpitz, R., Thiele, F., Rippe, K. P., & Grainger, D. W. (2007). Refining animal models in fracture research: Seeking consensus for changing the agenda in optimising both animal welfare and scientific validity for appropriate biomedical use. *BMC Musculoskeletal Disorders, 8*, 72.

Auerbach, J., Erlenmeyer-Kimling, L., Fish, B., Hans, S., Ingraham, L., Marcus, J., et al. (2009). Genetic risks in schizophrenia: Cross-national prospective longitudinal high-risk studies. *Handbook of behavior genetics* (pp. 487–500). New York: Springer Science + Business Media.

Aujoulat, I., Luminet, O., & Deccache, A. (2007). The perspective of patients on their experience of powerlessness. *Quality Health Research, 17*, 772–785.

Auld, F., Hyman, M., & Rudzinski, D. (2005). Theory and strategy of dream interpretation. In F. Auld & M. Hyman (Eds.), *Resolution of inner conflict: An introduction to psychoanalytic therapy* (2nd ed.). Washington, DC: American Psychological Association.

Aussilloux, C., & Baghdadli, A. (2006). Handicap mental et société: Soigner, éduquer, intégrer. Mental handicap and society. *Neuropsychiatrie de l'Enfance et de l'Adolescence, 54*, 336–340.

Austin, S., Ziyadeh, N., Forman, S., Prokop, L., Keliher, A., & Jacobs, D. (2008). Screening high school students for eating disorders: Results of a national initiative. *Preventing Chronic Disease, 5*, A114. Retrieved May 27, 2011, from http://www.cdc.gov/pcd/issues/2008/oct/07_0164.htm.

Averill, J. R. (1975). A semantic atlas of emotional concepts. *Catalog of Selected Documents in Psychology, 5*, 330.

Averill, J. R., Ekman, P., Panksepp, J., Scherer, K. R., Shweder, R. A., Davidson, R. J., et al. (1994). Are there basic emotions? In P. Ekman & R. J. Davidson (Eds.), *The nature of emotion: Fundamental questions.* New York: Oxford University Press.

Avolio, B., & Waldman, D. (1994, September). Variations in cognitive, perceptual, and psychomotor abilities across the working life span: Examining the effects of race, sex, experience, education, and occupational type. *Psychology and Aging, 9*(3), 430–442.

Awad, A., & Voruganti, L. (2007). Antipsychotic medications, schizophrenia and the issue of quality of life. *Quality of life impairment in schizophrenia, mood and anxiety disorders: New perspectives on research and treatment* (pp. 307–319). New York: Springer Science + Business Media.

B

Babkina, A. M., & Bondi, K. M. (Eds.). (2003). *Affirmative action: An annotated bibliography* (2nd ed.). New York: Nova Science.

Bacchiochi, J. R. (2006). Development and validation of the Malingering Discriminant Function Index (M-DFI) for the Minnesota Multiphasic Personality Inventory-2 (MMPI-2). *Dissertation Abstracts International: Section B: The Sciences and Engineering, 66(10-B)*, 5673.

Back, M., Stopfer, J., Vazire, S., Gaddis, S., Schmukle, S., Egloff, B., et al. (2010). Facebook profiles reflect actual personality, not self-idealization. *Psychological Science, 2*, 373–374.

Bäckman, L., Small, B., & Wahlin, Å. (2001). Aging and memory: Cognitive and biological perspectives. *Handbook of the psychology of aging* (5th ed.) (pp. 349–377). San Diego: Academic Press.

Baddeley, A. (2001). Is working memory still working? *American Psychologist, 56*, 849–864.

Baddeley, A., Chincotta, D., & Adlam, A. (2001). Working memory and the control of action: Evidence from task switching. *Journal of Experimental Psychology: General, 130*, 641–657.

Baddeley, A., Eyssenck, M., & Anderson, C. 2009. *Memory*. New York: Psychology Press.

Baddeley, A., & Wilson, B. (1985). Phonological coding and short-term memory in patients without speech. *Journal of Memory and Language, 24*, 490–502.

Baer, J. (1993). *Creativity and divergent thinking: A task-specific approach*. Hillsdale, NJ: Erlbaum.

Bagge, C., & Sher, K. (2008). Adolescent alcohol involvement and suicide attempts: Toward the development of a conceptual framework. *Clinical Psychology Review, 28*, 1283–1296.

Bai, L. (2005). Children at play: A childhood beyond the Confucian shadow. *Childhood: A Global Journal of Child Research, 12*, 9–32.

Bains, O. S. (2006). Insomnia: Difficulty falling and staying asleep. In N. F. Watson, & B. V. Bradley, *Clinician's guide to sleep disorders*. Philadelphia: Taylor & Francis.

Bair, D. (2003). *Jung: A biography*. New York: Little, Brown, and Company.

Baker, J., & Berenbaum, H. (2007). Emotional approach and problem-focused coping: A comparison of potentially adaptive strategies. *Cognition and Emotion, 21*, 95–118.

Baker, S. E., Johnson, P. J., & Slater, D. (2007). Learned food aversion with and without an odour cue for protecting untreated baits from wild mammal foraging. *Applied Animal Behaviour Science, 102, Special issue: Conservation, enrichment and animal behavior*, 410–428.

Balaban, C. D. (2002). Neural substrates linking balance control and anxiety [Special issue: The Pittsburgh special issue]. *Physiology and Behavior, 77*, 469–475.

Balaban, C. D., McBurney, D. H., & Affeltranger, M. A. (2005). Three distinct categories of time course of pain produced by oral capsaicin. *The Journal of Pain, 6*, 315–322.

Balbach, E. D., Gasior, R. J., & Barbeau, E. M. (2003). R. J. Reynolds' targeting of African Americans: 1988–2000. *American Journal of Public Health, 93*, 822–827.

Baldwin, C. L., & Ash, I. K. (2011). Impact of sensory acuity on auditory working memory span in young and older adults. *Psychology and Aging, 26*, 85–91.

Ball, D. (2004). Genetic approaches to alcohol dependence. *British Journal of Psychiatry, 185*, 449–451.

Ball, H., Arseneault, L., Taylor, A., Maughan, B., Caspi, A., & Moffitt, T. (2008, January). Genetic and environmental influences on victims, bullies and bully-victims in childhood. *Journal of Child Psychology and Psychiatry, 49*, 104–112.

Baltes, P. B., & Kunzmann, U. (2003). Wisdom. *Psychologist, 16*, 131–133.

Banaji, M., & Greenwald, A. (1994). Implicit stereotyping and prejudice. *The psychology of prejudice: The Ontario symposium* (Vol. 7) (pp. 55–76). Hillsdale, NJ: Lawrence Erlbaum Associates, Inc.

Bandura, A. (1977). *Social learning theory*. Englewood Cliffs, NJ: Prentice Hall.

Bandura, A. (1986). *Social foundations of thought and action: A social cognitive theory*. Englewood Cliffs, NJ: Prentice Hall.

Bandura, A. (1992). Social cognitive theory. *Six theories of child development: Revised formulations and current issues* (pp. 1-60). London: Jessica Kingsley Publishers.

Bandura, A. (1994). Social cognitive theory of mass communication. In J. Bryant & D. Zillmann (Eds.), *Media effects: Advances in theory and research: LEA's communication series*. Hillsdale, NJ: Erlbaum.

Bandura, A. (1999). Social cognitive theory of personality. In D. Cervone & Y. Shod (Eds.), *The coherence of personality*. New York: Guilford.

Bandura, A. (2000). Self-efficacy: The foundation of agency. In W. J. Perrig and A. Grob (Eds.), *Control of human behavior, mental processes, and consciousness: Essays in honor of the 60th birthday of August Flammer*. Mahwah, NJ: Erlbaum.

Bandura, A. (2001). Social cognitive theory: An agentic perspective. *Annual Review of Psychology, 52*, 1–26.

Bandura, A. (2004). Swimming against the mainstream: The early years from chilly tributary to transformative mainstream. *Behaviour Research and Therapy, 42*, 613–630.

Bandura, A., Grusec, J. E., & Menlove, F. L. (1967). Vicarious extinction of avoidance behavior. *Journal of Personality and Social Psychology, 5*, 16–23.

Bandura, A., & Locke, E. A. (2003). Negative self-efficacy and goal effects revisited. *Journal of Applied Psychology, 88*, 87–99.

Bandura, A., Ross, D., & Ross, S. (1963a). Imitation of film-mediated aggressive models. *Journal of Abnormal and Social Psychology, 66*, 3–11.

Bandura, A., Ross, D., & Ross, S. (1963b). Vicarious reinforcement and imitative learning. *Journal of Abnormal and Social Psychology, 67*, 601–607.

Banerjee, N. (2007, April 20). Massacre in Virginia: On a stunned campus, longing for the normal but enveloped by grief. *The Washington Post*, p. 20.

Banich, T., & Heller, W. (1998). Evolving perspectives on lateralization of function. *Current Directions in Psychological Science, 7*, 1–2.

Banks, J. A. (2006). Improving race relations in schools: From theory and research to practice. *Journal of Social Issues, 62*, 607–614.

Baraas, R. C., Foster, D. H., & Amano, K. (2006). Anomalous trichromats' judgments of surface color in natural scenes under different daylights. *Neuroscience, 23*, 629–635.

Barandiaran, A. A., Pascual, A. C., & Samaniego, C. M. (2006). Una aportación crítica a la teoría kohlberiana: El desarrollo moral en adultos e implicaciones educativas. [A criticism of the Kohlberg theory: The moral development in adults and educative implications.] *Revista de Psicología General y Aplicada, 59*, 165–182.

Bargh, J. A., & Chartrand, T. L. (2000). The mind in the middle: A practical guide to priming and automaticity research. In H. T. Reis & C. M. Judd (Eds.), *Handbook of research methods in social and personality psychology*. New York: Cambridge University Press.

Barkley, R. (2000). *Taking charge of ADHD* (rev. ed.). New York: Guilford Press.

Barkley, R. (2005). *ADHD and the nature of self-control*. New York: Guilford.

Barkow, J. H., Cosmides, L., & Tooby, J. (Eds.). (1992). *The adapted mind*. New York: Oxford University Press.

Barlow, D. H. (2007). *Clinical handbook of psychological disorders: A step-by-step treatment manual* (4th ed.). New York: Guilford Press.

Barmeyer, C. I. (2004). Learning styles and their impact on cross-cultural training: An international comparison in France, Germany and Quebec. *International Journal of Intercultural Relations, 28*, 577–594.

Barnes, V. A., Davis, H. C., Murzynowski, J., & Treiber, F. A. (2004). Impact of meditation on resting and ambulatory blood pressure and heart rate in youth. *Medicine, 66*, 909–914.

Barnett, J. (1978). Contradictory proverbs. In D. Wallechinsky, *The People's Almanac #2* (p. 1121). New York: Doubleday.

Barnett, J. E., Wise, E. H., & Johnson-Greene, D. (2007). Informed consent: Too much of a good thing or not enough? *Professional Psychology: Research and Practice, 38*, 179–186.

Baron, R. (2005). So right it's wrong: Groupthink and the ubiquitous nature of polarized group decision making. In M. P. Zanna (Ed.), *Advances in experimental social psychology* (Vol. 37). San Diego: Elsevier Academic Press.

Baron, R., Vandello, J., & Brunsman, B. (1996, November). The forgotten variable in conformity research: Impact of task importance on social influence. *Journal of Personality and Social Psychology, 71*(5), 915–927.

Barresi, J. (2007). Consciousness and intentionality. *Journal of Consciousness Studies, 14, Special issue: Concepts of Consciousness: Integrating an Emerging Science*, 77–93.

Barrett, L. F., & Salovey, P. (Eds.). (2002). *The wisdom in feeling: Psychological processes in emotional intelligence*. New York: Guilford Press.

Barrett, L. F., & Wager, T. D. (2006). *Current Directions in Psychological Science, 15*, 79–83.

Barron, F. (1990). *Creativity and psychological health: Origins of personal vitality and creative freedom*. Buffalo, NY: Creative Education Foundation.

Barron, G., & Yechiam, E. (2002). Private e-mail requests and the diffusion of responsibility. *Computers in Human Behavior, 18*, 507–520.

Bartecchi, C. E., MacKenzie, T. D., & Schrier, R. W. (1995, May). The global tobacco epidemic. *Scientific American*, 44–51.

Bartholow, B. D., & Anderson, C. A. (2002). Effects of violent video games on aggressive behavior: Potential sex differences. *Journal of Experimental Social Psychology, 38*, 283–290.

Bartholow, B. D., Bushman, B. J., & Sestir, M. A. (2006). Chronic violent video game exposure and desensitization to violence: Behavioral and event-related brain potential data. *Journal of Experimental Social Psychology, 42*, 532–539.

Bartlett, F. (1932). *Remembering: A study in experimental and social psychology*. Cambridge: Cambridge University Press.

Bartlett, M. Y., & DeSteno, D. (2006). Gratitude and prosocial behavior: Helping when it costs you. *Psychological Science, 17*, 319–325.

Bartocci, G. (2004). Transcendence techniques and psychobiological mechanisms underlying religious experience. *Mental Health, Religion and Culture, 7*, 171–181.

Bartoshuk, L. (2000, July/August). The bitter with the sweet. *APS Observer, 11*, 33.

Bartoshuk, L., & Lucchina, L. (1997, January 13). Are you a supertaster? *U.S. News & World Report*, pp. 58–59.

Bartzokis, G., Nuechterlein, K. H., Lu, P. H., Gitlin, M., Rogers, S., & Mintz, J. (2003). Dysregulated brain development in adult men with schizophrenia: A magnetic resonance imaging study. *Biological Psychiatry, 53*, 412–421.

Baruss, I. (2003). *Alterations of consciousness: An empirical analysis for social scientists*. Washington, DC: American Psychological Association.

Bassottdi, G., Villanacci, V., Fisogni, S., Rossi, E., Baronio, P., Clerici, C., Maurer, C. A., Cathomas, G., & Antonelli, E. (2007). Enteric glial cells and their role in gastrointestinal motor abnormalities: Introducing the neurogliopathies. *World Journal of Gastroenterology, 14*, 4035–4041.

Bates, E. (2005). Plasticity, localization, and language development. In S. T. Parker and J. Langer (Eds.), *Biology and knowledge revisited: From neurogenesis to psychogenesis*. Mahwah, NJ: Lawrence Erlbaum Associates.

Bates, P. E., Cuvo, T., Miner, C. A., & Korabek, C. A. (2001). Simulated and community-based instruction involving persons with mild and moderate mental retardation. *Research in Developmental Disabilities, 22*, 95–115.

Bates, R. (2002). Liking and similarity as predictors of multi-source ratings. *Personnel Review, 31*, 540–552.

Batson, C. D. (2006). "Not all self-interest after all": Economics of empathy-induced altruism. In D. De Cremer, M. Zeelenberg, & J. K. Murnighan, *Social psychology and economics*. Mahwah, NJ: Lawrence Erlbaum Associates.

Batson, C. D., & Powell, A. A. (2003). Altruism and prosocial behavior. In T. Millon & M. J. Lerner (Eds.), *Handbook of psychology: Personality and social psychology* (Vol. 5). New York: Wiley.

Bauer, P. (2008). Toward a neuro-developmental account of the development of declarative memory. *Developmental Psychobiology, 50*, 19–31.

Bauman, S., & Kopp, T. G. (2006). Integrating a humanistic approach in outpatient sex offender groups. *Journal for Specialists in Group Work, 31*, 247–261.

Baumeister, A., & Baumeister, A. (2000). Mental retardation: Causes and effects. *Advanced abnormal child psychology* (2nd ed.) (pp. 327–355). Mahwah, NJ: Lawrence Erlbaum Associates Publishers.

Baumeister, A., & Francis, J. L. (2002). Historical development of the dopamine hypothesis of schizophrenia. *Journal of the History of the Neurosciences, 11*, 265–277.

Baumeister, R. F., & Stillman, T. (2006). Erotic plasticity: nature, culture, gender, and sexuality. In R. D. McAnulty, & M. M. Burnette, *Sex and sexuality: Sexuality today: Trends and controversies* (Vol. 1). Westport, CT: Praeger Publishers/ Greenwood Publishing.

Baumeister, R. F., Twenge, J. M., & Nuss, C. K. (2002). Effects of social exclusion on cognitive processes: Anticipated aloneness reduces intelligent thought. *Journal of Personality and Social Psychology, 83*, 817–827.

Baumgartner, F. (2002). The effect of hardiness in the choice of coping strategies in stressful situations. *Studia Psychologica, 44*, 69–75.

Baumrind, D. (2005). Patterns of parental authority and adolescent autonomy. *New Directions for Child and Adolescent Development, 108*, 61–69.

Baumrind, D., Larzelere, R. E., & Cowan, P. A. (2002). Ordinary physical punishment: Is it harmful? Comment on Gershoff (2002). *Psychological Bulletin, 32*, 42–51.

Bayliss, D. M., Jarrold, C., Baddeley, A. D., & Gunn, D. M. (2005a). The relationship between short-term memory and working memory: Complex span made simple? *Memory, 13*, 414–421.

Bayliss, D. M., Jarrold, C., Baddeley, A. D., Gunn, D. M., & Leigh, E. (2005b). Mapping the developmental constraints on working memory span performance. *Developmental Psychology, 41*, 579–597.

Bayne, R. (2005). *Ideas and evidence: Critical reflections on MBTI® theory and practice.* Gainesville, FL: Center for Applications of Psychological Type, CAPT.

Bazalakov, M. H., Wright, J., Schneble, E. J., McDonald, M. P., Hellman, C. J., Levey, A. I., & Blakely, R. D. (2006). Deficits in acetylcholine homeostasis, receptors and behaviors in choline transporter heterozygous mice. *Genes, Brain and Behavior, 6*, 411–424.

BBC (2003). http://news.bbc.co.uk/2/hi/health/medical_notes/3256615.stm.

Beaman, A. (1983, June). Fifteen years of foot-in-the-door research: A meta-analysis. *Personality and Social Psychology Bulletin, 9*(2), 181–196.

Bearman, C. R., Ball, L. J., & Ormerod, T. C. (2007). The structure and function of spontaneous analogising in domain-based problem solving. *Thinking & Reasoning, 13*, 273–294.

Beatty, J. (2000). *The human brain: Essentials of behavioral neuroscience.* Thousand Oaks, CA: Sage.

Beatty, W. W. (2002). Sex difference in geographical knowledge: Driving experience is not essential. *Journal of the International Neuropsychological Society, 8*, 804–810.

Beck, A. P., & Lewis, C. M. (Eds.). (2000). *The process of group psychotherapy: Systems for analyzing change.* Washington, DC: American Psychological Association.

Beck, A. T. (1995). Cognitive therapy: Past, present, and future. In M. J. Mahoney (Ed.), *Cognitive and constructive psychotherapies: Theory, research, and practice.* New York: Springer.

Beck, A. T. (2004). Cognitive therapy, behavior therapy, psychoanalysis, and pharmacotherapy: A cognitive continuum. In A. Freeman, M. J. Mahoney, P. Devito, & D. Martin (Eds.), *Cognition and psychotherapy* (2nd ed.). New York: Springer.

Beck, A. T., Freeman, A., & Davis, D. D. (2004). *Cognitive therapy of personality disorders* (2nd ed.). New York: Guilford Press.

Beck, A. T., & Rector, N. A. (2005). Cognitive approaches to schizophrenia: theory and therapy. *Annual Review of Clinical Psychology, 1*, 577–606.

Beck, H. P., Levinson, S., & Irons, G. (2009). Finding little Albert: A journey to John B. Watson's infant laboratory. *American Psychologist, 64*, 605–614.

Becker, B. E., & Luthar, S. S. (2007). Peer-perceived admiration and social preference: Contextual correlates of positive peer regard among suburban and urban adolescents. *Journal of Research on Adolescence, 17*, 117–144.

Becker, T. (2003). Is emotional intelligence a viable concept? *Academy of Management Review, 28*, 192–195.

Bedard, W. W., & Parsinger, M. A. (1995). Prednisolone blocks extreme intermale social aggression in seizure-induced, brain-damaged rats: Implications for the amygdaloid central nucleus, corticotrophin-releasing factor, and electrical seizures. *Psychological Reports, 77*, 3–9.

Beersma, D. G. M., & Gordijn, M. C. M. (2007). Circadian control of the sleep-wake cycle. *Physiology & Behavior, 90*.

Begg, D., & Langley, J. (2001). Changes in risky driving behavior from age 21 to 26 years. *Journal of Safety Research, 32*, 491–499.

Begley, S. (2002, September 13). The memory of September 11 is seared in your mind; but is it really true? *The Wall Street Journal*, p. B1.

Begley, S. (2005a, April 29). Evolution psychology may not help explain our behavior after all. *The Wall Street Journal*, p. D1.

Begley, S. (2005b, August 19). A spotless mind may ease suffering but erase identity. *The Wall Street Journal*, p. B1.

Begley, S. (2009, February 16). Will the BlackBerry sink the presidency? *Newsweek*, p. 37.

Behrens, M., Lendon, C., & Roe, C. (2009). A common biological mechanism in cancer and Alzheimer's disease? *Current Alzheimer Research, 6*, 196–204.

Beidel, D. C., & Turner, S. M. (2007). Etiology of social anxiety disorder. In D. C. Beidel & S. M. Turner, *Shy children, phobic adults: Nature and treatment of social anxiety disorders* (2nd ed.). Washington, DC: American Psychological Association.

Beilock, S. L., & Carr, T. H. (2005). When high-powered people fail: Working memory and "choking under pressure" in math. *Psychological Science, 16*, 101–105.

Bellezza, F. S. (2000). Mnemonic devices. In A. E. Kazdin (Ed.), *Encyclopedia of psychology* (Vol. 5) (pp. 286–287). Washington, DC: American Psychological Association.

Belli, R. F., & Loftus, E. F. (1996). The pliabilityof autobiographical memory: Misinformation and the false memory problem. In D. C. Rubin (Ed.), *Remembering our past: Studies in autobiographical memory* (pp. 157–179). New York: Cambridge University Press.

Belsky, J. (2006). Determinants and consequences of infant-parent attachment. *Child psychology: A handbook of contemporary issues* (2nd ed.) (pp. 53–77). New York: Psychology Press.

Belsky, J., & Pluess, M. (2009). The nature (and nurture?) of plasticity in early human development. *Perspectives on Psychological Science, 4*, 345–351.

Bem, D. J. (1996). Exotic becomes erotic: A developmental theory of sexual orientation. *Psychological Review, 103*, 320–335.

Bem, D. J., & Honorton, C. (1994). Does psi exist? Replicable evidence for an anomalous process of information transfer. *Psychological Bulletin, 115*, 4–18.

Benca, R. M. (2005). Diagnosis and treatment of chronic insomnia: A review. *Psychiatric Services, 56*, 332–343.

Benderly, B. L. (2004). Looking beyond the SAT. *American Psychological Society, 17*, 12–18.

Benet-Martinez, V., Lee, F., & Leu, J. (2006). Biculturalism and cognitive complexity: Expertise in cultural representations. *Journal of Cross-Cultural Psychology, 37*, 386–407.

Bengston, V., Gans, D., Pulney, N., & Silverstein, M. (2009). *Handbook of theories of aging* (2nd ed.). New York: Springer Publishing Co.

Benham, G., Woody, E. Z., & Wilson, K. S. (2006). Expect the unexpected: Ability, attitude, and responsiveness to hypnosis. *Journal of Personality and Social Psychology, 91*, 342–350.

Benight, C. C. (2004). Collective efficacy following a series of natural disasters. *Stress and Coping: An International Journal, 17*, 401–420.

Benjamin, L. T., Jr. (1985). Defining aggression. An exercise for classroom discussion. *Teaching of Psychology, 12*, 40–42, Table 1, 41.

Benson, E. (2003, April). The science of sexual arousal. *Monitor on Psychology*, pp. 50–56.

Benson, H. (1993). The relaxation response. In D. Goleman & J. Guerin (Eds.), *Mindbody medicine: How to use your mind for better health.* Yonkers, NY: Consumer Reports Publications.

Benson, H., Kornhaber, A., Kornhaber, C., LeChanu, M. N., et al. (1994). Increases in positive psychological characteristics with a new relaxation-response curriculum in high school students. *Journal of Research and Development in Education, 27*, 226–231.

Bentley, R., Ormerod, P., & Batty, M. (2011). Evolving social influence in large populations. *Behavioral Ecology and Sociobiology, 65*, 537–546.

Benton, S. A., Robertson, J. M., Tseng, W. C., Newton, F. B., & Benton, S. L. (2003). Changes in counseling center client problems across 13 years. *Professional Psychology: Research and Practice, 34*, 66–72.

Beresnevaité, M., Taylor, G. J., & Bagby, R. M. (2007). Assessing alexithymia and type A behavior in coronary heart disease patients: A multimethod approach. *Psychotherapy and Psychosomatics, 76*, 186–192.

Bergeron, J. M. (2006). Self-serving bias: A possible contributor of construct-irrelevant variance in high-stakes testing. *Dissertation Abstracts International Section A: Humanities and Social Sciences, 67(1-A)*, 88.

Bergin, A. E., & Garfield, S. L. (Eds.). (1994). *Handbook of psychotherapy and behavior change* (4th ed.). New York: Wiley.

Berk, L. E. (2005). Why parenting matters. In S. Olfman (Ed.), *Childhood lost: How American culture is failing our kids* (pp. 19–53). Westport, CT: Praeger Publishers/ Greenwood Publishing Group.

Berko, A., & Yuval, E. (2007). *The path to paradise: The inner world of suicide bombers and their dispatchers.* Westport, CT: Praeger Security International.

Berkowitz, L. (2001). On the formation and regulation of anger and aggression: A cognitive-neoassociationistic analysis. In W. G. Parrott (Ed.), *Emotions in social psychology: Essential readings.* New York: Psychology Press.

Berman, A. L., Jobes, D. A., & Silverman, M. M. (2006). An integrative-eclectic approach to treatment. In A. L. Berman, D. A. Jobes, & M. M. Silverman, *Adolescent suicide: Assessment and intervention* (2nd ed.). Washington, DC: American Psychological Association.

Bernal, G., Trimble, J. E., Burlew, A. K., & Leong, F. T. (Eds.). (2002). *Handbook of racial and ethnic minority psychology.* Thousand Oaks, CA: Sage.

Bernard, L. L. (1924). *Instinct: A study in social psychology.* New York: Holt.

Bernstein, D., & Loftus, E. (2009a). How to tell if a particular memory is true or false. *Perspectives on Psychological Science, 4*, 370–374.

Bernstein, D., & Loftus, E. (2009b). The consequences of false memories for food preferences and choices. *Perspectives on Psychological Science, 4*, 135–139.

Bernstein, D. M., Loftus, G. R., & Meltzoff, A. N. (2005). Object identification in preschool children and adults. *Developmental Science, 8*, 151–161.

Bernston, G. G., Bechara, A., & Damasio, H. (2007). Amygdala contribution to selective dimensions of emotion. *Social Cognitive and Affective Neuroscience, 2*, 123–129.

Berntsen, D., & Rubin, D. C. (2004). Cultural life scripts structure recall from autobiographical memory. *Memory and Cognition, 32*, 427–442.

Berntsen, D., & Thomsen, D. K. (2005). Personal memories for remote historical events: Accuracy and clarity of flashbulb memories related to World War II. *Journal of Experimental Psychology: General, 134*, 242–257.

Berridge, K. C. (2004). Motivation concepts in behavioral neuroscience. *Physiology and Behavior, 81*, 179–209.

Berrios, G. E. (1996). *The history of mental symptoms: Descriptive psychopathology since the 19th century.* Cambridge: Cambridge University Press.

Berscheid, E. (2006). *The Changing Reasons for Marriage and Divorce.* Mahwah, NJ: Lawrence Erlbaum Associates Publishers.

Bertakis, K. (2009). The influence of gender on the doctor–patient interaction. *Patient Education and Counseling, 76,* 356–360.

Bertakis, K., Franks, P., & Epstein, R. (2009). Patient-centered communication in primary care: Physician and patient gender and gender concordance. *Journal of Women's Health, 18,* 539–545.

Berthoud, H. R. (2002). Multiple neural systems controlling food intake and body weight. *Neuroscience and Biobehavioral Reviews, 26,* 393–428.

Betz, N. (2007). Career self-efficacy: Exemplary recent research and emerging directions. *Journal of Career Assessment, 15,* 403–422.

Beven, Y., Gillis, C., & Lee, K. (2007). "I take the good with the bad, and I moisturize": Defying middle age in the new millennium. *Menopause, 14,* 734–741.

Bhar, S., Gelfand, L., Schmid, S., Gallop, R., DeRubeis, R., Hollon, S., et al. (2008). Sequence of improvement in depressive symptoms across cognitive therapy and pharmacotherapy. *Journal of Affective Disorders, 110,* 161–166.

Bhardwaj, R. D., Curtis, M. A., Spalding, K. L., Buchholz, B. A., Fink, D., Bjork-Eriksson, T., Nordborg, C., Gage, F. H., Druid, H., Eriksson, P. S., & Frisen, J. (2006). Neocortical neurogenesis in humans is restricted to development. *Proceedings of the National Academy of Sciences, 103,* 12564–12568.

Bhatia, S., & Dey, S. (2011). Gender differences in depressive symptoms: The role of daily hassles, coping styles, social support and personal mastery. *Journal of the Indian Academy of Applied Psychology, 37,* 86–97.

Bhugra, D., & Mastrogianni, A. (2004). Globalization and mental disorders. *Journal of Counseling & Values, 35(2),* 83–93.

Bialystok, E., & Martin, M. M. (2004). Attention and inhibition in bilingual children: Evidence from the dimensional change card sort task. *Developmental Science, 7,* 325–339.

Bianchi, S. M., & Casper, L. M. (2000). American families. *Population Bulletin, 55(4).*

Bidwell, D. R. (2011). Wanting to die: How to prevent suicide. In C. Franklin & R. Fong (Eds.), *The church leader's counseling resource book: A guide to mental health and social problems.* New York: Oxford University Press.

Billiard, M. (2008). Narcolepsy: Current treatment options and future approaches. *Neuropsychiatric Disease and Treatment, 4,* 557–566.

Bindemann, M., Burton, A., Leuthold, H., & Schweinberger, S. (2008, July). Brain potential correlates of face recognition: Geometric distortions and the N250r brain response to stimulus repetitions. *Psychophysiology, 45,* 535–544.

Binet, A., & Simon, T. (1916). *The development of intelligence in children (The Binet-Simon Scale).* Baltimore: Williams & Wilkins.

Bingenheimer, J. B., Brennan, R. T., & Earls, F. J. (2005, May 27). Firearm violence exposure and serious violent behavior. *Science, 308,* 1323–1327.

Binstock, R., & George, L. K. (Eds.). (1996). *Handbook of aging and the social sciences* (4th ed.). San Diego: Academic Press.

Birren, J. E. (Ed.). (1996). *Encyclopedia of gerontology: Age, aging and the aged.* San Diego: Academic Press.

Bishop, M. (2005). Quality of life and psychosocial adaptation to chronic illness and disability: Preliminary analysis of a conceptual and theoretical synthesis. *Rehabilitation Counseling Bulletin, 48,* 219–231.

Bitterman, M. E. (2006). Classical conditioning since Pavlov. *Review of General Psychology, 10,* 365–376.

Bittles, A. H., Bower, C., & Hussain, R. (2007). The four ages of Down syndrome. *European Journal of Public Health, 17,* 121–225.

Bizley, J., Walker, K., Silverman, B., King, A., & Schnupp, J. (2009, February). Interdependent encoding of pitch, timbre, and spatial location in auditory cortex. *Journal of Neuroscience, 29,* 2064–2075.

Bjorklund, D. F., & Ellis, B. J. (2005). *Evolutionary psychology and child development: An emerging synthesis.* New York: Guilford Press.

Bjornstad, R. (2006). Learned helplessness, discouraged workers, and multiple unemployment equilibria. *The Journal of Socio-Economics, 35,* 458–475.

Black, A. L., & McCafferty, D. (1998, July 3–5). The age of contentment. *USA Weekend,* 4–6.

Black, P. (2006). Thrust to wholeness: The nature of self-protection. *Review of General Psychology, 10,* 191–209.

Blagrove, M., Farmer, L., & Williams, E. (2004). The relationship of nightmare frequency and nightmare distress to well-being. *Journal of Sleep Research, 13,* 129–136.

Blair, C. A., Thompson, L. F., & Wuensch, K. L. (2005). Electronic helping behavior: The virtual presence of others makes a difference. *Basic and Applied Social Psychology, 27,* 171–178.

Blakeslee, S. (1992, August 11). Finding a new messenger for the brain's signals to the body. *The New York Times,* p. C3.

Blakeslee, S. (2000, January 4). A decade of discovery yields a shock about the brain. *The New York Times,* p. D1.

Blass, T. (1996). Attribution of responsibility and trust in the Milgram obedience experiment. *Journal of Applied Social Psychology, 26,* 1529–1535.

Blass, T. (2004). *The man who shocked the world: The life and legacy of Stanley Milgram.* New York: Basic Books.

Blass, T. (2009). From New Haven to Santa Clara: A historical perspective on the Milgram obedience experiments. *American Psychologist, 64,* 37–45.

Blass, T. (Ed.) (2000). *Obedience to authority: Current perspectives on the Milgram Paradigm.* Mahwah, NJ: Erlbaum.

Blatter, K., & Cajochen, C. (2007). Circadian rhythms in cognitive performance: Methodological constraints, protocols, theoretical underpinnings. *Physiology & Behavior, 90,* 196–208.

Blennow, K., & Vanmechelen, E. (2003). CSF markers for pathogenic processes in Alzheimer's disease: Diagnostic implications and use in clinical neurochemistry. *Brain Research Bulletin, 61,* 235–242.

Blixen, C. E., Singh, A., & Xu, M. (2006). What women want: Understanding obesity and preferences for primary care weight reduction interventions among African-American and Caucasian women. *Journal of the National Medical Association, 98,* 1160–1170.

Bloch, M., Rotenberg, N., Koren, D., & Ehud, K. (2006, January). Risk factors for early postpartum depressive symptoms. *General Hospital Psychiatry, 28(1),* 3–8.

Block, R. I., O'Leary, D. S., Ehrhardt, J. C., Augustinack, J. C., Ghoneim, M. M., Arndt, S., & Hall, J. A. (2000). Effects of frequent marijuana use on brain tissue volume and composition. *Neuroreport 11,* 491–496.

Bloom, P. N., McBride, C. M., & Pollak, K. I. (2006). Recruiting teen smokers in shopping malls to a smoking-cessation program using the foot-in-the-door technique. *Journal of Applied Social Psychology, 36,* 1129–1144.

Bloor, L., Uchino, B., Hicks, A., & Smith, T.W. (2004). Social relationships and physiological functions: The effects of recalling social relationships on cardiovascular reactivity. *Annals of Behavioral Medicine, 28,* 29–38.

Blum, D. (2002). *Love at goon park: Harry Harlow and the science of affection.* Cambridge, MA: Perseus.

Boahen, K. (2005, May). Neuromorphic micro-chips. *Scientific American,* 56–64.

Bock, R. (1991). Prediction of growth. *Best methods for the analysis of change: Recent advances, unanswered questions, future directions* (pp. 126–136). Washington, DC: American Psychological Association.

Bode, C., de Ridder, D. T., Kuijer, R. G., & Bensing, J. M. (2007). Effects of an intervention promoting proactive coping competencies in middle and late adulthood. *Gerontologist, 47,* 42–51.

Boden, J. M., Fergusson, D. M., & Horwood, L. J. (2007). Anxiety disorders and suicidal behaviours in adolescence and young adulthood: Findings from a longitudinal study. *Psychological Medicine, 37,* 431–440.

Bodin, G. (2006). Review of harvesting free association. *Psychoanalytic Quarterly, 75,* 629–632.

Bogart, R. K., McDaniel, R. J., Dunn, W. J., Hunter, C., Peterson, A. L., & Write, E. E. (2007). Efficacy of group cognitive behavior therapy for the treatment of masticatory myofascial pain. *Military Medicine, 172,* 169–174.

Bogenschutz, M. P., Geppert, C. M., & George, J. (2006). The role of twelve-step approaches in dual diagnosis treatment and recovery. *American Journal of Addiction, 15,* 50–60.

Bohart, A. C. (2006). Understanding person-centered therapy: A review of Paul Wilkins' Person-centered therapy in focus. *Person-Centered and Experiential Psychotherapies, 5,* 138–143.

Bohn, A., & Berntsen, D. (2007). Pleasantness bias in flashbulb memories: Positive and negative flashbulb memories of the fall of the Berlin Wall among East and West Germans. *Memory and Cognition, 35,* 565–577.

Boisvert, C. M., & Faust, D. (2003). Leading researchers' consensus on psychotherapy research findings: Implications for the teaching and conduct of psychotherapy. *Professional Psychology: Research and Practice, 34,* 508–513.

Boles, D. B. (2005). A large-sample study of sex differences in functional cerebral lateralization. *Journal of Clinical and Experimental Neuropsychology, 27,* 759–768.

Bolger, N., & Amarel, D. (2007). Effects of social support visibility on adjustment to stress: experimental evidence. *Journal of Personality and Social Psychology, 92,* 458–475.

Boller, F. (2004). Rational basis of rehabilitation following cerebral lesions: A review of the concept of cerebral plasticity. *Functional Neurology: New Trends in Adaptive and Behavioral Disorders, 19,* 65–72.

Bolonna, A. A., & Kerwin, R. W. (2005). Partial agonism and schizophrenia. *British Journal of Psychiatry, 186,* 7–10.

Bonanni, R., Pasqualetti, P., Caltagirone, C., & Carlesimo, G. (2007). Primacy and recency effects in immediate free recall of sequences of spatial positions. *Perceptual and Motor Skills, 105,* 483–500.

Bonanno, G. A. (2004). Loss, trauma, and human resilence: Have we underestimated the human capacity to thrive after extremely aversive events? *American Psychologist, 59,* 20–28.

Bond, M. (2006). Psychodynamic psychotherapy in the treatment of mood disorders. *Current Opinion in Psychiatry, 19,* 40–43.

Bond, R. (2005, October). Group Size and Conformity. *Group Processes & Intergroup Relations, 8(4),* 331–354.

Bonnardel, V. (2006). Color naming and categorization in inherited color vision deficiencies. *Visual Neuroscience, 23,* 637–643.

Borbély, A. (1986). *Secrets of Sleep.* English translation. New York: Basic Books.

Bordnick, P. S., Elkins, R. L., Orr, T. E., Walters, P., & Thyer, B. A. (2004). Evaluating the relative effectiveness of three aversion therapies designed to reduce craving among cocaine abusers. *Behavioral Interventions, 19,* 1–24.

Borisenko, J. (2007). Fatherhood as a personality development factor in men. *The Spanish Journal of Psychology, 10,* 82–90.

Bornstein, R. F. (2003). Psychodynamic models of personality. In T. Millon & M. J. Lerner (Eds.), *Handbook of psychology: Personality and social psychology* (Vol. 5). New York: Wiley.

Bosma, H., van Boxtel, M. P. J., Ponds, R. W. H. M., Houx, P. J. H., Burdorf, A., & Jolles, J. (2003). Mental work demands protect against cognitive impairment: MAAS prospective cohort study. *Experimental Aging Research, 29,* 33–45.

Botvinick, M. (2004, August 6). Probing the neural basis of body ownership. *Science, 305,* 782–783.

Bouchard, C., & Bray, G. A. (Eds.). (1996). *Regulation of body weight: Biological and behavioral mechanisms.* New York: Wiley.

Bouchard, T. J., Jr. (2004). Genetic influence on human psychological traits: A survey. *Current Directions in Psychological Science, 13,* 148–151.

Bouchard, T. J. Jr., Segal, N. L., Tellegen, A., McGue, M., Keyes, M. & Krueger, R. (2004). Genetic influence on social attitudes: Another challenge to psychology from behavior genetics. In L. F. DiLalla (Ed.), *Behavior genetics principles: Perspectives in development, personality, and psychopathology.* Washington, DC: American Psychological Association.

Bourne, L. E., Dominowski, R. L., Loftus, E. F., & Healy, A. F. (1986). *Cognitive processes* (2nd ed.). Englewood Cliffs, NJ: Prentice Hall.

Bouton, M. E., Todd, T. P., Vurbic, D., & Winterbauer, N. E. (2011). Renewal after the extinction of free operant behavior. *Learning & Behavior, 39,* 57–67.

Bower, G. H., Thompson, S. S., & Tulving, E. (1994). Reducing retroactive interference: An interference analysis. *Journal of Experimental Psychology Learning, Memory, and Cognition, 20,* 51–66.

Bower, J. M., & Parsons, L. M. (2007). Rethinking the "lesser brain." In F. E. Bloom, *Best of the brain from Scientific American.* Washington, DC: Dana Press.

Boxer, P., Huesmann, L., Bushman, B., O'Brien, M., & Moceri, D. (2009). The role of violent media preference in cumulative developmental risk for violence and general aggression. *Journal of Youth and Adolescence, 38,* 417–428.

Boyce, W. T., & Ellis, B. J. (2005). Biological sensitivity to context: An evolutionary-developmental theory of the origins and functions of stress reactivity. *Development and Psychopathology, 17,* 271–301.

Boyd-Wilson, B. M., McClure, J., & Walkey, F. H. (2004). Are well-being and illusory perceptions linked? The answer may be yes, but. . . . *Australian Journal of Psychology, 56,* 1–9.

Boyle, S. H., Williams, R. B., Mark, D. B., Brummett, B. H., Siegler, I. C., & Barefoot, J. C. (2005). Hostility, age, and mortality in a sample of cardiac patients. *American Journal of Cardiology, 96,* 64–72.

Bozarth, J. D., Zimring, F. M., & Tausch, R. (2002). Client-centered therapy: The evolution of a revolution. In D. J. Cain (Ed.), *Humanistic psychotherapies: Handbook of research and practice* (pp. 147–188). Washington, DC: American Psychological Association.

Braaten, E. B. (2011). Psychotherapy: Interpersonal and insight-oriented approaches. In E. B. Braaten (Ed.), *How to find mental health care for your child.* Washington, DC: American Psychological Association.

Brackett, M. A., Rivers, S. E., & Salovey, P. (2011). Emotional intelligence: Implications for personal, social, academic, and workplace success. *Social and Personality Psychology Compass, 5,* 88–103.

Bradley, M. M., Miccoli, L., Escrig, M. A., & Lang, P. J. (2008). The pupil as measure of emotional arousal and autonomic activation. *Psychophysiology, 45,* 602–607.

Brady, N., Campbell, M., & Flaherty, M. (2005). Perceptual asymmetries are preserved in memory for highly familiar faces of self and friend. *Brain and Cognition, 58,* 334–342.

Brainerd, C. (1978, June). The stage question in cognitive-developmental theory. *Behavioral and Brain Sciences, 1*(2), 173–213.

Brambilla, P., Cipriani, A., Hotopf, M., & Barbui, C. (2005). Side-effect profile of fluoxetine in comparison with other SSRIs, tricyclic and newer antidepressants: A meta-analysis of clinical trial data. *Pharmacopsychiatry, 38,* 69–77.

Brasic, J. R. (2002). Conversion disorder in childhood. *German Journal of Psychiatry, 5,* 54–61.

Braun, A. R., Balkin, T. J., Wesensten, N. J., Gwadry, F., Carson, R. E., Varga, M., Baldwin, P., Belenky, G., & Herscovitch, P. (1998). Dissociated pattern of activity in visual cortices and their projections during human rapid eye movement sleep. *Science, 279,* 91–95.

Brausch, A. M. & Gutierrez, P. M. (2009). Differences in non-suicidal self-injury and suicide attempts in adolescents. *Journal of Youth and Adolescence, 21,* 46–51.

Brazelton, T. B. (1969). *Infants and mothers: Differences in development.* New York: Dell.

Brefczynski-Lewis, J., Lutz, A., Schaefer, H. Levinson, D., & Davidson, R. (2007). Neural correlates of attentional expertise in long-term meditation practitioners. *Proceedings of the National Academy of Sciences, 104,* 11483–11488.

Brehm, S., Kassin, S., & Fein, S. (2005). *Social Psychology* (6th ed.). New York: Houghton Mifflin.

Brennen, T., Vikan, A., & Dybdahl, R. (2007). Are tip-of-the-tongue states universal? Evidence from the speakers of an unwritten language. *Memory, 15,* 167–176.

Brewer, J. B., Zhao, Z., Desmond, J. E., Glover, G. H., & Gabrieli, J. D. E. (1998, August 21). Making memories: Brain activity that predicts how well visual experience will be remembered. *Science, 281,* 1185–1187.

Brewer, M. B., & Hewstone, M. (Eds.). (2003). *Social cognition.* Malden, MA: Blackwell Publishers.

Brewer, N., & Wells, G. L. (2011). Eyewitness identification. *Current Directions in Psychological Science, 20,* 24–27.

Brienza, Victoria. The Ten Least Stressful Jobs of 2011. (2011). CareerCast. http://www.careercast.com/jobs-rated/10-least-stressful-jobs-2011.

Bright, P., Buckman, J., & Fradera, A. (2006). Retrograde amnesia in patients with hippo-campal, medial temporal, temporal lobe, or frontal pathology. *Learning & Memory, 13,* 545–557.

Brislin, R., Worthley, R., & MacNab, B. (2006). Cultural intelligence: understanding behaviors that serve people's goals. *Group & Organization Management, 31,* 40–55.

Britt, G., & McCance-Katz, E. (2005). A Brief Overview of the Clinical Pharmacology of "Club Drugs." *Substance Use & Misuse, 40*(9), 1189–1201.

Brock, T. C., & Green, M. C. (Eds.). (2005). *Persuasion: Psychological insights and perspectives* (2nd ed.). Thousand Oaks, CA: Sage Publications.

Bröder, A., & Schiffer, S. (2006). Stimulus format and working memory in fast and frugal strategy selection. *Journal of Behavioral Decision Making, 19,* 361–380.

Brody, J. (2008, May 20). Trying to break nicotine's grip. *The New York Times,* p. E9.

Broidy, L. M., Nagin, D. S., & Tremblay, R. E. (2003). Developmental trajectories of childhood disruptive behaviors and adolescent delinquency: A six-site, cross-national study. *Developmental Psychology, 39,* 222–245.

Broman, C. L. (2005). Stress, race and substance use in college. *College Student Journal, 39,* 340–352.

Bronson, P., & Merryman, A. (2009). *NurtureShock.* New York: Twelve.

Brooker, R. J., Widmaier, W. P., Graham, L., & Stiling, P. (2008). *Biology.* New York: McGraw-Hill.

Brooks, L., McCabe, P., & Schneiderman, N. (2011). Stress and cardiometabolic syndrome. In R. J. Contrada, A. Baum, R. J. Contrada, A. Baum (Eds.), *The handbook of stress science: Biology, psychology, and health.* New York: Springer.

Brown, D. (1994, November). Subgroup norming: Legitimate testing practice or reverse discrimination? *American Psychologist, 49*(11), 927–928.

Brown, D. C. (1994). Subgroup norming: Legitimate testing practice or reverse discrimination? *American Psychologist, 49,* 927–928.

Brown, E. (2001, September 17). The World Health Organization takes on big tobacco (but don't hold your breath): Anti-smoking advocates are mounting a global campaign: It's going to be a long, hard fight. *Forbes,* pp. 37–41.

Brown, J. (2006). Attribution: Theories, affect and evolution. *Dissertation Abstracts International: Section B: The Sciences and Engineering, 67*(2-B), 1201.

Brown, L. S., & Pope, K. S. (1996). *Recovered memories of abuse: Assessment, therapy, forensics.* Washington, DC: American Psychological Association.

Brown, P. K., & Wald, G. (1964). Visual pigments in single rod and cones of the human retina. *Science, 144,* 45–52.

Brown, R. (1958). How shall a thing be called? *Psychological Review, 65,* 14–21.

Brown, R. (1973, February). Development of the first language in the human species. *American Psychologist, 28*(2), 97–106.

Brown, R., & Robertson, E. (2007). Off-line processing: Reciprocal interactions between declarative and procedural memories. *The Journal of Neuroscience, 27*(39), 10468–10475.

Brown, R. D., Goldstein, E., & Bjorklund, D. F. (2000). The history and zeitgeist of the repressed-false-memory debate: Scientific and sociological perspectives on suggestibility and childhood memory. In D. F. Bjorklund (Ed.), *False-memory creation in children and adults: Theory, research, and implications* (pp. 1–30). Mahwah, NJ: Lawrence Erlbaum.

Brown, R. J. (2006). Different types of "dissociation" have different psychological mechanisms. *Journal of Trauma Dissociation, 6,* 7–28.

Brown, S., & Martinez, M. J. (2007). Activation of premotor vocal areas during musical discrimination. *Brain and Cognition, 63,* 9–69.

Brown, S., Martinez, M. J., & Parson, L. M. (2006). Music and language side by side in the brain: A PET study of the generation of melodies and sentences. *European Journal of Neuroscience, 23,* 2791–2803.

Brownlee, K. (2007). What works for whom? (2nd ed.). A critical review of psychotherapy research. *Psychiatric Rehabilitation Journal, 30,* 239–240.

Bruce, V., Green, P. R., & Georgeson, M. (1997). *Visual perception: Physiology, psychology and ecology* (3rd ed.). Mahwah, NJ: Erlbaum.

Bruggeman, H., Yonas, A., & Konczak, J. (2007). The processing of linear perspective and binocular information for action and perception. *Neuropsychologia, 45,* 1420–1426.

Brunet, A., Orr, S. P., Tremblay, J., Robertson, K., Nader, K., & Pitman, R. K. (2007). Effect of post-retrieval propranolol on psychophysiologic responding during subsequent script-driven traumatic imagery in post-traumatic stress disorder. *Journal of Psychiatric Research, 22,* 301–315.

Bryant, R. M., Coker, A. D., Durodoye, B. A., McCollum, V. J., Pack-Brown, S. P., Constantine, M. G., & O'Bryant, B. J. (2005). Having our say: African American women, diversity, and counseling. *Journal of Counseling and Development, 83,* 313–319.

Brydon, L., Edwards, S., Mohamed-Ali, V., & Steptoe, A. (2004). Socioeconomic status and stress-induced increases in interleukin-6. *Brain, Behavior, and Immunity, 18,* 281–290.

Brzustowicz, L. M., Hodgkinson, K. A., Chow, E. W. C., Honer, W. G., & Bassett, A. S. (2000, April 28). Location of major susceptibility locus for familial schizophrenia on chromosome 1q21–q22. *Science, 288,* 678–682.

Buchanan, J. J., & Wright, D. L. (2011). Generalization of action knowledge following observational learning. *Acta Psychologica, 136,* 167–178.

Buchanan, R. W., Javitt, D. C., Marder, S. R., Schooler, N. R., Gold, J. M., McMahon, R. P., Heresco-Levy, U., & Carpenter, W. T. (2007). The Cognitive and Negative Symptoms in Schizophrenia Trial (CONSIST): The efficacy of glutamatergic agents for negative symptoms and cognitive impairments. *American Journal of Psychiatry, 164,* 1593–1602.

Buchanan, T. W., & Adolphs, R. (2004). The neuroanatomy of emotional memory in humans. In D. Reisberg & P. Hertel (Eds.), *Memory and emotion* (pp. 42–75). London: Oxford University Press.

Buchert, R., Thomasius, R., Wilke, F., Petersen, K., Nebeling, B., Obrocki, J., Schulze, O., Schmidt, U., & Clausen, M. (2004). A voxel-based PET investigation of the long-term effects of "ecstasy" consumption on brain serotonin transporters. *American Journal of Psychiatry, 161*, 1181–1189.

Buchsbaum, B., & D'Esposito, M. (2009). Is there anything special about working memory?. *Neuroimaging of human memory: Linking cognitive processes to neural systems* (pp. 255–261). New York: Oxford University Press.

Buckley, C. (2007, January 3). A man down, a train arriving, and a stranger makes a choice. *The New York Times*, p. 1.

Buehner, M., Krumm, S., & Ziegler, M. (2006). Cognitive abilities and their interplay: Reasoning, crystallized intelligence, working memory components, and sustained attention. *Journal of Individual Differences, 27*, 57–72.

Buffardi, L. E., & Campbell, W. K. (2008). Narcissism and social networking websites. *Personality and Social Psychology Bulletin,34*:10, 1303–1314.

Buhs, E., Ladd, G., & Herald, S. (2006). Peer exclusion and victimization: Processes that mediate the relation between peer group rejection and children's classroom engagement and achievement? *Journal of Educational Psychology, 98*, 1–13.

Bukobza, G. (2009). Relations between rebelliousness, risk-taking behavior, and identity status during emerging adulthood. *Identity, 9*, 159–177.

Bulik, C. M., Tozzi, F., Anderson, C., Mazzeo, S. E., Aggen, S., & Sullivan, P. F. (2003). The relation between eating disorders and components of perfectionism. *American Journal of Psychiatry, 160*, 366–368.

Bunge, S. A., & Wallis, J. D. (2008). *Neuroscience of rule-guided behavior*. New York: Oxford University Press.

Bunting, M. (2006). Proactive interference and item similarity in working memory. *Journal of Experimental Psychology: Learning, Memory, and Cognition, 32*, 183–196.

Burbach, M. E., Matkin, G. S., & Fritz, S. M. (2004). Teaching critical thinking in an introductory leadership course utilizing active learning strategies: A confirmatory study. *College Student Journal, 38*, 482–493.

Burchinal, M. R., Roberts, J. E., & Riggins, R., Jr. (2000). Relating quality of center-based child care to early cognitive and language development longitudinally. *Child Development, 71*, 338–357.

Bureau of Labor Statistics. (2007). American Time Use Survey. Washington, DC: Bureau of Labor Statistics.

Burger, J. M. (2009). Replicating Milgram: Would people still obey today? *American Psychologist, 64*, 1–11.

Burger, J. M., & Caldwell, D. F. (2003). The effects of monetary incentives and labeling on the foot-in-the-door effect: Evidence for a self-perception process. *Basic and Applied Social Psychology, 25*, 235–241.

Burger, J. M., Reed, M., & DeCesare, K. (1999). The effects of initial request size on compliance: More about the that's-not-all technique. *Basic and Applied Social Psychology, 21*, 243–249.

Burgoon, J. K., Bonito, J. A., Ramirez, A. J. R., Dunbar, N. E., Kam, K., & Fischer, J. (2002). Testing the interactivity principle: Effects of mediation, propinquity, and verbal and non-verbal modalities in interpersonal interaction [Special Issue: Research on the relationship between verbal and nonverbal communication: Emerging integrations]. *Journal of Communication, 52*, 657–677.

Burke, C. & McDaniel, J. (2001). *A special kind of hero*. Lincoln, NE: Doubleday.

Burkhauser, R., Butler, J., & Holden, K. (1991, September). How the death of a spouse affects economic well-being after retirement: A hazard model approach. *Social Science Quarterly, 72*(3), 504–519.

Burns, J. W., Quartana, P. J., & Bruehl, S. (2007). Anger management style moderates effects of emotion suppression during initial stress on pain and cardiovascular responses during subsequent pain-induction. *Annals of Behavioral Medicine, 34*, 154–165.

Burns, N. J. R., Bryan, J., & Nettelbeck, T. (2006). Ginkgo biloba: No robust effect on cognitive abilities or mood in healthy young or older adults. *Human Psychopharmacology: Clinical and Experimental, 21*, 27–37.

Buschman, T. J., & Miller, E. K. (2007, March 30). Top-down versus bottom-up control of attention in the prefrontal and posterior parietal cortices. *Science, 315*, 1860–1862.

Busey, T. A., & Loftus, G. R. (2007). Cognitive science and the law. *Trends in Cognitive Science, 11*, 111–117.

Bush, J. (2008). Viability of virtual reality exposure therapy as a treatment alternative. *Computers in Human Behavior, 24*, 1032–1040.

Bushman, B., & Huesmann, R. (2006). Short-term and long-term effects of violent media on aggression in children and adults. *Archives of Pediatric and Adolescent Medicine, 160*, 348–352.

Bushman, B. J., & Anderson, C. A. (2001). Media violence and the American public: Scientific facts versus media misinformation. *American Psychologist, 56*, 477–489.

Bushman, B. J., & Anderson, C. A. (2002). Violent video games and hostile expectations: A test of the general aggression model. *Personality and Social Psychology Bulletin, 28*, 1679–1686.

Bushman, B. J., & Bonacci, A. M. (2002). Violence and sex impair memory for television ads. *Journal of Applied Psychology*, Vol. 87, No. 3.

Bushman, B. J., Wang, M. C., & Anderson, C. A. (2005). Is the curve relating temperature to aggression linear or curvilinear? Assaults and temperature in Minneapolis reexamined. *Journal of Personality and Social Psychology, 89*, 62–66.

Buss, D. (2009). How can evolutionary psychology successfully explain personality and individual differences? *Perspectives on Psychological Science, 4*, 359–366.

Buss, D. M. (2001). Human nature and culture: An evolutionary psychological perspective. *Journal of Personality, 69*, 955–978.

Buss, D. M. (2003a). *The evolution of desire: Strategies of human mating*. New York: Basic Books.

Buss, D. M. (2003b). Sexual strategies: A journey into controversy. *Psychological Inquiry, 14*, 219–226.

Buss, D. M. (2004). Sex differences in human mate preferences: Evolutionary hypotheses tested in 37 cultures. In H. T. Reis & C. E. Rusbult (Eds.), *Close relationships: Key readings*. Philadelphia, PA: Taylor & Francis.

Buss, D. M., Abbott, M., & Angleitner, A. (1990). International preferences in selecting mates: A study of 37 cultures. *Journal of Cross-Cultural Psychology, 21*, 5–47.

Butcher, J. N. (2005). *A beginner's guide to the MMPI-2* (2nd ed.). Washington, DC: American Psychological Association.

Butler, A. C., Chapman, J. E., Forman, E. M., & Beck, A. T. (2006). The empirical status of cognitive-behavioral therapy: A review of meta-analyses. *Clinical Psychology Review, 26*, 17–31.

Butler, L. D., Koopman, C., Neri, E., Giese-Davis, J., Palesh, O. Thorne-Yocam, K. A., et al. (2009). Effects of supportive-expressive group therapy on pain in women with metastatic breast cancer. *Health Psychology, 28*, 579–587.

Butler, L. T., & Berry, D. C. (2004). Understanding the relationship between repetition priming and mere exposure. *British Journal of Psychology, 95*, 467–487.

Byne, W. (1996). Biology and homosexuality: Implications of neuroendocrinological and neuroanatomical studies. In R. P. Cabaj & T. S. Stein (Eds.), *Textbook of homosexuality and mental health*. Washington, DC: American Psychiatric Press.

Byrne-Davis, L., & Vedhara, K. (2008). Psychoneuroimmunology. *Social and Personality Psychology Compass, 2*, 751–764.

C

Cabanac, M., & Frankham, P. (2002). Evidence that transient nicotine lowers the body weight set point. *Physiology & Behavior, 76*, 539–542.

Cabaniss, D. L., Cherry, S., Douglas, C. J., & Schwartz, A. R. (2011). *Psychodynamic psychotherapy: A clinical manual*. New York: Wiley-Blackwell.

Cabioglu, M., Ergene, N., & Tan, Ü. (2007, May). Smoking cessation after acupuncture treatment. *International Journal of Neuroscience, 117*, 571–578.

Cachelin, F. M., & Regan, P. C. (2006). Prevalence and correlates of chronic dieting in a multi-ethnic U.S. community sample. *Eating and Weight Disorders, 11*, 91–99.

Cacioppo, J. T., Berntson, G. G., & Crites, S. L., Jr. (1996). Social neuroscience: Principles of psychophysiological arousal and response. In E. T. Higgins & A. W. Kruglanski (Eds.), *Social psychology: Handbook of basic principles*. New York: Guilford.

Cacioppo, J. T., & Decety, J. (2009). What are the brain mechanisms on which psychological processes are based? *Perspectives on Psychological Science, 4*, 10–18.

Cacioppo, J. T., Visser, P. S., & Picket, C. L. (2005). *Social neuroscience: People thinking about thinking people*. Cambridge, MA: MIT Press.

Cacioppo, J., & Petty, R. (1989). The Elaboration Likelihood Model: The role of affect and affect-laden information processing in persuasion. *Cognitive and affective responses to advertising* (pp. 69–89). Lexington, MA England: Lexington Books/D. C. Heath and Com.

Cacioppo, J., Petty, R., & Morris, K. (1983, October). Effects of need for cognition on message evaluation, recall, and persuasion. *Journal of Personality and Social Psychology, 45*(4), 805–818.

Cacioppo, J., Petty, R., Kao, C., & Rodriguez, R. (1986, November). Central and peripheral routes to persuasion: An individual difference perspective. *Journal of Personality and Social Psychology, 51*(5), 1032–1043.

Cadwallader, E. (1991). Depression and religion: Realities, perspectives and directions.

Caelian, C. F. (2006).The role of perfectionism and stress in the suicidal behaviour of depressed adolescents. *Dissertation Abstracts International: Section B: The Sciences and Engineering, 66(12-B)*, 6915.

Cahill, J. (2011). Review of "The extremes of the bell curve: Excellent and poor school performance and risk for severe mental disorders." *Emotional & Behavioural Difficulties, 16*, 112–113.

Cahill, L. (2005, May). His brain, her brain. *Scientific American*, pp. 40–47.

Cain, D. J. (Ed.). (2002). *Humanistic psychotherapies: Handbook of research and practice*. Washington, DC: American Psychological Association.

Calin-Jageman, R. J., & Fischer, T. M. (2007). Behavioral adaptation of the aplysia siphon-withdrawal response is accompanied by sensory adaptation. *Behavioral Neuroscience, 121*, 200–211.

Cameron, O. G. (2002). *Visceral sensory neuroscience: Interoception*. London: Oxford University Press.

Campbell, J., & Feng, A. (2011). Comparing adult productivity of American mathematics, physics, and chemistry Olympians with Terman's longitudinal study. *Roeper Review: A Journal on Gifted Education, 33*, 18–25.

Campbell, T. S., Ditto, B., Seguin, J. R., Assad, J-M., Pihl, R. O., Nagin, D., Tremblay, R. E. A longitudinal study of pain sensitivity and blood pressure in adolescent boys: Results from a 5-year follow-up. *Health Psychology, 21*, 594–600.

Canderelli, R., Leccesse, L., & Miller, N. (2007, December). Benefits of hormone replacement therapy in postmenopausal women. *Journal of the American Academy of Nurse Practitioners, 19*(12), 635–641.

Cannon, W. B. (1929). Organization for physiological homeostatics. *Physiological Review, 9,* 280–289.

Canteras, N. S. (2002). The medial hypothalamic defensive system: Hodological organization and functional implications [Special issue: Functional role of specific systems within the extended amygdala and hypothalamus]. *Pharmacology, Biochemistry and Behavior, 71,* 481–491.

Cantwell, R. H., & Andrews, B. (2002). Cognitive and psychological factors underlying secondary school students' feelings towards group work. *Educational Psychology, 22,* 75–91.

Capaldi, E. D. (Ed.). (1996). *Why we eat what we eat: The psychology of eating.* Washington, DC: American Psychological Association.

Caplan, D., & Waters, G., & Kennedy, D. (2007). A study of syntactic processing in aphasia II: Neurological aspects. *Brain and Language, 101,* 151–177.

Caplan, D., Waters, G., & DeDe, G. (2007). A study of syntactic processing in aphasia I: Behavioral (psycholinguistic) aspects. *Brain and Language, 101,* 103–150.

Cardon, L. (1994). Height, weight, and obesity. *Nature and nurture during middle childhood* (pp. 165–172). Malden: Blackwell Publishing.

Cardoso, S. H., & Sabbatini, R. M. E. (2001). Learning who is your mother: The behavior of imprinting. *Brain & Mind,* www.cerebromente.org.br/n14/experimento/lorenz/index-lorenz.html.

Carey, B. (2004, December 21). When pressure is on, good students suffer. *The New York Times,* p. D7.

Carey, B. (2009c, November 27). Surgery for mental ills offers hope and risk. *New York Times,* p. A1.

Carhart-Harris, R., (2007). Speed > Ecstasy > Ritalin: The science of amphetamines. *Journal of Psychopharmacology, 21,* 225.

Carlo, G., Mestre, M., Samper, P., Tur, A., & Armenta, B. E. (2011). The longitudinal relations among dimensions of parenting styles, sympathy, prosocial moral reasoning, and prosocial behaviors. *International Journal of Behavioral Development, 35,* 116–124.

Carmody, T., Duncan, C., Simon, J., Solkowitz, S., Huggins, J., Lee, S., et al. (2008). Hypnosis for smoking cessation: A randomized trial. *Nicotine & Tobacco Research, 10,* 811–818.

Carnagey, N., Anderson, C., & Bartholow, B. (2007). Media violence and social neuroscience: New questions and new opportunities. *Current Directions in Psychological Science, 16,* 178–182.

Carnagey, N. L., Anderson, C. A., & Bushman, B. J. (2007). The effect of video game violence on physiological desensitization to real-life violence. *Journal of Experimental Social Psychology, 43,* 489–496.

Carney, D., Colvin, C., & Hall, J. (2007). A thin slice perspective on the accuracy of first impressions. *Journal of Research in Personality, 41,* 1054–1072.

Carney, R. N., & Levin, J. R. (1998). Coming to terms with the keyword method in introductory psychology: A "neuromnemonic" example. *Teaching of Psychology, 25,* 132–135.

Carney, R. N., & Levin, J. R. (2003). Promoting higher-order learning benefits by building lower-order mnemonic connections. *Applied Cognitive Psychology, 17,* 563–575.

Carpenter, S. (2001). Sleep deprivation may be undermining teen health. *APA Monitor, 32,* 42–45.

Carpenter, S. (2002, April). What can resolve the paradox of mental health disparities? *APA Monitor, 33,* 18.

Carr, A. (2009, February). The effectiveness of family therapy and systemic interventions for adult-focused problems. *Journal of Family Therapy, 31*(1), 46–74.

Carrillo, M., Ricci, L., Coppersmith, G., & Melloni, R. (2009, August). The effect of increased serotonergic neurotransmission on aggression: A critical meta-analytical review of preclinical studies. *Psychopharmacology, 205,* 349–368.

Carter, R. T. (2003). Becoming racially and culturally competent: The racial-cultural counseling laboratory. *Journal of Multicultural Counseling and Development, 31,* 20–30.

Cartwright, R. (2006). A neuroscientist looks at how the brain makes up our minds. *PsycCRITIQUES, 51,* 35–41.

Cartwright, R., Agargum, M. Y., & Kirkby, J. (2006). Relation of dreams to waking concerns. *Psychiatry Research, 141,* 261–270.

Caruso, E. (2008). Use of experienced retrieval ease in self and social judgments. *Journal of Experimental Social Psychology, 44,* 148–155.

Carvalho, F. M., Pereira, S. R., C., Pires, R. G. W., Ferraz, V. P., Romano-Silva, M. A., Oliveira-Silva, I. F., & Ribeiro, A. M. (2006). Thiamine deficiency decreases glutamate uptake in the prefrontal cortex and impairs spatial memory performance in a water maze test. *Pharmacology, Biochemistry and Behavior, 83,* 481–489.

Carver, C., & Scheier, M. (2002). Coping processes and adjustment to chronic illness. In A. Christensen and M. Antoni (Eds.), *Chronic physical disorders: Behavioral medicine's perspective.* Malden: Blackwell Publishers.

Cary, P. (2007). A brief history of the concept of free will: Issues that are and are not germane to legal reasoning. *Behavioral Sciences & the Law, 25, Special issue: Free will,* 165–181.

Case, R., & Okamoto, Y. (1996). The role of central conceptual structures in the development of children's thought. *Monographs of the Society for Research in Child Development, 61,* v–265.

Casey, D. (2006, Fall). Eyeing the future: One patient's story. *Artificial Retina News,* p. 1.

Casey, S. D., Cooper-Brown, L. J., & Wacher, D. P. (2006). The use of descriptive analysis to identify and manipulate schedules of reinforcement in the treatment of food refusal. *Journal of Behavioral Education, 15,* 41–52.

Cashon, C. H., & Cohen, L. B. (2004). Beyond U-shaped development in infants' processing of faces: An information-processing account. *Journal of Cognition and Development, 5,* 59–80.

Caspi, A., Harrington, H., & Milne, B. (2003). Children's behavioral styles at age 3 are linked to their adult personality traits at age 26. *Journal of Personality, 71,* 495–513.

Cassells, J. V. S. (2007). The virtuous roles of truth and justice in integral dialogue: Research, theory, and model practice of the evolution of collective consciousness. *Dissertation Abstracts International Section A: Humanities and Social Sciences, 67*(10-A), 4005.

Cattell, R. B. (1965). *The scientific analysis of personality.* Chicago: Aldine.

Cattell, R. B. (1998). Where is intelligence? Some answers from the triadic theory. In J. J. McArdle & R. W. Woodcock (Eds.), *Human cognitive abilities in theory and practice* (pp. 29–38). Mahwah, NJ: Lawrence Erlbaum.

Cattell, R. B., Cattell, A. K., & Catell, H. E. P. (1993). *Sixteen personality factor questionnaire (16PF)* (5th ed.). San Antonio, TX: Harcourt Brace.

Cattell, R. B., Cattell, A. K., & Cattell, H. E. P. (2000). *The sixteen personality factor™ (16PF®) questionnaire.* Champaign, IL: Institute for Personality and Ability Testing.

Cauce, A. M. (2007). Bringing community psychology home: The leadership, community and values initiative. *American Journal of Community Psychology, 39,* 1–11.

Cavallini, E., Pagnin, A., and Vecchi, T. (2003). Aging and everyday memory: The beneficial effect of memory training. *Archives of Gerontology & Geriatrics, 37,* 241–257.

Cavenett, T., & Nixon, R. D. V. (2006). The effect of arousal on memory for emotionally-relevant information: A study of skydivers. *Behaviour Research and Therapy, 44,* 1461–1469.

Centers for Disease Control (CDC). (2000a). *Suicide prevention fact sheet, National Center for Injury Prevention and Control.* Atlanta, GA: Centers for Disease Control and Prevention.

Centers for Disease Control and Prevention. (2000b). Cigarette smoking among adults—United States. *Morbidity and Mortality Weekly Report* [serial online] 2002; 51 (29): 642–645 [accessed 2009 Oct. 12].

Centers for Disease Control (CDC). (2004a). *Chlamydia—CDC fact sheet.* Washington, DC: Centers for Disease Control and Prevention.

Centers for Disease Control (CDC). (2004b, June 11). Suicide and attempted suicide. *MMWR, 53,* 471.

Centers for Disease Control and Prevention. (2007). Physical activity and good nutrition: Essential elements to prevent chronic diseases and obesity, 2007. http://www.cdc.gov/ nccdphp/publications/aag/pdf/dnpa.pdf.

Chamberlain, K., & Zika, S. (1990). The minor events approach to stress: Support for the use of daily hassles. *British Journal of Psychology, 81,* 469–481.

Chamberlain, S. R., Menzies, L., Hampshire, A., Suckling, J., Fineberg, N. A., del Campo, N., et al. (2008, July 18). Orbitofrontal dysfunction in patients with obsessive-compulsive disorder and their unaffected relatives. *Science, 321,* 421–422.

Chambless, D. L., Crits-Christoph, P., Wampold, B. E., Norcross, J. C., Lambert, M. J., Bohart, A. C., Beutler, L. E., & Johannsen, B. E. (2006). What should be validated? In J. C. Norcross, L. E. Beutler, & R. F. Levant (Eds.) *Evidence-based practices in mental health: Debate and dialogue on the fundamental questions.* Washington, DC: American Psychological Association.

Chandra, P. (2007). Review of Language, mind, and brain: Some psychological and neurological constraints on theories of grammar. *Cognitive Systems Research, 8,* 53–56.

Chandran, S., & Menon, G. (2004). When a day means more than a year: Effects of temporal framing on judgments of health risk. *Journal of Consumer Research, 31,* 375–389.

Chang, J., & Sue, S. (2005). Culturally sensitive research: Where have we gone wrong and what do we need to do now? In M. G. Constantine, *Strategies for building multicultural competence in mental health and educational settings.* Hoboken, NJ: John Wiley & Sons.

Chang, S. W., & Ansley, T. N. (2003). A comparative study of item exposure control methods in computerized adaptive testing. *Journal of Educational Measurement, 40,* 71–103.

Chanon, V., & Boettiger, C. (2009). Addiction and cognitive control. *The Praeger international collection on addictions, Vol 2: Psychobiological profiles* (pp. 273–285). Santa Barbara, CA: Praeger/ABC-CLIO.

Chapelot, D., Marmonier, C., Aubert, R., Gausseres, N., & Louis-Sylvestre, J. (2004). A role for glucose and insulin preprandial profiles to differentiate meals and snacks. *Physiology and Behavior, 80,* 721–731.

Chapkis, W., & Webb, R. (2008). *Dying to get high: Marijuana as medicine.* New York: New York University Press.

Chaplin, W. F., Phillips, J. B., Brown, J. D., Clanton, N. R., and Stein, J. L. (2000). Handshaking, gender, personality and first impressions. *Journal of Personality and Social Psychology 79*(1), 110–117.

Chapman, J. (2006). Anxiety and defective decision making: An elaboration of the group-think model. *Management Decision, 44,* 1391–1404.

Chapman, L. J., & Chapman, J. P. (1973). *Disordered thought in schizophrenia.* New York: Appleton-Century-Crofts.

Charman, D. P. (2004). *Core processes in brief psychodynamic psychotherapy: Advancing effective practice.* Mahwah, NJ: Lawrence Erlbaum Associates.

Chechil, R. A. (2003). Mathematical tools for hazard function analysis. *Journal of Mathematical Psychology, 47,* 478–494.

Chen, A., Zhou, Y., & Gong, H. (2004). Firing rates and dynamic correlated activities of ganglion cells both contribute to retinal information processing. *Brain Research, 1017*, 13–20.

Cheney, C. D. (1996). Medical non adherence: A behavior analysis. In J. R. Cautela & W. Ishaq (Eds.), *Contemporary issues in behavior therapy: Improving the human condition: Applied Clinical Psychology*. New York: Plenum Press.

Cheng, C., & Cheung, M. L. (2005). Cognitive processes underlying coping flexibility: Differentiation and integration. *Journal of Personality, 73*, 859–886.

Cheston, S. E. (2002). A new paradigm for teaching counseling theory and practice. *Counselor Education & Supervision, 39*, 254–269.

Chisholm, E., Bapat, U., Chisholm, C., Alusi, G., & Vassaux, G. (2007). Gene therapy in head and neck cancer: A review. *Postgraduate Medical Journal, 83*, 731–737.

Cho, A. (2000). Gene therapy could aid hearing. *ScienceNOW, 518*, 1.

Cho, S., Holyoak, K. J., & Cannon, T. D. (2007). Analogical reasoning in working memory: Resources shared among relational integration, interference resolution, and maintenance. *Memory & Cognition, 35*, 1445–1455.

Choi, Y., Yeo, S., Hong, Y., & Lim, S. (2011). Neuroprotective changes of striatal degeneration-related gene expression by acupuncture in an MPTP mouse model of Parkinsonism: Microarray analysis. *Cellular & Molecular Neurobiology, 31*, 377–391.

Choi, Y. S., Gray, H., & Ambady, N. (2004). Glimpses of others: Unintended communication and unintended perception. In J. Bargh, J. Uleman, & R. Hassin (Eds.), *Unintended thought* (2nd ed.). New York: Oxford University Press.

Chomsky, N. (1968). *Language and mind*. New York: Harcourt Brace Jovanovich.

Chomsky, N. (1969). *Language and mind*. New York: Harcourt Brace Jovanovich.

Chomsky, N. (1978). On the biological basis of language capacities. In G. A. Miller & E. Lennenberg (Eds.), *Psychology and biology of language and thought*. New York: Academic Press.

Chomsky, N. (1991). Linguistics and cognitive science: Problems and mysteries. In A. Kasher (Ed.), *The Chomskyan turn*. Cambridge, MA: Blackwell.

Chou, K. (2005). Everyday competence and depressive symptoms: Social support and sense of control as mediators or moderators? *Aging and Mental Health, 9*, 177–183.

Choy, Y., Fyer, A. J. & Lipsitz, J. D. (2007). Treatment of specific phobia in adults. *Clinical Psychology Review, 27*, 266–286.

Christ, S. E., Steiner, R. D., & Grange, D. K. (2006). Inhibitory control in children with phenylketonuria. *Developmental Neuropsychology, 30*, 845–864.

Christakis, N. A., & Fowler, J. H. (2008). The collective dynamics of smoking in a large social network. *The New England Journal of Medicine, 358*, 2249–2258.

Christensen, A. J., & Johnson, J. A. (2002). Patient adherence with medical treatment regimens: An interactive approach. *Current Directions in Psychological Science, 11*, 94–101.

Christian, C. J., Lencz, T., Robinson, D. G., Burdick, K. E., Ashtari, M., Malhotra, A. K., et al. (2008). Gray matter structural alterations in obsessive-compulsive disorder: Relationship to neuropsychological functions. *Neuroimaging, 164*, 123–131.

Chronicle, E. P., MacGregor, J. N., & Ormerod, T. C. (2004). What makes an insight problem? The roles of heuristics, goal conception, and solution recoding in knowledge-lean problems. *Journal of Experimental Psychology: Learning, Memory, and Cognition, 30*, 14–27.

Chrysikou, E. G. (2006). When a shoe becomes a hammer: Problem solving as goal-derived, ad hoc categorization. *Dissertation Abstracts International: Section B: The Sciences and Engineering, 67(1-B)*, 569.

Cialdini, R. B. (2006). *Influence: The psychology of persuasion*. New York: Collins.

Cialdini, R. B., & Sagarin, B. J. (2005). Principles of interpersonal influence. In T. C. Brock & M. C. Green (Eds.), *Persuasion: Psychological insights and perspectives* (2nd ed.). Thousand Oaks, CA: Sage Publications.

Cialdini, R. B., Schaller, M., Houlihan, D., Arps, K., Fultz, J., & Beaman, A. L. (1975). Reciprocal concessions procedure for inducing compliance: The door-in-the-face technique. *Journal of Personality and Social Psychology, 31*, 206–215.

Clark, D. A. (2004). *Cognitive-behavioral therapy for OCD*. New York: Guilford.

Clark, D. A. (2007). Obsessions and compulsions. In N. Kazantzis, & L. L'Abate, *Handbook of homework assignments in psychotherapy: Research, practice, prevention*. New York: Springer Science + Business Media.

Clarke-Stewart, K. A., Vandell, D. L., McCartney, K., Owen, M. T., & Booth C. (2000). Effects of parental separation and divorce on very young children. *Journal of Family Psychology, 14*, 304–326.

Clarkin, J. F., & Lenzenweger, M. F. (Eds.) (2004) *Major theories of personality disorders* (2nd ed.). New York: Guilford.

Clarkin, J. F., Levy, K. N., Lenzenweger, M. F., & Kernberg, O. F. (2007). Evaluating three treatments for borderline personality disorder: A multiwave study. *American Journal of Psychiatry, 164*, 922–928.

Clausen, L., Rosenvinge, J. H., Friborg, O., & Rokkedal, K. (2011). Validating the Eating Disorder Inventory-3 (EDI-3): A comparison between 561 female eating disorders patients and 878 females from the general population. *Journal of Psychopathology and Behavioral Assessment, 33*, 101–110.

Clay D. L. (2000). Commentary: Rethinking our interventions in pediatric chronic pain and treatment research. *Journal of Pediatric Psychology, 25*, 53–55.

Clayton, K., & Lundberg-Love, P. (2009). Caffeine: Pharmacology and effects of the world's most popular drug. *The Praeger international collection on addictions, Vol. 2: Psychobiological profiles*. Santa Barbara, CA: Praeger/ABC-CLIO.

Clayton, R., Segress, M., & Caudill, C. (2008). Prevention of substance abuse. *The American Psychiatric Publishing textbook of substance abuse treatment (4th ed.)* (pp. 681–688). Arlington, VA: American Psychiatric Publishing, Inc.

Cleary, A. M. (2006). Relating familiarity-based recognition and the tip-of-the-tongue phenomenon: Detecting a word's recency in the absence of access to the word. *Memory & Cognition, 34*, 804–816.

Clements, A., M., Rimrodt, S. L., & Abel, J. R. (2006). Sex differences in cerebral laterality of language and visuospatial processing. *Brain and Language, 98*, 150–158.

Clemons, T. L. (2006). Underachieving gifted students: A social cognitive model. *Dissertation Abstracts International Section A: Humanities and Social Sciences, 66(9-A)*, 3208.

Cloud, J. (2000, June 5). The lure of ecstasy. *Time*, pp. 60–68.

Cloud, J. (2009, January 19). Minds on the Edge. *Time*, pp. 40–46.

Coan, J. A., Schaefer, H. S., & Davidson, R. J. (2006). Lending a hand: Social regulation of the neural response to threat. *Psychological Science, 17*, 1032–1039.

Coates, S. L., Butler, L. T., & Berry, D. C. (2006). Implicit memory and consumer choice: The mediating role of brand familiarity. *Applied Cognitive Psychology, 20*, 1101–1116.

Cobos, P., Sanchez, M., Garcia, C., Vera, M. N., & Vila, J. (2002). Revisiting the James versus Cannon debate on emotion: Startle and autonomic modulation in patients with spinal cord injuries. *Biological Psychology, 61*, 251–269.

Cochran, S. D. (2000). Emerging issues in research on lesbians' and gay men's mental health: Does sexual orientation really matter? *American Psychologist, 56*, 33–41.

Coffman, S. J., Martell, C. R., Dimidjian, S., Gallop, R., & Holon, S. D. (2007). Extreme nonresponse in cognitive therapy: Can behavioral activation succeed where cognitive therapy fails? *Journal of Consulting Clinical Psychology, 75*, 531–545.

Cohen, B. H. (2002). *Explaining psychological statistics* (2nd ed.). New York: Wiley.

Cohen, J. (2003). Things I have learned (so far). In A. E. Kazdin (Ed.), *Methodological issues and strategies in clinical research* (3rd ed.). Washington, DC: American Psychological Association.

Cohen, L., & Cashon, C. (2003). Infant perception and cognition. In R. Lerner and M. Easterbrooks (Eds.), *Handbook of psychology: Developmental psychology* (Vol. 6). New York: Wiley.

Cohen, P., Slomkowski, C., & Robins, L. N. (Eds.). (1999). *Historical and geographical influences on psychopathology*. Mahwah, NJ: Erlbaum.

Cohen, S. (2004, November). Social relationships and health. *American Psychologist*, 676–684.

Cohen, S., Doyle, W. J., Turner, R., Alper, C. M., & Skoner, D. P. (2003). Sociability and susceptibility to the common cold. *Psychological Science, 14*, 389–395.

Cohen, S., Hamrick, N., & Rodriguez, M. (2002). Reactivity and vulnerability to stress-associated risk for upper respiratory illness. *Psychosomatic Medicine, 64*, 302–310.

Colarusso, C. (1998). Development and treatment in late adulthood. *The course of life, Vol. 7: Completing the journey* (pp. 285–317). Madison, CT: International Universities Press, Inc.

Cole, M., Levitin, K., & Luria, A. (2006). *The autobiography of Alexander Luria: A dialogue with the making of mind*. Mahwah, NJ: Erlbaum.

Coleman, E. (2002). Masturbation as a means of achieving sexual health. *Journal of Psychology and Human Sexuality, 14*, 5–16.

Coles, R. (1997). *The moral intelligence of children*. New York: Random House.

Colland, V. T., Van Essen-Zandvliet, L. E. M., Lans, C., Denteneer, A., Westers, P., & Brackel, H. J. L. (2004). Poor adherence to self-medication instructions in children with asthma and their parents. *Patient Education and Counseling, 55*, 416–421.

Collins, A. M., & Loftus, E. F. (1975). A spreading-activation theory of semantic processing. *Psychological Review, 82*, 407–428.

Collins, A. M., & Quillian, M. R. (1969). Retrieval times from semantic memory. *Journal of Verbal Learning and Verbal Behavior, 8*, 240–247.

Collins, S. L., & Izenwasser, S. (2004). Chronic nicotine differentially alters cocaine-induced locomotor activity in adolescent vs. adult male and female rats. *Neuropharmacology, 46*, 349–362.

Colom, R., Jung, R. E., & Haier, R. J. (2006). Finding the g-factor in brain structure using the method of correlated vectors. *Intelligence, 34*, 561–570.

Coltheart, M., Langdon, R., & McKay, R. (2007). Schizophrenia and monothematic delusions. *Schizophrenia Bulletin, 33*, 642–647.

Coltraine, S., & Messineo, M. (2000). The perpetuation of subtle prejudice: Race and gender imagery in 1990s television advertising. *Sex Roles, 42*, 363–389.

Colwell, M. J., & Lindsey, E. W. (2005). Preschool children's pretend and physical play and sex of play partner: Connections to peer competence. *Sex Roles, 52*, 497–509.

Combrink-Graham, L., & McKenna, S. B. (2006). Families with children with disrupted attachments. In L. Combrink-Graham, *Children in family contexts: Perspectives on treatment*. New York: Guilford Press.

Combs, D., Basso, M., Wanner, J., & Ledet, S. (2008). Schizophrenia. *Handbook of psychological assessment, case conceptualization, and treatment: Adults* (Vol. 1) (pp. 352–402). Hoboken, NJ: John Wiley & Sons Inc.

Combs, D., & Mueser, K. (2007). Schizophrenia. *Adult psychopathology and diagnosis* (5th ed.) (pp. 234–285). Hoboken, NJ: John Wiley & Sons Inc.

Compagni, A., & Manderscheid, R. W. (2006). A neuroscientist-consumer alliance to transform mental health care. *Journal of Behavioral Health Services & Research, 33*, 265–274.

Compas, B. E., & Wagner, B. M. (1991). Psychosocial stress during adolescence: Intrapersonal and interpersonal processes. Adolescent stress: Causes and consequences. In M. E. Colten, & S. Gore, Eds., *Adolescent stress: Causes and consequences. Social institutions and social change*. Hawthorne, NY: Aldine de Gruyter.

Compton, W., Conway, K., Stinson, F., & Grant, B. (2006, December). Changes in the prevalence of major depression and comorbid substance use disorders in the United States between 1991–1992 and 2001–2002. *American Journal of Psychiatry, 163*(12), 2141–2147.

Comuzzie, A. G., & Allison, D. B. (1998, May 29). The search for human obesity genes. *Science, 280,* 1374–1377.

Conduit, R., Crewther, S. G., & Coleman, G. (2004). Spontaneous eyelid movements (ELMS) during sleep are related to dream recall on awakening. *Journal of Sleep Research, 13,* 137–144.

Conger, R. D., Wallace, L. E., Sun, Y., Simons, R. L., McLoyd, V. C., & Brody, G. H. (2002). Economic pressure in African American families: A replication and extension of the family stress model. *Developmental Psychology, 38,* 179–193.

Conner, M., Povey, R., Sparks, P., James, R., & Shepherd, R. (2003). Moderating role of attitudinal ambivalence within the theory of planned behaviour. *British Journal of Social Psychology, 42,* 75–94.

Connolly, A. C. (2007). Concepts and their features: Can cognitive science make good on the promises of concept empiricism? *Dissertation Abstracts International: Section B—The Sciences and Engineering, 67*(7-B), 4125.

Consumer Reports (1995). Mental health: Does therapy help?

Conte, H. R., Plutchik, R., & Draguns, J. G. (2004). The measurement of ego defenses in clinical research. In U. Hentschel, et al. (Eds.). *Defense mechanisms: Theoretical research and clinical perspectives.* Oxford, England: Elsevier Science.

Conway, M. A. (Ed.) (2002). *Levels of processing 30 years on special issue of memory.* Hove: Psychology Press.

Cooke, J. R., & Ancoli-Israel, S. (2006). Sleep and its disorders in older adults. *Psychiatric Clinics of North America, 29,* 1077–1093.

Cooklin, A. (2000). Therapy, the family and others. In H. Maxwell, *Clinical psychotherapy for health professionals.* Philadelphia: Whurr Publishers.

Coolidge, F., & Wynn, T. (2009). *The rise of Homo sapiens: The evolution of modern thinking.* Wiley-Blackwell.

Cooper, C. (2011). Review of "Fat: A cultural history of obesity." *Sociology, 45,* 181–183.

Cooper, H., & Patall, E. (2009, June). The relative benefits of meta-analysis conducted with individual participant data versus aggregated data. *Psychological Methods, 14,* 165–176.

Cooper, J. (2007). *Cognitive dissonance: Fifty years of a classic theory.* Thousand Oaks, CA: Sage Publications.

Cooper, J., Mirabile, R., & Scher, S. J. (2005). Actions and attitudes: The theory of cognitive dissonance. In T. C. Brock & M. C. Green (Eds.), *Persuasion: Psychological insights and perspectives* (2nd ed.). Thousand Oaks, CA: Sage Publications.

Cooper, Z., & Shafran, R. (2008). Cognitive behaviour therapy for eating disorders. *Behavioural and Cognitive Psychotherapy, 36,* 713–722.

Coplan, R., Reichel, M., & Rowan, K. (2009). Exploring the associations between maternal personality, child temperament, and parenting: A focus on emotions. *Personality and Individual Differences, 46,* 241–246.

Copolov, D. L., Seal, M. L., Maruff, P., Ulusoy, R., Wong, M. T. H., TochonDanguy, H. J., & Egan, G. F. (2003). Cortical activation associated with the human experience of auditory hallucinations and perception of human speech in schizophrenia: A PET correlation study. *Psychiatry Research: Neuroimaging, 123,* 139–152.

Corcoran, J., & Pillai, V. (2009, March). A review of the research on solution-focused therapy. *British Journal of Social Work, 39*(2), 234–242.

Cordnoldi, C., De Beni, R., & Helstrup, T. (2007). Memory sensitivity in autobiographical memory. In S. Magnussen, & T. Helstrup, *Everyday memory.* New York: Psychology Press.

Coren, S. (1992). The moon illusion: A different view through the legs. *Perceptual and Motor Skills, 75,* 827–831.

Coren, S. (2004). Sensation and perception. In I. B. Weiner. *Handbook of Psychology, Vol. 1,* Hoboken, NJ: John Wiley & Sons.

Coren, S., & Ward, L. M. (1989). *Sensation and perception* (3rd ed.). San Diego, CA: Harcourt Brace Jovanovich.

Corkin, S. (2002). What's new with the amnesic patient H.M.? *Nature Reviews Neuroscience 3,* 153–160.

Corless, I., Germino, B., & Pittman, M. (2003). *Dying, death, and bereavement: A challenge for living* (2nd ed.). New York: Springer Publishing Co.

Cornelius, M. D., Taylor, P. M., Geva, D., & Day, N. L. (1995). Prenatal tobacco and marijuana use among adolescents: Effects on offspring gestational age, growth, and morphology. *Pediatrics, 95,* 57–68.

Cornell, C. B. (2006). A graduated scale for determining mental age. *Dissertation Abstracts International: Section B—The Sciences and Engineering, 66*(9-B), 5121.

Corsello, A. (2005). The wronged man. In *The best American magazine writing, 2005.* New York: Columbia University Press.

Cosmides, L., & Tooby, J. (2004). Social exchange: The evolutionary design of a neurocognitive system. In M. S. Gazzaniga (Ed.), *Cognitive neurosciences* (3rd ed.). Cambridge, MA: MIT.

Costa, P. T., & McCrae, R. R. (2008). The NEO inventories. In R. P. Archer & S. R. Smith *Personality Assessment.* New York: Routledge/Taylor & Francis Group.

Costa, P. T., Jr., & Widiger, T. A. (Eds.). (2002). *Personality disorders and the five-factor model of personality* (2nd ed.). Washington, DC: American Psychological Association.

Costa, P., & McCrae, R. (2008). The NEO Inventories. *Personality assessment* (pp. 213–245). New York: Routledge/Taylor & Francis Group.

Cotton, P. (1993, July 7). Psychiatrists set to approve DSM-IV. *Journal of the American Medical Association, 270,* 13–15.

Couturier, J., & Lock, J. (2006). Eating disorders: Anorexia nervosa, bulimia nervosa, and binge eating disorder. In T. G. Plante, *Mental disorders of the new millennium: Biology and function* (Vol 3.). Westport, CT: Praeger Publishers/Greenwood Publishing.

Coventry, K. R., Venn, S. F., Smith, G. D., & Morley, A. M. (2003). Spatial problem solving and functional relations. *European Journal of Cognitive Psychology, 15,* 71–99.

Cowan, N., Towse, J. N., Hamilton, Z., Saults, J. S., Elliott, E. M., Lacey, J. F., Moreno, M. V., & Hitch, G. J. (2003). Children's working-memory processes: A response-timing analysis. *Journal of Experimental Psychology: General, 132,* 113–132.

Cowley, G. (2000, January 31). Alzheimer's: Unlocking the mystery. *Time,* pp. 46–54.

Cowley, G. (2003, February 24). Our Bodies, Our Fears. *Newsweek,* pp. 43–44.

Cox, R., Baker, S. E., Macdonald, D. W., & Berdoy, M. (2004). Protecting egg prey from carrion crows: The potential of aversive conditioning. *Applied Animal Behaviour Science, 87,* 325–342.

Coyle, N. (2006). The hard work of living in the face of death. *Journal of Pain and Symptom Management, 32,* 266–274.

Coyle, T. R. (2006). Test-retest changes on scholastic aptitude tests are not related to *g. Intelligence, 34,* 15–27.

Coyne, S. M., & Archer, J. (2005). The relationship between indirect and physical aggression on television and in real life. *Social Development, 14,* 324–338.

Craik, F., & Lockhart, R. (2008). Levels of processing and Zinchenko's approach to memory research. *Journal of Russian & East European Psychology, 46,* 52–60.

Craik, F. I. M. (1990). Levels of processing. In M. E. Eysenck (Ed.), *The Blackwell dictionary of cognitive psychology.* London: Blackwell.

Cramer, J. A. (1995). Optimizing long-term patient compliance. *Neurology, 45,* s25–s28.

Cramer, P. (2007). Longitudinal study of defense mechanisms: Late childhood to late adolescence. *Journal of Personality, 75,* 1–23.

Crawford, N. (2002). Science-based program curbs violence in kids. *APA Monitor, 33,* 38–39.

Creasey, G. L. (2005). *Research methods in lifespan development* (6th ed.). Boston: Allyn & Bacon.

Creswell, J., & Landon, T. (2009, January 25). The talented Mr. Madoff. *The New York Times,* p. 1.

Crews, F. (1996). The verdict on Freud. *Psychological Science, 7,* 63–68.

Crits-Christoph, P. (1992). The efficacy of brief dynamic psychotherapy: A meta-analysis. *American Journal of Psychiatry, 149,* 151–158.

Crocker, J., & Park, L. E. (2004). The costly pursuit of self-esteem. *Psychological Bulletin, 130,* 392–414.

Crombag, H. S., & Robinson, R. E. (2004). Drugs, environment, brain, and behavior. *Current Directions in Psychological Science, 13,* 107–111.

Cropley, A. (2006). In praise of convergent thinking. *Creativity Research Journal, 18,* 391–404.

Crosnoe, R., & Elder, G. H., Jr. (2002). Successful adaptation in the later years: A life course approach to aging. *Social Psychology Quarterly, 65,* 309–328.

Crum, A. J., & Langer, E. J. (2007). Mind-set matters: Exercise and the placebo effect. *Psychological Science, 18,* 165–171.

Cruz, A., & Green, B. G. (2000). Thermal stimulation of taste. *Nature. 403,* 889–892.

Cuijpers, P., van Straten, A., Andersson, G., & van Oppen, P. (2008). Psychotherapy for depression in adults: A meta-analysis of comparative outcome studies. *Journal of Consulting and Clinical Psychology, 76,* 909–922.

Cuijpers, P., van Straten, A., Smit, F., Mihalopoulos, C., & Beekman, A. (2008, October). Preventing the onset of depressive disorders: A meta-analytic review of psychological interventions. *American Journal of Psychiatry, 165,* 1272–1280.

Culhane-Pera, K. A., Borkan, J. M., & Patten, S. (2007). Culture and ethnicity. In O. J. Z. Sahler, & J. E. Carr, *The behavioral sciences and health care* (2nd rev. and updated ed.). Ashland, OH: Hogrefe & Huber Publishers.

Cullinane, C. A., Chu, D. Z. J., & Mamelak, A. N. (2002). Current surgical options in the control of cancer pain. *Cancer Practice, 10,* s21–s26.

Cummings, A., Ceponiene, R., & Koyama, A. (2006). Auditory semantic networks for words and natural sounds. *Brain Research, 1115,* 92–107.

Cunningham, P. (2006). Early years teachers and the influence of Piaget: Evidence from oral history. *Early Years An International Journal of Research and Development, 26,* 5–16.

Curşeu, P. (2011). Need for cognition and active information search in small student groups. *Learning and Individual Differences, 21,* 88–94.

Cwikel, J., Behar, L., & Rabson-Hare, J. (2000). A comparison of a vote count and a meta-analysis review of intervention research with adult cancer patients. *Research on Social Work Practice, 10,* 139–158.

Cynkar, A. (2007). The changing gender composition of psychology. *Monitor on Psychology, 38,* 46–48.

Czopp, A. M., & Monteith, M. J. (2006). Thinking Well of African Americans: Measuring Complimentary Stereotypes and Negative Prejudice. *Basic and Applied Social Psychology, 28,* 233–250.

Czopp, A. M., Monteith, M. J. & Mark, A.Y. (2006). Standing up for a change: reducing bias through interpersonal confrontation. *Journal of Personality and Social Psychology, 90,* 784–803.

D

D'Arcy, R. C. N., Bolster, R. B., & Ryner, L. (2007). A site directed fMRI approach for evaluating functional status in the anterolateral temporal lobes. *Neuroscience Research, 57*, 120–128.

Daftary, F., & Meri, J. W. (2002). *Culture and memory in medieval Islam.* London: I. B. Tauris.

Dai, D. Y., & Wang, X. (2007). The role of need for cognition and reader beliefs in text comprehension and interest development. *Contemporary Educational Psychology, 32*, 332–347.

Daines, B. (2006). Violations of agreed and implicit sexual and emotional boundaries in couple relationships—some thoughts arising from Levine's "A clinical perspective on couple infidelity." *Sexual and Relationship Therapy, 21*, 45–53.

Daitz, B. (2002, December 3). A DOCTOR'S JOURNAL; In Pain Clinic, Fruit, Candy And Relief. *NY Times.*

Dalal, A. K., & Misra, G. (2006). Psychology of health and well-being: Some emerging perspectives. *Psychological Studies, 51, Special issue: Psychology of Health and Well-Being*, 91–104.

Dale, A. (2006). Quality issues with survey research. *International Journal of Social Research Methodology: Theory & Practice, 9, Special issue: Quality in Social Research*, 143–158.

Dale, J. W., & von Schantz, M. (2007). *From genes to genomes: Concepts and applications of DNA technology.* New York: John Wiley & Sons.

Dalla Barba, G., & Decaix, C. (2009). "Do you remember what you did on March 13, 1985?" A case study of confabulatory hypermnesia. Cortex 45 (5): 566.

Dalsgaro, O. J., Hansen, N. G., Soes-Petersen, U., Evald, T., Hoegholm, A., Barber, J., & Vestbo, J. (2004). A multicenter, randomized, double-blind, placebo-controlled, 6-month trial of bupropion hydrochloride sustained-release tablets as an aid to smoking cessation in hospital employees. *Nicotine and Tobacco Research, 6*, 55–61.

Damasio, A. (2003, May 15). Mental self: The person within. *Nature, 423*, 227.

Damasio, H., Grabowski, T., Frank, R., Galaburda, A. M., & Damasio, A. R. (1994). The return of Phineas Gage: Clues about the brain from the skill of a famous patient. *Science, 264*, 1102–1105.

D'Amico, E., Chinman, M., Stern, S., & Wandersman, A. (2009). Community prevention handbook on adolescent substance abuse prevention and treatment: Evidence-based practices. *Adolescent substance abuse: Evidence-based approaches to prevention and treatment* (pp. 213–249). New York: Springer Science + Business Media.

Damon, W. (1999, August). The moral development of children. *Scientific American*, 72–78.

Danaei, G., Vender Hoorn, S., Lopez, A.D., Murray, C. J. L. & Ezzati, M. (2005). Causes of cancer in the world: Comparative risk assessment of nine behavioural and environmental risk factors. Comparative Risk Assessment collaborating group (Cancers). *Lancet, 366*, 1784–1793.

Dani, J. A., & Montague, P. (2007). Disrupting addiction through the loss of drug-associated internal states. *Nature Neuroscience, 10*, 403–404.

Darley, J. M., & Latané, B. (1968). Bystanders intervention in emergencies: Diffusion of responsibility. *Journal of Personality and Social Psychology, 8*, 377–383.

Darwin, C. J., Turvey, M. T., & Crowder, R. G. (1972). An auditory analogue of the Sperling partial-report procedure: Evidence for brief auditory storage. *Cognitive Psychology, 3*, 255–267.

Das, A. (2007). Masturbation in the United States. *Journal of Sex & Marital Therapy, 33*, 301–317.

Davidson, J. E., Deuser, R., & Sternberg, R. J. (1994). The role of metacognition in problem solving. In J. Metcalfe & A. P. Shimamura (Eds.), *Metacognition: Knowing about knowing.* Cambridge, MA: MIT.

Davidson, P. S. R., & Glisky, E. L. (2002). Is flash-bulb memory a special instance of source memory? Evidence from older adults. *Memory, 10*, 99–111.

Davies, S., Jackson, P., Lewis, G., Hood, S., Nutt, D., & Potokar, J. (2008). Is the association of hypertension and panic disorder explained by clustering of autonomic panic symptoms in hypertensive patients? *Journal of Affective Disorders, 111*, 344–350.

Davis, O., Haworth, C., & Plomin, R. (2009, January). Learning abilities and disabilities: Generalist genes in early adolescence. *Cognitive Neuropsychiatry, 14*, 312–331.

Davis, P. (2007). *Shakespeare Thinking.* London: Continuum.

Davis, S. F. (2007). The nose knows best. *PsycCRITIQUES, 52*, 22–31.

Davolt, S. (2006, July 1). Employers got game: Tedium-battling businesses use online motivational games. *Employee Benefit News.* http://ebn.benefitnews.com/.

Day, A. L., & Livingstone, H. A. (2003). Gender differences in perceptions of stressors and utilization of social support among university students. *Canadian Journal of Behavioural Science/Revue, 35*, 73–83.

Day, R. D., & Lamb, M. E. (2004). *Conceptualizing and measuring father involvement.* Mahwah, NJ: Lawrence Erlbaum Associates.

de Araujo, I. E. T., Kringelbach, M. L., & Rolls, E. T. (2003). Representation of umami taste in the human brain. *Journal of Neurophysiology, 90*, 313–319.

De Bini, R., Pazzaglia, F., & Gardini, S. (2007). The generation and maintenance of visual mental images: Evidence from image type and aging. *Brain and Cognition, 63*, 271–278.

de Boysson-Bardies, B., & DeBevoise, M. (1999). *How language comes to children: From birth to two years.* Cambridge, MA: The MIT Press.

de Maat, S., de Jonghe, F., Schoevers, R., & Dekker, J. (2009, February). The effectiveness of long-term psychoanalytic therapy: A systematic review of empirical studies. *Harvard Review of Psychiatry, 17(1)*, 1–23.

De Mello, M. F., De Jesus Mari, J., Bacaltchuk, J., Verdeli, H., & Neugebauer, R. (2005). A systematic review of research findings on the efficacy of interpersonal therapy for depressive disorders. *European Archives of Psychiatry and Clinical Neuroscience, 255*, 75–82.

Dean, C., & Dresbach, T. (2006). Neuroligins and neurexins: Linking cell adhesion, synapse formation and cognitive function. *International Journal of Psychiatry in Clinical Practice, 10 (Suppl)*, 5–11.

Dean-Borenstein, M. T. (2007). The long-term psychosocial effects of trauma on survivors of human-caused extreme stress situations. *Dissertation Abstracts International: Section B—The Sciences and Engineering, 67(11-B)*, 6733.

DeAngelis, D., & Monahan, J. (2008). Professional credentials and professional regulations: Social work professional development. In B. W. White, K. M. Sowers, & C. N. Dulmus, (Eds.), *Comprehensive handbook of social work and social welfare, Vol. 1: The profession of social work.* Hoboken, NJ: John Wiley & Sons.

Deary, I. J., & Der, G. (2005). Reaction time, age, and cognitive ability: Longitudinal findings from age 16 to 63 years in representative population samples. *Aging, Neuropsychology, & Cognition, 12*, 187–215.

Deater-Deckard, K., Ivy, L., & Smith, J. (2005). Resilience in gene-environment transactions. In S. Goldstein and R. B. Brooks (Eds.), *Handbook of resilience in children* (pp. 49–63). New York: Kluwer Academic/Plenum Publishers.

Debiec, J., Doyère, V., and Nader, K. (2006). Directly reactivated, but not indirectly reactivated, memories undergo reconsolidation in the amygdala. *PNAS Proceedings of the National Academy of Sciences of the United States of America, 103*, 3428–3433.

Deci, E. L., Koestner, R., & Ryan, R. M. (2001). Extrinsic rewards and intrinsic motivation in education: Reconsidered once again. *Review of Educational Research, 71*, 1–27.

Deci, E. L., & Ryan, R. M. (2008). Facilitating optimal motivation and psychological well-being across life's domains. *Canadian Psychology/Psychologie Canadienne, 49*, 14–23.

DeCoster, V. A. (2003). Predicting emotions in everyday social interactions: A test and comparison of affect control and social interactional theories. *Journal of Human Behavior in the Social Environment, 6*, 53–73.

Dediu, D., & Ladd, D. R. (2007). From the Cover: Linguistic tone is related to the population frequency of the adaptive haplogroups of two brain size genes, ASPM and Microcephalin. *Proceedings of the National Academy of Sciences, 104*, 10944–10949.

deGroot, A. (1978). *Thought and choice in chess.* Paris: Mouton de Gruyter.

del Rosal, E., Alonso, L., & Moreno, R. (2006). Simulation of habituation to simple and multiple stimuli. *Behavioural Processes, 73*, 272–277.

DeLamater, J. D., & Sill, M. (2005). Sexual desire in later life. *Journal of Sex Research, 42*, 138–149.

Delgado, M. R., Labouliere, C. D., & Phelps, E. A. (2006). Fear of losing money? Aversive conditioning with secondary reinforcers. *Social Cognitive and Affective Neuroscience, 1, Special issue: Genetic, Comparative and Cognitive Studies of Social Behavior*, 250–259.

Delinsky, S. S., Latner, J. D., & Wilson, G. T. (2006). Binge eating and weight loss in a self-help behavior modification program. *Obesity, 14*, 1244–1249.

Della Sala, S. (2011). A daguerreotype of Phineas Gage? *Cortex: A Journal Devoted to the Study of the Nervous System and Behavior, 47*, 83–90.

Demaree, H. A., & Everhart, D. E. (2004). Healthy high-hostiles: Reduced parasympathetic activity and decreased sympathovagal flexibility during negative emotional processing. *Personality and Individual Differences, 36*, 457–469.

Dement, W. C., & Wolpert, E. A. (1958). The relation of eye movements, body mobility, and external stimuli to dream content. *Journal of Experimental Psychology, 55*, 543–553.

Denmark, G. L., & Fernandez, L. C. (1993). Historical development of the psychology of women. In F. L. Denmark & M. A. Paludi (Eds.), *A handbook of issues and theories.* Westport, CT: Greenwood Press.

Dennett, D. C. (2003). *Freedom evolves.* New York: Viking.

Dennis, I. (2007). Halo effects in grading student projects. *Journal of Applied Psychology, 92*, 1169–1176.

Dennis, T. A., Cole, P. M., Zahn-Waxler, C., & Mizuta, I. (2002). Self in context: Autonomy and relatedness in Japanese and U.S. mother-preschooler dyads. *Child Development, 73*, 1803–1817.

Denollet, J. (2005). DS14: standard assessment of negative affectivity, social inhibition, and Type D personality. *Psychosomatic Medicine, 67*, 89–97.

Denollet J., & Brutsaert, D. L. (1998). Personality, disease severity, and the risk of long-term cardiac events in patients with a decreased ejection fraction after myocardial infarction. *Circulation, 97*, 167–173.

Deouell, L. Y., Parnes, A., & Pickard, N. (2006). Spatial location is accurately tracked by human auditory sensory memory: Evidence from the mismatch negativity. *European Journal of Neuroscience, 24*, 1488–1494.

D'Eramo, K., & Francis, G. (2004). Cognitive-Behavioral Psychotherapy. *Anxiety disorders in children and adolescents* (2nd ed.) (pp. 305–328). New York: Guilford Press.

Deregowski, J. B. (1973). Illusion and culture. In R. L. Gregory & G. H. Combrich (Eds.), *Illusion in nature and art* (pp. 161–192). New York: Scribner.

Derryberry, W. P. (2006). Review of social motivation: conscious and unconscious processes. *Journal of Moral Education, 35*, 276–278.

DeRubeis, R., Hollon, S., & Shelton, R. (2003, May 23). Presentation, American Psychiatric Association meeting, Philadelphia.

Des Jarlis, D. C., Sloboda, A., Friedman, S. R., Tempakski, B., McKnight, C., & Braine, N. (2006). Diffusion of the *D.A.R.E* and Syringe Exchange Programs. *American Journal of Public Health, 96*, 1354–1357.

Deshields, T., Tibbs, T., Fan, M. Y., & Taylor, M. (2006). Differences in patterns of depression after treatment for breast cancer [Electronic article published August 12, 2005]. *Psycho-Oncology, 15(5)*, 398–406.

Desimone, R. (1992, October 9). The physiology of memory: Recordings of things past. *Science, 258*, 245–255.

Dessing, J. C., Peper, C. E., Bullock, D., & Beek, P. J. (2005). How position, velocity, and temporal information combine in the prospective control of catching: Data and model. *Journal of Cognitive Neuroscience, 17*, 668–686.

Detoledo-Morrell, L., Stoub, T. R., & Wang, C. (2007). Hippocampal atrophy and disconnection in incipient and mild Alzheimer's disease. *Progressive Brain Research, 163C*, 741–823.

Detterman, D. K., Gabriel, L. T., & Ruthsatz, J. M. (2000). Intelligence and mental retardation. In R. J. Sternberg, et al. (Eds.), *Handbook of intelligence.* New York: Cambridge University Press.

Devonport, J. J., & Lane, A. M. (2006). Relationships between self-efficacy, coping and student retention. *Social Behavior and Personality, 34*, 127–138.

DeVries, H., Kerrick, S., & Oetinger, M. (2007, June). Satisfactions and regrets of midlife parents: A qualitative analysis. *Journal of Adult Development, 14(1)*, 6–15.

Dhillon, S., Yang, L., & Curran, M. (2008). Spotlight on bupropion in major depressive disorder. *CNS Drugs, 22*, 613–617.

Di Fabio, A., & Palazzeschi, L. (2009). An in-depth look at scholastic success: Fluid intelligence, personality traits or emotional intelligence? *Personality and Individual Differences, 46*, 581–585.

Di Forti, M., Lappin, J., & Murray, R. (2007, March). Risk factors for schizophrenia—All roads lead to dopamine. *European Neuropsychopharmacology, 17*, S101–SS107.

Diamond, M. (2009). Human intersexuality: Difference or disorder? *Archives of Sexual Behavior, 38*, 172.

Díaz, E., & De la Casa, L. G. (2011). Extinction, spontaneous recovery and renewal of flavor preferences based on taste–taste learning. *Learning and Motivation, 42*, 64–75.

DiCano, P., & Everitt, B. J. (2002). Reinstatement and spontaneous recovery of cocaine-seeking following extinction and different durations of withdrawal. *Behavioural Pharmacology, 13*, 397–406.

Dickerson, S. S., Kemeny, M. E., Aziz, N., Kim, K. H., & Fahey, J. L. (2004). Immunological effects of induced shame and guilt. *Psychosomatic Medicine, 66*, 124–131.

Diener, E., & Biswas-Diener, R. (2002). Will money increase subjective well-being? *Social Indicators Research, 57*, 119–169.

Diener, E., & Biswas-Diener, R. (2008). *Happiness: Unlocking the mysteries of psychological wealth.* Malden: Blackwell Publishing.

Diener, E., & Clifton, D. (2002). Life satisfaction and religiosity in broad probability samples. *Psychological Inquiry, 13*, 206–209.

Diener, E., & Seligman, M. E. P. (2002). Very happy people. *Psychological Science, 18*, 81–84.

Diener, E., & Seligman, M. E. P. (2004). Beyond money: Toward an economy of well-being. *Psychological Science in the Public Interest, 5*, 1–31.

Diener, E., Lucas, R. E., & Oishi, S. (2002). Subjective well-being: The science of happiness and life satisfaction. In C. R. Snyder & S. J. Lopez (Eds.), *Handbook of positive psychology* (pp. 463–473). London: Oxford University Press.

Diener, E., Lucas, R. E., & Scollon, C. N. (2006). Beyond the hedonic treadmill: Revising the adaptation theory of well-being. *American Psychologist, 61*, 305–314.

Diener, M., Isabella, R., Behunin, M., & Wong, M. (2008). Attachment to mothers and fathers during middle childhood: Associations with child gender, grade, and competence. *Social Development, 17*, 84–101.

DiGiovanna, A. G. (1994). *Human aging: Biological perspectives.* New York: McGraw-Hill.

Dijksterhuis, A., Chartrand, T. L., & Aarts, H. (2007). Effects of priming and perception on social behavior and goal pursuit. In J. A. Bargh, *Social psychology and the unconscious: The automaticity of higher mental processes.* New York: Psychology Press.

Dillard, J. P., & Shen, L. (2004). On the nature of reactance and its role in persuasive health communication. *Communication Monographs, 72*, 144–168.

Dillard, J. P., & Shen, L. (2007). Self-report measures of discrete emotions. In R. A. Reynolds, R. Woods, & J. D. Baker, *Handbook of research on electronic surveys and measurements.* Hershey, PA: Idea Group Reference/IGI Global, 2007.

Dillon, J. (2008, April). Reclaiming humanistic psychology from modernity: Problems and solutions. *Journal of Humanistic Psychology, 48*, 221–242.

DiLorenzo, P. M., & Yougentob, S. L. (2003). Olfaction and taste. In M. Gallagher & R. J. Nelson, *Handbook of psychology: Biological psychology* (Vol. 3). New York: Wiley.

Dimitropoulou, M., Duñabeitia, J., & Carreiras, M. (2011). Phonology by itself: Masked phonological priming effects with and without orthographic overlap. *Journal of Cognitive Psychology, 23*, 185–203.

Dinges, D. F., Pack, F., Wiliams, K., Gillen, K. A., Powell, J. W., Ott, G. E., Aptowicz, C., & Pack, A. I. (1997). Cumulative sleepiness, mood disturbance, and psychomotor vigilance performance decrements during a week of sleep restricted to 4–5 hours per night. *Sleep, 20*, 267–273.

Dion, K., Berscheid, E., & Walster, E. (1972, December). What is beautiful is good. *Journal of Personality and Social Psychology, 24(3)*, 285–290.

Dixon, L., & Goldman, H. (2003, December). Forty years of progress in community mental health: The role of evidence-based practices. *Australian and New Zealand Journal of Psychiatry, 37(6)*, 668–673.

Dixon, R. A., & Cohen, A. L. (2003). Cognitive development in adulthood. In R. M. Lerner, M. A. Easterbrooks, et al. (Eds.), *Handbook of psychology: Developmental psychology* (Vol. 6) (pp. 443–461). New York: Wiley.

Dixon, R. A., Rust, T. B., & Feltmate, S. E. (2007). Memory and aging: Selected research directions and application issues. *Canadian Psychology Psychologie Canadienne, 48*, 67–76.

Do, V. T. (2006). Asian American men and the media: The relationship between ethnic identity, self-esteem, and the endorsement of stereotypes. *Dissertation Abstracts International: Section B—The Sciences and Engineering, 67(6-B)*, 3446.

Dobbins, A. C., Jeo, R. M., Fiser, J., & Allman, J. M. (1998, July 24). Distance modulation of neural activity in the visual cortex. *Science, 281*, 552–555.

Dodge, K. A. (2004). The nature-nurture debate and public policy. *Merrill-Palmer Quarterly, 50*, 418–427.

Dodgen, C. (2005). Nicotine and Addiction. *Nicotine dependence: Understanding and applying the most effective treatment interventions* (pp. 65–80). Washington, DC: American Psychological Association.

D'Odorico, L., & Jacob, V. (2006, May). Prosodic and lexical aspects of maternal linguistic input to late-talking toddlers. *International Journal of Language & Communication Disorders, 41(3)*, 293–311.

Dohnke, B., Weiss-Gerlach, E., & Spies, C. D. (2011). Social influences on the motivation to quit smoking: Main and moderating effects of social norms. *Addictive Behaviors, 36*, 286–293.

Dohrenwend, B. P., Turner, J. B., Turse, N. A., Adams, B. G., Koenen, K. C., & Marshall, R. (2006, August 18). The psychological risks of Vietnam for U.S. veterans: A revisit with new data and methods. *Science, 313*, 979–982.

Doi, T. (1990). The cultural assumptions of psychoanalysis. In J. W. Stigler, R. A. Shweder, & G. Herdt (Eds.), *Cultural psychology: Essays on comparative human development.* New York: Cambridge University Press.

Dolan, P., & White, M. P. (2007). How can measures of subjective well-being be used to inform public policy? *Perspectives on Psychological Science, 2*, 71–85.

Dolan, R. J. (2002, November 8). Emotion, cognition, and behavior. *Science, 298*, 1191–1194.

Dolbier, C. L., Smith, S. E., & Steinhardt, M. A. (2007). Relationships of protective factors to stress and symptoms of illness. *American Journal of Health Behavior, 31*, 423–433.

Dollinger, S. J. (2003). Need for uniqueness, need for cognition and creativity. *Journal of Creative Behavior, 37*, 99–116.

Domhoff, G. W. (1996). *Finding meaning in dreams: A quantitative approach.* New York: Plenum Press.

Donahoe, J. W. (2003). Selectionism. In K. A. Lattal, & P. N. Chase (Eds.), *Behavior theory and philosophy.* New York: Kluwer Academic/Plenum Publishers.

Donahoe, J. W., & Vegas, R. (2004). Pavlovian Conditioning: The CSUR Relation. *Journal of Experimental Psychology: Animal Behavior Processes, 30*, 17–33.

Dong, M., Giles, W., Felitti, V., Dube, S. Williams, J., Chapman, D., and Anda, R. (2004). Insights into causal pathways for ischemic heart disease: Adverse childhood experiences study. *Circulation, 110*, 1761–1766.

Dortch, S. (1996, October). Our aching heads. *American Demographics,* pp. 4–8.

Doty, R. L., Green, P. A., Ram, C., & Yankell, S. L. (1982). Communication of gender from human breath odors: Relationship to perceived intensity and pleasantness. *Hormones and Behavior, 16*, 13–22.

Dougall, A. L., & Baum, A. (2004). Psychoneuroimmunology and trauma. In P. P. Schnurr and B. L. Green (Eds.), *Trauma and health: Physical health consequences of exposure to extreme stress* (pp. 129–155). Washington, DC: American Psychological Association.

Douglas, O., Burton, K. S., & Reese-Durham, N. (2008). The effects of the multiple intelligence teaching strategy on the academic achievement of eighth grade math students. *Journal of Instructional Psychology, 35*, 182–187.

Dovidio, J. F. (2001). On the nature of contemporary prejudice: The third wave. *Journal of Social Issues, 57*, 829–849.

Dovidio, J. F., & Gaertner, S. L. (2006). A multilevel perspective on prejudice: Crossing disciplinary boundaries. In P. A. M. Van Lange, *Bridging social psychology: Benefits of transdisciplinary approaches.* Mahwah, NJ: Lawrence Erlbaum Associates.

Dovidio, J. F., Gaertner, S. L., & Kawakami, K. (2003). Intergroup contact: The past, present, and the future. *Group Processes and Intergroup Relations, 6*, 5–20.

Dovidio, J. F., Gaertner, S. L., & Pearson, A. R. (2005). On the nature of prejudice: The psychological foundations of hate. In R. J. Sternberg (Ed.), *Psychology of hate.* Washington, DC: American Psychological Association.

Dovidio, J. F., Piliavin, J. A., Schroeder, D. A., & Penner, L. A. (2006). *The social psychology of prosocial behavior.* Mahwah, NJ: Lawrence Erlbaum Associates.

Dowling, N., Jackson, A., & Thomas, S. (2008). Behavioral interventions in the treatment of pathological gambling: A review of activity scheduling and desensitization. *International Journal of Behavioral Consultation and Therapy, 4*, 172–187.

Doyle, K. A. (2002). Rational Emotive Behavior Therapy and its application to women's groups. In W. Dryden, & M. Neenan (Eds.), *Rational emotive behaviour group therapy.* London: Whurr Publishers.

Dreier, O. (2008). *Psychotherapy in everyday life.* New York: Cambridge University Press.

Drewes, A. A. (2005). Play in selected cultures: Diversity and universality. In E. Gil and A. A. Drewes, *Cultural issues in play therapy* (pp. 26–71). New York: Guilford Press.

Drob, S. (2005). The mystical symbol: Some comments on Ankor, Giegerich, Scholem, and Jung. *Journal of Jungian Theory & Practice, 7,* 25–29.

Druss, B. (2005, September). A new front in the tobacco wars. *General Hospital Psychiatry, 27*(5), 319–320.

Dryden, W. (1999). *Rational emotive behavior therapy: A training manual.* New York: Springer.

Dubovsky, S. (1999, February 25). Tuning in to manic depression. *HealthNews, 5,* 8.

Ducharme, J. M., Sanjuan, E., & Drain, T. (2007). Errorless compliance training: Success-focused behavioral treatment of children with Asperger syndrome. *Behavior Modification, 31,* 329–344.

Duesbury, E. M. (2011). *The counselor's guide for facilitating the interpretation of dreams: Family and other relationship systems perspectives.* New York: Routledge/ Taylor & Francis Group.

Duffy, M., Gillig, S. E., Tureen, R. M., & Ybarra, M. A. (2002). A critical look at the DSM-IV. *Journal of Individual Psychology, 58,* 363–373.

Dukakis, K., and Tye, L. (2006, September 18). I feel good, I feel fine. *Newsweek,* pp. 62–63.

Duke, M., & Nowicki, S., Jr. (1979). *Abnormal psychology: Perspectives on being different.* Monterey, CA: Brooks/Cole.

Dumont, M., & Dumont, D. (2008). Deinstitutionalization in the United States and Italy: A historical survey. *International Journal of Mental Health, 37,* 61–70.

Duncker, K. (1945). On problem solving. *Psychological Monographs, 58* (5, whole no. 270).

Duvarci, S., ben Mamou, C., and Nader, K. (2006). Extinction is not a sufficient condition to prevent fear memories from undergoing reconsolidation in the basolateral amygdala. *European Journal of Neuroscience, 24,* 249–260.

E

Eaker, E. D., Sullivan, L. M., Kelly-Hayes, M., D'Agostino, R. B., Sr., & Benjamin, E. J. (2004). Anger and hostility predict the development of atrial fibrillation in men in the Framingham Offspring Study. *Circulation, 109,* 1267–1271.

Ebbinghaus, H. (1885/1913). *Memory: A contribution to experimental psychology* (H. A. Roger & C. E. Bussenius, Trans.). New York: Columbia University Press.

Eberhard, K. M., Cutting, J. C., & Bock, K. (2005). Making syntax of sense: Number agreement in sentence production. *Psychological Review, 112,* 531–559.

Eberhardt, J. L., Goff, P. A., Purdie, V. J., & Davies, P. G. (2004). Seeing black: Race, crime, and visual processing. *Journal of Personality and Social Psychology, 87,* 876–893.

Eberling, J., Jagust, W., Christine, C., Starr, P., Larson, P., Bankiewicz, K., et al. (2008, May). Results from a phase I safety trial of hAADC gene therapy for Parkinson disease. *Neurology, 70*(21), 1980–1983.

Ebstein, R. P., Benjamin, J., & Belmaker, R. H. (2003). Behavioral genetics, genomics, and personality. In R. Plomin & J. C. DeFries (Eds.), *Behavioral genetics in the postgenomic era* (pp. 365–388). Washington, DC: American Psychological Association.

Ebster, C., & Neumayr, B. (2008). Applying the door-in-the-face compliance technique to retailing. *The International Review of Retail, Distribution and Consumer Research, 18,* 121–128.

Ecenbarger, W. (1993, April 1). America's new merchants of death. *The Reader's Digest,* 50.

Eckardt, M. H. (2005). Karen Horney: A portrait: The 120th anniversary, Karen Horney, September 16, 1885. *American Journal of Psychoanalysis, 65,* 95–101.

Edinger, J. D., Wohlgemuth, W. K., Radtke, R. A., Marsh, G. R., & Quillian, R. E. (2001). Cognitive behavioral therapy for treatment of chronic primary insomnia: A randomized controlled trial. *Journal of the American Medical Association, 285,* 1856–1864.

Edwards, R. R., & Fillingim, R. B. (2007). Self-reported pain sensitivity: Lack of correlation with pain threshold and tolerance. *European Journal of Pain, 11,* 594–598.

Egan, G., Mathai, M. L., Uschakov, A., Wade, J. D., Weisinger, R. S., & Oldfield, B. J. (2004). Physiological and pathophysiological influences on thirst. *Physiology and Behavior, 81,* 795–803.

Egan, K. (2005). Students' development in theory and practice: The doubtful role of research. *Harvard Educational Review, 75,* 25–41.

Egliston, K., & Rapee, R. (2007). Inhibition of fear acquisition in toddlers following positive modelling by their mothers. *Behaviour Research and Therapy, 45,* 1871–1882.

Eichenbaum, H. (2004). Toward an information processing framework for memory representation by the hippocampus. In M. S. Gazzaniga (Ed.), *Cognitive neurosciences* (3rd ed.) (pp. 679–690). Cambridge, MA: MIT.

Eisch, A., Cameron, H., Encinas, J., Meltzer, L., Ming, G., & Overstreet-Wadiche, L. (2008, November). Adult neurogenesis, mental health, and mental illness: Hope or hype? *Journal of Neuroscience, 28*(46), 11785–11791.

Eisenberg, N., Guthrie, I. K., & Cumberland, A. (2002). Prosocial development in early adulthood: A longitudinal study. *Journal of Personality and Social Psychology, 82,* 993–1006.

Eisenberger, N. I., & Bookheimer, S. Y. (2005). An fMRI investigation of race-related amygdala activity in African-American and Caucasian-American individuals. *Nature Neuroscience, 8,* 720–722.

Eizenman, M. M., & Zaslavsky, O. (2004). Students' verification strategies for combinatorial problems. *Mathematical Thinking and Learning, 6,* 15–36.

Ekman, P. (1972). Universals and cultural differences in facial expressions of emotion. In J. Cole (Ed.), *Darwin and facial expression: A century of research in review* (pp. 169–222). New York: Academic Press.

Ekman, P. (1994a). All emotions are basic. In P. Ekman & R. J. Davidson (Eds.), *The nature of emotion: Fundamental questions.* New York: Oxford University Press.

Ekman, P. (1994b). Strong evidence for universals in facial expressions: A reply to Russell's mistaken critique. *Psychological Bulletin, 115,* 268–287.

Ekman, P., Davidson, R. J., & Friesen, W. V. (1990). Emotional expression and brain physiology: II. The Duchenne smile. *Journal of Personality and Social Psychology, 58,* 342–353.

Ekman, P., Levenson, R. W., & Friesen, W. V. (1983, September 16). Autonomic nervous system activity distinguishes among emotions. *Science, 223,* 1208–1210.

Ekman, P., & O'Sullivan, M. (1991). Facial expression: Methods, means, and moues. In R. S. Feldman & B. Rimé (Eds.), *Fundamentals of nonverbal behavior.* Cambridge: Cambridge University Press.

Elfhag, K., Tynelius, P., & Rasmussen, F. (2007). Sugar-sweetened and artificially sweetened soft drinks in association to restrained, external and emotional eating. *Physiology & Behavior, 91,* 191–195.

El-Hai, J. (2005). *The lobotomist: A maverick medical genius and his tragic quest to rid the world of mental illness.* New York: Wiley.

Elkind, D. (1998). *All grown up and no place to go: Teenagers in crisis.* New York: Da Capo Press.

Elkins, G., Marcus, J., Bates, J., Hasan, R. M., & Cook, T. (2006). Intensive hypnotherapy for smoking cessation: A prospective study. *International Journal of Clinical Experimental Hypnosis, 54,* 303–315.

Ellason, J. W., & Ross, C. A. (2004). SCL-90-R norms for dissociative identity disorder. *Journal of Trauma and Dissociation, 5,* 85–91.

Ellins, E., Halcox, J., Donald, A., Field, B., Brydon, L., Deanfield, J., et al. (2008). Arterial stiffness and inflammatory response to psychophysiological stress. *Brain, Behavior, and Immunity, 22,* 941–948.

Elliott, A. (2002). *Psychoanalytic theory: An introduction* (2nd ed.). Durham, NC: Duke University Press.

Elliott, J., Berman, H., & Kim, S. (2002). Critical ethnography of Korean Canadian women's menopause experience. *Health Care for Women International, 23,* 377–388.

Ellis, A. (1974). *Growth through reason.* Hollywood, CA: Wilshire Books.

Ellis, A. (2002). *Overcoming resistance: A rational emotive behavior therapy integrated approach* (2nd ed.). New York: Springer.

Ellis, A. (2004). Expanding the ABCs of rational emotive behavior therapy. In A. Freeman, M. J. Mahoney, P. Devito, & D. Martin (Eds.), *Cognition and psychotherapy* (2nd ed.). New York: Springer Publishing Co.

Ellis, A., & Tsui, A. (2007). Survival of the fittest or the least fit? When psychology meets ecology in organizational demography. *Perspectives on organizational fit* (pp. 287–315). Mahwah, NJ: Lawrence Erlbaum Associates Publishers.

El-Mallakh, R. S., & Abraham, H. D. (2007). MDMA (Ecstasy). *Annals of Clinical Psychiatry, 19,* 45–52.

Emick, J., & Welsh, M. (2005). Association between formal operational thought and executive function as measured by the Tower of Hanoi-Revised. *Learning and Individual Differences, 15,* 177–188.

Endres, T., & Fendt, M. (2007). Conditioned behavioral responses to a context paired with the predator odor trimethylthiazoline. *Behavioral Neuroscience, 121,* 594–601.

Engen, T. (1987). Remembering odors and their names. *American Scientist, 75,* 497–503.

Engler, J., & Goleman, D. (1992). *The consumer's guide to psychotherapy.* New York: Simon & Schuster.

Epstein, R. (1996). *Cognition, creativity, and behavior: Selected essays.* Westport, CT: Praeger/Greenwood.

Eranti, S. V., & McLoughlin, D. M. (2003). Electroconvulsive therapy: State of the art. *British Journal of Psychiatry, 182,* 8–9.

Erickson, R. (2008, February). A study of the science of taste: On the origins and influence of the core ideas. *Behavioral and Brain Sciences, 31,* 59–75.

Erikson, E. H. (1963). *Childhood and society.* New York: Norton.

Ervik, S., Abdelnoor, M., & Heier, M. S. (2006). Health-related quality of life in narcolepsy. *Acta Neurologica Scandinavica, 114,* 198–204.

Etchegary, H. (2004). Psychological aspects of predictive genetic-test decision: What do we know so far? *Analyses of Social Issues and Public Policy, 4,* 13–31.

Evans, A. M. (2007). Transference in the nurse-patient relationship. *Journal of Psychiatric and Mental Health Nursing, 14,* 189–195.

Evans, D. E., & Rothbart, M. K. (2007). Developing a model for adult temperament. *Journal of Research in Personality, 41,* 868–888.

Evans, J. B. T. (2004). Informal reasoning: Theory and method. *Canadian Journal of Experimental Psychology, 58,* 69–74.

Evans, J. B. T., & Feeney, A. (2004). The role of prior belief in reasoning. In J. P. Leighton (Ed.), *Nature of reasoning*. New York: Cambridge University Press.

Evcik, D., Kavuncu, V., Cakir, T., Subasi, V., & Yaman, M. (2007). Laser therapy in the treatment of carpal tunnel syndrome: A randomized controlled trial. *Photomedical Laser Surgery, 25,* 34–39.

Everette, M. (2008). Gestational weight and dietary intake during pregnancy: Perspectives of African American women. *Maternal & Child Health Journal, 12,* 718–724.

Everly, G. S., Jr., & Lating, J. M. (2007). Psychotherapy: A cognitive perspective. In A. Monat, R. S. Lazarus, & G. Reevy, *The Praeger handbook on stress and coping* (Vol. 2). Westport, CT: Praeger Publishers/Greenwood Publishing.

Eysenck, H. (1991). Dimensions of personality: The biosocial approach to personality. *Explorations in temperament: International perspectives on theory and measurement* (pp. 87–103). New York: Plenum Press.

Eysenck, H. (1995). *Eysenck on extraversion*. New York: Wiley.

Eysenck, M. (2006). *Fundamentals of cognition*. Hove: Psychology Press/Taylor & Francis.

Ezzell, C. (September 2002). Clocking cultures. *Scientific American*, pp. 74–75.

Ezzati, M., Henley, S. J., Thun, M. J., & Lopez, A. D. (2005). Role of smoking in global and regional cardiovascular mortality. *Circulation, 112,* 489–497.

F

Fagan, J. F., & Holland, C. R. (2002). Equal opportunity and racial differences in IQ. *Intelligence, 30,* 361–387.

Fagan, J. F., & Holland, C. R. (2007). Racial equality in intelligence: Predictions from a theory of intelligence as processing. *Intelligence, 35,* 319–334.

Falck-Ytter, T., & Gredebäck, G. (2006). Infants predict other people's action goals. *Nature Neuroscience, 9,* 878–879.

Fallon, A. (2006). Informed consent in the practice of group psychotherapy. *International Journal of Group Psychotherapy, 56,* 431–453.

Fallon, B. A., & Feinstein, S. (2001). Hypochondriasis. In K. A. Phillips (Ed.), *Somatoform and factitious disorders*. Washington, DC: American Psychiatric Association.

Fanselow, M. S., & Poulos, A. M. (2005). The neuroscience of mammalian associative learning. *Annual Review of Psychology, 56,* 207–234.

Farmer, R., & Chapman, A. (2008). Changing behavior by changing the environment. *Behavioral interventions in cognitive behavior therapy: Practical guidance for putting theory into action* (pp. 105–139). Washington, DC: American Psychological Association.

Favazza, A. (1996). *Bodies under Siege: Self-Mutilation and Body Modification in Culture and Psychiatry* (2d ed.). Baltimore: The Johns Hopkins University Press.

Fazio, R., & Olson, M. (2003). Implicit measures in social cognition research: Their meaning and uses. *Annual Review of Psychology, 54,* 297–327.

Fearing, V. G., & Clark, J. (Eds.). (2000). *Individuals in context: A practical guide to client-centered practice*. Chicago: Slack Publishing.

Fedeli, A., Braconi, S., Economidou, D., Cannella, N., Kallupi, M., Guerrini, R., et al. (2009). The paraventricular nucleus of the hypothalamus is a neuroanatomical substrate for the inhibition of palatable food intake by neuropeptide S. *European Journal of Neuroscience, 30,* 1594–1602.

Fee, E., Brown, T. M., Lazarus, J., & Theerman, P. (2002). Exploring acupuncture: Ancient ideas, modern techniques. *American Journal of Public Health, 92,* 1592.

Fein, S., Goethals, G., & Kugler, M. (2007). Social influence on political judgments: The case of presidential debates. *Political Psychology, 28,* 165–192.

Feinberg, A. W. (2002, April). Homocysteine may raise Alzheimer's risk: A physician's perspective. *HealthNews*, p. 4.

Feldhusen, J. F., (2006). The role of the knowledge base in creative thinking. In J. C. Kaufman, & J. Baer, *Creativity and reason in cognitive development*. New York: Cambridge University Press.

Feldman, D. H. (2003). Cognitive development in childhood. In R. M. Lerner, M. A. Easterbrooks, et al. (Eds.), *Handbook of psychology: Developmental psychology* (Vol. 6) (pp. 195–210). New York: Wiley.

Feldman, D. H. (2004). Piaget's stages: The unfinished symphony of cognitive development. *New Ideas in Psychology, 22,* 175–231.

Feldman, R. S. (2003). *P.O.W.E.R. Learning* (2nd ed.). New York: McGraw-Hill.

Feldman, R. S. (2009). *P.O.W.E.R. Learning* (4th ed.). New York: McGraw-Hill.

Feldman, R. S. (2010). *P.O.W.E.R. Learning: Strategies for Success in College and Life* (5th ed). New York: McGraw-Hill.

Feldman, R. S. (Ed.). (1993). *Applications of nonverbal behavioral theories and research*. Hillsdale, NJ: Erlbaum.

Feldt, L. S. (2005). Estimating the reliability of a test battery composite or a test score based on weighted item scoring. *Measurement & Evaluation in Counseling & Development, 37,* 184–191.

Fenter, V. L. (2006). Concerns about Prozac and direct-to-consumer advertising of prescription drugs. *International Journal of Risk & Safety in Medicine, 18,* 1–7.

Feret, A., Steinweg, S., Griffin, H. C., & Glover, S. (2007). Macular degeneration: Types, causes, and possible interventions. *Geriatric Nursing, 28,* 387–392.

Fernander, A., Shavers, V., & Hammons, G. (2007, October). A biopsychosocial approach to examining tobacco-related health disparities among racially classified social groups. *Addiction, 102*(2), 43–57.

Festinger, L. (1957). *A theory of cognitive dissonance*. Stanford, CA: Stanford University Press.

Festinger, L., & Carlsmith, J. M. (1959). Cognitive consequences of forced compliance. *Journal of Abnormal and Social Psychology, 58,* 203–210.

Feuerstein, M. (2007). *Handbook of cancer survivorship*. New York: Springer Science + Business Media.

Fichtenberg, C. M., & Glantz, S. A. (2006). Association of the California tobacco control program with declines in cigarette consumption and mortality from heart disease. In K. E. Warner, *Tobacco control policy*. San Francisco: Jossey-Bass.

Fields, R. (2008, March). White Matter. *Scientific American, 298*(3), 54–61.

Fields, R. D. (2004, April). The other half of the brain. *Scientific American*, pp. 55–61.

Fields-Meyer, T. (1995, September 25). Having their say. *People*, pp. 50–60.

Fillingim, R. B. (2011). Review of 'Functional pain syndromes'. *The Clinical Journal of Pain, 27,* 82–84.

Fine, L. (1994). Personal communication.

Fine, R., & Fine, L. (2003). *Basic chess endings*. New York: Random House.

Fingelkurts, A., Fingelkurts, A. A., & Kallio, S. (2007). Hypnosis induces a changed composition of brain oscillations in EEG: A case study. *Contemporary Hypnosis, 24,* 3–18.

Fink, M. (2000). Electroshock revisited. *American Scientist, 88,* 162–167.

Finke, R. A. (1995). Creative insight and preinventive forms. In R. J. Sternberg & J. E. Davidson (Eds.), *The nature of insight*. Cambridge, MA: MIT.

Finkler, K. (2004). Traditional healers in Mexico: The effectiveness of spiritual practices. In U. P. Gielen, J. M. Fish, & J. G. Draguns (Eds.), *Handbook of culture, therapy, and healing*. Mahwah, NJ: Lawrence Erlbaum Associates.

Finlay, F. O., Jones, R., & Coleman, J. (2002). Is puberty getting earlier? The views of doctors and teachers. *Child: Care, Health and Development, 28,* 205–209.

Finley, C. L., & Cowley, B. J. (2005). The effects of a consistent sleep schedule on time taken to achieve sleep. *Clinical Case Studies, 4,* 304–311.

Finn, A. (2011). Jungian analytical theory. In D. Capuzzi, D. R. Gross, et al. (Eds.), *Counseling and psychotherapy* (5th ed.). Alexandria, VA: American Counseling Association.

Finney, M. L., Stoney, C. M., & Engebretson, T. O. (2002). Hostility and anger expression in African American and European American men is associated with cardiovascular and lipid reactivity. *Psychophysiology, 39,* 340–349.

Firestein, B. A. (Ed.). (1996). *Bisexuality: The psychology and politics of an invisible minority*. Thousand Oaks, CA: Sage.

Fishbach, A., Dhar, R., & Zhang, Y. (2006). Subgoals as substitutes or complements: The role of goal accessibility. *Journal of Personality and Social Psychology, 91,* 232–242.

Fisher, C. B. (2003). *Decoding the ethics code: A practical guide for psychologists*. Thousand Oaks, CA: Sage.

Fisher, C. B., Hoagwood, K., Boyce, C., Duster, T., Frank, D. A., Grisso, T., Levine, R. J., Macklin, R., Spencer, M. B., Takanishi, R., Trimble, J. E., & Zayas, L. H. (2002). Research ethics for mental health science involving ethnic minority children and youths. *American Psychologist, 57,* 1024–1040.

Fisher, E., Brown, L., Aron, A., Strong, G., & Mashek, D. (2010). Reward, addiction, and emotion regulation systems associated with rejection in love. *Journal of Neurophysiology, 104,* 51-60.

Fisher, J. E., & O'Donohue, W. T. (2006). *Practitioner's guide to evidence-based psychotherapy*. New York: Springer Science + Business Media.

Fisk, J. E., Bury, A. S., & Holden, R. (2006). Reasoning about complex probabilistic concepts in childhood. *Scandinavian Journal of Psychology, 47,* 497–504.

Fiske, S. T. (2002). What we know now about bias and intergroup conflict, the problem of the century. *Current Directions in Psychological Science, 11,* 123–128.

Fitch, K. L., & Sanders, R. E. (2005). *Handbook of language and social interaction*. Mahwah, NJ: Lawrence Erlbaum Associates.

Fitzgerald, P., & Daskalakis, Z. (2008, January). The use of repetitive transcranial magnetic stimulation and vagal nerve stimulation in the treatment of depression. *Current Opinion in Psychiatry, 21,* 25–29.

Flam, F. (1991, June 14). Queasy riders. *Science, 252,* 1488.

Flavell, S. W., Cowan, C. W., Kim, T., Greer, P. L., Lin, Y., Paradis, S., Griffith, E. C., Hu, L. S., Chen, C., & Greenberg, M. E. (2006, February 17). Activity-dependent regulation of MEF2 transcription factors suppresses excitatory synapse number. *Science, 311,* 1008–1010.

Fleeson, W. (2004). Moving personality beyond the person-situation debate: The challenge and the opportunity of within-person variability. *Current Directions in Psychological Science, 13,* 83–87.

Fleeson, W. (2004, April). Moving personality beyond the person-situation debate: The challenge and the opportunity of within-person variability. *Current Directions in Psychological Science, 13*(2), 83–87.

Fleischman, D. A., Wilson, R. S., Gabrieli, J. D. E., Bienias, J. L., & Bennett, D. A. (2004). A longitudinal study of implicit and explicit memory in old persons. *Psychology and Aging, 19,* 617–625.

Fleming, J. (2000). Affirmative action and standardized test scores. *Journal of Negro Education, 69,* 27–37.

Foderaro, L. W. (2006, February 16). Westchester lawyer, his memory lost, is found in Chicago shelter after 6 months. *The New York Times*, p. B3.

Fogarty, J. S., & Young, G. A., Jr. (2000). Patient-physician communication. *Journal of the American Medical Association, 289,* 92.

Folk, C., & Remington, R. (2008, January). Bottom-up priming of top-down attentional control settings. *Visual Cognition, 16,* 215–231.

Folkman, S., & Moskowitz, J. T. (2000). Stress, positive emotion, and coping. *Current Directions in Psychological Science, 9,* 115–118.

Folkman, S., & Moskowitz, J. T. (2004). Coping: Pitfalls and promise. *Annual Review of Psychology, 55,* 745–774.

Follett, K., & Hess, T. M. (2002). Aging, cognitive complexity, and the fundamental attribution error. *Journal of Gerontology: Series B: Psychological Sciences and Social Sciences, 57B*, P312–P323.

Fontaine, J., Scherer, K., Roesch, E., & Ellsworth, P. (2007, December). The world of emotions is not two-dimensional. *Psychological Science, 18*(12), 1050–1057.

Forer, B. (1949). The fallacy of personal validation: A classroom demonstration of gullibility. *Journal of Abnormal and Social Psychology, 44*, 118–123.

Forgas, J. P., & Laham, S. M. (2005). The interaction between affect and motivation in social judgments and behavior. In J. P. Forgas, K. P. Williams, S. M. Laham (Eds.), *Social motivation: Conscious and unconscious processes.* New York: Cambridge University Press.

Forlenza, M. J., & Baum, A. (2004). Psychoneuroimmunology. In T. J. Boll & R. G. Frank (Eds.), *Handbook of clinical health psychology: Models and perspectives in health psychology* (Vol. 3). Washington, DC: American Psychological Association.

Fosshage, J. L. (2011). How do we "know" what we "know"? And change what we "know"? *Psychoanalytic Dialogues, 21*, 55–74.

Foster, K. M. (2005). Introduction: John Uzo Ogbu (1939–2003): How do you ensure the fair consideration of a complex ancestor? Multiple approaches to assessing the work and legacy of John Uzo Ogbu. *International Journal of Qualitative Studies in Education, 18*, 559–564.

Foster, P., Drago, V., FitzGerald, D., Skoblar, B., Crucian, G., & Heilman, K. (2008). Spreading activation of lexical-semantic networks in Parkinson's disease. *Neuropsychologia, 46*, 1908–1914.

Foster, R., Fantoni, C., Caudek, C., & Domini, F. (2011). Integration of disparity and velocity information for haptic and perceptual judgments of object depth. *Acta Psychologica, 136*, 300–310.

Foulds, J., Gandhi, K. K., & Steinberg, M. B. (2006). Factors associated with quitting smoking at a tobacco dependence treatment clinic. *American Journal of Health Behavior, 30*, 400–412.

Fountas, K. N., & Smith, J. R. (2007). Historical evolution of stereotactic amygdalotomy for the management of severe aggression. *Journal of Neurosurgery, 106*, 716–713.

Fountoulakis, K. N., Vieta, E., Sanchez-Moreno, J., Kaprinis, S. G., Goikolea, J. M., & Kaprinis, G. S. (2005). Treatment guidelines for bipolar disorder: A critical review. *Journal of Affective Disorders, 86*, 1–10.

Fowler, C. A., & Galantucci, B. (2008). The relation of speech perception and speech production. In Pisoni, D. B. & Remez, R. E. (Eds.), *The handbook of speech perception.* Malden, MA: Blackwell Publishing.

Fox, C. R. (2006). The availability heuristic in the classroom: How soliciting more criticism can boost your course ratings. *Judgment and Decision Making, 1*, 86–90.

Fox, S., & Spector, P. E. (2000). Relations of emotional intelligence, practical intelligence, general intelligence, and trait affectivity with interview outcomes: It's not all just "G." *Journal of Organizational Behavior, 21*, 203–220.

Fraley, R. C., & Shaver, P. R. (1998). Airport separations: A naturalistic study of adult attachment dynamics in separating couples. *Journal of Personality and Social Psychology, 75*, 1198–1212, http://faculty.sjcny.edu/~treboux/documents/airportseparations.pdf.

Francis, G., & Beidel, D. (1995). Cognitive-behavioral psychotherapy. *Anxiety disorders in children and adolescents* (pp. 321–340). New York: Guilford Press.

Frank, L. R. (2002). Electroshock: A crime against the spirit. *Ethical Human Sciences and Services, 4*, 63–71.

Frankenberger, K. D. (2004). Adolescent egocentrism, risk perceptions, and sensation seeking among smoking and nonsmoking youth. *Journal of Adolescent Research, 19*, 576–590.

Franklin, A., Pilling, M., & Davies, I. (2005). The nature of infant color categorization: Evidence from eye movements on a target decision task. *Journal of Experimental Child Psychology, 91*, 227–248.

Franklin, M. E., March, J. S., & Garcia, A. (2007). Treating obsessive-compulsive disorder in children and adolescents. In C. Purdon, M. M. Antony, & L. J. Summerfeldt, (Eds.), *Psychological treatment of obsessive-compulsive disorder: Fundamentals and beyond.* Washington, DC: American Psychological Association.

Franko, D., and Striegel-Moore, R. (2002). The role of body dissatisfaction as a risk factor for depression in adolescent girls: Are the differences Black and White? *Journal of Psychosomatic Research, 53*, 975–983.

Franzek, E., & Beckmann, H. (1996). Gene-environment interaction in schizophrenia: Season-of-birth effect reveals etiologically different subgroups. *Psychopathology, 29*, 14–26.

Fraser, J., & Solovey, A. (2007). *Second-order change in psychotherapy: The golden thread that unifies effective treatments.* Washington, DC: American Psychological Association.

Frasure-Smith, N., Lesperance, F., & Talajic, M. (2000). The prognostic importance of depression, anxiety, anger, and social support following myocardial infarction: Opportunities for improving survival. In P. M McCabe, N. Schneiderman, T. M. Field, & A. R. Wellens (Eds.), *Stress, coping, and cardiovascular disease.* Mahwah, NJ: Erlbaum.

Frederickson, B. L., & Branigan, C. (2005). Positive emotions broaden the scope of attention and thought-action repertoires. *Cognition & Emotion, 19*, 313–332.

Freedle, R., Keeney, T., & Smith, N. (1970). Effects of mean depth and grammaticality on children's imitations of sentences. *Journal of Verbal Learning & Verbal Behavior, 9*(2), 149–154.

Freedman, D. S. (1995). The importance of body fat distribution in early life. *American Journal of the Medical Sciences, 310*, S72–S76.

Freedman, J., & Fraser, S. C. (1966). Compliance without pressure: The foot-in-the-door technique. *Journal of Personality and Social Psychology, 4*, 195–202.

Freeman, A., Mahoney, M., DeVito, P., & Martin, D. (2004). *Cognition and psychotherapy* (2nd ed.). New York: Springer Publishing Co.

Fregni, F., & Pascual-Leone, A. (2007). Technology insight: Noninvasive brain stimulation in neurology-perspectives on the therapeutic potential of rTMS and tDCS. *Nature Clinical Practice Neurology, 3*, 383–393.

Frensch, P. A., & Rünger, D. (2003). Implicit learning. *Current Directions in Psychological Science, 12*, 13–18.

Freud, S. (1900). *The interpretation of dreams.* New York: Basic Books.

Freud, S. (1920). *Beyond the pleasure principle: A study of death instinct in human aggression* (J. Strachey, Trans.). New York: Bantam Books.

Freud, S. (1922/1959). *Group psychology and the analysis of the ego.* London: Hogarth.

Freudenreich, O., & Goff, D. C. (2011). Treatment of psychotic disorders. In D. A. Ciraulo, R. Shader, D. A. Ciraulo, & R. Shader (Eds.), *Pharmacotherapy of depression* (2nd ed.). New York: Springer Science + Business Media.

Friborg, O., Barlaug, D., Martinussen, M., Rosenvinge, J. H., & Hjemdal, O. (2005). Resilience in relation to personality and intelligence. *International Journal of Methods in Psychiatric Research, 14*, 29–42.

Friedberg, R. D. (2006). A cognitive-behavioral approach to family therapy. *Journal of Contemporary Psychotherapy, 36*, 159–165.

Friedman, J. N. W., Oltmanns, T. F., & Turkheimer, E. (2007). Interpersonal perception and personality disorders: Utilization of a thin slice approach. *Journal of Research in Personality, 41*, 667–688.

Friedman, M. J. (2006). Posttraumatic stress disorder among military returnees from Afghanistan and Iraq. *American Journal of Psychiatry, 163*, 586–593.

Frijda, N. H. (2005). Emotion experience. *Cognition and Emotion, 19*, 473–497.

Frincke, J. L., & Pate, W. E, II. (2004, March). *Yesterday, today, and tomorrow. Careers in Psychology 2004, what students need to know.* Paper presented at the Annual Convention of the Southeastern Psychological Association, Atlanta, GA.

Frings, L., Wagner, K., Unterrainer, J., Spreer, J., Halsband, U., & Schulze-Bonhage, A. (2006). Gender-related differences in lateralization of hippocampal activation and cognitive strategy. *Neuroreport, 17*, 417–421.

Fritsch, T., McClendon, M. J., Smyth, K. A., Lerner, A. J., Friedland, R. P., & Larsen, J. D. (2007). Cognitive functioning in healthy aging: The role of reserve and lifestyle factors early in life. *Gerontologist, 47*, 307–322.

Frost, L. E., & Bonnie, R. J. (Eds.). (2001). *The evolution of mental health law.* Washington, DC: American Psychological Association.

Frost, R. O., & Steketee, G. (Eds.). (2002). *Cognitive approaches to obsessions and compulsions: Theory, assessment, and treatment.* New York: Pergamon Press.

Fry, D. (2005). Rough-and-Tumble Social Play in Humans. *The nature of play: Great apes and humans* (pp. 54–85). New York: Guilford Press.

Fu, G., Xu, F., Cameron, C., & Lee, K. (2007). Cross-cultural differences in children's choice, categorization and evaluation of truth and lies. *Developmental Psychology, 43*, 278–293.

Fuller, A. (2006). Hypnosis and ideomotor compliance in the treatment of smoking tobacco and cannabis. *Australian Journal of Clinical Hypnotherapy and Hypnosis, 27*, 14–18.

Funder, D. C. (1991). Global traits: A neoAllportian approach to personality. *Psychological Science, 2*, 31–39.

Furnham, A., & Crump, J. (2005). Personality traits, types, and disorders: An examination of the relationship between three self-report measures. *European Journal of Personality, 19*, 167–184.

Furumoto, L., & Scarborough, E. (2002). Placing women in the history of psychology: The first American women psychologists. In W. E. Pickren (Ed.), *Evolving perspectives on the history of psychology* (pp. 527–543). Washington, DC: American Psychological Association.

G

Gaab, J., Rohleder, N., Nater, U. M., & Ehlert, U. (2005). Psychological determinants of the cortisol stress response: The role of anticipatory cognitive appraisal. *Psychoneuroendocrinology, 30*, 599–610.

Gabbard, G. (2009). Psychoanalysis and psychodynamic psychotherapy. *Essentials of personality disorders* (pp. 185–207). Arlington, VA: American Psychiatric Publishing, Inc.

Galanter, E. (1962). Contemporary psychophysics. In R. Brown, E. Galanter, E. Hess, & G. Maroler (Eds.), *New directions in psychology* (pp. 87–157). New York: Holt.

Galanter, M. (2007). Spirituality and recovery in 12-step programs: an empirical model. *Journal of Substance Abuse Treatment, 33*, 265–272.

Galatzer-Levy, R. M., & Cohler, B. J. (1997). *Essential psychoanalysis: A contemporary introduction.* New York: Basic Books.

Galavotti, C., Saltzman, L. E., Sauter, S. L., & Sumartojo, E. (1997, February). Behavioral science activities at the Center for Disease Control and Prevention: A selected overview of exemplary programs. *American Psychologist, 52*, 154–166.

Galef, D. (2001, April 27). The information you provide is anonymous, but what was your name again? *The Chronicle of Higher Education, 47*, B5.

Gallup Poll. (2001, June 8). *American's belief in psychic and paranormal phenomena is up over last decade.* Washington, DC: The Gallup Organization.

Gami, A. S., Howard, D. E., Olson, E. J., Somers, V. K. (2005). Day-night pattern of sudden death in obstructive sleep apnea. *New England Journal of Medicine, 353*, 1206–1214.

Gangestad, S. W., Simpson, J. A., Cousins, A. J., Garver-Apgar, C. E., & Christensen, P. N. (2004). Women's preferences for male behavioral displays change across the menstrual cycle. *Psychological Science, 15*, 203–207.

Gangwisch, J., Heymsfield, S., Boden-Albala, B., Kreier, F., Pickering, T., Zammit, G., et al. (2008, August). Sleep duration associated with mortality in elderly, but not middle-aged adults in a large US sample. *Sleep: Journal of Sleep and Sleep Disorders Research, 31*(8), 1087–1096.

Ganio, M. S., Johnson, E. C., Lopez, R. M., Stearns, R. L., Emmanuel, H., Anderson, J. M., et al. (2011). Caffeine lowers muscle pain during exercise in hot but not cool environments. *Physiology & Behavior, 102*, 429–435.

Ganong, L. H., & Coleman, M. (1999). *Changing families, changing responsibilities: Family obligations following divorce and remarriage*. Mahwah, NJ: Erlbaum.

Garb, H. N., Wood, J. M., Lilenfeld, S. O., & Nezworski, M. T. (2005). Roots of the Rorschach controversy. *Clinical Psychology Review, 25*, 97–118.

Garber, J., & Horowitz, J. L. (2002). Depression in children. In I. H. Gotlib & C. L. Hammen (Eds.), *Handbook of depression*. New York: Guilford Press.

Garcia, J. (1990). Learning without memory. *Journal of Cognitive Neuroscience, 2*, 287–305.

Garcia, J. (2003). Psychology is not an enclave. In R. J. Sternberg (Ed.), *Psychologists defying the crowd: Stories of those who battled the establishment and won*. Washington, DC: American Psychological Association.

Garcia, S. M., Weaver, K., Moskowitz, G. B., & Darley, J. M. (2002). Crowded minds: The implicit bystander effect. *Journal of Personality and Social Psychology, 83*, 843–853.

Garcia-Andrade, C., Wall, T. L., & Ehlers, C. L. (1997). The firewater myth and response to alcohol in Mission Indians. *Journal of Psychiatry, 154*, 983–988.

Garcia-Palacios, A., Hoffman, H., & Carlin, A. (2002). Virtual reality in the treatment of spider phobia: A controlled study. *Behavior Research & Therapy, 40*, 983–993.

Gardini, S., Cornoldi, C., De Beni, R., & Venneri, A. (2009). Cognitive and neuronal processes involved in sequential generation of general and specific mental images. *Psychological Research/Psychologische Forschung, 73*, 633–643.

Gardner, B., & O'Connor, D. (2008). A review of the cognitive effects of electroconvulsive therapy in older adults. *The Journal of ECT, 24*, 68–80.

Gardner, E. P., & Kandel, E. R. (2000). Touch. In E. R. Kandel, J. H. Schwartz, & T. M. Jessell (Eds.), *Principles of neural science* (4th ed.). New York: McGraw-Hill.

Gardner, F., & Moore, Z. (2008). Understanding clinical anger and violence: The anger avoidance model. *Behavior Modification, 32*, 897–912.

Gardner, H. (1975). *The shattered mind: The person after brain damage*. New York: Knopf.

Gardner, H. (1999). *Intelligence reframed: Multiple intelligences for the 21st century*. New York: Basic Books.

Gardner, H. (2005). Scientific psychology: Should we bury it or praise it? In R. J. Sternberg (Ed.), *Unity in psychology: Possibility or pipe dream?* (pp. 77–90). Washington, DC: American Psychological Association.

Garland, J. (1999). Working with older adults. *What is clinical psychology?* (3rd ed.) (pp. 184–208). New York: Oxford University Press.

Garlow, S. J., Purselle, D. C., & Heninger, M. (2007). Cocaine and alcohol use preceding suicide in African American and White adolescents. *Journal of Psychiatric Research, 41*, 530–536.

Garrigan, P., & Kellman, P. (2008, February). Perceptual learning depends on perceptual constancy. *PNAS Proceedings of the National Academy of Sciences of the United States of America, 105*, 2248–2253.

Garwick, G. B. (2007). Intelligence-related terms in mental retardation, learning disability, and gifted/talented professional usage, 1983–2001: The 1992 mental retardation redefinition as natural experiment. *Dissertation Abstracts International Section A: Humanities and Social Sciences, 67*(9-A), 3296.

Garwood, C. L., & Potts, L. A. (2007). Emerging pharmacotherapies for smoking cessation. *American Journal of Health Systems Pharmacology, 64*, 1693–1698.

Garza-Guerrero, C. (2000). Idealization and mourning in love relationships: Normal and pathological spectra. *Psychoanalytic Quarterly, 69*, 121–150.

Gass, C. S., Luis, C. A., Meyers, T. L., & Kuljis, R. O. (2000). Familial Creutzfeldt-Jakob disease: A neuro-psychological case study. *Archives of Clinical Neuropsychology, 15*, 165–175.

Gatchel, R. J., & Oordt, M. S. (2003). Obesity. In R. J. Gatchel & M. S. Oordt, *Clinical health psychology and primary care: Practical advice and clinical guidance for successful collaboration* (pp. 149–167). Washington, DC: American Psychological Association.

Gatchel, R. J. & Weisberg, J. N. (2000). *Personality characteristics of patients with pain*. Washington, DC: APA Books.

Gathérias, F. (2006). Psychologie succincte des auteurs d'attentat suicide. Brief psychological analysis of suicide bombers. *Revue Francophone—Du Stress et du Trauma, 6*, 47–52.

Gazzaniga, M. S. (1998, July). The split brain revisited. *Scientific American*, pp. 50–55.

Gazzaniga, M. S., Ivry, R. B., & Mangun, G. R. (2002). *Cognitive neuroscience: The biology of the mind* (2nd ed.). New York: W. W. Norton.

Ge, X., Kim, I. J., Brody, G. H., Conger, R. D., Simons, R. L., Gibbons, F. X., & Cutrona, C. E. (2003). It's about timing and change: Pubertal transition effects on symptoms of major depression among African American youths. *Developmental Psychology, 39*, 430–439.

Gegax, T. (2005, June 6). An end to "power hour." *Newsweek*, p. 28.

Gegenfurtner, K. R. (2003). Color vision. *Annual Review of Neuroscience, 26*, 181–206.

Gelernter, J., & Stein, M. (2009). Heritability and genetics of anxiety disorders. *Oxford handbook of anxiety and related disorders* (pp. 87–96). New York: Oxford University Press.

Gelfand, M. M. (2000). Sexuality among older women. *Journal of Women's Health and Gender Based Medicine, 9*(Suppl. 1), S15–S20.

Gelman, R., & Baillargeon, R. (1983). A review of some Piagetian concepts. In J. H. Flavell & E. M. Markman (Eds.), *Handbook of child psychology: Cognitive development* (Vol. 3) (4th ed.). New York: Wiley.

Gelman, R., & Kit-Fong Au, T. (Eds.). (1996). *Perceptual and cognitive development*. New York: Academic Press.

Gennaro, R. J. (2004). *Higher-order theories of consciousness: An anthology*. Amsterdam, Netherlands: John Benjamins.

Genovese, J. E. C. (2006). Piaget, pedagogy, and evolutionary psychology. *Evolutionary Psychology, 4*, 2127–2137.

Gentile, B., Grabe, S., Dolan-Pascoe, B., Twenge, J., Wells, B., & Maitino, A. (2009). Gender differences in domain-specific self-esteem: A meta-analysis. *Review of General Psychology, 13*, 34–45.

Gentile, D., Mathieson, L., & Crick, N. (2011). Media violence associations with the form and function of aggression among elementary school children. *Social Development, 20*, 213–232.

Gentner, D., Goldin, S., & Goldin-Meadow, S. (Eds.). (2003). *Language in mind: Advances in the study of language and cognition*. Cambridge, MA: MIT.

Georgas, J. (2006). Families and family change. *Families across cultures: A 30-nation psychological study* (pp. 3–50). New York: Cambridge University Press.

George, M. S., Wassermann, E. M., Williams, W. A., Callahan, A., et al. (1995). Daily repetitive transcranial magnetic stimulations (rTMS) improves mood in depression. *Neuroreport: An International Journal for the Rapid Communication of Research in Neuroscience, 6*, 1853–1856.

George, S., & Moselhy, H. (2005). Cocaine-induced trichotillomania. *Addiction, 100*, 255–256.

George, T. P. (1999). Design, measurement, and analysis in developmental research. In M. Bornstein & M. Lamb, *Developmental psychology*. Mahwah, NJ: Erlbaum.

Georgiou, G. A., Bleakley, C., Hayward, J., Russo, R., Dutton, K., Eltiti, S., & Fox, E. (2005). Focusing on fear: Attentional disengagement from emotional faces. *Visual Cognition, 12*, 145–158.

Geraerts, E., Schooler, J., Merckelbach, H., Jelicic, M., Hauer, B., & Ambadar, Z. (2007, July). The reality of recovered memories: Corroborating continuous and discontinuous memories of childhood sexual abuse. *Psychological Science, 18*(7), 564–568.

German, T., & Defeyter, M. (2000, December). Immunity to functional fixedness in young children. *Psychonomic Bulletin & Review, 7*(4), 707–712.

Gershkoff-Stowe, L., Connell, B., & Smith, L. (2006). Priming overgeneralizations in two- and four-year-old children. *Journal of Child Language, 33*, 461–486.

Gershoff, A. D., & Johar, G. V. (2006). Do You Know Me? Consumer Calibration of Friends' Knowledge. *J. Consumer Research, 32*(4) 496–503.

Gerstel, N. (2005, April 8). In search of time. *Science, 308*, 204–205.

Getner, D., & Holyoak, K. J. (1997, January). Reasoning and learning by analogy. *American Psychologist, 52*, 32–34.

Giacobbi, P. R., Jr., Lynn, T. K., Wetherington, J. M., Jenkins, J., Bodendorf, M., & Langley, B. (2004). Stress and coping during the transition to university for first-year female athletes. *Sports Psychologist, 18*, 1–20.

Giacomini, M., Baylis, F., & Robert, J. (2007). Banking on it: Public policy and the ethics of stem cell research and development. *Social Sciences Medicine, 22*, 88–84.

Gibb, K., Tunbridge, D., Chua, A., & Frederickson, N. (2007). Pathways to inclusion: Moving from special school to mainstream. *Educational Psychology in Practice, 23*, 109–127.

Gibbons, R. D., Brown, C. H., Hur, K., Marcus, S. M., Bhamik, D. K., Erkens, J. A., Herrings, R. M. C., & Mann, J. J. (2007). Early evidence on the effects of regulators' suicidally warnings on SSRI prescriptions and suicide in children and adolescents. *American Journal of Psychiatry, 164*, 1356–1363.

Gibbs, N. (2005, August 8). Being 13. *Time*, pp. 41–55.

Gibbs, W. W. (2002, August.) From mouth to mind. *Scientific American*, p. 26.

Gilbert, D. T., McNulty, S. E., Guiliano, T. A., & Benson, J. E. (1992). Blurry words and fuzzy deeds: The attribution of obscure behavior. *Journal of Personality and Social Psychology, 62*, 18–25.

Gilbert, D. T., Miller, A. G., & Ross, L. (1998). Speeding with Ned: A personal view of the correspondence bias. In J. M. Darley & J. Cooper (Eds.), *Attribution and social interaction: The legacy of Edward E. Jones*. Washington, DC: American Psychological Association.

Gilbert, P. D. (2007). Spirituality and mental health: A very preliminary overview. *Current Opinions in Psychiatry, 20*, 594–598.

Gilboa, A., Winocur, G., & Rosenbaum, R. S. (2006). Hippocampal contributions to recollection in retrograde and anterograde amnesia. *Hippocampus, 16*, 966–980.

Gilchrist, A., Cowan, N., & Naveh-Benjamin, M. (2009). Investigating the childhood development of working memory using sentences: New evidence for the growth of chunk capacity. *Journal of Experimental Child Psychology, 104*, 252–265.

Gilligan, C. (1996). The centrality of relationships in psychological development: A puzzle, some evidence, and a theory. In G. G. Noam & K. W. Fischer (Eds.), *Development and vulnerability in close relationships*. Hillsdale, NJ: Erlbaum.

Gilligan, C. (2004). Recovering psyche: reflections on life-history and history. *The Annual of Psychoanalysis, 32*, 131–147.

Gilovich, T., Griffin, D., & Kahneman, D. (Eds.). (2002). *Heuristics and biases: The psychology of intuitive judgment*. Cambridge, England: Cambridge University Press.

Gintis, H. (2009). *The bounds of reason: Game theory and the unification of the behavioral sciences*. Princeton, NJ: Princeton University Press.

Gladwell, M. (2004, September 20). Annals of psychology: Personality, plus how corporations figure out who you are. *The New Yorker*, pp. 42–45.

Gladwin, T. (1964). Culture and logical process. In N. Goodenough (Ed.), *Explorations in cultural anthropology: Essays in honor of George Peter Murdoch*. New York: McGraw-Hill.

Glass, K., Flory, K., Hankin, B., Kloos, B., & Turecki, G. (2009). Are coping strategies, social support, and hope associated with psychological distress among Hurricane Katrina survivors? *Journal of Social and Clinical Psychology, 28*, 779–795.

Glickler, J. (2006). Advancing in advancement: A self-efficacy study of development practitioners in higher education. *Dissertation Abstracts International: Section B: The Sciences and Engineering, 67(2-B)*, 1190.

Glicksohn, J., & Nahari, G. (2007). Interacting personality traits? Smoking as a test case. *European Journal of Personality, 21*, 225–234.

Glisky, E. L. (2007). Changes in cognitive function in human aging. In D. R. Riddle, *Brain aging: Models, methods, and mechanisms*. Boca Raton, FL: CRC Press.

Godden, D., & Baddeley, A. (1975). Context dependent memory in two natural environments. *British Journal of Psychology, 66*, 325–331.

Goffin, R. D., Jelley, R. B., & Wagner, S. H. (2003). Is halo helpful? Effects of inducing halo on performance rating accuracy. *Social Behavior and Personality, 31*, 625–636.

Goin, M. K. (2005). A current perspective on the psychotherapies. *Psychiatric Services, 56*, 255–257.

Gold, L. (2006). Suicide and gender. *The American Psychiatric Publishing textbook of suicide assessment and management* (1st ed.) (pp. 77–106). Arlington, VA: American Psychiatric Publishing, Inc.

Gold, P. E., Cahill, L., & Wenk, G. L. (2002). Ginkgo biloba: A cognitive enhancer? *Psychological Science in the Public Interest, 3*, 2–7.

Goldberg. C. (2007, August 2). Implants offer hope in brain injury cases. *Boston Globe*, p. A1.

Golden, A. M., Daigleish, T., & Spinks, H. (2006). Dysfunctional attitudes in seasonal affective disorder. *Behaviour Research and Therapy, 44*, 1159–1164.

Golden, W. L. (2006). Hypnotherapy for anxiety, phobias and psychophysiological disorders. In R. A. Chapman, *The clinical use of hypnosis in cognitive behavior therapy: A practitioner's casebook*. New York: Springer Publishing.

Golimbet, V. E., Alfimova, M. V., Gritsenko, I. K., & Ebstein, R. P. (2007). Relationship between dopamine system genes and extraversion and novelty seeking. *Neuroscience Behavior and Physiology, 37*, 601–606.

Goldstein, I. (2000). Female sexual arousal disorder: New insights. *International Journal of Impotence Research, 12*(Suppl. 4), S152–S157.

Goldstein, J. (2003). People @ play: Electronic games. In van Oostendorp, H., *Cognition in a digital world* (pp. 25–45). Mahwah, NJ: Lawrence Erlbaum Associates.

Goldstein, S. N. (2006). The exploration of spirituality and identity status in adolescence. *Dissertation Abstracts International: Section B: The Sciences and Engineering, 67(6-B)*, 3481.

Goldstone, R. L., & Kersten, A. (2003). Concepts and categorization. In A. F. Healy & R. W. Proctor (Eds.), *Handbook of psychology: Experimental psychology* (Vol. 4) (pp. 599–621). New York: Wiley.

Goleman, D. (1993, July 21). "Expert" babies found to teach others. *The New York Times*, p. C-10.

Golimbet, V. E., Alfimova, M. V., Gritsenko, I. K., & Ebstein, R. P. (2007). Relationship between dopamine system genes and extraversion and novelty seeking. *Neuroscience Behavior and Physiology, 37*, 601–606.

Gonidakis, S., & Longo, V. (2009). Programmed longevity and programmed aging theories. *Handbook of theories of aging* (2nd ed.) (pp. 215–228). New York: Springer Publishing Co.

Gontier, N. (2008). Genes, brains, and language: An epistemological examination of how genes can underlie human cognitive behavior. *Review of General Psychology, 12*, 170–180.

Gontkovsky, S. T. (2005). Neurobiological bases and neuropsychological correlates of aggression and violence. In J. P. Morgan (Ed.), *Psychology of aggression*. Hauppauge, NY: Nova Science Publishers.

Gontkovsky, S. T., & Beatty, W. W. (2006). Practical methods for the clinical assessment of information processing speed. *International Journal of Neuroscience, 116*, 1317–1325.

Goode, E. (1999, April 13). If things taste bad, "phantoms" may be at work. *The New York Times*, pp. D1–D2.

Goodheart, C. D., Kazdin, A. E., & Sternberg, R. J. (Eds.). (2006). *Evidence-based psychotherapy: Where practice and research meet*. Washington, DC: American Psychological Association.

Goodman, G., & Quas, J. (2008). Repeated interviews and children's memory: It's more than just how many. *Current Directions in Psychological Science, 17*, 386–390.

Goodman, W. K., Rudorfer, M. V., & Maser, J. D. (2000). *Obsessive-compulsive disorder: Contemporary issues in treatment*. Mahwah, NJ: Lawrence Erlbaum Associates.

Goodnough, A., & O'Connor, A. (2009, April 22). Student at Boston U. may be tied to third case. *The New York Times*, A20.

Goodwin, R. D., & Hamilton, S. P. (2003). Lifetime comorbidity of antisocial personality disorder and anxiety disorders among adults in the community. *Psychiatry Research, 117*, 159–166.

Goodwin, R., Costa, P., & Adonu, J. (2004). Social support and its consequences: "Positive" and "deficiency" values and their implications for support and self-esteem. *British Journal of Social Psychology, 43*, 465–474.

Gooren, L. (2006). The biology of human psychosexual differentiation. *Hormones and Behavior, 50*, 589–601.

Gorfine, T., & Zisapel, N. (2009, February). Late evening brain activation patterns and their relation to the internal biological time, melatonin, and homeostatic sleep debt. *Human Brain Mapping, 30*(2), 541–552.

Gosling, S., Sandy, C., & Potter, J. (2010). Personalities of self-identified "Dog People" and "Cat People." *Anthrozoos, 23*, 213–222.

Gotlib, I. H., Krasnoperova, E., Yue, D. N., & Joorman, J. (2004). Attentional biases for negative interpersonal stimuli in clinical depression. *Journal of Abnormal Psychology, 113*, 127–135.

Gottesman, I. I. (1997, June 6). Twin: En route to QTLs for cognition. *Science, 276*, 1522–1523.

Gottesman, I. I., & Hanson, D. R. (2005). Human development: Biological and genetic processes. *Annual Review of Psychology, 56*, 263–286.

Gottfredson, L. (1994, November). The science and politics of race-norming. *American Psychologist, 49*(11), 955–963.

Gottfredson, L. S. (2004). Schools and the g factor. *Wilson Quarterly*, 35–45.

Gottfredson, L. S., & Deary, I. J. (2004). Intelligence predicts health and longevity, but why? *Current Directions in Psychological Science, 13*, 1–4.

Gottlieb, D. A. (2004). Acquisition with partial and continuous reinforcement in pigeon autoshaping. *Learning and Behavior, 32*, 321–334.

Gottlieb, D. A. (2006). Effects of partial reinforcement and time between reinforced trials on terminal response rate in pigeon autoshaping. *Behavioural Processes, 72*, 6–13.

Goubert, L., Vlaeyen, J. S., Crombez, G., & Craig, K. D. (2011). Learning about pain from others: An observational learning account. *The Journal of Pain, 12*, 167–174.

Gould, E., Reeves, A. J., Graziano, M. S. A., & Gross, C. G. (1999, October 15). Neurogenesis in the neocortex of adult primates. *Science*, 548–552.

Gould, R. L. (1978). *Transformations*. New York: Simon & Schuster.

Govindarajan, A., Kelleher, R. J., & Tonegawa, S. (2006). A clustered plasticity model of long-term memory engrams. *Nature Reviews Neuroscience, 7*, 575–583.

Grady, D., & Altman, L. K. (2008, December 29). Lessons for other smokers in Obama's efforts to quit. *The New York Times*, p. A12.

Graham, C. A., Bancroft, J., & Doll, H. A. (2007). Does oral contraceptive-induced reduction in free testosterone adversely affect the sexuality or mood of women? *Psychoneuroendocrinology, 32*, 246–255.

Graham, S. (1992). "Most of the subjects were white and middle class": Trends in published research on African Americans in selected APA journals, 1970–1989. *American Psychologist, 47*, 629–639.

Granic, I., Hollenstein, T., & Dishion, T. (2003). Longitudinal analysis of flexibility and reorganization in early adolescence: A dynamic systems study of family interactions. *Developmental Psychology, 39*, 606–617.

Grann, J. D. (2007). Confidence in knowledge past: An empirical basis for a differential decay theory of very long-term memory monitoring. *Dissertation Abstracts International Section A: Humanities and Social Sciences, 67*, 2462.

Gray, G. C. (2006). The regulation of corporate violations: punishment, compliance, and the blurring of responsibility. *British Journal of Criminology, 46*, 875–892.

Graziano, M. S., Taylor, C. S., & Moore, T. (2002). Complex movements evolved by microstimulation of precentral cortex. *Neuron, 34*, 841–851.

Graziano, W. G., Habashi, M. M., Sheese, B. E., & Tobin, R. M. (2007). Agreeableness, empathy, and helping: A person situation perspective. *Journal of Personality and Social Psychology, 93*, 583–599.

Greedorfer, S. (2002). Socialization processes and sport behavior. *Advances in sport psychology* (2nd ed.) (pp. 377–401). Champaign, IL: Human Kinetics.

Green, B. G., & George, P. (2004). 'Thermal Taste' Predicts Higher Responsiveness to Chemical Taste and Flavor. *Chemical Senses, 29*, 617–628.

Green, G., & Osborne, J. (1985, January). Does vicarious instigation provide support for observational learning theories? A critical review. *Psychological Bulletin, 97*(1), 3–17.

Green, J. S., Henderson, F. R., & Collinge, M. D. (2003). *Prevention and control of wildlife damage: Coyotes*. Lincoln: University of Nebraska, Institute of Agriculture and Natural Resources. Retrieved from http://wildlifedamage.unl.edu/handbook/handbook/carnivor/ca_c51.pdf.

Greenberg, R., & Goldman, E. (2009). Antidepressants, psychotherapy or their combination: Weighing options for depression treatments. *Journal of Contemporary Psychotherapy, 39*, 83–91.

Greenberg, R. M., & Kellner, C. H. (2005). Electroconvulsive therapy: A selected review. *American Journal of Geriatric Psychiatry, 13*, 268–281.

Greene, J. D., Sommerville, R. B., Nystrom, L. E., Darley, J. M., & Cohen, J. D. (2001, September 14). An fMRI investigation of emotional engagement in moral judgment. *Science, 293*, 2105–2108.

Greene, R. L., & Clopton, J. R. (2004). Minnesota Multiphasic Personality Inventory-2 (MMPI-2). In M. E. Maruish (Ed.), *Use of psychological testing for treatment planning and outcomes assessment: Instruments for adults* (Vol. 3) (3rd ed.). Mahwah, NJ: Lawrence Erlbaum Associates.

Greenspan, S. (2006). Functional concepts in mental retardation: Finding the natural essence of an artificial category. *Exceptionality, 14,* 205–224.

Greenwald, A. G., Draine S. C., & Abrams, R. L. (1996, September 20). Three cognitive markers of unconscious semantic activation. *Science, 272,* 1699–1702.

Greenwald, A. G., Nosek, B. A., & Banaji, M. R. (2003). Understanding and using the Implicit Association Test: 1. An improved scoring algorithm. *Journal of Personality and Social Psychology 85,* 197–216.

Greenwald, A. G., Nosek, B. A., & Sriram, N. (2006). Consequential validity of the implicit association test: Comment on Blanton and Jaccard. *American Psychologist, 61,* 56–61.

Greenwald, A. G., Rudman, L. A., Nosek, B. A., & Zayas, V. (2006). Why so little faith? A reply to Blanton and Jaccard's (2006) Skeptical view of testing pure multiplicative theories. *Psychological Review, 113,* 170–180.

Greer, R. D., Dudek-Singer, J., & Gautreaux, G. (2006). Observational learning. *International Journal of Psychology, 41,* 486–499.

Greer, S. (1999). Mind–body research in psychooncology. *Advances in Mind-Body Medicine, 15*(4), 236–244.

Gregg, J. P., Lit, L., Baron, C. A., Hertz-Picciotto, I., Walker, W., Davis, R. A., Croen, L. A., Ozonoff, S., Hansen, R., Pessah, I. N., & Sharp, F. R. (2007). Gene expression changes in children with autism. *Genomics, 12,* 88–97.

Gregory, R. L. (1978). *The psychology of seeing* (3rd ed.). New York: McGraw-Hill.

Greven, C. U., Rijsdijk, F. V., & Plomin, R. (2011). A twin study of ADHD symptoms in early adolescence: Hyperactivity-impulsivity and inattentiveness show substantial genetic overlap but also genetic specificity. *Journal of Abnormal Child Psychology: An official publication of the International Society for Research in Child and Adolescent Psychopathology, 39,* 265–275.

Grigorenko, E. (2009). Speaking genes or genes for speaking? Deciphering the genetics of speech and language. *Journal of Child Psychology and Psychiatry, 50,* 116–125.

Grigorenko, E. L. (2000). Heritability and intelligence. In R. J. Sternberg, et al. (Eds.), *Handbook of intelligence.* New York: Cambridge University Press.

Grigoriadis, S., & Ravitz, P. (2007). An approach to interpersonal psychotherapy for postpartum depression: Focusing on interpersonal changes. *Canadian Family Physician, 53,* 1469–1475.

Grilo, C M., Sanislow, C. A., Skodol, A. E., Gunderson, J. G., Stout, R. L., Shea, M. T., Zanarini, M. C., Bencer, D. S., Morey, L. C., Dyck, I. R., & McGlashan, T. H. (2003). Do eating disorders co-occur with personality disorders? Comparison groups matter. *International Journal of Eating Disorders, 33,* 155–164.

Grindstaff, J. S., & Fisher, L. A. (2006). Sport psychology consultants' experience of using hypnosis in their practice: An exploratory investigation. *The Sport Psychologist, 20,* 368–386.

Gronau, N., Cohen, A., & Ben-Shakhar, G. (2003). Dissociations of personally significant and task-relevant distractors inside and outside the focus of attention: A combined behavioral and psychophysiological study. *Journal of Experimental Psychology, 123,* 512–529.

Gronholm, P., Rinne, J. O., Vorobyev, V., & Laine, M. (2005). Naming of newly learned objects: A PET activation study. *Brain Research and Cognitive Brain Research, 14,* 22–28.

Gross, D. M. (2006). *The secret history of emotion: From Aristotle's Rhetoric to modern brain science.* Chicago: University of Chicago Press.

Grossmann, K., & Grossmann, K. (1990, January). The wider concept of attachment in cross-cultural research. *Human Development, 33*(1), 31–47.

Grossmann, T., Striano, T., & Friederici, A. D. (2007). Developmental changes in infants' processing of happy and angry facial expressions: A neurobehavioral study. *Brain and Cognition, 64,* 30–41.

Groves, R. M., Singer, E., Lepkowski, J. M., Heeringa, S. G., & Alwin, D. F. In S. J. House, F. T. Juster, R. L. Kahn, H. Schuman, & E. Singer (2004). *A telescope on society: Survey research and social science at the University of Michigan and beyond.* Ann Arbor, MI: University of Michgan Press.

Grucza, R., Norberg, K., & Bierut, L. (2009). Binge drinking among youths and young adults in the United States: 1979–2006. *Journal of the American Academy of Child & Adolescent Psychiatry, 48,* 692–702.

Grunwald, T., Boutros, N. N., Pezer, N., von Oertzen, J., Fernandez, G., Schaller, C., & Elger, C. E. (2003). Neuronal substrates of sensory gating within the human brain. *Biological Psychiatry, 15,* 511–519.

Guadagno, R. E., & Cialdini, R. B. (2002). Online persuasion: An examination of gender differences in computer-mediated interpersonal influence [Special issue: Groups and Internet]. *Group Dynamics, 6,* 38–51.

Guéguen, N., Marchand, M., Pascual, A., & Lourel, M. (2008). Foot-in-the-door technique using a courtship request: A field experiment. *Psychological Reports, 103,* 529–534.

Guerrero, L., La Valley, A., & Farinelli, L. (2008, October). The experience and expression of anger, guilt, and sadness in marriage: An equity theory explanation. *Journal of Social and Personal Relationships, 25,* 699–724.

Guilleminault, C., Kirisoglu, C., Bao, G., Arias, V., Chan, A., & Li, K. K. (2005). Adult chronic sleepwalking and its treatment based on polysomnography. *Brain, 128* (Pt. 5), 1062–1069.

Gunter, B. (2008). Media violence: Is there a case for causality? *American Behavioral Scientist, 51,* 1061–1122.

Gurin, P. (2006). Informing theory from practice and applied research. *Journal of Social Issues, 62,* 621–628.

Gurunjj, R., & Roethel-Wendorf, A. (2009). Stress and mental health. In S. Eshun, & R.A.R. Gurunjj, Eds. *Culture and mental health: Sociocultural influences, theory, and practice* (pp. 35–53). New York: Wiley-Blackwell.

Guthrie, R. V. (1998). *Even the rat was white: A historical view of psychology* (2nd ed.). Needham Heights, MA: Allyn & Bacon.

Gutierrez, P. M., Muehlenkamp, J. L., Konick, L. C., & Osman, A. (2005). What role does race play in adolescent suicidal ideation? *Archives of Suicide Research, 9,* 177–192.

Gwynn, M. I., & Spanos, N. P. (1996). Hypnotic responsiveness, nonhypnotic suggestibility, and responsiveness to social influence. In R. G. Kunzendorf, N. P. Spahos, & B. Wallace (Eds.), *Hypnosis and imagination.* Amityville, NY: Baywood.

H

Haberstick, B. C., Schmitz, S., Young, S. E., & Hewitt, J. K. (2005).Contributions of genes and environments to stability and change in externalizing and internalizing problems during elementary and middle school. *Behavior Genetics, 35,* 381–396.

Haberstick, B. C., Timberlake, D., & Ehringer, M. A. (2007). Genes, time to first cigarette and nicotine dependence in a general population sample of young adults. *Addiction, 102,* 655–665.

Hackam, D. G. (2007). Translating animal research into clinical benefit. *British Medical Journal, 334,* 163–164.

Hadjistavropoulos, T., Craig, K. D., & Fuchs-Lacelle, S. (2004). *Social influences and the communication of pain.* Mahwah, NJ: Lawrence Erlbaum Associates.

Haier, R. J., Colom, R., Schroeder, D. H., Condon, C. A., Tang, C., Eaves, E., et al. (2009). Gray matter and intelligence factors: Is there a neuro-g? *Intelligence, 37,* 136–144.

Haley, W. E., Clair, J. M., & Saulsberry, K. (1992). Family caregiver satisfaction with medical care of their demented relatives. *Gerontologist, 32,* 219–226.

Halford, S. (2006). Collapsing the boundaries? Fatherhood, organization and homeworking. *Gender, Work & Organization, 13,* 383–402.

Halkitis, P. (2009). *Methamphetamine addiction: Biological foundations, psychological factors, and social consequences.* Washington, DC: American Psychological Association.

Hall, R. E. (2002). *The Bell Curve*: Implications for the performance of black/white athletes. *Social Science Journal, 39,* 113–118.

Halle, M. (2009, August 4). Can drilling electrodes into your brain help you lose weight? *Daily Mail* (London).

Hallschmid, M., Benedict, C., Born, J., Fehm, H., & Kern, W. (2004). Manipulating central nervous mechanisms of food intake and body weight regulation by intranasal administration of neuropeptides in man. *Physiology and Behavior, 83,* 55–64.

Halpern, D. F. (2005). Psychology at the intersection of work and family: Recommendations for employers, working families, and policy-makers. *American Psychologist, 60,* 397–409.

Halpert, J. (2003, April 28). What do patients want? *Newsweek,* pp. 63–64.

Hamani, Y., Sciaki-Tamir, Y., Deri-Hasid, R., Miller-Pogrund, T., Milwidsky, A., & Haimov-Kochman, R. (2007). Misconceptions about oral contraception pills among adolescents and physicians. *Human Reproduction, 22,* 3078–3083.

Hamann, S. (2001). Cognitive and neural mechanisms of emotional memory. *Trends in Cognitive Sciences, 5,* 394–400.

Hamann, S., Ely, T. D., Hoffman, J. M., & Kilts, C. D. (2002). Ecstasy and agony: Activation of human amygdala in positive and negative emotion. *Psychological Science, 13,* 135–141.

Hamberg, K. (2005). Biology, Gender and Behaviour. A Critical Discussion of the Biological Models Used for Explaining Cognitive and Behavioural Gender Differences. *Psychology of gender identity* (pp. 127–144). Hauppauge, NY: Nova Biomedical Books.

Hambleton, R. K. (2006). Psychometric models, test designs and item types for the next generation of educational and psychological tests. In D. Bartram, & R. K. Hambleton, *Computer-based testing and the Internet: Issues and advances.* New York: John Wiley & Sons.

Hamer, D. H., Hu, S., Magnuson, V. L., Hu, N., & Pattatucci, A. M. L. (1993, July 16). A linkage between DNA markers on the X chromosome and male sexual orientation. *Science, 261,* 321–327.

Hamer, M., Taylor, A., & Steptoe, A. (2006). The effect of acute aerobic exercise on stress related blood pressure responses: A systematic review and meta-analysis. *Biological Psychology, 71,* 183–190.

Hamilton, A. C., & Martin, R. C. (2007). Semantic short-term memory deficits and resolution of interference: A case for inhibition? In D. S. Gorfein, & C. M. Macleod, *Inhibition in cognition.* Washington, DC: American Psychological Association.

Hamilton, W. L., Biener, L., & Brennan, R. T. (2007). Do local tobacco regulations influence perceived smoking norms? Evidence from adult and youth surveys in Massachusetts. *Health Education Research,* Health Education Research Advance Access published online on October 18, 2007, Health Education Research, doi:10.1093/her/cym054

Hammond, C., & Gold, M. (2008). Caffeine dependence, withdrawal, overdose and treatment: A review. *Directions in Psychiatry, 28,* 177–190.

Hammond, D. C. (2007). Review of the efficacy of clinical hypnosis with headaches and migraines. *International Journal of Clinical and Experimental Hypnosis, 55,* April 2007. Special issue: Evidence-based practice clinical hypnosis—part 1, 207–219.

Hampson, R. (2007, Oct 8). Dozens feel pinched by lobsterman's tale. *USA Today*, 3.

Haney, C., & Zimbardo, P. (2009). Persistent dispositionalism in interactionist clothing: Fundamental attribution error in explaining prison abuse. *Personality and Social Psychology Bulletin, 35*, 807–814.

Haney, J. (2008). Self-administration of cocaine, cannabis and heroin in the human laboratory: Benefits and pitfalls. *Addiction Biology, 14*, 9–21.

Hankins, F. (1925). Back to Rousseau. *Nation, 121*, 238–239.

Hanley, S. J., & Abell, S. C. (2002). Maslow and relatedness: Creating an interpersonal model of self-actualization. *Journal of Humanistic Psychology, 42*, 37–56.

Hannon, E. E., & Johnson, S. P. (2005). Infants use meter to categorize rhythms and melodies: Implications for musical structure learning. *Cognitive Psychology, 50*, 354–377.

Hansell, S. (2007, January 3). Google answer to filling jobs is an algorithm. *The New York Times*, p. A1.

Harding, D. J., & Jencks, C. (2003). Changing Attitudes toward premarital sex: Cohort, period, and aging effects. *The Public Opinion Quarterly, 67*, 211–226.

Hardison, D. M. (2006). Review of phonetics and phonology in language comprehension and production: Differences and similarities. *Studies in Second Language Acquisition, 28*, 138–140.

Hardt, J., Sidor, A., Nickel, R., Kappis, B., Petrak, P., & Egle, U. (2008). Childhood adversities and suicide attempts: A retrospective study. *Journal of Family Violence, 23*, 713–718.

Hardy, L. T., (2007). Attachment theory and reactive attachment disorder: theoretical perspectives and treatment implications. *Journal of Child and Adolescent Psychiatric Nursing, 20*, 27–39.

Harlaar, N., Spinath, F. M., Dale, P. S., & Plomin, R. (2005). Genetic influences on early word recognition abilities and disabilities: A study of 7-year-old twins. *Journal of Child Psychology and Psychiatry, 46*, 373–384.

Harlow, H. F., & Zimmerman, R. R. (1959). Affectional responses in the infant monkey. *Science, 130*, 421–432.

Harlow, J. M. (1869). Recovery from the passage of an iron bar through the head. *Massachusetts Medical Society Publication, 2*, 329–347.

Harmon-Jones, E., & Winkielman, P. (2007). *Social neuroscience: Integrating biological and psychological explanations of social behavior.* New York: Guilford Press.

Harold, G. T., Fincham, F. D., Osborne, L. N., & Conger, R. D. (1997). Mom and dad are at it again: Adolescent perceptions of marital conflict and adolescent psychological distress. *Developmental Psychology, 33*, 333–350.

Harper, T. (1978, November 15). It's not true about people 65 or over. *Green Bay Press-Gazette* (Wisconsin), p. D-1.

Harris, G. (2009). Flavors banned from cigarettes to deter youths. *The New York Times*, Sept. 23, p. A1.

Hart, B., & Risley, T. R. (1997). Use of language by three-year-old children. Courtesy of Drs. Betty Hart and Todd Risley, University of Kansas.

Hartung, C. M., & Widiger, T. A. (1998). Gender differences in the diagnosis of mental disorders: Conclusions and controversies of the DSM-IV. *Psychological Bulletin, 123*, 260–278.

Harvey, A., Nathens, A., Bandiera, G., & LeBlanc, V. (2010). Threat and challenge: Cognitive appraisal and stress responses in simulated trauma resuscitations. *Medical Education, 44*, 587–594.

Harvey, J. H., Wenzel, A., Sprecher, S. (2004). *The handbook of sexuality in close relationships.* Mahwah, NJ: Lawrence Erlbaum.

Haslam, C., & Lawrence, W. (2004). Health-related behavior and beliefs of pregnant smokers. *Health Psychology, 23*, 486–491.

Hauke, C. (2006). The unconscious: Personal and collective. In R. K. Papadopoulos, *The handbook of Jungian psychology: Theory, practice and applications.* New York: Routledge.

Hausenblas, H., & Downs, D. (2002). Relationship among sex, imagery and exercise dependence symptoms. *Psychology of Addictive Behaviors, 16*, 169–172.

Hauser, M. D. (2000). The sound and the fury: Primate vocalizations as reflections of emotion and thought. In N. L. Wallin & B. Merker (Eds.), *The origins of music.* Cambridge, MA: MIT.

Hauser, M. D., Chomsky, N., & Fitch, W. T. (2002, November, 22). The faculty for language: What is it, who has it, and how did it evolve? *Science, 298*, 1569–1579.

Havermans, R. C., Mulkens, S., Nederkoorn, C., & Jansen, A. (2007). The efficacy of cue exposure with response prevention in extinguishing drug and alcohol cue reactivity. *Behavioral Interventions, 22*, 121–135.

Haviland-Jones, J., & Chen, D. (1999, April 17). *Human olfactory perception.* Paper presented at the Association for Chemoreception Sciences, Sarasota, Florida.

Hawkes, Christopher H., & Doty, R. L. (2009). *The neurology of olfaction.* Cambridge, UK: Cambridge University Press.

Hayflick, L. (2007). Biological aging is no longer an unsolved problem. *Annals of the New York Academy of Sciences, 1100*, 1–13.

Hays, P. A. (2008). *Addressing cultural complexities in practice: Assessment, diagnosis, and therapy* (2nd ed.). Washington, DC: American Psychological Association.

Hayslip, B., Neumann, C. S., Louden, L., & Chapman, B. (2006). Developmental stage theories. In J. C. Thomas, D. L. Segal, & M. Hersen (Eds.). *Comprehensive Handbook of Personality and Psychopathology, Vol. 1: Personality and Everyday Functioning.* Hoboken, NJ: John Wiley & Sons.

Hayslip, B., Neumann, C., Louden, L., & Chapman, B. (2006). Developmental Stage Theories. *Comprehensive Handbook of Personality and Psychopathology: Personality and Everyday Functioning* (Vol. 1) (pp. 115–141). Hoboken, NJ: John Wiley & Sons Inc.

Hazlett, H., Hammer, J., Hooper, S. R., & Kamphaus, R. W. (2011). Down syndrome. In S. Goldstein, C. R. Reynolds, S. Goldstein, C. R. Reynolds (Eds.), *Handbook of neurodevelopmental and genetic disorders in children* (2nd ed.). New York: Guilford Press.

Heath, A. C., & Madden, P. A. F. (1995). Genetic influences on smoking behavior. In J. R. Turner, L. R. Cardon, & J. K. Hewitt (Eds.), *Behavior genetic approaches in behavioral medicine: Perspectives on individual differences.* New York: Plenum.

Heath, R. A. (2006). *The Praeger handbook of trans-sexuality: Changing gender to match mindset.* Westport, CT: Praeger Publishers/Greenwood Publishing.

Heatherton, T., & Sargent, J. (2009). Does watching smoking in movies promote teenage smoking? *Current Directions in Psychological Science, 18*, 63–67.

Hecht, J. M. (2007). The happiness myth: Why what we think is right is wrong. A history of what really makes us happy. New York: HarperSanFrancisco/HarperCollins.

Hedgepeth, E. (2005). Different lenses, different vision. *School Administrator, 62*, 36–39.

Hedges, D. W., Brown, B. L., Shwalk, D. A., Godfrey, K., & Larcher, A. M. (2007). The efficacy of selective serotonin reuptake inhibitors in adult social anxiety disorder: A meta-analysis of double-blind, placebo-controlled trials. *Journal of Psychopharmacology, 21*, 102–111.

Hegarty, P. (2007). From genius inverts to gendered intelligence: Lewis Terman and the power of the norm. *History of Psychology, 10*, Special issue: Power matters: Knowledge politics in the history of psychology, 132–155.

Hegarty, P., & Massey, S. (2007). Anti-homosexual prejudice . . . as opposed to what? Queer theory and the social psychology of anti-homosexual attitudes. *Journal of Homosexuality, 52*, 47–71.

Heinrichs, R. W. (2005). The primacy of cognition in schizophrenia. *American Psychologist, 60*, 229–242.

Helfand, S. J. (2011). Managing disruptive offenders: A behavioral perspective. In T. J. Fagan & R. K. Ax (Eds.), *Correctional mental health: From theory to best practice.* Thousand Oaks, CA: Sage Publications, Inc.

Heller, S. (2005). *Freud A to Z.* New York: Wiley. Helmuth, L. (2000, August 25). Synapses shout to overcome distance. *Science, 289*, 1273.

Helmbold, N., Troche, S. & Rammsayer, T. (2007). Processing of temporal and nontemporal information as predictors of psychometric intelligence: A structural-equation-modeling approach. *Journal of Personality, 75*, 985–1006.

Helson, R., & Soto, C. (2005, August). Up and Down in Middle Age: Monotonic and Nonmonotonic Changes in Roles, Status, and Personality. *Journal of Personality and Social Psychology, 89*(2), 194–204.

Henderlong, J., & Lepper, M. R. (2002). The effects of praise on children's intrinsic motivation: A review and synthesis. *Psychological Bulletin, 128*, 774–795.

Henderson, J., Kesmodel, U., & Gray, R. (2007). Systematic review of the fetal effects of prenatal binge-drinking. *Journal of Epidemiology and Community Health, 61*, 1069–1073.

Henderson, N. D. (1982). Correlations in IQ for pairs of people with varying degrees of genetic relatedness and shared environment. *Annual Review of Psychology, 33*, 219–243.

Hendrick, C., & Hendrick, S. S. (2003). Romantic love: Measuring cupid's arrow. In S. J. Lopez & C. R. Snyder (Eds.), *Positive psychological assessment: A handbook of models and measures.* Washington, DC: American Psychological Association.

Hendricks, P., & Spenader, J. (2005). When Production Precedes Comprehension: An Optimization Approach to the Acquisition of Pronouns. *Language Acquisition: A Journal of Developmental Linguistics, 13*(4), 319–348.

Henningsen, D. D., Henningsen, M. L., & Eden, J. (2006). Examining the symptoms of group-think and retrospective sensemaking. *Small Group Research, 37*, 36–64.

Henry, D., McClellen, D., Rosenthal, L., Dedrick, D., & Gosdin, M. (2008, February). Is sleep really for sissies? Understanding the role of work in insomnia in the US. *Social Science & Medicine, 66*, 715–726.

Hentschel, U., Smith, G., Draguns, J. G., & Elhers, W. (2004). *Defense mechanisms: Theoretical, research and clinical perspectives.* Oxford, England: Elsevier Science.

Herbenick, D., Reece, M., Sanders, S., Dodge, B., Ghassemi, A., & Fortenberry, J. (2009). Prevalence and characteristics of vibrator use by women in the United States: Results from a nationally representative study. *Journal of Sexual Medicine, 6*, 1857–1866.

Herrán, A., Carrera, M., & Sierra-Biddle, D. (2006). Panic disorder and the onset of agoraphobia. *Psychiatry and Clinical Neurosciences, 60*, 395–396.

Herrington, D. M., & Howard, T. D. (2003). From presumed benefit to potential harm—Hormone therapy and heart disease. *New England Journal of Medicine, 349*, 519–521.

Herrnstein, R. J., & Murray, D. (1994). *The bell curve.* New York: Free Press.

Hertzog, C., Kramer, A., Wilson, R., & Lindenberger, U. (2008). Enrichment effects on adult cognitive development: Can the functional capacity of older adults be preserved and enhanced? *Psychological Science in the Public Interest, 9*, 1–65.

Herzberg, L. (2009). Direction, causation, and appraisal theories of emotion. *Philosophical Psychology, 22*, 167–186.

Herzog, H. A. (2005). Dealing with the animal research controversy. In C. K. Akins & S. Panicker (Eds.), *Laboratory animals in research and teaching: Ethics, care, and methods.* Washington, DC: American Psychological Association.

Heshka, S., Anderson, J. W., Atkinson, R. L., Greenway, F. L., Hill, J. O., Phinney, S. D., Kolotkin, R. L., Miller-Kovach, K., & Pi-Sunyer, F. X. (2003). Weight loss with self-help compared with a structured commercial program: A randomized trial. *Journal of the American Medical Association, 289*, 1792–1798.

Hess, E. H., & Polt, J. M. (1960). Pupil size as related to interest value of visual stimuli. *Science, 132,* 249–350.

Hess, M. J., Houg, S., & Tammaro, E. (2007). The experience of four individuals with paraplegia enrolled in an outpatient interdisciplinary sexuality program. *Sexuality and Disability, 25,* 189–195.

Hess, T. M., Hinson, J. T., & Statham, J. A. (2004). Explicit and implicit stereotype activation effects on memory: Do age and awareness moderate the impact of priming? *Psychology and Aging, 19,* 495–505.

Hettema, J. (2005). Genetics of Anxiety Disorders. *Psychiatric genetics* (pp. 141–165). Arlington, VA: American Psychiatric Publishing, Inc.

Heuser, S. (2006, April 2). A case of mind over matter. *Boston Globe,* p. A1.

Heyman, G. D., & Diesendruck, G. (2002). The Spanish *ser/estar* distinction in bilingual children's reasoning about human psychological characteristics. *Developmental Psychology, 38,* 407–417.

Heywood, S., & McCabe, M. P. (2006). Negative affect as a mediator between body dissatisfaction and extreme weight loss and muscle gain behaviors. *Journal of Health Psychology, 11,* 833–844.

Hibbard, P. (2007, February). A statistical model of binocular disparity. *Visual Cognition, 15,* 149–165.

Hiby, E. F., Rooney, N. J., & Bradshaw, J. W. S. (2004). Dog training methods: Their use, effectiveness and interaction with behaviour and welfare. *Animal Welfare, 13,* 63–69.

Hicks, T. V., & Leitenberg, H. (2001). Sexual fantasies about one's partner versus someone else: Gender differences in incidence and frequency. *Journal of Sex Research, 38,* 43–50.

Hilarski, C. (2007). Antisocial personality disorder. In B. A. Thyer, & J. S. Wodarski, *Social work in mental health: An evidence-based approach.* Hoboken, NJ: John Wiley & Sons.

Hilgard, E. (1992). Disassociation and theories of hypnosis. In E. Fromm & M. E. Nash (Eds.), *Contemporary hypnosis research.* New York: Guilford.

Hill, J. O., Catenacci, V., & Wyatt, H. R. (2005). Obesity: Overview of an epidemic. *Psychiatric Clinics of North America, 28,* 1–23.

Hill, J. O., Wyatt, H. R., Reed, G. W., & Peters, J. C. (2003, February 7). Obesity and the environment: Where do we go from here? *Science, 299,* 853–855.

Hillix, W. A. (2007). The past, present, and possible futures of animal language research. In D. A. Washburn, *Primate perspectives on behavior and cognition.* Washington, DC: American Psychological Association.

Hines, M. (2004). *Brain gender.* New York: Oxford University Press.

Hinshaw, S. P., Zupan, B. A., Simmel, C., Nigg, J. T., & Melnick, S. (1997). Peer status in boys with and without attention-deficit hyperactivity disorder: Predictions from overt and covert antisocial behavior, social isolation, and authoritative parenting beliefs. *Child Development, 68,* 880–896.

Hirsh, I. J., & Watson, C. S. (1996). Auditory psychophysics and perception. *Annual Review of Psychology, 47,* 461–484.

Hirschler, B. (2007, May 1). Doctors test gene therapy to treat blindness. *Reuters,* p. 9.

Hirsh, I. J., & Watson, C. S. (1996). Auditory psychophysics and perception. *Annual Review of Psychology, 47,* 461–484.

Hjemdal, O., Aune, T., Reinfjell, T., Stiles, T.C., & Friborg, O. (2007). Resilience as a predictor of depressive symptoms: A correlational study with young adolescents. *Clinical Child Psychology and Psychiatry, 12,* 91–104.

Hjertaas, T. (2004). Adler and Binswanger: Individual psychology and existentialism. *Journal of Individual Psychology, 60,* 396–407.

Ho, S. M. Y., Saltel, P., Machavoine, J., Rapoport-Hubschman, N., & Spiegel, D. (2004). Cross-cultural aspects of cancer care. In National Institutes of Health and Stanford University School of Medicine, *Cancer, culture, and communication.* New York: Kluwer Academic/Plenum Publishers.

Ho, W. (2004). Using Kohonen neural network and principle component analysis to characterize divergent thinking. *Creativity Research Journal, 16,* 283–292.

Hobfoll, S. E., Freedy, J. R., Green B. L., & Solomon, S. D. (1996). Coping in reaction to extreme stress: The roles of resource loss and resource availability. In M. Zeidner & N. S. Endler (Eds.), *Handbook of coping: Theory, research, applications.* New York: Wiley.

Hobfoll, S. E., Hall, B. J., & Canetti-Nisim, D. (2007). Refining our understanding of traumatic growth in the face of terrorism: Moving from meaning cognitions to doing what is meaningful. *Applied Psychology: An International Review, 56,* 345–366.

Hobson, J. A. (2005). In bed with Mark Solms? What a nightmare! A reply to Domhoff (2005). *Dreaming, 15,* 21–29.

Hochschild, A. (2001, February). A generation without public passion. *Atlantic Monthly,* pp. 33–42.

Hock, H. S., & Ploeger, A. (2006) Linking dynamical perceptual decisions at different levels of description in motion pattern formation: Psychophysics. *Perception & Psychophysics, 68,* 505–514.

Hoff, E. (2003). Language development in childhood. In R. M. Lerner, M. A. Easterbrooks, et al. (Eds.), *Handbook of psychology: Developmental psychology* (Vol. 6) (pp. 171–193). New York: Wiley.

Hoff, E. (2008). *Language development.* New York: Wadsworth.

Hoffer, T. B., et al. (2005, March 8). *Doctorate recipients from United States universities: Summary report 2003.* Chicago: NORC at the University of Chicago.

Hoffman, E. (2001). *Psychological testing at work: How to use, interpret, and get the most out of the newest tests in personality, learning style, aptitudes, interests, and more!* New York: McGraw-Hill.

Hoffman, H. (1996). *Amorous turkeys and addicted ducklings: A search for the causes of social attachment.* Boston: Authors Cooperative.

Hofmann, S. G. (2007). Enhancing exposure-based therapy from a translational research perspective. *Behaviour Research and Therapy, 45,* 1987–2001.

Hofmann, W., Friese, M., Schmeichel, B. J., & Baddeley, A. D. (2011). Working memory and self-regulation. In K. D. Vohs, R. F. Baumeister, et al. (Eds.), *Handbook of self-regulation: Research, theory, and applications* (2nd ed.). New York: Guilford Press.

Hofmann, W., Gschwendner, T., Castelli, L., & Schmitt, M. (2008). Implicit and explicit attitudes and interracial interaction: The moderating role of situationally available control resources. *Group Processes & Intergroup Relations, 11,* 69–87.

Hogan, J., Davies, S., & Hogan, R. (2007). Generalizing personality-based validity evidence. In S. M. McPhail, *Alternative validation strategies: Developing new and leveraging existing validity evidence.* Hoboken, NJ: John Wiley & Sons.

Hoge, C. W., & Castro, C. A. (2006, September 2). Post-traumatic stress disorder in UK and US forces deployed to Iraq. *Lancet, 368,* 837.

Hogg, M. A. (2006). Social identity theory. In P. J. Burke, *Contemporary social psychological theories.* Stanford University Press.

Hogg, M. A., & Hains, S. C. (2001). Intergroup relations and group solidarity: Effects of group identification and social beliefs on depersonalized attraction. In M. A. Hogg & D. Abrams (Eds.), *Intergroup relations: Essential readings.* New York: Psychology Press.

Holden, C. (2003, January 17). Deconstructing schizophrenia. *Science, 299,* 333–335.

Holden, C. (2005, June 10). Sex and the suffering brain. *Science, 308,* 1574–1577.

Holden, C. (2007, June 29). Embryonic stem cells. Stem cell science advances as politics stall. *Science, 316,* 1825.

Holland, J. C., & Lewis, S. (2001). *The human side of cancer: Living with hope, coping with uncertainty.* New York: Quill.

Hollander, E, Zohar, J., Sirovatka, P., & Regier, D. (Eds.). (2011). *Obsessive-compulsive spectrum disorders: Refining the research agenda for DSM-V.* Washington, DC: American Psychiatric Association.

Holler, G. D. (2006). Relations of hypnotic susceptibility, absorption, imagery, sexual fantasy, sexual daydreaming, and social desirability to sexual satisfaction. *Dissertation Abstracts International: Section B: The Sciences and Engineering, 67,* 3453.

Holleran, S., Mehl, M., & Levitt, S. (2009). Eavesdropping on social life: The accuracy of stranger ratings of daily behavior from thin slices of natural conversations. *Journal of Research in Personality, 43,* 660–672.

Hollingworth, H. L. (1943/1990). *Leta Stetter Hollingworth: A biography.* Boston: Anker.

Hollins, K. (2007). Consequences of antenatal mental health problems for child health and development. *Current Opinions on Obstetric Gynecology, 19,* 568–573.

Hollis, K. L. (1997, September). Contemporary research on Pavlovian conditioning: A "new" functional analysis. *American Psychologist, 52,* 956–965.

Hollon, S. D., Thase, M. E., & Markowitz, J. C. (2002). Treatment and prevention of depression. *Psychological Science in the Public Interest, 3,* 39–77.

Holloway, L. (2000, December 16). Chief of New York City schools plans to revamp bilingual study. *The New York Times,* p. A1.

Holmes, A., Yang, R. J., Lesch, K. P., Crawley, J. N., & Murphy, D. L. (2003). Mice lacking the Serotonin Transporter Exhibit 5-HT-sub(1A) receptor-mediated abnormalities in tests for anxiety-like behavior. *Neuropsychopharmacology, 28,* 2077–2088.

Holmes, C., Ballard, C., Lehmann, D., Smith, A. D., Beaumont, H., Day, N., Khan, M. N., Lovestone, S., McCulley, M., Morris, C. M., Munoz, D. G., O'Brien, K., Russ, C., Del Ser, T., & Warden, D. (2006). Rate of progression of cognitive decline in Alzheimer's disease: Effect of butyrylcholinesterase K gene variation. *Journal of Neurology, Neurosurgery, and Psychiatry, 76,* 640–643.

Holowka, S., & Pettito, L. A. (2002, August 30). Left hemisphere cerebral specialization for babies while babbling. *Science, 297,* 1515.

Holt, M., & Jahn, R. (2004, March, 26). Synaptic vesicles in the fast lane. *Science, 303,* 1986–1987.

Holtzman, D., & Kulish, N. (1996). Nevermore: The hymen and the loss of virginity. *Journal of the American Psychoanalytic Association, 44,* 303–332.

Holy, T. E., Dulac, C., & Meister, M. (2000, September 1). Responses of vomeronasal neurons to natural stimuli. *Science, 289,* 1569–1572.

Hong, E., Milgram, R. M., & Gorsky, H. (1995). Original thinking as a predictor of creative performance in young children. *Roeper Review, 18,* 147–149.

Hongchun, W., & Ming, L. (2006). About the research on suggestibility and false memory. *Psychological Science (China), 29,* 905–908.

Hopkin, M. (2007, August 2). Implant boosts activity in injured brain. *Nature, 448,* 522.

Hopkins, W., & Cantalupo, C. (2008, June). Theoretical speculations on the evolutionary origins of hemispheric specialization. *Current Directions in Psychological Science, 17,* 233–237.

Hopton, A., & MacPherson, H. (2010). Acupuncture for chronic pain: Is acupuncture more than an effective placebo? A systematic review of pooled data from meta-analyses. *Pain Practice, 10,* 94–102.

Hopwood, C. J., Donnellan, M., Blonigen, D. M., Krueger, R. F., McGue, M., Iacono, W. G., et al. (2011). Genetic and environmental influences on personality trait stability and growth during the transition to adulthood: A three-wave longitudinal study. *Journal of Personality and Social Psychology, 100,* 545–556.

Hopwood, C., Newman, D., Donnellan, M., Markowitz, J., Grilo, C., Sanislow, C., et al. (2009). The stability of personality traits in individuals with borderline personality disorder. *Journal of Abnormal Psychology, 118,* 806–815.

Horínek, D., Varjassyová, A., & Hort, J. (2007). Magnetic resonance analysis of amyg-dalar volume in Alzheimer's disease. *Current Opinion in Psychiatry, 20,* 273–277.

Horn, J. L. (2002). Selections of evidence, misleading assumptions, and over-simplifications: The political message of *The Bell Curve.* In J. M. Fish (Ed.), *Race and intelligence: Separating science from myth* (pp. 297–325). Mahwah, NJ: Erlbaum.

Horney, K. (1937). *Neurotic personality of our times.* New York: Norton.

Horton, K. D., Wilson, D. E., Vonk, J., Kirby, S. L., & Nielsen, T. (2005). Measuring automatic retrieval: A comparison of implicit memory, process dissociation, and speeded response procedures. *Acta Psychologica, 119,* 235–263.

Horwath, E., Weissman, M. M. (2000). The epidemiology and cross-national presenta-tion of obsessive-compulsive disorder. *Psychiatric Clinics of North America, 23,* 493–507

Houghtalen, R. P., & Talbot, N. (2007). Dissociative disorders and cognitive disorders. In O. J. Z. Sahler, & J. E. Carr, *The behavioral sciences and health care* (2nd rev. and updated ed.). Ashland, OH: Hogrefe & Huber Publishers, 2007.

Howe, C. J. (2002). The countering of overgeneralization. *Journal of Child Language, 29,* 875–895.

Howells, J. G., & Osborn, M. L. (1984). *A reference companion to the history of abnor-mal psychology.* Westport, CT: Greenwood Press.

Howes, O., & Kapur, S. (2009). The dopamine hypothesis of schizophrenia: Version III—The final common pathway. *Schizophrenia Bulletin, 35,* 549–562.

Howitt, D., & Cramer, D. (2000). *First steps in research and statistics: A practical workbook for psychology students.* Philadelphia: Psychology Press.

Hrabosky, J. I., White, M. A., Masheb, R. M., & Grilo, C. M. (2007). Physical activity and its correlates in treatment-seeking obese patients with binge eating disorder. *International Journal of Eating Disorders, 40,* 72–76.

Hsu, B., Koing, A., Kessler, C., Knapke, K., et al. (1994). Gender differences in sexual fantasy and behavior in a college population: A ten-year replication. *Journal of Sex and Marital Therapy, 20,* 103–118.

Hu, F. B., Li, T. Y., Colditz, G. A., Willett, W. C., & Manson, J. E. (2003). Television watching and other sedentary behaviors in relation to risk of obesity and type 2 diabetes mellitus in women. *Journal of the American Medical Association, 289,* 1785–1791.

Huang, C., Yeh, T., Li, T., & Chang, C. (2010). The idea storming cube: Evaluating the effects of using game and computer agent to support divergent thinking. *Journal of Educational Technology & Society, 13,* 180–191.

Huang, Y. (2005). A copper rule versus the golden rule: A Daoist-Confucian proposal for global ethics. *Philosophy East and West, 55,* 394–425.

Hubbard, K., O'Neill, A., & Cheakalos, C. (1999, April 12). Out of control. *People,* 52–72.

Hubel, D. H., & Wiesel, T. N. (2004). *Brain and visual perception: The story of a 25-year collaboration.* New York: Oxford University Press.

Huber, F., Beckmann, S. C., & Herrmann, A. (2004). Means-end analysis: Does the affective state influence information processing style? *Psychology and Marketing, 21,* 715–737.

Hudson, W. (1960). Pictorial depth perception in subcultural groups in Africa. *Journal of Social Psychology, 52,* 183–208.

Hudson, J., Hiripi, E., Harrison, G., & Kessler, R. (2007). The prevalence and correlates of eating disorders in the National Comorbidity Survey Replication. *Biological Psychiatry, 61,* 348–358.

Hudspeth, A. J. (2000). Hearing. In E. R. Kandel, J. H. Schwartz, & T. M. Jessell (Eds.), *Principles of neural science* (4th ed.). New York: McGraw-Hill.

Hui, L., Hua, F., Diandong, H., & Hong, Y. (2007, March). Effects of sleep and sleep deprivation on immunoglobulins and complement in humans. *Brain, Behavior, and Immunity, 21*(3), 308–310.

Huijie, T. (2006). The measurement and assessment of mental health: A longitudinal and cross-sectional research on undergraduates, adults and patients. *Psychological Science (China), 29,* 419–422.

Huizinga, M., Cooper, L., Bleich, S., Clark, J., & Beach, M. (2009). Physician respect for patients with obesity. *Journal of General Internal Medicine, 24,* 1236–1239.

Hull, C. L. (1943). *Principles of behavior.* New York: Appleton-Century-Crofts.

Humayun, M., Dagnelie, G., Greenberg, R., Propst, R., & Phillips, D. (1966). Visual perception elicited by electrical stimulation of retina in blind humans. *Archive of Ophthalmology, 114,* 40–46.

Humphrey, N., Curran, A., & Morris, E. (2007). Emotional intelligence and education: A critical review. *Educational Psychology, 27,* 235–254.

Humphreys, G. W., & Müller, H. (2000). A search asymmetry reversed by figure-ground assignment. *Psychological Science, 11,* 196–200.

Humphreys, J. (2003). Resilience in sheltered battered women. *Issues in Mental Health Nursing, 24,* 137–152.

Hunt, E. (1994). Problem solving. In R. J. Sternberg (Ed.), *Thinking and problem solv-ing: Handbook of perception and cognition* (2nd ed.). San Diego: Academic Press.

Hunt, E. (2005). Information processing and intelligence: Where we are and where we are going. In R. J. Sternberg & J. E. Pretz, *Cognition and intelligence: Identifying the mechanisms of the mind.* New York: Cambridge University Press.

Hunt, J. S., Seifert, A. L., & Armenta, B. E. (2006). Stereotypes and prejudice as dynamic constructs: reminders about the nature of intergroup bias from the hurricane Katrina relief efforts. *Analyses of Social Issues and Public Policy (ASAP), 6,* 237–253.

Hunt, M. (1974). *Sexual behaviors in the 1970s.* New York: Dell.

Hunter, C. (2011). *Mastering the power of self-hypnosis: A practical guide to self-empowerment* (2nd ed.). Norwalk, CT: Crown House Publishing Limited.

Huprich, S. (2009). *Psychodynamic therapy: Conceptual and empirical foundations.* New York: Routledge/Taylor & Francis Group.

Hurt, C. S., Ganerjee, S., Tunnard, C., Whitehead, D. L., Tsolaki, M., Mecocci, P., et al. (2005). Insight, cognition and quality of life in Alzheimer's disease. *NeuroMed Consortium, Journal of Neurology, Neurosurgery & Psychiatry, 81,* 331–336.

Huston, A. C., Donnerstein, E., Fairchild, H. H., Feshback, N. D., Katz, P., Murray, J. P., Rubinstein, E. A., Wilcox, B. L., & Zuckerman, D. (1992). Big world, small screen: The role of television in American society. Omaha, NE: University of Nebraska Press.

Hutchinson, S. L., Baldwin, C. K., & Oh, S-S. (2006). Adolescent coping: Exploring adolescents' leisure-based responses to stress. *Leisure Sciences, 28,* 115–131.

Hyde, J., Mezulis, A., & Abramson, L. (2008, April). The ABCs of depression: Integrat-ing affective, biological, and cognitive models to explain the emergence of the gender difference in depression. *Psychological Review, 115*(2), 291–313.

Hyde, J. S. & Grabe, S. (2008). Meta-analysis in the psychology of women. In F. L. Denmark & M. A. Paludi (Eds.), *Psychology of women: A handbook of issues and theories* (2nd ed.). Westport, CT: Praeger Publishers/Greenwood Publishing Group.

Hyde, K., Peretz, I., & Zatorre, R. (2008, February). Evidence for the role of the right auditory cortex in fine pitch resolution. *Neuropsychologia, 46,* 632–639.

Hyman, R. (1994). Anomaly or artifact? Comments on Bem and Honorton. *Psychologi-cal Bulletin, 115,* 19–24.

Hyman, S. E. (2003, September). Diagnosing disorders. *Scientific American,* pp. 96–103.

I

Iachini, S. M. (2005). Mental images and the brain. *Cognitive Neuropsychology, 22,* 333–347.

Iachini, T., & Giusberti, F. (2004). Metric properties of spatial images generated from locomotion: The effect of absolute size on mental scanning. *European Journal of Cognitive Psychology, 16,* 573–596.

Iaria, G., Palermo, L., Committeri, G., & Barton, J. (2009). Age differences in the formation and use of cognitive maps. *Behavioural Brain Research, 196,* 187–191.

Ievers-Landis, C. E., Hoff, A. L., Brez, C., Cancilliere, M. K., McConnell, J., & Kerr, D. (2005). Situational analysis of dietary challenges of the treatment regimen for chil-dren and adolescents with phenylketonuria and their primary caregivers. *Journal of Developmental and Behavioral Pediatrics, 26,* 186–193.

Iglesias, A. (2005). Awake-alert hypnosis in the treatment of panic disorder: A case report. *American Journal of Clinical Hypnosis, 47,* 249–257.

Igo, S. E. (2006). Review of A telescope on society: Survey research and social science at the University of Michigan and beyond. *Journal of the History of the Behavioral Sciences, 42,* 95–96.

Ihler, E. (2003). Patient-physician communication. *Journal of the American Medical Association, 289,* 92.

Ikonomidou, C., Bittigau, P., Ishimaru, M. J., Wozniak, D. F., Koch, C., Genz, K., Price, M. T., Stefovska, V., Hörster, F., Tenkova, T., Dikranian, K., & Olney, J. W. (2000, February 11). Ethanol-induced apoptotic neurodegeneration and fetal alcohol syndrome. *Science, 287,* 1056–1060.

Ilies, R., Arvey, R. D., & Bouchard, T. J., Jr. (2006). Darwinism, behavioral genetics, and organizational behavior: A review and agenda for future research. *Journal of Organizational Behavior, 27,* Special issue: Darwinian Perspectives on Behavior in Organizations, 96–141.

Imamura, M., & Nakamizo, S. (2006). An empirical test of formal equivalence between Emmert's Law and the size-distance invariance hypothesis. *The Spanish Journal of Psychology, 9*(2), 295–299.

Imhof, L., Wallhagen, M., Mahrer-Imhof, R., & Monsch, A. (2006, October). Becoming Forgetful: How Elderly People Deal with Forgetfulness in Everyday Life. *American Journal of Alzheimer's Disease and Other Dementias, 21*(5), 347–353.

Innocenti, G. M. (2007). Subcortical regulation of cortical development: Some effects of early, selective deprivations. *Progressive Brain Research, 164,* 23–37.

Interlandi, J. (2008, March 3). What addicts need. *Newsweek,* p. 31–16.

Irwin, M. (2008). Human psychoneuroimmunology: 20 years of discovery. *Brain, Behavior, and Immunity, 22,* 129–139.

Irwin, R. R. (2006). Spiritual development in adulthood: Key concepts and models. In C. Hoare, *Handbook of adult development and learning.* New York: Oxford University Press.

Isacson, O., & Kordower, J. (2008). Future of cell and gene therapies for Parkinson's disease. *Annals of Neurology, 64,* S122–SS138.

Isaksen, S. G., Dorval, K., & Treffinger, D. J. (2011). *Creative approaches to problem solving: A framework for innovation and change* (3rd ed.). Thousand Oaks, CA: Sage Publications, Inc.

Isay, R. A. (1994). *Being homosexual: Gay men and their development.* Lanham, MD: Jason Aronson.

Isbell, L. M., & Tyler, J. M. (2003). Teaching students about in-group favoritism and the minimal groups paradigm. *Teaching of Psychology, 30,* 127–130.

Iverson, L. (2000). *The science of marijuana.* Oxford, England: Oxford University Press.

Iverson, P., Kuhl, P. K., Reiko, A. Y., Diesch, E., Tohkura, Y., Ketterman, A., & Siebert, C. (2003). A perceptual interference account of acquisition difficulties for non-native phonemes. *Cognition, 87,* B47–B57.

Iverson, S. D., & Iversen, L. L. (2007). Dopamine: 50 years in perspective. *Trends in Neurosciences, 30,* 188–191.

Izard, C. E. (1990). Facial expressions and the regulation of emotions. *Journal of Personality and Social Psychology, 58,* 487–498.

Izard, C. E. (1994). Innate and universal facial expressions: Evidence from developmental and cross-cultural research. *Psychological Bulletin, 115,* 288–299.

Izard, C. E., & Abe, J. A. (2004). Developmental changes in facial expressions of emotions in the strange situation during the second year of life. *Emotion, 4,* 251–265.

J

Jackson, J. D. (2006). Trauma, attachment, and coping: Pathways to resilience. *Dissertation Abstracts International: Section B: The Sciences and Engineering, 67(1-B),* 547.

Jackson, L. M. (2011). *The psychology of prejudice: From attitudes to social action.* Washington, DC: American Psychological Association.

Jacobs, J. A., & Gerson, K. (2004). *The time divide: Work, family, and gender inequality.* Cambridge, MA: Harvard University Press.

Jacobs, M., Roesch, S., Wonderlich, S., Crosby, R., Thornton, L., Wilfley, D., et al. (2009). Anorexia nervosa trios: Behavioral profiles of individuals with anorexia nervosa and their parents. *Psychological Medicine, 39,* 451–461.

Jacoby, L. L., Bishara, A. J., Hessels, S., & Hughes, A. (2007). Probabilistic retroactive interference: The role of accessibility bias in interference effects. *Journal of Experimental Psychology: General, 136,* 200–216.

Jaffé, A., Prasad, S. A., & Larcher, V. (2006). Gene therapy for children with cystic fibrosis—Who has the right to choose? *Journal of Medical Ethics, 32,* 361–364.

Jain, S., Mills, P. J., & Von Känel, R. (2007). Effects of perceived stress and uplifts on inflammation and coagulability. *Psychophysiology, 44,* 154–160.

James, H. S., Jr. (2005). Why did you do that? An economic examination of the effect of extrinsic compensation on intrinsic motivation and performance. *Journal of Economic Psychology, 26,* 549–566.

James, W. (1890). *The principles of psychology.* New York: Holt.

Jamieson, G. A. (2007). *Hypnosis and conscious states: The cognitive neuroscience perspective.* New York: Oxford University Press.

Jamison, K. R. (1995). *An unquiet mind: A memoir of moods and madness.* New York: Knopf.

Jang, H., Reeve, J., Ryan, R. M., & Kim, A. (2009, August). Can self-determination theory explain what underlies the productive, satisfying learning experiences of collectivistically oriented Korean students? *Journal of Educational Psychology, 101,* 644–661.

Jang, S. J., You, S. H., & Ahn, S. H. (2007). Neurorehabilitation-induced cortical reorganization in brain injury: A 14-month longitudinal follow-up study. *NeuroRehabilitation, 22,* 117–122.

Janicki-Deverts, D., Cohen, S., Adler, N. E., Schwartz, J. E., Matthews, K. A., & Seeman, T. E. (2007). Socioeconomic status is related to urinary catecholamines in the Coronary Artery Risk Development in Young Adults (CARDIA) study. *Psychosomatic Medicine, 69,* 514–520.

Janis, I. L. (1997). Groupthink. In R. P. Vecchio, *Leadership: Understanding the dynamics of power and influence in organizations.* Notre Dame, IN: University of Notre Dame Press.

Janssen, D. (2007, May). First stirrings: Cultural notes on orgasm, ejaculation, and wet dreams. *Journal of Sex Research, 44(2),* 122–134.

Jaret, P. (1992, November/December). Mind over malady. *Health,* pp. 87–94.

Jarlais, D. C. D., Arasteh, K., & Perlis, T. (2007). The transition from injection to non-injection drug use: Long-term outcomes among heroin and cocaine users in New York City. *Addiction, 102,* 778–785.

Javitt, D. C., & Coyle, J. T. (January 2004). Decoding schizophrenia. *Scientific American,* pp. 46–55.

Jayson, S. (2006, August 21). Gen Nexters have their hands full. *USA Today,* p. 1D.

Jefferson, D. J. (2005, August 8). American's most dangerous drug. *Newsweek,* pp. 41–47.

Jeffrey, S. A., & Adomdza, G. K. (2011). Incentive salience and improved performance. *Human Performance, 24,* 47–59.

Jenkins, A. M., Albee, G. W., Paster, V. S., Sue, S., Baker, D. B., Comas-Dias, L., Puente, A. E., Suinn, R. M., Caldwell-Colbert, A. T., Williams, V. M., & Root, M. P. P. (2003). Ethnic minorities. In D. K. Freedheim, Handbook of psychology: *History of Psychology,* Vol. 1. Hoboken, NJ: John Wiley & Sons.

Jenkins, S. (2004, October 29). Mystics all-star cites depression for her absence. *The Washington Post,* p. A1.

Jenkins, S. R. (1994). Need for power and women's careers over 14 years: Structural power, job satisfaction, and motive change. *Journal of Personality and Social Psychology, 66,* 155–165.

Jensen, A. R. (2002). Galton's legacy to research on intelligence. *Journal of Biosocial Science, 34,* 145–172.

Jensen, A. R. (2003). Do age-group differences on mental tests imitate racial differences? *Intelligence, 31,* 107–121.

Jensen, A. R. (2005). Psychometric g and mental chronometry. *Cortex, 41,* 230–231.

Jequier, E. (2002). Pathways to obesity. *International Journal of Obesity and Related Metabolic Disorders, 26,* S12–S17.

Jetten, J., Hornsey, M. J., & Adarves-Yorno, I. (2006). When group members admit to being conformist: The role of relative intragroup status in conformity self-reports. *Personality and Social Psychology Bulletin, 32,* 162–173.

Jha, A. (2006, February 3). Pill could make painful memories a thing of past: Common drug may help to fight post traumatic stress. *The Guardian* (London), p. 15.

Jhally, S., Goldman, R., Cassidy, M., Katula, R., Seiter, E., Pollay, R. W., Lee, J. S., Carter-Whitney, D., Steinem, G., et al. (1995). Advertising. In G. Dines & J. M. Humez (Eds.), *Gender, race, and class in media: A text-reader.* Thousand Oaks, CA: Sage.

Joe, G. W., Flynn, P. M., & Broome, K. M. (2007). Patterns of drug use and expectations in methadone patients. *Addictive Behaviors, 32,* 1640–1656.

John, O., & Srivastava, S. (1999). The Big Five Trait taxonomy: History, measurement, and theoretical perspectives. *Handbook of personality: Theory and research* (2nd ed.) (pp. 102–138). New York: Guilford Press.

Johnson, H. D. (2004). Gender, grade and relationship differences in emotional closeness within adolescent friendships. *Adolescence, 39,* 243–255.

Johnson, J. G., Cohen, P., Smailes, E. M., Kasen, S., & Brook, J. S. (2002, March 29). Television viewing and aggressive behavior during adolescence and adulthood. *Science, 295,* 2468–2471.

Johnson, S. P. (2004). Development of perceptual completion in infancy. *Psychological Science, 15,* 769–775.

Johnson, S., Fulford, D., & Eisner, L. (2009). Psychosocial mechanisms in bipolar disorder. *Behavioral mechanisms and psychopathology: Advancing the explanation of its nature, cause, and treatment* (pp. 77–106). Washington, DC: American Psychological Association.

Johnson, S., Gruber, J., & Eisner, L. (2007). Emotion and Bipolar Disorder. *Emotion and psychopathology: Bridging affective and clinical science* (pp. 123–150). Washington, DC: American Psychological Association.

John-Steiner, V., & Mahn, H. (2003). Sociocultural contexts for teaching and learning. In W. M. Reynolds & G. E. Miller (Eds.), *Handbook of psychology: Educational psychology* (Vol. 7) (pp. 125–151). New York: Wiley.

Johnston, L.D., O'Malley, P. M., Bachman, J.G., & Schulenberg, J.E. (2007). *Monitoring the Future: National results on adolescent drug use: Overview of key findings, 2006.* (NIH Publication No. 07-6202). Bethesda, MD: National Institute on Drug Abuse.

Johnston, L. D., O'Malley, P. M., Bachman, J. G., & Schulenberg, J. E. (2004, December 21). *Overall teen drug use continues gradual decline; but use of inhalants rises.* University of Michigan News and Information Services: Ann Arbor, MI. Retrieved August 23, 2005, from www.monitoringthefuture.org.

Johnston, L. D., O'Malley, P. M., Bachman, J. G., & Schulenberg, J. E. (2007). *Monitoring the Future national results on adolescent drug use: Overview of key findings, 2007.* Ann Arbor, MI: University of Michigan.

Johnston, L. D., O'Malley, P. M., Bachman, J. G., & Schulenberg, J. E. (2009). *Monitoring the future national results on adolescent drug use; overview of key findings, 2008* (NIH Publication No. 09-7401). Bethesda, MD: National Institute on Drug Abuse.

Johnston, M. V. (2004). Clinical disorders of brain plasticity. *Brain and Development, 26,* 73–80.

Jokela, M., Elovainio, M., Kivimäki, M., Keltikangas-Järvinen, L. (2008). Temperament and migration patterns in Finland. *Psychological Science* 19(9): 831–837.

Jones, A. L. (2006). The contemporary psychoanalyst: Karen Horney's theory applied in today's culture. *PsycCRITIQUES, 51,* 127–134.

Jones, J. C., & Barlow, D. H. (1990). Self-reported frequency of sexual urges, fantasies, and masturbatory fantasies in heterosexual males and females. *Archives of Sexual Behavior, 19,* 269–279.

Jones, J. E., & Corp, E. S. (2003). Effect of naltrexone on food intake and body weight in Syrian hamsters depends on metabolic status. *Physiology and Behavior, 78,* 67–72.

Jones, J. M. (2007). Exposure to chronic community violence: Resilience in African American children. *Journal of Black Psychology, 33,* 125–149.

Jones, K., Callen, F., Blagrove, M., & Parrott, A. (2008). Sleep, energy and self rated cognition across 7 nights following recreational ecstasy/MDMA use. *Sleep and Hypnosis, 10,* 2–38.

Jones, R. K., Darroch, J. E., Singh, S. (2005). Religious differentials in the sexual and reproductive behaviors of young women in the United States. *Journal of Adolescent Health, 36,* 279–288.

Jonides, J., Lewis, R., Nee, D., Lustig, C., Berman, M., & Moore, K. (2008). The mind and brain of short-term memory. *Annual Review of Psychology, 59,* 193–224.

Jonides, J., Sylvester, C., Lacey, S., Wager, T., Nichols, T., & Awh, E. (2003). Modules of working memory. *Principles of learning and memory* (pp. 113–134). Cambridge, MA: Birkhäuser.

Jorgensen, G. (2006). Kohlberg and Gilligan: Duet or duel? *Journal of Moral Education, 35,* 179–196.

Joshanloo, M., & Afshari, S. (2011). Big Five personality traits and self-esteem as predictors of life satisfaction in Iranian Muslim university students. *Journal of Happiness Studies, 12,* 105–113.

Joyce, J. (1934). *Ulysses.* New York: Random House.

Joyce, N., & Baker, D. (2008). The lip key. *The Observer, 21,* 14.

Joyce, P., Light, K., Rowe, S., Cloninger, R., & Kennedy, M. (2010). Self-mutilation and suicide attempts: Relationships to bipolar disorder, borderline personality disorder, temperament and character. *Australian & New Zealand Journal of Psychiatry, 44,* 250-257.

Juliano, L. M., & Griffiths, R. R. (2004). A critical review of caffeine withdrawal: Empirical validation of symptoms and signs, incidence, severity, and associated features. *Psychopharmacology, 176,* 1–29.

Julien, R. M. (2001). *A primer of drug action* (9th ed.). New York: Freeman.

Jung, C. G. (1961). *Freud and psychoanalysis.* New York: Pantheon.

Jung, J. (2002). *Psychology of alcohol and other drugs: A research perspective.* Thousand Oaks, CA: Sage.

Jussim, L. (1989). Teacher expectations: Self-fulfilling prophecies, perceptual biases, and accuracy. *Journal of Personality and Social Psychology, 57*(3), 469–480.

Juster, F. T., Ono, H., & Stafford, F. (2002). *Report on housework and division of labor.* Ann Arbor, MI: Institute for Social Research.

Jylha, M. (2004). Old age and loneliness: Cross-sectional and longitudinal analyses in the Tampere longitudinal study on aging. *Canadian Journal on Aging/La Revue canadienne du vieillissement, 23,* 157–168.

K

Kaasinen, V., & Rinne, J. O. (2002). Functional imaging studies of dopamine system and cognition in normal aging and Parkinson's disease. *Neuroscience & Biobehavioral Reviews, 26,* 785–793.

Kadosh, R., Henik, A., & Walsh, V. (2009, May). Synaesthesia: Learned or lost? *Developmental Science, 12,* 484–491.

Kadzin, A. (1988). The token economy: A decade later. *Human operant conditioning and behavior modification* (pp. 119–137). Oxford, England: John Wiley & Sons.

Kagan, J. (2003). Biology, context and developmental inquiry. *Annual Review of Psychology, 54,* 1–23.

Kahneman, D., & Tversky, A. (1973, July). On the psychology of prediction. *Psychological Review, 80*(4), 237–251.

Kahneman, D., Diener, E., & Schwarz, N. (1998). *Well-being: The foundations of hedonic psychology.* New York: Russell Sage Foundation.

Kalarchian, M. A., Levine, M. D., Klem, M. L., Burke, L. E., Soulakova, J. N., & Marcus, M. D. (2011). Impact of addressing reasons for weight loss on behavioral weight-control outcome. *American Journal of Preventive Medicine, 40,* 18–24.

Kalb, C. (2001a, April 9). Playing with pain killers. *Newsweek,* pp. 45–48.

Kalb, C. (2001b, February 26). DARE checks into rehab. *Newsweek,* p. 56.

Kalb, C. (2003, May 19). Taking a new look at pain. *Newsweek,* p. 32.

Kaller, C. P., Unterrainer, J. M., Rahm, B., & Halsband, U. (2004). The impact of problem structure on planning: Insights from the Tower of London task. *Cognitive Brain Research, 20,* 462–472.

Kallio, S., & Revonsuo, A. (2003). Hypnotic phenomena and altered states of consciousness: A multilevel framework of description and explanation. *Contemporary Hypnosis, 20,* 111–164.

Kamin, L. (2006). African IQ and mental retardation. *South African Journal of Psychology, 36,* 1–9

Kaminski, P., Chapman, B. P., Haynes, S. D., & Own, L. (2005). Body image, eating behaviors, and attitudes toward exercise among gay and straight men. *Eating Behaviors, 6,* 179–187.

Kandel, E. R., Schwartz, J. H., & Jessell, T. M. (Eds.) (2000). *Principles of neural science* (4th ed.). New York: McGraw-Hill.

Kane, M. J., & Engle, R. W. (2002). The role of prefrontal cortex in working-memory capacity, executive attention, and general fluid intelligence: An individual-differences perspective. *Psychonomic Bulletin and Review, 9,* 637–671.

Kantrowitz, B. (2006, April 24). The quest for rest. *Newsweek,* p. 51.

Kantrowitz, B., & Underswood, A. (2007, June 25). The teen drinking dilemma. *Newsweek,* pp. 36–37.

Kaplan, M. S., Huguer, N., McFarland, B. H., & Newsom, J. T. (2007). Suicide among male veterans: A prospective population-based study. *Journal of Epidemiological Community Health, 61,* 619–624.

Kaplan, R. M., & Saccuzzo, D. P. (2001). *Psychological testing: Principles, applications, and issues* (5th ed.). Belmont, CA: Wadsworth/Thomson Learning.

Kappas, A. (2011). Emotion and regulation are one! *Emotion Review, 3,* 17–25.

Kara, P., & Boyd, J. (2009, April). A micro-architecture for binocular disparity and ocular dominance in visual cortex. *Nature, 458*(7238), 627–631.

Karatsoreos, I. N., Bhagat, S., Bloss, E. B., Morrison, J. H., & McEwen, B. S. (2011). Disruption of circadian clocks has ramifications for metabolism, brain, and behavior. PNAS *Proceedings of the National Academy of Sciences of the United States of America, 108,* 1657–1662.

Karim, A., Hinterberger, T., Richter, J., Mellinger, J., Neumann, N., Flor, H., Kubler, A., and Birnaumer, N. (2006). Neural Internet: Web surfing with brain potentials for the completely paralyzed. *Neurorehabilitation and Neural Repair, 20,* 508–515.

Karni, A., Tanne, D., Rubenstein, B. S., Askenazy, J. J. M., & Sagi, D. (1992, October). No dreams—no memory: The effect of REM sleep deprivation on learning a new perceptual skill. *Society for Neuroscience Abstracts, 18,* 387.

Kassel, J. D., Evatt, D. P., Greenstein, J. E., Wardle, M. C., Yates, M. C., & Veilleux, J. C. (2007). The acute effects of nicotine on positive and negative affect in adolescent smokers. *Journal of Abnormal Psychology, 116,* 543–553.

Kassin, S. M. (2005). On the psychology of confessions: Does innocence put innocents at risk? *American Psychologist, 60,* 215–228.

Kaštelan, A., Franciškovic, A., Tanja, M., & Moro, L. (2007). Psychotic symptoms in combat-related post-traumatic stress disorder. *Military Medicine, 172,* 273–277.

Kato, K., & Pedersen, N. L. (2005). Personality and coping: A study of twins reared apart and twins reared together. *Behavior Genetics, 35,* 147–158.

Kato, N. (2009). Neurophysiological mechanisms of electroconvulsive therapy for depression. *Neuroscience Research, 64,* 3–11.

Kato, T. (2007). Molecular genetics of bipolar disorder and depression. *Psychiatry and Clinical Neurosciences, 61,* 3–19.

Katsiyannis, A., Zhang, D., & Woodruff, N. (2005). Transition supports to students with mental retardation: An examination of data from the national longitudinal transition study 2. *Education and Training in Developmental Disabilities, 40,* 109–116.

Katz, M. (2001). The implications of revising Freud's empiricism for drive theory. *Psychoanalysis and Contemporary Thought, 24,* 253–272.

Kaufman, A., Johnson, C., & Liu, X. (2008). A CHC theory-based analysis of age differences on cognitive abilities and academic skills at ages 22 to 90 years. *Journal of Psychoeducational Assessment, 26,* 350–381.

Kaufman, A. S. & Lichtenberger, E.O. (1999). *Essentials of WAIS-III assessment.* Hoboken, NJ: John Wiley & Sons Inc.

Kaufman, A. S., & Lichtenberger, E. O. (2000). *Essentials of WISC-III and WPPSI-R assessment.* New York: Wiley.

Kaufman, J., & Needham, A. (2011). Spatial expectations of young human infants, following passive movement. *Developmental Psychobiology, 53,* 23–36.

Kaufman, J. C., & Baer, J. (2005). *Creativity across domains: Faces of the muse.* Mahwah, NJ: Lawrence Erlbaum Associates.

Kaufman, J. C., & Baer, J. (2006). Creativity and reason in cognitive development. New York: Cambridge University Press.

Kawasaki, C., Nugent, J. K., Miyashita, H., Miyahara, H., et al. (1994). The cultural organization of infants' sleep [Special issue: Environments of birth and infancy]. *Children's Environment, 11,* 135–141.

Kawashima, H., Izaki, Y., & Grace, A. A. (2006). Cooperativity between hippocampal-pre-frontal short-term plasticity through associative long-term potentiation. *Brain Research, 1109,* 37–44.

Kay, P., & Regier, T. (2007). Color naming universals: the case of Berinmo. *Cognition, 102,* 289–298.

Kazar, D. B. (2006). Forensic psychology: Did we leave anything out? *PsycCRITIQUES, 51,* 88–97.

Kearns, K. P. (2005). Broca's aphasia. In L. L. LaPointe (Ed.), *Aphasia and related neurogenic language disorders* (3rd ed.). New York: Thieme New York.

Keating, D. P., & Clark, L. V. (1980). Development of physical and social reasoning in adolescence. *Developmental Psychology, 16,* 23–30.

Keck, P., & McElroy, S. (2007). Pharmacological treatments for bipolar disorder. *A guide to treatments that work (3rd ed.)* (pp. 323–350). New York: Oxford University Press.

Keillor, J. M., Barrett, A. M., Crucian, G. P., Kortenkamp, S., & Heilman, K. M. (2002). Emotional experience and perception in the absence of facial feedback. *Journal of the International Neuropsychological Society, 8,* 130–135.

Keller, W. R., Fischer, B. A., & Carpenter, W. R. (2011). Revisiting the diagnosis of schizophrenia: Where have we been and where are we going? *CNS Neuroscience & Therapeutics, 17,* 83–88.

Kelley, H. (1950). The warm-cold variable in first impressions of persons. *Journal of Personality and Social Psychology, 18,* 431–439.

Kellman, P., & Banks, M. (1998). Infant visual perception. *Handbook of child psychology: Cognition, perception, and language* (Vol. 2) (pp. 103–146). Hoboken, NJ: John Wiley & Sons Inc.

Kellner, C., Pritchett, J., Beale, M., & Coffey, C. (1997). *Handbook of ECT.* Washington, DC: American Psychiatric Association.

Kelly, J. B. (2000). Children's adjustment in conflicted marriage and divorce: A decade review of research. *Journal of the American Academy of Child & Adolescent Psychiatry, 39,* 963–973.

Keltikangas-Järvinen, L., Räikkönen, K., Ekelund, J., & Peltonen, L. (2004). Nature and nurture in novelty seeking. *Molecular Psychiatry, 9,* 308–311.

Keltner, N. L., & Grant, J. S. (2006). Smoke, smoke, smoke that cigarette. *Perspectives in Psychiatric Care, 42,* 256–261.

Kemeny, M. E. (2003). The psychobiology of stress. *Current Directions in Psychological Science, 12,* 124–129.

Kemeny, M. E. (2007). Psycho neuroimmunology. In H. S. Friedman, & R. C. Silver, *Foundations of health psychology.* New York: Oxford University Press.

Kempermann, G., & Gage, F. H. (1999, May). New nerve cells for the adult brain. *Scientific American,* pp. 48–53.

Kemps, E., & Tiggemann, M. (2007). Reducing the vividness and emotional impact of distressing autobiographical memories: The importance of modality-specific interference. *Memory, 15,* 412–422.

Kendler, K., Halberstadt, L., Butera, F., Myers, J., Bouchard, T., & Ekman, P. (2008). The similarity of facial expressions in response to emotion-inducing films in reared-apart twins. *Psychological Medicine, 38*(10), 1475–1483.

Kendler, K. S., Gatz, M., & Gardner, C. O. (2006). Personality and major depression. *Archives of General Psychiatry, 63,* 1113–1120.

Kendler, K. S., Myers, J., & Gardner, C. O. (2006). Caffeine intake, toxicity and dependence and lifetime risk for psychiatric and substance use disorders: An epidemiologic and co-twin control analysis. *Psychological Medicine, 36,* 1717–1725.

Kenneally, C. (2006, July 3). The deepest cut. How can someone live with only half a brain?

Kennedy, J. E. (2004). A proposal and challenge for proponents and skeptics of psi. *Journal of Parapsychology, 68,* 157–167.

Kenway, L., & Wilson, M. A. (2001). Temporally structured replay of awake hippocampal ensemble activity during rapid eye movement sleep. *Neuron, 29,* 145–156.

Kesebir, P., & Diener, E. (2008). In pursuit of happiness: Empirical answers to philosophical questions. *Perspectives on Psychological Science, 3,* 117–125.

Kess, J. F., & Miyamoto, T. (1994). *Japanese psycholinguistics.* Amsterdam, Netherlands: John Benjamins.

Kessler, R. C., Berglund, P., & Demler, O. (2005). Lifetime prevalence and age-of-onset distributions of DSM-IV disorders in the National Comorbidity Survey replication. *Archives of General Psychiatry, 62,* 593–602.

Kessler, R. C., & Wang, P. S. (2008). The descriptive epidemiology of commonly occurring mental disorders in the United States. *Annual Review of Public Health, 29,* 115–129.

Kettenmann, H., & Ransom, B. R. (2005). *Neuroglia* (2nd ed.). New York: Oxford University Press.

Key, W. B. (2003). Subliminal sexuality: The fountainhead for America's obsession. In T. Reichert & J. Lambaiase (Eds.), *Sex in advertising: Perspectives on the erotic appeal. LEA's communication series* (pp. 195–212). Mahwah, NJ: Lawrence Erlbaum.

Khazaal, Y., Chatton, A., Claeys, F., Ribordy, F., Zullino, D., & Cabanac, M. (2008). Antipsychotic drug and body weight set-point. *Physiology & Behavior, 95,* 157–160.

Kidd, E., & Lum, J. (2008). Sex differences in past tense overregularization. *Developmental Science, 11,* 882–889.

Kiecolt, J. K. (2003). Satisfaction with work and family life: No evidence of a cultural reversal. *Journal of Marriage and Family, 65,* 23–35.

Kiefer, A. K., & Sekaquaptewa, D. (2006). Implicit stereotypes and women's math performance: How implicit gender-math stereotypes influence women's susceptibility to stereotype threat. *Journal of Experimental Social Psychology, 43,* 825–832.

Kihlstrom, J. F. (2005a). Dissociative disorders. *Annual Review of Clinical Psychology, 1,* 227–253.

Kihlstrom, J. F. (2005b). Is hypnosis an altered state of consciousness or what? Comment. *Contemporary Hypnosis, 22,* 34–38.

Kihlstrom, J. F., Schacter, D. L., Cork, R. C., Hurt, C. A., & Behr, S. E. (1990). Implicit and explicit memory following surgical anesthesia. *Psychological Science, 1,* 303–306.

Kim, D. R., Pesiridou, A., & O'Reardon, J. P. (2009). Transcranial magnetic stimulation in the treatment of psychiatric disorders. *Current Psychiatry Reports, 11,* 447– 452.

Kim, H., Clark, D., & Dionne, R. (2009, July). Genetic contributions to clinical pain and analgesia: Avoiding pitfalls in genetic research. *The Journal of Pain, 10,* 663–693.

Kim, H. S. (2002). We talk, therefore we think? A cultural analysis of the effect of talking on thinking. *Journal of Personality and Social Psychology, 83,* 828–842.

Kim, J., & Grunig, J. E. (2011). Problem solving and communicative action: A situational theory of problem solving. *Journal of Communication, 61,* 120–149.

Kim, J., & Mueller, C. (1978). *Introduction to factor analysis: What it is and how to do it.* New York: Sage Publications.

Kim, K. H., Relkin, N. R., Lee, K. M., & Hirsch, J. (1997, July 10). Distinct cortical areas associated with native and second languages. *Nature, 388,* 171–174.

Kim, S-E., Kim, J-W, & Kim, J-J. (2007). The neural mechanism of imagining facial affective expression. *Brain Research, 1145,* 128–137.

Kimbrel, N. A. (2007). A model of the development and maintenance of generalized social phobia. *Clinical Psychological Review, 8,* 69–75.

Kim-Cohen, J., Caspi, A., & Moffitt, T. E. (2003). Prior juvenile diagnoses in adults with mental disorder: Developmental follow-back of a prospective-longitudinal cohort. *Archives of General Psychiatry, 60,* 709–717.

Kim-Cohen, J., Moffitt, T. E., Taylor, A., Pawlby, S. J., & Caspi, A. (2005). Maternal depression and children's antisocial behavior: Nature and nurture effects. *Archives of General Psychiatry, 62,* 173–181.

King-Casas, B., Sharp, C., Lomax-Bream, L., Lohrenz, T., Fonagy, P., & Montague, P. R. (2008, August, 8). The rupture and repair of cooperation in borderline personality disorder. *Science, 321,* 806–810.

Kinsey, A., Pomeroy, W., & Martin, C. (1948). *Sexual behavior in the human male.* Oxford, England: Saunders.

Kinsey, A., Pomeroy, W., Martin, C., & Gebhard, P. (1953). *Sexual behavior in the human female.* Oxford, England: Saunders.

Kirk, K. M., Bailey, J. M., & Martin, N. G. (2000). Etiology of male sexual orientation in an Australian twin sample. *Psychology, Evolution & Gender, 2,* 301–311.

Kirsch, I., & Braffman, W. (2001). Imaginative suggestibility and hypnotizability. *Current Directions in Psychological Science, 10,* 57–61.

Kirsch, I., Lynn, S. J., Vigorito, M. & Miller, R. R. (2004). The role of cognition in classical and operant conditioning. *Journal of Clinical Psychology, 60,* 369–392.

Kirschenbaum, H. (2004). Carl Rogers's life and work: An assessment on the 100th anniversary of his birth. *Journal of Counseling and Development, 82,* 116–124.

Kirschenbaum, H., & Jourdan, A. (2005). The current status of Carl Rogers and the person-centered approach. *Psychotherapy: Theory, Research, Practice, Training, 42,* 37–51.

Kish, S., Fitzmaurice, P., Boileau, I., Schmunk, G., Ang, L., Furukawa, Y., et al. (2009). Brain serotonin transporter in human methamphetamine users. *Psychopharmacology, 202,* 649–661.

Kishore, R., & Dutt, K. (1986, March). Electrically induced aversion therapy in alcoholics. *Indian Journal of Clinical Psychology, 13*(1), 39–43.

Kisilevsky, B., Hains, S., Brown, C., Lee, C., Cowperthwaite, B., Stutzman, S., et al. (2009). Fetal sensitivity to properties of maternal speech and language. *Infant Behavior & Development, 32,* 59–71.

Kiss, A. (2004). Does gender have an influence on the patient-physician communication? *Journal of Men's Health and Gender, 1,* 77–82.

Klein, S. M., Giovino, G. A., Barker, D. C., Tworek, C., Cummings, K. M., & O'Connor, R. J. (2008). Use of flavored cigarettes among older adolescent and adult smokers: United States, 2004–2005. *Nicotine &Tobacco Research, 10:*7, 1209–214.

Kleinman, A. (1996). How is culture important for DSM-IV? In J. E. Mezzich, A. Kleinman, H. Fabrega, Jr., & D. L. Parron (Eds.), *Culture and psychiatric diagnosis: A DSM-IV perspective* Washington, DC: American Psychiatric Press.

Klötz, F., Garle, M., & Granath, F. (2006). Criminality among individuals testing positive for the presence of anabolic androgenic steroids. *Archives of General Psychiatry, 63,* 1274–1279.

Kluck, A. (2008). Family factors in the development of disordered eating: Integrating dynamic and behavioral explanations. *Eating Behaviors, 9,* 471–483.

Kluger, J. (2001, April 2). Fear not! *Time,* pp. 51–62.

Kluger, J. (2006, December 4). Why we worry about the things we shouldn't and ignore the things we should. *Time,* pp. 64–71.

Klump, K., & Culbert, K. (2007). Molecular genetic studies of eating disorders: Current status and future directions. *Current Directions in Psychological Science, 16,* 37–41.

Knight, S. C., & Meyer, R. G. (2007). Forensic hypnosis. In A. M. Goldstein, *Forensic psychology: Emerging topics and expanding roles.* Hoboken, NJ: John Wiley & Sons.

Knoblich, G., & Sebanz, N. (2006). The social nature of perception and action. *Current Directions in Psychological Science, 15,* 99–111.

Kobayashi, F., Schallert, D. L., & Ogren, H. A. (2003). Japanese and American folk vocabularies for emotions. *Journal of Social Psychology, 143,* 451–478.

Kohlberg, L. (1984). *The psychology of moral development: Essays on moral development* (Vol. 2). San Francisco: Harper & Row.

Kohlberg, L., & Ryncarz, R. A. (1990). Beyond justice reasoning: Moral development and consideration of a seventh stage. In C. N. Alexander & E. J. Langer (Eds.), *Higher stages of human development: Perspectives on adult growth.* New York: Oxford University Press.

Kohler, C. G., Turner, T., Stolar, N. M., Bilker, W. B., Brensinger, C. M., Gur, R. E., & Gur, R. C. (2004). Differences in facial expressions of four universal emotions. *Psychiatry Research, 128,* 235–244.

Köhler, W. (1927). *The mentality of apes.* London: Routledge & Kegan Paul.

Kojima, M., & Kangawa, K. (2008). Structure and function of ghrelin. *Results & Problems in Cell Differentiation, 46,* 89–115.

Kolata, G. (2002, December 2). With no answers on risks, steroid users still say "yes." *The New York Times,* p. 1A.

Kolb, B., Gibb, R., & Robinson, T. E. (2003). Brain plasticity and behavior. *Current Directions in Psychological Science, 12,* 1–5.

Kong, D., Soon, C., & Chee, M. L. (2011). Reduced visual processing capacity in sleep deprived persons. *NeuroImage, 55,* 629–634.

Konig, R. (2005). Introduction: Plasticity, learning, and cognition. In R. Konig., P. Heil., E. Budinger & H. Scheich (Eds.), *The auditory cortex: A synthesis of human and animal research.* Mahwah, NJ: Lawrence Erlbaum Associates Publishers, 2005.

Konijn, E., Bijvank, M. N., & Bushman, B. J. (2007). I wish I were a warrior: The role of wishful identification in the effects of violent video games on aggression in adolescent boys. *Developmental Psychology, 43,* 1038–1044.

Koocher, G. P., Norcross, J. C., & Hill, S. S. (2005). *Psychologists' desk reference* (2nd ed.). New York: Oxford University Press.

Kopelman, M. D., & Fleminger, S. (2002). Experience and perspectives on the classification of organic mental disorders. *Psychopathology, 35,* 76–81.

Koper, R. J., & Jaasma, M. A. (2001). Interpersonal style: are human social orientations guided by generalized interpersonal needs? *Communications Reports, 14,* 117–129.

Koplewicz, H. (2002). *More than moody: Recognizing and treating adolescent depression.* New York: Putnam.

Korecka, J. A., Verhaagen, J., & Hol, E. M. (2007). Cell-replacement and gene-therapy strategies for Parkinson's and Alzheimer's disease. *Regenerative Medicine, 2,* 425–426.

Kosfeld, M., Heinrich, M., Zak, P. J., Fischbacher, U., & Fehr, E. (2005, June 2). Oxytocin increases trust in humans. *Nature, 435,* 673–676.

Kosslyn, S. M., Cacioppo, J. T., Davidson, R. J., Hugdahl, K., Lovallo, W. R., Spiegel, D., & Rose, R. (2002). Bridging psychology and biology. *American Psychologist, 57,* 341–351.

Kosslyn, S. M., & Shin, L. M. (1994). Visual mental images in the brain: Current issues. In M. J. Farah & G. Ratcliff (Eds.), *The neuropsychology of high-level vision: Collected tutorial essays. Carnegie Mellon symposia on cognition.* Hillsdale, NJ: Erlbaum.

Kotre, J., & Hall, E. (1990). *Seasons of life.* Boston: Little, Brown.

Kowert, P. A. (2002). *Groupthink or deadlock: When do leaders learn from their advisors? SUNY Series on the Presidency.* Albany: State University of New York Press.

Kovács, T., Szabó, P., & Pászthy, B. (2011). Reduced specificity of autobiographical memory in anorexia nervosa. *Journal of Cognitive and Behavioral Psychotherapies, 11,* 57–66.

Kozaric-Kovacic, D., & Borovecki, A. (2005). Prevalence of psychotic comorbidity in combat-related post-traumatic stress disorder. *Military Medicine, 170,* 223–226.

Kozulin, A., Gindis, B., Ageyev, V. S., & Miller, S. M. (2003). *Vygotsky's educational theory in cultural context.* New York: Cambridge University Press.

Kramer, P. (1993). *Listening to Prozac.* New York: Viking.

Kreher, D., Holcomb, P., Goff, D., & Kuperberg, G. (2008). Neural evidence for faster and further automatic spreading activation in schizophrenic thought disorder. *Schizophrenia Bulletin, 34,* 473–482.

Kremen, A., & Lyons, M. J. (2011). Behavioral genetics of aging. In K. Schaie, S. L. Willis, K. Schaie, S. L. Willis (Eds.), *Handbook of the psychology of aging* (7th ed.). San Diego, CA: Elsevier Academic Press.

Kreuger, A. (2007). Are we having fun yet? Categorizing and evaluating changes in time allocation. *Brookings Papers on Economic Activity* (Vol. 2), 193–218.

Krijn, M., Emmelkamp, P. M. G., Olafsson, R. P., & Biemond, R. (2004). Virtual reality exposure therapy of anxiety disorders: A review. *Clinical Psychology Review, 24,* 259–281.

Kring, A., & Earnst, K. (2003). Nonverbal Behavior in Schizophrenia. *Nonverbal behavior in clinical settings* (pp. 263–285). New York: Oxford University Press.

Kring, A., & Moran, E. (2008, September). Emotional response deficits in schizophrenia: Insights from affective science. *Schizophrenia Bulletin, 34*(5), 819–834.

Krueger, K., & Dayan, P. (2009). Flexible shaping: How learning in small steps helps. *Cognition, 110,* 380–394.

Krueger, R. G., Hicks, B. M., & McGue, M. (2001). Altruism and antisocial behavior: Independent tendencies, unique personality correlates, distinct etiologies. *Psychological Science, 12,* 397–402.

Krusemark, E., Campbell, W., & Clementz, B. (2008). Attributions, deception, and event related potentials: An investigation of the self-serving bias. *Psychophysiology, 45,* 511–515.

Kubler, A., Winter, S., and Ludolph, A. (2005). Severity of depressive symptoms and quality of life in patients with amyotrophic lateral sclerosis. *Neurorehabilitation and Neural Repair, 19,* 182–193.

Kübler-Ross, E. (1969). *On death and dying.* New York: Macmillan.

Kubovy, M., Epstein, W., & Gepshtein, S. (2003). Foundations of visual perception. In A. F. Healy, & R. W. Proctor (Eds.). *Handbook of psychology: Experimental psychology* (Vol. 4). New York: Wiley.

Kudler, H., Krupnick, J., Blank, A., Herman, J., & Horowitz, M. (2009). Psychodynamic therapy for adults. *Effective treatments for PTSD: Practice guidelines from the International Society for Traumatic Stress Studies* (2nd ed.) (pp. 346–369). New York: Guilford Press.

Kuhn, D. (2002). What is scientific thinking, and how does it develop?. *Blackwell handbook of childhood cognitive development* (pp. 371–393). Malden: Blackwell Publishing.

Kuo, L. J. (2007). Effects of bilingualism on development of facets of phonological competence (China). *Dissertation Abstracts International Section A: Humanities and Social Sciences, 67(11-A),* 4095.

Kuppens, P., Ceulemans, E., Timmerman, M. E., Diener, E., & Kim-Prieto, C. (2006). Universal intracultural and intercultural dimensions of the recalled frequency of emotional experience. *Journal of Cross Cultural Psychology, 37,* 491–515.

Kuriyama, K., Stickgold, R., & Walker, M. P. (2004). Sleep-dependent learning and motor-skill complexity. *Learning and Memory, 11,* 705–713.

Kuther, T. L. (2003). *Your career in psychology: Psychology and the law.* New York: Wadsworth.

Kvavilashvili, L., & Fisher, L. (2007). Is time-based prospective remembering mediated by self-initiated rehearsals? Role of incidental cues, ongoing activity, age, and motivation. *Journal of Experimental Psychology: General, 136,* 112–132.

Kwon, P., & Laurenceau, J. P. (2002). A longitudinal study of the hopelessness theory of depression: Testing the dia-thesis-stress model within a differential reactivity and exposure framework [Special issue: Reprioritizing the role of science in a realistic version of the scientist-practitioner model]. *Journal of Clinical Psychology, 50,* 1305–1321.

L

Laas, I. (2006). Self-actualization and society: A new application for an old theory. *Journal of Humanistic Psychology, 46,* 77–91.

Lacerda, F., von Hofsten, C., & Heimann, M. (2001). *Emerging cognitive abilities in early infancy.* Mahwah, NJ: Lawrence Erlbaum Associates.

Laederach-Hofmann, K., & Messerli-Buergy, N. (2007). Chest pain, angina pectoris, panic disorder, and Syndrome X. In J. Jordan, B. Barde, & A. M. Zeiher, *Contributions toward evidence-based psychocardiology: A systematic review of the literature.* Washington, DC: American Psychological Association.

Lagacé-Séguin, D. G., & d'Entremont, M. L. (2006). The role of child negative affect in the relations between parenting styles and play. *Early Child Development and Care, 176,* 461–477.

Lahti, J., Räikkönen, K., Ekelund, J., Peltonen, L., Raitakari, O. T., & Keltikangas-Järvinen, L. (2005). Novelty seeking: Interaction between parental alcohol use and dopamine D4 receptor gene exon III polymorphism over 17 years. *Psychiatric Genetics, 15,* 133–139.

Laird, J. D., & Bressler, C. (1990). William James and the mechanisms of emotional experience. *Personality and Social Psychology Bulletin, 16,* 636–651.

Lakhan, S., & Vieira, K. (2009, May 15). Schizophrenia pathophysiology: Are we any closer to a complete model? *Annals of General Psychiatry, 8.*

Lal, S. (2002). Giving children security: Mamie Phipps Clark and the racialization of child psychology. *American Psychologist, 57,* 20–28.

Lamal, P. A. (1979). College students' common beliefs about psychology. *Teaching of Psychology, 6,* 155–158.

Lamb, H. R., & Weinberger, L. E. (2005). One-year follow-up of persons discharged from a locked intermediate care facility. *Psychiatric Services, 56,* 198–201.

Lamb, M. E., & Garretson, M. E. (2003). The effects of interviewer gender and child gender on the informativeness of alleged child sexual abuse victims in forensic interviews. *Law and Human Behavior, 27,* 157–171.

Lamborn, S. D., & Groh, K. (2009). A four-part model of autonomy during emerging adulthood: Associations with adjustment. *International Journal of Behavioral Development, 33,* 393–401.

Lana, R. E. (2002). The cognitive approach to language and thought [Special issue: Choice and chance in the formation of society: Behavior and cognition in social theory]. *Journal of Mind and Behavior, 23,* 51–57.

Lanctot, K. L., Herrmann, N. & Mazzotta, P. (2001). Role of serotonin in the behavioral and psychological symptoms of dementia. *Journal of Neuropsychiatry & Clinical Neurosciences, 13,* 5–21.

Lane, K. A., Banaji, M. R., Nosek, B. A., & Greenwald, A. G. (Eds.). (2007).Understanding and using the implicit association test: iv: what we know (so far) about the method. In B. Wittenbrink, & N. Schwarz, *Implicit measures of attitudes.* New York: Guilford Press.

Lane, S. D., Cherek, D. R., & Tcheremissine, O. V. (2007). Response preseveration and adaptation in heavy marijuana-smoking adolescents. *Addictive Behaviors, 32,* 977–990.

Lang, A. J., Sorrell, J. T., & Rodgers, C. S. (2006). Anxiety sensitivity as a predictor of labor pain. *European Journal of Pain, 10,* 263–270.

Langan-Fox, J., & Grant, S. (2006). The Thematic Apperception Test: Toward a standard measure of the big three motives. *Journal of Personality Assessment, 87,* 277–291.

Langdridge, D., & Butt, T. (2004). The fundamental attribution error: A phenomenological critique. *British Journal of Social Psychology, 43,* 357–369.

Langlois, J. H., Kalakanis, L., Rubenstein, A. J., Larson, A., Hallam, M. & Smoot, M. (2000). Maxims or myths of beauty? A meta-analytic and theoretical review. *Psychological Bulletin, 126,* 390–423.

Langreth, R. (2000, May 1). Every little bit helps: How even moderate exercise can have a big impact on your health. *The Wall Street Journal,* p. R5.

Lankov, A. (2004). The dawn of modern Korea: Changes for better or worse. *The Korea Times,* p. A1.

Lanza, S. T., & Collins, L. M. (2002). Pubertal timing and the onset of substance use in females during early adolescence. *Prevention Science, 3,* 69–82.

LaPiere, R. (1938). The sociological significance of measurable attitudes. *American Sociological Review, 3,* 175–182.

Laqueur, T. W. (2003). *Solitary sex: A cultural history of masturbation.* New York: Zone.

Larsen, R. J., & Buss, D. M. (2006). *Personality psychology: Domains of knowledge about human nature with PowerWeb* (2nd ed.). New York: McGraw-Hill.

Lascaratos, G., Ji, D., & Wood, J. P. (2007). Visible light affects mitochondrial function and induces neuronal death in retinal cell cultures. *Vision Research, 47,* 1191–1201.

Latané, B., & Darley, J. M. (1970). *The unresponsive bystander: Why doesn't he help?* New York: Appleton-Century-Crofts.

Latané, B., & Nida, S. (1981). Ten years of research on group size and helping.

Laugharne, J., Janca, A., & Widiger, T. (2007). Posttraumatic stress disorder and terrorism: 5 years after 9/11. *Current Opinion in Psychiatry, 20,* 36–41.

Lavelli, M., & Fogel, A. (2005). Developmental changes in the relationship between the infant's attention and emotion during early face-to-face communication. *Developmental Psychology, 41,* 265–280.

Lavenex, P., & Lavenex, P. (2009). Spatial memory and the monkey hippocampus: Not all space is created equal. *Hippocampus, 19,* 8–19.

Lazarus, A. A. (1997). *Brief but comprehensive psychotherapy: The multimodal way.* New York: Springer.

Lazarus, R. S. (1995). Emotions express a social relationship, but it is an individual mind that creates them. *Psychological Inquiry, 6,* 253–265.

Lazarus, R. S. (2000). Toward better research on stress and coping. *American Psychologist, 55,* 665–673.

Leahy, R. L. (2003). *Roadblocks in cognitive-behavioral therapy: Transforming challenges into opportunities for change.* New York: Guilford Press.

Leary, C., Kelley, M., Morrow, J., & Mikulka, P. (2008). Parental use of physical punishment as related to family environment, psychological well-being, and personality in undergraduates. *Journal of Family Violence, 23,* 1–7.

LeBoutillier, N., & Marks, D. (2003, February). Mental imagery and creativity: A meta-analytic review study. *British Journal of Psychology, 94*(1), 29–44.

Leckman, J. F., & King, R. A. (2007). A developmental perspective on the controversy surrounding the use of SSRIs to treat pediatric depression. *American Journal of Psychiatry, 164,* 1304–1306.

Lecrubier, Y. (2001). Prescribing patterns for depression and anxiety worldwide. *Journal of Clinical Psychiatry, 62*(13), 31–36.

Lee, A., Isaac, M. & Janca, A. (2007). Posttraumatic stress disorder and terrorism. In A. Monat, R.S. Lazarus et al. (Eds.), *The Praeger handbook on stress and coping* (Vol.1). Westport, CT: Praeger Publishers/Greenwood Publishing Group.

Lee, A. Y., & Aaker, J. L. (2004). Bringing the frame into focus: The influence of regulatory fit on processing fluency and persuasion. *Journal of Personality and Social Psychology, 86,* 205–218.

Lee, D., Kleinman, J., and Kleinman, A. (2007). Rethinking depression: An ethnographic study of the experiences of depression among Chinese. *Harvard Review of Psychiatry, 15,* 1–8.

Lee, H. J., & Kwon, S. M. (2003). Two different types of obsession: Autogenous obsessions and reactive obsessions. *Behaviour Research & Therapy, 41,* 11–29.

Lee, H. J., Kwon, S. M., Kwon, J. S., & Telch, M. J. (2005). Testing the autogenous reactive model of obsessions. *Depress Anxiety, 21,* 118–129.

Lee, K., & Ashton, M. C. (2007). Factor analysis in personality research. In R. W. Robins, R. C. Fraley, & R. F. Krueger, *Handbook of research methods in personality psychology* (pp. 424–443). New York: Guilford Press.

Lee, M. J., Hust, S., Zhang, L., & Zhang, Y. (2011). Effects of violence against women in popular crime dramas on viewers' attitudes related to sexual violence. *Mass Communication & Society, 14,* 25–44.

Lee, S. H., Ahn, S. C., & Lee, Y. J. (2007). Effectiveness of a meditation-based stress management program as an adjunct to pharmacotherapy in patients with anxiety disorder. *Journal of Psychosomatic Research, 62,* 189–195.

Lee-Chai, A. Y., Bargh, J. A. (Eds.). (2001). *The use and abuse of power: Multiple perspectives on the causes of corruption*. Philadelphia: Psychology Press.

Lee-Chiong, T. L. (2006). *Sleep: A comprehensive handbook*. New York: Wiley-Liss.

Lefaucheur, J. P., Brugieres, P., Menard-Lefaucheur, I., Wendling, S., Pommier, M., & Bellivier, F. (2007). The value of navigation-guided rTMS for the treatment of depression: An illustrative case. *Neurophysiologic Clinics, 37*, 265–271.

Lehar, S. (2003). *The world in your head: A gestalt view of the mechanism of conscious experience*. Mahwah, NJ: Erlbaum.

Lehman, D. R., & Taylor, S. E. (1988). Date with an earthquake: Coping with a probable, unpredictable disaster. *Personality and Social Psychology Bulletin, 13*, 546–555.

Lehrman, S. (2007). Going beyond X and Y. *Scientific American*, pp. 40–41.

Leib, J. R., Gollust, S. E., Hull, S. C., & Wilfond, B. S. (2005). Carrier screening panels for Ashkenazi Jews: is more better? *Genetic Medicine, 7*, 185–190.

Leibel, R. L., Rosenbaum, M., Hirsch, J. (1995, March 9). Changes in energy expenditure resulting from altered body. *New England Journal of Medicine, 332*, 621–628.

Leiblum, S. R. & Chivers, M. L. (2007). Normal and persistent genital arousal in women: New perspectives. *Journal of Sex & Marital Therapy, 33*, 357–373.

Leigh, J. H., Zinkhan, G. M. & Swaminathan, V. (2006). Dimensional relationships of recall and recognition measures with selected cognitive and affective aspects of print ads. *Journal of Advertising, 35*, 105–122.

Leiter, S., & Leiter, W. M. (2003). *Affirmative action in antidiscrimination law and policy: An overview and synthesis. SUNY series in American constitutionalism*. Albany: State University of New York Press.

Leitner, L. M. (2007). Diversity issues, postmodernism, and psychodynamic therapy. *PsycCRITIQUES, 52*, No pagination specified.

Leland, J. (1999, May 10). The secret life of teens. *Newsweek*, pp. 44–50.

Lemay, E., & Clark, M. (2008). How the head liberates the heart: Projection of communal responsiveness guides relationship promotion. *Journal of Personality and Social Psychology, 94*, 647–671.

Lemay, E. P., Jr., Clark, M. S., & Feeney, B. C. (2007). Projection of responsiveness to needs and the construction of satisfying communal relationships. *Journal of Personality and Social Psychology, 92*, 834–853.

Lemonick, M. D. (2000, December 11). Downey's downfall. *Time*, p. 97.

Lengua, L. J., & Kovacs, E. A. (2005). Bidirectional associations between temperament and parenting and the prediction of adjustment problems in middle childhood. *Journal of Applied Developmental Psychology, 26*, 21–38.

Lengua, L. J, & Long, A. C. (2002). The role of emotionality and self-regulation in the appraisal-coping process: Tests of direct and moderating effects. *Journal of Applied Developmental Psychology, 23*, 471–493.

Lenzenweger, M. F., & Dworkin, R. H. (Eds.). (1998). *The origins and development of schizophrenia: Advances in experimental psychopathology*. Washington, DC: American Psychological Association.

Leo, R. J., & Latif, T. (2007). Repetitive transcranial magnetic stimulation (rTMS) in experimentally induced and chronic neuropathic pain: A review. *The Journal of Pain, 8*, 453-459.

Leonard, E. (2009, May 18). Kirstie Alley: I've let myself go. *People*, p. 50.

Leong, F. T. I., & Blustein, D. L. (2000). Toward a global vision of counseling psychology. *Counseling Psychology, 28*, 5–9.

Lepage, J. F., & Theoret, H. (2007). The mirror neuron system: grasping others' actions from birth? *Developmental Science, 10*, 513–523.

Leppanen, J. M., Moulson, M. C., Vogel-Farley, V. K. & Nelson, C. A. (2007). An ERP study of emotional face processing in the adult and infant brain. *Child Development, 78*, 232–245.

Lepper, M. R., Corpus, J. H., & Iyengar, S. S. (2005). Intrinsic and extrinsic motivational orientations in the classroom: Age differences and academic correlates. *Journal of Educational Psychology, 97*, 184–196.

Leu, J., Wang, J., & Koo, K. (2011). Are positive emotions just as "positive" across cultures? *Emotion*. http://www.ncbi.nlm.nih.gov/pubmed/21443338.

LeVay, S. (1993). *The sexual brain*. Cambridge, MA: MIT.

LeVay, S. (1999). *The Sexual Brain*. Cambridge, MA: MIT.

LeVay, S. (2011). *Gay, straight, and the reason why: The science of sexual orientation*. New York: Oxford University Press.

Levenson, R. W. (1994). The search for autonomic specificity. In P. Ekman & R. J. Davidson (Eds.), *The nature of emotion: Fundamental questions*. New York: Oxford University Press.

Levi, A., Chan, K. K., & Pence, D. (2006). Real men do not read labels: the effects of masculinity and involvement on college students' food decisions. *Journal of American College Health, 55*, 91–98.

Levin, B. E., (2006). Metabolic sensing neurons and the control of energy homeostasis. *Physiology & Behavior, 89*, 486–489.

Levin, R. J. (2007). Sexual activity, health and well-being—the beneficial roles of coitus and masturbation. *Sexual and Relationship Therapy, 22*, 135–148.

Levine, J. M., & Moreland, R. L. (2006). Small groups: An overview. In J. M. Levine & R. L. Moreland (Eds.), *Small groups*. New York: Psychology Press.

Levine, M., & Crowther, S. (2008, December). The responsive bystander: How social group membership and group size can encourage as well as inhibit bystander intervention. *Journal of Personality and Social Psychology, 95*(6), 1429–1439.

Levine, S. Z., & Rabinowitz, J. (2007). Revisiting the 5 dimensions of the Positive and Negative Syndrome Scale. *Journal of Clinical Psychopharmacology, 27*, 431–436.

Levinson, D. (1992). *The seasons of a woman's life*. New York: Knopf.

Levinson, D. J. (1990). A theory of life structure development in adulthood. In C. N. Alexander & E. J. Langer (Eds.), *Higher stages of human development: Perspectives on adult growth*. New York: Oxford University Press.

Levy, B. (1996). Improving memory in old age through implicit self-stereotyping. *Journal of Personality and Social Psychology, 71*, 1092–1107.

Levy, B. R., & Myers, L. M. (2004). Preventive health behaviors influenced by self-perceptions of aging. *Preventive Medicine: An International Journal Devoted to Practice and Theory, 39*, 625–629.

Levy, B. R., Slade, M. D., Kunkel, S. R., & Kasl, S. V. (2002). Longevity increased by positive self-perceptions of aging. *Journal of Personality & Social Psychology, 83*, 261–270. Levy, S. (2004, April 12). All eyes on Google. *Newsweek*, p. 40.

Levy, Y. S., Stroomza, M., Melamed, E., & Offen, D. (2004). Embryonic and adult stem cells as a source for cell therapy in Parkinson's disease. *Journal of Molecular Neuroscience, 24*, 353–386.

Lewandowski, S., Stritzke, W. G. K., & Oberauer, K. (2005). Memory for fact, fiction and misinformation: The Iraq War 2003. *Psychological Science, 16*, 190–195.

Lewin, T. (2006, July 9). At colleges, women are leaving men in the dust. *The New York Times*, p. 1.

Lewinsohn, P. M., & Essau, C. A. (2002). Depression in adolescents. In I. H. Gotlib & C. L. Hammen (Eds.), *Handbook of depression* (pp. 541–559). New York: Guilford Press.

Lewinsohn, P. M., Petit, J. W., Joiner, T. E., Jr., & Seeley, J. R. (2003). The symptomatic expression of major depressive disorder in adolescents and young adults. *Journal of Abnormal Psychology, 112*, 244–252.

Lewis, M., & Haviland-Jones, J. M. (2000). *Handbook of emotions* (2nd ed.). New York: Guilford Press.

Li, J. (2011). Cultural frames of children's learning beliefs. In L. Jensen, L. Jensen (Eds.), *Bridging cultural and developmental approaches to psychology: New syntheses in theory, research, and policy*. New York: Oxford University Press.

Li, J., Wang, L., & Fischer, K. W. (2004). The organization of Chinese shame concepts. *Cognition and Emotion, 18*, 767–797.

Li, M. D., Cheng, R., Ma, J. Z., & Swan, G. E. (2003). A meta-analysis of estimated genetic and environmental effects on smoking behavior in male and female adult twins. *Addiction, 98*, 23–31.

Li, S., Sun, Y., & Wang, Y. (2007). 50% off or buy one get one free? Frame preference as a function of consumable nature in dairy products. *The Journal of Social Psychology, 147*, 413–421.

Li, T-K., Volkow, N. D., & Baler, R. D. (2007). The biological bases of nicotine and alcohol co-addiction. *Biological Psychiatry, 61*, 1–3.

Liang, K. A. (2007). Acculturation, ambivalent sexism, and attitudes toward women who engage in premarital sex among Chinese American young adults. *Dissertation Abstracts International: Section B: The Sciences and Engineering, 67(10-B)*, 6065.

Lidz, J., & Gleitman, L. R. (2004). Argument structure and the child's contribution to language learning. *Trends in Cognitive Sciences, 8*, 157–161.

Lieberman, M. D. (2007). Social cognitive neuro-science: A review of core processes. *Annual Review of Psychology, 58*, 259–289.

Lieberman, M. D., Hariri, A., Jarcho, J. M., Lien, Y-W., Chu, R-L., Jen, C-H., & Wu, C-H. (2006). Do Chinese commit neither fundamental attribution error nor ultimate attribution error? *Chinese Journal of Psychology, 48*, 163–181.

Lilienfeld, S. O. (2007). Psychological treatments that cause harm. *Perspectives on Psychological Science, 2*, 53–58.

Lin, C-H., & Lin, H-M. (2007). What price do you ask for the 'extra one'?: A social value orientation perspective. *Social Behavior and Personality, 35*, 9–18.

Lin, S., Huang, M., Lin, H., & Pan, C. (2010). Deterioration of intelligence in methamphetamine-induced psychosis: Comparison with alcohol dependence on WAIS-III. *Psychiatry & Clinical Neurosciences, 64*, 4–9.

Lin, Y. Y., Chen, W. T., Liao, K. K., Yeh, T. C., Wu, Z. Z., & Ho, L. T. (2005). Hemispheric balance in coding speech and non-speech sounds in Chinese participants. *Neuroreport, 16*, 469–473.

Lindblad, F., Lindahl, M., & Theorell, T. (2006). Physiological stress reactions in 6th and 9th graders during test performance. *Stress and Health: Journal of the International Society for the Investigation of Stress, 22*, 189–195.

Lindh-Astrand, L., Brynhildsen, J., & Hoffmann, M. (2007). Attitudes towards the menopause and hormone therapy over the turn of the century. *Maturitas, 56*, 12–20.

Lindley, L. D. (2006). The paradox of self-efficacy: Research with diverse populations. *Journal of Career Assessment, 14*, 143–160.

Lindorff, M. (2005). Determinants of received social support: Who gives what to managers? *Journal of Social and Personal Relationships, 22*, 323–337.

Lindsay, P., Maynard, I., & Thomas, O. (2005). Effects of hypnosis on flow states and cycling performance. *Sport Psychologist, 19*, 164–177.

Lindsay, P. H., & Norman, D. A. (1977). *Human information processing* (2nd ed.). New York: Academic Press.

Lindsey, E., & Colwell, M. (2003). Preschoolers' emotional competence: Links to pretend and physical play. *Child Study Journal, 33*, 39–52.

Linehan, M. M., Cochran, B., & Kehrer, C. A. (2001a). Borderline personality disorder. In D. H. Barlow (Ed.), *Clinical handbook of psychological disorder* (3rd ed) New York: Guilford Press.

Linehan, M. M., Cochran, B. N., & Kehrer, C. A. (2001b). Dialectical behavior therapy for borderline personality disorder. In D. H. Barlow (Ed.), *Clinical handbook of psychological disorders: A step-by-step treatment manual* (3rd ed.) (pp. 470–522). New York: Guilford Press.

Links, P. S., Eynan, R., & Heisel, M. J. (2007). Affective instability and suicidal ideation and behavior in patients with borderline personality disorder. *Journal of Personality Disorders, 21*, 72–86.

Lipman, M. (2003). *Thinking in education* (2nd ed.). New York: Cambridge University Press.

Lippa, R. A. (2005). *Gender, nature, and nurture* (2nd ed.). Mahwah, NJ: Erlbaum.

Litowitz, B. E. (2007). Unconscious fantasy: A once and future concept. *Journal of the American Psychoanalytic Association, 55*, 199–228.

Little, A., Burt, D. M., & Perrett, D. I. (2006). What is good is beautiful: Face preference reflects desired personality. *Personality and Individual Differences, 41*, 1107–1118.

Little, K., Ramssen, E., Welchko, R., Volberg, V., Roland, C., & Cassin, B. (2009). Decreased brain dopamine cell numbers in human cocaine users. *Psychiatry Research, 168*, 173–180.

Liu, J. H., & Mills, D. (2006). Modern racism and neo-liberal globalization: The discourses of plausible deniability and their multiple functions. *Journal of Community & Applied Social Psychology, 16*, 83–99.

Liu, L., He, S-Z., & Wu, Y. (2007). An analysis of the characteristics of single parent families with different structures and their children. *Chinese Journal of Clinical Psychology, 15*, 68–70.

Livesley, W., & Jang, K. (2008). The behavioral genetics of personality disorder. *Annual Review of Clinical Psychology, 4*, 247–274.

Lobato, M. I., Koff, W. J., & Manenti, C. (2006). Follow-up of sex reassignment surgery in transsexuals: A Brazilian cohort. *Archives of Sexual Behavior, 35*, 711–715.

Lobban, F., Barrowclough, C., & Jones, S. (2006). Does expressed emotion need to be understood within a more systemic framework? An examination of discrepancies in appraisals between patients diagnosed with schizophrenia and their relatives. *Social Psychiatry and Psychiatric Epidemiology, 41*, 50–55.

Locke, J. L. (2006). Parental selection of vocal behavior: Crying, cooking, babbling, and the evolution of language. *Human Nature, 17*, 155–168.

Lockl, K., & Schneider, W. (2007). Knowledge about the mind: Links between theory of mind and later metamemory. *Child Development, 78*, 148–167.

Lofthouse, N., McBurnett, K., Arnold, L., & Hurt, E. (2011). Biofeedback and neurofeedback treatment for ADHD. *Psychiatric Annals, 41*, 42–48.

Loftus, E. F. (1993). Psychologists in the eyewitness world. *American Psychologist, 48*, 550–552.

Loftus, E. F. (2004). Memories of things unseen. *Current Directions in Psychological Science, 13*, 145–147.

Loftus, E. F., & Bernstein, D. M. (2005). Rich false memories: The royal road to success. In A. F. Healy, *Experimental cognitive psychology and its applications*. Washington, DC: American Psychological Association.

Loftus, E. F., & Palmer, J. C. (1974). Reconstruction of automobile destruction: An example of the interface between language and memory. *Journal of Verbal Learning and Verbal Behavior, 13*, 585–589.

Loftus, E., & Cahill, L. (2007). Memory Distortion: From Misinformation to Rich False Memory. *The foundations of remembering: Essays in honor of Henry L. Roediger, III* (pp. 413–25). New York: Psychology Press.

Long, A., (1987, December). What is this thing called sleep? *National Geographic, 172*, 786–821.

Long, G. M., & Beaton, R. J. (1982). The case for peripheral persistence: Effects of target and background luminance on a partial-report task. *Journal of Experimental Psychology: Human Perception and Performance, 8*, 383–391.

Lopes, A. C., Greenberg, B. D., Noren, G., Canteras, M. M., Busatto, G. F. de Mathis, et al. (2009). Treatment of resistant obsessive-compulsive disorder with ventral capsular/ventral striatal gamma capsulotomy: A pilot prospective study. *The Journal of Neuropsychiatry and Clinical Neurosciences, 21*, 381–392.

López, S. R., & Guarnaccia, P. J. (2000). Cultural psychopathology: Uncovering the social world of mental illness. *Annual Review of Psychology, 51*, 571–598.

López, S. R., & Guarnaccia, P. J. (2005). Cultural dimensions of psychopathology: The social world's impact on mental illness. In J. E. Maddux & B. A. Winstead (Eds.), *Foundations for a contemporary understanding*. Mahwah, NJ: Lawrence Erlbaum Associates.

Lorenz, K. (1966). *On aggression*. New York: Harcourt Brace Jovanovich.

Lorenz, K. (1974). *Civilized man's eight deadly sins*. New York: Harcourt Brace Jovanovich.

Lothane, Z. (2005). Jung, A biography. *Journal of the American Psychoanalytic Association, 53*, 317–324.

Loving, T., Crockett, E., & Paxson, A. (2009). Passionate love and relationship thinkers: Experimental evidence for acute cortisol elevations in women. *Psychoneuroendocrinology, 34*, 939–946.

Lowe, P., Humphreys, C., & Williams, S. J. (2007). Night terrors: Women's experiences of (not) sleeping where there is domestic violence. *Violence Against Women, 13*, 549–561.

Lowery, D., Fillingim, R. B., & Wright, R. A. (2003). Sex differences and incentive effects on perceptual and cardiovascular responses to cold pressor pain. *Psychosomatic Medicine, 65*, 284–291.

Lu, J., Sherman, D., Devor, M., & Saper, C. B. (2006). A putative flip-flop switch for control of REM sleep. *Nature, 441*, 589–594.

Lubell, K. M., Swahn, M. H., Crosby, A. E., & Kegler, S. R. (2004). Methods of suicide among persons aged 10–19 years—United States, 1992–2001. *MMWR, 53*, 471–473. Retrieved from www.cdc.gov/ mmwr/PDF/wk/mm5322.pdf.

Lubinski, D., Benbow, C. P., Webb, R. M., & Bleske-Rechek, A. (2006). Tracking exceptional human capital over two decades. *Psychological Science, 17*, 194–199.

Lublin, H., Eberhard, J., & Levander, S. (2005). Current therapy issues and unmet clinical needs in the treatment of schizophrenia: A review of the new generation antipsychotics. *International Clinical Psychopharmacology, 20*, 183–198.

Luchins, A. S. (1946). Classroom experiments on mental set. *American Journal of Psychology, 59*, 295–298.

Lucki, I., & O'Leary, O. F. (2004). Distinguishing roles for norepinephrine and serotonin in the behavioral effects of antidepressant drugs. *Journal of Clinical Psychiatry, 65*, 11–24.

Luders, E., Narr, K. L., Zaidel, E., Thompson, P. M., & Toga, A. W. (2006). Gender effects on callosal thickness in scaled and unscaled space. *Neuroreport, 17*, 1103–1106.

Ludwig, A. M. (1996, March). Mental disturbances and creative achievement. *The Harvard Mental Health Letter*, pp. 4–6.

Lueken, U., Kruschwitz, J., Muehlhan, M., Siegert, J., Hoyer, J., & Wittchen, H. (2011). How specific is specific phobia? Different neural response patterns in two subtypes of specific phobia. *NeuroImage, 56*, 363–72.

Lun, V. M., & Bond, M. H. (2006). Achieving relationship harmony in groups and its consequence for group performance. *Asian Journal of Social Psychology, 9*, 195–202.

Lundberg, U. (2011). Neuroendocrine measures. In R. J. Contrada, A. Baum, R. J. Contrada, A. Baum (Eds.), *The handbook of stress science: Biology, psychology, and health*. New York: Springer Publishing Co.

Luo, S., & Zhang, G. (2009). What leads to romantic attraction: Similarity, reciprocity, security, or beauty? Evidence from a speed-dating study. *Journal of Personality, 77*, 933–964.

Luria, A. R. (1968). *The mind of a mnemonist*. Cambridge, MA: Basic Books.

Luthar, S. S., Cicchetti, D., & Becker, B. (2000). The construct of resilience: A critical evaluation and guidelines for future work. *Child Development, 71*, 543–562.

Lutz, C. K. & Novak, M. A. (2005). Environmental enrichment for nonhuman primates: theory and application. *ILAR Journal, 46*, 178–191.

Lutz, W., Lambert, M. J., Harmon, S. C., Tschitsaz, A., Schurch, E., & Stulz, N. (2006). The probability of treatment success, failure and duration—What can be learned from empirical data to support decision making in clinical practice? *Clinical Psychology & Psychotherapy, 13*, 223–232.

Ly, D. H., Lockhart, D. J., Lerner, R. A., & Schultz, P. G. (2000, March 31). Mitotic mis-regulation and human aging. *Science, 287*, 2486–2492.

Lykken, D. T. (1995). *The antisocial personalities*. Mahwah, NJ: Erlbaum.

Lymberis, S. C., Parhar, P. K., Katsoulakis, E., & Formenti, S. C. (2004). Pharmacogenomics and breast cancer. *Pharmacogenomics, 5*, 31–55.

Lynch, T. R., Trost, W. T, Salsman, N., & Linehan, M. M. (2007). Dialectical behavior therapy for borderline personality disorder. *Annual Review of Clinical Psychology, 3*, 181–205.

Lynn, S. J., Fassler, O., & Knox, J. (2005). Hypnosis and the altered state debate: Something more or nothing more? Comment. *Contemporary Hypnosis, 22*, 39–45.

Lynn, S. J., Kirsch, I., Barabasz, A., Cardena, E., & Patterson, D. (2000). Hypnosis as an empirically supported clinical intervention: The state of the evidence and a look to the future.

Lynn, S. J., Lock, T., Loftus, E. F., Krackow, E., & Lilienfeld, S. O. (2003). The remembrance of things past: Problematic memory recovery techniques in psychotherapy. In S. O. Lilienfeld, S. J. Lynn, & J. M. Lohr (Eds.) *Science and pseudoscience in clinical psychology*. New York: Guilford Press.

Lynn, S. J., Neufeld, V., Green, J. P., Sandberg, D., et al. (1996). Daydreaming, fantasy, and psychopathology. In R. G. Kunzendorf, N. P. Spanos, & B. Wallace (Eds.), *Hypnosis and imagination. Imagery and human development series*. Amityville, NY: Baywood.

Lyon, G. J., Abi-Dargham, A., Moore, H., Lieberman, J. A., Javitch, J. A., & Sulzer, D. (2011). Presynaptic regulation of dopamine transmission in schizophrenia. *Schizophrenia Bulletin, 37*, 108–117.

M

Macaluso, E., & Driver, J. (2005). Multisensory spatial interactions: a window onto functional integration in the human brain. *Trends in Neurosciences, 28, Issue 5*, 264–271.

Macaluso, E., Frith, C. D., & Driver, J. (2000, August 18). Modulation of human visual cortex by crossmodal spatial attention. *Science, 289*, 1206–1208.

Macduff, I. (2006). Your pace or mine? Culture, time and negotiation. *Negotiation Journal, 22*, 31–45.

Mace, J. (2007). Involuntary memory: Concept and theory. *Involuntary memory* (pp. 1–19). Malden: Blackwell Publishing.

MacFarlane, G., Blomberg, S., & Vasey, P. (2010). Homosexual behaviour in birds: Frequency of expression is related to parental care disparity between the sexes. *Animal Behaviour, 80*, 375–390.

Machado, R. B., Suchecki, D., & Tufik, S. (2005). Sleep homeostasis in rats assessed by a long-term intermittent paradoxical sleep deprivation protocol. *Behavioural Brain Research, 160*, 356–364.

Macht, M., & Simons, G. (2011). Emotional eating. In I. Nyklíček, A. Vingerhoets, et al. (Eds.), *Emotion regulation and well-being*. New York: Springer Science + Business Media.

MacIntyre, T., Moran, A., & Jennings, D. J. (2002). Is controllability of imagery related to canoe-slalom performance? *Perceptual & Motor Skills, 94*, 1245–1250.

Mack, J. (2003). *The museum of the mind*. London: British Museum Publications.

Mackay, J., & Eriksen, M. (2002). *The tobacco atlas*. Geneva, Switzerland: World Health Organization.

Mackay, P., Donovan, D., & Marlatt, G. (1991). Cognitive and behavioral approaches to alcohol abuse. *Clinical textbook of addictive disorders* (pp. 452–481). New York: Guilford Press.

MacLennan, A. (2009, June). Evidence-based review of therapies at the menopause. *International Journal of Evidence-Based Healthcare, 7*(2), 112–123.

Macmillan, M. (1996). *Freud evaluated: The completed arc*. Cambridge, MA: MIT.

MacNeilage, P. F., Rogers, L. J., & Vallortigara, G. (2009, July). Origins of the left & right brain. *Scientific American*, 60–67.

Madden, D. J. (2007). Aging and visual attention. *Current Directions in Psychological Science, 16*, 70–74.

Maddi, S. R. (2007). The story of hardiness: Twenty years of theorizing, research, and practice. In A. Monat, R. S. Lazarus, & G. Reevy, *The Praeger handbook on stress and coping* (Vol. 2). Westport, CT: Praeger Publishers/Greenwood Publishing.

Madon, S., Willard, J., & Guyll, M. (2006). Self-fulfilling prophecy effects of mothers' beliefs on children's alcohol use: accumulation, dissipation, and stability over time. *Journal of Personality and Social Psychology, 90*, 911–926.

Magida, A. J. (2006). *Opening the doors of wonder: Reflections on religious rites of passage*. Berkeley, CA: University of California Press.

Magoni, M., Bassani, L., Okong, P., Kituuka, P., Germinario, E. P., Giuliano, M., & Vella, S. (2005). Mode of infant feeding and HIV infection in children in a program for prevention of mother-to-child transmission in Uganda. *AIDS, 19*, 433–437.

Magoon, M., & Critchfield, T. (2008). Concurrent schedules of positive and negative reinforcement: Differential-impact and differential-outcomes hypotheses. *Journal of the Experimental Analysis of Behavior, 90*, 1–22.

Magruder, K., & Yeager, D. (2009). The prevalence of PTSD across war eras and the effect of deployment on PTSD: A systematic review and meta-analysis. *Psychiatric Annals, 39*, 778–788.

Maguire, E. A., Gadian, D. G., Johnsrude, I. S., Good, C. D., Ashburner, J., Frackowiak, R. S. J., & Frith, C. D. (2000). Navigation-related structural change in the hippocampi of taxi drivers. *Proceedings of the National Academy of Sciences, 97*, 4398–4403.

Maguire, E. A., Woollett, K., & Spiers, H. J. (2006). London taxi drivers and bus drivers: A structural MRI and neuropsychological analysis. *Hippocampus, 16*, 1091–1101.

Mahmood, M., & Black, J. (2005). Narcolepsy-cataplexy: How does recent understanding help in evaluation and treatment. *Current Treatment Options in Neurology, 7*, 363–371.

Maier, S. F., & Watkins, L. R. (2000). Learned helplessness. In A. E. Kazdin, *Encyclopedia of psychology* (Vol. 4). Washington, DC: American Psychological Association.

Majdandzic, M., & van den Boom, D. C. (2007). Multimethod longitudinal assessment of temperament in early childhood. *Journal of Personality, 75*, 121–167.

Majeres, R. L. (2007). Sex differences in phono-logical coding: Alphabet transformation speed. *Intelligence, 35*, 335–346.

Majorano, M., & D'Odorico, L. (2011). The transition into ambient language: A longitudinal study of babbling and first word production of Italian children. *First Language, 31*, 47–66.

Maldonado, J. R., & Spiegel, D. (2003). Dissociative disorders. In R. E. Hales & S. C. Yudofsky, *The American Psychiatric Publishing textbook of clinical psychiatry* (4th ed.). Washington, DC: American Psychiatric Publishing.

Malle, B. F. (2004). *How the mind explains behavior: Folk explanations, meaning, and social interaction*. Cambridge, MA: MIT.

Malouff, J. M., Thorsteinsson, E. B., & Schutte, N. S. (2007). The efficacy of problem solving therapy in reducing mental and physical health problems: A meta-analysis. *Clinical Psychology Review, 27*, 46–57.

Malpas, P. (2008, April). Predictive genetic testing of children for adult-onset diseases and psychological harm. *Journal of Medical Ethics, 34*, 275–278.

Mamassis, G., & Doganis, G. (2004). The effects of a mental training program on juniors pre-competitive anxiety, self-confidence, and tennis performance. *Journal of Applied Sport Psychology, 16*, 118–137.

Mampe, B., Friederici, A., Christophe, A., & Wermke, K. (2009). Newborns' cry melody is shaped by their native language. *Current Biology, 19*, 1994–1997.

Mancinelli, R., Binetti, R., & Ceccanti, M. (2007). Woman, alcohol and environment: Emerging risks for health. *Neuroscience & Biobehavioral Reviews, 31*, 246–253.

Mancuso, F., Horan, W. P., Kern, R. S., & Green, M. F. (2011). Social cognition in psychosis: Multidimensional structure, clinical correlates, and relationship with functional outcome. *Schizophrenia Research, 125*, 143–151.

Manly, J. J. (2005). Advantages and disadvantages of separate norms for African Americans. *Clinical Neuropsychologist, 19*, 270–275.

Manly, J. J. (2006). Deconstructing race and ethnicity: implications for measurement of health outcomes. *Medical Care, 44, Special issue: Measurement in a multi-ethnic society*, S10–S16.

Mann, K. (2004). Pharmacotherapy of Alcohol Dependence A Review of the Clinical Data. *CNS Drugs, 18*(8), 485–504.

Mann, K., Ackermann, K., Croissant, B., Mundle, G., Nakovics, H., Diehl, A. (2005). Neuroimaging of gender differences in alcohol dependence: are women more vulnerable? *Alcoholism: Clinical & Experimental Research, 29*, 896–901.

Mann, T. (2007). Medicare's search for effective obesity treatments: Diets are not the answer. *American Psychologist, 62*, 220–233.

Manning, M. A., & Hoyme, E. H. (2007). Fetal alcohol spectrum disorders: A practical clinical approach to diagnosis. *Neuroscience & Biobehavioral Reviews, 31*, 230–238.

Manning, S. Y. (2005). Dialectical behavior therapy of severe and chronic problems. In L. VandeCreek (Ed.), *Innovations in clinical practice: Focus on adults*. Sarasota, FL: Professional Resource Press/Professional Resource Exchange.

Manor, J. K., & Gailliot, M. T. (2007). Altruism and egoism: Prosocial motivations for helping depend on relationship context. *European Journal of Social Psychology, 37*, 347–358.

Manstead, A. S. R., & Wagner, H. L. (2004). *Experience emotion*. Cambridge, England: Cambridge University Press.

Manstead, A. S. R., Frijda, N., & Fischer, A. H. (Eds.) (2003). *Feelings and emotions: The Amsterdam Symposium*. Cambridge, England: Cambridge University Press.

Marcaurelle, R., Bélanger, C., & Marchand, A. (2003). Marital relationship and the treatment of panic disorder with agoraphobia: A critical review. *Clinical Psychology Review, 23*, 247–276.

Marcaurelle, R., Bélanger, C., & Marchand, A. (2005). Marital predictors of symptom severity in panic disorder with agoraphobia. *Journal of Anxiety Disorders, 19*, 211–232.

Marcus-Newhall, A., Pedersen, W. C., & Carlson, M. (2000). Displaced aggression is alive and well: A meta-analytic review. *Journal of Personality and Social Psychology, 78*, 670–689.

Markowitz, J., & Patrick, K. (2008, June). Introduction. *Journal of Clinical Psychopharmacology, 28*(32), S37–SS38.

Marks, I. M. (2004). The Nobel prize award in physiology to Ivan Petrovich Pavlov–1904. *Australian and New Zealand Journal of Psychiatry, 38*, 674–677.

Markus, H. R., & Hamedani, M. G. (2007). Sociocultural psychology: The dynamic interdependence among self systems and social systems. In S. Kitayama & D. Cohen (Eds.) *Handbook of cultural psychology*. New York: Guilford Press.

Markus, H. R., & Kitayama, S. (2003). Models of agency: Sociocultural diversity in the construction of action. In V. Murphy-Berman & J. J. Berman (Eds.), *Cross-cultural differences in perspectives on the self*. Lincoln, NE: University of Nebraska Press.

Marmar, C. (2009). Mental health impact of Afghanistan and Iraq deployment: Meeting the challenge of a new generation of veterans. *Depression and Anxiety, 26*, 493–497.

Maroda, K. J. (2004). A relational perspective on women and power. *Psychoanalytic Psychology, 21*, 428–435.

Marsh, B. (2008, February 24). A growing cloud over the planet. *The New York Times*, p. WK4.

Marsh, H. W., Hau, K. T., & Sung, R. Y. T. (2007). Childhood obesity, gender, actual-ideal body image discrepancies, and physical self-concept in Hong Kong children: Cultural differences in the value of moderation. *Developmental Psychology, 43*, 647–662.

Marshall, J. R. (2011). Ultimate causes and the evolution of altruism. *Behavioral Ecology and Sociobiology, 65*, 503–512.

Marshall, K., Laing, D. G., & Jinks, A. L. (2006). The capacity of humans to identify components in complex odor-taste mixtures. *Chemical Senses, 31*, 539–545.

Marshall, M. K. (2007). The critical factors of coaching practice leading to successful coaching outcomes. *Dissertation Abstracts International: Section B: The Sciences and Engineering, 67*(7-B), 4092.

Marshall, R. D., Bryant, R. A., Amsel, L., Suh, E. J., Cook, J. M., & Neria, Y. (2007). The psychology of ongoing threat: Relative risk appraisal, the September 11 attacks and terrorism-related fears. *American Psychologist, 62*, 304–316.

Marszalek, J. (2007). Computerized adaptive testing and the experience of flow in examinees. *Dissertation Abstracts International Section A: Humanities and Social Sciences, 67*(7-A), 2465.

Martelle, S., Hanley, C., & Yoshino K. (2003, January 28). "Sopranos" scenario in slaying? *Los Angeles Times*, p. B1.

Martin, A. J., & Marsh, H. W. (2002). Fear of failure: Friend or foe? *Australian Psychologist, 38*, 31–38.

Martin, H. (2006, July 3). New heights. *Los Angeles Times*. p. 1, Part E.

Martin, L., & Pullum, G. K. (1991). *The great Eskimo vocabulary hoax*. Chicago: University of Chicago Press.

Martin, P. D., & Brantley, P. J. (2004). Stress, coping, and social support in health and behavior. In J. M. Raczynski & L. C. Leviton (Eds.), *Handbook of clinical health psychology: Disorders of behavior and health* (Vol. 2). Washington, DC: American Psychological Association.

Martin, R. C. (2005). Components of short-term memory and their relation to language processing. *Current Directions in Psychological Science, 14*, 204–208.

Martindale, C. (1981). *Cognition and consciousness*. Homewood, IL: Dorsey.

Martire, K. A., & Kemp, R. I. (2011). Can experts help jurors to evaluate eyewitness evidence? A review of eyewitness expert effects. *Legal and Criminological Psychology, 16*, 24–36.

Mascia, K., & Servis, R. (2009, August 24). Mail carriers to the rescue. *People*, 108–110.

Marx, J. (2004, July 16). Prolonging the agony. *Science, 305*, 326–328.

Mashour, G. A., Walker, E. E., & Martuza, R. L. (2005). Psychosurgery: Past, present, and future. *Brain Research Reviews, 48*, 409–419.

Mashour, G., Walker, E., & Martuza, R. (2005, June). Psychosurgery: Past, present, and future. *Brain Research Reviews, 48*(3), 409–419.

Maslow, A. H. (1970). *Motivation and personality*. New York: Harper & Row.

Maslow, A. H. (1987). *Motivation and personality* (3rd ed.). New York: Harper & Row.

Massaro, D. W., & Chen, T. H. (2008). The motor theory of speech perception revisited. *Psychonomic Bulletin & Review, 15*, 453–457.

Mast, F. W., & Kosslyn, S. M. (2002). Visual mental images can be ambiguous: Insights from individual differences in spatial transformation abilities. *Cognition, 86*, 57–70.

Masters, W. H., & Johnson, V. E. (1979). *Homosexuality in perspective.* Boston: Little, Brown.

Masuda, M. (2003). Meta-analyses of love scales: Do various love scales measure the same psychological constructs? *Japanese Psychological Research, 45,* 25–37.

Mataix-Cols, D., & Bartres-Faz, D. (2002). Is the use of the wooden and computerized versions of the Tower of Hanoi Puzzle equivalent? *Applied Neuropsychology, 9,* 117–120.

Matlin, M. W. (2000). *The psychology of women* (4th ed.). Ft. Worth: Harcourt.

Maton, K. I., Kohout, J. L., Wicherski, M., Leary, G. E., & Vinokurov, A. (2006). Minority students of color and the psychology graduate pipeline. *American Psychologist, 61,* 117–131.

Matson, J., & LoVullo, S. (2008). A review of behavioral treatments for self-injurious behaviors of persons with autism spectrum disorders. *Behavior Modification, 32,* 61–76.

Matsumoto, D. (2002). Methodological requirements to test a possible in-group advantage in judging emotions across cultures: Comment on Elfenbein and Ambady (2002) and evidence. *Psychological Bulletin, 128,* 236–242.

Matthews, G., & Funke, G. J. (2006). Worry and information-processing. In G. C. L. Davey & A. Wells, *Worry and its psychological disorders: Theory, assessment and treatment.* Hoboken, NJ: Wiley Publishing.

Matthews, K. A., (2005). Psychological perspectives on the development of coronary heart disease. *American Psychologist, 60,* 783–796.

Maurer, D., Lewis, T. L., Brent, H. P., & Levin, A. V. (1999, October 1). Rapid improvement in the acuity of infants after visual input. *Science, 286,* 108–110.

Maxwell, J., Bohman, T., & Spence, R. (2004, May). Differences in Characteristics of Heroin Inhalers and Heroin Injectors at Admission to Treatment: A Preliminary Study Using a Large Database of Client Records. *Substance Use & Misuse, 39*(6), 993–1012.

Mayer, J. D., Salovey, P., & Caruso, D. R. (2004). Emotional intelligence: Theory, findings, and implications. *Psychological Inquiry, 15,* 197–215.

Maynard, A. E., & Martini, M. I. (2005). *Learning in cultural context: Family, peers, and school.* New York: Kluwer Academic/Plenum Publishers.

Mazard, A., Laou, L., Joliot, M., & Mellet, E. (2005). Neural impact of the semantic content of visual mental images and visual percepts. *Brain Research and Cognitive Brain Research, 24,* 423–435.

McAdams, D. (1989). Intimacy: The need to be close. New York: Doubleday.

McAdams, D. P., Diamond, A., de St. Aubin, E., & Mansfield, E. (1997). Stories of commitment: The psychosocial construction of generative lives. *Journal of Personality and Social Psychology, 72,* 678–694.

McCabe, C., & Rolls, E. T. (2007). Umami: A delicious flavor formed by convergence of taste and olfactory pathways in the human brain. *European Journal of Neuroscience, 25,* 1855–1864.

McCarthy, J. (2005). Individualism and collectivism: What do they have to do with counseling? *Journal of Multicultural Counseling and Development, 33,* 108–117.

McCaul, K. D., Johnson, R. J., & Rothman, A. J. (2003). The effects of framing and action instructions on whether older adults obtain flu shots. *Health Psychology.*

McCauley, C. (2007). Psychological issues in understanding terrorism and the response to terrorism. Psychological aspects of suicide terrorism. In B. Bongar, L. M. Brown, & L. E. Beutler, *Psychology of terrorism.* New York: Oxford University Press.

McCleary, L., and Sanford, M. (2002). Parental expressed emotion in depressed adolescents: prediction of clinical course and relationship to comorbid disorders and social functioning. *Journal of child psychology and psychiatry and allied disciplines, 43*(5), 587–595.

McClelland, D. C. (1985). How motives, skills, and values determine what people do. *American Psychologist, 40,* 812–825.

McClelland, D. C. (1993). Intelligence is not the best predictor of job performance. *Current Directions in Psychological Research, 2,* 5–8.

McClelland, D. C., Atkinson, J. W., Clark, R. A., & Lowell, E. L. (1953). *The achievement motive.* New York: Appleton-Century-Crofts.

McClelland, L. E., & Pilcher, J. J. (2007). Assessing subjective sleepiness during a night of sleep deprivation: Examining the internal state and behavioral dimensions of sleepiness. *Behavioral Medicine, 33,* 17–26.

McClure, J., Sutton, R. M., Sibley, C. G. (2007). Listening to reporters or engineers? How instance-based messages about building design affect earthquake fatalism. *Journal of Applied Social Sciences, 37,* 1956–1973.

McCormick, C. G. (2003). Metacognition and learning. In W. M. Reynolds & G. E. Miller (Eds.), *Handbook of psychology: Educational psychology* (Vol. 7, pp. 79–102). New York: Wiley.

McCrae, R. R., & Costa, P. T. (1990). *Personality in adulthood.* New York: Guilford Press.

McCrae, R., Terracciano, A., and 79 Members of the Personality Profiles of Cultures Project. (2005a). Personality profiles of cultures: Aggregate personality traits. *Journal of Personality and Social Psychology, 89,* 407–425.

McCrae R. R., Terracciano A., & 78 Members of the Personality Profiles of Cultures Project. (2005b). Universal features of personality traits from the observer's perspective: Data from 50 cultures. *Journal of Personality and Social Psychology, 88,* 547–561.

McCrink, K., & Wynn, K. (2007). Ratio abstraction by 6-month-old infants. *Psychological Science, 18,* 740–745.

McDaniel, M. A., Maier, S. F., & Einstein, G. O. (2002). "Brain specific" nutrients: A memory cure? *Psychological Science in the Public Interest, 3,* 12–18.

McDonald, C., & Murray, R. M. (2004). Can structural magnetic resonance imaging provide an alternative phenotype for genetic studies of schizophrenia? In M. S. Keshavan, J. L. Kennedy, & R. M. Murray (Eds.), *Neurodevelopment and schizophrenia.* New York: Cambridge University Press.

McDonald, H. E., & Hirt, E. R. (1997). When expectancy meets desire: Motivational effects in reconstructive memory. *Journal of Personality and Social Psychology, 72,* 5–23.

McDougall, W. (1908). *Introduction to social psychology.* London: Methuen.

McDowell, D. M., & Spitz, H. I. (1999). *Substance abuse.* New York: Brunner/Mazel.

McEwen, B. S. (1998, January 15). Protective and damaging effects of stress mediators [Review article]. *New England Journal of Medicine, 338,* 171–179.

McGaugh, J. L. (2003). *Memory and emotion: The making of lasting memories.* New York: Columbia University Press.

McGilvray, J. (Ed.). (2004). *The Cambridge companion to Chomsky.* Oxford, England: Cambridge University Press.

McGinn, D. (2003, June 9). Testing, testing: The new job search. *Time,* pp. 36–38.

McGlynn, F. D., Smitherman, T. A., & Gothard, K. D. (2004). Comment on the status of systematic desensitization. *Behavior Modification, 28,* 194–205.

McGregor, K. K., & Capone, N. C. (2004). Genetic and environmental interactions in determining the early lexicon: Evidence from a set of tri-zygotic quadruplets. *Journal of Child Language, 31,* 311–337.

McGuire, W. J. (1997). Creative hypothesis generating in psychology: Some useful heuristics. *Annual Review of Psychology, 48,* 1–30.

McIntyre, K., Korn, J., & Matsuo, H. (2008). Sweating the small stuff: How different types of hassles result in the experience of stress. *Stress and Health: Journal of the International Society for the Investigation of Stress, 24,* 383–392.

McKeever, V. M., & Huff, M. E. (2003). A diathesis-stress model of post-traumatic stress disorder: Ecological, biological, and residual stress pathways. *Review of General Psychology, 7,* 237–250.

McKenzie-McLean, J. (2006, August 3). On the scent of a new detector. *The Press* (Christchurch, New Zealand), 7.

McKinley, M. J., Cairns, M. J., Denton, D. A., McLaughlin, T., & Williams, R. (1988). The token economy. *Handbook of behavior therapy in education* (pp. 469–487). New York: Plenum Press.

McLellan, A., & Childress, A. (1985). Aversive therapies for substance abuse: Do they work?. *Journal of Substance Abuse Treatment, 2*(3), 187–191.

McManus, C. (2004). *Right hand, left hand: The origins of asymmetry in brains, bodies, atoms and cultures.* Cambridge, MA: Harvard University Press.

McMurtray, A. M., Licht, E., Yeo, T., Krisztal, E., Saul, R. E., & Mendez, M. F. (2007). Positron emission tomography facilitates diagnosis of early-onset Alzheimer's disease. *European Neurology, 59,* 31–37.

McNamara, P. (2004). *An evolutionary psychology of sleep and dreams.* Westport, CT: Praeger Publishers/Greenwood Publishing Group. Mead, M. (1949). *Male and female.* New York: Morrow.

Mead, M. (1949). *Male and female.* New York: Morrow.

Medeiros, R., Prediger, R.D.S., Passos, G.F., Pandolfo, P., et al. (2007). Connecting TNF-Î± signaling pathways to iNOS expression in a mouse model of Alzheimer's disease: Relevance for the behavioral and synaptic deficits induced by amyloid Î2 protein. *Journal of Neuroscience, 27,* 5394–5404.

Meeter, M., & Murre, J. M. J. (2004). Consolidation of long-term memory: Evidence and alternatives. *Psychological Bulletin, 130,* 843–857.

Mehl-Madrona, L. E. (2004). Hypnosis to facilitate uncomplicated birth. *American Journal of Clinical Hypnosis, 46,* 299–312.

Meinlschmidt, G., & Heim, C. (2007). Sensitivity to intranasal oxytocin in adult men with early parental separation. *Biological Psychiatry, 61,* 1109–1111.

Mel, B. W. (2002, March 8). What the synapse tells the neuron. *Science, 295,* 1845–1846.

Mel'nikov, K. S. (1993, October–December). On some aspects of the mechanistic approach to the study of processes of forgetting. *Vestnik Moskovskogo Universiteta Seriya 14 Psikhologiya,* pp. 64–67.

Meltzer, H. Y. (2000). Genetics and etiology of schizophrenia and bipolar disorder. *Biological Psychiatry, 47,* 171–173.

Meltzoff, A. N. (1996). The human infant as imitative generalist: A 20-year progress report on infant imitation with implications for comparative psychology. In C. M. Heyes & B. G. Galef, Jr. (Eds.), *Social learning in animals: The roots of culture.* San Diego: Academic Press.

Melzack, R., & Katz, J. (2004). *The gate control theory: Reaching for the brain.* Mahwah, NJ: Lawrence Erlbaum Associates. Mendelsohn, J. (2003, November 7–9). What we know about sex. *USA Weekend,* pp. 6–9.

Merari, A. (2007). Psychological aspects of suicide terrorism. In B. Bongar, L. M. Brown, & L. E. Beutler, *Psychology of terrorism.* New York: Oxford University Press.

Merikangas, K. R., Ames, M., Cui, L., Stang, P. E., Ustun, T. B., VonKorff, M., & Kessler, R. C. (2007). The impact of comorbidity of mental and physical conditions on role disability in the US adult household population. *Archives of General Psychiatry, 64,* 1180–1188.

Messer, S. B., & McWilliams, N. (2003). The impact of Sigmund Freud and *The Interpretation of Dreams.* In R. J. Sternberg (Ed.), *The anatomy of impact: What makes the great works of psychology great* (pp. 71–88). Washington, DC: American Psychological Association.

Messner, M., Reinhard, M., & Sporer, S. (2008). Compliance through direct persuasive appeals: The moderating role of communicator's attractiveness in interpersonal persuasion. *Social Influence, 3,* 67–83.

Meyer, I., & Ladewig, J. (2008). The relationship between number of training sessions per week and learning in dogs. *Applied Animal Behaviour Science, 111,* 311–320.

Meyer, R. G., & Osborne, Y. V. H. (1987). *Case studies in abnormal behavior* (2nd ed.). Boston: Allyn & Bacon.

Meyer-Bahlburg, H. (1997). The role of prenatal estrogens in sexual orientation. In L. Ellis & L. Ebertz (Eds.), *Sexual orientation: Toward biological understanding.* Westport, CT: Praeger.

Meyerowitz, J. (2004). *How sex changed: A history of transsexuality in the United States.* Cambridge, MA: Harvard University Press.

Meyers-Levy, J., & Zhu, R. (2007) The influence of ceiling height: The effect of priming on the type of processing that people use. *Journal of Consumer Research, 34,* 174–186.

Mialet, J. P., Pope, H. G., & Yurgelun, T. D. (1996). Impaired attention in depressive states: A non-specific deficit? *Psychological Medicine, 26(5),* 1009–1020.

Michael, R. T., Gagnon, J. H., Laumann, E. O., & Kolata, G. (1994). *Sex in America: A definitive survey.* Boston: Little, Brown.

Midanik, L. T., Tam, T. W., & Weisner, C. (2007). Concurrent and simultaneous drug and alcohol use: Results of the 2000 national alcohol survey. *Drug and Alcohol Dependence, 90,* 72–80.

Middlebrooks, J. C., Furukawa, S., Stecker, G. C., & Mickey, B. J. (2005). Distributed representation of sound-source location in the auditory cortex. In R. König, P. Heil, E. Budinger, & H. Scheich (Eds.), *Auditory cortex: A synthesis of human and animal research.* Mahwah, NJ: Lawrence Erlbaum Associates.

Mifflin, L. (1998, January 14). Study finds a decline in TV network violence. *The New York Times,* A14.

Mignon, A., & Mollaret, P. (2002). Applying the affordance conception of traits: A person perception study. *Personality and Social Psychology Bulletin, 28,* 1327–1334.

Mika, V. S., Wood, P. R., Weiss, B. D., & Trevino, L. (2007). Ask Me 3: Improving communication in a Hispanic pediatric outpatient practice. *American Journal of Behavioral Health, 31,* S115–S121.

Miklowitz, D. J., & Thompson, M. C. (2003). Family variables and interventions in schizophrenia. In G. Sholevar & G. Pirooz (Eds.), *Textbook of family and couples therapy: Clinical applications* (pp. 585–617). Washington, DC: American Psychiatric Publishing.

Mikulincer, M., & Shaver, P. R. (2005). Attachment security, compassion, and altruism. *Current Directions in Psychological Science, 14,* 34–38.

Miletic, M. P. (2002). The introduction of a feminine psychology to psychoanalysis: Karen Horney's legacy [Special issue: Interpersonal psychoanalysis and feminism]. *Contemporary Psychoanalysis, 38,* 287–299.

Milgram, S. (1963, October). Behavioral Study of obedience. *The Journal of Abnormal and Social Psychology, 67(4),* 371–378.

Milgram, S. (1974). *Obedience to authority: An experimental view.* New York: Harper & Row.

Milgram, S. (2005). *Obedience to authority.* Pinter & Martin: New York.

Millar, M. (2002). Effects of guilt induction and guilt reduction on door-in-the-face. *Communication Research, 29,* 666–680.

Miller, D. W. (2000, February 25). Looking askance at eyewitness testimony. *The Chronicle of Higher Education,* pp. A19–A20.

Miller, G. (2006a). A spoonful of medicine—and a steady diet of normalcy. *Science, 311,* 464–465.

Miller, G. (2006b). China: Healing the metaphorical heart. *Science, 311,* 462–463.

Miller, G. A. (1956). The magical number seven, plus or minus two: Some limits on our capacity for processing information. *Psychology Review, 63,* 81–97.

Miller, G. F., & Penke, L. (2007). The evolution of human intelligence and the coefficient of additive genetic variance in human brain size. *Intelligence, 35,* 97–114.

Miller, J. (1984, May). Culture and the development of everyday social explanation. *Journal of Personality and Social Psychology, 46(5),* 961–978.

Miller, J. A., & Leffard, S. A. (2007). Behavioral assessment. In S. R. Smith & L. Handler, *The clinical assessment of children and adolescents: A practitioner's handbook.* Mahwah, NJ: Lawrence Erlbaum Associates.

Miller, J. G. (1984). Culture and the development of everyday social explanation. *Journal of Personality and Social Psychology, 46,* 961–978.

Miller, L., Gur, M., Shanok, A., & Weissman, M. (2008). Interpersonal psychotherapy with pregnant adolescents: Two pilot studies. *Journal of Child Psychology and Psychiatry, 49,* 733–742.

Miller, L. A., Taber, K. H., Gabbard, G. O., Hurley, R. A. (2005). Neural underpinnings of fear and its modulation: Implications for anxiety disorders. *Journal of Neuropsychiatry and Clinical Neurosciences, 17,* 1–6.

Miller, M. (2005). *Divergent effects of laughter and mental stress on endothelial function: Potential impact of entertainment.* Paper presented at the 54th Annual Scientific Session of the American College of Cardiology, Orlando, Florida.

Miller, M. N., & Pumariega, A. J. (2001). Culture and eating disorders: A historical and cross-cultural review. *Psychiatry: Interpersonal and Biological Processes, 64,* 93–110.

Miller, N. E., & Magruder, K. M. (Eds.). (1999). *Cost-effectiveness of psychotherapy: A guide for practitioners, researchers, and policymakers.* New York: Oxford University Press.

Miller, W. R., & Thoresen, C. E. (2003). Spirituality, religion, and health: An emerging research field. *American Psychologist, 58,* 24–35.

Miller-Jones, D. (1991). Informal reasoning in inner-city children. In J. F. Voss & D. N. Perkins (Eds.), *Informal reasoning and education.* Hillsdale, NJ: Lawrence Erlbaum.

Miller-Perrin, C., Perrin, R., & Kocur, J. (2009). Parental physical and psychological aggression: Psychological symptoms in young adults. *Child Abuse & Neglect, 33,* 1–11.

Milling, L., Chau, P., & Mills-Baxter, M. (2006). A Review of Psychopathology. *Your practicum in psychology: A guide for maximizing knowledge and competence* (pp. 105–127). Washington, DC: American Psychological Association.

Millner, D. (April, 2007). Little mean girls. *Parenting, 21,* 47.

Millon, T., & Davis, R. O. (1996). *Disorders of personality: DSM-IV and beyond* (2nd ed.). New York: Wiley.

Millon, T., Davis, R., & Millon, C. (2000). *Personality disorders in modern life.* New York: Wiley.

Millon, T., Simonsen, E., Birket-Smith, M., & Davis, R. (1998). *Psychopathy: Antisocial, criminal, and violent behavior.* New York: Guilford Press.

Milner, B. (1966). Amnesia following operation on temporal lobes. In C. W. M. Whitty & P. Zangwill (Eds.), *Amnesia.* London: Butterworth.

Milner, B. (2005). The medial temporal-lobe amnesic syndrome. *Psychiatric Clinics of North America, 28,* 599–611.

Miltenberger, R. (2008). Behavior modification. *Handbook of clinical psychology: Children and adolescents* (Vol. 2) (pp. 626–652). Hoboken, NJ: John Wiley & Sons Inc.

Milton, J., & Wiseman, R. (1999). Does psi exist? Lack of replication of an anomalous process of information transfer. *Psychological Bulletin, 125,* 387–391.

Milyavskaya, M., & Koestner, R. (2011). Psychological needs, motivation, and well-being: A test of self-determination theory across multiple domains. *Personality and Individual Differences, 50,* 387–391.

Miner, J., & Clarke-Stewart, K. (2008). Trajectories of externalizing behavior from age 2 to age 9: Relations with gender, temperament, ethnicity, parenting, and rater. *Developmental Psychology, 44,* 771–786.

Miner-Rubino, K., Winter, D. G., & Stewart, A. J. (2004). Gender, social class, and the subjective experience of aging: Self-perceived personality change from early adulthood to late midlife. *Personality and Social Psychology Bulletin, 30,* 1599–1610.

Mintle, L. (2011). To eat or not to eat: Eating disorders. In C. Franklin, R. Fong et al. (Eds.), *The church leader's counseling resource book: A guide to mental health and social problems.* New York: Oxford University Press.

Minuchin, S. (1999). Retelling, reimagining, and re-searching: A continuing conversation. *Journal of Marital and Family Therapy, 25,* 9–14.

Miquel, J. (2006). Integración de teorías del envejecimiento (parte I). Integration of theories of ageing. *Revista Espanola de Geriatria y Gerontologia, 41,* 55–63.

Mischel, W. (2004). Toward an integrative science of the person. *Annual Review of Psychology, 55,* 1–22.

Mischel, W. (2009). From Personality and Assessment (1968) to Personality Science, 2009. *Journal of Research in Personality, 43,* 282–290.

Miserando, M. (1991). Memory and the seven dwarfs. *Teaching of Psychology, 18,* 169–171.

Mitchell, D. B., & Schmitt, F. A. (2006). Short-and long-term implicit memory in aging and Alzheimer's disease. *Neuropsychological Development and Cognition, B, Aging and Neuropsychological Cognition, 13,* 611–635.

Mitte, K. (2005). Meta-analysis of cognitive-behavioral treatments for generalized anxiety disorder: A comparison with pharmacotherapy. *Psychological Bulletin, 131,* 785–795.

Moffitt, T. E., & Caspi, A. (2007). Evidence from behavioral genetics for environmental contributions to antisocial conduct. In J. E. Grusec, & P. D. Hastings, *Handbook of socialization: Theory and research.* New York: Guilford Press.

Moffitt, T. E., Caspi, A., & Rutter, M. (2006). Measured gene-environment interactions in psychopathology: Concepts, research strategies, and implications for research, intervention, and public understanding of genetics. *Perspectives on Psychological Science, 1,* 5–27.

Moghaddam, F. M. (2007). The staircase to terrorism: A psychological exploration. Psychological aspects of suicide terrorism. In B. Bongar, L. M. Brown, & L. E. Beutler, *Psychology of terrorism.* New York: Oxford University Press.

Mohapel, P., Leanza, G., Kokaia, M., & Lindvall, O. (2005). Forebrain acetylcholine regulates adult hippo-campal neurogenesis and learning. *Neurobiology of Aging, 26,* 939–946.

Moher, C., Gould, D., Hegg, E., & Mahoney, A. (2008). Non-generalized and generalized conditioned reinforcers: Establishment and validation. *Behavioral Interventions, 23,* 13–38.

Mokdad, A. H., Brewer, R. D., & Naimi, T. (2007). Binge drinking is a problem that cannot be ignored. *Preventive Medicine: An International Journal Devoted to Practice and Theory, 44,* 303–304.

Mol, M., Carpay, M., Ramakers, I., Rozendaal, N., Verhey, F., & Jolles, J. (2007, May). The effect of perceived forgetfulness on quality of life in older adults: A qualitative review. *International Journal of Geriatric Psychiatry, 22(5),* 393–400.

Montgomery, C., Fisk, J. E., Newcombe, R., Wareing, M., & Murphy, P. N. (2005). Syllogistic reasoning performance in MDMA (Ecstasy) users. *Experimental and Clinical Psychopharmacology, 13,* 137–145.

Montgomery, S. (2006). Serotonin noradrenaline reuptake inhibitors: Logical evolution of antidepressant development. *International Journal of Psychiatry in Clinical Practice, 10,* 5–11.

Montoya, R., & Insko, C. (2008). Toward a more complete understanding of the reciprocity of liking effect. *European Journal of Social Psychology, 38,* 477–498.

Moody, H. R. (2000). *Aging: Concepts and controversies.* Thousand Oaks, CA: Sage.

Mooney, S. M., & Varlinskaya, E. I. (2011). Acute prenatal exposure to ethanol and social behavior: Effects of age, sex, and timing of exposure. *Behavioural Brain Research, 216*, 358–364.

Moore, D., Aveyard, P., Connock, M., Wang, D., Fry-Smith, A., & Barton, P. (2009, April). Effectiveness and safety of nicotine replacement therapy assisted reduction to stop smoking: Systematic review and meta-analysis. *BMJ: British Medical Journal, 338*(7699), 1–9.

Moore, D. G., Goodwin, J. E., & George, R. (2007). Infants perceive human point-light displays as solid forms. *Cognition, 104*, 377–396.

Moore, M. M. (2002). Behavioral observation. In M. W. Wiederman & B. E. Whitley (Eds.), *Handbook for conducting research on human sexuality* Mahwah, NJ: Lawrence Erlbaum.

Moorey, J., Davidson, K., Evans, M., & Feigenbaum, J. (2006). Psychological therapies for personality disorder. *Personality disorder and community mental health teams: A practitioner's guide* (pp. 91–123). New York: John Wiley & Sons Ltd.

Moorey, S. (2007). Cognitive therapy. In W. Dryden, *Dryden's handbook of individual therapy* (5th ed.). Thousand Oaks, CA: Sage Publications.

Morad, Y., Barkana, Y., Zadok, D., Hartstein, M., Pras, E., & Bar-Dayan, Y. (2009, July). Ocular parameters as an objective tool for the assessment of truck drivers fatigue. *Accident Analysis and Prevention, 41*, 856–860.

Mora-Giral, M., Raich-Escursell, R. M., Segues, C.V., Torras-Claras, A. J., & Huon, G. (2004). Bulimia symptoms and risk factors in university students. *Eating and Weight Disorders, 9*, 163–169.

Moretz, M., & McKay, D. (2009). The role of perfectionism in obsessive-compulsive symptoms: "Not just right" experiences and checking compulsions. *Journal of Anxiety Disorders, 23*, 640–644.

Morgan, A. A., Marsiske, M., & Whitfield, K. E. (2008). Characterizing and explaining differences in cognitive test performance between African American and European American older adults. *Experimental Aging Research, 34*, 80–100.

Morley, K., Lynskey, M., Madden, P., Treloar, S., Heath, A., & Martin, N. (2007, September). Exploring the inter-relationship of smoking age-at-onset, cigarette consumption and smoking persistence: Genes or environment?. *Psychological Medicine, 37*(9), 1357–1367.

Morone, N. E., & Greco, C. M. (2007). Mind-body interventions for chronic pain in older adults: A structured review. *Pain Medicine, 8*, 359–375.

Morris, J. F., Waldo, C. R., & Rothblum, E. D. (2001). A model of predictors and outcomes of outness among lesbian and bisexual women. *American Journal of Orthopsychiatry, 71*, 61–71.

Morrissey, S. (2006, March 12). Microbe-busting bandages. *Time*.

Morrone, A. S., & Pintrich, P. R. (2006). Achievement motivation. In G. G. Bear & K. M. Minke, *Children's needs III: Development, prevention, and intervention*. Washington, DC: National Association of School Psychologists.

Morrow, J., & Wolff, R. (1991, May). Wired for a miracle. *Health*, 64–84.

Mosher, C. J., & Akins, S. (2007). *Drugs and drug policy: The control of consciousness alteration*. Thousand Oaks, CA: Sage Publications.

Moshman, D. (2011). *Adolescent rationality and development: Cognition, morality, and identity* (3rd ed.). New York: Psychology Press.

Moskowitz, G. B. (2004). *Social cognition: Understanding self and others*. New York: Guilford Press.

Motley, M. T. (1987, February). What I meant to say. *Psychology Today*, 25–28.

Muammar, O. M. (2007). An integration of two competing models to explain practical intelligence. *Dissertation Abstracts International: Section B: The Sciences and Engineering, 67*(7-B), 4128.

Mueller, C. E. (2009). Protective factors as barriers to depression in gifted and non-gifted adolescents. *Gifted Child Quarterly, 53*, 3–14.

Mueser, K., Salyers, M., and Mueser, P. (2001). A prospective analysis of work in schizophrenia. *Schizophrenia Bulletin, 27*, 281–296.

Mullen, B., & Rice, D. R. (2003). Ethnophaulisms and exclusion: The behavioral consequences of cognitive representation of ethnic immigrant groups. *Personality and Social Psychology Bulletin, 29*, 1056–1067.

Munakata, Y. (2006). Information processing approaches to development. In D. Kuhn, R. S. Siegler, W. Damon, & R. M. Lerner, *Handbook of child psychology: Cognition, perception, and language* (Vol. 2) (6th ed.). Hoboken, NJ: John Wiley & Sons.

Munger, D. (2009, April 20). Super-recognizers: people with an amazing ability to recognize faces. Retrieved from http://scienceblogs.com/cognitivedaily/2009/04/super-recognizers_people_with.php.

Murphy, E., Clegg, J., & Almack, K. (2011). Constructing adulthood in discussions about the futures of young people with moderate-profound intellectual disabilities. *Journal of Applied Research in Intellectual Disabilities, 24*, 61–73.

Murphy, G. (2004). The big book of concepts: Cambridge, MA: MIT Press.

Murphy, G. J., Glickfield, L. L., Balsen, Z., & Isaacson, J. S. (2004). Sensory neuron signaling to the brain: Properties of transmitter release from olfactory nerve terminals. *Journal of Neuroscience, 24*, 3023–3030.

Murphy, G. L. (2005). The study of concepts inside and outside the laboratory: Medin versus Medin. In W. Ahn, R. L. Goldstone,B. C. Love, A. B. Markman, & P. Wolff (Eds.), *Categorization inside and outside the laboratory: Essays in honor of Douglas L. Medin*. Washington, DC: American Psychological Association.

Murphy, R. T., Wismar, K., & Freeman, K. (2003). Stress symptoms among African-American college students after the September 11, 2001 terrorist attacks. *Journal of Nervous and Mental Disease, 191*, 108–114.

Murphy, S. T., & Zajonc, R. B. (1993). Affect, cognition, and awareness: Affective priming with optimal and suboptimal stimulus exposures. *Journal of Personality and Social Psychology, 64*, 723–739.

Murphy, S., et al. (1998). Interference under the influence. *Personality and Social Psychology Bulletin, 24*, 517–528.

Murray, R., Lappin, J., & Di Forti, M. (2008, August). Schizophrenia: From developmental deviance to dopamine dysregulation. *European Neuropsychopharmacology, 18*, S129–SS134.

Murray, S. L., Holmes, J. G., & Griffin, D. W. (2004). The benefits of positive illusions: Idealization and the construction of satisfaction in close relationships. In H. T. Reis & C. E. Rusbult (Eds.), *Close relationships: Key readings*. Philadelphia: Taylor & Francis.

Murthy, P., Kudlur, S., George, S., & Mathew, G. (2009). A clinical overview of fetal alcohol syndrome. *Addictive Disorders & Their Treatment, 8*(1), 1–12.

Myers, D. G. (2000). The funds, friends, and faith of happy people. *American Psychologist, 55*, 56–67.

Myers, D. G., & Diener, E. (1995, May). The pursuit of happiness: New research uncovers some anti-intuitive insights into how many people are happy—and why. *Scientific American*, pp. 70–72.

Myers, D., & Diener, E. (1995, January). Who is happy? *Psychological Science, 6*(1), 10–19.

Myers, L. L. (2007). Anorexia nervosa, bulimia nervosa, and binge eating disorder. In B. A. Thyer & J. S. Wodarski. *Social work in mental health: An evidence-based approach*. Hoboken, NJ: John Wiley & Sons.

Myerson, J., Adams, D. R., Hale, S., & Jenkins, L. (2003). Analysis of group differences in processing speed: Brinley plots, Q-Q plots, and other conspiracies. *Psychonomic Bulletin and Review, 10*, 224–237.

Myrtek, M. (2007). Type a behavior and hostility as independent risk factors for coronary heart disease. In J. Jordan, B. Barde, & A. M. Zeiher, *Contributions toward evidence-based psychocardiology: A systematic review of the literature*. Washington, DC: American Psychological Association.

Mytinger, C. (2001). *Headhunting in the Solomon Islands: Around the Coral Sea*. Santa Barbara, CA: Narrative Press.

N

Nadeem, E., & Graham, S. (2005). Early puberty, peer victimization, and internalizing symptoms in ethnic minority adolescents. *Journal of Early Adolescence, 25*, 197–222.

Nagai, Y., Goldstein, L. H., Fenwick, P. B. C., & Trimble, M. R. (2004). Clinical efficacy of galvanic skin response biofeedback training in reducing seizures in adult epilepsy: A preliminary randomized controlled study. *Epilepsy and Behavior, 5*, 216–223.

Nagda, B. A., Tropp, L. R., & Paluck, E. L. (2006). Looking back as we look ahead: Integrating research, theory, and practice on intergroup relations. *Journal of Social Research, 62*, 439–451.

Nagel, K., & Jones, K. (1992, Spr). Sociological factors in the development of eating disorders. *Adolescence, 27*(105), 107–113.

Nagy, T. F. (2011). *Essential ethics for psychologists: A primer for understanding and mastering core issues*. Washington, DC: American Psychological Association.

Naik, G. (2004, December 29). New obesity boom in Arab countries has old ancestry. *The Wall Street Journal*, p. A1.

Najman, J. M., Aird, R., Bor, W., O'Callaghan, M., Williams, G. M., & Shuttlewood, G. J. (2004). The generational transmission of socioeconomic inequalities in child cognitive development and emotional health. *Social Science and Medicine, 58*, 1147–1158.

Nakamura, Y. (2004). Isolation of p53-target genes and their functional analysis. *Cancer Science, 95*, 7–11.

Nakato, E., Otsuka, Y., Kanazawa, S., Yamaguchi, M. K., & Kakigi, R. (2011). Distinct differences in the pattern of hemodynamic response to happy and angry facial expressions in infants—A near-infrared spectroscopic study. *NeuroImage, 54*, 1600–1606.

Narrow, W. E., Rae, D. S., Robins, L. N., & Regier, D. A. (2002). Revised prevalence estimates of mental disorders in the United States: Using a clinical significance criterion to reconcile 2 surveys' estimates. *Archives of General Psychiatry, 59*, 115–123.

Nasir, N. S., & Hand, V. M. (2006). Exploring sociocultural perspectives on race, culture, and learning. *Review of Educational Research, 76*, 449–475.

Nasrallah, H., Black, D., Goldberg, J., Muzina, D., & Pariser, S. (2008). Issues associated with the use of atypical antipsychotic medications. *Annals of Clinical Psychiatry, 20*, S24–S29.

Nathan, P. E., Stuart, S. P., & Dolan, S. L. (2000). Research on psychotherapy efficacy and effectiveness: Between Scylla and Charybdis? *Psychological Bulletin, 126*, 964–981.

National Academy of Sciences (1999). *Marijuana and medicine: Assessing the science base*. Washington, DC: National Academy Press.

National Adolescent Health Information Center. (2003). *Fact Sheet on Demographics: Adolescents*. San Francisco, CA: University of California, San Francisco.

National Association for the Education of Young Children. (2005). *Position statements of the NAEYC*. http://www.naeyc.org/about/positions.asp#where.

National Institute of Mental Health. (2007). National survey tracks prevalence of personality disorders in U.S. population. http://www.nimh.nih.gov/science-news/2007/national-survey-tracks-prevalence-of-personality-disorders-in-us-population.shtml.

National Institute on Drug Abuse. (2000). *Principles of drug addiction treatment: A research-based guide.* Washington, DC: National Institute on Drug Abuse.

Natvig, G. K., Albrektsen, G., & Ovarnstrøm, U. (2003a). Methods of teaching and class participation in relation to perceived social support and stress: Modifiable factors for improving health and well-being among students. *Educational Psychology, 23,* 261–274.

Natvig, G. K., Albrektsen, G., & Qvamstrøm, U. (2003b). Associations between psychosocial factors and happiness among school adolescents. *International Journal of Nursing Practice, 9,* 166–175.

Naveh-Benjamin, M., Guez, J., & Sorek, S. (2007). The effects of divided attention on encoding processes in memory: Mapping the locus of interference. *Canadian Journal of Experimental Psychology, 61,* 1–12.

Nebenzahl, D. (2007, January 27). Creativity works: An environment that fosters creativity is more productive than a workplace plagued with a negative atmosphere. *The Gazette (Montreal),* p. G1.

Neber, H., & Heller, K. A. (2002). Evaluation of a summer-school program for highly gifted secondary-school students: The German Pupils Academy. *European Journal of Psychological Assessment, 18,* 214–228.

Nęcka, E., & Orzechowski, J. (2005). Higher-order cognition and intelligence. *Cognition and intelligence: Identifying the mechanisms of the mind* (pp. 122–141). New York: Cambridge University Press.

Neighbors, C., Lee, C., Lewis, M., Fossos, N., & Larimer, M. (2007). Are social norms the best predictor of outcomes among heavy-drinking college students? *Journal of Studies on Alcohol and Drugs, 68,* 556–565.

Neitz, J., Neitz, M., & Kainz, P. M. (1996, November 1). Visual pigment gene structure and the severity of color vision defects. *Science, 274,* 801–804.

Nelson, C., Morse, P., & Leavitt, L. (1979, December). Recognition of facial expressions by seven-month-old infants. *Child Development, 50*(4), 1239–1242.

Nelson, P. D. (2007). The globalization of psychology: What does it mean? *The Educator, 5,* 1–4.

Nelson, W. M., III, & Finch, A. J., Jr. (2000). Managing anger in youth: A cognitive-behavioral intervention approach. In P. C. Kendall, *Child & adolescent therapy: Cognitive-behavioral procedures* (2nd ed.). New York: Guilford Press.

Neron, S., & Stephenson, R. (2007). Effectiveness of hypnotherapy with cancer patients' trajectory: Emesis, acute pain, and analgesia and anxiolysis in procedures. *International Journal of Clinical Experimental Hypnosis, 55,* 336–354.

Nesdale, D., Maass, A., & Durkin, K. (2005). Group norms, threat, and children's racial prejudice. *Child Development, 76,* 652–663.

Nesheim, S., Henderson, S., Lindsay, M., Zuberi, J., Grimes, V., Buehler, J., Lindegren, M. L., & Bulterys, M. (2004). *Prenatal HIV testing and antiretroviral prophylaxis at an urban hospital— Atlanta, Georgia, 1997–2000.* Atlanta, GA: Centers for Disease Control.

Nesse, R. M. (2000). Is depression an adaptation? *Archives of General Psychiatry, 57,* 14–20.

Nestler, E. J. (2001, June 22). Total recall—the memory of addiction. *Science, 292,* 2266–2267.

Nestler, E. J., & Malenka, R. C. (2004, March). The addicted brain. *Scientific American,* pp. 78–83.

Nestoriuc, Y., & Martin, A. (2007, March). Efficacy of biofeedback for migraine: A meta-analysis. *Pain, 128,* 111–127.

Nestoriuc, Y., Martin, A., Rief, W., & Andrasik, F. (2008, September). Biofeedback treatment for headache disorders: A comprehensive efficacy review. *Applied Psychophysiology and Biofeedback, 33,* 125–140.

Neubauer, A. C., & Fink, A. (2005). Basic information processing and the psychophysiology of intelligence. In R. J. Sternberg & J. E. Pretz, *Cognition and intelligence: Identifying the mechanisms of the mind.* New York: Cambridge University Press.

Neuberg, S. (1989, March). The goal of forming accurate impressions during social interactions: Attenuating the impact of negative expectancies. *Journal of Personality and Social Psychology, 56*(3), 374–386.

Newby-Clark, I. R., & Ross, M. (2003). Conceiving the past and future. *Personality and Social Psychology Bulletin, 29,* 807–818.

Newell, A., & Simon, H. (1972). *Human problem solving.* Englewood Cliffs, NJ: Prentice Hall.

Newman, C. F., Leahy, R. L., Beck, A. T., Reilly-Harrington, N. A., & Gyulai, L. (2002). *Bipolar disorder: A cognitive therapy approach.* Washington, DC: American Psychological Association.

Newport, F., & Carroll, J. (2002, November 27). Battle of the bulge: Majority of Americans want to lose weight. *Gallup News Service,* 1–9.

Niccols, A. (2007). Fetal alcohol syndrome and the developing socio-emotional brain. *Brain Cognition, 65,* 135–142.

Niccols, A. (2007, October). Fetal alcohol syndrome and the developing socio-emotional brain. *Brain and Cognition, 65*(1), 135–142.

NICHD Early Child Care Research Network. (1998). Early child care and self-control, compliance and problem behavior at twenty-four and thirty-six months. *Child Development, 69,* 1145–1170.

NICHD Early Child Care Research Network. (1999). Child care and mother-child interaction in the first three years of life. *Developmental Psychology, 35,* 1399–1413.

NICHD Early Child Care Research Network. (2000). Characteristics and quality of child care for toddlers and preschoolers. *Applied Developmental Science, 4,* 116–135.

NICHD Early Child Care Research Network. (2001). Child-care and family predictors of preschool attachment and stability from infancy. *Developmental Psychology, 37,* 847–862.

NICHD Early Child Care Research Network. (2002). The interaction of child care and family risk in relation to child development at 24 and 36 months. *Applied Developmental Science, 6,* 144–156.

NICHD Early Child Care Research Network. (2006). Infant-mother attachment: Risk and protection in relation to changing maternal caregiving quality over time. *Developmental Psychology, 42* (1), 38–58.

Nicholson, I. A. M. (2003). *Inventing personality: Gordon Allport and the science of selfhood.* Washington, DC: American Psychological Association.

Nicotine manipulation confirmed [Editorial]. (2007, January 27). *The New York Times.* http://www.nytimes.com/2007/01/23/opinion/23tue3.html.

Niedenthal, P. M. (2007, May 18). Embodying emotion. *Science, 316,* 1002–1005.

Nielsen, C., Staud, R., & Price, D. (2009, March). Individual differences in pain sensitivity: Measurement, causation, and consequences. *The Journal of Pain, 10,* 231–237.

Nielsen, C., Stubhaug, A., Price, D., Vassend, O., Czajkowski, N., & Harris, J. (2008, May). Individual differences in pain sensitivity: Genetic and environmental contributions. *Pain, 136,* 21–29.

Nielsen, S. L., Smart, D. W., Isakson, R. L., Worthen, V. E., Gregersen, A. T., & Lambert, M. J. (2004). The *Consumer Reports* effectiveness score: What did consumers report? *Journal of Counseling Psychology, 51,* 25–37.

Nigg, J. T., & Goldsmith, H. H. (1994). Genetics of personality disorders: Perspectives from personality and psychopathology research. *Psychological Bulletin, 115,* 346–380.

Nightmare frequency as a function of age, gender, and September 11, 2001: Findings from an internet questionnaire. *Dreaming, 16,* 145–158.

Nikles, C. D., II, Brecht, D. L., Klinger, E., & Bursell, A. L. (1998). The effects of current concern- and nonconcern-related waking suggestions on nocturnal dream content. *Journal of Personality and Social Psychology, 75,* 242–255.

Nilsson, H., Juslin, P., & Olsson, H. (2008). Exemplars in the mist: The cognitive substrate of the representativeness heuristic. *Scandinavian Journal of Psychology, 49,* 201–212.

Nimrod, G., & Kleiber, D. A. (2007). Reconsidering change and continuity in later life: Toward an innovation theory of successful aging. *International Journal of Human Development, 65,* 1–22.

Nisbett, R. (2003). *The geography of thought.* New York: Free Press.

Nisbett, R. E. (2007, December 9). All brains are the same color. *New York Times,* p. E11.

Nisbett, R. E. (2009, February). All brains are the same color. *Association for Psychological Science Observer, 22*(3), 20–21.

Nishida, M., Pearsall, J., Buckner, R., & Walker, M. (2009, May). REM sleep, prefrontal theta, and the consolidation of human emotional memory. *Cerebral Cortex, 19,* 1158–1166.

Nishino, S. (2007, June). Clinical and neurobiological aspects of narcolepsy. *Sleep Medicine, 8,* 373–399.

Nissle, S., & Bschor, T. (2002). Winning the jackpot and depression: Money cannot buy happiness. *International Journal of Psychiatry in Clinical Practice, 6,* 183–186.

Nittrouer, S., Lowenstein, J. H. (2007). Children's weighting strategies for word-final stop voicing are not explained by auditory sensitivities. *Journal of Speech, Language, and Hearing Research, 50,* 58–73.

Nivoli, A. A., Colom, F., Murru, A., Pacchiarotti, I., Castro-Loli, P., González-Pinto, A., et al. (2011). New treatment guidelines for acute bipolar depression: A systematic review. *Journal of Affective Disorders, 129,* 14–26.

Noble, H. B. (1999, March 12). New from the smoking wars: Success. *The New York Times,* pp. D1–D2.

Noice, T., & Noice, H. (2002, April). Very long-term recall and recognition of well-learned material. *Applied Cognitive Psychology, 16*(3), 259–272.

Noland, R. W. (1999). *Sigmund Freud revisited.* New York: Twayne Publishers.

Nolen-Hoeksema, S. (2007). *Abnormal psychology* (4th ed.). New York: McGraw-Hill.

Noller, P. (2006). Marital Relationships. *Close relationships: Functions, forms and processes* (pp. 67–88). Hove: Psychology Press/Taylor & Francis.

Norcia, A. M., Pei, F., Bonneh, Y., Hou, C., Sampath, V., & Pettet, M. W. (2005). Development of sensitivity to texture and contour information in the human infant. *Journal of Cognitive Neuroscience, 17,* 569–579.

Norcross, J. C. (2002). Empirically supported therapy relationships. In J. C. Norcross, *Psychotherapy relationships that work: Therapist contributions and responsiveness to patients.* New York: Oxford University Press.

Norcross, J. C., Beutler, L. E., & Levant, R. F. (2006). *Evidence-based practices in mental health: Debate and dialogue on the fundamental questions.* Washington, DC: American Psychological Association.

Norlander, T., Von Schedvin, H., & Archer, T. (2005). Thriving as a function of affective personality: Relation to personality factors, coping strategies and stress. *Anxiety, Stress & Coping: An International Journal, 18,* 105–116.

Norman, P. (2011). The theory of planned behavior and binge drinking among undergraduate students: Assessing the impact of habit strength. *Addictive Behaviors, 36,* 107–116.

Northwestern University (2009, May 20). Exposure to two languages carries far-reaching benefits. *ScienceDaily.* Retrieved August 11, 2009, from www.sciencedaily.com/releases/2009/05/090519172157.htm.

Norton, P. J., & Price, E. C. (2007). A meta-analytic review of adult cognitive-behavioral treatment outcome across the anxiety disorders. *Journal of Nervous and Mental Disease, 195,* 521–531.

Novick, D., Swartz, H., & Frank, E. (2010). Suicide attempts in bipolar I and bipolar II disorder: A review and meta-analysis of the evidence. *Bipolar Disorders, 12,* 1–9.

Novick, L., & Bassok, M. (2005). Problem Solving. *The Cambridge handbook of thinking and reasoning* (pp. 321–349). New York: Cambridge University Press.

Nowak, A., Vallacher, R., & Miller, M. (2003). Social influence and group dynamics. *Handbook of psychology: Personality and social psychology* (Vol. 5) (pp. 383–417). Hoboken, NJ: John Wiley & Sons Inc.

Noy, V. M. (2006). A psychoneuroimmunology program for Hispanic women with stage I—II breast cancer. *Dissertation Abstracts International: Section B: The Sciences and Engineering, 66(11–B),* 6287.

Noyes, R., Jr., Stuart, S. P., Langbehn, D. R., Happel, R. L., Longley, S. L., Muller, B. A., & Yagla, S. J. (2003). Test of an interpersonal model of hypochondriasis. *Psychosomatic Medicine, 65,* 292–300.

Ntinas, K. M. (2007). Behavior modification and the principle of normalization: Clash or synthesis? *Behavioral Interventions, 22,* 165–177.

Nucci, L. P. (2002). The development of moral reasoning. In U. Goswami (Ed.), *Blackwell handbook of childhood cognitive development. Blackwell Handbooks of developmental psychology* (pp. 303–325). Malden, MA: Blackwell.

Nunes, A., & Kramer, A. F. (2009). Experience-based mitigation of age-related performance declines: Evidence from air traffic control, Journal of Experimental Psychology: Applied (Vol. 15, No. 1), www.apa.org/journals/releases/xap15112.pdf.

Nunes, J., Carr, J., & Sawchuk, C. (2007). Learning processes. *The behavioral sciences and health care* (2nd rev. and updated ed.) (pp. 63–72). Ashland, OH: Hogrefe & Huber Publishers.

Nurnberger, J. I., Jr., & Bierut, L. J. (2007, April). Seeking the connections: Alcoholism and our genes. *Scientific American,* pp. 46–53.

Nusbaum, E. C., & Silvia, P. J. (2011). Are intelligence and creativity really so different? Fluid intelligence, executive processes, and strategy use in divergent thinking. *Intelligence, 39,* 36–45.

Nussbaum, A. D. & Steele, C. M. (2007). Situational disengagement and persistence in the face of adversity. *Journal of Experimental Social Psychology, 43,* 127–134.

Nyberg, L., & Tulving, E. (1996). Classifying human long-term memory: Evidence from converging dissociations. *European Journal of Cognitive Psychology, 8,* 163–183.

O

O'Brien, K. M., & LeBow, M. D. (2007). Reducing maladaptive weight management practices: Developing a psychoeducational intervention program. *Eating Behaviors, 8,* 195–210. Occhionero, M. (2004). Mental processes and the brain during dreams. *Dreaming, 14,* 54–64.

O'Connor, D. B., & O'Connor, R. C. (2004). Perceived changes in food intake in response to stress: The role of conscientiousness. *Stress and Health: Journal of the International Society for the Investigation of Stress, 20,* 279–291.

O'Hair, D., Thompson, S. R., & Sparks, L. (2005). Negotiating cancer care through communication. In E. B. Ray, Ed., *Health communication in practice: A case study approach.* Mahwah, NJ: Lawrence Erlbaum Associates.

O'Keefe, T., & Fox, K. (Eds.). (2003). *Finding the real me: True tales of sex and gender diversity.* San Francisco: Jossey-Bass.

O'Malley, P., and Johnston, L. (2002). Epidemiology of alcohol and other drug use among American college students. *Journal of Studies on Alcohol, 14,* 23–39.

Oatley, K., Keltner, D., & Jenkins, J. M. (2006). *Understand emotions.* Blackwell.

Oberauer, K. (2007). In search of the magic number. *Experimental Psychology, 54,* 245–246.

Oberman, L. M., Pineda, J. A., & Ramachandran, V. S. (2007). The human mirror neuron system: A link between action observation and social skills. *Social Cognitive and Affective Neuroscience, 2,* 62–66.

Oehman, A., & Mineka, S. (2003). The malicious serpent: Snakes as a prototypical stimulus for an evolved module of fear. *Current Directions in Psychological Science, 12,* 5–9.

Oei, N., Everaerd, W., Elzinga, B., van Well, S., & Bermond, B. (2006). Psychosocial stress impairs working memory at high loads: An association with cortisol levels and memory retrieval. *The International Journal on the Biology of Stress, 9,* 133–141.

Offer, D., Kaiz, M., Howard, K. I., & Bennett, E. S. (2000). The altering of reported experiences. *Journal of the American Academy of Child & Adolescent Psychiatry, 39,* 735–742.

Ogbu, J. (1992). Understanding cultural diversity and learning. *Educational Researcher, 21,* 5–14.

Ogbu, J. (2003). *Black American students in an affluent suburb.* Mahwah, NJ: Lawrence Erlbaum Associates.

Ogren, K., & Sandlund, M. (2007). Lobotomy at a state mental hospital in Sweden. A survey of patients operated on during the period 1947–1958. *Nordic Journal of Psychiatry, 61,* 355–362.

Ohara, K. (2007). The n-3 polyunsaturated fatty acid/dopamine hypothesis of schizophrenia. *Progress in Neuro-Psychopharmacology & Biological Psychiatry, 31,* 469–474.

Ohira, T., Hozawa, A., Iribarren, C., Daviglus, M. L., Matthews, K. A., Gross, M. D., & Jacobs, D. R., Jr. (2007). Longitudinal association of serum carotenoids and tocopherols with hostility: The CARDIA study. *American Journal of Epidemiology, 18,* 235–241.

Ojha, H., & Pramanick, M. (2009). Effects of age on intensity and priority of life needs. *Journal of the Indian Academy of Applied Psychology, 35,* 131–136.

Olds, M. E., & Fobes, J. L. (1981). The central basis of motivation: Intracranial self-stimulation studies. *Annual Review of Psychology, 32,* 123–129.

Olfson, M., & Marcus, S. (2008). A case-control study of antidepressants and attempted suicide during early phase treatment of major depressive episodes. *Journal of Clinical Psychiatry, 69,* 425–432.

Olijslagers, J. E., Werkman, T. R., & McCreary, A. C. (2006). Modulation of midbrain dopamine neurotransmission by serotonin, a versatile interaction between neurotransmitters and significance for antipsychotic drug action. *Current Neuropharmacology, 4,* 59–68.

Olivardia, R., & Pope, H. (2002). Body image disturbance in childhood and adolescence. In D. Castle & K. Phillips (Eds.), *Disorders of body image.* Petersfield: Wrightson Biomedical Publishing.

Olivares-Olivares, P., Rosa-Alcázar, A., & Olivares-Rodríguez, J. (2008, May). Does individual attention improve the effect of group treatment of adolescents with social phobia? *International Journal of Clinical and Health Psychology, 8(2),* 465–481.

Oliver, M. B., & Hyde, J. S. (1993). Gender differences in sexuality: A meta-analysis. *Psychological Bulletin, 114,* 29–51.

Olson, D. (2006). Becoming responsible for who we are: The trouble with traits. *Howard Gardner under fire: The rebel psychologist faces his critics* (pp. 39–44). Chicago: Open Court Publishing.

Olson, D. H., & DeFrain, J. (2005). *Marriages and families: Intimacy, diversity, and strengths with PowerWeb.* New York: McGraw-Hill.

Olson, M. A., & Fazio, R. H. (2001). Implicit attitude formation through classical conditioning. *Psychological Science, 12,* 413–417.

Opler, M., Perrin, M., Kleinhaus, K., & Malaspina, D. (2008). Factors in the etiology of schizophrenia: Genes, parental age, and environment. *Primary Psychiatry, 15,* 37–45.

Oppenheimer, D. M. (2004). Spontaneous discounting of availability in frequency judgment tasks. *Psychological Science, 15,* 100–105.

Oren, D. A., & Terman, M. (1998, January 16). Tweaking the human circadian clock with light. *Science, 279,* 333–334.

Ornat, S., & Gallo, P. (2004). Acquisition, learning, or development of language? Skinner's "Verbal behavior" revisited. *Spanish Journal of Psychology, 7,* 161–170.

Orwin, R. G., & Condray, D. S. (1984). Smith and Glass' psychotherapy conclusions need further probing: On Landman and Dawes' re-analysis. *American Psychologist, 39,* 71–72.

Oskamp, S. (Ed.). (2000) *Reducing prejudice and discrimination.* Mahwah, NJ: Erlbaum.

Ost, J. (2006). Recovered memories. *Investigative interviewing: Rights, research, regulation* (pp. 259–291). Devon: Willan Publishing.

Otake, K., Shimai, S., & Tanaka-Matsumi, J. (2006). Happy people become happier through kindness: A counting kindnesses intervention. *Journal of Happiness Studies, 7,* 361–375.

Ouimet, A., Gawronski, B., & Dozois, D. (2009). Cognitive vulnerability to anxiety: A review and an integrative model. *Clinical Psychology Review, 29,* 459–470.

P

Pace, T. W., & Heim, C. M. (2011). A short review on the psychoneuroimmunology of posttraumatic stress disorder: From risk factors to medical comorbidities. *Brain, Behavior, and Immunity, 25,* 6–13.

Pachankis, J. E. & Goldfried, M. R. (2007). An integrative, principle-based approach to psychotherapy. In S. G. Hofmann & J. Weinberger (Eds.), *The art and science of psychotherapy.* New York: Routledge/Taylor & Francis Group.

Pagonis, T. A., Angelopoulos, N., & Koukoulis, G. N. (2006). Psychiatric side effects induced by supraphysiological doses of combinations of anabolic steroids correlate to the severity of abuse. *European Psychiatry, 21,* 551–562.

Pagoto, S. L., Kozak, A. T., & Spates, C. R (2006). Systematic desensitization for an older woman with a severe specific phobia: an application of evidenced-based practice. *Clinical Gerontologist, 30,* 89–98.

Paivio, A. (1971). *Imagery and verbal processes.* New York: Holt, Rinehart & Winston.

Palermo, G. B. (2006). Editorial: Those evil suicide bombers. *International Journal of Offender Therapy and Comparative Criminology, 50,* 119–120.

Pallanti, S., & Bernardi, S. (2009, July). Neurobiology of repeated transcranial magnetic stimulation in the treatment of anxiety: A critical review. *International Clinical Psychopharmacology, 24,* 163–173.

Palma, B., Tiba, P., Machado, R., Tufik, S., & Suchecki, D. (2007, May). Immune outcomes of sleep disorders: The hypothalamic-pituitary-adrenal axis as a modulatory factor. *Revista Brasileira de Psiquiatria, 29(1),* S33–S38.

Palmer, I. (2007). Terrorism, suicide bombing, fear and mental health. *International Review of Psychiatry, 19,* 289–296.

Pandit, S., Argyropoulos, S., & Nutt, D. (2001, March). Current status of anxiolytic drugs. *Primary Care Psychiatry, 7(1),* 1–5.

Pandya, M., Pozuelo, L., & Malone, D. (2007). Electroconvulsive therapy: What the internist needs to know. *Cleveland Clinic Journal of Medicine, 74,* 679–685.

Paniagua, F. A. (2000). *Diagnosis in a multicultural context: A casebook for mental health professionals.* Thousand Oaks, CA: Sage.

Papalia, D., Olds, S., & Feldman, R. (2007). *Human development* (10th ed.). New York: McGraw-Hill.

Paquette, D., Carbonneau, R., & Dubeau, D. (2003). Prevalence of father-child rough-and-tumble play and physical aggression in pre-school children. *European Journal of Psychology of Education, 18,* 171–189.

Paquier, P. F., & Mariën, P. (2005). A synthesis of the role of the cerebellum in cognition. *Aphasiology, 19,* 3–19.

Paris, J. (2000). Predispositions, personality traits, and posttraumatic stress disorder. *Harvard Review of Psychiatry, 8,* 175–183.

Parish, C. L., & Arenas, E. (2007). Stem-cell-based strategies for the treatment of Parkinson's disease. *Neurodegenerative Disease, 4,* 339–347.

Park, C. L., & Grant, C. (2005). Determinants of positive and negative consequences of alcohol consumption in college students: Alcohol use, gender, and psychological characteristics. *Addictive Behaviors, 30,* 755–765.

Park, D. C. (2007). Eating disorders: A call to arms. *American Psychologist, 62,* 158.

Park, H., & Antonioni, D. (2007). Personality, reciprocity, and strength of conflict resolution strategy. *Journal of Research in Personality, 41,* 110–125.

Park, S., Ko, C., Bae, H., Jung, W., Moon, S., Cho, K., et al. (2009). Short-term reactions to acupuncture treatment and adverse events following acupuncture: A cross-sectional survey of patient reports in Korea. *Journal of Alternative & Complementary Medicine, 15,* 1275–1283.

Park, W. W. (2000). A comprehensive empirical investigation of the relationships among variables of the group-think model. *Journal of Organizational Behavior, 21,* 873–887.

Parke, R. D. (2004). Development in the family. *Annual Review of Psychology, 55,* 365–399.

Parker, E. S., Cahill, L., & McGaugh, J. L. (2006). A case of unusual autobiographical remembering. *Neurocase, 12,* 35–49.

Parker-Pope, T. (2003, April 22). The diet that works. *The Wall Street Journal,* R1, R5.

Parmley, M. C. (2007). The effects of the confirmation bias on diagnostic decision making. *Dissertation Abstracts International: Section B: The Sciences and Engineering, 67*(8-B), 4719.

Parra, A., & Argibay, J. C. (2007). Comparing psychics and non-psychics through a 'token-object' forced-choice ESP test. *Journal of the Society for Psychical Research, 71,* 80–90.

Parrott, A. C. (2002). Recreational Ecstasy/MDMA, the serotonin syndrome, and serotonergic neurotoxicity [Special issue: Serotonin]. *Pharmacology, Biochemistry & Behavior, 71,* 837–844.

Parson, E. (1994). Post-traumatic stress disorder (PTSD): Its biopsychobehavioral aspects and management. *Anxiety and related disorders: A handbook* (pp. 226–285). Oxford, England: John Wiley & Sons.

Pary, R., Matuschka, P., Lewis, S., & Lippmann, S. (2006, February). Managing Bipolar Depression. *Psychiatry, 3*(2), 30–41.

Pascual, A., & Guéguen, N. (2005). Foot-in-the-door and door-in-the-face: A comparative meta-analytic study. *Psychological Reports, 96,* 122–128.

Pascual, A., & Guéguen, N. (2006). Door-in-the-face technique and monetary solicitation: An evaluation in a field setting. *Perceptual and Motor Skills, 103,* 974–978.

Pascual, M. A., & Rodriguez, M. A. (2006). Learning by operant conditioning as a nonlinear self-organized process. *Nonlinear Dynamics, Psychology, and Life Sciences, 10,* 341–364.

Pascual-Leone, A., et al. (1995). Modulation of muscle responses evoked by transcranial magnetic stimulation during the acquisition of new fine motor skills. *Journal of Neurophysiology 74,* 1037–1045.

Patterson, D. R. (2004). Treating pain with hypnosis. *Current Directions in Psychological Science, 13,* 252–255.

Paukert, A., Stagner, B., & Hope, K. (2004). The assessment of active listening skills in helpline volunteers. *Stress, Trauma, and Crisis: An International Journal, 7,* 61–76.

Paul, A. M. (2004). *Cult of personality: How personality tests are leading us to miseducate our children, mismanage our companies and misunderstand ourselves.* New York: Free Press.

Paulmann, S., Jessen, S., & Kotz, S. A. (2009). Investigating the multimodal nature of human communication: Insights from ERPs. *Journal of Psychophysiology, 23,* 63–76.

Paulozzi, L. J. (2006). Opioid analgesic involvement in drug abuse deaths in American metropolitan areas. *American Journal of Public Health, 96,* 1755–1757.

Pavitt, C. (2007). Impression formation. In B. B. Whaley & W. Samter, *Explaining communication: Contemporary theories and exemplars.* Mahwah, NJ: Lawrence Erlbaum Associates.

Pavlov, I. P. (1927). *Conditioned reflexes.* London: Oxford University Press.

Payne, D. G. (1986). Hyperamnesia for pictures and words: Testing the recall level hypothesis. *Journal of Experimental Psychology: Learning, Memory, and Cognition, 12,* 16–29.

Payne, K., & Marcus, D. (2008). The efficacy of group psychotherapy for older adult clients: A meta-analysis. *Group Dynamics: Theory, Research, and Practice, 12,* 268–278.

Pearce, J. M. S. (2007). Synaesthesia. *European Neurology, 57,* 120–124.

Pearlstein, T., & Steiner, M. (2008). Premenstrual dysphoric disorder: Burden of illness and treatment update. *Journal of Psychiatry & Neuroscience, 33,* 291–301.

Pearson, A. R., Dovidio, J. F., & Pratto, F. (2007). Racial prejudice, intergroup hate, and blatant and subtle bias of whites toward blacks in legal decision making in the United States. *International Journal of Psychology & Psychological Therapy, 7,* 125–134.

Pearson, J., & Clifford, C. W. G. (2005). When your brain decides what you see: Grouping across monocular, binocular, and stimulus rivalry. *Psychological Science, 16,* 516–519.

Pedersen, D. M. (2002). Intrinsic-extrinsic factors in sport motivation. *Perceptual & Motor Skills, 95,* 459–476.

Pedersen, P. B., Draguns, J. G., Lonner, W. J., & Trimble, J. E. (Eds.). (2002). *Counseling across cultures* (5th ed.). Thousand Oaks, CA: Sage.

Peiro, J. M., & Lunt, I. (2002). The context for a European framework for psychologists' training. *European Psychologist, 7,* 169–179.

Pell, M. D., Monetta, L., Paulmann, S., & Kotz, S. A. (2009). Recognizing emotions in a foreign language. *Journal of Nonverbal Behavior, 33,* 107–120.

Pellegrini, S., Muzio, R. N., Mustaca, A. E., & Papini, M. R. (2004). Successive negative contrast after partial reinforcement in the consummatory behavior of rats. *Learning and Motivation, 35,* 303–321.

Pelli, D. G., Burns, C. W., & Farell, B. (2006). Feature detection and letter identification. *Vision Research, 46,* 4646–4674.

Pellis, S. M. & Pellis, V. C. (2007). Rough-and-tumble play and the development of the social brain. *Current Directions in Psychological Science, 16,* 95–97.

Penley, J. A., Tomaka, J., & Wiebe, J. S. (2002). The association of coping to physical and psychological health outcomes: A meta-analytic review. *Journal of Behavioral Medicine, 25,* 551–603.

Penn, D. L., Corrigan, P. W., Bentall, R. P., Racenstein, J. M., & Newman, L. (1997). Social cognition in schizophrenia. *Psychological Bulletin, 121,* 114–132.

Penney, J. B., Jr. (2000). Neurochemistry. In B. S. Fogel, R. B. Schiffer, et al. (Eds.), *Synopsis of neuropsychiatry.* New York: Lippincott Williams & Wilkins.

Pennington, B. F. (2002). *The development of psychopathology: Nature and nurture.* New York: Guilford Press.

Pennington, B. F. (2003). Review of The Development of Psychopathology: Nature and Nurture. *American Journal of Orthopsychiatry, 73,* 235.

Pennington, D. (2003). *Essential personality.* London: Arnold.

Penzel, F. (2000). *Obsessive-compulsive disorders: A complete guide to getting well and staying well.* New York: Oxford University Press.

People. (2007, July 13). Love Stories You'll Never forget. *People,* p. 18.

People Weekly. (2000, May 8). Giant steps, p. 117.

Peretti-Watel, P., Halfen, S., & Grémy, I. (2007). Risk denial about smoking hazards and readiness to quit among French smokers: An exploratory study. *Addictive Behaviors, 32,* 377–383.

Perez, R. M., DeBord, K. A., & Bieschke, K. J. (Eds.). (2000). *Handbook of counseling and psychotherapy with lesbian, gay, and bisexual clients.* Washington, DC: American Psychological Association.

Perkins, K., Conklin, C., & Levine, M. (2008). *Cognitive-behavioral therapy for smoking cessation: A practical guidebook to the most effective treatments.* New York: Routledge/Taylor & Francis Group.

Perloff, R. M. (2003). *The dynamics of persuasion: Communication and attitudes in the 21st century* (2nd ed.). Mahwah, NJ: Erlbaum.

Perry, B. (2008, May 19). "I don't know how to forget." *People,* p. 143.

Perry, J., Felce, D., Allen, D., & Meek, A. (2011). Resettlement outcomes for people with severe challenging behaviour moving from institutional to community living. *Journal of Applied Research in Intellectual Disabilities, 24,* 1–17.

Pert, C. B. (2002). The wisdom of the receptors: Neuropeptides, the emotions, and body-mind. *Advances in Mind-Body Medicine, 18,* 30–35.

Pervin, L. A. (2003). *The science of personality* (2nd ed.). London: Oxford University Press.

Pesmen, C. (2006, March). Don't let pain get in your way. *Money,* p. 48.

Peters, E., Hess, T. M., Västfjäll, D., & Auman, C. (2007). Adult age differences in dual information processes. *Perspectives on Psychological Science, 2,* 1–23.

Peters, J., Suchan, B., Koster, O., & Daum, I. (2007). Domain-specific retrieval of source information in the medial temporal lobe. *European Journal of Neuroscience, 26,* 1333–1343.

Peterson, C. (2000). The future of optimism. *American Psychologist, 55,* 44–55.

Peterson, L. R., & Peterson, M. J. (1959). Short-term retention of individual items. *Journal of Experimental Psychology, 58,* 193–198.

Peterson, R. A., & Brown, S. P. (2005). On the use of beta coefficients in meta-analysis. *Journal of Applied Psychology, 90,* 175–181.

Petersson, K. M., Silva, C., Castro-Caldas, A., Ingvar, M., & Reis, A. (2007). Literacy: A cultural influence on functional left-right differences in the inferior parietal cortex. *European Journal of Neuroscience, 26,* 791–799.

Petrill, S. A. (2005). Introduction to this special issue: Genes, environment, and the development of reading skills. *Scientific Studies of Reading, 9,* 189–196.

Petrill, S. A., & Deater-Deckard, K. (2004). The heritability of general cognitive ability: A within-family adoption design. *Intelligence, 32,* 403–409.

Pettigrew, T. (2004). Racial Integration Today: Revisiting Kenneth B. Clark's Vision. In G. Philogene, (Ed), *Racial identity in context: The legacy of Kenneth B. Clark.* Washington, DC: American Psychological Association.

Pettigrew, T. F. (2004). Justice deferred: A half century after *Brown v. Board of Education. American Psychologist, 59,* 521–529.

Pettigrew, T. F., & L. R. Tropp. (2006). A meta-analytic test of intergroup contact theory. *Journal of Personality and Social Psychology, 90,* 751–783.

Pettingale, K. W., Morris, T., Greer, S., & Haybittle, J. L. (1985). Mental attitudes to cancer: An additional prognostic factor. *Lancet,* 750.

Pettito, L. A. (1993). On the ontogenetic requirements for early language acquisition. In B. de Boysson-Bardies, S. de Schonen, P. W. Jusczyk, P. McNeilage, & J. Morton (Eds.), *Developmental neurocognition: Speech and face processing in the first year of life. NATO ASI series D: Behavioural and social sciences* (Vol. 69). Dordrecht: Kluwer Academic.

Petty, R., Cacioppo, J., Strathman, A., & Priester, J. (1994). To think or not to think: Exploring two routes to persuasion. *Persuasion: Psychological insights and perspectives* (pp. 113–147). Needham Heights, MA: Allyn & Bacon.

Petty, R., Cacioppo, J. T., Strathman, A. J., & Priester, J. R. (2005). To think or not to think: Exploring two routes to persuasion. In T. C. Brock & M. C. Green (Eds.), *Persuasion: Psychological insights and perspectives* (2nd ed.). Thousand Oaks, CA: Sage Publications.

Pfeffer, C. R. (2006). An evolutionary perspective on childhood depression. In P. S. Jensen, P. Knapp, & D. A. Mrazek, *Toward a new diagnostic system for child psychopathology: Moving beyond the DSM*. New York: Guilford Press.

Phelps, R. P. (2005). *Defending standardized testing*. Mahwah, NJ: Lawrence Erlbaum Associates.

Philip, P., Sagaspe, P., Moore, N., Taillard, J., Charles, A., Guilleminault, C., & Bioulac, B. (2005). Fatigue, sleep restriction and driving performance. *Accident Analysis and Prevention, 37*, 473–478.

Piaget, J. (1970). Piaget's theory. In P. H. Mussen (Ed.), *Carmichael's manual of child psychology* (3rd ed.) (Vol. I). New York: Wiley.

Picchioni, D., Goeltzenleucher, B., Green, D. N., Convento, M. J., Crittenden, R., Hallgren, M., & Hick, R. A. (2002). Nightmares as a coping mechanism for stress. *Dreaming: Journal of the Association for the Study of Dreams, 12*, 155–169.

Pickel, K. (2009). The weapon focus effect on memory for female versus male perpetrators. *Memory, 17*, 664–678.

Pickering, G. J., & Gordon, R. (2006). Perception of mouthfeel sensations elicited by red wine are associated with sensitivity to 6-N-propylthiouracil. *Journal of Sensory Studies, 21*, 249–265.

Pickersgill, M. (2011). "Promising" therapies: Neuroscience, clinical practice, and the treatment of psychopathy. *Sociology of Health & Illness, 33*, 448–464.

Piechowski, M. M. (2003). From William James to Maslow and Dabrowski: Excitability of character and self-actualization. In D. Ambrose, L. M. Cohen, et al. (Eds.), *Creative intelligence: Toward theoretic integration: Perspectives on creativity* (pp. 283–322). Cresskill, NJ: Hampton Press.

Pietarinen, A-V. (2006). The evolution of semantics and language-games for meaning. *Interaction Studies: Social Behaviour and Communication in Biological and Artificial Systems, 7*, 79–104.

Pillay, S. S., Gruber, S. A., Rogowska, J., Simpson, N., & Yurgelun-Todd, D. A. (2006). fMRI of fearful facial affect recognition in panic disorder: the cingulate gyrus-amygdala connection.

Pillay, S. S., Rogowska, J., Gruber, S. A., Simpson, N., & Yurgelun-Todd, D. A. (2007). Recognition of happy facial affect in panic disorder: an fMRI study. *Journal of Anxiety Disorders, 21*, 381–393.

Pilotti, M., Chodorow, M., & Shono, Y. (2009). The benefits and costs of prior exposure: A large-scale study of interference effects in stimulus identification. *American Journal of Psychology, 122*, 191–208.

Pincemy, G., Dobson, F., & Jouventin, Pierre. (2010). Homosexual mating displays in penguins. *Ethology, 116*, 1210–1216.

Pincus, T., & Morley, S. (2001). Cognitive-processing bias in chronic pain: A review and integration. *Psychological Bulletin, 127*, 599–617.

Pineda, J. A., Giromini, L., Porcelli, P., Parolin, L., & Viglione, D. J. (2011). Mu suppression and human movement responses to the Rorschach test. *NeuroReport: For Rapid Communication of Neuroscience Research, 22*, 223–226.

Pinel, J. P. J., Assanand, S., & Lehman, D. R. (2000). Hunger, eating and ill health. *American Psychologist, 55*, 1105–1116.

Pinker, S. (1994). *The language instinct.* New York: William Morrow.

Pinker, S. (2002). *The blank slate: The modern denial of human nature.* New York: Viking.

Pinker, S. (2004). *How the mind works.* New York: Gardner Books.

Pinker, S., & Jackendoff, R. (2005). The faculty of language: What's special about it? *Cognition, 96*, 201–236.

Pinkerton, S. D., Bogart, L. M., Cecil, H., & Abramson, P. R. (2002). Factors associated with masturbation in a collegiate sample. *Journal of Psychology and Human Sexuality, 14*, 103–121.

Pinquart, M., Duberstein, P. R., & Lyness J. M. (2006). Treatments for later-life depressive conditions: a meta-analytic comparison of pharmacotherapy and psychotherapy. *American Journal of Psychiatry, 163*, 1493–1501.

Pinquart, M., & Sörensen, S. (2001, December). Influences on loneliness in older adults: A meta-analysis. *Basic and Applied Social Psychology, 23*(4), 245–266.

Pi-Sunyer, X. (2003). A clinical view of the obesity problem. *Science, 299*, 859–860.

Pitman, R. K., & Delahanty, D. L. (2005). Conceptually driven pharmacologic approaches to acute trauma. *CNS Spectrums, 10*, 99–106.

Platek, S., & Kemp, S. (2009, February). Is family special to the brain? An event-related fMRI study of familiar, familial, and self-face recognition. *Neuropsychologia, 47*, 849–858.

Plomin, R. (2003a). 50 years of DNA: What it has meant to psychological science. *American Psychological Society, 16*, 7–8.

Plomin, R. (2003b). General cognitive ability. In R. Pomin, J. C. DeFries, et al. (Eds.), *Behavioral genetics in the postgenomic era*. Washington, DC: American Psychological Association.

Plomin, R. (2009). The nature of nurture. In K. McCartney & R. A. Weinberg, (Eds.). *Experience and development: A festschrift in honor of Sandra Wood Scarr.* New York: Psychology Press.

Plomin, R., & Caspi, R. (1999). Behavioral genetics and personality. In L. A. Pervin & O. P. John (Eds.), *Handbook of personality: Theory and research.* (2nd ed.). New York: Guilford.

Plomin, R., & Davis, O. (2009, January). The future of genetics in psychology and psychiatry: Microarrays, genome-wide association, and non-coding RNA. *Journal of Child Psychology and Psychiatry, 50*, 63–71.

Plomin, R., DeFries, J. C., Craig, I. W., & McGuffin, P. (2003). *Behavioral genetics in the postgenomic era*. Washington, DC: American Psychological Association.

Plomin, R., & Kovas, Y. (2005). Generalist genes and learning disabilities. *Psychological Bulletin, 131*, 592–617.

Plomin, R., & McGuffin, P. (2003). Psychopathology in the postgenomic era. *Annual Review of Psychology, 54*, 205–228.

Plonczynski, D. J., & Plonczynski, K. J. (2007). Hormone therapy in perimenopausal and postmenopausal women: examining the evidence on cardiovascular disease risks. *Journal of Gerontological Nursing, 33*, 48–55.

Plous, S., & Herzog, H. A. (2000, October 27). Poll shows researchers favor lab animal protection. *Science, 290*, 711.

Plous, S., & Zimbardo, P. G. (2004, September 10). How social science can reduce terrorism. *The Chronicle of Higher Education*, B9–B10.

Plowright, C. M. S., Simonds, V. M., & Butler, M. A. (2006). How bumblebees first find flowers: Habituation of visual pattern preferences, spontaneous recovery, and dishabituation. *Learning and Motivation, 37*, 66–78.

Pogarsky, G., & Piquero, A. R. (2003). Can punishment encourage offending? Investigating the "resetting" effect. *Journal of Research in Crime and Delinquency, 40*, 95–120.

Pole, N. (2007). The psychophysiology of post-traumatic stress disorder: A meta-analysis. *Psychological Bulletin, 133*, 34–45.

Polivy, J., & Herman, C. P. (2002). Causes of eating disorders. *Annual Review of Psychology, 53*, 187–213.

Polivy, J., Herman, C. P., & Boivin, M. (2005). Eating disorders. In J. E. Maddux and B. A. Winstead, *Psychopathology: Foundations for a contemporary understanding* (pp. 229–254). Mahwah, NJ: Lawrence Erlbaum Associates.

Polk, N. (1997, March 30). The trouble with school testing systems. *The New York Times*, p. CN3.

Polonsky, D. C. (2006). Review of the big book of masturbation: From angst to zeal. *Journal of Sex & Marital Therapy, 32*, 75–78.

Pomerantz, E., & Wang, Q. (2009). The role of parental control in children's development in western and East Asian countries. *Current Directions in Psychological Science, 18*, 285–289.

Pomerlau, O. F. (1995). Individual differences in sensitivity to nicotine: Implications of genetic research on nicotine dependence [Special issue: Genetic, environmental, and situational factors mediating the effects of nicotine]. *Behavior Genetics, 25*, 161–177.

Ponterotto, J. G., Gretchen, D., & Chauhan, R. V. (2001). Cultural identity and multicultural assessment: Quantitative and qualitative tools for the clinician. In L. A. Suzuki, & J. G. Ponterotto (Eds.), *Handbook of multicultural assessment: Clinical, psychological, and educational applications* (2nd ed.). San Francisco: Jossey-Bass/Pfeiffer.

Ponterotto, J. G., Utsey, S. O., & Pedersen, P. B. (2006). *Preventing prejudice: A guide for counselors, educators, and parents*. Thousand Oaks, CA: Sage Publications.

Poo, C. & Isaacson, J. S. (2007). An early critical period for long-term plasticity and structural modification of sensory synapses in olfactory cortex. *Journal of Neuroscience, 27*, 7553–7558.

Popa, D., Léna, C., Alexandre, C., & Adrien, J. (2008). Lasting syndrome of depression produced by reduction in serotonin uptake during postnatal development: Evidence from sleep, stress, and behavior. *The Journal of Neuroscience, 28*, 88–97.

Porkka-Heiskanen, T., Strecker, R. E., Thakkar, M., Bjorkum, A. A., Greene, R. W., & McCarley, R. W. (1997, May 23). Adenosine: A mediator of the sleep-inducing effects of prolonged wakefulness. *Science, 276*, 1265–1268.

Porte, H. S., & Hobson, J. A. (1996). Physical motion in dreams: One measure of three theories. *Journal of Abnormal Psychology, 105*, 329–335.

Porter, C. L., & Hsu, H. C. (2003). First-time mothers' perceptions of efficacy during the transition to motherhood: Links to infant temperament. *Journal of Family Psychology, 17*, 54–64.

Porto, R. R. (2011). The placebo effect: Its importance in treatment. *Sexologies: European Journal of Sexology and Sexual Health/Revue européenne de sexologie et de santé sexuelle, 20*, 15–19.

Posner, M. I., & DiGirolamo, G. J. (2000). Cognitive neuroscience: Origins and promise. *Psychological Bulletin, 126*, 873–889.

Post, J. M. (2011). Crimes of obedience: "Groupthink" at Abu Ghraib. *International Journal of Group Psychotherapy, 61*, 49–66.

Pottick, K. J., Kirk, S. A., Hsieh, D. K., & Tian, X. (2007). Judging mental disorder in youths: Effects of client, clinician, and contextual differences. *Journal of Consulting Clinical Psychology, 75*, 1–8.

Povinelli, D. J., & Vonk, J. (2004). We don't need a microscope to explore the chimpanzee's mind. *Mind and Language, 19*, 1–28.

Powell, L. H. (2006). Review of marital and sexual lifestyles in the U.S.: attitudes, behaviors, and relationships in social context. *Family Relations, 55*, 149.

Powell, L. H, Shahabi, L, & Thoresen, C. E. (2003). Religion and spirituality: Linkages to physical health. *American Psychology, 58*, 36–52.

Powers, K. D. (2006). An analysis of Kohlbergian moral development in relationship to biblical factors of morality in seminary students (Lawrence Kohlberg). *Dissertation Abstracts International: Section B: The Sciences and Engineering, 67(6-B)*, 3485.

Powers, M., & Emmelkamp, P. (2008). Virtual reality exposure therapy for anxiety disorders: A meta-analysis. *Journal of Anxiety Disorders, 22*, 561–569.

Pratkanis, A. R. (2007). Social influence analysis: An index of tactics. In A. R. Prat-kanis, *The science of social influence: Advances and future progress.* New York: Psychology Press.

Pratkanis, A. R., Epley, N. & Savitsky, K. (2007). Issue 12: Is subliminal persuasion a myth? In J. A. Nier, *Taking sides: Clashing views in social psychology* (2nd ed.) New York: McGraw-Hill.

Pratt, H. D., Phillips, E. L., Greydanus, D. E., & Patel, D. R. (2003). Eating disorders in the adolescent population: Future directions [Special issue: Eating disorders in adolescents]. *Journal of Adolescent Research, 18,* 297–317.

Predicting psychosocial consequences of homophobic victimization in middle school students. *Journal of Early Adolescence, 27*(2), 175–191.

Presbury, J., McKee, J., & Echterling, L. (2007). Person-centered approaches. *Counseling and psychotherapy with children and adolescents: Theory and practice for school and clinical settings* (4th ed.) (pp. 180–240). Hoboken, NJ: John Wiley & Sons Inc.

Pressley, M. P., & Harris., K. R. (2006). Cognitive strategies instruction: from basic research to classroom instruction. In P. A. Alexander, & P. H. Winne, *Handbook of educational psychology.* Mahwah, NJ: Erlbaum.

Pretzer, J. L., & Beck, A. T. (2005). A cognitive theory of personality disorders. In M. F. Lenzenweger & J. F. Clarkin (Eds.), *Major theories of personality disorder* (2nd ed.). New York: Guilford Press.

Price, M. (2008. September). Against doctors' orders. *Monitor on Psychology,* pp. 34–36.

Prince, C.V. (2005). Homosexuality, transvestism and transsexuality: Reflections on their etymology and differentiation. *International Journal of Transgenderism, 8,* 15–18.

Prinz, J. J. (2007). Emotion: Competing theories and philosophical issues. In P. Tha-gard, *Philosophy of psychology and cognitive science.* Amsterdam: North Holland/Elsevier.

Prior, A., & MacWhinney, B. (2010). A bilingual advantage in task switching. *Bilin-gualism: Language & Cognition, 13,* 253–262.

Prislin, R., Brewer, M., & Wilson, D. J. (2002). Changing majority and minority positions within a group versus an aggregate. *Personality and Social Psychology Bulletin, 28,* 650–647.

Proffitt, D. R. (2006). Distance perception. *Current Directions in Psychological Sci-ence, 15,* 131–139.

Prohovnik, I., Skudlarski, P., Fulbright, R. K., Gore, J. C., & Wexler, B. E. (2004). Functional MRI changes before and after onset of reported emotions. *Psychiatry Research: Neuroimaging, 132,* 239–250.

Puca, R. M. (2005). The influence of the achievement motive on probability estimates in pre- and post-decisional action phases. *Journal of Research in Personality, 39,* 245–262.

Puetz, T., Flowers, S., & O'Connor, P. (2008). A randomized controlled trial of the effect of aerobic exercise training on feelings of energy and fatigue in sedentary young adults with persistent fatigue. *Psychotherapy & Psychosomatics, 77,* 167–174.

Puhl, R., & Latner, J. (2007). Stigma, obesity, and the health of the nation's children. *Psychological Bulletin, 133,* 557–580.

Puller, C., & Haverkamp, S. (2011). Bipolar cell pathways for color vision in non-primate dichromats. *Visual Neuroscience, 28,* 51–60.

Putnam, F. W. (2000). Dissociative disorders. In A. J. Sameroff, M. Lewis (Eds.), *Handbook of developmental psychopathology* (2nd ed.). Dordrecht: Kluwer Academic Publishers.

Q

Quadros, P. S., Goldstein, A. Y. N., DeVries, G. J., & Wagner, C. K. (2002). Regula-tion of sex differences in progesterone receptor expression in the medial preoptic nucleus of post-natal rats. *Journal of Neuroendocrinology, 14,* 761–767.

Quartana, P. J., & Burns, J. W. (2007). Painful consequences of anger suppression. *Emotion, 7,* 400–414.

Quas, J. A., Malloy, L. C., & Melinder, A. (2007). Developmental differences in the effects of repeated interviews and interviewer bias on young children's event memory and false reports. *Developmental Psychology, 43,* 823–837.

Quenot, J. P., Boichot, C., Petit, A., Falcon-Eicher, S., d'Athis, P., Bonnet, C., Wolf, J. E., Louis, P., & Brunotte, F. (2005). Usefulness of MRI in the follow-up of patients with repaired aortic coarctation and bicuspid aortic valve. *International Journal of Cardiology, 103,* 312–316.

Quinn, D. M., Kahng, S. K., & Crocker, J. (2004). Discreditable: Stigma effects of revealing a mental illness history on test performance. *Personality and Social Psychology Bulletin, 30,* 803–815.

Quintana, S. M., Aboud, F. E., Chao, R. K., (2006). Race, ethnicity, and culture in child development: Contemporary research and future directions. *Child Development, 77,* 1129–1141.

R

Rabin, J. (2004). Quantification of color vision with cone contrast sensitivity. *Visual Neuroscience, 21,* 483–485.

Rachman, S., & deSilva, P. (2004). *Panic disorders: The facts.* Oxford, England: Oxford University Press.

Rado, J., Dowd, S., & Janicak, P. (2008). The emerging role of transcranial magnetic stimulation (TMS) for treatment of psychiatric disorders. *Directions in Psychiatry, 28,* 314–332.

Raffaele, P. (2006, November). Speaking Bonobo. *Smithsonian Magazine.*

Rahman, Q., Kumari, V., & Wilson, G. D. (2003). Sexual orientation-related differences in pre-pulse inhibition of the human startle response. *Behavioral Neuroscience, 117,* 1096–1102.

Rajagopal, S. (2006). The placebo effect. *Psychiatric Bulletin, 30,* 185–188.

Ralston, A. (2004). *Between a rock and a hard place.* New York: Simon & Schuster.

Ramachandran, V. S. (2004). *A brief tour of human consciousness: From impostor poodles to purple numbers.* New York: Pi Press.

Ramachandran, V. S., & Hubbard, E. M. (2001). Synesthesia—a window into percep-tion, thought and language. *Journal of Consciousness Studies, 8,* 3–34.

Ramachandran, V. S., Hubbard, E. M., & Butcher, P. A. (2004). Synesthesia, cross-activation and the foundations of neuroepistemology. In G. A. Calvert, C. Spence, & B. E. Stein, *The handbook of multisensory processes.* Cambridge, MA: MIT Press.

Rambaud, C., & Guilleminault, C. (2004). "Back to sleep" and unexplained death in infants. *Journal of Sleep and Sleep Disorders, 27,* 1359–1366.

Ramos, R. T. (2006). Antidepressants and dizziness. *Journal of Psychopharmacology, 20,* 708–713.

Ramsay, M. C., Reynolds, C. R., & Kamphaus, R. W. (2002). *Essentials of behavioral assessment.* New York: Wiley.

Ramus, F. (2006). Genes, brain, and cognition: A roadmap for the cognitive scientist. *Cognition, 101,* 247–269.

Ranganath, C., & Blumenfeld, R. (2005, August). Doubts about double dissociations between short- and long-term memory. *Trends in Cognitive Sciences, 9*(8), 374–380.

Rangell, L. (2007). *The road to unity in psychoanalytic theory.* Lanham, MD: Jason Aronson.

Rapport, R. L. (2005). *Nerve endings: The discovery of the synapse.* New York: W. W. Norton.

Raskin, N. J., & Rogers, C. R. (1989). Person-centered therapy. In R. J. Corsini, & D. Wedding (Eds.), *Current psychotherapies* (4th ed.). Itasca, IL: F. E. Peacock.

Raskin, N., & Rogers, C. (1989). Person-centered therapy. *Current psychotherapies* (4th ed.) (pp. 155–194). Itasca, IL: F. E. Peacock Publishers.

Rassin, E. (2008). Individual differences in the susceptibility to confirmation bias. *Netherlands Journal of Psychology, 64,* 87–93.

Rassin, E., & Muris, P. (2007). Abnormal and normal obsessions: A reconsideration. *Behaviour Research and Therapy, 45,* 1065–1070.

Rattazzi, M. C., LaFuci, G., & Brown, W. T. (2004). Prospects for gene therapy in the Fragile X Syndrome. *Mental Retardation and Developmental Disabilities Research Reviews, 10,* 75–81.

Ravindran, A. V., Matheson, K., Griffiths, J., Merali, Z., & Anisman, H. (2002). Stress, coping, uplifts, and quality of life in subtypes of depression: A conceptual frame-work and emerging data. *Journal of Affective Disorders, 71,* 121–130.

Ray, L., Bryan, A., MacKillop, J., McGeary, J., Hesterberg, K., & Hutchison, K. (2009). The dopamine D_4 receptor gene exon III polymorphism, problematic alcohol use and novelty seeking: Direct and mediated genetic effects. *Addiction Biology, 14,* 238–244.

Ray, L. A., & Hutchison, K. E. (2007). Effects of naltrexone on alcohol sensitivity and genetic moderators of medication response: a double-blind placebo-controlled study. *Archives of General Psychiatry, 64,* 1069–1077.

Ray, R., et al. (2008). Neuroimaging, genetics and the treatment of nicotine addiction. *Behavioural Brain Research, 193,* 159–169.

Raz, A. (2007). Suggestibility and hypnotizability: Mind the gap. *American Journal of Clinical Hypnosis, 49,* 205–210.

Read, J., Beattie, M., Chamberlain, R., & Merrill, J. (2008). Beyond the "binge" thresh-old: Heavy drinking patterns and their association with alcohol involvement indices in college students. *Addictive Behaviors, 33,* 225–234.

Rechtschaffen, A., Bergmann, B., Everson, C., Gilliland, M., & Kushida, C. (2002, Feb-ruary). Sleep deprivation in the rat: X. Integration and discussion of the findings. *Sleep: Journal of Sleep and Sleep Disorders Research, 25*(1), 68–87.

Redding, G. M. (2002). A test of size-scaling and relative-size hypotheses for the moon illusion. *Perception and Psychophysics, 64,* 1281–1289.

Redding, G. M., & Hawley, E. (1993). Length illusion in fractional Müller-Lyer stimuli: An object-perception approach. *Perception, 22,* 819–828.

Redish, A. D. (2004). Addiction as a computational process gone awry. *Science, 306,* 1944–1947.

Reed, P. (2007). Response rate and sensitivity to the molar feedback function relating response and reinforcement rate on VI+ schedules of reinforcement. *Journal of Experimental Psychology: Animal Behavior Processes, 33,* 428–439.

Reed, P., & Morgan, T. (2008). Effect on subsequent fixed-interval schedule perfor-mance of prior exposure to ratio and interval schedules of reinforcement. *Learning & Behavior, 36,* 82–91.

Reed, S. K. (1996). *Cognition: Theory and applications* (4th ed.). Pacific Grove, CA: Brooks/Cole.

Reese, R. J., Conoley, C. W., & Brossart, D. F. (2002). Effectiveness of telephone coun-seling: A field-based investigation. *Journal of Counseling Psychology, 49,* 233–242.

Regan, P. C. (2006). Love. In R. D. McAnulty, & M. M. Burnette, *Sex and sexuality: Sexual function and dysfunction* (Vol. 2). Westport, CT: Praeger Publishers/Greenwood Publishing.

Reichenberg, A., & Harvey, P. D. (2007). Neuropsychological impairments in schizo-phrenia: Integration of performance-based and brain imaging findings. *Psychologi-cal Bulletin, 133,* 212–223.

Reif, A., & Lesch, K. P. (2003). Toward a molecular architecture of personality. *Behavioural Brain Research, 139,* 1–20.

Reijonen, J. H., Pratt, H. D., Patel, D. R., & Greydanus, D. E. (2003). Eating disorders in the adolescent population: An overview [Special issue: Eating disorders in adolescents]. *Journal of Adolescent Research, 18,* 209–222.

Reilly, T., & Waterhouse, J. (2007). Altered sleep-wake cycles and food intake: The Ramadan model. *Physiology & Behavior, 90,* 219–228.

Reinecke, A., Cooper, M., Favaron, E., Massey-Chase, R., & Harmer, C. (2011). Attentional bias in untreated panic disorder. *Psychiatry Research, 185,* 387–393.

Reiner, R. (2008, March). Integrating a portable biofeedback device into clinical practice for patients with anxiety disorders: Results of a pilot study. *Applied Psychophysiology and Biofeedback, 33,* 55–61.

Reisberg, D. (1997). *Cognition: Exploring the science of the mind.* New York: W. W. Norton. Reiss, S., & Havercamp, S. M. (2005). Motivation in developmental context: A new method for studying self-actualization. *Journal of Humanistic Psychology, 45,* 41–53.

Reisberg, D. (2009). *Cognition: Exploring the science of the mind.* New York: Norton.

Reitman, D., Murphy, M., Hupp, S., & O'Callaghan, P. (2004). Behavior Change and Perceptions of Change: Evaluating the Effectiveness of a Token Economy. *Child & Family Behavior Therapy, 26(2),* 17–36.

Reitman, J. S. (1965). *Cognition and thought.* New York: Wiley.

Relier, J. P. (2001). Influence of maternal stress on fetal behavior and brain development. *Biology of the Neonate, 79,* 168–171.

Remington, G. (2003). Understanding antipsychotic 'atypicality': A clinical and pharmacological moving target. *Journal of Psychiatry & Neuroscience, 28,* 275–284.

Rende, R. (2007). Thinking inside and outside the (black) box: Behavioral genetics and human development. *Human Development, 49,* 343–346.

Renshaw, D. C. (2006). Male and female circumcision today. *The Family Journal, 14,* 283–285.

Repp, B. H., & Knoblich, G. (2007). Action can affect auditory perception. *Psychological Science, 18,* 6–7.

Rescorla, R. A. (1988). Pavlovian conditioning: It's not what you think it is. *American Psychologist, 43,* 151–160.

Reynolds, C. R., & Ramsay, M. C. (2003). Bias in psychological assessment: An empirical review and recommendations. In J. R. Graham & J. A. Naglieri (Eds.), *Handbook of psychology: Assessment psychology* (Vol. 10) (pp. 67–93). New York: Wiley.

Reynolds, R. I., & Takooshian, H. (1988, January). Where were you August 8, 1985? *Bulletin of the Psychonomic Society, 26,* 23–25.

Ricciuti, H. N. (1993). Nutrition and mental development. *Current Directions in Psychological Science, 2,* 43–46.

Rice, C. (2009, December 18). Prevalence of Autism Spectrum Disorders—Autism and Developmental Disabilities Monitoring Network, United States, 2006. *MMWR, 58*(SS10), 1–20.

Rice, L., & Greenberg, L. (1992). Humanistic approaches to psychotherapy. *History of psychotherapy: A century of change* (pp. 197–224). Washington, DC: American Psychological Association.

Rice, M. L., Tomblin, J. B., Hoffman, L., Richman, W. A., & Marquis, J. (2004). Grammatical tense deficits in children with SLI and nonspecific language impairment: Relationships with non-verbal IQ over time. *Journal of Speech, Language, and Hearing Research, 47,* 816–834.

Rich, E. L., & Shapiro, M. L. (2007). Prelimbic/infralimbic inactivation impairs memory for multiple task switches, but not flexible selection of familiar tasks. *Journal of Neuroscience, 27,* 4747–4755.

Richard, D. C. S., & Lauterbach, D. (Eds.). (2006). *Handbook of exposure therapies.* New York: Academic Press.

Richard, M. (2005). Effective treatment of eating disorders in Europe: Treatment outcome and its predictors. *European Eating Disorders Review, 13,* 169–179.

Richards, R. (2006). Frank Barron and the study of creativity: A voice that lives on. *Journal of Humanistic Psychology, 46,* 352–370.

Richardson, A. S., Bergen, H. A., Martin, G., Roeger, L., & Allison, S. (2005). Perceived academic performance as an indicator of risk of attempted suicide in young adolescents. *Archives of Suicide Research, 9,* 163–176.

Richardson, B. (2002, September 30). Light-bulb moments. *The Wall Street Journal,* p. R7.

Richardson, J. E. (2011). The academic engagement of White and ethnic minority students in distance education. *Educational Psychology, 31,* 123–139.

Richgels, D. J. (2004). Paying attention to language. *Reading Research Quarterly, 39,* 470–477.

Rieber, R. W., & Robinson, D. K. (2006). Review of the essential Vygotsky. *Journal of the History of the Behavioral Sciences, 42,* 178–180.

Riedel, G., Platt, B., & Micheau, J. (2003). Glutamate receptor function in learning and memory. *Behavioural Brain Research, 140,* 1–47.

Rieder, R. O., Kaufmann, C. A., & Knowles, J. A. (1996). Genetics. In R. E. Hales & S. C. Yudofsky (Eds.), *The American Psychiatric Press synopsis of psychiatry.* Washington, DC: American Psychiatric Press.

Rigby, L., & Waite, S. (2007). Group therapy for self-esteem, using creative approaches and metaphor as clinical tools. *Behavioural and Cognitive Psychotherapy, 35,* 361–364.

Ringold, D. J. (1996). Social criticisms of target marketing: Process or product? In R. P. Hill (Ed.), *Marketing and consumer research in the public interest.* Thousand Oaks, CA: Sage.

Riniolo, T. C., Koledin, M., Drakulic, G. M., & Payne, R. A. (2003). An archival study of eyewitness memory of the Titanic's final plunge. *Journal of General Psychology, 130,* 89–95.

Rinn, W. E. (1984). The neuropsychology of facial expression: A review of neurological and psychological mechanisms for producing facial expressions. *Psychological Bulletin, 95,* 52–77.

Rinn, W. E. (1991). Neuropsychology of facial expression. In R. S. Feldman & B. Rimé (Eds.), *Fundamentals of non-verbal behavior.* Cambridge: Cambridge University Press.

Riolo, F. (2007). Ricordare, ripetere e rielaborare: Un lascito di Freud alla psicoanalisi futura. Remembering, repeating, and working through: Freud's legacy to the psychoanalysis of the future. *Rivista di Psicoanalisi, 53,* 439–446.

Rivera-García, A., Ramírez-Salado, I., Corsi-Cabrera, M., & Calvo, J. (2011). Facial muscle activation during sleep and its relation to the rapid eye movements of REM sleep. *Journal of Sleep Research, 20,* 82–91.

Rivera-Gaxiola, M., Klarman, L., Garcia-Sierra, A., & Kuhl, P. K. (2005). Neural patterns to speech and vocabulary growth in American infants. *Neuroreport: For Rapid Communication of Neuroscience Research, 16,* 495–498.

Robbins, B. (2008). What is the good life? Positive psychology and the renaissance of humanistic psychology. *The Humanistic Psychologist, 36,* 96–112.

Roberts, M. (2010). Emotional intelligence, empathy and the educative power of poetry: A Deleuzo-Guattarian perspective. *Journal of Psychiatric and Mental Health Nursing, 17,* 236–241.

Roberts, M. E., Moore, S. D., & Beckham, J. C. (2007). Post-traumatic stress disorder and substance use disorders. In M. Al'bsi *Stress and Addiction: Biological and Psychological Mechanisms.* San Diego, CA: Elsevier Academic Press.

Robins, R. W. (2005, October 7). The nature of personality: Genes, culture, and national character. *Science, 310,* 62–63.

Robinson, D. N. (2007). Theoretical psychology: What is it and who needs it? *Theory & Psychology, 17,* 187–198.

Robinson, D. S. (2007). Antidepressant drugs: Early onset of therapeutic effect. *Primary Psychiatry, 14,* 23–24.

Rock, A. (1999, January). Quitting time for smokers. *Money,* pp. 139–141.

Rodd, Z. A., Bell, R. L., Sable, H. J. K., Murphy, J. M., & McBride, W. J. (2004). Recent advances in animal models of alcohol craving and relapse. *Pharmacology, Biochemistry and Behavior, 79,* 439–450.

Roediger, H. L., III, & McDermott, K. B. (2000). Tricks of memory. *Current Directions in Psychological Science, 9,* 123–127.

Roediger, H., Balota, D., & Watson, J. (2001). Spreading activation and arousal of false memories. *The nature of remembering: Essays in honor of Robert G. Crowder* (pp. 95–115). Washington, DC: American Psychological Association.

Roesch, S. C., Adams, L., Hines, A., Palmores, A., Vyas, P., Tran, C., Pekin, S., & Vaughn, A. A. (2005). Coping with prostate cancer: A meta-analytic review. *Journal of Behavioral Medicine, 28,* 281–293.

Rogers, C. R. (1951). *Client-centered therapy.* Boston: Houghton-Mifflin.

Rogers, C. R. (1971). A theory of personality. In S. Maddi (Ed.), *Perspectives on personality.* Boston: Little, Brown.

Rogers, C. R. (1995). *A way of being.* Boston: Houghton Mifflin.

Rogers, J. M. (2009). Tobacco and pregnancy: Overview of exposures and effects. *Birth Defects Res. C. Embryo Today, 84,* 152–160.

Rogers, L. J. (2011). Review of "The master and his emissary: The divided brain and the making of the western world." *Laterality: Asymmetries of Body, Brain and Cognition, 16,* 125–128.

Rogers, M. B., Loewenthal, K. M., Lewis, C. A., Amlot, R., Cinnirella, M., & Humayan, A. (2007). The role of religious fundamentalism in terrorist violence: A social psychological analysis. *International Review of Psychiatry, 19,* 253–262.

Rogers, P. (2002, August 2). Too much, too soon. *People,* pp. 79–82.

Rogers, P., & Eftimiades, M. (1995, July 24). Bearing witness. *People Weekly,* pp. 42–43.

Rogers, S. (2007). The underlying mechanisms of semantic memory loss in Alzheimer's disease and semantic dementia. *Dissertation Abstracts International: Section B: The Sciences and Engineering, 67(10-B),* 5591.

Rohan, K. J., Roecklein, K. A., & Tierney Lindsey, K. (2007). A randomized controlled trial of cognitive-behavioral therapy, light therapy, and their combination for seasonal affective disorder. *Journal of Consulting and Clinical Psychology, 75,* 489–500.

Roid, G., Nellis, L. & McLellan, M. (2003). Assessment with the Leiter International Performance Scale—Revised and the S-BIT. In R.S. McCallum & R. Steve (Eds.), *Handbook of nonverbal assessment.* New York: Kluwer Academic/ Plenum Publishers.

Roisman, G. I., Collins, W. A. Sroufe, L. A., & Egeland, B. (2005). Predictors of young adults' representations of and behavior in their current romantic relationship: Prospective tests of the prototype hypothesis. *Attachment and Human Development, 7,* 105–121.

Roizen, N. J., & Patterson, D. (2003). Down's syndrome. *Lancet, 361,* 1281–1289.

Rollman, G. B. (2004). *Ethnocultural variations in the experience of pain.* Mahwah, NJ: Lawrence Erlbaum Associates.

Rom, S. A., Miller, L., & Peluso, J. (2009). Playing the game: Psychological factors in surviving cancer. *International Journal of Emergency Mental Health, 11,* 25–36.

Romeu, P. F. (2006). Memories of the terrorist attacks of September 11, 2001: A study of the consistency and phenomenal characteristics of flashbulb memories. *The Spanish Journal of Psychology, 9,* 52–60.

Room, R., Babor, T., & Rehm, J. (2005, February). Alcohol and public health. *Lancet, 365*(9458), 519–530.

Rorschach, H. (1924). *Psychodiagnosis: A diagnostic test based on perception.* New York: Grune & Stratton.

Rosch, E. (1975). Cognitive representation of semantic categories. *Journal of Experimental Psychology, 104,* 192–233.

Rosch, E., & Mervis, C. (1975). Family resemblances: Studies in the internal structure of categories. *Cognitive Psychology, 7*(4), 573–605.

Rose, N., & Blackmore, S. (2002). Horses for courses: Tests of a psychic claimant. *Journal of the Society for Psychical Research, 66,* 29–40.

Rosen, H. (2000). The creative evolution of the theoretical foundations for cognitive therapy. *Journal of Cognitive Psychotherapy, 14, Special issue: Creativity in the context of cognitive therapy,* 123–134.

Rosen, J. (2005, August 28.) The future v. Roberts. *New York Times Magazine,* pp. 24–29, 44, 50–51.

Rosenbloom, T., & Wolf, Y. (2002). Sensation seeking and detection of risky road signals: A developmental perspective. *Accident Analysis and Prevention, 34,* 569–580.

Rosenhan, D. L. (1973). On being sane in insane places. *Science, 179,* 250–258.

Rosenman, R. H., Brand, R. J., Jenkins, C. D., Friedman, M., Straus, R., & Wurm, M. (1994). Coronary heart disease in the Western Collaborative Group Study: Final follow-up experience of 8¹/₂ years. In A. Steptoe, & J. Wardle, Eds., *Psychosocial processes and health: A reader.* New York: Cambridge University Press.

Rosenstein, D. S., & Horowitz, H. A. (1996). Adolescent attachment and psychopathology. *Journal of Consulting and Clinical Psychology, 64,* 244–253.

Rosenthal, A. M. (2008). *Thirty-eight witnesses: The Kitty Genovese case.* Hoboken, NJ: Melville House Publishing.

Rosenthal, R. (2002). Covert communication in classrooms, clinics, courtrooms and cubicles. *American Psychologist, 57,* 838–849.

Rosenthal, R. (2003). Covert communication in laboratories, classrooms, and the truly real world. *Current Directions in Psychological Science, 12,* 151–154.

Rosov, A. (1993a). Striving for superiority as a fundamental drive. *Psikhologicheskiy Zhurnal, 14*(6), 133–141.

Rosov, A. (1993b). Striving for superiority as a fundamental drive. *Psikhologicheskiy Zhurnal, 14,* 133–141.

Ross, H. E. (2000). Sensation and perception. In D. S. Gupta, S. Deepa, & R. M. Gupta, et al. (Eds.), *Psychology for psychiatrists* (pp. 20–40). London: Whurr Publishers.

Ross, H. E., & Plug, C. (2002). *The mystery of the moon illusion: Exploring size perception.* Oxford: University Press.

Ross, J. (2006). Sleep on a problem . . . It works like a dream. *The Psychologist, 19,* 738–740.

Ross, L. (1977). The intuitive psychologist and his shortcomings: Distortions in the attribution process. In L.Berkowitz (Ed.), *Advances in experimental social psychology* (Vol. 10) (pp. 173–240). Orlando, FL: Academic Press.

Ross, P. E. (2004, April). Draining the language out of color. *Scientific American,* pp. 46–51.

Rossato, M., Pagano, C., & Vettor, R. (2008). The cannabinoid system and male reproductive functions. *Journal of Neuroendocrinology, 20,* 90–93.

Rossell, S. L., Bullmore, E. T., Williams, S. C. R., & David, A. S. (2002). Sex differences in functional brain activation during a lexical visual field task. *Brain and Language, 80,* 97–105.

Rossi, J. J., June, C. H., & Kohn, D. B. (2007). Genetic therapies against HIV. *Natural Biotechnology, 25,* 1444–1454.

Rossier J, Dahourou D., McCrae, R. R. (2005). Structural and mean level analyses of the Five-Factor Model and locus of control: Further evidence from Africa. *Journal of Cross-Cultural Psychology, 36,* 227–246.

Rossouw, J. E., Prentice, R. L., Manson, J. E., Wu, L., Barad, D., Barnabei, V. M., Ko, M., LaCroix, A. Z., Margolis, K. L., & Stefanick, M. L. (2007). Postmenopausal hormone therapy and risk of cardiovascular disease by age and years since menopause. *Journal of the American Medical Association, 297,* 1465–1477.

Rotan, L. W., & Ospina-Kammerer, V. (2007). *Mindbody medicine: Foundations and practical applications.* New York: Routledge/Taylor & Francis Group.

Roter, D. L., Hall, J. A., & Aoki, Y. (2002). Physician gender effects in medical communication: A meta-analytic review. *Journal of the American Medical Association, 288,* 756–764.

Rothgänger, H. (2003, December). Analysis of the sounds of the child in the first year of age and a comparison to the language. *Early Human Development, 75*(1), 55–69.

Rothman, A. J., & Salovey, P. (1997). Shaping perceptions to motivate healthy behavior: The role of message framing. *Psychological Bulletin, 121,* 3–19.

Roughton, R. E. (2002). Rethinking homosexuality: What it teaches us about psychoanalysis. *Journal of the American Psychoanalytic Association, 50,* 733–763.

Roush, W. (1995, September 1). Can "resetting" hormonal rhythms treat illness? *Science, 269,* 1220–1221.

Routtenberg, A., & Lindy, J. (1965). Effects of the availability of rewarding septal and hypothalamic stimulation on bar pressing for food under conditions of deprivation. *Journal of Comparative and Physiological Psychology, 60,* 158–161.

Rowe, J. B., Toni, I., Josephs, O., Frackowiak, R. S. J., & Passingham, R. E. (2000, June 2). The prefrontal cortex: Response selection or maintenance within working memory? *Science, 288,* 1656–1660.

Rowley, S. J., Sellers, R. M., Chavous, T. M., & Smith, M. A. (1998). The relationship between racial identity and self-esteem in African American college and high school students. *Journal of Personality and Social Psychology, 74,* 715–724.

Røysamb, E., Kendler, K. S., Tambs, K., Ørstavik, R. E., Neale, M. C., Aggen, S. H., et al. (2011). The joint structure of DSM-IV Axis I and Axis II disorders. *Journal of Abnormal Psychology, 120,* 198–209.

Royzman, E. B., Cassidy, K. W., & Baron, J. (2003). "I know, you know": Epistemic egocentrism in children and adults. *Review of General Psychology, 7,* 38–65.

Rozencwajg, P., Cherfi, M., Ferrandez, A. M., Lautrey, J., Lemoine, C., & Loarer, E. (2005). Age-related differences in the strategies used by middle aged adults to solve a block design task. *International Journal of Aging and Human Development, 60,* 159–182.

Rozin, P., Kabnick, K., Pete, E., Fischler, C., & Shields, C. (2003). The ecology of eating: Smaller portion sizes in France than in the United States help explain the French paradox. *Psychological Science, 14,* 450–454.

Rubichi, S., Ricci, F., Padovani, R., & Scaglietti, L. (2005). Hypnotic susceptibility, baseline attentional functioning, and the Stroop task. *Consciousness and Cognition: An International Journal, 14,* 296–303.

Rubin, D. C. (1999). *Remembering our past: Studies in autobiographical memory.* New York: Cambridge University Press.

Rubin, D. C., Schrauf, R. W., Gulgoz, S., & Naka, M. (2007). Cross-cultural variability of component processes in autobiographical remembering: Japan, Turkey, and the USA. *Memory, 15,* 536–547.

Rudman, L. A. & Ashmore, R. D. (2007). Discrimination and the Implicit Association Test. *Group Processes & Intergroup Relations, 10,* 359–372.

Rudner, M., & Rönnberg, J. (2008). The role of the episodic buffer in working memory for language processing. *Cognitive Processing, 9,* 19–28.

Ruggs, E. N., Martinez, L. R., & Hebl, M. R. (2011). How individuals and organizations can reduce interpersonal discrimination. *Social and Personality Psychology Compass, 5,* 29–42.

Runco, M. A. (2006). Introduction to the special issue: divergent thinking. *Creativity Research Journal, 18,* 249–250.

Runco, M. A., & Sakamoto, S. O. (1993). Reaching creatively gifted students through their learning styles. In R. M. Milgram, R. S. Dunn, & G. E. Price (Eds.), *Teaching and counseling gifted and talented adolescents: An international learning style perspective.* Westport, CT: Praeger/Greenwood.

Rusche, B. (2003). The 3Rs and animal welfare–conflict or the way forward? *ALTEX, 20, (Suppl. 1),* 63–76.

Ruscher, J. B., Fiske, S. T., & Schnake, S. B. (2000). The motivated tactician's juggling act: Compatible vs. incompatible impression goals. *British Journal of Social Psychology, 39,* 241–256.

Rushton, J. P. & Jensen, A. R. (2006). The totality of available evidence shows the race IQ gap still remains. *Psychological Science, 17,* 921–922.

Russell, J. A., & Sato, K. (1995). Comparing emotion words between languages. *Journal of Cross Cultural Psychology, 26,* 384–391.

Russell, R., Duchaine, B., & Nakayama, K. (2009). Super-recognizers: People with extraordinary face recognition ability. *Psychonomic Bulletin & Review, 16,* 252–257.

Russo, N. (1981). Women in psychology. In L. T. Benjamin, Jr. & K. D. Lowman (Eds.), *Activities handbook for the teaching of psychology.* Washington, DC: American Psychological Association.

Rustin, M. (2006). Infant observation research: What have we learned so far? *Infant Observation, 9,* 35–52.

Rutherford, B., Rose, S., Sneed, J., & Roose, S. (2009, April). Study design affects participant expectations: A survey. *Journal of Clinical Psychopharmacology, 29,* 179–181.

Rutter, M. (2002). Nature, nurture, and development: From evangelism through science toward policy and practice. *Child Development, 73,* 1–21.

Rutter, M. (2006). *Genes and behavior: Nature-nurture interplay explained.* Malden, MA: Blackwell Publishing.

Rychlak, J. (1997). *In defense of human consciousness.* Washington, DC: American Psychological Association.

Rydell, R., McConnell, A., & Mackie, D. (2008). Consequences of discrepant explicit and implicit attitudes: Cognitive dissonance and increased information processing. *Journal of Experimental Social Psychology, 44,* 1526–1532.

Rymer, R. (1994). *Genie: A scientific tragedy.* New York: Penguin.

S

Saarni, C. (1999). *Developing emotional competence.* New York: Guilford.

Sabbagh, K. (2009). *Remembering our childhood: How memory betrays us.* New York: Oxford University Press.

Sachs-Ericsson, N., Joiner, T., Plant, E. A., & Blazer, D. G. (2005). The influence of depression on cognitive decline in community-dwelling elderly persons. *American Journal of Geriatric Psychiatry, 13,* 402–408.

Sackeim, H. A., Haskett, R. F., Mulsant, B. H., Thase, M. E., Mann, J. J., Pettinati, H. M., Greenberg, R. M., Crowe, R. R., Cooper, T. B., & Prudic, J. (2001). Continuation pharmaco-therapy in the prevention of relapse following electroconvulsive therapy: A randomized controlled trial. *Journal of the American Medical Association, 285,* 1299–1307.

Sacks, O. (2003, July 28). The mind's eye. *The New Yorker,* pp. 48–59.

Saczynski, J., Willis, S., and Schaie, K. (2002). Strategy use in reasoning training with older adults. *Aging, Neuropsychology, & Cognition, 9,* 48–60.

Saggino, A., Perfetti, B., & Spitoni, G. (2006). Fluid intelligence and executive functions: New perspectives. In L. V. Wesley, *Intelligence: New research.* Hauppauge, NY: Nova Science Publishers.

Sahin, N. T., Pinker, S., & Halgren, E. (2006). Abstract grammatical processing of nouns and verbs in Broca's area: Evidence from fMRI. *Cortex, 42,* 540–562.

Sakai, K. L. (2005, November 4). Language acquisition and brain development. *Science, 310,* 815–817.

Salgado, D. M., Quinlin, K. J., & Zlotnick, C. (2007). The relationship of lifetime polysubstance dependence to trauma exposure, symptomatology, and psychosocial functioning in incarcerated women with comorbid PTSD and substance use disorder. *Journal of Trauma Dissociation, 8,* 9–26.

Salmela-Aro, K., & Nurmi, J-E. (2007). Self-esteem during university studies predicts career characteristics 10 years later. *Journal of Vocational Behavior, 70,* 463–477.

Salsman, N. L. (2006). Interpersonal change as an outcome of Time-Limited Interpersonal Therapy. *Dissertation Abstracts International: Section B—The Sciences and Engineering, 66(9-B),* 5103.

Salvi, V., Fagiolini, A., Swartz, H., Maina, G., & Frank, E. (2008). The use of antidepressants in bipolar disorder. *Journal of Clinical Psychiatry, 69,* 1307–1318.

Salvy, S. J., Mulick, J. A., & Butter, E. (2004). Contingent electric shock (SIBIS) and a conditioned punisher eliminate severe head banging in a preschool child. *Behavioral Interventions, 19,* 59–72.

Salzman, L. (1964). Psychoanalysis in evolution. *Comprehensive Psychiatry, 5(6),* 364–373.

Samantaray, S. K., Srivastava, M., & Mishra, P. K. (2002). Fostering self concept and self actualization as bases for empowering women in national development: A challenge for the new millennium. *Social Science International, 18,* 58–63.

Samoilov, V., & Zayas, V. (2007). Ivan Petrovich Pavlov (1849–1936). *Journal of the History of the Neurosciences, 16,* 74–89.

Sampson, M., McCubbin, R., & Tyrer, P. (2006). *Personality disorder and community mental health teams: A practitioner's guide.* New York: John Wiley & Sons Ltd.

Sampson, S. M., Solvason, H., B., Husain, M. M. (2007). Envisioning transcranial magnetic stimulation (TMS) as a clinical treatment option for depression. *Psychiatric Annals, 37, Special issue: Neuromodulation: Patients with depression may benefit from treatment with vagus nerve and transcranial magnetic stimulation,* 189–196.

Sams, M., Hari, R., Rif, J., & Knuutila, J. (1993). The human auditory memory trace persists about 10 sec: Neuromagnetic evidence. *Journal of Cognitive Neuroscience, 5,* 363–370.

Samuel, D. B., & Widiger, T. A. (2006). Differentiating normal and abnormal personality from the perspective of the DSM. S. Strack, *Differentiating normal and abnormal personality* (2nd ed.). New York: Springer Publishing.

Sanderson, M. (2007). Assessment of manic symptoms in different cultures. *British Journal of Psychiatry, 190,* 178.

Sandomir, R. (2007, July 17). W. W. E.'s testing is examined after Bennoit murder-suicide. *The New York Times,* S3.

Sandoval, J., Frisby, C. L., Geisinger, K. F., Scheuneman, J. D., & Grenier, J. R. (Eds.). (1998). *Test interpretation and diversity: Achieving equity in assessment.* Washington, DC: American Psychological Association.

Santel, S., Baving, L., Krauel, K., Munte, T. F. & Rotte, M. (2006). Hunger and satiety in anorexia nervosa: fMRI during cognitive processing of food pictures. *Brain Research, 1114,* 138–148.

Saper, C. B., Lu, J., Chou, T. C., & Gooley, J. (2005). The hypothalamic integrator for circadian rhythms. *Trends in Neuroscience, 28,* 152–157.

Sapolsky, R. M. (2003). Gene therapy for psychiatric disorders. *American Journal of Psychiatry, 160,* 208–220.

Sargent, J. D., Stoolmiller, M., Worth, K. A., Cal, C. S., Wills, T. A., Gibbons, F. X., Gerrard, M., & Tanski, S. (2007). Exposure to smoking depictions in movies: Its association with established adolescent smoking. *Archives of Pediatric Adolescent Medicine, 161,* 849–856.

Satel, S. (2006). Is caffeine addictive?—A review of the literature. *American Journal of Drug and Alcohol Abuse, 32,* 493–502.

Sato, N., Shimamura, M., & Takeuchi, D. (2007). Gene therapy for ischemic brain disease with special reference to vascular dementia. *Geriatrics & Gerontology International, 7,* 1–14.

Saucier, D. A., & Cain, M. E. (2006). The foundations of attitudes about animal research. *Ethics & Behavior, 16,* 117–133.

Savage, J. (2008). The role of exposure to media violence in the etiology of violent behavior: A criminologist weighs in. *American Behavioral Scientist, 51,* 1123–1136.

Savage, J., & Yancey, C. (2008). The effects of media violence exposure on criminal aggression: A meta-analysis. *Criminal Justice and Behavior, 35,* 772–791.

Savage-Rumbaugh, E. S., Toth, N., & Schick, K. (2007). Kanzi learns to knap stone tools. In D. A. Washburn, *Primate perspectives on behavior and cognition.* Washington, DC: American Psychological Association.

Savas, H. A., Yumru, M., & Kaya, M. C. (2007). Atypical antipsychotics as "mood stabilizers": A retrospective chart review. *Progress in Neuro-Psychopharmacology & Biological Psychiatry, 31,* 1064–1067.

Savazzi, S., Fabri, M., Rubboli, G., Paggi, A., Tassinari, C. A., Marzi, C. A. (2007). Interhemispheric transfer following callosotomy in humans: Role of the superior colliculus, *Neuropsychologia, 45,* 2417–2427.

Saville, B. (2009). Performance under competitive and self-competitive fixed-interval schedules of reinforcement. *The Psychological Record, 59,* 21–38.

Sawa, A., & Snyder, S. H. (2002, April 26). Schizophrenia: Diverse approaches to a complex disease. *Science, 296,* 692–695.

Sayette, M. A. (1993). An appraisal disruption model of alcohol's effects on stress responses in social drinkers. *Psychological Bulletin, 114,* 459–476.

Saywitz, K., & Goodman, G. (1990). Unpublished study reported in Goleman, D. (1990, November 6). Doubts rise on children as witnesses. *The New York Times,* pp. C-1, C-6.

Scarr, S. (1993). Genes, experience, and development. In D. Magnusson, P. Jules, & M. Casaer (Eds.), *Longitudinal research on individual development: Present status and future perspectives. European network on longitudinal studies on individual development, 8.* Cambridge: Cambridge University Press.

Scarr, S. (1998). American child care today. *American Psychologist, 53,* 95–108.

Scaturo, D. J. (2004). Fundamental clinical dilemmas in contemporary group psychotherapy. *Group Analysis, 37,* 201–217.

Scelfo, J. (2007, February 26). Men & depression: Facing darkness. *Newsweek,* pp. 43–50.

Schachter, S., & Singer, J. E. (1962). Cognitive, social, and physiological determinants of emotional state. *Psychological Review, 69,* 379–399.

Schacter, D. L., & Badgaiyan, R. D. (2001). Neuroimaging of priming: New perspectives on implicit and explicit memory. *Current Directions in Psychological Science, 10,* 1–4.

Schacter, D. L., Dobbins, I. G., & Schnyer, D. M. (2004). Specificity of priming: A cognitive neuroscience perspective. *Nature Reviews Neuroscience, 5,* 853–862.

Schacter, D. L., Wagner, A. D., & Buckner, R. L. (2000). Memory systems of 1999. In E. Tulving, F. I. Craik, I. M. Fergus, et al. (Eds.), *The Oxford handbook of memory.* New York: Oxford University Press.

Schaefer, R. T. (2000). *Sociology: A brief introduction* (3rd ed.). Boston: McGraw-Hill.

Schaie, K., & Willis, S. (Eds.). (2011). *Handbook of the psychology of aging* (7th ed.). San Diego: Elsevier Academic Press.

Schaie, K. W. (2005). *Developmental influences on adult intelligence: The Seattle Longitudinal Study.* New York: Oxford University Press.

Schaller, M., & Crandall, C. S. (Eds.) (2004). *The psychological foundations of culture.* Mahwah, NJ: Lawrence Erlbaum Associates.

Schechter, T., Finkelstein, Y., Koren, G. (2005). Pregnant "DES daughters" and their offspring. *Canadian Family Physician, 51,* 493–494.

Schedlowski, M., & Tewes, U. (Eds.) (1999). *Psychoneuroimmunology: An interdisciplinary introduction.* New York: Plenum.

Scheele, B., & DuBois, F. (2006). Catharsis as a moral form of entertainment. In J. Bryant, & P. Vorderer, *Psychology of entertainment.* Mahwah, NJ: Lawrence Erlbaum Associates Publishers.

Scheff, T. J. 1984. *Being mentally ill: A sociological theory* (3rd ed.). Hawthorne, NY: Aldine de Gruyter.

Scheier, M. F., Carver, C. S., & Bridges, M. W. (1994). Distinguishing optimism from neuroticism (and trait anxiety, self-mastery, and self-esteem): A revision of the Life Orientation Test. *Journal of Personality and Social Psychology, 67,* 1063–1078.

Scheier, M., & Carver, C. (1993, February). On the power of positive thinking: The benefits of being optimistic. *Current Directions in Psychological Science, 2(1),* 26–30.

Schenone, M. H., Aquin, E., Li, Y., Lee, C., Kruger, M., & Bahado-Songh, R. O. (2010). Prenatal prediction of neonatal survival at the borderline viability. *Journal of Maternal-Fetal Neonatal Medicine, 12,* 31–38.

Schepers, P., & van den Berg, P. T. (2007). Social factors of work-environment creativity. *Journal of Business and Psychology, 21,* 407–428.

Schieber, F. (2006). Vision and aging. In J. E. Birren, & K. W. Schaire, *Handbook of the psychology of aging* (6th ed.). Amsterdam, Netherlands: Elsevier.

Schiff, N. D., Giacino, J. T., Kalmar, K., Victor, J. D., Baker, K., Gerber, M., Fritz, B., Eisenberg, B., O'Connor, J., Kobylarz, E. J., Farris, A., Machado, A., McCagg, C., Plum, F., Fins, J. J., & Resai, A. R. (2007, August 2). Behavioral improvements with thalamic stimulation after severe traumatic brain injury. *Nature, 448,* 600–603.

Schiffer, A. A., Pedersen, S. S., Widdershoven, J. W., Hendriks, E. H., Winter, J. B., & Denollet, J. (2005). The distressed (type D) personality is independently associated with impaired health status and increased depressive symptoms in chronic heart failure. *European Journal of Cardiovascular Prevention and Rehabilitation, 12,* 341–346.

Schillinger, D., Bindman, A., Wang, F., Stewart, A., & Piette, J. (2004). Functional health literacy and the quality of physician-patient communication among diabetes patients. *Patient Education and Counseling, 52,* 315–323.

Schmidt, J. P. (2006). The discovery of neurotransmitters: A fascinating story and a scientific object lesson. *PsycCRITIQUES, 61,* 101–115.

Schmidt, N. B., Kotov, R., & Joiner, T. E., Jr. (2004). *Taxometrics: Toward a new diagnostic scheme for psychopathology.* Washington, DC: American Psychological Association.

Schmitt, D., Realo, A., Voracek, M., & Allik, J. (2008). Why can't a man be more like a woman? Sex differences in Big Five personality traits across 55 cultures. *Journal of Personality and Social Psychology, 94,* 168–182.

Schmitt, D. P., Allik, J., & Mccrae, R. R. (2007). The geographic distribution of big five personality traits: patterns and profiles of human self-description across 56 nations. *Journal of Cross-Cultural Psychology, 38,* 173–212.

Schnatz, P. F., Murphy, J. L., O'Sullivan, D. M., & Sorosky, J. I. (2007). Patient choice: comparing criteria for selecting an obstetrician-gynecologist based on image, gender, and professional attributes. *American Journal of Obstetrics and Gynecology, 197,* 548–561.

Schneider, D. J. (2003). *The psychology of stereotyping.* New York: Guilford Press.

Schneider, D., & Logan, G. (2009, January). Selecting a response in task switching: Testing a model of compound cue retrieval. *Journal of Experimental Psychology: Learning, Memory, and Cognition, 35*(1), 122–136.

Schofield, A. T. & Vaughan-Jackson, P. (1914). *What a boy should know; Cassell* London (2nd ed.). In J. Harvey, A. Wenzel, & S. Sprecher (Eds.), *The handbook of sexuality in close relationships* (385–409). Mahwah, NJ: Lawrence Erlbaum Associates, Inc.

Schredl, M., & Piel, E. (2005). Gender differences in dreaming: Are they stable over time? *Personality and Individual Differences, 39,* 309–316.

Schredl, M., Barthold, C., & Zimmer, J. (2006). Dream recall and nightmare frequency: A family study. *Perceptual and Motor Skills, 102,* 878–880.

Schretlen, D., Pearlson, G. D., Anthony, J. C., Aylward, E. H., Augustine, A. M., Davis, A., & Barta, P. (2000). Elucidating the contributions of processing speed, executive ability, and frontal lobe volume to normal age-related differences in fluid intelligence. *Journal of the International Neuropsychological Society, 6,* 52–61.

Schroers, M., Prigot, J., & Fagen, J. (2007, December). The effect of a salient odor context on memory retrieval in young infants. *Infant Behavior & Development, 30,* 685–689.

Schulte-Ruther, M., Markowitsch, J. J., Fink, G. R., & Piefke, M. (2007). Mirror neuron and theory of mind mechanisms involved in face-to-face interactions: A functional magnetic resonance imaging approach to empathy. *Journal of Cognitive Neuroscience, 19,* 1354–1372.

Schutt, R. K. (2001). *Investigating the social world: The process and practice of research.* Thousand Oaks, CA: Sage.

Schwartz, B. (2008). Working memory load differentially affects tip-of-the-tongue states and feeling-of-knowing judgments. *Memory & Cognition, 36,* 9–19.

Schwartz, B. L. (2001). The relation of tip-of-the-tongue states and retrieval time. *Memory & Cognition, 29,* 117–126.

Schwartz, B. L. (2002). The phenomenology of naturally-occurring tip-of-the-tongue states: A diary study. In S. P. Shohov (Ed.), *Advances in psychology research* (Vol. 8) (pp. 73–84). Huntington, NY: Nova.

Schwartz, J., & Wald, M. L. (2003). NASA's curse?: "Groupthink" is 30 years old, and still going strong. *The New York Times,* p. C1.

Schwartz, J. M., & Begley, S. (2002). *The mind and the brain: Neuroplasticity and the power of mental force.* (2002). New York: Regan Books/Harper Collins.

Schwartz, S. J., Cote, J. E., & Arnett, J. J. (2005). Identity and agency in emerging adulthood: Two developmental routes in the individualization process. *Youth & Society, 37,* 201–229.

Schwenkreis, P., El Tom, S., Ragert, P., Pleger, B., Tegenthoff, M., & Dinse, H. (2007, December). Assessment of sensorimotor cortical representation asymmetries and motor skills in violin players. *European Journal of Neuroscience, 26,* 3291–3302.

Scollon, C., & King, L. A. (2011). What people really want in life and why it matters: Contributions from research on folk theories of the good life. In R. Biswas-Diener, R. Biswas-Diener (Eds.), *Positive psychology as social change.* New York: Springer Science + Business Media.

Scullin, M. H., Kanaya, T., & Ceci, S. J. (2002). Measurement of individual differences in children's suggestibility across situations. *Journal of Experimental Psychology: Applied, 8,* 233–246.

Seamon, M. J., Fass, J. A., Maniscalco-Feichtl, M., & Abu-Shraie, N. A. (2007). Medical marijuana and the developing role of the pharmacist. *American Journal of Health System Pharmacy, 64,* 1037–1044.

Sebel, P. S., Bonke, B., & Winograd, E. (Eds.). (1993). *Memory and awareness in anesthesia.* Englewood Cliffs, NJ: Prentice Hall.

Sebire, S. J., Standage, M., & Vansteenkiste, M. (2009) Examining intrinsic versus extrinsic exercise goals: Cognitive, affective, and behavioral outcomes. *Journal of Sport Exercise Psychology, 31,* 189–210.

Sefcek, J. A., Brumbach, B. H., & Vasquez, G. (2007). The evolutionary psychology of human mate choice: How ecology, genes, fertility, and fashion influence mating strategies. *Journal of Psychology & Human Sexuality, 18,* 125–182.

Segal, D. (2006, March 22). A trip down memory lane. *Washington Post,* p. C01.

Segall, M. H., Campbell, D. T., & Herskovits, M. J. (1966). *The influence of culture on visual perception.* New York: Bobbs-Merrill.

Segerstrom, S. C., & Miller, G. E. (2004). Psychological stress and the human immune system: A meta-analytic study of 30 years of inquiry. *Psychological Bulletin, 130,* 601–630.

Sehulster, J. (1995, Spr.). Memory styles and related abilities in presentation of self. *American Journal of Psychology, 108*(1), 67–88.

Seibt, B., & Förster, J. (2005). Stereotype threat and performance: How self-stereotypes influence processing by inducing regulatory foci. *Journal of Personality and Social Psychology, 87,* 38–56.

Seli, H. (2007). 'Self' in self-worth protection: The relationship of possible selves to achievement motives and self-worth protective strategies. *Dissertation Abstracts International Section A: Humanities and Social Sciences, 67*(9-A), 3302.

Seligman, M. E. (1975). *Helplessness: On depression, development, and death.* San Francisco: Freeman.

Seligman, M. E. (1995, December). The effectiveness of psychotherapy: The *Consumer Reports* study. *American Psychologist, 50,* 965–974.

Seligman, M. E. (1996, October). Science as an ally of practice. *American Psychologist, 51,* 1072–1079.

Seligman, M. E. (2007). *What you can change . . . and what you can't: The complete guide to successful self-improvement.* New York: Vintage.

Seligman, M. E. P., & Fowler, R. D. (2011). Comprehensive Soldier Fitness and the future of psychology. *American Psychologist, 66,* 82–86.

Seligman, M. E. P., & Maier, S. F. (1967). Failure to escape traumatic shock. *Journal of Experimental Psychology, 74,* 1–9.

Selkoe, D. (2008). Soluble oligomers of the amyloid β-protein impair synaptic plasticity and behavior. *Behavioural Brain Research, 192,* 106–113.

Selkoe, D. J. (1997, January 31). Alzheimer's disease: Genotypes, phenotype, and treatments. *Science, 275,* 630–631.

Selkoe, D. J. (2002). Alzheimer's disease is a synaptic failure. *Science, 298,* 789–791.

Sellbom, M., & Ben-Porath, Y. S. (2006). The Minnesota Multiphasic Personality Inventory-2. In R. P. Archer, *Forensic uses of clinical assessment instruments* (pp. 19–55). Mahwah, NJ: Lawrence Erlbaum Associates.

Sellbom, M., Fischler, G., & Ben-Porath, Y. (2007). Identifying MMPI-2 Predictors of police officer integrity and misconduct. *Criminal Justice and Behavior, 34,* 985–1004.

Sells, R. (1994, August). *Homosexuality study.* Paper presented at the annual meeting of the American Statistical Association, Toronto.

Selove, R. (2007). The glass is half full: Current knowledge about pediatric cancer and sickle cell anemia. *PsycCRITIQUES, 52,* 88–99.

Selsky, A. (1997, February 16). African males face circumcision rite. *The Boston Globe,* p. C7.

Selye, H. (1976). *The stress of life.* New York: McGraw-Hill.

Selye, H. (1993). History of the stress concept. In L. Goldberger & S. Breznitz (Eds.), *Handbook of stress: Theoretical and clinical aspects* (2nd ed.). New York: Free Press.

Semler, C. N., & Harvey, A. G. (2005). Misperception of sleep can adversely affect daytime functioning in insomnia. *Behaviour Research and Therapy, 43,* 843–856.

Semykina, A., & Linz, S. J. (2007). Gender differences in personality and earnings: Evidence from Russia. *Journal of Economic Psychology, 28,* 387–410.

Sen, B., Sinha, S., Ahmed, S., Ghosh, S. Gangopadhyay, P. K., & Usha, R. (2007). Lack of association of HOXA1 and HOXB1 variants with autism in the Indian population. *Psychiatric Genetics, 17,* 22–36.

Serences, J., Ester, E., Vogel, E., & Awh, E. (2009). Stimulus-specific delay activity in human primary visual cortex. *Psychological Science, 20,* 207–214.

Seroczynski, A. D., Jacquez, F. M., & Cole, D. A. (2003). Depression and suicide during adolescence. In G. R. Adams, M. D. Berzonsky (Eds.), *Blackwell handbook of adolescence.* Malden, MA: Blackwell Publishers.

Serpell, R. (2000). Intelligence and culture. In R. Sternberg (Ed.), *Handbook of intelligence.* Cambridge, England: Cambridge University Press.

Serrano, E., & Warnock, J. (2007, October). Depressive disorders related to female reproductive transitions. *Journal of Pharmacy Practice, 20*(5), 385–391.

Seventh U.S. Circuit Court of Appeals. (2001). *Chicago Firefighters Local 2, et al. v. City of Chicago, et al.* Nos. 00–1272, 00–1312, 00–1313, 00–1314, and 00–1330. Chicago.

Seymour, B. (2006). Carry on eating: Neural pathways mediating conditioned potentiation of feeding. *Journal of Neuroscience, 26,* 1061–1062.

Shafer, V. L. & Garrido-Nag, K. (2007). The neurodevelopmental bases of language. In E. Hoff & M. Shatz, *Blackwell handbook of language development.* Malden, MA: Blackwell Publishing 21–45.

Shah, D. B., Pesiridou, A., Baltuch, G. H., Malone, D. A. & O'Reardon, J. P. (2008). Functional neurosurgery in the treatment of severe obsessive compulsive disorder and major depression: Overview of disease circuits and therapeutic targeting for the clinician. *Psychiatry, 5,* 24–33.

Shaikholeslami, R., & Khayyer, M. (2006). Intrinsic motivation, extrinsic motivation, and learning English as a foreign language. *Psychological Reports, 99,* 813–818.

Shankar, G., & Simmons, A. (2009, January). Understanding ethics guidelines using an internet-based expert system. *Journal of Medical Ethics, 35,* 65–68.

Shapiro, L. R. (2006). Remembering September 11th: The role of retention interval and rehearsal on flashbulb and event memory. *Memory, 14,* 129–147.

Sharif, Z., Bradford, D., Stroup, S., & Lieberman, J. (2007). Pharmacological treatment of schizophrenia. *A guide to treatments that work* (3rd ed.) (pp. 203–241). New York: Oxford University Press.

Sharma, H. S., Sjoquist, P. O., & Ali, S. F. (2007). Drugs of abuse-induced hyperthermia, blood-brain barrier dysfunction and neurotoxicity: Neuroprotective effects of a new antioxidant compound h-290/51. *Current Pharmaceutical Design, 13,* 1903–1923.

Shaver, P., & Mikulincer, M. (Eds.). (2011). *Human aggression and violence: Causes, manifestations, and consequences.* Washington, DC: American Psychological Association.

Shea, A., & Steiner, M. (2008). Cigarette smoking during pregnancy. *Nicotine & Tobacco Research, 10,* 267–278.

Sheehan, S. (1982). *Is there no place on earth for me?* New York, NY: Houghton Mifflin.

Shelton, R. C., Keller, M. B., Gelenberg, A., Dunner, D. L., Hirschfeld, R. M. A., Thase, M. E., Russell, J., Lydiard, R. B., Crits-Cristoph, P., Gallop, R., Todd, L., Hellerstein, D., Goodnick, P., Keitner, G., Stahl, S. M., & Halbreich, R. U. (2002). The effectiveness of St. John's wort in major depression: A multi-center, randomized placebo-controlled trial. *Journal of the American Medical Association, 285,* 1978–1986.

Shepard, R. N., Metzler, J., Bisiach, E., Luzzati, C., Kosslyn, S. M., Thompson, W. L., Kim, I., & Alpert, N. M. (2000). Part IV: Imagery. In M. S. Gazzaniga et al. (Eds.), *Cognitive neuro-science: A reader.* Malden, MA: Blackwell.

Sheppard, L. D., & Vernon, P. A. (2008). Intelligence and speed of information-processing: A review of 50 years of research. *Personality and Individual Differences, 44,* 535–551.

Shepperd, J., Malone, W., & Sweeny, K. (2008). Exploring causes of the self-serving bias. *Social and Personality Psychology Compass, 2,* 895–908.

Sherblom, S. (2008). The legacy of the "care challenge": Re-envisioning the outcome of the justice-care debate. *Journal of Moral Education, 37,* 81–98.

Sherman, S. L., Allen, E. G., Bean, L. H., & Freeman, S. B. (2007). Epidemiology of Down syndrome [Special issue: Down syndrome]. *Mental Retardation and Developmental Disabilities Research Reviews, 13,* 221–227.

Shi, P., Huang, J. F., & Zhang, Y. P. (2005). Bitter and sweet/umami taste receptors with differently evolutionary pathways. *Yi Chuan Xue Bao, 32,* 346–353.

Shiffman, S. (2007). Use of more nicotine lozenges leads to better success in quitting smoking. *Addiction, 102,* 809–814.

Shimono, K., & Wade N. J. (2002). Monocular alignment in different depth planes. *Vision Research, 42,* 1127–1135.

Shinn, M., Gottlieb, J., Wett, J. L., Bahl, A., Cohen, A., & Baron, E. D. (2007). Predictors of homelessness among older adults in New York city: disability, economic, human and social capital and stressful events. *Journal of Health Psychology, 12,* 696–708.

Shochet, I., Smyth, T., & Homel, R. (2007). The impact of parental attachment on adolescent perception of the school environment and school connectedness. *Australian & New Zealand Journal of Family Therapy, 28,* 109–118.

Shoda, Y., & Mischel, W. (2006). Applying meta-theory to achieve generalisability and precision in personality science. *Applied Psychology: An International Review, 55,* 439–452.

Shohov, S. (2002). *Trends in cognitive psychology.* Hauppauge, NY: Nova Science Publishers.

Shors, T. J. (2009, March). Saving new brain cells. *Scientific American,* pp. 47–54.

Shulman, J. L., & Horne, S. G. (2006). Guilty or not? A path model of women's sexual force fantasies. *Journal of Sex Research, 43,* 368–377.

Shurkin, J. N. (1992). *Terman's kids: The ground-breaking study of how the gifted grow up.* Boston: Little, Brown.

Shweder, R.A. & Haidt, J. (1994). The future of moral psychology: Truth, intuition, and the pluralist way. In B. Puka (Ed), *Reaching out: Caring, altruism, and prosocial behavior.* New York: Garland Publishing.

Sidman, M. (2006). The distinction between positive and negative reinforcement: Some additional considerations. *Behavior Analyst, 29,* 135–139.

Siegal, M. (1991). A clash of conversational worlds: Interpreting cognitive development through communication. *Perspectives on socially shared cognition* (pp. 23–40). Washington, DC: American Psychological Association.

Siegel, J. M. (2003, November). Why we sleep. *Scientific American,* 92–97.

Siegel, J. M. (2005). The incredible, shrinking sleep-learning connection. *Behavioral and Brain Sciences, 28,* 82–83.

Siegel, L., & Davis, L. (2008). Somatic disorders. In R. J. Morris, & T. R. Kratochwill, Eds., *The practice of child therapy* (4th ed.) (pp. 249–298). Mahwah, NJ: Lawrence Erlbaum Associates.

Siegel, R. (2005). Psychophysiological Disorders: Embracing Pain. *Mindfulness and psychotherapy* (pp. 173–196). New York: Guilford Press.

Siegert, R. J., & Ward, T. (2002). Clinical psychology and evolutionary psychology: Toward a dialogue. *Review of General Psychology, 6,* 235–259.

Siemer, M., Mauss I., & Gross, J. J. (2007). Same situation—Different emotions: How appraisals shape our emotions. *Emotion, 7,* 592–600.

Sifrit, K. J. (2006). The effects of aging and cognitive decrements on simulated driving performance. *Dissertation Abstracts International: Section B: The Sciences and Engineering, 67,* 2863.

Sigman, M. (1995). Nutrition and child development: More food for thought. *Current Directions in Psychological Science, 4,* 52–55.

Sigurðardóttir, Z., & Sighvatsson, M. (2006). Operant conditioning and errorless learning procedures in the treatment of chronic aphasia. *International Journal of Psychology, 41,* 527–540.

Silva, M. T. A., Gonçalves, F. L., & Garcia-Mijares, M. (2007). Neural events in the reinforcement contingency. *Behavior Analyst, 30,* 17–30.

Silverstein, M. L. (2007). Rorschach test findings at the beginning of treatment and 2 years later, with a 30-year follow-up. *Journal of Personality Assessment, 88,* 131–143.

Simcock, G., & Hayne, H. (2002). Breaking the barrier? Children fail to translate their pre-verbal memories into language. *Psychological Science, 13,* 225–231.

Simon, G., Ludman, E., Unützer, J., Operskalski, B., & Bauer, M. (2008). Severity of mood symptoms and work productivity in people treated for bipolar disorder. *Bipolar Disorders, 10,* 718–725.

Simon, H. (2003). The uses of mental imagery in thinking. *Cognitive Processing, 4(2),* 87–97.

Simon, S., & Hoyt, C. (2008). Exploring the gender gap in support for a woman for president. *Analyses of Social Issues and Public Policy (ASAP), 8,* 157–181.

Simons, W., & Dierick, M. (2005). Transcranial magnetic stimulation as a therapeutic tool in psychiatry. *World Journal of Biological Psychiatry, 6,* 6–25.

Simonton, D. K. (2000a). Archival research. In A. E. Kazdin (Ed.), *Encyclopedia of psychology* (Vol. 1). Washington, DC: American Psychological Association.

Simonton, D. K. (2000b). Creativity: Cognitive, personal, developmental, and social aspects. *American Psychologist, 55,* 151–158.

Simonton, D. K. (2003). Scientific creativity as constrained stochastic behavior: the integration of product, person, and process perspectives. *Psychological Bulletin, 129,* 475–494.

Singer, J. L. (2006). Why imagery, personal memories, and daydreams matter. In J. L. Singer, *Imagery in psychotherapy.* Washington, DC: American Psychological Association.

Singh, S., Wulf, D., Samara, R, & Cuca, Y. P. (2000). Gender differences in the timing of first intercourse: Data from 14 countries. *International Family Planning Perspectives, 26,* 21–28, 43.

Sininger, Y. S., & Cone-Wesson, B. (2004, September 10). Asymmetric cochlear processing mimics hemispheric specialization. *Science, 305,* 1581.

Sininger, Y. S., & Cone-Wesson, B. (2006). Lateral asymmetry in the ABR of neonates: evidence and mechanisms. *Hearing Research, 212,* 203–211.

Skinner, B. F. (1957). *Verbal behavior.* New York: Appleton-Century-Crofts.

Skinner, B. F. (1975). The steep and thorny road to a science of behavior. *American Psychologist, 30,* 42–49.

Skinner, N., & Fox-Francoeur, C. (2010). Personality implications of adaption-innovation: V. birth order as a determinant of cognitive style. *Social Behavior & Personality, 38,* 237–240.

Skolnick, P., Popik, P., Trullas, R. (2009). Glutamate-based antidepressants: 20 years on. *Trends in Pharmacological Science, 30,* 563–569.

Sledz, M., Oddy, M., & Beaumont, J. G. (2007). Psychological adjustment to locked-in syndrome. *Journal of Neurological Neurosurgery and Psychiatry, 12,* 33–37.

Sleek, S. (1997, June). Can "emotional intelligence" be taught in today's schools? *APA Monitor,* 25.

Sloan, E. P., Hauri, P., Bootzin, R., Morin, C., et al. (1993). The nuts and bolts of behavioral therapy for insomnia. *Journal of Psychosomatic Research, 37* (Suppl.), 19–37.

Smeets, T. (2011). Acute stress impairs memory retrieval independent of time of day. *Psychoneuroendocrinology, 36,* 495–501.

Smetana, J. (2005). Adolescent-parent conflict: Resistance and subversion as developmental process. In L. Nucci (Ed.), *Conflict, contradiction, and contrarian elements in moral development and education.* (pp. 69–91). Mahwah, NJ: Lawrence Erlbaum Associates.

Smetana, J. B. (2007). Strategies for understanding archetypes and the collective unconscious of an organization. *Dissertation Abstracts International Section A: Humanities and Social Sciences, 67(12-A),* 4714.

Smetana, J., Daddis, C., and Chuang, S. (2003). "Clean your room!" A longitudinal investigation of adolescent-parent conflict and conflict resolution in middle-class African American families. *Journal of Adolescent Research, 18,* 631–650.

Smith, B. H., Barkley, R. A., & Shapiro, C. J. (2006). Attention-Deficit/Hyperactivity Disorder. In E. J. Mash & R. A. Barkley, *Treatment of childhood disorders* (3rd. ed). New York: Guilford Press.

Smith, C. (2006). Symposium V—Sleep and learning: New developments. *Brain and Cognition, 60, Special issue: Methods and Learning in Functional MRI,* 331–332.

Smith, C. A., & Lazarus, R. S. (2001). Appraisal components, core relational themes, and the emotions. In W. G. Parrott (Ed.), *Emotions in social psychology: Essential readings* (pp. 94–114). Philadelphia: Psychology Press.

Smith, C. D., Chebrolu, J., Wekstein, D. R., Schmitt, F. A., & Markesbery, W. R. (2007). Age and gender effects on human brain anatomy: a voxel-based morphometric study in healthy elderly. *Neurobiology of Aging, 28,* 1057–1087.

Smith, D. (October 2001). Can't get your 40 winks? Here's what the sleep experts advise. *Monitor on Psychology, 37.*

Smith, D. E., Springer, C. M., & Barrett, S. (2011). Physical discipline and socioemotional adjustment among Jamaican adolescents. *Journal of Family Violence, 26,* 51–61.

Smith, E. (1988, May). Fighting cancerous feelings. *Psychology Today,* pp. 22–23.

Smith, E. E. (2000). Neural bases of human working memory. *Current Directions in Psychological Science, 9,* 45–49.

Smith, E. R., & Semin, G. R. (2007). Situated social cognition. *Current Directions in Psychological Science, 16,* 132–135.

Smith, K., Miner, J., Wiegmann, D., & Newman, S. (2009). Individual differences in exploratory and antipredator behaviour in juvenile small mouth bass (Micropterus dolomieru). *Behaviour, 146,* 283–294.

Smith, L., Cornelius, V., Warnock, A., Bell, A., & Young, A. (2007). Effectiveness of mood stabilizers and antipsychotics in the maintenance phase of bipolar disorder: A systematic review of randomized controlled trials. *Bipolar Disorders, 9,* 394–412.

Smith, M. B. (2003). Moral foundations in research with human participants. In A. E. Kazdin (Ed.), *Methodological issues & strategies in clinical research* (3rd ed.). Washington, DC: American Psychological Association.

Smith, M. L., Glass, G. V., & Miller, T. J. (1980). *The benefits of psychotherapy.* Baltimore: Johns Hopkins University Press.

Smith, R. A., & Weber, A. L. (2005). Applying social psychology in everyday life. In F. W. Schneider, J. A. Gruman, & L. M. Coutts, *Applied social psychology: Understanding and addressing social and practical.* Thousand Oaks, CA: Sage Publications.

Smith, W. B. (2007). Karen Horney and psychotherapy in the 21st century. *Clinical Social Work Journal, 35,* 57–66.

Smolowe, J. (2008, June 23). Medical miracle surgery for an unborn child. *People,* p. 96.

Snyder, D. J., Fast, K., & Bartoshuk, L. M. (2004). Valid comparisons of suprathreshold sensations. *Journal of Consciousness Studies, 11,* 96–112.

Snyder, J., Cramer, A., & Afrank, J. (2005). The contributions of ineffective discipline and parental hostile attributions of child misbehavior to the development of conduct problems at home and school. *Developmental Psychology, 41*, 30–41.

Snyder, M. (2002). Applications of Carl Rogers' theory and practice to couple and family therapy: A response to Harlene Anderson and David Bott. *Journal of Family Therapy, 24*, 317–325.

Sobel, K., Gerrie, M., Poole, B., & Kane, M. (2007, October). Individual differences in working memory capacity and visual search: The roles of top-down and bottom-up processing. *Psychonomic Bulletin & Review, 14*, 840–84

Society for Personality Assessment. (2005). The status of Rorschach in clinical and forensic practice: An official statement by the board of trustees of the Society for Personality Assessment. *Journal of Personality Assessment, 85*, 219–237.

Sohr-Preston, S.L. & Scaramella, L. V. (2006). Implications of timing of maternal depressive symptoms for early cognitive and language development. *Clinical Child Care and Family Review, 9*, 65–83.

Soken, N., & Pick, A. (1999, November). Infants' perception of dynamic affective expressions: Do infants distinguish specific expressions? *Child Development, 70*(6), 1275–1282.

Sokolove, M. (2003, November 16). Should John Hinckley go free? *The New York Times Magazine*, pp. 52–54, 92.

Solomon, P. R., Adams, F., Silver, A., Zimmer, J., & Deveaux, R. (2002). Ginkgo for memory enhancement: A randomized controlled trial. *JAMA, 88*, 835–840.

Sommer, R., & Sommer, B. (2001). *A practical guide to behavioral research: Tools and techniques* (5th ed.). New York: Oxford University Press.

Sorbring, E., Deater-Deckard, K., & Palmerus, K. (2006). Girls' and boys' perception of mothers' intentions of using physical punishment and reasoning as discipline methods. *European Journal of Developmental Psychology, 3*, 142–162.

Sori, C. F. (Ed.). (2006). *Engaging children in family therapy: Creative approaches to integrating theory and research in clinical practice*. New York: Routledge/Taylor & Francis Group.

Soussignan, R. (2002). Duchenne smile, emotional experience, and automatic reactivity: A test of the facial feedback hypothesis. *Emotion, 2*, 52–74.

Souter, E., and Wong, M. (2006, May 15). Exercise almost killed her. *People*, p. 165–170.

South, S., & Krueger, R. (2008). An interactionist perspective on genetic and environmental contributions to personality. *Social and Personality Psychology Compass, 2*, 929–948.

Spackman, M. P., Fujiki, M., & Brinton, B. (2006). Understanding emotions in context: The effects of language impairment on children's ability to infer emotional reactions. *International Journal of Language & Communication Disorders, 41*, 173–188.

Spangler, W. D. (1992). Validity of questionnaire and TAT measures of need for achievement: Two meta-analyses. *Psychological Bulletin, 112*, 140–154.

Spanos, N. P., Barner, T. X., & Lang, G. (2005). Cognition and self-control: Cognitive control of painful sensory input. *Integrative Physiological & Behavioral Science, 40*, 119–128.

Sparks, S. D. (2007, October 2). Foundation: Gifted poor students given short shrift. *Education Daily, 40*, 3.

Spataro, P., Mulligan, N. W., & Rossi-Arnaud, C. (2011). Attention and implicit memory: The role of the activation of multiple representations. *Experimental Psychology, 58*, 110–116.

Spearman, C. (1927). *The abilities of man*. London: Macmillan.

Speirs Neumeister, K. L., & Finch, H. (2006). Perfectionism in high-ability students: Relational precursors and influences on achievement motivation. *Gifted Child Quarterly, 50*, 238–251.

Spence, M. J., & DeCasper, A. J. (1982, March). *Human fetuses perceive maternal speech*. Paper presented at the meeting of the International Conference on Infant Studies, Austin, TX.

Spencer, S. J., Fein, S., Zanna, M. P., & Olson, J. M. (Eds.) (2003). *Motivated social perception: The Ontario Symposium* (Vol. 9). Mahwah, NJ: Erlbaum.

Spencer-Rodgers, J., Peng, K., Wang, L., & Hou, Y. (2004). Dialectical self-esteem and East-West differences in psychological well-being. *Personality and Social Psychology Bulletin, 30*, 1416–1432.

Sperry, L. (2009). Cancer. *Treatment of chronic medical conditions: Cognitive-behavioral therapy strategies and integrative treatment protocols* (pp. 119–133). Washington, DC: American Psychological Association.

Sperry, R. (1982). Some effects of disconnecting the cerebral hemispheres. *Science, 217*, 1223–1226.

Spiegel, D. (1993). Social support: How friends, family, and groups can help. In D. Goleman & J. Gurin (Eds.), *Mind-body medicine*. Yonkers, NY: Consumer Reports Books.

Spiegel, D. (1996). Hypnosis. In R. E. Hales & S. C. Yudofsky (Eds.), *The American Psychiatric Press synopsis of psychiatry*. Washington, DC: American Psychiatric Press.

Spiegel, D. (Ed.). (1999). *Efficacy and cost-effectiveness of psychotherapy*. New York: American Psychiatric Press.

Spiers, H. J., & Maguire, F. A. (2007). Decoding human brain activity during real-world experiences. *Trends in Cognitive Science, 11*, 356–365.

Spiller, L. D., & Wymer, W. W., Jr. (2001). Physicians' perceptions and use of commercial drug information sources: An examination of pharmaceutical marketing to physicians. *Health Marketing Quarterly, 19*, 91–106.

Spindler, H., Kruse, C., Zwisler, A., & Pedersen, S. (2009). Increased anxiety and depression in Danish cardiac patients with a type D personality: Cross-validation of the Type D Scale (DS14). *International Journal of Behavioral Medicine, 16*, 98–107.

Spinella, M., & Lester, D. (2006). Can money buy happiness? *Psychological Reports, 99*, 992.

Spitz, H. H. (1987). Problem-solving processes in special populations. In J. G. Borkowski & J. D. Day (Eds.), *Cognition in special children: Comparative approaches to retardation, learning disabilities, and giftedness*. Norwood, NJ: Ablex.

Spitzer, R. L., Skodol, A. E., Gibbon, M., & Williams, J. B. W. (1983). *Psychopathology: A case book*. New York: McGraw-Hill.

Sprecher, S., & Regan, P. C. (2002). Liking some things (in some people) more than others: Partner preferences in romantic relationships and friendships. *Journal of Social and Personal Relationships, 19*, 436–481.

Sprender, M. (2007). *Memory 101 for educators*. Thousand Oaks, CA: Corwin Press.

Sprenkle, D. H., & Moon, S. M. (Eds.). (1996). *Research methods in family therapy*. New York: Guilford Press.

Springen, K. (2004, August 9) Anxiety: Sweet and elusive sleep. *Newsweek*, p. 21.

Squire, L. R., Clark, R. E., & Bayley, P. J. (2004). Medial temporal lobe function and memory. In M. S. Gazzaniga (Ed.), *Cognitive neurosciences* (3rd ed.) (pp. 691–708). Cambridge, MA: MIT.

St. Dennis, C., Hendryx, M., Henriksen, A. L., Setter, S. M., & Singer, B. (2006). Postdischarge treatment costs following closure of a state geropsychiatric ward: Comparison of 2 levels of community care. *Primary Care Companion Journal of Clinical Psychiatry, 8*, 279–284.

St. Jacques, P. L., & Levine, B. (2007). Ageing and autobiographical memory for emotional and neutral events. *Memory, 15*, 129–144.

Staddon, J. E. R., & Cerutti, D. T. (2003). Operant conditioning. *Annual Review of Psychology, 54*, 115–144.

Staley, J. K., & Sanacora, G., & Tamagnan, G. (2006). Sex differences in diencephalon serotonin transporter availability in major depression. *Biological Psychiatry, 59*, 40–47.

Stankov, L. (2003). Complexity in human intelligence. In R. J. Sternberg, J. Lautrey, et al. (Eds.), *Models of intelligence: International perspectives* (pp. 27–42). Washington, DC: American Psychological Association.

Stanojevic, S., Mitic, K., & Vujic, V. (2007). Exposure to acute physical and psychological stress alters the response of rat macrophages to corticosterone, neuropeptide Y and beta-endorphin. *International Journal on the Biology of Stress, 10*, 65–73.

Stanton, A. L., Danoff-Burg, S., Cameron, C. L., Bishop, M., Collins, C. A., Kirk, S. B., Sworowski, L. A., & Twillman, R. (2000). Emotionally expressive coping predicts psychological and physical adjustment to breast cancer. *Journal of Consulting and Clinical Psychology, 68*, 875–882.

Stapel, D. A., & Semin, G. R. (2007). The magic spell of language: Linguistic categories and their perceptual consequences. *Journal of Personality and Social Psychology, 93*, 23–33.

Starcevic, V., Berle, D., Milicevic, D., Hannan, A., Pamplugh, C., & Eslick, G. D. (2007). Pathological worry, anxiety disorders and the impact of co-occurrence with depressive and other anxiety disorders. *Journal of Anxiety Disorders, 21*, 1016–1027.

Startup, M., Bucci, S., & Langdon, R. (2009). Delusions of reference: A new theoretical model. *Cognitive Neuropsychiatry, 14*, 110–126.

Steblay, N., Dysart, J., Fulero, S., & Lindsay, R. C. L. (2003). Eyewitness accuracy rates in police showup and lineup presentations: A meta-analytic comparison. *Law & Human Behavior, 27*, 523–540.

Stedenfeld, K. A., Clinton, S. M., Kerman, I. A., Akil, H., Watson, S. J., & Sved, A. F. (2011). Novelty-seeking behavior predicts vulnerability in a rodent model of depression. *Physiology & Behavior*, In Press.

Steele, C. M., & Josephs, R. A. (1990). Alcohol myopia: Its prized and dangerous effects. *American Psychologist, 45*, 921–933.

Steele, J. D., Christmas, D., Eljamel, M. S., & Matthews, K. (2007). Anterior cingulotomy for major depression: clinical outcome and relationship to lesion characteristics. *Biological Psychiatry, 12*, 127–134.

Stegerwald, F., & Janson, G. R. (2003). Conversion therapy: Ethical considerations in family counseling. *Family Journal—Counseling and Therapy for Couples and Families, 11*, 55–59.

Steiger, A. (2007). Neurochemical regulation of sleep. *Journal of Psychiatric Research, 41*, 537–552.

Stein, L. A. R., & Graham, J. R. (2005). Ability of substance abusers to escape detection on the Minnesota Multiphasic Personality Inventory-Adolescent (MMPI-A) in a juvenile correctional facility. *Assessment, 12*, 28–39.

Steinberg, L. (2007). Risk taking in adolescence. *Current Directions in Psychological Science, 16*, 55–59.

Steiner, B., Wolf, S., & Kempermann, G. (2006). Adult neurogenesis and neurodegenerative disease. *Regenerative Medicine, 1*, 15–28.

Steiner, J. (2008). Transference to the analyst as an excluded observer. *The International Journal of Psychoanalysis, 89*, 39–54.

Stemler, S. E., & Sternberg, R. J. (2006). Using situational judgment tests to measure practical intelligence. In J. A. Weekley, & R. E. Ployhart, *Situational judgment tests: Theory, measurement, and application*. Mahwah, NJ: Erlbaum.

Stemler, S. E., Sternberg, R. J., Grigorenko, E. L., Jarvin, L., & Sharpes, K. (2009). Using the theory of successful intelligence as a framework for developing assessments in AP physics. *Contemporary Educational Psychology, 34*, 195–209.

Stenbacka, L., & Vanni, S. (2007). fMRI of peripheral visual field representation. *Clinical Neurophysiology, 108*, 1303–1314.

Stenklev, N. C., & Laukli, E. (2004). Cortical cognitive potentials in elderly persons. *Journal of the American Academy of Audiology, 15*, 401–413.

Stephens, M., & Townsend, A. (1997, June). Stress of parent care: Positive and negative effects of women's other roles. *Psychology and Aging, 12*(2), 376–386.

Stephenson, R. H., & Banet-Weiser, S. (2007). Super-sized kids: Obesity, children, moral panic, and the media. In J. A. Bryant, *The children's television community.* Mahwah, NJ: Lawrence Erlbaum Associates.

Stepp, L. (2007, April 24). For Virginia Tech survivors, memories will be powerful. *Washington Post,* p. HE01.

Stern, E., & Silbersweig, D. A. (2001). Advances in functional neuroimaging methodology for the study of brain systems underlying human neuropsychological function and dysfunction. In D. A. Silbersweig & E. Stern (Eds.), *Neuropsychology and functional neuro-imaging: Convergence, advances and new directions.* Amsterdam: Swets and Zeitlinger.

Stern, R. M., & Koch, K. L. (1996). Motion sickness and differential susceptibility. *Current Directions in Psychological Science, 5,* 115–120.

Sternberg, E. M. (2002). Walter B. Cannon and Voodoo Death: A perspective from 60 years on. *American Journal of Public Health, 92,* 1564–1566.

Sternberg, R. J. (1990). *Metaphors of mind: Conceptions of the nature of intelligence.* New York: Cambridge University Press. Sternberg, R. J. (1998). *Successful intelligence: How practical and creative intelligence determine success in life.* New York: Plume.

Sternberg, R. J. (1998). *Successful intelligence: How practical and creative intelligence determine success in life.* New York: Plume.

Sternberg, R. J. (2000). Intelligence and wisdom. In R. J. Sternberg et al. (Eds.), *Handbook of intelligence.* New York: Cambridge University Press.

Sternberg, R. J. (2001). What is the common thread of creativity? Its dialectical relation to intelligence and wisdom. *American Psychologist, 56,* 360–362.

Sternberg, R. J. (2002a). Individual differences in cognitive development. In U. Goswami (Ed.), *Blackwell handbook of childhood cognitive development. Blackwell handbooks of developmental psychology* (pp. 600–619). Malden, MA: Blackwell.

Sternberg, R. J. (Ed.). (2002b). *Why smart people can be so stupid.* New Haven, CT: Yale University Press.

Sternberg, R. J. (2004a). A triangular theory of love. In H. T. Reis & C. E. Rusbult (Eds.), *Close relationships: Key readings.* Philadelphia, PA: Taylor & Francis.

Sternberg, R. J. (2004b). Culture and intelligence. *American Psychologist, 59,* 325–338.

Sternberg, R. J. (2004c). Theory-based university admissions testing for a new millennium. *Educational Psychologist, 39,* 185–198.

Sternberg, R. J. (2006). A duplex theory of love. In R. J. Sternberg, Ed., *The new psychology of love.* New Haven, CT: Yale University Press.

Sternberg, R. J., & Beall, A. E. (1991). How can we know what love is? An epistemological analysis. In G. J. O. Fletcher & F. D. Fincham (Eds.), *Cognition in close relationships.* Hillsdale, NJ: Erlbaum.

Sternberg, R. J., & Grigorenko, E. L. (2005). Cultural explorations of the nature of intelligence. In A. F. Healy (Ed.), *Experimental cognitive psychology and its applications.* Washington, DC: American Psychological Association.

Sternberg, R. J., & Hedlund, J. (2002). Practical intelligence, "g," and work psychology. *Human Performance, 15,* 143–160.

Sternberg, R. J., & Jarvin, L. (2003). Alfred Binet's contributions as a paradigm for impact in psychology. In R. J. Sternberg (Ed.), *The anatomy of impact: What makes the great works of psychology great* (pp. 89–107). Washington, DC: American Psychological Association.

Sternberg, R. J., Kaufman, J. C., & Pretz, J. E. (2004). A propulsion model of creative leadership [Special issue: Creativity in the workplace]. *Creativity and Innovation Management, 13,* 145–153.

Sternberg, R. J., & O'Hara, L. A. (2000). Intelligence and creativity. In R. Sternberg et al. (Eds.), *Handbook of intelligence.* New York: Cambridge University Press.

Sternberg, R. J., & Pretz, J. E. (2005). *Cognition and intelligence: Identifying the mechanisms of the mind.* New York: Cambridge University Press, 2005.

Sternberg, R. J., Grigorenko, E. L., & Kidd, K. K. (2005). Intelligence, race, and genetics. *American Psychologist, 60,* 46–59.

Sternberg, R. J., Hojjat, M., & Barnes, M. L. (2001). Empirical aspects of a theory of love as a story. *European Journal of Personality, 15,* 1–20.

Stettler, N., Stallings, V. A., Troxel, A. B., Zhao. J., Z., Schinnar, R., Nelson, S. E., Ziegler, E. E., Strom, B. L. (2005). Weight gain in the first week of life and overweight in adulthood. *Circulation, 111,* 1897–1903.

Stevens, G., & Gardner, S. (1982). *The women of psychology: Pioneers and innovators* (Vol. 1). Cambridge, MA: Schenkman.

Stevens, M. J., & Gielen, U. P. (Eds.) (2007). *Toward a global psychology: Theory, research, intervention, and pedagogy.* Mahwah, NJ: Lawrence Erlbaum.

Stevens, P. & Harper, D. J. (2007). Professional accounts of electroconvulsive therapy: A discourse analysis. *Social Science & Medicine, 64,* 1475–1486.

Stevenson, H. W., Lee, S., & Mu, X. (2000). Successful achievement in mathematics: China and the United States. In C. F. M. van Lieshout & P. G. Heymans (Eds.), *Developing talent across the life span.* New York: Psychology Press.

Stevenson, R. J., & Case, T. I. (2005). Olfactory imagery: A review. *Psychonomic Bulletin and Review, 12,* 244–264.

Stevenson-Hinde, J., & Verschueren, K. (2002). Attachment in childhood. *Blackwell handbook of childhood social development* (pp. 182–204). Malden: Blackwell Publishing.

Stickgold, R. A., Winkelman, J. W., & Wehrwein, P. (2004, January 19). You will start to feel very sleepy . . . *Newsweek,* pp. 58–60.

Stickgold, R., Hobson, J. A., Fosse, R., & Fosse, M. (2001, November 2). Sleep, learning, and dreams: Off-line memory reprocessing. *Science, 294,* pp. 1052–1057.

Stickley, T., & Nickeas, R. (2006). Becoming one person: Living with dissociative identity disorder. *Journal of Psychiatric and Mental Health Nursing, 13,* 180–187.

Stier, H., & Lewin-Epstein, N. (2000). Women's part-time employment and gender inequality in the family. *Journal of Family Issues, 21,* 390–410.

Stimson, G., Grant, M., Choquet, M., & Garrison, P. (2007). *Drinking in context: Patterns, interventions, and partnerships.* New York: Routledge/Taylor & Francis Group.

Stocks, E., Lishner, D., & Decker, S. (2009). Altruism or psychological escape: Why does empathy promote prosocial behavior? *European Journal of Social Psychology, 39,* 649–665.

Stockton, R., Morran, D. K., & Krieger, K. M. (2004). An overview of current research and best practices for training beginning group leaders. In J. L. DeLucia-Waack, D. A. Gerrity, C. R. Kalodner, & M. T. Riva (Eds.), *Handbook of group counseling and psychotherapy.* Thousand Oaks, CT: Sage Publications.

Stompe, T., Ortwein-Swoboda, G., Ritter, K., & Schanda, H. (2003). Old wine in new bottles? Stability and plasticity of the contents of schizophrenic delusions. *Psychopathology, 36,* 6–12.

Storm, L., & Ertel, S. (2001). Does psi exist? Comments on Milton and Wiseman's (1999) meta-analysis of Ganzfeld's research. *Psychological Bulletin, 127,* 424–433.

Stouffer, E. M., & White, N. M. (2006). Neural circuits mediating latent learning and conditioning for salt in the rat. *Neurobiology of Learning and Memory, 86,* 91–99.

Strange, D., Clifasefi, S., & Garry, M. (2007). False memories. In M. Garry, & H. Hayne, *Do justice and let the sky fall: Elizabeth Loftus and her contributions to science, law, and academic freedom.* Mahwah, NJ: Lawrence Erlbaum Associates.

Strathern, A., & Stewart, P. J. (2003). *Landscape, memory and history: Anthropological perspectives.* London: Pluto Press.

Strauss, E. (1998, May 8). Writing, speech separated in split brain. *Science, 280,* 287.

Strayer, D. L., & Drews, F. A. (2007). Cell-phone-induced driver distraction. *Current Directions in Psychological Science, 16,* 128–131.

Strayer, D. L., Drews, F. A., Crouch, D. J., & Johnston, W. A. (2005). Why do cell phone conversations interfere with driving? In W. R. Walker and D. Herrmann (Eds.) *Cognitive technology: Transforming thought and society.* Jefferson, NC: McFarland & Company.

Street, R. L., & Haidet, P. (2011). How well do doctors know their patients? Factors affecting physician understanding of patients' health beliefs. *Journal of General Internal Medicine, 26,* 21–27.

Striano, T., & Vaish, A. (2006). Seven- to 9-month-old infants use facial expressions to interpret others' actions. *British Journal of Developmental Psychology, 24,* 753–760.

Striegel-Moore, R., & Bulik, C. M. (2007). Risk factors for eating disorders. *American Psychologist, 62,* 181–198.

Strobel, M., Tumasjan, A., & Spörrle, M. (2011). Be yourself, believe in yourself, and be happy: Self-efficacy as a mediator between personality factors and subjective well being. *Scandinavian Journal of Psychology, 52,* 43–48.

Strong, T., & Tomm, K. (2007). Family therapy as re-coordinating and moving on together. *Journal of Systemic Therapies, 26,* 42–54.

Stronski, S. M., Ireland, M., & Michaud, P. (2000). Protective correlates of stages in adolescent substance use: A Swiss national study. *Journal of Adolescent Health, 26,* 420–427.

Stroup, T., Kraus, J., & Marder, S. (2006). Pharmacotherapies. *The American Psychiatric Publishing Textbook of Schizophrenia* (pp. 303–325). Arlington, VA: American Psychiatric Publishing, Inc.

Strupp, H. H. (1996, October). The tripartite model and the *Consumer Reports* study. *American Psychologist, 51,* 1017–1024.

Strupp, H. H., & Binder, J. L. (1992). Current developments in psychotherapy. *The Independent Practitioner, 12,* 119–124.

Sue, D. W., Sue, D., & Sue, S. (1990). *Understanding abnormal behavior* (3rd ed.). Boston: Houghton-Mifflin.

Suh, E. M. (2002). Culture, identity consistency, and subjective well-being. *Journal of Personality & Social Psychology, 83,* 1378–1391.

Suhail, K., & Chaudhry, H. R. (2004). Predictors of subjective well-being in an Eastern Muslim culture. *Journal of Social and Clinical Psychology, 23,* 359–376.

Suizzo, M-A., & Bornstein, M. H. (2006). French and European American child-mother play: Culture and gender considerations. *International Journal of Behavioral Development, 30,* 498–508.

Sullivan, J., Riccio, C., & Reynolds, C. (2008, September). Variations in students' school- and teacher-related attitudes across gender, ethnicity, and age. *Journal of Instructional Psychology, 35,* 296–305.

Summers, M. (2000) *Everything in its place.* New York: Putnam.

Sumner, J. A., Griffith, J. W., & Mineka, S. (2011). Examining the mechanisms of overgeneral autobiographical memory: Capture and rumination, and impaired executive control. *Memory, 19,* 169–183.

Sun, S., Schubert, C., Liang, R., Roche, A., Kulin, H., Lee, P., et al. (2005, November). Is sexual maturity occurring earlier among U.S. children? *Journal of Adolescent Health, 37*(5), 345–355.

Sun, T., Patoine, C., Abu-Khalil, A., Visvader, J., Sum, E., Cherry, T. J., Orkink, S. H., Geschwind, D. H., & Walsh, C. A. (2005, June 17). Early asymmetry of gene transcriptions in embryonic human left and right cerebral cortex. *Science, 308,* 1794–1796.

Super, C. M. (1980). Cognitive development: Looking across at growing up. In C. M. Super & S. Harakness (Eds.), *New directions for child development: Anthropological perspectives on child development* (pp. 59–69). San Francisco: Jossey-Bass.

Surette, R. (2002). Self-reported copycat crime among a population of serious and violent juvenile offenders. *Crime & Delinquency, 48,* 46–69.

Susser, E. S., Herman, D. B., & Aaron, B. (2002, August). Combating the terror of terrorism. *Scientific American,* pp. 70–77.

Sutin, A. R., & Robins, R. W. (2007). Phenomenology of autobiographical memories: The Memory Experiences Questionnaire. *Memory, 15,* 390–411.

Svarstad, B. (1976). Physician-patient communication and patient conformity with medical advice. In D. Mechanic (Ed.), *The growth of bureaucratic medicine.* New York: Wiley.

Svartdal, F. (2003). Extinction after partial reinforcement: Predicted vs. judged persistence. *Scandinavian Journal of Psychology, 44,* 55–64.

Swain, P. I. (2006). *New developments in eating disorders research.* Hauppauge, NY: Nova Science Publishers.

Swales, M. A., & Heard, H. L. (2007). The therapy relationship in dialectical behaviour therapy. In P. Gilbert & R. L. Leahy, *The therapeutic relationship in the cognitive behavioral psychotherapies.* New York: Routledge/Taylor & Francis.

Swann, W. B., Jr., Chang-Schneider, C., & Larsen McClarty, K. (2007). Do people's self-views matter? Self-concept and self-esteem in everyday life. *American Psychologist, 62,* 84–94.

Swanson, H. L., Harris, K. R., & Graham, S. (Eds.). (2003). *Handbook of learning disabilities.* New York: Guilford Press.

Swets, J. A., & Bjork, R.A. (1990). Enhancing human performance: An evaluation of "new age" techniques considered by the U.S. Army. *Psychological Science, 1,* 85–96.

Szasz, T. (1994). *Cruel compassion: Psychiatric control of society's unwanted.* New York: Wiley.

Szasz, T. (2004). "Knowing what ain't so": R. D. Laing and Thomas Szasz. *Psychoanalytic Review, 91,* 331–346.

Szasz, T. (2006). The pretense of psychology as science: The myth of mental illness in statu nascendi. *Current Psychology: Developmental, Learning, Personality, Social, 25,* 42–49.

Szegedy Maszak, M. (2003, January 13). The sound of unsound minds. *U.S. News & World Report,* pp. 45–46.

T

Tadmor, C. T. (2007). Biculturalism: The plus side of leaving home? The effects of second-culture exposure on integrative complexity and its consequences for overseas performance. *Dissertation Abstracts International Section A: Humanities and Social Sciences, 67(8-A),* 3068.

Taggi, F., Crenca, A., Cedri, C., Giustini, M., Dosi, G., & Marturano, P. (2007). Road safety and the tsunami of cell phones. *Ann Ig, 19,* 269–274.

Tajfel, H., & Turner, J. C. (2004). The social identity theory of intergroup behavior. In J. T. Jost & J. Sidanius (Eds.), *Political psychology: Key readings.* New York: Psychology Press.

Takahashi, M., Nakata, A., Haratani, T., Ogawa, Y., & Arito, H. (2004). Post-lunch nap as a worksite intervention to promote alertness on the job. *Ergonomics, 47,* 1003–1013.

Takahashi, T., & Washington, W. (1991, January). A group-centered object relations approach to group psychotherapy with severely disturbed patients. *International Journal of Group Psychotherapy, 41*(1), 79–96.

Takizawa, T., Kondo, T., & Sakihara, S. (2007). Stress buffering effects of social support on depressive symptoms in middle age: Reciprocity and community mental health: Corrigendum. *Psychiatry and Clinical Neurosciences, 61,* 336–337.

Talarico, J. (2009). Freshman flashbulbs: Memories of unique and first-time events in starting college. *Memory, 17,* 256–265.

Talarico, J., & Rubin, D. (2007). Flashbulb memories are special after all; in phenomenology, not accuracy. *Applied Cognitive Psychology, 21,* 557–578.

Talmi, D., Anderson, A., Riggs, L., Caplan, J., & Moscovitch, M. (2008). Immediate memory consequences of the effect of emotion on attention to pictures. *Learning & Memory, 15,* 172–182.

Tal-Or, N., & Papirman, Y. (2007). The fundamental attribution error in attributing fictional figures' characteristics to the actors. *Media Psychology, 9,* 331–345.

Talukdar, S., & Shastri, J. (2006). Contributory and adverse factors in social development of young children. *Psychological Studies, 51,* 294–303.

Tamis-LeMonda, C. (2004, July). Conceptualizing Fathers' Roles: Playmates and More. *Human Development, 47*(4), 220–227.

Tan, L., & Ward, G. (2008). Rehearsal in immediate serial recall. *Psychonomic Bulletin & Review, 15,* 535–542.

Tan, W., Lo, C., Jong, A., Xing, L., Fitzgerald, M., Vollmer, W., et al. (2009). Marijuana and chronic obstructive lung disease: A population-based study. *Canadian Medical Association Journal, 180,* 814–820.

Tanner, J. M. (1990). *Foetus into man: Physical growth from conception to maturity* (rev. ed.). Cambridge, MA: Harvard University Press.

Taras, H., & Potts-Datema, W. (2005). Chronic health conditions and student performance at school. *Journal of School Health, 75,* 255–266.

Tasker, F. & Golombok, S. (1995). Adults raised as children in lesbian families. *American Journal of Orthopsychiatry, 65,* 203–215.

Tasker, F. (2005). Lesbian mothers, gay fathers, and their children: A review. *Journal of Developmental and Behavioral Pediatrics, 26,* 224–240.

Tavniers, J., Ruysseveldt, J., Smeets, T., & Von Grumbkow, J. (2010). High-intensity stress elicits robust cortisol increases, and impairs working memory and visuo-spatial declarative memory in Special Forces candidates: A field experiment. *The International Journal on the Biology of Stress, 13,* 323–333.

Taylor, C. (2004, November 29). The sky's the limit. *Time,* pp. 15–17.

Taylor, F., & Bryant, R. A. (2007). The tendency to suppress, inhibiting thoughts, and dream rebound. *Behaviour Research and Therapy, 45,* pp. 163–168.

Taylor, S. (2003). Anxiety sensitivity and its implications for understanding and treating PTSD. *Journal of Cognitive Psychotherapy, 17,* 179–186.

Taylor, S. E. (1995). Quandary at the crossroads: Paternalism versus advocacy surrounding end-of-treatment decisions. *American Journal of Hospital Palliatory Care, 12,* 43–46.

Taylor, S. E., Kemeny, M. E., Reed, G. M., Bower, J. E., & Gruenewald, T. L. (2000). Psychological resources, positive illusions, and health. *American Psychologist, 55,* 99–109.

Teff, K. L., Petrova, M., & Havel, P. J. (2007). 48-h Glucose infusion in humans: Effect on hormonal responses, hunger and food intake. *Physiology & Behavior, 90,* 733–743.

Tellegen, A., Lykken, D. T., Bouchard, T. J., Jr., Wilcox, K. J., Segal, N. L., & Rich, S. (1988). Personality similarity in twins reared apart and together. *Journal of Personality and Social Psychology, 54,* 1031–1039.

Templer, D. I., & Arkawa, H. (2006). Association of race and color with mean IQ across nations. *Psychological Reports, 99,* 191–196.

Tenenbaum, H. R., & Ruck, M. D. (2007). Are teachers' expectations different for racial minority than for European American students? A meta-analysis. *Journal of Educational Psychology, 99,* 253–273.

Tenopyr, M. L. (2002). Theory versus reality: Evaluation of 'g' in the workplace. *Human Performance, 15,* 107–122.

Teodorov, E., Salzgerber, S. A., Felicio, L. F., Varolli, F. M. F., & Bernardi, M. M. (2002). Effects of perinatal picrotoxin and sexual experience on heterosexual and homosexual behavior in male rats. *Neurotoxicology and Teratology, 24,* 235–245.

Terman, L. (1997). The discovery and encouragement of exceptional talent (1954). *The evolution of psychology: Fifty years of the American Psychologist* (pp. 306–320). Washington, DC: American Psychological Association.

Terman, L., & Oden, M. (1947). *The gifted child grows up: twenty-five years' follow-up of a superior group.* Oxford: Stanford Univ. Press.

Terracciano, A., Abdel-Khalek, A., Adam, N., Adamovova, L., and 83 additional authors. (2005). National character does not reflect mean personality trait levels in 49 cultures. *Science, 310,* 96–100.

Terry, W. S. (2003). *Learning and memory: Basic principles, processes, and procedures* (2nd ed.). Boston: Allyn & Bacon.

Tervaniemi, M., Jacobsen, T., & Röttger, S. (2006). Selective tuning of cortical sound-feature processing by language experience. *European Journal of Neuroscience, 23,* 2538–2541.

Tesoriero, H. (July 5, 2007). Mysteries of the "faceblind" could illuminate the brain. *Wall Street Journal,* A1.

Tetlock, P. E. (1997). Psychological perspectives on international conflict and cooperation. In D. F. Halpern & A. E. Voiskounsky (Eds.), *States of mind: American and post-Soviet perspectives on contemporary issues in psychology.* London: Oxford University Press.

Thachil, A. F., Mohan, R., & Bhugra, D. (2007). The evidence base of complementary and alternative therapies in depression. *Journal of Affective Disorders, 97,* 23–35.

Thara, R. (2004). Twenty-year course of schizophrenia: The Madras longitudinal study. *Canadian Journal of Psychiatry, 49,* 564–569.

Tharp, R. G. (1989). Psychocultural variables and constants: Effects on teaching and learning in schools [Special issue: Children and their development: Knowledge base, research agenda, and social policy application]. *American Psychologist, 44,* 349–359.

Thatcher, D. L., & Clark, D. B., (2006). Adolescent alcohol abuse and dependence: Development, diagnosis, treatment and outcomes. *Current Psychiatry Reviews, 2,* 159–177.

Thomas, D. (1991). Context as a retrieval cue in pigeon long-term memory. *Memory mechanisms: A tribute to G. V. Goddard* (pp. 329–352). Hillsdale, NJ: Lawrence Erlbaum Associates, Inc.

Thomas, P., Mathur, P., Gottesman, I. I., Nagpal, R., Nimgaonkar, V. L., & Deshpande, S. N. (2007). Correlates of hallucinations in schizophrenia: A cross-cultural evaluation. *Schizophrenia Research, 92,* 41–49.

Thomason, M., Race, E., Burrows, B., Whitfield-Gabrieli, S., Glover, G., & Gabrieli, J. (2009). Development of spatial and verbal working memory capacity in the human brain. *Journal of Cognitive Neuroscience, 21,* 316–332.

Thompson, J. (2000, June 18). "I was certain, but I was wrong." *The New York Times,* p. E14.

Thompson, P. M., Hayaski, K. M., Simon, S. L., Geaga, J. A., Hong, M. S., Sui, Y., Lee, J. Y., Toga, A. W., Ling, W., & London, E. D. (2004, June 30). Structural abnormalities in the brains of human subjects who use methamphetamine. *The Journal of Neuroscience, 24*(26), 6028–6036.

Thompson, R., Braun, K., Grossmann, K., Gunnar, M., Heinrichs, M., Keller, H., et al. (2005). Group Report: Early Social Attachment and Its Consequences: The Dynamics of a Developing Relationship. *Attachment and bonding: A new synthesis* (pp. 349–384). Cambridge, MA: MIT Press.

Thompson, R. D., Goldsmith, A. A., & Tran, G. Q. (2011). Alcohol and drug use in socially anxious young adults. In C. A. Alfano, D. C. Beidel, C. A. Alfano, D. C. Beidel (Eds.), *Social anxiety in adolescents and young adults: Translating developmental science into practice.* Washington, DC: American Psychological Association.

Thompson, W. L., Hsiao, Y., & Kosslyn, S. M. (2011). Dissociation between visual attention and visual mental imagery. *Journal of Cognitive Psychology, 23,* 256–263.

Thorkildsen, T. A. (2006). An empirical exploration of language and thought. *Psyc-CRITIQUES, 51,* No pagination specified.

Thorndike, E. L. (1932). *The fundamentals of learning.* New York: Teachers College.

Thornton, A., & McAuliffe, K. (2006, July 14). Teaching in wild meerkats. *Science, 313,* 227–229.

Thornton, A., & Young-DeMarco, L. (2001). Four decades of trends in attitudes toward family issues in the United States: The 1960s through the 1990s. *Journal of Marriage and the Family, 63,* 1009–1017.

Thrash, T. M., & Elliot, A. J. (2002). Implicit and self-attributed achievement motives: Concordance and predictive validity. *Journal of Personality, 70,* 729–755.

Tian, F. F., Tu, S. S., Qiu, J. J., Lu, J. Y., Wei, D. T., Su, Y. H., et al. (2011). Neural correlates of mental preparation for successful insight problem solving. *Behavioural Brain Research, 216,* 626–630.

Tippin, J., Sparks, J., & Rizzo, M. (2009, August). Visual vigilance in drivers with obstructive sleep apnea. *Journal of Psychosomatic Research, 67,* 143–151.

Tirri, K., & Nokelainen, P. (2008). Identification of multiple intelligences with the Multiple Intelligence Profiling Questionnaire III [Special issue: High-ability assessment]. *Psychology Science, 50,* 206–221.

Titone, D. A. (2002). Memories bound: The neuroscience of dreams. *Trends in Cognitive Science, 6,* 4–5.

Tolman, E. C., & Honzik, C. H. (1930). Introduction and removal of reward and maze performance in rats. *University of California Publications in Psychology, 4,* 257–275.

Tommasi, L. (2009). Mechanisms and functions of brain and behavioural asymmetries. *Philosophical Transactions of the Royal Society B, 364,* 855–859.

Toole, L. M., DeLeon, I. G., Kahng, S., Ruffin, G. E., Pletcher, C. A., & Bowman, L. G. (2004). Re-evaluation of constant versus varied punishers using empirically derived consequences. *Research in Developmental Disabilities, 25,* 577–586.

Toth, J. P., & Daniels, K. A. (2002). Effects of prior experience on judgments of normative word frequency: Automatic bias and correction. *Journal of Memory and Language, 46,* 845–874.

Touhara, K. (2007). Molecular biology of peptide pheromone production and reception in mice. *Advanced Genetics, 59,* 147–171.

Townsend, E. (2007). Suicide terrorists: Are they suicidal? *Suicide and Life-Threatening Behavior, 37,* 35–49.

Tov, W., & Diener, E. (2007). Culture and subjective well-being. In S. Kitayama (Ed.), *Handbook of cultural psychology* (pp. 691–713). New York: Guilford Press.

Tracy, J. L., & Robins, R. W. (2004). Show your pride: Evidence for a discrete emotion expression. *Psychological Science, 15,* 194–197.

Tranter, L. J., Koutstaal, W. (2008). Age and flexible thinking: An experimental demonstration of the beneficial effects of increased cognitively stimulating activity on fluid intelligence in healthy older adults. *Neuropsychology, and Cognition, 15,* 184–207.

Travis, F. (2006). From I to I: Concepts of self on a object-referral/self-referral continuum. In A. P. Prescott, *The concept of self in psychology.* Hauppauge, NY: Nova Science Publishers.

Travis, F., et al. (2009, February). Effects of transcendental meditation practice on brain functioning and stress reactivity in college students. *International Journal of Psychophysiology, 71,* 170–176.

Treas, J. (2004). Sex and Family: Changes and Challenges. *The blackwell companion to the sociology of families* (pp. 397–415). Malden: Blackwell Publishing.

Tremblay, A. (2004). Dietary fat and body weight set point. *Nutrition Review, 62* (7 Pt 2), S75–S77.

Tresniowski, A. & Smolowe, J. (2009, April 27). Dramatic high-seas rescue captain courageous. *People Magazine, 71,* 57.

Triesch, J., Jasso, H., & Deak, G. O. (2007). Emergence of mirror neurons in a model of gaze following. *Adaptive Behavior, 15,* 149–165.

Tropp, L. R., & Bianchi, R. A. (2006). Valuing diversity and interest in intergroup contact. *Journal of Social Issues, 62,* 533–551.

Tropp, L. R., & Pettigrew, T. F. (2005). Differential relationships between intergroup contact and affective and cognitive dimensions of prejudice. *Personality and Social Psychology Bulletin, 31,* 1145–1158.

Troyer, A. K., Häfliger, A., & Cadieux, M. J. (2006). Name and face learning in older adults: Effects of level of processing, self-generation, and intention to learn. *Journals of Gerontology: Series B: Psychological Sciences and Social Sciences, 61,* P67–P74.

Trudel, G. (2002). Sexuality and marital life: Results of a survey. *Journal of Sex and Marital Therapy, 28,* 229–249.

Trull, T. J, Solhan, M.B., and Watson, D. (2008). Affective instability: Measuring a core feature of borderline personality disorder with ecological momentary assessment. *Journal of Abnormal Psychology, 117*(3): 647–661.

Trull, T. J., Stepp, S. D., & Durrett, C. A. (2003). Research on borderline personality disorder: An update. *Current Opinion in Psychiatry, 16,* 77–82.

Trull, T. J., & Widiger, T. A. (2003). Personality disorders. In G. Stricker, T. A. Widiger, et al. (Eds.), *Handbook of psychology: Clinical psychology* (Vol. 8) (pp. 149–172). New York: Wiley.

Tryon, W. W. (2005). Possible mechanisms for why desensitization and exposure therapy work. *Clinical Psychology Review, 25,* 67–95.

Tsai, K. J., Tsai, Y. C., & Shen, C. K. (2007). GCSF rescues the memory impairment of animal models of Alzheimer's disease. *Journal of Experimental Medicine, 11,* 1273–1289.

Tsaousis, I., Nikolaou, I., & Serdaris, N. (2007). Do the core self-evaluations moderate the relationship between subjective well-being and physical and psychological health? *Personality and Individual Differences, 42,* 1441–1452.

Tse, W. S., & Bond, A. J. (2004). The impact of depression on social skills: A review. *Journal of Nervous and Mental Disease, 192*(4), 260–268.

Tseng, W. S. (2003). *Clinician's guide to cultural psychiatry.* San Diego: Elsevier Publishing.

Tsukasaki, T., & Ishii, K. (2004). Linguistic-cultural relativity of cognition: Rethinking the Sapir-Whorf hypothesis. *Japanese Psychological Review, 47,* 173–186.

Tsunoda, T. (1985). *The Japanese brain: Uniqueness and universality.* Tokyo: Taishukan Publishing.

Tucker Blackwell, V. G. (2006). Factors which influence the academic motivation and disengagement of adolescent, African American males within a social-historical and psychological context. *Dissertation Abstracts International, 67,* 1654A.

Tudor, K. (2008). Person-centred therapy, a cognitive behaviour therapy. *Against and for CBT: Towards a constructive dialogue?* (pp. 118–136). Ross-on-Wye: PCCS Books.

Tuerlinckx, F., De Boeck, P., & Lens, W. (2002). Measuring needs with the Thematic Apperception Test: A psychometric study. *Journal of Personality and Social Psychology, 82,* 448–461.

Tugay, N., Akbayrak, T., Demirturk, F., Karakaya, I. C., Kocaacar, O., Tugay, U., Karakay, M. G., & Demirturk, F. (2007). Effectiveness of transcutaneous electrical nerve stimulation and interferential current in primary dysmenorrhea. *Pain Medicine, 8,* 295–300.

Tulving, E. (2000). Concepts of memory. In E. Tulving, F. I. M. Craik, et al. (Eds.). *The Oxford handbook of memory.* New York: Oxford University Press.

Tulving, E. (2002). Episodic memory and common sense: How far apart? In A. Baddeley & J. P. Aggleton (Eds.), *Episodic memory: New directions in research* (pp. 269–287). London: Oxford University Press.

Tulving, E., & Psotka, J. (1971). Retroactive inhibition in free recall: Inaccessibility of information available in the memory store. *Journal of Experimental Psychology, 87,* 1–8.

Tulving, E., & Thompson, D. M. (1983). Encoding specificity and retrieval processes in episodic memory. *Psychological Review, 80,* 352–373.

Turk, D. C. (1994). Perspectives on chronic pain: The role of psychological factors. *Current Directions in Psychological Science, 3,* 45–49.

Turkewitz, G. (1993). The origins of differential hemispheric strategies for information processing in the relationships between voice and face perception. In B. de Boysson-Bardies, S. de Schonen, P. W. Jusczyk, P. McNeilage, & J. Morton (Eds.), *Developmental neurocognition: Speech and face processing in the first year of life. NATO ASI series D: Behavioural and social sciences* (Vol. 69). Dordrecht: Kluwer Academic.

Turnbull, C. (1961). Some observations regarding the experiences and behavior of the BaMbuti Pygmies. Urbana-Champaign, IL: University of Illinois Press.

Turnbull, O., & Solms, M. (2007). Awareness, desire, and false beliefs: Freud in the light of modern neuropsychology. *Cortex, 43,* 1083–1090.

Turner, M., Tamborini, R., Limon, M., & Zuckerman-Hyman, C. (2007). The moderators and mediators of door-in-the-face requests: Is it a negotiation or a helping experience? *Communication Monographs, 74,* 333–356.

Turner, M. E., Pratkanis, A. R., Struckman, C. K. (2007). Groupthink as social identity maintenance. In C. K. Struckman, *The science of social influence: Advances and future progress.* New York: Psychology Press.

Turner, W. J. (1995). Homosexuality, Type 1: An Xq28 phenomenon. *Archives of Sexual Behavior, 24,* 109–134.

Tuszynski, M. H. (2007). Nerve growth factor gene therapy in Alzheimer disease. *Alzheimer's Disease and Associated Disorders, 21,* 179–189.

Tversky, A., & Kahneman, D. (1973, September). Availability: A heuristic for judging frequency and probability. *Cognitive Psychology, 5*(2), 207–232.

Tversky, A., & Kahneman, D. (1987). Rational choice and the framing of decisions. In R. Hogarth & M. Reder (Eds.), *Rational choice: The contrast between economics and psychology.* Chicago: University of Chicago Press.

Tversky, A., & Kahneman, D. (1990). Judgment under uncertainty: Heuristics and biases. *Rationality in action: Contemporary approaches* (pp. 171–188). New York: Cambridge University Press.

Tydgat, I., & Grainger, J. (2009). Serial position effects in the identification of letters, digits, and symbols. *Journal of Experimental Psychology: Human Perception and Performance, 35,* 480–498.

U

U.S. Bureau of the Census. (2000). *Census 2000.* Retrieved from American Fact Finder http://factfinder.census.gov/servlet/BasicFactsServlet.

U.S. Bureau of the Census. (2001). *Census 2000.* Retrieved from American Fact Finder http://factfinder.census.gov/servlet/BasicFactsServlet.

U.S. Census Bureau. (2011). Age and sex composition: 2010. *2010 Census Briefs.* Retrieved June 4, 2011, from http://www.census.gov/prod/cen2010/briefs/c2010br-03.pdf.

U.S. Department of Labor, Bureau of Labor Statistics, "Highlight of Women's Earnings in 2004," Report 987, September 2005.

Ubell, E. (1993, January 10). Could you use more sleep? *Parade,* 16–18.

Uematsu, A., Tsurugizawa, T., Kitamura, A., Ichikawa, R., Iwatsuki, K., Uneyama, H., et al. (2011). Evaluation of the "liking" and "wanting" properties of umami compound in rats. *Physiology & Behavior, 102,* 553–558.

Umphress, E. E., Smith-Crowe, K., & Brief, A. P. (2007). When birds of a feather flock together and when they do not: Status composition, social dominance orientation, and organizational attractiveness. *Journal of Applied Psychology, 92,* 396–409.

Underwood, A. (2003, April 7). Shining a light on pain. *Newsweek,* p. 31.

Underwood, A. (2005, October 3). The Good Heart. *Newsweek,* p. 49.

Unsworth, N., & Engle, R. W. (2005). Individual differences in working memory capacity and learning: Evidence from the serial reaction time task. *Memory and Cognition, 33,* 213–220.

Updegraff, K. A., Helms, H. M., McHale, S. M., Crouter, A. C., Thayer, S. M., & Sales, L. H. (2004). Who's the boss? Patterns of perceived control in adolescents' friendships. *Journal of Youth & Adolescence, 33,* 403–420.

Ursprung, W. W., Sanouri, A., & DiFranza, J. R. (2009). The loss of autonomy over smoking in relation to lifetime cigarette consumption. *Addictive Behaviors, 22,* 12–19.

Uttl, B., Graf, P., & Cosentino, S. (2003). Implicit memory for new associations: Types of conceptual representations. In J. S. Bowers & C. J. Marsolek (Eds.), *Rethinking implicit memory* (pp. 302–323). London: Oxford University Press.

Uylings, H. B. M. (2006). Development of the human cortex and the concept of 'critical' or 'sensitive' periods. *Language Learning, 56,* 59–90.

V

Vagg, R., & Chapman, S. (2005, May). Nicotine analogues: A review of tobacco industry research interests. *Addiction, 100*(5), 701–712.

Vaillant, G. E., & Vaillant, C. O. (1990). Natural history of male psychological health: XII. A 46-year study of predictors of successful aging at age 65. *American Journal of Psychiatry, 147,* 31–37.

Vaitl, D., Schienle, A., & Stark, R. (2005). Neurobiology of fear and disgust. *International Journal of Psychophysiology, 57,* 1–4.

Valencia, R. R., & Suzuki, L. A. (2003). *Intelligence testing and minority students: Foundations, performance factors, and assessment issues.* Thousand Oaks, CA: Sage.

Valente, S. M. (1991). Electroconvulsive therapy. *Archives of Psychiatric Nursing, 5,* 223–228.

Valsiner, J., Diriwächter, R., & Sauck, C. (2005). Diversity in unity: Standard questions and nonstandard interpretations. In *Science and medicine in dialogue: Thinking through particulars and universals* (pp. 289–307). Westport, CT: Praeger Publishers/Greenwood Publishing Group.

Van Beekum, S. (2005). The therapist as a new object. *Transactional Analysis Journal, 35,* 187–191.

van den Bosch, L. M., Koeter, M. W., Stijnen, T., Verheul, R., & van den Brink, W. (2005). Sustained efficacy of dialectical behaviour therapy for borderline personality disorder. *Behavioral Research Therapy, 43,* 1231–1241.

van den Brink, W., & van Ree, J. (2003, December). Pharmacological treatments for heroin and cocaine addiction. *European Neuropsychopharmacology, 13*(6), 476–487.

Van den Wildenberg, W. P. M., & Van der Molen, M. W. (2004). Developmental trends in simple and selective inhibition of compatible and incompatible responses. *Journal of Experimental Child Psychology, 87,* 201–220.

van der Helm, P. A. (2006). Review of perceptual dynamics: Theoretical foundations and philosophical implications of gestalt psychology. *Philosophical Psychology, 19,* 274–279.

Van der Zee, E. A., Platt, B. B., & Riedel, G. G. (2011). Acetylcholine: Future research and perspectives. *Behavioural Brain Research.* In Press.

van Hooren, S. A. H., Valentijn, A. M., & Bosma, H. (2007). Cognitive functioning in healthy older adults aged 64–81: a cohort study into the effects of age, sex, and education. *Aging, Neuropsychology, and Cognition, 14,* 40–54.

van Marle, K., & Wynn, K. (2009). Infants' auditory enumeration: Evidence for analog magnitudes in the small number range. *Cognition, 111,* 302–316.

Van Overwalle, F., & Siebler, F. (2005). A Connecticut model of attitude formation and change. *Personality and Social Psychology Review, 9,* 231–274.

van Wel, F., Linssen, H., & Abma, R. (2000). The parental bond and the well-being of adolescents and young adults. *Journal of Youth & Adolescence, 29,* 307–318.

Vanasse, A., Niyonsenga, T., & Courteau, J. (2004). Smoking cessation within the context of family medicine: Which smokers take action? *Preventive Medicine: An International Journal Devoted to Practice and Theory, 38,* 330–337.

Vandell, D. L., Burchinal, M. R., Belsky, J., Owen, M. T., Friedman, S. L., Clarke-Stewart, A., McCartney, K., & Weinraub, M. (2005). *Early child care and children's development in the primary grades: Follow-up results from the NICHD Study of Early Child Care.* Paper presented at the biennial meeting of the Society for Research in Child Development, Atlanta.

vanDellen, M. R., Hoy, M. B., Fernandez, K., & Hoyle, R. H. (2011). Academic-contingent self-worth and the social monitoring system. *Personality and Individual Differences, 50,* 59–63.

Vandervert, L. R., Schimpf, P. H., & Liu, H. (2007). How working memory and the cerebellum collaborate to produce creativity and innovation. *Creativity Research Journal, 19,* 1–18.

Vanheule, S., Desmet, M., Rosseel, Y., & Meganck, R. (2006). Core transference themes in depression. *Journal of Affective Disorders, 91,* 71–75.

Varma, S. (2007). A computational model of Tower of Hanoi problem solving. *Dissertation Abstracts International: Section B: The Sciences and Engineering, 67*(8-B), 4736.

Vartanian, O. (2009). Variable attention facilitates creative problem solving. *Psychology of Aesthetics, Creativity, and the Arts, 3,* 57–59.

Vasey, P., & Jiskoot, H. (2010). The biogeography and evolution of female homosexual behavior in Japanese macaques. *Archives of Sexual Behavior, 39,* 1439–1441.

Vaughn, L. A., & Weary, G. (2002). Roles of the availability of explanations, feelings of ease, and dysphoria in judgments about the future. *Journal of Science and Clinical Psychology, 21,* 686–704.

Veasey, S., Rosen, R., Barzansky, B., Rosen, I., & Owens, J. (2002). Sleep loss and fatigue in residency training: A reappraisal. *Journal of the American Medical Association, 288,* 1116–1124.

Vedantam, S. (2005, January 23). See no bias. *Washington Post,* p. W12.

Vega, C. P. (2006). The effects of therapeutic components on at-risk middle school children's grades and attendance: An archival study of an after-school prevention program. *Dissertation Abstracts International: Section B: The Sciences and Engineering, 66,* 4504.

Vellacott, J. (2007). Resilience: A psychoanalytic exploration. *British Journal of Psychotherapy, 23,* 163–170.

Veltman, M. W. M., & Browne, K. D. (2001). Three decades of child mal-treatment research: Implications for the school years. *Trauma Violence and Abuse, 2,* 215–239.

Veniegas, R. C. (2000). Biological research on women's sexual orientations: Evaluating the scientific evidence. *Journal of Social Issues, 56,* 267–282.

Venning, A., Kettler, L., Eliott, J., & Wilson, A. (2009, March). The effectiveness of cognitive–behavioural therapy with hopeful elements to prevent the development of depression in young people: A systematic review. *International Journal of Evidence-Based Healthcare, 7*(1), 15–33.

Verdejo, A., Toribio, I., & Orozco, C. (2005). Neuropsychological functioning in methadone maintenance patients versus abstinent heroin abusers. *Drug and Alcohol Dependence, 78,* 283–288.

Verfaellie, M., & Keane, M. M. (2002). Impaired and preserved memory processes in amnesia. In L. R. Squire & D. L. Schacter (Eds.), *Neuropsychology of memory* (3rd ed.). New York: Guilford Press.

Vernon, P., Villani, V., Vickers, L., & Harris, J. (2008, January). A behavioral genetic investigation of the Dark Triad and the Big 5. *Personality and Individual Differences, 44,* 445–452.

Verona, E., & Sullivan, E. (2008). Emotional catharsis and aggression revisited: Heart rate reduction following aggressive responding. *Emotion, 8,* 331–340.

Victor, S. B., & Fish, M. C. (1995). Lesbian mothers and the children: A review for school psychologists. *School Psychology Review, 24,* 456–479.

Viding, E., Blair, R. J., Moffitt, T. E., & Plomin, R. (2005). Evidence for substantial genetic risk for psychopathy in 7-year-olds. *Journal of Child Psychology and Psychiatry, 46,* 592–597.

Vieira, E. M., & Freire, J. C. (2006). Alteridade e Psicologia Humanista: Uma leitura ética da abordagem centrada na pessoa. Alterity and humanistic psychology: An ethical reading of the Person-Centered Approach. *Estudos de Psicologia, 23,* 425–432.

Vignatelli, L., Plazzi, G., Peschechera, F., Delaj, L., & D'Alessandro, R. (2011). A 5-year prospective cohort study on health-related quality of life in patients with narcolepsy. *Sleep Medicine, 12,* 19–23.

Villablanca, J., de Andrés, I., & Garzón, M. (2003, September). Debating how rapid eye movement sleep is regulated (and by what). *Journal of Sleep Research, 12*(3), 259–262.

Villemure, C., Slotnick, B. M., & Bushnell, M. C. (2003). Effects of odors on pain perception: Deciphering the roles of emotion and attention. *Pain, 106,* 101–108.

Vitaro, F., Brendgen, M., & Arseneault, L. (2009). Methods and measures: The discordant MZ-twin method: One step closer to the holy grail of causality. *International Journal of Behavioral Development, 33,* 376–382.

Vitiello, A. L., Bonello, R. P., & Pollard, H. P. (2007). The effectiveness of ENAR(R) for the treatment of chronic neck pain in Australian adults: A preliminary single-blind, randomised controlled trial. *Chiropractic Osteopathology, 9,* 9.

Vleioras, G., & Bosma, H. A. (2005). Are identity styles important for psychological well-being? *Journal of Adolescence, 28,* 397–409.

Voicu, H., & Schmajuk, N. (2002). Latent learning, shortcuts and detours: A computational model. *Behavioural Processes, 59,* 67–86.

Volterra, V., Caselli, M. C., Capirci, O., Tonucci, F., & Vicari, S. (2003). Early linguistic abilities of Italian children with Williams syndrome [Special issue: Williams syndrome]. *Developmental Neuropsychology, 23,* 33–58.

Voruganti, L. P., Awad, A. G., Parker, B., Forrest, C., Usmani, Y., Fernando, M. L. D., & Senthilal, S. (2007). Cognition, functioning and quality of life in schizophrenia treatment: Results of a one-year randomized controlled trial of olanzapine and quetiapine. *Schizophrenia Research, 96,* 146–155.

Voss, J., & Paller, K. (2008). Brain substrates of implicit and explicit memory: The importance of concurrently acquired neural signals of both memory types. *Neuropsychologia, 46*(13), 3021–3029.

Vygotsky, L. S. (1926/1997). *Educational psychology.* Delray Beach, FL: St. Lucie Press.

W

Waber, R. L., Shiv, B., Carmon, Z., & Ariely, D. (2008), Commercial Features of Placebo and Therapeutic Efficiency. *Journal of the American Medical Association, 299,* 1016–1017.

Wachs, T. D., Pollitt, E., Cueto, S., & Jacoby, E. (2004). Structure and cross-contextual stability of neonatal temperament. *Infant Behavior and Development, 27,* 382–396.

Waddell, J., & Shors, T. J. (2008). Neurogenesis, learning and associative strength. *European Journal of Neurosciences, 27,* 3020–3028.

Wadden, T. A., Crerand, C. E., & Brock, J. (2005). Behavioral treatment of obesity. *Psychiatric Clinics of North America, 28,* 151–170.

Wade, K. A., Sharman, S. J., & Garry, M. (2007). False claims about false memory research. *Consciousness and Cognition: An International Journal, 16,* 18–28.

Wager, T. D (2005). The neural bases of placebo effects in pain. *Current Directions in Psychological Science, 14,* 175–180.

Wagner, A. W., Rizvi, S. L., & Harned, M. S. (2007). Applications of dialectical behavior therapy to the treatment of complex trauma-related problems: when one case formulation does not fit all. *Journal of Trauma Stress, 20,* 391–400.

Wagner, E. F., & Atkins, J. H. (2000). Smoking among teenage girls. *Journal of Child & Adolescent Substance Abuse, 9,* 93–110.

Wagner, H. J., Bollard, C. M., Vigouroux, S., Huls, M. H., Anderson, R., Prentice, H. G., Brenner, M. K., Heslop, H. E., & Rooney, C. M. (2004). A strategy for treatment of Epstein Barr virus-positive Hodgkin's disease by targeting interleukin 12 to the tumor environment using tumor antigen-specific T cells. *Cancer Gene Therapy, 2,* 81–91.

Wagner, R. K. (2002). Smart people doing dumb things: The case of managerial incompetence. In R. J. Sternberg (Ed.), *Why smart people can be so stupid* (pp. 42–63). New Haven, CT: Yale University Press.

Wagstaff, G. (2009, January). Is there a future for investigative hypnosis? *Journal of Investigative Psychology and Offender Profiling, 6,* 43–57.

Wain, H. J., Grammer, G. G., & Stasinos, J. (2006). Psychiatric intervention for medical and surgical patients following traumatic injuries. In E. C. Ritchie, P. J. Watson, & M. J. Friedman, *Interventions following mass violence and disasters: Strategies for mental health practice.* New York: Guilford Press.

Wainer, H., Dorans, N. J., Eignor, D., Flaugher, R., Green, B. E., Mislevy, R. J., Steinberg, L., & Thissen D. (2000). *Computerized adaptive testing: A primer* (2nd ed.). Mahwah, NJ: Erlbaum.

Waisbren, S. E. (2011). Phenylketonuria. In S. Goldstein, C. R. Reynolds, S. Goldstein, C. R. Reynolds (Eds.), *Handbook of neurodevelopmental and genetic disorders in children* (2nd ed.). New York: Guilford Press.

Walker, L. J., & Frimer, J. A. (2007). Moral personality of brave and caring exemplars. *Journal of Personality and Social Psychology, 93,* 845–860.

Walker, L., & Frimer, J. (2009). The song remains the same: Rebuttal to Sherblom's re-envisioning of the legacy of the care challenge. *Journal of Moral Education, 38,* 53–68.

Walker, M. P., & van der Helm, E. (2009). Overnight therapy? The role of sleep in emotional brain processing. *Psychological Bulletin, 135,* 731–748.

Walker, W. R., Skowronski, J. J., & Thompson, C. P. (2003). Consolidation of long-term memory: Evidence and alternatives. *Review of General Psychology, 7,* 203–210.

Waller, B., Cray, J., & Burrows, A. (2008, June). Selection for universal facial emotion. *Emotion, 8,* 435–439.

Wallerstein, J. S., Lewis, J., Blakeslee, S., & Lewis, J. (2000). *The unexpected legacy of divorce.* New York: Hyperion.

Walsh, B. T., Kaplan, A. S., Attia, E., Olmstead, M., Parides, M., Carter, J. C., Pike, K. M., Devlin, M. J., Woodside, B., Robert, C. A., & Rockert, W. (2006). Fluoxetine after weight restoration in anorexia nervosa: A randomized controlled trial. *JAMA: Journal of the American Medical Association, 295,* 2605–2612.

Walsh, R., & Shapiro, S. L. (2006). The meeting of meditative disciplines and western psychology. *American Psychologist, 61,* 227–239.

Wang, A., & Clark, D. A. (2002). Haunting thoughts: The problem of obsessive mental intrusions [Special issue: Intrusions in cognitive behavioral therapy]. *Journal of Cognitive Psychotherapy, 16,* 193–208.

Wang, O. (2003). Infantile amnesia reconsidered: A cross-cultural analysis. *Memory, 11,* 65–80.

Wang, P. S., Aguilar-Gaxiola, S., Alonso, J., Angermeyer, M. C., Borges, G., Bromet, E. J., Bruffaerts, R., deGirolamo, G., deGraaf, R., Gureje, O., Haro, J. M., Karam, E. G., Kessler, R. C., Kovess, V., Lane, M. C., Lee, S., Levinson, D., Ono, Y., Petukhova, M., Posada-Villa, J., Seedat, S., & Wells, J. E. (2007, September 8). Use of mental health services for anxiety, mood, and substance disorders in 17 countries in the WHO world mental health surveys. *Lancet, 370,* 841–850.

Wang, Q. (2004). The emergence of cultural self-constructs: autobiographical memory and self-description in European American and Chinese children. *Developmental Psychology, 40,* 3–15.

Wang, Q., & Conway, M. A. (2006). Autobiographical memory, self, and culture. In L-G. Nilsson & N. Ohta, *Memory and society: Psychological perspectives.* New York: Psychology Press.

Wang, Q., & Ross, M. (2007). Culture and memory. *Handbook of cultural psychology* (pp. 645–667). New York: Guilford Press.

Wang, X., Lu, T., Snider, R. K., & Liang, L. (2005). Sustained firing in auditory cortex evoked by preferred stimuli. *Nature, 435,* 341–346.

Ward, L. M. (2004). Wading through the stereotypes: Positive and negative associations between media use and Black adolescents' conceptions of self. *Developmental Psychology, 40,* 284–294.

Ward, W. C., Kogan, N., & Pankove, E. (1972). Incentive effects in children's creativity. *Child Development, 43,* 669–677.

Ward-Baker, P. D. (2007). The remarkable oldest old: A new vision of aging. *Dissertation Abstracts International Section A: Humanities and Social Sciences, 67*(8-A), 3115.

Warden, C. A., Wu, W-Y., & Tsai, D. (2006). Online shopping interface components: relative importance as peripheral and central cues. *CyberPsychology & Behavior, 9,* 285–296.

Warford, M. K. (2011). The zone of proximal teacher development. *Teaching and Teacher Education, 27,* 252–258.

Warriner, A.B., & Humphreys, K. (2008). Learning to fail: Reoccurring tip-of-the-tongue states. *The Quarterly Journal of Experimental Psychology, 61*(4), 535–542.

Wass, T. S., Mattson, S. N., & Riley, E. P. (2004). Neuroanatomical and neurobehavioral effects of heavy prenatal alcohol exposure. In J. Brick (Ed.), *Handbook of the medical consequences of alcohol and drug abuse.* (pp. 139–169). New York: Haworth Press.

Wasserman, E. A., & Miller, R. R. (1997). What's elementary about associative learning? *Annual Review of Psychology, 48,* 573–607.

Watson, D., Hubbard, B., & Wiese, D. (2000). Self-other agreement in personality and affectivity: The role of acquaintanceship, trait visibility, and assumed similarity. *Journal of Personality and Social Psychology, 78,* 546–558.

Watson, J. & Rayner, R. (1920). Conditioned emotional responses. *Journal of Experimental Psychology, 3,* 1–14.

Watson, J. B. (1924). *Behaviorism.* New York: Norton.

Watson, M., Haviland, J. S., Greer, S., Davidson, J., & Bliss, J. M. (1999). Influence of psychological response on survival in breast cancer: a population-based cohort study. *Lancet, 354,* 1331–1336.

Waxman, S. (2009). Learning from infants' first verbs. *Monographs of the Society for Research in Child Development, 74,* 127–132.

Weber, R., Ritterfeld, U., & Kostygina, A. (2006). Aggression and violence as effects of playing violent video games? In P. Vorderer & J. Bryant, *Playing video games: Motives, responses, and consequences.* Mahwah, NJ: Lawrence Erlbaum Associates.

Wechsler, H., Davenport, A., Dowdall, G., Moeykens, B., & Castillo, S. (1994). Health and behavioral consequences of binge drinking in college. A national survey of students at 140 campuses. *Journal of the American Medical Association, 272,* 1672–1677.

Wechsler, H., Kuo, M., Lee, H., & Dowdall, G. W. (2000). *Environmental correlates of underage alcohol use and related problems of college students.* Cambridge, MA: Harvard School of Public Health.

Wechsler, H., Lee, J. E., Nelson, T. F., & Kuo, M. (2002). Underage college students' drinking behavior, access to alcohol, and the influence of deterrence policies. *Journal of American College Health, 50,* 223–236.

Weeks, M., & Lupfer, M. B. (2004). Complicating race: The relationship between prejudice, race, and social class categorizations. *Personality and Social Psychology Bulletin, 30,* 972–984.

Wegener, D. T., Petty, R. E., Smoak, N. D., & Fabrigar, L. R. (2004). Multiple routes to resisting attitude change. In E. S. Knowles & J. A. Linn (Eds.), *Resistance and persuasion.* Mahwah, NJ: Lawrence Erlbaum Associates.

Wehrle, R., Kaufmann, C., Wetter, T. C., Holsboer, F., Auer, D. P., Pollmacher, T., & Czisch, M. (2007). Functional microstates within human REM sleep: First evidence from fMRI of a thalamocortical network specific for phasic REM periods. *European Journal of Neuroscience, 25,* 863–871.

Weinberg, M. S., Williams, C. J., & Pryor, D. W. (1991, February 27). Personal communication. Indiana University, Bloomington.

Weiner, B. A., & Wettstein, R. (1993). *Legal issues in mental health care.* New York: Plenum Press.

Weiner, I. B. (2004a). Monitoring psychotherapy with performance-based measures of personality functioning. *Journal of Personality Assessment, 83,* 323–331.

Weiner, I. B. (2004b). Rorschach Inkblot method. In M. E. Maruish (Ed.), *Use of psychological testing for treatment planning and outcomes assessment: Instruments for adults* (Vol. 3) (3rd ed.). Mahwah, NJ: Lawrence Erlbaum Associates.

Weinstein, L. (2007). Selected genetic disorders affecting Ashkenazi Jewish families. *Family & Community Health, 30,* 50–62.

Weinstein, M., Glei, D. A., Yamazaki, A., & Ming-Cheng, C. (2004). The role of intergenerational relations in the association between life stressors and depressive symptoms. *Research on Aging, 26,* 511–530.

Weis, R., Crockett, T. E., & Vieth, S. (2004). Using MMPI-A profiles to predict success in a military-style residential treatment program for adolescents with academic and conduct problems. *Psychology in the Schools, 41,* 563–574.

Weiss, W. M., & Weiss, M. R. (2003). Attraction- and entrapment-based commitment among competitive female gymnasts. *Journal of Sport & Exercise Psychology, 25,* 229–247.

Weissman, M., Bland, R. C., Canino, G. J., Faravelli, C., Greenwald, S., Hwu, H. G., Joyce, P. R., Karam, E. G., Lee, C. K., Lellouch, J., Lepine, J. P., Newman, S. C., Rubio-Stipec, M., Wells, J. E., Wickramarante, P. J., Wittchen, H., & Yeh, E. K. (1997, July 24–31). Cross-national epidemiology of major depression and bipolar disorder. *Journal of the American Medical Association, 276,* 293–299.

Weissman, M., Markowitz, J., & Klerman, G. L. (2007). *Clinician's quick guide to interpersonal psychotherapy.* New York: Oxford University Press.

Weisz, A., & Black, B. (2002). Gender and moral reasoning: African American youth respond to dating dilemmas. *Journal of Human Behavior in the Social Environment, 5,* 35–52.

Welkowitz, L. A., Struening, E. L., Pittman, J., Guardino, M., & Welkowitz, J. (2000). Obsessive-compulsive disorder and comorbid anxiety problems in a national anxiety screening sample. *Journal of Anxiety Disorders, 14,* 471–482.

Wells, G. L., Olson, E. A., & Charman, S. D. (2002). The confidence of eyewitnesses in their identifications from lineups. *Current Directions in Psychological Science, 11,* 151–154.

Wenar, C. (1994). *Developmental psychopathology: From infancy through adolescence* (3rd ed.). New York: McGraw-Hill.

Wenzel, A., Zetocha, K., & Ferraro, R. F. (2007). Depth of processing and recall of threat material in fearful and nonfearful individuals. *Anxiety, Stress & Coping: An International Journal, 20*, 223–237.

Werblin, F., & Roska, B. (2007, April). The movies in our eyes. *Scientific American*, 73–77.

Werker, J. F., & Tees, R. C. (2005). Speech perception as a window for understanding plasticity and commitment in language systems of the brain. *Developmental Psychobiology, 46*, 233–234.

Werner, J. S., Pinna, B., & Spillmann, L. (2007, March). Illusory color and the brain. *Scientific American*, 90–96.

Wertheimer, M. (1923). Untersuchungen zur Lehre von der Gestalt, II. *Psychologische Forschung, 5*, 301–350. In R. Beardsley and M. Wertheimer (Eds.) (1958), *Readings in perception*. New York: Van Nostrand.

West, D. S., Harvey-Berino, J., & Raczynski, J. M. (2004). Behavioral aspects of obesity, dietary intake, and chronic disease. In J. M. Raczynski and L. C. Leviton (Eds.), *Handbook of clinical health psychology: Disorders of behavior and health* (Vol. 2) (pp. 9–41). Washington, DC: American Psychological Association.

West, J. R., & Blake, C. A. (2005). Fetal alcohol syndrome: An assessment of the field. *Experimental Biological Medicine, 6*, 354–356.

West, R. L., Bagwell, D. K., & Dark-Freudeman, A. (2007). Self-efficacy and memory aging: The impact of a memory intervention based on self-efficacy. *Neuropsychological Development and Cognition, B, Aging and Neuropsychological Cognition, 14*, 1–28.

West, S. L., & O'Neal, K. K. (2004). Project D. A.R.E. outcome effectiveness revisited. *American Journal of Public Health, 94*, 1027–1029.

West, T. V., & Kenny, D. A. (2011). The truth and bias model of judgment. *Psychological Review, 118*, 357–378.

Westen, D., & Gabbard, G. O. (1999). Psychoanalytic approaches to personality. In L. A. Pervin & O. P. John (Eds.), *Handbook of personality: Theory and research* (2nd ed.). New York: Guilford.

Westen, D., Novotny, C. M., & Thompson-Brenner, H. (2004). The empirical status of empirically supported psychotherapies: Assumptions, findings, and reporting in controlled clinical trials. *Psychological Bulletin, 130*, 631–663.

Westerhausen, R., Moosmann, M., Alhø, K., Medvedev, S., Hämäläinen, H., & Hugdahl, K. (2009, January). Top-down and bottom-up interaction: Manipulating the dichotic listening ear advantage. *Brain Research, 1250*, 183–189.

Westerterp, K. R. (2006). Perception, passive overfeeding and energy metabolism. *Physiology & Behavior, 89*, 62–65.

Wetter, D. W., Fiore, M. C., Gritz, E. R., Lando, H. A., Stitzer, M. L., Hasselblad, V., & Baker, T. B. (1998). The Agency for Health Care Policy and Research. Smoking cessation clinical practice guideline: Findings and implications for psychologists. *American Psychologist, 53*, 657–669.

Whaley, B. B. (Ed.). (2000). *Explaining illness: Research, theory, and strategies*. Mahwah, NJ: Erlbaum.

Whalley, M., & Books, G. (2009). Enhancement of suggestibility and imaginative ability with nitrous oxide. *Psychopharmacology, 203*, 745–752.

Whiffen, V., & Demidenko, N. (2006). Mood Disturbance Across the Life Span. *Handbook of girls' and women's psychological health: Gender and well-being across the lifespan* (pp. 51–59). New York: Oxford University Press.

Whipple, N., Bernier, A., & Mageau, G. A. (2011). Broadening the study of infant security of attachment: Maternal autonomy-support in the context of infant exploration. *Social Development, 20*, 17–32.

Whisman, M., & Snyder, D. (2007). Sexual infidelity in a national survey of American women: Differences in prevalence and correlates as a function of method of assessment. *Journal of Family Psychology, 21*, 14–154.

Whitbourne, S. (2001). The physical aging process in midlife: Interactions with psychological and sociocultural factors. *Handbook of midlife development* (pp. 109–155). Hoboken, NJ: John Wiley & Sons Inc.

Whitbourne, S. (2010). *The search for fulfillment*. New York: Ballantine.

Whitbourne, S. K. (2000). The normal aging process. In S. K. Whitbourne & S. Krauss (Eds.), *Psychopathology in later adulthood*. New York: Wiley.

Whitbourne, S. K., & Wills, K. (1993). Psychological issues in institutional care of the aged. In S. B. Goldsmith (Ed.), *Long-term care*. Gaithersburg, MD: Aspen Press.

Whitbourne, S. K., Zuschlag, M. K., Elliot, L. B., & Waterman, A. S. (1992). Psychosocial development in adulthood: A 22-year sequential study. *Journal of Personality and Social Psychology, 63*, 260–271.

Whitchurch, E. R., Wilson, T. D., & Gilbert, D. T. (2011). "He loves me, he loves me not . . .": Uncertainty can increase romantic attraction. *Psychological Science, 22*, 172–175.

White, C. A., & Macleod, U. (2002, August). ABC of psychological medicine: Cancer. *BMJ: British Medical Journal, 325*(7360), 377–380.

White, L. (2007). Linguistic theory, universal grammar, and second language acquisition. In B. Van Patten, & J. Williams, *Theories in second language acquisition: An introduction*. Mahwah, NJ: Lawrence Erlbaum Associates.

Whitebread, D., Coltman, P., Jameson, H., & Lander, R. (2009). Play, cognition and self-regulation: What exactly are children learning when they learn through play? *Educational and Child Psychology, 26*, 40–52.

Whitehouse, W. G., Orne, E. C., Dinges, D. F., Bates, B. L., Nadon, R., & Orne, M. T. (2005). The cognitive interview: Does it successfully avoid the dangers of forensic hypnosis? *American Journal of Psychology, 118*, 213–234.

Whitfield, J. B., Zhu, G., Madden, P. A., Neale, M. C., Heath, A. C., & Martin, N. G. (2004). The genetics of alcohol intake and of alcohol dependence. *Alcoholism: Clinical and Experimental Research, 28*, 1153–1160.

Whitton, E. (2003). *Humanistic approach to psychotherapy*. Philadelphia: Whurr Publishers.

WHO World Mental Health Survey Consortium. (2004). Prevalence, severity, and unmet need for treatment of mental disorders in the World Health Organization World Mental Health Surveys. *Journal of the American Medical Association, 291*, 2581–2590.

Whorf, B. L. (1956). *Language, thought, and reality*. New York: Wiley.

Wickelgren, E. A. (2004). Perspective distortion of trajectory forms and perceptual constancy in visual event identification. *Perception and Psychophysics, 66*, 629–641.

Wickelgren, I. (2006, May 26). A vision for the blind. *Science, 312*, 1124–1126.

Wickens, C. D. (1984). *Engineering psychology and human performance*. Columbus, OH: Merrill.

Widaman, K. (2009). Phenylketonuria in children and mothers: Genes, environments, behavior. *Current Directions in Psychological Science, 18*, 48–52.

Widiger, T. A., & Clark, L. A. (2000). Toward *DSM-V* and the classification of psychopathology. *Psychological Bulletin, 126*, 946–963.

Widiger, T., & Mullins-Sweatt, S. (2008). Classification. *Handbook of clinical psychology: Adults* (Vol. 1) (pp. 341–370). Hoboken, NJ: John Wiley & Sons Inc.

Widmeyer, W. N., & Loy, J. W. (1988). When you're hot, you're hot! Warm-cold effects in first impressions of persons and teaching effectiveness. *Journal of Educational Psychology, 80*, 118–121.

Wielgosz, A. T., & Nolan, R. P. (2000). Biobehavioral factors in the context of ischemic cardiovascular disease. *Journal of Psychosomatic Research, 48*, 339–345.

Wiggins, J. S. (2003). *Paradigms of personality assessment*. New York: Guilford Press.

Wildavsky, B. (2000, September 4). A blow to bilingual education. *U.S. News & World Report*, 22–28.

Wiley. Altman, N. (1996). The accommodation of diversity in psychoanalysis. In R. P. Foster, M. Moskowitz, & R. A. Javier (Eds.), *Reaching across boundaries of culture and class: Widening the scope of psychotherapy*. Northvale, NJ: Jason Aronson.

Wilgoren, J. (1999, October 22). Quality day care, early, is tied to achievements as an adult. *The New York Times*, A16.

Wilkinson, H. A. (2009). Cingulotomy. *Journal of Neurosurgery, 110*, 607–611.

Willert, V., & Eggert, J. (2011). Modeling short-term adaptation processes of visual motion detectors. *Neurocomputing: An International Journal, 74*, 1329–1339.

Williams, C. L., & Butcher, J. N. (2011). History and development of the MMPI-A. In C. L. Williams, J. N. Butcher (Eds.), *A beginner's guide to the MMPI—A*. Washington, DC: American Psychological Association.

Williams, L., O'Connor, R. C., Grubb, N. R., & O'Carroll, R. E. (2011). Type D personality and illness perceptions in myocardial infarction patients. *Journal of Psychosomatic Research, 70*, 141–144.

Wilkinson, L., & Olliver-Gray, Y. (2006). The significance of silence: Differences in meaning, learning styles, and teaching strategies in cross-cultural settings. *Psychologia, 49*, 74–88.

Willander, J., & Larsson, M. (2006). Smell your way back to childhood: Autobiographical odor memory. *Psychonomic Bulletin & Review, 13*, 240–244.

Willems, R. M., & Hagoort, P. (2007). Neural evidence for the interplay between language, gesture, and action: a review. *Brain Language, 101*, 278–289.

Williams, J. E., Paton, C. C., Siegler, I. C., Eigenbrodt, M. L., Nieto, F. J., & Tyroler, H. A. (2000). Anger proneness predicts coronary heart disease risk: Prospective analysis from the Atherosclerosis Risk in Communities (ARIC) Study. *Circulation, 101*, 2034–2039.

Williams, J. W., Mulrow, C. D., Chiquette, E., Noel, P. H., Aguilar, C., & Cornell, J. (2000). A systematic review of newer pharmacotherapies for depression in adults: Evidence report summary. *Annals of Internal Medicine, 132*, 743–756.

Willis, G. L. (2005). The therapeutic effects of dopamine replacement therapy and its psychiatric side effects are mediated by pineal function. *Behavioural Brain Research, 160*, 148–160.

Willis, S. L., & Schaie, K. W. (1994). In C. B. Fisher & R. M. Lerner (Eds.), *Applied developmental psychology*. New York: McGraw-Hill.

Wills, T., Sargent, J., Stoolmiller, M., Gibbons, F., & Gerrard, M. (2008). Movie smoking exposure and smoking onset: A longitudinal study of mediation processes in a representative sample of U.S. adolescents. *Psychology of Addictive Behaviors, 22*, 269–277.

Wilmshurst, L. (2009). *Abnormal child psychology: A developmental perspective*. New York: Routledge/Taylor & Francis Group.

Wilson, M. A. (2002). Hippocampal memory formation, plasticity and the role of sleep. *Neurobiology of Learning & Memory, 78*, 565–569.

Wilson, R. S., Barral, S., Lee, J. H., Leurgans, S. E., Foroud, T. M., Sweet, R. A., et al. (2011). Heritability of different forms of memory in the late onset Alzheimer's disease family study. *Journal of Alzheimer's Disease, 23*, 249–255.

Wilson, T. G., Grilo, C. M., & Vitousek, K. M. (2007). Psychological treatment of eating disorders. *American Psychologist, 62*, Special issue: Eating disorders, 199–216.

Windholz, G., & Lamal, P. A. (2002). Koehler's insight revisited. In R. A. Griggs (Ed.), *Handbook for teaching introductory psychology: With an emphasis on assessment* (Vol. 3) (pp. 80–81). Mahwah, NJ: Erlbaum.

Winerman, L. (2005, June). ACTing up. *Monitor on Psychology*, 44–45.

Wines, M. (2004, March 18). For sniffing out land mines, a platoon of twitching noses. *New York Times*, A1, A4.

Winik, L. W. (2006, October 1). The true cost of depression. *Parade*, 7.

Winner, E. (2003). Creativity and talent. In M. H. Bornstein & L. Davidson (Eds.), *Well-being: Positive development across the life course* (pp. 371–380). Mahwah, NJ: Lawrence Erlbaum.

Winsler, A., Madigan, A. L., & Aquilino, S. A. (2005). Correspondence between maternal and paternal parenting styles in early childhood. *Early Childhood Research Quarterly, 20*, 1–12.

Winson, J. (1990, November). The meaning of dreams. *Scientific American*, pp. 86–96.

Winstead, B. A., & Sanchez, A. (2005). Gender and psychopathology. In J. E. Maddux & B. A. Winstead, *Psychopathology: Foundations for a contemporary understanding.* Mahwah, NJ: Lawrence Erlbaum Associates.

Winston, A. S. (2004). *Defining difference: Race and racism in the history of psychology.* Washington, DC: American Psychological Association.

Winston, J. S., O'Doherty, J., & Kilner, J. M. (2006). Brain systems for assessing facial attractiveness. *Neuropsychologia, 45*, 195–206.

Winter, D. G. (1988). The power motive in women—and men. *Journal of Personality and Social Psychology, 54*, 510–519.

Winter, D. G. (1995). *Personality: Analysis and interpretation of lives.* New York: McGraw-Hill.

Winter, D. G. (2007). The role of motivation, responsibility, and integrative complexity in crisis escalation: Comparative studies of war and peace crises. *Journal of Personality and Social Psychology, 92*, 920–937.

Winters, B. D., & Bussey, T. J. (2005). Glutamate receptors in perirhinal cortex mediate encoding, retrieval, and consolidation of object recognition memory. *Journal of Neuroscience, 25*, 4243–4251.

Wiseman, R., & Greening, E. (2002). The mind machine: A mass participation experiment into the possible existence of extra-sensory perception. *British Journal of Psychology, 93*, 487–499.

Wiseman, R., Greening, E., & Smith, M. D. (2003). Belief in the paranormal and suggestion in the séance room. *British Journal of Psychology, 94*, 285–297.

Witt, C. M., Jena, S., & Brinkhaus, B. (2006). Acupuncture for patients with chronic neck pain. *Pain, 125*, 98–106.

Wittchen, H., Nocon, A., Beesdo, K., Pine, D., Höfler, M., Lieb, R., et al. (2008). Agoraphobia and panic. *Psychotherapy and Psychosomatics, 77*, 147–157.

Wittenbrink, B, & Schwarz, N. (Eds.). (2007). *Implicit measures of attitudes.* New York: Guilford Press.

Wixted, J. (2005, February). A theory about why we forget what we once knew. *Current Directions in Psychological Science, 14*(1), 6–9.

Wixted, J. T., & Carpenter, S. K. (2007). The Wickelgren Power Law and the Ebbinghaus Savings Function. *Psychological Science, 18*, 133–134.

Wolf, M., van Doorn, G. S., Leimar, O., & Weissing, F. J. (2007). Life-history trade-offs favour the evolution of animal personalities. *Nature 447*, 581–584.

Wolfe, J. (2011). A new era at attention, perception, & psychophysics. *Attention, Perception, & Psychophysics, 73*, 72–78.

Wolfe, M. S. (2006). Shutting down Alzheimer's. *Scientific American, 294*, 72–79.

Wolff, N. (2002). Risk, response, and mental health policy: learning from the experience of the United Kingdom. *Journal of Health Politic and Policy Law, 27*, 801–802.

Wolitzky, D. L. (2006). Psychodynamic theories. In J. C. Thomas, D. L. Segal, & M. Hersen, *comprehensive handbook of personality and psychopathology: Personality and everyday functioning* (Vol. 1). Hoboken, NJ: John Wiley & Sons.

Wood, J. M., Nezworski, M. T., Lilienfeld, S. O., & Garb, H. N. (2003). *What's wrong with the Rorschach? Science confronts the controversial inkblot test.* New York: Wiley.

Wood, W. (2000). Attitude change: Persuasion and social influence. *Annual Review of Psychology, 51*, 539–570.

Woodruff, S. I., Conway, T. L., & Edwards, C. C. (2007). Sociodemographic and smoking-related psychosocial predictors of smoking behavior change among high school smokers. *Addictive Behaviors, 33*, 354–358.

Woods, S. C., & Seeley, R. J. (2002). Hunger and energy homeostasis. In H. Pashler & R. Gallistel (Eds.). *Steven's handbook of experimental psychology: Learning, motivation, and emotion* (3rd ed.) (Vol. 3) (pp. 633–668). New York: Wiley.

Woods, S. C., Schwartz, M. W., Baskin, D. G., & Seeley, R. J. (2000). Food intake and the regulation of body weight. *Annual Review of Psychology, 51*, 255–277.

Woods, S. C., Seeley, R. J., Porte, D., Jr., & Schwartz, M. W. (1998, May 29). Signals that regulate food intake and energy homeostasis. *Science, 280*, 1378–1383.

Woodson, S. R. J. (2006). Relationships between sleepiness and emotion experience: An experimental investigation of the role of subjective sleepiness in the generation of positive and negative emotions. *Dissertation Abstracts International: Section B—The Sciences and Engineering, 67*(5–B), 2849.

World Health Organization. (2011). Obesity and overweight: Factsheet #311. Retrieved May 27, 2011, from http://www.who.int/mediacentre/factsheets/fs311/en/index.html.

Wren, A. M., & Bloom, S. R. (2007). Gut hormones and appetite control. *Gastroenterology, 132*, 2116–2130.

Wright, K. (September 2002). Times of our lives. *Scientific American*, 59–65.

Wrosch, C., Bauer, I., & Scheier, M. F. (2005). Regret and quality of life across the adult life span: The influence of disengagement and available future goals. *Psychology and Aging, 20*, 657–670.

Wrzesniewski, K., & Chylinska, J. (2007). Assessment of coping styles and strategies with school-related stress. *School Psychology International, 28*, 179–194.

Wu, L-T., Schlenger, W. E., & Galvin, D. M. (2006). Concurrent use of methamphetamine, MDMA, LSD, ketamine, GHB, and flunitrazepam among American youths. *Drug and Alcohol Dependence, 84*, 102–113.

Wuethrich, B. (2001, March 16). Does alcohol damage female brains more? *Science, 291*, 2077–2079.

Wurtz, R. H., & Kandel, E. R. (2000). Central visual pathways. In E. R. Kandel, J. H. Schwartz, & T. M. Jessell (Eds.), *Principles of neural science* (4th ed.). New York: McGraw-Hill.

Wynn, K. (1995). Infants possess a system of numerical knowledge. *Current Directions in Psychological Science, 4*, 172–177.

Wynn, K. (2000). Findings of addition and subtraction in infants are robust and consistent: Reply to Wakeley, Rivera, and Langer. *Child Development, 71*, 1535–1536.

Wynn, K., Bloom, P., & Chiang, W. C. (2002). Enumeration of collective entities by 5-month-old infants. *Cognition, 83*, B55–B62.

Wyra, M., Lawson, M. J. & Hungi, N. (2007). The mnemonic keyword method: The effects of bidirectional retrieval training and of ability to image on foreign language vocabulary recall. *Learning and Instruction, 17*(3) 360–371.

X

Xiao, Z., Yan, H., Wang, Z., Zou, Z., Xu, Y., Chen, J., Zhang, H., Ross, C. A., & Keyes, B. B. (2006). Trauma and dissociation in China. *American Journal of Psychiatry, 163*, 1388–1391.

Y

Yanai, D., Weiland, J., Mahadevappa, M., Greenberg, R., Fine, I., & Humayun, M. (2007). Visual performance using retinal prosthesis in three subjects with retinitis pigmentosa. *American Journal of Ophthalmology, 143*, 820–827.

Yanovski, S. Z., & Yanovski, J. A. (2011). Obesity prevalence in the United States—Up, down, or sideways? *The New England Journal of Medicine, 364*, 987–989.

Yao, S-Q., Zhour, Y-H., & Jiang, L. (2006). The intelligence scale for Chinese adults: item analysis, reliability and validity. *Chinese Journal of Clinical Psychology, 14*, 441–445.

Yapko, M. D. (2006). Utilizing hypnosis in addressing ruminative depression-related insomnia. In M. D. Yapko, *Hypnosis and treating depression: Applications in clinical practice.* New York: Routledge/Taylor & Francis Group.

Yeomans, M. R., Tepper, B. J., & Ritezschel, J. (2007). Human hedonic responses to sweetness: Role of taste genetics and anatomy. *Physiology & Behavior, 91*, 264–273.

Yesilyaprak, B., Kisac, I., & Sanlier, N. (2007). Stress symptoms and nutritional status among survivors of the Marmara region earthquakes in Turkey. *Journal of Loss & Trauma, 12*, 1–8.

Yokoyama, H., Uchida, H., Kuroiwa, H., Kasahara, J., & Araki, T. (2011). Role of glial cells in neurotoxin-induced animal models of Parkinson's disease. *Neurological Sciences, 32*, 1–7.

Young, M. W. (2000, March). The tick-tock of the biological clock. *Scientific American*, 64–71.

Yu, C. (2011). The mechanisms of defense and dreaming. *Dreaming, 21*, 51–69.

Yusuf, S., Hawken, S., Ôunpuu, S., Dans, T., Avezum, A., Lanas, F., McQueen, M., Budaj, A., Pais, P., Varigos, J., and Lisheng, L. (2004). Effect of potentially modifiable risk factors associated with myocardial infarction in 52 countries (the INTERHEART study): Case-control study. *Lancet, 364*, 937–952.

Z

Zacks, J. (2008). Neuroimaging studies of mental rotation: A meta-analysis and review. *Journal of Cognitive Neuroscience, 20*, 1–19.

Zaitsu, W. (2007). The effect of fear on eyewitness' retrieval in recognition memory. *Japanese Journal of Psychology, 77*, 504–511.

Zajac, K., & Kobak, R. (2006). Attachment. *Children's needs III: Development, prevention, and intervention* (pp. 379–389). Washington, DC: National Association of School Psychologists.

Zajonc, R. B. (2001). Mere exposure: A gateway to the subliminal. *Current Directions in Psychological Science, 10*, 224–228.

Zalsman, G., & Apter, A. (2002). Serotonergic metabolism and violence/aggression. In J. Glicksohn (Ed.), *The neurobiology of criminal behavior: Neurobiological foundation of aberrant behaviors* (pp. 231–250). Dordrecht: Kluwer Academic.

Zaragoza, M. S., Belli, R. F., & Payment, K. E. (2007). Misinformation effects and the suggestibility of eyewitness memory. In M. Garry, & H. Hayne, *Do justice and let the sky fall: Elizabeth Loftus and her contributions to science, law, and academic freedom.* Mahwah, NJ: Lawrence Erlbaum Associates.

Zarate, C., & Manji, H. (2009). Potential novel treatments for bipolar depression. *Bipolar depression: Molecular neurobiology, clinical diagnosis and pharmacotherapy* (pp. 191–209). Cambridge: Birkhäuser.

Zarren, J. I., & Eimer, B. N. (2002). *Brief cognitive hypnosis: Facilitating the change of dysfunctional behavior.* New York: Springer.

Zaslow, M., Halle, T., & Martin, L. (2006). Child outcome measures in the study of child care quality. *Evaluation Review, 30*, 577–610.

Zebrowitz, L. A., & Montepare, J. M. (2005, June 10). Appearance DOES matter. *Science, 308,* 1565–1566.

Zebrowitz-McArthur, L. (1988). Person perception in cross-cultural perspective. In M. H. Bond (Ed.), *The cross-cultural challenge to social psychology.* Newbury Park, CA: Sage.

Zeidner, M., Matthews, G., & Roberts, R. D. (2004). Emotional intelligence in the workplace: A critical review. *Applied Psychology: An International Review, 53,* 371–399.

Zeigler, D. W., Wang, C. C., Yoast, R. A., Dickinson, B. D., McCaffree, M. A., Robinowitz, C. B., & Sterling, M. L. (2005). The neurocognitive effects of alcohol on adolescents and college students. *Preventive Medicine: An International Journal Devoted to Practice and Theory, 40,* 23–32.

Zevon, M., & Corn, B. (1990). Paper presented at the annual meeting of the American Psychological Association, Boston.

Zhang, F., Chen, Y., Heiman, M., & Dimarchi, R. (2005). Leptin: Structure, function and biology. *Vitamins and Hormones: Advances in Research and Applications, 71,* 345–372.

Zhang, Q., He, X., & Zhang, J. (2007). A comparative study on the classification of basic color terms by undergraduates from Yi nationality, Bai nationality and Naxi nationality. *Acta Psychologica Sinica, 39,* 18–26.

Zhou, Z. & Buck, L. B. (2006, March, 10). Combinatorial effects of odorant mixes in olfactory cortex. *Science,* 1477–1481.

Zhou, Z., Liu, Q., & Davis, R. L. (2005). Complex regulation of spiral ganglion neuron firing patterns by neurotrophin-3. *Journal of Neuroscience, 25,* 7558–7566.

Zians, J. (2007). A comparison of trait anger and depression on several variables: Attribution style, dominance, submissiveness, "need for power," efficacy and dependency. *Dissertation Abstracts International: Section B: The Sciences and Engineering, 67*(7-B), 4124.

Ziegler, R., Diehl, M., & Ruther, A. (2002). Multiple source characteristics and persuasion: Source inconsistency as a determinant of message scrutiny. *Personality and Social Psychology Bulletin, 28,* 496–508.

Zigler, E. F., Finn-Stevenson, M., & Hall, N. W. (2002). The first three years and beyond: Brain development and social policy. In E. F. Zigler, M. Finn-Stevenson, & N. W. Hall, *Current perspectives in psychology.* New Haven, CT: Yale University Press.

Zigler, E., Bennett-Gates, D., Hodapp, R., & Henrich, C. (2002). Assessing personality traits of individuals with mental retardation. *American Journal on Mental Retardation, 107,* 181–193.

Zimbardo, P. G. (1973). On the ethics of intervention in human psychological research: With special reference to the Stanford Prison Experiment. *Cognition, 2,* 243–256.

Zimbardo, P. G. (2004a). Does psychology make a significant difference in our lives? *American Psychologist, 59,* 339–351.

Zimbardo, P. G. (2004b). A situationist perspective on the psychology of evil: Understanding how good people are transformed into perpetrators. In A. G. Miller, *Social psychology of good and evil.* New York: Guilford Press.

Zimbardo, P. G. (2007). *The Lucifer effect: Understanding how good people turn evil.* New York: Random House.

Zimbardo, P. G., Maslach, C., & Haney, C. (2000). Reflections on the Stanford Prison Experiment: Genesis, transformations, consequences. In T. Blass (Ed.), *Obedience to Authority: Current Perspectives on the Milgram Paradigm.* Mahwah, NJ: Lawrence Erlbaum Associates.

Zimmermann, U. S., Blomeyer, D., & Laucht, M. (2007). How gene- and stress-behavior interactions can promote adolescent alcohol use: The roles of predrinking allostatic load and childhood behavior disorders. *Pharmacology, Biochemistry and Behavior, 86, Special issue: Adolescents, drug abuse and mental disorders,* 246–262.

Zito, J. M. (1993). *Psychotherapeutic drug manual* (3rd ed., rev.). New York: Wiley.

Zolotor, A., Theodore, A., Chang, J., Berkoff, M., & Runyan, D. (2008). Speak softly— and forget the stick: Corporal punishment and child physical abuse. *American Journal of Preventive Medicine,* 35, 364–369. Zuckerman, M. (1978). The search for high sensation. *Psychology Today,* pp. 30–46.

Zuckerman, M. (2002). Genetics of sensation seeking. In J. Benjamin, R. P. Ebstein, et al. (Eds.), *Molecular genetics and the human personality* (pp. 193–210). Washington, DC: American Psychiatric Publishing.

Zuckerman, M., & Kuhlman, D. M. (2000). Personality and risk-taking: Common biosocial factors [Special issue: Personality processes and problem behavior]. *Journal of Personality:, 68,* 999–1029.

Zuger, A. (2005, November 10). Doctors learn how to say what no one wants to hear. *The New York Times,* p. S1.

Chapter 1

Fackler, M. (2011, March 12). Japanese town reels from chaos left by Tsunami. *The New York Times*, p. 1.

Chapter 2

Halle, M. (2009, August 4). Can drilling electrodes into your brain help you lose weight? *Daily Mail* (London).

Chapter 3

Russell, R., Duchaine, B., & Nakayama, K. (2009). Super-recognizers: People with extraordinary face recognition ability. *Psychonomic Bulletin & Review, 16,* p. 252–257.

Chapter 4

Interlandi, J. (2008, March 3). What addicts need. *Newsweek*, p. 31–36.

Chapter 5

Begley, S. (2009, February 16). Will the BlackBerry sink the presidency? *Newsweek*, p. 37.

Chapter 6

Perry, B. (2008, May 19). I don't know how to forget. *People*, p. 143.

Chapter 7

Richardson, B. (2002, September 30). Light-bulb moments. *The Wall Street Journal*, p. R7.

Chapter 8

Leonard, E. (2009, May 18). Kirstie Alley: I've let myself go. *People*, p. 50.

Chapter 9

Smolowe, J. (2008, June 23). Medical miracle surgery for an unborn child. *People*, p. 96.

Chapter 10

Creswell, J., & Landon, T. (2009, January 25). The talented Mr. Madoff. *The New York Times*, p. 1.

Chapter 11

Feldman, R. (2011). *P.O.W.E.R. Learning: Strategies for Success in College and Life (5th Ed)*. New York: McGraw-Hill.

Chapter 12

Cloud, J. (2009, January 19). Minds on the Edge. *Time*, pp. 40–46.

Chapter 13

Mascia, K., & Servis, R. (2009, August 24). Mail carriers to the rescue. *People*, p. 108–110.

Photo Credits

Front Matter

p. i (top): © DNY59/iStockphoto; **p. i (center left):** © Fuse/Getty Images; **p. i (center right):** © Ingvar Björk/Alamy; **p. i (bottom left):** © CMCD/Getty Images; **p. iii (Ch. 3):** © Stockbyte/Getty Images; **p. iii (Ch. 5):** © Bounce/Getty Images; **p. iii (Ch. 9):** © Blend Images/Getty Images; **p. iii (Ch. 7):** © Image Source/Getty Images; **p. v (top):** © Thinkstock Images/Jupiterimages; **p. v (bottom):** © Digital Vision/Punchstock; **p. vi:** © Lifesize/Getty Images; **p. viii:** © Jose Luis Pelaez Inc/Blend Images LLC; **p. ix:** © Ron Yue/Alamy

Chapter 1

Opener: © Asahi Shimbun/Getty Images; **p. 4 (left):** © Reuters/Corbis; **p. 4 (center):** © Anna Clopet/Corbis; **p. 4 (right):** © Douglas Faulkner/Photo Researchers; **p. 6 (bottom):** © James Devaney/WireImage/Getty Images; **p. 7 (center):** © SSPL/The Image Works; **p. 8 (top left):** © **p. 8 (top right):** Courtesy, Wellesley College Archives. Photographed by Notman; **p. 8 (center left):** © Photo Researchers; **p. 8 (center):** © The Granger Collection; **p. 8 (center right):** © Bettmann/Corbis; **p. 8 (Cup):** © Pixtal/SuperStock; **p. 8 (Wundt):** © Bettmann/Corbis; **p. 9 (top left):** © Nina Leen/Time Life Pictures/Getty Images; **p. 9 (top right):** © The Granger Collection; **p. 9 (center left):** The Granger Collection; **p. 9 (center right):** Courtesy, Elizabeth Loftus; **p. 10:** © Reuters/Corbis; **p. 11 (Left-Rt.):** © David Sanger/Getty Images, © Ryan McVay/Getty Images, © White Packert/Getty Images, © Royalty-Free/Corbis; **p. 12 (top):** © AJ Photo/Photo Researchers; **p. 12 (bottom):** © Arthur Mount; **p. 13 (Left-Rt.):** © David Sanger/Getty Images, © Ryan McVay/Getty Images, © White Packert/Getty Images, © Royalty-Free/Corbis; **p. 14:** © Top-Pet-Pics/Alamy; **p. 17:** © Anna Clopet/Corbis; **p. 18 (top):** © Stockdisc; **p. 18 (bottom):** © Royalty-Free/Corbis; **p. 21 (bottom):** © Ed Bock/Corbis; **p. 22 (bottom):** © Dennis Wise/Getty Images; **p. 23 (top):** © Spencer Grant/PhotoEdit; **p. 23 (center):** © Hill Street Studios/Getty Images; **p. 23 (bottom):** © Rolf Haid/dpa/Corbis; **p. 24 (top):** © Adam Crowley/Getty Images; **p. 24 (bottom):** © Douglas Faulkner/Photo Researchers; **p. 25 (top):** © Erica Simone Leeds; **p. 29:** © BananaStock/JupiterImages

Chapter 2

Opener: PhotoAlto/Alix Minde/Getty Images; **p. 32 (top left):** © Jamie McCarthy/Getty Images; **p. 32 (top center):** © Comstock/JupiterImages; **p. 32 (top right):** © Ed Mulholland/WireImage/Getty Images; **p. 32 (center):** © Stephane De Sakutin/AFP/Getty Images; **p. 32 (bottom):** © UpperCut Images/Getty Images; **p. 33:** © Dennis Kunkel/Visuals Unlimited; **p. 38 (top):** © Jamie McCarthy/Getty Images; **p. 38 (bottom):** © Comstock/JupiterImages; **p. 39 (top):** © Mark Andersen/Getty Images; **p. 39 (bottom):** © Larry Williams/Blend Images/Getty Images; **p. 40:** © Doug Menuez/Digital Vision/Getty Images; **p. 41:** © Punchstock/Image Source; **p. 42:** © Ed Mulholland/WireImage/Getty Images; **p. 44:** © Stockbyte/Picture Quest; **p. 45 (top left):** © Hank Morgan/Photo Researchers; **p. 45 (left):** © Volker Steger/PhotoLibrary; **p. 45 (center):** © Bryan Christie Design; **p. 45 (right):** © Roger Ressmeyer/Corbis Images; **p. 46:** © Dana Neely/Getty Images; **p. 48:** © Royalty-Free/Corbis; **p. 49 (top):** Courtesy, Trustees of the British Museum, Natural History; **p. 49 (bottom):** From: Damasio, H., Grabowski, T., Frank, R., Galaburda, A. M., Damasio, A. R.: The return of Phineas Gage: Clues about the brain from the skull of a famous patient. Science, 264:1102–1105, 1994. Department of Neurology and Image Analysis Facility, University of Iowa. © AAAS; **p. 50:** © Christopher Stubbs/Alamy; **p. 52 (bottom):** © RubberBall Productions; **p. 57:** © BananaStock/JupiterImages

Chapter 3

Opener: © Jay Reilly/UpperCut Images/Getty Images; **p. 60 (top left):** © AP Photo/The Green Bay News-Chronicle, Boyd Fellows; **p. 60 (top right):** © Jeff Greenberg/Stock Boston; **p. 60 (center):** © NASA; **p. 60 (bottom):** © Matthew Leete/Photodisc/Getty Images; **p. 61 (top):** © AP Photo/Marco Garcia; **p. 63 (bottom):** © AP Photo/The Green Bay News-Chronicle, Boyd Fellows; **p. 64 (both):** © Biophoto Associates/Photo Researchers; **p. 65 (bottom):** © Dynamic Graphics/JupiterImages; **p. 66:** © Omikrom/Photo Researchers; **p. 67:** © Lars Niki; **p. 68 (bottom):** © Royalty-Free/Corbis; **p. 70:** © Tyler Edwards/Getty Images; **p. 72 (top):** © NASA; **p. 72 (center):** © Reed Kaestner/Royalty-Free/Corbis; **p. 73 (top):** © Omikron/Photo Researchers; **p. 73 (bottom):** © Photodisc/PunchStock; **p. 74 (bottom):** © Anthony Bradshaw/Getty Images; **p. 75 (bottom):** © Liu Yang/Redlink/Royalty-Free/Corbis; **p. 75 (top):** © Chase Jarvis/Getty Images; **p. 77 (a-b):** From Macalusoa, E. and Jon Driver, J.: Multisensory spatial interactions: a window onto functional integration in the human brain. Trends in Neurosciences, Volume 28, Issue 5, May 2005, pp. 264–271, Figure 1. Reprinted with permission from Elsevier; **p. 80 (top):** © Cary Wolinsky/Stock Boston; **p. 80 (bottom):** © Jeff Greenberg/Stock Boston; **p. 81:** © John G. Ross/Photo Researchers

Chapter 4

Opener: © Bloom Image/Getty Images; **p. 88 (top left):** © Nick Norman/Getty Images; **p. 88 (top right):** © Wolfgang Kaehler/Alamy; **p. 88 (center):** © AP Photo/Midland Daily News, Erin Painter; **p. 88 (bottom):** © The McGraw-Hill Companies, Inc./Photo by David Planchet; **p. 89 (bottom):** © Rob Melnychuk/Getty Images; **p. 90 (center):** © Photodisc/Getty Images; **p. 91 (top):** © Dynamic Graphics/JupiterImages; **p. 91 (bottom):** © Nick Norman/Getty Images; **p. 92 (1):** © Brand X Pictures/PunchStock; **p. 92 (2):** © DAJ/Getty Images; **p. 92 (3):** © Flying Colours Ltd./Getty Images; **p. 92 (4):** © Hamels/Photoalto/PictureQuest; **p. 92 (5):** © Brand X Pictures/PunchStock; **p. 92 (6):** © Purestock/PunchStock; **p. 93:** © Thinkstock/Getty Images; **p. 94 (bottom):** © CMCD/Getty Images; **p. 95 (top):** © Photodisc/Getty Images; **p. 96:** © AP Photo/Midland Daily News, Erin Painter; **p. 97 (top):** © Liquidlibrary/PictureQuest; **p. 98 (a-c):** From Brefczynski-Lewis, J. A., Lutz, A., Schaefer, H. S., Levinson, D. B. and Davidsoni, R. J.: Neural correlates of attentional expertise in long-term meditation practitioners. PNAS, Vol. 104, no. 17, pp. 11483–11488; **p. 100:** © Wolfgang Kaehler/Alamy; **p. 101 (top):** © iStockphoto.com/Aleaimage; **p. 101 (bottom):** © Photodisc Collection/Getty Images; **p. 102 (left):** © Stockbyte/Punchstock; **p. 102 (center):** © Jonnie Miles/Getty Images; **p. 102 (right):** © Per-Anders Pettersson/Getty Images; **p. 105 (left):** © iStockphoto.com/Jail Free; **p. 105 (right):** © iStockphoto.com/Token image; **p. 106 (bottom):** iStockphoto.com/Miroslava Holasová; **p. 107:** © Dennis Wise/Digital Vision/Getty Images

Chapter 5

Opener: © Mike Harrington/Getty Images; **p. 112 (top left):** Scott T. Baxter/Getty Images; **p. 112 (top center):** © Tim Hall/Getty Images; **p. 112 (top right):** © Gary Salter/Corbis; **p. 112 (bottom):** © David Frazier/The Image Works; **p. 113:** © Nathalie Walker; **p. 115 (top):** © Scott T. Baxter/Getty Images; **p. 115 (bottom):** © Amos Morgan/Getty Images; **p. 116:** © Photodisc/Getty Images; **p. 117:** © Brand X Pictures/PunchStock; **p. 118 (top):** © Nina Leen/Time Life Pictures/Getty Images; **p. 119 (top):** © Tim Hall/Getty Images; **p. 119 (bottom):** © Getty Images/Photodisc; **p. 120 (top left):** © Ryan McVay/Getty Images; **p. 120 (top right):** © Royalty-Free/Corbis; **p. 120 (center left):** © Masterfile; **p. 120 (center right):** © Amy Etra/Photo Edit; **p. 121:** © Tony Freeman/PhotoEdit; **p. 122:** © Studio 101/Alamy; **p. 124:** © Beau Lark/Corbis; **p. 125 (left):** © Getty Images; **p. 125 (right):** © Veer; **p. 127:** © Ariel Skelley/Corbis; **p. 128 (top center):** © Punchstock/BananaStock; **p. 128 (top right):** © Digital Vision/Getty Images; **p. 128 (center):** © Arthur Mount; **p. 129 (top):** © Gary Salter/Corbis; **p. 131:** © Image Source/Getty Images

Chapter 6

Opener: © Dan Tuffs/Getty Images; **p. 138 (top left):** © Paul Avis/Getty Images; **p. 138 (top center):** © Kathy McLaughlin/The Image Works; **p. 138 (top right):** © Joseph Nettis/Photo Researchers; **p. 138 (bottom):** © Ron Yue/Alamy; **p. 139 (center):** © D. Hurst/Alamy; **p. 139 (bottom left):** © The McGraw-Hill Companies, Inc./Gary He, photographer; **p. 139 (bottom right):** © Paul Avis/Getty Images; **p. 140:** © C Squared Studios/Getty Images; **p. 143:** © Kathy McLaughlin/The Image Works; **p. 146:** © Greatstock Photographic Library/Alamy; **p. 146 (frame):** © C Squared Studios/Getty Images; **p. 147 (left):** © G. K. & Vikki Hart/Getty Images; **p. 147 (right):** © Purestock/Getty Images; **p. 148:** © Amos Morgan/Getty Images; **p. 149:** © Ralf-Finn Hestoft/Corbis; **p. 151 (center):** © Siede Preis/Getty Images; **p. 152 (bottom):** © Monkey Business Images Ltd/Getty Images; **p. 153 (bottom):** © Joseph Nettis/Photo Researchers; **p. 155 (center):** © Masterfile; **p. 157:** Courtesy of Paul Thompson, Laboratory of Neuroimaging, UCLA; **p. 161:** © BananaStock/JupiterImages

Chapter 7

Opener: © Hill Street Studios/Getty Images; **p. 164 (left):** © Leon Neal/AFP/Getty Images; **p. 164 (center):** © Photodisc/Getty Images; **p. 164 (right):** © David Hiser/Still Media; **p. 165 (top):** © Leon Neal/AFP/Getty Images; **p. 165 (bottom left):** © Bettmann/Corbis; **p. 165 (bottom right):** © Jonathan Brady/epa/Corbis; **p. 166:** © AP Images/Julie Jacobson; **p. 169 (top):** © Photodisc/Getty Images; **p. 169 (bottom left):** © Hoby Finn/Getty Images; **p. 169 (bottom right):** © Stockbyte/PunchStock; **p. 173:** © Ryan McVay/Getty Images; **p. 174:** © Rob Crandall/Stock Connection Blue/Alamy; **p. 175:** © Aflo Foto Agency/Alamy; **p. 176:** © Image Source Black/Alamy; **p. 177:** © David Hiser/Still Media; **p. 179 (1):** © Harold Holt/Hulton Archive/Getty Images; **p. 179 (2):** © Bettmann/Corbis; **p. 179 (3):** Courtesy, Cold Spring Harbor Laboratory; **p. 179 (4):** © Bettmann/Corbis; **p. 179 (5):** © David Hiser/Still Media; **p. 179 (6):** © Bettmann/Corbis; **p. 179 (7):** © George C. Beresford/Getty Images; **p. 179 (8):** © Vera Anderson/Getty Images; **p. 180:** © Bob Daemmrich/The Image Works; **p. 181:** © Andersen Ross/Digital Vision/Getty Images; **p. 183:** © Doug Menuez/Digital Vision/Getty Images; **p. 187:** © AP Photo/Gregory Bull

Chapter 8

Opener: © Photo by Brian Doben/Contour/Getty Images; **p. 193 (inset):** © ABC/Photofest; **p. 194 (center):** © Vera Anderson/WireImage/Getty Images; **p. 194 (left):** © AP Photo/Gautam Singh; **p. 194 (top center):** © AP Photo/Eugenio Savio; **p. 194 (top right):** © Galen Rowell/Corbis; **p. 195 (top):** © Chase Swift/Corbis; **p. 195 (bottom):** © Reuters/Corbis; **p. 197 (top center):** © iStockphoto.com/Photogl; **p. 197 (top):** © Photodisc/Getty Images; **p. 197 (center top):** © Digital Vision; **p. 197 (center):** © Brand X Pictures/PunchStock; **p. 197 (bottom left):** © Brooke Fasani/Corbis; **p. 197 (bottom right):** © Brand X Pictures; **p. 198 (top):** © AP Photo/Gautam Singh; **p. 198 (bottom):** © D. Hurst/Alamy; **p. 199 (top):** © DoD photo by Cpl. Brian M. Henner, U.S. Marine Corps; **p. 199 (bottom):** © Doable/amanaimages/Corbis; **p. 200 (bottom):** © Burke Triolo Productions/Getty Images; **p. 201:** © Ellen

B. Senisi/The Image Works; **p. 202:** Reprint from Brain Research, Vol. 1114, (1), Santel, S., Baving, L., Krauel, K., Muente, T. F.: Hunger and Satiety in Anorexia Nervosa: fMRI during cognitive processing of food pictures. Fig. 4, pp. 138–148. 2006, with permission from Elsevier; **p. 204 (top):** © AP Photo/Eugenio Savio; **p. 204 (bottom):** © Andrew Unangst/Getty Images; **p. 205:** © Andrew Darrington/Alamy; **p. 206 (top):** © ballyscanlon/Digital Vision/Getty Images; **p. 206 (center):** © mauritius images GmbH/Alamy; **p. 206 (bottom):** © Amos Morgan/Getty Images; **p. 209 (center):** © AP Photo/J. Scott Applewhite; **p. 209 (bottom):** © AP Photo/Volker Wiciok; **p. 210 (bottom):** © Comstock Images; **p. 211:** © Stockbyte/Getty Images; **p. 212:** © Galen Rowell/Corbis; **p. 214 (top):** © Todd Headington/iStockphoto; **p. 214 (bottom):** © Matsumoto & Ekman, 1988

Chapter 9

Opener: © Marcy Maloy/Getty Images; **p. 220 (top right):** © Deborah Davis/PhotoEdit; **p. 220 (top center):** © AP Photo/Ed Andrieski; **p. 220 (top left):** © Ethno Images, Inc./Alamy; **p. 220 (bottom):** © Peter Byron; **p. 221:** © Digital Vision/Getty Images; **p. 222:** © Dave King/Dorling Kindersley/Getty Images; **p. 223:** © D.W. Fawcett/Photo Researchers; **p. 224 (left):** © Lennart Nilsson/Scanpix; **p. 224 (right):** © Petit Format/Science Source/Photo Researchers; **p. 225:** © Brand X Pictures/PunchStock; **p. 226:** © Picture Partners/Alamy; **p. 228 (all):** From Meltzhoff, A. N. (1988). Imitation of Televised Models by Infants. Child Development, 59, pp. 1221–1229. Photo Courtesy of A. N. Meltzhoff & M. Hanak; **p. 229 (left):** © Richard Hutchings/Digital Light Source; **p. 229 (right):** © Ethno Images, Inc./Alamy; **p. 230:** Courtesy Helen A. LeRoy, Harlow Primate Laboratory, University of Wisconsin; **p. 231 (top):** © Image Club; **p. 232 (top left):** © FotoKIA/Index Stock/Photolibrary; **p. 232 (top right):** © Digital Vision/PunchStock; **p. 233:** © David Tipling/Alamy; **p. 234 (top):** © Flying Colours Ltd./Getty Images; **p. 234 (center left):** © Laurence Mouton/Photoalto/PictureQuest; **p. 234 (center right):** © image100/Royalty-Free/Corbis; **p. 234 (bottom left):** © Stockbyte/Getty Images; **p. 234 (bottom right):** © Royalty-Free/Corbis; **p. 235:** © Laura Dwight/Photolibrary; **p. 238 (top left):** © Syracuse Newspapers/Gary Walts/The Image Works; **p. 238 (bottom):** © Stockbyte/Getty Images; **p. 240:** © Corbis Images/JupiterImages; **p. 242 (1):** © iStockphoto/Tarinoel; **p. 242 (2):** © BananaStock/PunchStock; **p. 242 (3):** © Ariel Skelley/Getty Images; **p. 242 (4):** © Jon Feingersh/Blend Images/Getty Images; **p. 242 (5):** © Mel Curtis/Getty Images; **p. 245 (top):** © AP Photo/Ed Andrieski; **p. 245 (center):** © Jose Luis Pelaez Inc./Blend Images/Corbis; **p. 246:** © Granger Wootz/Blend Images/Corbis; **p. 247:** © Randy Faris/Corbis; **p. 248 (left):** © Zave Smith/UpperCut Images/Getty Images; **p. 248 (right):** © Jose Luis Pelaez Inc./Blend Images/Getty Images; **p. 249 (top):** © Harry Scull, Jr./Buffalo News; **p. 249 (bottom):** © Deborah Davis/PhotoEdit; **p. 252:** © Dennis Wise/Digital Vision/Getty Images; **p. 242 (6):** © Blue Moon Stock/Alamy Images; **p. 242 (7):** © Comstock Images/Jupiter Images/Alamy; **p. 242 (8):** © Ryan McVay/Getty Images

Chapter 10

Opener: © Justin Lane/epa/Corbis; **p. 258 (top left):** © Warner Bros./Photofest; **p. 258 (top center):** © BananaStock/PunchStock; **p. 258 (top right):** © Michael Newman/PhotoEdit; **p. 258 (bottom):** © Getty Images; **p. 261 (top):** © Guy Gillette/Photo Researchers; **p. 261 (bottom):** © Arthur Mount; **p. 263 (top):** © Warner Bros./Photofest; **p. 263 (bottom):** © Arthur Mount; **p. 268:** © BananaStock/PunchStock; **p. 269:** © Michael Newman/PhotoEdit; **p. 273 (top):** © Brand X Pictures/Punchstock; **p. 273 (bottom):** © Royalty-Free/Corbis; **p. 277:** © Goodshoot/Punchstock

Chapter 11

Opener: © Andrew Brett Wallis/Getty Images; **p. 280 (top left):** © Barry Lewis/Corbis; **p. 280 (top center):** © AP Photo/Mark Humphrey; **p. 280 (top right):** © Lucas Jackson/Reuters; **p. 280 (bottom):** © J.J.Guillen/epa/Corbis; **p. 282:** © Barry Lewis/Corbis; **p. 286 (bottom):** © Ned Frisk Photography/Brand X/Corbis; **p. 287:** © Dr. David Phillips/Visuals Unlimited; **p. 288:** © Nick Daly/Getty Images; **p. 289:** © AP Photo/Mark Humphrey; **p. 290:** © Lucas Jackson/Reuters; **p. 291:** © Digital Vision/PunchStock; **p. 292 (top):** © Dennis Wise/Digital Vision/Getty Images; **p. 294:** © Thomas Barwick/Getty Images; **p. 296:** © Jose Luis Pelaez/Corbis; **p. 299:** © Stockbyte/Getty Images

Chapter 12

Opener: © Radius Images/Corbis; **p. 302 (left):** © Rino Gropuzzo/age fotostock; **p. 302 (center):** © Michael Newman/Photo Edit; **p. 302 (right):** © The McGraw-Hill Companies, Inc./Luke David, photographer; **p. 303:** © Ryan McVay/Getty Images; **p. 304:** Reprinted with permission from the Diagnostic and Statistical Manual of Mental Disorders, Text Revision, Copyright 2000; **p. 306 (top left):** © PhotoAlto/PictureQuest; **p. 306 (top right):** © Rino Gropuzzo/age fotostock; **p. 306 (center):** © Royalty-Free/Corbis; **p. 306 (bottom):** © Alamy Images; **p. 306 (spider):** © Photodisc/Getty Images; **p. 307 (right):** © Kevin Winter/Getty Images for Nickelodeon; **p. 309:** Vincent van Gogh. Portrait of Dr. Gachet. 1890. Musee d'Orsay, Paris, France. Scala/Art Resource NY; **p. 310 (both):** Courtesy, Ian H. Gotlib, Ph.D; **p. 311:** © Chad Baker/Ryan McVay/Getty Images; **p. 319:** © HBO/The Kobal Collection; **p. 321:** © Colin Young-Wolff/PhotoEdit; **p. 322 (top):** © Photodisc/PunchStock; **p. 322 (bottom):** © Giantstep Inc./Digital Vision/Getty Images; **p. 323:** © Michael Newman/Photo Edit; **p. 326:** © Jon Bradley/Getty Images; **p. 328:** © Comstock Images/PictureQuest; **p. 331 (top):** © The McGraw-Hill Companies, Inc./Luke David, photographer; **p. 331 (bottom):** © Doug Menuez/Digital Vision/Getty Images

Chapter 13

Opener: © Gregg Segal; **p. 336 (bottom):** © Feng Li/Getty Images; **p. 336 (top left):** © Paul Barton/Corbis; **p. 336 (top center):** © Barbara Burnes/Photo Researchers; **p. 336 (top right):** © Reuters NewMedia Inc./Corbis Images; **p. 339 (top):** © David J. Green Studio/Alamy; **p. 339 (bottom):** © PhotoAlto/Alix Minde/Getty Images; **p. 341:** © PhotoAlto/PunchStock; **p. 342:** © Paul Barton/Corbis; **p. 343:** © Masterfile Royalty-Free; **p. 347:** From the film OBEDIENCE © 1965 by Stanley Milgram and distributed by Penn. State Media Sales. Permission granted by Alexandra Milgram; **p. 348:** © Barbara Burnes/Photo Researchers; **p. 349:** © CMCD/Getty Images; **p. 357:** © Reuters NewMedia Inc./Corbis Images.

Text/Line Art credits

Chapter 1

p. 12: Drawing of Sigmund Freud from Gregory Feist and Erika Rosenberg, *Psychology: Making Connections*, 1st ed., p. 15. Copyright © 2010 by The McGraw-Hill Companies, Inc. Reprinted with permission.

Chapter 2

p. 33: Structure of a Neuron from Kent Van De Graaff, *Human Anatomy*, updated 5th ed. Copyright © 2000 by The McGraw-Hill Companies, Inc. Reprinted with permission. **p. 35 (top):** Changes in Electrical Charge in a Neuron During an Action Potential from Sylvia S. Mader, *Human Biology*, 6th ed., p. 250. Copyright © 2000 by The McGraw-Hill Companies, Inc. Reprinted with permission. **p. 35 (bottom):** How Synapses and Neurotransmitters Work from Sylvia S. Mader, *Human Biology*, 6th ed. Copyright © 2000 by The McGraw-Hill Companies, Inc. Reprinted with permission. **p. 41:** The Major Functions of the Autonomic Nervous System adapted from Michael W. Passer and Ronald E. Smith, *Psychology*, p. 91. Copyright © 2001 by The McGraw-Hill Companies, Inc. Reprinted with permission. **p. 44:** Major Endocrine Glands adapted from Robert Brooker, Eric Widmaier, Linda Graham, and Peter Stiling, *Biology*, 1st ed., p. 1062. Copyright © 2008 by The McGraw-Hill Companies, Inc. Reprinted with permission. **p. 46 (top):** Cross Section of the Brain from Rod R. Seeley, Trent D. Stephens, and Philip Tate, *Anatomy & Physiology*, 5th ed. Copyright © 2000 by The McGraw-Hill Companies, Inc. Reprinted with permission. **p. 46 (bottom):** Major Structures in the Brain from George Johnson and Thomas Emmel, *The Living World*, 2nd ed. Copyright © 2000 by The McGraw-Hill Companies, Inc. Reprinted with permission. **p. 51:** Try It! Assessing Brain Lateralization: "Assessing Brain Lateralization" adapted from *Brain and Cognition*, vol. 51, no. 3, B. E. Morton, "Asymmetry questionnaire outcomes correlate with several hemisphericity measures," pp. 372–374, Copyright © 2003, with permission from Elsevier. http://www.sciencedirect.com/science/journal/02782626. **p. 53:** The Split Brain from Robert Brooker, Eric Widmaier, Linda Graham, and Peter Stiling, *Biology*, 1st ed., p. 943. Copyright © 2008 by The McGraw-Hill Companies, Inc. Reprinted with permission.

Chapter 3

p. 64: The Electromagnetic Spectrum and the Visible Spectrum from Camille B. Wortman, Elizabeth F. Loftus, and Charles Weaver, *Psychology*, 5th ed., p. 113. Copyright © 1999 by The McGraw-Hill Companies, Inc. Reprinted with permission. **p. 66:** Receptor Cells, Rods and Cones, in the Eye from David Shier, Jackie Butler, and Ricki Lewis, *Hole's Essentials of Human Anatomy and Physiology*, 7th ed., p. 283. Copyright © 2000 by The McGraw-Hill Companies, Inc. Reprinted with permission. **p. 67:** Optic Nerve/Visual Fields from Sylvia S. Mader, *Biology*, 7th ed. Copyright © 2001 by The McGraw-Hill Companies, Inc. Reprinted with permission. **p. 70:** Parts of the Ear from Robert J. Brooker, Eric P. Widmaier, Linda Graham, and Peter Stiling, *Biology*, Figure 45.6, p. 956. Copyright © 2008 by The McGraw-Hill Companies, Inc. Reprinted with permission. **p. 79:** Top-Down Processing from Stanley Coren and Lawrence M. Ward, *Sensation & Perception*, 3rd ed. (1989), p. 329. Reprinted with permission of John Wiley & Sons, Inc. **p. 81:** Parthenon line drawings from Stanley Coren and Lawrence M. Ward, *Sensation & Perception*, 3rd ed. (1989), p. 5. Reprinted with permission of John Wiley & Sons, Inc.

Chapter 4

p. 89: The Sleep Cycle: "Brain wave patterns/sleep cycle table" from the book *Sleep* by J. Allan Hobson. Copyright © 1989 by J. Allan Hobson. Reprinted by permission of Henry Holt and Company, LLC. **p. 91:** Number of Hours People Sleep Each Night from Borbély, A. (1986). *Secrets of Sleep*, Figure 3.4 (p. 43). English translation, Copyright © 1986 by Basic Books. © 1984 by Deutsche Verlags-Anstalt GmbH, Stuttgart. Reprinted by permission of Basic Books, a member of the Perseus Books Group. **p. 99:** Different Drugs Affect Different Parts of the Nervous System from Sylvia S. Mader, *Human Biology*, 6th ed., p. 250. Copyright © 2000 by The McGraw-Hill Companies, Inc. Reprinted with permission. **p. 100:** Drug Use by High School Seniors from Johnston, L. D., O'Malley, P. M., Bachman, J. G., & Schulenberg, J. E. (2009). *Monitoring the Future national survey results on drug use, 1975–2008*. Volume I: Secondary school students (NIH Publication No. 09-7402). Bethesda, MD: National Institute on Drug Abuse, 721 pp. **p. 106:** Teenage Marijuana Use from Robert S. Feldman, *Understanding Psychology*, 10th ed., Figure 7, p. 168. Copyright © 2011 by The McGraw-Hill Companies, Inc. Reprinted with permission.

Chapter 5

p. 128: Drawing of Albert Bandura from Gregory Feist and Erika Rosenberg, *Psychology: Making Connections*, 1st ed., p. 319. Copyright © 2010 by The McGraw-Hill Companies, Inc. Reprinted with permission. **p. 131:** Analytical versus Relational Approaches to Learning from Anderson, J. A., & Adams, M. (1992). Acknowledging the learning styles of diverse student populations: Implications for instructional design. *New Directions for Teaching and Learning*, 49, pp. 19–33. Copyright © 1992 by Jossey-Bass, Inc. Reprinted by permission of John Wiley & Sons, Inc.

Chapter 6

p. 144: Semantic Memory Networks for Fire Engine from Collins, A. M., & Loftus, E. F. (1975). A spreading-activation theory of semantic processing. *Psychological Review*, 82, 407–428 (Figure 1, p. 412). Published by The American Psychological Association, adapted with permission. **p. 145:** Memory Consolidation in the Brain from Kent Van De Graaff, *Human Anatomy*, updated 5th ed. Copyright © 2000 by The McGraw-Hill Companies, Inc. Reprinted with permission. **p. 151:** Accuracy of Eyewitness Testimony Affected by Interviewer's Word Choice reprinted from *Journal of Verbal Learning and Verbal Behavior*, vol. 13, Loftus, E. F., & Palmer, J. C., "Reconstruction of automobile destruction: An example of the interface between language and memory," pp. 585–589, Copyright 1974, with permission from Elsevier. http://www.science-direct.com/science/journal/00225371. **p. 152:** Autobiographical Memories of Grades Recalled by College Students from Table 2 (p. 266) from Bahrick, H. P., Hall, L. K., & Berger, S. A. (1996). Accuracy and distortion in memory for high school grades. *Psychological Science*, 7, no, 5, 265–269. Copyright © 1996 Association for Psychological Science. Reprinted by permission of Sage Publications. **p. 155:** Pennies reprinted from *Cognitive Psychology*, vol. 11, Nickerson, R. S., & Adams, M. J., "Long-term memory for a common object," pp. 287–307, Copyright © 1979, with permission from Elsevier. http://www.sciencedirect.com/science/journal/00100285.

Chapter 7

p. 179: Gardner's Multiple Intelligences: Text from Gardner, H. (2006). *Multiple Intelligences: New Horizons in Theory and Practice*, pp. 8, 9–10, 11, 13, 15, 16. Copyright © 2006 by Howard Gardner. First edition © 1993 by Howard Gardner. Reprinted by permission of Basic Books, a member of the Perseus Books Group.

Chapter 8

p. 211: Hierarchy of Emotions from Shaver, P., Schwartz, J., Kirson, D., & O'Connor, C. (1987). Emotion knowledge: Further exploration of a prototype approach. *Journal of Personality and Social Psychology*, 52, 1061–1086 (Figure 1, p. 1067). Published by The American Psychological Association, adapted with permission.

Chapter 9

p. 236: Principles of Conservation from Judith Schickedanz et al., *Understanding Children & Adolescents*, Fig. 13.1, p. 440 "Tests of the Principle of Conservation Chart," © 2001 Judith Schickedanz, David Schickedanz, and Peggy Forsyth. Reproduced by permission of Pearson Education, Inc. **p. 237:** Memory Span Increases with Age for Both Numbers and Letter from Dempster, F. N. (1981). Memory span: Sources for individual and developmental differences. *Psychological Bulletin*, 89, 63–100. Published by The American Psychological Association, adapted with permission. **p. 240:** Kohlberg's Three Levels of Moral Development: Rest, J. Developmental hierarchy in preference and comprehension of moral judgment. Unpublished doctoral dissertation, University of Chicago, 1968, from Kohlberg, L. (1969). Stage and sequence: The cognitive-developmental approach to socialization. In D. Goslin (Ed.), *Handbook of Socialization Theory and Research* (pp. 381–382). Chicago: Rand McNally.

Chapter 10

p. 265: Eysenck's Three Dimensions of Personality from Eysenck, H. J. (1990). Biological dimensions of personality. In L. A. Pervin (Ed.), *Handbook of Personality: Theory and Research* (p. 246). New York: Guilford. Reprinted by permission of The Guilford Press. **p. 265:** The Big Five Personality Factors and Dimension of Sample Traits from L. A. Pervin (Ed.), (1990). *Handbook of Personality: Theory and Research* (chapter 3). New York: Guilford. Reprinted by permission of The Guilford Press. **p. 269:** Genetic Influences on Personality from Tellegen, A., Lykken, D. T., Bouchard, T. J., Jr., Wilcox, K. J., Segal, N. L., & Rich, S. (1988). Personality similarity in twins reared apart and together. *Journal of Personality and Social Psychology*, 54, 1031–1039. Published by The American Psychological Association, reprinted with permission.

Chapter 11

p. 283: Selye's General Adaptation Syndrome (GAS) from *The Stress of Life* by Hans Selye. Copyright © 1976 by The McGraw-Hill Companies, Inc. Reprinted by permission. **p. 284:** Try It! How Stressful Is Your Life? "Perceived Stress Scale" (pp. 394–395) adapted from Cohen, S., Kamarck, T., & Mermelstein, R. (1983). A global measure of perceived stress. *Journal of Health and Social Behavior*, 24, 385–396. Reprinted by permission of the American Sociological Association. **p. 288:** Relationship Between Patient Attitude and Cancer Survival reprinted from *The Lancet*, vol. 325, no. 8431, Pettingale, K. W., Morris, T., Greer, S., & Haybittle, J. L., "Mental attitudes to cancer: An additional prognostic factor," p. 750, Copyright 1985, with permission from Elsevier. http://www.sciencedirect.com/science/journal/01406736.

Chapter 12

p. 306: Types of Phobias adapted from Susan Nolen-Hoeksema, *Abnormal Psychology*, 4th ed., Figure 7.7, p. 232. Copyright © 2007 by The McGraw-Hill Companies, Inc. Reprinted with permission. **p. 307:** The Most Common Psychological Disorders from Laura A. King, *Experience Psychology*, 1st ed., Figure 12-12, p. 443. Copyright © 2010 by The McGraw-Hill Companies, Inc. Reprinted with permission. **p. 313:** "Table: Risk of Developing Schizophrenia" from the book *Schizophrenia Genesis: The Origins of Madness* by Irving I. Gottesman. Copyright © 1990 by Irving I. Gottesman. Reprinted by permission of Henry Holt and Company, LLC. **p. 315:** Problems Reported by Students Visiting a College Counseling Center from Benton, S. A., et al. (2003). Changes in counseling center client problems across 13 years. *Professional Psychology: Research and Practice*, 34, 66–72 (Table 1, p. 69). Published by The American Psychological Association. Adapted with permission.

Chapter 13

p. 338: Try It! The Need for Cognition from Cacioppo, J. T., Berntson, G. G., & Crites, S. L., Jr. (1996). Social neuroscience: Principles of psychophysiological arousal and response. In E. T. Higgins & A. W. Kruglanski (Eds.), *Social Psychology: Handbook of Basic Principles*. © 1996 The Guilford Press. Reprinted by permission of the publisher. **p. 341:** The Process We Use to Explain the Behavior of Others adapted from Anderson, C. A., Krull, D. S., & Weiner, B. (1996). Explanations: Processes and consequences. In E. T. Higgins & A. W. Kruglanski (Eds.), *Social Psychology: Handbook of Basic Principles* (p. 274). © 1996 The Guilford Press. Reprinted by permission of the publisher. **p. 351:** Sternberg's Three Types of Love from Sternberg, R. J. (1986). A triangular theory of love. *Psychological Review*, 93, 119–135 (Table 2, p. 123). Published by The American Psychological Association, adapted with permission. **p. 354:** Try It! Is This Aggression? excerpts from Table 1 "Aggression Questionnaire" (p. 41) from Benjamin, L. T., Jr. (1985). Defining aggression. An exercise for classroom discussion. *Teaching of Psychology*, 12, no. 1, pp. 40–42. Copyright © 1985 Society for the Teaching of Psychology, reprinted by permission of Sage Publications.

Bright, P., 158
Brinkhaus, B., 75
Brinton, B., 211
Brislin, R., 178
Britt, G., 105
Brock, J., 126
Brock, T. C., 337
Bröder, A., 142
Brody, J., 291
Broman, C. L., 286
Bronson, P., 348
Brooks, G., 97
Brooks, L., 283
Broome, K. M., 106
Brossart, D. F., 331
Brown, 293
Brown, E., 292
Brown, L. S., 152
Brown, P. K., 68
Brown, R., 143
Brown, R. J., 341
Brown, R. Douglas, 151
Brown, S., 48
Browne, K. D., 175
Bruce, V., 68, 81
Bruehl, S., 356
Bruggeman, H., 81
Bryant, R. A., 92
Bryant, R. M., 6
Brydon, L., 282
Brzustowicz, L. M., 313
Bucci, S., 312
Buchanan, J. J., 128
Buchanan, R. W., 313
Buchanan, T. W., 145
Buchert, R., 107
Buchsbaum, B., 141
Buck, L. B., 72
Buckman, J., 158
Buehner, M., 178
Buffardi, L. E., 314
Bukobza, G., 245
Bulik, C. M., 201
Bunge, S. A., 15
Bunting, M., 155
Burger, J. M., 345, 346, 347
Burgoon, J. K., 350
Burns, C. W., 67
Burns, J. W., 356
Burrows, A., 16
Burt, D. M., 350
Burton, K. S., 180
Bury, A. S., 166
Bush, J., 322
Bushman, B., 115
Bushman, B. J., 130, 352
Bushnell, M. C., 75
Buss, D. M., 221, 266, 268
Butcher, J. N., 272, 273
Butcher, P. A., 76
Butler, A. C., 324
Butler, L. D., 289
Butler, L. T., 148, 350
Butler, M. A., 116
Byne, W., 207
Byrne, G., 319
Byrne-Davis, L., 286

C

Cabanac, M., 200
Cabaniss, D. L., 320
Cachelin, F. M., 203
Cacioppo, J., 337
Cacioppo, J. T., 15, 338
Cadieux, M. J., 146
Caelian, C. F., 244
Cahill, J., 189
Cahill, L., 52, 137, 151
Cain, D. J., 271, 325
Cain, M. E., 24
Cajochen, C., 95
Calabrese, J. R., 329
Caldwell, D. F., 345
Calin-Jageman, R. J., 63
Calkins, M., 10

Cameron, O. G., 213
Campbell, D. T., 82
Campbell, J., 187
Campbell, T. S., 76
Campbell, W., 342
Campbell, W. K., 314
Canetti-Nisim, D., 15
Cannon, T. D., 53
Cannon, W. B., 213
Cantalupo, C., 50
Cantwell, R. H., 209
Capaldi, E. D., 200
Capone, N. C., 221
Carey, B., 330
Carhart-Harris, R., 103
Carlo, G., 231
Carlsmith, J. M., 339
Carlson, M., 353
Carmody, T., 97
Carnagey, 130
Carnagey, N., 353
Carney, D., 340
Carney, R. N., 156
Carpenter, S. K., 154
Carr, A., 326
Carreiras, M., 174
Carrillo, M., 38
Carroll, J., 203
Carroll, L., 173
Cartwright, R., 93
Caruso, D. R., 181
Caruso, E., 166
Carver, C., 252
Case, R., 237
Case, T. I., 72
Casey, S. D., 121
Cashon, C., 237
Caspi, A., 6, 221
Cassells, J. V. S., 262
Cassidy, K. W., 231
Castro, C. A., 290
Catenacci, V., 199
Cattell, A. K., 264
Cattell, H. E. P., 264
Cattell, R. B., 264, 271
Cauce, A. M., 331
Caudill, C., 101
Cavallini, E., 250
Cavenett, T., 195
Ceccanti, M., 104
Ceci, S. J., 151
Centers for Disease Control and
    Prevention, 243, 244
Ceponiene, R., 144
Cerutti, D. T., 121
Chamberlain, K., 282
Chambless, D. L., 327
Chan, K. K., 338
Chandra, P., 177
Chandran, S., 168
Chang, C., 172
Chang, J., 15
Chang-Schneider, C., 267
Chanon, V., 315
Chao, R. K., 15
Chapkis, W., 107
Chapman, A., 323
Chapman, J. P., 312
Chapman, L. J., 312
Chapman, S., 291
Charles, Joseph, 238
Charman, D. P., 320
Charman, S. D., 150
Chartrand, T. L., 340
Chaudhry, H. R., 296
Chauhan, R. V., 327
Chechil, R. A., 61
Chen, 75
Chen, A., 69
Cheng, C., 293
Cheston, S. E., 327
Cheung, M. L., 293
Chiang, W. C., 237
Childress, A., 321
Chincotta, D., 142
Chivers, M. L., 205

Cho, A., 71
Cho, K., 76
Cho, S., 53
Chodorow, M., 155
Choi, Y., 76
Chomsky, N., 176, 177
Chou, K., 289
Choy, Y., 321, 323
Christ, S. E., 225
Christakis, N. A., 291
Christophe, A., 228
Chronicle, E. P., 167
Chrysikou, E. G., 169
Chylinska, J., 284
Cialdini, R. B., 345, 346
Clark, D., 75
Clark, D. A., 303
Clark, D. B., 104
Clark, J., 325
Clark, L. A., 304
Clark, L. V., 236
Clark, M., 342
Clark, M. P., 10
Clark, M. S., 342
Clarke-Stewart, K. A., 232, 247
Clarkin, J. F., 314
Clausen, L., 201
Clay, D. L., 320
Clayton, K., 101
Clayton, R., 101
Cleary, A. M., 145
Clegg, J., 186
Clements, A. M., 51
Clementz, B., 342
Clemons, T. L., 187
Clifasefi, S., 152
Clifton, D., 296
Cloud, J., 107
Coan, J. A., 293
Coates, S. L., 148
Cobos, P., 212
Cochran, S. D., 208
Cochran, Thad, 111
Coffman, S. J., 327
Cohen, 107
Cohen, A. L., 250
Cohen, B. H., 21
Cohen, J., 280
Cohen, L. B., 237
Cohen, P., 318
Cohen, S., 286, 293
Cohler, B. J., 320
Coleman, E., 205
Coleman, G., 90
Coleman, J., 239
Coleman, M., 248
Coles, R., 241
Collins, A. M., 144
Collins, L. M., 239
Colom, R., 178
Coltheart, M., 312
Coltraine, S., 348
Colvin, C., 340
Colwell, M. J., 231
Combrink-Graham, L., 230
Combs, D., 312, 313
Compagni, A., 32
Compas, B. E., 282
Comuzzie, A. G., 201
Conduit, R., 90
Conklin, C., 324
Connell, B., 175
Conner, P., 338
Connolly, A. C., 165
Conoley, C. W., 331
Consentino, S., 148
Conte, H. R., 261
Conway, M. A., 147, 153
Conway, T. L., 291
Cooke, J. R., 94
Cooklin, A., 326
Cooper, C., 201
Cooper, H., 21
Cooper, J., 339
Cooper, Z., 204
Cooper-Brown, L. J., 121

Coplan, R., 232
Copolov, D. L., 312
Corcoran, J., 326
Cordnoldi, C., 152
Corkin, S., 144
Cornell, C. B., 182
Corp, E. S., 199
Corpus, J. H., 197
Corsello, A., 150
Costa, P., 265, 344
Costa, P. T., Jr., 314
Côté, J. E., 245
Cotton, P., 318
Cotton, W. L., 205
Courteau, J., 291
Couturier, J., 202, 204
Coventry, K. R., 167
Cowan, N., 237
Cowley, B. J., 96
Cowley, G., 157
Cox, 194
Coyle, N., 184, 252
Craik, F. I. M., 146
Cramer, A., 232
Cramer, P., 261
Crandall, C. S., 238
Cray, J., 16
Creasey, G. L., 222
Crerand, C. E., 126
Crews, F., 262
Crewther, S. G., 90
Crick, N., 130
Critchfield, T., 119
Crites, S. L., 338
Crockett, E., 351
Cropley, A., 173
Crosnoe, R., 251
Crowder, R. G., 140
Crowther, S., 353
Crum, A. J., 25
Crump, J., 263
Cruz, A., 77
Cuijpers, P., 327
Culbert, K., 204
Culhane-Pera, K. A., 294
Cumberland, A., 357
Cummings, A., 144
Curran, A., 181
Curran, M., 329
Curseu, P., 338
Cutting, J. C., 174
Cwikel, J., 21
Cynkar, A., 6
Czopp, A. M., 349

D

D'Amico, 101
D'Arcy, R. C. N., 45
D'Eramo, K., 323
Daftary, F., 152
Dai, D. Y., 338
Daines, B., 206
Dalai Lama, 180
Dale, J. W., 42
Damasio, A., 49
Damon, Matt, 318
Damon, W., 241
Dani, J. A., 291
Daniels, K. A., 148
Darley, J. M., 353, 354, 355
Darling, J., 73
Darroch, J. E., 206
Darth Vader, 263
Darwin, C. J., 140
Daskalakis, Z., 45
Davidson, 199
Davidson, J. E., 213
Davidson, R. J., 293
Davies, S., 274
Davis, D. D., 324
Davis, L., 280
Davis, O., 42
Davis, R., 315
Davis, R. L., 71
Davis, R. O., 314

Garza-Guerrero, C., 351
Gatchel, R. J., 75, 203
Gates, Bill, 14
Gautreaux, G., 323, 353
Gazzaniga, M. S., 32, 53
Ge, X., 239
Gebhard, P., 207
Gegenfurtner, K. R., 69
Gelfand, M. M., 249
Gelman, R., 227, 237
Gentile, B., 267
Gentile, D., 130
George, L. K., 251
George, P., 77
George, R., 227
George, S., 103
Georgeson, M., 68, 81
Geraerts, E., 151
Gershkoff-Stowe, L., 175
Giacobbi, P. R., Jr., 281
Gibb, K., 187
Gibb, R., 50
Gibbons, 337
Gibbons, R. D., 329
Gibbs, N., 238
Gibbs, W. W., 174
Gilbert, D. T., 264, 350
Gilboa, A., 158
Gilligan, C., 241, 243, 254
Gillis, C., 246
Giusberti, F., 164
Gladwell, M., 263, 274
Gladwin, T., 177
Glantz, S. A., 291
Glass, K., 285
Gleitman, L. R., 176
Glickler, J., 267
Glicksohn, J., 264, 340
Glisky, E. L., 251
Godden, D., 155
Goff, D. C., 329
Goffin, R. D., 342
Goin, M. K., 319
Gold, M., 101
Goldfried, M. R., 327
Goldman, E., 330
Goldman, H., 331
Goldsmith, A. A., 101
Goldsmith, H. H., 314
Goldstein, E., 151
Goldstein, I., 204
Goldstein, S., 225
Goldstein, S. N., 242
Goldstone, R. L., 165
Goleman, D., 294, 316
Golimbet, V. E., 42, 268
Golosheykin, S., 98
Gong, H., 69
Gontier, N., 177
Gontkovsky, S. T., 47, 180
Goode, E., 72, 320
Goodman, G., 151
Goodwin, J. E., 227
Goodwin, R., 344
Goodwin, R. D., 314
Gooren, L., 207
Gordijn, M. C. M., 95
Gordon, R., 73
Gorfine, T., 88
Gorsky, H., 173
Goslin, S., 265
Gottesman, I. I., 221, 313
Gottfredson, L. S., 187
Gottlieb, D. A., 121, 122
Goubert, L., 323
Gould, E., 51
Gould, R. L., 246
Govindarajan, A., 145
Grabe, S., 207, 208
Gradinaru, 45
Grady, D., 291
Graf, P., 148
Graham, J. R., 273
Graham, S., 239, 315
Grainger, J., 142
Grandin, T., 179

Grann, J. D., 154
Grant, 197
Grant, J. S., 291
Grant, S., 273
Gray, G. C., 353
Gray, R., 226
Graziano, W. G., 357
Green, B. G., 77
Green, G., 353
Green, M. C., 337
Green, P. R., 68, 81
Greenberg, L., 325
Greenberg, R., 330
Greenberg, R. M., 329
Greene, J. D., 214
Greenspan, S., 186
Greenwald, A. G., 148, 348
Greer, R. D., 288, 323, 353
Gregory, R. L., 82
Grémy, I., 339
Gretchen, D., 327
Greven, C. U., 222
Griffin, D. W., 351
Griffith, J. W., 152
Grigorenko, E. L., 177, 181, 189
Grigoriadis, S., 326
Grilo, C. M., 204
Grinspoon, Stuart, 292
Groh, K., 245
Gronholm, P., 45
Gross, D. M., 210
Gross, J. J., 210
Grossman, T., 227
Grucza, R., 103
Grunig, J. E., 167
Grunwald, T., 227
Grusec, J. E., 323
Guarnaccia, P. J., 318
Guéguen, N., 345
Guerrero, L., 16
Guez, J., 155
Guilleminault, C., 95
Gunter, B., 130
Gurunjj, R., 282
Guthrie, I. K., 357
Gutierrez, P. M., 243, 244
Guyll, M., 348
Gwynn, M. I., 97

H

Haberstick, B. C., 101, 223
Hackam, D. G., 24
Häfliger, A., 146
Hagoort, P., 177
Haidet, P., 294
Haidt, J., 211
Haier, R. J., 178
Hains, S. C., 344
Halfen, S., 339
Halford, S., 231
Halgren, E., 177
Halkitis, P., 103
Hall, B. J., 15
Hall, E., 248
Hall, J., 340
Hall, J. A., 294
Hall, N. W., 187, 225
Hall, R. E., 189
Hallschmid, M., 200
Halpern, D. F., 248
Halpert, J., 293
Hamann, S., 145
Hamberg, K., 52
Hambleton, R. K., 271
Hamer, D. H., 207
Hamer, M., 293
Hamilton, A. C., 140
Hamilton, S. P., 314
Hamilton, W. L., 291
Hammond, C., 101
Hammons, G., 290
Hamrick, N., 286
Haney, C., 345
Haney, J., 106
Hankins, F., 194

Hanley, C., 130
Hanley, S. J., 198
Hannon, E. E., 227
Hanson, D. R., 221, 313
Harding, D. J., 205
Hardison, D. M., 174
Hardy, L. T., 231
Harlow, H. F., 229, 230
Harold, G. T., 247
Harper, D. J., 329
Harper, T., 248
Harris, G., 291
Harris, K. R., 180, 315
Harrison, G., 202
Hart, B., 176
Hartung, C. M., 318
Harvey, A., 283
Harvey, J. H., 206
Harvey-Berino, J., 201
Haslam, C., 226
Hauke, C., 263
Hausenblas, H., 202
Hauser, M. D., 177
Havercamp, S., 69
Havercamp, S. M., 198
Havermans, R. C., 322
Haw, S., 291
Hawkes, C. H., 72
Hawley, E., 82
Hayflick, L., 249
Haynes, 99
Hays, P. A., 327
Hayslip, B., 262
Hazlett, H., 187
He, S-Z., 247
Heath, R. A., 208
Heatherton, T., 290
Hecht, J. M., 296
Hedgepeth, E., 241
Hedges, D. W., 328
Hedlund, J., 181
Hegarty, P., 187, 337
Heier, M. S., 94
Heim, C. M., 290
Heimann, M., 237
Heinrichs, R. W., 312
Heisel, M. J., 315
Helfand, S. J., 12
Heller, S., 262
Heller, W., 51
Helmbold, N., 180
Helstrup, T., 152
Henderlong, J., 197
Henderson, J., 226
Henik, A., 76
Henrich, 83
Henry, D., 94
Henry (sick woman's husband), 240
Hentschel, U., 261
Herbenick, D., 205
Herman, C. P., 202, 204
Herman, D. B., 290
Herrmann, A., 169
Herrnstein, R. J., 188–189
Herskovits, M. J., 82
Hertzog, C., 251
Herzberg, J., 213
Herzog, H. A., 24
Heshka, S., 203
Hess, D. W., 250
Hess, M. J., 53
Hewstone, M., 340
Heywood, S., 202
Hibbard, P., 80
Hiby, E. F., 121
Hicks, B. M., 357
Higgins, 12
Hilarski, C., 314
Hilgard, E., 97
Hill, J. O., 199, 203
Hill, S. S., 23
Hines, M., 51
Hinson, J. T., 250
Hiripi, E., 202
Hirsch, I. J., 71
Hirsch, J., 201

Hirschler, B., 42
Hirt, E. R., 150
Hjertaas, T., 263
Ho, S. M. Y., 294
Hobfoll, S. E., 15, 281
Hobson, J., 93
Hobson, J. A., 94
Hock, H. S., 61
Hoff, E., 173, 176, 177
Hoffman, E., 184
Hoffmann, S. G., 322
Hofmann, W., 142, 148
Hogan, J., 274
Hogan, R., 274
Hoge, C. W., 290
Hogg, M. A., 344, 348
Hojjat, M., 351
Holden, C., 312
Holden, R., 166
Holland, C. R., 188, 189
Holleran, S., 340
Hollingworth, H. L., 10
Hollingworth, L. S., 10
Hollon, S., 330
Hollon, S. D., 330
Holmes, J. G., 351
Holowka, S., 51
Holtzman, D., 205
Holy, T. E., 72
Holyoak, K. J., 53
Homel, R., 230
Hong, E., 173
Hong, Y., 76
Hongchun, W., 97
Honzik, C. H., 127
Hope, K., 331
Hopkins, W., 50
Hopton, A., 76
Hopwood, C., 315
Hopwood, C. J., 268
Horínek, D., 157
Horn, J. L., 189
Horney, K., 10, 259, 263, 271
Hornsey, M. J., 337, 343
Horowitz, H. A., 314
Hort, J., 157
Horton, K. D., 148
Horwath, E., 317
Horwood, L. J., 244
Houg, S., 53
Howe, C. J., 175
Howells, J. G., 302
Howes, O., 38
Hoyme, E. H., 186
Hoyt, C., 337
Hrabosky, J. I., 202
Hsiao, Y., 164
Hu, F. B., 203
Huang, C., 172
Huang, M., 104
Huang, Y., 240
Hubbard, E. M., 75, 76
Hubel, D. H., 67
Huber, F., 169
Hudson, J., 202
Hudson, W., 83
Hudspeth, A. J., 48, 71
Huesmann, R., 115
Hui, L., 91
Huijie, T., 222
Huizinga, M., 295
Hull, C. L., 195
Humphrey, N., 181
Humphreys, G. W., 79
Humphreys, K., 145
Hungi, N., 156
Hunt, E., 180
Hunt, M., 205, 207
Hunter, C., 97
Huprich, S., 319, 320
Hurt, C. S., 250
Hussain, R., 187
Hutchinson, K. E., 101
Hutchinson, S. L., 285
Hyde, J., 206
Hyde, J. S., 207, 208

Prince, C. V., 208
Prinz, J. J., 213
Prior, A., 175
Prislin, R., 344
Proffitt, D. R., 81
Prokop, L., 199
Pryor, D. W., 207
Psotka, J., 157
Puca, R. M., 209
Puetz, T., 204
Puller, C., 69
Purdom, Katie, 335

Q

Quartana, P. J., 356
Quas, J. A., 151
Quenot, J. P., 45
Quillian, M. R., 144
Quinlan, K. J., 315
Quintana, S. M., 15

R

Rabin, J., 68
Rabin, Yitzhak, 137
Rabinowitz, J., 313
Rabson-Hare, J., 21
Raczynski, J. M., 201
Rado, J., 45
Rahman, Q., 207
Rainville, 75
Rajagopal, S., 25
Ralston, A., 194, 198
Ramachandran, V. S., 75, 76
Rammsayer, T., 180
Ramsay, M. C., 188
Ramus, F., 223
Ranganath, C., 141
Ransom, B. R., 33
Rapee, R., 323
Raskin, N., 325
Rasmussen, F., 201
Rassin, E., 171
Ravindran, A. V., 282
Ravitz, P., 326
Ray, L., 268
Ray, L. A., 101
Ray, R., 101
Ray, Rachael, 336
Rayner, R., 115
Raz, A., 97
Read, J., 103
Rechtschaffen, A., 91
Rector, N. A., 324
Redding, G. M., 80, 82
Redish, A. D., 103
Reed, M., 345
Reed, P., 121, 122
Reed, S. K., 170
Reese, R. J., 331
Reese-Durham, N., 180
Regan, P. C., 203, 351
Rehm, J., 107
Reichel, M., 232
Reif, A., 221
Reijonen, J. H., 315
Reilly, T., 95
Reinhard, M., 337
Reisberg, D., 173
Reiss, S., 198
Reitman, J. S., 167
Remington, R., 79
Rende, R., 6
Repp, B. H., 83
Reston, Ana Carolina, 204
Revonsuo, A., 97
Reynolds, C., 17
Reynolds, C. R., 188, 225
Reynolds, R. I., 144
Riccio, C., 17
Rice, C., 315
Rice, L., 325
Rice, M. L., 175
Rich, E. L., 47
Richard, D. C. S., 323
Richards, R., 173

Richardson, A. S., 244
Richardson, J. E., 131
Richgels, D. J., 174
Rieber, R. W., 238
Riedel, G. G., 37
Rigby, L., 326
Rijsdijk, F. V., 222
Rinn, W. E., 215
Riolo, F., 262
Risley, T. R., 176
Ritezschel, J., 73
Ritterfeld, U., 130
Rivera-Garcia, A., 90
Rivers, S. E., 181
Rizzo, M., 94
Robbins, B., 13
Robert, J., 174
Roberts, M., 178
Robertson, E., 143
Robins, L. N., 318
Robins, R. W., 152, 211, 268
Robinson, D. K., 238
Robinson, D. N., 69, 329
Robinson, T. E., 50
Roch-Locours, L. A., 51
Rock, A., 291
Rodd, Z. A., 116
Rodriguez, M., 286
Rodriguez, M. A., 118
Roe, C., 250
Roesch, S. C., 285
Roethel-Wendorf, A., 282
Rogers, C. R., 13, 269–270, 271, 325
Rogers, J. M., 226
Rogers, L. J., 50, 51
Rogers, S., 250
Roid, G., 183
Roisman, G. I., 231
Roizen, N. J., 225
Roll, 12
Rolls, E. T., 73
Rom, S. A., 289
Romeu, P. F., 148
Rönnberg, J., 142
Room, R., 107
Rooney, N. J., 121
Roosevelt, E., 197
Rorschach, H., 273
Rosa-Alcazar, A., 326
Rosch, E., 165
Rosen, H., 324
Rosenbaum, M., 201
Rosenbaum, R. S., 158
Rosenbloom, T., 195
Rosenhan, D. L., 304
Rosenman, R. H., 287
Rosenstein, D. S., 314
Rosenthal, R., 24, 340
Roska, B., 68
Rosov, A., 263
Ross, D., 128
Ross, H. E., 76
Ross, J., 93
Ross, L., 264, 342
Ross, M., 150, 340
Ross, S., 128
Rossato, M., 106
Rossell, S. L., 52
Rossi-Arnaud, C., 148
Roter, D. L., 294
Rothblum, E. D., 208
Rothman, A. J., 295
Roughton, R. E., 207
Routtenberg, A., 47
Rowan, K., 232
Rowe, J. B., 49
Roy, 75
Røysamb, E., 304
Royzman, E. B., 231
Rozencwajg, P., 250
Rubichi, S., 97
Rubin, D. C., 149, 152, 153
Ruck, M. D., 21
Rudman, L. A., 348
Rudner, M., 142
Rudzinski, D., 320
Runco, M. A., 173

Rünger, D., 128
Rusche, B., 23
Ruscher, J. B., 340
Russell, J. A., 211
Rust, T. B., 250
Rustin, M., 17
Ruth, Babe, 179
Rutherford, B., 24
Ruthsatz, J. M., 186
Rutter, M., 221
Ryan, Richard, 198
Rydell, R., 339
Rymer, R., 175
Ryncarz, R. A., 241
Ryner, L., 45

S

Saarni, C., 232
Sabbagh, K., 151
Saccuzzo, D. P., 271
Sachs-Ericsson, N., 251
Sackeim, H. A., 329
Sacks, O., 37
Saczynski, J., 250
Sagarin, B. J., 345
Saggino, A., 178
Sahin, N. T., 177
Sakai, K. L., 177
Salgado, D. M., 315
Salmela-Aro, K., 267
Salovey, P., 181, 295
Salsman, N. L., 326
Salvi, V., 329
Samaniego, C. M., 241
Samantaray, S. K., 198
Samoilov, V., 113
Sampson, M., 319
Sams, M., 140
Sandlund, M., 330
Sandoval, J., 188
Sandy, C., 265
Sanford, M., 313
Sanjuan, E., 120
Sanlier, N., 54, 281
Sanouri, A., 291
Santel, S., 202, 204
Saper, C. B., 95
Sapolsky, R. M., 330
Sargent, J., 290
Sargent, J. D., 290
Sato, K., 211
Saucier, D. A., 24
Savas, H. A., 328
Savazzi, S., 53
Saville, B., 123
Sawa, A., 328
Sayette, M. A., 104
Saywitz, K., 151
Scaramella, L. V., 224
Scarborough, E., 10
Scarr, Sandra, 189
Scaturo, D. J., 326
Schachter, S., 213
Schacter, D. L., 148
Schaefer, H. S., 293
Schaefer, R. T., 247
Schaie, K., 248, 249, 250
Schaller, M., 238
Schallert, D. L., 211
Schechter, T., 225
Scheele, B., 352
Scheier, M. F., 251, 252
Schenone, M. H., 224
Schepers, P., 172, 173
Scher, S. J., 339
Schieber, F., 248
Schiffer, A., 142
Schiffer, A. A., 288
Schimpf, P. H., 46
Schlenger, W. E., 107
Schmeichel, B. J., 142
Schmitt, D. P., 265
Schnake, S. B., 340
Schnatz, P. F., 294
Schneider, A., 146
Schneider, W., 237

Schneiderman, N., 283
Schnyer, D. M., 148
Schredl, M., 92
Schrier, R. W., 292
Schroers, M., 72
Schultz, 289
Schutt, R. K., 17
Schutte, N. S., 327
Schwartz, B. L., 145
Schwartz, E. R., 38
Schwartz, J. M., 50
Schwartz, S. J., 245
Schwarz, N., 296, 349
Schwenkreis, P., 48
Scollon, C. N., 296
Scullin, M. H., 151
Seamon, M. J., 107
Sebanz, N., 83
Sebel, P. S., 147
Seeley, R. J., 200
Segall, M. H., 82
Segerstrom, S. C., 286
Segress, M., 101
Seibt, B., 348
Seifert, A. L., 347
Seli, H., 195
Seligman, M. E., 327
Seligman, M. E. P., 15, 289, 295, 296
Selkoe, D., 157
Selkoe, D. J., 251
Sellbom, M., 272
Sells, R., 207
Selove, R., 225
Selye, H., 282–283
Semin, G. R., 173, 340
Semykina, A., 209
Serdaris, N., 295
Serences, J., 140
Serpell, R., 188
Sestir, M. A., 130
Seymour, B., 200
Shafer, V. L., 175
Shafran, R., 204
Shah, D. B., 330
Shaikholeslami, R., 197
Shankar, G., 24
Shapiro, C. J., 315
Shapiro, L. R., 149
Shapiro, M. L., 47
Sharif, Z., 328
Sharma, H. S., 103
Sharman, S. J., 151
Shastri, J., 231
Shaver, P., 352
Shaver, P. R., 231
Shavers, V., 290
Shea, A., 226
Shelley, Mary, 90
Shelton, R., 330
Shen, C. K., 50
Shen, L., 210
Sheppard, L. D., 180
Shepperd, J., 342
Sherblom, S., 241
Sherman, S. L., 225
Shiffman, S., 291
Shiffrin, R. M., 139
Shimai, S., 295
Shimono, K., 81
Shinn, M., 331
Shochet, I., 230
Shoda, Y., 267
Shono, Y., 155
Shors, T. J., 50
Shurkin, J. N., 187
Shweder, R. A., 211
Sibley, C. G., 337
Sidman, M., 121
Siebler, F., 338
Siegel, 99
Siegel, J. M., 91, 280
Siegel, L., 280
Siemer, M., 210
Sifrit, K. J., 142
Sighvatsson, M., 118
SigurXardóttir, Z., 118
Sill, M., 249